Literature to Go

Literature to Go

THIRD EDITION

MICHAEL MEYER

University of Connecticut

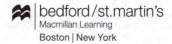
bedford/st.martin's
Macmillan Learning
Boston | New York

For Bedford/St. Martin's

Vice President, Editorial, Macmillan Learning Humanities: Edwin Hill
Editorial Director, English: Karen S. Henry
Executive Editor: Vivian Garcia
Senior Editor: Christina Gerogiannis
Senior Production Editor: Deborah Baker
Assistant Editor: Cara Kaufman
Media Producer: Allison Hart
Production Supervisor: Joe Ford
Marketing Manager: Sophia LaTorre-Zengierski
Copyeditor: Arthur Johnson
Permissions Manager: Kalina Ingham
Photo Editor: Martha Friedman
Photo Researcher: Susan Doheny
Permissions Editor: Arthur Johnson
Senior Art Director: Anna Palchik
Cover Design: John Callahan
Cover Art: Patti Mollica/Superstock
Composition: Jouve
Printing and Binding: Edwards Brothers Malloy, Inc.

Manufactured in the United States of America.

1 0 9 8 7 6
f e d c b a

For information, write: Bedford/St. Martin's, 75 Arlington Street, Boston, MA 02116
(617-399-4000)

ISBN 978-1-319-03726-0

Acknowledgments

FICTION

Toni Cade Bambara. "Sweet Town" from *Gorilla, My Love* by Toni Cade Bambara. Copyright © 1959, 1960, 1963, 1964, 1965, 1968, 1970, 1971, 1972 by Toni Cade Bambara. Used by permission of Random House, an imprint and division of Penguin Random House LLC. All rights reserved. Any third party use of this material, outside of this publication, is prohibited. Interested parties must apply directly to Penguin Random House LLC for permission.

Text acknowledgments and copyrights continue at the back of the book on pages 938–44, which constitute an extension of the copyright page. Art acknowledgments and copyrights appear on the same page as the art selections they cover.

For My Wife
Regina Barreca

About Michael Meyer

Michael Meyer, Emeritus Professor of English, taught writing and literature courses for more than thirty years — since 1981 at the University of Connecticut and before that at the University of North Carolina at Charlotte and the College of William and Mary. In addition to being an experienced teacher, Meyer is a highly regarded literary scholar. His scholarly articles have appeared in distinguished journals such as *American Literature, Studies in the American Renaissance*, and *Virginia Quarterly Review*. An internationally recognized authority on Henry David Thoreau, Meyer is a former president of the Thoreau Society and coauthor (with Walter Harding) of *The New Thoreau Handbook*, a standard reference source. His first book, *Several More Lives to Live: Thoreau's Political Reputation in America*, was awarded the Ralph Henry Gabriel Prize by the American Studies Association. He is also the editor of *Frederick Douglass: The Narrative and Selected Writings*. He has lectured on a variety of American literary topics from Cambridge University to Peking University. His other books for Bedford / St. Martin's include *The Bedford Introduction to Literature*, Eleventh Edition, *The Compact Bedford Introduction to Literature*, Eleventh Edition; *Thinking and Writing about Poetry*; *Poetry: An Introduction*, Seventh Edition; and *Thinking and Writing about Literature*, Second Edition.

Preface for Instructors

Like its predecessors, the third edition of *Literature to Go* assumes that reading and understanding literature offers a valuable means of apprehending life in its richness and diversity. This book also reflects the hope that its selections will inspire students to become lifelong readers of imaginative literature, as well as more thoughtful and skillful writers.

As before, the text is flexibly organized into four parts focusing on fiction, poetry, drama, and critical thinking and writing. The first three parts explain the literary elements of each genre and how to write about them. These three parts also explore several additional approaches to reading literature and conclude with an anthology of literary works. The fourth part provides detailed instruction on thinking, reading, and writing about literature that can be assigned selectively throughout the course. Sample student papers and hundreds of assignments appear in the text, offering students the support they need to read and write about literature.

Literature to Go accommodates many different teaching styles. New to the third edition are sixty-six carefully chosen stories, poems, and plays — as well as new art throughout the book.

FEATURES OF *LITERATURE TO GO*, THIRD EDITION

A wide and well-balanced selection of literature

39 stories, 209 poems, and 14 plays represent a variety of periods, nationalities, cultures, styles, and voices — from the serious to the humorous, and from the traditional to the contemporary. Each selection has been chosen for its appeal to students and for its effectiveness in demonstrating the elements, significance, and pleasures of literature. As in previous editions, canonical works by Ernest Hemingway, John Keats, Susan Glaspell, and many others are generously represented. In addition, there are many contemporary selections from well-regarded writers including Kay Ryan, Martín Espada, Lydia Davis, and David Ives.

Many options for teaching and learning about literature

In an effort to make literature come to life for students and the course a plea-sure to teach for instructors, *Literature to Go* offers these innovative features:

PERSPECTIVES ON LITERATURE   Intriguing documents — including critical essays, interviews, and contextual images — appear throughout the book to stimulate class discussion and writing.

CONNECTIONS BETWEEN "POPULAR" AND "LITERARY" CULTURE   The poetry and drama introductions incorporate examples from popular culture, effectively introducing students to the literary elements of a given genre through what they already know. For example, students are introduced to the elements of poetry through greeting card verse and to elements of drama through a television script from *Seinfeld*. Lively visuals throughout the anthology demonstrate how literature is woven into the fabric of popu-lar culture and art. These images help students recognize the imprint of lit-erature on their everyday lives.

CASE STUDIES THAT TREAT AUTHORS IN DEPTH Each genre section includes one or more chapters that focus closely on a major literary figure. Chapters on Flannery O'Connor, Dagoberto Gilb, Billy Collins, and William Shakespeare are complemented by bio-graphical introductions (with author photographs); critical perspectives; cultural documents (such as let-ters and draft manuscript pages); and a generous col-lection of images that serve to contextualize the works. A variety of critical thinking and writing questions follow the selections to stimulate student responses. All these supplementary materials engage students more fully with the writers and their works.

From Chapter 9: A Study of Flannery O'Connor
© Corbis.

Plenty of help with reading, writing, and research

CRITICAL READING*   Advice on how to read literature appears at the begin-ning of each genre section. Sample Close Readings of selections including Kate Chopin's "The Story of an Hour" (Fiction), William Hathaway's "Oh, Oh" (Poetry), and Susan Glaspell's *Trifles* (Drama) provide analyses of the lan-guage, images, and other literary elements at work in these selections. Interpre-tive annotations clearly show students the process of close reading and provide examples of the kind of critical thinking that leads to strong academic writing.

---

*A reference chart on the book's inside front cover outlines all of the book's help for read-ing and writing about literature.

Later in the book, Chapter 29, "Reading and the Writing Process," provides more instruction on how to read a work closely, annotate a text, take notes, keep a reading journal, and develop a topic into a thesis, with a section on arguing persuasively about literature. An Index of Terms appears at the back of the book, and a glossary provides thorough explanations of more than two hundred terms central to the study of literature.

THE WRITING AND RESEARCH PROCESS   Five chapters (29–33) cover every step of the writing process — from generating topics to documenting sources — while sample student papers model the results.

Of these chapters, three — "Writing about Fiction" (30), "Writing about Poetry" (31), and "Writing about Drama" (32) — focus on genre-specific writing assignments.

Five sample student papers — all with 2016 MLA-style documentation — model how to analyze and argue about literature and how to support ideas by citing examples. The papers are integrated throughout the book, as are "Questions for Writing" units that guide students through particular writing tasks: reading and writing responsively; developing a topic into a revised thesis; and writing about multiple works by an author.

Chapter 33, "The Literary Research Paper," offers detailed advice for finding, evaluating, and incorporating sources in a paper and includes current, detailed MLA documentation guidelines.

QUESTIONS FOR CRITICAL READING AND WRITING   Hundreds of questions and assignments — "Considerations for Critical Thinking and Writing," "Connections to Other Selections," "First Response" prompts, and "Creative Response" assignments — spark students' interest, sharpen their thinking, and improve their reading, discussion, and writing skills.

NEW TO THIS EDITION

66 classic and contemporary selections

10 STORIES, 52 POEMS, AND 4 PLAYS   representing canonical, multicultural, contemporary, and popular literature are new to this edition. Complementing the addition of several classic literary works are numerous stories, poems, and plays not

Wendy Wasserstein
Jack Mitchell / Getty Images.

frequently anthologized. These include stories by Gavin Ford Kovite, Geoff Wyss, and Lydia Davis; poems by Willa Cather, Seamus Heaney, and Martín Espada; and plays by Rich Orloff and Wendy Wasserstein. The stories, poems, and plays new to this edition are a rich collection of traditional, contemporary, and multicultural literature — works that will make classroom discussion come alive.

ACKNOWLEDGMENTS

This book has benefited from the ideas, suggestions, and corrections of scores of careful readers who helped transform various stages of an evolving manuscript into a finished book and into subsequent editions. I remain grateful to those I have thanked in previous prefaces, particularly the late Robert Wallace of Case Western Reserve University. In addition, many instructors who have used my anthologies responded to a questionnaire. For their valuable comments and advice, I am grateful to James Aubrey, Metropolitan State University of Denver; Eileen Baland, Mountain View College; Anita Baxter, Rowlett High School; Keri Bell, Harmony Public Schools; Miriam Bellis, University of Alabama at Birmingham; Mary Bradley, Eastern Florida State College; Janice Brantley, University of Arkansas at Pine Bluff; Akilah Brown, Santa Fe College; David Calonne, Eastern Michigan University; Denise Coulter, Atlantic Cape Community College; Jennifer Eble, Cleveland State Community College; Julie Gibson, Greenville Technical College; Dianna Hyde, Jefferson State Community College; Jennifer Jordan-Henley, Roane State Community College; Tamara Kuzmenkov, Tacoma Community College; Debbie Lelekis, Florida Institute of Technology; James Machor, Kansas State University; Debra Magai, Stuarts Draft High School; Diann Mason, Paris Junior College; James Minor, South Piedmont Community College; Paul Nagy, Clovis Community College; Troy Nordman, Butler Community College; Joe Payne, Centennial High School; David Pulling, Louisiana State University Eunice; Nancy Risch, Caldwell Community College and Technical Institute; Deborah Rosenthal, Massasoit Community College; Cathy Rusco, Muskegon Community College; Susan Saiter, Borough of Manhattan Community College, CUNY; Zahir Small, Santa Fe College; Joel Sperber, Seton Hall University; Susan Topping, Three Rivers Community College; John Valliere, Eastern Florida State College; Joette Waddle, Roane State Community College; Fontaine Wallace, Florida Institute of Technology; Rita Weeks, Spartanburg Community College; Jenny Williams, Spartanburg Community College; and Joyce Williams, University of Alabama at Birmingham.

I would also like to give special thanks to the following instructors who contributed teaching tips to *Resources for Teaching Literature to Go*: Sandra Adickes, Helen J. Aling, Sr. Anne Denise Brenann, Robin Calitri, James H. Clemmer, Robert Croft, Thomas Edwards, Elizabeth Kleinfeld, Olga Lyles, Timothy Peters, Catherine Rusco, Robert M. St. John, Richard Stoner, Nancy Veiga, Karla Walters, and Joseph Zeppetello.

I am also indebted to those who cheerfully answered questions and generously provided miscellaneous bits of information. What might have seemed to them like inconsequential conversations turned out to be important leads. Among these friends and colleagues are Raymond Anselment, Barbara Campbell, Ann Charters, Karen Chow, John Christie, Eleni Coundouriotis, Irving Cummings, William Curtin, Patrick Hogan, Lee Jacobus, Thomas Jambeck, Bonnie Januszewski-Ytuarte, Greta Little, George Monteiro, Brenda Murphy, Joel Myerson, Rose Quiello, Thomas Recchio, William Sheidley, Stephanie Smith, Milton Stern, Kenneth Wilson, and the dedicated reference librarians at the Homer Babbidge Library, University of Connecticut. I am particularly happy to acknowledge the tactful help of Roxanne Cody, owner of R. J. Julia Booksellers in Madison, Connecticut, whose passion for books authorizes her as the consummate matchmaker for writers, readers, and titles. It's a wonder that somebody doesn't call the cops.

I continue to be grateful for what I have learned from teaching my students and for the many student papers I have received over the years that I have used in various forms to serve as good and accessible models of student writing. I am also indebted to Valerie Duff-Strautmann for her extensive work on the third edition of *Resources for Teaching Literature to Go.*

At Bedford/St. Martin's, my debts once again require more time to acknowledge than the deadline allows. Charles H. Christensen and Joan E. Feinberg initiated this project and launched it with their intelligence, energy, and sound advice. This book has also benefited from the savvy insights of Denise Wydra, Edwin Hill, Vivian Garcia, Maura Shea, and Steve Scipione. Earlier editions of *The Bedford Introduction to Literature*, from which this book is adapted, were shaped by editors Karen Henry, Kathy Retan, Alanya Harter, Aron Keesbury, and Ellen Thibault; their work was as first rate as it was essential. As my development editor, Christina Gerogiannis expertly kept the book on track and made the journey a pleasure to the end; her valuable contributions richly remind me of how fortunate I am to be a Bedford/St. Martin's author. Cara Kaufman, assistant editor, gracefully handled a variety of editorial tasks. Permissions were deftly arranged by Kalina Ingham, Arthur Johnson, Martha Friedman, and Susan Doheny. The difficult tasks of production were skillfully managed by Deborah Baker, whose attention to details and deadlines was essential to the completion of this project. Arthur Johnson also provided careful copyediting, and Anne True did meticulous proofreading. I thank all of the people at Bedford/St. Martin's — including John Callahan, who designed the cover, and Sophia LaTorre-Zengierski, the marketing manager — who helped to make this formidable project a manageable one.

Finally, I am grateful to my sons Timothy and Matthew for all kinds of help, but mostly I'm just grateful they're my sons. And for making all the difference, I thank my wife, Regina Barreca.

— Michael Meyer

GET THE MOST OUT OF YOUR COURSE WITH *LITERATURE TO GO*

Literature to Go doesn't stop with a book. Bedford/St. Martin's offers resources that help you and your students get even more out of your book and course. You'll also find convenient instructor resources, and even a nationwide community of teachers. To learn more about or to order any of the following products, contact your Bedford/St. Martin's sales representative, or visit **macmillanlearning.com**.

Assign LaunchPad Solo for Literature — *the online, interactive, guide to close reading*

macmillanlearning.com

To get the most out of *Literature to Go*, assign it with *LaunchPad Solo for Literature*, which can be packaged at **a significant discount.** With easy-to-use and easy-to-assign modules, reading comprehension quizzes, and engaging author videos, *LaunchPad Solo for Literature* guides students through three common assignment types: responding to a reading, drawing connections between two or more texts, and instructor-led collaborative close reading. Get all of our great resources and activities in one fully customizable space online; then use our tools with your own content. To learn more about how you can use *LaunchPad Solo for Literature* in your course, please see pages xiv–xv of this Preface.

Package one of our best-selling brief handbooks at a discount

Do you need a pocket-sized handbook for your course? Package *Easy Writer* by Andrea Lunsford or *A Pocket Style Manual* by Diana Hacker and Nancy Sommers with this text at a 20% discount. For more information, go to **macmillanlearning.com**.

Teach longer works at a nice price

Volumes from our Literary Reprint series — the Case Studies in Contemporary Criticism series, Bedford Cultural Edition series, the Bedford Shakespeare series, and the Bedford College Editions — can be shrink-wrapped with *Literature to Go* at a discount. For a complete list of available titles, visit **macmillanlearning.com**.

Trade Up and save 50%

Add more value and choice to your students' learning experiences by packaging their Bedford/St. Martin's textbook with one of a thousand titles from our sister publishers, including Farrar, Straus and Giroux and St. Martin's Press — at a discount of 50% off the regular price. Visit **macmillanlearning.com** for details.

Access your instructor resources and get teaching ideas you can use today

Are you looking for professional resources for teaching literature and writing? How about some help with planning classroom activities?

REQUEST OR DOWNLOAD YOUR INSTRUCTOR'S MANUAL This comprehensive manual offers teaching support for every selection, useful for new and experienced instructors alike. Resources include commentaries, biographical information, and writing assignments, as well as teaching tips from instructors who have taught with the book, additional suggestions for connections among the selections, and thematic groupings with questions for discussion and writing. The manual is available in print and online at **macmillanlearning.com**.

JOIN OUR COMMUNITY The Macmillan English Community is home to Bedford/St. Martin's professional resources, featuring content to support the teaching of literature — including our popular blog, *LitBits*, as well as articles, research studies, and testimonials on the importance of literature in our classrooms and in our lives. Community members may also review projects and ideas in the pipeline. Join at **community.macmillan.com**.

ENGAGE YOUR STUDENTS WITH DIGITAL ASSIGNMENTS *Teaching Literature with Digital Technology* is a collection of digital assignments, each created by a contributor in the fields of literature and composition. Edited by Seattle-based scholar and teacher Tim Hetland and available as a print text or PDF e-book, this resource for instructors invites students to become knowledge-makers as it introduces creative uses of social media, digital tools, podcasts, multimodal assignments, and digital archives to learn about literature. Sample assignments can be viewed in the Professional Resources folder on the Macmillan English Community site. To order the print text, use ISBN: 978-1-4576-2948-8; to order the PDF e-book, use ISBN: 978-1-3190-7643-6.

ORDER CONTENT FOR YOUR COURSE MANAGEMENT SYSTEM Content cartridges for the most common course management systems — Blackboard, Canvas, Angel, Moodle, Sakai, and Desire2Learn — allow you to easily download Bedford/St. Martin's digital materials for your course. For more information, visit **macmillanlearning.com**.

LaunchPad Solo
macmillan learning

PAIRING *LITERATURE TO GO* WITH *LAUNCHPAD SOLO FOR LITERATURE* HELPS STUDENTS SUCCEED.

Available for free when packaged with *Literature to Go*, *LaunchPad Solo for Literature* gets to the heart of close reading. It offers a set of online materials that help beginning literature students learn and practice close reading and critical thinking skills in an interactive environment.

To package *LaunchPad Solo for Literature*, use ISBN 978-1-319-07714-3.

How can LaunchPad Solo for Literature *enhance your course?*

IT HELPS STUDENTS COME PREPARED TO CLASS   Assign one of almost 500 reading comprehension quizzes on commonly taught stories, poems, plays, and essays to ensure that your students complete and understand their reading. For homework assignments, have students work through close reading modules that will prepare them for lively, informed classroom discussions.

IT GIVES STUDENTS HANDS-ON PRACTICE IN CLOSE READING   Easy-to-use and easy-to-assign modules based on widely taught literary selections guide students through three common assignment types:

- **Respond to a Reading**
  Marginal questions that refer to specific passages in a publisher-provided literary work prompt students to read carefully and think critically about key issues raised by the text.

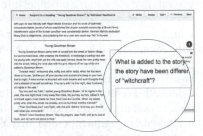

- **Draw Connections**
  Students read and compare two or more publisher-provided texts that illuminate each other. Students can download these texts, which have been annotated to highlight key moments and

To explore *LaunchPad Solo for Literature*,
visit **macmillanhighered.com/launchpadsolo/literature**.

contextual information, and respond in writing to a series of questions that highlight important similarities and differences between and among the texts.

- *Collaborate on a Reading*
Instructors can upload their favorite text or choose from over 200 publisher-provided texts to create a customized lesson on close reading. Using the highlighting tools and Notes feature in LaunchPad, the instructor can post notes or questions about specific passages or issues in a text, prompting students to respond with their own comments, questions, or observations. Students can also respond to each other, further collaborating and deepening their understanding of a text.

IT LETS YOU CREATE MULTIMEDIA ASSIGNMENTS ABOUT LITERATURE *LaunchPad Solo for Literature* enables you to embed videos, including favorite selections from YouTube, directly into your digital course. Whether you want students to analyze a Shakespearean scene, listen to W. B. Yeats reading his poems, or compare *The Great Gatsby* in print and on film, the tools are at your fingertips. You can annotate these videos for your students, or ask them to leave their own comments directly on the video content itself. Consider some of these assignment suggestions:

- *Create a Dialogue around an Assignment*
Some projects are complicated because they involve many choices and stages. Record yourself explaining the project, and upload the video to the Video Assignment tool. Require students to comment by asking a question or by proposing a topic.

- *Critique a Video as a Group*
Embed a video from YouTube or from another source. In your assignment instructions, provide discussion questions. Require students to add 2–3 comments on the video that respond to the prompt. You may grade this assignment with a rubric.

- *Collaborate on Acting out a Scene from a Play*
Although students most often study plays as written texts, it can be fun and informative to have them act out scenes for their classmates. Assign small groups of students to record themselves acting out their favorite scene from a play and upload the video for the class to watch. You can add your feedback and comments directly on the video.

- *Compare and Share Poems Your Students Read Aloud*
  Sound is essential in poetry, and how a poem is read can be as important to understanding as the words themselves. Invite students to record themselves — either using video, or audio only — and share the results with the class. Consider giving each student a "mood" for their reading, so that the class can hear how different tones and interpretations affect their response to the poem.

Brief Contents

Contents

A Collection of Stories   **293**

POETRY   **319**

The Elements of Poetry   **321**

16. Symbol, Allegory, and Irony   411

22. A Thematic Case Study: The World of Work   522

A Collection of Poems   **531**

23. Poems for Further Reading   533

DRAMA   559

The Study of Drama   561

24. Reading Drama   563

Reading Drama Responsively   563

Susan Glaspell • TRIFLES   565

Did Mrs. Wright kill her husband? While the men investigate, Mrs. Peters and Mrs. Hale reach their own conclusions.

A SAMPLE CLOSE READING
An Annotated Section of Trifles   575

Elements of Drama   577

Joan Ackermann • QUIET TORRENTIAL SOUND   581

Two sisters in their thirties order at a café: one a hot fudge sundae and a Coke, the other a decaf. In short order, the conversation turns to appetites.

Drama in Popular Forms   588

CRITICAL THINKING AND WRITING   853

Introduction

Reading
Imaginative Literature

To seek the source, the impulse of a
story is like tearing a flower to pieces
for wantonness.

— KATE CHOPIN

THE NATURE OF LITERATURE

Literature does not lend itself to a single tidy definition because the making of it over the centuries has been as complex, unwieldy, and natural as life itself. Is literature everything that has been written, from ancient prayers to graffiti? Does it include songs and stories that were not written down until many years after they were recited? Does literature include the television scripts from *Modern Family* as well as Shakespeare's *King Lear*? Is literature only writing that has permanent value and continues to move people? Must literature be true or beautiful or moral? Should it be socially useful?

Although these kinds of questions are not conclusively answered in this book, they are implicitly raised by the stories, poems, and plays included here. No definition of literature, particularly a brief one, is likely to satisfy everyone because definitions tend to weaken and require qualification when confronted by the uniqueness of individual works. In this context it is worth recalling Herman Melville's humorous use of a definition of a whale in *Moby-Dick* (1851). In the course of the novel

1

Melville presents his imaginative and symbolic whale as inscrutable, but he begins with a quotation from Georges Cuvier, a French naturalist who defines a whale in his nineteenth-century study *The Animal Kingdom* this way: "The whale is a mammiferous animal without hind feet." Cuvier's description is technically correct, of course, but there is little wisdom in it. Melville understood that the reality of the whale (which he describes as the "ungraspable phantom of life") cannot be caught by isolated facts. If the full meaning of the whale is to be understood, it must be sought on the open sea of experience, where the whale itself is, rather than in exclusionary definitions. Facts and definitions are helpful; however, they do not always reveal the whole truth.

Despite Melville's reminder that a definition can be too limiting and even comical, it is useful for our purposes to describe literature as a fiction consisting of carefully arranged words designed to stir the imagination. Stories, poems, and plays are fictional. They are made up — imagined — even when based on actual historic events. Such imaginative writing differs from other kinds of writing because its purpose is not primarily to transmit facts or ideas. Imaginative literature is a source more of pleasure than of information, and we read it for basically the same reasons we listen to music or view a dance: enjoyment, delight, and satisfaction. Like other art forms, imaginative literature offers pleasure and usually attempts to convey a perspective, mood, feeling, or experience. Writers transform the facts the world provides — people, places, and objects — into experiences that suggest meanings.

Consider, for example, the difference between the following factual description of a snake and a poem on the same subject. Here is *Webster's Eleventh New Collegiate Dictionary's* definition:

> any of numerous limbless scaled reptiles (suborder Serpentes syn. Ophidia) with a long tapering body and with salivary glands often modified to produce venom which is injected through grooved or tubular fangs.

Contrast this matter-of-fact definition with Emily Dickinson's poetic evocation of a snake in "A narrow Fellow in the Grass":

A narrow Fellow in the Grass
Occasionally rides —
You may have met Him — did you not
His notice sudden is —

The Grass divides as with a Comb —   5
A spotted shaft is seen —
And then it closes at your feet
And opens further on —

He likes a Boggy Acre
A floor too cool for Corn —   10

Yet when a Boy, and Barefoot —
I more than once at Noon

Have passed, I thought, a Whip lash
Unbraiding in the Sun
When stooping to secure it   15
It wrinkled, and was gone —

Several of Nature's People
I know, and they know me —
I feel for them a transport
Of cordiality —   20

But never met this Fellow
Attended, or alone
Without a tighter breathing
And Zero at the Bone —

The dictionary provides a succinct, anatomical description of what a snake is, while Dickinson's poem suggests what a snake can mean. The definition offers facts; the poem offers an experience. The dictionary would probably allow someone who had never seen a snake to sketch one with reasonable accuracy. The poem also provides some vivid subjective descriptions — for example, the snake dividing the grass "as with a Comb" — yet it offers more than a picture of serpentine movements. The poem conveys the ambivalence many people have about snakes — the kind of feeling, for example, so evident on the faces of visitors viewing the snakes at a zoo. In the poem there is both a fascination with and a horror of what might be called snakehood; this combination of feelings has been coiled in most of us since Adam and Eve.

A good deal more could be said about the numbing fear that undercuts the affection for nature at the beginning of this poem, but the point here is that imaginative literature gives us not so much the full, factual proportions of the world as some of its experiences and meanings. Instead of defining the world, literature encourages us to try it out in our imaginations.

THE VALUE OF LITERATURE

Mark Twain once shrewdly observed that a person who chooses not to read has no advantage over a person who is unable to read. In industrialized societies today, however, the question is not who reads, because nearly everyone can and does, but what is read. Why should anyone spend precious time with literature when there is so much reading material available that provides useful information about everything from the daily news to personal computers? Why should a literary artist's imagination compete for attention that could be spent on the firm realities that constitute everyday life? In fact, national best-seller lists much less often include collections of stories, poems, or plays than they do cookbooks and, not surprisingly, diet books. Although such fare may be filling, it doesn't stay with you. Most people have other appetites too.

Certainly one of the most important values of literature is that it nourishes our emotional lives. An effective literary work may seem to speak directly to us, especially if we are ripe for it. The inner life that good writers reveal in their characters often gives us glimpses of some portion of ourselves. We can be moved to laugh, cry, tremble, dream, ponder, shriek, or rage with a character by simply turning a page instead of turning our lives upside down. Although the experience itself is imagined, the emotion is real. That's why the final chapters of a good adventure novel can make a reader's heart race as much as a 100-yard dash or why the repressed love of Hester Prynne in *The Scarlet Letter* by Nathaniel Hawthorne is painful to a sympathetic reader. Human emotions speak a universal language regardless of when or where a work was written.

In addition to appealing to our emotions, literature broadens our perspectives on the world. Most of the people we meet are pretty much like ourselves, and what we can see of the world even in a lifetime is astonishingly limited. Literature allows us to move beyond the inevitable boundaries of our own lives and culture because it introduces us to people different from ourselves, places remote from our neighborhoods, and times other than our own. Reading makes us more aware of life's possibilities as well as its subtleties and ambiguities. Put simply, people who read literature experience more life and have a keener sense of a common human identity than those who do not. It is true, of course, that many people go through life without reading imaginative literature, but that is a loss rather than a gain. They may find themselves troubled by the same kinds of questions that reveal Daisy Buchanan's restless, vague discontentment in F. Scott Fitzgerald's *The Great Gatsby*: "What'll we do with ourselves this afternoon?" cried Daisy, "and the day after that, and the next thirty years?"

Sometimes students mistakenly associate literature more with school than with life. Accustomed to reading it in order to write a paper or pass an examination, students may perceive such reading as a chore instead of a pleasurable opportunity, something considerably less important than studying for the "practical" courses that prepare them for a career. The study of literature, however, is also practical because it engages you in the kinds of problem solving of vital importance in a variety of fields of study, from philosophy to science and technology. The interpretation of literary texts requires you to deal with uncertainties, value judgments, and emotions; these are unavoidable aspects of life.

People who make the most significant contributions to their professions — whether in business, engineering, teaching, or some other area — tend to be challenged rather than threatened by multiple possibilities. Instead of retreating to the way things have always been done, they bring freshness and creativity to their work. F. Scott Fitzgerald once astutely described the "test of a first-rate intelligence" as "the ability to hold two opposed ideas in the mind at the same time, and still retain the ability to function." People with such intelligence know how to read situations, shape questions, interpret details, and evaluate competing points of view. Equipped with a healthy respect for facts, they also understand the value of pursuing hunches and exercising their imaginations. Reading literature encourages a suppleness of mind that is helpful in any discipline or work.

Once the requirements for your degree are completed, what ultimately matters are not the courses listed on your transcript but the sensibilities and habits of mind that you bring to your work, friends, family, and, indeed, the rest of your life. A healthy economy changes and grows with the times; people do too if they are prepared for more than simply filling a job description. The range and variety of life that literature affords can help you to interpret your own experiences and the world in which you live.

To discover the insights that literature reveals requires careful reading and sensitivity. One of the purposes of a college introduction to literature class is to cultivate the analytic skills necessary for reading well. Class discussions often help establish a dialogue with a work that perhaps otherwise would not speak to you. Analytic skills can also be developed by writing about what you read. Writing is an effective means of clarifying your responses and ideas because it requires you to account for the author's use of language as well as your own. This book is based on two premises: that reading literature is pleasurable and that reading and understanding a work sensitively by thinking, talking, or writing about it increases the pleasure of the experience of it.

Understanding its basic elements — such as point of view, symbol, theme, tone, irony, and so on — is a prerequisite to an informed appreciation of literature. This kind of understanding allows you to perceive more in a literary work in much the same way that a spectator at a tennis match sees more if he or she understands the rules and conventions of the game. But literature is not simply a spectator sport. The analytic skills that open up literature also have their uses when you watch a television program or film and, more important, when you attempt to sort out the significance of the people, places, and events that constitute your own life. Literature enhances and sharpens your perceptions. What could be more lastingly practical as well as satisfying?

THE CHANGING LITERARY CANON

Perhaps the best reading creates some kind of change in us: we see more clearly; we're alert to nuances; we ask questions that previously didn't occur to us. Henry David Thoreau had that sort of reading in mind when he remarked in *Walden* that the books he valued most were those that caused him to date "a new era in his life from the reading." Readers are sometimes changed by literature, but it is also worth noting that the life of a literary work can also be affected by its readers. Melville's *Moby-Dick*, for example, was not valued as a classic until the 1920s, when critics rescued the novel from the obscurity of being cataloged in many libraries (including Yale's) not under fiction but under cetology, the study of whales. Indeed, many writers contemporary to Melville who were important and popular in the nineteenth century — William Cullen Bryant, Henry Wadsworth Longfellow, and James Russell Lowell, to name a few — are now mostly unread; their names appear more often on elementary schools built early in the twentieth century than in anthologies. Clearly, literary reputations and what is valued as great literature change over time and in the eyes of readers.

Such changes have steadily accelerated as the literary *canon* — those works considered by scholars, critics, and teachers to be the most important to read and study — has undergone a significant series of shifts. Writers who previously were overlooked, undervalued, neglected, or studiously ignored have been brought into focus in an effort to create a more diverse literary canon, one that recognizes the contributions of the many cultures that make up American society. Since the 1960s, for example, some critics have reassessed writings by women who had been left out of the standard literary traditions dominated by male writers. Many more female writers are now read alongside the male writers who traditionally populated literary history. Hence, a reader of Mark Twain and Stephen Crane is now just as likely to encounter Kate Chopin in a literary anthology. Until fairly recently Chopin was mostly regarded as a minor local colorist of Louisiana life. In the 1960s, however, the feminist movement helped to establish her present reputation as a significant voice in American literature owing to the feminist concerns so compellingly articulated by her female characters. This kind of enlargement of the canon also resulted from another reform movement of the 1960s. The civil rights movement sensitized literary critics to the political, moral, and esthetic necessity of rediscovering African American literature, and more recently Asian and Hispanic writers have been making their way into the canon. Moreover, on a broader scale the canon is being revised and enlarged to include the works of writers from parts of the world other than the West, a development that reflects the changing values, concerns, and complexities of recent decades, when literary landscapes have shifted as dramatically as the political boundaries of much of the world.

No semester's reading list — or anthology — can adequately or accurately echo all the new voices competing to be heard as part of the mainstream literary canon, but recent efforts to open up the canon attempt to sensitize readers to the voices of women, minorities, and writers from all over the world. This development has not occurred without its urgent advocates or passionate dissenters. It's no surprise that issues about race, gender, and class often get people off the fence and on their feet. Although what we regard as literature — whether it's called great, classic, or canonical — continues to generate debate, there is no question that such controversy will continue to reflect readers' values as well as the writers they admire.

FICTION

The Elements
of Fiction

1

Reading Fiction

You don't find out you're an artist because you do something really well. You find out you're an artist because when you fail you have something within you — strength or belief or just craziness — that picks you back up again.

— JUNOT DÍAZ

© Scott Lituchy/Star Ledger/
Corbis.

READING FICTION RESPONSIVELY

Reading a literary work responsively can be an intensely demanding activity. Henry David Thoreau — about as intense and demanding a reader and writer as they come — insists that "books must be read as deliberately and reservedly as they were written." Thoreau is right about the necessity for a conscious, sustained involvement with a literary work. Imaginative literature does demand more from us than, say, browsing through *People* magazine in a dentist's waiting room, but Thoreau makes the process sound a little more daunting than it really is. For when we respond to the demands of responsive reading, our efforts are usually rewarded with pleasure as well as understanding. Careful, deliberate reading — the kind that engages a reader's imagination as it calls forth the writer's — is a means of exploration that can take a reader outside whatever circumstance or experience previously defined his or her world. Just as we respond moment by moment to people and situations in our lives, we also respond to literary works as we read them, though we may not be fully aware of how we are affected at each point along the way. The more

13

conscious we are of how and why we respond to works in particular ways, the more likely we are to be imaginatively engaged in our reading.

In a very real sense both the reader and the author create the literary work. How a reader responds to a story, poem, or play will help to determine its meaning. The author arranges the various elements that constitute his or her craft — elements such as plot, character, setting, point of view, symbolism, theme, and style, which you will be examining in subsequent chapters and which are defined in the Glossary of Literary Terms (p. 915) — but the author cannot completely control the reader's response any more than a person can absolutely predict how a remark or action will be received by a stranger, a friend, or even a family member. Few authors *tell* readers how to respond. Our sympathy, anger, confusion, laughter, sadness, or whatever the feeling might be is left up to us to experience. Writers may have the talent to evoke such feelings, but they don't have the power and authority to enforce them. Because of the range of possible responses produced by imaginative literature, there is no single, correct, definitive response or interpretation. There can be readings that are wrongheaded or foolish, and some readings are better than others — that is, more responsive to a work's details and more persuasive — but that doesn't mean there is only one possible reading of a work.

Experience tells us that different people respond differently to the same work. Consider, for example, how often you've heard Melville's *Moby-Dick* described as one of the greatest American novels. This, however, is how a reviewer in *New Monthly Magazine* described the book when it was published in 1851: it is "a huge dose of hyperbolical slang, maudlin sentimentalism, and tragi-comic bubble and squeak." Melville surely did not intend or desire this response; but there it is, and it was not a singular, isolated reaction. This reading — like any reading — was influenced by the values, assumptions, and expectations that the readers brought to the novel from both previous readings and life experiences. The reviewer's refusal to take the book seriously may have caused him to miss the boat from the perspective of many other readers of *Moby-Dick*, but it indicates that even "classics" (perhaps especially those kinds of works) can generate disparate readings.

Consider the following brief story by Kate Chopin, a writer whose fiction (like Melville's) sometimes met with indifference or hostility in her own time. As you read, keep track of your responses to the central character, Mrs. Mallard. Write down your feelings about her in a substantial paragraph when you finish the story. Think, for example, about how you respond to the emotions she expresses concerning news of her husband's death. What do you think of her feelings about marriage? Do you think you would react the way she does under similar circumstances?

KATE CHOPIN (1851–1904)

The Story of an Hour 1894

Missouri Historical Society, St. Louis.

Knowing that Mrs. Mallard was afflicted with a heart trouble, great care was taken to break to her as gently as possible the news of her husband's death.

It was her sister Josephine who told her, in broken sentences; veiled hints that revealed in half concealing. Her husband's friend Richards was there, too, near her. It was he who had been in the newspaper office when intelligence of the railroad disaster was received, with Brently Mallard's name leading the list of "killed." He had only taken the time to assure himself of its truth by a second telegram, and had hastened to forestall any less careful, less tender friend in bearing the sad message.

She did not hear the story as many women have heard the same, with a paralyzed inability to accept its significance. She wept at once, with sudden, wild abandonment, in her sister's arms. When the storm of grief had spent itself she went away to her room alone. She would have no one follow her.

There stood, facing the open window, a comfortable, roomy armchair. Into this she sank, pressed down by a physical exhaustion that haunted her body and seemed to reach into her soul.

She could see in the open square before her house the tops of trees that 5 were all aquiver with the new spring life. The delicious breath of rain was in the air. In the street below a peddler was crying his wares. The notes of a distant song which some one was singing reached her faintly, and countless sparrows were twittering in the eaves.

There were patches of blue sky showing here and there through the clouds that had met and piled one above the other in the west facing her window.

She sat with her head thrown back upon the cushion of the chair, quite motionless, except when a sob came up into her throat and shook her, as a child who has cried itself to sleep continues to sob in its dreams.

She was young, with a fair, calm face, whose lines bespoke repression and even a certain strength. But now there was a dull stare in her eyes, whose gaze was fixed away off yonder on one of those patches of blue sky. It was not a glance of reflection, but rather indicated a suspension of intelligent thought.

There was something coming to her and she was waiting for it, fearfully. What was it? She did not know; it was too subtle and elusive to name. But she felt it, creeping out of the sky, reaching toward her through the sounds, the scents, the color that filled the air.

Now her bosom rose and fell tumultuously. She was beginning to recog- 10 nize this thing that was approaching to possess her, and she was striving to beat it back with her will—as powerless as her two white slender hands would have been.

When she abandoned herself a little whispered word escaped her slightly parted lips. She said it over and over under her breath: "free, free, free!" The vacant stare and the look of terror that had followed it went from her eyes. They stayed keen and bright. Her pulses beat fast, and the coursing blood warmed and relaxed every inch of her body.

She did not stop to ask if it were or were not a monstrous joy that held her. A clear and exalted perception enabled her to dismiss the suggestion as trivial.

She knew that she would weep again when she saw the kind, tender hands folded in death; the face that had never looked save with love upon her, fixed and gray and dead. But she saw beyond that bitter moment a long procession of years to come that would belong to her absolutely. And she opened and spread her arms out to them in welcome.

There would be no one to live for her during those coming years; she would live for herself. There would be no powerful will bending hers in that blind persistence with which men and women believe they have a right to impose a private will upon a fellow-creature. A kind intention or a cruel intention made the act seem no less a crime as she looked upon it in that brief moment of illumination.

And yet she had loved him — sometimes. Often she had not. What did 15 it matter! What could love, the unsolved mystery, count for in face of this possession of self-assertion which she suddenly recognized as the strongest impulse of her being!

"Free! Body and soul free!" she kept whispering.

Josephine was kneeling before the closed door with her lips to the keyhole, imploring for admission. "Louise, open the door! I beg; open the door — you will make yourself ill. What are you doing, Louise? For heaven's sake open the door."

"Go away. I am not making myself ill." No; she was drinking in a very elixir of life through that open window.

Her fancy was running riot along those days ahead of her. Spring days, and summer days, and all sorts of days that would be her own. She breathed a quick prayer that life might be long. It was only yesterday she had thought with a shudder that life might be long.

She arose at length and opened the door to her sister's importunities. 20 There was a feverish triumph in her eyes, and she carried herself unwittingly like a goddess of Victory. She clasped her sister's waist, and together they descended the stairs. Richards stood waiting for them at the bottom.

Some one was opening the front door with a latchkey. It was Brently Mallard who entered, a little travel-stained, composedly carrying his gripsack and umbrella. He had been far from the scene of accident, and did not even know there had been one. He stood amazed at Josephine's piercing cry; at Richards' quick motion to screen him from the view of his wife.

But Richards was too late.

When the doctors came they said she had died of heart disease — of joy that kills.

A SAMPLE CLOSE READING

An Annotated Section of "The Story of an Hour"

Even as you read a story for the first time, you can highlight passages, circle or underline words, and write responses in the margins. Subsequent readings will yield more insights once you begin to understand how various elements such as plot, characterization, and wording build toward the conclusion and what you perceive to be the story's central ideas. The following annotations for the first eleven paragraphs of "The Story of an Hour" provide a perspective written by someone who had read the work several times. Your own approach might, of course, be quite different — as the sample paper that follows the annotated passage amply demonstrates.

KATE CHOPIN (1851–1904)

The Story of an Hour   1894

> The title could point to the brevity of the story — only 23 short paragraphs — or to the decisive nature of what happens in a very short period of time. Or both.

Knowing that Mrs. Mallard was afflicted with a heart trouble, great care was taken to break to her as gently as possible the news of her husband's death.

> Mrs. Mallard's first name (Louise) is not given until paragraph 17, yet her sister Josephine is named immediately. This emphasizes Mrs. Mallard's married identity.

It was her sister Josephine who told her, in broken sentences; veiled hints that revealed in half concealing. Her husband's friend Richards was there, too, near her. It was he who had been in the newspaper office when intelligence of the railroad disaster was received, with Brently Mallard's name leading the list of "killed." He had only taken the time to assure himself of its truth by a second telegram, and had hastened to forestall any less careful, less tender friend in bearing the sad message.

> Given the nature of the cause of Mrs. Mallard's death at the story's end, it's worth noting the ambiguous description that she "was afflicted with a heart trouble." Is this one of Chopin's (rather than Josephine's) "veiled hints"?

She did not hear the story as many women have heard the same, with a paralyzed inability to accept its significance. She wept at once, with sudden, wild abandonment, in her sister's arms. When the storm of grief had spent itself she went away to her room alone. She would have no one follow her.

> When Mrs. Mallard weeps with "wild abandonment," the reader is again confronted with an ambiguous phrase: she grieves in an overwhelming manner yet seems to express relief at being abandoned by Brently's death.

There stood, facing the open window, a comfortable, roomy armchair. Into this she sank, pressed down by a physical exhaustion that haunted her body and seemed to reach into her soul.

She could see in the open square before her house the 5
tops of trees that were all aquiver with the new spring life. The delicious breath of rain was in the air. In the street below a peddler was crying his wares. The notes of a distant song which some one was singing reached her faintly, and countless sparrows were twittering in the eaves.

> These 3 paragraphs create an increasingly "open" atmosphere that leads to the "delicious" outside where there are inviting sounds and "patches of blue sky."

There's a definite tension between the inside and outside worlds.

Though still stunned by grief, Mrs. Mallard begins to feel a change come over her owing to her growing awareness of a world outside her room. What that change is remains "too subtle and elusive to name."

Mrs. Mallard's conflicted struggle is described in passionate, physical terms as if she is "possess[ed]" by a lover she is "powerless" to resist.

Once she has "abandoned" herself (see the "abandonment" in paragraph 3), the reader realizes that her love is to be "free, free, free." Her recognition is evident in the "coursing blood [that] warmed and relaxed every inch of her body."

There were patches of blue sky showing here and there through the clouds that had met and piled one above the other in the west facing her window.

She sat with her head thrown back upon the cushion of the chair, quite motionless, except when a sob came up into her throat and shook her, as a child who has cried itself to sleep continues to sob in its dreams.

She was young, with a fair, calm face, whose lines bespoke repression and even a certain strength. But now there was a dull stare in her eyes, whose gaze was fixed away off yonder on one of those patches of blue sky. It was not a glance of reflection, but rather indicated a suspension of intelligent thought.

There was something coming to her and she was waiting for it, fearfully. What was it? She did not know; it was too subtle and elusive to name. But she felt it, creeping out of the sky, reaching toward her through the sounds, the scents, the color that filled the air.

Now her bosom rose and fell tumultuously. She was 10
beginning to recognize this thing that was approaching to possess her, and she was striving to beat it back with her will — as powerless as her two white slender hands would have been.

When she abandoned herself a little whispered word escaped her slightly parted lips. She said it over and over under her breath: "free, free, free!" The vacant stare and the look of terror that had followed it went from her eyes. They stayed keen and bright. Her pulses beat fast, and the coursing blood warmed and relaxed every inch of her body. . . .

Do you find Mrs. Mallard a sympathetic character? Some readers think that she is callous, selfish, and unnatural — even monstrous — because she ecstatically revels in her newly discovered sense of freedom so soon after learning of her husband's presumed death. Others read her as a victim of her inability to control her own life in a repressive, male-dominated society. Is it possible to hold both views simultaneously, or are they mutually exclusive? Are your views in any way influenced by your being male or female? Does your age affect your perception? What about your social and economic background? Does your nationality, race, or religion in any way shape your attitudes? Do you have particular views about the institution of marriage that inform your assessment of Mrs. Mallard's character? Have other reading experiences — perhaps a familiarity with some of Chopin's other stories — predisposed you one way or another to Mrs. Mallard?

Understanding potential influences might be useful in determining whether a particular response to Mrs. Mallard is based primarily on the story's details and their arrangement or on an overt or a subtle bias that is brought to the story. If you unconsciously project your beliefs and assumptions onto a literary work, you run the risk of distorting it to accommodate your prejudice. Your feelings can be a reliable guide to interpretation, but you should be aware of what those feelings are based on.

Often specific questions about literary works cannot be answered definitively. For example, Chopin does not explain why Mrs. Mallard suffers a heart attack at the end of this story. Is the shock of seeing her "dead" husband simply too much for this woman "afflicted with a heart trouble"? Does she die of what the doctors call a "joy that kills" because she is so glad to see her husband? Is she so profoundly guilty about feeling "free" at her husband's expense that she has a heart attack? Is her death a kind of willed suicide in reaction to her loss of freedom? Your answers to these questions will depend on which details you emphasize in your interpretation of the story and the kinds of perspectives and values you bring to it. If, for example, you read the story from a feminist perspective, you would be likely to pay close attention to Chopin's comments about marriage in paragraph 14. Or if you read the story as an oblique attack on the insensitivity of physicians of the period, you might want to find out whether Chopin wrote elsewhere about doctors (she did) and compare her comments with historic sources.

Reading responsively makes you an active participant in the process of creating meaning in a literary work. The experience that you and the author create will most likely not be identical to another reader's encounter with the same work, but then that's true of nearly any experience you'll have, and it is part of the pleasure of reading. Indeed, talking and writing about literature is a way of sharing responses so that they can be enriched and deepened.

A SAMPLE PAPER

Differences in Responses to Kate Chopin's "The Story of an Hour"

The following paper was written in response to an assignment that called for a three- to four-page discussion of how different readers might interpret Mrs. Mallard's character.

Villa 1

Wally Villa
Professor Brian
English 210
12 January 2016

Differences in Responses to
Kate Chopin's "The Story of an Hour"

Kate Chopin's "The Story of an Hour" appears merely to explore a woman's unpredictable reaction to her husband's assumed death and reappearance, but actually Chopin offers Mrs. Mallard's bizarre story to reveal problems that are inherent in the institution of marriage. By offering this depiction of a marriage that stifles the woman to the point that she celebrates the death of her kind and loving husband, Chopin challenges her readers to examine their own views of marriage and relationships between men and women. Each reader's judgment of Mrs. Mallard and her behavior inevitably stems from his or her own personal feelings about marriage and the influences of societal expectations. Readers of differing genders, ages, and marital experiences are, therefore, likely to react differently to Chopin's startling portrayal of the Mallards' marriage, and that certainly is true of my response to the story compared to my father's and grandmother's responses.

Marriage often establishes boundaries between people that make them unable to communicate with each other. The Mallards' marriage was evidently crippled by both their inability to talk to one another and Mrs. Mallard's conviction that her marriage was defined by a "powerful will bending hers in that blind persistence with which men and women believe they have a right to impose a private will upon a fellow-creature" (16). Yet she does not recognize that it is not just men who impose their will upon women and that the problems inherent in marriage affect men and women equally. To me, Mrs. Mallard is a somewhat sympathetic character, and I appreciate her longing to live out the "years to come that would belong to her absolutely" (16). However, I also believe that she could have tried to improve her own situation somehow, either by reaching out to her husband or by abandoning the marriage altogether. Chopin uses Mrs. Mallard's tragedy to illuminate aspects of marriage that are harmful and, in this case, even deadly. Perhaps the Mallards' relationship should be taken as a warning to others: sacrificing one's own

[margin notes:]

Thesis providing writer's interpretation of story's purpose

Introduction setting up other reader responses discussed later in paper

Analysis of story's portrayal of marriage, with textual evidence

Analysis of character and plot, connecting with story's purpose

Villa 2

happiness in order to satisfy societal expectations can poison one's life and even
destroy entire families.

When my father read "The Story of an Hour," his reaction to Mrs. Mallard
was more antagonistic than my own. He sees Chopin's story as a timeless
"battle of the sexes," serving as further proof that men will never really be able
to understand what it is that women want. Mrs. Mallard endures an obviously
unsatisfying marriage without ever explaining to her husband that she feels
trapped and unfulfilled. Mrs. Mallard dismisses the question of whether or
not she is experiencing a "monstrous joy" (16) as trivial, but my father does
not think that this is a trivial question. He believes Mrs. Mallard is guilty of a
monstrous joy because she selfishly celebrates the death of her husband without
ever having allowed him the opportunity to understand her feelings. He believes
that, above all, Brently Mallard should be seen as the most victimized character
in the story. Mr. Mallard is a good, kind man, with friends who care about him
and a marriage that he thinks he can depend on. He "never looked save with
love" (16) upon his wife, his only "crime" (16) was his presence in the house,
and yet he is the one who is bereaved at the end of the story, for reasons he
will never understand. Mrs. Mallard's passion for her newly discovered freedom is
perhaps understandable, but according to my father, Mr. Mallard is the character
most deserving of sympathy.

> Contrasting summary and analysis of another reader's response

Maybe not surprisingly, my grandmother's interpretation of "The Story
of an Hour" was radically different from both mine and my father's. My
grandmother was married in 1936 and widowed in 1959 and therefore can
identify with Chopin's characters, who live at the turn of the twentieth century.
Her first reaction, aside from her unwavering support for Mrs. Mallard and her
predicament, was that this story demonstrates the differences between the
ways men and women related to each other a century ago and the way they
relate today. Unlike my father, who thinks Mrs. Mallard is too passive, my
grandmother believes that Mrs. Mallard doesn't even know that she is feeling
repressed until after she is told that Brently is dead. In 1894, divorce was so
scandalous and stigmatized that it simply wouldn't have been an option for
Mrs. Mallard, and so her only way out of the marriage would have been one

> Contrasting summary and analysis of another reader's response

> Cultural and historical background providing context for response and story itself

Villa 3

of their deaths. Being relatively young, Mrs. Mallard probably considered herself doomed to a long life in an unhappy marriage. My grandmother also feels that, in spite of all we know of Mrs. Mallard's feelings about her husband and her marriage, she still manages to live up to everyone's expectations of her as a woman both in life and in death. She is a dutiful wife to Brently, as she is expected to be. She weeps "with sudden, wild abandonment" when she hears the news of his death; she locks herself in her room to cope with her new situation, and she has a fatal heart attack upon seeing her husband arrive home. Naturally the male doctors would think that she died of the "joy that kills" (16)—nobody could have guessed that she was unhappy with her life, and she would never have wanted them to know.

Analysis supported with textual evidence

Interpretations of "The Story of an Hour" seem to vary according to the gender, age, and experience of the reader. While both male and female readers can certainly sympathize with Mrs. Mallard's plight, female readers—as was evident in our class discussions—seem to relate more easily to her predicament and more quickly exonerate her of any responsibility for her unhappy situation. Conversely, male readers are more likely to feel compassion for Mr. Mallard, who loses his wife for reasons that will always remain entirely unknown to him. Older readers probably understand more readily the strength of social forces and the difficulty of trying to deny societal expectations concerning gender roles in general and marriage in particular. Younger readers seem to feel that Mrs. Mallard is too passive and that she could have improved her domestic life immeasurably if she had taken the initiative to either improve or end her relationship with her husband. Ultimately, how each individual reader responds to Mrs. Mallard's story reveals his or her own ideas about marriage, society, and how men and women communicate with each other.

Conclusion summarizing reader responses explored in the paper

Villa 4

Work Cited

Chopin, Kate. "The Story of an Hour." *Literature to Go*, edited by Michael Meyer, 3rd ed., Bedford/St. Martin's, 2017, pp. 15–16.

Before beginning your own writing assignment on fiction, you should review Chapter 30, "Writing about Fiction," as well as Chapter 29, "Reading and the Writing Process," which provides a step-by-step explanation of how to choose a topic, develop a thesis, and organize various types of writing assignments. If you use outside sources, you should also be familiar with the conventional documentation procedures described in Chapter 33, "The Literary Research Paper."

EXPLORATIONS AND FORMULAS

Each time we pick up a work of fiction, go to the theater, or turn on the television, we have a trace of the same magical expectation that can be heard in the voice of a child who begs, "Tell me a story." Human beings have enjoyed stories ever since they learned to speak. Whatever the motive for creating stories — even if simply to delight or instruct — the basic human impulse to tell and hear stories existed long before the development of written language. Myths about the origins of the world and legends about the heroic exploits of demigods were among the earliest forms of storytelling to develop into oral traditions, which were eventually written down. These narratives are the ancestors of the stories we read on the printed page today.

The stories that appear in anthologies for college students are generally chosen for their high literary quality. Such stories can affect us at the deepest emotional level, reveal new insights into ourselves or the world, and stretch us by exercising our imaginations. The following chapters on plot, character, setting, and the other elements of literature are designed to provide the terms and concepts that can help you understand how a work of fiction achieves its effects and meanings. It is worth acknowledging, however, that many people buy and read fiction that is quite different from the stories usually anthologized in college texts. What about all those paperbacks with exciting, colorful covers near the cash registers in shopping malls and corner drugstores?

These books, known as **formula fiction**, are the adventure, western, detective, science fiction, and romance novels that entertain millions of readers annually. What makes them so popular? What do their characters, plots, and themes offer readers that accounts for the tremendous sales of stories with titles like *Caves of Doom*, *Silent Scream*, *Colt .45*, and *Forbidden Ecstasy*? Many of the writers included in this book have enjoyed wide popularity and written best-sellers, but there are more readers of formula fiction than there are readers of Ernest Hemingway, William Faulkner, or Joyce Carol Oates, to name only a few. Formula novels do provide entertainment, of course, but that makes them no different from serious stories, if entertainment means pleasure. Any of the stories in this or any other anthology can be read for pleasure.

Formula fiction, though, is usually characterized as escape literature. There are sensible reasons for this description. Adventure stories about soldiers of fortune are eagerly read by men who live pretty average lives doing ordinary jobs. Romance novels about attractive young women falling in love with tall, dark, handsome men are read mostly by women who dream themselves out of their familiar existences. The excitement, violence, and passion that such stories provide are a kind of reprieve from everyday experience.

And yet readers of serious fiction may also use it as a refuge, a liberation from monotony and boredom. Mark Twain's humorous stories have, for example, given countless hours of pleasurable relief to readers who would rather spend time in Twain's light and funny world than in their own. Others might prefer the terror of Edgar Allan Poe's fiction or the painful predicament of two lovers in a Joyce Carol Oates story.

Although the specific elements of formula fiction differ depending on the type of story, some basic ingredients go into all westerns, mysteries, adventures, science fiction, and romances. From the very start, a reader can anticipate a happy ending for the central character, with whom he or she will identify. There may be suspense, but no matter what or how many the obstacles, complications, or near defeats, the hero or heroine succeeds and reaffirms the values and attitudes the reader brings to the story. Virtue triumphs, love conquers all, honesty is the best policy, and hard work guarantees success. Hence, the villains are corralled, the wedding vows are exchanged, the butler confesses, and gold is discovered at the last moment. The visual equivalents of such formula stories are readily available at movie theaters and in television series. Some are better than others, but all are relatively limited by the writer's goal of giving an audience what will sell.

Although formula fiction may not offer many surprises, it provides pleasure to a wide variety of readers. College professors, for example, are just as likely to be charmed by formula stories as anyone else. Readers of serious fiction who revel in exploring more challenging imaginative worlds can also enjoy formulaic stories, which offer little more than an image of the world as a simple place in which our assumptions and desires are confirmed. The familiarity of a given formula is emotionally satisfying because we are secure in our expectations of it. We know at the start of a Sherlock Holmes story that the mystery will be solved by that famous detective's relentless scientific analysis of the clues, but we take pleasure in seeing how Holmes unravels the mystery before us. Similarly, we know that James Bond's wit, grace, charm, courage, and skill will ultimately prevail over the diabolic schemes of eccentric villains, but we volunteer for the mission anyway.

Perhaps that happens for the same reason that we climb aboard a roller coaster: no matter how steep and sharp the curves, we stay on a track that is both exciting and safe. Although excitement, adventure, mystery, and romance are major routes to escape in formula fiction, most of us make that trip only temporarily, for a little relaxation and fun. Momentary relief from our everyday concerns is as healthy and desirable as an occasional daydream or fantasy. Such reading is a form of play because we — like spectators of or participants in a game — experience a formula of excitement, tension, and then release that can fascinate us regardless of how many times the game is played.

Many publishers of formula fiction — such as romance, adventure, or detective stories — issue a set number of new novels each month. Readers can buy them in stores or subscribe to them through the mail. These same publishers send "tip sheets" on request to authors who want to write for a particular series. The details of the formula differ from one series to another, but each tip sheet covers the basic elements that go into a story.

The following composite tip sheet summarizes the typical advice offered by publishers of romance novels. These are among the most popular titles published in the United States; it has been estimated that four out of every ten paperbacks sold are romance novels. The categories and the tone of the language in this composite tip sheet are derived from a number of publishers and provide a glimpse of how formula fiction is written and what the readers of romance novels are looking for in their escape literature.

A Composite of a Romance Tip Sheet

PLOT

The story focuses on the growing relationship between the heroine and hero. After a number of complications, they discover lasting love and make a permanent commitment to each other in marriage. The plot should move quickly. Background information about the heroine should be kept to a minimum. The hero should appear as early as possible (preferably in the first chapter and no later than the second), so that the hero's and heroine's feelings about each other are in the foreground as they cope with misperceptions that keep them apart until the final pages of the story. The more tension created by their uncertainty about each other's love, the greater the excitement and anticipation for the reader.

Love is the major interest. Do not inject murder, extortion, international intrigue, hijacking, horror, or supernatural elements into the plot. Controversial social issues and politics, if mentioned at all, should never be allowed a significant role. Once the heroine and hero meet, they should clearly be interested in each other, but that interest should be complicated by some kind of misunderstanding. He, for example, might find her too ambitious, an opportunist, cold, or flirtatious; or he might assume that she is attached to someone else. She might think he is haughty, snobbish, power hungry, indifferent, or contemptuous of her. The reader knows what they do not: that eventually these obstacles will be overcome. Interest is sustained by keeping the lovers apart until very near the end so that the reader will stay with the plot to see how they get together.

HEROINE

The heroine is a modern American woman between the ages of nineteen and twenty-eight who reflects today's concerns. The story is told in the third person from her point of view. She is attractive and nicely dressed but not glamorous; glitter and sophistication should be reserved for the other woman (the heroine's rival for the hero), whose flashiness will compare unfavorably with the heroine's modesty. When the heroine does dress up, however, her beauty should be stunningly apparent. Her trim figure is appealing but not abundant; a petite healthy appearance is desirable. Both her looks and her clothes should be generously detailed.

Her personality is spirited and independent without being pushy or stubborn because she knows when to give in. Although sensitive, she doesn't cry every time she is confronted with a problem (though she might cry in private moments). A sense of humor is helpful. Because she is on her own, away from parents (usually deceased) or other protective relationships, she is self-reliant as well as vulnerable. The story may begin with her on the verge of an important decision about her life. She is clearly competent but not entirely certain of her own qualities. She does not take her attractiveness for granted or realize how much the hero is drawn to her.

Common careers for the heroine include assistant, nurse, teacher, interior designer, assistant manager, department store buyer, travel expert, or struggling photographer (no menial work). She can also be a doctor, lawyer, or other professional. Her job can be described in some detail and made exciting, but it must not dominate her life. Although she is smart, she is not extremely intellectual or defined by her work. Often she meets the hero through work, but her major concerns center on love, marriage, home, and family. White wine is okay, but she never drinks alone — or uses drugs. She may be troubled, frustrated, threatened, and momentarily thwarted in the course of the story, but she never totally gives in to despair or desperation. She has strengths that the hero recognizes and admires. 5

HERO

The hero should be about ten years older than the heroine and can be foreign or American. He needn't be handsome in a traditional sense, but he must be strongly masculine. Always tall and well built (not brawny or thick) and usually dark, he looks as terrific in a three-piece suit as he does in sports clothes. His clothes reflect good taste and an affluent life-style. Very successful professionally and financially, he is a man in charge of whatever work he's engaged in (financier, doctor, publisher, architect, business executive, airline pilot, artist, etc.). His wealth is manifested in his sophistication and experience.

His past may be slightly mysterious or shrouded by some painful moment (perhaps with a woman) that he doesn't want to discuss. Whatever the circumstance — his wife's death or divorce are common — it was not his fault. Avoid chronic problems such as alcoholism, drug addiction, or sexual dysfunctions. To others he may appear moody, angry, unpredictable, and explosively passionate, but the heroine eventually comes to realize his warm, tender side. He should be attractive not only as a lover but also as a potential husband and father.

SECONDARY CHARACTERS

Because the major interest is in how the heroine will eventually get together with the hero, the other characters are used to advance the action. There are three major types:

(1) *The Other Woman:* Her vices serve to accent the virtues of the heroine; immediately beneath her glamorous sophistication is a deceptive, selfish, mean-spirited, rapacious predator. She may seem to have the hero in her clutches, but she never wins him in the end.

(2) *The Other Man:* He usually falls into two types: (a) the decent sort who is there when the hero isn't around and (b) the selfish sort who schemes rather than loves. Neither is a match for the hero.

(3) *Other Characters:* Like furniture, they fill in the background and are useful for positioning the hero and heroine. These characters are familiar types such as the hero's snobbish aunt, the heroine's troubled younger siblings, the loyal friend, or the office gossip. They should be realistic, but they must not be allowed to obscure the emphasis on the lovers. The hero may have children from a previous marriage, but they should rarely be seen or heard. It's usually simpler and better not to include them.

SETTING

The setting is usually contemporary. Romantic, exciting places are best: New York City, London, Paris, Rio, the mountains, the ocean — wherever it is exotic and love's possibilities are the greatest. Marriage may take the heroine and hero to a pretty suburb or small town.

LOVE SCENES

The hero and heroine may make love before marriage. The choice will depend largely on the heroine's sensibilities and circumstances. She should reflect modern attitudes. If the lovers do engage in premarital sex, it should be made clear that neither is promiscuous, especially the heroine. Even if their relationship is consummated before marriage, their lovemaking should not occur until late in the story. There should be at least several passionate scenes, but complications, misunderstandings, and interruptions should keep the couple from actually making love until they have made a firm commitment to each other. Descriptions should appeal to the senses; however, detailed, graphic close-ups are unacceptable. Passion can be presented sensually but not clinically; the lovemaking should be seen through a soft romantic lens. Violence and any out-of-the-way sexual acts should not even be hinted at. No coarse language.

WRITING

Avoid extremely complex sentences, very long paragraphs, and lengthy descriptions. Use concise, vivid details to create the heroine's world. Be sure to include full descriptions of the hero's and heroine's physical features and clothes. Allow the reader to experience the romantic mood surrounding the lovers. Show how the heroine feels; do not simply report her feelings. Dialogue should sound like ordinary conversation, and the overall writing should be contemporary English without slang, difficult foreign expressions, strange dialects, racial epithets, or obscenities (*hell, damn*, and a few other mild swears are all right).

LENGTH

55,000 to 65,000 words in ten to twelve chapters.   15

CONSIDERATIONS FOR CRITICAL THINKING AND WRITING

1. FIRST RESPONSE. Given the expectations implied by the tip sheet, what generalizations can you make about those likely to write formula fiction? Does the tip sheet change the way you think about romantic fiction or other kinds of formula fiction?

2. Who is the intended audience for this type of romance? Try to describe the audience in detail: How does a romance novel provide escape for these readers?

3. Why should the hero be "about ten years older than the heroine"? If he is divorced, why is it significant that "it was not his fault"?

4. Why do you think the hero and heroine are kept apart by complications until the end of the story? Does the outline of the plot sound familiar to you or remind you of any other stories?

5. Why do you think restrictions are placed on the love scenes?

6. Why are "extremely complex sentences, very long paragraphs, and lengthy descriptions" discouraged?

7. Explain how the tip sheet confirms traditional views of male and female roles in society. Does it accommodate any broken traditions?

8. CREATIVE RESPONSE. Try writing a scene for a formula romance, or read the excerpt from Edgar Rice Burroughs's *Tarzan of the Apes* (p. 46) and try an adventure scene.

A COMPARISON OF TWO STORIES

Each of the following contemporary pieces of fiction is about a woman who experiences deep sorrow. The first, from *A Secret Sorrow* by Karen van der Zee, is an excerpt from a romance by Harlequin Books, a major publisher of formula fiction that has sold well over a billion copies of its romance titles — enough for about 20 percent of the world's population. The second piece, Gail Godwin's "A Sorrowful Woman," is a complete short story that originally appeared in *Esquire*; it is not a formula story.

Read each selection carefully and look for evidence of formulaic writing in the chapters from *A Secret Sorrow*. Pay particular attention to the advice on plotting and characterization offered in the composite tip sheet. As you read Godwin's short story, think about how it is different from van der Zee's excerpt; note also any similarities. The questions that follow the stories should help you consider how the experiences of reading the two are different.

KAREN VAN DER ZEE (B. 1947)

By permission of the author.

Born and raised in Holland, Karen van der Zee lives in the United States, where she has become a successful romance writer, contributing more than thirty novels to the popular Harlequin series. This excerpt consists of the final two chapters of *A Secret Sorrow*. This is what has happened so far: the central character, Faye, is recuperating from the psychological effects of a serious car accident in which she received a permanent internal injury. After the accident, she quits her job and breaks her engagement to Greg. She moves into her brother Chuck's house and falls in love with Kai, a visiting Texan and good friend of her brother. At the end of Chapter 10, Kai insists on knowing why she will not marry him and asks, "Who is Doctor Jaworski?"

From *A Secret Sorrow*   *1981*

Chapter Eleven

Faye could feel the blood drain from her face and for one horrifying moment she thought she was going to faint right in Kai's arms. The room tilted and everything swirled around in a wild madman's dance. She clutched at him for support, fighting for control, trying to focus at some point beyond his shoulder. Slowly, everything steadied.

"I . . . I don't know him," she murmured at last. "I . . ."

He reached in the breast pocket of his shirt, took out a slip of paper, and held it out for her to see. One glance and Faye recognized it as the note from Doctor Martin with Doctor Jaworski's name scrawled on it, thickly underlined.

"How did you get that?" Her voice was a terrified whisper. She was still holding on, afraid she would fall if she let go.

"I found it on the floor in my bedroom. It must have fallen out of your   5
wallet along with everything else on Saturday morning."

Yes — oh God! Her legs were shaking so badly, she knew it was only his
arms that kept her from falling.

"Who is Doctor Jaworski, Faye?" His voice was patiently persistent.

"I . . . he . . ." Her voice broke. "Let me go, please let me go." She felt as if
she were suffocating in his embrace and she struggled against him, feebly, but
it was no use.

"He's a psychiatrist, isn't he?" His voice was gentle, very gentle, and she
looked up at him in stunned surprise.

He knew, oh God, he knew. She closed her eyes, a helpless sense of inevi-   10
tability engulfing her.

"You know," she whispered. "How do you know?"

"Simple. Two minutes on the phone to Chicago." He paused. "Doctor
Martin — was he one of the doctors who treated you at the hospital?"

"Yes."

"Why did he give you Doctor Jaworski's name? Did he want you to make
an appointment with him?"

"Yes." Despondency overtook her. There was no going back now. No   15
escape from the truth. No escape from his arms. Resistance faded and she felt
numbed and lifeless. It didn't matter any more. Nothing mattered.

"Did you?" Kai repeated.

"Did I what?"

"See him — Doctor Jaworski."

"No."

"Why did Doctor Martin want you to see a psychiatrist?"   20

"I . . ." Faye swallowed miserably. "It's . . . it's therapy for grieving . . .
mourning." She made a helpless gesture with her hand. "When people lose
a . . . a wife, or husband for instance, they go through a more or less predictable pattern of emotions . . ." She gave him a quick glance, then looked away.
"Like denial, anger . . ."

". . . depression, mourning, acceptance," Kai finished for her, and she
looked back at him in surprise.

"Yes."

His mouth twisted in a little smile. "I'm not totally ignorant about subjects other than agronomy." There was a momentary pause as he scrutinized
her face. "Why did you need that kind of therapy, Faye?"

And then it was back again, the resistance, the revolt against his prob-   25
ing questions. She stiffened in defense — her whole body growing rigid with
instinctive rebellion.

"It's none of your business!"

"Oh, yes, it is. We're talking about our life together. Your life and mine."

She strained against him, hands pushing against his chest. "Let me go!
Please let me go!" Panic changed into tears. She couldn't take his nearness any
more, the feel of his hard body touching hers, the strength of him.

"No, Faye, no. You're going to tell me. Now. I'm not letting you go until
you've told me everything. Everything, you hear?"

"I can't!" she sobbed. "I can't!"   30

"Faye," he said slowly, "you'll *have* to. You told me you love me, but you don't want to marry me. You have given me no satisfactory reasons, and I'll be damned if I'm going to accept your lack of explanations."

"You have no right to demand an explanation!"

"Oh, yes, I have. You're part of me, Faye. Part of my life."

"You talk as if you own me!" She was trembling, struggling to get away from him. She couldn't stand there, so close to him with all the pent-up despair inside her, the anger, the fear of what she knew not how to tell him.

His hands were warm and strong on her back, holding her steady. Then,   35
with one hand, he tilted back her head and made her look at him. "You gave me your love — I own that," he said softly. "True loving involves commitment, vulnerability, trust. Don't you trust me, Faye?"

New tears ran silently down her cheeks. "If I told you," she blurted out, "you wouldn't . . . you wouldn't . . ."

"I wouldn't *what?*"

"You wouldn't want me any more!" The words were wrenched from her in blind, agonizing grief. "You wouldn't *want* me any more!"

He shook his head incredulously. "What makes you think you can make that decision for me? Do you have so little trust in my love for you?"

Faye didn't answer, couldn't answer. Through a mist of tears he was noth-   40
ing but a blur in front of her eyes.

"What is so terrible that you can't tell me?"

She shrank inwardly, as if shriveling away in pain. "Let me go," she whispered. "Please let me go and I'll tell you."

After a moment's hesitation Kai released her. Faye backed away from him, feeling like a terrified animal. She stood with her back against the wall, glad for the support, her whole body shaking. She took a deep breath and wiped her face dry with her hand.

"I'm afraid . . . afraid to marry you."

"Afraid?" He looked perplexed. "Afraid of what? Of me? Of marriage?"   45

Faye closed her eyes, taking another deep breath. "I can't be what you want me to be. We can't have the kind of life you want." She looked at him, standing only a few feet away, anguish tearing through her. "I'm so afraid . . . you'll be disappointed," she whispered.

"Oh God, Faye," he groaned, "I love you." He came toward her and panic surged through her as he held her against the wall, his hands reaching up to catch her face between them.

"Don't," she whispered. "Please, don't touch me." But it was no use. His mouth came down on hers and he kissed her with a hard, desperate passion.

"I love you," he said huskily. "I love you."

Faye wrenched her face free from his hands. "Don't touch me! Please   50
don't touch me!" She was sobbing now, her words barely audible. Her knees gave way and her back slid down along the wall until she crumpled on to the floor, face in her hands.

Kai took a step backward and pulled her up. "Stand up, Faye. For God's sake stand up!" He held her against the wall and she looked at him, seeing every line in his dark face, the intense blue of his eyes, and knew that this was the moment, that there was no more waiting.

And Kai knew it too. His eyes held hers locked in unrelenting demand. "Why should I be disappointed, Faye? *Why?*"

Her heart was thundering in her ears and it seemed as if she couldn't breathe, as if she were going to drown.

"Because . . . because I can't give you children! Because I can't get pregnant! I can't have babies! That's why!" Her voice was an agonized cry, torn from the depths of her misery. She yanked down his arms that held her locked against the wall and moved away from him. And then she saw his face.

It was ashen, gray under his tan. He stared at her as if he had never seen 55 her before.

"Oh my God, Faye . . ." His voice was low and hoarse. "Why didn't you tell me, why . . ."

Faye heard no more. She ran out the door, snatching her bag off the chair as she went by. The only thought in her mind was to get away — away from Kai and what was in his eyes.

She reached for Kai's spare set of car keys in her bag, doing it instinctively, knowing she couldn't walk home alone in the dark. How she managed to get the keys in the door lock and in the ignition she never knew. Somehow, she made it home.

The phone rang as Faye opened the front door and she heard Chuck answer it in the kitchen.

"She's just got in," he said into the mouthpiece, smiling at Faye as she 60 came into view. He listened for a moment, nodded. "Okay, fine with me."

Faye turned and walked up the stairs, taking deep breaths to calm her shattered nerves. Kai hadn't wasted any time checking up on her. She didn't care what he was telling Chuck, but she wasn't going to stand there listening to a one-sided conversation. But only a second later Chuck was behind her on the stairs.

"Kai wanted to know whether you'd arrived safely."

"I did, thank you," she said levelly, her voice surprisingly steady.

"I take it you ran out and took off with his car?"

"Did he say that?"   65

"No. He was *worried* about you. He wanted to make sure you went home." He sounded impatient, and she couldn't blame him. She was making life unbearable for everyone around her. Everybody worried about her. Everybody loved her. Everything should be right. Only it wasn't.

"Well, I'm home now, and I'm going to bed. Good night."

"Good night, Faye."

Faye lay in bed without any hope of sleep. Mechanically she started to sort through her thoughts and emotions, preparing mentally for the next confrontation. There would be one, she didn't doubt it for a moment. But she needed time — time to clear her head, time to look at everything in a reasonable, unemotional way.

It was a temptation to run — get in the car and keep driving, but it would   70
be a stupid thing to do. There was no place for her to go, and Kai would find
her, no matter what. If there was one thing she knew about Kai it was his stubbornness and his persistence. She had to stick it out, right here, get it over
with, deal with it. Only she didn't know how.

She lay listening to the stillness, just a few sounds here and there — the
house creaking, a car somewhere in the distance, a dog barking. She had
to think, but her mind refused to cooperate. She *had* to think, decide what
to say to Kai the next time she saw him, but she couldn't think, she *couldn't
think*.

And then, as she heard the door open in the silence, the quiet footsteps
coming up the stairs, she knew it was too late, that time had run out.

Without even knocking he came into her room and walked over to the
bed. She could feel the mattress sag as his weight came down on it. Her heart
was pounding like a sledgehammer, and then his arms came around her and
he drew her against him.

"Faye," he said quietly, "please marry me."

"No," she said thickly. "No." She could feel him stiffen against her and she   75
released herself from his arms and slid off the bed. She switched on the light
and stood near the window, far from the bed, far from Kai. "I don't expect you
to play the gentleman, I don't expect you to throw out a life of dreams just for
the sake of chivalry. You don't have to marry me, Kai." She barely recognized
her own voice. It was like the cool calm sound of a stranger, unemotional, cold.
"You don't have to marry me," she repeated levelly, giving him a steady look.

Her words were underlined by the silence that followed, a silence loaded
with a strange, vibrating energy, a force in itself, filling the room.

Kai rose to his feet, slowly, and the face that looked at her was like that
of a stranger, a dangerous, angry stranger. Never before had she seen him so
angry, so full of hot, fuming fury.

"Shut up," he said in a low, tight voice. "Shut up and stop playing the
martyr!"

The sound of his voice and the words he said shocked Faye into silence.
She stared at him open-mouthed, and then a slow, burning anger arose
inside her.

"How dare you! How . . ."   80

He strode toward her and took her upper arms and shook her. "Shut up
and listen to me! What the hell are you thinking? What the hell did you expect
me to do when you told me? You throw me a bomb and then walk out on me!
What did you expect my reaction to be? Was I supposed to stay cool and calm
and tell you it didn't matter? Would you have married me then? Well, let me
tell you something! It matters! It matters to me! I am not apologizing for my
reaction!" He paused, breathing hard. "You know I always wanted children,
but what in God's name makes you think you're the only one who has the
right to feel bad about it? I have that right too, you hear! I love you, dammit,
and I want to marry you, and if we can't have children I have all the right in
the world to feel bad about it!"

He stopped talking. He was still breathing hard and he looked at her with stormy blue eyes. Faye felt paralyzed by his tirade and she stared at him, incapable of speech. She couldn't move, she couldn't think.

"Why do you think I want you for my wife?" he continued on a calmer note. "Because you're some kind of baby factory? What kind of man do you think I am? I love *you*, not your procreating ability. So we have a problem. Well, we'll learn to deal with it, one way or another."

There was another silence, and still Faye didn't speak, and she realized she was crying, soundlessly, tears slowly dripping down her cheeks. She was staring at his chest, blindly, not knowing what to think, not thinking at all.

He lifted her chin, gently. "Look at me, Faye."   85

She did, but his face was only a blur.

"Faye, we're in this together — you and I. Don't you see that? It's not just *your* problem, it's *ours*."

"No," she whispered. "No!" She shook her head wildly. "You have a choice, don't you see that? You don't have to marry me. You could marry someone else and have children of your own."

"Oh, God, Faye," he groaned, "you're wrong. Don't you know? Don't you see? I *don't* have a choice. I never did have a choice, or a chance. Not since I met you and fell in love with you. I don't *want* anybody else, don't you understand that? I want you, only you."

She wanted to believe it, give in to him. Never before had she wanted   90
anything more desperately than she wanted to give in to him now. But she couldn't, she couldn't . . . She closed her eyes, briefly, fighting for reason, common sense.

"Kai, I . . . I can't live all my life with your regret and your disappointment. Every time we see some pregnant woman, every time we're with somebody else's children I'll feel I've failed you! I . . ." Her voice broke and new sobs came unchecked.

He held her very tightly until she calmed down and then he put her from him a little and gave her a dark, compelling look.

"It's not *my* regret, or *my* disappointment," he said with quiet emphasis. "It's *ours*. We're not talking about *you* or *me*. We're talking about *us*. I love you, and you love me, and that's the starting point, that comes first. From then on we're in it together."

Faye moved out of his arms, away from him, but her legs wouldn't carry her and she sank into a chair. She covered her face with her hands and tried desperately to stop the crying, to stop the tears from coming and coming as if they would never end.

"How . . . how can I ever believe it?"   95

"Because I'm asking you to," he said quietly. He knelt in front of her, took her hands away from her wet face. "Look at me, Faye. No other woman can give me what you can — yourself, your love, your warmth, your sense of humor. All the facets of your personality that make up the final you. I've known other women, Faye, but none of them have ever stirred in me any feelings that come close to what I feel for you. You're an original, remember?

There's no replacement for an original. There are only copies, and I don't want a copy. To me you're special, and you'll have to believe it, take it on faith. That's what love is all about."

He was holding her hands in his, strong brown hands, and she was looking down on them, fighting with herself, fighting with everything inside her to believe what he was saying, to accept it, to give in to it.

Leaning forward, Kai kissed her gently on the mouth and smiled. "It's all been too much too soon for you, hasn't it? You never really got a chance to get over the shock, and when I fell in love with you it only made things worse." He smiled ruefully and Faye was surprised at his insight.

"Yes," she said. "It all happened too fast."

"Bad timing. If only we could have met later, after you'd sorted it all out   100
in your mind, then it would never have been such a crisis."

She looked at him doubtfully. "It wouldn't have changed the facts."

"No, but it might have changed your perspective."

Would it have? she wondered. Could she ever feel confident and secure in her worth as a woman? Or was she at this moment too emotionally bruised to accept that possibility?

"I don't understand," he said, "why I never guessed what was wrong. Now that I know, it all seems so obvious." He looked at her thoughtfully. "Faye," he said gently, "I want you to tell me exactly what happened to you, what Doctor Martin told you."

She stared at him, surprised a little. A thought stirred in the back of her   105
mind. Greg. He had never even asked. The why and the what had not interested him. But Kai, he wanted to know. She swallowed nervously and began the story, slowly, word for word, everything Doctor Martin had said. And he listened, quietly, not interrupting. "So you see," she said at last, "we don't have to hope for any miracles either."

"We'll make our own miracles," he said, and smiled. "Come here," he said then, "kiss me."

She did, shyly almost, until he took over and lifted her up and carried her to the bed. He looked down on her, eyes thoughtful. "I won't pretend I understand your feelings about this, the feelings you have about yourself as a woman, but I'll try." He paused for a moment. "Faye," he said then, speaking with slow emphasis, "don't *ever*, not for a single moment, think that you're not good enough for me. You're the best there is, Faye, the very best."

His mouth sought hers and he kissed her with gentle reassurance at first, then with rising ardor. His hands moved over her body, touching her with sensual, intimate caresses.

"You're my woman, Faye, you're mine . . ."

Her senses reeled. She could never love anyone like she loved him. No   110
one had ever evoked in her this depth of emotion. This was real, this was forever. Kai wanted her as much as ever. No chivalry, this, no game of pretense, she was very sure of that. And when he lifted his face and looked at her, it was all there in his eyes and the wonder of it filled her with joy.

"Do you believe me now?" he whispered huskily. "Do you believe I love you and want you and need you?"

She nodded wordlessly, incapable of uttering a sound.

"And do you love me?"

Again she nodded, her eyes in his.

"Okay, then." In one smooth flowing movement he got to his feet. He 115 crossed to the closet, opened it, and took out her suitcases. He put one on the end of the bed and began to pile her clothes in it, taking armfuls out of the closet.

Faye watched incredulously. "What are you doing?" she managed at last.

Kai kept on moving around, opening drawers, taking out her things, filling the suitcase until it could hold no more. "Get dressed. We're going home."

"Home . . . ?"

For a moment he stopped and he looked at her with a deep blue glitter in his eyes. "Yes, *home* — where you belong. With me, in my house, in my bed, in my arms."

"Oh, Kai," she said tremulously, smiling suddenly. "It's midnight!" 120

His eyes were very dark. "I've waited long enough, I'm not waiting any more. You're coming with me, now. And I'm not letting you out of my sight until we're safely married. I don't want you getting any crazy ideas about running off to save me from myself, or some such notion."

Her throat was dry. "Please, let's not rush into it! Let's think about it first!"

Calmly he zipped up the full suitcase, swung it off the bed, and put it near the door. "I'm not rushing into anything," he said levelly. "I've wanted to marry you for quite a while, remember?"

He crossed to the bed, sat down next to her, and put his arm around her. "Faye, I wish you wouldn't worry so. I'm not going to change my mind. And I haven't shelved my hopes for a family, either." There was a brief silence. "When we're ready to have kids, we'll have them. We'll adopt them. There are orphanages the world over, full of children in need of love and care. We'll do whatever it takes. We'll get them, one way or another."

Faye searched his face, faint hope flickering deep inside her. 125

"Would you want that?"

"Why not?"

"I don't know, really. I thought you . . . it isn't the same."

"No," he said levelly, "it isn't. Adoption is a different process from pregnancy and birth, but the kids will be ours just the same and we'll love them no less."

"Yes," she said, "yes." And suddenly it seemed as if a light had been 130 turned on inside her, as if suddenly she could see again, a future with Kai, a future with children.

A bronzed hand lifted her face. "Look, Faye, I'll always be sorry. I'll always be sorry not to see you pregnant, not to see you with a big stomach knowing you're carrying my child, but I'll live."

Faye lowered her eyes and tears threatened again. With both his hands he cupped her face.

"Look at me, Faye. I want you to stop thinking of yourself as a machine with a defect. You're not a damaged piece of merchandise, you hear? You're a living, breathing human being, a warm-blooded female, and I love you."

Through a haze of tears she looked at him, giving a weak smile. "I love you too." She put her arms around him and he heaved an unsteady breath.

"Faye," he said huskily, "you're my first and only choice."   135

Chapter Twelve

Kai and Faye had their family, two girls and a boy. They came to them one at a time, from faraway places, with small faces and large dark eyes full of fear. In their faces Faye could read the tragedies of war and death and poverty. They were hungry for love, hungry for nourishment and care. At night they woke in terror, screaming, their memories alive in sleep.

Time passed, and in the low white ranch house under the blue skies of Texas they flourished like the crops in the fields. They grew tall and straight and healthy and the fear in their dark eyes faded. Like their father they wore jeans and boots and large-brimmed hats, and they rode horses and played the guitar. They learned to speak English with a Southern twang.

One day Kai and Faye watched them as they played in the garden, and joy and gratitude overflowed in Faye's heart. Life was good and filled with love.

"They're all ours," she said. Even now after all these years she sometimes still couldn't believe it was really so.

Kai smiled at her. His eyes, still very blue, crinkled at the corners. "Yes,   140 and you're all mine."

"They don't even look like us," she said. "Not even a tiny little bit." No blondes, no redheads.

Taking her in his arms, Kai kissed her. "They're true originals, like their mother. I wouldn't want it any other way."

There was love in his embrace and love in his words and in her heart there was no room now for doubt, no room for sorrow.

Sometimes in the night he would reach for her and she would wake to his touch, his hands on her breast, her stomach, searching. In the warm darkness of their bed she would come to him and they would hold each other close and she knew he had been dreaming.

She knew the dream. She was walking away from him, calling out that   145 she couldn't marry him, the words echoing all around. "*I can't marry you! I can't marry you!*" And Kai was standing there watching her go, terrified, unable to move, his legs frozen to the ground. He wanted to follow her, keep her from leaving, but his legs wouldn't move.

Kai had told her of the dream, of the panic that clutched at him as he watched her walk out of his life. And always he would wake and search for her in the big bed, and she knew of only one way to reassure him. And in the warm afterglow of lovemaking, their bodies close together, she knew that to him she was everything, to him she was the only woman, beautiful, complete, whole.

GAIL GODWIN (B. 1937)

Born in Birmingham, Alabama, Gail Godwin was educated at the University of North Carolina and the University of Iowa, where she earned a Ph.D. in English in 1971. She is a full-time writer who has won grants from the National Endowment for the Arts, the Guggenheim Foundation, and the American Institute for the Arts and Letters. Among her novels are *Glass People* (1971), *A Mother and Two Daughters* (1981), *The Finishing School* (1985), *Evensong* (1999), *Queen of the Underworld* (2006), and *Flora* (2015). Her short stories have been collected in several volumes including *Dream Children* (1976) and *Mr. Bedford and the Muses* (1983).

Alan Carey / The Image Works.

A Sorrowful Woman   1971

Once upon a time there was a wife and mother one too many times

One winter evening she looked at them: the husband durable, receptive, gentle; the child a tender golden three. The sight of them made her so sad and sick she did not want to see them ever again.

She told the husband these thoughts. He was attuned to her; he understood such things. He said he understood. What would she like him to do? "If you could put the boy to bed and read him the story about the monkey who ate too many bananas, I would be grateful." "Of course," he said. "Why, that's a pleasure." And he sent her off to bed.

The next night it happened again. Putting the warm dishes away in the cupboard, she turned and saw the child's gray eyes approving her movements. In the next room was the man, his chin sunk in the open collar of his favorite wool shirt. He was dozing after her good supper. The shirt was the gray of the child's trusting gaze. She began yelping without tears, retching in between. The man woke in alarm and carried her in his arms to bed. The boy followed them up the stairs, saying, "It's all right, Mommy," but this made her scream. "Mommy is sick," the father said, "go wait for me in your room."

The husband undressed her, abandoning her only long enough to root beneath the eiderdown for her flannel gown. She stood naked except for her bra, which hung by one strap down the side of her body; she had not the impetus to shrug it off. She looked down at the right nipple, shriveled with chill, and thought, How absurd, a vertical bra. "If only there were instant sleep," she said, hiccuping, and the husband bundled her into the gown and went out and came back with a sleeping draught guaranteed swift. She was to drink a little glass of cognac followed by a big glass of dark liquid and afterwards there was just time to say Thank you and could you get him a clean pair of pajamas out of the laundry, it came back today.

The next day was Sunday and the husband brought her breakfast in bed 5 and let her sleep until it grew dark again. He took the child for a walk, and when they returned, red-cheeked and boisterous, the father made supper. She heard them laughing in the kitchen. He brought her up a tray of buttered toast, celery sticks, and black bean soup. "I am the luckiest woman," she said, crying real tears. "Nonsense," he said. "You need a rest from us," and went to prepare the sleeping draught, find the child's pajamas, select the story for the night.

She got up on Monday and moved about the house till noon. The boy, delighted to have her back, pretended he was a vicious tiger and followed her from room to room, growling and scratching. Whenever she came close, he would growl and scratch at her. One of his sharp little claws ripped her flesh, just above the wrist, and together they paused to watch a thin red line materialize on the inside of her pale arm and spill over in little beads. "Go away," she said. She got herself upstairs and locked the door. She called the husband's office and said, "I've locked myself away from him. I'm afraid." The husband told her in his richest voice to lie down, take it easy, and he was already on the phone to call one of the baby-sitters they often employed. Shortly after, she heard the girl let herself in, heard the girl coaxing the frightened child to come and play.

After supper several nights later, she hit the child. She had known she was going to do it when the father would see. "I'm sorry," she said, collapsing on the floor. The weeping child had run to hide. "What has happened to me, I'm not myself anymore." The man picked her tenderly from the floor and looked at her with much concern. "Would it help if we got, you know, a girl in? We could fix the room downstairs. I want you to feel freer," he said, understanding these things. "We have the money for a girl. I want you to think about it."

And now the sleeping draught was a nightly thing, she did not have to ask. He went down to the kitchen to mix it, he set it nightly beside her bed. The little glass and the big one, amber and deep rich brown, the flannel gown and the eiderdown.

The man put out the word and found the perfect girl. She was young, dynamic, and not pretty. "Don't bother with the room, I'll fix it up myself." Laughing, she employed her thousand energies. She painted the room white, fed the child lunch, read edifying books, raced the boy to the mailbox, hung her own watercolors on the fresh-painted walls, made spinach soufflé, cleaned a spot from the mother's coat, made them all laugh, danced in stocking feet to music in the white room after reading the child to sleep. She knitted dresses for herself and played chess with the husband. She washed and set the mother's soft ash-blonde hair and gave her neck rubs, offered to.

The woman now spent her winter afternoons in the big bedroom. She 10 made a fire in the hearth and put on slacks and an old sweater she had loved at school, and sat in the big chair and stared out the window at snow-ridden branches, or went away into long novels about other people moving through other winters.

The girl brought the child in twice a day, once in the later afternoon when he would tell of his day, all of it tumbling out quickly because there was not much time, and before he went to bed. Often now, the man took his wife to dinner. He made a courtship ceremony of it, inviting her beforehand so she could get used to the idea. They dressed and were beautiful together again and went out into the frosty night. Over candlelight he would say, "I think you are better, you know." "Perhaps I am," she would murmur. "You look . . . like a cloistered queen," he said once, his voice breaking curiously.

One afternoon the girl brought the child into the bedroom. "We've been out playing in the park. He found something he wants to give you, a surprise." The little boy approached her, smiling mysteriously. He placed his cupped hands in hers and left a live dry thing that spat brown juice in her palm and leapt away. She screamed and wrung her hands to be rid of the brown juice. "Oh, it was only a grasshopper," said the girl. Nimbly she crept to the edge of the curtain, did a quick knee bend, and reclaimed the creature, led the boy competently from the room.

"The girl upsets me," said the woman to her husband. He sat frowning on the side of the bed he had not entered for so long. "I'm sorry, but there it is." The husband stroked his creased brow and said he was sorry too. He really did not know what they would do without that treasure of a girl. "Why don't you stay here with me in bed," the woman said.

Next morning she fired the girl who cried and said, "I loved the little boy, what will become of him now?" But the mother turned away her face and the girl took down the watercolors from the walls, sheathed the records she had danced to, and went away.

"I don't know what we'll do. It's all my fault, I know. I'm such a burden, I 15 know that."

"Let me think. I'll think of something." (Still understanding these things.)

"I know you will. You always do," she said.

With great care he rearranged his life. He got up hours early, did the shopping, cooked the breakfast, took the boy to nursery school. "We will manage," he said, "until you're better, however long that is." He did his work, collected the boy from the school, came home and made the supper, washed the dishes, got the child to bed. He managed everything. One evening, just as she was on the verge of swallowing her draught, there was a timid knock on her door. The little boy came in wearing his pajamas. "Daddy has fallen asleep on my bed and I can't get in. There's not room."

Very sedately she left her bed and went to the child's room. Things were much changed. Books were rearranged, toys. He'd done some new drawings. She came as a visitor to her son's room, wakened the father and helped him to bed. "Ah, he shouldn't have bothered you," said the man, leaning on his wife. "I've told him not to." He dropped into his own bed and fell asleep with a moan. Meticulously she undressed him. She folded and hung his clothes. She covered his body with the bedclothes. She flicked off the light that shone in his face.

The next day she moved her things into the girl's white room. She put   20 her hairbrush on the dresser; she put a note pad and pen beside the bed. She stocked the little room with cigarettes, books, bread, and cheese. She didn't need much.

At first the husband was dismayed. But he was receptive to her needs. He understood these things. "Perhaps the best thing is for you to follow it through," he said. "I want to be big enough to contain whatever you must do."

All day long she stayed in the white room. She was a young queen, a virgin in a tower; she was the previous inhabitant, the girl with all the energies. She tried these personalities on like costumes, then discarded them. The room had a new view of streets she'd never seen that way before. The sun hit the room in late afternoon and she took to brushing her hair in the sun. One day she decided to write a poem. "Perhaps a sonnet." She took up her pen and pad and began working from words that had lately lain in her mind. She had choices for the sonnet, ABAB or ABBA for a start. She pondered these possibilities until she tottered into a larger choice: she did not have to write a sonnet. Her poem could be six, eight, ten, thirteen lines, it could be any number of lines, and it did not even have to rhyme.

She put down the pen on top of the pad.

In the evenings, very briefly, she saw the two of them. They knocked on her door, a big knock and a little, and she would call Come in, and the husband would smile though he looked a bit tired, yet somehow this tiredness suited him. He would put her sleeping draught on the bedside table and say, "The boy and I have done all right today," and the child would kiss her. One night she tasted for the first time the power of his baby spit.

"I don't think I can see him anymore," she whispered sadly to the   25 man. And the husband turned away, but recovered admirably and said, "Of course, I see."

So the husband came alone. "I have explained to the boy," he said. "And we are doing fine. We are managing." He squeezed his wife's pale arm and put the two glasses on her table. After he had gone, she sat looking at the arm.

"I'm afraid it's come to that," she said. "Just push the notes under the door; I'll read them. And don't forget to leave the draught outside."

The man sat for a long time with his head in his hands. Then he rose and went away from her. She heard him in the kitchen where he mixed the draught in batches now to last a week at a time, storing it in a corner of the cupboard. She heard him come back, leave the big glass and the little one outside on the floor.

Outside her window the snow was melting from the branches, there were more people on the streets. She brushed her hair a lot and seldom read anymore. She sat in her window and brushed her hair for hours, and saw a boy fall off his new bicycle again and again, a dog chasing a squirrel, an old woman peek slyly over her shoulder and then extract a parcel from a garbage can.

In the evening she read the notes they slipped under her door. The 30 child could not write, so he drew and sometimes painted his. The notes were painstaking at first; the man and boy offering the final strength of their day to her. But sometimes, when they seemed to have had a bad day, there were only hurried scrawls.

One night, when the husband's note had been extremely short, loving but short, and there had been nothing from the boy, she stole out of her room as she often did to get more supplies, but crept upstairs instead and stood outside their doors, listening to the regular breathing of the man and boy asleep. She hurried back to her room and drank the draught.

She woke earlier now. It was spring, there were birds. She listened for sounds of the man and the boy eating breakfast; she listened for the roar of the motor when they drove away. One beautiful noon, she went out to look at her kitchen in the daylight. Things were changed. He had bought some new dish towels. Had the old ones worn out? The canisters seemed closer to the sink. She got out flour, baking powder, salt, milk (he bought a different brand of butter), and baked a loaf of bread and left it cooling on the table.

The force of the two joyful notes slipped under her door that evening pressed her into the corner of the little room; she had hardly space to breathe. As soon as possible, she drank the draught.

Now the days were too short. She was always busy. She woke with the first bird. Worked till the sun set. No time for hair brushing. Her fingers raced the hours.

Finally, in the nick of time, it was finished one late afternoon. Her veins 35 pumped and her forehead sparkled. She went to the cupboard, took what was hers, closed herself into the little white room and brushed her hair for a while.

The man and boy came home and found: five loaves of warm bread, a roast stuffed turkey, a glazed ham, three pies of different fillings, eight molds of the boy's favorite custard, two weeks' supply of fresh-laundered sheets and shirts and towels, two hand-knitted sweaters (both of the same gray color), a sheath of marvelous watercolor beasts accompanied by mad and fanciful stories nobody could ever make up again, and a tablet full of love sonnets addressed to the man. The house smelled redolently of renewal and spring. The man ran to the little room, could not contain himself to knock, flung back the door.

"Look, Mommy is sleeping," said the boy. "She's tired from doing all our things again." He dawdled in a stream of the last sun for that day and watched his father roll tenderly back her eyelids, lay his ear softly to her breast, test the delicate bones of her wrist. The father put down his face into her fresh-washed hair.

"Can we eat the turkey for supper?" the boy asked.

Considerations for Critical Thinking and Writing

1. FIRST RESPONSE. How did you respond to the excerpt from *A Secret Sorrow* and to "A Sorrowful Woman"? Do you like one more than the other? Is one of the women — Faye or Godwin's unnamed wife — more likable than the other? Why do you think you respond the way you do to the characters and the stories — is your response intellectual, emotional, a result of authorial intent, a mix of these, or something else entirely?

2. Describe what you found appealing in each story. Can you point to passages in both that strike you as especially well written or interesting? Was there anything in either story that did not appeal to you? Why?

3. How do the two women's attitudes toward family life differ? How does that difference constitute the problem in each story?

4. How would you describe the theme — the central point and meaning — in each story?

5. To what extent might "A Sorrowful Woman" be regarded as an unromantic sequel to *A Secret Sorrow*?

6. Can both stories be read a second or third time and still be interesting? Why or why not?

7. Explain how you think a romance formula writer would end "A Sorrowful Woman," or write the ending yourself.

8. Contrast what marriage means in the two stories.

2

Plot

Ermeni Studio, Milan.
Courtesy of the Ernest
Hemingway Photographic
Collection, John Fitzgerald
Kennedy Library, Boston.

Never mistake motion for action.
—ERNEST HEMINGWAY

Created by a writer's imagination, a work of fiction need not be factual or historically accurate. Although actual people, places, and events may be included in fiction, facts are not as important as is the writer's use of them. We can learn much about Russian life in the early part of the nineteenth century from Leo Tolstoy's *War and Peace*, but that historical information is incidental to Tolstoy's exploration of human nature. Tolstoy, like most successful writers, makes us accept as real the world in his novel no matter how foreign it may be to our own reality. One of the ways a writer achieves this acceptance and engagement—and one of a writer's few obligations—is to interest us in what is happening in the story. We are carried into the writer's fictional world by the plot.

   Plot is the author's arrangement of incidents in a story. It is the organizing principle that controls the order of events. This structure is, in a sense, what remains after a writer edits out what is irrelevant to the story being told. What is told takes on meaning as it is brought into focus by a skillful writer who selects and orders the events that constitute the story's plot.

44

Events can be presented in a variety of orders. A chronological arrangement begins with what happens first, then second, and so on, until the last incident is related. The events in William Faulkner's "A Rose for Emily," however, are not arranged in chronological order because that would give away the story's surprise ending; instead, Faulkner moves back and forth between the past and present to provide information that leads up to the final startling moment (which won't be given away here either; the story begins on p. 54).

Some stories begin at the end and then lead up to why or how events worked out as they did. If you read the first paragraph of Ralph Ellison's "Battle Royal" (p. 177), you'll find an example of this arrangement that will make it difficult for you to stop reading. Stories can also begin in the middle of things (the Latin term for this common plot strategy is *in medias res*). In this kind of plot we enter the story on the verge of some important moment. John Updike's "A & P" (p. 149) begins with the narrator, a teenager working at a checkout counter in a supermarket, telling us: "In walks these three girls in nothing but bathing suits." Right away we are brought into the middle of a situation that will ultimately create the conflict in the story.

Another common strategy is the *flashback*, a device that informs us about events that happened before the opening scene of a work. Nearly all of Ellison's "Battle Royal" takes the form of a flashback as the narrator recounts how his identity as a black man was shaped by the circumstances that attended a high-school graduation speech he delivered twenty years earlier in a hotel ballroom before a gathering of the town's leading white citizens, most of whom were "quite tipsy." Whatever the plot arrangement, you should be aware of how the writer's conscious ordering of events affects your responses to the action.

EDGAR RICE BURROUGHS (1875–1950)

A great many stories share a standard plot pattern. The following excerpt from Edgar Rice Burroughs's novel *Tarzan of the Apes* provides a conventional plot pattern in which the *character*, an imagined person in the story, is confronted with a problem leading to a climactic struggle that is followed by a resolution of the problem. The elements of a conventional plot are easily recognizable to readers familiar with fast-paced, action-packed mysteries, spy thrillers, westerns, or adventure stories. These page-turners are carefully plotted so that the reader is swept up by the action.

Although Burroughs wrote *Tarzan of the Apes* some one hundred years ago, the novel and its subsequent films, television shows, comic books, and numerous other spin-offs continue to thrive in the undergrowth of American popular culture. Curiously, one such by-product even includes a pseudo-autobiography titled *Me Cheeta: My Life in Hollywood* (2009), a memoir allegedly written by the chimpanzee that appeared in the Tarzan movies but never in the novels, an oddity that suggests the action continues in the Tarzan trade.

Burroughs's novel, published in 1914 and the first in the series, charts the growth to manhood of a child raised in the African jungle by great apes. Tarzan struggles to survive his primitive beginnings and to reconcile what he has learned in the jungle with his equally powerful instincts to be a civilized human being. One of the more exciting moments in Tarzan's development is his final confrontation with his old enemy, Terkoz, a huge tyrannical ape that has kidnapped Jane, a pretty nineteen-year-old from Baltimore, Maryland, who has accompanied her father on an expedition to the jungle.

Burroughs Memorial Collection, Rare Books, Archives & Special Collections, University of Louisville.

In the chapter preceding this excerpt, Tarzan falls in love with Jane and writes this pointed, if not eloquent, note to her: "I am Tarzan of the Apes. I want you. I am yours. You are mine." Just as he finishes the note, he hears "the agonized screams of a woman" and rushes into the jungle to find their source. Meanwhile, Esmeralda, Jane's maid, hysterical with fear and grief, reports that Jane, the fair and gentle embodiment of civilization in the story, has been carried off by a gorilla. Here is the first half of the next chapter, which illustrates how Burroughs plots the sequence of events so that the emphasis is on physical action.

From *Tarzan of the Apes*   1914

From the time Tarzan left the tribe of great anthropoids in which he had been raised, it was torn by continual strife and discord. Terkoz proved a cruel and capricious king, so that, one by one, many of the older and weaker apes, upon whom he was particularly prone to vent his brutish nature, took their families and sought the quiet and safety of the far interior.

But at last those who remained were driven to desperation by the continued truculence of Terkoz, and it so happened that one of them recalled the parting admonition of Tarzan:

"If you have a chief who is cruel, do not do as the other apes do, and attempt, any one of you, to pit yourself against him alone. But, instead, let two or three or four of you attack him together. Then, if you will do this, no chief will dare to be other than he should be, for four of you can kill any chief who may ever be over you."

And the ape who recalled this wise counsel repeated it to several of his fellows, so that when Terkoz returned to the tribe that day he found a warm reception awaiting him.

There were no formalities. As Terkoz reached the group, five huge, hairy 5
beasts sprang upon him.

At heart he was an arrant coward, which is the way with bullies among
apes as well as among men; so he did not remain to fight and die, but tore
himself away from them as quickly as he could and fled into the sheltering
boughs of the forest.

Two more attempts he made to rejoin the tribe, but on each occasion he
was set upon and driven away. At last he gave it up, and turned, foaming with
rage and hatred, into the jungle.

For several days he wandered aimlessly, nursing his spite and looking for
some weak thing on which to vent his pent anger.

It was in this state of mind that the horrible, manlike beast, swinging
from tree to tree, came suddenly upon two women in the jungle.

He was right above them when he discovered them. The first intimation 10
Jane Porter had of his presence was when the great hairy body dropped to the
earth beside her, and she saw the awful face and the snarling, hideous mouth
thrust within a foot of her.

One piercing scream escaped her lips as the brute hand clutched her
arm. Then she was dragged toward those awful fangs which yawned at
her throat. But ere they touched that fair skin another mood claimed the
anthropoid.

The tribe had kept his women. He must find others to replace them. This
hairless white ape would be the first of his new household, and so he threw
her roughly across his broad, hairy shoulders and leaped back into the trees,
bearing Jane away.

Esmeralda's scream of terror had mingled once with that of Jane, and
then, as was Esmeralda's manner under stress of emergency which required
presence of mind, she swooned.

But Jane did not once lose consciousness. It is true that that awful face,
pressing close to hers, and the stench of the foul breath beating upon her
nostrils, paralyzed her with terror; but her brain was clear, and she comprehended all that transpired.

With what seemed to her marvelous rapidity the brute bore her through 15
the forest, but still she did not cry out or struggle. The sudden advent of the
ape had confused her to such an extent that she thought now that he was
bearing her toward the beach.

For this reason she conserved her energies and her voice until she could
see that they had approached near enough to the camp to attract the succor
she craved.

She could not have known it, but she was being borne farther and farther
into the impenetrable jungle.

The scream that had brought Clayton and the two older men stumbling through the undergrowth had led Tarzan of the Apes straight to where
Esmeralda lay, but it was not Esmeralda in whom his interest centered,
though pausing over her he saw that she was unhurt.

For a moment he scrutinized the ground below and the trees above, until the ape that was in him by virtue of training and environment, combined with the intelligence that was his by right of birth, told his wondrous wood-craft the whole story as plainly as though he had seen the thing happen with his own eyes.

And then he was gone again into the swaying trees, following the high-flung spoor which no other human eye could have detected, much less translated.   20

At boughs' ends, where the anthropoid swings from one tree to another, there is most to mark the trail, but least to point the direction of the quarry; for there the pressure is downward always, toward the small end of the branch, whether the ape be leaving or entering a tree. Nearer the center of the tree, where the signs of passage are fainter, the direction is plainly marked.

Here, on this branch, a caterpillar has been crushed by the fugitive's great foot, and Tarzan knows instinctively where that same foot would touch in the next stride. Here he looks to find a tiny particle of the demolished larva, oft-times not more than a speck of moisture.

Again, a minute bit of bark has been upturned by the scraping hand, and the direction of the break indicates the direction of the passage. Or some great limb, or the stem of the tree itself has been brushed by the hairy body, and a tiny shred of hair tells him by the direction from which it is wedged beneath the bark that he is on the right trail.

Nor does he need to check his speed to catch these seemingly faint records of the fleeing beast.

To Tarzan they stand out boldly against all the myriad other scars and bruises and signs upon the leafy way. But strongest of all is the scent, for Tarzan is pursuing up the wind, and his trained nostrils are as sensitive as a hound's.   25

There are those who believe that the lower orders are specially endowed by nature with better olfactory nerves than man, but it is merely a matter of development.

Man's survival does not hinge so greatly upon the perfection of his senses. His power to reason has relieved them of many of their duties, and so they have, to some extent, atrophied, as have the muscles which move the ears and scalp, merely from disuse.

The muscles are there, about the ears and beneath the scalp, and so are the nerves which transmit sensations to the brain, but they are underdeveloped because they are not needed.

Not so with Tarzan of the Apes. From early infancy his survival had depended upon acuteness of eyesight, hearing, smell, touch, and taste far more than upon the more slowly developed organ of reason.

The least developed of all in Tarzan was the sense of taste, for he could eat luscious fruits, or raw flesh, long buried, with almost equal appreciation; but in that he differed but slightly from more civilized epicures.   30

Almost silently the ape-man sped on in the track of Terkoz and his prey, but the sound of his approach reached the ears of the fleeing beast and spurred it on to greater speed.

Three miles were covered before Tarzan overtook them, and then Terkoz, seeing that further flight was futile, dropped to the ground in a small open glade, that he might turn and fight for his prize or be free to escape unhampered if he saw that the pursuer was more than a match for him.

He still grasped Jane in one great arm as Tarzan bounded like a leopard into the arena which nature had provided for this primeval-like battle.

When Terkoz saw that it was Tarzan who pursued him, he jumped to the conclusion that this was Tarzan's woman, since they were of the same kind — white and hairless — and so he rejoiced at this opportunity for double revenge upon his hated enemy.

To Jane the strange apparition of this godlike man was as wine to sick   35
nerves.

From the description which Clayton and her father and Mr. Philander had given her, she knew that it must be the same wonderful creature who had saved them, and she saw in him only a protector and a friend.

But as Terkoz pushed her roughly aside to meet Tarzan's charge, and she saw the great proportions of the ape and the mighty muscles and the fierce fangs, her heart quailed. How could any vanquish such a mighty antagonist?

Like two charging bulls they came together, and like two wolves sought each other's throat. Against the long canines of the ape was pitted the thin blade of the man's knife.

Jane — her lithe, young form flattened against the trunk of a great tree, her hands tight pressed against her rising and falling bosom, and her eyes wide with mingled horror, fascination, fear, and admiration — watched the primordial ape battle with the primeval man for possession of a woman — for her.

As the great muscles of the man's back and shoulders knotted beneath   40
the tension of his efforts, and the huge biceps and forearm held at bay those mighty tusks, the veil of centuries of civilization and culture were swept from the blurred vision of the Baltimore girl.

When the long knife drank deep a dozen times of Terkoz's heart's blood, and the great carcass rolled lifeless upon the ground, it was a primeval woman who sprang forward with outstretched arms toward the primeval man who had fought for her and won.

And Tarzan?

He did what no red-blooded man needs lessons in doing. He took his woman in his arms and smothered her upturned, panting lips with kisses.

For a moment Jane lay there with half-closed eyes. For a moment — the first in her young life — she knew the meaning of love.

But as suddenly as the veil had been withdrawn it dropped again, and   45
an outraged conscience suffused her face with its scarlet mantle, and a

mortified woman thrust Tarzan of the Apes from her and buried her face in her hands.

Tarzan had been surprised when he had found the girl he had learned to love after a vague and abstract manner a willing prisoner in his arms. Now he was surprised that she repulsed him.

He came close to her once more and took hold of her arm. She turned upon him like a tigress, striking his great breast with her tiny hands.

Tarzan could not understand it.

A moment ago, and it had been his intention to hasten Jane back to her people, but that little moment was lost now in the dim and distant past of things which were but can never be again, and with it the good intention had gone to join the impossible.

Since then Tarzan of the Apes had felt a warm, lithe form close pressed to his. Hot, sweet breath against his cheek and mouth had fanned a new flame to life within his breast, and perfect lips had clung to his in burning kisses that had seared a deep brand into his soul — a brand which marked a new Tarzan.

Again he laid his hand upon her arm. Again she repulsed him. And then Tarzan of the Apes did just what his first ancestor would have done.

He took his woman in his arms and carried her into the jungle.

This episode begins with **exposition**, the background information the reader needs to make sense of the situation in which the characters are placed. The first eight paragraphs let us know that Terkoz has been overthrown as leader of the ape tribe and that he is roaming the jungle "looking for some weak thing on which to vent his pent anger." This exposition is in the form of a flashback. (Recall that the previous chapter ended with Esmeralda's report of the kidnapping; now we will see what happened.)

Once this information supplies a context for the characters, the plot gains momentum with the **rising action**, a complication that intensifies the situation: Terkoz, looking for a victim, discovers the vulnerable Esmeralda and Jane. His first impulse is to kill Jane, but his "mood" changes when he remembers that he has no woman of his own after having been forced to leave the tribe (more exposition). Hence, there is a further complication in the rising action when he decides to carry her off. Just when it seems that the situation could not get any worse, it does. The reader is invited to shudder even more than if Terkoz had made a meal of Jane because she may have to endure the "awful face," "foul breath," and lust of this beast.

When Tarzan finally catches up to Terkoz, the **conflict** of this episode fully emerges. Tarzan must save the woman he loves by defeating his long-standing enemy, while Terkoz seeks to achieve a "double revenge" by killing Tarzan and taking his woman. Terkoz's assumption that Jane is Tarzan's woman is a **foreshadowing**, a suggestion of what is yet to come. In this conflict Tarzan is the **protagonist** or **hero**, the central character who engages our interest and empathy. *Protagonist* is often a more useful term than *hero*

or *heroine*, however, because the central character of a story can be despi-
cable as well as heroic. Terkoz is the *antagonist*, the force that opposes the
protagonist.

The battle between Tarzan and Terkoz creates *suspense* because the
reader is made anxious about what is going to happen. Burroughs makes
certain that the reader will worry about the outcome by having Jane wonder, "How could any vanquish such a mighty antagonist?" If we are caught
up in the moment, we watch the battle, as Jane does, with "mingled horror, fascination, fear, and admiration" to see what will happen next. The
moment of greatest emotional tension, the *climax*, occurs when Tarzan kills
Terkoz. Tarzan's victory is the *resolution* of the conflict, also known as the
dénouement (a French word meaning the "untying of the knot"). This could
have been the conclusion to the episode except that Jane and Tarzan simultaneously discover their "primeval" selves sexually drawn to each other.
Burroughs resolves one conflict — the battle with Terkoz — but then immediately creates another — by raising the question of what a respectable professor's daughter from Baltimore is doing in the sweaty arms of a panting,
half-naked man.

For a brief moment the cycle of conflict, suspense, and resolution begins
again as Jane passionately kisses Tarzan; then her "outraged conscience"
causes her to regain her sense of propriety and she pushes him away. Although
Tarzan succeeds in the encounter with Terkoz, he is not successful with Jane.
However, Burroughs creates suspense for a third time at the very end of the
episode, when the "new Tarzan," having been transformed by this sexual
awakening, "took his woman in his arms and carried her into the jungle."
What will he do next? Despite the novel's implausibility (beginning with the
premise that apes could raise a human child) and its heavy use of coincidences
(not the least of which is Tarzan's donning a loincloth for the first time only
four pages before he meets Jane), the story is difficult to put down. The plot
swings us swiftly and smoothly from incident to incident, even if there is an
occasional interruption, such as Burroughs's discussion of evolution, in the
flow of the action.

The primary conflict that Tarzan experiences in his battle with Terkoz is
external. External conflict is popular in adventure stories because the protagonist's physical struggles with a formidable foe or the ever-present dangers
of a dense jungle echoing wild screams provide plenty of excitement. External conflicts may place the protagonist in opposition to another individual,
nature, or society. Tarzan's battle with societal values begins the moment he
instinctively takes Jane in his arms to carry her off into the jungle. He will
learn that an individual's conflict with society can be as frustrating as it is
complex, which is why so many plots in serious fiction focus on this conflict.
It can be seen, to cite only two examples, in a mysterious stranger's alienation
from a materialistic culture in Herman Melville's "Bartleby, the Scrivener"
(p. 99) and in a young black man's struggle with racism in Ellison's "Battle
Royal" (p. 177).

Conflict may also be internal; in such a case some moral or psychological issue must be resolved within the protagonist. Inner conflicts frequently accompany external ones, as in Godwin's "A Sorrowful Woman" (p. 38). Godwin's story is quiet and almost uneventful compared with *Tarzan of the Apes*. The conflict, though puzzling, is more significant in "A Sorrowful Woman" because that story subtly explores some troubling issues that cannot be resolved simply by "huge biceps" or a "lithe, young form." The protagonist struggles with both internal and external forces. We are not told why she withdraws from her considerate husband and beautiful son. There is no exposition to explain why she is hopelessly "sad and sick" of them. There is no readily identifiable antagonist in her way, but there are several possibilities. Her antagonist is some part of herself that cannot find satisfaction in playing the roles of wife and mother, yet her husband and child also seem to bear some of the responsibility, as does the domestic environment that defines her.

Although Burroughs makes enormous demands on Tarzan to survive the perils of the jungle, the author makes few demands on the reader. In part, that's why *Tarzan of the Apes* is so much fun: we sit back while Tarzan does all the work, struggling heroically through all the conflicts Burroughs has planted along his jungle paths. Godwin's story, in contrast, illustrates that there are other kinds of plots, less dependent on action but equally full of conflict. This kind of reading is more demanding, but ultimately more satisfying, because as we confront conflicts in serious fiction we read not only absorbing stories but also ourselves. We are invited not to escape life but to look long and hard at it. Although serious fiction can be as diverting and pleasurable as most standard action-packed plots, serious fiction offers an additional important element: a perspective on experience that reflects rather than deflects life.

The following three stories — Lydia Davis's "Negative Emotions," William Faulkner's "A Rose for Emily," and Andre Dubus's "Killings" — are remarkable for the different kinds of tension produced in each by a subtle use of plot.

Lydia Davis (b. 1947)

Born in Northampton, Massachusetts, Lydia Davis graduated from Barnard College in 1970, after which she began work as a translator of French literature. Her success as a translator can be measured in part by the French government's awarding her the Chevalier of the Order of Arts. She has won high praise particularly for her translations of Marcel Proust. As a fiction

© Colin McPherson/Corbis.

writer, Davis has appeared in numerous literary periodicals while publishing one novel, *The End of the Story* (1995), and a number of collections of short stories, including *Break It Down* (1986); *Almost No Memory* (1997); *Samuel Johnson Is Indignant* (2001); *Varieties of Disturbances: Stories* (2007); *The Collected Stories of Lydia Davis* (2009); and *Can't and Won't* (2014), the collection from which "Negative Emotions" is reprinted. Among the prestigious literary prizes that Davis has been awarded are fellowships from the MacArthur and Guggenheim foundations, a Lannan Literary Award, and a Whiting Writer's Award. She has taught at several schools, including Bard College and the University at Albany. Davis is well known for her brief, compact, sharp, and often humorous fictions that survey contemporary life. "In such a form," she observes, "each word has to be right."

Negative Emotions   2014

A well-meaning teacher, inspired by a text he had been reading, once sent all the other teachers in his school a message about negative emotions. The message consisted entirely of advice quoted from a Vietnamese Buddhist monk.

Emotion, said the monk, is like a storm: it stays for a while and then it goes. Upon perceiving the emotion (like a coming storm), one should put oneself in a stable position. One should sit or lie down. One should focus on one's abdomen. One should focus, specifically, on the area just below one's navel, and practice mindful breathing. If one can identify the emotion as an emotion, it may then be easier to handle.

The other teachers were puzzled. They did not understand why their colleague had sent them a message about negative emotions. They resented the message, and they resented their colleague. They thought he was accusing them of having negative emotions and needing advice about how to handle them. Some of them were, in fact, angry.

The teachers did not choose to regard their anger as a coming storm. They did not focus on their abdomens. They did not focus on the area just below their navels. Instead, they wrote back immediately, declaring that because they did not understand why he had sent it, his message had filled them with negative emotions. They told him that it would take a lot of practice for them to get over the negative emotions caused by his message. But, they went on, they did not intend to do this practice. Far from being troubled by their negative emotions, they said, they in fact liked having negative emotions, particularly about him and his message.

Considerations for Critical Thinking and Writing

1. **first response.** Why does it make sense that the author of this story is also a professional translator? What does that fact suggest about her sensitivity to diction and tone?

2. Describe the movement of the story's plot. What elements of a typical plot (see the glossary entry for *plot*) can you find in the story?

3. Which paragraphs seem particularly humorous to you? Explain why the story does or doesn't make a serious point.

4. To what extent do you think these paragraphs constitute a short story?

5. CONNECTION TO ANOTHER SELECTION. Compare the style, tone, and irony of Davis's story with those of Annie Proulx's "55 Miles to the Gas Pump" (p. 314).

WILLIAM FAULKNER (1897–1962)

Cofield Collection, Archives and Special Collections, University of Mississippi Libraries.

Born into an old Mississippi family that had lost its influence and wealth during the Civil War, William Faulkner lived nearly all his life in the South writing about Yoknapatawpha County, an imagined Mississippi county similar to his home in Oxford. Among his novels based on this fictional location are *The Sound and the Fury* (1929), *As I Lay Dying* (1930), *Light in August* (1932), and *Absalom, Absalom!* (1936). Although his writings are regional in their emphasis on local social history, his concerns are broader. In his 1950 acceptance speech for the Nobel Prize for Literature, he insisted that the "problems of the human heart in conflict with itself . . . alone can make good writing because only that is worth writing about, worth the agony and the sweat." This commitment is evident in his novels and in *The Collected Stories of William Faulkner* (1950).

A Rose for Emily   1931

I

When Miss Emily Grierson died, our whole town went to her funeral: the men through a sort of respectful affection for a fallen monument, the women mostly out of curiosity to see the inside of her house, which no one save an old manservant — a combined gardener and cook — had seen in at least ten years.

It was a big, squarish frame house that had once been white, decorated with cupolas and spires and scrolled balconies in the heavily lightsome style of the seventies, set on what had once been our most select street. But garages and cotton gins had encroached and obliterated even the august names of that neighborhood; only Miss Emily's house was left, lifting its stubborn and coquettish decay above the cotton wagons and the gasoline pumps — an eyesore among eyesores. And now Miss Emily had gone to join the representatives of those august names where they lay in the cedar-bemused cemetery among the ranked and anonymous graves of Union and Confederate soldiers who fell at the battle of Jefferson.

Alive, Miss Emily had been a tradition, a duty, and a care; a sort of hereditary obligation upon the town, dating from that day in 1894 when Colonel Sartoris, the mayor — he who fathered the edict that no Negro woman should appear on the streets without an apron — remitted her taxes, the dispensation dating from the death of her father on into perpetuity. Not that Miss Emily would have accepted charity. Colonel Sartoris invented an involved tale to the effect that Miss Emily's father had loaned money to the town, which the town, as a matter of business, preferred this way of repaying. Only a man of Colonel Sartoris' generation and thought could have invented it, and only a woman could have believed it.

When the next generation, with its more modern ideas, became mayors and aldermen, this arrangement created some little dissatisfaction. On the first of the year they mailed her a tax notice. February came, and there was no reply. They wrote her a formal letter, asking her to call at the sheriff's office at her convenience. A week later the mayor wrote her himself, offering to call or to send his car for her, and received in reply a note on paper of an archaic shape, in a thin, flowing calligraphy in faded ink, to the effect that she no longer went out at all. The tax notice was also enclosed, without comment.

They called a special meeting of the Board of Aldermen. A deputation 5 waited upon her, knocked at the door through which no visitor had passed since she ceased giving china-painting lessons eight or ten years earlier. They were admitted by the old Negro into a dim hall from which a stairway mounted into still more shadow. It smelled of dust and disuse — a close, dank smell. The Negro led them into the parlor. It was furnished in heavy, leather-covered furniture. When the Negro opened the blinds of one window, they could see that the leather was cracked; and when they sat down, a faint dust rose sluggishly about their thighs, spinning with slow motes in the single sun-ray. On a tarnished gilt easel before the fireplace stood a crayon portrait of Miss Emily's father.

They rose when she entered — a small, fat woman in black, with a thin gold chain descending to her waist and vanishing into her belt, leaning on an ebony cane with a tarnished gold head. Her skeleton was small and spare; perhaps that was why what would have been merely plumpness in another was obesity in her. She looked bloated, like a body long submerged in motionless water, and of that pallid hue. Her eyes, lost in the fatty ridges of her face, looked like two small pieces of coal pressed into a lump of dough as they moved from one face to another while the visitors stated their errand.

She did not ask them to sit. She just stood in the door and listened quietly until the spokesman came to a stumbling halt. Then they could hear the invisible watch ticking at the end of the gold chain.

Her voice was dry and cold. "I have no taxes in Jefferson. Colonel Sartoris explained it to me. Perhaps one of you can gain access to the city records and satisfy yourselves."

"But we have. We are the city authorities, Miss Emily. Didn't you get a notice from the sheriff, signed by him?"

"I received a paper, yes," Miss Emily said. "Perhaps he considers himself the sheriff . . . I have no taxes in Jefferson." 10

"But there is nothing on the books to show that, you see. We must go by the—"

"See Colonel Sartoris. I have no taxes in Jefferson."

"But, Miss Emily—"

"See Colonel Sartoris." (Colonel Sartoris had been dead almost ten years.) "I have no taxes in Jefferson. Tobe!" The Negro appeared. "Show these gentlemen out."

II

So she vanquished them, horse and foot, just as she had vanquished their 15 fathers thirty years before about the smell. That was two years after her father's death and a short time after her sweetheart—the one we believed would marry her—had deserted her. After her father's death she went out very little; after her sweetheart went away, people hardly saw her at all. A few of the ladies had the temerity to call, but were not received, and the only sign of life about the place was the Negro man—a young man then—going in and out with a market basket.

"Just as if a man—any man—could keep a kitchen properly," the ladies said; so they were not surprised when the smell developed. It was another link between the gross, teeming world and the high and mighty Griersons.

A neighbor, a woman, complained to the mayor, Judge Stevens, eighty years old.

"But what will you have me do about it, madam?" he said.

"Why, send her word to stop it," the woman said. "Isn't there a law?"

"I'm sure that won't be necessary," Judge Stevens said. "It's probably 20 just a snake or a rat that nigger of hers killed in the yard. I'll speak to him about it."

The next day he received two more complaints, one from a man who came in diffident deprecation. "We really must do something about it, Judge. I'd be the last one in the world to bother Miss Emily, but we've got to do something." That night the Board of Aldermen met—three graybeards and one younger man, a member of the rising generation.

"It's simple enough," he said. "Send her word to have her place cleaned up. Give her a certain time to do it in, and if she don't . . ."

"Dammit, sir," Judge Stevens said, "will you accuse a lady to her face of smelling bad?"

So the next night, after midnight, four men crossed Miss Emily's lawn and slunk about the house like burglars, sniffing along the base of the brickwork and at the cellar openings while one of them performed a regular sowing motion with his hand out of a sack slung from his shoulder. They broke open the cellar door and sprinkled lime there, and in all the outbuildings. As they recrossed the lawn, a window that had been dark was lighted and Miss Emily sat in it, the light behind her, and her upright torso motionless as that of an idol. They crept quietly across the lawn and into the shadow of the locusts that lined the street. After a week or two the smell went away.

That was when people had begun to feel really sorry for her. People in our town, remembering how old lady Wyatt, her great-aunt, had gone completely crazy at last, believed that the Griersons held themselves a little too high for what they really were. None of the young men were quite good enough for Miss Emily and such. We had long thought of them as a tableau, Miss Emily a slender figure in white in the background, her father a spraddled silhouette in the foreground, his back to her and clutching a horsewhip, the two of them framed by the back-flung front door. So when she got to be thirty and was still single, we were not pleased exactly, but vindicated; even with insanity in the family she wouldn't have turned down all of her chances if they had really materialized.

When her father died, it got about that the house was all that was left to her; and in a way, people were glad. At last they could pity Miss Emily. Being left alone, and a pauper, she had become humanized. Now she too would know the old thrill and the old despair of a penny more or less.

The day after his death all the ladies prepared to call at the house and offer condolence and aid, as is our custom. Miss Emily met them at the door, dressed as usual and with no trace of grief on her face. She told them that her father was not dead. She did that for three days, with the ministers calling on her, and the doctors, trying to persuade her to let them dispose of the body. Just as they were about to resort to law and force, she broke down, and they buried her father quickly.

We did not say she was crazy then. We believed she had to do that. We remembered all the young men her father had driven away, and we knew that with nothing left, she would have to cling to that which had robbed her, as people will.

III

She was sick for a long time. When we saw her again, her hair was cut short, making her look like a girl, with a vague resemblance to those angels in colored church windows — sort of tragic and serene.

The town had just let the contracts for paving the sidewalks, and in the summer after her father's death they began the work. The construction company came with niggers and mules and machinery, and a foreman named Homer Barron, a Yankee — a big, dark, ready man, with a big voice and eyes lighter than his face. The little boys would follow in groups to hear him cuss the niggers, and the niggers singing in time to the rise and fall of picks. Pretty soon he knew everybody in town. Whenever you heard a lot of laughing anywhere about the square, Homer Barron would be in the center of the group. Presently we began to see him and Miss Emily on Sunday afternoons driving in the yellow-wheeled buggy and the matched team of bays from the livery stable.

At first we were glad that Miss Emily would have an interest, because the ladies all said, "Of course a Grierson would not think seriously of a Northerner, a day laborer." But there were still others, older people, who said that even grief could not cause a real lady to forget *noblesse oblige*° — without calling it *noblesse oblige*. They just said, "Poor Emily. Her kinsfolk should come to her." She had some kin in Alabama; but years ago her father had fallen out with them over the estate of old lady Wyatt, the crazy woman, and there was no communication between the two families. They had not even been represented at the funeral.

And as soon as the old people said, "Poor Emily," the whispering began. "Do you suppose it's really so?" they said to one another. "Of course it is. What else could . . ." This behind their hands; rustling of craned silk and satin behind jalousies closed upon the sun of Sunday afternoon as the thin, swift clop-clop-clop of the matched team passed: "Poor Emily."

She carried her head high enough — even when we believed that she was fallen. It was as if she demanded more than ever the recognition of her dignity as the last Grierson; as if it had wanted that touch of earthiness to reaffirm her imperviousness. Like when she bought the rat poison, the arsenic. That was over a year after they had begun to say "Poor Emily," and while the two female cousins were visiting her.

"I want some poison," she said to the druggist. She was over thirty then, still a slight woman, though thinner than usual, with cold, haughty black eyes in a face the flesh of which was strained across the temples and about the eye-sockets as you imagine a lighthouse-keeper's face ought to look. "I want some poison," she said.

"Yes, Miss Emily. What kind? For rats and such? I'd recom —"   35

"I want the best you have. I don't care what kind."

The druggist named several. "They'll kill anything up to an elephant. But what you want is —"

"Arsenic," Miss Emily said. "Is that a good one?"

"Is . . . arsenic? Yes, ma'am. But what you want —"

"I want arsenic."   40

The druggist looked down at her. She looked back at him, erect, her face like a strained flag. "Why, of course," the druggist said. "If that's what you want. But the law requires you to tell what you are going to use it for."

Miss Emily just stared at him, her head tilted back in order to look him eye for eye, until he looked away and went and got the arsenic and wrapped it up. The Negro delivery boy brought her the package; the druggist didn't come back. When she opened the package at home there was written on the box, under the skull and bones: "For rats."

IV

So the next day we all said, "She will kill herself"; and we said it would be the best thing. When she had first begun to be seen with Homer Barron, we

---

noblesse oblige: The obligation of people of high social position.

had said, "She will marry him." Then we said, "She will persuade him yet," because Homer himself had remarked—he liked men, and it was known that he drank with the younger men in the Elks' Club—that he was not a marrying man. Later we said, "Poor Emily" behind the jalousies as they passed on Sunday afternoon in the glittering buggy, Miss Emily with her head high and Homer Barron with his hat cocked and a cigar in his teeth, reins and whip in a yellow glove.

Then some of the ladies began to say that it was a disgrace to the town and a bad example to the young people. The men did not want to interfere, but at last the ladies forced the Baptist minister—Miss Emily's people were Episcopal—to call upon her. He would never divulge what happened during that interview, but he refused to go back again. The next Sunday they again drove about the streets, and the following day the minister's wife wrote to Miss Emily's relations in Alabama.

So she had blood-kin under her roof again and we sat back to watch   45 developments. At first nothing happened. Then we were sure that they were to be married. We learned that Miss Emily had been to the jeweler's and ordered a man's toilet set in silver, with the letters H. B. on each piece. Two days later we learned that she had bought a complete outfit of men's clothing, including a nightshirt, and we said, "They are married." We were really glad. We were glad because the two female cousins were even more Grierson than Miss Emily had ever been.

So we were not surprised when Homer Barron—the streets had been finished some time since—was gone. We were a little disappointed that there was not a public blowing-off, but we believed that he had gone on to prepare for Miss Emily's coming, or to give her a chance to get rid of the cousins. (By that time it was a cabal, and we were all Miss Emily's allies to help circumvent the cousins.) Sure enough, after another week they departed. And, as we had expected all along, within three days Homer Barron was back in town. A neighbor saw the Negro man admit him at the kitchen door at dusk one evening.

And that was the last we saw of Homer Barron. And of Miss Emily for some time. The Negro man went in and out with the market basket, but the front door remained closed. Now and then we would see her at a window for a moment, as the men did that night when they sprinkled the lime, but for almost six months she did not appear on the streets. Then we knew that this was to be expected too; as if that quality of her father which had thwarted her woman's life so many times had been too virulent and too furious to die.

When we next saw Miss Emily, she had grown fat and her hair was turning gray. During the next few years it grew grayer and grayer until it attained an even pepper-and-salt iron-gray, when it ceased turning. Up to the day of her death at seventy-four it was still that vigorous iron-gray, like the hair of an active man.

From that time on her front door remained closed, save for a period of six or seven years, when she was about forty, during which she gave lessons in china-painting. She fitted up a studio in one of the downstairs rooms, where the daughters and granddaughters of Colonel Sartoris' contemporaries were sent to her with the same regularity and in the same spirit that they were sent to church on Sundays with a twenty-five-cent piece for the collection plate. Meanwhile her taxes had been remitted.

Then the newer generation became the backbone and the spirit of the town, and the painting pupils grew up and fell away and did not send their children to her with boxes of color and tedious brushes and pictures cut from the ladies' magazines. The front door closed upon the last one and remained closed for good. When the town got free postal delivery, Miss Emily alone refused to let them fasten the metal numbers above her door and attach a mailbox to it. She would not listen to them.

Daily, monthly, yearly we watched the Negro grow grayer and more stooped, going in and out with the market basket. Each December we sent her a tax notice, which would be returned by the post office a week later, unclaimed. Now and then we would see her in one of the downstairs windows — she had evidently shut up the top floor of the house — like the carven torso of an idol in a niche, looking or not looking at us, we could never tell which. Thus she passed from generation to generation — dear, inescapable, impervious, tranquil, and perverse.

And so she died. Fell ill in the house filled with dust and shadows, with only a doddering Negro man to wait on her. We did not even know she was sick; we had long since given up trying to get information from the Negro. He talked to no one, probably not even to her, for his voice had grown harsh and rusty, as if from disuse.

She died in one of the downstairs rooms, in a heavy walnut bed with a curtain, her gray head propped on a pillow yellow and moldy with age and lack of sunlight.

V

The Negro met the first of the ladies at the front door and let them in, with their hushed, sibilant voices and their quick, curious glances, and then he disappeared. He walked right through the house and out the back and was not seen again.

The two female cousins came at once. They held the funeral on the second day, with the town coming to look at Miss Emily beneath a mass of bought flowers, with the crayon face of her father musing profoundly above the bier and the ladies sibilant and macabre; and the very old men — some in their brushed Confederate uniforms — on the porch and the lawn, talking of Miss Emily as if she had been a contemporary of theirs, believing that they had danced with her and courted her perhaps, confusing time with its mathematical progression, as the old do, to whom all the past is not a diminishing road but, instead, a huge meadow which no winter ever quite touches, divided from them now by the narrow bottle-neck of the most recent decade of years.

Already we knew that there was one room in that region above stairs which no one had seen in forty years, and which would have to be forced. They waited until Miss Emily was decently in the ground before they opened it.

The violence of breaking down the door seemed to fill this room with pervading dust. A thin, acrid pall as of the tomb seemed to lie everywhere upon this room decked and furnished as for a bridal: upon the valance curtains of faded rose color, upon the rose-shaded lights, upon the dressing table, upon the delicate array of crystal and the man's toilet things backed with tarnished silver, silver so tarnished that the monogram was obscured. Among them lay a collar and tie, as if they had just been removed, which, lifted, left upon the surface a pale crescent in the dust. Upon a chair hung the suit, carefully folded; beneath it the two mute shoes and the discarded socks.

The man himself lay in the bed.

For a long while we just stood there, looking down at the profound and fleshless grin. The body had apparently once lain in the attitude of an embrace, but now the long sleep that outlasts love, that conquers even the grimace of love, had cuckolded him. What was left of him, rotted beneath what was left of the nightshirt, had become inextricable from the bed in which he lay; and upon him and upon the pillow beside him lay that even coating of the patient and biding dust.

Then we noticed that in the second pillow was the indentation of a head. One of us lifted something from it, and leaning forward, that faint and invisible dust dry and acrid in the nostrils, we saw a long strand of iron-gray hair. 60

CONSIDERATIONS FOR CRITICAL THINKING AND WRITING

1. FIRST RESPONSE. How might this story be rewritten as a piece of formula fiction? You could write it as a romance, detective, or horror story — whatever strikes your fancy. Does Faulkner's version have elements of formulaic fiction?

2. What is the effect of the final paragraph of the story? How does it contribute to your understanding of Emily? Why is it important that we get this information last rather than at the beginning of the story?

3. Contrast the order of events as they happen in the story with the order in which they are told. How does this plotting create interest and suspense?

4. Faulkner uses a number of gothic elements in this plot: the imposing decrepit house, the decayed corpse, and the mysterious secret horrors connected with Emily's life. How do these elements forward the plot and establish the atmosphere?

5. In what sense does the narrator's telling of the story serve as "A Rose for Emily"? Why do you think the narrator uses *we* rather than *I*?

6. Explain how Emily's reasons for murdering Homer are related to her personal history and to the ways she handled previous conflicts.

7. Discuss how Faulkner's treatment of the North and South contributes to the meaning of the story.

Andre Dubus (1936–1999)

© Marion Ettlinger.

Though a native of Louisiana, where he attended the Christian Brothers School and McNeese State College, Andre Dubus lived much of his life in Massachusetts; many of his stories are set in the Merrimack Valley north of Boston. After college Dubus served as an officer for five years in the Marine Corps. He then took an M.F.A. at the University of Iowa in 1966 and began teaching at Bradford College in Massachusetts. His fiction earned him numerous awards, and he was both a Guggenheim and a MacArthur Fellow. Among his collections of fiction are *Separate Flights* (1975); *Adultery and Other Choices* (1977); *Finding a Girl in America* (1980), from which "Killings" is taken; *The Last Worthless Evening* (1986); *Collected Stories* (1988); and *Dancing after Hours* (1996). In 1991 he published *Broken Vessels*, a collection of autobiographical essays. His stories are often tense with violence, anger, tenderness, and guilt; they are populated by characters who struggle to understand and survive their experiences, painful with failure and the weight of imperfect relationships. In "Killings," the basis for a 2001 film titled *In the Bedroom*, Dubus offers a powerful blend of intimate domestic life and shocking violence.

Killings   1979

On the August morning when Matt Fowler buried his youngest son, Frank, who had lived for twenty-one years, eight months, and four days, Matt's older son, Steve, turned to him as the family left the grave and walked between their friends, and said: "I should kill him." He was twenty-eight, his brown hair starting to thin in front where he used to have a cowlick. He bit his lower lip, wiped his eyes, then said it again. Ruth's arm, linked with Matt's, tightened; he looked at her. Beneath her eyes there was swelling from the three days she had suffered. At the limousine Matt stopped and looked back at the grave, the casket, and the Congregationalist minister who he thought had probably had a difficult job with the eulogy though he hadn't seemed to, and the old funeral director who was saying something to the six young pallbearers. The grave was on a hill and overlooked the Merrimack, which he could not see from where he stood; he looked at the opposite bank, at the apple orchard with its symmetrically planted trees going up a hill.

Next day Steve drove with his wife back to Baltimore where he managed the branch office of a bank, and Cathleen, the middle child, drove with her husband back to Syracuse. They had left the grandchildren with friends. A month after the funeral Matt played poker at Willis Trottier's because Ruth, who knew this was the second time he had been invited, told him to go, he couldn't sit home with her for the rest of her life, she was all right. After the game Willis went outside to tell everyone good night and, when the others had driven away, he walked with Matt to his car. Willis was a short, silver-haired man who had opened a diner after World War II, his trade then mostly very early breakfast, which he cooked, and then lunch for the men who worked at the leather and shoe factories. He now owned a large restaurant.

"He walks the Goddamn streets," Matt said.

"I know. He was in my place last night, at the bar. With a girl."

"I don't see him. I'm in the store all the time. Ruth sees him. She sees 5 him too much. She was at Sunnyhurst today getting cigarettes and aspirin, and there he was. She can't even go out for cigarettes and aspirin. It's killing her."

"Come back in for a drink."

Matt looked at his watch. Ruth would be asleep. He walked with Willis back into the house, pausing at the steps to look at the starlit sky. It was a cool summer night; he thought vaguely of the Red Sox, did not even know if they were at home tonight; since it happened he had not been able to think about any of the small pleasures he believed he had earned, as he had earned also what was shattered now forever: the quietly harried and quietly pleasurable days of fatherhood. They went inside. Willis's wife, Martha, had gone to bed hours ago, in the rear of the large house which was rigged with burglar and fire alarms. They went downstairs to the game room: the television set suspended from the ceiling, the pool table, the poker table with beer cans, cards, chips, filled ashtrays, and the six chairs where Matt and his friends had sat, the friends picking up the old banter as though he had only been away on vacation; but he could see the affection and courtesy in their eyes. Willis went behind the bar and mixed them each a Scotch and soda; he stayed behind the bar and looked at Matt sitting on the stool.

"How often have you thought about it?" Willis said.

"Every day since he got out. I didn't think about bail. I thought I wouldn't have to worry about him for years. She sees him all the time. It makes her cry."

"He was in my place a long time last night. He'll be back." 10

"Maybe he won't."

"The band. He likes the band."

"What's he doing now?"

"He's tending bar up to Hampton Beach. For a friend. Ever notice even the worst bastard always has friends? He couldn't get work in town. It's just tourists and kids up to Hampton. Nobody knows him. If they do, they don't care. They drink what he mixes."

"Nobody tells me about him." 15

"I hate him, Matt. My boys went to school with him. He was the same then. Know what he'll do? Five at the most. Remember that woman about seven years ago? Shot her husband and dropped him off the bridge in the Merrimack with a hundred-pound sack of cement and said all the way through it that nobody helped her. Know where she is now? She's in Lawrence now, a secretary. And whoever helped her, where the hell is he?"

"I've got a .38 I've had for years, I take it to the store now. I tell Ruth it's for the night deposits. I tell her things have changed: we got junkies here now too. Lots of people without jobs. She knows though."

"What does she know?"

"She knows I started carrying it after the first time she saw him in town. She knows it's in case I see him, and there's some kind of a situation —"

He stopped, looked at Willis, and finished his drink. Willis mixed him 20 another.

"What kind of situation?"

"Where he did something to me. Where I could get away with it."

"How does Ruth feel about that?"

"She doesn't know."

"You said she does, she's got it figured out." 25

He thought of her that afternoon: when she went into Sunnyhurst, Strout was waiting at the counter while the clerk bagged the things he had bought; she turned down an aisle and looked at soup cans until he left.

"Ruth would shoot him herself, if she thought she could hit him."

"You got a permit?"

"No."

"I do. You could get a year for that." 30

"Maybe I'll get one. Or maybe I won't. Maybe I'll just stop bringing it to the store."

Richard Strout was twenty-six years old, a high school athlete, football scholarship to the University of Massachusetts where he lasted for almost two semesters before quitting in advance of the final grades that would have forced him not to return. People then said: Dickie can do the work; he just doesn't want to. He came home and did construction work for his father but refused his father's offer to learn the business; his two older brothers had learned it, so that Strout and Sons trucks going about town, and signs on construction sites, now slashed wounds into Matt Fowler's life. Then Richard married a young girl and became a bartender, his salary and tips augmented and perhaps sometimes matched by his father, who also posted his bond. So his friends, his enemies (he had those: fist fights or, more often, boys and then young men who had not fought him when they thought they should have), and those who simply knew him by face and name, had a series of images of him which they recalled when they heard of the killing: the high school running back, the young drunk in bars, the oblivious hard-hatted young man eating lunch at a counter, the bartender who could perhaps be called courteous but not more than that: as he tended bar, his dark eyes and dark, wide-jawed face appeared less sullen, near blank.

One night he beat Frank. Frank was living at home and waiting for September, for graduate school in economics, and working as a lifeguard at Salisbury Beach, where he met Mary Ann Strout, in her first month of separation. She spent most days at the beach with her two sons. Before ten o'clock one night Frank came home; he had driven to the hospital first, and he walked into the living room with stitches over his right eye and both lips bright and swollen.

"I'm all right," he said, when Matt and Ruth stood up, and Matt turned off the television, letting Ruth get to him first: the tall, muscled but slender suntanned boy. Frank tried to smile at them but couldn't because of his lips.

"It was her husband, wasn't it?" Ruth said. 35

"Ex," Frank said. "He dropped in."

Matt gently held Frank's jaw and turned his face to the light, looked at the stitches, the blood under the white of the eye, the bruised flesh.

"Press charges," Matt said.

"No."

"What's to stop him from doing it again? Did you hit him at all? Enough 40 so he won't want to next time?"

"I don't think I touched him."

"So what are you going to do?"

"Take karate," Frank said, and tried again to smile.

"That's not the problem," Ruth said.

"You know you like her," Frank said. 45

"I like a lot of people. What about the boys? Did they see it?"

"They were asleep."

"Did you leave her alone with him?"

"He left first. She was yelling at him. I believe she had a skillet in her hand."

"Oh for God's sake," Ruth said. 50

Matt had been dealing with that too: at the dinner table on evenings when Frank wasn't home, was eating with Mary Ann; or, on the other nights — and Frank was with her every night — he talked with Ruth while they watched television, or lay in bed with the windows open and he smelled the night air and imagined, with both pride and muted sorrow, Frank in Mary Ann's arms. Ruth didn't like it because Mary Ann was in the process of divorce, because she had two children, because she was four years older than Frank, and finally — she told this in bed, where she had during all of their marriage told him of her deepest feelings: of love, of passion, of fears about one of the children, of pain Matt had caused her or she had caused him — she was against it because of what she had heard: that the marriage had gone bad early, and for most of it Richard and Mary Ann had both played around.

"That can't be true," Matt said. "Strout wouldn't have stood for it."

"Maybe he loves her."

"He's too hot-tempered. He couldn't have taken that."

But Matt knew Strout had taken it, for he had heard the stories too. 55 He wondered who had told them to Ruth; and he felt vaguely annoyed and isolated: living with her for thirty-one years and still not knowing what she talked about with her friends. On these summer nights he did not so much argue with her as try to comfort her, but finally there was no difference between the two: she had concrete objections, which he tried to overcome. And in his attempt to do this, he neglected his own objections, which were the same as hers, so that as he spoke to her he felt as disembodied as he sometimes did in the store when he helped a man choose a blouse or dress or piece of costume jewelry for his wife.

"The divorce doesn't mean anything," he said. "She was young and maybe she liked his looks and then after a while she realized she was living with a bastard. I see it as a positive thing."

"She's not divorced yet."

"It's the same thing. Massachusetts has crazy laws, that's all. Her age is no problem. What's it matter when she was born? And that other business: even if it's true, which it probably isn't, it's got nothing to do with Frank, and it's in the past. And the kids are no problem. She's been married six years; she ought to have kids. Frank likes them. He plays with them. And he's not going to marry her anyway, so it's not a problem of money."

"Then what's he doing with her?"

"She probably loves him, Ruth. Girls always have. Why can't we just leave it at that?"   60

"He got home at six o'clock Tuesday morning."

"I didn't know you knew. I've already talked to him about it."

Which he had: since he believed almost nothing he told Ruth, he went to Frank with what he believed. The night before, he had followed Frank to the car after dinner.

"You wouldn't make much of a burglar," he said.

"How's that?"   65

Matt was looking up at him; Frank was six feet tall, an inch and a half taller than Matt, who had been proud when Frank at seventeen outgrew him; he had only felt uncomfortable when he had to reprimand or caution him. He touched Frank's bicep, thought of the young taut passionate body, believed he could sense the desire, and again he felt the pride and sorrow and envy too, not knowing whether he was envious of Frank or Mary Ann.

"When you came in yesterday morning, I woke up. One of these mornings your mother will. And I'm the one who'll have to talk to her. She won't interfere with you. Okay? I know it means—" But he stopped, thinking: I know it means getting up and leaving that suntanned girl and going sleepy to the car, I know—

"Okay," Frank said, and touched Matt's shoulder and got into the car.

There had been other talks, but the only long one was their first one: a night driving to Fenway Park, Matt having ordered the tickets so they could talk, and knowing when Frank said yes, he would go, that he knew the talk was coming too. It took them forty minutes to get to Boston, and they talked about Mary Ann until they joined the city traffic along the Charles River, blue in the late sun. Frank told him all the things that Matt would later pretend to believe when he told them to Ruth.

"It seems like a lot for a young guy to take on," Matt finally said.   70

"Sometimes it is. But she's worth it."

"Are you thinking about getting married?"

"We haven't talked about it. She can't for over a year. I've got school."

"I *do* like her," Matt said.

He did. Some evenings, when the long summer sun was still low in the 75
sky, Frank brought her home; they came into the house smelling of suntan
lotion and the sea, and Matt gave them gin and tonics and started the charcoal in the backyard, and looked at Mary Ann in the lawn chair: long and
very light brown hair (Matt thinking that twenty years ago she would have
dyed it blonde), and the long brown legs he loved to look at; her face was
pretty; she had probably never in her adult life gone unnoticed into a public
place. It was in her wide brown eyes that she looked older than Frank; after a
few drinks Matt thought what he saw in her eyes was something erotic, testament to the rumors about her; but he knew it wasn't that, or all that: she had,
very young, been through a sort of pain that his children, and he and Ruth,
had been spared. In the moments of his recognizing that pain, he wanted
to tenderly touch her hair, wanted with some gesture to give her solace and
hope. And he would glance at Frank, and hope they would love each other,
hope Frank would soothe that pain in her heart, take it from her eyes; and
her divorce, her age, and her children did not matter at all. On the first two
evenings she did not bring her boys, and then Ruth asked her to bring them
the next time. In bed that night Ruth said, "She hasn't brought them because
she's embarrassed. She shouldn't feel embarrassed."

Richard Strout shot Frank in front of the boys. They were sitting on the living room floor watching television, Frank sitting on the couch, and Mary
Ann just returning from the kitchen with a tray of sandwiches. Strout came
in the front door and shot Frank twice in the chest and once in the face with
a 9 mm automatic. Then he looked at the boys and Mary Ann, and went
home to wait for the police.

It seemed to Matt that from the time Mary Ann called weeping to tell him
until now, a Saturday night in September, sitting in the car with Willis, parked
beside Strout's car, waiting for the bar to close, that he had not so much moved
through his life as wandered through it, his spirit like a dazed body bumping into furniture and corners. He had always been a fearful father: when his
children were young, at the start of each summer he thought of them drowning in a pond or the sea, and he was relieved when he came home in the evenings and they were there; usually that relief was his only acknowledgment of
his fear, which he never spoke of, and which he controlled within his heart.
As he had when they were very young and all of them in turn, Cathleen too,
were drawn to the high oak in the backyard, and had to climb it. Smiling, he
watched them, imagining the fall: and he was poised to catch the small body
before it hit the earth. Or his legs were poised; his hands were in his pockets
or his arms were folded and, for the child looking down, he appeared relaxed
and confident while his heart beat with the two words he wanted to call out
but did not: *Don't fall.* In winter he was less afraid: he made sure the ice would
hold him before they skated, and he brought or sent them to places where they

could sled without ending in the street. So he and his children had survived their childhood, and he only worried about them when he knew they were driving a long distance, and then he lost Frank in a way no father expected to lose his son, and he felt that all the fears he had borne while they were growing up, and all the grief he had been afraid of, had backed up like a huge wave and struck him on the beach and swept him out to sea. Each day he felt the same and when he was able to forget how he felt, when he was able to force himself not to feel that way, the eyes of his clerks and customers defeated him. He wished those eyes were oblivious, even cold; he felt he was withering in their tenderness. And beneath his listless wandering, every day in his soul he shot Richard Strout in the face; while Ruth, going about town on errands, kept seeing him. And at nights in bed she would hold Matt and cry, or sometimes she was silent and Matt would touch her tightening arm, her clenched fist.

As his own right fist was now, squeezing the butt of the revolver, the last of the drinkers having left the bar, talking to each other, going to their separate cars which were in the lot in front of the bar, out of Matt's vision. He heard their voices, their cars, and then the ocean again, across the street. The tide was in and sometimes it smacked the sea wall. Through the windshield he looked at the dark red side wall of the bar, and then to his left, past Willis, at Strout's car, and through its windows he could see the now-emptied parking lot, the road, the sea wall. He could smell the sea.

The front door of the bar opened and closed again and Willis looked at Matt then at the corner of the building; when Strout came around it alone Matt got out of the car, giving up the hope he had kept all night (and for the past week) that Strout would come out with friends, and Willis would simply drive away; thinking: *All right then. All right*; and he went around the front of Willis's car, and at Strout's he stopped and aimed over the hood at Strout's blue shirt ten feet away. Willis was aiming too, crouched on Matt's left, his elbow resting on the hood.

"Mr. Fowler," Strout said. He looked at each of them, and at the guns. 80
"Mr. Trottier."

Then Matt, watching the parking lot and the road, walked quickly between the car and the building and stood behind Strout. He took one leather glove from his pocket and put it on his left hand.

"Don't talk. Unlock the front and back and get in."

Strout unlocked the front door, reached in and unlocked the back, then got in, and Matt slid into the back seat, closed the door with his gloved hand, and touched Strout's head once with the muzzle.

"It's cocked. Drive to your house."

When Strout looked over his shoulder to back the car, Matt aimed at his 85
temple and did not look at his eyes.

"Drive slowly," he said. "Don't try to get stopped."

They drove across the empty front lot and onto the road, Willis's headlights shining into the car; then back through town, the sea wall on the left hiding the beach, though far out Matt could see the ocean; he uncocked the revolver; on the right were the places, most with their neon signs off, that did so much business in summer: the lounges and cafés and pizza houses, the street itself empty of traffic, the way he and Willis had known it would be when they decided to take Strout at the bar rather than knock on his door at two o'clock one morning and risk that one insomniac neighbor. Matt had not told Willis he was afraid he could not be alone with Strout for very long, smell his smells, feel the presence of his flesh, hear his voice, and then shoot him. They left the beach town and then were on the high bridge over the channel: to the left the smacking curling white at the breakwater and beyond that the dark sea and the full moon, and down to his right the small fishing boats bobbing at anchor in the cove. When they left the bridge, the sea was blocked by abandoned beach cottages, and Matt's left hand was sweating in the glove. Out here in the dark in the car he believed Ruth knew. Willis had come to his house at eleven and asked if he wanted a nightcap; Matt went to the bedroom for his wallet, put the gloves in one trouser pocket and the .38 in the other and went back to the living room, his hand in his pocket covering the bulge of the cool cylinder pressed against his fingers, the butt against his palm. When Ruth said good night she looked at his face, and he felt she could see in his eyes the gun, and the night he was going to. But he knew he couldn't trust what he saw. Willis's wife had taken her sleeping pill, which gave her eight hours — the reason, Willis had told Matt, he had the alarms installed, for nights when he was late at the restaurant — and when it was all done and Willis got home he would leave ice and a trace of Scotch and soda in two glasses in the game room and tell Martha in the morning that he had left the restaurant early and brought Matt home for a drink.

"He was making it with my wife." Strout's voice was careful, not pleading.

Matt pressed the muzzle against Strout's head, pressed it harder than he wanted to, feeling through the gun Strout's head flinching and moving forward; then he lowered the gun to his lap.

"Don't talk," he said.

Strout did not speak again. They turned west, drove past the Dairy Queen closed until spring, and the two lobster restaurants that faced each other and were crowded all summer and were now also closed, onto the short bridge crossing the tidal stream, and over the engine Matt could hear through his open window the water rushing inland under the bridge; looking to his left he saw its swift moonlit current going back into the marsh which, leaving the bridge, they entered: the salt marsh stretching out on both sides, the grass tall in patches but mostly low and leaning earthward as though windblown, a large dark rock sitting as though it rested on nothing but itself, and shallow pools reflecting the bright moon.

Beyond the marsh they drove through woods, Matt thinking now of the hole he and Willis had dug last Sunday afternoon after telling their wives they were going to Fenway Park. They listened to the game on a transistor radio, but heard none of it as they dug into the soft earth on the knoll they had chosen because elms and maples sheltered it. Already some leaves had fallen. When the hole was deep enough they covered it and the piled earth with dead branches, then cleaned their shoes and pants and went to a restaurant

90

farther up in New Hampshire where they ate sandwiches and drank beer and watched the rest of the game on television. Looking at the back of Strout's head he thought of Frank's grave; he had not been back to it; but he would go before winter, and its second burial of snow.

He thought of Frank sitting on the couch and perhaps talking to the children as they watched television, imagined him feeling young and strong, still warmed from the sun at the beach, and feeling loved, hearing Mary Ann moving about in the kitchen, hearing her walking into the living room; maybe he looked up at her and maybe she said something, looking at him over the tray of sandwiches, smiling at him, saying something the way women do when they offer food as a gift, then the front door opening and this son of a bitch coming in and Frank seeing that he meant the gun in his hand, this son of a bitch and his gun the last person and thing Frank saw on earth.

When they drove into town the streets were nearly empty: a few slow cars, a policeman walking his beat past the darkened fronts of stores. Strout and Matt both glanced at him as they drove by. They were on the main street, and all the stoplights were blinking yellow. Willis and Matt had talked about that too: the lights changed at midnight, so there would be no place Strout had to stop and where he might try to run. Strout turned down the block where he lived and Willis's headlights were no longer with Matt in the back seat. They had planned that too, had decided it was best for just the one car to go to the house, and again Matt had said nothing about his fear of being alone with Strout, especially in his house: a duplex, dark as all the houses on the street were, the street itself lit at the corner of each block. As Strout turned into the driveway Matt thought of the one insomniac neighbor, thought of some man or woman sitting alone in the dark living room, watching the all-night channel from Boston. When Strout stopped the car near the front of the house, Matt said: "Drive it to the back."

He touched Strout's head with the muzzle.   95

"You wouldn't have it cocked, would you? For when I put on the brakes."

Matt cocked it, and said: "It is now."

Strout waited a moment; then he eased the car forward, the engine doing little more than idling, and as they approached the garage he gently braked. Matt opened the door, then took off the glove and put it in his pocket. He stepped out and shut the door with his hip and said: "All right."

Strout looked at the gun, then got out, and Matt followed him across the grass, and as Strout unlocked the door Matt looked quickly at the row of small backyards on either side, and scattered tall trees, some evergreens, others not, and he thought of the red and yellow leaves on the trees over the hole, saw them falling soon, probably in two weeks, dropping slowly, covering. Strout stepped into the kitchen.

"Turn on the light."   100

Strout reached to the wall switch, and in the light Matt looked at his wide back, the dark blue shirt, the white belt, the red plaid pants.

"Where's your suitcase?"

"My suitcase?"

"Where is it?"

"In the bedroom closet."   105

"That's where we're going then. When we get to a door you stop and turn on the light."

They crossed the kitchen, Matt glancing at the sink and stove and refrigerator: no dishes in the sink or even the dish rack beside it, no grease splashings on the stove, the refrigerator door clean and white. He did not want to look at any more but he looked quickly at all he could see: in the living room magazines and newspapers in a wicker basket, clean ashtrays, a record player, the records shelved next to it, then down the hall where, near the bedroom door, hung a color photograph of Mary Ann and the two boys sitting on a lawn — there was no house in the picture — Mary Ann smiling at the camera or Strout or whoever held the camera, smiling as she had on Matt's lawn this summer while he waited for the charcoal and they all talked and he looked at her brown legs and at Frank touching her arm, her shoulder, her hair; he moved down the hall with her smile in his mind, wondering: was that when they were both playing around and she was smiling like that at him and they were happy, even sometimes, making it worth it? He recalled her eyes, the pain in them, and he was conscious of the circles of love he was touching with the hand that held the revolver so tightly now as Strout stopped at the door at the end of the hall.

"There's no wall switch."

"Where's the light?"

"By the bed."   110

"Let's go."

Matt stayed a pace behind, then Strout leaned over and the room was lighted: the bed, a double one, was neatly made; the ashtray on the bedside table clean, the bureau top dustless, and no photographs; probably so the girl — who *was* she? — would not have to see Mary Ann in the bedroom she believed was theirs. But because Matt was a father and a husband, though never an ex-husband, he knew (and did not want to know) that this bedroom had never been theirs alone. Strout turned around; Matt looked at his lips, his wide jaw, and thought of Frank's doomed and fearful eyes looking up from the couch.

"Where's Mr. Trottier?"

"He's waiting. Pack clothes for warm weather."

"What's going on?"   115

"You're jumping bail."

"Mr. Fowler —"

He pointed the cocked revolver at Strout's face. The barrel trembled but not much, not as much as he had expected. Strout went to the closet and got the suitcase from the floor and opened it on the bed. As he went to the bureau, he said: "He was making it with my wife. I'd go pick up my kids and he'd be there. Sometimes he spent the night. My boys told me."

He did not look at Matt as he spoke. He opened the top drawer and Matt stepped closer so he could see Strout's hands: underwear and socks, the socks rolled, the underwear folded and stacked. He took them back to the bed, arranged them neatly in the suitcase, then from the closet he was taking shirts and trousers and a jacket; he laid them on the bed and Matt followed him to the bathroom and watched from the door while he packed those things a person accumulated and that became part of him so that at times in the store Matt felt he was selling more than clothes.

"I wanted to try to get together with her again." He was bent over the   120
suitcase. "I couldn't even talk to her. He was always with her. I'm going to jail for it; if I ever get out I'll be an old man. Isn't that enough?"

"You're not going to jail."

Strout closed the suitcase and faced Matt, looking at the gun. Matt went to his rear, so Strout was between him and the lighted hall; then using his handkerchief he turned off the lamp and said: "Let's go."

They went down the hall, Matt looking again at the photograph, and through the living room and kitchen, Matt turning off the lights and talking, frightened that he was talking, that he was telling this lie he had not planned: "It's the trial. We can't go through that, my wife and me. So you're leaving. We've got you a ticket, and a job. A friend of Mr. Trottier's. Out west. My wife keeps seeing you. We can't have that anymore."

Matt turned out the kitchen light and put the handkerchief in his pocket, and they went down the two brick steps and across the lawn. Strout put the suitcase on the floor of the back seat, then got into the front seat and Matt got in the back and put on his glove and shut the door.

"They'll catch me. They'll check passenger lists."   125

"We didn't use your name."

"They'll figure that out too. You think I wouldn't have done it myself if it was that easy?"

He backed into the street, Matt looking down the gun barrel but not at the profiled face beyond it.

"You were alone," Matt said. "We've got it worked out."

"There's no planes this time of night, Mr. Fowler."   130

"Go back through town. Then north on 125."

They came to the corner and turned, and now Willis's headlights were in the car with Matt.

"Why north, Mr. Fowler?"

"Somebody's going to keep you for a while. They'll take you to the air-port." He uncocked the hammer and lowered the revolver to his lap and said wearily: "No more talking."

As they drove back through town, Matt's body sagged, going limp with   135
his spirit and its new and false bond with Strout, the hope his lie had given Strout. He had grown up in this town whose streets had become places of apprehension and pain for Ruth as she drove and walked, doing what she had to do; and for him too, if only in his mind as he worked and chatted six days a week in his store; he wondered now if his lie would have worked, if sending

Strout away would have been enough; but then he knew that just thinking of Strout in Montana or whatever place lay at the end of the lie he had told, thinking of him walking the streets there, loving a girl there (who *was* she?) would be enough to slowly rot the rest of his days. And Ruth's. Again he was certain that she knew, that she was waiting for him.

They were in New Hampshire now, on the narrow highway, passing the shopping center at the state line, and then houses and small stores and sandwich shops. There were few cars on the road. After ten minutes he raised his trembling hand, touched Strout's neck with the gun, and said: "Turn in up here. At the dirt road."

Strout flicked on the indicator and slowed.

"Mr. Fowler?"

"They're waiting here."

Strout turned very slowly, easing his neck away from the gun. In the   140 moonlight the road was light brown, lighter and yellowed where the headlights shone; weeds and a few trees grew on either side of it, and ahead of them were the woods.

"There's nothing back here, Mr. Fowler."

"It's for your car. You don't think we'd leave it at the airport, do you?"

He watched Strout's large, big-knuckled hands tighten on the wheel, saw Frank's face that night: not the stitches and bruised eye and swollen lips, but his own hand gently touching Frank's jaw, turning his wounds to the light. They rounded a bend in the road and were out of sight of the highway: tall trees all around them now, hiding the moon. When they reached the abandoned gravel pit on the left, the bare flat earth and steep pale embankment behind it, and the black crowns of trees at its top, Matt said: "Stop here."

Strout stopped but did not turn off the engine. Matt pressed the gun hard against his neck, and he straightened in the seat and looked in the rearview mirror, Matt's eyes meeting his in the glass for an instant before looking at the hair at the end of the gun barrel.

"Turn it off."   145

Strout did, then held the wheel with two hands, and looked in the mirror.

"I'll do twenty years, Mr. Fowler; at least. I'll be forty-six years old."

"That's nine years younger than I am," Matt said, and got out and took off the glove and kicked the door shut. He aimed at Strout's ear and pulled back the hammer. Willis's headlights were off and Matt heard him walking on the soft thin layer of dust, the hard earth beneath it. Strout opened the door, sat for a moment in the interior light, then stepped out onto the road. Now his face was pleading. Matt did not look at his eyes, but he could see it in the lips.

"Just get the suitcase. They're right up the road."

Willis was beside him now, to his left. Strout looked at both guns. Then   150 he opened the back door, leaned in, and with a jerk brought the suitcase out. He was turning to face them when Matt said: "Just walk up the road. Just ahead."

Strout turned to walk, the suitcase in his right hand, and Matt and Willis followed; as Strout cleared the front of his car he dropped the suitcase and, ducking, took one step that was the beginning of a sprint to his right. The gun kicked in Matt's hand, and the explosion of the shot surrounded him, isolated him in a nimbus of sound that cut him off from all his time, all his history, isolated him standing absolutely still on the dirt road with the gun in his hand, looking down at Richard Strout squirming on his belly, kicking one leg behind him, pushing himself forward, toward the woods. Then Matt went to him and shot him once in the back of the head.

Driving south to Boston, wearing both gloves now, staying in the middle lane and looking often in the rearview mirror at Willis's headlights, he relived the suitcase dropping, the quick dip and turn of Strout's back, and the kick of the gun, the sound of the shot. When he walked to Strout, he still existed within the first shot, still trembled and breathed with it. The second shot and the burial seemed to be happening to someone else, someone he was watching. He and Willis each held an arm and pulled Strout face-down off the road and into the woods, his bouncing sliding belt white under the trees where it was so dark that when they stopped at the top of the knoll, panting and sweating, Matt could not see where Strout's blue shirt ended and the earth began. They pulled off the branches then dragged Strout to the edge of the hole and went behind him and lifted his legs and pushed him in. They stood still for a moment. The woods were quiet save for their breathing, and Matt remembered hearing the movements of birds and small animals after the first shot. Or maybe he had not heard them. Willis went down to the road. Matt could see him clearly out on the tan dirt, could see the glint of Strout's car and, beyond the road, the gravel pit. Willis came back up the knoll with the suitcase. He dropped it in the hole and took off his gloves and they went down to his car for the spades. They worked quietly. Sometimes they paused to listen to the woods. When they were finished Willis turned on his flashlight and they covered the earth with leaves and branches and then went down to the spot in front of the car, and while Matt held the light Willis crouched and sprinkled dust on the blood, backing up till he reached the grass and leaves, then he used leaves until they had worked up to the grave again. They did not stop. They walked around the grave and through the woods, using the light on the ground, looking up through the trees to where they ended at the lake. Neither of them spoke above the sounds of their heavy and clumsy strides through low brush and over fallen branches. Then they reached it: wide and dark, lapping softly at the bank, pine needles smooth under Matt's feet, moonlight on the lake, a small island near its middle, with black, tall evergreens. He took out the gun and threw for the island: taking two steps back on the pine needles, striding with the throw and going to one knee as he followed through, looking up to see the dark shapeless object arcing downward, splashing.

They left Strout's car in Boston, in front of an apartment building on Commonwealth Avenue. When they got back to town Willis drove slowly over the bridge and Matt threw the keys into the Merrimack. The sky was turning light. Willis let him out a block from his house, and walking home he listened for sounds from the houses he passed. They were quiet. A light was on in his living room. He turned it off and undressed in there, and went softly toward the bedroom; in the hall he smelled the smoke, and he stood in the bedroom doorway and looked at the orange of her cigarette in the dark. The curtains were closed. He went to the closet and put his shoes on the floor and felt for a hanger.

"Did you do it?" she said.

He went down the hall to the bathroom and in the dark he washed his   155
hands and face. Then he went to her, lay on his back, and pulled the sheet up to his throat.

"Are you all right?" she said.

"I think so."

Now she touched him, lying on her side, her hand on his belly, his thigh.

"Tell me," she said.

He started from the beginning, in the parking lot at the bar; but soon   160
with his eyes closed and Ruth petting him, he spoke of Strout's house: the order, the woman presence, the picture on the wall.

"The way she was smiling," he said.

"What about it?"

"I don't know. Did you ever see Strout's girl? When you saw him in town?"

"No."

"I wonder who she was."   165

Then he thought: *not was: is. Sleeping now she is his girl.* He opened his eyes, then closed them again. There was more light beyond the curtains. With Ruth now he left Strout's house and told again his lie to Strout, gave him again that hope that Strout must have for a while believed, else he would have to believe only the gun pointed at him for the last two hours of his life. And with Ruth he saw again the dropping suitcase, the darting move to the right: and he told of the first shot, feeling her hand on him but his heart isolated still, beating on the road still in that explosion like thunder. He told her the rest, but the words had no images for him, he did not see himself doing what the words said he had done; he only saw himself on that road.

"We can't tell the other kids," she said. "It'll hurt them, thinking he got away. But we mustn't."

"No."

She was holding him, wanting him, and he wished he could make love with her but he could not. He saw Frank and Mary Ann making love in her bed, their eyes closed, their bodies brown and smelling of the sea; the other girl was faceless, bodiless, but he felt her sleeping now; and he saw Frank and Strout, their faces alive; he saw red and yellow leaves falling on the earth, then snow: falling and freezing and falling; and holding Ruth, his cheek touching her breast, he shuddered with a sob that he kept silent in his heart.

CONSIDERATIONS FOR CRITICAL THINKING AND WRITING

1. **FIRST RESPONSE.** How do you feel about Matt's act of revenge? Trace the emotions his character produces in you as the plot unfolds.

2. Discuss the significance of the title. Why is "Killings" a more appropriate title than "Killers"?

3. What are the effects of Dubus's ordering of events in the story? How would the effects be different if the story were told in a chronological order?

4. Describe the Fowler family before Frank's murder. How does the murder affect Matt?

5. What is learned about Richard from the flashback in paragraphs 32 through 75? How does this information affect your attitude toward him?

6. What is the effect of the description of Richard shooting Frank in paragraph 76?

7. How well planned is Matt's revenge? Why does he lie to Richard about sending him out west?

8. Describe Matt at the end of the story when he tells his wife about the killing. How do you think this revenge killing will affect the Fowler family?

9. How might "Killings" be considered a love story as well as a murder story?

10. **CONNECTION TO ANOTHER SELECTION.** Compare and contrast Matt's motivation for murder with Emily's in "A Rose for Emily" (p. 54). Which character made you feel more empathy and sympathy for his or her actions? Why?

3

Character

When I find a well-drawn character in fiction or biography, I generally take a warm personal interest in him, for the reason that I have known him before—met him on the river.

—MARK TWAIN

© Bettmann/CORBIS.

Character is essential to plot. Without characters Burroughs's *Tarzan of the Apes* would be a travelogue through the jungle and Faulkner's "A Rose for Emily" little more than a faded history of a sleepy town in the South. If stories were depopulated, the plots would disappear because characters and plots are interrelated. A dangerous jungle is important only because we care what effect it has on a character. Characters are influenced by events just as events are shaped by characters. Tarzan's physical strength is the result of his growing up in the jungle, and his strength, along with his inherited intelligence, allows him to be master there.

The methods by which a writer creates people in a story so that they seem actually to exist are called ***characterization***. Huck Finn never lived yet those who have read Mark Twain's novel about his adventures along the Mississippi River feel as if they know him. A good writer gives us the illusion that a character is real, but we should also remember that a character is not an actual person but instead has been created by the author. Though we might walk out of a room in which Huck Finn's Pap talks racist nonsense, we would not throw away the book in a similar fit of anger. This illusion of reality is the magic that allows us to move beyond the circumstances of our own lives into a writer's fictional world, where we can encounter everyone from royalty to paupers, murderers, lovers, cheaters, martyrs, artists, destroyers, and, nearly always, some part of ourselves. To understand our response to a story, we should be able to recognize the methods of characterization the author uses.

CHARLES DICKENS (1812–1870)

Charles Dickens is well known for creating characters who have stepped off the pages of his fictions into the imaginations and memories of his readers. His characters are successful not because readers might have encountered such people in their own lives, but because his characterizations are vivid and convincing. He manages to make strange and eccentric people appear familiar. The following excerpt from *Hard Times* is the novel's entire first chapter. In it Dickens introduces and characterizes a school principal addressing a classroom full of children.

© Bettmann/CORBIS.

From *Hard Times*   1854

"Now, what I want is, Facts. Teach these boys and girls nothing but Facts. Facts alone are wanted in life. Plant nothing else, and root out everything else. You can only form the minds of reasoning animals upon Facts: nothing else will ever be of any service to them. This is the principle on which I bring up my own children, and this is the principle on which I bring up these children. Stick to Facts, sir!"

The scene was a plain, bare, monotonous vault of a schoolroom, and the speaker's square forefinger emphasized his observations by underscoring every sentence with a line on the schoolmaster's sleeve. The emphasis was helped by the speaker's square wall of a forehead, which had his eyebrows for its base, while his eyes found commodious cellarage in two dark caves, overshadowed by the wall. The emphasis was helped by the speaker's mouth, which was wide, thin, and hard set. The emphasis was helped by the speaker's voice, which was inflexible, dry, and dictatorial. The emphasis was helped by the speaker's hair, which bristled on the skirts of his bald head, a plantation of firs to keep the wind from its shining surface, all covered with knobs, like the crust of a plum pie, as if the head had scarcely warehouse-room for the hard facts stored inside. The speaker's obstinate carriage, square coat, square legs, square shoulders — nay, his very neckcloth, trained to take him by the throat with an unaccommodating grasp, like a stubborn fact, as it was — all helped the emphasis.

"In this life, we want nothing but Facts, sir; nothing but Facts!"

The speaker, and the schoolmaster, and the third grown person present, all backed a little, and swept with their eyes the inclined plane of little vessels then and there arranged in order, ready to have imperial gallons of facts poured into them until they were full to the brim.

Dickens withholds his character's name until the beginning of the second chapter; he calls this fact-bound educator Mr. Gradgrind. Authors sometimes put as much time and effort into naming their characters as parents invest in naming their children. Names can be used to indicate qualities that the writer associates with the characters. Mr. Gradgrind is precisely what his name suggests. The "schoolmaster" employed by Gradgrind is Mr. M'Choakumchild. Pronounce this name aloud and you have the essence of this teacher's educational philosophy. In Nathaniel Hawthorne's *The Scarlet Letter*, Chillingworth is cold and relentless in his single-minded quest for revenge. The innocent and youthful protagonist in Herman Melville's *Billy Budd* is nipped in the bud by the evil Claggart, whose name simply sounds unpleasant. Of course, not every name is suggestive of the qualities a character may embody, but it is frequently worth determining what is in a name.

The only way to tell whether a name reveals character is to look at the other information the author supplies about the character. We evaluate fictional characters in much the same way we understand people in our own lives. By piecing together bits of information, we create a context that allows us to interpret their behavior. We can predict, for instance, that an acquaintance who is a chronic complainer is not likely to have anything good to say about a roommate. We interpret words and actions in the light of what we already know about someone, and that is why keeping track of what characters say (and how they say it) along with what they do (and don't do) is important.

Authors reveal characters by other means too. Physical descriptions can indicate important inner qualities; disheveled clothing, a crafty smile, or a blush might communicate as much as or more than what a character says. Characters can also be revealed by the words and actions of others who respond to them. In literature, moreover, we have one great advantage that life cannot offer; a work of fiction can give us access to a person's thoughts. Although in Herman Melville's "Bartleby, the Scrivener" (p. 99) we learn about Bartleby primarily through descriptive details, words, actions, and his relationships with the other characters, Melville allows us to enter the lawyer's consciousness.

Authors have two major methods of presenting characters: **showing** and **telling**. Characters shown in dramatic situations reveal themselves indirectly by what they say and do. In the first paragraph of the excerpt from *Hard Times*, Dickens shows us some of Gradgrind's utilitarian educational principles by having him speak. We can infer the kind of person he is from his reference to boys and girls as "reasoning animals," but we are not told what to think of him until the second paragraph. It would be impossible to admire Gradgrind after reading the physical description of him and the school that he oversees. The adjectives in the second paragraph make the author's evaluation of Gradgrind's values and personality clear: everything about him is rigidly "square"; his mouth is "thin, and hard set"; his voice is "inflexible, dry, and dictatorial"; and he presides over a "plain, bare, monotonous vault of a schoolroom." Dickens directly lets us know how to feel about Gradgrind, but he does so artistically. Instead of simply being presented with a statement that Gradgrind is destructively practical, we get a detailed and amusing description.

We can contrast Dickens's direct presentation in this paragraph with the indirect showing that Gail Godwin uses in "A Sorrowful Woman." Godwin avoids telling us how we should think about the characters. Their story includes little description and no evaluations or interpretations by the author. To determine the significance of the events, the reader must pay close attention to what the characters say and do. Like Godwin, many twentieth-century authors favor showing over telling because showing allows readers to discover the meanings, which modern authors are often reluctant to impose on an audience for whom fixed meanings and values are not as strong as they once were. However, most writers continue to reveal characters by telling as well as showing when the technique suits their purposes — when, for example, a minor character must be sketched economically or when a long time has elapsed, causing changes in a major character. Telling and showing complement each other.

Characters can be convincing whether they are presented by telling or showing, provided their actions are *motivated*. There must be reasons for how they behave and what they say. If adequate motivation is offered, we can understand and find *plausible* their actions no matter how bizarre. In "A Rose for Emily" (p. 54), Faulkner makes Emily Grierson's intimacy with a corpse credible by preparing us with information about her father's death along with her inability to leave the past and live in the present. Emily turns out to be *consistent*. Although we are surprised by the ending of the story, the behavior it reveals is compatible with her temperament.

Some kinds of fiction consciously break away from our expectations of traditional realistic stories. Consistency, plausibility, and motivation are not very useful concepts for understanding and evaluating characterizations in modern *absurdist literature*, for instance, in which characters are often alienated from themselves and their environment in an irrational world. In this world there is no possibility for traditional heroic action; instead we find an *antihero* who has little control over events. Yossarian from Joseph Heller's *Catch-22* is an example of a protagonist who is thwarted by the absurd terms on which life offers itself to many twentieth-century characters.

In most stories we expect characters to act plausibly and in ways consistent with their personalities, but that does not mean that characters cannot develop and change. A *dynamic* character undergoes some kind of change because of the action of the plot. Huck Finn's view of Jim, the runaway slave in Mark Twain's novel, develops during their experiences on the raft. Huck discovers

Jim's humanity and, therefore, cannot betray him because Huck no longer sees his companion as merely the property of a white owner. On the other hand, Huck's friend, Tom Sawyer, is a *static* character because he does not change. He remains interested only in high adventure, even at the risk of Jim's life. As static characters often do, Tom serves as a foil to Huck; his frivolous concerns are contrasted with Huck's serious development. A *foil* helps to reveal by contrast the distinctive qualities of another character.

The extent to which a character is developed is another means by which character can be analyzed. The novelist E. M. Forster coined the terms *flat* and *round* to distinguish degrees of character development. A *flat character* embodies one or two qualities, ideas, or traits that can be readily described in a brief summary. For instance, Mr. M'Choakumchild in Dickens's *Hard Times* stifles students instead of encouraging them to grow. Flat characters tend to be one-dimensional. They are readily accessible because their characteristics are few and simple; they are not created to be psychologically complex.

Some flat characters are immediately recognizable as *stock characters*. These stereotypes are particularly popular in formula fiction, television programs, and action movies. Stock characters are types rather than individuals. The poor but dedicated writer falls in love with a hard-working understudy, who gets nowhere because the corrupt producer favors his boozy, pampered mistress for the leading role. Characters such as these — the loyal servant, the mean stepfather, the henpecked husband, the dumb blonde, the sadistic army officer, the dotty grandmother — are prepackaged; they lack individuality because their authors have, in a sense, not imaginatively created them but simply summoned them from a warehouse of clichés and social prejudices. Stock characters can become fresh if a good writer makes them vivid, interesting, or memorable, but too often a writer's use of these stereotypes is simply weak characterization.

Round characters are more complex than flat or stock characters. Round characters have more depth and require more attention. They may surprise us or puzzle us. Although they are more fully developed, round characters are also more difficult to summarize because we are aware of competing ideas, values, and possibilities in their lives. As a flat character, Huck Finn's alcoholic, bigoted father is clear to us; we know that Pap is the embodiment of racism and irrationality. But Huck is considerably less predictable because he struggles with what Twain calls a "sound heart and a deformed conscience."

In making distinctions between flat and round characters, you must understand that an author's use of a flat character — even as a protagonist — does not necessarily represent an artistic flaw. Moreover, both flat and round characters can be either dynamic or static. Each plot can be made most effective by its own special kind of characterization. Terms such as *round* and *flat* are helpful tools to use to determine what we know about a character, but they are not an infallible measurement of the quality of a story.

The next three stories — May-lee Chai's "Saving Sourdi," Ron Carlson's "Max," and Herman Melville's "Bartleby, the Scrivener" — offer character studies worthy of close analysis. As you read them, notice the methods of characterization used to bring each to life.

MAY-LEE CHAI (B. 1967)

May-lee Chai, the first of her family to be born in the United States, is a San Francisco author and graduate of Yale University. Chai has worked as a reporter for the Associated Press and taught creative writing at San Francisco State University, the University of Wyoming, and Amherst College. She is the author of *My Lucky Face* (1997), a novel about a woman's marriage in contemporary China, and *Glamorous Asians: Short Stories and Essays* (2004), and she is coauthor, with her father, Winberg Chai, of *The Girl from Purple Mountain* (2001), a family memoir about her grandparents' journey from China to America. *Hapa Girl: A Memoir* (2007) describes the bigotry her family encountered in rural South Dakota. Her novels *Dragon Chica* (2010) and *Tiger Girl* (2013) are about the characters in "Saving Sourdi."

Jason Doiy.

WHEN I WRITE "When I was a teenager, I lived on a farm. I'd get up early in the morning while it was still dark and write bad sci-fi stories for 20 minutes before I had to go out for chores. That was my escape. The stories were terrible, but the act of writing was my salvation."   — MAY-LEE CHAI

Saving Sourdi

2001

Once, when my older sister, Sourdi, and I were working alone in our family's restaurant, just the two of us and the elderly cook, some men got drunk and I stabbed one of them. I was eleven.

I don't remember where Ma had gone that night. But I remember we were tired and it was late. We were one of the only restaurants that stayed open past nine in those days. The men had been growing louder, until they were our only customers, and, finally, one of them staggered up and put his arm across Sourdi's shoulders. He called her his "China doll," and his friends hooted at this.

Sourdi looked distressed and tried to remove his arm, but he held her tighter. She said, "Please," in her incense-sweet voice, and he smiled and said, "Say it again nice and I might just have to give you a kiss."

That summer we'd just moved to South Dakota. After all the crummy jobs Ma had had to take in Texas, where we'd first come to the U.S., where our sponsors lived, we were so proud to be working in our own restaurant. When we moved to South Dakota, I thought we'd find the real America, the one where we were supposed to be, not the hot sweaty America where we lived packed together in an apartment with bars on the windows on a street where angry boys in cars played loud music and shot guns at each other in the night. The summer we moved to join my uncle's family to run the Silver Palace, I was certain we would at last find the life we deserved.

Now I was panicked. I wanted Ma to be there. Ma would know what to 5 do. She always did. I stood there, chewing my nails, wishing I could make them go away. The men's voices were so loud in my ears, I was drowning in the sound.

I ran into the kitchen. I had this idea to get the cook and the cleaver, but the first thing that caught my eye was this little paring knife on the counter next to a bowl of oranges. I grabbed the knife and ran back out to Sourdi.

"Get away from my sister!" I shouted, waving the paring knife.

The men were silent for about three seconds, then they burst into laughter.

I charged and stabbed the man in the sleeve.

In a movie or a television show this kind of scene always unfolds in slow 10 motion, but everything happened so fast. I stabbed the man, Sourdi jumped free, Ma came rushing in the front door waving her arms. "Omigod! What happen?"

"Jesus Christ!" The man shook his arm as though it were on fire, but the paring knife was stuck in the fabric of his jeans jacket.

I thought Ma would take care of everything now. And I was right, she did, but not the way I had imagined. She started apologizing to the man, and she helped him take off his jacket. She made Sourdi get the first-aid kit from the bathroom, "Quick! Quick!" Ma even tried to put some ointment on his cut, but he just shrugged her off.

I couldn't believe it. I wanted to take the knife back and stab myself. That's how I felt when I heard her say, "No charge, on the house," for their dinner, despite the $50-worth of pitchers they'd had.

Ma grabbed me by the shoulders. "Say you sorry. Say it." I pressed my lips firmly together and hung my head. Then she slapped me.

I didn't start crying until after the men had left. "But, Ma," I said, "he was 15 hurting Sourdi!"

"Then why Sourdi not do something?" Ma twisted my ear. "You not thinking. That your problem. You always not think!"

Afterwards, Sourdi said I was lucky. The knife had only grazed the man's skin. They could have sued us. They could have pressed charges.

"I don't care!" I hissed then. "I shoulda killed him! I shoulda killed that sucker!"

Sourdi's face changed. I'd never seen my sister look like that. Not ever. Especially not at me. I was her favorite. But she looked then the way I felt inside. Like a big bomb was ticking behind her eyes.

We were sitting together in the bathroom. It was late at night, and every- 20
one else was asleep. Sometimes we locked ourselves in the bathroom then,
just the two of us, so we could talk about things like boys at school or who
was the cutest actor on television shows we liked or how we felt when our
family fought, when Uncle and Auntie yelled at each other, or when Ma grew
depressed and smoked too much and looked at us as though she wished we'd
never been born.

This night, however, Sourdi looked at me grimly. "Oh, no, Nea. Don't
ever say that. Don't ever talk like that."

I was going to smile and shrug and say something like "I was just kidding," but something inside me couldn't lie tonight. I crossed my arms over
my flat chest, and I stuck out my lower lip, like I'd seen the tough girls at
school do. "Anyone mess like that with me, I'm gonna kill him!"

Sourdi took me by the shoulders then and shook me so hard I thought
she was going to shake my head right off my body. She wouldn't stop even after
I started to cry.

"Stop, stop!" I begged. "I'll be good! I promise, I'll be good!"

Finally, she pushed me away from her and sat on the toilet, with her head 25
in her hands. Although she'd been the one hurting me, she looked as though
she'd been beaten up, the way she sat like that, her shoulders hunched over
her lap, as though she were trying to make herself disappear.

"I was trying to protect you," I said through my tears. "I was trying to
save you. You're so stupid! I should just let that man diss you!"

Sourdi's head shot up and I could see that she had no patience left. Her eyes
were red and her nostrils flared. She stood up and I took a step back quickly.
I thought she was going to grab me and shake me again, but this time she just
put her hand on my arm. "They could take you away. The police, they could
put you in a foster home. All of us."

A chill ran through my whole body, like a live current. We all knew about
foster homes. Rudy Gutierrez in third grade was taken away from his parents after the teacher noticed some bruises on his back. He'd tried to shoplift
some PayDays from the 7-Eleven and got caught. When his dad got home
that weekend, he let him have it. But after the school nurse took a look at him,
Rudy was taken away from his parents and sent to live in a foster home. His
parents couldn't speak English so good and didn't know what was happening until too late. Anyway, what kind of lawyer could they afford? We heard
later from his cousin in Mrs. Chang's homeroom that Rudy's foster-dad had
molested him. The cousin said Rudy ran away from that home, but he got
caught. At any rate, none of us ever saw him again.

"You want to go to a foster home?" Sourdi asked me.

"No," I whispered.   30

"Then don't be so stupid!"

I started crying again, because I realized Sourdi was right. She kissed me
on the top of my head and hugged me to her. I leaned my head against her
soft breasts that had only recently emerged from her chest and pretended that
I was a good girl and that I would always obey her. What I didn't tell Sourdi

was that I was still a wicked girl. I was glad I'd stabbed that man. I was crying only because life was so unfair.

We used to say that we'd run away, Sourdi and me. When we were older. After she graduated. She'd be my legal guardian. We'd go to California to see the stars. Paris. London. Cambodia even, to light incense for the bones of our father. We'd earn money working in Chinese restaurants in every country we visited. We had enough experience; it had to be worth something.

We'd lie awake all night whispering back and forth. I'd climb into Sourdi's bed, claiming that I couldn't sleep, curling into a ball beside my older sister, the smell of her like salt and garlic and a sweet scent that emanated directly from her skin. Sometimes I'd stroke Sourdi's slick hair, which she plaited into a thick wet braid so that it would be wavy in the morning. I would stay awake all night, pinching the inside of Sourdi's arm, the soft flesh of her thigh, to keep my sister from falling asleep and leaving me alone.

When she first started seeing Duke, I used to think of him as something 35 like a bookmark, just holding a certain space in her life until it was time for her to move on. I never thought of him as a fork in the road, dividing my life with Sourdi from Sourdi's life with men.

In those days, I didn't understand anything.

Ma had hired Duke to wash dishes at the Palace that first summer. At first, we paid him no mind. He was just this funny-looking white kid, hair that stuck up straight from his head when he wasn't wearing his silly baseball cap backwards, skinny as a stalk of bamboo, long legs and long arms that seemed to move in opposition to each other. Chopstick-boy I called him, just to be mean. He took it as a compliment.

I could see why he fell in love with Sourdi. My sister was beautiful. Really beautiful, not like the girls in magazines with their pale, pinched faces, pink and powdery, brittle girls. Sourdi looked like a statue that had been rescued from the sea. She was smooth where I had angles and soft where I was bone. Sourdi's face was round, her nose low and wide, her eyes crescent-shaped like the quarter moon, her hair sleek as seaweed. Her skin was a burnished cinnamon color. Looking at Sourdi, I could pretend I was beautiful, too. She had so much to spare.

At first, Duke and Sourdi only talked behind the Palace, pretending to take a break from the heat of the kitchen. I caught them looking at the stars together.

The first time they kissed, I was there, too. Duke was giving us a ride 40 after school in his pickup. He had the music on loud and the windows were open. It was a hot day for October, and the wind felt like a warm ocean that we could swim in forever. He was going to drop us off at the Palace, but then Duke said he had something to show us, and we circled around the outskirts of town, taking the gravel road that led to the open fields, beyond the highway where the cattle ranches lay. Finally, he pulled off the gravel road and parked.

"You want us to look at cows?" I asked impatiently, crossing my arms.

He laughed at me then and took Sourdi by the hand. We hiked through a ditch to the edge of an empty cornfield long since harvested, the stubble of cornstalks poking up from the black soil, pale and bonelike. The field was laced with a barbed-wire fence to keep the cattle in, though I couldn't see any cows at all. The whole place gave me the creeps.

Duke held the strands of barbed wire apart for Sourdi and me and told us to crawl under the fence.

"Just trust me," he said.

We followed him to a spot in the middle of the field. "It's the center of the world," Duke said. "Look." And he pointed back to where we'd come from, and suddenly I realized the rest of the world had disappeared. The ground had appeared level, but we must have walked into a tiny hollow in the plains, because from where we stood there was only sky and field for as far as our eyes could see. We could no longer see the road or Duke's pickup, our town, or even the green smudge of cottonwoods that grew along the Yankton River or the distant hills of Nebraska. There was nothing overhead, either; the sky was unbroken by clouds, smooth as an empty rice bowl. "It's just us here," Duke said. "We're alone in the whole universe."

All at once, Sourdi began to breathe funny. Her face grew pinched, and she wiped at her eyes with the back of her hand.

"What's wrong?" Duke asked stupidly.

Then Sourdi was running wildly. She took off like an animal startled by a gunshot. She was trying to head back to the road, but she tripped over the cornstalks and fell onto her knees. She started crying for real.

I caught up to her first — I've always been a fast runner. As Duke approached, I put my arms around Sourdi.

"I thought you'd like it," Duke said.

"We're city girls," I said, glaring at him. "Why would we like this hick stuff?"

"I'm sorry," Sourdi whispered. "I'm so sorry."

"What are you sorry for? It's his fault!" I pointed out.

Now Duke was kneeling next to Sourdi. He tried to put his arm over her shoulder, too. I was going to push him away, when Sourdi did something very surprising. She put both her arms around his neck and leaned against him, while Duke said soft, dumb-sounding things that I couldn't quite hear. Then they were kissing.

I was so surprised, I stared at them before I forced myself to look away. Then I was the one who felt like running, screaming, for the road.

On the way back to the Palace, Duke and Sourdi didn't talk, but they held hands. The worst part was I was sitting between them.

Ma didn't seem to notice anything for a while, but then with Ma it was always hard to know what she was thinking, what she knew and what she didn't. Sometimes she seemed to go through her days like she was made of stone. Sometimes she erupted like a volcano.

Uncle fired Duke a few weeks later. He said it was because Duke had dropped a tray of dishes. It was during the Saturday lunch rush when Sourdi and I weren't working and couldn't witness what had happened.

"He's a clumsy boy," Ma agreed after work that night, when we all sat around in the back booths and ate our dinner.

Sourdi didn't say anything. She knew Ma knew.   60

She kept seeing Duke, of course. They were both juniors, and there was only one high school in town. Now when I crept into Sourdi's bed at night, when she talked about running away, she meant Duke and her. I was the one who had to pipe up that I was coming with them, too. What we didn't know was that Ma was making plans as well.

Uncle first introduced his friend Mr. Chhay in the winter. I'd had a strange dream the night before. I hadn't remembered it at all until Mr. Chhay walked into the Palace, with his hangdog face and his suit like a salesman's. He sat in a corner booth with Uncle and, while they talked, he shredded a napkin, then took the scraps of paper and rolled them between his thumb and index finger into a hundred tiny red balls. He left them in the ashtray, like a mountain of fish eggs. Seeing them, I remembered my dream.

I was swimming in the ocean. I was just a small child, but I wasn't afraid at all. The sea was liquid turquoise, the sunlight yellow as gold against my skin. Fish were swimming alongside me. I could see through the clear water to the bottom of the sea. The fish were schooling around me and below me, and they brushed against my feet when I kicked the water. Their scales felt like bones scraping my toes. I tried to push them away, but the schools grew more dense, until I was swimming amongst them under the waves.

The fish began to spawn around me and soon the water was cloudy with eggs. I tried to break through the film, but the eggs clung to my skin. The water darkened as we entered a sea of kelp. I pushed against the dark slippery strands like Sourdi's hair. I realized I was pushing against my sister, wrapped in the kelp, suspended just below the surface of the water. Then I woke up.

I thought about that dream seeing that old guy Mr. Chhay with Uncle   65
and I knew they were up to no good. I wanted to warn Sourdi, but she seemed to understand without my having to tell her anything.

Uncle called over to her and introduced her to his friend. But Sourdi wouldn't even look at Mr. Chhay. She kept her eyes lowered, though he tried to smile and talk to her. She whispered so low in reply that no one could understand a word she said. I could tell the man was disappointed when he left. His shoulders seemed barely able to support the weight of his jacket.

Mr. Chhay wrote letters to Uncle, to Ma. He thanked them for their hospitality and enclosed pictures of his business and his house, plus a formal portrait of himself looking ridiculous in another suit, standing in front of some potted plants, his hair combed over the bald spot in the middle of his head.

The next time he came to visit the Palace, he brought gifts. A giant Chinese vase for Ma, Barbie dolls for my younger sisters and cousin, a Christian music cassette tape for me, and a bright red leather purse for Sourdi.

Ma made Sourdi tell him thank you.

And that was all she said to him.

But this old guy was persistent. He took us all out to eat at a steakhouse once. He said he wanted to pay back Uncle for some good deed he'd done a long time ago when they both first came to America. I could have told him, Sourdi hated this kind of food. She preferred Mexican, tacos, not this Midwest cowboy stuff. But Ma made us all thank him.

"Thank you, Mr. Chhay," we said dutifully. He'd smiled so all his yellow teeth showed at once. "Oh, please, call me Older Brother," he said.

It was the beginning of the end. I should have fought harder then. I should have stabbed this man, too.

I saw Duke at Sourdi's wedding. She invited him for the ceremony proper, the reception, too, but he didn't show up until the end. I almost didn't see him at all. He was slouching through the parking lot of St. Agnes, wearing his best hightops and the navy-blue suit that his mother had insisted upon buying for graduation. I wasn't used to him looking like a teenage undertaker, but I recognized his loping gait immediately. That afternoon of Sourdi's wedding, he was holding a brown bag awkwardly behind his back, as if trying to conceal the fact that he was drinking as conspicuously as possible.

I was standing inside the bingo hall, before the row of squat windows, my

back turned to the festivities, the exploding flash capturing the tipsy toasts, the in-laws singing off-key to the rented karaoke machine.

Then it really became too much to bear, and I had to escape the terrible heat, the flickering fluorescent lights. I slipped from the church into the ferocious March wind and gave it my best shot, running across the hard lawn, but the too-tight heels pinched my toes and the stiff taffeta bodice of the cotton-candy-pink bridesmaid's dress might as well have been a vise around my rib cage. I had intended to make it off church property, run to the empty field that stretched low and dark all the way to the horizon, but I only made it to the end of the walk near the rectory before vomiting into Sister Kevin's over-tended tulip patch.

Duke came over and sat on his haunches beside me, while I puked. I let him hold back my hair, while the wedding cake and wine cooler that I'd tried poured from my mouth.

Finally, I spat a few times to clear my mouth, then sat back on my rear end. After a few minutes, I could take a sip from Duke's beer.

We didn't talk.

I took out the pack of cigarettes I'd stolen from Ma's purse and lit one. It took five puffs before I could mask the taste of bile and sugar.

The wind was blowing fiercely from the northwest, whipping my hair about my face like a widow's veil, throwing dust from the parking lot around us like wedding rice.

After a long while, Duke stood up and walked back down the sidewalk lined with yellow daffodils. He walked bow-legged, like all the boys in our town, farmers' sons, no matter how cool Duke tried to be. I buried my head in my arms and watched him from under one polyester-covered armpit as he climbed back into his pickup and pulled away with a screech. As he left the parking lot, he tossed the brown bag with the empty bottle of Bud out the window. It fell into the street, where it rolled and rolled until it disappeared into a ditch.

Ma liked Sourdi's husband. He had a steady job, a house. She didn't mind he was so old and Sourdi just eighteen when they married. In her eyes, eighteen was a good age to start a family. "I was younger than Sourdi when I get married," Ma liked to say.

When Sourdi sent pictures home for the holidays, Ma ooohed and 85 aaahed as though they were winning lottery tickets. My sister and her old husband in front of a listing Christmas tree, a pile of presents at their feet. Then, the red-faced baby sprawled on a pink blanket on the living room carpet, drooling in its shiny high chair, slumped in its Snugli like a rock around Sourdi's neck.

"Look. Sony," Ma pointed at the big-screen television in the background of the New Year's pictures. "Sourdi say they got all new washer/dryer, too. Maytag."

When I looked at my sister's pictures, I could see that she looked tired.

Sourdi always said that Ma used to be a very brave woman. She also said that Ma used to be a beautiful woman who liked to have her hair fixed in salons, who wore pretty dresses and knew how to dance in all the fashionable styles. I don't remember this mother. I remember the mother who worked two jobs for us.

I might never have seen Duke again if it were not for Sourdi's strange phone call one Saturday evening nearly two years after her wedding. I was fourteen and a half.

At first, I hadn't recognized my older sister's voice. 90

"Who is this?" I demanded, thinking: heavy breathing, prank caller.

"Who d'you think?" Sourdi was crying, a tiny crimped sound that barely crept out of the receiver. Then her voice steadied with anger and grew familiar. "Is Ma there?"

"What's the matter? What happened?"

"Just let me speak to Ma, O.K.?" There was a pause, as Sourdi blew her nose. "Tell her it's important."

I lured Ma from the TV room without alerting my younger sisters. Ma 95 paced back and forth in the kitchen between the refrigerator and the stove, nodding and muttering, "Mmm, mmm, uh-hmm." I could just hear the tinny squeak of Sourdi's panicked voice.

I sat on the floor, hugging my knees, in the doorway to the hall, just out of Ma's line of sight.

Finally, Ma said, in the tone normally reserved for refusing service to the unruly or arguing with a customer who had a complaint, "It's always like this. Every marriage is hard. Sometimes there is nothing you can do —"

Then Ma stopped pacing. "Just minute," she said and she took the phone with her into the bathroom, shutting the door firmly behind her.

When she came out again, twenty-two minutes later, she ignored me completely. She set the phone back on the counter without saying a word.

"So?" I prompted.   100

"I'm tired." Ma rubbed her neck with one hand. "Just let me rest. You girls, it's always something. Don't let your old mother rest."

She yawned extravagantly. She claimed she was too tired to watch any more TV. She had to go to bed, her eyes just wouldn't stay open.

I tried calling Sourdi, but the phone only rang and rang.

The next morning, Sunday, I called first thing, but then *he* picked up, my sister's husband.

"Oh, is this Nea?" he said, so cheerfully it was obvious he was hiding   105
something.

"Yes, I'd like to speak to my sister."

"I'm sorry, Little Sister." I just hated when he called me that. "My wife is out right now. But I'll tell her you called. She'll be sorry she missed you."

It was eight o'clock in the morning, for Chrissake.

"Oh, thank you," I said, sweet as pie. "How's the baby?"

"So well!" Then he launched into a long explanation about his daugh-   110
ter's eating habits, her rather average attempts to crawl, the simple words she was trying to say. For all I knew, Sourdi could have been right there, fixing his breakfast, washing his clothes, cleaning up his messes. I thought of my sister's voice in my ear, the tiny sound like something breaking.

It was all I could do to disguise the disdain in my voice. "Be sure to tell Sourdi to call back. Ma found that recipe she wanted. That special delicious recipe she was looking for. I can't tell you what it is, Ma's secret recipe, but you'll really be surprised."

"Oh, boy," the jerk said. "I didn't know about any secret recipe."

"That's why it's a secret." I hung up. I couldn't breathe. My chest hurt. I could feel my swollen heart pressing against my ribs.

The next afternoon, I tried calling back three more times, but no one answered.

At work that evening, Ma was irritable. She wouldn't look me in the   115
eyes when I tried to get her attention. Some little kid spilled his Coke into a perfectly good plate of House Special Prawns and his parents insisted they be given a new order — and a new Coke — on the house. There was a minor grease fire around quarter to nine — the smoke alarms all went off at the same time — and then the customers started complaining about the cold, too, once we had opened all the doors and windows to clear the air. Fairly average as far as disasters went, but they put Ma in a sour mood.

Ma was taking a cigarette break out back by the dumpsters, smoke curling from her nostrils, before I could corner her. She wasn't in the mood to talk, but after the nicotine fix took hold, she didn't tell me to get back to work, either.

I asked Ma if I could have a smoke. She didn't get angry. She smiled in her tired way, the edges of her mouth twitching upwards just a little, and said, "Smoking will kill you." Then she handed me her pack.

"Maybe Sourdi should come back home for a while," I suggested.

"She's a married woman. She has her own family now."

"She's still part of our family."   120

Ma didn't say anything, just tilted her head back and blew smoke at the stars, so I continued, "Well, don't you think she might be in trouble? She was crying, you know. It's not like Sourdi." My voice must have slipped a tad, just enough to sound disrespectful, because Ma jerked upright, took the cigarette out of her mouth and glared at me.

"What you think? You so smart? You gonna tell me what's what?" Ma threw her cigarette onto the asphalt. "You not like your sister. Your sister know how to bear things!"

She stormed back into the kitchen, and Ma ignored me for the rest of the evening.

I called Sourdi one more time, after Ma and my sisters had gone to bed and I finally had the kitchen to myself, the moon spilling from the window onto the floor in a big, blue puddle. I didn't dare turn on the lights.

This time, my sister answered. "Mmm . . . Hello?"   125

"Sourdi?"

"What time is it?"

"Sssh." My heart beat so loudly, I couldn't hear my own voice. "How are you doing?"

"Oh, we're fine. The baby, she's doing real good. She's starting to talk —"

"No, no, no. I mean, what happened the other night?"   130

"What?"

Another voice now, low, a man's voice, just beneath the snow on the line. Then suddenly a shriek.

"Uh-oh. I just woke her up." Sourdi's voice grew fainter as she spoke to him: "Honey, can you check the baby's diaper?" Then she said to me, "I have to go. The baby, she's hungry, you know."

"Let him handle it. I have to talk to you a minute, O.K.? Just don't go, Sourdi. What's going on? What did you say to Ma?"

Sourdi sighed, like a balloon losing its air. "Oh . . . nothing. Look, I really   135
have to go. Talk to you later, Nea." She hung up.

I called back in twenty minutes, surely long enough to change a diaper, but the phone only rang forlornly, ignored.

I considered taking Ma's car, but then Ma wouldn't be able to get to work and I wasn't sure how long I needed to be gone. Then I thought of Duke.

Even though it was far too late in the night, I called Duke. He was still in town, two years after graduation. I'd heard he was working as a mechanic at the Standard station. I found his number in the phone book.

"It's Nea. Pick up your phone, Duke," I hissed into his machine. "It's an emergency!"

"Nea?!" He was yawning. "My God. What time is it?"   140

"Duke! It's important! It's Sourdi, she's in trouble."

There was a pause while I let him absorb all this.

"You have to drive me to Des Moines. We have to get her."

"What happened?"

"Look, I don't have time to explain. We have to go tonight. It's an emer-   145
gency. A matter of life and death."

"Did you call the police?"

"Don't be stupid. Sourdi would never call the cops. She loves that jerk."

"What?" Duke whispered, "Her husband, he beat her up?"

"Duke, I told you, I can't say anything right now. But you have to help me."

He agreed to meet me at the corner, where there'd be no chance Ma could   150
hear his truck. I'd be waiting.

It was freezing. The wind stung my cheeks, which wasn't a good sign. Could
be rain coming, or worse, snow. Even when the roads were clear, it was a
good six-hour drive. I didn't want to think how long it would take if we ran
into a late-season blizzard.

There was the roar of a souped-up engine and then a spray of gravel.
Snoop Doggy Dogg growled over the wind.

"Duke! What took you?"

He put his hand over the door, barring me from climbing up. "You want
me to help or not?"

"Don't joke."   155

I pulled myself inside and then made Duke back up rather than run in
front of the house. Just in case Ma woke up.

"How come your Ma didn't want to come?"

"She doesn't know."

"Sourdi didn't want to worry her?"

"Mmm." There was no point trying to shout above Snoop Dogg.   160

He was obviously tired. When Duke was tired, he turned his music up
even louder than normal. I'd forgotten that. Now the bass underneath the rap
was vibrating in my bones. But at least he did as I asked and took off toward
the highway.

Soon the squat buildings of town, the used-car lots on the route in from
the interstate with their flapping colored flags, and the metal storage units
of the Sav-U-Lot passed from view, and there was nothing before us but the
black sky and the highway and the patches of snow on the shoulders glowing
briefly in the wake of the headlights.

I must have fallen asleep, though I don't remember feeling tired. I was standing on the deck of a boat in an inky ocean, trying to read the stars, but every
time I found one constellation, the stars began to blink and fade. I squinted
at them, but the stars would not stay in place. Then my head snapped forward as the pickup careened off the shoulder.

The pickup landed in a ditch. Metal glittered in the headlights; the fields
on this side of the highway were strung with barbed wire.

We got out by sacrificing our jackets, stuffing them under the back tires   165
until we had enough traction to slide back onto the pavement.

I insisted upon driving. "I got my license," I lied. "And I'm not tired at all."

Duke settled into the passenger seat, his arms folded across his chest, his head tilted back, preparing to go to sleep again.

"D'ya think she'll be happy to see me?" he said out of the blue. "Sourdi sent me a Christmas card with a picture of the baby. Looks just like . . . But I didn't write back or nothing. She probably thought I was angry. She mad at me, you think?"

"Sourdi's never mad at anybody."

"She must be mad at her husband if she wants you to come get her."   170

"She doesn't know we're coming."

"What!"

"I didn't have time to explain to her."

"You're not running away from home, are you?" Duke's eyes narrowed and his voice grew slow as if he thought he was suddenly being clever.

"Yeah, I'm running away to Des Moines."   175

Once upon a time, in another world, a place almost unimaginable to me sitting in the pickup with Madonna singing "Lucky Star" on the radio, Sourdi had walked across a minefield, carrying me on her back. She was nine and I was four. Because she'd told me, I could see it all clearly, better than if I actually remembered: the startled faces of people who'd tripped a mine, their limbs in new arrangements, the bones peeking through the earth. Sourdi had said it was safest to step on the bodies; that way you knew a mine was no longer there.

This was nothing I would ever tell Duke. It was our own personal story, just for Sourdi and me to share. Nobody's business but ours.

I would walk on bones for my sister, I vowed. I would put my bare feet on rotting flesh. I would save Sourdi.

We found the house in West Des Moines after circling for nearly an hour through the identical streets with their neat lawns and boxy houses and chain link fences. I refused to allow Duke to ask for directions from any of the joggers or the van that sputtered by, delivering the *Register*. He figured people in the neighborhood would know, just ask where the Oriental family lived. I told him to go to hell. Then we didn't talk for a while.

But as soon as we found Locust Street, I recognized the house. I knew it   180
was Sourdi's even though it had been painted a different color since the last set of pictures. The lace undercurtains before the cheerful flowered draperies, the flourishing plants in the windows, next to little trinkets, figurines in glass that caught the light. Every space crammed with something sweet.

The heater in Duke's truck began to make a high-pitched, sick-cat whine as we waited, parked across the street, staring at Sourdi's house.

"So, are we going to just sit here?"

"Shh," I said irritably. "Just wait a minute." Somehow I had imagined that Sourdi would sense our presence, the curtains would stir, and I'd only have to wait a moment for my sister to come running out the front door. But we sat patiently, shivering, staring at Sourdi's house. Nothing moved.

"Her husband's home," I said stupidly. "He hasn't gone to work yet."

"He wouldn't dare try anything. Not with the both of us here. We should just go and knock."   185

"They're probably still asleep."

"Nea, what's the matter with you? What are you afraid of all of a sudden?"

I'd had it with Duke. He just didn't understand anything. I hopped out of the truck and ran through the icy air, my arms wrapped around my body. The sidewalk was slick beneath my sneakers, still damp from the ditch, and I slid onto my knees on the driveway. My right hand broke the fall. A sharp jagged pain shot up to my elbow and stayed there, throbbing. I picked myself up and ran limping to the door and rang.

No one answered for a minute, and then it was him.

"What on earth? Nea!" Sourdi's husband was dressed for work, but he hadn't shaved yet. He looked even older than I remembered, his thinning hair flat across his skull, his bloodshot eyes and swollen lids still heavy from sleep. He might have been handsome once, decades ago, but I saw no evidence of it now. He held the door open and I slipped into the warmth without even removing my shoes first. "How did you get here? Is your mother coming, too?"   190

My eyes started to water, the transition from cold to heat. Slowly the room came into focus. It was a mess. Baby toys on the carpet, shoes in a pile by the door, old newspapers scattered on an end table anchored by a bowl of peanut shells. The TV was blaring somewhere, and a baby was crying.

Sourdi emerged from the kitchen, dressed in a bright pink sweatsuit emblazoned with the head of Minnie Mouse, pink slippers over her feet, the baby on her hip. She had a bruise across her cheekbone and the purple remains of a black eye. Sourdi didn't say anything for a few seconds as she stared at me, blinking, her mouth falling open. "Where's Ma?"

"Home."

"Oh, no." Sourdi's face crumpled. "Is everything all right?"

I couldn't believe how dense my sister had become. We used to be able to communicate without words. "Everything's fine . . . at home. Of course." I tried to give her a look so that she'd understand that I had come to rescue her, but Sourdi stood rigidly in place in the doorway to the kitchen, her mouth twitching, puzzled.   195

"Please, Little Sister, sit down," her husband said. "Let me make you some tea."

Someone banged on the front door, three times. Before I could begin to feel annoyed that Duke couldn't even wait five minutes, that he just had to ruin everything, my sister's husband opened the door again. I didn't bother to turn, instead I watched Sourdi's eyes widen and her wide mouth pucker into an O as she gasped, "Duke!"

"What's goin' on?" Duke said.

Then everyone stared at me with such identical expressions of noncomprehension that I had to laugh. Then I couldn't stop, because I hadn't slept and it was so cold and my nose was running and I didn't have any Kleenex.

"I said, what the hell is going on?" Duke repeated.   200

Sourdi's husband approached Duke. He smiled. "You must be Nea's —"

But by now, Duke had seen Sourdi's bruises. His mouth twisted into a sneer. "You bastard! I oughtta —" He punched Sourdi's husband in the nose. Sourdi screamed, her husband bent over double. Duke drew back his fist again, but Sourdi ran forward and grabbed him. She was punching him on the chest, "Out! Out! You! I'll call the police!" She tried to claw him with her nails, but Duke threw his arms up around his head.

Sourdi's husband stood up. Blood gushed from his nose all over his white shirt and tie.

"Come on!" I said stupidly. "Come on, Sourdi, let's go!"

But it was pretty obvious that she didn't want to leave.   205

The baby began shrieking.

I started crying, too.

After everyone had calmed down, Duke went down the street to the 7-Eleven to get a bag of ice for Mr. Chhay, who kept saying "I'm fine, don't worry," even though his nose had turned a deep scarlet and was starting to swell.

It turned out Sourdi's husband hadn't beaten her up. An economy-size box of baby wipes had fallen off the closet shelf and struck her full in the eye.

While Mr. Chhay went into the bedroom to change his clothes, I sat with 210
Sourdi in the kitchen as she tried to get the squawling baby to eat its breakfast.

"Nea, what's wrong with you?"

"What's wrong with me? Don't you get it? I was trying to help you!"

Sourdi sighed as the baby spat a spoonful of the glop onto the table. "I'm a married woman. I'm not just some girl anymore. I have my own family. You understand that?"

"You were crying." I squinted at my sister. "I heard you."

"I'm gonna have another baby, you know. That's a big step. That's a big   215
thing." She said this as though it explained everything.

"You sound like an old lady. You're only twenty, for Chrissake. You don't have to live like this. Ma is wrong. You can be anything, Sourdi."

Sourdi pinched her nose between two fingers. "Everything's gonna be fine. We just had a little argument, but it's O.K. We had a good talk. He understands now. I'm still gonna go to school. I haven't changed my mind. After the baby gets a little bigger, I mean, both babies. Maybe when they start preschool."

Just then her husband came back into the kitchen. He had to use the phone to call work. His face looked like a gargoyle's.

Sourdi looked at me then, so disappointed. I knew what she was thinking. She had grown up, and I had merely grown unworthy of her love.

After Duke got back with the ice, he and Sourdi's husband shook hands.   220
Duke kept saying, "Gosh, I'm so sorry," and Mr. Chhay kept repeating, "No problem, don't worry."

Then Sourdi's husband had to go. We followed him to the driveway. My sister kissed him before he climbed into his Buick. He rolled down the window, and she leaned in and kissed him again.

I turned away. I watched Duke standing in the doorway, holding the baby in his arms, cooing at its face. In his tough wannabe clothes, the super-wide jeans and his fancy sneakers and the chain from his wallet to his belt loops, he looked surprisingly young.

Sourdi lent us some blankets and matching his-and-hers Donald and Daisy Duck sweatshirts for the trip back, since our coats were still wet and worthless.

"Don't tell Ma I was here, O.K.?" I begged Sourdi. "We'll be home by afternoon. She'll just think I'm with friends or something. She doesn't have to know, O.K.?"

Sourdi pressed her full lips together into a thin line and nodded in a way 225 that seemed as though she were answering a different question. And I knew that I couldn't trust my sister to take my side anymore.

As we pulled away from Sourdi's house, the first icy snowflakes began to fall across the windshield.

Sourdi stood in the driveway with the baby on her hip. She waved to us as the snow swirled around her like ashes.

She had made her choice, and she hadn't chosen me.

Sourdi told me a story once about a magic serpent, the Naga, with a mouth so large, it could swallow people whole. Our ancestors carved Naga into the stones of Angkor Wat to scare away demons. Sourdi said people used to believe they could come alive in times of great evil and protect the temples. They could eat armies.

I wished I was a Naga. I would have swallowed the whole world in one gulp. 230 But I have no magic powers. None whatsoever.

CONSIDERATIONS FOR CRITICAL THINKING AND WRITING

1. FIRST RESPONSE. How does your response to Nea develop over the course of the story? Is she a dynamic or a static character?

2. Explain how Nea and Sourdi serve as character foils to one another.

3. Discuss whether you think Duke is a flat or a round character.

4. What is the effect of the story's being told from Nea's perspective? How might the story be different if it were told from the mother's point of view?

5. Do you think Mr. Chhay is a good or bad husband?

6. How does the information about Nea and Sourdi's trip through the minefield affect your understanding of Nea's relationship with her sister?

7. Comment on the title. Why wouldn't an alternative like "Nea the Troublemaker" be appropriate?

8. CONNECTION TO ANOTHER SELECTION. Compare the characterization of Nea in "Saving Sourdi" and of Sammy in John Updike's "A & P" (p. 149). In what sense do both characters see themselves as rescuers?

Ron Carlson (b. 1947)

Born in Logan, Utah, Ron Carlson is emeritus professor of English at Arizona State University. He has published his fiction widely in magazines such as the *New Yorker, Esquire,* and *Harper's.* To date he has published four novels, the most recent being *The Signal* (2010), and five collections of short stories, the last *The Blue Box* (2014). On his own work Carlson has commented: "I think all stories, long and short, require astonishing attention . . . Attention is the ruler of craft." And for a discussion of his own short story writing, see *Ron Carlson Writes a Story* (2007).

> **When I Write** "After I finish a story, I wait a few days and make sure I've got every beat, every moment that I wanted. I look for the thing I've omitted or hurried past. I also read everything I write aloud." —RON CARLSON

Max   1986

Max is a crotch dog. He has powerful instinct and insistent snout, and he can ruin a cocktail party faster than running out of ice. This urge of his runs deeper than any training can reach. He can sit, heel, fetch; he'll even fetch a thrown snowball from a snowfield, bringing a fragment of it back to you delicately in his mouth. And then he'll poke your crotch, and be warned: it is no gentle nuzzling.

So when our friend Maxwell came by for a drink to introduce us to his new girlfriend, our dog Max paddled up to him and jabbed him a sharp one, a stroke so clean and fast it could have been a boxing glove on a spring. Maxwell, our friend, lost his breath and sat on the couch suddenly and heavily, unable to say anything beyond a hoarse whisper of "*Scotch.* Just *scotch.* No ice."

Cody put Max out on the back porch, of course, where he has spent a good measure of this long winter, and Maxwell took a long nourishing sip on his scotch and began recovering. He's not athletic at all, but I admired the way he had folded, crumpling just like a ballplayer taking an inside pitch in the nuts. It wasn't enough to change my whole opinion of him, but it helped me talk to him civilly for five minutes while Cody calmed the dog. I think I had seen a sly crocodile smile on Max's face after he'd struck, pride in a job well done, possibly, and then again, possibly a deeper satisfaction. He had heard Cody and me talk about Maxwell before, and Max is a smart dog.

Maxwell, his color returning, was now explaining that his new girlfriend, Laurie, would be along in a minute; she had been detained at aerobics class. Life at the museum was hectic and lovely, he was explaining. It was frustrating for him to be working with folk so ignorant of what made a good show, of counterpoint, of even the crudest elements of art. Let alone business, the business of curating, the business of public responsibility, the business in general. I was hoping to get him on his arch tirade about how the average intelligence in his department couldn't make a picture by connecting the dots, a routine which Cody could dial up like a phone number. But I wasn't going to get it tonight; he was already on business, his favorite topic.

The truth is that Maxwell is a simple crook. He uses his office to travel   5 like a pasha; he damages borrowed work, sees to the insurance, and then buys some of it for himself; he only mounts three shows a year; and he only goes in four days a week.

Cody came in for one of her favorite parts, Maxwell's catalogue (including stores and prices) of the clothing and jewelry he was wearing tonight. Cody always asked about the clerks, and so his glorious monologue was sprinkled with diatribes about the help. Old Maxwell.

When his girlfriend, Laurie, finally did arrive, breathless and airy at the same time, Maxwell had all three rings on the coffee table and he was showing Cody his new watch. Laurie tossed her head three times taking off her coat; we were in for a record evening.

Maxwell would show her off for a while, making disparaging remarks about exercise *of any kind*, and she would admire his rings, ranking them like tokens on the table, going into complex and aesthetic reasons for her choices. I would fill her full of the white wine that all of Maxwell's girlfriends drink, and then when she asked where the powder room was, I would rise with her and go into the kitchen, wait, count to twenty-five while selecting another Buckhorn out of the fridge, and let Max in.

CONSIDERATIONS FOR CRITICAL THINKING AND WRITING

1. FIRST RESPONSE. Why do you think the story is titled "Max" rather than "Maxwell"?

2. What details are especially effective in characterizing Maxwell and his girlfriend?

3. How does the narrator serve as an implicit foil to Maxwell?

4. CREATIVE RESPONSE. Write an additional final paragraph that describes what happens when Max is let back into the house, a paragraph that is worthy of the humor in the rest of the story.

5. Why do you think Carlson didn't write that paragraph?

HERMAN MELVILLE (1819–1891)

Hoping to improve his distressed financial situation, Herman Melville left New York and went to sea as a young common sailor. He returned to become an uncommon writer. His experiences at sea became the basis for his early novels: *Typee* (1846), *Omoo* (1847), *Mardi* (1849), *Redburn* (1849), and *White-Jacket* (1850). Ironically, with the publication of his masterpiece, *Moby-Dick* (1851), Melville lost the popular success he had enjoyed with his earlier books because his readers were not ready for its philosophical complexity. Although he wrote more, Melville's works were read less and slipped into obscurity. His final short novel, *Billy Budd*, was not published until the 1920s, when critics rediscovered him. In "Bartleby, the Scrivener," Melville presents a quiet clerk in a law office whose baffling "passive resistance" disrupts the life of his employer, a man who attempts to make sense of Bartleby's refusal to behave reasonably.

Library of Congress, Prints and Photographs Division.

Bartleby, the Scrivener   1853

A Story of Wall Street

I am a rather elderly man. The nature of my avocations, for the last thirty years, has brought me into more than ordinary contact with what would seem an interesting and somewhat singular set of men, of whom, as yet, nothing, that I know of, has ever been written — I mean, the law-copyists, or scriveners. I have known very many of them, professionally and privately, and, if I pleased, could relate diverse histories, at which good-natured gentlemen might smile, and sentimental souls might weep. But I waive the biographies of all other scriveners, for a few passages in the life of Bartleby, who was a scrivener, the strangest I ever saw, or heard of. While, of other law-copyists, I might write the complete life, of Bartleby nothing of that sort can be done. I believe that no materials exist, for a full and satisfactory biography of this man. It is an irreparable loss to literature. Bartleby was one of those beings of whom nothing is ascertainable, except from the original sources, and, in his case, those are very small. What my own astonished eyes saw of Bartleby, *that* is all I know of him, except, indeed, one vague report, which will appear in the sequel.

Ere introducing the scrivener, as he first appeared to me, it is fit I make some mention of myself, my *employés*, my business, my chambers, and general surroundings, because some such description is indispensable to an adequate understanding of the chief character about to be presented. Imprimis:° I am a man who, from his youth upwards, has been filled with a profound conviction that the easiest way of life is the best. Hence, though I belong to a profession proverbially energetic and nervous, even to turbulence, at times, yet nothing of that sort have I ever suffered to invade my peace. I am one of those

Imprimis: In the first place.

unambitious lawyers who never address a jury, or in any way draw down public applause; but, in the cool tranquillity of a snug retreat, do a snug business among rich men's bonds, and mortgages, and title-deeds. All who know me, consider me an eminently *safe* man. The late John Jacob Astor,° a personage little given to poetic enthusiasm, had no hesitation in pronouncing my first grand point to be prudence; my next, method. I do not speak it in vanity, but simply record the fact, that I was not unemployed in my profession by the late John Jacob Astor; a name which, I admit, I love to repeat; for it hath a rounded and orbicular sound to it, and rings like unto bullion. I will freely add, that I was not insensible to the late John Jacob Astor's good opinion.

Some time prior to the period at which this little history begins, my avocations had been largely increased. The good old office, now extinct in the State of New York, of a Master in Chancery, had been conferred upon me. It was not a very arduous office, but very pleasantly remunerative. I seldom lose my temper; much more seldom indulge in dangerous indignation at wrongs and outrages; but I must be permitted to be rash here and declare, that I consider the sudden and violent abrogation of the office of Master in Chancery, by the new Constitution, as a — premature act; inasmuch as I had counted upon a life-lease of the profits, whereas I only received those of a few short years. But this is by the way.

My chambers were up stairs, at No. — Wall Street. At one end, they looked upon the white wall of the interior of a spacious skylight shaft, penetrating the building from top to bottom.

This view might have been considered rather tame than otherwise, 5 deficient in what landscape painters call "life." But, if so, the view from the other end of my chambers offered, at least, a contrast, if nothing more. In that direction, my windows commanded an unobstructed view of a lofty brick wall, black by age and everlasting shade; which wall required no spyglass to bring out its lurking beauties, but, for the benefit of all near-sighted spectators, was pushed up to within ten feet of my window-panes. Owing to the great height of the surrounding buildings, and my chambers being on the second floor, the interval between this wall and mine not a little resembled a huge square cistern.

At the period just preceding the advent of Bartleby, I had two persons as copyists in my employment, and a promising lad as an office-boy. First, Turkey; second, Nippers; third, Ginger Nut. These may seem names, the like of which are not usually found in the Directory. In truth, they were nicknames, mutually conferred upon each other by my three clerks, and were deemed expressive of their respective persons or characters. Turkey was a short, pursy Englishman, of about my own age — that is, somewhere not far from sixty. In the morning, one might say, his face was of a fine florid hue, but after twelve o'clock, meridian — his dinner hour — it blazed like a grate full of Christmas coals; and continued blazing — but, as it were, with a gradual wane — till six o'clock, P.M., or thereabouts; after which, I saw no more of the proprietor of the face, which, gaining its meridian with the sun, seemed to set with it, to

<hr />

John Jacob Astor (1763–1848): An enormously wealthy American capitalist.

rise, culminate, and decline the following day, with the like regularity and undiminished glory. There are many singular coincidences I have known in the course of my life, not the least among which was the fact, that, exactly when Turkey displayed his fullest beams from his red and radiant countenance, just then, too, at that critical moment, began the daily period when I considered his business capacities as seriously disturbed for the remainder of the twenty-four hours. Not that he was absolutely idle, or averse to business then; far from it. The difficulty was, he was apt to be altogether too energetic. There was a strange, inflamed, flurried, flighty recklessness of activity about him. He would be incautious in dipping his pen into his inkstand. All his blots upon my documents were dropped there after twelve o'clock, meridian. Indeed, not only would he be reckless, and sadly given to making blots in the afternoon, but, some days, he went further, and was rather noisy. At such times, too, his face flamed with augmented blazonry, as if cannel coal had been heaped on anthracite. He made an unpleasant racket with his chair; spilled his sand-box; in mending his pens, impatiently split them all to pieces, and threw them on the floor in a sudden passion; stood up, and leaned over his table, boxing his papers about in a most indecorous manner, very sad to behold in an elderly man like him. Nevertheless, as he was in many ways a most valuable person to me, and all the time before twelve o'clock, meridian, was the quickest, steadiest creature, too, accomplishing a great deal of work in a style not easily to be matched — for these reasons, I was willing to overlook his eccentricities, though, indeed, occasionally, I remonstrated with him. I did this very gently, however, because, though the civilest, nay, the blandest and most reverential of men in the morning, yet, in the afternoon, he was disposed, upon provocation, to be slightly rash with his tongue — in fact, insolent. Now, valuing his morning services as I did, and resolved not to lose them — yet, at the same time, made uncomfortable by his inflamed ways after twelve o'clock — and being a man of peace, unwilling by my admonitions to call forth unseemly retorts from him, I took upon me, one Saturday noon (he was always worse on Saturdays) to hint to him, very kindly, that, perhaps, now that he was growing old, it might be well to abridge his labors; in short, he need not come to my chambers after twelve o'clock, but, dinner over, had best go home to his lodgings, and rest himself till tea-time. But no; he insisted upon his afternoon devotions. His countenance became intolerably fervid, as he oratorically assured me — gesticulating with a long ruler at the other end of the room — that if his services in the morning were useful, how indispensable, then, in the afternoon?

"With submission, sir," said Turkey, on this occasion, "I consider myself your right-hand man. In the morning I but marshal and deploy my columns; but in the afternoon I put myself at their head, and gallantly charge the foe, thus" — and he made a violent thrust with the ruler.

"But the blots, Turkey," intimated I.

"True; but, with submission, sir, behold these hairs! I am getting old. Surely, sir, a blot or two of a warm afternoon is not to be severely urged against gray hairs. Old age — even if it blot the page — is honorable. With submission, sir, we *both* are getting old."

This appeal to my fellow-feeling was hardly to be resisted. At all events,   10
I saw that go he would not. So, I made up my mind to let him stay, resolving,
nevertheless, to see to it that, during the afternoon, he had to do with my less
important papers.

Nippers, the second on my list, was a whiskered, sallow, and, upon
the whole, rather piratical-looking young man, of about five-and-twenty.
I always deemed him the victim of two evil powers — ambition and indigestion. The ambition was evinced by a certain impatience of the duties of
a mere copyist, an unwarrantable usurpation of strictly professional affairs
such as the original drawing up of legal documents. The indigestion seemed
betokened in an occasional nervous testiness and grinning irritability, causing the teeth to audibly grind together over mistakes committed in copying;
unnecessary maledictions, hissed, rather than spoken, in the heat of business; and especially by a continual discontent with the height of the table
where he worked. Though of a very ingenious mechanical turn, Nippers
could never get this table to suit him. He put chips under it, blocks of various sorts, bits of pasteboard, and at last went so far as to attempt an exquisite adjustment, by final pieces of folded blotting-paper. But no invention
would answer. If, for the sake of easing his back, he brought the table-lid at
a sharp angle well up towards his chin, and wrote there like a man using the
steep roof of a Dutch house for his desk, then he declared that it stopped
the circulation in his arms. If now he lowered the table to his waistbands,
and stooped over it in writing, then there was a sore aching in his back. In
short, the truth of the matter was, Nippers knew not what he wanted. Or, if
he wanted anything, it was to be rid of a scrivener's table altogether. Among
the manifestations of his diseased ambition was a fondness he had for receiving visits from certain ambiguous-looking fellows in seedy coats, whom he
called his clients. Indeed, I was aware that not only was he, at times, considerable of a ward-politician, but he occasionally did a little business at the
justices' courts, and was not unknown on the steps of the Tombs.° I have
good reason to believe, however, that one individual who called upon him
at my chambers, and who, with a grand air, he insisted was his client, was
no other than a dun, and the alleged title-deed, a bill. But, with all his failings, and the annoyances he caused me, Nippers, like his compatriot Turkey,
was a very useful man to me; wrote a neat, swift hand; and, when he chose,
was not deficient in a gentlemanly sort of deportment. Added to this, he
always dressed in a gentlemanly sort of way; and so, incidentally, reflected
credit upon my chambers. Whereas, with respect to Turkey, I had much
ado to keep him from being a reproach to me. His clothes were apt to
look oily, and smell of eating-houses. He wore his pantaloons very loose
and baggy in summer. His coats were execrable, his hat not to be handled. But while the hat was a thing of indifference to me, inasmuch as his
natural civility and deference, as a dependent Englishman, always led him
to doff it the moment he entered the room, yet his coat was another matter.

the Tombs: A jail in New York City.

Concerning his coats, I reasoned with him; but with no effect. The truth was, I suppose, that a man with so small an income could not afford to sport such a lustrous face and a lustrous coat at one and the same time. As Nippers once observed, Turkey's money went chiefly for red ink. One winter day, I presented Turkey with a highly respectable-looking coat of my own — a padded gray coat, of a most comfortable warmth, and which buttoned straight up from the knee to the neck. I thought Turkey would appreciate the favor, and abate his rashness and obstreperousness of afternoons. But no; I verily believe that buttoning himself up in so downy and blanket-like a coat had a pernicious effect upon him — upon the same principle that too much oats are bad for horses. In fact, precisely as a rash, restive horse is said to feel his oats, so Turkey felt his coat. It made him insolent. He was a man whom prosperity harmed.

Though, concerning the self-indulgent habits of Turkey, I had my own private surmises, yet, touching Nippers, I was well persuaded that, whatever might be his faults in other respects, he was, at least, a temperate young man. But indeed, nature herself seemed to have been his vintner, and, at his birth, charged him so thoroughly with an irritable, brandy-like disposition, that all subsequent potations were needless. When I consider how, amid the stillness of my chambers, Nippers would sometimes impatiently rise from his seat, and stooping over his table, spread his arms wide apart, seize the whole desk, and move it, and jerk it, with a grim, grinding motion on the floor, as if the table were a perverse voluntary agent, intent on thwarting and vexing him, I plainly perceive that, for Nippers, brandy-and-water were altogether superfluous.

It was fortunate for me that, owing to its peculiar cause — indigestion — the irritability and consequent nervousness of Nippers were mainly observable in the morning, while in the afternoon he was comparatively mild. So that, Turkey's paroxysms only coming on about twelve o'clock, I never had to do with their eccentricities at one time. Their fits relieved each other, like guards. When Nippers' was on, Turkey's was off; and *vice versa*. This was a good natural arrangement, under the circumstances.

Ginger Nut, the third on my list, was a lad, some twelve years old. His father was a carman, ambitious of seeing his son on the bench instead of a cart, before he died. So he sent him to my office, as student at law, errand-boy, cleaner, and sweeper, at the rate of one dollar a week. He had a little desk to himself, but he did not use it much. Upon inspection, the drawer exhibited a great array of the shells of various sorts of nuts. Indeed, to this quick-witted youth, the whole noble science of the law was contained in a nutshell. Not the least among the employments of Ginger Nut, as well as one which he discharged with the most alacrity, was his duty as cake and apple purveyor for Turkey and Nippers. Copying lawpapers being proverbially a dry, husky sort of business, my two scriveners were fain to moisten their mouths very often with Spitzenbergs, to be had at the numerous stalls nigh the Custom House and Post Office. Also, they sent Ginger Nut very frequently for that peculiar cake — small, flat, round, and very spicy — after which he had been named by them. Of a cold morning, when business was but dull, Turkey would gobble up scores of these cakes, as if they were mere wafers — indeed, they sell them at the rate of six or eight for a penny — the scrape of his pen blending with the crunching of the crisp particles in his mouth. Of all the fiery afternoon blunders and flurried rashness of Turkey, was his once moistening a ginger-cake between his lips, and clapping it on to a mortgage, for a seal. I came within an ace of dismissing him then. But he mollified me by making an oriental bow, and saying —

"With submission, sir, it was generous of me to find you in stationery on   15 my own account."

Now my original business — that of a conveyancer and title hunter, and drawer-up of recondite documents of all sorts — was considerably increased by receiving the Master's office. There was now great work for scriveners. Not only must I push the clerks already with me, but I must have additional help.

In answer to my advertisement, a motionless young man one morning stood upon my office threshold, the door being open, for it was summer. I can see that figure now — pallidly neat, pitiably respectable, incurably forlorn! It was Bartleby.

After a few words touching his qualifications, I engaged him, glad to have among my corps of copyists a man of so singularly sedate an aspect, which I thought might operate beneficially upon the flighty temper of Turkey, and the fiery one of Nippers.

I should have stated before that ground-glass folding-doors divided my premises into two parts, one of which was occupied by my scriveners, the other by myself. According to my humor, I threw open these doors, or closed them. I resolved to assign Bartleby a corner by the folding-doors, but on my side of them, so as to have this quiet man within easy call, in case any trifling thing was to be done. I placed his desk close up to a small side-window in that part of the room, a window which originally had afforded a lateral view of certain grimy brickyards and bricks, but which, owing to subsequent erections, commanded at present no view at all, though it gave some light. Within three feet of the panes was a wall, and the light came down from far above, between two lofty buildings, as from a very small opening in a dome. Still further to a satisfactory arrangement, I procured a high green folding screen, which might entirely isolate Bartleby from my sight, though not remove him from my voice. And thus, in a manner, privacy and society were conjoined.

At first, Bartleby did an extraordinary quantity of writing. As if long   20 famishing for something to copy, he seemed to gorge himself on my documents. There was no pause for digestion. He ran a day and night line, copying by sunlight and by candle-light. I should have been quite delighted with his application, had he been cheerfully industrious. But he wrote on silently, palely, mechanically.

It is, of course, an indispensable part of a scrivener's business to verify the accuracy of his copy, word by word. Where there are two or more scriveners in an office, they assist each other in this examination, one reading from the copy, the other holding the original. It is a very dull, wearisome, and lethargic affair. I can readily imagine that, to some sanguine temperaments, it would be altogether intolerable. For example, I cannot credit that the mettlesome poet, Byron, would have contentedly sat down with Bartleby to examine a law document of, say five hundred pages, closely written in a crimpy hand.

Now and then, in the haste of business, it had been my habit to assist in comparing some brief document myself, calling Turkey or Nippers for this purpose. One object I had, in placing Bartleby so handy to me behind the screen, was, to avail myself of his services on such trivial occasions. It was on the third day, I think, of his being with me, and before any necessity had arisen for having his own writing examined, that, being much hurried to complete a small affair I had in hand, I abruptly called to Bartleby. In my haste and natural expectancy of instant compliance, I sat with my head bent over the original on my desk, and my right hand sideways, and somewhat nervously extended with the copy, so that, immediately upon emerging from his retreat, Bartleby might snatch it and proceed to business without the least delay.

In this very attitude did I sit when I called to him, rapidly stating what it was I wanted him to do — namely, to examine a small paper with me. Imagine my surprise, nay, my consternation, when, without moving from his privacy, Bartleby, in a singularly mild, firm voice, replied, "I would prefer not to."

I sat awhile in perfect silence, rallying my stunned faculties. Immediately it occurred to me that my ears had deceived me, or Bartleby had entirely misunderstood my meaning. I repeated my request in the clearest tone I could assume; but in quite as clear a one came the previous reply, "I would prefer not to."

"Prefer not to," echoed I, rising in high excitement, and crossing the   25 room with a stride. "What do you mean? Are you moonstruck? I want you to help me compare this sheet here — take it," and I thrust it towards him.

"I would prefer not to," said he.

I looked at him steadfastly. His face was leanly composed; his gray eye dimly calm. Not a wrinkle of agitation rippled him. Had there been the least uneasiness, anger, impatience, or impertinence in his manner; in other words, had there been anything ordinarily human about him, doubtless I should have violently dismissed him from the premises. But as it was, I should have as soon thought of turning my pale plaster-of-paris bust of Cicero out of doors. I stood gazing at him awhile, as he went on with his own writing, and then reseated myself at my desk. This is very strange, thought I. What had one best do? But my business hurried me. I concluded to forget the matter for the present, reserving it for my future leisure. So, calling Nippers from the other room, the paper was speedily examined.

A few days after this, Bartleby concluded four lengthy documents, being quadruplicates of a week's testimony taken before me in my High Court of Chancery. It became necessary to examine them. It was an important suit, and great accuracy was imperative. Having all things arranged, I called Turkey, Nippers, and Ginger Nut, from the next room, meaning to place the four copies in the hands of my four clerks, while I should read from the original. Accordingly, Turkey, Nippers, and Ginger Nut had taken their seats in a row, each with his document in his hand, when I called to Bartleby to join this interesting group.

"Bartleby! quick, I am waiting."

I heard a slow scrape of his chair legs on the uncarpeted floor, and soon he appeared standing at the entrance of his hermitage.

"What is wanted?" said he, mildly.

"The copies, the copies," said I, hurriedly. "We are going to examine them. There" — and I held towards him the fourth quadruplicate.

"I would prefer not to," he said, and gently disappeared behind the screen.

For a few moments I was turned into a pillar of salt, standing at the head of my seated column of clerks. Recovering myself, I advanced towards the screen, and demanded the reason for such extraordinary conduct.

"*Why* do you refuse?"

"I would prefer not to."

With any other man I should have flown outright into a dreadful passion, scorned all further words, and thrust him ignominiously from my presence. But there was something about Bartleby that not only strangely disarmed me, but, in a wonderful manner, touched and disconcerted me. I began to reason with him.

"These are your own copies we are about to examine. It is labor saving to you, because one examination will answer for your four papers. It is common usage. Every copyist is bound to help examine his copy. Is it not so? Will you not speak? Answer!"

"I prefer not to," he replied in a flute-like tone. It seemed to me that, while I had been addressing him, he carefully revolved every statement that I made; fully comprehended the meaning; could not gainsay the irresistible conclusion; but, at the same time, some paramount consideration prevailed with him to reply as he did.

"You are decided, then, not to comply with my request — a request made according to common usage and common sense?"

He briefly gave me to understand, that on that point my judgment was sound. Yes: his decision was irreversible.

It is not seldom the case that, when a man is browbeaten in some unprecedented and violently unreasonable way, he begins to stagger in his own plainest faith. He begins, as it were, vaguely to surmise that, wonderful as it may be, all the justice and all the reason is on the other side. Accordingly, if any disinterested persons are present, he turns to them for some reinforcement for his own faltering mind.

"Turkey," said I, "what do you think of this? Am I not right?"

"With submission, sir," said Turkey, in his blandest tone, "I think that you are."

"Nippers," said I, "what do *you* think of it?"

"I think I should kick him out of the office."

(The reader of nice perceptions will have perceived that, it being morning, Turkey's answer is couched in polite and tranquil terms, but Nippers replies in ill-tempered ones. Or, to repeat a previous sentence, Nippers' ugly mood was on duty, and Turkey's off.)

"Ginger Nut," said I, willing to enlist the smallest suffrage in my behalf, "what do *you* think of it?"

"I think, sir, he's a little *luny*," replied Ginger Nut, with a grin.

"You hear what they say," said I, turning towards the screen, "come forth 50 and do your duty."

But he vouchsafed no reply. I pondered a moment in sore perplexity. But once more business hurried me. I determined again to postpone the consideration of this dilemma to my future leisure. With a little trouble we made out to examine the papers without Bartleby, though at every page or two Turkey deferentially dropped his opinion, that this proceeding was quite out of the common; while Nippers, twitching in his chair with a dyspeptic nervousness, ground out, between his set teeth, occasional hissing maledictions against the stubborn oaf behind the screen. And for his (Nippers') part, this was the first and the last time he would do another man's business without pay.

Meanwhile Bartleby sat in his hermitage, oblivious to everything but his own peculiar business there.

Some days passed, the scrivener being employed upon another lengthy work. His late remarkable conduct led me to regard his ways narrowly. I observed that he never went to dinner; indeed, that he never went anywhere. As yet I had never, of my personal knowledge, known him to be outside of my office. He was a perpetual sentry in the corner. At about eleven o'clock though, in the morning, I noticed that Ginger Nut would advance toward the opening in Bartleby's screen, as if silently beckoned thither by a gesture invisible to me where I sat. The boy would then leave the office, jingling a few pence, and reappear with a handful of ginger-nuts, which he delivered in the hermitage, receiving two of the cakes for his trouble.

He lives, then, on ginger-nuts, thought I; never eats a dinner, properly speaking; he must be a vegetarian, then, but no; he never eats even vegetables, he eats nothing but ginger-nuts. My mind then ran on in reveries concerning the probable effects upon the human constitution of living entirely on ginger-nuts. Ginger-nuts are so called, because they contain ginger as one of their peculiar constituents, and the final flavoring one. Now, what was ginger? A hot, spicy thing. Was Bartleby hot and spicy? Not at all. Ginger, then, had no effect upon Bartleby. Probably he preferred it should have none.

Nothing so aggravates an earnest person as a passive resistance. If the 55 individual so resisted be of a not inhumane temper, and the resisting one perfectly harmless in his passivity, then, in the better moods of the former, he will endeavor charitably to construe to his imagination what proves impossible to be solved by his judgment. Even so, for the most part, I regarded Bartleby and his ways. Poor fellow! thought I, he means no mischief; it is plain he intends no insolence; his aspect sufficiently evinces that his eccentricities are involuntary. He is useful to me. I can get along with him. If I turn him away, the chances are he will fall in with some less indulgent employer, and then he will be rudely treated, and perhaps driven forth miserably to starve. Yes. Here I can cheaply purchase a delicious self-approval. To befriend Bartleby; to humor him in his strange wilfulness, will cost me little or nothing, while I lay up in my soul what will eventually prove a sweet morsel for my conscience. But this mood was not invariable with me. The passiveness of Bartleby sometimes irritated me. I felt strangely goaded on to encounter him in new opposition — to elicit some angry spark from him answerable to my own. But, indeed, I might as well have essayed to strike fire with my knuckles against a bit of Windsor soap. But one afternoon the evil impulse in me mastered me, and the following little scene ensued:

"Bartleby," said I, "when those papers are all copied, I will compare them with you."

"I would prefer not to."

"How? Surely you do not mean to persist in that mulish vagary?"

No answer.

I threw open the folding-doors nearby, and turning upon Turkey and Nippers, exclaimed:

"Bartleby a second time says, he won't examine his papers. What do you think of it, Turkey?"

It was afternoon, be it remembered. Turkey sat glowing like a brass boiler; his bald head steaming; his hands reeling among his blotted papers.

"Think of it?" roared Turkey. "I think I'll just step behind his screen, and black his eyes for him!"

So saying, Turkey rose to his feet and threw his arms into a pugilistic position. He was hurrying away to make good his promise, when I detained him, alarmed at the effect of incautiously rousing Turkey's combativeness after dinner.

"Sit down, Turkey," said I, "and hear what Nippers has to say. What do you think of it, Nippers? Would I not be justified in immediately dismissing Bartleby?"

"Excuse me, that is for you to decide, sir. I think his conduct quite unusual, and, indeed, unjust, as regards Turkey and myself. But it may only be a passing whim."

"Ah," exclaimed I, "you have strangely changed your mind, then — you speak very gently of him now."

"All beer," cried Turkey; "gentleness is effects of beer — Nippers and I dined together to-day. You see how gentle *I* am, sir. Shall I go and black his eyes?"

"You refer to Bartleby, I suppose. No, not to-day, Turkey," I replied; "pray, put up your fists."

I closed the doors, and again advanced towards Bartleby. I felt additional incentives tempting me to my fate. I burned to be rebelled against again. I remembered that Bartleby never left the office.

"Bartleby," said I, "Ginger Nut is away; just step around to the Post Office, won't you?" (it was but a three minutes' walk) "and see if there is anything for me."

"I would prefer not to."

"You *will* not?"

"I *prefer* not."

I staggered to my desk, and sat there in a deep study. My blind invet-   75
eracy returned. Was there any other thing in which I could procure myself to
be ignominiously repulsed by this lean, penniless wight? — my hired clerk?
What added thing is there, perfectly reasonable, that he will be sure to refuse
to do?

"Bartleby!"

No answer.

"Bartleby," in a louder tone.

No answer.

"Bartleby," I roared.   80

Like a very ghost, agreeably to the laws of magical invocation, at the
third summons, he appeared at the entrance of his hermitage.

"Go to the next room, and tell Nippers to come to me."

"I prefer not to," he respectfully and slowly said, and mildly disappeared.

"Very good, Bartleby," said I, in a quiet sort of serenely-severe self-
possessed tone, intimating the unalterable purpose of some terrible retribution very close at hand. At the moment I half intended something of the kind.
But upon the whole, as it was drawing towards my dinner-hour, I thought it
best to put on my hat and walk home for the day, suffering much from perplexity and distress of mind.

Shall I acknowledge it? The conclusion of this whole business was, that it   85
soon became a fixed fact of my chambers, that a pale young scrivener, by the
name of Bartleby, had a desk there; that he copied for me at the usual rate of
four cents a folio (one hundred words); but he was permanently exempt from
examining the work done by him, that duty being transferred to Turkey and
Nippers, out of compliment, doubtless, to their superior acuteness; moreover,
said Bartleby was never, on any account, to be dispatched on the most trivial
errand of any sort; and that even if entreated to take upon him such a matter,
it was generally understood that he would "prefer not to" — in other words,
that he would refuse point-blank.

As days passed on, I became considerably reconciled to Bartleby. His
steadiness, his freedom from all dissipation, his incessant industry (except
when he chose to throw himself into a standing revery behind his screen),
his great stillness, his unalterableness of demeanor under all circumstances,
made him a valuable acquisition. One prime thing was this — *he was always
there* — first in the morning, continually through the day, and the last at night.
I had a singular confidence in his honesty. I felt my most precious papers perfectly safe in his hands. Sometimes, to be sure, I could not, for the very soul of
me, avoid falling into sudden spasmodic passions with him. For it was exceeding difficult to bear in mind all the time those strange peculiarities, privileges,
and unheard-of exemptions, forming the tacit stipulations on Bartleby's part
under which he remained in my office. Now and then, in the eagerness of
dispatching pressing business, I would inadvertently summon Bartleby, in a
short, rapid tone, to put his finger, say, on the incipient tie of a bit of red tape

with which I was about compressing some papers. Of course, from behind the screen the usual answer, "I prefer not to," was sure to come; and then, how could a human creature, with the common infirmities of our nature, refrain from bitterly exclaiming upon such perverseness—such unreasonableness? However, every added repulse of this sort which I received only tended to lessen the probability of my repeating the inadvertence.

Here it must be said, that, according to the custom of most legal gentlemen occupying chambers in densely populated law buildings, there were several keys to my door. One was kept by a woman residing in the attic, which person weekly scrubbed and daily swept and dusted my apartments. Another was kept by Turkey for convenience sake. The third I sometimes carried in my own pocket. The fourth I knew not who had.

Now, one Sunday morning I happened to go to Trinity Church, to hear a celebrated preacher, and finding myself rather early on the ground I thought I would walk round to my chambers for a while. Luckily I had my key with me; but upon applying it to the lock, I found it resisted by something inserted from the inside. Quite surprised, I called out; when to my consternation a key was turned from within; and thrusting his lean visage at me, and holding the door ajar, the apparition of Bartleby appeared, in his shirt-sleeves, and otherwise in a strangely tattered *deshabille*, saying quietly that he was sorry, but he was deeply engaged just then, and—preferred not admitting me at present. In a brief word or two, he moreover added, that perhaps I had better walk round the block two or three times, and by that time he would probably have concluded his affairs.

Now, the utterly unsurmised appearance of Bartleby, tenanting my law-chambers of a Sunday morning, with his cadaverously gentlemanly *nonchalance*, yet withal firm and self-possessed, had such a strange effect upon me, that incontinently I slunk away from my own door, and did as desired. But not without sundry twinges of impotent rebellion against the mild effrontery of this unaccountable scrivener. Indeed, it was his wonderful mildness chiefly, which not only disarmed me, but unmanned me, as it were. For I consider that one, for the time, is sort of unmanned when he tranquilly permits his hired clerk to dictate to him, and order him away from his own premises. Furthermore, I was full of uneasiness as to what Bartleby could possibly be doing in my office in his shirt-sleeves, and in an otherwise dismantled condition of a Sunday morning. Was anything amiss going on? Nay, that was out of the question. It was not to be thought of for a moment that Bartleby was an immoral person. But what could he be doing there?—copying? Nay again, whatever might be his eccentricities, Bartleby was an eminently decorous person. He would be the last man to sit down to his desk in any state approaching to nudity. Besides, it was Sunday; and there was something about Bartleby that forbade the supposition that he would by any secular occupation violate the proprieties of the day.

Nevertheless, my mind was not pacified; and full of a restless curiosity, at last I returned to the door. Without hindrance I inserted my key, opened it, and entered. Bartleby was not to be seen. I looked round anxiously, peeped

90

behind his screen; but it was very plain that he was gone. Upon more closely examining the place, I surmised that for an indefinite period Bartleby must have ate, dressed, and slept in my office, and that too without plate, mirror, or bed. The cushioned seat of a rickety old sofa in one corner bore the faint impress of a lean, reclining form. Rolled away under his desk, I found a blanket; under the empty grate, a blacking box and brush; on a chair, a tin basin, with soap and a ragged towel; in a newspaper a few crumbs of ginger-nuts and a morsel of cheese. Yes, thought I, it is evident enough that Bartleby has been making his home here, keeping bachelor's hall all by himself. Immediately then the thought came sweeping across me, what miserable friendlessness and loneliness are here revealed! His poverty is great; but his solitude, how horrible! Think of it. Of a Sunday, Wall Street is deserted as Petra;° and every night of every day it is an emptiness. This building, too, which of weekdays hums with industry and life, at nightfall echoes with sheer vacancy, and all through Sunday is forlorn. And here Bartleby makes his home; sole spectator of a solitude which he has seen all populous—a sort of innocent and transformed Marius brooding among the ruins of Carthage?°

For the first time in my life a feeling of overpowering stinging melancholy seized me. Before, I had never experienced aught but a not unpleasing sadness. The bond of a common humanity now drew me irresistibly to gloom. A fraternal melancholy! For both I and Bartleby were sons of Adam. I remembered the bright silks and sparkling faces I had seen that day, in gala trim, swan-like sailing down the Mississippi of Broadway; and I contrasted them with the pallid copyist, and thought to myself, Ah, happiness courts the light, so we deem the world is gay; but misery hides aloof, so we deem that misery there is none. These sad fancyings—chimeras, doubtless, of a sick and silly brain—led on to other and more special thoughts, concerning the eccentricities of Bartleby. Presentiments of strange discoveries hovered round me. The scrivener's pale form appeared to me laid out, among uncaring strangers, in its shivering winding-sheet.

Suddenly I was attracted by Bartleby's closed desk, the key in open sight left in the lock.

I mean no mischief, seek the gratification of no heartless curiosity, thought I; besides, the desk is mine, and its contents, too, so I will make bold to look within. Everything was methodically arranged, the papers smoothly placed. The pigeon-holes were deep, and removing the files of documents, I groped into their recesses. Presently I felt something there, and dragged it out. It was an old bandanna handkerchief, heavy and knotted. I opened it, and saw it was a saving's bank.

I now recalled all the quiet mysteries which I had noted in the man. I remembered that he never spoke but to answer; that, though at intervals he

---

Petra: An ancient Arabian city whose ruins were discovered in 1812.
Marius . . . of Carthage: Gaius Marius (157–86 B.C.), an exiled Roman general, sought refuge in the African city-state of Carthage, which had been destroyed by the Romans in the Third Punic War. Later writers, describing his arrival, compared the ruins of Marius's political career to the devastated city.

had considerable time to himself, yet I had never seen him reading — no, not even a newspaper; that for long periods he would stand looking out, at his pale window behind the screen, upon the dead brick wall; I was quite sure he never visited any refectory or eating-house; while his pale face clearly indicated that he never drank beer like Turkey; or tea and coffee even, like other men; that he never went anywhere in particular that I could learn; never went out for a walk, unless, indeed, that was the case at present; that he had declined telling who he was, or whence he came, or whether he had any relatives in the world; that though so thin and pale, he never complained of ill-health. And more than all, I remembered a certain unconscious air of pallid — how shall I call it? — of pallid haughtiness, say, or rather an austere reserve about him, which had positively awed me into my tame compliance with his eccentricities, when I had feared to ask him to do the slightest incidental thing for me, even though I might know, from his long-continued motionlessness, that behind his screen he must be standing in one of those dead-wall reveries of his.

Revolving all these things, and coupling them with the recently discovered fact, that he made my office his constant abiding place and home, and not forgetful of his morbid moodiness; revolving all these things, a prudential feeling began to steal over me. My first emotions had been those of pure melancholy and sincerest pity; but just in proportion as the forlornness of Bartleby grew and grew to my imagination, did that same melancholy merge into fear, that pity into repulsion. So true it is, and so terrible, too, that up to a certain point the thought or sight of misery enlists our best affections; but, in certain special cases, beyond that point it does not. They err who would assert that invariably this is owing to the inherent selfishness of the human heart. It rather proceeds from a certain hopelessness of remedying excessive and organic ill. To a sensitive being, pity is not seldom pain. And when at last it is perceived that such pity cannot lead to effectual succor, common sense bids the soul be rid of it. What I saw that morning persuaded me that the scrivener was the victim of innate and incurable disorder. I might give alms to his body; but his body did not pain him; it was his soul that suffered, and his soul I could not reach.

I did not accomplish the purpose of going to Trinity Church that morning. Somehow, the things I had seen disqualified me for the time from church-going. I walked homeward, thinking what I would do with Bartleby. Finally, I resolved upon this — I would put certain calm questions to him the next morning, touching his history, etc., and if he declined to answer them openly and unreservedly (and I supposed he would prefer not), then to give him a twenty dollar bill over and above whatever I might owe him, and tell him his services were no longer required; but that if in any other way I could assist him, I would be happy to do so, especially if he desired to return to his native place, wherever that might be, I would willingly help to defray the expenses. Moreover, if, after reaching home, he found himself at any time in want of aid, a letter from him would be sure of a reply.

The next morning came.

"Bartleby," said I, gently calling to him behind his screen.

No reply.

"Bartleby," said I, in a still gentler tone, "come here; I am not going to ask you to do anything you would prefer not to do — I simply wish to speak to you." 100

Upon this he noiselessly slid into view.

"Will you tell me, Bartleby, where you were born?"

"I would prefer not to."

"Will you tell me *anything* about yourself?"

"I would prefer not to." 105

"But what reasonable objection can you have to speak to me? I feel friendly towards you."

He did not look at me while I spoke, but kept his glance fixed upon my bust of Cicero, which, as I then sat, was directly behind me, some six inches above my head.

"What is your answer, Bartleby?" said I, after waiting a considerable time for a reply, during which his countenance remained immovable, only there was the faintest conceivable tremor of the white attenuated mouth.

"At present I prefer to give no answer," he said, and retired into his hermitage.

It was rather weak in me I confess, but his manner, on this occasion, 110 nettled me. Not only did there seem to lurk in it a certain calm disdain, but his perverseness seemed ungrateful, considering the undeniable good usage and indulgence he had received from me.

Again I sat ruminating what I should do. Mortified as I was at his behavior, and resolved as I had been to dismiss him when I entered my office, nevertheless I strangely felt something superstitious knocking at my heart, and forbidding me to carry out my purpose, and denouncing me for a villain if I dared to breathe one bitter word against this forlornest of mankind. At last, familiarly drawing my chair behind his screen, I sat down and said: "Bartleby, never mind, then, about revealing your history; but let me entreat you, as a friend, to comply as far as may be with the usages of this office. Say now, you will help to examine papers tomorrow or next day: in short, say now, that in a day or two you will begin to be a little reasonable: — say so, Bartleby."

"At present I would prefer not to be a little reasonable," was his mildly cadaverous reply.

Just then the folding-doors opened, and Nippers approached. He seemed suffering from an unusually bad night's rest, induced by severer indigestion than common. He overheard those final words of Bartleby.

"*Prefer not*, eh?" gritted Nippers — "I'd *prefer* him, if I were you, sir," addressing me — "I'd *prefer* him; I'd give him preferences, the stubborn mule! What is it, sir, pray, that he *prefers* not to do now?"

Bartleby moved not a limb. 115

"Mr. Nippers," said I, "I'd prefer that you would withdraw for the present."

Somehow, of late, I had got into the way of involuntarily using this word "prefer" upon all sorts of not exactly suitable occasions. And I trembled to think that my contact with the scrivener had already and seriously affected me in a mental way. And what further and deeper aberration might it not yet produce? This apprehension had not been without efficacy in determining me to summary measures.

As Nippers, looking very sour and sulky, was departing, Turkey blandly and deferentially approached.

"With submission, sir," said he, "yesterday I was thinking about Bartleby here, and I think that if he would but prefer to take a quart of good ale every day, it would do much towards mending him, and enabling him to assist in examining his papers."

"So you have got the word, too," said I, slightly excited.   120

"With submission, what word, sir?" asked Turkey, respectfully crowding himself into the contracted space behind the screen, and by so doing, making me jostle the scrivener. "What word, sir?"

"I would prefer to be left alone here," said Bartleby, as if offended at being mobbed in his privacy.

"*That's* the word, Turkey," said I — "*that's* it."

"Oh, *prefer*? oh yes — queer word. I never use it myself. But, sir, as I was saying, if he would but prefer —"

"Turkey," interrupted I, "you will please withdraw."   125

"Oh certainly, sir, if you prefer that I should."

As he opened the folding-door to retire, Nippers at his desk caught a glimpse of me, and asked whether I would prefer to have a certain paper copied on blue paper or white. He did not in the least roguishly accent the word "prefer." It was plain that it involuntarily rolled from his tongue. I thought to myself, surely I must get rid of a demented man, who already has in some degree turned the tongues, if not the heads of myself and clerks. But I thought it prudent not to break the dismission at once.

The next day I noticed that Bartleby did nothing but stand at his window in his dead-wall revery. Upon asking him why he did not write, he said that he had decided upon doing no more writing.

"Why, how now? what next?" exclaimed I, "do no more writing?"

"No more."   130

"And what is the reason?"

"Do you not see the reason for yourself?" he indifferently replied.

I looked steadfastly at him, and perceived that his eyes looked dull and glazed. Instantly it occurred to me, that his unexampled diligence in copying by his dim window for the first few weeks of his stay with me might have temporarily impaired his vision.

I was touched. I said something in condolence with him. I hinted that of course he did wisely in abstaining from writing for a while; and urged him to embrace that opportunity of taking wholesome exercise in the open air. This, however, he did not do. A few days after this, my other clerks being absent, and being in a great hurry to dispatch certain letters by the mail, I thought that, having nothing else earthly to do, Bartleby would surely be less inflexible than usual, and carry these letters to the Post Office. But he blankly declined. So, much to my inconvenience, I went myself.

Still added days went by. Whether Bartleby's eyes improved or not, I 135
could not say. To all appearance, I thought they did. But when I asked him
if they did, he vouchsafed no answer. At all events, he would do no copying.
At last, in replying to my urgings, he informed me that he had permanently
given up copying.

"What!" exclaimed I; "suppose your eyes should get entirely well — better
than ever before — would you not copy then?"

"I have given up copying," he answered, and slid aside.

He remained as ever, a fixture in my chamber. Nay — if that were
possible — he became still more of a fixture than before. What was to be
done? He would do nothing in the office; why should he stay there? In plain
fact, he had now become a millstone to me, not only useless as a necklace, but
afflictive to bear. Yet I was sorry for him. I speak less than truth when I say
that, on his own account, he occasioned me uneasiness. If he would but have
named a single relative or friend, I would instantly have written, and urged
their taking the poor fellow away to some convenient retreat. But he seemed
alone, absolutely alone in the universe. A bit of wreck in the mid-Atlantic. At
length, necessities connected with my business tyrannized over all other considerations. Decently as I could, I told Bartleby that in six days' time he must
unconditionally leave the office. I warned him to take measures, in the interval, for procuring some other abode. I offered to assist him in this endeavor,
if he himself would but take the first step towards a removal. "And when you
finally quit me, Bartleby," added I, "I shall see that you go not away entirely
unprovided. Six days from this hour, remember."

At the expiration of that period, I peeped behind the screen, and lo!
Bartleby was there.

I buttoned up my coat, balanced myself; advanced slowly towards him, 140
touched his shoulder, and said, "The time has come; you must quit this place;
I am sorry for you; here is money; but you must go."

"I would prefer not," he replied, with his back still towards me.

"You *must*."

He remained silent.

Now I had an unbounded confidence in this man's common honesty.
He had frequently restored to me sixpences and shillings carelessly dropped
upon the floor, for I am apt to be very reckless in such shirt-button affairs.
The proceeding, then, which followed will not be deemed extraordinary.

"Bartleby," said I, "I owe you twelve dollars on account; here are thirty- 145
two, the odd twenty are yours — Will you take it?" and I handed the bills
towards him.

But he made no motion.

"I will leave them here, then," putting them under a weight on the table.
Then taking my hat and cane and going to the door, I tranquilly turned and
added — "After you have removed your things from these offices, Bartleby,
you will of course lock the door — since every one is now gone for the day but
you — and if you please, slip your key underneath the mat, so that I may have
it in the morning. I shall not see you again; so good-bye to you. If, hereafter,

in your new place of abode, I can be of any service to you, do not fail to advise me by letter. Good-bye, Bartleby, and fare you well."

But he answered not a word; like the last column of some ruined temple, he remained standing mute and solitary in the middle of the otherwise deserted room.

As I walked home in a pensive mood, my vanity got the better of my pity. I could not but highly plume myself on my masterly management in getting rid of Bartleby. Masterly I call it, and such it must appear to any dispassionate thinker. The beauty of my procedure seemed to consist in its perfect quietness. There was no vulgar bullying, no bravado of any sort, no choleric hectoring, and striding to and fro across the apartment, jerking out vehement commands for Bartleby to bundle himself off with his beggarly traps. Nothing of the kind. Without loudly bidding Bartleby depart — as an inferior genius might have done — I *assumed* the ground that depart he must; and upon that assumption built all I had to say. The more I thought over my procedure, the more I was charmed with it. Nevertheless, next morning, upon awakening, I had my doubts — I had somehow slept off the fumes of vanity. One of the coolest and wisest hours a man has, is just after he awakes in the morning. My procedure seemed as sagacious as ever — but only in theory. How it would prove in practice — there was the rub. It was truly a beautiful thought to have assumed Bartleby's departure; but, after all, that assumption was simply my own, and none of Bartleby's. The great point was, not whether I had assumed that he would quit me, but whether he would prefer to do so. He was more a man of preferences than assumptions.

After breakfast, I walked down town, arguing the probabilities *pro* and 150 *con*. One moment I thought it would prove a miserable failure, and Bartleby would be found all alive at my office as usual; the next moment it seemed certain that I should find his chair empty. And so I kept veering about. At the corner of Broadway and Canal Street, I saw quite an excited group of people standing in earnest conversation.

"I'll take odds he doesn't," said a voice as I passed.

"Doesn't go? — done!" said I, "put up your money."

I was instinctively putting my hand in my pocket to produce my own, when I remembered that this was an election day. The words I had overheard bore no reference to Bartleby, but to the success or non-success of some candidate for the mayoralty. In my intent frame of mind, I had, as it were, imagined that all Broadway shared in my excitement, and were debating the same question with me. I passed on, very thankful that the uproar of the street screened my momentary absent-mindedness.

As I had intended, I was earlier than usual at my office door. I stood listening for a moment. All was still. He must be gone. I tried the knob. The door was locked. Yes, my procedure had worked to a charm; he indeed must be vanished. Yet a certain melancholy mixed with this: I was almost sorry for my brilliant success. I was fumbling under the door mat for the key, which Bartleby was to have left there for me, when accidentally my knee knocked against a panel, producing a summoning sound, and in response a voice came to me from within — "Not yet; I am occupied."

It was Bartleby.

I was thunderstruck. For an instant I stood like the man who, pipe in mouth, was killed one cloudless afternoon long ago in Virginia, by summer lightning; at his own warm open window he was killed, and remained leaning out there upon the dreamy afternoon, till some one touched him, when he fell.

"Not gone!" I murmured at last. But again obeying that wondrous ascendancy which the inscrutable scrivener had over me, and from which ascendancy, for all my chafing, I could not completely escape, I slowly went down stairs and out into the street, and while walking round the block, considered what I should next do in this unheard-of perplexity. Turn the man out by an actual thrusting I could not; to drive him away by calling him hard names would not do; calling in the police was an unpleasant idea; and yet, permit him to enjoy his cadaverous triumph over me — this, too, I could not think of. What was to be done? or, if nothing could be done, was there anything further that I could *assume* in the matter? Yes, as before I had prospectively assumed that Bartleby would depart, so now I might retrospectively assume that departed he was. In the legitimate carrying out of this assumption, I might enter my office in a great hurry, and pretending not to see Bartleby at all, walk straight against him as if he were air. Such a proceeding would in a singular degree have the appearance of a home-thrust. It was hardly possible that Bartleby could withstand such an application of the doctrine of assumption. But upon second thoughts the success of the plan seemed rather dubious. I resolved to argue the matter over with him again.

"Bartleby," said I, entering the office, with a quietly severe expression, "I am seriously displeased. I am pained, Bartleby. I had thought better of you. I had imagined you of such a gentlemanly organization, that in any delicate dilemma a slight hint would suffice — in short, an assumption. But it appears I am deceived. Why," I added, unaffectedly starting, "you have not even touched that money yet," pointing to it, just where I had left it the evening previous.

He answered nothing.

"Will you, or will you not, quit me?" I now demanded in a sudden passion, advancing close to him.

"I would prefer *not* to quit you," he replied, gently emphasizing the *not*.

"What earthly right have you to stay here? Do you pay any rent? Do you pay my taxes? Or is this property yours?"

He answered nothing.

"Are you ready to go on and write now? Are your eyes recovered? Could you copy a small paper for me this morning? or help examine a few lines? or step round to the Post Office? In a word, will you do anything at all, to give a coloring to your refusal to depart the premises?"

He silently retired into his hermitage.

I was now in such a state of nervous resentment that I thought it but prudent to check myself at present from further demonstrations. Bartleby and I were alone. I remembered the tragedy of the unfortunate Adams and the still more unfortunate Colt° in the solitary office of the latter; and how poor Colt, being dreadfully incensed by Adams, and imprudently permitting himself to get wildly excited, was at unawares hurried into his fatal act — an act which certainly no man could possibly deplore more than the actor himself. Often it had occurred to me in my ponderings upon the subject that had that altercation taken place in the public street, or at a private residence, it would not have terminated as it did. It was the circumstance of being alone in a solitary office, up stairs, of a building entirely unhallowed by humanizing domestic associations — an uncarpeted office, doubtless, of a dusty, haggard sort of appearance — this it must have been, which greatly helped to enhance the irritable desperation of the hapless Colt.

But when this old Adam of resentment rose in me and tempted me concerning Bartleby, I grappled him and threw him. How? Why, simply by recalling the divine injunction: "A new commandment give I unto you, that ye love one another." Yes, this it was that saved me. Aside from higher considerations, charity often operates as a vastly wise and prudent principle — a great safeguard to its possessor. Men have committed murder for jealousy's sake, and anger's sake, and hatred's sake, and selfishness' sake, and spiritual pride's sake; but no man, that ever I heard of, ever committed a diabolical murder for sweet charity's sake. Mere self-interest, then, if no better motive can be enlisted, should, especially with high-tempered men, prompt all beings to charity and philanthropy. At any rate, upon the occasion in question, I strove to drown my exasperated feelings towards the scrivener by benevolently construing his conduct. Poor fellow, poor fellow! thought I, he don't mean anything; and besides, he has seen hard times, and ought to be indulged.

I endeavored, also, immediately to occupy myself, and at the same time to comfort my despondency. I tried to fancy, that in the course of the morning, at such time as might prove agreeable to him, Bartleby, of his own free accord, would emerge from his hermitage and take up some decided line of march in the direction of the door. But no. Half-past twelve o'clock came; Turkey began to glow in the face, overturn his inkstand, and become generally obstreperous; Nippers abated down into quietude and courtesy; Ginger Nut munched his noon apple; and Bartleby remained standing at his window in one of his profoundest dead-wall reveries. Will it be credited? Ought I to acknowledge it? That afternoon I left the office without saying one further word to him.

Some days now passed, during which, at leisure intervals I looked a little into "Edwards on the Will," and "Priestley on Necessity."° Under the

---

Adams . . . Colt: Samuel Adams was killed by John C. Colt, brother of the gun maker, during a quarrel in 1842. After a sensational court case, Colt committed suicide just before he was to be hanged.

"Edwards . . . Necessity": Jonathan Edwards, in Freedom of the Will (1754), and Joseph Priestley, in Doctrine of Philosophical Necessity (1777), both argued that human beings do not have free will.

circumstances, those books induced a salutary feeling. Gradually I slid into the persuasion that these troubles of mine, touching the scrivener, had been all predestined from eternity, and Bartleby was billeted upon me for some mysterious purpose of an all-wise Providence, which it was not for a mere mortal like me to fathom. Yes, Bartleby, stay there behind your screen, thought I; I shall persecute you no more; you are harmless and noiseless as any of these old chairs; in short, I never feel so private as when I know you are here. At last I see it, I feel it; I penetrate to the predestined purpose of my life. I am content. Others may have loftier parts to enact; but my mission in this world, Bartleby, is to furnish you with office-room for such period as you may see fit to remain.

I believe that this wise and blessed frame of mind would have contin- 170 ued with me, had it not been for the unsolicited and uncharitable remarks obtruded upon me by my professional friends who visited the rooms. But thus it often is, that the constant friction of illiberal minds wears out at last the best resolves of the more generous. Though to be sure, when I reflected upon it, it was not strange that people entering my office should be struck by the peculiar aspect of the unaccountable Bartleby, and so be tempted to throw out some sinister observations concerning him. Sometimes an attorney, having business with me, and calling at my office, and finding no one but the scrivener there, would undertake to obtain some sort of precise information from him touching my whereabouts; but without heeding his idle talk, Bartleby would remain standing immovable in the middle of the room. So after contemplating him in that position for a time, the attorney would depart, no wiser than he came.

Also, when a reference was going on, and the room full of lawyers and witnesses, and business driving fast, some deeply-occupied legal gentleman present, seeing Bartleby wholly unemployed, would request him to run round to his (the legal gentleman's) office and fetch some papers for him. Thereupon, Bartleby would tranquilly decline, and yet remain idle as before. Then the lawyer would give a great stare, and turn to me. And what could I say? At last I was made aware that all through the circle of my professional acquaintance, a whisper of wonder was running round, having reference to the strange creature I kept at my office. This worried me very much. And as the idea came upon me of his possibly turning out a long-lived man, and keeping occupying my chambers, and denying my authority; and perplexing my visitors; and scandalizing my professional reputation; and casting a general gloom over the premises; keeping soul and body together to the last upon his savings (for doubtless he spent but half a dime a day), and in the end perhaps outlive me, and claim possession of my office by right of his perpetual occupancy: as all these dark anticipations crowded upon me more and more, and my friends continually intruded their relentless remarks upon the apparition in my room; a great change was wrought in me. I resolved to gather all my faculties together, and forever rid me of this intolerable incubus.

Ere revolving any complicated project, however, adapted to this end, I first simply suggested to Bartleby the propriety of his permanent departure. In a calm and serious tone, I commended the idea to his careful and mature consideration. But, having taken three days to meditate upon it, he apprised me, that his original determination remained the same; in short, that he still preferred to abide with me.

What shall I do? I now said to myself, buttoning up my coat to the last button. What shall I do? what ought I to do? what does conscience say I *should* do with this man, or, rather, ghost. Rid myself of him, I must; go, he shall. But how? You will not thrust him, the poor, pale, passive mortal — you will not thrust such a helpless creature out of your door? you will not dishonor yourself by such cruelty? No, I will not, I cannot do that. Rather would I let him live and die here, and then mason up his remains in the wall. What, then, will you do? For all your coaxing, he will not budge. Bribes he leaves under your own paper-weight on your table; in short, it is quite plain that he prefers to cling to you.

Then something severe, something unusual must be done. What! surely you will not have him collared by a constable, and commit his innocent pallor to the common jail? And upon what ground could you procure such a thing to be done? — a vagrant, is he? What! he a vagrant, a wanderer, who refuses to budge? It is because he will *not* be a vagrant, then, that you seek to count him *as* a vagrant. That is too absurd. No visible means of support: there I have him. Wrong again: for indubitably he *does* support himself, and that is the only unanswerable proof that any man can show of his possessing the means so to do. No more, then. Since he will not quit me, I must quit him. I will change my offices; I will move elsewhere, and give him fair notice, that if I find him on my new premises I will then proceed against him as a common trespasser.

Acting accordingly, next day I thus addressed him: "I find these chambers too far from the City Hall; the air is unwholesome. In a word, I propose to remove my offices next week, and shall no longer require your services. I tell you this now, in order that you may seek another place." 175

He made no reply, and nothing more was said.

On the appointed day I engaged carts and men, proceeded to my chambers, and having but little furniture, everything was removed in a few hours. Throughout, the scrivener remained standing behind the screen, which I directed to be removed the last thing. It was withdrawn; and, being folded up like a huge folio, left him the motionless occupant of a naked room. I stood in the entry watching him a moment, while something from within me upbraided me.

I re-entered, with my hand in my pocket — and — and my heart in my mouth.

"Good-bye, Bartleby; I am going — good-bye, and God some way bless you; and take that," slipping something in his hand. But it dropped upon the floor, and then — strange to say — I tore myself from him whom I had so longed to be rid of.

Established in my new quarters, for a day or two I kept the door locked,   180
and started at every footfall in the passages. When I returned to my rooms,
after any little absence, I would pause at the threshold for an instant, and
attentively listen, ere applying my key. But these fears were needless. Bartleby
never came nigh me.

I thought all was going well, when a perturbed-looking stranger visited
me, inquiring whether I was the person who had recently occupied rooms at
No. — Wall Street.

Full of forebodings, I replied that I was.

"Then, sir," said the stranger, who proved a lawyer, "you are responsible
for the man you left there. He refuses to do any copying; he refuses to do anything; he says he prefers not to; and he refuses to quit the premises."

"I am very sorry, sir," said I, with assumed tranquillity, but an inward
tremor, "but, really, the man you allude to is nothing to me — he is no relation
or apprentice of mine, that you should hold me responsible for him."

"In mercy's name, who is he?"   185

"I certainly cannot inform you. I know nothing about him. Formerly I
employed him as a copyist; but he has done nothing for me now for some
time past."

"I shall settle him, then — good morning, sir."

Several days passed, and I heard nothing more; and, though I often felt
a charitable prompting to call at the place and see poor Bartleby, yet a certain
squeamishness, of I know not what, withheld me.

All is over with him, by this time, thought I, at last, when, through
another week, no further intelligence reached me. But, coming to my room
the day after, I found several persons waiting at my door in a high state of
nervous excitement.

"That's the man — here he comes," cried the foremost one, whom I rec-   190
ognized as the lawyer who had previously called upon me alone.

"You must take him away, sir, at once," cried a portly person among them,
advancing upon me, and whom I knew to be the landlord of No. — Wall
Street. "These gentlemen, my tenants, cannot stand it any longer; Mr. B —,"
pointing to the lawyer, "has turned him out of his room, and he now persists
in haunting the building generally, sitting upon the banisters of the stairs by
day, and sleeping in the entry by night. Everybody is concerned; clients are
leaving the offices; some fears are entertained of a mob; something you must
do, and that without delay."

Aghast at this torrent, I fell back before it, and would fain have locked
myself in my new quarters. In vain I persisted that Bartleby was nothing to
me — no more than to any one else. In vain — I was the last person known to
have anything to do with him, and they held me to the terrible account. Fearful, then, of being exposed in the papers (as one person present obscurely
threatened), I considered the matter, and, at length, said, that if the lawyer
would give me a confidential interview with the scrivener, in his (the lawyer's) own room, I would, that afternoon, strive my best to rid them of the
nuisance they complained of.

Going up stairs to my old haunt, there was Bartleby silently sitting upon the banister at the landing.

"What are you doing here, Bartleby?" said I.

"Sitting upon the banister," he mildly replied. 195

I motioned him into the lawyer's room, who then left us.

"Bartleby," said I, "are you aware that you are the cause of great tribulation to me, by persisting in occupying the entry after being dismissed from the office?"

No answer.

"Now one of two things must take place. Either you must do something, or something must be done to you. Now what sort of business would you like to engage in? Would you like to re-engage in copying for some one?"

"No; I would prefer not to make any change." 200

"Would you like a clerkship in a dry-goods store?"

"There is too much confinement about that. No, I would not like a clerkship; but I am not particular."

"Too much confinement," I cried, "why, you keep yourself confined all the time!"

"I would prefer not to take a clerkship," he rejoined, as if to settle that little item at once.

"How would a bar-tender's business suit you? There is no trying of the 205 eyesight in that."

"I would not like it at all; though, as I said before, I am not particular."

His unwonted wordiness inspirited me. I returned to the charge.

"Well, then, would you like to travel through the country collecting bills for the merchants? That would improve your health."

"No, I would prefer to be doing something else."

"How, then, would going as a companion to Europe, to entertain some 210 young gentleman with your conversation — how would that suit you?"

"Not at all. It does not strike me that there is anything definite about that. I like to be stationary. But I am not particular."

"Stationary you shall be, then," I cried, now losing all patience, and, for the first time in all my exasperating connection with him, fairly flying into a passion. "If you do not go away from these premises before night, I shall feel bound — indeed, I *am* bound — to — to quit the premises myself!" I rather absurdly concluded, knowing not with what possible threat to try to frighten his immobility into compliance. Despairing of all further efforts, I was precipitately leaving him, when a final thought occurred to me — one which had not been wholly unindulged before.

"Bartleby," said I, in the kindest tone I could assume under such exciting circumstances, "will you go home with me now — not to my office, but my dwelling — and remain there till we can conclude upon some convenient arrangement for you at our leisure? Come, let us start now, right away."

"No: at present I would prefer not to make any change at all."

I answered nothing; but, effectually dodging every one by the sudden- 215 ness and rapidity of my flight, rushed from the building, ran up Wall Street towards Broadway, and, jumping into the first omnibus, was soon removed from pursuit. As soon as tranquillity returned, I distinctly perceived that I had now done all that I possibly could, both in respect to the demands of the landlord and his tenants, and with regard to my own desire and sense of duty, to benefit Bartleby, and shield him from rude persecution. I now strove to be entirely care-free and quiescent; and my conscience justified me in the attempt; though, indeed, it was not so successful as I could have wished. So fearful was I of being again hunted out by the incensed landlord and his exasperated tenants, that, surrendering my business to Nippers, for a few days, I drove about the upper part of the town and through the suburbs, in my rockaway; crossed over to Jersey City and Hoboken, and paid fugitive visits to Manhattanville and Astoria. In fact, I almost lived in my rockaway for the time.

When again I entered my office, lo, a note from the landlord lay upon the desk. I opened it with trembling hands. It informed me that the writer had sent to the police, and had Bartleby removed to the Tombs as a vagrant. Moreover, since I knew more about him than any one else, he wished me to appear at that place, and make a suitable statement of the facts. These tidings had a conflicting effect upon me. At first I was indignant; but, at last, almost approved. The landlord's energetic, summary disposition, had led him to adopt a procedure which I do not think I would have decided upon myself; and yet, as a last resort, under such peculiar circumstances, it seemed the only plan.

As I afterwards learned, the poor scrivener, when told that he must be conducted to the Tombs, offered not the slightest obstacle, but, in his pale, unmoving way, silently acquiesced.

Some of the compassionate and curious by-standers joined the party; and headed by one of the constables arm-in-arm with Bartleby, the silent procession filed its way through all the noise, and heat, and joy of the roaring thoroughfares at noon.

The same day I received the note, I went to the Tombs, or, to speak more properly, the Halls of Justice. Seeking the right officer, I stated the purpose of my call, and was informed that the individual I described was, indeed, within. I then assured the functionary that Bartleby was a perfectly honest man, and greatly to be compassionated, however unaccountably eccentric. I narrated all I knew, and closed by suggesting the idea of letting him remain in as indulgent confinement as possible, till something less harsh might be done — though, indeed, I hardly knew what. At all events, if nothing else could be decided upon, the almshouse must receive him. I then begged to have an interview.

Being under no disgraceful charge, and quite serene and harmless in 220 all his ways, they had permitted him freely to wander about the prison, and, especially, in the inclosed grass-platted yards thereof. And so I found him there, standing all alone in the quietest of the yards, his face towards a high wall, while all around, from the narrow slits of the jail windows, I thought I saw peering out upon him the eyes of murderers and thieves.

"Bartleby!"

"I know you," he said, without looking round — "and I want nothing to say to you."

"It was not I that brought you here, Bartleby," said I, keenly pained at his implied suspicion. "And to you, this should not be so vile a place. Nothing reproachful attaches to you by being here. And see, it is not so sad a place as one might think. Look, there is the sky, and here is the grass."

"I know where I am," he replied, but would say nothing more, and so I left him.

As I entered the corridor again, a broad meat-like man, in an apron, accosted me, and, jerking his thumb over his shoulder, said — "Is that your friend?"

"Yes."

"Does he want to starve? If he does, let him live on the prison fare, that's all."

"Who are you?" asked I, not knowing what to make of such an unofficially speaking person in such a place.

"I am the grub-man. Such gentlemen as have friends here, hire me to provide them with something good to eat."

"Is this so?" said I, turning the turnkey.

He said it was.

"Well, then," said I, slipping some silver into the grub-man's hands (for so they called him), "I want you to give particular attention to my friend there; let him have the best dinner you can get. And you must be as polite to him as possible."

"Introduce me, will you?" said the grub-man, looking at me with an expression which seemed to say he was all impatience for an opportunity to give a specimen of his breeding.

Thinking it would prove of benefit to the scrivener, I acquiesced; and, asking the grub-man his name, went up with him to Bartleby.

"Bartleby, this is a friend; you will find him very useful to you."

"Your sarvant, sir, your sarvant," said the grub-man, making a low salutation behind his apron. "Hope you find it pleasant here, sir; nice grounds — cool apartments — hope you'll stay with us some time — try to make it agreeable. What will you have for dinner to-day?"

"I prefer not to dine to-day," said Bartleby, turning away. "It would disagree with me; I am unused to dinners." So saying, he slowly moved to the other side of the inclosure, and took up a position fronting the deadwall.

"How's this?" said the grub-man, addressing me with a stare of astonishment. "He's odd, ain't he?"

"I think he is a little deranged," said I, sadly.

"Deranged? deranged is it? Well, now, upon my word, I thought that friend of yourn was a gentleman forger; they are always pale and genteel-like, them forgers. I can't help pity 'em — can't help it, sir. Did you know Monroe Edwards?" he added, touchingly, and paused. Then, laying his hand piteously on my shoulder, sighed, "he died of consumption at Sing-Sing. So you weren't acquainted with Monroe?"

"No, I was never socially acquainted with any forgers. But I cannot stop longer. Look to my friend yonder. You will not lose by it. I will see you again."

Some few days after this, I again obtained admission to the Tombs, and went through the corridors in quest of Bartleby; but without finding him.

"I saw him coming from his cell not long ago," said a turnkey, "may be he's gone to loiter in the yards."

So I went in that direction.

"Are you looking for the silent man?" said another turnkey, passing me. 245
"Yonder he lies — sleeping in the yard there. 'Tis not twenty minutes since I saw him lie down."

The yard was entirely quiet. It was not accessible to the common prisoners. The surrounding walls, of amazing thickness, kept off all sounds behind them. The Egyptian character of the masonry weighed upon me with its gloom. But a soft imprisoned turf grew under foot. The heart of the eternal pyramids, it seemed, wherein, by some strange magic, through the clefts, grass-seed, dropped by birds, had sprung.

Strangely huddled at the base of the wall, his knees drawn up, and lying on his side, his head touching the cold stones, I saw the wasted Bartleby. But nothing stirred. I paused; then went close up to him; stooped over, and saw that his dim eyes were open; otherwise he seemed profoundly sleeping. Something prompted me to touch him. I felt his hand, when a tingling shiver ran up my arm and down my spine to my feet.

The round face of the grub-man peered upon me now. "His dinner is ready. Won't he dine to-day, either? Or does he live without dining?"

"Lives without dining," said I, and closed the eyes.

"Eh! — He's asleep, ain't he?" 250

"With kings and counselors,"° murmured I.

There would seem little need for proceeding further in this history. Imagination will readily supply the meagre recital of poor Bartleby's interment. But, ere parting with the reader, let me say, that if this little narrative has sufficiently interested him, to awaken curiosity as to who Bartleby was, and what manner of life he led prior to the present narrator's making his acquaintance, I can only reply, that in such curiosity I fully share, but am wholly unable to gratify it. Yet here I hardly know whether I should divulge one little item of rumor, which came to my ear a few months after the scrivener's decease. Upon what basis it rested, I could never ascertain; and hence, how true it is I cannot now tell. But, inasmuch as this vague report has not been without a certain suggestive interest to me, however sad, it may prove the same with some others; and so I will briefly mention it. The report was this: that Bartleby had been a subordinate clerk in the Dead Letter Office at Washington, from which he had been suddenly removed by a change in the administration. When I think over this rumor, hardly can I express the emotions which seize me. Dead letters! does it not sound like dead men?

"With kings and counselors": From Job 3:13–14: "then had I been at rest, / With kings and counselors of the earth, / which built desolate places for themselves."

Conceive a man by nature and misfortune prone to a pallid hopelessness, can any business seem more fitted to heighten it than that of continually handling these dead letters, and assorting them for the flames? For by the cart-load they are annually burned. Sometimes from out the folded paper the pale clerk takes a ring — the finger it was meant for, perhaps, moulders in the grave; a bank-note sent in swiftest charity — he whom it would relieve, nor eats nor hungers any more; pardon for those who died despairing; hope for those who died unhoping; good tidings for those who died stifled by unrelieved calamities. On errands of life, these letters speed to death.

Ah, Bartleby! Ah, humanity!

CONSIDERATIONS FOR CRITICAL THINKING AND WRITING

1. FIRST RESPONSE. How does the lawyer's description of himself serve to characterize him? Why is it significant that he is a lawyer? Are his understandings and judgments about Bartleby and himself always sound?

2. Why do you think Turkey, Nippers, and Ginger Nut are introduced to the reader before Bartleby?

3. Describe Bartleby's physical characteristics. How is his physical description a foreshadowing of what happens to him?

4. How does Bartleby's "I would prefer not to" affect the routine of the lawyer and his employees?

5. What is the significance of the subtitle: "A Story of Wall Street"?

6. Who is the protagonist? Whose story is it?

7. Does the lawyer change during the story? Does Bartleby? Who is the antagonist?

8. What motivates Bartleby's behavior? Why do you think Melville withholds the information about the Dead Letter Office until the end of the story? Does this background adequately explain Bartleby?

9. Does Bartleby have any lasting impact on the lawyer?

10. Do you think Melville sympathizes more with Bartleby or with the lawyer?

11. Describe the lawyer's changing attitudes toward Bartleby.

12. Consider how this story could be regarded as a kind of protest with nonnegotiable demands.

13. Discuss the story's humor and how it affects your response to Bartleby.

14. Trace your emotional reaction to Bartleby as he is revealed in the story.

15. CONNECTION TO ANOTHER SELECTION. Compare Bartleby's withdrawal from life with that of the protagonist in Gail Godwin's "A Sorrowful Woman" (p. 38). Why does each character choose death?

4

Setting

© Steve Ellison / Corbis.

My role is to look at the world, get a true, not an idealized vision of it and hand it over to you in fictional form.

— FAY WELDON

Setting is the context in which the action of a story occurs. The major elements of setting are time, place, and the social environment that frames the characters. These elements establish the world in which the characters act. In most stories they also serve as more than backgrounds and furnishings. If we are sensitive to the contexts provided by setting, we are better able to understand the behavior of the characters and the significance of their actions. It may be tempting to read quickly through a writer's descriptions and ignore the details of the setting once a geographic location and a historic period are established. But if you read a story so impatiently, the significance of the setting may slip by you. That kind of reading is similar to traveling on interstate highways: a lot of ground gets covered, but very little is seen along the way.

If we ask why a writer chooses to include certain details in a work, then we are likely to make connections that relate the details to some larger purpose, such as the story's meaning. The final scene in Godwin's "A Sorrowful Woman" (p. 38) occurs in the spring, an ironic time for the action to be set because instead of rebirth for the protagonist there is only death. There is usually a reason for placing a story in a particular time or location.

Melville's "Bartleby, the Scrivener" (p. 99), for example, takes on meaning as Bartleby's "dead-wall reveries" begin to reflect his shattered vision of life. He is surrounded by walls. A folding screen separates him from others in the office; he is isolated. The office window faces walls; there is no view to relieve the deadening work. Bartleby faces a wall at the prison where he dies; the final wall is death. As the subtitle indicates, this is "A Story of Wall Street." Unless the geographic location or the physical details of a story are used merely as necessary props, they frequently shed light on character and action. All offices have walls, but Melville transforms the walls into an antagonist that represents the limitations Bartleby sees and feels all around him but does not speak of.

Time, location, and the physical features of a setting can all be relevant to the overall purpose of a story. So too is the social environment in which the characters are developed. In Faulkner's "A Rose for Emily" (p. 54) the changes in her southern town serve as a foil for Emily's tenacious hold on a lost past. She is regarded as a "fallen monument," as old-fashioned and peculiar as the "stubborn and coquettish decay" of her house. Neither she nor her house fits into the modern changes that are paving and transforming the town. Without the social context, this story would be mostly an account of a bizarre murder rather than an exploration of the conflicts Faulkner associated with the changing South. Setting enlarges the meaning of Emily's actions.

Not every story uses setting as a means of revealing mood, idea, meaning, or characters' actions. Some stories have no particularly significant setting. It is entirely possible to envision a story in which two characters speak to each other about a conflict between them and little or no mention is made of the time or place they inhabit. If, however, a shift in setting would make a serious difference to our understanding of a story, then the setting is probably an important element in the work. Consider how different "Bartleby, the Scrivener" would be if it were set in a relaxed, pleasant, sunny town in the South rather than in the grinding, limiting materialism of Wall Street. Bartleby's withdrawal from life would be less comprehensible and meaningful in such a setting. The setting is integral to that story.

The following three stories — Ernest Hemingway's "Soldier's Home," Fay Weldon's "IND AFF, or Out of Love in Sarajevo," and Mark Halliday's "Young Man on Sixth Avenue" — include settings that serve to shape their meanings.

ERNEST HEMINGWAY (1899–1961)

In 1918, a year after graduating from high school in Oak Park, Illinois, Ernest Hemingway volunteered as an ambulance driver in World War I. At the Italian front, he was seriously wounded. This experience haunted him and many of the characters in his short stories and novels. *In Our Time* (1925) is a collection of short stories, including "Soldier's Home," that reflect some of Hemingway's own attempts to read-just to life back home after the war. *The Sun Also Rises* (1926), *A Farewell to Arms* (1929), and *For Whom the Bell Tolls* (1940) are also about war and its impact on people's lives. Hemingway courted violence all his life — in war, the bullring, the boxing ring, and big game hunting. When he was sixty-two years old and terminally ill with cancer, he committed suicide by shooting himself with a shotgun. "Soldier's Home" takes place in a small town in Oklahoma; the war, however, is never distant from the protagonist's mind as he struggles to come home again.

Soldier's Home   1925

Ermeni Studio, Milan. Courtesy of the Ernest Hemingway Photographic Collection, John Fitzgerald Kennedy Library, Boston.

Krebs went to the war from a Methodist college in Kansas. There is a picture which shows him among his fraternity brothers, all of them wearing exactly the same height and style collar. He enlisted in the Marines in 1917 and did not return to the United States until the second division returned from the Rhine in the summer of 1919.

There is a picture which shows him on the Rhine with two German girls and another corporal. Krebs and the corporal look too big for their uniforms. The German girls are not beautiful. The Rhine does not show in the picture.

By the time Krebs returned to his home town in Oklahoma the greeting of heroes was over. He came back much too late. The men from the town who had been drafted had all been welcomed elaborately on their return. There had been a great deal of hysteria. Now the reaction had set in. People seemed to think it was rather ridiculous for Krebs to be getting back so late, years after the war was over.

At first Krebs, who had been at Belleau Wood, Soissons, the Champagne, St. Mihiel, and in the Argonne° did not want to talk about the war at all. Later he felt the need to talk but no one wanted to hear about it. His town had heard too many atrocity stories to be thrilled by actualities. Krebs found that to be listened to at all he had to lie, and after he had done this twice he, too, had a reaction against the war and against talking about it. A distaste for everything that had happened to him in the war set in because of the lies he had told. All of the times that had been able to make him feel cool and clear inside himself when he thought of them; the times so long back when he had done the one

---

Belleau Wood . . . Argonne: Sites of battles in World War I in which American troops were instrumental in pushing back the Germans.

thing, the only thing for a man to do, easily and naturally, when he might have done something else, now lost their cool, valuable quality and then were lost themselves.

His lies were quite unimportant lies and consisted in attributing to him- 5
self things other men had seen, done, or heard of, and stating as facts certain apocryphal incidents familiar to all soldiers. Even his lies were not sensational at the pool room. His acquaintances, who had heard detailed accounts of German women found chained to machine guns in the Argonne forest and who could not comprehend, or were barred by their patriotism from interest in, any German machine gunners who were not chained, were not thrilled by his stories.

Krebs acquired the nausea in regard to experience that is the result of untruth or exaggeration, and when he occasionally met another man who had really been a soldier and they talked a few minutes in the dressing room at a dance he fell into the easy pose of the old soldier among other soldiers: that he had been badly, sickeningly frightened all the time. In this way he lost everything.

During this time, it was late summer, he was sleeping late in bed, getting up to walk down town to the library to get a book, eating lunch at home, reading on the front porch until he became bored, and then walking down through the town to spend the hottest hours of the day in the cool dark of the pool room. He loved to play pool.

In the evening he practiced on his clarinet, strolled down town, read, and went to bed. He was still a hero to his two young sisters. His mother would have given him breakfast in bed if he had wanted it. She often came in when he was in bed and asked him to tell her about the war, but her attention always wandered. His father was noncommittal.

Before Krebs went away to the war he had never been allowed to drive the family motor car. His father was in the real estate business and always wanted the car to be at his command when he required it to take clients out into the country to show them a piece of farm property. The car always stood outside the First National Bank building where his father had an office on the second floor. Now, after the war, it was still the same car.

Nothing was changed in the town except that the young girls had grown 10
up. But they lived in such a complicated world of already defined alliances and shifting feuds that Krebs did not feel the energy or the courage to break into it. He liked to look at them, though. There were so many good-looking young girls. Most of them had their hair cut short. When he went away only little girls wore their hair like that or girls that were fast. They all wore sweaters and shirt waists with round Dutch collars. It was a pattern. He liked to look at them from the front porch as they walked on the other side of the street. He liked to watch them walking under the shade of the trees. He liked the round Dutch collars above their sweaters. He liked their silk stockings and flat shoes. He liked their bobbed hair and the way they walked.

When he was in town their appeal to him was not very strong. He did not like them when he saw them in the Greek's ice cream parlor. He did not want them themselves really. They were too complicated. There was something else. Vaguely he wanted a girl but he did not want to have to work to get her. He would have liked to have a girl but he did not want to have to spend a long time getting her. He did not want to get into the intrigue and the politics. He did not want to have to do any courting. He did not want to tell any more lies. It wasn't worth it.

He did not want any consequences. He did not want any consequences ever again. He wanted to live alone without consequences. Besides he did not really need a girl. The army had taught him that. It was all right to pose as though you had to have a girl. Nearly everybody did that. But it wasn't true. You did not need a girl. That was the funny thing. First a fellow boasted how girls mean nothing to him, that he never thought of them, that they could not touch him. Then a fellow boasted that he could not get along without girls, that he had to have them all the time, that he could not go to sleep without them.

That was all a lie. It was all a lie both ways. You did not need a girl unless you thought about them. He learned that in the army. Then sooner or later you always got one. When you were really ripe for a girl you always got one. You did not have to think about it. Sooner or later it would come. He had learned that in the army.

Now he would have liked a girl if she had come to him and not wanted to talk. But here at home it was all too complicated. He knew he could never get through it all again. It was not worth the trouble. That was the thing about French girls and German girls. There was not all this talking. You couldn't talk much and you did not need to talk. It was simple and you were friends. He thought about France and then he began to think about Germany. On the whole he had liked Germany better. He did not want to leave Germany. He did not want to come home. Still, he had come home. He sat on the front porch.

He liked the girls that were walking along the other side of the street. He liked the look of them much better than the French girls or the German girls. But the world they were in was not the world he was in. He would like to have one of them. But it was not worth it. They were such a nice pattern. He liked the pattern. It was exciting. But he would not go through all the talking. He did not want one badly enough. He liked to look at them all, though. It was not worth it. Not now when things were getting good again. ^15

He sat there on the porch reading a book on the war. It was a history and he was reading about all the engagements he had been in. It was the most interesting reading he had ever done. He wished there were more maps. He looked forward with a good feeling to reading all the really good histories when they would come out with good detail maps. Now he was really learning about the war. He had been a good soldier. That made a difference.

One morning after he had been home about a month his mother came into his bedroom and sat on the bed. She smoothed her apron.

"I had a talk with your father last night, Harold," she said, "and he is willing for you to take the car out in the evenings."

"Yeah?" said Krebs, who was not fully awake. "Take the car out? Yeah?"

"Yes. Your father has felt for some time that you should be able to take 20 the car out in the evenings whenever you wished but we only talked it over last night."

"I'll bet you made him," Krebs said.

"No. It was your father's suggestion that we talk the matter over."

"Yeah. I'll bet you made him," Krebs sat up in bed.

"Will you come down to breakfast, Harold?" his mother said.

"As soon as I get my clothes on," Krebs said.   25

His mother went out of the room and he could hear her frying something downstairs while he washed, shaved, and dressed to go down into the dining-room for breakfast. While he was eating breakfast his sister brought in the mail.

"Well, Hare," she said. "You old sleepyhead. What do you ever get up for?"

Krebs looked at her. He liked her. She was his best sister.

"Have you got the paper?" he asked.

She handed him the Kansas City *Star* and he shucked off its brown wrap- 30 per and opened it to the sporting page. He folded the *Star* open and propped it against the water pitcher with his cereal dish to steady it, so he could read while he ate.

"Harold," his mother stood in the kitchen doorway, "Harold, please don't muss up the paper. Your father can't read his *Star* if it's been mussed."

"I won't muss it," Krebs said.

His sister sat down at the table and watched him while he read.

"We're playing indoor over at school this afternoon," she said. "I'm going to pitch."

"Good," said Krebs. "How's the old wing?"   35

"I can pitch better than lots of the boys. I tell them all you taught me. The other girls aren't much good."

"Yeah?" said Krebs.

"I tell them all you're my beau. Aren't you my beau, Hare?"

"You bet."

"Couldn't your brother really be your beau just because he's your 40 brother?"

"I don't know."

"Sure you know. Couldn't you be my beau, Hare, if I was old enough and if you wanted to?"

"Sure. You're my girl now."

"Am I really your girl?"

"Sure."   45

"Do you love me?"

"Uh, huh."

"Will you love me always?"

"Sure."

"Will you come over and watch me play indoor?"   50

"Maybe."

"Aw, Hare, you don't love me. If you loved me, you'd want to come over and watch me play indoor."

Krebs's mother came into the dining-room from the kitchen. She carried a plate with two fried eggs and some crisp bacon on it and a plate of buckwheat cakes.

"You run along, Helen," she said. "I want to talk to Harold."

She put the eggs and bacon down in front of him and brought in a jug 55 of maple syrup for the buckwheat cakes. Then she sat down across the table from Krebs.

"I wish you'd put down the paper a minute, Harold," she said.

Krebs took down the paper and folded it.

"Have you decided what you are going to do yet, Harold?" his mother said, taking off her glasses.

"No," said Krebs.

"Don't you think it's about time?" His mother did not say this in a mean 60 way. She seemed worried.

"I hadn't thought about it," Krebs said.

"God has some work for everyone to do," his mother said. "There can be no idle hands in His Kingdom."

"I'm not in His Kingdom," Krebs said.

"We are all of us in His Kingdom."

Krebs felt embarrassed and resentful as always. 65

"I've worried about you so much, Harold," his mother went on. "I know the temptations you must have been exposed to. I know how weak men are. I know what your own dear grandfather, my own father, told us about the Civil War and I have prayed for you. I pray for you all day long, Harold."

Krebs looked at the bacon fat hardening on his plate.

"Your father is worried, too," his mother went on. "He thinks you have lost your ambition, that you haven't got a definite aim in life. Charley Simmons, who is just your age, has a good job and is going to be married. The boys are all settling down; they're all determined to get somewhere; you can see that boys like Charley Simmons are on their way to being really a credit to the community."

Krebs said nothing.

"Don't look that way, Harold," his mother said. "You know we love you 70 and I want to tell you for your own good how matters stand. Your father does not want to hamper your freedom. He thinks you should be allowed to drive the car. If you want to take some of the nice girls out riding with you, we are only too pleased. We want you to enjoy yourself. But you are going to have to settle down to work, Harold. Your father doesn't care what you start in at. All work is honorable as he says. But you've got to make a start at something. He asked me to speak to you this morning and then you can stop in and see him at his office."

"Is that all?" Krebs said.

"Yes. Don't you love your mother, dear boy?"

"No," Krebs said.

His mother looked at him across the table. Her eyes were shiny. She started crying.

"I don't love anybody," Krebs said.   75

It wasn't any good. He couldn't tell her, he couldn't make her see it. It was silly to have said it. He had only hurt her. He went over and took hold of her arm. She was crying with her head in her hands.

"I didn't mean it," he said. "I was just angry at something. I didn't mean I didn't love you."

His mother went on crying. Krebs put his arm on her shoulder.

"Can't you believe me, mother?"

His mother shook her head.   80

"Please, please, mother. Please believe me."

"All right," his mother said chokily. She looked up at him. "I believe you, Harold."

Krebs kissed her hair. She put her face up to him.

"I'm your mother," she said. "I held you next to my heart when you were a tiny baby."

Krebs felt sick and vaguely nauseated.   85

"I know, Mummy," he said. "I'll try and be a good boy for you."

"Would you kneel and pray with me, Harold?" his mother asked.

They knelt down beside the dining-room table and Krebs's mother prayed.

"Now, you pray, Harold," she said.

"I can't," Krebs said.

"Try, Harold."   90

"I can't."

"Do you want me to pray for you?"

"Yes."

So his mother prayed for him and then they stood up and Krebs kissed   95
his mother and went out of the house. He had tried so to keep his life from being complicated. Still, none of it had touched him. He had felt sorry for his mother and she had made him lie. He would go to Kansas City and get a job and she would feel all right about it. There would be one more scene maybe before he got away. He would not go down to his father's office. He would miss that one. He wanted his life to go smoothly. It had just gotten going that way. Well, that was all over now, anyway. He would go over to the schoolyard and watch Helen play indoor baseball.

Considerations for Critical Thinking and Writing

1. **FIRST RESPONSE.** The title, "Soldier's Home," focuses on the setting. Do you have a clear picture of Krebs's home? Describe it, filling in missing details from your associations of home, Krebs's routine, or anything else you can use.

2. What does the photograph of Krebs, the corporal, and the German girls reveal?

3. Belleau Wood, Soissons, the Champagne, St. Mihiel, and the Argonne were the sites of fierce and bloody fighting. What effect have these battles had on Krebs? Why do you think he won't talk about them to the people at home?

4. Why does Krebs avoid complications and consequences? How has the war changed his attitudes toward work and women? How is his hometown different from Germany and France? What is the conflict in the story?

5. Why do you think Hemingway refers to the protagonist as Krebs rather than Harold? What is the significance of his sister calling him "Hare"?

6. How does Krebs's mother embody the community's values? What does Krebs think of those values?

7. What is the resolution to Krebs's conflict?

8. Comment on the appropriateness of the story's title.

9. Explain how Krebs's war experiences are present throughout the story even though we get no details about them.

10. CONNECTION TO ANOTHER SELECTION. Contrast the attitudes toward domestic life implicit in this story with those in Gail Godwin's "A Sorrowful Woman" (p. 38). How do the stories' settings help to account for the differences between them?

11. CONNECTION TO ANOTHER SELECTION. How might Krebs's rejection of his community's values be related to Sammy's relationship to his supermarket job in John Updike's "A & P" (p. 149)? What details does Updike use to make the setting in "A & P" a comic, though nonetheless serious, version of Krebs's hometown?

FAY WELDON (B. 1933)

Born in England and raised in New Zealand, Fay Weldon graduated from St. Andrew's University in Scotland. She wrote advertising copy for various companies and was a propaganda writer for the British Foreign Office before turning to fiction. She has written novels, short stories, plays, and radio scripts. In 1971 her script for an episode of *Upstairs, Downstairs* won an award from the Society of Film and Television Arts. She has written more than thirty novels, including *The Fat Woman's Joke* (1967), *Down Among the Women* (1971), *Praxis* (1978), *The Life and Loves of a She-Devil* (1983), *Life Force* (1991), *The Bulgari Connection* (2001), *She May Not Leave* (2005), *The Stepmother's*

© Steve Ellison / Corbis.

Diary (2008), *Chalcot Crescent* (2010), *Kehua!* (2011), and *Habits of the House* (2012), and an equal number of plays and scripts. Her collections of short stories include *Moon over Minneapolis* (1992), *Wicked Women* (American edition, 1997), *A Hard Time to Be a Father* (1998), and *Nothing to Wear and Nowhere to Hide* (2002). Weldon often uses ironic humor to portray carefully drawn female characters coming to terms with the facts of their lives. Awarded a CBE (Commander of the Order of the British Empire) in 2001, Weldon currently teaches creative writing at Bath Spa University in Bath, England.

IND AFF   1988

or Out of Love in Sarajevo

This is a sad story. It has to be. It rained in Sarajevo, and we had expected fine weather.

The rain filled up Sarajevo's pride, two footprints set into a pavement which mark the spot where the young assassin Princip stood to shoot the Archduke Franz Ferdinand and his wife. (Don't forget his wife: everyone forgets his wife, the archduchess.) That was in the summer of 1914. Sarajevo is a pretty town, Balkan style, mountain-rimmed. A broad, swift, shallow river runs through its center, carrying the mountain snow away, arched by many bridges. The one nearest the two footprints has been named the Princip Bridge. The young man is a hero in these parts. Not only does he bring in the tourists — look, look, the spot, the very spot! — but by his action, as everyone knows, he lit a spark which fired the timber which caused World War I which crumbled the Austro-Hungarian Empire, the crumbling of which made modern Yugoslavia possible. Forty million dead (or was it thirty?) but who cares? So long as he loved his country.

The river, they say, can run so shallow in the summer it's known derisively as "the wet road." Today, from what I could see through the sheets of falling rain, it seemed full enough. Yugoslavian streets are always busy — no one stays home if they can help it (thus can an indecent shortage of housing space create a sociable nation) and it seemed as if by common consent a shield of bobbing umbrellas had been erected two meters high to keep the rain off the streets. It just hadn't worked around Princip's corner.

"Come all this way," said Peter, who was a professor of classical history, "and you can't even see the footprints properly, just two undistinguished puddles." Ah, but I loved him. I shivered for his disappointment. He was supervising my thesis on varying concepts of morality and duty in the early Greek States as evidenced in their poetry and drama. I was dependent upon him for my academic future. He said I had a good mind but not a first-class mind and somehow I didn't take it as an insult. I had a feeling first-class minds weren't all that good in bed.

Sarajevo is in Bosnia, in the center of Yugoslavia, that grouping of ⁵ unlikely states, that distillation of languages into the phonetic reasonableness of Serbo-Croatian. We'd sheltered from the rain in an ancient mosque in Serbian Belgrade; done the same in a monastery in Croatia; now we spent a wet couple of days in Sarajevo beneath other people's umbrellas. We planned to go on to Montenegro, on the coast, where the fish and the artists come from, to swim and lie in the sun, and recover from the exhaustion caused by the sexual and moral torments of the last year. It couldn't possibly go on raining forever. Could it? Satellite pictures showed black clouds swishing gently all over Europe, over the Balkans, into Asia — practically all the way from Moscow to London, in fact. It wasn't that Peter and myself were being singled out. No. It was raining on his wife, too, back in Cambridge.

Peter was trying to decide, as he had been for the past year, between his wife and myself as his permanent life partner. To this end we had gone away, off the beaten track, for a holiday; if not with his wife's blessing, at least with her knowledge. Were we really, truly suited? We had to be sure, you see, that this was more than just any old professor-student romance; that it was the Real Thing, because the longer the indecision went on the longer Mrs. Piper would be left dangling in uncertainty and distress. They had been married for twenty-four years; they had stopped loving each other a long time ago, of course — but there would be a fearful personal and practical upheaval entailed if he decided to leave permanently and shack up, as he put it, with me. Which I certainly wanted him to do. I loved him. And so far I was winning hands down. It didn't seem much of a contest at all, in fact. I'd been cool and thin and informed on the seat next to him in a Zagreb theater (Mrs. Piper was sweaty and only liked telly); was now eager and anxious for social and political instruction in Sarajevo (Mrs. Piper spat in the face of knowledge, he'd once told me); and planned to be lissome (and I thought topless but I hadn't quite decided: this might be the area where the age difference showed) while I splashed and shrieked like a bathing belle in the shallows of the Montenegrin coast. (Mrs. Piper was a swimming coach: I imagined she smelt permanently of chlorine.)

In fact so far as I could see, it was no contest at all between his wife and myself. But Peter liked to luxuriate in guilt and indecision. And I loved him with an inordinate affection.

Princip's prints are a meter apart, placed as a modern cop on a training shoot-out would place his feet — the left in front at a slight outward angle, the right behind, facing forward. There seemed great energy focused here. Both hands on the gun, run, stop, plant the feet, aim, fire! I could see the footprints well enough, in spite of Peter's complaint. They were clear enough to me.

We went to a restaurant for lunch, since it was too wet to do what we loved to do: that is, buy bread, cheese, sausage, wine, and go off somewhere in our hired car, into the woods or the hills, and picnic and make love. It was a private restaurant—Yugoslavia went over to a mixed capitalist-communist economy years back, so you get either the best or worst of both systems, depending on your mood—that is to say, we knew we would pay more but be given a choice. We chose the wild boar.

"Probably ordinary pork soaked in red cabbage water to darken it," said   10
Peter. He was not in a good mood.

Cucumber salad was served first.

"Everything in this country comes with cucumber salad," complained Peter. I noticed I had become used to his complaining. I supposed that when you had been married a little you simply wouldn't hear it. He was forty-six and I was twenty-five.

"They grow a lot of cucumber," I said.

"If they can grow cucumbers," Peter then asked, "why can't they grow *mange-tout*°?" It seemed a why-can't-they-eat-cake sort of argument to me, but not knowing enough about horticulture not to be outflanked if I debated the point, I moved the subject on to safer ground.

"I suppose Princip's action couldn't really have started World War I," I   15
remarked. "Otherwise, what a thing to have on your conscience! One little shot and the deaths of thirty million."

"Forty," he corrected me. Though how they reckon these things and get them right I can't imagine. "Of course he didn't start the war. That's just a simple tale to keep the children quiet. It takes more than an assassination to start a war. What happened was that the buildup of political and economic tensions in the Balkans was such that it had to find some release."

"So it was merely the shot that lit the spark that fired the timber that started the war, et cetera?"

"Quite," he said. "World War I would have had to have started sooner or later."

"A bit later or a bit sooner," I said, "might have made the difference of a million or so; if it was you on the battlefield in the mud and the rain you'd notice; exactly when they fired the starting-pistol; exactly when they blew the final whistle. Is that what they do when a war ends; blow a whistle? So that everyone just comes in from the trenches."

But he wasn't listening. He was parting the flesh of the soft collapsed   20
orangey-red pepper which sat in the middle of his cucumber salad; he was carefully extracting the pips. His nan had once told him they could never be digested, would stick inside and do terrible damage. I loved him for his dexterity and patience with his knife and fork. I'd finished my salad yonks ago, pips and all. I was hungry. I wanted my wild boar.

Peter might be forty-six, but he was six foot two and grizzled and muscled with it, in a dark-eyed, intelligent, broad-jawed kind of way. I adored him. I loved to be seen with him. "Muscular academic, not weedy academic" as my younger sister Clare once said. "Muscular academic is just a generally

---

mange-tout: A sugar pea or bean (French).

superior human being: everything works well from the brain to the toes. Weedy academic is when there isn't enough vital energy in the person, and the brain drains all the strength from the other parts." Well, Clare should know. Clare is only twenty-three, but of the superior human variety kind herself, vividly pretty, bright and competent — somewhere behind a heavy curtain of vibrant red hair, which she only parts for effect. She had her first degree at twenty. Now she's married to a Harvard professor of economics seconded to the United Nations. She can even cook. I gave up competing yonks ago. Though she too is capable of self-deception. I would say her husband was definitely of the weedy academic rather than the muscular academic type. And they have to live in Brussels.

The archduke's chauffeur had lost his way, and was parked on the corner trying to recover his nerve when Princip came running out of a café, planted his feet, aimed, and fired. Princip was nineteen — too young to hang. But they sent him to prison for life and, since he had TB to begin with, he only lasted three years. He died in 1918, in an Austrian prison. Or perhaps it was more than TB: perhaps they gave him a hard time, not learning till later, when the Austro-Hungarian Empire collapsed, that he was a hero. Poor Princip, too young to die — like so many other millions. Dying for love of a country.

"I love you," I said to Peter, my living man, progenitor already of three children by his chlorinated, swimming-coach wife.

"How much do you love me?"

"Inordinately! I love you with inordinate affection." It was a joke between us. Ind Aff!   25

"Inordinate affection is a sin," he'd told me. "According to the Wesleyans. John Wesley° himself worried about it to such a degree he ended up abbreviating it in his diaries, Ind Aff. He maintained that what he felt for young Sophy, the eighteen-year-old in his congregation, was not Ind Aff, which bears the spirit away from God towards the flesh: he insisted that what he felt was a pure and spiritual, if passionate, concern for her soul."

Peter said now, as we waited for our wild boar, and he picked over his pepper, "Your Ind Aff is my wife's sorrow, that's the trouble." He wanted, I knew, one of the long half-wrangles, half soul-sharings that we could keep going for hours, and led to piercing pains in the heart which could only be made better in bed. But our bedroom at the Hotel Europa was small and dark and looked out into the well of the building — a punishment room if ever there was one. (Reception staff did sometimes take against us.) When Peter had tried to change it in his quasi-Serbo-Croatian, they'd shrugged their Bosnian shoulders and pretended not to understand, so we'd decided to put up with it. I did not fancy pushing hard single beds together — it seemed easier not to have the pain in the heart in the first place. "Look," I said, "this holiday is supposed to be just the two of us, not Mrs. Piper as well. Shall we talk about something else?"

John Wesley (1703–1791): English religious leader and founder of Methodism.

Do not think that the archduke's chauffeur was merely careless, an inefficient chauffeur, when he took the wrong turning. He was, I imagine, in a state of shock, fright, and confusion. There had been two previous attempts on the archduke's life since the cavalcade had entered town. The first was a bomb which got the car in front and killed its driver. The second was a shot fired by none other than young Princip, which had missed. Princip had vanished into the crowd and gone to sit down in a corner café and ordered coffee to calm his nerves. I expect his hand trembled at the best of times — he did have TB. (Not the best choice of assassin, but no doubt those who arrange these things have to make do with what they can get.) The archduke's chauffeur panicked, took the wrong road, realized what he'd done, and stopped to await rescue and instructions just outside the café where Princip sat drinking his coffee.

"What shall we talk about?" asked Peter, in even less of a good mood.

"The collapse of the Austro-Hungarian Empire?" I suggested. "How does an empire collapse? Is there no money to pay the military or the police, so everyone goes home? Or what?" He liked to be asked questions. 30

"The Hungro-Austrarian Empire," said Peter to me, "didn't so much collapse as fail to exist any more. War destroys social organizations. The same thing happened after World War II. There being no organized bodies left between Moscow and London — and for London read Washington, then as now — it was left to these two to put in their own puppet governments. Yalta, 1944. It's taken the best part of forty-five years for nations of West and East Europe to remember who they are."

"Austro-Hungarian," I said, "not Hungro-Austrarian."

"I didn't say Hungro-Austrarian," he said.

"You did," I said.

"Didn't," he said. "What the hell are they doing about our wild boar? Are they out in the hills shooting it?" 35

My sister Clare had been surprisingly understanding about Peter. When I worried about him being older, she pooh-poohed it; when I worried about him being married, she said, "Just go for it, sister. If you can unhinge a marriage, it's ripe for unhinging, it would happen sooner or later, it might as well be you. See a catch, go ahead and catch! Go for it!"

Princip saw the archduke's car parked outside, and went for it. Second chances are rare in life: they must be responded to. Except perhaps his second chance was missing in the first place? Should he have taken his cue from fate, and just sat and finished his coffee, and gone home to his mother? But what's a man to do when he loves his country? Fate delivered the archduke into his hands: how could he resist it? A parked car, a uniformed and medaled chest, the persecutor of his country — how could Princip not, believing God to be on his side, but see this as His intervention, push his coffee aside and leap to his feet?

Two waiters stood idly by and watched us waiting for our wild boar. One was young and handsome in a mountainous Bosnian way — flashing eyes, hooked nose, luxuriant black hair, sensuous mouth. He was about my age. He smiled. His teeth were even and white. I smiled back, and instead of the pain in the heart I'd become accustomed to as an erotic sensation, now felt, quite violently, an associated yet different pang which got my lower stomach. The true, the real pain of Ind Aff!

"Fancy him?" asked Peter.

"No," I said. "I just thought if I smiled the wild boar might come quicker." 40

The other waiter was older and gentler: his eyes were soft and kind. I thought he looked at me reproachfully. I could see why. In a world which for once, after centuries of savagery, was finally full of young men, unslaughtered, what was I doing with this man with thinning hair?

"What are you thinking of?" Professor Piper asked me. He liked to be in my head.

"How much I love you," I said automatically, and was finally aware how much I lied. "And about the archduke's assassination," I went on, to cover the kind of tremble in my head as I came to my senses, "and let's not forget his wife, she died too — how can you say World War I would have happened anyway. If Princip hadn't shot the archduke, something else, some undisclosed, unsuspected variable, might have come along and defused the whole political/military situation, and neither World War I nor II ever happened. We'll just never know, will we?"

I had my passport and my travelers' checks with me. (Peter felt it was less confusing if we each paid our own way.) I stood up, and took my raincoat from the peg.

"Where are you going?" he asked, startled.   45

"Home," I said. I kissed the top of his head, where it was balding. It smelt gently of chlorine, which may have come from thinking about his wife so much, but might merely have been that he'd taken a shower that morning. ("The water all over Yugoslavia, though safe to drink, is unusually chlorinated": Guide Book.) As I left to catch a taxi to the airport the younger of the two waiters emerged from the kitchen with two piled plates of roasted wild boar, potatoes duchesse, and stewed peppers. ("Yugoslavian diet is unusually rich in proteins and fats": Guide Book.) I could tell from the glisten of oil that the food was no longer hot, and I was not tempted to stay, hungry though I was. Thus fate — or was it Bosnian willfulness? — confirmed the wisdom of my intent.

And that was how I fell out of love with my professor, in Sarajevo, a city to which I am grateful to this day, though I never got to see very much of it, because of the rain.

It was a silly sad thing to do, in the first place, to confuse mere passing academic ambition with love: to try and outdo my sister Clare. (Professor Piper was spiteful, as it happened, and did his best to have my thesis refused, but I went to appeal, which he never thought I'd dare, and won. I had a first-class mind after all.) A silly sad episode, which I regret. As silly and sad as Princip, poor young man, with his feverish mind, his bright tubercular cheeks, and his inordinate affection for his country, pushing aside his cup of coffee, leaping to his feet, taking his gun in both hands, planting his feet, aiming, and firing — one, two, three shots — and starting World War I. The first one missed, the second got the wife (never forget the wife), and the third got the archduke and a whole generation, and their children, and their children's children, and on and on forever. If he'd just hung on a bit, there in Sarajevo, that June day, he might have come to his senses. People do, sometimes quite quickly.

CONSIDERATIONS FOR CRITICAL THINKING AND WRITING

1. FIRST RESPONSE. Do you agree with Weldon's first line, "This is a sad story"? Explain why or why not.

2. How does the rain establish the mood for the story in the first five paragraphs?

3. Characterize Peter. What details concerning him reveal his personality?

4. Describe the narrator's relationship with Peter. How do you think he regards her? Why is she attracted to him?

5. Why is Sarajevo important for the story's setting? What is the effect of having the story of Princip's assassination of the Archduke Franz Ferdinand and his wife woven through the plot?

6. Describe Mrs. Piper. Though she doesn't appear in the story, she does have an important role. What do you think her role is?

7. What is "Ind Aff"? Why is it an important element of this story?

8. What is the significance of the two waiters (paras. 38–41)? How do they affect the narrator?

9. Why does the narrator decide to go home (para. 46)? Do you think she makes a reasoned or an impulsive decision? Explain why you think so.

10. CONNECTION TO ANOTHER SELECTION. Compare and contrast "IND AFF" and David Updike's "Summer" (p. 155) as love stories. Do you think that the stories end happily or the way you would want them to? Are the endings problematic?

MARK HALLIDAY (B. 1949)

Born in Ann Arbor, Michigan, Mark Halliday earned a B.A. and an M.A. from Brown University and a Ph.D. from Brandeis University. A teacher at Ohio University, his short stories and poems have appeared in a variety of periodicals, including the *Massachusetts Review, Michigan Quarterly Review, Chicago Review*, and the *New Republic*. Among his six collections of poetry, *Little Star* was selected by the National Poetry Series for publication in 1987. He has also written a critical study on poet Wallace Stevens titled *Stevens and the Interpersonal* (1991).

WHEN I WRITE "After fifty, a year can seem strangely brief, and even a decade can vanish like a dream. I wrote this story when I was around forty, thinking about my father and how mysterious to him the racing away of his youth must seem. Now that I'm over sixty, the story's feeling has come closer to home." —MARK HALLIDAY

Young Man on Sixth Avenue   1995

He was a young man in the big city. He was a young man in the biggest, the most overwhelming city—and he was not overwhelmed. For see, he strode across Fifth Avenue just before the light changed, and his head was up in the sharp New York wind and he was thriving upon the rock of Manhattan, in 1938. His legs were long and his legs were strong; there was no question about his legs; they were unmistakable in their length and strength; they were as bold and dependable as any American machine, moving him across Fifth just in time, his brown shoes attaining the sidewalk without any faltering, his gait unaware of the notion that legs might ever want to rest. Forty-ninth Street! He walked swiftly through the haste and blare, through the chilly exclamation points of taxis and trucks and people. He was a man! In America, '38, New York, two o'clock in the afternoon, sunlight chopping down between buildings, Forty-ninth Street. And his hair was so dark, almost black, and it had a natural wave in it recognized as a handsome feature by everyone, recognized universally, along with his dark blue eyes and strong jaw. Women saw him, they all had to see him, all the young women had to perceive him reaching the corner of Forty-ninth and Sixth, and they had to know he was a candidate. He knew they knew. He knew they knew he would *get* some of them, and he moved visibly tall with the tall potential of the not-finite twentieth-century getting that would be his inheritance; and young women who glanced at him on Sixth Avenue knew that he knew. They felt that they or their sisters would have to take him into account, and they touched their scarves a little nervously.

He was twenty-five years old, and this day in 1938 was the present. It was so obviously and totally the present, so unabashed and even garish with its presentness, beamingly right there right now like Rita Hayworth,° all Sixth Avenue was in fact at two o'clock a thumping bright Rita Hayworth and the young man strode south irresistibly. If there was only one thing he knew, crossing Forty-eighth, it was that this day was the present, out of which uncounted glories could and must blossom—when?—in 1938, or in 1939, soon, or in the big brazen decade ahead, in 1940, soon; so he walked with fistfuls of futures that could happen in all his pockets.

And his wavy hair was so dark, almost black. And he knew the right restaurant for red roast beef, not too expensive. And in his head were some sharp ideas about Dreiser, and Thomas Wolfe, and John O'Hara.

On Forty-seventh between two buildings (buildings taller even than him) there was an unexpected zone of deep shade. He paused for half a second, and he shivered for some reason. Briskly then, briskly he moved ahead.

In the restaurant on Seventh Avenue he met his friend John for a witty   5
late lunch. Everything was—the whole lunch was good. It was right. And what they said was both hilarious and notably well informed. And then soon he was taking the stairs two at a time up to an office on Sixth for his interview.

Rita Hayworth (1918–1987): A Hollywood movie star.

The powerful lady seemed to like his sincerity and the clarity of his eyes — a hard combination to beat — and the even more powerful man in charge sized him up and saw the same things, and he got the job.

That job lasted three years, then came the War, then another job, then Judy, and the two kids, and a better job in Baltimore, and those years — those years. And those years. "Those years" — and the kids went to college with new typewriters. In the blue chair, with his work on his lapboard, after a pleasant dinner of macaroni and sausage and salad, he dozed off. Then he was sixty. Sixty? Then he rode back and forth on trains, Judy became ill, doctors offered opinions, comas were deceptive, Judy died. But the traffic on Coleytown Road next morning still moved casually too fast. And in a minute he was seventy-five and the phone rang with news that witty John of the great late lunches was dead. The house pulsed with silence.

Something undone? What? The thing that would have saved — what? Waking in the dark — maybe something unwritten, that would have made people say "*Yes* that's why you matter so much." Ideas about Wolfe. Dreiser. Or some lost point about John O'Hara.

Women see past him on the street in this pseudo-present and he feels they are so stupid and walks fierce for a minute but then his shoulders settle closer to his skeleton with the truth about these women: not especially stupid; only young. In this pseudo-present he blinks at a glimpse of that young man on Sixth Avenue, young man as if still out there in the exclamation of Sixth Avenue — that young man ready to stride across — but a taxi makes him step back to the curb, he'll have to wait a few more seconds, he can wait.

Considerations for Critical Thinking and Writing

1. **FIRST RESPONSE.** Do you identify with the young man as he is described in the first paragraph? Is he appealing to you? Why or why not?

2. Why do you think this story opens in 1938? Why is the Manhattan setting important?

3. The American novelists Theodore Dreiser, Thomas Wolfe, and John O'Hara are mentioned in paragraphs 3 and 7. Of what significance are these novelists in this story? You may have to research these writers to answer this question.

4. What is the conflict in the story?

5. Locate the climax in the story. Is there a resolution to the conflict? Explain.

6. **CONNECTION TO ANOTHER SELECTION.** Write an essay comparing the ending of Halliday's story with that of Raymond Carver's "Popular Mechanics" (p. 216). What is the effect of the ending on your reading of each story?

5

Point of View

It is not necessary to portray many characters. The center of gravity should be in two persons: him and her.

— ANTON CHEKHOV

© Austrian Archives / CORBIS.

Because one of the pleasures of reading fiction consists of seeing the world through someone else's eyes, it is easy to overlook the eyes that control our view of the plot, characters, and setting. *Point of view* refers to who tells us the story and how it is told. What we know and how we feel about the events in a story are shaped by the author's choice of a point of view. The teller of a story, the *narrator*, inevitably affects our understanding of the characters' actions by filtering what is told through his or her own perspective. The narrator should not be confused with the author who has created the narrative voice because the two are usually distinct (more on this point later).

If the narrative voice is changed, the story will change. Consider, for example, how different "Bartleby, the Scrivener" (p. 99) would be if Melville had chosen to tell the story from Bartleby's point of view instead of the lawyer's. With Bartleby as narrator, much of the mystery concerning his behavior would be lost. The peculiar force of his saying "I would prefer not to" would be lessened amid all the other things he would have to say as narrator. Moreover, the lawyer's reaction — puzzled, upset, outraged, and finally sympathetic to Bartleby — would be lost too. It would be entirely possible, of course, to write a story from Bartleby's point of view, but it would not be the story Melville wrote.

The possible ways of telling a story are many, and more than one point of view can be worked into a single story. However, the various points of view that storytellers draw on can be conveniently grouped into two broad categories: (1) the third-person narrator and (2) the first-person narrator. The third-person narrator uses *he*, *she*, or *they* to tell the story and does not participate in the action. The first-person narrator uses *I* and is a major or minor participant in the action. A second-person narrator, *you*, is possible but is rarely used because of the awkwardness in thrusting the reader into the story, as in "You are minding your own business on a park bench when a drunk steps out of the bushes and demands your lunch bag."

Let's look now at the most important and most often used variations within first- and third-person narrations.

THIRD-PERSON NARRATOR   (Nonparticipant)

1. Omniscient (the narrator takes us inside the character[s])
2. Limited omniscient (the narrator takes us inside one or two characters)
3. Objective (the narrator is outside the character[s])

No type of third-person narrator appears as a character in a story. The **omniscient narrator** is all-knowing. From this point of view, the narrator can move from place to place and pass back and forth through time, slipping into and out of characters as no human being possibly could in real life. This narrator can report the characters' thoughts and feelings as well as what they say and do. In the excerpt from *Tarzan of the Apes* (p. 46), Burroughs's narrator tells us about events concerning Terkoz in another part of the jungle that long preceded the battle between Terkoz and Tarzan. We also learn Tarzan's and Jane's inner thoughts and emotions during the episode. And Burroughs's narrator describes Terkoz as "an arrant coward" and a bully, thereby evaluating the character for the reader. This kind of intrusion is called **editorial omniscience**. In contrast, narration that allows characters' actions and thoughts to speak for themselves is known as **neutral omniscience**. Most modern writers use neutral omniscience so that readers can reach their own conclusions.

The **limited omniscient narrator** is much more confined than the omniscient narrator. With limited omniscience the author very often restricts the narrator to the single perspective of either a major or a minor character. Sometimes a narrator can see into more than one character, particularly in a longer work that focuses, for example, on two characters alternately from one chapter to the next. Short stories, however, frequently are restricted by length to a single character's point of view. The way people, places, and events appear to that character is the way they appear to the reader. The reader has access to the thoughts and feelings of the characters revealed by the narrator, but neither the reader nor the narrator has access to the inner lives of any of the other characters in the story. The events in James Joyce's "Eveline" (p. 309) are viewed entirely through the protagonist's eyes. She unifies the story by being present through all the action.

In Hemingway's "Soldier's Home" (p. 129), a limited omniscient narration is the predominant point of view. Krebs's thoughts and reaction to being home from the war are made available to the reader by the narrator, who tells us that Krebs "felt embarrassed and resentful" or "sick and vaguely nauseated" by the small-town life he has reentered. Occasionally, however, Hemingway uses an *objective point of view* when he dramatizes particularly tense moments in a detached impersonal manner between Krebs and his mother. In the following excerpt, Hemingway's narrator shows us Krebs's feelings instead of telling us what they are. Krebs's response to his mother's concerns is presented without comment. The external details of the scene reveal his inner feelings.

> "I've worried about you so much, Harold," his mother went on. "I know the temptations you must have been exposed to. I know how weak men are. I know what your own dear grandfather, my own father, told us about the Civil War and I have prayed for you. I pray for you all day long, Harold."
>
> Krebs looked at the bacon fat hardening on his plate.
>
> "Your father is worried, too," his mother went on. "He thinks you have lost your ambition, that you haven't got a definite aim in life. Charley Simmons, who is just your age, has a good job and is going to be married. The boys are all settling down; they're all determined to get somewhere; you can see that boys like Charley Simmons are on their way to being really a credit to the community."
>
> Krebs said nothing.
>
> "Don't look that way, Harold . . ."

When Krebs looks at the bacon fat, we can see him cooling and hardening too. Hemingway does not describe the expression on Krebs's face, yet we know it is a look that disturbs his mother as she goes on about what she thinks she knows. Krebs and his mother are clearly tense and upset; the details, action, and dialogue reveal that without the narrator telling the reader how each character feels.

FIRST-PERSON NARRATOR (Participant)

1. Major character
2. Minor character

With a *first-person narrator*, the *I* presents the point of view of only one character's consciousness. The reader is restricted to the perceptions, thoughts, and feelings of that single character. This is Melville's technique with the lawyer in "Bartleby, the Scrivener" (p. 99). Everything learned about the characters, action, and plot comes from the unnamed lawyer. Bartleby remains a mystery because we are limited to what the lawyer knows and reports. The lawyer cannot explain what Bartleby means because he does not entirely know himself. Melville's use of the first person encourages us to identify with the lawyer's confused reaction to Bartleby so that we pay attention not only to the scrivener but to the lawyer's response to him. We are as perplexed as the lawyer and share his effort to make sense of Bartleby.

The lawyer is an **unreliable narrator**, whose interpretation of events is different from the author's. We cannot entirely accept the lawyer's assessment of Bartleby because we see that the lawyer's perceptions are not totally to be trusted. Melville does not expect us, for example, to agree with the lawyer's suggestion that the solution to Bartleby's situation might be to "entertain some young gentleman with your conversation" on a trip to Europe. Given Bartleby's awful silences, this absurd suggestion reveals the lawyer's superficial understanding. The lawyer's perceptions frequently do not coincide with those Melville expects his readers to share. Hence, the lawyer's unreliability preserves Bartleby's mysterious nature while revealing the lawyer's sensibilities. The point of view is artistically appropriate for Melville's purposes because the eyes through which we perceive the plot, characters, and setting are also the subject of the story.

Narrators can be unreliable for a variety of reasons: they might lack self-knowledge, like Melville's lawyer, or they might be innocent and inexperienced, like Ralph Ellison's young narrator in "Battle Royal" (p. 177). Youthful innocence frequently characterizes a **naive narrator** such as Mark Twain's Huck Finn or Holden Caulfield, J. D. Salinger's twentieth-century version of Huck in *The Catcher in the Rye*. These narrators lack the sophistication to interpret accurately what they see; they are unreliable because the reader must go beyond their understanding of events to comprehend the situations described. Huck and Holden describe their respective social environments, but the reader, with more experience, supplies the critical perspective that each boy lacks. In "Battle Royal" that perspective is supplemented by Ellison's dividing the narration between the young man who experiences events and the mature man who reflects back on those events.

Few generalizations can be made about the advantages or disadvantages of using a specific point of view. What can be said with confidence, however, is that writers choose a point of view to achieve particular effects because point of view determines what we know about the characters and events in a story. We should, therefore, be aware of who is telling the story and whether the narrator sees things clearly and reliably.

The next four works warrant a careful examination of their points of view. In John Updike's "A & P," a teenager makes a significant decision about his future while at a supermarket checkout, and another young man in David Updike's "Summer" discovers an equally important truth about the present. After a strange turn of events, the protagonist in Charlotte Perkins

Gilman's "If I Were a Man" explores gender from a provocative point of view. And in Maggie Mitchell's "It Would Be Different If," a woman reflects upon an early rejection in her life.

JOHN UPDIKE (1932–2009)

Boston Globe / Getty Images.

John Updike grew up in the small town of Shillington, Pennsylvania, and on a family farm nearby. Academic success in school earned him a scholarship to Harvard, where he studied English and graduated in 1954. He soon sold his first story and poem to the *New Yorker*. Also an artist, Updike studied drawing in Oxford, England, and returned to take a position on the staff at the *New Yorker*. His first book, a collection of poems titled *The Carpentered Hen and Other Tame Creatures*, appeared in 1958, and the following year he published a book of stories and a novel, *The Poorhouse Fair*, which received the Rosenthal Foundation Award in 1960. Updike produced his second novel, *Rabbit, Run*, in the same year. The prolific Updike lived in Massachusetts the rest of his life and continued to publish essays, poems, a novel, or a book of stories nearly every year, including *The Centaur* (1963), winner of the National Book Award; *Rabbit Is Rich* (1981) and *Rabbit at Rest* (1990), both Pulitzer Prize winners; and *The Witches of Eastwick* (1984), which was made into a major motion picture (Warner Bros., 1987). His last novel was *Terrorist* (2006), and his last short story collection was *My Father's Tears and Other Stories* (2009). Updike's fiction is noted for its exemplary use of storytelling conventions, its unique prose style, and its engaging picture of middle-class American life.

A & P   1961

In walks these three girls in nothing but bathing suits. I'm in the third check-out slot, with my back to the door, so I don't see them until they're over by the bread. The one that caught my eye first was the one in the plaid green two-piece. She was a chunky kid, with a good tan and a sweet broad soft-looking can with those two crescents of white just under it, where the sun never seems to hit, at the top of the backs of her legs. I stood there with my hand on a box of HiHo crackers trying to remember if I rang it up or not. I ring it up again and the customer starts giving me hell. She's one of these cash-register-watchers, a witch about fifty with rouge on her cheekbones and no eyebrows, and I know it made her day to trip me up. She'd been watching cash registers for fifty years and probably never seen a mistake before.

By the time I got her feathers smoothed and her goodies into a bag — she gives me a little snort in passing, if she'd been born at the right time they would have burned her over in Salem — by the time I get her on her way the girls had circled around the bread and were coming back, without a push-cart, back my way along the counters, in the aisle between the checkouts and the Special bins. They didn't even have shoes on. There was this chunky one, with the two-piece — it was bright green and the seams on the bra were still sharp and her belly was still pretty pale so I guessed she just got it (the suit) — there was this one, with one of those chubby berry-faces, the lips all bunched together under her nose, this one, and a tall one, with black hair that hadn't quite frizzed right, and one of these sunburns right across under the eyes, and a chin that was too long — you know, the kind of girl other girls think is very "striking" and "attractive" but never quite makes it, as they very well know, which is why they like her so much — and then the third one, that wasn't quite so tall. She was the queen. She kind of led them, the other two peeking around and making their shoulders round. She didn't look around, not this queen, she just walked straight on slowly, on these long white prima-donna legs. She came down a little hard on her heels, as if she didn't walk in her bare feet that much, putting down her heels and then letting the weight move along to her toes as if she was testing the floor with every step, putting a little deliberate extra action into it. You never know for sure how girls' minds work (do you really think it's a mind in there or just a little buzz like a bee in a glass jar?) but you got the idea she had talked the other two into coming in here with her, and now she was showing them how to do it, walk slow and hold yourself straight.

She had on a kind of dirty-pink — beige maybe, I don't know — bathing suit with a little nubble all over it and, what got me, the straps were down. They were off her shoulders looped loose around the cool tops of her arms, and I guess as a result the suit had slipped a little on her, so all around the top of the cloth there was this shining rim. If it hadn't been there you wouldn't have known there could have been anything whiter than those shoulders. With the straps pushed off, there was nothing between the top of the suit and the top of her head except just *her*, this clean bare plane of the top of her chest down from the shoulder bones like a dented sheet of metal tilted in the light. I mean, it was more than pretty.

She had sort of oaky hair that the sun and salt had bleached, done up in a bun that was unraveling, and a kind of prim face. Walking into the A & P with your straps down, I suppose it's the only kind of face you *can* have. She held her head so high her neck, coming up out of those white shoulders, looked kind of stretched, but I didn't mind. The longer her neck was, the more of her there was.

She must have felt in the corner of her eye me and over my shoulder 5 Stokesie in the second slot watching, but she didn't tip. Not this queen. She kept her eyes moving across the racks, and stopped, and turned so slow it made my stomach rub the inside of my apron, and buzzed to the other two, who kind of huddled against her for relief, and then they all three of them went up the cat-and-dogfood-breakfast-cereal-macaroni-rice-raisins-seasonings-spreads-spaghetti-soft-drinks-crackers-and-cookies aisle. From the third slot I look straight up this aisle to the meat counter, and I watched them all the way. The fat one with the tan sort of fumbled with the cookies, but on second thought she put the package back. The sheep pushing their carts down the aisle — the girls were walking against the usual traffic (not that we have one-way signs or anything) — were pretty hilarious. You could see them, when Queenie's white shoulders dawned on them, kind of jerk, or hop, or hiccup, but their eyes snapped back to their own baskets and on they pushed. I bet you could set off dynamite in an A & P and the people would by and large keep reaching and checking oatmeal off their lists and muttering "Let me see, there was a third thing, began with A, asparagus, no, ah, yes, applesauce!" or whatever it is they do mutter. But there was no doubt, this jiggled them. A few houseslaves in pin curlers even looked around after pushing their carts past to make sure what they had seen was correct.

You know, it's one thing to have a girl in a bathing suit down on the beach, where what with the glare nobody can look at each other much anyway, and another thing in the cool of the A & P, under the fluorescent lights, against all those stacked packages, with her feet paddling along naked over our checker-board green-and-cream rubber-tile floor.

"Oh Daddy," Stokesie said beside me. "I feel so faint."

"Darling," I said. "Hold me tight." Stokesie's married, with two babies chalked up on his fuselage already, but as far as I can tell that's the only difference. He's twenty-two, and I was nineteen this April.

"Is it done?" he asks, the responsible married man finding his voice. I forgot to say he thinks he's going to be manager some sunny day, maybe in 1990 when it's called the Great Alexandrov and Petrooshki Tea Company or something.

What he meant was, our town is five miles from a beach, with a big summer colony out on the Point, but we're right in the middle of town, and the women generally put on a shirt or shorts or something before they get out of the car into the street. And anyway these are usually women with six children and varicose veins mapping their legs and nobody, including them, could care less. As I say, we're right in the middle of town, and if you stand at our front doors you can see two banks and the Congregational church and the newspaper store and three real-estate offices and about twenty-seven old freeloaders tearing up Central Street because the sewer broke again. It's not as if we're on the Cape, we're north of Boston and there's people in this town haven't seen the ocean for twenty years.

The girls had reached the meat counter and were asking McMahon something. He pointed, they pointed, and they shuffled out of sight behind a pyramid of Diet Delight peaches. All that was left for us to see was old McMahon patting his mouth and looking after them sizing up their joints. Poor kids, I began to feel sorry for them, they couldn't help it.

10

Now here comes the sad part of the story, at least my family says it's sad, but I don't think it's so sad myself. The store's pretty empty, it being Thursday afternoon, so there was nothing much to do except lean on the register and wait for the girls to show up again. The whole store was like a pinball machine and I didn't know which tunnel they'd come out of. After a while they come around out of the far aisle, around the light bulbs, records at discount of the Caribbean Six or Tony Martin Sings or some such gunk you wonder they waste the wax on, sixpacks of candy bars, and plastic toys done up in cellophane that fall apart when a kid looks at them anyway. Around they come, Queenie still leading the way, and holding a little gray jar in her hands. Slots Three through Seven are unmanned and I could see her wondering between Stokes and me, but Stokesie with his usual luck draws an old party in baggy gray pants who stumbles up with four giant cans of pineapple juice (what do these bums *do* with all that pineapple juice? I've often asked myself). So the girls come to me. Queenie puts down the jar and I take it into my fingers icy cold. Kingfish Fancy Herring Snacks in Pure Sour Cream: 49¢. Now her hands are empty, not a ring or a bracelet, bare as God made them, and I wonder where the money's coming from. Still with that prim look she lifts a folded dollar bill out of the hollow at the center of her nubbled pink top. The jar went heavy in my hand. Really, I thought that was so cute.

Then everybody's luck begins to run out. Lengel comes in from haggling with a truck full of cabbages on the lot and is about to scuttle into that door marked MANAGER behind which he hides all day when the girls touch his eye. Lengel's pretty dreary, teaches Sunday school and the rest, but he doesn't miss that much. He comes over and says, "Girls, this isn't the beach."

Queenie blushes, though maybe it's just a brush of sunburn I was noticing for the first time, now that she was so close. "My mother asked me to pick up a jar of herring snacks." Her voice kind of startled me, the way voices do when you see the people first, coming out so flat and dumb yet kind of tony, too, the way it ticked over "pick up" and "snacks." All of a sudden I slid right down her voice into the living room. Her father and the other men were standing around in ice-cream coats and bow ties and the women were in sandals picking up herring snacks on toothpicks off a big glass plate and they were all holding drinks the color of water with olives and sprigs of mint in them. When my parents have somebody over they get lemonade and if it's a real racy affair Schlitz in tall glasses with "They'll Do It Every Time" cartoons stenciled on.

"That's all right," Lengel said. "But this isn't the beach." His repeating this struck me as funny, as if it had just occurred to him, and he had been thinking all these years the A & P was a great big dune and he was the head lifeguard. He didn't like my smiling—as I say he doesn't miss much—but he concentrates on giving the girls that sad Sunday-school-superintendent stare. 15

Queenie's blush is no sunburn now, and the plump one in plaid, that I liked better from the back—a really sweet can—pipes up, "We weren't doing any shopping. We just came in for the one thing."

"That makes no difference," Lengel tells her, and I could see from the way his eyes went that he hadn't noticed she was wearing a two-piece before. "We want you decently dressed when you come in here."

"We *are* decent," Queenie says suddenly, her lower lip pushing, getting sore now that she remembers her place, a place from which the crowd that runs the A & P must look pretty crummy. Fancy Herring Snacks flashed in her very blue eyes.

"Girls, I don't want to argue with you. After this come in here with your shoulders covered. It's our policy." He turns his back. That's policy for you. Policy is what the kingpins want. What the others want is juvenile delinquency.

All this while, the customers had been showing up with their carts but, you know, sheep, seeing a scene, they had all bunched up on Stokesie, who shook open a paper bag as gently as peeling a peach, not wanting to miss a word. I could feel in the silence everybody getting nervous, most of all Lengel, who asks me, "Sammy, have you rung up their purchase?"

I thought and said "No" but it wasn't about that I was thinking. I go through the punches, 4, 9, GROC. TOT — it's more complicated than you think, and after you do it often enough, it begins to make a little song, that you hear words to, in my case "Hello *(bing)* there, you *(gung)* hap-py *pee*-pul *(splat)*!" — the *splat* being the drawer flying out. I uncrease the bill, tenderly as you may imagine, it just having come from between the two smoothest scoops of vanilla I had ever known were there, and pass a half and a penny into her narrow pink palm, and nestle the herrings in a bag and twist its neck and hand it over, all the time thinking.

The girls, and who'd blame them, are in a hurry to get out, so I say "I quit" to Lengel quick enough for them to hear, hoping they'll stop and watch me, their unsuspected hero. They keep right on going, into the electric eye; the door flies open and they flicker across the lot to their car, Queenie and Plaid and Big Tall Goony-Goony (not that as raw material she was so bad), leaving me with Lengel and a kink in his eyebrow.

"Did you say something, Sammy?"

"I said I quit."

"I thought you did."

"You didn't have to embarrass them."

"It was they who were embarrassing us."

I started to say something that came out "Fiddle-de-doo." It's a saying of my grandmother's, and I know she would have been pleased.

"I don't think you know what you're saying," Lengel said.

"I know you don't," I said. "But I do." I pull the bow at the back of my apron and start shrugging it off my shoulders. A couple customers that had been heading for my slot begin to knock against each other, like scared pigs in a chute.

Lengel sighs and begins to look very patient and old and gray. He's been a friend of my parents for years. "Sammy, you don't want to do this to your

Mom and Dad," he tells me. It's true, I don't. But it seems to me that once you begin a gesture it's fatal not to go through with it. I fold the apron, "Sammy" stitched in red on the pocket, and put it on the counter, and drop the bow tie on top of it. The bow tie is theirs, if you've ever wondered. "You'll feel this for the rest of your life," Lengel says, and I know that's true, too, but remembering how he made the pretty girl blush makes me so scrunchy inside I punch the No Sale tab and the machine whirs "pee-pul" and the drawer splats out. One advantage to this scene taking place in summer, I can follow this up with a clean exit, there's no fumbling around getting your coat and galoshes, I just saunter into the electric eye in my white shirt that my mother ironed the night before, and the door heaves itself open, and outside the sunshine is skating around on the asphalt.

I look around for my girls, but they're gone, of course. There wasn't anybody but some young married screaming with her children about some candy they didn't get by the door of a powder-blue Falcon station wagon. Looking back in the big windows, over the bags of peat moss and aluminum lawn furniture stacked on the pavement, I could see Lengel in my place in the slot, checking the sheep through. His face was dark gray and his back stiff, as if he'd just had an injection of iron, and my stomach kind of fell as I felt how hard the world was going to be to me hereafter.

Considerations for Critical Thinking and Writing

1. **FIRST RESPONSE.** Describe the setting. How accurate do you think Updike's treatment of the A & P is?

2. What kind of person is Sammy? How do his actions and speech constitute his own individual style?

3. Analyze the style of the first paragraph. How does it set the tone for the rest of the story?

4. What is the story's central conflict? Does it seem to be a serious or trivial conflict to you?

5. With what kind of values is Lengel associated? Do you feel any sympathy for him?

6. What do you think is Stokesie's function in the story?

7. Consider Sammy's treatment of the three girls. Do you think his account of them is sexist? Explain why or why not.

8. Locate the climax of the story. How does the climax affect your attitude toward Sammy?

9. How do you think the story would be different if it were told from another character's point of view instead of Sammy's?

10. Discuss the thematic significance of the story's final paragraph. Would you read the story differently if this last paragraph were eliminated?

11. **CONNECTION TO ANOTHER SELECTION.** Compare the tone established by the point of view in this story and in Maggie Mitchell's "It Would Be Different If" (p. 166).

DAVID UPDIKE (B. 1957)

Born in Ipswich, Massachusetts, David Updike is the son of author John Updike. David received his B.A. in art history at Harvard and his M.A. from Teachers College, Columbia University. His acclaimed children's books include *An Autumn Tale* (1988), *A Spring Story* (1989), *Seven Times Eight* (1990), *The Sounds of Summer* (1993), and *A Helpful Alphabet of Friendly Objects* (1998), which he coauthored with his father. "Summer," a poignant tale for adults, is part of *Out on the Marsh: Stories* (1988), a collection of his short fiction. A second collection, *Old Girlfriends*, appeared in 2009.

Jan Brown.

Summer   *1985*

It was the first week in August, the time when summer briefly pauses, shifting between its beginning and its end: the light had not yet begun to change, the leaves were still full and green on the trees, the nights were still warm. From the woods and fields came the hiss of crickets; the line of distant mountains was still dulled by the edge of summer haze, the echo of fireworks was replaced by the rumble of thunder and the hollow premonition of school, too far off to imagine though dimly, dully felt. His senses were consumed by the joy of their own fulfillment: the satisfying swat of a tennis ball, the dappled damp and light of the dirt road after rain, the alternating sensations of sand, mossy stone, and pine needles under bare feet. His days were spent in the adolescent pursuit of childhood pleasures: tennis, a haphazard round of golf, a variant of baseball adapted to the local geography: two pine trees as foul poles, a broomstick as the bat, the apex of the small, secluded house the dividing line between home runs and outs. On rainy days they swatted bottle tops across the living room floor, and at night vented budding cerebral energy with games of chess thoughtfully played over glasses of iced tea. After dinner they would paddle the canoe to the middle of the lake, and drift beneath the vast, blue-black dome of sky, looking at the stars and speaking softly in tones which, with the waning summer, became increasingly philosophical: the sky's blue vastness, the distance and magnitude of stars, an endless succession of numbers, gave way to a rising sensation of infinity, eternity, an imagined universe with no bounds. But the sound of the paddle hitting against the side of the canoe, the faint shadow of surrounding mountains, the cry of a nocturnal bird brought them back to the happy, cloistered finity of their world, and they paddled slowly home and went to bed.

Homer woke to the slant and shadow of a summer morning, dressed in their shared cabin, and went into the house where Mrs. Thyme sat alone, looking out across the flat blue stillness of the lake. She poured him a cup of coffee and they quietly talked, and it was then that his happiness seemed most tangible. In this summer month with the Thymes, freed from the complications of his own family, he had released himself to them and, as interim member — friend, brother, surrogate son — he lived in a blessed realm between two worlds.

From the cool darkness of the porch, smelling faintly of moldy books and kerosene and the tobacco of burning pipes, he sat looking through the screen to the lake, shimmering beneath the heat of a summer afternoon: a dog lay sleeping in the sun, a bird hopped along a swaying branch, sunlight came in through the trees and collapsed on the sandy soil beside a patch of moss, or mimicked the shade and cadence of stones as they stepped to the edge of a lake where small waves lapped a damp rock and washed onto a sandy shore. An inverted boat lay decaying under a tree, a drooping American flag hung from its gnarled pole, a haphazard dock started out across the cove toward distant islands through which the white triangle of a sail silently moved.

The yellowed pages of the book from which he occasionally read swam before him: ". . . Holmes clapped the hat upon his head. It came right over the forehead and settled on the bridge of his nose. 'It is a question of cubic capacity' said he . . ." Homer looked up. The texture of the smooth, unbroken air was cleanly divided by the sound of a slamming door, echoing up into the woods around him. Through the screen he watched Fred's sister Sandra as she came ambling down the path, stepping lightly between the stones in her bare feet. She held a towel in one hand, a book in the other, and wore a pair of pale blue shorts — faded relics of another era. At the end of the dock she stopped, raised her hands above her head, stretching, and then sat down. She rolled over onto her stomach and, using the book as a pillow, fell asleep.

Homer was amused by the fact, that although she did this every day, she 5 didn't get any tanner. When she first came in her face was faintly flushed, and there was a pinkish line around the snowy band where her bathing suit strap had been, but the back of her legs remained an endearing, pale white, the color of eggshells, and her back acquired only the softest, brownish blur. Sometimes she kept her shoes on, other times a shirt, or sweater, or just collapsed onto the seat of the boat, her pale eyelids turned upward toward the pale sun; and as silently as she arrived, she would leave, walking back through the stones with the same, casual sway of indifference. He would watch her, hear the distant door slam, the shower running in the far corner of the house. Other times he would just look up and she would be gone.

On the tennis court she was strangely indifferent to his heroics. When the crucial moment arrived — Homer serving in the final game of the final set — the match would pause while she left, walking across the court, stopping to call the dog, swaying out through the gate. Homer watched her as she went down the path, and, impetus suddenly lost, he double faulted, stroked a routine backhand over the back fence, and the match was over.

When he arrived back at the house she asked him who won, but didn't seem to hear his answer. "I wish I could go sailing," she said, looking distractedly out over the lake.

At night, when he went out to the cottage where he and Fred slept, he could see her through the window as she lay on her bed, reading, her arm folded beneath her head like a leaf. Her nightgown, pulled and buttoned to her chin, pierced him with a regret that had no source or resolution, and its imagined texture floated in the air above him as he lay in bed at night, suspended in the surrounding darkness, the scent of pine, the hypnotic cadence of his best friend's breathing.

Was it that he had known her all his life, and as such had grown up in the shadow of her subtle beauty? Was it the condensed world of the lake, the silent reverence of surrounding woods, mountains, which heightened his sense of her and brought the warm glow of her presence into soft, amorous focus? She had the hair of a baby, the freckles of a child, and the sway of motherhood. Like his love, her beauty rose up in the world which spawned and nurtured it, and found in the family the medium in which it thrived, and in Homer distilled to a pure distant longing for something he had never had.

One day they climbed a mountain, and as the components of family and friends strung out along the path on their laborious upward hike, he found himself tromping along through the woods with her with nobody else in sight. Now and then they would stop by a stream, or sit on a stump, or stone, and he would speak to her, and then they would set off again, he following her. But in the end this day exhausted him, following her pale legs and tripping sneakers over the ruts and stones and a thousand roots, all the while trying to suppress a wordless, inarticulate passion, and the last mile or so he left her, sprinting down the path in a reckless, solitary release, howling into the woods around him. He was lying on the grass, staring up into the patterns of drifting clouds when she came ambling down. "Wher'd you go? I thought I'd lost you," she said, and sat heavily down in the seat of the car. On the ride home, his elbow hopelessly held in the warm crook of her arm, he resolved to release his love, give it up, on the grounds that it was too disruptive to his otherwise placid life. But in the days to follow he discovered that his resolution had done little to change her, and her life went on its oblivious, happy course without him.

His friendship with Fred, meanwhile, continued on its course of athletic and boyhood fulfillment. Alcohol seeped into their diet, and an occasional cigarette, and at night they would drive into town, buy two enormous cans of Australian beer and sit at a small cove by the lake, talking. One night on the ride home Fred accelerated over a small bridge, and as the family station wagon left the ground their heads floated up to the ceiling, touched, and then came crashing down as the car landed and Fred wrestled the car back onto course. Other times they would take the motorboat out onto the lake and make sudden racing turns around buoys, sending a plume of water into the air and everything in the boat crashing to one side. But always with these adventures Homer felt a pang of absence, and was always relieved when they headed back toward the familiar cove, and home.

As August ran its merciless succession of beautiful days, Sandra drifted in and out of his presence in rising oscillations of sorrow and desire. She worked at a bowling alley on the other side of the lake, and in the evening Homer and Fred would drive the boat over, bowl a couple of strings, and wait for her to get off work. Homer sat at the counter and watched her serve up sloshing cups of coffee, secretly loathing the leering gazes of whiskered truck drivers, and loving her oblivious, vacant stare in answer, hip cocked, hand on counter, gazing up into the neon air above their heads. When she was finished, they would pile into the boat and skim through darkness the four or five miles home, and it was then, bundled beneath sweaters and blankets, the white hem of her waitressing dress showing through the darkness, their hair swept in the wind and their voices swallowed by the engine's slow, steady growl, that he felt most powerless to her attraction. As the boat rounded corners he would close his eyes and release himself to gravity, his body's warmth swaying into hers, guising his attraction in the thin veil of centrifugal force. Now and then he would lean into the floating strands of her hair and speak into her fragrance, watching her smile swell in the pale half-light of the moon, the umber glow of the boat's rear light, her laughter spilling backward over the swirling "V" of wake.

Into the humid days of August a sudden rain fell, leaving the sky a hard, unbroken blue and the nights clear and cool. In the morning when he woke, leaving Fred a heap of sighing covers in his bed, he stepped out into the first rays of sunlight that came through the branches of the trees and sensed, in the cool vapor that rose from damp pine needles, the piercing cry of a blue jay, that something had changed. That night as they ate dinner—hamburgers and squash and corn-on-the-cob—everyone wore sweaters, and as the sun set behind the undulating line of distant mountains—burnt, like a filament of summer into his blinking eyes—it was with an autumnal tint, a reddish glow. Several days later the tree at the end of the point bloomed with a sprig of russet leaves, one or two of which occasionally fell, and their lives became filled with an unspoken urgency. Life of summer went on in the silent knowledge that, with the slow, inexorable seepage of an hourglass, it was turning into fall. Another mountain was climbed, annual tennis matches were arranged and played. Homer and Fred became unofficial champions of the lake by trouncing the elder Dewitt boys, unbeaten in several years. "Youth, youth," glum Billy Dewitt kept saying over iced tea afterward, in jest, though Homer could tell he was hiding some greater sense of loss.

And the moment, the conjunction of circumstance that, through the steady exertion of will, minor adjustments of time and place, he had often tried to induce, never happened. She received his veiled attentions with a kind of amused curiosity, as if smiling back on innocence. One night they had been the last ones up, and there was a fleeting, shuddering moment before he stepped through the woods to his cabin and she went to her bed that he recognized, in a distant sort of way, as the moment of truth. But to touch her, or kiss her, seemed suddenly incongruous, absurd, contrary to something he could not put his finger on. He looked down at the floor and softly said goodnight. The screen door shut quietly behind him and he went out into the darkness and made his way through the unseen sticks and stones, and it was only then, tripping drunkenly on a fallen branch, that he realized he had never been able to imagine the moment he distantly longed for.

The Preacher gave a familiar sermon about another summer having run 15 its course, the harvest of friendship reaped, and a concluding prayer that, "God willing, we will all meet again in June." That afternoon Homer and Fred went sailing, and as they swept past a neighboring cove Homer saw in its sullen shadows a girl sitting alone in a canoe, and in an eternal, melancholy signal of parting, she waved to them as they passed. And there was something in the way that she raised her arm which, when added to the distant impression of her fullness, beauty, youth, filled him with longing as their boat moved inexorably past, slapping the waves, and she disappeared behind a crop of trees.

The night before they were to leave they were all sitting in the living room after dinner — Mrs. Thyme sewing, Fred folded up with the morning paper, Homer reading on the other end of the couch where Sandra was lying — when the dog leapt up and things shifted in such a way that Sandra's bare foot was lightly touching Homer's back. Mrs. Thyme came over with a roll of newspaper, hit the dog on the head and he leapt off. But to Homer's surprise Sandra's foot remained, and he felt, in the faint sensation of exerted pressure, the passive emanation of its warmth, a distant signal of acquiescence. And as the family scene continued as before it was with the accompanying drama of Homer's hand, shielded from the family by a haphazard wall of pillows, migrating over the couch to where, in a moment of breathless abandon, settled softly on the cool hollow of her arch. She laughed at something her mother had said, her toe twitched, but her foot remained. It was only then, in the presence of the family, that he realized she was his accomplice, and that, though this was as far as it would ever go, his love had been returned.

CONSIDERATIONS FOR CRITICAL THINKING AND WRITING

1. FIRST RESPONSE. How do you respond to this love story? Would the story be more satisfying if Homer and Sandra openly acknowledged their feelings for each other and kissed at the end? Why or why not?

2. What details in the first paragraph evoke particular feelings about August? What sort of mood is created by these details?

3. How is Homer's attraction to Sandra made evident in paragraphs 5 through 9?

4. Why do you think August is described as a "merciless succession of beautiful days" (para. 12)?

5. Analyze the images in paragraph 13 that evoke the impending autumn. What does Billy Dewitt's lament about "youth, youth" add to this description?

6. Discuss the transition between paragraphs 14 and 15. How is the mood effectively changed between the night and the next day?

7. What effect does Homer's friendship with Fred and his relationship with the Thyme family have on your understanding of his reticent attraction to Sandra?

8. What, if any, significance can you attach to the names of Homer, Sandra, Thyme, and the Dewitt boys?

9. How successful do you think Updike is in evoking youthful feeling about summer in this story? Explain why you responded positively or negatively to this evocation of summer.

10. **CONNECTION TO ANOTHER SELECTION.** Compare David Updike's treatment of summer as the setting of his story with John Updike's use of summer as the setting in "A & P" (p. 149).

11. **CONNECTION TO ANOTHER SELECTION.** Discuss "Summer" and Dagoberto Gilb's "Love in L.A." (p. 267) as love stories. Explain why you might prefer one over the other.

CHARLOTTE PERKINS GILMAN (1860–1935)

Born in Hartford, Connecticut, Charlotte Perkins Gilman was raised by her mother in strained economic circumstances because her father deserted the family soon after her birth. She briefly attended the Rhode Island School of Design and subsequently worked as an artist and teacher to support herself before her first marriage, which ended in divorce after she had a nervous breakdown following her daughter's birth. In California she remarried and became an influential writer, lecturer, and activist, focusing on feminist issues concerning labor, economics, ethics, and social reform. Among her books urging women to achieve financial autonomy in order to further social justice are *Women and Economics* (1898) and *The Man-Made World* (1900). Her best-known fiction is "The Yellow Wallpaper," a short story based on her mental breakdown and the problematic treatment she received. Her other works include a volume of poetry, *In This Our World* (1893); a utopian novel *Herland* (1915); and numerous short stories, novels, and essays on social reform.

If I Were a Man   1914

"If I were a man, . . ." that was what pretty little Mollie Mathewson always said when Gerald would not do what she wanted him to — which was seldom.

That was what she said this bright morning with a stamp of her little high-heeled slipper, just because he had made a fuss about that bill, the long one with the "account rendered," which she had forgotten to give him the first time and been afraid to the second — and now he had taken it from the post-man himself.

Mollie was "true to type." She was a beautiful instance of what is reverentially called "a true woman." Little, of course — no true woman may be big. Pretty, of course — no true woman could possibly be plain. Whimsical, capricious, charming, changeable, devoted to pretty clothes and always "wearing them well," as the esoteric phrase has it. (This does not refer to the clothes — they do not wear well in the least — but to some special grace of putting them on and carrying them about, granted to but few, it appears.)

She was also a loving wife and a devoted mother possessed of "the social gift" and the love of "society" that goes with it, and, with all these was fond and proud of her home and managed it as capably as — well, as most women do.

If ever there was a true woman it was Mollie Mathewson, yet she was   5 wishing heart and soul she was a man.

And all of a sudden she was!

She was Gerald, walking down the path so erect and square-shouldered, in a hurry for his morning train, as usual, and, it must be confessed, in something of a temper.

Her own words were ringing in her ears — not only the "last word," but several that had gone before, and she was holding her lips tight shut, not to say something she would be sorry for. But instead of acquiescence in the position taken by that angry little figure on the veranda, what she felt was a sort of superior pride, a sympathy as with weakness, a feeling that "I must be gentle with her," in spite of the temper.

A man! Really a man — with only enough subconscious memory of herself remaining to make her recognize the differences.

At first there was a funny sense of size and weight and extra thickness,   10 the feet and hands seemed strangely large, and her long, straight, free legs swung forward at a gait that made her feel as if on stilts.

This presently passed, and in its place, growing all day, wherever she went, came a new and delightful feeling of being *the right size*.

Everything fitted now. Her back snugly against the seat-back, her feet comfortably on the floor. Her feet? . . . His feet! She studied them carefully. Never before, since her early school days, had she felt such freedom and comfort as to feet — they were firm and solid on the ground when she walked; quick, springy, safe — as when, moved by an unrecognizable impulse, she had run after, caught, and swung aboard the car.

Another impulse fished in a convenient pocket for change — instantly, automatically, bringing forth a nickel for the conductor and a penny for the newsboy.

These pockets came as a revelation. Of course she had known they were there, had counted them, made fun of them, mended them, even envied them; but she never had dreamed of how it *felt* to have pockets.

Behind her newspaper she let her consciousness, that odd mingled con-   15 sciousness, rove from pocket to pocket, realizing the armored assurance of having all those things at hand, instantly get-at-able, ready to meet emergencies. The cigar case gave her a warm feeling of comfort — it was full; the firmly held fountain pen, safe unless she stood on her head; the keys, pencils, letters, documents, notebook, checkbook, bill folder — all at once, with a deep rushing sense of power and pride, she felt what she had never felt before in all her life — the possession of money, of her own earned money — hers to give or to withhold, not to beg for, tease for, wheedle for — hers.

That bill — why, if it had come to her — to him, that is — he would have paid it as a matter of course, and never mentioned it — to her.

Then, being he, sitting there so easily and firmly with his money in his pockets, she wakened to his life-long consciousness about money. Boyhood — its desires and dreams, ambitions. Young manhood — working tremendously for the wherewithal to make a home — for her. The present years with all their net of cares and hopes and dangers; the present moment, when he needed every cent for special plans of great importance, and this bill, long overdue and demanding payment, meant an amount of inconvenience wholly unnecessary if it had been given him when it first came; also, the man's keen dislike of that "account rendered."

"Women have no business sense!" she found herself saying. "And all that money just for hats — idiotic, useless, ugly things!"

With that she began to see the hats of the women in the car as she had never seen hats before. The men's seemed normal, dignified, becoming, with enough variety for personal taste, and with distinction in style and in age, such as she had never noticed before. But the women's —

With the eyes of a man and the brain of a man; with the memory of a   20 whole lifetime of free action wherein the hat, close-fitting on cropped hair, had been no handicap; she now perceived the hats of women.

The massed fluffed hair was at once attractive and foolish, and on that hair, at every angle, in all colors, tipped, twisted, tortured into every crooked shape, made of any substance chance might offer, perched these formless objects. Then, on their formlessness the trimmings — these squirts of stiff feathers, these violent outstanding bows of glistening ribbon, these swaying, projecting masses of plumage which tormented the faces of bystanders.

Never in all her life had she imagined that this idolized millinery could look, to those who paid for it, like the decorations of an insane monkey.

And yet, when there came into the car a little woman, as foolish as any, but pretty and sweet-looking, up rose Gerald Mathewson and gave her his seat. And, later, when there came in a handsome red-cheeked girl, whose hat was wilder, more violent in color and eccentric in shape than any other — when she stood nearby and her soft curling plumes swept his cheek once and again — he felt a sense of sudden pleasure at the intimate tickling touch — and she, deep down within, felt such a wave of shame as might well drown a thousand hats forever.

When he took his train, his seat in the smoking car, she had a new surprise. All about him were the other men, commuters too, and many of them friends of his.

To her, they would have been distinguished as "Mary Wade's husband," "the man Belle Grant is engaged to," "that rich Mr. Shopworth," or "that pleasant Mr. Beale." And they would all have lifted their hats to her, bowed, made polite conversation if near enough — especially Mr. Beale.

Now came the feeling of open-eyed acquaintance, of knowing men — as they were. The mere amount of this knowledge was a surprise to her — the whole background of talk from boyhood up, the gossip of barber-shop and club, the conversation of morning and evening hours on trains, the knowledge of political affiliation, of business standing and prospects, of character — in a light she had never known before.

They came and talked to Gerald, one and another. He seemed quite popular. And as they talked, with this new memory and new understanding, an understanding which seemed to include all these men's minds, there poured in on the submerged consciousness beneath a new, a startling knowledge — what men really think of women.

Good, average, American men were there; married men for the most part, and happy — as happiness goes in general. In the minds of each and all there seemed to be a two-story department, quite apart from the rest of their ideas, a separate place where they kept their thoughts and feelings about women.

In the upper half were the tenderest emotions, the most exquisite ideals, the sweetest memories, all lovely sentiments as to "home" and "mother," all delicate admiring adjectives, a sort of sanctuary, where a veiled statue, blindly adored, shared place with beloved yet commonplace experiences.

In the lower half — here that buried consciousness woke to keen distress — they kept quite another assortment of ideas. Here, even in this clean-minded husband of hers, was the memory of stories told at men's dinners, of worse ones overheard in street or car, of base traditions, coarse epithets, gross experiences — known, though not shared.

And all these in the department "woman," while in the rest of the mind — here was new knowledge indeed.

The world opened before her. Not the world she had been reared in — where Home had covered all the map, almost, and the rest had been "foreign," or "unexplored country," but the world as it was — man's world, as made, lived in, and seen, by men.

It was dizzying. To see the houses that fled so fast across the car window, in terms of builders' bills, or of some technical insight into materials and methods; to see a passing village with lamentable knowledge of who "owned it" and of how its Boss was rapidly aspiring in state power, or of how that kind of paving was a failure; to see shops, not as mere exhibitions of desirable objects, but as business ventures, many were sinking ships, some promising a profitable voyage — this new world bewildered her.

She — as Gerald — had already forgotten about that bill, over which she — as Mollie — was still crying at home. Gerald was "talking business" with this man, "talking politics" with that, and now sympathizing with the carefully withheld troubles of a neighbor.

Mollie had always sympathized with the neighbor's wife before.

She began to struggle violently with this large dominant masculine consciousness. She remembered with sudden clearness things she had read, lectures she had heard, and resented with increasing intensity this serene masculine preoccupation with the male point of view.

Mr. Miles, the little fussy man who lived on the other side of the street, was talking now. He had a large complacent wife; Mollie had never liked her much, but had always thought him rather nice — he was so punctilious in small courtesies.

And here he was talking to Gerald — such talk!

"Had to come in here," he said. "Gave my seat to a dame who was bound to have it. There's nothing they won't get when they make up their minds to it — eh?"

"No fear!" said the big man in the next seat. "They haven't much mind to   40
make up, you know — and if they do, they'll change it."

"The real danger," began the Rev. Alfred Smythe, the new Episcopal clergyman, a thin, nervous, tall man with a face several centuries behind the times, "is that they will overstep the limits of their God-appointed sphere."

"Their natural limits ought to hold 'em, I think," said cheerful Dr. Jones. "You can't get around physiology, I tell you."

"I've never seen any limits, myself, not to what they want, anyhow," said Mr. Miles. "Merely a rich husband and a fine house and no end of bonnets and dresses, and the latest thing in motors, and a few diamonds — and so on. Keeps us pretty busy."

There was a tired gray man across the aisle. He had a very nice wife, always beautifully dressed, and three unmarried daughters, also beautifully dressed — Mollie knew them. She knew he worked hard, too, and she looked at him now a little anxiously.

But he smiled cheerfully.   45

"Do you good, Miles," he said. "What else would a man work for? A good woman is about the best thing on earth."

"And a bad one's the worst, that's sure," responded Miles.

"She's a pretty weak sister, viewed professionally," Dr. Jones averred with solemnity, and the Rev. Alfred Smythe added, "She brought evil into the world."

Gerald Mathewson sat up straight. Something was stirring in him which he did not recognize — yet could not resist.

"Seems to me we all talk like Noah," he suggested drily. "Or the ancient   50
Hindu scriptures. Women have their limitations, but so do we, God knows. Haven't we known girls in school and college just as smart as we were?"

"They cannot play our games," coldly replied the clergyman.

Gerald measured his meager proportions with a practiced eye.

"I never was particularly good at football myself," he modestly admitted, "but I've known women who could outlast a man in all-round endurance. Besides — life isn't spent in athletics!"

This was sadly true. They all looked down the aisle where a heavy ill-dressed man with a bad complexion sat alone. He had held the top of the columns once, with headlines and photographs. Now he earned less than any of them.

"It's time we woke up," pursued Gerald, still inwardly urged to unfamiliar 55 speech. "Women are pretty much *people*, seems to me. I know they dress like fools — but who's to blame for that? We invent all those idiotic hats of theirs, and design their crazy fashions, and, what's more, if a woman is courageous enough to wear common-sense clothes — and shoes — which of us wants to dance with her?

"Yes, we blame them for grafting on us, but are we willing to let our wives work? We are not. It hurts our pride, that's all. We are always criticizing them for making mercenary marriages, but what do we call a girl who marries a chump with no money? Just a poor fool, that's all. And they know it.

"As for Mother Eve — I wasn't there and can't deny the story, but I will say this. If she brought evil into the world, we men have had the lion's share of keeping it going ever since — how about that?"

They drew into the city, and all day long in his business, Gerald was vaguely conscious of new views, strange feelings, and the submerged Mollie learned and learned.

Considerations for Critical Thinking and Writing

1. **FIRST RESPONSE.** Describe where the shift in point of view occurs in the story. How did you respond to it?

2. To what extent do you think the descriptions of what constitutes "a true woman" in 1914 (paragraphs 3 and 4) reflect attitudes today?

3. How convincing do you find Mollie's description of what it is like to be a man?

4. What is the thematic significance of the overdue bill and money in the story?

5. How does her description of what constitutes a man's identity differ from that of a woman's?

6. Consider whether or not the gender issues raised by Gilman seem to you dated or contemporary.

7. **CREATIVE RESPONSE.** Write two substantial paragraphs from the point of view of Gerald in which he suddenly discovers that he's a woman. What would you have him say about what it is like to be a woman? Choose either 1914 or the twenty-first century as your frame of reference.

Maggie Mitchell (b. 1970)

Maggie Mitchell grew up in a small town in the northernmost part of New York State, on the Canadian border. She received an undergraduate degree in English from Cornell University and a Ph.D. from the University of Connecticut, and she now teaches English at the University of West Georgia. Her first novel, *Pretty Is* (2015), has been widely translated. Mitchell's short fiction has appeared in a number of literary magazines, including *New*

Ohio Review, American Literary Review, and *Green Mountains Review.* The stark landscape of her childhood often finds its way into her short stories, as it does in "It Would Be Different If," which originally appeared in *New South.*

Photo courtesy of Jill Sutton.

It Would Be Different If   2011

Here's what I remember. If I could hate you, this is what I would hate you for. It's a summer night, humid, starry. It's already pretty late but we're all heading over to Canada, to a bar called the Shipyard. She is there, which surprises me, because the Shipyard is the kind of place where people crack beer bottles over each other's heads, and I wouldn't have thought it was her scene. But she's been hanging out with your sister Megan all summer, working down at the restaurant, back when it was still the Riverside. She's always around. She annoys me, but I don't suspect anything yet. There are two boats; we're splitting into groups. I'm standing on the dock, a beer in my hand. I've had a little too much to drink already, probably, because everything seems very dark, slightly confused. I'm trying to figure out which boat you're in so I don't get stuck in the other one. Just then a car happens to go by on Water Street and its headlights flicker across us. You're already in the first boat, and you're reaching your hand up toward the dock, smiling. I move blindly in your direction, thinking you're reaching for me, when another flash of light shows me that she is grabbing for your hand, you're swinging her down, the smile is for her, it's not a mistake. I stand on the dock in a mini-skirt and a very skimpy cropped top, my hair sprayed into a sort of stiff gold cloud because it is the 80s. I feel, for the first time in my life, completely ridiculous. There's no turning back, though. I can't just announce, like a little kid, that I'm going home, I don't want to play anymore, though that's exactly what I feel.

The first boat is full. The headlights veer away: everything is dark again. I tumble somehow into the second boat, wishing I had something to cover myself with: I feel naked, although back then I always dressed like that, we all did. At the Shipyard I mostly stay in the bathroom, drinking and crying. I don't remember the boat ride home. But that's it, that's the end of it. That much I remember.

I've heard variations on this story from everyone, over the years. I'm always the victim, the one people feel sorry for. Maybe there are other versions where I get what's coming to me, where I've always needed to be put in my place, something like that, but I doubt it. People have never liked Amber much; they tend to be on my side. Or at least they did: as the years go by, I notice, that's less true. It's so long ago that people can't get too worked up about it anymore. Now they talk as if it was somehow inevitable, and we just didn't know it yet — you know, isn't life funny, but look how it all works out in the end. Except when it doesn't.

It would be different if we lived in the kind of place where people can disappear, never see each other again. It would be different if I could pretend you didn't exist. But there you are: you are at the post office, peering into your mailbox, pulling out a stack of envelopes and catalogues while I drop my electric bill in the mail slot; I wait till you turn around, to make sure you see me. You would rather not see me. You're at the table on the other side of the restaurant, bending forward to speak to her, or wiping food off your kid's face. You're getting gas, staring off into the distance, forgetting what you are doing. You don't notice that I'm driving by. What are you thinking of? You're everywhere. I think you have ruined my life.

And now she's the one they feel sorry for. Yes, of course I know what you've 5 been up to. Everyone knows. I see your truck in the parking lot at Jude's every night, and they say you don't tend to leave alone. I see her sometimes: Amber. She looks smaller, paler, less pretty. I could almost feel sorry for her myself, to tell you the truth. I don't blame you, of course. It's just because it's all wrong. I could have told you it would happen.

I wasn't supposed to be one of those people, the unmarryable ones. I never expected to be. I had you, and we had plans, ever since our junior year: Nikki and Jeff. Nikki Gilbert. It sounded right. We joked about getting old, how you would go bald and I'd go pure white, and we'd go fishing in the summer, cross-country skiing in the winter, with our dog. It was a beagle. I had a bit of a stoop; you had put on some weight. You can't cancel that out.

It wasn't fair. She had gone away — to college, the city, whatever. She was the kind of person who goes away, doesn't come back: that's what everyone expected. But she did come back and she chose you, of all people. Why you? You're not like her. You are like us.

Well. Here's what I imagine. It's the best I can do. I am working, finishing up someone's hair. It's late afternoon — that quiet time when the sun starts to come in sideways. Whose hair? Someone like Deb White, not much of a talker, but lots of hair, complicated hair, ever since Don got his job back and they gave up on that hippie phase. I'm finished with the cut and now I'm styling it, taking my time because I don't have any more appointments that day, blowing it out section by section, working through the layers. Her eyes are half closed, I hum a little. It's nice.

Then I hear the door clang as it swings shut behind someone. I glance over and it's you. I am calm; we say nothing. I just nod, and you pick up a magazine and sit down on the couch to wait. Like anyone else. I don't rush Deb. If anything I slow down, taking extra time with each wave, making it perfect. You're just sitting there but somehow you fill the air, you're everywhere and invisible. I breathe you, I walk on you, I curl you into Deb's frosted waves. But I don't shake, or sweat. I'm not nervous. You're like a birthday, a red X on the calendar. Sooner or later you'll happen, one way or the other: it doesn't matter what I do. Eventually Deb rises to her feet, admires herself in the mirror. She writes a check; I don't take credit cards. It seems to take her forever, like one of those women in line at the grocery store. In the meantime I sweep up the heap of doll-like hair around the chair, straighten up the station. She makes an appointment for the next month. Finally she drifts toward the door and I follow her, because she is chatting about something, telling me a story about one of her daughters; she always does this. I wave as she maneuvers herself into her car, careful not to disturb her hair.

When I return to the shop you have seated yourself in the chair that is   10
probably still warm from its contact with Deb White's bony behind. I think of this, for some reason. I see myself smile in the mirror and our eyes, for the first time, meet each other's reflections. I drape a hunter green smock across you, attach it behind your neck with velcro straps.

I cut your hair. I use four different kinds of scissors, a razor, two combs, a touch of mousse. I used to cut your hair in high school, for practice. Now I do it better. Mostly I keep my eyes focused on your head, like an artist putting the final touches on some life-sized sculpture, but every now and then I look up, and there you are in the mirror. We always look at the same moment. We know exactly how long to wait between looks; we know not to overdo it. Your eyes are still the same blue as always but there are crinkles, now, at the corners. I think you are better looking than ever. My work does you justice: this is the best haircut you will ever, ever get.

I remove the smock when it's over. You do not pay. You don't speak. You look at me one more time, and you touch my hand — so far, given the circumstances, I have been the one to do all the touching — and then you leave. I wait until your truck has pulled away to sweep up the short brown hairs. I can't throw them away, so I tilt the contents of the dustpan into one of the nice creamy envelopes I use for gift certificates.

I don't know what happens after that. Probably you don't leave her right away. But sooner or later I know you'll come. I'll be waiting. For now I'll settle for the trimmings, glossy and shampoo-scented, and for the traces of your reflection that you seem to have left in the mirror. You flicker endlessly between the stiff curls of middle-aged ladies in pastel pantsuits, the long doomed locks of small terrified boys, the towering, glittery updos of girls on their way to the prom. You remind me to wait, promise that things will be different. I believe you.

Considerations for Critical Thinking and Writing

1. FIRST RESPONSE. What actually happens in this story? What is the status of the present in relation to memory and imagination?

2. How does the narrator invite the reader's sympathy? Is it important that we sympathize with her?

3. How trustworthy is the narrator's version of events? What specific lines or passages reinforce or undermine her perspective?

4. What kind of resolution does this story offer? Would you say that the conflict has been resolved, in any sense?

5. What does the narrator's way of relating this story — not *what* she says, but the way she says it — reveal about her world or about her character?

6. What sense do you get of the town in which this story is set? How important is the setting to your understanding of the story and the characters?

7. What is the significance of the final line of the story?

8. CREATIVE RESPONSE. Use what you think you can infer about the narrator from this story to craft a paragraph from a third-person point of view in which Nikki is portrayed unsympathetically.

6

Symbolism

Everett Collection / Newscom.

Now mind, I recognize no dichotomy
between art and protest.
— RALPH ELLISON

A *symbol* is a person, object, or event that suggests more than its literal meaning. This basic definition is simple enough, but the use of symbol in literature makes some students slightly nervous because they tend to regard it as a booby trap, a hidden device that can go off during a seemingly harmless class discussion. "I didn't see that when I was reading the story" is a frequently heard comment. This sort of surprise and recognition is both natural and common. Most readers go through a story for the first time getting their bearings, figuring out what is happening to whom and so on. Patterns and significant details often require a second or third reading before they become evident—before a symbol sheds light on a story. Then the details of a work may suddenly fit together, and its meaning may be reinforced, clarified, or enlarged by the symbol. Symbolic meanings are usually embedded in the texture of a story, but they are not "hidden"; instead, they are carefully placed. Reading between the lines (where there is only space) is unnecessary. What is needed is a careful consideration of the elements of the story, a sensitivity to its language, and some common sense.

Common sense is a good place to begin. Symbols appear all around us; anything can be given symbolic significance. Without symbols our lives would be stark and vacant. Awareness of a writer's use of symbols is not all that different from the kinds of perceptions and interpretations that allow us to make sense of our daily lives. We know, for example, that a ring used in a wedding is more than just a piece of jewelry because it suggests the unity and intimacy of a closed circle. The bride's gown may be white because we tend to associate innocence and purity with that color. Or consider the meaning of a small polo pony sewn on a shirt or some other article of clothing. What started as a company trademark has gathered around it a range of meanings suggesting everything from quality and money to preppiness and silliness. The ring, the white gown, and the polo pony trademark are symbolic because each has meanings that go beyond its specific qualities and functions.

Symbols such as these that are widely recognized by a society or culture are called *conventional symbols*. The Christian cross, the Star of David, a swastika, or a nation's flag all have meanings understood by large groups of people. Certain kinds of experiences also have traditional meanings in Western cultures. Winter, the setting sun, and the color black suggest death, while spring, the rising sun, and the color green evoke images of youth and new beginnings. (It is worth noting, however, that individual cultures sometimes have their own conventions; some Eastern cultures associate white rather than black with death and mourning. And obviously the polo pony trademark would mean nothing to anyone totally unfamiliar with American culture.) These broadly shared symbolic meanings are second nature to us.

Writers use conventional symbols to reinforce meanings. Kate Chopin, for example, emphasizes the spring setting in "The Story of an Hour" (p. 15) as a way of suggesting the renewed sense of life that Mrs. Mallard feels when she thinks herself free from her husband.

A *literary symbol* can include traditional, conventional, or public meanings, but it may also be established internally by the total context of the work in which it appears. In "Soldier's Home" (p. 129), Hemingway does not use Krebs's family home as a conventional symbol of safety, comfort, and refuge from the war. Instead, Krebs's home becomes symbolic of provincial, erroneous presuppositions compounded by blind innocence, sentimentality, and smug middle-class respectability. The symbolic meaning of his home reveals that Krebs no longer shares his family's and town's view of the world. Their notions of love, the value of a respectable job, and a belief in God seem to him petty, complicated, and meaningless. The significance of Krebs's home is determined by the events within the story, which reverse and subvert the traditional associations readers might bring to it. Krebs's interactions with his family and the people in town reveal what home has come to mean to him.

A literary symbol can be a setting, character, action, object, name, or anything else in a work that maintains its literal significance while suggesting other meanings. Symbols cannot be restricted to a single meaning; they are suggestive rather than definitive. Their evocation of multiple meanings allows a writer to say more with less. Symbols are economical devices for evoking complex ideas without having to resort to painstaking explanations that would make a story more like an essay than an experience. The many walls in Melville's "Bartleby, the Scrivener" (p. 99) cannot be reduced to one idea. They have multiple meanings that unify the story. The walls are symbols of the deadening, dehumanizing, restrictive repetitiveness of the office routine, as well as of the confining, materialistic sensibilities of Wall Street. They suggest whatever limits and thwarts human aspirations, including death itself. We don't know precisely what shatters Bartleby's will to live, but the walls in the story, through their symbolic suggestiveness, indicate the nature of the limitations that cause the scrivener to slip into hopelessness and his "dead-wall reveries."

When a character, object, or incident indicates a single, fixed meaning, the writer is using **allegory** rather than symbol. Whereas symbols have literal functions as well as multiple meanings, the primary focus in allegory is on the abstract idea called forth by the concrete object. John Bunyan's *Pilgrim's Progress*, published during the seventeenth century, is a classic example of allegory because the characters, action, and setting have no existence beyond their abstract meanings. Bunyan's purpose is to teach his readers the exemplary way to salvation and heaven. The protagonist, named Christian, flees the City of Destruction in search of the Celestial City. Along the way he encounters characters who either help or hinder his spiritual journey. Among them are Mr. Worldly Wiseman, Faithful, Prudence, Piety, and a host of others named after the virtues or vices they display. These characters, places, and actions exist solely to illustrate religious doctrine. Allegory tends to be definitive rather than suggestive. It drives meaning into a corner and keeps it there. Most modern writers prefer the exploratory nature of symbol to the reductive nature of pure allegory.

Stories often include symbols that you may or may not perceive on a first reading. Their subtle use is a sign of a writer's skill in weaving symbols into the fabric of the characters' lives. Symbols may sometimes escape you, but that is probably better than finding symbols where only literal meanings are intended. Allow the text to help you determine whether a symbolic reading is appropriate.

By keeping track of the total context of the story, you should be able to decide whether your reading is reasonable and consistent with the other facts; plenty of lemons in literature yield no symbolic meaning even if they are squeezed. Be sensitive to the meanings that the author associates with people, places, objects, and actions. You may not associate home with provincial innocence as Hemingway does in "Soldier's Home," but a close reading of the story will permit you to see how and why he constructs that symbolic meaning. If you treat stories like people — with tact and care — they ordinarily are accessible and enjoyable.

The next three stories — Tobias Wolff's "That Room," Ralph Ellison's "Battle Royal," and Michael Oppenheimer's "The Paring Knife" — rely on symbols to convey meanings that go far beyond the specific incidents described in their plots.

TOBIAS WOLFF (B. 1945)

Born in Birmingham, Alabama, Tobias Wolff grew up in the state of Washington. After quitting high school, he worked on a ship and for a carnival. In the army he served four years as a paratrooper, after which he studied to pass the entrance exams for Oxford University, from which he graduated with high honors. He has published two memoirs — *This Boy's Life* (1989) and *In Pharaoh's Army: Memories of the Lost War* (1994). In addition to his two novels, *The Barracks Thief* (1984) and *Old School* (2003), he has published four short story collections: *In the Garden of North American Martyrs* (1981), *Back in the World* (1985), *The Night in Question* (1996), and *Our Story Begins* (2008). Wolff has taught literature and creative writing courses at Stanford University since 1997.

> **WHEN I WRITE** "I revise until I can't see a way to make a story better. Only then do I show it to a few trusted readers. If they spot a real weakness, I'll go back to work. Knowing when it's finished is a matter of instinct — an instinct that grows sharper with time and experience." —TOBIAS WOLFF

That Room   *2008*

The summer after my first year of high school, I got a case of independence and started hitchhiking to farms up and down the valley for daywork picking berries and mucking out stalls. Then I found a place where the farmer paid me ten cents an hour over minimum wage, and his plump, childless wife fed me lunch and fussed over me while I ate, so I stayed on there until school started.

While shoveling shit or hacking weeds out of a drainage ditch, I'd sometimes stop to gaze out toward the far fields, where the hands, as the farmer called them, were bucking bales of hay into a wagon, stacking them to teetering heights. Now and then a bark of laughter reached me, a tag end of conversation. The farmer hadn't let me work in the hay because I was too small, but I beefed up over the winter, and the following summer he let me join the crew.

So I was a hand. A hand! I went a little crazy with that word, with the pleasure of applying it to myself. Having a job like this changed everything. It delivered you from the reach of your parents, from the caustic scrutiny of your friends. It set you free among strangers in the eventful world, where you could practice being someone else until you *were* someone else. It put money in your pocket and allowed you to believe that your other life — your inessential, parenthetical life at home and school — was just a sop to those deluded enough to imagine you still needed them.

There were three others working the fields with me: the farmer's shy, muscle-bound nephew, Clemson, who was in my class at school but to whom I condescended because he was just an inexperienced kid, and two Mexican brothers, Miguel and Eduardo. Miguel, short and stolid and solitary, spoke very little English, but rakish Eduardo did the talking for both of them. While the rest of us did the heavy work, Eduardo provided advice about girls and told stories in which he featured as a trickster and deft, indefatigable swords-man. He played it for laughs, but in the very materials of his storytelling — the dance halls and bars, the bumbling border guards, the clod-brained farmers and their insatiable wives, the larcenous cops, the whores who loved him — I felt the actuality of a life I knew nothing about yet somehow contrived to want for myself: a real life in a real world.

While Eduardo talked, Miguel labored silently beside us, now and then grunting with the weight of a bale, his acne-scarred face flushed with heat, narrow eyes narrowed even tighter against the sun. Clemson and I sprinted and flagged, sprinted and flagged, laughing at Eduardo's stories, goading him with questions. Miguel never flagged, and never laughed. He sometimes watched his brother with what appeared to be mild curiosity; that was all.

The farmer, who owned a big spread with a lot of hay to bring in, should have hired more hands. He had only the four of us, and there was always the danger of rain. He was a relaxed, amiable man, but as the season wore on he grew anxious and began to push us harder and keep us longer. During the last week or so I spent the nights with Clemson's family, just down the road, so I could get to the farm with the others at sunup and work until dusk. The bales were heavy with dew when we started bringing them in. The air in the loft turned steamy from fermentation, and Eduardo warned the farmer that the hay might combust, but he held us to his schedule. Limping, sunburned, covered with scratches, I could hardly get out of bed in the morning. But although I griped with Clemson and Eduardo, I was secretly glad to take my place beside them, to work as if I had no choice.

Eduardo's car broke down toward the end of the week, and Clemson started driving him and Miguel to and from the decrepit motel where they lived with other seasonal workers. Sometimes, pulling up to their door, we'd all just sit there, saying nothing. We were that tired. Then one night Eduardo asked us in for a drink. Clemson, being a good boy, tried to beg off, but I got out with Miguel and Eduardo, knowing he wouldn't leave me. "Come on, Clem," I said, "don't be a homo." He looked at me, then turned the engine off.

That room. Jesus. The brothers had done their best, making their beds, keeping their clothes neatly folded in open suitcases, but you got swamped by the smell of mildew the moment you stepped inside. The floor was mushy underfoot and shedding squares of drab linoleum, the ceiling bowed and stained. The overhead light didn't quite reach the corners. Behind the mildew was another, unsettling smell. Clemson was a fastidious guy and writhed in distress as I made a show of being right at home.

We poured rye into our empty stomachs and listened to Eduardo, and before long we were all drunk. Someone came to the door and spoke to him in Spanish, and Eduardo went outside and didn't come back. Miguel and I kept drinking. Clemson was half asleep, his chin declining slowly toward his chest and snapping up again. Then Miguel looked at me. He slitted his eyes and looked at me hard, without blinking, and began to protest an injustice done him by our boss, or maybe another boss. I could barely understand his English, and he kept breaking into Spanish, which I didn't understand at all. But he was angry — I understood that much.

At some point he went across the room and came back and put a pistol 10 on the table, right in front of him. A revolver, long barrel, most of the bluing worn off. Miguel stared at me over the pistol and resumed his complaint, entirely in Spanish. He was looking at me, but I knew he was seeing someone else. I had rarely heard him speak before. Now the words poured out in an aggrieved singsong, and I saw that his own voice was lashing him on somehow, the very sound of his indignation proving that he had been wronged, feeding his rage, making him hate whoever he thought I was. I was too afraid to speak. All I could do was smile.

That room — once you enter it, you never really leave. You can forget you're there, you can go on as if you hold the reins, that the course of your life, yea even its *length*, will reflect the force of your character and the wisdom of your judgments. And then you hit an icy patch on a turn one sunny March day and the wheel in your hands becomes a joke and you no more than a spectator to your own dreamy slide toward the verge, and then you remember where you are.

Or you board a bus with thirty other young men. It's early, just before dawn. That's when the buses always leave, their lights dimmed, to avoid the attention of the Quakers outside the gate, but it doesn't work and they're waiting, silently holding up their signs, looking at you not with reproach but with sadness and sympathy as the bus drives past them and on toward the airport and the plane that will take you where you would not go — and at this moment you know exactly what your desires count for, and your plans, and all your strength of body and will. Then you know where you are, as you will know where you are when those you love die before their time — the time you had planned for them, for yourself with them — and when your daily allowance of words and dreams is withheld from you, and when your daughter drives the car straight into a tree. And if she walks away without a scratch you still feel that dark ceiling close overhead, and know where you are. And what can you do but what you did back in this awful room, with Miguel hating you for nothing and a pistol ready to hand? Smile and hope for a change of subject.

It came, this time. Clemson bolted up from his chair, bent forward, and puked all over the table. Miguel stopped talking. He stared at Clemson as if he'd never seen him before, and when Clemson began retching again Miguel jumped up and grabbed him by the shirt and pushed him toward the door. I took over and helped Clemson outside while Miguel looked on, shrieking his disgust. Disgust! Now *he* was the fastidious one. Revulsion had trumped rage, had trumped even hatred. Oh, how sweetly I tended Clemson that night! I thought he'd saved my life. And maybe he had.

The farmer's barn burned to the ground that winter. When I heard about it, I said, "Didn't I tell him? I did, I told that stupid sumbitch not to put up wet hay."

CONSIDERATIONS FOR CRITICAL THINKING AND WRITING

1. FIRST RESPONSE. Why does the narrator describe his "life at home and school" as "inessental, parenthetical" (para. 3) in comparison to "a real life in a real world" (para. 4)?

2. Why is the work the narrator does on the farm important to him?

3. How are Eduardo and Miguel foils to one another?

4. Why is Miguel so angry?

5. How does the motel room and what happens in it take on symbolic meaning in this plot?

6. Discuss the significance of paragraphs 11 through 12. Why do you think they appear where they do and are set off from the rest of the story?

7. How is the bus trip described in paragraph 12 relevant to the narrator's experience? What kind of perspective on life is expressed in this paragraph?

8. Discuss your reading of the story's final paragraph and how it relates to the rest of the narration.

9. CONNECTION TO ANOTHER SELECTION. Discuss the similarities and differences related to the nature of what the protagonist learns about life in "That Room" and in either John Updike's "A & P" (p. 149) or Ralph Ellison's "Battle Royal" (p. 177).

RALPH ELLISON (1914–1994)

Born in Oklahoma and educated at the Tuskegee Institute in Alabama, where he studied music, Ralph Ellison gained his reputation as a writer on the strength of his only published novel, *Invisible Man* (1952). He also published some scattered short stories and two collections of essays, *Shadow and Act* (1964) and *Going to the Territory* (1986). Although his writing was not extensive, it is important because Ellison

Everett Collection / Newscom.

wrote about race relations in the context of universal human concerns. *Invisible Man* is the story of a young black man who moves from the South to the North and discovers what it means to be black in America. "Battle Royal," published in 1947 as a short story, became the first chapter of *Invisible Man*. It concerns the beginning of the protagonist's long struggle for an adult identity in a world made corrupt by racial prejudice.

Battle Royal   1947

It goes a long way back, some twenty years. All my life I had been looking
for something, and everywhere I turned someone tried to tell me what it
was. I accepted their answers too, though they were often in contradiction
and even self-contradictory. I was naive. I was looking for myself and asking everyone except myself questions which I, and only I, could answer. It
took me a long time and much painful boomeranging of my expectations
to achieve a realization everyone else appears to have been born with: That I
am nobody but myself. But first I had to discover that I am an invisible man!

And yet I am no freak of nature, nor of history. I was in the cards, other
things having been equal (or unequal) eighty-five years ago. I am not ashamed
of my grandparents for having been slaves. I am only ashamed of myself for
having at one time been ashamed. About eighty-five years ago they were told
that they were free, united with others of our country in everything pertain-
ing to the common good, and, in everything social, separate like the fingers of
the hand. And they believed it. They exulted in it. They stayed in their place,
worked hard, and brought up my father to do the same. But my grandfather is
the one. He was an odd old guy, my grandfather, and I am told I take after him.
It was he who caused the trouble. On his deathbed he called my father to him
and said, "Son, after I'm gone I want you to keep up the good fight. I never
told you, but our life is a war and I have been a traitor all my born days, a spy
in the enemy's country ever since I gave up my gun back in the Reconstruction. Live with your head in the lion's mouth. I want you to overcome 'em
with yeses, undermine 'em with grins, agree 'em to death and destruction,
let 'em swoller you till they vomit or bust wide open." They thought the old
man had gone out of his mind. He had been the meekest of men. The younger
children were rushed from the room, the shades drawn and the flame of the
lamp turned so low that it sputtered on the wick like the old man's breathing.
"Learn it to the young-uns," he whispered fiercely; then he died.

But my folks were more alarmed over his last words than over his dying.
It was as though he had not died at all, his words caused so much anxiety. I
was warned emphatically to forget what he had said and, indeed, this is the
first time it has been mentioned outside the family circle. It had a tremendous
effect upon me, however. I could never be sure of what he meant. Grandfather
had been a quiet old man who never made any trouble, yet on his deathbed
he had called himself a traitor and a spy, and he had spoken of his meekness
as a dangerous activity. It became a constant puzzle which lay unanswered in
the back of my mind. And whenever things went well for me I remembered
my grandfather and felt guilty and uncomfortable. It was as though I was carrying out his advice in spite of myself. And to make it worse, everyone loved
me for it. I was praised by the most lily-white men of the town. I was considered an example of desirable conduct — just as my grandfather had been.
And what puzzled me was that the old man had defined it as *treachery*. When
I was praised for my conduct I felt a guilt that in some way I was doing something that was really against the wishes of the white folks, that if they had

understood they would have desired me to act just the opposite, that I should have been sulky and mean, and that that really would have been what they wanted, even though they were fooled and thought they wanted me to act as I did. It made me afraid that some day they would look upon me as a traitor and I would be lost. Still I was more afraid to act any other way because they didn't like that at all. The old man's words were like a curse. On my graduation day I delivered an oration in which I showed that humility was the secret, indeed, the very essence of progress. (Not that I believed this — how could I, remembering my grandfather? — I only believed that it worked.) It was a great success. Everyone praised me and I was invited to give the speech at a gathering of the town's leading white citizens. It was a triumph for our whole community.

It was in the main ballroom of the leading hotel. When I got there I discovered that it was on the occasion of a smoker, and I was told that since I was to be there anyway I might as well take part in the battle royal to be fought by some of my schoolmates as part of the entertainment. The battle royal came first.

All of the town's big shots were there in their tuxedoes, wolfing down   5 the buffet foods, drinking beer and whiskey and smoking black cigars. It was a large room with a high ceiling. Chairs were arranged in neat rows around three sides of a portable boxing ring. The fourth side was clear, revealing a gleaming space of polished floor. I had some misgivings over the battle royal, by the way. Not from a distaste for fighting, but because I didn't care too much for the other fellows who were to take part. They were tough guys who seemed to have no grandfather's curse worrying their minds. No one could mistake their toughness. And besides, I suspected that fighting a battle royal might detract from the dignity of my speech. In those pre-invisible days I visualized myself as a potential Booker T. Washington. But the other fellows didn't care too much for me either, and there were nine of them. I felt superior to them in my way, and I didn't like the manner in which we were all crowded together into the servants' elevator. Nor did they like my being there. In fact, as the warmly lighted floors flashed past the elevator we had words over the fact that I, by taking part in the fight, had knocked one of their friends out of a night's work.

We were led out of the elevator through a rococo hall into an anteroom and told to get into our fighting togs. Each of us was issued a pair of boxing gloves and ushered out into the big mirrored hall, which we entered looking cautiously about us and whispering, lest we might accidentally be heard above the noise of the room. It was foggy with cigar smoke. And already the whiskey was taking effect. I was shocked to see some of the most important men of the town quite tipsy. They were all there — bankers, lawyers, judges, doctors, fire chiefs, teachers, merchants. Even one of the more fashionable pastors. Something we could not see was going on up front. A clarinet was vibrating sensuously and the men were standing up and moving eagerly forward. We were a small tight group, clustered together, our bare upper bodies touching and shining with anticipatory sweat; while up front the big shots were becoming increasingly excited over something we still could not see. Suddenly I heard the school superintendent, who had told me to come, yell, "Bring up the shines, gentlemen! Bring up the little shines!"

We were rushed up to the front of the ballroom, where it smelled even more strongly of tobacco and whiskey. Then we were pushed into place. I almost wet my pants. A sea of faces, some hostile, some amused, ringed around us, and in the center, facing us, stood a magnificent blonde — stark naked. There was dead silence. I felt a blast of cold air chill me. I tried to back away, but they were behind me and around me. Some of the boys stood with lowered heads, trembling. I felt a wave of irrational guilt and fear. My teeth chattered, my skin turned to goose flesh, my knees knocked. Yet I was strongly attracted and looked in spite of myself. Had the price of looking been blindness, I would have looked. The hair was yellow like that of a circus kewpie doll, the face heavily powdered and rouged, as though to form an abstract mask, the eyes hollow and smeared a cool blue, the color of a baboon's butt. I felt a desire to spit upon her as my eyes brushed slowly over her body. Her breasts were firm and round as the domes of East Indian temples, and I stood so close as to see the fine skin texture and beads of pearly perspiration glistening like dew around the pink and erected buds of her nipples. I wanted at one and the same time to run from the room, to sink through the floor, or go to her and cover her from my eyes and the eyes of the others with my body; to feel the soft thighs, to caress her and destroy her, to love her and murder her, to hide from her, and yet to stroke where below the small American flag tattooed upon her belly her thighs formed a capital V. I had a notion that of all in the room she saw only me with her impersonal eyes.

And then she began to dance, a slow sensuous movement; the smoke of a hundred cigars clinging to her like the thinnest of veils. She seemed like a fair bird-girl girdled in veils calling to me from the angry surface of some gray and threatening sea. I was transported. Then I became aware of the clarinet playing and the big shots yelling at us. Some threatened us if we looked and others if we did not. On my right I saw one boy faint. And now a man grabbed a silver pitcher from a table and stepped close as he dashed ice water upon him and stood him up and forced two of us to support him as his head hung and moans issued from his thick bluish lips. Another boy began to plead to go home. He was the largest of the group, wearing dark red fighting trunks much too small to conceal the erection which projected from him as though in answer to the insinuating low-registered moaning of the clarinet. He tried to hide himself with his boxing gloves.

And all the while the blonde continued dancing, smiling faintly at the big shots who watched her with fascination, and faintly smiling at our fear. I noticed a certain merchant who followed her hungrily, his lips loose and drooling. He was a large man who wore diamond studs in a shirtfront which swelled with the ample paunch underneath, and each time the blonde swayed her undulating hips he ran his hand through the thin hair of his bald head and, with his arms upheld, his posture clumsy like that of an intoxicated panda, wound his belly in a slow and obscene grind. This creature was completely hypnotized. The music had quickened. As the dancer flung herself about with a detached expression on her face, the men began reaching out to touch her. I could see their beefy fingers sink into the soft flesh. Some of the others tried to stop them as she began to move around the floor in grace- ful circles, as they gave chase, slipping and sliding over the polished floor. It was mad. Chairs went crashing, drinks were spilt, as they ran laughing and howling after her. They caught her just as she reached a door, raised her from the floor, and tossed her as college boys are tossed at a hazing, and above her red, fixed-smiling lips I saw the terror and disgust in her eyes, almost like my own terror and that which I saw in some of the other boys. As I watched, they tossed her twice and her soft breasts seemed to flatten against the air and her legs flung wildly as she spun. Some of the more sober ones helped her to escape. And I started off the floor, heading for the anteroom with the rest of the boys.

Some were still crying in hysteria. But as we tried to leave we were stopped 10 and ordered to get into the ring. There was nothing to do but what we were told. All ten of us climbed under the ropes and allowed ourselves to be blind- folded with broad bands of white cloth. One of the men seemed to feel a bit sympathetic and tried to cheer us up as we stood with our backs against the ropes. Some of us tried to grin. "See that boy over there?" one of the men said. "I want you to run across at the bell and give it to him right in the belly. If you don't get him, I'm going to get you. I don't like his looks." Each of us was told the same. The blindfolds were put on. Yet even then I had been going over my speech. In my mind each word was as bright as flame. I felt the cloth pressed into place, and frowned so that it would be loosened when I relaxed.

But now I felt a sudden fit of blind terror. I was unused to darkness. It was as though I had suddenly found myself in a dark room filled with poison- ous cottonmouths. I could hear the bleary voices yelling insistently for the battle royal to begin.

"Get going in there!"

"Let me at that big nigger!"

I strained to pick up the school superintendent's voice, as though to squeeze some security out of that slightly more familiar sound.

"Let me at those black sonsabitches!" someone yelled.   15

"No, Jackson, no!" another voice yelled. "Here, somebody, help me hold Jack."

"I want to get at that ginger-colored nigger. Tear him limb from limb," the first voice yelled.

I stood against the ropes trembling. For in those days I was what they called ginger-colored, and he sounded as though he might crunch me between his teeth like a crisp ginger cookie.

Quite a struggle was going on. Chairs were being kicked about and I could hear voices grunting as with a terrific effort. I wanted to see, to see more desperately than ever before. But the blindfold was tight as a thick skin- puckering scab and when I raised my gloved hands to push the layers of white aside a voice yelled, "Oh, no you don't, black bastard! Leave that alone!"

"Ring the bell before Jackson kills him a coon!" someone boomed in the 20
sudden silence. And I heard the bell clang and the sound of the feet scuffling
forward.

A glove smacked against my head. I pivoted, striking out stiffly as someone went past, and felt the jar ripple along the length of my arm to my shoulder. Then it seemed as though all nine of the boys had turned upon me at
once. Blows pounded me from all sides while I struck out as best I could. So
many blows landed upon me that I wondered if I were not the only blindfolded fighter in the ring, or if the man called Jackson hadn't succeeded in
getting me after all.

Blindfolded, I could no longer control my motions. I had no dignity.
I stumbled about like a baby or a drunken man. The smoke had become
thicker and with each new blow it seemed to sear and further restrict my
lungs. My saliva became like hot bitter glue. A glove connected with my head,
filling my mouth with warm blood. It was everywhere. I could not tell if the
moisture I felt upon my body was sweat or blood. A blow landed hard against
the nape of my neck. I felt myself going over, my head hitting the floor. Streaks
of blue light filled the black world behind the blindfold. I lay prone, pretending that I was knocked out, but felt myself seized by hands and yanked to
my feet. "Get going, black boy! Mix it up!" My arms were like lead, my head
smarting from blows. I managed to feel my way to the ropes and held on,
trying to catch my breath. A glove landed in my mid-section and I went over
again, feeling as though the smoke had become a knife jabbed into my guts.
Pushed this way and that by the legs milling around me, I finally pulled erect
and discovered that I could see the black, sweat-washed forms weaving in the
smoky-blue atmosphere like drunken dancers weaving to the rapid drumlike
thuds of blows.

Everyone fought hysterically. It was complete anarchy. Everybody fought
everybody else. No group fought together for long. Two, three, four, fought
one, then turned to fight each other, were themselves attacked. Blows landed
below the belt and in the kidney, with the gloves open as well as closed, and
with my eye partly opened now there was not so much terror. I moved carefully, avoiding blows, although not too many to attract attention, fighting from
group to group. The boys groped about like blind, cautious crabs crouching
to protect their mid-sections, their heads pulled in short against their shoulders, their arms stretched nervously before them, with their fists testing the
smoke-filled air like the knobbed feelers of hypersensitive snails. In one corner
I glimpsed a boy violently punching the air and heard him scream in pain as
he smashed his hand against a ring post. For a second I saw him bent over
holding his hand, then going down as a blow caught his unprotected head.
I played one group against the other, slipping in and throwing a punch then
stepping out of range while pushing the others into the melee to take the blows
blindly aimed at me. The smoke was agonizing and there were no rounds, no
bells at three minute intervals to relieve our exhaustion. The room spun round
me, a swirl of lights, smoke, sweating bodies surrounded by tense white faces. I
bled from both nose and mouth, the blood spattering upon my chest.

The men kept yelling, "Slug him, black boy! Knock his guts out!"

"Uppercut him! Kill him! Kill that big boy!"   25

Taking a fake fall, I saw a boy going down heavily beside me as though we were felled by a single blow, saw a sneaker-clad foot shoot into his groin as the two who had knocked him down stumbled upon him. I rolled out of range, feeling a twinge of nausea.

The harder we fought the more threatening the men became. And yet, I had begun to worry about my speech again. How would it go? Would they recognize my ability? What would they give me?

I was fighting automatically when suddenly I noticed that one after another of the boys was leaving the ring. I was surprised, filled with panic, as though I had been left alone with an unknown danger. Then I understood. The boys had arranged it among themselves. It was the custom for the two men left in the ring to slug it out for the winner's prize. I discovered this too late. When the bell sounded two men in tuxedos leaped into the ring and removed the blindfold. I found myself facing Tatlock, the biggest of the gang. I felt sick at my stomach. Hardly had the bell stopped ringing in my ears than it clanged again and I saw him moving swiftly toward me. Thinking of nothing else to do I hit him smash on the nose. He kept coming, bringing the rank sharp violence of stale sweat. His face was a black blank of a face, only his eyes alive — with hate of me and aglow with a feverish terror from what had happened to us all. I became anxious. I wanted to deliver my speech and he came at me as though he meant to beat it out of me. I smashed him again and again, taking his blows as they came. Then on a sudden impulse I struck him lightly and as we clinched, I whispered, "Fake like I knocked you out, you can have the prize."

"I'll break your behind," he whispered hoarsely.

"For *them*?"   30

"For *me*, sonofabitch!"

They were yelling for us to break it up and Tatlock spun me half around with a blow, and as a joggled camera sweeps in a reeling scene, I saw the howling red faces crouching tense beneath the cloud of blue-gray smoke. For a moment the world wavered, unraveled, flowed, then my head cleared and Tatlock bounced before me. That fluttering shadow before my eyes was his jabbing left hand. Then falling forward, my head against his damp shoulder, I whispered,

"I'll make it five dollars more."

"Go to hell!"

But his muscles relaxed a trifle beneath my pressure and I breathed,   35
"Seven?"

"Give it to your ma," he said, ripping me beneath the heart.

And while I still held him I butted him and moved away. I felt myself bombarded with punches. I fought back with hopeless desperation. I wanted to deliver my speech more than anything else in the world, because I felt that only these men could judge truly my ability, and now this stupid clown was ruining my chances. I began fighting carefully now, moving in to punch him and out again with my greater speed. A lucky blow to his chin and I had him going too — until I heard a loud voice yell, "I got my money on the big boy."

Hearing this, I almost dropped my guard. I was confused: Should I try to win against the voice out there? Would not this go against my speech, and was not this a moment for humility, for nonresistance? A blow to my head as I danced about sent my right eye popping like a jack-in-the-box and settled my dilemma. The room went red as I fell. It was a dream fall, my body languid and fastidious as to where to land, until the floor became impatient and smashed up to meet me. A moment later I came to. An hypnotic voice said FIVE emphatically. And I lay there, hazily watching a dark red spot of my own blood shaping itself into a butterfly, glistening and soaking into the soiled gray world of the canvas.

When the voice drawled TEN I was lifted up and dragged to a chair. I sat dazed. My eye pained and swelled with each throb of my pounding heart and I wondered if now I would be allowed to speak. I was wringing wet, my mouth still bleeding. We were grouped along the wall now. The other boys ignored me as they congratulated Tatlock and speculated as to how much they would be paid. One boy whimpered over his smashed hand. Looking up front, I saw attendants in white jackets rolling the portable ring away and placing a small square rug in the vacant space surrounded by chairs. Perhaps, I thought, I will stand on the rug to deliver my speech.

Then the M.C. called to us, "Come on up here boys and get your money." 40 We ran forward to where the men laughed and talked in their chairs, waiting. Everyone seemed friendly now.

"There it is on the rug," the man said. I saw the rug covered with coins of all dimensions and a few crumpled bills. But what excited me, scattered here and there, were the gold pieces.

"Boys, it's all yours," the man said. "You get all you grab."

"That's right, Sambo," a blond man said, winking at me confidentially.

I trembled with excitement, forgetting my pain. I would get the gold and the bills, I thought. I would use both hands. I would throw my body against the boys nearest me to block them from the gold.

"Get down around the rug now," the man commanded, "and don't any- 45 one touch it until I give the signal."

"This ought to be good," I heard.

As told, we got around the square rug on our knees. Slowly the man raised his freckled hand as we followed it upward with our eyes.

I heard, "These niggers look like they're about to pray!"

Then, "Ready," the man said. "Go!"

I lunged for a yellow coin lying on the blue design of the carpet, touch- 50 ing it and sending a surprised shriek to join those rising around me. I tried frantically to remove my hand but could not let go. A hot, violent force tore through my body, shaking me like a wet rat. The rug was electrified. The hair bristled up on my head as I shook myself free. My muscles jumped, my nerves jangled, writhed. But I saw that this was not stopping the other boys. Laughing in fear and embarrassment, some were holding back and scooping up the coins knocked off by the painful contortions of the others. The men roared above us as we struggled.

"Pick it up, goddamnit, pick it up!" someone called like a bass-voiced parrot. "Go on, get it!"

I crawled rapidly around the floor, picking up the coins, trying to avoid the coppers and to get greenbacks and the gold. Ignoring the shock by laughing, as I brushed the coins off quickly, I discovered that I could contain the electricity—a contradiction, but it works. Then the men began to push us onto the rug. Laughing embarrassedly, we struggled out of their hands and kept after the coins. We were all wet and slippery and hard to hold. Suddenly I saw a boy lifted into the air, glistening with sweat like a circus seal, and dropped, his wet back landing flush upon the charged rug, heard him yell and saw him literally dance upon his back, his elbows beating a frenzied tattoo upon the floor, his muscles twitching like the flesh of a horse stung by many flies. When he finally rolled off, his face was gray and no one stopped him when he ran from the floor amid booming laughter.

"Get the money," the M.C. called. "That's good hard American cash!"

And we snatched and grabbed, snatched and grabbed. I was careful not to come too close to the rug now, and when I felt the hot whiskey breath descend upon me like a cloud of foul air I reached out and grabbed the leg of a chair. It was occupied and I held on desperately.

"Leggo, nigger! Leggo!"

The huge face wavered down to mine as he tried to push me free. But my body was slippery and he was too drunk. It was Mr. Colcord, who owned a chain of movie houses and "entertainment palaces." Each time he grabbed me I slipped out of his hands. It became a real struggle. I feared the rug more than I did the drunk, so I held on, surprising myself for a moment by trying to topple *him* upon the rug. It was such an enormous idea that I found myself actually carrying it out. I tried not to be obvious, yet when I grabbed his leg, trying to tumble him out of the chair, he raised up roaring with laughter, and, looking at me with soberness dead in the eye, kicked me viciously in the chest. The chair leg flew out of my hand and I felt myself going and rolled. It was as though I had rolled through a bed of hot coals. It seemed a whole century would pass before I would roll free, a century in which I was seared through the deepest levels of my body to the fearful breath within me and the breath seared and heated to the point of explosion. It'll all be over in a flash, I thought as I rolled clear. It'll all be over in a flash.

But not yet, the men on the other side were waiting, red faces swollen as though from apoplexy as they bent forward in their chairs. Seeing their fingers coming toward me I rolled away as a fumbled football rolls off the receiver's fingertips, back into the coals. That time I luckily sent the rug sliding out of place and heard the coins ringing against the floor and the boys scuffling to pick them up and the M.C. calling, "All right, boys, that's all. Go get dressed and get your money."

55

I was limp as a dish rag. My back felt as though it had been beaten with wires.

When we had dressed the M.C. came in and gave us each five dollars, except Tatlock, who got ten for being last in the ring. Then he told us to leave. I was not to get a chance to deliver my speech, I thought. I was going out into the dim alley in despair when I was stopped and told to go back. I returned to the ballroom, where the men were pushing back their chairs and gathering in groups to talk.

The M.C. knocked on a table for quiet. "Gentlemen," he said, "we almost forgot an important part of the program. A most serious part, gentlemen. This boy was brought here to deliver a speech which he made at his graduation yesterday . . ."

"Bravo!"

"I'm told that he is the smartest boy we've got out there in Greenwood. I'm told that he knows more big words than a pocket-sized dictionary."

Much applause and laughter.

"So now, gentlemen, I want you to give him your attention."

There was still laughter as I faced them, my mouth dry, my eye throbbing. I began slowly, but evidently my throat was tense, because they began shouting, "Louder! Louder!"

"We of the younger generation extol the wisdom of that great leader and educator," I shouted, "who first spoke these flaming words of wisdom: 'A ship lost at sea for many days suddenly sighted a friendly vessel. From the mast of the unfortunate vessel was seen a signal: "Water, water; we die of thirst!" The answer from the friendly vessel came back: "Cast down your bucket where you are." The captain of the distressed vessel, at last heeding the injunction, cast down his bucket, and it came up full of fresh sparkling water from the mouth of the Amazon River.' And like him I say, and in his words, 'To those of my race who depend upon bettering their condition in a foreign land, or who underestimate the importance of cultivating friendly relations with the Southern white man, who is his next-door neighbor, I would say: "Cast down your bucket where you are" — cast it down in making friends in every manly way of the people of all races by whom we are surrounded . . .'"

I spoke automatically and with such fervor that I did not realize that the men were still talking and laughing until my dry mouth, filling up with blood from the cut, almost strangled me. I coughed, wanting to stop and go to one of the tall brass, sand-filled spittoons to relieve myself, but a few of the men, especially the superintendent, were listening and I was afraid. So I gulped it down, blood, saliva, and all, and continued. (What powers of endurance I had during those days! What enthusiasm! What a belief in the rightness of things!) I spoke even louder in spite of the pain. But still they talked and still they laughed, as though deaf with cotton in dirty ears. So I spoke with greater emotional emphasis. I closed my ears and swallowed blood until I was nauseated. The speech seemed a hundred times as long as before, but I could not leave out a single word. All had to be said, each memorized nuance considered, rendered. Nor was that all. Whenever I uttered a word of three or more syllables a group of voices would yell for me to repeat it. I used the phrase "social responsibility" and they yelled:

"What's that word you say, boy?"

"Social responsibility," I said.

"What?"   70

"Social . . ."

"Louder."

". . . responsibility."

"More!"

"Respon —"   75

"Repeat!"

"— sibility."

The room filled with the uproar of laughter until, no doubt, distracted by having to gulp down my blood, I made a mistake and yelled a phrase I had often seen denounced in newspaper editorials, heard debated in private.

"Social . . ."

"What?" they yelled.   80

". . . equality —"

The laughter hung smokelike in the sudden stillness. I opened my eyes, puzzled. Sounds of displeasure filled the room. The M.C. rushed forward. They shouted hostile phrases at me. But I did not understand.

A small dry mustached man in the front row blared out, "Say that slowly, son!"

"What, sir?"

"What you just said!"   85

"Social responsibility, sir," I said.

"You weren't being smart, were you, boy?" he said, not unkindly.

"No, sir!"

"You sure that about 'equality' was a mistake?"

"Oh, yes, sir," I said. "I was swallowing blood."   90

"Well, you had better speak more slowly so we can understand. We mean to do right by you, but you've got to know your place at all times. All right, now, go on with your speech."

I was afraid. I wanted to leave but I wanted also to speak and I was afraid they'd snatch me down.

"Thank you, sir," I said, beginning where I had left off, and having them ignore me as before.

Yet when I finished there was a thunderous applause. I was surprised to see the superintendent come forth with a package wrapped in white tissue paper, and, gesturing for quiet, address the men.

"Gentlemen, you see that I did not overpraise this boy. He makes a   95
good speech and some day he'll lead his people in the proper paths. And I don't have to tell you that that is important in these days and times. This is a good, smart boy, and so to encourage him in the right direction, in the name of the Board of Education I wish to present him a prize in the form of this . . ."

He paused, removing the tissue paper and revealing a gleaming calfskin brief case.

". . . in the form of this first-class article from Shad Whitmore's shop."

"Boy," he said, addressing me, "take this prize and keep it well. Consider it a badge of office. Prize it. Keep developing as you are and some day it will be filled with important papers that will help shape the destiny of your people."

I was so moved that I could hardly express my thanks. A rope of bloody saliva forming a shape like an undiscovered continent drooled upon the leather and I wiped it quickly away. I felt an importance that I had never dreamed.

"Open it and see what's inside," I was told.   100

My fingers a-tremble, I complied, smelling the fresh leather and finding an official-looking document inside. It was a scholarship to the state college for Negroes. My eyes filled with tears and I ran awkwardly off the floor.

I was overjoyed; I did not even mind when I discovered that the gold pieces I had scrambled for were brass pocket tokens advertising a certain make of automobile.

When I reached home everyone was excited. Next day the neighbors came to congratulate me. I even felt safe from grandfather, whose deathbed curse usually spoiled my triumphs. I stood beneath his photograph with my brief case in hand and smiled triumphantly into his stolid black peasant's face. It was a face that fascinated me. The eyes seemed to follow everywhere I went.

That night I dreamed I was at a circus with him and that he refused to laugh at the clowns no matter what they did. Then later he told me to open my brief case and read what was inside and I did, finding an official envelope stamped with the state seal; and inside the envelope I found another and another, endlessly, and I thought I would fall of weariness. "Them's years," he said. "Now open that one." And I did and in it I found an engraved document containing a short message in letters of gold. "Read it," my grandfather said. "Out loud!"

"To Whom It May Concern," I intoned. "Keep This Nigger-Boy Running."   105
I awoke with the old man's laughter ringing in my ears.

(It was a dream I was to remember and dream again for many years after. But at that time I had no insight into its meaning. First I had to attend college.)

Considerations for Critical Thinking and Writing

1. **First response.** Discuss how the protagonist's expectations are similar to what has come to be known as the American dream — the assumption that ambition, hard work, perseverance, intelligence, and virtue always lead to success. Do you believe in the American dream?

2. How does the first paragraph of the story sum up the conflict that the narrator confronts? In what sense is he "invisible"?

3. What is the symbolic significance of the naked blonde? What details reveal that she represents more than a sexual tease in the story?

4. How does the battle in the boxing ring and the scramble for money afterward suggest the kind of control whites have over blacks in the story?

5. How can the dream at the end of the story be related to the major incidents that precede it?

6. Given the grandfather's advice, explain how "meekness" can be a "dangerous activity" and a weapon against oppression.

7. Imagine the story as told from a third-person point of view. How would this change the story? Do you think the story would be more or less effective told from a third-person point of view? Explain your answer.

8. CONNECTION TO ANOTHER SELECTION. Compare and contrast Ellison's view of the South with William Faulkner's in "A Rose for Emily" (p. 54).

MICHAEL OPPENHEIMER (B. 1943)

Born in Berkeley, California, Michael Oppenheimer grew up on a cattle ranch in the Rocky Mountains of southwest Colorado. He graduated from Antioch College and earned a master of arts in English and art at Lone Mountain College / University of San Francisco. Oppenheimer has published short stories and worked as a reporter, teacher, and publisher of a press; he currently lives in Bellingham, Washington, where he creates kinetic environmental art.

The Paring Knife   *1982*

I found a knife under the refrigerator while the woman I love and I were cleaning our house. It was a small paring knife that we lost many years before and had since forgotten about. I showed the knife to the woman I love and she said, "Oh. Where did you find it?" After I told her, she put the knife on the table and then went into the next room and continued to clean. While I cleaned the kitchen floor, I remembered something that happened four years before that explained how the knife had gotten under the refrigerator.

We had eaten a large dinner and had drunk many glasses of wine. We turned all the lights out, took our clothing off, and went to bed. We thought we would make love, but something happened and we had an argument while making love. We had never experienced such a thing. We both became extremely angry. I said some very hurtful things to the woman I love. She kicked at me in bed and I got out and went into the kitchen. I fumbled for a chair and sat down. I wanted to rest my arms on the table and then rest my head in my arms, but I felt the dirty dishes on the table and they were in the way. I became incensed. I swept everything that was on the table onto the floor. The noise was tremendous, but then the room was very quiet and I suddenly felt sad. I thought I had destroyed everything. I began to cry. The woman I love came into the kitchen and asked if I was all right. I said, "Yes." She turned the light on and we looked at the kitchen floor. Nothing much was broken, but the floor was very messy. We both laughed and then went back to bed and made love. The next morning we cleaned up the mess, but obviously overlooked the knife.

I was about to ask the woman I love if she remembered that incident when she came in from the next room and without saying a word, picked up the knife from the table and slid it back under the refrigerator.

CONSIDERATIONS FOR CRITICAL THINKING AND WRITING

1. FIRST RESPONSE. Why do you think the woman slides the knife back under the refrigerator at the end of the story?

2. Consider whether the knife is used as a conventional symbol or as a literary symbol in the story.

3. Discuss the significance of the title.

4. How does the flashback in the second paragraph provide the necessary exposition to create the elements of a complex plot?

5. CREATIVE RESPONSE. Rewrite the second paragraph without revising the first and third paragraphs so that the woman's motivation for sliding the knife under the refrigerator must be read in a very different way than you read it now.

6. CONNECTION TO ANOTHER SELECTION. Compare the narrator's emotions at the end of this story and in Maggie Mitchell's "It Would Be Different If" (p. 166).

7. CONNECTION TO ANOTHER SELECTION. Explain how symbolism is central to understanding the resolution of the conflicts in "The Paring Knife" and in Raymond Carver's "Popular Mechanics" (p. 216).

7

Theme

To produce a mighty book, you must choose a mighty theme.

— HERMAN MELVILLE,
from *Moby-Dick,* 1851

Theme is the central idea or meaning of a story. It provides a unifying point around which the plot, characters, setting, point of view, symbols, and other elements of a story are organized. In some works the theme is explicitly stated. Nathaniel Hawthorne's "Wakefield," for example, begins with the author telling the reader that the point of his story is "done up neatly, and condensed into the final sentence." Most modern writers, however, present their themes implicitly (as Hawthorne does in the majority of his stories), so determining the underlying meaning of a work often requires more effort than it does from the reader of "Wakefield." One reason for the difficulty is that the theme is fused into the elements of the story, and these must be carefully examined in relation to one another as well as to the work as a whole. But then that's the value of determining the theme, for it requires a close analysis of all the elements of a work. Such a close reading often results in sharper insights into this overlooked character or that seemingly unrelated incident. Accounting for the details and seeing how they fit together result in greater understanding of the story.

Themes are not always easy to express, but some principles can aid you in articulating the central meaning of a work. First distinguish between the theme of a story and its subject. They are not equivalents. Many stories share identical subjects, such as fate, death, innocence, youth, loneliness, racial prejudice, and disillusionment. Karen van der Zee's "A Secret Sorrow" (p. 29) and Gail Godwin's "A Sorrowful Woman" (p. 38) both focus on marriage. Yet each story usually makes its own statement about the subject and expresses a different view of life.

Although readers may differ in their interpretations of a story, that does not mean that *any* interpretation is valid. If we were to assert that Krebs's dissatisfactions in Hemingway's "Soldier's Home" (p. 129) could be readily eliminated by his settling down to marriage and a decent job (his mother's solution), we would have missed Hemingway's purposes in writing the story; we would have failed to see how Krebs's war experiences have caused him to reexamine the assumptions and beliefs that previously nurtured him but now seem unreal to him. We would have to ignore much in the story in order to arrive at such a reading. To be valid, the statement of the theme should be responsive to the details of the story. It must be based on evidence within the story rather than solely on experiences, attitudes, or values the reader brings to the work—such as personally knowing a war veteran who successfully adjusted to civilian life after getting a good job and marrying. Familiarity with the subject matter of a story can certainly be an aid to interpretation, but it should not get in the way of seeing the author's perspective.

Sometimes readers too hastily conclude that a story's theme always consists of a moral, some kind of lesson that is dramatized by the various elements of the work. There are stories that do this—Hawthorne's "Wakefield," for example. Here are the final sentences in his story about a middle-aged man who drops out of life for twenty years:

> He has left us much food for thought, a portion of which shall lend its wisdom to a moral, and be shaped into a figure. Amid the seeming confusion of our mysterious world, individuals are so nicely adjusted to a system, and systems to one another and to a whole, that, by stepping aside for a moment, a man exposes himself to a fearful risk of losing his place forever. Like Wakefield, he may become, as it were, the Outcast of the Universe.

Most stories, however, do not include such direct caveats about the conduct of life. A tendency to look for a lesson in a story can produce a reductive and inaccurate formulation of its theme. Consider the damage done to Godwin's "A Sorrowful Woman" (p. 38) if its theme is described as this: "The woman in the story is too selfish to cope with the responsibilities of marriage." Godwin's focus in this story is on the woman's desperate response to her domestic identity rather than on her inability to be a good wife. In fact, a good many stories go beyond traditional social values to explore human behavior instead of condemning or endorsing it.

There is no precise formula that can take you to the center of a story's meaning and help you to articulate it. However, several strategies are practical and useful once you have read the story. Apply these pointers during a second or third reading:

1. Pay attention to the title of the story. It often provides a lead to a major symbol (Hemingway's "Soldier's Home," p. 129) or to the subject around which the theme develops (Godwin's "A Sorrowful Woman," p. 38).

2. Look for details in the story that have potential for symbolic meanings. Careful consideration of names, places, objects, minor characters, and incidents can lead you to the central meaning — for example, think of the stripper in Ellison's "Battle Royal" (p. 177). Be especially attentive to elements you did not understand on the first reading.

3. Decide whether the protagonist changes or develops some important insight as a result of the action. Carefully examine any generalizations the protagonist or narrator makes about the events in the story.

4. When you formulate the theme of the story in your own words, write it down in one or two complete sentences that make some point about the subject matter. Revenge may be the subject of a story, but its theme should make a statement about revenge: "Instead of providing satisfaction, revenge defeats the best in one's self " is one possibility.

5. Be certain that your expression of the theme is a generalized statement rather than a specific description of particular people, places, and incidents in the story. Contrast the preceding statement of a theme on revenge with this too-specific one: "In Nathaniel Hawthorne's *The Scarlet Letter*, Roger Chillingworth loses his humanity owing to his single-minded attempts to punish Arthur Dimmesdale for fathering a child with Chillingworth's wife, Hester." Hawthorne's theme is not restricted to a single fictional character named Chillingworth but to anyone whose life is ruined by revenge.

6. Be wary of using clichés as a way of stating theme. They tend to short-circuit ideas instead of generating them. It may be tempting to resort to something like "an eye for an eye" as a statement of the theme of *The Scarlet Letter*; however, even the slightest second thought reveals how much more ambiguous and complicated that story is.

7. Be aware that some stories emphasize theme less than others. Stories that have as their major purpose adventure, humor, mystery, or terror may have little or no theme. In Edgar Allan Poe's "The Pit and the Pendulum," for example, the protagonist is not used to condemn torture; instead, he becomes a sensitive gauge to measure the pain and horror he endures at the hands of his captors.

What is most valuable about articulating the theme of a work is the process by which the theme is determined. Ultimately, the theme is expressed by the story itself and is inseparable from the experience of reading the story. Tim O'Brien's explanation of one of his short stories, "How to Tell a True War Story," is probably true of most kinds of stories: "In a true war story, if there's a moral [or theme] at all, it's like the thread that makes the cloth. You can't tease it out. You can't extract the meaning without unraveling the deeper meaning." Describing the theme should not be a way to consume a story, to be done with it. It is a means of clarifying our thinking about what we've read and probably felt intuitively.

Edgar Allan Poe's "The Cask of Amontillado," Gavin Ford Kovite's "When Engaging Targets, Remember," and Joyce Carol Oates's "Hi Howya Doin" are three stories whose themes emerge from the authors' skillful use of plot, character, setting, and symbol.

EDGAR ALLAN POE (1809–1849)

Library of Congress, Prints and Photographs Division.

Edgar Allan Poe grew up in the home of John Allan, in Richmond, Virginia, after his mother died in 1811, and he was educated in Scotland and England for five years before completing his classical education in Richmond. After a short stint at the University of Virginia, Poe went to Boston, where he began publishing his poetry. His foster father sent him to West Point Military Academy, but Poe was expelled and moved on to New York, where he published a book of poems inspired by the Romantic movement. Moving among editorial jobs in Baltimore, Richmond, and New York, Poe married his thirteen-year-old cousin Virginia Clemm. Early in his story-writing career, Poe published his only novel-length piece, *The Narrative of Arthur Gordon Pym* (1838), and the following year, he began to work in the genre of the supernatural and horrible, with the stories "William Wilson" and "The Fall of the House of Usher." He gained publicity with the detective story "The Murders in the Rue Morgue," became nationally famous with the publication of his poem "The Raven" in 1845, and died four years later in Baltimore after a drinking binge. Poe theorized that the short story writer should plan every word toward the achievement of a certain effect, and that stories should be read in a single sitting. Morbidity and dreamlike flights of fancy, for which Poe is often recognized, do not detract from his lucid crafting of suspense and his erudite control of language and symbol.

The Cask of Amontillado 1846

The thousand injuries of Fortunato I had borne as I best could; but when he ventured upon insult, I vowed revenge. You, who so well know the nature of my soul, will not suppose, however, that I gave utterance to a threat. *At length* I would be avenged; this was a point definitely settled — but the very definitiveness with which it was resolved precluded the idea of risk.

I must not only punish, but punish with impunity. A wrong is unredressed when retribution overtakes its redresser. It is equally unredressed when the avenger fails to make himself felt as such to him who has done the wrong.

It must be understood, that neither by word nor deed had I given Fortunato cause to doubt my good-will. I continued, as was my wont, to smile in his face, and he did not perceive that my smile *now* was at the thought of his immolation.

He had a weak point — this Fortunato — although in other regards he was a man to be respected and even feared. He prided himself on his connoisseurship in wine. Few Italians have the true virtuoso spirit. For the most part their enthusiasm is adopted to suit the time and opportunity — to practise imposture upon the British and Austrian *millionnaires*. In painting and gemmary Fortunato, like his countrymen, was a quack — but in the matter of old wines he was sincere. In this respect I did not differ from him materially: I was skilful in the Italian vintages myself, and bought largely whenever I could.

It was about dusk, one evening during the supreme madness of the carnival season, that I encountered my friend. He accosted me with excessive warmth, for he had been drinking much. The man wore motley. He had on a tight-fitting parti-striped dress, and his head was surmounted by the conical cap and bells. I was so pleased to see him, that I thought I should never have done wringing his hand.

I said to him: "My dear Fortunato, you are luckily met. How remarkably   5
well you are looking to-day! But I have received a pipe° of what passes for Amontillado, and I have my doubts."

"How?" said he. "Amontillado? A pipe? Impossible! And in the middle of the carnival!"

"I have my doubts," I replied; "and I was silly enough to pay the full Amontillado price without consulting you in the matter. You were not to be found, and I was fearful of losing a bargain."

"Amontillado!"

"I have my doubts."

"Amontillado!"

"And I must satisfy them."   10

"Amontillado!"

"As you are engaged, I am on my way to Luchesi. If any one has a critical turn, it is he. He will tell me ——"

"Luchesi cannot tell Amontillado from Sherry."

"And yet some fools will have it that his taste is a match for your own."   15

"Come, let us go."

"Whither?"

"To your vaults."

"My friend, no; I will not impose upon your good nature. I perceive you have an engagement. Luchesi ——"

"I have no engagement; — come."   20

pipe: A large keg.

"My friend, no. It is not the engagement, but the severe cold with which I perceive you are afflicted. The vaults are insufferably damp. They are encrusted with nitre."

"Let us go, nevertheless. The cold is merely nothing. Amontillado! You have been imposed upon. And as for Luchesi, he cannot distinguish Sherry from Amontillado."

Thus speaking, Fortunato possessed himself of my arm. Putting on a mask of black silk, and drawing a *roquelaire*° closely about my person, I suffered him to hurry me to my palazzo.

There were no attendants at home; they had absconded to make merry in honor of the time. I had told them that I should not return until the morning, and had given them explicit orders not to stir from the house. These orders were sufficient, I well knew, to insure their immediate disappearance, one and all, as soon as my back was turned.

I took from their sconces two flambeaux, and giving one to Fortunato, 25 bowed him through several suites of rooms to the archway that led into the vaults. I passed down a long and winding staircase, requesting him to be cautious as he followed. We came at length to the foot of the descent, and stood together on the damp ground of the catacombs of the Montresors.

The gait of my friend was unsteady, and the bells upon his cap jingled as he strode.

"The pipe?" said he.

"It is farther on," said I; "but observe the white web-work which gleams from these cavern walls."

He turned toward me, and looked into my eyes with two filmy orbs that distilled the rheum of intoxication.

"Nitre?" he asked, at length.   30

"Nitre," I replied. "How long have you had that cough?"

"Ugh! ugh! ugh! — ugh! ugh! ugh! — ugh! ugh! ugh! — ugh! ugh! ugh! — ugh! ugh! ugh!"

My poor friend found it impossible to reply for many minutes.

"It is nothing," he said, at last.

"Come," I said, with decision, "we will go back; your health is precious. 35 You are rich, respected, admired, beloved; you are happy, as once I was. You are a man to be missed. For me it is no matter. We will go back; you will be ill, and I cannot be responsible. Besides, there is Luchesi ——"

"Enough," he said; "the cough is a mere nothing; it will not kill me. I shall not die of a cough."

"True — true," I replied; "and, indeed, I had no intention of alarming you unnecessarily; but you should use all proper caution. A draught of this Medoc will defend us from the damps."

Here I knocked off the neck of a bottle which I drew from a long row of its fellows that lay upon the mould.

"Drink," I said, presenting him the wine.

---

roquelaire: A short cloak.

He raised it to his lips with a leer. He paused and nodded to me famil- 40
iarly, while his bells jingled.

"I drink," he said, "to the buried that repose around us."

"And I to your long life."

He again took my arm, and we proceeded.

"These vaults," he said, "are extensive."

"The Montresors," I replied, "were a great and numerous family." 45

"I forget your arms."

"A huge human foot d'or,° in a field azure; the foot crushes a serpent ram-
pant whose fangs are imbedded in the heel."

"And the motto?"

"Nemo me impune lacessit."°

"Good!" he said. 50

The wine sparkled in his eyes and the bells jingled. My own fancy grew
warm with the Medoc. We had passed through walls of piled bones, with
casks and puncheons intermingling into the inmost recesses of the catacombs. I paused again, and this time I made bold to seize Fortunato by an
arm above the elbow.

"The nitre!" I said; "see, it increases. It hangs like moss upon the vaults.
We are below the river's bed. The drops of moisture trickle among the bones.
Come, we will go back ere it is too late. Your cough ——"

"It is nothing," he said; "let us go on. But first, another draught of the
Medoc."

I broke and reached him a flagon of De Grâve. He emptied it at a breath.
His eyes flashed with a fierce light. He laughed and threw the bottle upward
with a gesticulation I did not understand.

I looked at him in surprise. He repeated the movement — a gro- 55
tesque one.

"You do not comprehend?" he said.

"Not I," I replied.

"Then you are not of the brotherhood."

"How?"

"You are not of the masons." 60

"Yes, yes," I said; "yes, yes."

"You? Impossible! A mason?"

"A mason," I replied.

"A sign," he said.

"It is this," I answered, producing a trowel from beneath the folds of my 65
roquelaire.

"You jest," he exclaimed, recoiling a few paces. "But let us proceed to the
Amontillado."

"Be it so," I said, replacing the tool beneath the cloak, and again offering
him my arm. He leaned upon it heavily. We continued our route in search

d'or: Of gold.
Nemo . . . lacessit (Latin): No one wounds me with impunity.

of the Amontillado. We passed through a range of low arches, descended, passed on, and descending again, arrived at a deep crypt, in which the foulness of the air caused our flambeaux rather to glow than flame.

At the most remote end of the crypt there appeared another less spacious. Its walls had been lined with human remains, piled to the vault overhead, in the fashion of the great catacombs of Paris. Three sides of this interior crypt were still ornamented in this manner. From the fourth the bones had been thrown down, and lay promiscuously upon the earth, forming at one point a mound of some size. Within the wall thus exposed by the displacing of the bones, we perceived a still interior recess, in depth about four feet, in width three, in height six or seven. It seemed to have been constructed for no especial use within itself, but formed merely the interval between two of the colossal supports of the roof of the catacombs, and was backed by one of their circumscribing walls of solid granite.

It was in vain that Fortunato, uplifting his dull torch, endeavored to pry into the depth of the recess. Its termination the feeble light did not enable us to see.

"Proceed," I said; "herein is the Amontillado. As for Luchesi ——" 70

"He is an ignoramus," interrupted my friend, as he stepped unsteadily forward, while I followed immediately at his heels. In an instant he had reached the extremity of the niche, and finding his progress arrested by the rock, stood stupidly bewildered. A moment more and I had fettered him to the granite. In its surface were two iron staples, distant from each other about two feet, horizontally. From one of these depended a short chain, from the other a padlock. Throwing the links about his waist, it was but the work of a few seconds to secure it. He was too much astounded to resist. Withdrawing the key I stepped back from the recess.

"Pass your hand," I said, "over the wall; you cannot help feeling the nitre. Indeed it is *very* damp. Once more let me *implore* you to return. No? Then I must positively leave you. But I must first render you all the little attentions in my power."

"The Amontillado!" ejaculated my friend, not yet recovered from his astonishment.

"True," I replied; "the Amontillado."

As I said these words I busied myself among the pile of bones of which 75 I have before spoken. Throwing them aside, I soon uncovered a quantity of building stone and mortar. With these materials and with the aid of my trowel, I began vigorously to wall up the entrance of the niche.

I had scarcely laid the first tier of the masonry when I discovered that the intoxication of Fortunato had in a great measure worn off. The earliest indication I had of this was a low moaning cry from the depth of the recess. It was *not* the cry of a drunken man. There was then a long and obstinate silence. I laid the second tier, and the third, and the fourth; and then I heard the furious vibrations of the chain. The noise lasted for several minutes, during which, that I might hearken to it with the more satisfaction, I ceased my labors and sat down upon the bones. When at last the clanking subsided, I resumed the trowel, and finished without interruption the fifth, the sixth, and the seventh tier. The wall was now nearly upon a level with my breast. I again paused, and holding the flambeaux over the masonwork, threw a few feeble rays upon the figure within.

A succession of loud and shrill screams, bursting suddenly from the throat of the chained form, seemed to thrust me violently back. For a brief moment I hesitated — I trembled. Unsheathing my rapier, I began to grope with it about the recess; but the thought of an instant reassured me. I placed my hand upon the solid fabric of the catacombs, and felt satisfied. I reapproached the wall. I replied to the yells of him who clamored. I reechoed — I aided — I surpassed them in volume and in strength. I did this, and the clamorer grew still.

It was now midnight, and my task was drawing to a close. I had completed the eighth, the ninth, and the tenth tier. I had finished a portion of the last and the eleventh; there remained but a single stone to be fitted and plastered in. I struggled with its weight; I placed it partially in its destined position. But now there came from out the niche a low laugh that erected the hairs upon my head. It was succeeded by a sad voice, which I had difficulty in recognizing as that of the noble Fortunato. The voice said —

"Ha! ha! ha! — he! he! — a very good joke indeed — an excellent jest. We will have many a rich laugh about it at the palazzo — he! he! he! — over our wine — he! he! he!"

"The Amontillado!" I said.   80

"He! he! he! — he! he! he! — yes, the Amontillado. But is it not getting late? Will not they be awaiting us at the palazzo, the Lady Fortunato and the rest? Let us be gone."

"Yes," I said, "let us be gone."

"For the love of God, Montresor!"

"Yes," I said, "for the love of God!"

But to these words I hearkened in vain for a reply. I grew impatient. I   85
called aloud:

"Fortunato!"

No answer. I called again:

"Fortunato!"

No answer still, I thrust a torch through the remaining aperture and let it fall within. There came forth in return only a jingling of the bells. My heart grew sick — on account of the dampness of the catacombs. I hastened to make an end of my labor. I forced the last stone into its position; I plastered it up. Against the new masonry I re-erected the old rampart of bones. For the half of a century no mortal has disturbed them. *In pace requiescat!*°

Considerations for Critical Thinking and Writing

1. **FIRST RESPONSE.** How does this narrative compare as a "horror story" with versions of that genre you might have seen or read?

In pace requiescat! (Latin): In peace may he rest!

2. Explain how Poe creates suspense in this plot.

3. Characterize the narrator. What motivates his behavior?

4. Why do you think Poe never reveals Fortunato's original insult to the narrator?

5. Discuss the moments of irony in the story. How do they affect its tone?

6. How do you account for the narrator's sick feeling in the final paragraph? What does this suggest about the story's possible themes?

7. **CONNECTION TO ANOTHER SELECTION.** Compare the treatment of revenge in "The Cask of Amontillado" and in one of the following: William Faulkner's "A Rose for Emily" (p. 54), Andre Dubus's "Killings" (p. 62), or Joyce Carol Oates's "Hi Howya Doin" (p. 209).

GAVIN FORD KOVITE (B. 1981)

Gavin Ford Kovite led an infantry platoon in Iraq from 2004 to 2005. He attended New York University Law School and has served as an army lawyer. His writing career began with the NYU Veterans Writing Workshop, where his work was published in its journal *Nine Lives*. With Christopher Robinson, he has cowritten a novel, *War of the Encyclopaedists* (2015), that focuses on two friends whose lives go in different directions after college, one fighting in Iraq, the other studying at a Boston graduate school. "When Engaging Targets, Remember" appeared in *Fire and Forget* (2013), an anthology of war fiction written by veterans. In the story Kovite employs a choose-your-own-adventure narrative point of view to achieve powerful effects.

When Engaging Targets, Remember   2013

(1) On the Road

You are a United States infantryman. An Imperial Grunt. The emblem of American militarism. Your rank is: Specialist. It is late 2004, and you are behind a machine gun in al-Anbar, Iraq, swathed in bulky armor and expensive gear and sitting — almost reclining — in a wide nylon sling slung across the roof of a Humvee that's as cartoonishly bulky as you. Your job as a Humvee gunner is to provide rear security for a convoy of fuel tankers that's currently wending its way from the Baghdad airport to a Forward Operating Base one hundred miles east.

You're no fool; you're a college kid. You were just about to declare a polisci major at UC Riverside when you got the letter ordering you to active duty for Iraq, along with the rest of your California National Guard brigade. You're smart, and you get the joke. The fuel will be used to fill the vehicles and generators of the combat and combat support units at the base, whose main task is to secure the area around Kut, the security of which presumably increases the security of the country and then the region, which helps to secure the world in general and the United States in particular. It's tough to make a direct connection between what you're doing right now and the peace and prosperity of your hometown of Riverside, but that's no surprise because global security is all about action that's collective as well as synergistic, as far as you understand it.

As you think this, you reach into one of the nylon pouches of your vest. You pull out a Met-RX Big 100 protein bar and unwrap it with your teeth while your left hand rests on the handle of the Browning .50 caliber machine gun mounted to a swivel in front of you. The air smells of dust and burning garbage. The sky is eggshell white with brown and black highlights. You're about to see some action, although you don't know it quite yet.

At the front of your field of vision is the enormous black barrel of an M2 .50 caliber machine gun, a weapon that's longer than you are tall and that shoots rounds the size of small dildos. In the middle range of your vision, fifty meters away, is a pack of cars following your convoy. Any one of them could be a suicide car bomb, but they're probably just average Joes, day-to-day Iraqis trying to get somewhere. The reason they're all fifty meters away is that there's a large, white, bilingual sign affixed to your Humvee's rear that reads "US CONVOY DO NOT APPROACH WITHIN 50 METERS OR YOU WILL BE FIRED UPON," the Operation Iraqi Freedom version of the good old "IF YOU CAN READ THIS YOU'RE DRIVING TOO CLOSE." And of course, there's you, crouched in the gunner's hatch menacing everyone with the .50 cal.

It doesn't always work. Some hajjis are weirdly — almost nihilistically, you think — unresponsive to menacing. You wonder if nihilistic is the right word to use. Your PHIL 101 Intro to Western Philosophy course went over nihilism last semester, but thanks to the letter you got sending you here, you never finished it. Your PHIL 101 professor was nice about you leaving midway through, although he kept on saying he was, "So, so sorry," as if someone you loved had contracted a terminal illness.   5

Your thoughts drift. You know the importance of vigilance and constant scanning, but you are perhaps too imaginative for sentry work or rolling down Baghdad highways day in and day out. Consider: there is a large crater in the intersection outside your unit's walled-off living area on the edge of the Green Zone where a silver BMW exploded, beheading rush-hour commuters and landing a guy from 1st Cavalry Division in the ICU with "polytrauma," which is the new buzzword for injuries sustained in the kind of blast that would kill anyone lacking 100 pounds of Kevlar and ceramic armor and twenty-first-century surgical care. Thanks to a recent mop-up operation, you can now mentally produce a photorealistic image of what your own body would look like after such an explosion, and this image comes unbidden to your mind during long stretches of highway.

The protein bar is incredibly dry and needs to be washed down frequently with rubbery-tasting water from the hose of your CamelBak. You think about going back to UC Riverside and enrolling in ENGL 302 with no lower jaw or tongue, having to write out your conversation or type through some text-to-speech thing like a twenty-year-old Stephen Hawking, your old roommates looking at you with kindness and awkwardness and pity, no one really wanting to talk to you in that condition, and you not wanting to talk to anyone either. Sex with the Riverside coeds would be out of the question, with you looking like either the Phantom of the Opera or that Marine in the *New York Times Magazine* with his face and scalp totally burned off and scarred over, a too-scary-for-PG version of the guy in *Goonies*. And that's just what could happen to your head. A bomb could leave you dickless and castrated too, which would probably take at least one leg off pretty close, which would lead the few girls you have gotten with to suspect that it's worse than it looks and to have nightmares of what's become of you "down there." Your buddies wouldn't be able to take you out for drinks without acknowledging it and thinking about it, the worst thing that could happen to a guy, your catheter filling your bag with fluid after a few Heinekens and one of your friends, most of whom front like they're assholes but are actually really nice guys, changing it out for you, trying to decide whether wisecracking about it or refraining from wisecracking would make you feel worse.

You're not a worrywart, though. You cut that train of thought off and start mouthing Jay-Z lyrics while swiveling the Fifty around and aiming at cars and windows and the rooftops of the drab apartment buildings that line the highways. One interesting tidbit you heard from the 3rd Infantry Division troops, whom you relieved, is that some gunners have been ordered to crouch way down in the hatch, like too far down to really be able to see anything, since the main danger is IEDs, which you won't see anyway, but which will take your head off in a close blast or in a rollover if you're standing up tall and trying to scan this way and that.

In your (albeit limited) army experience, this is the kind of decision that sergeants or officers make for you, but you haven't been instructed either way, probably because your sergeants and officers, being new here themselves, either haven't thought of it or aren't sure whether it's wise. You figure you're probably justified in going either way, even though you're the rear security and are supposed to be keeping an eye out for threats coming from the rear of the convoy. You can crouch down low, popping up for a quick scan every fifteen or twenty seconds. You might miss the telltale lumps of a roadside IED that didn't detonate, but this also means you'd avoid taking the blast in your face if it does. All in all it seems prudent. On the other hand, there are things you know you don't know and things you don't know you don't know. And as long as you're crouched down, you're not watching the convoy's six.

DO YOU:

Crouch down in the turret and pop up to scan every twenty seconds? TURN TO SECTION (2).

Remain standing and scanning as before? TURN TO SECTION (3).

(2) Turtle Down

Here's the worst situation: after having mulled over keeping your head down, you decide to keep it up, and then you get hit with an IED, which burns your face off or gives you the kind of brain trauma that disables you for the rest of your life but doesn't erase the memory of mulling over and then failing to take a simple precaution that could have saved you. You feel around for a comfortable sitting position and then settle into it, figuring out by trial and error the best method for hauling your heavily armored self up at twenty-second intervals for a quick scan. Your armor and equipment increase your body weight by about seventy pounds, and human nature and muscle fatigue being what they are, the twenty-second intervals become more like thirty seconds as the hours wear on. The convoy is keeping speed and making good time. The traffic is staying fifty meters away from you. You pass a billboard advertising Mr. Brown Canned Iced Coffee, which has actually become a personal favorite and is sold by the case by Ali at a kiosk he set up at the outskirts of your Forward Operating Base. Body armor is uncomfortable to move around in, but the immobility (along with the drone of the engine) can be somewhat sleep inducing in the heat, hence the regular drinking of Mr. Browns. The cartoon Mr. Brown himself looks jolly and avuncular. Popping back down into a sitting position on the turret's swinging foot-sling, you dig a strawberry-yogurt-flavored protein bar (that you've added for snack purposes) out of the extra ammo pouch on your flak vest and take a bite. Guardo, the medic, is sitting in the right rear seat looking troglodytic and pudgy-faced in his helmet and armor. Your boots have been resting on his trauma bag since you've assumed your new, protected position. Guardo does not seem to object to this. He holds a fist up, and you give it a bump.

The explosion sounds like a huge beam of hardwood snapping in half. The driver and your squad leader, Staff Sergeant Boyle, call out, "IED." Your gun truck runs over a large pothole almost immediately, smacking your neck painfully against the edge of the turret and pushing your Kevlar down over your eyes. Your platoon leader is yelling something indecipherable on the radio, and Guardo is yanking at the bag under your feet. You hear some of the gunners farther up in the column open fire. You untangle your feet and yank yourself back up behind the Fifty.

You are surprised to see a black BMW sedan passing you on the left at a high rate of speed and headed straight for the fuel trucks about fifty meters up in the middle of the convoy. Your Rules of Engagement (ROE) card, which you are required to keep in your left chest pocket at all times, reads: 15

THESE RULES APPLY AT ALL TIMES AND ON ALL OPERATIONS

1. **Positive Identification (PID) is required prior to engagement.** PID is a reasonable certainty that the target you are engaging is exhibiting hostile intent or committing a hostile act. Once you have PID, you may use escalated force up to and including deadly force, to eliminate the threat.

2. **When engaging targets, remember:**

   a. Escalation of force. Always use the minimum amount of force necessary to eliminate the threat. If time and circumstances permit, use the following degrees of
   force when responding to hostile act or hostile intent:

   - Shout verbal warnings to halt.
   - Show your weapon and demonstrate intent to use it.
   - Shoot a warning shot (vehicles only).
   - Shoot a disabling shot (vehicles only).
   - Shoot to eliminate target.

In bold is the caveat:

**NOTHING ON THIS CARD PREVENTS YOU FROM USING ALL FORCE
NECESSARY TO DEFEND YOURSELF.**

By the time you get the barrel swung around, the BMW has passed you.
The time for warning or disabling shots is over, given that a shot going into
the engine block at this angle would also go through the driver's head. You
either engage the BMW or let it drive right into the middle of the convoy.

DO YOU:

Fire on the BMW? TURN TO (5).

Let the BMW pass into the convoy? TURN TO (6).

20

(3) Look Out

You'll try and find a way to broach the subject with your squad leader tomorrow in a way that doesn't sound like you're just being a pussy. For now, your
job is rear security and you have to be scanning at all times. You stay standing and facing the rear like a good trooper, only every once in a while allowing half of your mind to slip into a daydream about mom's kitchen or the
Riverside coeds, and *you* wonder if thinking about whether you're a wartime
cliché prevents you from being a wartime cliché.

About an hour after you made your decision to stand, an IED goes off at
the front of the column. You can feel it as well as hear it: a pocket of stiffened
air busting by with a sound like an enormous firecracker.* As soon as the IED

---

*Most people have only seen large explosions in movies and so understandably assume
that a large bomb makes a sort of loud but sort of wet and rumbly sound, because this
is the sound it makes in theaters. But theater explosions are made by the vibrations of
speaker cones, whereas an actual explosion is the sound of air expanding at like twenty
thousand feet per second, which for obvious legal as well as technical reasons even the
fanciest Dolby-surround-sound systems cannot reproduce. If you've never heard a
large explosion go off nearby, just think of one of those little Black Cat firecrackers that
tween boys like to light and throw on the street around the Fourth of July, then multiply it
by a thousand or ten thousand until it's a loud, sharp, and pretty scary sound that you can
feel as well as hear, and (because you can feel it) always seems surprisingly close.

goes off, your truck swerves slightly and hits a pothole, jolting you against the rear of the turret and pushing your Kevlar forward over your eyes. You push it back up and see that a black BMW about fifty meters away has floored it in the left lane and looks like it's going to try to pass you. After about a second's worth of deer-in-the-headlights hesitation, you remember your Rules of Engagement, which are printed on a small, yellow folding card that you keep in your left chest pocket. The card reads:

THESE RULES APPLY AT ALL TIMES AND ON ALL OPERATIONS

1. **Positive Identification (PID) is required prior to engagement:** PID is a reasonable certainty that the target you are engaging is exhibiting hostile intent or committing a hostile act. Once you have PID, you may use escalated force up to and including deadly force, to eliminate the threat.

2. **When engaging targets, remember:**

   a. Escalation of force. Always use the minimum amount of force necessary to eliminate the threat. If time and circumstances permit, use the following degrees of force when responding to hostile act or hostile intent:

   - Shout verbal warnings to halt.
   - Show your weapon and demonstrate intent to use it.
   - Shoot a warning shot (vehicles only).
   - Shoot a disabling shot (vehicles only).
   - Shoot to eliminate target.

In bold is the caveat:

NOTHING ON THIS CARD PREVENTS YOU FROM USING ALL FORCE NECESSARY TO DEFEND YOURSELF.

Many would have seized up in a situation like this, but you remember the ROE and go by the numbers as per your training, first yelling Hey and Stay Back. The meaning of this should be obvious by the context, even to non-English speakers, but the BMW keeps coming and is now within thirty meters. The next step in the ROE — Show (show your presence and weapon) — is a constant, given the huge DO NOT APPROACH sign, not to mention the enormous and unmistakable Fifty. Next is Shoot (a warning shot), which you now do, fully aware that gunfire at the rear of the column is going to freak out the rest of the group, but whatever, he's at twenty-five meters now, and you lower the Fifty and fire into the concrete behind your truck, not trusting yourself to be able to put it close to but not in the car, given that your truck's starting to hit potholes and swerve around, and a single round could take ten people's heads off if they were lined up right.

The car seems to hesitate for a moment, then continues ahead. It'll be   25
past your bumper in a few seconds. You're probably within blast radius right
now, and the thought that you should just duck pops into your head. You
push it away. The ROE is all about your personal subjective threat assessment, an assessment that, given al-Qaeda's well-known tactic of impersonat-
ing civilians, is very hard to make. The ROE card makes clear however, that
NOTHING ON THIS CARD PREVENTS YOU FROM USING ALL FORCE
NECESSARY TO DEFEND YOURSELF, which is either a smart reminder of
priorities or an end-run around the rules themselves. Your NCOs have made
it clear to you that you are absolutely permitted and expected to light up a
hajji that's intent on plowing into the convoy and won't respond to shouts,
warning shots, and so on. The step now is to walk fire up into the engine block
and then into the driver. You've just about committed to blow the BMW away
when you remember the two-liter water bottle next to you and wonder if you
can just fling it onto their windshield, like maybe the driver is too dense to
realize that you're going to shoot him unless he stops, or is spooked and needs
to be snapped out of it. You're out of time.

DO YOU:

Try and fling the water bottle onto the BMW's windshield? TURN
TO (4).

Engage the BMW with the .50 caliber? TURN TO (5).

(4) Water

You grab the water bottle in one of your green, fuzzy gloves and chuck it. Your
aim is true. The bottle caroms off the windshield right in front of the driver.
This would get a reaction out of you for sure. But instead of stopping, the BMW
driver steps on it and speeds past you in the next lane while you're trying to get
the Fifty around. There's no longer a question of warning shots, but you could
still stop the vehicle before it reaches the tankers. If you blow it away, you run
the risk of Swiss-cheesing a family. If you don't stop it and it's a VBIED and it
gets to one of the JP-4 Tankers, it could wipe out half the convoy.

DO YOU: 30

Fire on the BMW? TURN TO (5).

Let the BMW pass into the convoy? TURN TO (6).

(5) Fire

The M2 Browning .50 caliber machine gun was designed near the end of the
First World War, and its design reflects its heritage. It is black and 100 percent steel and more than five feet long, weighing well over one hundred
pounds loaded. Each round is almost half a foot long, and they are clipped
together in long steel belts that disintegrate into shell casing and projectile with a sound that is described as "barking" but of course doesn't sound
like anything else except for the repeated detonations of about 250 grains
of propellant reverberating through a four-foot-long steel barrel. There is

a widespread misconception among American combat soldiers that its use against human targets is banned by a number of treaties, and recruits have been told by generations of drill sergeants to aim a Fifty at enemy soldiers' "equipment" rather than their bodies. The persistence of this myth can probably be explained by the fact that while smaller bullets punch holes in humans, the Fifty takes them apart.

You draw a bead at the piece of concrete just in front of the BMW and depress the butterfly trigger. It is terrifically loud. You struggle to keep the muzzle from moving up and right as it spits out five huge slugs per second — the BMW is right next to the trucks and heaven forfend you put a round into one of your buddies or a tanker. Your grandmother used to say "heaven forfend," and the phrase is repeated in your panic brain in a queer voice that is somewhere between your grandmother's and your own. You quit firing after three bursts, unwilling to continue to shoot alongside (heaven forfend) your own column. You watch gratefully as another gunner a few trucks down opens up as well.

The riddled BMW swerves to the left and slows. Your ribcage expands, as it seems like a physical weight has been lifted. You have not killed your friends, either with a bullet or through inaction. No one will suffer poly-trauma because of you, you think, and to know that after a few seconds of not knowing it gives you a euphoria almost palpably chemical, the dopamine hitting your brain and a wave of pleasure moving from your scalp to your balls. 35

The column is moving slowly forward and your truck follows. The BMW slows and lists to port. It has no remaining windows. There is no blood visible, though of course there must be a sea of blood. A Browning .50 caliber round puts a hole in a human body the size of a grapefruit. The hole is much larger than the slug itself because of the kinetic force of the slug hitting flesh at approximately 2,910 feet per second.

It is afternoon and the sun is at about a forty-five-degree angle from the ground and very bright. Through the lattice of complex shadows you can see what is probably a human body in the back seat. One of the silhouette's hands is up by its shoulder, as though it is calling a waiter. You can see into the car more easily because all of the bullets make the shadow cast by the car's roof and sides somewhat translucent. You are convinced for a second that the person sitting up in the backseat is alive and unharmed. There are now a few thin streams of blood running from a bullet hole low in the passenger door and onto the concrete. The smell of burned-up ammunition propellant is acrid and strong. You briefly remember that the BMW could still be a bomb and duck back into your hatch after making a quick 360-degree scan. You then pass the location of the IED explosion and are out on the open road again, picking up speed, the radio buzzing furiously.

TURN TO (7).

(6) Denouement (I)

You have about two seconds to make this decision. Your heart tightens up, and your thumbs clench a bit, but you do not press the trigger. Maybe you decided at the time that the statistical probability of any black BMW sprint-ing into a US convoy in al-Anbar being an actual suicide bomber was low enough that the risk of death should be borne by your comrades rather than the BMW's occupants. More probably you just froze up in the moment and couldn't bring yourself to fire on a human being—a normal enough prob-lem for troops throughout history. You're a smart person, and you'll have years to rationalize the decision.

The BMW floors it up through the convoy until it gets to the fourth 40 truck, where Boyce sees it and is faster on the trigger than you. He yells at the BMW and puts a few rounds into the concrete in front of it. The BMW keeps going. As per SOP, Boyce then puts down a steady stream of fire in front of the vehicle, and the car drives right through it like a pole of fresh timber though a mill saw. The car swings to the left and smashes up against the median. The convoy's radios are all going furiously. Drivers don't know whether to drive in the right lane closest to the IED and the dirt berm that was drawing the convoy's fire, or in the left lane closest to the now-smoking BMW that everyone assumes is a possible VBIED.

You have gone back to scanning the rear, but allow yourself a long glance at the BMW as it passes by your right shoulder. Aside from the scat-tered dents in the roof, it looks from the rear like the driver just parked it up against the median for some inscrutable reason. You think you see at least one other person in the vehicle besides the driver. Soon the convoy clears the IED, and the spread-out broken glass and parked-looking, corpse-filled vehicle recede into the distance as you pick up speed.

You'll be chewed out but good for letting some random car come right into the convoy like that. You'll get a lot of meaningful glances from the other members of your platoon, too, who also spend time thinking about getting their jaws or dicks blown off, and who depend on you to fend off bombers. The next morning, your squad leader informs you that he's swapping you out with the driver. You'll be behind the wheel for the rest of the rotation.

THE END

(7) Denouement (II)

They do not ask how you knew that BMW was a VBIED; the whole crux of the terrorist tactic is to take what looks like an innocent civilian family sedan or produce truck and rig it to blow. The idea is to use your own human-ity against you—if you are fast on the trigger, you will end up stopping car bombers but killing civilians, doing al-Qaeda's work for it. If you hold your fire past the point of no return, you will start to get hit more often as al-Qaeda realizes that convoys are soft targets. It is the other asymmetry of this type of asymmetric warfare: heads they win, tails you lose.

It was a good shoot—the vehicle was speeding into the convoy. The LT 45 arranges for you to see the chaplain anyway, because he suspects (with what you imagine is near certainty) that the BMW was full of civilians, the driver maybe having been spooked by the IED and thinking the thing to do was just step on it. Possibly he was drunk, unusual at midafternoon, but who knows? You shot them, regardless. You accept this, at first, as an unfortunate happenstance that is sort of the by-product of a landscape in which every enemy appears by design to be a civilian, which means that every civilian appears as a possible enemy. It will become a small hard nut of guilt and self-pity that you carry around, and that will, in subtle ways, color your opinions about yourself and the government and the people around you. You will find it hard to concentrate and your mind will frequently wander. You will stew in anger over insults that you imagine in daydreams. You will want to kill again, for a time. You will never quite be the same, although of course, no one can be certain whether or not this is a bad thing.

THE END

Considerations for Critical Thinking and Writing

1. FIRST RESPONSE. Describe the point of view. If the story were told from a different point of view, how do you think your response might change?

2. Select a substantial paragraph that reveals the narrator's character and analyze how the details, tone, and action contribute to his characterization.

3. To what extent is the setting used as an antagonist in the story?

4. What do you think is the effect and the purpose of the narrator's detailed description of the Browning .50 caliber machine gun?

5. How does Kovite create suspense in the plot?

6. What kind of choices did you make at the end of each numbered section? Did you read straight through or choose to turn to subsequent sections? What difference in your ordering of the plot did those choices make?

7. What function do the Rules of Engagement serve in the story? How are they related to the conflict?

8. Compare the alternative endings in sections 6 and 7. Consider how the theme(s) of the story differs depending upon which ending you choose. What themes emerge when you combine both?

JOYCE CAROL OATES (B. 1938)

Raised in upstate New York, Joyce Carol Oates earned degrees at Syracuse University and the University of Wisconsin. Both the range and volume of her writing are extraordinarily extensive. A writer of novels, plays, short stories, poetry, and literary criticism, she has published over eighty books. Oates has described the subject matter of her fiction as "real people in a real society," but her method of expression ranges from the realistic to the experimental. Her novels include *them* (1969), *Do with Me What You Will* (1973), *Child-wold* (1976), *Bellefleur* (1980), *A Bloodsmoor Romance* (1982), *Marya: A Life* (1986), *You Must Remember This* (1987), *Black Water* (1992), *I'll Take*

You There (2003), *Missing Mom* (2005),
Mudwoman (2012), *Carthage* (2014), and
Sacrifice (2015). Among her collections of
short stories are *Marriages and Infidelities*
(1972), *Raven's Wing* (1986), *The Assigna-
tion* (1988), *Heat* (1991), *Haunted: Tales
of the Grotesque* (1994), *Will You Always
Love Me? and Other Stories* (1996), *The Col-
lector of Hearts* (1998), *Small Avalanches
and Other Stories* (2004), *High Lonesome:
New and Selected Stories 1966–2006* (2006),
Dear Husband (2009), *The Corn Maiden
and Other Stories* (2011), and *Lovely,
Dark, Deep: Stories* (2014). Oates teaches at
Princeton University.

© Beth Gwinn.

Hi Howya Doin   2007

Good-looking husky guy six-foot-four in late twenties or early thirties,
Caucasian male, as the initial police report will note, he's solid-built as a fire
hydrant, carries himself like an athlete, or an ex-athlete just perceptibly
thickening at the waist, otherwise in terrific condition like a bronze figure in
motion, sinewy arms pumping as he runs, long muscled legs, chiseled-
muscled calves, he's hurtling along the moist woodchip path at the western
edge of the university arboretum at approximately six P.M., Thursday evening, and there comes, from the other direction, a woman jogger on the
path, female in her late thirties, flushed face, downturned eyes, dark hair
threaded with gray like cobwebs, an awkward runner, fleshy lips parted,
holds her arms stiff at her sides, in a shrunken pullover shirt with a faded
tiger cat on its front, not-large but sizable breasts shaking as she runs, mimicked in the slight shaking of her cheeks, and her hips in carrot-colored
sweatpants, this is Madeline Hersey frowning at the woodchip path before
her, Madeline's exasperating habit of staring at the ground when she runs,
oblivious of the arboretum, though at this time in May it's dazzling with
white dogwood, pink dogwood, vivid yellow forsythia, Madeline is a lab
technician at Squibb, lost in a labyrinth of her own tangled thoughts (career,
lover, lover's "learning disabled" child), startled out of her reverie by the
loud aggressive-friendly greeting *Hi! Howya doin!* flung out at her like a
playful slap on the buttocks as the tall husky jogger passes Madeline with the
most fleeting of glances, big-toothed bemused smile, and Madeline loses her
stride, in a faltering voice *Fine — thank you —* but the other jogger is past,
unhearing and now on the gravel path behind the university hospital, now on
the grassy towpath beside the old canal, in the greenly lushness of University
Dells Park where, in the late afternoon, into dusk joggers are running singly
and in couples, in groups of three or more, track-team runners from the

local high school, college students, white-haired older runners both male and female, to these the husky jogger in skin-tight mustard-yellow T-shirt, short navy-blue shorts showing his chiseled thigh muscles, size-twelve Nikes calls out *Hi Howya doin* in a big bland booming voice, *Hi Howya doin* and a flash of big horsy teeth, long pumping legs, pumping arms, it's his practice to come up close behind a solitary jogger, a woman maybe, a girl, or an older man, so many "older" men (forties, fifties, sixties, and beyond) in the university community, sometimes a younger guy who's sweated through his clothes, beginning to breathe through his mouth, size-twelve Nikes striking the earth like mallets, *Hi! Howya doin!* jolting Kyle Lindeman out of dreamy-sexy thoughts, jolting Michelle Rossley out of snarled anxious thoughts, there's Diane Hendricks who'd been an athlete in high school now twenty pounds overweight, divorced, no kid, replaying in her head a quarrel she'd had with a woman friend, goddamn she's angry! goddamn she's not going to call Ginny back, this time! trying to calm her rush of thoughts like churning roiling water, trying to measure her breaths Zen-fashion, inhale, exhale, inhale and out of nowhere into this reverie a tall husky hurtling figure bears down upon her, toward her, veering into her line of vision, instinctively Diane bears to the right to give him plenty of room to pass her, hopes this is no one she knows from work, no one who knows her, trying not to look up at him, tall guy, husky, must weigh two-twenty, works out, has got to be an athlete, or ex-athlete, a pang of sexual excitement courses through her, or is it sexual dread even as *Hi! Howya doin!* rings out loud and bemused like an elbow in Diane's left breast as the stranger pounds past her, in his wake an odor of male sweat, acrid-briny male sweat and an impression of big glistening teeth bared in a brainless grin or is it a mock-grin, death's-head grin? — thrown off stride, self-conscious and stumbling, Diane manages to stammer *Fine — I'm fine* as if the stranger brushing past her is interested in her, or in her well-being, in the slightest, what a fool Diane is! — yet another day, moist-bright morning in the university dells along the path beside the seed-stippled lagoon where amorous-combative male mallard ducks are pursuing female ducks with much squawking, flapping of wings, and splashing water, there comes the tall husky jogger, Caucasian male six-foot-four, two-twenty pounds, no ID as the initial police report will note, on this occasion the jogger is wearing a skin-tight black Judas Priest T-shirt, very short white-nylon shorts revealing every surge, ripple, sheen of chiseled thigh muscles, emerging out of a shadowy pathway at the edge of the birch woods to approach Dr. Rausch of the university's geology department, older man, just slightly vain of being "fit," dark-tinted aviator glasses riding the bridge of his perspiring nose, Dr. Rausch panting as he runs, not running so fast as he'd like, rivulets of sweat like melting grease down his back, sides, sweating through his shirt, in baggy khaki shorts to the knee, Dr. Rausch grinding his jaws in thought (departmental budget cuts! his youngest daughter's wrecked marriage! his wife's biopsy next morning at seven A.M., he will drive her to the medical center and wait for her, return her home and yet somehow get to the tenure committee meeting he's chairing at eleven A.M.) when *Hi! Howya doin!* jolts Dr. Rausch as if the husky jogger in the black Judas Priest T-shirt has extended a playful size-twelve foot into Dr. Rausch's path to trip him, suddenly he's thrown off-stride, poor old guy, hasn't always been sixty-four years old, sunken-chested, skinny white legs sprouting individual hairs like wires, hard little pot belly straining at the unbelted waistline of the khaki shorts, Dr. Rausch looks up squinting, is this someone he knows? should know? who knows *him*? across the vertiginous span of thirty years in the geology department Dr. Rausch has had so many students, but before he can see who this is, or make a panting effort to reply in the quick-casual way of youthful joggers, the husky jogger has passed by Dr. Rausch without a second glance, legs like pistons of muscle, shimmering sweat-film like a halo about his body, fair-brown, russet-brown hair in curls like wood shavings lifting halo-like from his large uplifted head, big toothy smile, large broad nose made for deep breathing, enormous dark nostrils that look as if thumbs have been shoved into them, soon again this shimmering male figure appears on the far side of the dells, another afternoon on the Institute grounds, hard-pounding feet, muscled arms pumping, on this day a navy blue T-shirt faded from numerous launderings, another time the very short navy-blue shorts, as he runs he exudes a yeasty body odor, sighting a solitary male jogger ahead he quickens his pace to overtake him, guy in his early twenties, university student, no athlete, about five-eight, skinny guy, running with some effort, breathing through his mouth, and in his head a swirl of numerals, symbols, equations, quantum optics, quantum noise, into this reverie *Hi! Howya doin* is like a firecracker tossed by a prankish kid, snappishly the younger jogger replies *I'm okay* as his face flushes, how like high school, junior high kids pushing him around, in that instant he's remembering, almost now limping, lost the stride, now life seems pointless, you know it's pointless, you live, you die, look how his grandfather died, what's the point, there is none, as next day, next week, late Friday afternoon of the final week in May along the canal tow-path past Linden Road where there are fewer joggers looming up suddenly in your line of vision, approaching you, a tall husky male jogger running in the center of the path, instinctively you bear to the right, instinctively you turn your gaze downward, no eye contact on the towpath, you've been lost in thought, coils of thought like electric currents burning-hot, scalding-hot, the very pain, anguish, futility of your thoughts, for what is your soul but your thoughts, upright flame cupped between your hands silently pleading *Don't speak to me, respect my privacy please* even as the oncoming jogger continues to approach, in the center of the path, inexorably, unstoppably, curly hairs on his arms shimmering with a bronze-roseate glow, big teeth bared in a smile *Hi! Howya doing!* loud and bland and booming mock-friendly, and out of the pocket of your nylon jacket you fumble to remove the snub-nosed, twenty-two-caliber Smith & Wesson revolver you'd stolen from your stepfather's lodge in Jackson Hole, Wyoming, three years before, hateful of the old drunk asshole you'd waited for him to ask if you'd taken it, were you the one to take his gun that's unlicensed, and your stepfather never asked, and you never told, and you lift the toy-like gun in a hand trembling with excitement, with trepidation, with anticipation, aim at the face looming at you like a balloon-face up close and fire and the bullet leaps like magic from the toy-weapon with unexpected force and short-range accuracy and enters the face at the forehead directly above the big-nostriled nose, in an instant the husky jogger in the mustard-yellow T-shirt drops to his knees on the path, already the mustard-yellow T-shirt is splashed with blood, on his belly now and brawny arms outspread, face flattened against the path fallen silent and limp as a cloth puppet when the puppeteer has lost interest and dropped the puppet, he's dead, *That's how I'm doin.*

Considerations for Critical Thinking and Writing

1. **First response.** How is the style of this story particularly suited to jogging?

2. What is the effect of the narrator's mentioning the "initial police report" in the second line?

3. Explain how the male jogger is a character foil to Madeline Hersey. How do the other joggers' responses to him further define his character?

4. How might this story be regarded as a kind of sociology of jogging? Consider whether or not it seems like an accurate rendition of it to you.

5. How does Oates subtly convey the passage of time in the narrative?

6. The inevitable question: Is this story funny? Why or why not?

7. **Connection to another selection.** Comment on the ways in which style is related to content in "Hi Howya Doin" and in Rick Moody's "Boys" (p. 226).

8

Style, Tone, and Irony

I like it when there is some feeling of threat or sense of menace in short stories. I think a little menace is fine to have in a story.

— RAYMOND CARVER

© Marion Ettlinger.

STYLE

Style is a concept that everyone understands on some level because in its broadest sense it refers to the particular way in which anything is made or done. Style is everywhere around us. The world is saturated with styles in cars, clothing, buildings, teaching, dancing, music, politics — in anything that reflects a distinctive manner of expression or design. Consider, for example, how a tune sung by the Beatles differs from the same tune performed by a string orchestra. There's no mistaking the two styles.

Authors also have different characteristic styles. *Style* refers to the distinctive manner in which a writer arranges words to achieve particular effects. That arrangement includes individual word choices and matters such as the length of sentences, their structure and tone, and the use of irony.

Diction refers to a writer's choice of words. Because different words evoke different associations in a reader's mind, the writer's choice of words is crucial in controlling a reader's response. The diction must be appropriate for the characters and the situations in which the author places them. Consider how inappropriate it would have been if Melville had had Bartleby respond to the lawyer's requests with "Hell no!" instead of "I would prefer not to." The word *prefer* and the tentativeness of *would* help reinforce the scrivener's mildness, his dignity, and even his seeming reasonableness — all of which frustrate the lawyer's efforts to get rid of him. Bartleby, despite his passivity, seems to be in control of the situation. If he were to shout "Hell no!" he would appear angry, aggressive, desperate, and too informal, none of which would fit with his solemn, conscious decision to die. Melville makes the lawyer the desperate party by carefully choosing Bartleby's words.

Sentence structure is another element of a writer's style. Hemingway's terse, economical sentences are frequently noted and readily perceived. Here are the concluding sentences of Hemingway's "Soldier's Home" (p. 129), in which Krebs decides to leave home:

> He had tried so to keep his life from being complicated. Still, none of it had touched him. He had felt sorry for his mother and she had made him lie. He would go to Kansas City and get a job and she would feel all right about it. There would be one more scene maybe before he got away. He would not go down to his father's office. He would miss that one. He wanted his life to go smoothly. It had just gotten going that way. Well, that was all over now, anyway. He would go over to the schoolyard and watch Helen play indoor baseball.

Hemingway expresses Krebs's thought the way Krebs thinks. The style avoids any "complicated" sentence structures. Seven of the eleven sentences begin with the word *He*. There are no abstractions or qualifications. We feel as if we are listening not only to *what* Krebs thinks but to *how* he thinks. The style reflects his firm determination to make, one step at a time, a clean, unobstructed break from his family and the entangling complications they would impose on him.

Contrast this straightforward style with Vladimir Nabokov's description of a woman in his short story "The Vane Sisters." The sophisticated narrator teaches French literature at a women's college and is as observant as he is icily critical of the woman he describes in this passage:

> Her fingernails were gaudily painted, but badly bitten and not clean. Her lovers were a silent young photographer with a sudden laugh and two older men, brothers, who owned a small printing establishment across the street. I wondered at their tastes whenever I glimpsed, with a secret shudder, the higgledy-piggledy striation of black hairs that showed all along her pale shins through the nylon of her stockings with the scientific distinctness of a preparation flattened under glass; or when I felt, at her every movement, the dullish, stalish, not particularly conspicuous but all-pervading and depressing emanation that her seldom bathed flesh spread from under weary perfumes and creams.

This portrait — etched with a razor blade — is restrained but devastating. Hemingway's and Nabokov's uses of language are very different, yet each style successfully fuses what is said with how it is said. We could write summaries of both passages, but our summaries, owing to their styles, would not have the same effect as the originals. And that makes all the difference.

TONE

Style reveals *tone*, the author's implicit attitude toward the people, places, and events in a story. When we speak, tone is conveyed by our voice inflections, our wink of an eye, or some other gesture. A professor who says "You're going to fail the next exam" may be indicating concern, frustration, sympathy, alarm, humor, or indifference, depending on the tone of voice. In a literary work that spoken voice is unavailable; instead we must rely on the context in which a statement appears to interpret it correctly.

In Chopin's "The Story of an Hour" (p. 15), for example, we can determine that the author sympathizes with Mrs. Mallard despite the fact that her grief over her husband's assumed death is mixed with joy. Though Mrs. Mallard thinks she's lost her husband, she experiences relief because she feels liberated from an oppressive male-dominated life. That's why she collapses when she sees her husband alive at the end of the story. Chopin makes clear in the final line ("When the doctors came they said she had died of heart disease — of joy that kills") that the men misinterpret both her grief and joy, for in the larger context of Mrs. Mallard's emotions we see, unlike the doctors, that her death may well have been caused not by a shock of joy but by an overwhelming recognition of her lost freedom. We discover that through the tone. This stylistic technique is frequently an important element for interpreting a story. An insensitivity to tone can lead a reader astray in determining the theme of a work. Regardless of who is speaking in a story, it is wise to listen for the author's voice too.

IRONY

One of the enduring themes in literature is that things are not always what they seem to be. What we see — or think we see — is not always what we get. The unexpected complexity that often surprises us in life — what Herman Melville in *Moby-Dick* called the "universal thump" — is fertile ground for writers of imaginative literature. They cultivate that ground through the use of *irony*, a device that reveals a reality different from what appears to be true.

Verbal irony consists of a person saying one thing but meaning the opposite. If a student driver smashes into a parked car and the angry instructor turns to say "You sure did well today," the statement is an example of verbal irony. What is meant is not what is said. Verbal irony that is calculated to hurt someone by false praise is commonly known as **sarcasm**. In literature, however, verbal irony is usually not openly aggressive; instead, it is more subtle and restrained though no less intense.

In Godwin's "A Sorrowful Woman" (p. 38), a woman retreats from her family because she cannot live in the traditional role that her husband and son expect of her. When the husband tries to be sympathetic about her withdrawal from family life, the narrator tells us three times that "he understood such things" and that in "understanding these things" he tried to be patient by "still understanding these things." The narrator's repetition of these phrases constitutes verbal irony because they call attention to the fact that the husband doesn't understand his wife at all. His "understanding" is really only a form of condescension that represents part of her problem rather than a solution.

Situational irony exists when there is an incongruity between what is expected to happen and what actually happens. For instance, the protagonist in Godwin's "A Sorrowful Woman" seems, by traditional societal standards, to have all that a wife and mother could desire in a family, but, given her needs, that turns out not to be enough to sustain even her life, let alone her happiness. The ironic situation creates a distinction between appearances and realities and brings the reader closer to the central meaning of the story.

As you read Raymond Carver's "Popular Mechanics," Susan Minot's "Lust," Rick Moody's "Boys," and Geoff Wyss's "How to Be a Winner," pay attention to the authors' artful use of style, tone, and irony to convey meanings.

Raymond Carver (1938–1988)

Born in 1938 in Clatskanie, Oregon, to working-class parents, Carver grew up in Yakima, Washington, was educated at Humboldt State College in California, and did graduate work at the University of Iowa. He married at age nineteen and during his college years worked at a series of low-paying jobs to help support his family. These difficult years eventually ended in divorce. He taught at a number of universities, among them the University of California, Berkeley; the University of Iowa; the University of Texas, El Paso; and Syracuse University. Carver's collections of stories include *Will You Please Be Quiet,*

© Marion Ettlinger.

Please? (1976); *What We Talk about When We Talk about Love* (1981), from which "Popular Mechanics" is taken; *Cathedral* (1984); and *Where I'm Calling From: New and Selected Stories* (1988). Though extremely brief, "Popular Mechanics" describes a stark domestic situation with a startling conclusion.

Popular Mechanics   1981

Early that day the weather turned and the snow was melting into dirty water. Streaks of it ran down from the little shoulder-high window that faced the backyard. Cars slushed by on the street outside, where it was getting dark. But it was getting dark on the inside too.

He was in the bedroom pushing clothes into a suitcase when she came to the door.

I'm glad you're leaving! I'm glad you're leaving! she said. Do you hear?

He kept on putting his things into the suitcase.

Son of a bitch! I'm so glad you're leaving! She began to cry. You can't even look me in the face, can you?   5

Then she noticed the baby's picture on the bed and picked it up.

He looked at her and she wiped her eyes and stared at him before turning and going back to the living room.

Bring that back, he said.

Just get your things and get out, she said.

He did not answer. He fastened the suitcase, put on his coat, looked around   10
the bedroom before turning off the light. Then he went out to the living room.

She stood in the doorway of the little kitchen, holding the baby.

I want the baby, he said.

Are you crazy?

No, but I want the baby. I'll get someone to come by for his things.

You're not touching this baby, she said.   15

The baby had begun to cry and she uncovered the blanket from around his head.

Oh, oh, she said, looking at the baby.

He moved toward her.

For God's sake! she said. She took a step back into the kitchen.

I want the baby.   20

Get out of here!

She turned and tried to hold the baby over in a corner behind the stove.

But he came up. He reached across the stove and tightened his hands on the baby.

Let go of him, he said.

Get away, get away! she cried.   25

The baby was red-faced and screaming. In the scuffle they knocked down a flowerpot that hung behind the stove.

He crowded her into the wall then, trying to break her grip. He held on to the baby and pushed with all his weight.

Let go of him, he said.

Don't, she said. You're hurting the baby, she said.

I'm not hurting the baby, he said.   30

The kitchen window gave no light. In the near-dark he worked on her fisted fingers with one hand and with the other hand he gripped the screaming baby up under an arm near the shoulder.

She felt her fingers being forced open. She felt the baby going from her.

No! she screamed just as her hands came loose.

She would have it, this baby. She grabbed for the baby's other arm. She caught the baby around the wrist and leaned back.

But he would not let go. He felt the baby slipping out of his hands and he   35
pulled back very hard.

In this manner, the issue was decided.

Considerations for Critical Thinking and Writing

1. **FIRST RESPONSE.** Discuss the story's final lines. What is the "issue" that is "decided"?

2. Though there is little description of the setting in this story, how do the few details that are provided help to establish the tone?

3. How do small actions take on larger significance in the story? Consider the woman picking up the baby's picture and the knocked-down flowerpot.

4. Why is this couple splitting up? Do we know? Does it matter? Explain your response.

5. Discuss the title of the story. The original title was "Mine." Which do you think is more effective?

6. Explain how Carver uses irony to convey theme.

7. **CONNECTION TO ANOTHER SELECTION.** Compare Carver's style with Ernest Hemingway's in "Soldier's Home" (p. 129).

Susan Minot (B. 1956)

Born and raised in Massachusetts, Susan Minot earned a B.A. at Brown University and an M.F.A. at Columbia University. Before devoting herself full-time to writing, Minot worked as an assistant editor at *Grand Street* magazine. Her stories have appeared in the *Atlantic*, *Harper's*, the *New Yorker*, *Mademoiselle*, and *Paris Review*. Her short stories have been collected in *Lust and Other Stories* (1989), and she has published five novels — *Monkeys* (1986), *Folly* (1992), *Evening* (1998), *Rapture* (2002), and *Thirty Girls* (2014), as well as one volume of poetry, *Poems 4 A.M.* (2002).

Ulf Andersen/Getty Images.

Lust   1984

Leo was from a long time ago, the first one I ever saw nude. In the spring before the Hellmans filled their pool, we'd go down there in the deep end, with baby oil, and like that. I met him the first month away at boarding school. He had a halo from the campus light behind him. I flipped.

Roger was fast. In his illegal car, we drove to the reservoir, the radio blaring, talking fast, fast, fast. He was always going for my zipper. He got kicked out sophomore year.

By the time the band got around to playing "Wild Horses," I had tasted Bruce's tongue. We were clicking in the shadows on the other side of the amplifier, out of Mrs. Donovan's line of vision. It tasted like salt, with my neck bent back, because we had been dancing so hard before.

Tim's line: "I'd like to see you in a bathing suit." I knew it was his line when he said the exact same thing to Annie Hines.

You'd go on walks to get off campus. It was raining like hell, my sweater 5 as sopped as a wet sheep. Tim pinned me to a tree, the woods light brown and dark brown, a white house half hidden with the lights already on. The water was as loud as a crowd hissing. He made certain comments about my forehead, about my cheeks.

We started off sitting at one end of the couch and then our feet were squished against the armrest and then he went over to turn off the TV and came back after he had taken off his shirt and then we slid onto the floor and he got up again to close the door, then came back to me, a body waiting on the rug.

You'd try to wipe off the table or to do the dishes and Willie would untuck your shirt and get his hands up under in front, standing behind you, making puffy noises in your ear.

He likes it when I wash my hair. He covers his face with it and if I start to say something, he goes, "Shush."

For a long time, I had Philip on the brain. The less they noticed you, the more you got them on the brain.

My parents had no idea. Parents never really know what's going on, 10 especially when you're away at school most of the time. If she met them, my mother might say, "Oliver seems nice" or "I like that one" without much of an opinion. If she didn't like them, "He's a funny fellow, isn't he?" or "Johnny's perfectly nice but a drink of water." My father was too shy to talk to them at all unless they played sports and he'd ask them about that.

The sand was almost cold underneath because the sun was long gone. Eben piled a mound over my feet, patting around my ankles, the ghostly surf rumbling behind him in the dark. He was the first person I ever knew who died, later that summer, in a car crash. I thought about it for a long time.

"Come here," he says on the porch.
I go over to the hammock and he takes my wrist with two fingers.
"What?"
He kisses my palm then directs my hand to his fly. 15

Songs went with whichever boy it was. "Sugar Magnolia" was Tim, with the line "Rolling in the rushes / down by the riverside." With "Darkness

Darkness," I'd picture Philip with his long hair. Hearing "Under My Thumb" there'd be the smell of Jamie's suede jacket.

We hid in the listening rooms during study hall. With a record cover over the door's window, the teacher on duty couldn't look in. I came out flushed and heady and back at the dorm was surprised how red my lips were in the mirror.

One weekend at Simon's brother's, we stayed inside all day with the shades down, in bed, then went out to Store 24 to get some ice cream. He stood at the magazine rack and read through *MAD* while I got butterscotch sauce, craving something sweet.

I could do some things well. Some things I was good at, like math or painting or even sports, but the second a boy put his arm around me, I forgot about wanting to do anything else, which felt like a relief at first until it became like sinking into a muck.

It was different for a girl.   20

When we were little, the brothers next door tied up our ankles. They held the door of the goat house and wouldn't let us out till we showed them our underpants. Then they'd forget about being after us and when we played whiffle ball, I'd be just as good as they were.

Then it got to be different. Just because you have on a short skirt, they yell from the cars, slowing down for a while, and if you don't look, they screech off and call you a bitch.

"What's the matter with me?" they say, point-blank.
Or else, "Why won't you go out with me? I'm not asking you to get married," about to get mad.

Or it'd be, trying to be reasonable, in a regular voice, "Listen, I just want   25
to have a good time."
So I'd go because I couldn't think of something to say back that wouldn't be obvious, and if you go out with them, you sort of have to do something.

I sat between Mack and Eddie in the front seat of the pickup. They were having a fight about something. I've a feeling about me.

Certain nights you'd feel a certain surrender, maybe if you'd had wine. The surrender would be forgetting yourself and you'd put your nose to his neck and feel like a squirrel, safe, at rest, in a restful dream. But then you'd start to slip from that and the dark would come in and there'd be a cave. You make out the dim shape of the windows and feel yourself become a cave, filled absolutely with air, or with a sadness that wouldn't stop.

Teenage years. You know just what you're doing and don't see the things that start to get in the way.

Lots of boys, but never two at the same time. One was plenty to keep 30 you in a state. You'd start to see a boy and something would rush over you like a fast storm cloud and you couldn't possibly think of anyone else. Boys took it differently. Their eyes perked up at any little number that walked by. You'd act like you weren't noticing.

The joke was that the school doctor gave out the pill like aspirin. He didn't ask you anything. I was fifteen. We had a picture of him in assembly, holding up an IUD shaped like a T. Most girls were on the pill, if anything, because they couldn't handle a diaphragm. I kept the dial in my top drawer like my mother and thought of her each time I tipped out the yellow tablets in the morning before chapel.

If they were too shy, I'd be more so. Andrew was nervous. We stayed up with his family album, sharing a pack of Old Golds. Before it got light, we turned on the TV. A man was explaining how to plant seedlings. His mouth jerked to the side in a tic. Andrew thought it was a riot and kept imitating him. I laughed to be polite. When we finally dozed off, he dared to put his arm around me, but that was it.

You wait till they come to you. With half fright, half swagger, they stand one step down. They dare to touch the button on your coat then lose their nerve and quickly drop their hand so you — you'd do anything for them. You touch their cheek.

The girls sit around in the common room and talk about boys, smoking their heads off.

"What are you complaining about?" says Jill to me when we talk about 35 problems.

"Yeah," says Giddy. "You always have a boyfriend."

I look at them and think, As if.

I thought the worst thing anyone could call you was a cock-teaser. So, if you flirted, you had to be prepared to go through with it. Sleeping with someone was perfectly normal once you had done it. You didn't really worry about it. But there were other problems. The problems had to do with something else entirely.

Mack was during the hottest summer ever recorded. We were renting a house on an island with all sorts of other people. No one slept during the heat wave, walking around the house with nothing on which we were used to because of the nude beach. In the living room, Eddie lay on top of a coffee table to cool off. Mack and I, with the bedroom door open for air, sweated and sweated all night.

"I can't take this," he said at three A.M. "I'm going for a swim." He and   40
some guys down the hall went to the beach. The heat put me on edge. I sat on
a cracked chest by the open window and smoked and smoked till I felt even
worse, waiting for something — I guess for him to get back.

One was on a camping trip in Colorado. We zipped our sleeping bags
together, the coyotes' hysterical chatter far away. Other couples murmured in
other tents. Paul was up before sunrise, starting a fire for breakfast. He wasn't
much of a talker in the daytime. At night, his hand leafed about in the hair at
my neck.

There'd be times when you overdid it. You'd get carried away. All the next
day, you'd be in a total fog, delirious, absent-minded, crossing the street and
nearly getting run over.

The more girls a boy has, the better. He has a bright look, having reaped
fruits, blooming. He stalks around, sure-shouldered, and you have the feeling
he's got more in him, a fatter heart, more stories to tell. For a girl, with each
boy it's as though a petal gets plucked each time.

Then you start to get tired. You begin to feel diluted, like watered-down stew.

Oliver came skiing with us. We lolled by the fire after everyone had gone   45
to bed. Each creak you'd think was someone coming downstairs. The silver
loop bracelet he gave me had been a present from his girlfriend before.

On vacations, we went skiing, or you'd go south if someone invited you.
Some people had apartments in New York that their families hardly ever used.
Or summer houses, or older sisters. We always managed to find someplace to go.

We made the plan at coffee hour. Simon snuck out and met me at Main
Gate after lights-out. We crept to the chapel and spent the night in the balcony. He tasted like onions from a submarine sandwich.

The boys are one of two ways: either they can't sit still or they don't move.
In front of the TV, they won't budge. On weekends they play touch football
while we sit on the sidelines, picking blades of grass to chew on, and watch.
We're always watching them run around. We shiver in the stands, knocking
our boots together to keep our toes warm, and they whizz across the ice,
chopping their sticks around the puck. When they're in the rink, they refuse
to look at you, only eyeing each other beneath low helmets. You cheer for
them but they don't look up, even if it's a face-off when nothing's happening,
even if they're doing drills before any game has started at all.

Dancing under the pink tent, he bent down and whispered in my ear. We
slipped away to the lawn on the other side of the hedge. Much later, as he was

leaving the buffet with two plates of eggs and sausage, I saw the grass stains on the knees of his white pants.

Tim's was shaped like a banana, with a graceful curve to it. They're all 50 different. Willie's like a bunch of walnuts when nothing was happening, another's as thin as a thin hot dog. But it's like faces; you're never really surprised.

Still, you're not sure what to expect.

I look into his face and he looks back. I look into his eyes and they look back at mine. Then they look down at my mouth so I look at his mouth, then back to his eyes then, backing up, at his whole face. I think, Who? Who are you? His head tilts to one side.

I say, "Who are you?"

"What do you mean?"

"Nothing."

55

I look at his eyes again, deeper. Can't tell who he is, what he thinks.

"What?" he says. I look at his mouth.

"I'm just wondering," I say and go wandering across his face. Study the chin line. It's shaped like a persimmon.

"Who are you? What are you thinking?"

He says, "What the hell are you talking about?"

60

Then they get mad after, when you say enough is enough. After, when it's easier to explain that you don't want to. You wouldn't dream of saying that maybe you weren't really ready to in the first place.

Gentle Eddie. We waded into the sea, the waves round and plowing in, buffalo-headed, slapping our thighs. I put my arms around his freckled shoulders and he held me up, buoyed by the water, and rocked me like a sea shell.

I had no idea whose party it was, the apartment jam-packed, stepping over people in the hallway. The room with the music was practically empty, the bare floor, me in red shoes. This fellow slides onto one knee and takes me around the waist and we rock to jazzy tunes, with my toes pointing heavenward, and waltz and spin and dip to "Smoke Gets in Your Eyes" or "I'll Love You Just for Now." He puts his head to my chest, runs a sweeping hand down my inside thigh and we go loose-limbed and sultry and as smooth as silk and I stamp my red heels and he takes me into a swoon. I never saw him again after that but I thought, I could have loved that one.

You wonder how long you can keep it up. You begin to feel as if you're showing through, like a bathroom window that only lets in grey light, the kind you can't see out of.

They keep coming around. Johnny drives up at Easter vacation from 65
Baltimore and I let him in the kitchen with everyone sound asleep. He has
friends waiting in the car.

"What are you, crazy? It's pouring out there," I say.

"It's okay," he says. "They understand."

So he gets some long kisses from me, against the refrigerator, before he
goes because I hate those girls who push away a boy's face as if she were made
out of Ivory soap, as if she's that much greater than he is.

The note on my cubby told me to see the headmaster. I had no idea for
what. He had received complaints about my amorous displays on the town
green. It was Willie that spring. The headmaster told me he didn't care what I
did but that Casey Academy had a reputation to uphold in the town. He lowered his glasses on his nose. "We've got twenty acres of woods on this campus," he said. "If you want to smooch with your boyfriend, there are twenty
acres for you to do it out of the public eye. You read me?"

Everybody'd get weekend permissions for different places, then we'd all 70
go to someone's house whose parents were away. Usually there'd be more boys
than girls. We raided the liquor closet and smoked pot at the kitchen table
and you'd never know who would end up where, or with whom. There were
always disasters. Ceci got bombed and cracked her head open on the banister
and needed stitches. Then there was the time Wendel Blair walked through
the picture window at the Lowes' and got slashed to ribbons.

He scared me. In bed, I didn't dare look at him. I lay back with my eyes
closed, luxuriating because he knew all sorts of expert angles, his hands never
fumbling, going over my whole body, pressing the hair up and off the back of
my head, giving an extra hip shove, as if to say *There*. I parted my eyes slightly,
keeping the screen of my lashes low because it was too much to look at him,
his mouth loose and pink and parted, his eyes looking through my forehead, or
kneeling up, looking through my throat. I was ashamed but couldn't look him
in the eye.

You wonder about things feeling a little off-kilter. You begin to feel like a
piece of pounded veal.

At boarding school, everyone gets depressed. We go in and see the
housemother, Mrs. Gunther. She got married when she was eighteen.
Mr. Gunther was her high school sweetheart, the only boyfriend she ever had.

"And you knew you wanted to marry him right off?" we ask her.

She smiles and says, "Yes." 75

"They always want something from you," says Jill, complaining about her
boyfriend.

"Yeah," says Giddy. "You always feel like you have to deliver something."

"You do," says Mrs. Gunther. "Babies."

After sex, you curl up like a shrimp, something deep inside you ruined, slammed in a place that sickens at slamming, and slowly you fill up with an overwhelming sadness, an elusive gaping worry. You don't try to explain it, filled with the knowledge that it's nothing after all, everything filling up finally and absolutely with death. After the briskness of loving, loving stops. And you roll over with death stretched out alongside you like a feather boa, or a snake, light as air, and you . . . you don't even ask for anything or try to say something to him because it's obviously your own damn fault. You haven't been able to — to what? To open your heart. You open your legs but can't, or don't dare anymore, to open your heart.

It starts this way: 80
You stare into their eyes. They flash like all the stars are out. They look at you seriously, their eyes at a low burn and their hands no matter what starting off shy and with such a gentle touch that the only thing you can do is take that tenderness and let yourself be swept away. When, with one attentive finger they tuck the hair behind your ear, you —
You do everything they want.
Then comes after. After when they don't look at you. They scratch their balls, stare at the ceiling. Or if they do turn, their gaze is altogether changed. They are surprised. They turn casually to look at you, distracted, and get a mild distracted surprise. You're gone. Their blank look tells you that the girl they were fucking is not there anymore. You seem to have disappeared.

Considerations for Critical Thinking and Writing

1. **FIRST RESPONSE.** What do you think of the narrator? Why? Do you agree with the definition the story offers for *lust*?

2. How effective is the narrator's description of teenage sex? What do you think she means when she says, "You know just what you're doing and don't see the things that start to get in the way" (para. 29)?

3. Discuss the story's tone. Is it what you expected from the title?

4. What do you think is the theme of "Lust"? Does its style carry its theme?

5. What is the primary setting for the story? What does it reveal about the nature of the narrator's economic and social class?

6. In a *Publishers Weekly* interview (November 6, 1992), Minot observed, "There's more fictional material in unhappiness and disappointment and frustration than there is in happiness. Who was it that said, 'Happiness is like a blank page'?" What do you think of this observation?

7. **CONNECTION TO ANOTHER SELECTION.** Compare the treatments of youthful sexuality in "Lust" and David Updike's "Summer" (p. 155). Do you prefer one story to the other? Why?

8. **CONNECTION TO ANOTHER SELECTION.** Write an essay explaining the sort of advice the narrator of Fay Weldon's "IND AFF, or Out of Love in Sarajevo" (p. 136) might give to the narrator of "Lust." You might try writing this in the form of a letter.

RICK MOODY (B. 1961)

Born in New York City, Rick Moody grew up in Connecticut and earned his undergraduate degree at Brown University and his M.F.A. at Columbia University. His first of five novels, *Garden State* (1992), won the Pushcart Editor's Choice Award. *The Ice Storm* (1994) was made into a popular film directed by Ang Lee in 1997 and was followed by three more novels: *Purple America* (1996), *The Diviners* (2005), and *The Four Fingers of Death* (2010). Moody has also published three collections of short stories and novellas: *The Ring of Brightest Angels Along Heaven* (1995); *Demonology* (2001), which collects "Boys"; and

© Colin McPherson/Corbis.

Right Livelihoods (2007). "Boys" was included in *The Best American Short Stories 2001*, in which Moody describes how this experimental story began. He had heard a fellow writer, Max Steele, use the phrase "Then the boys entered the house" at a reading and found himself "preoccupied" with what is "perhaps the most essential gesture in a boy's life." He then "started playing around with the sentence."

Boys   2000

Boys enter the house, boys enter the house. Boys, and with them the ideas of boys (ideas leaden, reductive, inflexible), enter the house. Boys, two of them, wound into hospital packaging, boys with infant-pattern baldness, slung in the arms of parents, boys dreaming of breasts, enter the house. Twin boys, kettles on the boil, boys in hideous vinyl knapsacks that young couples from Edison, N.J., wear on their shirt fronts, knapsacks coated with baby saliva and staphylococcus and milk vomit, enter the house. Two boys, one striking the other with a rubberized hot dog, enter the house. Two boys, one of them striking the other with a willow switch about the head and shoulders, the other crying, enter the house. Boys enter the house speaking nonsense. Boys enter the house calling for mother. On a Sunday, in May, a day one might nearly describe as perfect, an ice cream truck comes slowly down the lane, chimes inducing salivation, and children run after it, not long after which boys dig a hole in the back yard and bury their younger sister's dolls two feet down, so that she will never find these dolls and these dolls will rot in hell, after which boys enter the house. Boys, trailing after their father like he is the Second Goddamned Coming of Christ Goddamned Almighty, enter the house, repair to the basement to watch baseball. Boys enter the house, site of devastation, and repair immediately to the kitchen, where they mix lighter fluid, vanilla pudding, drain-opening lye, balsamic vinegar, blue food coloring, calamine lotion, cottage cheese, ants, a plastic lizard one of them received in his Christmas stocking, tacks, leftover mashed potatoes, Spam, frozen lima beans, and chocolate syrup in a medium-sized saucepan and heat over a low flame until thick, afterward transferring the contents of this saucepan into a Pyrex lasagna dish, baking the Pyrex lasagna dish in the oven for nineteen minutes before attempting to persuade their sister that she should eat the mixture; later they smash three family heirlooms (the last, a glass egg, intentionally) in a two-and-a-half-hour stretch, whereupon they are sent to their bedroom until freed, in each case thirteen minutes after. Boys enter the house, starchy in pressed shirts and flannel pants that itch so bad, fresh from Sunday school instruction, blond and brown locks (respectively) plastered down but even so with a number of cowlicks protruding at odd angles, disconsolate and humbled, uncertain if boyish things — such as shooting at the neighbor's dog with a pump-action BB gun and gagging the fat boy up the street with a bandanna and showing their shriveled boy-penises to their younger sister — are exempted from the commandment to *Love the Lord thy God with all thy heart and with all thy soul and with all thy mind, and thy neighbor as thyself.* Boys enter the house in baseball gear (only one of the boys can hit): in their spikes, in mismatched tube socks that smell like Stilton cheese. Boys enter the house in soccer gear. Boys enter the house carrying skates. Boys enter the house with lacrosse sticks, and soon after, tossing a lacrosse ball lightly in the living room, they destroy a lamp. One boy enters the house sporting basketball clothes, the other wearing jeans and a sweatshirt. One boy enters the house bleeding profusely and is taken out to get stitches, the other watches. Boys enter the house at the end of term carrying report cards, sneak around the house like spies of foreign nationality, looking for a place to hide the report cards for the time being (under a toaster? in a medicine cabinet?). One boy with a black eye enters the house, one boy without. Boys with acne enter the house and squeeze and prod large skin blemishes in front of their sister. Boys with acne-treatment products hidden about their persons enter the house. Boys, standing just up the street, sneak cigarettes behind a willow in the Elys' yard, wave smoke away from their natural fibers, hack terribly, experience nausea, then enter the house. Boys call each other *Retard, Homo, Geek,* and, later, *Neckless Thug, Theater Fag,* and enter the house exchanging further epithets. Boys enter house with nose-hair clippers, chase sister around house threatening to depilate her eyebrows. She cries. Boys attempt to induce girls to whom they would not have spoken only six or eight months prior to enter the house with them. Boys enter the house with girls efflorescent and homely and attempt to induce girls to sneak into their bedroom, as they still share a single bedroom; girls refuse. Boys enter the house, go to separate bedrooms. Boys, with their father (an arm around each of them), enter the house, but of the monologue preceding and succeeding this entrance, not a syllable is preserved. Boys enter the house having masturbated in a variety of locales. Boys enter the house having masturbated in train-station bathrooms, in forests, in beach houses, in football bleachers at night under the stars, in cars (under a blanket), in the shower, backstage, on a plane, the boys masturbate constantly, identically, three times a day in some cases, desire like a madness upon them, at the mere sound of certain words, words that sound like other words, *interrogative* reminding them of *intercourse*, *beast* reminding them of *breast*, *sects* reminding them of *sex*, and so forth, the boys are not very smart yet, and as they enter the house they feel, as always, immense shame at the scale of this self-abusive cogitation, seeing a classmate, seeing a billboard, seeing a fire hydrant, seeing things that should not induce thoughts of masturbation (their sister, e.g.) and then thinking of masturbation anyway. Boys enter the house, go to their rooms, remove sexually explicit magazines from hidden stashes, put on loud music, feel despair. Boys enter the house worried; they argue. The boys are ugly, they are failures, they will never be loved, they enter the house. Boys enter the house and kiss their mother, who feels differently now they have outgrown her. Boys enter the house, kiss their mother, she explains the seriousness of their sister's difficulty, her diagnosis. Boys enter the house, having attempted to locate the spot in their yard where the dolls were buried, eight or nine years prior, without success; they go to their sister's room, sit by her bed. Boys enter the house and tell their completely bald sister jokes about baldness. Boys hold either hand of their sister, laying aside differences, having trudged grimly into the house. Boys skip school, enter house, hold vigil. Boys enter the house after their parents have both gone off to work, sit with their sister and with their sister's nurse. Boys enter the house carrying cases of beer. Boys enter the house, very worried now, didn't know more worry was possible. Boys enter the house carrying controlled substances, neither having told the other that he is carrying a controlled substance, though an intoxicated posture seems appropriate under the circumstances. Boys enter the house weeping and hear weeping around them. Boys enter the house embarrassed, silent, anguished, keening, afflicted, angry, woeful, grief-stricken. Boys enter the house on vacation, each clasps the hand of the other with genuine warmth, the one wearing dark colors and having shaved a portion of his head, the other having grown his hair out longish and wearing, uncharacteristically, a tie-dyed shirt. Boys enter the house on vacation and argue bitterly about politics (other subjects are no longer discussed), one boy supporting the Maoist insurgency in a certain Southeast Asian country, one believing that to change the system you need to work inside it; one boy threatens to beat the living shit out of the other, refuses crème brûlée, though it is created by his mother in order to keep the peace. One boy writes home and thereby enters the house only through a mail slot: he argues that the other boy is crypto-fascist, believing that the market can seek its own level on questions of ethics and morals; boys enter the house on vacation and announce future professions; boys enter the house on vacation and change their minds about professions; boys enter the house on vacation, and one boy brings home a sweetheart but throws a tantrum when it is suggested that the sweetheart will have to retire on the folding bed in the basement; the other boy, having no sweetheart, is distant and withdrawn, preferring to talk late into the night about family members gone from this world. Boys enter the house several weeks apart. Boys enter the house on days of heavy rain. Boys enter the house, in different calendar years, and upon entering, the boys seem to do nothing but compose manifestos, for the benefit of parents; they follow their mother around the place, having fashioned these manifestos in celebration of brand-new independence: *Mom, I like to lie in bed late into the morning watching game shows*, or, *I'm never going to date anyone but artists from now on, mad girls, dreamers, practicers of black magic*, or, *A man should eat bologna, sliced meats are important*, or, *An American should bowl at least once a year*, but these manifestos apply only for brief spells, after which they are reversed or discarded. Boys don't enter the house at all, except as ghostly afterimages of younger selves, fleeting images of sneakers dashing up a staircase; soggy towels on the floor of the bathroom; blue jeans coiled like asps in the basin of the washing machine; boys as an absence of boys, blissful at first, you put a thing down on a spot, put this book down, come back later, it's still there; you buy a box of cookies, eat three, later three are missing. Nevertheless, when boys next enter the house, which they ultimately must do, it's a relief, even if it's only in preparation for weddings of acquaintances from boyhood, one boy has a beard, neatly trimmed, the other has rakish sideburns, one boy wears a hat, the other boy thinks hats are ridiculous, one boy wears khakis pleated at the waist, the other wears denim, but each changes into his suit (one suit fits well, one is a little tight), as though suits are the liminary marker of adulthood. Boys enter the house after the wedding and they are slapping each other on the back and yelling at anyone who will listen, *It's a party!* One boy enters the house, carried by friends, having been arrested (after the wedding) for driving while intoxicated, complexion ashen; the other boy tries to keep his mouth shut: the car is on its side in a ditch, the car has the top half of a tree broken over its bonnet, the car has struck another car, which has in turn struck a third, *Everyone will have seen*. One boy misses his brother horribly, misses the past, misses a time worth being nostalgic over, a time that never existed, back when they set their sister's playhouse on fire; the other boy avoids all mention of that time; each of them is once the boy who enters the house alone, missing the other, each is devoted and each callous, and each plays his part on the telephone, over the course of months. Boys enter the house with fishing gear, according to prearranged date and time, arguing about whether to use lures or live bait, in order to meet their father for the fishing adventure, after which boys enter the house again, almost immediately, with live bait, having settled the question; boys boast of having caught fish in the past, though no fish has ever been caught: *Remember when the blues were biting?* Boys enter the house carrying their father, slumped. Happens so fast. Boys rush into the house leading EMTs to the couch in the living room where the body lies, boys enter the house, boys enter the house, boys enter the house. Boys hold open the threshold, awesome threshold that has welcomed them when they haven't even been able to welcome themselves, that threshold which welcomed them when they had to be taken in, here is its tarnished knocker, here is its euphonious bell, here's where the boys had to sand the door down because it never would hang right in the frame, here are the scuff marks from when boys were on the wrong side of the door demanding, here's where there were once milk bottles for the milkman, here's where the newspaper always landed, here's the mail slot, here's the light on the front step, illuminated, here's where the boys are standing, as that beloved man is carried out. Boys, no longer boys, exit.

Considerations for Critical Thinking and Writing

1. **FIRST RESPONSE.** Write a paragraph that describes in detail the style of this story. In what ways is it conventional as well as unconventional?

2. What is the story's basic plot? What actually happens? Does it have any kind of pattern to it?

3. Who are the major characters? Is there an antagonist who produces a conflict? Explain why or why not.

4. How well do you think Moody captures boys' lives?

5. How is the plot related to the story's style?

6. What do you think is the significance of the final sentence?

7. **CONNECTION TO ANOTHER SELECTION.** Discuss how time is conveyed stylistically in this narrative and in Mark Halliday's "Young Man on Sixth Avenue" (p. 143).

GEOFF WYSS (B. 1968)

Raised in Peoria, Illinois, Geoff Wyss moved to teach high school English in New Orleans, where many of his stories are set. He has a degree in creative writing from Kansas State University. The author of a novel, *Tiny Clubs* (2007), and *How* (2012), a collection of short stories and winner of the Ohio State University Fiction Prize, he has also published short stories in *Image*, *Painted Bride Quarterly*, *Northwest Review*, *Tin House*, and *Glimmer Train*. In "How to Be a Winner," Wyss combines humor and satire in an ironically detailed style.

© 2011, Samantha Scheel.

How to Be a Winner   **2012**

The first thing is, it takes guts. Let me hear you say it! Guts!

Men, when you have gotten to know me better, you will understand I am an individual who I am prepared to repeatedly demand or ask a question until I get my desired response. I am an individual who in my mind and heart there is constant focus on a goal. When you boys have locked up your pads and you're on your way home to Mommy or maybe you're quote kicking it with friends, I am a person who odds are almost a hundred percent I am still in my office devising a punishing, foolproof offense. I have in my office there's a coffee maker for late nights and film of you name the coverage or blocking scheme and I've got film of it, and this is me choosing to excel. Or sometimes, for health reasons and what have you, I drink green tea.

So my prerequisite question I'm asking is, are you able to look in the mirror and say this is a person with guts? Not am I a cruel person. Not am I unsportsmanlike in terms of hits to the knee or do I fall into the trap of performance-enhancing drugs, that whole spectrum. But am I a person who could fashion my own tourniquet in a war setting and return to battle? Am I a person who the Ten Commandments is my guiding code, which things like the Internet make it harder for you as young people than it was for me? Am I man enough to befriend a homosexual or a retarded individual despite I am a looked-up-to athlete, because everyone is deserving of respect? If you can say yes to these integrity benchmarks, my vow here today is that maybe you are five-foot-one like this gentleman in the front row, and maybe you have a, what is that, son, an eye patch? over your eye, but I will teach you how to be a winner.

So you are 0-5, 0-2 in district play. OK. Your coach has contacted me for the purpose of we're going to rectify that. My name is Cleveland Miller, and I am what is known as a sports behavior consultant, or simply a consultant. As a coach, my players referred to me as *Coach Killer* for the style of play I harped. I had a trademark of everyone in the state knew I was going to run the football and I ran the football anyway. In my last three years at Meequeepanassatommee High School, Storrs, Connecticut, my teams compiled a record of 36-1 and brought home two state titles. For the last four years, I have been an individual brought into various programs and et cetera, work environments and even governments, for mental toughness and success orientation. You may recall in your memory a period when Jay Cutler of the NFL Denver Broncos lost confidence in his mid-range game, specifically over the middle. This was widely reported. The person called in on that matter to restore Jay's way of thinking vis-à-vis throw with your eyes, not with your arm was me, and I induced him with anecdotes of let's look at how the greats did it and a visualization mini-retreat, which the next week he threw three touchdown passes. My moniker or what have you is I mix modern technology with old-fashioned I know what makes people tick. But I want to let you know that in your case today, I have waived my fee because I have watched the tapes your coach sent me and heard his cry from the wilderness. Men, be not afraid. Follow me. I have come to lead you forth.

Specifics of you're doing this wrong and you're doing that wrong we'll   5
save for the field. But what the tapes are showing as a general sphere are
missed tackles and confusion about where do I line up for the play in question, which these are mental or will-power mistakes. My notes indicate a
recurring facet of it basically looks like you're handing the ball to the opposing team, which this is like giving candy to a girl who's already trying to kick
you in the nuts. I saw individuals in this room trip and fall purposely to avoid
physical contact. Then there are what you would call the football stupidity or
a nicer word would be lack of knowledge issues. The offensive unit lined up
on the wrong side of the ball not once this season but twice. That's five yards
right there. I had to make a new category in Excel for plays you ran with only
ten men on the field. Then, number three, there are the issues of lack of self-
caring about yourself and your teammates. One particular individual whose
number I won't state but whose position involves predominantly running
the ball with stamina was captured for posterity lighting a cigarette under the
bleachers and slowly enjoying the rich tobacco flavor. Let me guess that the
reason I hear giggling in the back of the room is listen now and see if I've got
it is because you have told yourself if we are going to lose anyway, then losing
will not hurt as much if I put myself in a passive or female position, go ahead,
other team, eff me and get it over with. See, here's the thing is, I have coached
losers before. I know and sympathize the mentality. I have coached many losers successfully, and this is what qualifies me to aggress and incent you. At
Meequeepanassatommee High School, Storrs, Connecticut, I took young men
whose major yearn was huffing chemicals and self-touching themselves in the
lavatory, and I turned them into *yes-ma'am*, *yes-sir* type of people who would
have eaten my enemy's heart off a spear. Did I have my critics, so to say? Yes, I
did. But a rule of life you can say Cleveland Miller taught you is your critics are
people who secretly wish they could be you. They are frequently English teachers and Math teachers, and they sit on school boards and whisper-campaign
about what they call abusive and coercive treatment. They are people who
according to a tape measure may be the size of a full-size person, but they pre-
side in your memory as approximately a midget. They never played the game,
and they will never know the inner joy and feeling of hit or be hit. They notify
their decisions to you on the letterhead of a law firm instead of we're going to
speak to you face to face and fire you as a man. Son, look at me. Spit out that
gum, look at me, and listen as I tell you the story of Michael Wiltonberry.

There are many types of loser. Michael Wiltonberry was the kind where
the word I use for it is smug. This is a word that means clever combined with a
sort of facial look that is begging authority figures to punch you in the mouth.
I knew Michael as a student in my health class with leather wrist bracelets
on his wrists and hair over his eyes, which that was his message he wanted
to send and I got the message. His main hobby in class was writing offensive material on small pieces of paper, this would be female vaginas and jokes
about my teaching approach, and passing them to other students. But all that
changed the day I entered the student lavatory on what they call a whim and
intercessed Michael handing a plastic bag of narcotics to a fellow student. If

there is a national or international drug of people everywhere who have no goals, it is marijuana or weed, which was the contents of this bag, which I plucked into my keeping. But: did I see this incident as this is a bad or negative moment in life, no good can come of it? Something to get downhearted? No: because winners are never downhearted, this is a hallmark. Because fate may have given Michael Wiltonberry a father who only saw the sun when the law dragged him out into it, but it also gave him a six-foot-three frame with high physical I.Q. and surprising foot speed. I took the plastic bag like this, and I placed it in the toilet like so, and I applied the flushing mechanism. And I looked at Michael the same way I am looking at you, young man, as an individual of infinite potential. And I expressed my hope that he would show up for spring football practice the next morning with cleats and a hairstyle suitable to a young man of the male gender.

This seventeen-year-old boy had the lungs of a coal miner, but I addressed that situation by making him throw up his old lungs every day until he developed new ones. Experience had taught Michael he could remedy a cure for everything by crying, and I provided him a new experience where crying gave him more things to cry about. I saw Michael's car entering a McDonald's one night after practice, a cry-for-help mobile with heavy metal or maybe the lingo is goth markings, and I took him home so my wife could make him a proper supper. A sit-down meal is one of my messages to you, men. Plates you can't fold and forks made out of metal, you report to your parents regarding I learned this or that about the world today, what wisdom do you have for me, your loving son. My wife served I'll always remember it was pot roast that night, and Michael took seconds. His favorite dish in the long run was this baked chicken with my wife puts bread crumbs on it, which Michael came to my residence for every Monday night, Monday being the night his mother was pre-engaged committing adultery in various taverns. How anyone could become so wasteful with what God has given them, which you would think loving and caring for your child would be universal, this is the question I ask myself. My wife was unable to have children personally. There was a medical term we were given. But — but my point I'm trying to express to you young men here today is how I ran Michael at practice and fed him at home and dragged him out of parties by the neck to reverse-motivate his bad habits and, yes, a couple times at the beginning I let my players teach him lessons of respect in the locker room. And eventually the outside loser was washed away to reveal the inside winner of Michael James Wiltonberry. This was remarked by everyone who crossed his path, including his grades went up in his core subjects. And next fall he led my team to the state finals, where he played the last nine minutes of the fourth quarter with a torn ACL. So when I tell you this is a winner and that is a winner, and when I use a word like son in the context of that's how I saw Michael, you will understand certain things the school board did not, such as maybe there is a good reason a player would spend the night at a coach's house. Such as maybe human life doesn't always fit your rule book. So I had to leave that job. But I still speak to Michael by phone, and I want you to know that he excelled in Division II college football until he was reinjured and today is a grocery store manager or is on that track is what they call it, and he has two healthy children.

I sometimes consider that today's world possibly makes young people afraid to win. Whether there is something to that. That there is a sense of everything is dirty, everyone is lying. That there is a so-called hedonism of I have to always be enjoying myself. But, men, please understand, and there is no doubt in my mind or should be in yours about this: the world is broken down into half the world is winners and half the world is losers. We have what is known as a locked struggle. The losers are trying to make losers of us all. This is their armageddon goal, and they are constantly attaining toward this goal with persuasive this and attractive that, mostly things of the body. But if we winners surrender, the world can say good-bye to the following. The precision excellence of football. American military superiority. Inventions to improve the daily lives of people from caveman times to now. Trust among humans based on here is my word and handshake. And hello to the following. Constant sex jokes in films, suck you, suck me. Everyone is obese. Cities are you can't even go into them without a machine gun. And one day when we're all watching TV, Ayatollah Busybody gets elected President of the World. It's a locked struggle. The championship of the world is at stake. You can take the first step toward winning that championship when we go out onto the field today.

So grab your helmets, men. I am going to teach you speed concepts, and I am going to teach you pre-game. I have studied Buddhist meditation, and tomorrow I will insert that component. I asked you to spit out that gum, son. Only losers have to always be doing something with their mouths. That's the main organ of losers, their mouths. Ours is our guts, men. Say it with me! Guts!

CONSIDERATIONS FOR CRITICAL THINKING AND WRITING

1. FIRST RESPONSE. To what extent is Cleveland Miller similar or dissimilar to coaches you have known? Is his characterization credible to you?

2. Cite specific examples of how diction, grammar, sentence structure, and logic reveal the coach's character.

3. How is Cleveland Miller's coaching style similar to his style of teaching?

4. What was the coach's experience in his previous job?

5. Why does the coach tell the story about Michael Wiltonberry? Why do you think the author includes it?

6. How does the penultimate paragraph suggest the coach's politics and world view?

7. Discuss the nature of the satire in this story. Explain why you found it humorous — or why you did not.

8. CONNECTION TO ANOTHER SELECTION. Compare the treatment of the boys' lives in Wyss's story and in Rick Moody's "Boys" (p. 226).

9. CONNECTION TO ANOTHER SELECTION. Write an essay that compares how style reveals character in "How to Be a Winner" and in the excerpt from Charles Dickens's *Hard Times* (p. 78).

Fiction in Depth

9

A Study of Flannery O'Connor

Everett Collection / Newscom.

In most English classes the short story has become a kind of literary specimen to be dissected. Every time a story of mine appears in a Freshman anthology, I have a vision of it, with its little organs laid open, like a frog in a bottle.

— FLANNERY O'CONNOR

I am always having it pointed out to me that life in Georgia is not at all the way I picture it, that escaped criminals do not roam the roads exterminating families, nor Bible salesmen prowl about looking for girls with wooden legs.

— FLANNERY O'CONNOR

When Flannery O'Connor (1925–1964) died of lupus before her fortieth birthday, her work was cruelly cut short. Nevertheless, she had completed two novels, *Wise Blood* (1952) and *The Violent Bear It Away* (1960), as well as thirty-one short stories. Despite her brief life and relatively modest output, her work is regarded as among the most distinguished American fiction of the mid-twentieth century. Her two collections of short stories, *A Good Man Is Hard to Find* (1955) and *Everything That Rises Must Converge* (1965), were included in *The Complete Stories of Flannery O'Connor* (1971), which won the National Book Award. The stories included in this chapter offer a glimpse into the work of this important twentieth-century writer.

Cheers,
Flannery

A BRIEF BIOGRAPHY AND INTRODUCTION

O'Connor's fiction grapples with living a spiritual life in a secular world. Although this major concern is worked into each of her stories, she takes a broad approach to spiritual issues by providing moral, social, and psychological contexts that offer a wealth of insights and passion that her readers have found both startling and absorbing. Her stories are challenging because her characters, who initially seem radically different from people we know, turn out to be, by the end of each story, somehow familiar — somehow connected to us.

O'Connor inhabited simultaneously two radically different worlds. The world she created in her stories is populated with bratty children, malcontents, incompetents, pious frauds, bewildered intellectuals, deformed cynics, rednecks, hucksters, racists, perverts, and murderers who experience dramatically intense moments that surprise and shock readers. Her personal life, however, was largely uneventful. She humorously acknowledged its quiet nature in 1958 when she claimed that "there won't be any biographies of me because, for only one reason, lives spent between the house and the chicken yard do not make exciting copy."

A broad outline of O'Connor's life may not offer very much "exciting copy," but it does provide clues about why she wrote such powerful fiction. The only child of Catholic parents, O'Connor was born in Savannah, Georgia, where she attended a parochial grammar school and high school. When she was thirteen, her father became ill with disseminated lupus, a rare, incurable blood disease, and had to abandon his real-estate business. The family moved to Milledgeville in central Georgia, where her mother's family had lived for generations. Because there were no Catholic schools in Milledgeville, O'Connor attended a public high school. In 1942, the year after her father died of lupus, O'Connor graduated from high school and enrolled in Georgia State College for Women. There she wrote for the literary magazine until receiving her diploma in 1945. Her stories earned her a fellowship to the Writers' Workshop at the University of Iowa, and for two years she learned to write steadily and seriously. She sold her first story to *Accent* in 1946 and earned her master of fine arts degree in 1947. She wrote stories about life in the rural South, and this subject matter, along with her devout Catholic perspective, became central to her fiction.

With her formal education behind her, O'Connor was ready to begin her professional career at the age of twenty-two. Equipped with determination ("No one can convince me that I shouldn't rewrite as much as I do") and offered the opportunity to be around other practicing writers, she moved to New York, where she worked on her first novel, *Wise Blood*. In 1950, however, she was diagnosed as having lupus, and, returning to Georgia for treatment, she took up permanent residence on her mother's farm in Milledgeville. There she lived a severely restricted but productive life, writing stories and raising peacocks.

Flannery O'Connor (above left) as a child at Andalusia farm and (above right) in her teens (age sixteen or seventeen). O'Connor, whose youth was marked by the declining health and death of her father, once wrote, "[A]nybody who has survived childhood has enough information about life to last him the rest of the days."

Flannery O'Connor and a Self-Portrait. The author poses in front of an accurate, if rather fierce, self-portrait with one of her beloved ring-necked pheasants. As a child, O'Connor enjoyed raising birds, a passion that was sparked when one of her chickens, "a buff Cochin Bantam [that] had the distinction of being able to walk either forward or backward," was reported on in the press. "I had to have more and more chickens. . . . I wanted one with three legs or three wings but nothing in that line turned up. . . . My quest, whatever it was for, ended with peacocks," she wrote.

The *Corinthian* Staff. Flannery O'Connor (seated, center) as editor of the *Corinthian*, the literary magazine at Georgia State College for Women (now Georgia College and State University). O'Connor attended the college from 1942 through 1945 and earned a B.A. in social science.
Courtesy of Ina Dillard Russell Library Special Collections, Georgia College and State University.

With the exception of O'Connor's early years in Iowa and New York and some short lecture trips to other states, she traveled little. Although she made a pilgrimage to Lourdes (apparently more for her mother's sake than for her own) and then to Rome for an audience with the pope, her life was centered in the South. Like those of William Faulkner and many other southern writers, O'Connor's stories evoke the rhythms of rural southern speech and manners in insulated settings where widely diverse characters mingle. Also like Faulkner, she created works whose meanings go beyond their settings. She did not want her fiction to be seen in the context of narrowly defined regionalism: she complained that "in almost every hamlet you'll find at least one old lady writing epics in Negro dialect and probably two or three old gentlemen who have impossible historical novels on the way." Refusing to be caricatured, she knew that "the woods are full of regional writers, and it is the great horror of every serious Southern writer that he will become one of them." O'Connor's stories are rooted in rural southern culture, but in a larger sense they are set within the psychological and spiritual landscapes of the human soul. This interior setting universalizes local materials in much the same way that Nathaniel Hawthorne's New England stories do. Indeed, O'Connor once described herself as "one of his descendants": "I feel more of a kinship with him than any other American."

O'Connor's deep spiritual convictions coincide with the traditional emphasis on religion in the South, where, she said, there is still the belief "that man has fallen and that he is only perfectible by God's grace, not by his own unaided efforts." Although O'Connor's Catholicism differs from the prevailing Protestant fundamentalism of the South, the religious ethos so pervasive even in rural southern areas provided fertile ground for the spiritual crises her characters experience. In a posthumous collection of her articles, essays, and reviews aptly titled *Mystery and Manners* (1969), she summarized her basic religious convictions:

> I am no disbeliever in spiritual purpose and no vague believer. I see from the standpoint of Christian orthodoxy. This means that for me the meaning of life is centered in our Redemption by Christ and what I see in the world I see in its relation to that. I don't think that this is a position that can be taken halfway or one that is particularly easy in these times to make transparent in fiction.

O'Connor realized that she was writing against the grain of the readers who discovered her stories in the *Partisan Review, Sewanee Review, Mademoiselle,* or *Harper's Bazaar.* Many readers thought that Christian dogma would make her writing doctrinaire, but she insisted that the perspective of Christianity allowed her to interpret the details of life and guaranteed her "respect for [life's] mystery." O'Connor's stories contain no prepackaged prescriptions for living, no catechisms that lay out all the answers. Instead, her characters struggle with spiritual questions in bizarre, incongruous situations. Their lives are grotesque — even comic — precisely because they do not understand their own spiritual natures. Their actions are extreme and abnormal. O'Connor explains the reasons for this in *Mystery and Manners*; she says she sought to expose the "distortions" of "modern life" that appear "normal" to her audience. Hence, she used "violent means" to convey her vision to a "hostile audience." "When you can assume that your audience holds the same beliefs you do, you can relax a little and use more normal means of talking to it." But when the audience holds different values, "you have to make your vision apparent by shock — to the hard of hearing you shout, and for the almost-blind you draw large and startling figures." O'Connor's characters lose or find their soul-saving grace in painful, chaotic circumstances that bear little or no resemblance to the slow but sure progress to the Celestial City of repentant pilgrims in traditional religious stories.

Because her characters are powerful creations who live convincing, even if ugly, lives, O'Connor's religious beliefs never supersede her storytelling. One need not be either Christian or Catholic to appreciate her concerns about human failure and degradation and her artistic ability to render fictional lives that are alternately absurdly comic and tragic. The ironies that abound in her work leave plenty of room for readers of all persuasions. O'Connor's work is narrow in the sense that her concerns are emphatically spiritual, but her compassion and her belief in human possibilities — even among the most unlikely characters — afford her fictions a capacity for wonder that is exhilarating. Her precise, deft use of language always reveals more than it seems to tell.

O'Connor's stories present complex experiences that cannot be tidily summarized; it takes the entire story to suggest the meanings. Read "A Good Man Is Hard to Find" for the pleasure of entering the remarkable world O'Connor creates. You're in for some surprises.

A Good Man Is Hard to Find   1953

The grandmother didn't want to go to Florida. She wanted to visit some of her connections in east Tennessee and she was seizing at every chance to change Bailey's mind. Bailey was the son she lived with, her only boy. He was sitting on the edge of his chair at the table, bent over the orange sports section of the *Journal*. "Now look here, Bailey," she said, "see here, read this," and she stood with one hand on her thin hip and the other rattling the newspaper at his bald head. "Here this fellow that calls himself The Misfit is aloose from the Federal Pen and headed toward Florida and you read here what it says he did to these people. Just you read it. I wouldn't take my children in any direction with a criminal like that aloose in it. I couldn't answer to my conscience if I did."

Bailey didn't look up from his reading so she wheeled around then and faced the children's mother, a young woman in slacks, whose face was as broad and innocent as a cabbage and was tied around with a green head-kerchief that had two points on the top like a rabbit's ears. She was sitting on the sofa, feeding the baby his apricots out of a jar. "The children have been to Florida before," the old lady said. "You all ought to take them somewhere else for a change so they would see different parts of the world and be broad. They never have been to east Tennessee."

The children's mother didn't seem to hear her but the eight-year-old boy, John Wesley, a stocky child with glasses, said, "If you don't want to go to Florida, why dontcha stay at home?" He and the little girl, June Star, were reading the funny papers on the floor.

"She wouldn't stay at home to be queen for a day," June Star said without raising her yellow head.

"Yes and what would you do if this fellow, The Misfit, caught you?" the   5 grandmother asked.

"I'd smack his face," John Wesley said.

"She wouldn't stay at home for a million bucks," June Star said. "Afraid she'd miss something. She has to go everywhere we go."

"All right, Miss," the grandmother said. "Just remember that the next time you want me to curl your hair."

June Star said her hair was naturally curly.

The next morning the grandmother was the first one in the car, ready to   10 go. She had her big black valise that looked like the head of a hippopotamus in one corner, and underneath it she was hiding a basket with Pitty Sing, the cat, in it. She didn't intend for the cat to be left alone in the house for three days because he would miss her too much and she was afraid he might brush against one of the gas burners and accidentally asphyxiate himself. Her son, Bailey, didn't like to arrive at a motel with a cat.

She sat in the middle of the back seat with John Wesley and June Star on either side of her. Bailey and the children's mother and the baby sat in front and they left Atlanta at eight forty-five with the mileage on the car at 55890. The grandmother wrote this down because she thought it would be interesting to say how many miles they had been when they got back. It took them twenty minutes to reach the outskirts of the city.

The old lady settled herself comfortably, removing her white cotton gloves and putting them up with her purse on the shelf in front of the back window. The children's mother still had on slacks and still had her head tied up in a green kerchief, but the grandmother had on a navy blue straw sailor hat with a bunch of white violets on the brim and a navy blue dress with a small white dot in the print. Her collars and cuffs were white organdy trimmed with lace and at her neckline she had pinned a purple spray of cloth violets containing a sachet. In case of an accident, anyone seeing her dead on the highway would know at once that she was a lady.

She said she thought it was going to be a good day for driving, neither too hot nor too cold, and she cautioned Bailey that the speed limit was fifty-five miles an hour and that the patrolmen hid themselves behind billboards and small clumps of trees and sped out after you before you had a chance to slow down. She pointed out interesting details of the scenery: Stone Mountain; the blue granite that in some places came up to both sides of the highway; the brilliant red clay banks slightly streaked with purple; and the various crops that made rows of green lace-work on the ground. The trees were full of silver-white sunlight and the meanest of them sparkled. The children were reading comic magazines and their mother had gone back to sleep.

"Let's go through Georgia fast so we won't have to look at it much," John Wesley said.

"If I were a little boy," said the grandmother, "I wouldn't talk about my 15 native state that way. Tennessee has the mountains and Georgia has the hills."

"Tennessee is just a hillbilly dumping ground," John Wesley said, "and Georgia is a lousy state too."

"You said it," June Star said.

"In my time," said the grandmother, folding her thin veined fingers, "children were more respectful of their native states and their parents and everything else. People did right then. Oh look at the cute little pickaninny!" she said and pointed to a Negro child standing in the door of a shack. "Wouldn't that make a picture, now?" she asked and they all turned and looked at the little Negro out of the back window. He waved.

"He didn't have any britches on," June Star said.

"He probably didn't have any," the grandmother explained. "Little nig- 20 gers in the country don't have things like we do. If I could paint, I'd paint that picture," she said.

The children exchanged comic books.

The grandmother offered to hold the baby and the children's mother passed him over the front seat to her. She set him on her knee and bounced him and told him about the things they were passing. She rolled her eyes and screwed up her mouth and stuck her leathery thin face into his smooth bland one. Occasionally he gave her a faraway smile. They passed a large cotton field with five or six graves fenced in the middle of it, like a small island. "Look at the graveyard!" the grandmother said, pointing it out. "That was the old family burying ground. That belonged to the plantation."

"Where's the plantation?" John Wesley asked.

"Gone With the Wind," said the grandmother. "Ha. Ha."

When the children finished all the comic books they had brought, they 25 opened the lunch and ate it. The grandmother ate a peanut butter sandwich and an olive and would not let the children throw the box and the paper napkins out the window. When there was nothing else to do they played a game by choosing a cloud and making the other two guess what shape it suggested. John Wesley took one the shape of a cow and June Star guessed a cow and John Wesley said, no, an automobile, and June Star said he didn't play fair, and they began to slap each other over the grandmother.

The grandmother said she would tell them a story if they would keep quiet. When she told a story, she rolled her eyes and waved her head and was very dramatic. She said once when she was a maiden lady she had been courted by a Mr. Edgar Atkins Teagarden from Jasper, Georgia. She said he was a very good-looking man and a gentleman and that he brought her a watermelon every Saturday afternoon with his initials cut in it, E.A.T. Well, one Saturday, she said, Mr. Teagarden brought the watermelon and there was nobody at home and he left it on the front porch and returned in his buggy to Jasper, but she never got the watermelon, she said, because a nigger boy ate it when he saw the initials, E.A.T.! This story tickled John Wesley's funny bone and he giggled and giggled but June Star didn't think it was any good. She said she wouldn't marry a man that just brought her a watermelon on Saturday. The grandmother said she would have done well to marry Mr. Teagarden because he was a gentleman and had bought Coca-Cola stock when it first came out and that he had died only a few years ago, a very wealthy man.

They stopped at The Tower for barbecued sandwiches. The Tower was a part stucco and part wood filling station and dance hall set in a clearing outside of Timothy. A fat man named Red Sammy Butts ran it and there were signs stuck here and there on the building and for miles up and down the highway saying, TRY RED SAMMY'S FAMOUS BARBECUE. NONE LIKE FAMOUS RED SAMMY'S! RED SAM! THE FAT BOY WITH THE HAPPY LAUGH. A VETERAN! RED SAMMY'S YOUR MAN!

Red Sammy was lying on the bare ground outside The Tower with his head under a truck while a gray monkey about a foot high, chained to a small chinaberry tree, chattered nearby. The monkey sprang back into the tree and got on the highest limb as soon as he saw the children jump out of the car and run toward him.

Inside, The Tower was a long dark room with a counter at one end and tables at the other and dancing space in the middle. They all sat down at a board table next to the nickelodeon and Red Sam's wife, a tall burnt-brown woman with hair and eyes lighter than her skin, came and took their order. The children's mother put a dime in the machine and played "The Tennessee Waltz," and the grandmother said that tune always made her want to dance. She asked Bailey if he would like to dance but he only glared at her. He didn't have a naturally sunny disposition like she did and trips made him nervous. The grandmother's brown eyes were very bright. She swayed her head from side to side and pretended she was dancing in her chair. June Star said play something she could tap to so the children's mother put in another dime and played a fast number and June Star stepped out onto the dance floor and did her tap routine.

"Ain't she cute?" Red Sam's wife said, leaning over the counter. "Would you like to come be my little girl?"   30

"No I certainly wouldn't," June Star said. "I wouldn't live in a broken-down place like this for a million bucks!" and she ran back to the table.

"Ain't she cute?" the woman repeated, stretching her mouth politely.

"Aren't you ashamed?" hissed the grandmother.

Red Sam came in and told his wife to quit lounging on the counter and hurry up with these people's order. His khaki trousers reached just to his hip bones and his stomach hung over them like a sack of meal swaying under his shirt. He came over and sat down at a table nearby and let out a combination sigh and yodel. "You can't win," he said. "You can't win," and he wiped his sweating red face off with a gray handkerchief. "These days you don't know who to trust," he said. "Ain't that the truth?"

"People are certainly not nice like they used to be," said the grandmother.   35

"Two fellers come in here last week," Red Sammy said, "driving a Chrysler. It was a old beat-up car but it was a good one and these boys looked all right to me. Said they worked at the mill and you know I let them fellers charge the gas they bought? Now why did I do that?"

"Because you're a good man!" the grandmother said at once.

"Yes'm, I suppose so," Red Sam said as if he were struck with this answer.

His wife brought the orders, carrying the five plates all at once without a tray, two in each hand and one balanced on her arm. "It isn't a soul in this green world of God's that you can trust," she said. "And I don't count nobody out of that, not nobody," she repeated, looking at Red Sammy.

"Did you read about that criminal, The Misfit, that's escaped?" asked the grandmother.   40

"I wouldn't be a bit surprised if he didn't attack this place right here," said the woman. "If he hears about it being here, I wouldn't be none surprised to see him. If he hears it's two cent in the cash register, I wouldn't be a tall surprised if he. . . ."

"That'll do," Red Sam said. "Go bring these people their Co'-Colas," and the woman went off to get the rest of the order.

"A good man is hard to find," Red Sammy said. "Everything is getting terrible. I remember the day you could go off and leave your screen door unlatched. Not no more."

He and the grandmother discussed better times. The old lady said that in her opinion Europe was entirely to blame for the way things were now. She said the way Europe acted you would think we were made of money and Red Sam said it was no use talking about it, she was exactly right. The children ran outside into the white sunlight and looked at the monkey in the lacy chinaberry tree. He was busy catching fleas on himself and biting each one carefully between his teeth as if it were a delicacy.

They drove off again into the hot afternoon. The grandmother took 45 cat naps and woke up every few minutes with her own snoring. Outside of Toombsboro she woke up and recalled an old plantation that she had visited in this neighborhood once when she was a young lady. She said the house had six white columns across the front and that there was an avenue of oaks leading up to it and two little wooden trellis arbors on either side in front where you sat down with your suitor after a stroll in the garden. She recalled exactly which road to turn off to get to it. She knew that Bailey would not be willing to lose any time looking at an old house, but the more she talked about it, the more she wanted to see it once again and find out if the little twin arbors were still standing. "There was a secret panel in this house," she said craftily, not telling the truth but wishing that she were, "and the story went that all the family silver was hidden in it when Sherman° came through but it was never found. . . ."

"Hey!" John Wesley said. "Let's go see it! We'll find it! We'll poke all the woodwork and find it! Who lives there? Where do you turn off at? Hey Pop, can't we turn off there?"

"We never have seen a house with a secret panel!" June Star shrieked. "Let's go to the house with the secret panel! Hey Pop, can't we go see the house with the secret panel!"

"It's not far from here, I know," the grandmother said. "It won't take over twenty minutes."

Bailey was looking straight ahead. His jaw was as rigid as a horseshoe. "No," he said.

The children began to yell and scream that they wanted to see the house 50 with the secret panel. John Wesley kicked the back of the front seat and June Star hung over her mother's shoulder and whined desperately into her ear that they never had any fun even on their vacation, that they could never do what THEY wanted to do. The baby began to scream and John Wesley kicked the back of the seat so hard that his father could feel the blows in his kidney.

"All right!" he shouted and drew the car to a stop at the side of the road. "Will you all shut up? Will you all just shut up for one second? If you don't shut up, we won't go anywhere."

"It would be very educational for them," the grandmother murmured.

"All right," Bailey said, "but get this: this is the only time we're going to stop for anything like this. This is the one and only time."

"The dirt road that you have to turn down is about a mile back," the grandmother directed. "I marked it when we passed."

Sherman: William Tecumseh Sherman (1820–1891), Union Army commander who led infamous marches through the South during the Civil War.

"A dirt road," Bailey groaned.   55

After they had turned around and were headed toward the dirt road, the grandmother recalled other points about the house, the beautiful glass over the front doorway and the candle-lamp in the hall. John Wesley said that the secret panel was probably in the fireplace.

"You can't go inside this house," Bailey said. "You don't know who lives there."

"While you all talk to the people in front, I'll run around behind and get in a window," John Wesley suggested.

"We'll all stay in the car," his mother said.

They turned onto the dirt road and the car raced roughly along in a swirl   60
of pink dust. The grandmother recalled the times when there were no paved roads and thirty miles was a day's journey. The dirt road was hilly and there were sudden washes in it and sharp curves on dangerous embankments. All at once they would be on a hill, looking down over the blue tops of trees for miles around, then the next minute, they would be in a red depression with the dust-coated trees looking down on them.

"This place had better turn up in a minute," Bailey said, "or I'm going to turn around."

The road looked as if no one had traveled on it for months.

"It's not much farther," the grandmother said and just as she said it, a horrible thought came to her. The thought was so embarrassing that she turned red in the face and her eyes dilated and her feet jumped up, upsetting her valise in the corner. The instant the valise moved, the newspaper top she had over the basket under it rose with a snarl and Pitty Sing, the cat, sprang onto Bailey's shoulder.

The children were thrown to the floor and their mother, clutching the baby, was thrown out the door onto the ground; the old lady was thrown into the front seat. The car turned over once and landed right-side-up in a gulch off the side of the road. Bailey remained in the driver's seat with the cat — gray-striped with a broad white face and an orange nose — clinging to his neck like a caterpillar.

As soon as the children saw they could move their arms and legs, they   65
scrambled out of the car, shouting, "We've had an ACCIDENT!" The grandmother was curled up under the dashboard, hoping she was injured so that Bailey's wrath would not come down on her all at once. The horrible thought she had before the accident was that the house she had remembered so vividly was not in Georgia but in Tennessee.

Bailey removed the cat from his neck with both hands and flung it out the window against the side of a pine tree. Then he got out of the car and started looking for the children's mother. She was sitting against the side of the red gutted ditch, holding the screaming baby, but she only had a cut down her face and a broken shoulder. "We've had an ACCIDENT!" the children screamed in a frenzy of delight.

"But nobody's killed," June Star said with disappointment as the grandmother limped out of the car, her hat still pinned to her head but the broken front brim standing up at a jaunty angle and the violet spray hanging off the side. They all sat down in the ditch, except the children, to recover from the shock. They were all shaking.

"Maybe a car will come along," said the children's mother hoarsely.

"I believe I have injured an organ," said the grandmother, pressing her side, but no one answered her. Bailey's teeth were clattering. He had on a yellow sport shirt with bright blue parrots designed in it and his face was as yellow as the shirt. The grandmother decided that she would not mention that the house was in Tennessee.

The road was about ten feet above and they could see only the tops of 70 the trees on the other side of it. Behind the ditch they were sitting in there were more woods, tall and dark and deep. In a few minutes they saw a car some distance away on top of a hill, coming slowly as if the occupants were watching them. The grandmother stood up and waved both arms dramatically to attract their attention. The car continued to come on slowly, disappeared around a bend and appeared again, moving even slower, on top of the hill they had gone over. It was a big black battered hearse-like automobile. There were three men in it.

It came to a stop just over them and for some minutes, the driver looked down with a steady expressionless gaze to where they were sitting, and didn't speak. Then he turned his head and muttered something to the other two and they got out. One was a fat boy in black trousers and a red sweat shirt with a silver stallion embossed on the front of it. He moved around on the right side of them and stood staring, his mouth partly open in a kind of loose grin. The other had on khaki pants and a blue striped coat and a gray hat pulled down very low, hiding most of his face. He came around slowly on the left side. Neither spoke.

The driver got out of the car and stood by the side of it, looking down at them. He was an older man than the other two. His hair was just beginning to gray and he wore silver-rimmed spectacles that gave him a scholarly look. He had a long creased face and didn't have on any shirt or undershirt. He had on blue jeans that were too tight for him and was holding a black hat and a gun. The two boys also had guns.

"We've had an ACCIDENT!" the children screamed.

The grandmother had the peculiar feeling that the bespectacled man was someone she knew. His face was as familiar to her as if she had known him all her life but she could not recall who he was. He moved away from the car and began to come down the embankment, placing his feet carefully so that he wouldn't slip. He had on tan and white shoes and no socks, and his ankles were red and thin. "Good afternoon," he said. "I see you all had you a little spill."

"We turned over twice!" said the grandmother.   75

"Oncet," he corrected. "We seen it happen. Try their car and see will it run, Hiram," he said quietly to the boy with the gray hat.

"What you got that gun for?" John Wesley asked. "Whatcha gonna do with that gun?"

"Lady," the man said to the children's mother, "would you mind calling them children to sit down by you? Children make me nervous. I want all you all to sit down right together there where you're at."

"What are you telling US what to do for?" June Star asked.

Behind them the line of woods gaped like a dark open mouth. "Come 80 here," said their mother.

"Look here now," Bailey said suddenly, "we're in a predicament! We're in. . . ."

The grandmother shrieked. She scrambled to her feet and stood staring. "You're The Misfit!" she said. "I recognized you at once!"

"Yes'm," the man said, smiling slightly as if he were pleased in spite of himself to be known, "but it would have been better for all of you, lady, if you hadn't of reckernized me."

Bailey turned his head sharply and said something to his mother that shocked even the children. The old lady began to cry and The Misfit reddened.

"Lady," he said, "don't you get upset. Sometimes a man says things he 85 don't mean. I don't reckon he meant to talk to you thataway."

"You wouldn't shoot a lady, would you?" the grandmother said and removed a clean handkerchief from her cuff and began to slap at her eyes with it.

The Misfit pointed the toe of his shoe into the ground and made a little hole and then covered it up again. "I would hate to have to," he said.

"Listen," the grandmother almost screamed, "I know you're a good man. You don't look a bit like you have common blood. I know you must come from nice people!"

"Yes mam," he said, "finest people in the world." When he smiled he showed a row of strong white teeth. "God never made a finer woman than my mother and my daddy's heart was pure gold," he said. The boy with the red sweat shirt had come around behind them and was standing with his gun at his hip. The Misfit squatted down on the ground. "Watch them children, Bobby Lee," he said. "You know they make me nervous." He looked at the six of them huddled together in front of him and he seemed to be embarrassed as if he couldn't think of anything to say. "Ain't a cloud in the sky," he remarked, looking up at it. "Don't see no sun but don't see no cloud neither."

"Yes, it's a beautiful day," said the grandmother. "Listen," she said, "you 90 shouldn't call yourself The Misfit because I know you're a good man at heart. I can just look at you and tell."

"Hush!" Bailey yelled. "Hush! Everybody shut up and let me handle this!" He was squatting in the position of a runner about to sprint forward but he didn't move.

"I pre-chate that, lady," The Misfit said and drew a little circle in the ground with the butt of his gun.

"It'll take a half a hour to fix this here car," Hiram called, looking over the raised hood of it.

"Well, first you and Bobby Lee get him and that little boy to step over yonder with you," The Misfit said, pointing to Bailey and John Wesley. "The boys want to ast you something," he said to Bailey. "Would you mind stepping back in them woods there with them?"

"Listen," Bailey began, "we're in a terrible predicament! Nobody realizes 95 what this is," and his voice cracked. His eyes were as blue and intense as the parrots in his shirt and he remained perfectly still.

The grandmother reached up to adjust her hat brim as if she were going to the woods with him but it came off in her hand. She stood staring at it and after a second she let it fall to the ground. Hiram pulled Bailey up by the arm as if he were assisting an old man. John Wesley caught hold of his father's hand and Bobby Lee followed. They went off toward the woods and just as they reached the dark edge, Bailey turned and supporting himself against a gray naked pine trunk, he shouted, "I'll be back in a minute, Mamma, wait on me!"

"Come back this instant!" his mother shrilled but they all disappeared into the woods.

"Bailey Boy!" the grandmother called in a tragic voice but she found she was looking at The Misfit squatting on the ground in front of her. "I just know you're a good man," she said desperately. "You're not a bit common!"

"Nome, I ain't a good man," The Misfit said after a second as if he had considered her statement carefully, "but I ain't the worst in the world neither. My daddy said I was a different breed of dog from my brothers and sisters. 'You know,' Daddy said, 'it's some that can live their whole life out without asking about it and it's others has to know why it is, and this boy is one of the latters. He's going to be into everything!'" He put on his black hat and looked up suddenly and then away deep into the woods as if he were embarrassed again. "I'm sorry I don't have on a shirt before you ladies," he said, hunching his shoulders slightly. "We buried our clothes that we had on when we escaped and we're just making do until we can get better. We borrowed these from some folks we met," he explained.

"That's perfectly all right," the grandmother said. "Maybe Bailey has an 100 extra shirt in his suitcase."

"I'll look and see terrectly," The Misfit said.

"Where are they taking him?" the children's mother screamed.

"Daddy was a card himself," The Misfit said. "You couldn't put anything over on him. He never got in trouble with the Authorities though. Just had the knack of handling them."

"You could be honest too if you'd only try," said the grandmother. "Think how wonderful it would be to settle down and live a comfortable life and not have to think about somebody chasing you all the time."

The Misfit kept scratching in the ground with the butt of his gun as if he 105 were thinking about it. "Yes'm, somebody is always after you," he murmured.

The grandmother noticed how thin his shoulder blades were just behind his hat because she was standing up looking down on him. "Do you ever pray?" she asked.

He shook his head. All she saw was the black hat wiggle between his shoulder blades. "Nome," he said.

There was a pistol shot from the woods, followed closely by another. Then silence. The old lady's head jerked around. She could hear the wind move through the tree tops like a long satisfied insuck of breath. "Bailey Boy!" she called.

"I was a gospel singer for a while," The Misfit said. "I been most everything. Been in the arm service, both land and sea, at home and abroad, been twict married, been an undertaker, been with the railroads, plowed Mother Earth, been in a tornado, seen a man burnt alive oncet," and he looked up at the children's mother and the little girl who were sitting close together, their faces white and their eyes glassy; "I even seen a woman flogged," he said.

"Pray, pray," the grandmother began, "pray, pray. . . ."   110

"I never was a bad boy that I remember of," The Misfit said in an almost dreamy voice, "but somewheres along the line I done something wrong and got sent to the penitentiary. I was buried alive," and he looked up and held her attention to him by a steady stare.

"That's when you should have started to pray," she said. "What did you do to get sent to the penitentiary that first time?"

"Turn to the right, it was a wall," The Misfit said, looking up again at the cloudless sky. "Turn to the left, it was a wall. Look up it was a ceiling, look down it was a floor. I forget what I done, lady. I set there and set there, trying to remember what it was I done and I ain't recalled it to this day. Oncet in a while, I would think it was coming to me, but it never come."

"Maybe they put you in by mistake," the old lady said vaguely.

"Nome," he said. "It wasn't no mistake. They had the papers on me."   115

"You must have stolen something," she said.

The Misfit sneered slightly. "Nobody had nothing I wanted," he said. "It was a head-doctor at the penitentiary said what I had done was kill my daddy but I known that for a lie. My daddy died in nineteen ought nineteen of the epidemic flu and I never had a thing to do with it. He was buried in the Mount Hopewell Baptist churchyard and you can see for yourself."

"If you would pray," the old lady said, "Jesus would help you."

"That's right," The Misfit said.

"Well then, why don't you pray?" she asked trembling with delight   120 suddenly.

"I don't want no hep," he said. "I'm doing all right by myself."

Bobby Lee and Hiram came ambling back from the woods. Bobby Lee was dragging a yellow shirt with bright blue parrots in it.

"Throw me that shirt, Bobby Lee," The Misfit said. The shirt came flying at him and landed on his shoulder and he put it on. The grandmother couldn't name what the shirt reminded her of. "No, lady," The Misfit said while he was buttoning it up, "I found out the crime don't matter. You can do one thing or you can do another, kill a man or take a tire off his car, because sooner or later you're going to forget what it was you done and just be punished for it."

The children's mother had begun to make heaving noises as if she couldn't get her breath. "Lady," he asked, "would you and that little girl like to step off yonder with Bobby Lee and Hiram and join your husband?"

"Yes, thank you," the mother said faintly. Her left arm dangled helplessly 125
and she was holding the baby, who had gone to sleep, in the other. "Hep that
lady up, Hiram," The Misfit said as she struggled to climb out of the ditch,
"and Bobby Lee, you hold onto that little girl's hand."

"I don't want to hold hands with him," June Star said. "He reminds me
of a pig."

The fat boy blushed and laughed and caught her by the arm and pulled
her off into the woods after Hiram and her mother.

Alone with The Misfit, the grandmother found that she had lost her
voice. There was not a cloud in the sky nor any sun. There was nothing
around her but woods. She wanted to tell him that he must pray. She opened
and closed her mouth several times before anything came out. Finally she
found herself saying, "Jesus, Jesus," meaning Jesus will help you, but the way
she was saying it, it sounded as if she might be cursing.

"Yes'm," The Misfit said as if he agreed. "Jesus thown everything off balance. It was the same case with Him as with me except He hadn't committed
any crime and they could prove I had committed one because they had the
papers on me. Of course," he said, "they never shown me my papers. That's
why I sign myself now. I said long ago, you get your signature and sign everything you do and keep a copy of it. Then you'll know what you done and you
can hold up the crime to the punishment and see do they match and in the
end you'll have something to prove you ain't been treated right. I call myself
The Misfit," he said, "because I can't make what all I done wrong fit what all I
gone through in punishment."

There was a piercing scream from the woods, followed closely by a pis- 130
tol report. "Does it seem right to you, lady, that one is punished a heap and
another ain't punished at all?"

"Jesus!" the old lady cried. "You've got good blood! I know you wouldn't
shoot a lady! I know you come from nice people! Pray! Jesus, you ought not
to shoot a lady. I'll give you all the money I've got!"

"Lady," The Misfit said, looking beyond her far into the woods, "there
never was a body that give the undertaker a tip."

There were two more pistol reports and the grandmother raised her head
like a parched old turkey hen crying for water and called, "Bailey Boy, Bailey
Boy!" as if her heart would break.

"Jesus was the only One that ever raised the dead," The Misfit continued, "and He shouldn't have done it. He thown everything off balance. If He
did what He said, then it's nothing for you to do but thow away everything
and follow Him, and if He didn't, then it's nothing for you to do but enjoy
the few minutes you got left the best way you can — by killing somebody or
burning down his house or doing some other meanness to him. No pleasure but meanness," he said and his voice had become almost a snarl.

"Maybe He didn't raise the dead," the old lady mumbled, not knowing 135
what she was saying and feeling so dizzy that she sank down in the ditch with
her legs twisted under her.

"I wasn't there so I can't say He didn't," The Misfit said. "I wisht I had of
been there," he said, hitting the ground with his fist. "It ain't right I wasn't

there because if I had of been there I would of known. Listen lady," he said in a high voice, "if I had of been there I would of known and I wouldn't be like I am now." His voice seemed about to crack and the grandmother's head cleared for an instant. She saw the man's face twisted close to her own as if he were going to cry and she murmured, "Why you're one of my babies. You're one of my own children!" She reached out and touched him on the shoulder. The Misfit sprang back as if a snake had bitten him and shot her three times through the chest. Then he put his gun down on the ground and took off his glasses and began to clean them.

Hiram and Bobby Lee returned from the woods and stood over the ditch, looking down at the grandmother who half sat and half lay in a puddle of blood with her legs crossed under her like a child's and her face smiling up at the cloudless sky.

Without his glasses, The Misfit's eyes were red-rimmed and pale and defenseless-looking. "Take her off and thow her where you thown the others," he said, picking up the cat that was rubbing itself against his leg.

"She was a talker, wasn't she?" Bobby Lee said, sliding down the ditch with a yodel.

"She would of been a good woman," The Misfit said, "if it had been somebody there to shoot her every minute of her life." 140

"Some fun!" Bobby Lee said.

"Shut up, Bobby Lee," The Misfit said. "It's no real pleasure in life."

CONSIDERATIONS FOR CRITICAL THINKING AND WRITING

1. FIRST RESPONSE. How does O'Connor portray the family? What is comic about them? What qualities about them are we meant to take seriously? Are you shocked by what happens to them? Does your attitude toward them remain constant during the course of the story?

2. How do the grandmother's concerns about the trip to Florida foreshadow events in the story?

3. Describe the grandmother. How does O'Connor make her the central character?

4. Characterize The Misfit. What makes him so? Can he be written off as simply insane? How does the grandmother respond to him?

5. Why does The Misfit say that "Jesus thown everything off balance" (para. 129)? What does religion have to do with the brutal action of this story?

6. What does The Misfit mean at the end when he says about the grandmother, "She would of been a good woman . . . if it had been somebody there to shoot her every minute of her life"?

7. Describe the story's tone. Is it consistent? What is the effect of O'Connor's use of tone?

8. How is coincidence used to advance the plot? How do coincidences lead to ironies in the story?

9. Explain how the title points to the story's theme.

Perspectives on O'Connor

FLANNERY O'CONNOR

On the Use of Exaggeration and Distortion   1969

When I write a novel in which the central action is a baptism, I am very well aware that for a majority of my readers, baptism is a meaningless rite, and so in my novel I have to see that this baptism carries enough awe and mystery to jar the reader into some kind of emotional recognition of its significance. To this end I have to bend the whole novel — its language, its structure, its action. I have to make the reader feel, in his bones if nowhere else, that something is going on here that counts. Distortion in this case is an instrument; exaggeration has a purpose, and the whole structure of the story or novel has been made what it is because of belief. This is not the kind of distortion that destroys; it is the kind that reveals, or should reveal.

From "Novelist and Believer" in *Mystery and Manners*

CONSIDERATIONS FOR CRITICAL THINKING AND WRITING

1. O'Connor says that exaggeration and distortion reveal something in her stories. What is the effect of such exaggeration and distortion in "A Good Man Is Hard to Find"? What is revealed by it?

2. Do you think that O'Connor's story has anything to offer a reader who has no religious faith? Explain why or why not.

JOSEPHINE HENDIN (B. 1946)

On O'Connor's Refusal to "Do Pretty"   1970

There is, in the memory of one Milledgeville matron, the image of O'Connor at nineteen or twenty who, when invited to a wedding shower for an old family friend, remained standing, her back pressed against the wall, scowling at the group of women who had sat down to lunch. Neither the devil nor her mother could make her say yes to this fiercely gracious female society, but Flannery O'Connor could not say no even in a whisper. She could not refuse the invitation but she would not accept it either. She did not exactly "fuss" but neither did she "do pretty."

From *The World of Flannery O'Connor*

CONSIDERATIONS FOR CRITICAL THINKING AND WRITING

1. How is O'Connor's personality revealed in this anecdote about her ambivalent response to society? Allow the description to be suggestive for you, and flesh out a brief portrait of her.

2. Consider how this personality makes itself apparent in "A Good Man Is Hard to Find." How does the anecdote help to characterize the narrator's voice in the story?

3. To what extent do you think biographical details such as this — assuming the Milledgeville matron's memory to be accurate — can shed light on a writer's works?

CLAIRE KATZ (B. 1935)

The Function of Violence in O'Connor's Fiction   *1974*

From the moment the reader enters O'Connor's backwoods, he is poised on the edge of a pervasive violence. Characters barely contain their rage; images reflect a hostile nature; and even the Christ to whom the characters are ultimately driven is a threatening figure . . . full of the apocalyptic wrath of the Old Testament.

O'Connor's conscious purpose is evident enough . . . . : to reveal the need for grace in a world grotesque without a transcendent context. "I have found that my subject in fiction is the action of grace in territory largely held by the devil," she wrote [in *Mystery and Manners*], and she was not vague about what the devil is: "an evil intelligence determined on its own supremacy." It would seem that for O'Connor, given the fact of original Sin, any intelligence determined on its own supremacy was intrinsically evil. For in each work, it is the impulse toward secular autonomy, the smug confidence that human nature is perfectible by its own efforts, that she sets out to destroy, through an act of violence so intense that the character is rendered helpless, a passive victim of a superior power. Again and again she creates a fiction in which a character attempts to live autonomously, to define himself and his values, only to be jarred back to what she calls "reality" — the recognition of helplessness in the face of contingency, and the need for absolute submission to the power of Christ.

From "Flannery O'Connor's Rage of Vision"
in *American Literature*

CONSIDERATIONS FOR CRITICAL THINKING AND WRITING

1. Which O'Connor characters can be accurately described as having an "evil intelligence determined on its own supremacy" (para. 2)? Choose one character, and write an essay explaining how this description is central to the conflict of the story.

2. Compare this O'Connor story with one of Hawthorne's "in which a character attempts to live autonomously, to define himself and his values, only to be jarred back to . . . 'reality' — the recognition of helplessness in the face of contingency . . ." (para. 2).

Time *Magazine, on* A Good Man Is Hard to Find and Other Stories

1962

Highly unladylike . . . a brutal irony, a slam-bang humor, and a style of writing as balefully direct as a death sentence.

> From a *Time* magazine blurb quoted on the cover of the second American edition of *A Good Man Is Hard to Find and Other Stories*

CONSIDERATIONS FOR CRITICAL THINKING AND WRITING

1. How adequate do you think this blurb is in characterizing the story?
2. CREATIVE RESPONSE. Write your own blurb for the story and be prepared to justify your pithy description.

10

A Study of
Dagoberto Gilb: The Author
Reflects on Three Stories

For me, fiction is life transformed and
fueled by imagination.
— DAGOBERTO GILB

Courtesy of Dagoberto Gilb.

INTRODUCTION

Dagoberto Gilb chose the three short stories in this chapter and provides commentary on each of them. Along with his personal observations on the stories are relevant images and documents that offer perspectives for interpreting and appreciating his fiction. Gilb's candid comments on the stories are written specifically for readers who are interested in why and how the stories were composed. He reveals some of the biographical contexts and circumstances that led him to become an avid reader and then a successful writer (despite the dismal grade he received for his first college English

Courtesy of Dagoberto Gilb.

paper) and how he managed to build a fictional world while working full time on construction sites.

In addition to the stories and commentaries, this chapter also offers contexts for the stories, including photographs of his family and his life as a construction carpenter in Los Angeles, California, and El Paso, Texas. Also included are a draft manuscript page from an essay collection, an edited galley from the short story "Uncle Rock" originally published in the *New Yorker*, Gilb's comments on physical labor and popular perceptions of Mexican American culture, and an interview with Michael Meyer that ranges from issues of political correctness to how "advocacy" is embedded in Gilb's literary art. You'll find this ex-carpenter to be a straightforward storyteller who makes a point of being on the level.

A BRIEF BIOGRAPHY

Born in Los Angeles in 1950, Dagoberto Gilb worked as a construction worker and a journeyman high-rise carpenter with the United Brotherhood of Carpenters for some sixteen years as he began hammering out his fiction. Though born and raised in California, he considered both Los Angeles and El Paso to be home. His Anglo father was a laconic, hardened World War II Marine Corps veteran who worked for nearly fifty years in a Los Angeles industrial laundry, his mother was an undocumented Mexican immigrant, and their marriage ended early. Gilb's life, like his fiction, is grounded by working-class circumstances in which laborers sweat to pay bills and put food on the table. He does not list any unpaid internships on his résumé.

As Gilb acknowledges in *Gritos*, a collection of essays, he was not in his youth "precocious in matters of literature, even to the end of my teenage years when I still thought of 'book' more as a verb." He did, however, read on the job and make his way to junior college and then to the University of California, Santa Barbara, where he earned a B.A. and an M.A. studying philosophy and religious studies. In college, he devoured canonical American and European writers and then discovered Chicano literature, works that ultimately inspired him to write about his own experiences. After graduate school, he followed construction jobs between Los Angeles and El Paso, making a living and finding the material for framing much of his writing.

Following some success in publishing a number of short stories in literary journals, a chapbook-size collection of stories, *Winners on the Pass Line*, appeared in 1985. Gilb's first full collection, the critically acclaimed book *The Magic of Blood* (1993), won the PEN/Ernest Hemingway Award as well as the Jesse Jones Award from the Texas Institute of Letters and was a finalist for the PEN/Faulkner Award. On the heels of a National Endowment for the Arts Fellowship, he published a novel, *The Last Known Residence of Mickey Acuña* (1994), which was followed by a Guggenheim Foundation Fellowship. *Gritos* (2003), consisting of essays previously published in such venues as the *New Yorker*, the *New York Times*, the *Los Angeles Times*, and the *Nation*, along with commentaries written for National Public Radio's

(*Top*) Dagoberto
Gilb's mother. Los
Angeles, California,
late 1940s.
Courtesy of Dagoberto Gilb.

(*Right*) Dagoberto
Gilb with his older
son, Antonio. El Paso,
Texas, 1978.
Courtesy of Dagoberto Gilb

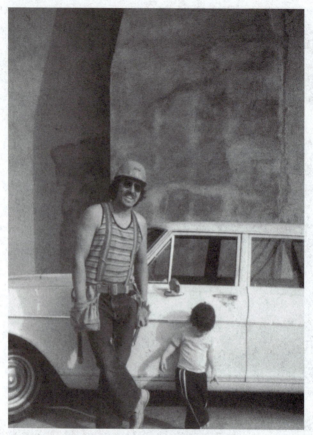

The author with his son Antonio. Los Angeles, California, 1981. The '62 Chevy pictured here is the very one mentioned on page 269.
Courtesy of Dagoberto Gilb.

Fresh Air, offers a perspective on how a Mexican American working man became a nationally recognized working writer. Another novel, *The Flowers* (2008), and two more collections of stories, *Woodcuts of Women* (2001) and *Before the End, After the Beginning* (2011), have solidified his reputation as a highly regarded fiction writer. His works have been translated into Spanish, French, German, Italian, Japanese, Chinese, and Turkish, and he has been invited to be a visiting writer at a number of schools, including the University of Texas at Austin, the University of Wyoming, the University of Arizona, and Vassar College.

Previously a tenured professor in the Creative Writing Program at Texas State University in San Marcos, Gilb is currently writer-in-residence and executive director of Centro Victoria, a center for Mexican American literature and culture at the University of Houston in Victoria, Texas,

Dagoberto Gilb at work. Los Angeles, California, 1986.
Courtesy of Dagoberto Gilb.

where the undergraduate student body is primarily Latino; he describes the school as "the smallest, most just barely at its beginning university in the country." Located equidistant from Houston, Austin, San Antonio, and Corpus Christi, in a state that in several years will be 50 percent Latino, Centro Victoria was founded, in part, to educate Texans of all ethnicities and educational levels — and others outside the state — about the history and culture of Mexican Americans, who make up two-thirds of the Latino population in the United States. The purpose of the center is to foster an understanding and appreciation of Mexican American literature and art in Texas and beyond.

One of Centro Victoria's major projects is to provide Texas students and teachers with lesson plans based on *Hecho en Tejas: An Anthology of Texas Mexican Literature* (2006), edited by Gilb, which ranges from sixteenth-century exploration narratives to twenty-first-century poetry and prose. By integrating Mexican American arts into the curriculum, the program elevates the vicissitudes of Latinos' lives — satisfactions as well as challenges — to an art and helps to validate the very existence and presence of Latinos in the United States who never before had the opportunity to read about their own unique experiences. Gilb makes clear in his introduction to *Hecho en Tejas* that the predominant popular attitude toward people of Mexican descent in the United States, whether legitimate citizens or the undocumented — what some in the media call "illegals" — is shaped by cultural distortions:

> The kindest attitude portrays the culture as an homage in a children's museum, or as in a folklorico dance show, and the prevailing images, framed

(*Left*) The author in 2002, at the Brownsville, Texas–Matamoros, Mexico, border.
Courtesy of Dagoberto Gilb.

(*Below*) Dagoberto Gilb with his younger son, Ricardo. Uruapan, Mexico, 2005.
Courtesy of Dagoberto Gilb.

(*Top*) The author at the Pirámedes del
Sol y Luna. Mexico, 2008.
Courtesy of Dagoberto Gilb.

(*Right*) Dagoberto Gilb at a PEN /
Faulkner reading at the Folger
Shakespeare Library. Washington,
D.C., 2012.
Courtesy of Dagoberto Gilb.

and shelved in the state's unconscious, are of men in sombreros and serapes walking burros, women patting tortillas or stuffing tamales in color-frilled white housedresses, while the stories of Mexican adventures are of border whorehouses and tequila drunks—not meant as harmful, only fascinating, and wild.

Gilb insists on moving beyond such patronizing images and passionately announces as the anthology's major theme: "We have been here, we are still here." (For a brief, provocative comparison of Mexican American and African American cultural experiences in the West and South, see Gilb's "On Distortions of Mexican American Culture," p. 283.)

Furthering his goal of making Mexican Americans apparent in American culture, in 2011 Gilb founded *Huizache: The Magazine of Latino Literature*, published by Centro Victoria at the University of Houston–Victoria. Featuring literary works from mostly Latino writers who are largely neglected or ignored, the magazine also opens its pages to all fiction, poetry, and essays that challenge ethnic, gender, or social stereotyping. "A huizache," as explained on the title page, "is an acacia tree that is native to Mexico but also grows wild in South and East Texas. It irritates the regional farmers because, no matter what they do, it keeps growing and populating." The editor, Diana López, asks readers to "think of this journal as the nursery that fosters this tree and any species considered 'invasive.'" *Huizache* is founded on the energy, ambition, and neglected talent of Latino and Latina writers in Texas and the Southwest. Additionally, Gilb has edited with his son Ricardo Angel Gilb *Mexican American Literature* (2016), an anthology of poetry, fiction, drama, and essays by fifty writers responding to and reflecting upon their Mexican American cultural experiences.

Gilb's own writing offers a broad landscape of Mexican American experience in a direct, straightforward style that is energized by his unapologetically hearty and robust take on ordinary life. His characters work pretty hard in the face of ugly inequities, make money but not enough of it, get fired, find work, fall in love, desire marriage, settle on divorce, suffer loss, maintain dignity, strive to succeed, frequently fail, raise kids, embody fear, and stubbornly persevere—all of them serially engaged in the disorderly conduct of being human.

Dagoberto Gilb

How Books Bounce

2012

Many have asked me, how did you become a writer? This is one of those ordinary questions that comes at Q&A's, but at mine I sometimes catch a snarky or world-weary, all-caps emphasis on the *you*. I could snap off a couple of words in defense, but the truth is that I, too, find me a curious representative of literature. Real writers are bred like champion racehorses, the offspring of Seabiscuit and Secretariat. When real writers discuss their careers, they refer back (modestly, of course) to what they published before their double-digit birthdays. They had books at home (that's all I need to say there). The very classiest universities begged them to be under-grads, and while there they briefly thought they might become a molecu-lar chemist or an avant-garde sculptor. Now, modestly, these real writers will say they were probably better at one of those. Whereas, in contrast, I read my first book when I was seventeen because, in a less than advanced English class for we special few (I worked a full-time, graveyard shift job as a janitor), one day the teacher mentioned a novel hippies were reading. I wanted to know what hippies read because they seemed to have all kinds of easy goings-on that weren't like mine. And nothing in mine included any books. My pre-janitor years I can't say were busy with any poetic forms other than chrome spokes on wheels and girls who didn't read poetry either. Where I came up, balls were as close to books as I got. I bounced them, hit them, threw them, caught them, guarded them, blocked them, kicked them, jump-shot them. They weren't books. Nobody expected me to read them. I didn't. Neither was it suggested that maybe I try an actual volume with unrounded corners, though if anyone had, I would have made it bounce too.

I was not, in other words, born a writer. And then I went to a junior col-lege. Much of that incentive was not so much improving my brains as not los-ing them, or my legs, walking point in Vietnam (older friends, drafted, came back not doing great). My first freshman comp paper I got a D. The teacher told me she was being generous. When I failed the class, I was smart enough to know who took night classes — on the curve with the most tired day job students (mine was full-time too, a department store stock boy), this time, at a lesser community college, I got a B. I did not consider a major in chemistry. The only sculpture I knew of came from Mexico, which, cool-looking and deep, I couldn't say I understood any better than what was taught in art his-tory (nothing Mexican, indigenous, colonial, or modern). I tried a business law class. I liked math but too much homework. Sociology, political science, geography, history, philosophy — each offered original news to me. I was learning. Excited, I began eating it all up. Though I still feared English. That second semester requirement, when you study literature, I remember having to look up a word in virtually every sentence of Melville's *Billy Budd*. Suppos-edly American, I thought it had to be from a foreign language, and I wasn't sure if I understood what exactly happened to Mr. Budd. I took the teacher at his word for the explanation of it. Great story!

Oh, how I then fell in love. In the beginning it was any books I called on or which called on me. Books stacked and piled and neatly lined up in rows, new or used or checked out (I even stole them, yes, I here confess!). There were the small ones forgotten in quirky, cramped bottom corners, and ones that took tall ladders to touch, and ones that saw so little light their covers seemed to have recast inward — I loved them the most, these difficult ones, hard to get to know, to understand, odd, too quiet and bashful, secret. When suddenly I became furtive: though I would never take a lit class again, I was reading novels and poetry.

How did I become a writer? Something happened, that's pretty clear. Did lightning strike and skip the ears hearing, override the memory but alter the brain? Am I the product of some secret government experiment that maybe went wrong? How did a boy who cared only about sports — what little reading I would do young was from a newspaper sports page — become a man who would idealize books like classic teams and then become one of its professional "athletes"?

I've always been obsessed with story. Whether it's nature or nurture, or what I like to call my family mess, I cannot recall a time when I wasn't listening to a story being told. Maybe because I have only a single blurry memory of my father leaving my childhood home, it opens with ones about him and my mother. Of German descent, he was born in Kentucky but came to Los Angeles young. She was baptized in Mexico City at the Basílica de Guadalupe. He joined the Marines to fight the Japanese at Pearl Harbor. She kept the rising sun flag he'd captured as an advanced scout. Older, he watched her growing up next door to the industrial laundry where he started working when he was thirteen, where she eventually did too as a teenager (not for long). She grew up in that house next door with her mother, who was my grandmother, who was the mistress of the owner of the laundry who owned the house (what in Spanish is known as *la casa chica*). My grandmother came to the United States after her husband, my grandfather, was killed. By knife, went the story, and in the back. My grandmother came to the United States following her sister, my great-aunt, whose mother — this story! — had been married at fourteen to a man in his sixties and she had . . . not sure how many but a number of children by him. When my great-aunt turned eighteen, her mother traveled from Xalapa and in the capital rented the finest limousine for a visit to the presidential palace. And thus, my great-aunt represented Mexico on a tour to Europe and the United States as an opera singer. She wound up in Hollywood, married to a minor French director. My grandmother died young, making my mother closer to my great-aunt. By the time I am old enough to first see her — old, a widow for years, hard for a young person to imagine any glamorous youth attaching to her — she is nothing but a seamstress who needed money, a job, one of fifty at the industrial laundry where my father had become the floor supervisor. She repaired the elastic on bras, my father, bitter by divorce and who knows, enjoyed pointing out. He gave me a job there when I too turned thirteen. And this was when I begin to have stories.

When I think about being a writer now, I can't help but think of the improbable travel that my genes have made to get here. This journey. And to think we *each* have one, no matter to what breeding or privilege we were born. Why we perk up to listen, why we are driven to, I have no idea. It's so fun to bounce books on your ride — it's a necessary skill. But go, get out there, and what I know is you'll meet people, you'll see places, you'll hear stories that only you will be able to tell.

—D.G.

Dagoberto Gilb

Love in L.A.   *1993*

Jake slouched in a clot of near motionless traffic, in the peculiar gray of
concrete, smog, and early morning beneath the overpass of the Hollywood
Freeway on Alvarado Street. He didn't really mind because he knew how
much worse it could be trying to make a left onto the onramp. He certainly
didn't do that every day of his life, and he'd assure anyone who'd ask that he
never would either. A steady occupation had its advantages and he couldn't
deny thinking about that too. He needed an FM radio in something better than this '58 Buick he drove. It would have crushed velvet interior with
electric controls for the L.A. summer, a nice warm heater and defroster for
the winter drives at the beach, a cruise control for those longer trips, mellow
speakers front and rear of course, windows that hum closed, snuffing out
that nasty exterior noise of freeways. The fact was that he'd probably have to
change his whole style. Exotic colognes, plush, dark nightclubs, maitais and
daiquiris, necklaced ladies in satin gowns, misty and sexy like in a tequila
ad. Jake could imagine lots of possibilities when he let himself, but none that
ended up with him pressed onto a stalled freeway.

Jake was thinking about this freedom of his so much that when he
glimpsed its green light he just went ahead and stared bye bye to the steadily
employed. When he turned his head the same direction his windshield faced,
it was maybe one second too late. He pounced the brake pedal and steered
the front wheels away from the tiny brakelights but the smack was unavoidable. Just one second sooner and it would only have been close. One second
more and he'd be crawling up the Toyota's trunk. As it was, it seemed like only
a harmless smack, much less solid than the one against his back bumper.

Jake considered driving past the Toyota but was afraid the traffic ahead
would make it too difficult. As he pulled up against the curb a few carlengths
ahead, it occurred to him that the traffic might have helped him get away
too. He slammed the car door twice to make sure it was closed fully and to
give himself another second more, then toured front and rear of his Buick
for damage on or near the bumpers. Not an impressionable scratch even in the
chrome. He perked up. Though the car's beauty was secondary to its ability to
start and move, the body and paint were clean except for a few minor dings.
This stood out as one of his few clearcut accomplishments over the years.

Before he spoke to the driver of the Toyota, whose looks he could see
might present him with an added complication, he signaled to the driver of
the car that hit him, still in his car and stopped behind the Toyota, and waved
his hands and shook his head to let the man know there was no problem as
far as he was concerned. The driver waved back and started his engine.

"It didn't even scratch my paint," Jake told her in that way of his. "So how   5
you doin? Any damage to the car? I'm kinda hoping so, just so it takes a little
more time and we can talk some. Or else you can give me your phone number now and I won't have to lay my regular b.s. on you to get it later."

He took her smile as a good sign and relaxed. He inhaled her scent like it was clean air and straightened out his less than new but not unhip clothes.

"You've got Florida plates. You look like you must be Cuban."

"My parents are from Venezuela."

"My name's Jake." He held out his hand.

"Mariana." 10

They shook hands like she'd never done it before in her life.

"I really am sorry about hitting you like that." He sounded genuine. He fondled the wide dimple near the cracked taillight. "It's amazing how easy it is to put a dent in these new cars. They're so soft they might replace waterbeds soon." Jake was confused about how to proceed with this. So much seemed so unlikely, but there was always possibility. "So maybe we should go out to breakfast somewhere and talk it over."

"I don't eat breakfast."

"Some coffee then."

"Thanks, but I really can't." 15

"You're not married, are you? Not that that would matter that much to me. I'm an openminded kinda guy."

She was smiling. "I have to get to work."

"That sounds boring."

"I better get your driver's license," she said.

Jake nodded, disappointed. "One little problem," he said. "I didn't bring 20 it. I just forgot it this morning. I'm a musician," he exaggerated greatly, "and, well, I dunno, I left my wallet in the pants I was wearing last night. If you have some paper and a pen I'll give you my address and all that."

He followed her to the glove compartment side of her car.

"What if we don't report it to the insurance companies? I'll just get it fixed for you."

"I don't think my dad would let me do that."

"Your dad? It's not your car?"

"He bought it for me. And I live at home." 25

"Right." She was slipping away from him. He went back around to the back of her new Toyota and looked over the damage again. There was the trunk lid, the bumper, a rear panel, a taillight.

"You do have insurance?" she asked, suspicious, as she came around the back of the car.

"Oh yeah," he lied.

"I guess you better write the name of that down too."

He made up a last name and address and wrote down the name of an 30 insurance company an old girlfriend once belonged to. He considered giving a real phone number but went against that idea and made one up.

"I act too," he lied to enhance the effect more. "Been in a couple of movies."

She smiled like a fan.

"So how about your phone number?" He was rebounding maturely.

She gave it to him.

"Mariana, you are beautiful," he said in his most sincere voice. 35

"Call me," she said timidly.

Jake beamed. "We'll see you, Mariana," he said holding out his hand. Her hand felt so warm and soft he felt like he'd been kissed.

Back in his car he took a moment or two to feel both proud and sad about his performance. Then he watched the rear view mirror as Mariana pulled up behind him. She was writing down the license plate numbers on his Buick, ones that he'd taken off a junk because the ones that belonged to his had expired so long ago. He turned the ignition key and revved the big engine and clicked into drive. His sense of freedom swelled as he drove into the now moving street traffic, though he couldn't stop the thought about that FM stereo radio and crushed velvet interior and the new car smell that would even make it better.

DAGOBERTO GILB

On Writing "Love in L.A."   2012

I was unemployed when I wrote "Love in L.A." I wasn't happy about that. I had two young sons and a wife and a landlord and utility companies I supported and I drove an older car that needed, at the very least, springs and shocks and often gas. When I'd come back to L.A. in the early '80s after many years here and there but mostly El Paso, I did so with dreams of good money as a construction worker with high-rise skills. I'd joined the carpenter's union, and I was a journeyman, and there were cranes in the skyline everywhere. I was good at it. And work was great when I was working, but a job ended, and it always ended too fast. . . . As I was saying, I drove an old car, a 1962 Chevy II wagon. I used to joke around that it was a vintage classic. It came with a red vinyl interior its previous owner had done pretty in Juárez, and I kept the rest up. It roared with a rebuilt six-cylinder, and I did the tune-ups myself. I'd gotten it super cheap and the best you could say about it, years later, was that it still ran. I had no money for anything else. And I was, again, unemployed, close to broke.

I'd been going like this for years by then, surviving. Only surviving. Should I be trying to find some better line of work? Not to say that I hadn't tried before. Physically able, I could do this if there were regular paychecks. The last time there were no checks for too long, we lost our apartment. Could be this is nothing but the way life is. Lots of my friends didn't do much better. But with me there was also this: was it really that I was trying to be a writer? If I stopped wanting that, maybe even construction work would get easier for me to find because I would give in to it only. They were parallel dream worlds, one where I made a good living as a carpenter, another where I made a living as a writer. Most thought the writer one was fantasy. I didn't, but then I didn't know any better. I did know that I was having a hard time.

Were mine dreams that you have to push forward to reach, or were they fantasies that you get over?

Writing is like having a fever: your brain can't shy away, won't stop. It's a few lines of a lyric or melody that you can't shut down, a word or lover's name that follows you, whether you're talking to who you know or overhearing strangers, an image that has superimposed itself so equally on the familiar and not, that it can't be "out there," only in you. It won't quit you until you write it.

Her: I do not remember where I was driving from one day when I was inching along in some ridiculous street traffic caused by a minor accident. Except nothing in this part of Los Angeles, on Melrose Avenue, is minor, right? And it wasn't really so minor, as car-only damage goes. It was an elderly man, nondescript, whose little car had been rear-ended. He was standing there. A tall, leggy, too curvy woman in the bigger car (her hood wouldn't shut) was pacing and going on, upset as though it weren't her fault. She wore the highest heels and the slinkiest dress. It wasn't three in the morning, it was three in the afternoon. Like everyone else crawling by, it didn't seem like the man knew how to respond other than to stare at her.

Him: many years earlier, I knew a creepy guy who pretended his occupation was connected to Hollywood movies and that he had money. Since he was dark, he saw himself in an ethnic category of an Anthony Quinn or even a Charles Bronson, though more leading man — he would say that people thought he looked like Omar Sharif. Really only he saw Dr. Zhivago in his mirror. He combed his hair with a quality mousse once he began to share an apartment with an older dude who had done some TV show westerns, who knows what else, and drove a red Corvette convertible. Only slightly dangerous (low-level Tony Montana), he scored his women with props — he might lay out a black book to a certain page, incidentally, where no one could miss the famous names he had fake numbers for.

I worried I was as messed up as him, worse in a way, because I had a family. No I wasn't. Yes I was. No. Yes. Was I a construction worker pretending to be a writer? Writing was this full of it dude who was getting me. Or was I this man looking in a mirror, not seeing the screws tightening or falling out under my hardhat? Was I doing the right thing? Did I know what the right thing was? I worried that writing was that woman in the accident — excessive, spoiled, flashy, gaudy, not responsible for the wreck. Writing was beautiful, and sexy, and dramatic. Writing was fun even when there was a minor accident. Writing was L.A., cruising Melrose, a neighborhood where rich people lived lives unlike mine, drove Mercedes.

Then I wrote this story. I'd lived alone for a bit over by 3rd and Alvarado, an older *mexicano* part of town. I made her Venezuelan because I wanted her to be the fairy tale Latina beauty. I wanted her to be driving an economical Toyota. I wanted her to smile. I wanted her to have a family and be getting an education. I didn't want her to be a fool. Him, surviving, I wanted in an old luxury car with dreams, or fantasies, of a better one without dings, a little lost, a little scared, not in the system. I wanted them both in a brief moment together. The writer, I didn't know which of the two characters I was. The carpenter, I got another job out of the union hall soon after.

Dagoberto Gilb

Shout   *2001*

He beat on the screen door. "Will somebody open this?!" Unlike most men, he didn't leave his hard hat in his truck, he took it inside his home, and he had it in his hand. His body was dry now, at least wasn't like it was two hours ago at work, when he wrung his T-shirt of sweat, made it drool between the fingers of his fist, he and his partner making as much of a joke out of it as they could. That's how hot it was, how humid, and it'd been like this, in the nineties and hundreds, for two weeks, and it'd been hot enough before that. All he could think about was unlacing his dirty boots, then peeling off those stinky socks, then the rest. He'd take a cold one into the shower. The second one. He'd down the first one right at the refrigerator. "Come on!" Three and four were to be appreciated, five was mellow, and six let him nap before bed.

"I didn't hear you," his wife said.

"Didn't *hear* me? How *couldn't* you hear me? And why's it locked any-ways? When I get here I don't feel like waiting to come in. Why can't you leave the thing unlocked?"

"Why do you think?"

"Well don't let the baby open it. I want this door open when I get home."   5
He carried on in Spanish, *hijos de* and *putas* and *madres* and *chingadas*. This was the only Spanish he used at home. He tossed the hard hat near the door, relieved to be inside, even though it was probably hotter than outside, even though she was acting mad. He took it that she'd been that way all day already.

Their children, three boys, were seven, four, and almost two, and they were, as should be expected, battling over something.

"Everybody shut up and be quiet!" he yelled. Of course that worsened the situation, because when he got mad he scared the baby, who immediately started crying.

"I'm so tired," he muttered.

She glared at him, the baby in her arms.

"You know sometimes I wish you were a man cuz I wouldn't let you get   10
away with looks like that. I wouldn't take half the shit I take from you." He fell back into the wooden chair nobody sat in except him when he laced the high-top boots on, or off, as he already had. "You know how hot it was today? A hundred and five. It's unbelievable." He looked at her closely, deeply, which he didn't often do, especially this month. She was trying to settle down the baby and turned the TV on to distract the other two.

"It's too hard to breathe," he said to her. He walked bare-footed for the beer and took out two. They were in the door tray of the freezer and almost frozen.

"So nothing happened today?" she asked. Already she wasn't mad at him. It was how she was, why they could get along.

"Nothing else was said. Maybe nothing's gonna happen. God knows this heat's making everybody act unnatural. But tomorrow's check day. If he's gonna get me most likely it'll be tomorrow." He finished a beer leaning against the tile near the kitchen sink, enjoying a peace that had settled into the apartment. The baby was content, the TV was on, the Armenians living an arm's reach away were chattering steadily, there was a radio on from an apartment in a building across from them, Mexican TV upstairs, pigeons, a dog, traffic noise, the huge city out there groaning its sound — all this silence in the apartment.

"There's other jobs," he said. "All of 'em end no matter what anyways."

It was a job neither of them wanted to end too soon. This year he'd been   15
laid up for months after he fell and messed up his shoulder and back. He'd been drunk — a happy one that started after work — but he did it right there at his own front door, playing around. At the same time the duplex apartment they'd been living in for years had been sold and they had to move here. It was all they could get, all they were offered, since so few landlords wanted three children, boys no less, at a monthly rent they could afford. They were lucky to find it and it wasn't bad as places went, but they didn't like it much. They felt like they were starting out again, and that did not seem right. They'd talked this over since they'd moved in until it degenerated into talk about separation. And otherwise, in other details, it also wasn't the best year of their lives.

He showered in warm water, gradually turning the hot water down until it came out as cold as the summer allowed, letting the iced beer do the rest.

She was struggling getting dinner together, the boys were loud and complaining about being hungry, and well into the fifth beer, as he sat near the bright color and ever-happy tingle of the TV set, his back stiffening up, he snapped.

"Everybody has to shut up! I can't stand this today! I gotta relax some!"

She came back at him screaming too. "I can't stand *you*!"

He leaped. "You don't talk to me like that!"   20

She came right up to him. "You gonna hit me?!" she dared him.

The seven-year-old ran to his bed but the other two froze up, waiting for the tension to ease enough before their tears squeezed out.

"Get away from me," he said trying to contain himself. "You better get away from me right now. You know, just go home, go to your mother's, just go."

"*You* go! *You* get out! We're gonna stay!"

He looked through her, then slapped a wall, rocking what seemed like   25
the whole building. "You don't know how close you are."

He wouldn't leave. He walked into the bedroom, then walked out, sweating. He went into the empty kitchen — they were all in the children's room, where there was much crying — and he took a plate and filled it with what she'd made and went in front of the tube and he clicked on a ball game, told himself to calm himself and let it all pass at least tonight, at least while the weather was like it was and while these other things were still bothering both of them, and then he popped the sixth beer. He wasn't going to fall asleep on the couch tonight.

Eventually his family came out, one by one peeking around a corner to see what he looked like. Then they ate in a whisper, even cutting loose here and there with a little giggle or gripe. Eventually the sun did set, though that did nothing to wash off the glue of heat.

And eventually the older boys felt comfortable enough to complain about bedtime. Only the baby cried — he was tired and wanted to sleep but couldn't because a cold had clogged his nose. Still, they were all trying to maintain the truce when from outside, a new voice came in: SHUT THAT FUCKING KID UP YOU FUCKING PEOPLE! HEY! SHUT THAT FUCKING KID UP OVER THERE!

It was like an explosion except that he flew toward it. He shook the window screen with his voice. "You fuck yourself, asshole! You stupid asshole, you shut your mouth!" He ran out the other way, out the screen door and around and under the heated stars. "Come on out here, mouth! Come out and say that to my face!" He squinted at all the windows around him, no idea where it came from. "So come on! Say it right now!" There was no taker, and he turned away, his blood still bright red.

When he came back inside, the children had gone to bed and she was 30 lying down with the baby, who'd fallen asleep. He went back to the chair. The game ended, she came out, half-closing the door behind her, and went straight to their bed. He followed.

"I dunno," he said after some time. He'd been wearing shorts and nothing else since his shower, and it shouldn't have taken him so long, yet he just sat there on the bed. Finally he turned on the fan and it whirred, ticking as it pivoted left and right. "It doesn't do any good, but it's worse without it." He looked at her like he did earlier. "I'm kinda glad nobody came out. Afterwards I imagined some nut just shooting me, or a few guys coming. I'm getting too old for that shit."

She wasn't talking.

"So what did they say?" he asked her. "At the clinic?"

"Yes."

"Yes what?" 35

"That I am."

They both listened to the fan and to the mix of music from the Armenians and that TV upstairs.

"I would've never thought it could happen," he said. "That one time, and it wasn't even good."

"Maybe for you. I knew it then."

"You did?" 40

She rolled on her side.

"I'm sorry about all the yelling," he said.

"I was happy you went after that man. I always wanna do stuff like that." He rolled to her.

"I'm too sticky. It's too hot." 45

"I have to. We do. It's been too long, and now it doesn't matter."

"It does matter," she said. "I love you."

"I'm sorry," he said, reaching over to touch her breast. "You know I'm sorry."

He took another shower afterward. A cold shower. His breath sputtered and noises hopped from his throat. He crawled into the bed naked, onto the sheet that seemed as hot as ever, and listened to outside, to that mournful Armenian music mixing with Spanish, and to the fan, and it had stilled him. It was joy, and it was so strange. She'd fallen asleep and so he resisted kissing her, telling her. He thought he should hold on to this as long as he could, until he heard the pitch of the freeway climb, telling him that dawn was near and it was almost time to go back to work.

Dagoberto Gilb

On Writing "Shout"   2012

I suspect that younger readers — though older ones too — believe that a writer would enjoy going back and reading his earlier work. Probably a few do. I do not. It's like going back and looking at old photographs. I see a younger me, and I think of all the decisions I made, or didn't, because I didn't know what I didn't know. Worse, I read these stories and see what I would cut over there and add right here. And who am I to do that now to these full-grown stories? I think about where I was in my head when I wrote them . . . but let me give you this easier where: when I wrote "Shout," we were living in an East Hollywood apartment building beneath an elderly Armenian couple who grew parsley in the cracks of the cement pathways, who were miserable whenever my two baby boys rode their noisy Big Wheels. If the horrible thing about construction work was those times I didn't have a job, one of the great things was those times when I didn't have a job — not banging nails meant, instead, me getting to stay home at my wooden desk. (I still had the one I bought used in college. Beside me then was a Mexican calavera who oversaw whatever was on it, which it does to this day, on a newer wood desk.) That was when I allowed myself to write "officially" these pages I wanted published, the ones crafted, the ones you read. Not to say I was not always writing. Even working eleven hours, six days a week for as many months as a job would hold me, I wrote every day, but it would be in a notebook, recording conversations, incidents, descriptions, deep philosophical insights, and dear diary type boo-hoos or longings. Thousands of pages accumulated. My best writing hours were when my sons were asleep, and there was quiet, though once I got onto something, I could work anytime, in any noise.

It's surely obvious that much of my fiction comes from my own life and experiences. "Shout," for instance, could be said to have come out of the same period of my life as "Love in L.A." Hard to avoid what lasted over a decade. It used to be that most writers wrote out of their lived experience. Herman Melville, of *Moby Dick* (and *Billy Budd*), was a whaler. Nowadays people expect fiction to be nothing but mental creation and research, drawn on the page. Art is the imagination, goes this view, is the writer's desk alone, and the discipline there. That's not untrue, and it alone works well for very many. Gustave Flaubert, imagining a life as a woman, is said to have written one of the greatest novels of a woman, *Madame Bovary*. For me, fiction is life transformed and fueled by imagination. Experience often teaches by surprise — what cannot be predicted by the best reader in the library. My own favorite writers are out there, feeling the wind, on an adventure. Fiction I admire the most captures what, like life, smacks you when and where you're not looking, and the blow can seem so small, and it's so big.

Which brings up the subject of the small and the big, the short story and the novel. In many respects, a novel is simply a short story that is made larger, fuller, with more characters, more involved situations, a longer and more casual read. Thus, many short stories can be expanded into novels, or become segments of one. But I want to say that the best short fiction has more kinship with poetry: the goal is to reduce words and condense, and it is driven more by image than plot, both contrary to the novel. War can be described in a hundred pages of a battle scene, but might be more lastingly understood in an image of a tear falling, red itself or what is seen through it. There are never enough pages for love, but isn't it only the neighbor's *gallo* waking you up angry until you see, sound asleep next to you. . . .

The small. If novels are often about epic sweeps of history and issues, the big ideas of big egos, characters who are larger than whole nations and journeys that are bold, short fiction goes for what's left off-screen, following characters who would be minor against the headliners in those novels, but whose conclusions, The Ends, if less grandiose and more subtle, are anything shy of large.

And so, my own stories are about the small things and the people who aren't seen much in literature. There was a time when characters like those who populate my fiction were written about more, just not very much in recent decades. By that I mean common Americans, what many call working people, be they employed or looking to be. There are not a lot of stories about men like the main character in "Shout." I have found over the years that many know them as fathers and uncles, brothers and husbands, but they are not in the books they read. What you see in "Shout" as well is this man in a Mexican American family, yet another huge segment of American culture seldom read about. What I hoped to offer was not a simple portrayal of a construction worker coming home from work exhausted from a long day in the heat, not just a domestic squabble he causes with a patient wife, the mother of their three children. Left there, it would be a working-class cliché, the macho stereotype not only of that kind of man but also of a Mexican male. What I wanted seen was the same bullish rage he had in his home being used to defend his family when a stranger screams at them. And then the intimacy, what is hidden in the broad, usual expectation, what is forgotten when you don't know characters as living people, that the man and woman are lovers.

DAGOBERTO GILB

Uncle Rock   2011

In the morning, at his favorite restaurant, Erick got to order his favorite American food, sausage and eggs and hash-brown *papitas*° fried crunchy on top. He'd be sitting there, eating with his mother, not bothering anybody, and life was good, when a man started changing it all. Lots of times it was just a man staring too much — but then one would come over. Friendly, he'd put his thick hands on the table as if he were touching water, and squat low, so that he was at sitting level, as though he were so polite, and he'd smile, with coffee-and-tobacco-stained teeth. He might wear a bolo tie and speak in a drawl. Or he might have on a tan uniform, a company logo on the back, an oval name patch on the front. Or he'd be in a nothing-special work shirt, white or striped, with a couple of pens clipped onto the left side pocket, tucked into a pair of jeans or chinos that were morning-clean still, with a pair of scuffed work boots that laced up higher than regular shoes. He'd say something about her earrings, or her bracelet, or her hair, or her eyes, and if she had on her white uniform how nice it looked on her. Or he'd come right out with it and tell her how pretty she was, how he couldn't keep himself from walking up, speaking to her directly, and could they talk again? Then he'd wink at Erick. Such a fine-looking boy! How old is he, eight or nine? Erick wasn't even small for an eleven-year-old. He tightened his jaw then, slanted his eyes up from his plate at his mom and not the man, definitely not this man he did not care for. Erick drove a fork into a goopy American egg yolk and bled it into his American potatoes. She wouldn't offer the man Erick's correct age either, saying only that he was growing too fast.

She almost always gave the man her number if he was wearing a suit. Not a sports coat but a buttoned suit with a starched white shirt and a pinned tie meant something to her. Once in a while, Erick saw one of these men again at the front door of the apartment in Silverlake. The man winked at Erick as if they were buddies. Grabbed his shoulder or arm, squeezed the muscle against the bone. What did Erick want to be when he grew up? A cop, a jet-airplane mechanic, a travel agent, a court reporter? A dog groomer? Erick stood there, because his mom said that he shouldn't be impolite. His mom's date said he wanted to take Erick along with them sometime. The three of them. What kind of places did Erick think were fun? Erick said nothing. He never said anything when the men were around, and not because of his English, even if that was what his mother implied to explain his silence. He didn't talk to any of the men and he didn't talk much to his mom either. Finally they took off, and Erick's night was his alone. He raced to the grocery store and bought half a gallon of chocolate ice cream. When he got back, he turned on the TV, scooted up real close, as close as he could, and ate his dinner with a soup

---

papitas: Potatoes.

spoon. He was away from all the men. Even though a man had given the TV to them. He was a salesman in an appliance store who'd bragged that a rich customer had given it to him and so why shouldn't he give it to Erick's mom, who couldn't afford such a good TV otherwise?

When his mom was working as a restaurant hostess, and was going to marry the owner, Erick ate hot-fudge sundaes and drank chocolate shakes. When she worked at a trucking company, the owner of all the trucks told her he was getting a divorce. Erick climbed into the rigs, with their rooms full of dials and levers in the sky. Then she started working in an engineer's office. There was no food or fun there, but even he could see the money. He was not supposed to touch anything, but what was there to touch — the tubes full of paper? He and his mom were invited to the engineer's house, where he had two horses and a stable, a swimming pool, and two convertible sports cars. The engineer's family was there: his grown children, his gray-haired parents. They all sat down for dinner in a dining room that seemed bigger than Erick's apartment, with three candelabras on the table, and a tablecloth and cloth napkins. Erick's mom took him aside to tell him to be well mannered at the table and polite to everyone. Erick hadn't said anything. He never spoke anyway, so how could he have said anything wrong? She leaned into his ear and said that she wanted them to know that he spoke English. That whole dinner he was silent, chewing quietly, taking the smallest bites, because he didn't want them to think he liked their food.

When she got upset about days like that, she told Erick that she wished they could just go back home. She was tired of worrying. "Back," for Erick, meant mostly the stories he'd heard from her, which never sounded so good to him: she'd had to share a room with her brothers and sisters. They didn't have toilets. They didn't have electricity. Sometimes they didn't have enough food. He saw this Mexico as if it were the backdrop of a movie on afternoon TV, where children walked around barefoot in the dirt or on broken sidewalks and small men wore wide-brimmed straw hats and baggy white shirts and pants. The women went to church all the time and prayed to alcoved saints and, heads down, fearful, counted rosary beads. There were rocks everywhere, and scorpions and tarantulas and rattlesnakes, and vultures and no trees and not much water, and skinny dogs and donkeys, and ugly bad guys with guns and bullet vests who rode laughing into town to drink and shoot off their pistols and rifles, driving their horses all over like dirt bikes on desert dunes. When they spoke English, they had stupid accents — his mom didn't have an accent like theirs. It didn't make sense to him that Mexico would only be like that, but what if it was close? He lived on paved, lighted city streets, and a bicycle ride away were the Asian drugstore and the Armenian grocery store and the corner where black Cubans drank coffee and talked Dodgers baseball.

When he was in bed, where he sometimes prayed, he thanked God for 5 his mom, who he loved, and he apologized for not talking to her, or to anyone, really, except his friend Albert, and he apologized for her never going to church and for his never taking Holy Communion, as Albert did — though only to God would he admit that he wanted to only because Albert did. He prayed for good to come, for his mom and for him, since God was like magic, and happiness might come the way of early morning, in the trees and bushes full of sparrows next to his open window, louder and louder when he listened hard, eyes closed.

The engineer wouldn't have mattered if Erick hadn't told Albert that he was his dad. Albert had just moved into the apartment next door and lived with both his mother and his father, and since Albert's mother already didn't like Erick's mom, Erick told him that his new dad was an engineer. Erick actually believed it, too, and thought that he might even get his own horse. When that didn't happen, and his mom was lying on her bed in the middle of the day, blowing her nose, because she didn't have the job anymore, that was when Roque came around again. Roque was nobody — or he was anybody. He wasn't special, he wasn't not. He tried to speak English to Erick, thinking that was the reason Erick didn't say anything when he was there. And Erick had to tell Albert that Roque was his uncle, because the engineer was supposed to be his new dad any minute. Uncle Rock, Erick said. His mom's brother, he told Albert. Roque worked at night and was around during the day, and one day he offered Erick and Albert a ride. When his mom got in the car, she scooted all the way over to Roque on the bench seat. Who was supposed to be her brother, Erick's Uncle Rock. Albert didn't say anything, but he saw what had happened, and that was it for Erick. Albert had parents, grandparents, and a brother and a sister, and he'd hang out only when one of his cousins wasn't coming by. Erick didn't need a friend like him.

What if she married Roque, his mom asked him one day soon afterward. She told Erick that they would move away from the apartment in Silverlake to a better neighborhood. He did want to move, but he wished that it weren't because of Uncle Rock. It wasn't just because Roque didn't have a swimming pool or horses or a big ranch house. There wasn't much to criticize except that he was always too willing and nice, too considerate, too generous. He wore nothing flashy or expensive, just ordinary clothes that were clean and ironed, and shoes he kept shined. He combed and parted his hair neatly. He didn't have a buzzcut like the men who didn't like kids. He moved slow, he talked slow, as quiet as night. He only ever said yes to Erick's mom. How could she not like him for that? He loved her so much — anybody could see his pride when he was with her. He signed checks and gave her cash. He knocked on their door carrying cans and fruit and meat. He was there when she asked, gone when she asked, back whenever, grateful. He took her out to restaurants on Sunset, to the movies in Hollywood, or on drives to the beach in rich Santa Monica.

Roque knew that Erick loved baseball. Did Roque like baseball? It was doubtful that he cared even a little bit — he didn't listen to games on the radio or TV, and he never looked at a newspaper. He loved boxing though. He knew the names of all the Mexican fighters as if they lived here, as if they were Dodgers players like Steve Yeager, Dusty Baker, Kenny Landreaux or Mike Marshall, or Pedro Guerrero. Roque did know about Fernando Valenzuela, everyone did, even his mom, which is why she agreed to let Roque take them to a game. What Mexican didn't love Fernando? Dodger Stadium was close to their apartment. He'd been there once with Albert and his family — well, outside it, on a nearby hill, to see the fireworks for Fourth of July. His mom decided that all three of them would go on a Saturday afternoon, since Saturday night, Erick thought, she might want to go somewhere else, even with somebody else.

Roque, of course, didn't know who the Phillies were. He knew nothing about the strikeouts by Steve Carlton or the homeruns by Mike Schmidt. He'd never heard of Pete Rose. It wasn't that Erick knew very much either, but there was nothing that Roque could talk to him about, if they were to talk.

If Erick showed his excitement when they drove up to Dodger Stadium and parked, his mom and Roque didn't really notice it. They sat in the bleachers, and for him the green of the field was a magic light; the stadium decks surrounding them seemed as far away as Rome. His body was somewhere it had never been before. The fifth inning? That's how late they were. Or were they right on time, because they weren't even sure they were sitting in the right seats yet when he heard the crack of the bat, saw the crowd around them rising as it came at them. Erick saw the ball. He had to stand and move and stretch his arms and want that ball until it hit his bare hands and stayed there. Everybody saw him catch it with no bobble. He felt all the eyes and voices around him as if they were every set of eyes and every voice in the stadium. His mom was saying something, and Roque, too, and then, finally, it was just him and that ball and his stinging hands. He wasn't even sure if it had been hit by Pete Guerrero. He thought for sure it had been, but he didn't ask. He didn't watch the game then — he couldn't. He didn't care who won. He stared at his official National League ball, reimagining what had happened. He ate a hot dog and drank a soda and he sucked the salted peanuts and the wooden spoon from his chocolate-malt ice cream. He rubbed the bumpy seams of his homerun ball.

Game over, they were the last to leave. People were hanging around, not going straight to their cars. Roque didn't want to leave. He didn't want to end it so quickly, Erick thought, while he still had her with him. Then one of the Phillies came out of the stadium door and people swarmed — boys mostly, but also men and some women and girls — and they got autographs before the player climbed onto the team's bus. Joe Morgan, they said. Then Garry Maddox appeared. Erick clutched the ball but he didn't have a pen. He just watched, his back to the gray bus the Phillies were getting into.

Then a window slid open. *Hey, big man,* a voice said. Erick really wasn't sure. *Gimme the ball, la pelota,*° the face in the bus said. *I'll have it signed, comprendes?*° *Échalo,*° *just toss it to me.* Erick obeyed. He tossed it up to the hand that was reaching out. The window closed. The ball was gone a while,

la pelota: The ball.
comprendes?: Understand?
Échalo: Throw it.

so long that his mom came up to him, worried that he'd lost it. The window slid open again and the voice spoke to her. *We got the ball, Mom. It's not lost, just a few more.* When the window opened once more, this time the ball was there. *Catch.* There were all kinds of signatures on it, though none that he could really recognize except for Joe Morgan and Pete Rose.

Then the voice offered more, and the hand threw something at him. *For your mom, okay? Comprendes?* Erick stared at the asphalt lot where the object lay, as if he'd never seen a folded-up piece of paper before. *Para tu mamá, bueno?* He picked it up, and he started to walk over to his mom and Roque, who were so busy talking they hadn't noticed anything. Then he stopped. He opened the note himself. No one had said he couldn't read it. It said, *I'd like to get to know you. You are muy linda. Very beautiful and sexy. I don't speak Spanish very good, may be you speak better English, pero No Importa.°² Would you come by tonite and let me buy you a drink?* There was a phone number and a hotel room number. A name, too. A name that came at him the way that the homerun had.

Erick couldn't hear. He could see only his mom ahead of him. She was talking to Roque, Roque was talking to her. Roque was the proudest man, full of joy because he was with her. It wasn't his fault he wasn't an engineer. Now Erick could hear again. Like sparrows hunting seed, boys gathered round the bus, calling out, while the voice in the bus was yelling at him, *Hey, big guy! Give it to her!* Erick had the ball in one hand and the note in the other. By the time he reached his mom and Roque, the note was already somewhere on the asphalt parking lot. *Look*, he said in a full voice. *They all signed my ball.*

pero No Importa: It doesn't matter.

Dagoberto Gilb

On Writing "Uncle Rock"   2012

Mostly I don't like talking about my work. What can I say without implying a boast that it is fine writing you will want to know at least as well as me, if not better? (Of course it is!) Not only tasteless, it's a little questionable. Because, of course, this is somebody else's occupation, not my mirror's. Do you go to a restaurant telling you that it has "The Best Mexican Food in Texas!" (Of course it does, right?) All this aside, "Uncle Rock" might be one of my easiest stories to disassemble to see how it was put together.

As a craft, what I do isn't that much different than what a tile setter does. My fictional tiles, however, are broken, chipped, cracked, and come in different sizes and proportions and colors, and what I do is make a mosaic. There are sentences based on experience of my own years ago, and there are graphs which are what I remember doing with my sons when they were children; there are objects much like I owned, and a character who is memories of two people on the body of a third I worked with. Even within a single sentence, the imaginary is beside the Googled. The drama is invention. "Uncle Rock" appears to be a story of an eleven-year-old boy's life in the '80s, when really it is a set of disconnected images from several decades flipped through so quickly that it gives the illusion of movement (yes, like a "movie"), a story of a single experience. People read this story and assume it must be autobiographical. A compliment to my craft. You now know it was written willfully, by design.

Where the shards of tiles come from is what distinguishes what's mine from another writer's. And no doubt there are all sorts of piles to go through. I studied religion in college. That wasn't because I made a mistake and picked a degree plan that I thought I would cash in on. It's that I learned we live on a circling planet and noticed that I am alive and conscious. My curiosity about this has driven me to where I am. What I write is called literary fiction. The purpose of commercial fiction is, besides making money, to pass the time pleasantly, to get some relief from the grind — to entertain. Though this used to be more the function of reading in the past, now that is primarily handled by television and film. Literary fiction intends to entertain as well (and I say it does, more and especially so when it's great), and wishes to make money, but its goal — as is mine — is to reach out from the ordinary to realize the extraordinary. To point to the mystery that is being alive, in a strange place, in a time — a reader's, a writer's — that is not only in time. Is Erick's story about the '60s, '80s, these teens? Is his mom or Roque only a product of a class or culture? Is this story about males and single women, about the boundaries of love between a fatherless boy and a mother?

Don't think I'm denying that my fiction has autobiography in it. But this is true of most works of art, no more mine than many. Still, "Uncle Rock" could be used to do a clinical, psychological take on me through my work, digging out the root troubles haunting me. Most likely not wrong. It could be pointed out that, for instance, how the too wild single mother theme and character comes up here as it does in other pieces by me. That I have a *mami* issue. Probably true. But in my defense, my mom really did create some stories. Say you were the littlest broke, or even felt like splurging, treating yourself, or just felt like making life easy for yourself, and you knew where there was a chest of gold coins. Wouldn't you go there and grab one? It's only one here, and another couple in the past, not like I got greedy and grabbed the whole suitcase.

It's easiest for me to talk about my work when it has to do with advocacy. I would argue that all art advocates, like it or not, and that a writer represents a group of people and their interests. My fiction is very much about the common people in America, those who work and support families with their hands and bodies for hourly wages, who go about their lives hidden from media and celebrity links. Characters with "careers" like Erick's mother or Roque are not read about. Which brings up the American West — it is still unusual to read literary work set in and written by those who live west of the Mississippi. But it is more than rare to read stories set in the American Southwest, and more so still when they are about Mexican American people in their historical homeland — why the mountains and rivers and cities have names in Spanish. And I do that. My stories represent the Chicano story. It could be said that this is unavoidable for me, and that's not wrong, but my advocacy began only vaguely when I was young. In college I was lucky enough to see Luis Valdez's plays performed by his Teatro Campesino. I went to events supporting, and featuring, César Chávez. Both were synonymous with the farm workers' movement. Broccoli, to me, only came from a Safeway grocery store, and other people ate that kind of food. But the urban Mexican American was, obviously, always there too. There was simply little to no publicly documented evidence of it. Many call this an "invisibility" of the culture and history in the United States. I don't see it that way, not when what's loved about the Mexican American West, from cowboys to adobes, from margaritas to enchiladas, tacos, and burritos, are now as American as an iPod and a hamburger. I say Mexican Americans are being ignored willfully, an ignorance that has gotten worse in the past decade as a seismic demographic shift is altering the region's, and nation's, political landscape.

Which finally brings me back to "Uncle Rock." Take it apart, and you find a description of the Mexican American situation: Roque, a working man who struggles with English, an anybody, nobody special, who only works hard and is steady, is the only one who treats Erick's mother well. He adores her. But, despite the humiliation she endures, she wants more than what he is able to offer. She is beautiful and attracts all kinds of attention, so how can she not want more than what everyone else accepts? Her American dream. Erick is as embarrassed by his mom as he is attached to her. He is bothered so much that he has gone mute — he does not want to talk to anyone but God and his friend Albert. From the outside, it would appear that his is a struggle with the English language. One day he realizes a dream. In the days of Fernandomania, Roque takes him and his mom to a Dodgers game. Not only does he get to go to his first professional baseball game, not only does he catch a homerun ball, but a famous baseball player wants to meet his mother. At first thrilled, as young as he is Erick knows the offer is disrespectful and crude. And when he walks back to the two of them, who are unaware of what happened, he speaks to them. I want Erick's voice to get louder, smarter, and more confident.

Perspectives

DAGOBERTO GILB

On Physical Labor   2003

From "Work Union," *Gritos*

Not everybody wants to sit at a desk for a living. So many of us come from cultures where it is expected that we will move our bodies in the wind and sun, at dawn and into dusk. Many of us have been taught by family that physical work feels good and is good — when the day is over, we know what we did because we see it, we feel the efforts in our feet and hands and bones, and when we go home, when the wife puts food on the table and the family sits down and eats, there is unmistakable pride that all of it is because we have done our job.

It is human to work, to bend and grip, to lift and pull. It's never about getting tired or dirty. There is nothing wrong with sweat and toil. It is only about conditions and decent wages that there can come complaint. This is what so many people don't understand, especially those who sit in chairs in offices. They see us tired, they see us worried. They say, Well, if you don't like your situation, why don't you get a better job? Because it isn't the job, the kind of work. The job is good. Being a carpenter, an electrician, a plumber, an iron-worker, a laborer, those are all good. What isn't good is to be earning a living that can't bring in enough money to raise a healthy family, buy a home, go to a dentist and doctor, and be around comfortably for grandchildren.

A writer from Detroit who worked years for the Fisher Body Plant in Flint, Michigan, has recently been profiled in the newspapers because he won a prize for his writing. In the exultation of winning, he has been quoted often about those years he worked on the assembly line, saying, "I can't stress to you enough how much I hated it." This writer, he is certainly a good man, but like so many, he simply forgot what a joy employment is, what a job means to people and their families. There is only good in work, and the very best people are those who work hard.

DAGOBERTO GILB

On Distortions of Mexican American Culture   *2011*

From "La Próxima Parada Is Next," *American Book Review*

When Americans think of the South, some might think of its white society, Antebellum and post, its white literature, its wealth, yet the black culture is undeniably ever there, present. Others might discuss the history of the South in terms of black people, their history of slavery, their struggle with poverty, as the homeland of African Americans. This binary is a permanent overlay on the topography of the Southeast region, that quadrangle of the U.S. It is a black-white that has come to define much of America's internal history. Now consider a comparable Southwest quadrangle, one whose historical binary could be called — should be called — brown and white. We are all taught passionately about the American expansion into the West, cattle drives, cowboys and Indians, John Wayne movies, but if someone were to say it is the homeland of Mexican Americans, would anyone associate that with populations in Los Angeles, the state of New Mexico, El Paso, San Antonio, the Rio Grande Valley? Visitors thrill at oversized enchilada plates and the bountiful bowls of tortilla chips (Americanisms, both), visits to seventeenth- and early eighteenth-century missions, and they see and hear the vast numbers of "Mexican" people who speak to them in homegrown English at shops, stores, and stations — and yet somehow, relaxing in adobe-themed motels or new Spanish Villa homes, the binary here is not brown and white but *blank* and white, the dominant Mexican culture as if from an uninhabited ghost town. Meanwhile, what brown people they encounter — what articles appear in the media — are recent immigrants, invaders from the border. Part of American history? Curiously, if we were to assert that we are part of Mexico's history — which nobody here or there ever has or does — that would be far more of an outrage than lament that, unless photographed in folklorico costume, we have no images in our nation's history other than as foreigners.

Michael Meyer Interviews Dagoberto Gilb   2012

Meyer: Here is a potentially annoying but sincere usage question concerning a simple matter of terms that has caused me and my students to sometimes stumble: Do we (do you) use Chicano or Latino, Hispanic or Mexican American or Tex Mex to describe your writings? Should I even bring up feminine endings and hyphens as well? Do the terms define important distinctions? Is there a single umbrella term? Can you help sort this out for us?

Gilb: Aww, the rage of the nomenclature. All these words are better than the ones when I was young — "beaner" and "wetback" are the hit oldies, but just the word "Mexican," with but a soft decibel of racist tone, could clear the bench. The Chicano period was the beginning of the alternative. The problem with that became the masculine "o" at the end. Since the linguistic rules of Spanish reflected a macho boys' club mentality that did rule beyond usage, Chicanas rightfully fought for the equal status of the feminine "a," which has since created the slash usage, Chicana / o. It was the Nixon administration which came in with the word "Hispanic" as a "non-political" term (Chicanos and Chicanas, college-educated, did not vote Republican). It is a word now predominantly used in Republican circles. Latino, Latina, and Latina / o are the alternative to that. For me the problem with this is its application in the West. While Mexican Americans are close to 70 percent of the national demographic, Latinas and Latinos in the West are 95 percent Mexican American. One may note that neither do I love the hyphen that can be used in "Mexican American" (as in, the diminutive, hyphenated American). Me being me, I don't love the exhausting bureaucracy of slash world, and me being as American as the rest of us, I want nicknames of one or at most two syllables, so I've been going with the gender-neutral "MexAm" when it fits in easily. Sorry for the extra cap. And so it goes.

Meyer: It's not likely that any of your characters subscribe to the *American Book Review*, because they are mostly working-class, hard-working individuals struggling to earn a living. Do you think your work reaches an audience that includes the kind of characters that you write about? Do you worry about making the connection?

Gilb: Sadly, yes, improbable that an under-educated community would read or receive suggestions to read any of my writing, fiction or nonfiction. Is that because reading has become a luxury item? Is education a luxury item? Historically this has been true in most countries, in Europe, in Mexico, in Latin America. It was just less true in ours. At least as ideals went. Today, it would seem that's our direction. But putting that aside, my writing does reach a segment of the population that does care. And it touches enough even in my own community of people who recognize family members in the stories, who recognize their own voices through hearing mine. And I was invited into a literary world that has rewarded me. Not only have my books been published by Grove Press (the house whose books I was most infatuated with as a young reader), but my work has been in the most honored pages of the literary establishment — the *New Yorker* and *Harper's* magazines — and has been granted their finer awards. That doesn't mean that the mainstream public cares about what I do enough to make me a rich author, but it does mean that there is a respect in our country's literary marketplace for the ideas that pass through me and the people those ideas intend to honor. I am proud that this is true.

Meyer: In your comments about "Uncle Rock" you write that "It's easiest for me to talk about my work when it has to do with advocacy." Which of the stories that you've chosen to include in this anthology do you think most fully seems to be an "advocacy story"?

Gilb: All art advocates. The one who says his doesn't, he's someone who's advocating for the way things are, someone who's comfortable. I'm not saying that's right or wrong (though I'm sure I would pick a better or worse), only that it is a stance. For those who are less than comfortable, that status of ghosts, in situations that are less romantic or sitcom popular. I myself have gone through stages of understanding about the role of advocacy. I used to think that, like Dostoevsky, it — the politics, the spirituality — was contained in the art of the fiction alone, not in tracts or marches. A writer writes quietly alone, no option. It's in the finished work, and readers who are ready to find it, will. But I have changed. Maybe because I became a parent. Maybe because, as a journeyman, I worked with an apprentice often. Maybe because I was a coach for nine years and both yelled at and encouraged boys and girls who needed the coaching and got better. Once I became a teacher, a professor even, I found that, being in front of a class, students knowing that it was real and could be earned and I'd come from where they did, their learning altered their views, broke down their clichés and stereotypes. How many Chicano professors of English have you had? Why should it be surprising, even, that Mexican Americans have as many professional and personal complexities as others? As to the stories in this anthology, I don't really think of any one of them having more or less advocacy than another. Choose any of mine anywhere. A different emphasis in that one as opposed to this

Hecho en Tejas: An Anthology of Texas Mexican Literature was edited by Gilb and published in 2006 by the University of New Mexico Press.

From *Hecho en Tejas* by Dagoberto Gilb
© 2006, University of New Mexico Press.

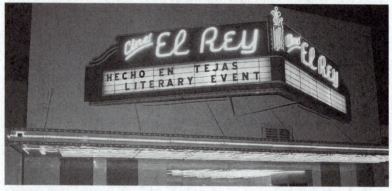

An event celebrating the anthology at the historic Cine El Rey Theatre. McAllen, Texas, 2007.
Courtesy of Dagoberto Gilb.

one, that's it. As to me, I am simply more aware of saying aloud, maybe saying louder, HEY! LOOK! Not sure if that's me, or survival in noisy times.

Meyer: In interviews and essays you have described the disadvantages of not being a northeastern writer snugly situated in the New York literary scene. Are there any encouraging advantages to being a southwestern writer in today's literary market?

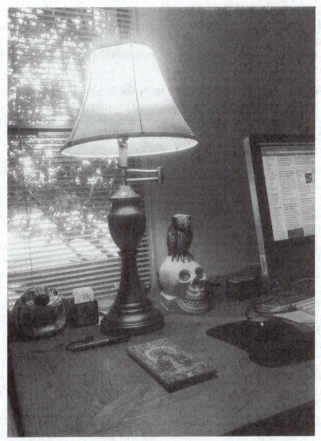

Dagoberto Gilb's desk—and the Mexican *calavera* that oversees it, mentioned in his essay "On Writing 'Shout'" (p. 274).
Courtesy of Dagoberto Gilb.

Gilb: If you're from San Francisco, you're a Bay Area writer. From Oregon or Washington, a writer from the Pacific Northwest. Colorado, Utah, Wyoming, Montana, a western writer. If you're from the Southeast, a southern writer. If you live in New York, even Boston, you're a national writer. Hard to argue with the economic demographics and the number of readers who live in those cities and the history of colleges and universities there, as well as magazines and publishers. Traditions groove permanent paths. Hard for anyone to not follow the money, and that's where the money is, too. Also hard not to be born where you're born. The Southwest has always had an exoticized legacy. D. H. Lawrence and Georgia O'Keeffe are New Mexico. Meanwhile, the MexAm Southwest has barely registered on an art stat, but no doubt that too has to change. The Apaches came to learn the force of America's westward expansion onto their land. Mexican Americans — though probably less, are no more immigrant than those from European descent, despite the demagoguery — will be 50 percent of the American Southwest soon, and its beautiful culture and epic history is unavoidably blending into the American mainstream.

Meyer: You suffered a debilitating stroke in 2009 from which you have since remarkably recovered, but if you were to write a short story about that experience, the fact that it is your writing hand that remains impaired seems to conjure all kinds of symbolic meanings. What has that stroke meant to you as a writer?

Gilb: A story titled "please, thank you," first published in *Harper's* and then collected in *Before the End, After the Beginning*, does deal with a character, Mr. Sanchez, who suffered a stroke similar to the one I did. He and I have had to learn how to type only, first one-handed, then slowly with one finger on the other hand, instead of using a pen to write. I can't say I like it a lot, so I do not recommend anyone use the technique to gain insights or to seek material. Yes, it's hard not to consider the metaphor: a writer losing the use of his writing hand. Add to that it happening the night he is celebrating the beginning of a new future as a full-time writer. But that metaphor is only one. Another is the obstacle it is for many of us to be writers. To be artists. To do what we dream, not what is expected, not what we accept. What we have to work hard for. That has always been me, and so adding this new element is not really new. When I wrote the stories for my last collection (mentioned above), for me it was an act of calm defiance — no, I am not done yet — but also gratitude for the generous gifts still given. I'm lucky I can do what I always wanted to do, that I am a writer, and I only need a keyboard. That's not so bad.

gilb / story
8

I don't want that, but then again, yes, that'd probably be better, because, then again, I don't believe that's the explanation. This is a campus where my work can be taught in a Chicano lit course only. I ~~a third Mexican American~~ wonder when, if ever, we ~~would~~ will be considered gourmet enough, talented enough, important enough.

I am guilty too because I don't think I'm smart enough. Flawed in a couple of personal areas, I wish I could claim to be better here, I wish instead of wanting to collapse and watch HBO (even, I admit, those cheap ~~TV~~ judge shows), I could read another book. I know those kind of writers. My God, they are so brilliant and articulate. I ~~even~~ know a couple who are geniuses. But what I ~~can~~ only hope might be seen is what gets undervalued: Not only has writing saved my life, projected it into New York and European fantasylands I'd never know otherwise, ~~but~~ and Washington, D.C., has offered me joy and fun. ~~In this,~~ there are limits to how much that might be seen in these essays. I assure you, everyone of them has given me such pleasure and satisfaction, the same kind I ~~have~~ had when I used to cut wood with my skilsaw and drive nails and build, watch a building rise ~~high~~ huge, a fun of the kind that trowels the back of a tile with adhesive and sets it in, the pattern mounting. Each word is rock I've placed personally into a wall—five go in and I pick through a pile and find another, shift them around until I like it then it's right I've chipped and knicked at most so ~~that~~ they look to me like good sentences, good paragraphs. If I don't think of myself as the smartest, I do feel a strength in my working the craft, so that everytime I maybe too finish something I'm impressed proud of myself, can hardly believe I did it, that I could. ~~Because it's~~ The words are almost as though ~~it came from another~~ consciousness, beyond my own physical self or nature, because ~~I don't think~~ not I was born to be a writer, I've just done it anyway. Often this work is outright fun, almost as fun as it ~~would be~~ at a good construction job where we were all muscles sweating and laughing and building shit and getting paid ~~all~~ at the same time—living and working—except writing work is alone, only an imaginary crew. Sometimes you see that laughter in these essays, but even

A draft manuscript page for the introduction to Gilb's essay collection, *Gritos*, published in 2003 by Grove Press.
Courtesy of Dagoberto Gilb.

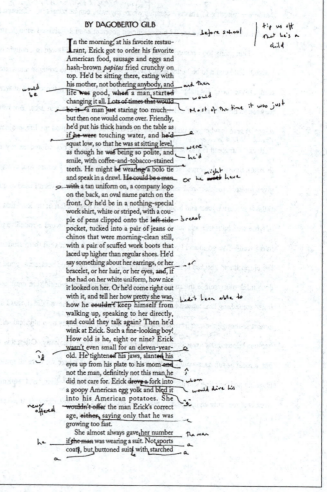

FICTION

UNCLE ROCK

BY DAGOBERTO GILB

In the morning, at his favorite restaurant, Erick got to order his favorite American food, sausage and eggs and hash-brown *papitas* fried crunchy on top. He'd be sitting there, eating with his mother, not bothering anybody, and life was good, when a man started changing it all. Lots of times that would be it, a man just staring too much—but then one would come over. Friendly, he'd put his thick hands on the table and if he were touching water, and he'd squat low, so that he was at sitting level, as though he was being so polite, and smile, with coffee-and-tobacco-stained teeth. He might be wearing a bolo tie and speak in a drawl. He could be a man with a tan uniform on, a company logo on the back, an oval name patch on the front. Or he'd be in a nothing-special work shirt, white or striped, with a couple of pens clipped onto the left side pocket, tucked into a pair of jeans or chinos that were morning-clean still, with a pair of scuffed work boots that laced up higher than regular shoes. He'd say something about her earrings, or her bracelet, or her hair, or her eyes, and, if she had on her white uniform, how nice it looked on her. Or he'd come right out with it, and tell her how pretty she was, how he couldn't keep himself from walking up, speaking to her directly, and could they talk again? Then he'd wink at Erick. Such a fine-looking boy! How old is he, eight or nine? Erick wasn't even small for an eleven-year-old. He tightened his jaws, slanted his eyes up from his plate to his mom and not the man, definitely not this man he did not care for. Erick drove a fork into a goopy American egg yolk and bled it into his American potatoes. She wouldn't offer the man Erick's correct age, either, saying only that he was growing too fast.

She almost always gave her number if the man was wearing a suit. Not sports coat, but buttoned suits with starched

---

Edited galleys from *The New Yorker* for "Uncle Rock."
Courtesy of Dagoberto Gilb.

Considerations for Critical Thinking and Writing

1. Gilb describes two "parallel dream worlds" in his autobiographical commentary on "Love in L.A.": "one where I made a good living as a carpenter, another where I made a living as a writer" (p. 269). How do you think this tension informs Jake's behavior and character in the story?

2. In his reflections on "Shout," Gilb posits that "the best short fiction has more kinship with poetry: the goal is to reduce words and condense, and it is driven more by image than plot, both contrary to the novel" (p. 275). How does the final paragraph of "Shout" serve as an example of how images can supersede plot in this short story?

3. Gilb argues in his discussion of "Uncle Rock" that "all art advocates, like it or not, and that a writer represents a group of people and their interests" (pp. 281–82). Explain to what extent you think that "Uncle Rock," in particular, fulfills this description of Gilb's writing.

4. In "How Books Bounce" (p. 264) and in the three Gilb stories in this anthology, the life exhibited is often fraught with volatile economic and domestic instabilities, and yet these challenges are typically met by shrewd strength, sound sturdiness, and determination. Do you think this ultimately adds up to a grim or positive perspective on life? Discuss two stories along with "How Books Bounce" to consider this question.

5. In his comments "On Distortions of Mexican American Culture" (p. 283), Gilb contrasts how black culture in the South has had deep roots in America's history and consciousness compared to the ways in which Mexican American culture in the Southwest is largely overlooked or distorted. Consider how Mexicans are portrayed in popular American culture and discuss whether or not you agree with Gilb's observations.

6. CONNECTION TO ANOTHER SELECTION. How might "Love in L.A." or "Shout" be considered love stories but very different from John Updike's "A & P" (p. 149) or David Updike's "Summer" (p. 155)? Choose one of Gilb's stories and one of the Updikes' stories to compare the social setting, conflicts, protagonists, and tone.

7. CONNECTION TO ANOTHER SELECTION. Explain how Gilb's perspective "On Physical Labor" (p. 282) can be used as a means of tracing some shared themes about work among the poems in Chapter 22, "A Thematic Case Study: The World of Work" (p. 522).

Suggested Topics for Longer Papers

1. "My own stories are about the small things and the people who aren't seen much in literature" ("On Writing 'Shout,'" p. 274). How do the three stories in this collection portray the details of working people's lives? What common themes emerge from those portrayals?

2. As executive director of Centro Victoria, Gilb has worked diligently to advance Mexican American literature and culture. Discuss the ways in which you think Gilb's three stories challenge social stereotyping.

A Collection
of Stories

11

Stories for Further Reading

I mean to live and die by my own mind.

— ZORA NEALE HURSTON

Library of Congress, Prints and
Photographs Division.

TONI CADE BAMBARA (1939–1995)

Raised in New York City's Harlem and Bedford-Stuyvesant communities,
Toni Cade Bambara graduated from Queens College in 1959, studied in Florence and Paris, and earned her M.A. at City College of New York in 1964.
She also studied dance, linguistics, and filmmaking and worked a variety of
jobs in welfare, recreation, and community housing, in addition to teaching
at various schools, including Rutgers University and Spelman College. She
described her writing as "straight-up fiction . . . 'cause I value my family and
friends, and mostly 'cause I lie a lot anyway." Her fiction has been collected
in *Gorilla, My Love* (1972) and *The Sea Birds Are Still Alive* (1977), and in
1980 she published her first novel, *The Salt Eaters*, followed by *If Blessing
Comes* (1987). Her most recent books, *Deep Sightings and Rescue Missions*
(1996) and *These Bones Are Not My Child* (1999), were published posthumously. A number of her screenplays have been produced, including *Epitaph for Willie* and *Tar Baby*. In the following story an adolescent reflects on
a memorable summer.

Sweet Town   1959

It is hard to believe that there was only one spring and one summer apiece that year, my fifteenth year. It is hard to believe that I so quickly squandered my youth in the sweet town playground of the sunny city, that wild monkey-bardom of my fourth-grade youthhood. However, it was so.

"Dear Mother" — I wrote one day on her bathroom mirror with a candle sliver — "please forgive my absence and my decay and overlook the freckled dignity and pockmarked integrity plaguing me this season."

I used to come on even wilder sometimes and write her mad cryptic notes on the kitchen sink with charred matches. Anything for a bit, we so seldom saw each other. I even sometimes wrote her a note on paper. And then one day, having romped my soul through the spectrum of sunny colors, I dashed up to her apartment to escape the heat and found a letter from her which eternally elated my heart to the point of bursture and generally endeared her to me forever. Written on the kitchen table in cake frosting was the message, "My dear, mad, perverse young girl kindly take care and paint the fire escape in your leisure . . ." All the *i*'s were dotted with marmalade, the *t*'s were crossed with orange rind. Here was a sight to carry with one forever in the back of the screaming eyeballs somewhere. I howled for at least five minutes out of sheer madity and vowed to love her completely. Leisure. As if bare-armed spring ever let up from its invitation to perpetuate the race. And as if we ever owned a fire escape. "Zweep," I yelled, not giving a damn for intelligibility and decided that if ever I was to run away from home, I'd take her with me. And with that in mind, and with Penelope splintering through the landscape and the pores secreting animal champagne, I bent my youth to the season's tempo and proceeded to lose my mind.

There is a certain glandular disturbance all beautiful, wizardly, great people have second sight to, that trumpets through the clothes, sets the nerves up for the kill, and torments the senses to orange explosure. It has something to do with the cosmic interrelationship between the cellular atunement of certain designated organs and the firmental correlation with the axis shifts of the globe. My mother calls it sex and my brother says it's groin-fever time. But then, they were always ones for brevity. Anyway, that's the way it was. And in this spring race, the glands always win and the muses and the brain core must step aside to ride in the trunk with the spare tire. It was during this sweet and drugged madness time that I met B. J., wearing his handsomeness like an article of clothing, for an effect, and wearing his friend Eddie like a necessary pimple of adolescence. It was on the beach that we met, me looking great in a pair of cut-off dungarees and them with beards. Never mind the snows of yesteryear, I told myself, I'll take the sand and sun blizzard any day.

"Listen, Kit," said B. J. to me one night after we had experienced such 5
we-encounters with the phenomenal world at large as a two-strawed mocha, duo-jaywalking summons, twosome whistling scenes, and other such like we-experiences, "the thing for us to do is hitch to the Coast and get into films."

"Righto," said Ed. "And soon."

"Sure thing, honeychile," I said, and jumped over an unknown garbage can. "We were made for celluloid — beautifully chiseled are we, not to mention well-buffed." I ran up and down somebody's stoop, whistling "Columbia the Gem of the Ocean" through my nose. And Eddie made siren sounds and walked a fence. B. J. grasped a parking-sign pole and extended himself parallel to the ground. I applauded, not only the gymnastics but also the offer. We liked to make bold directionless overtures to action like those crazy teenagers you're always running into on the printed page or MGM movies.

"We could buy a sleeping bag," said B. J., and challenged a store cat to duel.

"We could buy a sleeping bag," echoed Eddie, who never had any real contribution to make in the say of statements.

"Three in a bag," I said while B. J. grasped me by the belt and we went flying 10 down a side street. "Hrumph," I coughed, and perched on a fire hydrant. "Only one bag?"

"Of course," said B. J.

"Of course," said Ed. "And hrumph."

We came on like this the whole summer, even crazier. All of our friends abandoned us, they couldn't keep the pace. My mother threatened me with disinheritance. And my old roommate from camp actually turned the hose on me one afternoon in a fit of Florence Nightingale therapy. But hand in hand, me and Pan, and Eddie too, whizzed through the cement kaleidoscope making our own crazy patterns, singing our own song. And then one night a crazy thing happened. I dreamt that B. J. was running down the street howling, tearing his hair out and making love to the garbage cans on the boulevard. I was there laughing my head off and Eddie was spinning a beer bottle with a faceless person I didn't even know. I woke up and screamed for no reason I know of and my roommate, who was living with us, threw a Saltine cracker at me in way of saying something about silence, peace, consideration, and sleepdom. And then on top of that another crazy thing happened. Pebbles were flying into my opened window. The whole thing struck me funny. It wasn't a casement window and there was no garden underneath. I naturally laughed my head off and my roommate got really angry and cursed me out viciously. I explained to her that pebbles were coming in, but she wasn't one for imagination and turned over into sleepdom. I went to the window to see who I was going to share my balcony scene with, and there below, standing on the milkbox, was B. J. I climbed out and joined him on the stoop.

"What's up?" I asked, ready to take the world by storm in my mixed-match baby-doll pajamas. B. J. motioned me into the foyer and I could see by the distraught mask that he was wearing that serious discussion was afoot.

"Listen, Kit," he began, looking both ways with unnecessary caution. 15 "We're leaving, tonight, now. Me and Eddie. He stole some money from his grandmother, so we're cutting out."

"Where're ya going?" I asked. He shrugged. And just then I saw Eddie dash across the stoop and into the shadows. B. J. shrugged and he made some kind of desperate sound with his voice like a stifled cry. "It's been real great. The summer and you . . . but . . . "

"Look here," I said with anger. "I don't know why the hell you want to hang around with that nothing." I was really angry but sorry too. It wasn't at all what I wanted to say. I would have liked to have said, "Apollo, we are the only beautiful people in the world. And because our genes are so great, our kid can't help but burst through the human skin into cosmic significance." I wanted to say, "You will bear in mind that I am great, brilliant, talented, good-looking, and am going to college at fifteen. I have the most interesting complexes ever, and despite Freud and Darwin I have made a healthy adjustment as an earthworm." But didn't tell him this. Instead, I revealed that petty, small, mean side of me by saying "Eddie is a shithead."

B. J. scratched his head, swung his foot in an arc, groaned and took off. "Maybe next summer . . ." he started to say but his voice cracked and he and Eddie went dashing down the night street, arm in arm. I stood there with my thighs bare and my soul shook. Maybe we will meet next summer, I told the mailboxes. Or maybe I'll quit school and bum around the country. And in every town I'll ask for them as the hotel keeper feeds the dusty, weary traveler that I'll be. "Have you seen two guys one great, the other acned? If you see 'em, tell 'em Kit's looking for them." And I'd bandage up my cactus-torn feet and sling the knapsack into place and be off. And in the next town, having endured dust storms, tornadoes, earthquakes, and coyotes, I'll stop at the saloon and inquire. "Yeh, they travel together," I'd say in a voice somewhere between W. C. Fields and Gladys Cooper. "Great buddies. Inseparable. Tell 'em for me that Kit's still a great kid."

And legends'll pop up about me and my quest. Great long twelve-bar blues ballads with eighty-nine stanzas. And a strolling minstrel will happen into the feedstore where B. J.'ll be and hear and shove the farmer's daughter off his lap and mount up to find me. Or maybe we won't meet ever, or we will but I won't recognize him cause he'll be an enchanted frog or a bald-headed, fat man and I'll be God knows what. No matter. Days other than the here and now, I told myself, will be dry and sane and sticky with the rotten apricots oozing slowly in the sweet time of my betrayed youth.

STEPHEN CRANE (1871–1900)

Born in Newark, New Jersey, Stephen Crane attended Lafayette College and Syracuse University and then worked as a freelance journalist in New York City. He wrote newspaper pieces, short stories, poems, and novels for his entire, brief adult life. His first book, *Maggie: A Girl of the Streets* (1893), is a story about New York slum life and prostitution. His most famous novel, *The Red Badge of Courage* (1895), gives readers a vivid, convincing re-creation of Civil War battles, even though Crane had never been to war.

An Episode of War   1899

The lieutenant's rubber blanket lay on the ground, and upon it he had poured the company's supply of coffee. Corporals and other representatives of the grimy and hot-throated men who lined the breast-work had come for each squad's portion.

The lieutenant was frowning and serious at this task of division. His lips pursed as he drew with his sword various crevices in the heap, until brown squares of coffee, astoundingly equal in size, appeared on the blanket. He was on the verge of a great triumph in mathematics, and the corporals were thronging forward, each to reap a little square, when suddenly the lieutenant cried out and looked quickly at a man near him as if he suspected it was a case of personal assault. The others cried out also when they saw blood upon the lieutenant's sleeve.

He had winced like a man stung, swayed dangerously, and then straightened. The sound of his hoarse breathing was plainly audible. He looked sadly, mystically, over the breast-work at the green face of a wood, where now were many little puffs of white smoke. During this moment the men about him gazed statue-like and silent, astonished and awed by this catastrophe which happened when catastrophes were not expected — when they had leisure to observe it.

As the lieutenant stared at the wood, they too swung their heads, so that for another instant all hands, still silent, contemplated the distant forest as if their minds were fixed upon the mystery of a bullet's journey.

The officer had, of course, been compelled to take his sword into his left 5 hand. He did not hold it by the hilt. He gripped it at the middle of the blade, awkwardly. Turning his eyes from the hostile wood, he looked at the sword as he held it there, and seemed puzzled as to what to do with it, where to put it. In short, this weapon had of a sudden become a strange thing to him. He looked at it in a kind of stupefaction, as if he had been endowed with a trident, a sceptre, or a spade.

Finally he tried to sheathe it. To sheathe a sword held by the left hand, at the middle of the blade, in a scabbard hung at the left hip, is a feat worthy of a sawdust ring. This wounded officer engaged in a desperate struggle with the sword and the wobbling scabbard, and during the time of it he breathed like a wrestler.

But at this instant the men, the spectators, awoke from their stone-like poses and crowded forward sympathetically. The orderly-sergeant took the sword and tenderly placed it in the scabbard. At the time, he leaned nervously backward, and did not allow even his finger to brush the body of the lieutenant. A wound gives strange dignity to him who bears it. Well men shy from his new and terrible majesty. It is as if the wounded man's hand is upon the curtain which hangs before the revelations of all existence — the meaning of ants, potentates, wars, cities, sunshine, snow, a feather dropped from a bird's wing; and the power of it sheds radiance upon a bloody form, and makes the other men understand sometimes that they are little. His comrades look at him with large eyes thoughtfully. Moreover, they fear vaguely that the weight of a finger upon him might send him headlong, precipitate the tragedy, hurl him at once into the dim, gray unknown. And so the orderly-sergeant, while sheathing the sword, leaned nervously backward.

There were others who proffered assistance. One timidly presented his shoulder and asked the lieutenant if he cared to lean upon it, but the latter waved him away mournfully. He wore the look of one who knows he is the victim of a terrible disease and understands his helplessness. He again stared over the breast-work at the forest, and then, turning, went slowly rearward. He held his right wrist tenderly in his left hand as if the wounded arm was made of very brittle glass.

And the men in silence stared at the wood, then at the departing lieutenant; then at the wood, then at the lieutenant.

As the wounded officer passed from the line of battle, he was enabled 10 to see many things which as a participant in the fight were unknown to him. He saw a general on a black horse gazing over the lines of blue infantry at the green woods which veiled his problems. An aide galloped furiously, dragged his horse suddenly to a halt, saluted, and presented a paper. It was, for a wonder, precisely like a historical painting.

To the rear of the general and his staff a group, composed of a bugler, two or three orderlies, and the bearer of the corps standard, all upon maniacal horses, were working like slaves to hold their ground, preserve their respectful interval, while the shells boomed in the air about them, and caused their chargers to make furious quivering leaps.

A battery, a tumultuous and shining mass, was swirling toward the right. The wild thud of hoofs, the cries of the riders shouting blame and praise, menace and encouragement, and, last, the roar of the wheels, the slant of the glistening guns, brought the lieutenant to an intent pause. The battery swept in curves that stirred the heart; it made halts as dramatic as the crash of a wave on the rocks, and when it fled onward this aggregation of wheels, levers, motors had a beautiful unity, as if it were a missile. The sound of it was a war-chorus that reached into the depths of man's emotion.

The lieutenant, still holding his arm as if it were of glass, stood watching this battery until all detail of it was lost, save the figures of the riders, which rose and fell and waved lashes over the black mass.

Later, he turned his eyes toward the battle, where the shooting sometimes crackled like bush fires, sometimes sputtered with exasperating irregularity, and sometimes reverberated like the thunder. He saw the smoke rolling upward and saw crowds of men who ran and cheered, or stood and blazed away at the inscrutable distance.

He came upon some stragglers, and they told him how to find the field   15
hospital. They described its exact location. In fact, these men, no longer
having part in the battle, knew more of it than others. They told the performance of every corps, every division, the opinion of every general. The
lieutenant, carrying his wounded arm rearward, looked upon them with
wonder.

At the roadside a brigade was making coffee and buzzing with talk like
a girls' boarding school. Several officers came out to him and inquired concerning things of which he knew nothing. One, seeing his arm, began to
scold. "Why, man, that's no way to do. You want to fix that thing." He appro-
priated the lieutenant and the lieutenant's wound. He cut the sleeve and laid
bare the arm, every nerve of which softly fluttered under his touch. He bound
his handkerchief over the wound, scolding away in the meantime. His tone
allowed one to think that he was in the habit of being wounded every day. The
lieutenant hung his head, feeling, in this presence, that he did not know how
to be correctly wounded.

The low white tents of the hospital were grouped around an old schoolhouse. There was here a singular commotion. In the foreground two ambu-
lances interlocked wheels in the deep mud. The drivers were tossing the
blame of it back and forth, gesticulating and berating, while from the ambu-
lances, both crammed with wounded, there came an occasional groan. An
interminable crowd of bandaged men were coming and going. Great numbers sat under the trees nursing heads or arms or legs. There was a dispute
of some kind raging on the steps of the schoolhouse. Sitting with his back
against a tree a man with a face as gray as a new army blanket was serenely
smoking a corncob pipe. The lieutenant wished to rush forward and inform
him that he was dying.

A busy surgeon was passing near the lieutenant. "Good morning," he said,
with a friendly smile. Then he caught sight of the lieutenant's arm, and his face
at once changed. "Well, let's have a look at it." He seemed possessed suddenly
of a great contempt for the lieutenant. This wound evidently placed the latter
on a very low social plane. The doctor cried out impatiently: "What mutton-
head tied it up that way anyhow?" The lieutenant answered, "Oh, a man."

When the wound was disclosed the doctor fingered it disdainfully.
"Humph," he said, "You come along with me and I'll tend to you." His voice
contained the same scorn as if he were saying, "You will have to go to jail."

The lieutenant had been very meek, but now his face flushed, and he   20
looked into the doctor's eyes. "I guess I won't have it amputated," he said.

"Nonsense, man! Nonsense! Nonsense!" cried the doctor. "Come along,
now. I won't amputate it. Come along. Don't be a baby."

"Let go of me," said the lieutenant, holding back wrathfully, his glance
fixed upon the door of the old schoolhouse, as sinister to him as the portals
of death.

And this is the story of how the lieutenant lost his arm. When he reached
home, his sisters, his mother, his wife, sobbed for a long time at the sight of

the flat sleeve. "Oh, well," he said, standing shamefaced amid these tears, "I don't suppose it matters so much as all that."

NATHANIEL HAWTHORNE (1804–1864)

Born in Salem, Massachusetts, Nathaniel Hawthorne came from a family that traced its roots back to the Puritans. After graduating from Bowdoin College in 1825, he returned home to Salem, where for the next twelve years he read and taught himself how to write. He published his first collection of stories, *Twice-Told Tales*, in 1837, followed by a second edition in 1842, and *Mosses from an Old Manse* in 1846. In 1849 he lost his job at the Salem Custom House and focused on his writing. In addition to *The Scarlet Letter* (1850), he wrote *The House of Seven Gables*

© Peabody Essex Museum, Salem, Massachusetts.

(1851); *The Blithedale Romance* (1852); *The Snow-Image, and Other Twice-Told Tales* (1852); a campaign biography of his Bowdoin classmate, *The Life of Franklin Pierce* (1852); and two collections of stories for children, *A Wonder Book* (1852) and *Tanglewood Tales* (1853).

Wakefield

1835

In some old magazine or newspaper I recollect a story, told as truth, of a man—let us call him Wakefield—who absented himself for a long time from his wife. The fact, thus abstractedly stated, is not very uncommon, nor—without a proper distinction of circumstances—to be condemned either as naughty or nonsensical. Howbeit, this, though far from the most aggravated, is perhaps the strangest instance on record of marital delinquency; and, moreover, as remarkable a freak as may be found in the whole list of human oddities. The wedded couple lived in London. The man, under pretense of going a journey, took lodgings in the next street to his own house, and there, unheard of by his wife or friends, and without the shadow of a reason for such self-banishment, dwelt upwards of twenty years. During that period, he beheld his home every day, and frequently the forlorn Mrs. Wakefield. And after so great a gap in his matrimonial felicity—when his death was reckoned certain, his estate settled, his name dismissed from memory, and his wife, long, long ago, resigned to her autumnal widowhood—he entered the door one evening, quietly, as from a day's absence, and became a loving spouse till death.

   This outline is all that I remember. But the incident, though of the purest originality, unexampled, and probably never to be repeated, is one, I think, which appeals to the generous sympathies of mankind. We know, each for himself, that none of us would perpetrate such a folly, yet feel as if some other might. To my own contemplations, at least, it has often recurred, always exciting wonder, but with a sense that the story must be true, and a conception of its hero's character. Whenever any subject so forcibly affects the mind, time is well spent in thinking of it. If the reader choose, let him do his own meditation; or if he prefer to ramble with me through the twenty years of Wakefield's vagary, I bid him welcome; trusting that there will be a pervading spirit and a moral, even should we fail to find them, done up neatly, and condensed into the final sentence. Thought has always its efficacy, and every striking incident its moral.

What sort of a man was Wakefield? We are free to shape out our own idea, and call it by his name. He was now in the meridian of life; his matrimonial affections, never violent, were sobered into a calm, habitual sentiment; of all husbands, he was likely to be the most constant, because a certain sluggishness would keep his heart at rest, wherever it might be placed. He was intellectual, but not actively so; his mind occupied itself in long and lazy musings, that ended to no purpose, or had not vigor to attain it; his thoughts were seldom so energetic as to seize hold of words. Imagination, in the proper meaning of the term, made no part of Wakefield's gifts. With a cold but not depraved nor wandering heart, and a mind never feverish with riotous thoughts, nor perplexed with originality, who could have anticipated that our friend would entitle himself to a foremost place among the doers of eccentric deeds? Had his acquaintances been asked, who was the man in London the surest to perform nothing today which should be remembered on the morrow, they would have thought of Wakefield. Only the wife of his bosom might have hesitated. She, without having analyzed his character, was partly aware of a quiet selfishness, that had rusted into his inactive mind; of a peculiar sort of vanity, the most uneasy attribute about him; of a disposition to craft, which had seldom produced more positive effects than the keeping of petty secrets, hardly worth revealing; and, lastly, of what she called a little strangeness, sometimes, in the good man. This latter quality is indefinable, and perhaps nonexistent.

Let us now imagine Wakefield bidding adieu to his wife. It is the dusk of an October evening. His equipment is a drab great-coat, a hat covered with an oilcloth, top-boots, an umbrella in one hand, and a small portmanteau in the other. He has informed Mrs. Wakefield that he is to take the night coach into the country. She would fain inquire the length of his journey, its object, and the probable time of his return; but, indulgent to his harmless love of mystery, interrogates him only by a look. He tells her not to expect him positively by the return coach, nor to be alarmed should he tarry three or four days; but, at all events, to look for him at supper on Friday evening. Wakefield himself, be it considered, has no suspicion of what is before him. He holds out his hand, she gives her own, and meets his parting kiss in the matter-of-course way of a ten years' matrimony; and forth goes the middle-aged Mr. Wakefield, almost resolved to perplex his good lady by a whole week's absence. After the door has closed behind him, she perceives it thrust partly open, and a vision of her husband's face, through the aperture, smiling on her, and gone in a moment. For the time, this little incident is dismissed without a thought. But, long afterwards, when she has been more years a widow than wife, that smile recurs, and flickers across all her reminiscences of Wakefield's visage. In her many musings, she surrounds the original smile with a multitude of fantasies, which make it strange and awful: as, for instance, if she imagines him in a coffin, that parting look is frozen on his pale features; or, if she dreams of him in heaven, still his blessed spirit wears a quiet and crafty smile. Yet, for its sake, when all others have given him up for dead, she sometimes doubts whether she is a widow.

But our business is with the husband. We must hurry after him along 5 the street, ere he lose his individuality, and melt into the great mass of London life. It would be vain searching for him there. Let us follow close at his heels, therefore, until, after several superfluous turns and doublings, we find him comfortably established by the fireside of a small apartment, previously bespoken. He is in the next street to his own, and at his journey's end. He can scarcely trust his good fortune, in having got thither unperceived — recollecting that, at one time, he was delayed by the throng, in the very focus of a lighted lantern; and, again, there were footsteps that seemed to tread behind his own, distinct from the multitudinous tramp around him; and, anon, he heard a voice shouting afar, and fancied that it called his name. Doubtless, a dozen busybodies had been watching him, and told his wife the whole affair. Poor Wakefield! Little knowest thou thine own insignificance in this great world! No mortal eye but mine has traced thee. Go quietly to thy bed, foolish man; and, on the morrow, if thou wilt be wise, get thee home to good Mrs. Wakefield, and tell her the truth. Remove not thyself, even for a little week, from thy place in her chaste bosom. Were she, for a single moment, to deem thee dead, or lost, or lastingly divided from her, thou wouldst be woefully conscious of a change in thy true wife forever after. It is perilous to make a chasm in human affections; not that they gape so long and wide — but so quickly close again!

Almost repenting of his frolic, or whatever it may be termed, Wakefield lies down betimes, and starting from his first nap, spreads forth his arms into the wide and solitary waste of the unaccustomed bed. "No," — thinks he, gathering the bedclothes about him, — "I will not sleep alone another night."

In the morning he rises earlier than usual, and sets himself to consider what he really means to do. Such are his loose and rambling modes of thought that he has taken this very singular step with the consciousness of a purpose, indeed, but without being able to define it sufficiently for his own contemplation. The vagueness of the project, and the convulsive effort with which he plunges into the execution of it, are equally characteristic of a feebleminded man. Wakefield sifts his ideas, however, as minutely as he may, and finds himself curious to know the progress of matters at home — how his exemplary wife will endure her widowhood of a week; and, briefly, how the little sphere of creatures and circumstances, in which he was a central object, will be affected by his removal. A morbid vanity, therefore, lies nearest the bottom of the affair. But, how is he to attain his ends? Not, certainly, by keeping close in this comfortable lodging, where, though he slept and awoke in the next street to his home, he is as effectually abroad as if the stage-coach had been whirling him away all night. Yet, should he reappear, the whole project is knocked in the head. His poor brains being hopelessly puzzled with this dilemma, he at length ventures out, partly resolving to cross the head of the street, and send one hasty glance towards his forsaken domicile. Habit — for he is a man of habits — takes him by the hand, and guides him, wholly unaware, to his own door, where, just at the critical moment, he is aroused by the scraping of his foot upon the step. Wakefield! whither are you going?

At that instant his fate was turning on the pivot. Little dreaming of the doom to which his first backward step devotes him, he hurries away, breathless with agitation hitherto unfelt, and hardly dares turn his head at the distant corner. Can it be that nobody caught sight of him? Will not the whole household — the decent Mrs. Wakefield, the smart maid-servant, and the dirty little footboy — raise a hue and cry, through London streets, in pursuit of their fugitive lord and master? Wonderful escape! He gathers courage to pause and look homeward, but is perplexed with a sense of change about the familiar edifice, such as affects us all, when, after a separation of months or years, we again see some hill or lake, or work of art, with which we were friends of old. In ordinary cases, this indescribable impression is caused by the comparison and contrast between our imperfect reminiscences and the reality. In Wakefield, the magic of a single night has wrought a similar transformation, because, in that brief period, a great moral change has been effected. But this is a secret from himself. Before leaving the spot, he catches a far and momentary glimpse of his wife, passing athwart the front window, with her face turned towards the head of the street. The crafty nincompoop takes to his heels, scared with the idea that, among a thousand such atoms of mortality, her eye must have detected him. Right glad is his heart, though his brain be somewhat dizzy, when he finds himself by the coal fire of his lodgings.

So much for the commencement of this long whimwham. After the initial conception, and the stirring up of the man's sluggish temperament to put it in practice, the whole matter evolves itself in a natural train. We may suppose him, as the result of deep deliberation, buying a new wig, of reddish hair, and selecting sundry garments, in a fashion unlike his customary suit of brown, from a Jew's old-clothes bag. It is accomplished. Wakefield is another man. The new system being now established, a retrograde movement to the old would be almost as difficult as the step that placed him in his unparalleled position. Furthermore, he is rendered obstinate by a sulkiness occasionally incident to his temper, and brought on at present by the inadequate sensation which he conceives to have been produced in the bosom of Mrs. Wakefield. He will not go back until she be frightened half to death. Well; twice or thrice has she passed before his sight, each time with a heavier step, a paler cheek, and more anxious brow; and in the third week of his nonappearance he detects a portent of evil entering the house, in the guise of an apothecary. Next day the knocker is muffled. Towards nightfall comes the chariot of a physician, and deposits its big-wigged and solemn burden at Wakefield's door, whence, after a quarter of an hour's visit, he emerges, perchance the herald of a funeral! Dear woman! Will she die? By this time, Wakefield is excited to something like energy of feeling, but still lingers away from his wife's bedside, pleading with his conscience that she must not be disturbed at such a juncture. If aught else restrains him, he does not know it. In the course of a few weeks she gradually recovers; the crisis is over; her heart is sad, perhaps, but quiet; and, let him return soon or late, it will never be feverish for him again. Such ideas glimmer through the mist of Wakefield's mind, and render him indistinctly conscious that an almost impassable gulf divides his hired apartment from his former home. "It is but in the next street!" he sometimes says. Fool! it is in another world. Hitherto, he has put off his return from one particular day to another; henceforward, he leaves the precise time undetermined. Not tomorrow — probably next week — pretty soon. Poor man! The dead have nearly as much chance of revisiting their earthly homes as the self-banished Wakefield.

Would that I had a folio to write, instead of an article of a dozen pages! Then might I exemplify how an influence beyond our control lays its strong hand on every deed which we do, and weaves its consequences into an iron tissue of necessity. Wakefield is spellbound. We must leave him, for ten years or so, to haunt around his house, without once crossing the threshold, and to be faithful to his wife, with all the affection of which his heart is capable, while he is slowly fading out of hers. Long since, it must be remarked, he had lost the perception of singularity in his conduct.   10

Now for a scene! Amid the throng of a London street we distinguish a man, now waxing elderly, with few characteristics to attract careless observers, yet bearing, in his whole aspect, the handwriting of no common fate, for such as have the skill to read it. He is meager; his low and narrow forehead is deeply wrinkled; his eyes, small and lusterless, sometimes wander apprehensively about him, but oftener seem to look inward. He bends his head, and moves with an indescribable obliquity of gait, as if unwilling to display his full front to the world. Watch him long enough to see what we have described, and you will allow that circumstances — which often produce remarkable men from nature's ordinary handiwork — have produced one such here. Next, leaving him to sidle along the footwalk, cast your eyes in the opposite direction, where a portly female, considerably in the wane of life, with a prayer-book in her hand, is proceeding to yonder church. She has the placid mien of settled widowhood. Her regrets have either died away, or have become so essential to her heart, that they would be poorly exchanged for joy. Just as the lean man and well-conditioned woman are passing, a slight obstruction occurs, and brings these two figures directly in contact. Their hands touch; the pressure of the crowd forces her bosom against his shoulder; they stand face to face, staring into each other's eyes. After a ten years' separation, thus Wakefield meets his wife!

The throng eddies away, and carries them asunder. The sober widow, resuming her former pace, proceeds to church, but pauses in the portal, and throws a perplexed glance along the street. She passes in, however, opening her prayer-book as she goes. And the man! with so wild a face that busy and selfish London stands to gaze after him, he hurries to his lodgings, bolts the door, and throws himself upon the bed. The latent feelings of years break out; his feeble mind acquires a brief energy from their strength; all the miserable strangeness of his life is revealed to him at a glance; and he cries out, passionately, "Wakefield! Wakefield! You are mad!"

Perhaps he was so. The singularity of his situation must have so molded him to himself, that, considered in regard to his fellow creatures and the business of life, he could not be said to possess his right mind. He had contrived, or rather he had happened, to dissever himself from the world — to vanish — to give up his place and privileges with living men, without being admitted among the dead. The life of a hermit is nowise parallel to his. He was in the bustle of the city, as of old; but the crowd swept by and saw him not; he was, we may figuratively say, always beside his wife and at his hearth, yet must never feel the warmth of the one nor the affection of the other. It was Wakefield's unprecedented fate to retain his original share of human sympathies, and to be still involved in human interests, while he had lost his reciprocal influence on them. It would be a most curious speculation to trace out the effect of such circumstances on his heart and intellect, separately, and in unison. Yet, changed as he was, he would seldom be conscious of it, but deem himself the same man as ever; glimpses of the truth, indeed, would come, but only for the moment; and still he would keep saying, "I shall soon go back!" — nor reflect that he had been saying so for twenty years.

I conceive, also, that these twenty years would appear, in the retrospect, scarcely longer than the week to which Wakefield had at first limited his absence. He would look on the affair as no more than interlude in the main business of his life. When, after a little while more, he should deem it time to re-enter his parlor, his wife would clap her hands for joy, on beholding the middle-aged Mr. Wakefield. Alas, what a mistake! Would Time but await the close of our favorite follies, we should be young men, all of us, and till Dooms-day.

One evening, in the twentieth year since he vanished, Wakefield is taking his customary walk towards the dwelling which he still calls his own. It is a gusty night of autumn, with frequent showers that patter down upon the pavement, and are gone before a man can put up his umbrella. Pausing near the house, Wakefield discerns, through the parlor windows of the second floor, the red glow and the glimmer and fitful flash of a comfortable fire. On the ceiling appears a grotesque shadow of good Mrs. Wakefield. The cap, the nose and chin, and the broad waist from an admirable caricature, which dances, moreover, with the up-flickering and down-sinking blaze, almost too merrily for the shade of an elderly widow. At this instant a shower chances to fall, and is driven, by the unmannerly gust, full into Wakefield's face and bosom. He is quite penetrated with its autumnal chill. Shall he stand wet and shivering here, when his own hearth has a good fire to warm him, and his own wife will run to fetch the gray coat and small-clothes, which, doubtless, she has kept carefully in the closet of their bedchamber? No! Wakefield is no such fool. He ascends the steps — heavily! — for twenty years have stiffened his legs since he came down — but he knows it not. Stay, Wakefield! Would you go to the sole home that is left you? Then step into your grave! The door opens. As he passes in, we have a parting glimpse of his visage, and recognize the crafty smile, which was the precursor of the little joke that he has ever since been playing off at his wife's expense. How unmercifully has he quizzed the poor woman! Well, a good night's rest to Wakefield!

This happy event — supposing it to be such — could only have occurred at an unpremeditated moment. We will not follow our friend across the threshold. He has left us much food for thought, a portion of which shall lend its wisdom to a moral, and be shaped into a figure. Amid the seeming confusion of our mysterious world, individuals are so nicely adjusted to a system, and systems to one another and to a whole, that, by stepping aside for a moment, a man exposes himself to a fearful risk of losing his place forever. Like Wakefield, he may become, as it were, the Outcast of the Universe.

JAMES JOYCE (1882–1941)

James Joyce was born in Dublin, Ireland, in 1882 and, in an imaginative sense, he never left that city. He received a strict Jesuit education, but once he began to doubt his faith during his final year at Belvedere College, Dublin, he felt his calling as a writer more and more strongly. Joyce studied modern languages at University College, Dublin, and taught himself Norwegian so he could read the plays of Henrik Ibsen in their original language. Ibsen's depiction of individual rebellion against community values resonated deeply for Joyce and contributed to his resolution to leave Ireland for Paris after he received his B.A. degree in 1902.

Courtesy of the Poetry / Rare Books Collection, UB Libraries, State University of New York at Buffalo.

Joyce returned to Dublin when his mother contracted a fatal illness, and he stayed on for a brief time, working as a schoolteacher. He departed for Switzerland, leaving Ireland for good, in 1904. Nora Barnacle, an uneducated young woman with little interest in literature, went with him. The couple lived in Trieste and Zurich, where Joyce taught school and wrote. He published *Dubliners* in 1914; "Eveline" is taken from this collection of short stories. *A Portrait of the Artist as a Young Man* followed in 1916. He and Nora moved to Paris in 1920 and remained there until World War II forced them back to Switzerland. He published *Ulysses* in Paris in 1922, but the book was banned in America and Britain until 1933. *Finnegan's Wake*, which Joyce considered his crowning achievement, took fourteen years to write and was published in 1939.

Eveline   *1914*

She sat at the window watching the evening invade the avenue. Her head was leaned against the window curtains and in her nostrils was the odor of dusty cretonne. She was tired.

Few people passed. The man out of the last house passed on his way home; she heard his footsteps clacking along the concrete pavement and afterwards crunching on the cinder path before the new red houses. One time there used to be a field there in which they used to play every evening with other people's children. Then a man from Belfast bought the field and built houses in it — not like their little brown houses but bright brick houses with shining roofs. The children of the avenue used to play together in that field — the Devines, the Waters, the Dunns, little Keogh the cripple, she and her brothers and sisters. Ernest, however, never played: he was too grown up. Her father used often to hunt them in out of the field with his blackthorn stick; but usually little Keogh used to keep *nix* and call out when he saw her father coming. Still they seemed to have been rather happy then. Her father was not so bad then; and besides, her mother was alive. That was a long time ago; she and her brothers and sisters were all grown up; her mother was dead. Tizzie Dunn was dead, too, and the Waters had gone back to England. Everything changes. Now she was going to go away like the others, to leave her home.

Home! She looked round the room, reviewing all its familiar objects which she had dusted once a week for so many years, wondering where on earth all the dust came from. Perhaps she would never see again those familiar objects from which she had never dreamed of being divided. And yet during all those years she had never found out the name of the priest whose yellowing photograph hung on the wall above the broken harmonium beside the colored print of the promises made to Blessed Margaret Mary Alacoque. He had been a school friend of her father. Whenever he showed the photograph to a visitor her father used to pass it with a casual word:

— He is in Melbourne now.

She had consented to go away, to leave her home. Was that wise? She 5 tried to weigh each side of the question. In her home anyway she had shelter and food; she had those whom she had known all her life about her. Of course she had to work hard both in the house and at business. What would they say of her in the Stores when they found out that she had run away with a fellow? Say she was a fool, perhaps; and her place would be filled up by advertisement. Miss Gavan would be glad. She had always had an edge on her, especially whenever there were people listening.

— Miss Hill, don't you see these ladies are waiting?

— Look lively, Miss Hill, please.

She would not cry many tears at leaving the Stores.

But in her new home, in a distant unknown country, it would not be like that. Then she would be married — she, Eveline. People would treat her with respect then. She would not be treated as her mother had been. Even now, though she was over nineteen, she sometimes felt herself in danger of her father's violence. She knew it was that that had given her the palpitations. When they were growing up he had never gone for her, like he used to go for Harry and Ernest, because she was a girl; but latterly he had begun to threaten her and say what he would do to her only for her dead mother's sake. And now she had nobody to protect her. Ernest was dead and Harry, who was in the church decorating business, was nearly always down somewhere in the country. Besides, the invariable squabble for money on Saturday nights had begun to weary her unspeakably. She always gave her entire wages — seven shillings — and Harry always sent up what he could but the trouble was to get any money from her father. He said she used to squander the money, that she had no head, that he wasn't going to give her his hard-earned money to throw about the streets, and much more, for he was usually fairly bad of a Saturday night. In the end he would give her the money and ask her had she any intention of buying Sunday's dinner. Then she had to rush out as quickly as she could and do her marketing, holding her black leather purse tightly in her hand as she elbowed her way through the crowds and returning home late under her load of provisions. She had hard work to keep the house together and to see that the two young children who had been left to her charge went to school regularly and got their meals regularly. It was hard work — a hard life — but now that she was about to leave it she did not find it a wholly undesirable life.

She was about to explore another life with Frank. Frank was very kind,   10
manly, open-hearted. She was to go away with him by the night-boat to be his wife and to live with him in Buenos Aires where he had a home waiting for her. How well she remembered the first time she had seen him; he was lodging in a house on the main road where she used to visit. It seemed a few weeks ago. He was standing at the gate, his peaked cap pushed back on his head and his hair tumbled forward over a face of bronze. Then they had come to know each other. He used to meet her outside the Stores every evening and see her home. He took her to see *The Bohemian Girl* and she felt elated as she sat in an unaccustomed part of the theater with him. He was awfully fond of music and sang a little. People knew that they were courting and, when he sang about the lass that loves a sailor, she always felt pleasantly confused. He used to call her Poppens out of fun. First of all it had been an excitement for her to have a fellow and then she had begun to like him. He had tales of distant countries. He had started as a deck boy at a pound a month on a ship of the Allan Line going out to Canada. He told her the names of the ships he had been on and the

names of the different services. He had sailed through the Straits of Magellan and he told her stories of the terrible Patagonians. He had fallen on his feet in Buenos Aires, he said, and had come over to the old country just for a holiday. Of course, her father had found out the affair and had forbidden her to have anything to say to him.

— I know these sailor chaps, he said.

One day he had quarreled with Frank and after that she had to meet her lover secretly.

The evening deepened in the avenue. The white of two letters in her lap grew indistinct. One was to Harry; the other was to her father. Ernest had been her favorite but she liked Harry too. Her father was becoming old lately, she noticed; he would miss her. Sometimes he could be very nice. Not long before, when she had been laid up for a day, he had read her out a ghost story and made toast for her at the fire. Another day, when their mother was alive, they had all gone for a picnic to the Hill of Howth. She remembered her father putting on her mother's bonnet to make the children laugh.

Her time was running out but she continued to sit by the window, leaning her head against the window curtain, inhaling the odor of dusty cretonne. Down far in the avenue she could hear a street organ playing. She knew the air. Strange that it should come that very night to remind her of the promise to her mother, her promise to keep the home together as long as she could. She remembered the last night of her mother's illness; she was again in the close dark room at the other side of the hall and outside she heard a melancholy air of Italy. The organ-player had been ordered to go away and given sixpence. She remembered her father strutting back into the sickroom saying:

— Damned Italians! coming over here!   15

As she mused the pitiful vision of her mother's life laid its spell on the very quick of her being — that life of commonplace sacrifices closing in final craziness. She trembled as she heard again her mother's voice saying constantly with foolish insistence:

— Derevaun Seraun! Derevaun Seraun!°

She stood up in a sudden impulse of terror. Escape! She must escape! Frank would save her. He would give her life, perhaps love, too. But she wanted to live. Why should she be unhappy? She had a right to happiness. Frank would take her in his arms, fold her in his arms. He would save her.

She stood among the swaying crowd in the station at the North Wall. He held her hand and she knew that he was speaking to her, saying something about the passage over and over again. The station was full of soldiers with brown baggages. Through the wide doors of the sheds she caught a glimpse of the black mass of the boat, lying in beside the quay wall, with illumined portholes. She answered nothing. She felt her cheek pale and cold and, out of a maze of distress, she prayed to God to direct her, to show her what was

---

Derevaun Seraun!: (Gaelic) "The end of pleasure is pain!"

her duty. The boat blew a long mournful whistle into the mist. If she went, tomorrow she would be on the sea with Frank, steaming toward Buenos Aires. Their passage had been booked. Could she still draw back after all he had done for her? Her distress awoke a nausea in her body and she kept moving her lips in silent fervent prayer.

A bell clanged upon her heart. She felt him seize her hand: 20

— Come!

All the seas of the world tumbled about her heart. He was drawing her into them: he would drown her. She gripped with both hands at the iron railing.

— Come!

No! No! No! It was impossible. Her hands clutched the iron in frenzy. Amid the seas she sent a cry of anguish!

— Eveline! Evvy!   25

He rushed beyond the barrier and called to her to follow. He was shouted at to go on but he still called to her. She set her white face to him, passive, like a helpless animal. Her eyes gave him no sign of love or farewell or recognition.

JAMAICA KINCAID (B. 1949)

Trix Rosen.

Jamaica Kincaid was born Elaine Potter Richardson on the Caribbean island of Antigua. She moved to New York in 1965 to work as an au pair, studied photography at both the New School for Social Research and Franconia College, and changed her name to Jamaica Kincaid in 1973 with her first publication, "When I Was 17," a series of interviews. Over the next few years, she wrote for the *New Yorker* magazine, first as a freelancer and then as a staff writer. In 1978, Kincaid wrote her first piece of fiction, "Girl," published in the *New Yorker* and included in her debut short story collection, *At the Bottom of the River* (1983), which won an award from the Academy and Institute of Arts and Letters and was nominated for the PEN/Faulkner Award. Her other work includes *Annie John* (1985), *Lucy* (1990), *Autobiography of My Mother* (1994), *See Now Then* (2013), and three nonfiction books, *A Small Place* (1988), *My Brother* (1997), and *Mr. Potter* (2002). Whether autobiographical fiction or nonfiction, her work usually focuses on the perils of postcolonial society, paralleled by an examination of rifts in mother-daughter relationships.

Girl   1978

Wash the white clothes on Monday and put them on the stone heap; wash the color clothes on Tuesday and put them on the clothesline to dry; don't walk barehead in the hot sun; cook pumpkin fritters in very hot sweet oil; soak your little cloths right after you take them off; when buying cotton to make yourself a nice blouse, be sure that it doesn't have gum on it, because that way it won't hold up well after a wash; soak salt fish overnight before you cook it; is it true that you sing benna° in Sunday school?; always eat your food in such a way that it won't turn someone else's stomach; on Sundays try to walk like a lady and not like the slut you are so bent on becoming; don't sing benna in Sunday school; you mustn't speak to wharf-rat boys, not even to give directions; don't eat fruits on the street — flies will follow you; *but I don't sing benna on Sundays at all and never in Sunday school;* this is how to sew on a button; this is how to make a buttonhole for the button you have just sewed on; this is how to hem a dress when you see the hem coming down and so to prevent yourself from looking like the slut I know you are so bent on becoming; this is how you iron your father's khaki shirt so that it doesn't have a crease; this is how you iron your father's khaki pants so that they don't have a crease; this is how you grow okra — far from the house, because okra tree harbors red ants; when you are growing dasheen,° make sure it gets plenty of water or else it makes your throat itch when you are eating it; this is how you sweep a corner; this is how you sweep a whole house; this is how you sweep a yard; this is how you smile to someone you don't like too much; this is how you smile to someone you don't like at all; this is how you smile to someone you like completely; this is how you set a table for tea; this is how you set a table for dinner; this is how you set a table for dinner with an important guest; this is how you set a table for lunch; this is how you set a table for breakfast; this is how to behave in the presence of men who don't know you very well, and this way they won't recognize immediately the slut I have warned you against becoming; be sure to wash every day, even if it is with your own spit; don't squat down to play marbles — you are not a boy, you know; don't pick people's flowers — you might catch something; don't throw stones at blackbirds, because it might not be a blackbird at all; this is how to make a bread pudding; this is how to make doukona;° this is how to make pepper pot;° this is how to make a good medicine for a cold; this is how to make a good medicine to throw away a child before it even becomes a child; this is how to catch a fish; this is how to throw back a fish you don't like, and that way something bad won't fall on you; this is how to bully a man; this is how a man bullies you; this is

benna: Calypso music.
dasheen: The edible rootstock of taro, a tropical plant.
doukona: A spicy plantain pudding.
pepper pot: A stew.

how to love a man, and if this doesn't work there are other ways, and if they don't work don't feel too bad about giving up; this is how to spit up in the air if you feel like it, and this is how to move quick so that it doesn't fall on you; this is how to make ends meet; always squeeze bread to make sure it's fresh; *but what if the baker won't let me feel the bread?*; you mean to say that after all you are really going to be the kind of woman who the baker won't let near the bread?

ANNIE PROULX (B. 1935)

John Harding / The Life Images Collection / Getty Images.

Annie Proulx was born in 1935 and did not finish her first book until 1988. She received a B.A. from the University of Vermont in 1969 and a master's degree from Sir George Williams University, both in history, and later became a freelance writer of articles for magazines in the United States. She published short stories occasionally until she had enough to make her first collection, *Heart Songs and Other Stories* (1988), which she followed with the novel *Postcards* in 1992. Her breakthrough novel was *The Shipping News* (1993), which won both the Pulitzer Prize and the National Book Award, and she has since produced two novels, *Accordion Crimes* (1996) and *The Old Ace in the Hole* (2003), and three books of short stories, *Close Range: Wyoming Stories* (1999), *Bad Dirt: Wyoming Stories 2* (2004), and *Fine Just the Way It Is: Wyoming Stories 3* (2008). Setting her works in places as distant as Newfoundland and Wyoming, Proulx conveys her dark, comic stories by creating a strong sense of place, using her talent for keen detail and for reproducing the peculiarities of local speech. *The Shipping News* and the short story "Brokeback Mountain" from *Close Range* were made into popular films. In 2011, Proulx published *Bird Cloud: A Memoir*, about her life in Wyoming.

55 Miles to the Gas Pump   1999

Rancher Croom in handmade boots and filthy hat, that walleyed cattleman, stray hairs like curling fiddle string ends, that warm-handed, quick-foot dancer on splintery boards or down the cellar stairs to a rack of bottles of his own strange beer, yeasty, cloudy, bursting out in garlands of foam, Rancher Croom at night galloping drunk over the dark plain, turning off at a place he knows to arrive at a canyon brink where he dismounts and looks down on tumbled rock, waits, then steps out, parting the air with his last roar, sleeves surging up windmill arms, jeans riding over boot tops, but before he hits he rises again to the top of the cliff like a cork in a bucket of milk.

Mrs. Croom on the roof with a saw cutting a hole into the attic where she has not been for twelve years thanks to old Croom's padlocks and warnings, whets to her desire, and the sweat flies as she exchanges the saw for a chisel and hammer until a ragged slab of peak is free and she can see inside: just as she thought: the corpses of Mr. Croom's paramours — she recognizes them from their photographs in the paper: MISSING WOMAN — some desiccated as jerky and much the same color, some moldy from lying beneath roof leaks, and all of them used hard, covered with tarry handprints, the marks of boot heels, some bright blue with the remnants of paint used on the shutters years ago, one wrapped in newspaper nipple to knee.

When you live a long way out you make your own fun.

MARK TWAIN (1835–1910)

© Bettmann / CORBIS.

Mark Twain is the pen name of Samuel Clemens, born in Missouri in 1835. Twain spent most of his childhood in Hannibal, Missouri, on the Mississippi River, and after the death of his father when he was eleven, he worked at a series of jobs to help support his family. A newspaper job prepared him to wander east working for papers and exploring St. Louis, New York, and Philadelphia. Later he trained as a steamboat pilot on the Mississippi and piloted boats professionally until the onset of the Civil War. Clemens had used a couple of different pseudonyms for minor publications before this point, but in 1863 he signed a travel narrative "Mark Twain," from a boating term that means "two fathoms deep," and the name for the great American humorist was created. Twain gained fame in 1865 with his story "The Celebrated Jumping Frog of Calaveras County," which appeared in the New York–based *Saturday Press*. He then became a traveling correspondent, writing pieces on his travels to Europe and the Middle East, and returned to the United States in 1870, when he married and moved to Connecticut. Twain produced *Roughing It* (1872) and *The Gilded Age* (1873) while he toured the country lecturing, and in 1876 published *The Adventures of Tom Sawyer*, an instant hit. His subsequent publications include *A Tramp Abroad* (1880), *The Prince and the Pauper* (1881), and the masterpiece *The Adventures of Huckleberry Finn* (1884). Often traveling and lecturing, Twain wrote several more books, including story collections, *The Tragedy of Pudd'nhead Wilson* (1894), and *Tom Sawyer, Detective* (1896), before he died in Italy in 1910. His work is noted for the combination of rough humor and vernacular language it often uses to convey keen social insights. In "The Story of the Good Little Boy" Twain offers his version of a Sunday-school lesson.

The Story of the Good Little Boy   1870

Once there was a good little boy by the name of Jacob Blivens. He always obeyed his parents, no matter how absurd and unreasonable their demands were; and he always learned his book, and never was late at Sabbath-school. He would not play hookey, even when his sober judgment told him it was the most profitable thing he could do. None of the other boys could ever make that boy out, he acted so strangely. He wouldn't lie, no matter how convenient it was. He just said it was wrong to lie, and that was sufficient for him. And he was so honest that he was simply ridiculous. The curious ways that that Jacob had, surpassed everything. He wouldn't play marbles on Sunday, he wouldn't rob birds' nests, he wouldn't give hot pennies to organ-grinders' monkeys; he didn't seem to take any interest in any kind of rational amusement. So the other boys used to try to reason it out and come to an understanding of him, but they couldn't arrive at any satisfactory conclusion. As I said before, they could only figure out a sort of vague idea that he was "afflicted," and so they took him under their protection, and never allowed any harm to come to him.

This good little boy read all the Sunday-school books; they were his greatest delight. This was the whole secret of it. He believed in the good little boys they put in the Sunday-school books; he had every confidence in them. He longed to come across one of them alive once; but he never did. They all died before his time, maybe. Whenever he read about a particularly good one he turned over quickly to the end to see what became of him, because he wanted to travel thousands of miles and gaze on him; but it wasn't any use; that good little boy always died in the last chapter, and there was a picture of the funeral, with all his relations and the Sunday-school children standing around the grave in pantaloons that were too short, and bonnets that were too large, and everybody crying into handkerchiefs that had as much as a yard and a half of stuff in them. He was always headed off in this way. He never could see one of those good little boys on account of his always dying in the last chapter.

Jacob had a noble ambition to be put in a Sunday-school book. He wanted to be put in, with pictures representing him gloriously declining to lie to his mother, and her weeping for joy about it; and pictures representing him standing on the doorstep giving a penny to a poor beggar-woman with six children, and telling her to spend it freely, but not to be extravagant, because extravagance is a sin; and pictures of him magnanimously refusing to tell on the bad boy who always lay in wait for him around the corner as he came from school, and welted him over the head with a lath, and then chased him home, saying, "Hi! hi!" as he proceeded. That was the ambition of young Jacob Blivens. He wished to be put in a Sunday-school book. It made him feel a little uncomfortable sometimes when he reflected that the good little boys always died. He loved to live, you know, and this was the most unpleasant feature about being a Sunday-school-book boy. He knew it was not healthy to be good. He knew it was more fatal than consumption to be so supernaturally good as the boys in the books were; he knew that none of them had ever been able to stand it long, and it pained him to think that if they put him in a book he wouldn't ever see it, or even if they did get the book out before he died it wouldn't be popular without any picture of his funeral in the back part of it. It couldn't be much of a Sunday-school book that couldn't tell about the advice he gave to the community when he was dying. So at last, of course, he had to make up his mind to do the best he could under the circumstances — to live right, and, hang on as long as he could, and have his dying speech all ready when his time came.

But somehow nothing ever went right with this good little boy; nothing ever turned out with him the way it turned out with the good little boys in the books. They always had a good time, and the bad boys had the broken legs; but in his case there was a screw loose somewhere, and it all happened just the other way. When he found Jim Blake stealing apples, and went under the tree to read to him about the bad little boy who fell out of a neighbor's apple tree and broke his arm, Jim fell out of the tree, too, but he fell on *him* and broke *his* arm, and Jim wasn't hurt at all. Jacob couldn't understand that. There wasn't anything in the books like it.

And once, when some bad boys pushed a blind man over in the mud, and Jacob ran to help him up and receive his blessing, the blind man did not give him any blessing at all, but whacked him over the head with his stick and said he would like to catch him shoving *him* again, and then pretending to help him up. This was not in accordance with any of the books. Jacob looked them all over to see.

One thing that Jacob wanted to do was to find a lame dog that hadn't any place to stay, and was hungry and persecuted, and bring him home and pet him and have that dog's imperishable gratitude. And at last he found one and was happy; and he brought him home and fed him, but when he was going to pet him the dog flew at him and tore all the clothes off him except those that were in front, and made a spectacle of him that was astonishing. He examined authorities, but he could not understand the matter. It was of the same breed of dogs that was in the books, but it acted very differently. Whatever this boy did he got into trouble. The very things the boys in the books got rewarded for turned out to be about the most unprofitable things he could invest in.

Once, when he was on his way to Sunday-school, he saw some bad boys starting off pleasuring in a sailboat. He was filled with consternation, because he knew from his reading that boys who went sailing on Sunday invariably got drowned. So he ran out on a raft to warn them, but a log turned with him and slid him into the river. A man got him out pretty soon, and the doctor pumped the water out of him, and gave him a fresh start with his bellows, but he caught cold and lay sick abed nine weeks. But the most unaccountable thing about it was that the bad boys in the boat had a good time all day, and then reached home alive and well in the most surprising manner. Jacob Blivens said there was nothing like these things in the books. He was perfectly dumbfounded.

When he got well he was a little discouraged, but he resolved to keep on trying anyhow. He knew that so far his experiences wouldn't do to go in a book, but he hadn't yet reached the allotted term of life for good little boys, and he hoped to be able to make a record yet if he could hold on till his time was fully up. If everything else failed he had his dying speech to fall back on.

He examined his authorities, and found that it was now time for him to go to sea as a cabin-boy. He called on a ship-captain and made his application, and when the captain asked for his recommendations he proudly drew out a tract and pointed to the word, "To Jacob Blivens, from his affectionate teacher." But the captain was a coarse, vulgar man, and he said, "Oh, that be blowed! *that* wasn't any proof that he knew how to wash dishes or handle a slush-bucket, and he guessed he didn't want him." This was altogether the most extraordinary thing that ever happened to Jacob in all his life. A compliment from a teacher, on a tract, had never failed to move the tenderest emotions of ship-captains, and open the way to all offices of honor and profit in their gift — it never had in any book that ever *he* had read. He could hardly believe his senses.

This boy always had a hard time of it. Nothing ever came out according to   10
the authorities with him. At last, one day, when he was around hunting up bad little boys to admonish, he found a lot of them in the old iron-foundry fixing up a little joke on fourteen or fifteen dogs, which they had tied together in long procession, and were going to ornament with empty nitroglycerin cans made fast to their tails. Jacob's heart was touched. He sat down on one of those cans (for he never minded grease when duty was before him), and he took hold of the foremost dog by the collar, and turned his reproving eye upon wicked Tom Jones. But just at that moment Alderman McWelter, full of wrath, stepped in. All the bad boys ran away, but Jacob Blivens rose in conscious innocence and began one of those stately little Sunday-school-book speeches which always commence with "Oh, sir!" in dead opposition to the fact that no boy, good or bad, ever starts a remark with "Oh, sir." But the alderman never waited to hear the rest. He took Jacob Blivens by the ear and turned him around, and hit him a whack in the rear with the flat of his hand; and in an instant that good little boy shot out through the roof and soared away toward the sun, with the fragments of those fifteen dogs stringing after him like the tail of a kite. And there wasn't a sign of that alderman or that old iron-foundry left on the face of the earth; and, as for young Jacob Blivens, he never got a chance to make his last dying speech after all his trouble fixing it up, unless he made it to the birds; because, although the bulk of him came down all right in a tree-top in an adjoining county, the rest of him was apportioned around among four townships, and so they had to hold five inquests on him to find out whether he was dead or not, and how it occurred. You never saw a boy scattered so.[1]

Thus perished the good little boy who did the best he could, but didn't come out according to the books. Every boy who ever did as he did prospered except him. His case is truly remarkable. It will probably never be accounted for.

---

[1] This glycerin catastrophe is borrowed from a floating newspaper item, whose author's name I would give if I knew it. M.T.

POETRY

The Elements
of Poetry

12

Reading Poetry

Ink runs from the corners of my mouth.
There is no happiness like mine.
I have been eating poetry.
— MARK STRAND

© Christopher Felver / Corbis.

READING POETRY RESPONSIVELY

Perhaps the best way to begin reading poetry responsively is not to allow yourself to be intimidated by it. Come to it, initially at least, the way you might listen to a song on the radio. You probably listen to a song several times before you hear it all, before you have a sense of how it works, where it's going, and how it gets there. You don't worry about analyzing a song when you listen to it, even though after repeated experiences with it you know and anticipate a favorite part and know, on some level, why it works for you. Give yourself a chance to respond to poetry. The hardest work has already been done by the poet, so all you need to do at the start is listen for the pleasure produced by the poet's arrangement of words.

Try reading the following poem aloud. Read it aloud before you read it silently. You may stumble once or twice, but you'll make sense of it if you pay attention to its punctuation and don't stop at the end of every line where there is no punctuation. The title gives you an initial sense of what the poem is about.

LISA PARKER (B. 1972)

Snapping Beans   *1998*

For Fay Whitt

I snapped beans into the silver bowl
that sat on the splintering slats
of the porchswing between my grandma and me.
I was home for the weekend,
from school, from the North,   5
Grandma hummed "What A Friend We Have In Jesus"
as the sun rose, pushing its pink spikes
through the slant of cornstalks,
through the fly-eyed mesh of the screen.
We didn't speak until the sun overcame   10
the feathered tips of the cornfield
and Grandma stopped humming. I could feel
the soft gray of her stare
against the side of my face
when she asked, *How's school a-goin'?*   15
I wanted to tell her about my classes,
the revelations by book and lecture,
as real as any shout of faith
and potent as a swig of strychnine.
She reached the leather of her hand   20
over the bowl and cupped
my quivering chin; the slick smooth of her palm
held my face the way she held tomatoes
under the spigot, careful not to drop them,
and I wanted to tell her   25
about the nights I cried into the familiar
heartsick panels of the quilt she made me,
wishing myself home on the evening star.
I wanted to tell her
the evening star was a planet,   30
that my friends wore noserings and wrote poetry
about sex, about alcoholism, about Buddha.
I wanted to tell her how my stomach burned
acidic holes at the thought of speaking in class,
speaking in an accent, speaking out of turn,   35
how I was tearing, splitting myself apart
with the slow-simmering guilt of being happy
despite it all.
I said, *School's fine.*
We snapped beans into the silver bowl between us   40

and when a hickory leaf, still summer green,
skidded onto the porchfront,
Grandma said,
It's funny how things blow loose like that.

CONSIDERATIONS FOR CRITICAL THINKING AND WRITING

1. FIRST RESPONSE. Describe the speaker's feelings about starting a life at college. How do those feelings compare with your own experiences?

2. How does the grandmother's world differ from the speaker's at school? What details especially reveal those differences?

3. Discuss the significance of the grandmother's response to the hickory leaf in line 44. How do you read the last line?

The next poem creates a different kind of mood. Think about the title, "Those Winter Sundays," before you begin reading the poem. What associations do you have with winter Sundays? What emotions does the phrase evoke in you?

ROBERT HAYDEN (1913–1980)

Those Winter Sundays   *1962*

Sundays too my father got up early
and put his clothes on in the blueblack cold,
then with cracked hands that ached
from labor in the weekday weather made
banked fires blaze. No one ever thanked him.   5

I'd wake and hear the cold splintering, breaking.
When the rooms were warm, he'd call,
and slowly I would rise and dress,
fearing the chronic angers of that house,

Speaking indifferently to him,   10
who had driven out the cold
and polished my good shoes as well.
What did I know, what did I know
of love's austere and lonely offices?

Does the poem match the feelings you have about winter Sundays? Either way, your response can be useful in reading the poem. For most of us, Sundays are days at home; they might be cozy and pleasant experiences or they might be dull and depressing. Whatever they are, Sundays are more evocative than, say, Tuesdays. Hayden uses that response to call forth a sense of missed opportunity in the poem. The person who reflects

on those winter Sundays didn't know until much later how much he had to
thank his father for "love's austere and lonely offices." This is a poem about
a cold past and a present reverence for his father — elements brought together by the phrase "Winter Sundays." *His* father? You may have noticed
that the poem doesn't use a masculine pronoun; hence the voice could be
a woman's. Does the gender of the voice make any difference to your reading? Would it make any difference about which details are included or what
language is used?

What is most important about your initial readings of a poem is that
you ask questions. If you read responsively, you'll find yourself asking all
kinds of questions about the words, descriptions, sounds, and structure of
a poem. The specifics of those questions will be generated by the particular
poem. We don't, for example, ask how humor is achieved in "Those Winter
Sundays" because there is none, but it is worth asking what kind of tone
is established by the description of "the chronic angers of that house." The
remaining chapters in this part of the book will help you formulate and
answer questions about a variety of specific elements in poetry, such as
speaker, image, metaphor, symbol, rhyme, and rhythm. For the moment,
however, read the following poem several times and note your response at
different points in the poem. Then write down a half-dozen or so questions
about what produces your response to the poem. To answer questions, it's
best to know first what the questions are, and that's what the rest of this
chapter is about.

JOHN UPDIKE (1932–2009)

Dog's Death   1969

She must have been kicked unseen or brushed by a car.
Too young to know much, she was beginning to learn
To use the newspapers spread on the kitchen floor
And to win, wetting there, the words, "Good dog! Good dog!"

We thought her shy malaise was a shot reaction.   5
The autopsy disclosed a rupture in her liver.
As we teased her with play, blood was filling her skin
And her heart was learning to lie down forever.

Monday morning, as the children were noisily fed
And sent to school, she crawled beneath the youngest's bed.   10
We found her twisted and limp but still alive.
In the car to the vet's, on my lap, she tried

To bite my hand and died. I stroked her warm fur
And my wife called in a voice imperious with tears.
Though surrounded by love that would have upheld her,   15
Nevertheless she sank and, stiffening, disappeared.

Back home, we found that in the night her frame,
Drawing near to dissolution, had endured the shame
Of diarrhoea and had dragged across the floor
To a newspaper carelessly left there. *Good dog.*   20

Here's a simple question to get started with your own questions: What would the poem's effect have been if Updike had titled it "Good Dog" instead of "Dog's Death"?

THE PLEASURE OF WORDS

The impulse to create and appreciate poetry is as basic to human experience as language itself. Although no one can point to the precise origins of poetry, it is one of the most ancient of the arts, because it has existed ever since human beings discovered pleasure in language. The tribal ceremonies of peoples without written languages suggest that the earliest primitive cultures incorporated rhythmic patterns of words into their rituals. These chants, very likely accompanied by the music of a simple beat and the dance of a measured step, expressed what people regarded as significant and memorable in their lives. They echoed the concerns of the chanters and the listeners by chronicling acts of bravery, fearsome foes, natural disasters, mysterious events, births, deaths, and whatever else brought people pain or pleasure, bewilderment or revelation. Later cultures, such as the ancient Greeks, made poetry an integral part of religion.

Thus, from its very beginnings, poetry has been associated with what has mattered most to people. These concerns — whether natural or supernatural — can, of course, be expressed without vivid images, rhythmic patterns, and pleasing sounds, but human beings have always sensed a magic in words that goes beyond rational, logical understanding. Poetry is not simply a method of communication; it is a unique experience in itself.

What is special about poetry? What makes it valuable? Why should we read it? How is reading it different from reading prose? To begin with, poetry pervades our world in a variety of forms, ranging from advertising jingles to song lyrics. These may seem to be a long way from the chants heard around a primitive campfire, but they serve some of the same purposes. Like poems printed in a magazine or book, primitive chants, catchy jingles, and popular songs attempt to stir the imagination through the carefully measured use of words.

Although reading poetry usually makes more demands than does the kind of reading we use to skim a magazine or newspaper, the appreciation of poetry comes naturally enough to anyone who enjoys playing with words. Play is an important element of poetry. Consider, for example, how the following words appeal to the children who gleefully chant them in playgrounds:

I scream, you scream
We all scream
For ice cream.

These lines are an exuberant evocation of the joy of ice cream. Indeed, chanting the words turns out to be as pleasurable as eating ice cream. In poetry, the expression of the idea is as important as the idea expressed.

But is "I scream..." poetry? Some poets and literary critics would say that it certainly is one kind of poem because the children who chant it experience some of the pleasures of poetry in its measured beat and repeated sounds. However, other poets and critics would define poetry more narrowly and insist, for a variety of reasons, that this isn't true poetry but merely *doggerel*, a term used for lines whose subject matter is trite and whose rhythm and sounds are monotonously heavy-handed.

Although probably no one would argue that "I scream..." is a great poem, it does contain some poetic elements that appeal, at the very least, to children. Does that make it poetry? The answer depends on one's definition, but poetry has a way of breaking loose from definitions. Because there are nearly as many definitions of poetry as there are poets, Edwin Arlington Robinson's succinct observations are useful: "[P]oetry has two outstanding characteristics. One is that it is undefinable. The other is that it is eventually unmistakable."

This comment places more emphasis on how a poem affects a reader than on how a poem is defined. By characterizing poetry as "undefinable," Robinson acknowledges that it can include many different purposes, subjects, emotions, styles, and forms. What effect does the following poem have on you?

WILLIAM HATHAWAY (B. 1944)

Oh, Oh   *1982*

My girl and I amble a country lane,
moo cows chomping daisies, our own
sweet saliva green with grass stems.
"Look, look," she says at the crossing,
"the choo-choo's light is on." And sure
enough, right smack dab in the middle
of maple dappled summer sunlight
is the lit headlight — so funny.
An arm waves to us from the black window.
We wave gaily to the arm. "When I hear
trains at night I dream of being president,"
I say dreamily. "And me first lady," she
says loyally. So when the last boxcars,
named after wonderful, faraway places,
and the caboose chuckle by we look
eagerly to the road ahead. And there,
poised and growling, are fifty Hell's Angels.

William Hathaway.

15

A SAMPLE CLOSE READING

An Annotated Version of "Oh, Oh"

After you've read a poem two or three times, a deeper, closer reading—line by line, word by word, syllable by syllable—will help you discover even more about the poem. Ask yourself: What happens (or does not happen) in the poem? What are the poem's central ideas? How do the poem's words, images, and sounds, for example, contribute to its meaning? What is the poem's overall tone? How is the poem put together?

You can flesh out your close reading by writing your responses in the margins of the page. The following interpretive notes offer but one way to read Hathaway's poem.

The title offers an interjection expressing strong emotion and foreboding.

WILLIAM HATHAWAY (B. 1944)

Oh, Oh 1982

The informal language conjures up an idyllic picture of a walk in the country, where the sights, sounds, and tastes are full of pleasure.

The carefully orchestrated *d*'s, *m*'s, *p*'s, and *s*'s of lines 6–8 create sounds that are meant to be savored.

Filled with confidence and hope, the couple imagines a successful future together in exotic locations. Even the train is happy for them as it "chuckle[s]" in approval of their dreams.

The visual effect of the many o's in lines 1–5 (and 15) suggests an innocent, wide-eyed openness to experience while the repetitive *oo* sounds echo a kind of reassuring, satisfied cooing.

"Right smack dab in the middle" of the poem, the "black window" hints that all is not well.

Not until the very last line does "the road ahead" yield a terrifying surprise. The strategically "poised" final line derails the leisurely movement of the couple and brings their happy story to a dead stop. The emotional reversal parked in the last few words awaits the reader as much as it does the couple. The sight and sound of the motorcycle gang signal that what seemed like heaven is, in reality, hell: Oh, oh.

My girl and I amble a country lane,
moo cows chomping daisies, our own
sweet saliva green with grass stems.
"Look, look," she says at the crossing,
"the choo-choo's light is on." And sure   5
enough, right smack dab in the middle
of maple dappled summer sunlight
is the lit headlight — so funny.
An arm waves to us from the black window.
We wave gaily to the arm. "When I hear   10
trains at night I dream of being president,"
I say dreamily. "And me first lady," she
says loyally. So when the last boxcars,
named after wonderful, faraway places,
and the caboose chuckle by we look   15
eagerly to the road ahead. And there,
poised and growling, are fifty Hell's Angels.

Hathaway's poem serves as a convenient reminder that poetry can be full of surprises. Full of confidence, this couple, like the reader, is unprepared for the shock to come. When we see those "fifty Hell's Angels," we are confronted with something like a bucket of cold water in the face.

But even though our expectations are abruptly and powerfully reversed, we are finally invited to view the entire episode from a safe distance — the distance provided by the delightful humor in this poem. After all, how seriously can we take a poem that is titled "Oh, Oh"? The poet has his way with us, but we are brought in on the joke, too. The terror takes on comic proportions as the innocent couple is confronted by no fewer than *fifty* Hell's Angels. This is the kind of raucous overkill that informs a short animated film produced some years ago titled *Bambi Meets Godzilla*: you might not have seen it, but you know how it ends. The poem's good humor comes through when we realize how pathetically inadequate the response of "Oh, Oh" is to the circumstances.

As you can see, reading a description of what happens in a poem is not the same as experiencing a poem. The exuberance of "I scream . . ." and the surprise of Hathaway's "Oh, Oh" are in the hearing or reading rather than in the retelling. A ***paraphrase*** is a prose restatement of the central ideas of a poem in your own language. Consider the difference between the following poem and the paraphrase that follows it. What is missing from the paraphrase?

ROBERT FRANCIS (1901–1987)

Catch   1950

Two boys uncoached are tossing a poem together,
Overhand, underhand, backhand, sleight of hand, every hand,
Teasing with attitudes, latitudes, interludes, altitudes,
High, make him fly off the ground for it, low, make him stoop,
Make him scoop it up, make him as-almost-as-possible miss it,   5
Fast, let him sting from it, now, now fool him slowly,
Anything, everything tricky, risky, nonchalant,
Anything under the sun to outwit the prosy,
Over the tree and the long sweet cadence down,
Over his head, make him scramble to pick up the meaning,   10
And now, like a posy, a pretty one plump in his hands.

Paraphrase: A poet's relationship to a reader is similar to a game of catch. The poem, like a ball, should be pitched in a variety of ways to challenge and create interest. Boredom and predictability must be avoided if the game is to be engaging and satisfying.

A paraphrase can help us achieve a clearer understanding of a poem, but, unlike a poem, it misses all the sport and fun. It is the poem that "outwit[s] the prosy" because the poem serves as an example of what it suggests poetry should be. Moreover, the two players—the poet and the reader—are "uncoached." They know how the game is played, but their expectations do not preclude spontaneity and creativity or their ability to surprise and be surprised. The solid pleasure of the workout—of reading poetry—is the satisfaction derived from exercising your imagination and intellect. Perhaps the best way to approach a poem is similar to what Francis's "Catch" implies: expect to be surprised, stay on your toes, and concentrate on the delivery.

A SAMPLE STUDENT ANALYSIS

Tossing Metaphors Together in Robert Francis's "Catch"

The following sample paper on Robert Francis's "Catch" was written in response to an assignment that asked students to discuss the use of metaphor in the poem. Notice that Chris Leggett's paper is clearly focused and well organized. His discussion of the use of metaphor in the poem stays on track from beginning to end without any detours concerning unrelated topics (for a definition of *metaphor*, see p. 396). His title draws on the central metaphor of the poem, and he organizes the paper around four key words used in the poem: "attitudes, latitudes, interludes, altitudes." These constitute the heart of the paper's four substantive paragraphs, and they are effectively framed by introductory and concluding paragraphs. Moreover, the transitions between paragraphs clearly indicate that the author was not merely tossing a paper together.

Chris Leggett

Professor Lyles

English 203-1

9 November 2015

Tossing Metaphors Together in Robert Francis's "Catch"

Exploration of the meaning of the word catch.

The word *catch* is an attention getter. It usually means something is about to be hurled at someone and that he or she is expected to catch it. *Catch* can also signal a challenge to another player if the toss is purposefully difficult. Robert Francis, in his poem "Catch,"

Thesis statement identifying purpose of the poem's metaphors.

uses the extended metaphor of two boys playing catch to explore the considerations a poet makes when "tossing a poem together" (line 1). Line 3 of "Catch" enumerates these considerations metaphorically as

Reference to specific language in the poem, around which the paper is organized.

"attitudes, latitudes, interludes, [and] altitudes." While regular prose is typically straightforward and easily understood, poetry usually takes great effort to understand and appreciate. To exemplify this, Francis presents the reader not with a normal game of catch with the ball flying back and forth in a repetitive and predictable fashion, but with a physically challenging game in which one must concentrate, scramble, and exert oneself to catch the ball, as one must stretch the intellect to truly grasp

Introductory analysis of the poem's purpose.

a poem.

Analysis of the meaning of attitude *in the poem.*

The first consideration mentioned by Francis is attitude. Attitude, when applied to the game of catch, indicates the ball's pitch in flight—upward, downward, or straight. It could also describe the players' attitudes toward each other or toward the game in general. Below this literal level lies *attitude's* meaning in relation to poetry. Attitude in this case represents a poem's tone.

Discussion of how the attitude metaphor contributes to the poem's tone.

A poet may "Teas[e] with attitudes" (3) by experimenting with different tones to achieve the desired mood. The underlying tone of "Catch" is a playful one, set and reinforced by the use of a game. This playfulness is further reinforced by such words and phrases as "[t]easing" (3), "outwit" (8), and "fool him" (6).

Analysis of the meaning of latitude *in the poem.*

Considered also in the metaphorical game of catch is latitude, which, when applied to the game, suggests the range the object may be thrown— how high, how low, or how far. Poetic latitude, along similar lines, concerns a poem's breadth, or the scope of topic. Taken one level further, latitude suggests freedom from normal restraints or limitations, indicating the ability to

Leggett 2

go outside the norm to find originality of expression. The entire game of
catch described in Francis's poem reaches outside the normal expectations
of something being merely tossed back and forth in a predictable manner.
The ball is thrown in almost every conceivable fashion, "Overhand,
underhand . . . every hand" (2). Other terms describing the throws—such
as "tricky," "risky," "Fast," "slowly," and "Anything under the sun"
(6-8)—express endless latitude for avoiding predictability in Francis's game
of catch and metaphorically in writing poetry.

> Discussion of how the latitude metaphor contributes to the poem's scope and message.

During a game of catch the ball may be thrown at different intervals,
establishing a steady rhythm or a broken, irregular one. Other intervening
features, such as the field being played on or the weather, could also affect
the game. These features of the game are alluded to in the poem by the use
of the word *interludes*. *Interlude* in the poetic sense represents the poem's
form, which can similarly establish or diminish rhythm or enhance meaning.
Lines 6 and 9, respectively, show a broken and a flowing rhythm. Line 6
begins rapidly as a hard toss that stings the catcher's hand is described.
The rhythm of the line is immediately slowed, however, by the word "now"
followed by a comma, followed by the rest of the line. In contrast, line 9
flows smoothly as the reader visualizes the ball flying over the tree and
sailing downward. The words chosen for this line function perfectly. The
phrase "the long sweet cadence down" establishes a sweet rhythm that reads
smoothly and rolls off the tongue easily. The choice of diction not only
affects the poem's rhythmic flow but also establishes through connotative
language the various levels at which the poem can be understood,
represented in "Catch" as altitude.

> Analysis of the meaning of *interlude* in the poem.

> Discussion of how the interlude metaphor contributes to the poem's form and rhythm.

While *altitudes* when referring to the game of catch means how high
an object is thrown, in poetry it could refer to the level of diction, lofty or
down-to-earth, formal or informal. It suggests also the levels at which a poem
can be comprehended, the literal as well as the interpretive. In Francis's game
of catch, the ball is thrown high to make the player reach, low to "make him
stoop" (4), or "Over his head [to] make him scramble" (10), implying that the
player should have to exert himself to catch it. So too, then, should the reader
of poetry put great effort into understanding the full meaning of a poem. Francis
exemplifies this consideration in writing poetry by giving "Catch" not only an
enjoyable literal meaning concerning the game of catch, but also a rich

> Analysis of the meaning of *altitudes* in the poem.

metaphorical meaning—reflecting the process of writing poetry. Francis uses several phrases and words with multiple meanings. The phrase "tossing a poem together" (1) can be understood as tossing something back and forth or the process of constructing a poem. While "prosy" (8) suggests prose itself, it also means the mundane or the ordinary. In the poem's final line the word *posy* of course represents a flower, while it is also a variant of the word *poesy*, meaning poetry, or the practice of composing poetry.

Francis effectively describes several considerations to be taken in writing poetry in order to "outwit the prosy" (8). His use of the extended metaphor in "Catch" shows that a poem must be unique, able to be comprehended on multiple levels, and a challenge to the reader. The various rhythms in the lines of "Catch" exemplify the ideas they express. While achieving an enjoyable poem on the literal level, Francis has also achieved a rich metaphorical meaning. The poem offers a good workout both physically and intellectually.

Discussion of how the altitude metaphor contributes to the poem's literal and symbolic meanings, with references to specific language.

Conclusion summarizing ideas explored in the paper.

Work Cited

Francis, Robert. "Catch." *Literature to Go,* edited by Michael Meyer, 3rd ed, Bedford/St. Martin's, 2017, p. 330.

Before beginning your own writing assignment on poetry, you should review Chapter 31, "Writing about Poetry," and Chapter 29, "Reading and the Writing Process," which provides a step-by-step overview of how to choose a topic, develop a thesis, and organize various types of writing assignments. If you are using outside sources in your paper, you should make sure that you are familiar with the conventional documentation procedures described in Chapter 33, "The Literary Research Paper."

How does the speaker's description in Francis's "Catch" of what readers might expect from reading poetry compare with the speaker's expectations concerning fiction in the next poem by Philip Larkin?

Philip Larkin (1922–1985)
A Study of Reading Habits   *1964*

When getting my nose in a book
Cured most things short of school,
It was worth ruining my eyes
To know I could still keep cool,
And deal out the old right hook   5
To dirty dogs twice my size.

Later, with inch-thick specs,
Evil was just my lark:
Me and my cloak and fangs
Had ripping times in the dark.   10
The women I clubbed with sex!
I broke them up like meringues.

Don't read much now: the dude
Who lets the girl down before
The hero arrives, the chap   15
Who's yellow and keeps the store,
Seem far too familiar. Get stewed:
Books are a load of crap.

In "A Study of Reading Habits," Larkin distances himself from a speaker whose sensibilities he does not wholly share. The poet—and many readers—might identify with the reading habits described by the speaker in the first twelve lines, but Larkin uses the last six lines to criticize the speaker's attitude toward life as well as reading. The speaker recalls in lines 1–6 how as a schoolboy he identified with the hero, whose virtuous strength always triumphed over "dirty dogs," and in lines 7–12 he recounts how his schoolboy fantasies were transformed by adolescence into a fascination with violence and sex. This description of early reading habits is pleasantly amusing, because many readers of popular fiction will probably recall having moved through similar stages, but at the end of the poem the speaker provides more information about himself than he intends to.

As an adult the speaker has lost interest in reading because it is no longer an escape from his own disappointed life. Instead of identifying with heroes or villains, he finds himself identifying with minor characters who are irresponsible and cowardly. Reading is now a reminder of his failures, so he turns to alcohol. His solution, to "Get stewed" because "Books are a load of crap," is obviously self-destructive. The speaker is ultimately exposed by Larkin as someone who never grew beyond fantasies. Getting drunk is consistent with the speaker's immature reading habits. Unlike the speaker, the poet understands that life is often distorted by escapist fantasies, whether through a steady diet of popular fiction or through alcohol. The speaker in this poem, then, is not Larkin but a created identity whose voice is filled with disillusionment and delusion.

The problem with Larkin's speaker is that he misreads books as well as his own life. Reading means nothing to him unless it serves as an escape from himself. It is not surprising that Larkin has him read fiction rather than poetry because poetry places an especially heavy emphasis on language. Fiction, indeed any kind of writing, including essays and drama, relies on carefully chosen and arranged words, but poetry does so to an even greater extent. Notice, for example, how Larkin's deft use of trite expressions and slang characterizes the speaker so that his language reveals nearly as much about his dreary life as what he says. Larkin's speaker would have no use for poetry.

Here is a poem that looks quite different from most *verse*, a term used for lines composed in a measured rhythmical pattern, which are often, but not necessarily, rhymed.

Robert Morgan (b. 1944)

Mountain Graveyard   1979

for the author of "Slow Owls"

Spore Prose

stone	notes
slate	tales
sacred	cedars
heart	earth
asleep	please
hated	death

Though unconventional in its appearance, this is unmistakably poetry because of its concentrated use of language. The poem demonstrates how serious play with words can lead to some remarkable discoveries. At first glance "Mountain Graveyard" may seem intimidating. What, after all, does this list of words add up to? How is it in any sense a poetic use of language? But if the words are examined closely, it is not difficult to see how they work. The wordplay here is literally in the form of a game. Morgan uses a series of **anagrams** (words made from the letters of other words, such as *read* and *dare*) to evoke feelings about death. "Mountain Graveyard" is one of several poems that Morgan has called "Spore Prose" (another anagram) because he finds in individual words the seeds of poetry. He wrote the poem in honor of the fiftieth birthday of another poet, Jonathan Williams, the author of "Slow Owls," whose title is also an anagram.

The title, "Mountain Graveyard," indicates the poem's setting, which is also the context in which the individual words in the poem interact to provide a larger meaning. Morgan's discovery of the words on the stones of a graveyard is more than just clever. The observations he makes among the silent graves go beyond the curious pleasure a reader experiences in finding that the words *sacred cedars*, referring to evergreens common in cemeteries, consist of the same letters. The surprise and delight of realizing the connection between *heart* and *earth* are tempered by the more sober recognition that everyone's story ultimately ends in the ground. The hope that the dead are merely asleep is expressed with a plea that is answered grimly by a hatred of death's finality.

The following poem also involves a startling discovery about words. With the peculiar title "l(a," the poem cannot be read aloud, so there is no sound, but is there sense, a **theme** — a central idea or meaning — in the poem?

E. E. Cummings (1894–1962)

l(a   *1958*

l(a

le
af
fa

ll

s)
one
l

iness

© Bettmann/Corbis.

Considerations for Critical Thinking and Writing

1. FIRST RESPONSE. Discuss the connection between what appears inside and outside the parentheses in this poem.

2. What does Cummings draw attention to by breaking up the words? How do this strategy and the poem's overall shape contribute to its theme?

3. Which seems more important in this poem — what is expressed or the way it is expressed?

Although "Mountain Graveyard" and "l(a" do not resemble the kind of verse that readers might recognize immediately as poetry on a page, both are actually a very common type of poem, called the **lyric**, usually a brief poem that expresses the personal emotions and thoughts of a single speaker. Lyrics are often written in the first person, but sometimes — as in "Mountain Graveyard" and "l(a" — no speaker is specified. Lyrics present a subjective mood, emotion, or idea. Very often they are about love or death, but almost any subject or experience that evokes some intense emotional response can be found in lyrics. In addition to brevity and emotional intensity, lyrics are also frequently characterized by their musical qualities. The word *lyric* derives from the Greek word *lyre*, meaning a musical instrument that originally accompanied the singing of a lyric. Lyric poems can be organized in a variety of ways, such as the sonnet, elegy, and ode (see Chapter 19), but it is enough to point out here that lyrics are an extremely popular kind of poetry with writers and readers.

The following anonymous lyric was found in a sixteenth-century manuscript.

ANONYMOUS

Western Wind

ca. 1500

Western wind, when wilt thou blow,
The small rain down can rain?
Christ, if my love were in my arms,
And I in my bed again!

This speaker's intense longing for his lover is characteristic of lyric poetry. He impatiently addresses the western wind that brings spring to England and could make it possible for him to be reunited with the woman he loves. We do not know the details of these lovers' lives because this poem focuses on the speaker's emotion. We do not learn why the lovers are apart or if they will be together again. We don't even know if the speaker is a man. But those issues are not really important. The poem gives us a feeling rather than a story.

A poem that tells a story is called a ***narrative poem***. Narrative poetry may be short or very long. An ***epic***, for example, is a long narrative poem on a serious subject chronicling heroic deeds and important events. Among the most famous epics are Homer's *Iliad* and *Odyssey*, the Old English *Beowulf*, Dante's *Divine Comedy*, and John Milton's *Paradise Lost*. More typically, however, narrative poems are considerably shorter, as is the case with the following poem, which tells the story of a child's memory of her father.

WHEN I WRITE "There are lots of things that are going on in the world, in your room, or in that book you didn't read for class that could set you on fire if you gave them a chance. Poetry isn't only about what you feel, it's about what you think, and about capturing the way the world exists in one particular moment." —REGINA BARRECA

Regina Barreca (b. 1957)

Nighttime Fires   1986

© Nicolette Theriault.

When I was five in Louisville
we drove to see nighttime fires. Piled seven of us,
all pajamas and running noses, into the Olds,
drove fast toward smoke. It was after my father
lost his job, so not getting up in the morning
gave him time: awake past midnight, he read
    old newspapers
with no news, tried crosswords until he split the
    pencil
between his teeth, mad. When he heard
the wolf whine of the siren, he woke my mother,
and she pushed and shoved   10
us all into waking. Once roused we longed for burnt wood
and a smell of flames high into the pines. My old man liked
driving to rich neighborhoods best, swearing in a good mood
as he followed fire engines that snaked like dragons
and split the silent streets. It was festival, carnival.   15

If there were a Cadillac or any car
in a curved driveway, my father smiled a smile
from a secret, brittle heart.
His face lit up in the heat given off by destruction
like something was being made, or was being set right.   20
I bent my head back to see where sparks
ate up the sky. My father who never held us
would take my hand and point to falling cinders that
covered the ground like snow, or, excited, show us
the swollen collapse of a staircase. My mother   25
watched my father, not the house. She was happy
only when we were ready to go, when it was finally over
and nothing else could burn.
Driving home, she would sleep in the front seat
as we huddled behind. I could see his quiet face in the   30
rearview mirror, eyes like hallways filled with smoke.

This narrative poem could have been a short story if the poet had wanted to say more about the "brittle heart" of this unemployed man whose daughter so vividly remembers the desperate pleasure he took in watching fire consume other people's property. Indeed, a reading of William Faulkner's famous short story "Barn Burning" suggests how such a character can be further developed and how his child responds to him. The similarities between Faulkner's angry character and the poem's father, whose "eyes [are] like hallways filled with smoke," are coincidental, but the characters' sense of "something . . . being set right" by flames is worth comparing. Although we do not know everything about this man and his family, we have a much firmer sense of their story than we do of the story of the couple in "Western Wind."

Although narrative poetry is still written, short stories and novels have largely replaced the long narrative poem. Lyric poems tend to be the predominant type of poetry today. Regardless of whether a poem is a narrative or a lyric, however, the strategies for reading it are somewhat different from those for reading prose. Try these suggestions for approaching poetry.

Suggestions for Approaching Poetry

1. Assume that it will be necessary to read a poem more than once. Give yourself a chance to become familiar with what the poem has to offer. Like a piece of music, a poem becomes more pleasurable with each encounter.

2. Pay attention to the title; it will often provide a helpful context for the poem and serve as an introduction to it. Larkin's "A Study of Reading Habits" is precisely what its title describes.

3. As you read the poem for the first time, avoid becoming entangled in words or lines that you don't understand. Instead, give yourself a chance to take in the entire poem before attempting to resolve problems encountered along the way.

4. On a second reading, identify any words or passages that you don't understand. Look up words you don't know; these might include names, places, historical and mythical references, or anything else that is unfamiliar to you.

5. Read the poem aloud (or perhaps have a friend read it to you). You'll probably discover that some puzzling passages suddenly fall into place when you hear them. You'll find that nothing helps, though, if the poem is read in an artificial, exaggerated manner. Read in as natural a voice as possible, with slight pauses at line breaks. Silent reading is preferable to imposing a te-tumpty-te-tum reading on a good poem.

6. Read the punctuation. Poems use punctuation marks—in addition to the space on the page—as signals for readers. Be especially careful not to assume that the end of a line marks the end of a sentence, unless it is concluded by punctuation. Consider, for example, the opening lines of Hathaway's "Oh, Oh":

> My girl and I amble a country lane,
> moo cows chomping daisies, our own
> sweet saliva green with grass stems.

Line 2 makes little or no sense if a reader stops after "own." Keeping track of the subjects and verbs will help you find your way among the sentences.

7. Paraphrase the poem to determine whether you understand what happens in it. As you work through each line of the poem, a paraphrase will help you to see which words or passages need further attention.

8. Try to get a sense of who is speaking and what the setting or situation is. Don't assume that the speaker is the author; often it is a created character.

9. Assume that each element in the poem has a purpose. Try to explain how the elements of the poem work together.

10. Be generous. Be willing to entertain perspectives, values, experiences, and subjects that you might not agree with or approve of. Even if baseball bores you, you should be able to comprehend its imaginative use in Francis's "Catch."

11. Don't expect to produce a definitive reading. Many poems do not resolve all the ideas, issues, or tensions in them, and so it is not always possible to drive their meaning into an absolute corner. Your reading will explore rather than define the poem. Poems are not trophies to be stuffed and mounted. They're usually more elusive. And don't be afraid that a close reading will damage the poem. Poems aren't hurt when we analyze them; instead, they come alive as we experience them and put into words what we discover through them.

These strategies should be a useful means for getting inside poems to understand how they work. Furthermore, because reading poetry inevitably increases sensitivity to language, you're likely to find yourself a better reader of words in any form — whether in a novel, a newspaper editorial, an advertisement, a political speech, or a conversation — after having studied poetry. In short, many of the reading skills that make poetry accessible also open up the world you inhabit.

BILLY COLLINS (B. 1941)

Introduction to Poetry 1988

I ask them to take a poem
and hold it up to the light
like a color slide

or press an ear against its hive.

I say drop a mouse into a poem   5
and watch him probe his way out,

or walk inside the poem's room
and feel the walls for a light switch.

I want them to water-ski
across the surface of a poem   10
waving at the author's name on the shore.

But all they want to do
is tie the poem to a chair with rope
and torture a confession out of it.

They begin beating it with a hose   15
to find out what it really means.

CONSIDERATIONS FOR CRITICAL THINKING AND WRITING

1. FIRST RESPONSE. In what sense does this poem offer suggestions for approaching poetry? What advice does the speaker provide in lines 1–11?

2. How does the mood of the poem change beginning in line 12? What do you make of the shift from "them" to "they"?

3. Paraphrase the poem. How is your paraphrase different from what is included in the poem?

POETRY IN POPULAR FORMS

Before you try out these strategies for reading on a few more poems, it is worth acknowledging that the verse that enjoys the widest readership appears not in collections, magazines, or even anthologies for students, but in greeting cards. A significant amount of the personal daily mail delivered in the United States consists of greeting cards. That represents millions of lines of verse going by us on the street and in planes over our heads. These verses share some similarities with the poetry included in this anthology, but there are also important differences that indicate the need for reading serious poetry closely rather than casually.

The popularity of greeting cards is easy to explain: just as many of us have neither the time nor the talent to make gifts for birthdays, weddings, anniversaries, graduations, Valentine's Day, Mother's Day, and other holidays, we are unlikely to write personal messages when cards conveniently say them for us. Although impersonal, cards are efficient and convey an important message no matter what the occasion for them: I care. These greetings are rarely serious poetry; they are not written to be. Nevertheless, they demonstrate the impulse in our culture to generate and receive poetry.

In a handbook for greeting-card freelancers, a writer and past editor of such verse began with this advice:

> Once you determine what you want to say — and in this regard it is best to stick to one basic idea — you must choose your words to do several things at the same time:
>
> 1. Your idea must be expressed as a complete idea; it must have a beginning, a middle, and an end.
> 2. There must be coherence in your verse. Every line must be linked logically and smoothly with its neighbors.
> 3. Your expressions . . . must be conversational. High-flown language rarely comes off successfully in greeting-card writing.
> 4. You must write with emphasis — and something else: enthusiasm. It's necessary to create interest in that all-important first line. From that point on, writing your verse is a matter of developing your idea and bringing it to a peak of emphasis in the last line. Occasionally you will find that you have shot your wad too early in the verse, and whatever you say after that point sounds like an afterthought.
> 5. You must do all of the above and at the same time make everything come out right in the meter-and-rhyme department.[1]

This advice is followed by a list of approximately fifty of the most frequently used rhyme sounds accompanied by rhyming words, such as *love*, *of*, *above* for the sound *uv*. The point of these prescriptions is that the verse must be written so that it is immediately accessible — consumable — by both the buyer and the recipient. Writers of these cards are expected to avoid any complexity.

Compare the following greeting-card verse with the poem that comes after it. "Magic of Love," by Helen Farries, has been a longtime favorite in a major greeting-card company's "wedding line"; with different endings it has been used also in valentines and friendship cards.

HELEN FARRIES (1918–2008)

Magic of Love   *date unknown*

There's a wonderful gift that can give you a lift,
It's a blessing from heaven above!
It can comfort and bless, it can bring happiness —
It's the wonderful MAGIC OF LOVE!

Like a star in the night, it can keep your faith bright,   5
Like the sun, it can warm your hearts, too —
It's a gift you can give every day that you live,
And when given, it comes back to you!

---

[1] Chris Fitzgerald, "Conventional Verse: The Sentimental Favorite," *The Greeting Card Writer's Handbook*, ed. H. Joseph Chadwick (Cincinnati: Writer's Digest, 1975), 13, 17.

When love lights the way, there is joy in the day
And all troubles are lighter to bear,   10
Love is gentle and kind, and through love you will find
There's an answer to your every prayer!

May it never depart from your two loving hearts,
May you treasure this gift from above —
You will find if you do, all your dreams will come true,   15
In the wonderful MAGIC OF LOVE!

JOHN FREDERICK NIMS (1913–1999)

Love Poem   1947

My clumsiest dear, whose hands shipwreck vases,
At whose quick touch all glasses chip and ring,
Whose palms are bulls in china, burs in linen,
And have no cunning with any soft thing

Except all ill-at-ease fidgeting people: 5
The refugee uncertain at the door
You make at home; deftly you steady
The drunk clambering on his undulant floor.

Unpredictable dear, the taxi drivers' terror,
Shrinking from far headlights pale as a dime   10
Yet leaping before red apoplectic streetcars —
Misfit in any space. And never on time.

A wrench in clocks and the solar system. Only
With words and people and love you move at ease.
In traffic of wit expertly maneuver   15
And keep us, all devotion, at your knees.

Forgetting your coffee spreading on our flannel,
Your lipstick grinning on our coat,
So gaily in love's unbreakable heaven
Our souls on glory of spilt bourbon float.   20

Be with me, darling, early and late. Smash glasses —
I will study wry music for your sake.
For should your hands drop white and empty
All the toys of the world would break.

CONSIDERATIONS FOR CRITICAL THINKING AND WRITING

1. FIRST RESPONSE. Read these two works aloud. How are they different?
   How the same?

2. To what extent does the advice to would-be greeting-card writers apply to each work?

3. Compare the two speakers. Which do you find more appealing? Why?

4. How does Nims's description of love differ from Farries's?

In contrast to poetry, which transfigures and expresses an emotion or experience through an original use of language, the verse in "Magic of Love" relies on *clichés* — ideas or expressions that have become tired and trite from overuse, such as describing love as "a blessing from heaven above." Clichés anesthetize readers instead of alerting them to the possibility of fresh perceptions. They are used to draw out *stock responses* — predictable, conventional reactions to language, characters, symbols, or situations; God, heaven, the flag, motherhood, hearts, puppies, and peace are some often-used objects of stock responses. Advertisers manufacture careers from this sort of business.

Clichés and stock responses are two of the major ingredients of sentimentality in literature. *Sentimentality* exploits the reader by inducing responses that exceed what the situation warrants. This pejorative term should not be confused with *sentiment*, which is synonymous with *emotion* or *feeling*. Sentimentality cons readers into falling for the mass murderer who is devoted to stray cats, and it requires that we not think twice about what we're feeling because those tears shed for the little old lady, the rage aimed at the vicious enemy soldier, and the longing for the simple virtues of poverty might disappear under the slightest scrutiny. The experience of sentimentality is not unlike biting into a swirl of cotton candy; it's momentarily sweet but wholly insubstantial.

Clichés, stock responses, and sentimentality are generally the hallmarks of weak writing. Poetry — the kind that is unmistakable — achieves freshness, vitality, and genuine emotion that sharpen our perceptions of life.

POEMS FOR FURTHER STUDY

CORNELIUS EADY (B. 1954)

The Supremes

1991

We were born to be gray. We went to school,
Sat in rows, ate white bread,
Looked at the floor a lot. In the back
Of our small heads

A long scream. We did what we could,   5
And all we could do was
Turn on each other. How the fat kids suffered!
Not even being jolly could save them.

And then there were the anal retentives,
The terrified brown-noses, the desperately   10
Athletic or popular. This, of course,
Was training. At home

Our parents shook their heads and waited.
We learned of the industrial revolution,
The sectioning of the clock into pie slices.   15
We drank cokes and twiddled our thumbs. In the
Back of our minds

A long scream. We snapped butts in the showers,
Froze out shy girls on the dance floor,
Pin-pointed flaws like radar.   20
Slowly we understood: this was to be the world.

We were born insurance salesmen and secretaries,
Housewives and short order cooks,
Stock room boys and repairmen,
And it wouldn't be a bad life, they promised,   25
In a tone of voice that would force some of us
To reach in self-defense for wigs,
Lipstick,

Sequins.

Considerations for Critical Thinking and Writing

1. **FIRST RESPONSE.** Who were the Supremes? Why is the title so crucial for this poem?

2. Explain how the meanings and mood of this poem would change if it ended with line 25.

3. How does the speaker's recollection of school experiences compare with your own?

4. **CONNECTION TO ANOTHER SELECTION.** Discuss the speakers' memories of school in "The Supremes" and in Judy Page Heitzman's "The Schoolroom on the Second Floor of the Knitting Mill" (p. 405).

TED KOOSER (B. 1939)

Selecting a Reader   1974

First, I would have her be beautiful,
and walking carefully up on my poetry
at the loneliest moment of an afternoon,
her hair still damp at the neck
from washing it. She should be wearing   5

a raincoat, an old one, dirty
from not having money enough for the cleaners.
She will take out her glasses, and there
in the bookstore, she will thumb
over my poems, then put the book back   10
up on its shelf. She will say to herself,
"For that kind of money, I can get
my raincoat cleaned." And she will.

CONSIDERATIONS FOR CRITICAL THINKING AND WRITING

1. **FIRST RESPONSE.** What do the descriptive details in this poem reveal
   about the kind of reader the poet desires?

2. Based on this description of the poet's desired reader, write a one-
   paragraph description of the poem's speaker. Try to include some imaginative details that suggest his personality.

ALBERTO RÍOS (B. 1952)

Seniors   *1985*

William cut a hole in his Levi's pocket
so he could flop himself out in class
behind the girls so the other guys
could see and shit what guts we all said.
All Konga wanted to do over and over   5
was the rubber band trick, but he showed
everyone how, so nobody wanted to see
anymore and one day he cried, just cried
until his parents took him away forever.
Maya had a Hotpoint refrigerator standing   10
in his living room, just for his family to show
anybody who came that they could afford it.

Me, I got a French kiss, finally, in the catholic
darkness, my tongue's farthest half vacationing
loudly in another mouth like a man in Bermudas,   15
and my body jumped against a flagstone wall,
I could feel it through her thin, almost
nonexistent body: I had, at that moment, that moment,
a hot girl on a summer night, the best of all
the things we tried to do. Well, she   20
let me kiss her, anyway, all over.

Or it was just a flagstone wall
with a flaw in the stone, an understanding cavity

Alberto Ríos.

for burning young men with smooth dreams —
the true circumstance is gone, the true   25
circumstances about us all then
are gone. But when I kissed her, all water,
she would close her eyes, and they into somewhere
would disappear. Whether she was there
or not, I remember her, clearly, and she moves   30
around the room, sometimes, until I sleep.

I have lain on the desert in watch
low in the back of a pick-up truck
for nothing in particular, for stars, for
the things behind stars, and nothing comes   35
more than the moment: always now, here in a truck,
the moment again to dream of making love and sweat,
this time to a woman, or even to all of them
in some allowable way, to those boys, then,
who couldn't cry, to the girls before they were   40
women, to friends, me on my back, the sky over me
pressing its simple weight into her body
on me, into the bodies of them all, on me.

Considerations for Critical Thinking and Writing

1. **First response.** Comment on the use of slang in the poem. Does it surprise you? How does it characterize the speaker?

2. How does the language of the final stanza differ from that of the first stanza? To what purpose?

3. Write an essay that discusses the speaker's attitudes toward sex and life. How are they related?

4. **Connection to another selection.** Think about "Seniors" as a kind of love poem and compare the speaker's voice here with the one in T. S. Eliot's "The Love Song of J. Alfred Prufrock" (p. 537). How are these two voices used to evoke different cultures? Of what value is love in these cultures?

Willa Cather (1873–1947)

Prairie Spring   *1913*

Evening and the flat land,
Rich and sombre and always silent;
The miles of fresh-plowed soil,
Heavy and black, full of strength and harshness;
The growing wheat, the growing weeds,   5
The toiling horses, the tired men;

The long empty roads,
Sullen fires of sunset, fading,
The eternal, unresponsive sky.
Against all this, Youth,   10
Flaming like the wild roses,
Singing like the larks over the plowed fields,
Flashing like a star out of the twilight;
Youth with its insupportable sweetness,
Its fierce necessity,   15
Its sharp desire,
Singing and singing,
Out of the lips of silence,
Out of the earthy dusk.

Considerations for Critical Thinking and Writing

1. FIRST RESPONSE. To what extent do lines 1–9 present competing perspectives on the prairie?

2. Compare the poet's description of youth with that of the prairie.

3. Discuss the appropriateness of the title.

4. CONNECTION TO ANOTHER SELECTION. How might the themes in Mary Oliver's "The Poet with His Face in His Hands" (p. 351) indicate what she might have to say about "Prairie Spring"?

Alfred, Lord Tennyson (1809–1892)

The Eagle   1851

Fragment

He clasps the crag with crooked hands;
Close to the sun in lonely lands,
Ringed with the azure world, he stands.

The wrinkled sea beneath him crawls:
He watches from his mountain walls,
And like a thunderbolt he falls.

Considerations for Critical Thinking and Writing

1. FIRST RESPONSE. How does the speaker distinguish between the eagle's movements in the second stanza and those in the first stanza?

2. Although this poem is considered to be a fragment by Tennyson, how might it also be considered as a kind of complete portrait of an eagle?

3. CONNECTION TO ANOTHER SELECTION. Why can "The Eagle" and the anonymously written "Western Wind" (p. 338) be accurately described as lyric poems?

ROBERT FROST (1874–1963)

Design   *1936*

I found a dimpled spider, fat and white,
On a white heal-all,° holding up a moth
Like a white piece of rigid satin cloth —
Assorted characters of death and blight
Mixed ready to begin the morning right,   5
Like the ingredients of a witches' broth —
A snow-drop spider, a flower like a froth,
And dead wings carried like a paper kite.

What had the flower to do with being white,
The wayside blue and innocent heal-all?   10
What brought the kindred spider to that height,
Then steered the white moth thither in the night?
What but design of darkness to appall? —
If design govern in a thing so small.

CONSIDERATIONS FOR CRITICAL THINKING AND WRITING

1. FIRST RESPONSE. What kinds of speculations are raised in the poem's final two lines? Consider the meaning of the title. Is there more than one way to read it?

2. How does the division of the octave and sestet in this sonnet serve to organize the speaker's thoughts and feelings? What is the predominant rhyme? How does that rhyme relate to the poem's meaning?

3. Which words seem especially rich in connotative meanings? Explain how they function in the sonnet.

4. CONNECTION TO ANOTHER SELECTION. Compare the ironic tone of "Design" with the tone of William Hathaway's "Oh, Oh" (p. 328). What would you have to change in Hathaway's poem to make it more like Frost's?

EDGAR ALLAN POE (1809–1849)

Sonnet — To Science   *1845*

Science! true daughter of Old Time thou art!
    Who alterest all things with thy peering eyes.
Why preyest thou thus upon the poet's heart,
    Vulture, whose wings are dull realities?
How should he love thee? or how deem thee wise,   5
    Who wouldst not leave him in his wandering

---

² *heal-all:* A common flower, usually blue, once used for medicinal purposes.

To seek for treasure in the jewelled skies,
   Albeit he soared with an undaunted wing?
Hast thou not dragged Diana° from her car?   *goddess of hunting and the moon*
   And driven the Hamadryad° from the wood   *tree nymph*   10
To seek a shelter in some happier star?
   Hast thou not torn the Naiad° from her flood,   *water nymph*
The Elfin from the green grass, and from me
The summer dream beneath the tamarind tree?°   *exotic Asian tree*

CONSIDERATIONS FOR CRITICAL THINKING AND WRITING

1. FIRST RESPONSE. How is science characterized in lines 1–4? Which words are particularly revealing?

2. Given the references to Diana, the Hamadryad, the Naiad, the Elfin, and the tamarind tree, how would you describe the poet's world compared to the scientist's?

3. How do you think a scientist might respond to this poem?

4. CONNECTION TO ANOTHER SELECTION. Compare the speaker's attitudes toward what Poe calls in this poem "peering eyes" with the speaker's attitude toward the readers in Billy Collins's "Introduction to Poetry" (p. 341).

MARY OLIVER (B. 1935)

The Poet with His Face in His Hands   2005

You want to cry aloud for your
mistakes. But to tell the truth the world
doesn't need any more of that sound.

So if you're going to do it and can't
stop yourself, if your pretty mouth can't   5
hold it in, at least go by yourself across

the forty fields and the forty dark inclines
of rocks and water to the place where
the falls are flinging out their white sheets

like crazy, and there is a cave behind all that   10
jubilation and water fun and you can
stand there, under it, and roar all you

want and nothing will be disturbed; you can
drip with despair all afternoon and still,
on a green branch, its wings just lightly touched   15

by the passing foil of the water, the thrush,
puffing out its spotted breast, will sing
of the perfect, stone-hard beauty of everything.

Considerations for Critical Thinking and Writing

1. FIRST RESPONSE. Describe the kind of poet the speaker characterizes. What is the speaker's attitude toward that sort of poet?

2. Explain which single phrase used by the speaker to describe the poet most reveals for you the speaker's attitude toward the poet.

3. How is nature contrasted with the poet?

4. CONNECTION TO ANOTHER SELECTION. Compare the thematic use of nature in Oliver's poem and in Robert Frost's "Design" (p. 350).

13

Word Choice, Word Order, and Tone

I still feel that a poet has a duty to words, and that words can do wonderful things. And it's too bad to just let them lie there without doing anything with and for them.
— GWENDOLYN BROOKS

The Granger Collection.

WORD CHOICE

Diction

Like all good writers, poets are keenly aware of *diction*, their choice of words. Poets, however, choose words especially carefully because the words in poems call attention to themselves. Characters, actions, settings, and symbols may appear in a poem, but in the foreground, before all else, is the poem's language. Also, poems are usually briefer than other forms of writing. A few inappropriate words in a 200-page novel (which would have about 100,000 words) create fewer problems than they would in a 100-word poem. Functioning in a compressed atmosphere, the words in a poem must convey meanings gracefully and economically. Readers therefore have to be alert to the ways in which those meanings are released.

Although poetic language is often more intensely charged than ordinary speech, the words used in poetry are not necessarily different from everyday speech. Inexperienced readers may sometimes assume that language must be high-flown and out-of-date to be included in a poem: instead of reading about a boy "enjoying a swim," they expect to read about a boy "disporting with pliant arm o'er a glassy wave." During the eighteenth century this kind of *poetic diction* — the use of elevated language rather than ordinary language — was highly valued in English poetry, but since the nineteenth century poets have generally overridden the distinctions that were once made between words used in everyday speech and those used in poetry. Today all levels of diction can be found in poetry.

A poet, like any writer, has several levels of diction from which to choose; they range from formal to middle to informal. *Formal diction* consists of a dignified, impersonal, and elevated use of language. Notice, for example, the formality of Thomas Hardy's description of the sunken luxury liner *Titanic* in this stanza from "The Convergence of the Twain" (the entire poem appears on pp. 369–70):

> In a solitude of the sea
> Deep from human vanity,
> And the Pride of Life that planned her, stilly couches she.

There is nothing casual or relaxed about these lines. Hardy's use of "stilly," meaning "quietly" or "calmly," is purely literary; the word rarely, if ever, turns up in everyday English.

The language used in Sharon Olds's "Last Night" (p. 367) represents a less formal level of diction; the speaker uses a *middle diction* spoken by most educated people. Consider how Olds's speaker struggles the next day to comprehend her passion:

> Love? It was more like dragonflies
>
> in the sun, 100 degrees at noon,
>
> the ends of their abdomens stuck together, I
>
> close my eyes when I remember.

The words used to describe this encounter are common enough, yet it is precisely Olds's use of language that evokes the extraordinary nature of this couple's connection.

Informal diction is evident in Philip Larkin's "A Study of Reading Habits" (p. 335). The speaker's account of his early reading is presented *colloquially*, in a conversational manner that in this instance includes slang expressions not used by the culture at large:

> When getting my nose in a book
>
> Cured most things short of school,
>
> It was worth ruining my eyes
>
> To know I could still keep cool,
>
> And deal out the old right hook
>
> To dirty dogs twice my size.

This level of diction is clearly not that of Hardy's or Olds's speakers.

Poets may also draw on another form of informal diction, called **dialect.** Dialects are spoken by definable groups of people from a particular geographic region, economic group, or social class. New England dialects are often heard in Robert Frost's poems, for example. Gwendolyn Brooks uses a black dialect in "We Real Cool" (p. 375) to characterize a group of pool players. Another form of diction related to particular groups is *jargon*, a category of language defined by a trade or profession. Sociologists, photographers, carpenters, baseball players, and dentists, for example, all use words that are specific to their fields. Sally Croft offers an appetizing dish of cookbook jargon in "Home-Baked Bread" (p. 391).

Many levels of diction are available to poets. The variety of diction to be found in poetry is enormous, and that is how it should be. No language is foreign to poetry because it is possible to imagine any human voice as the speaker of a poem. When we say a poem is formal, informal, or somewhere in between, we are making a descriptive statement rather than an evaluative one. What matters in a poem is not only which words are used but how they are used.

Denotations and Connotations

One important way that the meaning of a word is communicated in a poem is through sound: snakes *hiss*, saws *buzz*. This and other matters related to sound are discussed in Chapter 17. Individual words also convey meanings through denotations and connotations. **Denotations** are the literal, dictionary meanings of a word. For example, *bird* denotes a feathered animal with wings (other denotations for the same word include a shuttlecock, an airplane, or an odd person), but in addition to its denotative meanings, *bird* also carries *connotations* — associations and implications that go beyond a word's literal meanings. Connotations derive from how a word has been used and the associations people make with it. Therefore, the connotations of *bird* might include fragility, vulnerability, altitude, the sky, or freedom, depending on the context in which the word is used. Consider also how different the connotations are for the following types of birds: hawk, dove, penguin, pigeon, chicken, peacock, duck, crow, turkey, gull, owl, goose, coot, and vulture. These words have long been used to refer to types of people as well as birds. They are rich in connotative meanings.

Connotations derive their resonance from a person's experiences with a word. Those experiences may not always be the same, especially when the people having them are in different times and places. *Theater*, for instance, was once associated with depravity, disease, and sin, whereas today the word usually evokes some sense of high culture and perhaps visions of elegant opulence. In several ethnic communities in the United States many people would find *squid* appetizing, but elsewhere the word is likely to produce negative connotations. Readers must recognize, then, that words written in other times and places may have unexpected connotations. Annotations usually help in these matters, which is why it makes sense to pay attention to them when they are available.

Ordinarily, though, the language of poetry is accessible, even when the circumstances of the reader and the poet are different. Although connotative language may be used subtly, it mostly draws on associations experienced by many people. Poets rely on widely shared associations rather than on the idiosyncratic response that an individual might have to a word. Someone who has received a severe burn from a fireplace accident may associate the word *hearth* with intense pain instead of home and family life, but that reader must not allow a personal experience to undermine the response the poet intends to evoke. Connotative meanings are usually public meanings.

Perhaps this can be seen most clearly in advertising, where language is also used primarily to convey moods and feelings rather than information. For instance, three decades of increasing interest in nutrition and general fitness have created a collective consciousness that advertisers have capitalized on successfully. Knowing that we want to be slender or lean or slim (not *spare* or *scrawny* and certainly not *gaunt*), advertisers have created a new word to describe beers, wines, sodas, cheeses, canned fruits, and other products that tend to overload what used to be called sweatclothes and sneakers. The word is *lite*. The assumed denotative meaning of *lite* is "low in calories," but as close readers of ingredient labels know, some *lites* are heavier than regularly prepared products. There can be no doubt about the connotative meaning of *lite*, however. Whatever is *lite* cannot hurt you; less is more. Even the word is lighter than *light*; there is no unnecessary droopy *g* or plump *h*. *Lite* is a brilliantly manufactured use of connotation.

Connotative meanings are valuable because they allow poets to be economical and suggestive simultaneously. In this way emotions and attitudes are carefully woven into the texture of the poem's language. Read the following poem and pay close attention to the connotative meanings of its words.

RANDALL JARRELL (1914–1965)

The Death of the Ball Turret Gunner   1945

From my mother's sleep I fell into the State
And I hunched in its belly till my wet fur froze.
Six miles from earth, loosed from its dream of life,
I woke to black flak and the nightmare fighters.
When I died they washed me out of the turret with a hose.

The title of this poem establishes the setting and the speaker's situation. Like the setting of a short story, the setting of a poem is important when the time and place influence what happens. "The Death of the Ball Turret Gunner" is set in the midst of a war and, more specifically, in a ball turret — a Plexiglas sphere housing machine guns on the underside of a bomber. The speaker's situation obviously places him in extreme danger; indeed, his fate is announced in the title.

Although the poem is written in the first-person singular, its speaker is clearly not the poet. Jarrell uses a **persona**, a speaker created by the poet. In this poem the persona is a disembodied voice that makes the gunner's story all the more powerful. What is his story? A paraphrase might read something like this:

> After I was born, I grew up to find myself at war, cramped into the turret of a bomber's belly some 31,000 feet above the ground. Below me were exploding shells from antiaircraft guns and attacking fighter planes. I was killed, but the bomber returned to base, where my remains were cleaned out of the turret so the next man could take my place.

This paraphrase is accurate, but its language is much less suggestive than the poem's. The first line of the poem has the speaker emerge from his "mother's sleep," the anesthetized sleep of her giving birth. The phrase also suggests the comfort, warmth, and security he knew as a child. This safety was left behind when he "fell," a verb that evokes the danger and involuntary movement associated with his subsequent "State" (*fell* also echoes, perhaps, the fall from innocence to experience related in the Bible).

Several dictionary definitions appear for the noun *state*; it can denote a territorial unit, the power and authority of a government, a person's social status, or a person's emotional or physical condition. The context provided by the rest of the poem makes clear that "State" has several denotative meanings here: because it is capitalized, it certainly refers to the violent world of a government at war, but it also refers to the gunner's vulnerable status as well as his physical and emotional condition. By having "State" carry more than one meaning, Jarrell has created an intentional ambiguity. **Ambiguity** allows for two or more simultaneous interpretations of a word, a phrase, an action, or a situation, all of which can be supported by the context of a work. Through his ambiguous use of "State," Jarrell connects the horrors of war not just to bombers and gunners but to the governments that control them.

Related to this ambiguity is the connotative meaning of "State" in the poem. The context demands that the word be read with a negative charge. The word is used not to indicate patriotic pride but to suggest an anonymous, impersonal "State" that kills rather than nurtures the life in its "belly." The state's "belly" is a bomber, and the gunner is "hunched" like a fetus in the cramped turret, where, in contrast to the warmth of his mother's womb, everything is frozen, even the "wet fur" of his flight jacket (newborn infants have wet fur too). The gunner is not just 31,000 feet from the ground but "Six miles from earth." *Six miles* has roughly the same denotative meaning as 31,000 feet, but Jarrell knew that the connotative meaning of *six miles* makes the speaker's position seem even more remote and frightening.

When the gunner is born into the violent world of war, he finds himself waking up to a "nightmare" that is all too real. The poem's final line is grimly understated, but it hits the reader with the force of an exploding shell: what the State-bomber-turret gives birth to is a gruesome death that is merely one of an endless series. It may be tempting to reduce the theme of this poem to the idea that "war is hell," but Jarrell's target is more specific. He implicates the "State," which routinely executes such violence, and he does so without preaching or hysterical denunciations. Instead, his use of language conveys his theme subtly and powerfully.

WORD ORDER

Meanings in poems are conveyed not only by denotations and connotations but also by the poet's arrangement of words into phrases, clauses, and sentences to achieve particular effects. The ordering of words into meaningful verbal patterns is called *syntax*. A poet can manipulate the syntax of a line to place emphasis on a word; this is especially apparent when a poet varies normal word order. In Emily Dickinson's "A narrow Fellow in the Grass" (p. 2), for example, the speaker says about the snake that "His notice sudden is." Ordinarily, that would be expressed as "his notice is sudden." By placing the verb *is* unexpectedly at the end of the line, Dickinson creates the sense of surprise we feel when we suddenly come upon a snake. Dickinson's inversion of the standard word order also makes the final sound of the line a hissing *is*.

TONE

Tone is the writer's attitude toward the subject, the mood created by all the elements in the poem. Writing, like speech, can be characterized as serious or light, sad or happy, private or public, angry or affectionate, bitter or nostalgic, or by any other attitudes and feelings that human beings experience. In Jarrell's "The Death of the Ball Turret Gunner," the tone is clearly serious; the voice in the poem even sounds dead. Listen again to the persona's final words: "When I died they washed me out of the turret with a hose." The brutal, restrained matter-of-factness of this line is effective because the reader is called on to supply the appropriate anger and despair — a strategy that makes those emotions all the more convincing.

Consider how tone is used to convey meaning in the next poem, inspired by the poet's contemplation of mortality.

ANGELA ALAIMO O'DONNELL (B. 1960)

Messenger   2013

5PM
& again

you're calling
me to supper.

Across the red fence   5
you sing my name —

An-ge-la —
three notes

that rise and fall,
each a bright bell   10

knelling *now*.
Though I know

you are dead
as those days,

as that small girl   15
I used to be,

I'm still
running,

And you're still
calling me.   20

Considerations for Critical Thinking and Writing

1. **FIRST RESPONSE.** Describe the speaker's relationship to her mother in the past and now.

2. Is the tone of the poem consistent throughout? Why or why not?

3. How does the diction transform the ordinary experience of a child being called for supper into something more significant?

The next work is a ***dramatic monologue,*** a type of poem in which a character — the speaker — addresses a silent audience in such a way as to reveal unintentionally some aspect of his or her temperament or personality. What tone is created by Machan's use of a persona?

KATHARYN HOWD MACHAN (B. 1952)

Hazel Tells LaVerne   1976

last night
im cleanin out my
howard johnsons ladies room
when all of a sudden
up pops this frog
musta come from the sewer
swimmin aroun an tryin ta
climb up the sida the bowl

> **WHEN I WRITE** "When a poem begins to find its shape and form and voice inside you, let your heart and your head join to give it the best life you can: passion! imagery! music! And if it will let you, humor: ah, the world needs all it can get." —KATHARYN HOWD MACHAN

so i goes ta flushm down
but sohelpmegod he starts talkin   10
bout a golden ball
an how i can be a princess
me a princess
well my mouth drops
all the way to the floor   15
an he says
kiss me just kiss me
once on the nose
well i screams
ya little green pervert   20
an i hitsm with my mop
an has ta flush
the toilet down three times
me
a princess   25

CONSIDERATIONS FOR CRITICAL THINKING AND WRITING

1. FIRST RESPONSE. What do you imagine the situation and setting are for
   this poem? Do you like this revision of the fairy tale "The Frog Prince"?

2. What creates the poem's humor? How does Hazel's use of language
   reveal her personality? Is her treatment of the frog consistent with her
   character?

3. What is the theme? Is it conveyed through denotative or connotative
   language?

4. CREATIVE RESPONSE. Write what you think might be LaVerne's reply to
   Hazel. First, write LaVerne's response as a series of ordinary sentences,
   and then try editing and organizing them into poetic lines.

5. CONNECTION TO ANOTHER SELECTION. Although Robert Browning's "My
   Last Duchess" (p. 426) is a more complex poem than Machan's, both
   use dramatic monologues to reveal character. How are the strategies in
   each poem similar?

MARTÍN ESPADA (B. 1957)

Latin Night at the Pawnshop   1987

Chelsea, Massachusetts
Christmas, 1987

The apparition of a salsa band
gleaming in the Liberty Loan
pawnshop window:

WHEN I WRITE "As a poet and a
reader, I am most interested in
the theme of justice. I am
interested in poems that
address justice vividly,
concretely, specifically. Poets
are, as Shelley put it, the
'unacknowledged legislators of
the world.' We shouldn't leave
justice to the lawyers and the
politicians." —MARTÍN ESPADA

Golden trumpet,
silver trombone,
congas, maracas, tambourine,

all with price tags dangling
like the city morgue ticket
on a dead man's toe.

CONSIDERATIONS FOR CRITICAL THINKING AND WRITING

1. FIRST RESPONSE. What is "Latin" about this night at the pawnshop?
2. What kind of tone is created by the poet's word choice and by the poem's rhythm?
3. Does it matter that this apparition occurs on Christmas night? Why or why not?
4. What do you think is the central point of this poem? How do the speaker's attitude and tone change during the course of this next poem?

PAUL LAURENCE DUNBAR (1872–1906)

To a Captious Critic 1903

Dear critic, who my lightness so deplores,
Would I might study to be prince of bores,
Right wisely would I rule that dull estate —
But, sir, I may not; till you abdicate.

CONSIDERATIONS FOR CRITICAL THINKING AND WRITING

1. FIRST RESPONSE. How do Dunbar's vocabulary and syntax signal the level of diction used in the poem?
2. Describe the speaker's tone. How does it characterize the speaker as well as the critic?
3. CREATIVE RESPONSE. Using "To a Captious Critic" as a model, try writing a four-line witty reply to someone in your own life — perhaps a roommate, coach, teacher, waiter, dentist, or anyone else who provokes a strong response in you.

DICTION AND TONE IN FOUR LOVE POEMS

The first three of these love poems share the same basic situation and theme: a male speaker addresses a female (in the first poem it is a type of female) urging that love should not be delayed because time is short. This theme is as familiar in poetry as it is in life. In Latin this tradition is known as *carpe diem,* "seize the day." Notice how the poets' diction helps create a distinctive tone in each poem, even though the subject matter and central ideas are similar (although not identical) in all three.

ROBERT HERRICK (1591–1674)

To the Virgins, to Make Much of Time   1648

Gather ye rose-buds while ye may,
  Old Time is still a-flying;
And this same flower that smiles today,
  Tomorrow will be dying.

The glorious lamp of heaven, the sun,
  The higher he's a-getting,
The sooner will his race be run,
  And nearer he's to setting.

That age is best which is the first,
  When youth and blood are warmer;
But being spent, the worse, and worst
  Times still succeed the former.

Then be not coy, but use your time,
  And while ye may, go marry;
For having lost but once your prime,
  You may for ever tarry.

© Hulton-Deutsch Collection / Corbis.

CONSIDERATIONS FOR CRITICAL THINKING AND WRITING

1. FIRST RESPONSE. Would there be any change in meaning if the title of this poem were "To Young Women, to Make Much of Time"? Do you think the poem can apply to young men, too?

2. What do the virgins have in common with the flowers (lines 1–4) and the course of the day (5–8)?

3. How does the speaker develop his argument? What will happen to the virgins if they don't "marry"? Paraphrase the poem.

4. What is the tone of the speaker's advice?

The next poem was also written in the seventeenth century, but it includes some words that have changed in usage and meaning over the past three hundred years. The title of Andrew Marvell's "To His Coy Mistress" requires some explanation. "Mistress" does not refer to a married man's illicit lover but to a woman who is loved and courted — a sweetheart. Marvell uses "coy" to describe a woman who is reserved and shy rather than coquettish or flirtatious. Often such shifts in meanings over time are explained in the notes that accompany reprintings of poems. You should keep in mind, however, that it is helpful to have a reasonably thick dictionary available when you are reading poetry. The most thorough is the *Oxford English Dictionary* (*OED*), which provides histories of words. The *OED* is a multivolume leviathan, but there are other useful unabridged dictionaries and desk dictionaries and many are available online.

Knowing a word's original meaning can also enrich your understanding of why a contemporary poet chooses a particular word. In "Design" (p. 350), Robert Frost raises provocative questions about the nature of evil and the existence of God in his dark examination of a moth's death, all presented in unexpected images of whiteness. He ends the poem with a series of questions concerning what causes "death and blight," wondering if it is a "design of darkness to appall" or no design at all, a universe informed only by random meaninglessness. Frost's precise contemporary use of "appall" captures the sense of consternation and dismay that such a frightening contemplation of death might evoke, but a dictionary reveals some further relevant insights. The dictionary's additional information about the history of *appall* shows us why it is the perfect word to establish the overwhelming effect of the poem. The word comes from the Middle English *appallen*, meaning "to grow faint," and in Old French *apalir* means "to grow pale" or white. These meanings reinforce the powerful sense of death buried in the images of whiteness throughout the poem. Moreover, Frost's "appall" also echoes a funereal pall, or coffin, allowing the word to bear even more connotative weight. Knowing the origin of *appall* gives us the full heft of the poet's word choice.

Although some of the language in "To His Coy Mistress" requires annotations for the modern reader, this poem continues to serve as a powerful reminder that time is a formidable foe, even for lovers.

© Michael Nicholson / CORBIS.

Andrew Marvell (1621–1678)

To His Coy Mistress　　　1681

Had we but world enough, and time,
This coyness, lady, were no crime.
We would sit down, and think which way
To walk, and pass our long love's day.
Thou by the Indian Ganges'° side　　　　　　　　　　　　　5
Shouldst rubies find; I by the tide
Of Humber° would complain.° I would　　　　　　*write love songs*
Love you ten years before the Flood,
And you should, if you please, refuse
Till the conversion of the Jews.　　　　　　　　　　　　10
My vegetable love should grow°
Vaster than empires, and more slow;

---

5 *Ganges*: A river in India sacred to the Hindus.　7 *Humber*: A river that flows through Marvell's native town, Hull.　11 *My vegetable love . . . grow*: A slow, unconscious growth.

An hundred years should go to praise
Thine eyes and on thy forehead gaze,
Two hundred to adore each breast,   15
But thirty thousand to the rest:
An age at least to every part,
And the last age should show your heart.
For, lady, you deserve this state,
Nor would I love at lower rate.   20
   But at my back I always hear
Time's wingèd chariot hurrying near;
And yonder all before us lie
Deserts of vast eternity.
Thy beauty shall no more be found,   25
Nor in thy marble vault shall sound
My echoing song; then worms shall try
That long preserved virginity,
And your quaint honor turn to dust,
And into ashes all my lust.   30
The grave's a fine and private place,
But none, I think, do there embrace.
   Now, therefore, while the youthful hue
Sits on thy skin like morning dew,
And while thy willing soul transpires°   *breathes forth*   35
At every pore with instant fires,
Now let us sport us while we may,
And now, like amorous birds of prey,
Rather at once our time devour
Than languish in his slow-chapped° power.   *slow-jawed*   40
Let us roll all our strength and all
Our sweetness up into one ball,
And tear our pleasures with rough strife
Thorough° the iron gates of life.   *through*
Thus, though we cannot make our sun   45
Stand still, yet we will make him run.

CONSIDERATIONS FOR CRITICAL THINKING AND WRITING

1. **FIRST RESPONSE.** Do you think this *carpe diem* poem is hopelessly dated, or does it speak to our contemporary concerns?

2. This poem is divided into a three-part argument. Briefly summarize each section: if (lines 1–20), but (21–32), therefore (33–46).

3. What is the speaker's tone in lines 1–20? How much time would he spend adoring his mistress? Is he sincere? How does he expect his mistress to respond to these lines?

4. How does the speaker's tone change beginning with line 21? What is his view of time in lines 21–32? What does this description do to the lush and leisurely sense of time in lines 1–20? How do you think his mistress would react to lines 21–32?

5. In the final lines of Herrick's "To the Virgins, to Make Much of Time" (p. 362), the speaker urges the virgins to "go marry." What does Marvell's speaker urge in lines 33–46? How is the pace of these lines (notice the verbs) different from that of the first twenty lines of the poem?

6. This poem is sometimes read as a vigorous but simple celebration of flesh. Is there more to the theme than that?

The third in this series of *carpe diem* poems is a twenty-first-century work. The language of Ann Lauinger's "Marvell Noir" is more immediately accessible than that of Marvell's "To His Coy Mistress"; an ordinary dictionary will quickly identify any words unfamiliar to a reader. But the title might require an online search or a dictionary of biography for the reference to Marvell, as well as a dictionary of allusions to provide a succinct description that explains the reference to film noir. An ***allusion*** is a brief cultural reference to a person, a place, a thing, an event, or an idea in history or literature. Allusive words, like connotative words, are both suggestive and economical; poets use allusions to conjure up biblical authority, scenes from Shakespeare's plays, historic figures, wars, great love stories, and anything else that might serve to deepen and enrich their own work. The title of "Marvell Noir" makes two allusions that an ordinary dictionary may not explain, because it alludes to Marvell's most famous poem, "To His Coy Mistress," and to dark crime films (*noir* is "black" in French) of the 1940s that were often filmed in black and white featuring tough-talking, cynical heroes—such as those portrayed by Humphrey Bogart—and hardened, cold women—like the characters played by Joan Crawford. Lauinger assumes that her reader will understand the allusions.

Allusions imply reading and cultural experiences shared by the poet and the reader. Literate audiences once had more in common than they do today because more people had similar economic, social, and educational backgrounds. But a judicious use of specialized dictionaries, encyclopedias, and online reference tools such as Google Search can help you decipher allusions that grow out of this body of experience. As you read more, you'll be able to make connections based on your own experiences with literature. In a sense, allusions make available what other human beings have deemed worth remembering, and that is certainly an economical way of supplementing and enhancing your own experience.

Lauinger's version of the *carpe diem* theme follows. What strikes you as particularly modern about it?

ANN LAUINGER (B. 1948)

Marvell Noir   2005

Sweetheart, if we had the time,
A week in bed would be no crime.
I'd light your Camels, pour your Jack;
You'd do shiatsu on my back.

> **WHEN I READ** "As a writer, my best friends are some very dead poets. Reading them is what made me want to write, and re-reading them keeps me writing." —ANN LAUINGER

When you got up to scramble eggs,   5
I'd write a sonnet to your legs,
And you could watch my stubble grow.
Yes, gorgeous, we'd take it slow.
I'd hear the whole sad tale again:
A roadhouse band; you can't trust men;   10
He set you up; you had to eat,
And bitter with the bittersweet
Was what they dished you; Ginger lied;
You weren't there when Sanchez died;
You didn't know the pearls were fake . . .   15
Aw, can it, sport! Make no mistake,
You're in it, doll, up to your eyeballs!
Tears? Please! You'll dilute our highballs,
And make that angel face a mess
For the nice Lieutenant. I confess   20
I'm nuts for you — but take the rap?
You must think I'm some other sap!
And, precious, I kind of wish I was.
Well, when they spring you, give a buzz;
Guess I'll get back to Archie's wife,   25
And you'll get twenty-five to life.
You'll have time then, more than enough,
To reminisce about the stuff
That dreams are made of, and the men
You suckered. Sadly, in the pen   30
Your kind of talent goes to waste.
But Irish bars are more my taste
Than iron ones: stripes ain't my style.
You're going down; I promise I'll
Come visit every other year.   35
Now kiss me, sweet — the squad car's here.

CONSIDERATIONS FOR CRITICAL THINKING AND WRITING

1. **FIRST RESPONSE.** How does Lauinger's poem evoke Marvell's *carpe diem* poem (p. 363) and the tough-guy tone of a "noir" narrative, a crime story or thriller that is especially dark?

2. Discuss the ways in which time is a central presence in the poem.

3. Explain the allusion to dreams in lines 28–29.

4. **CONNECTION TO ANOTHER SELECTION.** Compare the speaker's voice in this poem with that of the speaker in "To His Coy Mistress" (p. 363). What significant similarities and differences do you find?

This fourth love poem is a twentieth-century work in which the speaker's voice is a woman's. How does it sound different from the way the men speak in the previous three poems?

SHARON OLDS (B. 1942)

Last Night   *1996*

The next day, I am almost afraid.
Love? It was more like dragonflies
in the sun, 100 degrees at noon,
the ends of their abdomens stuck together, I
close my eyes when I remember. I hardly   5
knew myself, like something twisting and
twisting out of a chrysalis,
enormous, without language, all
head, all shut eyes, and the humming
like madness, the way they writhe away,   10
and do not leave, back, back,
away, back. Did I know you? No kiss,
no tenderness — more like killing, death-grip
holding to life, genitals
like violent hands clasped tight   15
barely moving, more like being closed
in a great jaw and eaten, and the screaming
I groan to remember it, and when we started
to die, then I refuse to remember,
the way a drunkard forgets. After,   20
you held my hands extremely hard as my
body moved in shudders like the ferry when its
axle is loosed past engagement, you kept me
sealed exactly against you, our hairlines
wet as the arc of a gateway after   25
a cloudburst, you secured me in your arms till I slept —
that was love, and we woke in the morning
clasped, fragrant, buoyant, that was
the morning after love.

CONSIDERATIONS FOR CRITICAL THINKING AND WRITING

1. FIRST RESPONSE. How is your response to this poem affected by the
   fact that the speaker is female? Explain why this is or isn't a *carpe diem*
   poem.

2. Comment on the descriptive passages of "Last Night." Which images
   seem especially vivid to you? How do they contribute to the poem's
   meaning?

3. Explain how the poem's tone changes from beginning to end.

4. CONNECTIONS TO OTHER SELECTIONS. How does the speaker's description of intimacy compare with Herrick's and Marvell's?

Perspective

GENE WEINGARTEN (B. 1951), DAN WEINGARTEN (B. 1984), AND DAVID CLARK (B. 1960)

Barney & Clyde   2012

cartoonistgroup.com.

CONSIDERATIONS FOR CRITICAL THINKING AND WRITING

1. Did you get the joke? Probably not, but how does a Google search help you?

2. Additional strips of *Barney & Clyde* can be found on the Internet, which provides information about the comic's characters as well as its writers and illustrator. How does that information serve to characterize the type of humor in the strip?

3. Choose a poem from Chapter 23, "Poems for Further Reading," that is rich in allusions and use the Internet to explain their function in the poem.

POEMS FOR FURTHER STUDY

WALT WHITMAN (1819–1892)

The Dalliance of the Eagles   1880

Skirting the river road, (my forenoon walk, my rest,)
Skyward in air a sudden muffled sound, the dalliance of the eagles,
The rushing amorous contact high in space together,
The clinching interlocking claws, a living, fierce, gyrating wheel,
Four beating wings, two beaks, a swirling mass tight grappling,   5
In tumbling turning clustering loops, straight downward falling,
Till o'er the river pois'd, the twain yet one, a moment's lull,

A motionless still balance in the air, then parting, talons loosing,
Upward again on slow-firm pinions slanting, their separate diverse flight,
She hers, he his, pursuing.   10

CONSIDERATIONS FOR CRITICAL THINKING AND WRITING

1. FIRST RESPONSE. Why do you think Whitman chose the word *dalliance* rather than, perhaps, *mating*?

2. List the verbs in the poem and comment on their effects in evoking the scene.

3. CONNECTION TO ANOTHER SELECTION. Compare Whitman's treatment of the eagles with Tennyson's description of "The Eagle" (p. 349). Which do you find more powerful? Why?

THOMAS HARDY (1840–1928)

The Convergence of the Twain   1912

Lines on the Loss of the "Titanic"°

I

In a solitude of the sea
Deep from human vanity,
And the Pride of Life that planned her, stilly couches she.

II

Steel chambers, late the pyres
Of her salamandrine fires,°   5   *thread*
Cold currents thrid,° and turn to rhythmic tidal lyres.

III

Over the mirrors meant
To glass the opulent
The sea-worm crawls — grotesque, slimed, dumb, indifferent.

IV

Jewels in joy designed   10
To ravish the sensuous mind
Lie lightless, all their sparkles bleared and black and blind.

"Titanic": A luxurious ocean liner, reputed to be unsinkable, which sank after hitting an iceberg on its maiden voyage in 1912. Only a third of the 2,200 passengers survived.

5 *salamandrine fires:* Salamanders were, according to legend, able to survive fire; hence the ship's fires burned even though under water.

V

Dim moon-eyed fishes near
Gaze at the gilded gear
And query: "What does this vaingloriousness down here?"   15

VI

Well: while was fashioning
This creature of cleaving wing,
The Immanent Will that stirs and urges everything

VII

Prepared a sinister mate
For her — so gaily great —   20
A Shape of Ice, for the time far and dissociate.

VIII

And as the smart ship grew
In stature, grace, and hue,
In shadowy silent distance grew the Iceberg too.

IX

Alien they seemed to be: 25
No mortal eye could see
The intimate welding of their later history,

X

Or sign that they were bent
By paths coincident
On being anon twin halves of one august event,   30

XI

Till the Spinner of the Years
Said "Now!" And each one hears,
And consummation comes, and jars two hemispheres.

Considerations for Critical Thinking and Writing

1. FIRST RESPONSE. Describe a contemporary disaster comparable to the sinking of the *Titanic*. How was your response to it similar to or different from the speaker's response to the fate of the *Titanic*?

2. How do the words used to describe the ship in this poem reveal the speaker's attitude toward the *Titanic*?

3. The diction of the poem suggests that the *Titanic* and the iceberg participate in something like an arranged marriage. What specific words imply this?

4. Who or what causes the disaster? Does the speaker assign responsibility?

DAVID R. SLAVITT (B. 1935)

Titanic   1983

Who does not love the *Titanic*?
If they sold passage tomorrow for that same crossing,
who would not buy?

To go down . . . We all go down, mostly
alone. But with crowds of people, friends, servants,   5
well fed, with music, with lights! Ah!

And the world, shocked, mourns, as it ought to do
and almost never does. There will be the books and movies
to remind our grandchildren who we were
and how we died, and give them a good cry.   10

Not so bad, after all. The cold
water is anesthetic and very quick.
The cries on all sides must be a comfort.

We all go: only a few, first-class.

CONSIDERATIONS FOR CRITICAL THINKING AND WRITING

1. FIRST RESPONSE. What, according to the speaker in this poem, is so compelling about the *Titanic*? Do you agree?

2. Discuss the speaker's tone. Is "Titanic" merely a sarcastic poem?

3. What is the effect of the poem's final line? What emotions does it elicit?

4. CONNECTION TO ANOTHER SELECTION. How does "Titanic" differ in its attitude toward opulence from "The Convergence of the Twain" (p. 369)?

5. CONNECTION TO ANOTHER SELECTION. Which poem, "Titanic" or "The Convergence of the Twain," is more emotionally satisfying to you? Explain why.

6. CONNECTION TO ANOTHER SELECTION. Compare the speakers' tones in "Titanic" and "The Convergence of the Twain."

Danusha Laméris (b. 1971)

Names   2014

What happens to the ones that fall out of favor:
the Dorises and Archibalds,
the Theodores and Eunices?
They all had their day,
once roamed the earth in multitudes   5
alongside Gerties and Wyatts —
at least one in every classroom.
Names written in neat block print,
scratched into tree bark,
engraved on heart-shaped lockets,   10
filling the morning paper
with weddings and engagements.
How could they have known
that one-by-one the Constances
and Clydes would disappear,   15
replaced by Jennifers, Jacobs,
Ashleys and Aidens.
That few would ever dance again,
corsages pinned to their breasts
or hear their names on the radio   20
whispered in dedication,
or uttered in darkness
by a breathless voice,
or even shouted out in anger —
"Seymour!"—   25
as they grabbed the keys and stormed out the door.
Each name fading quietly from daily life
as though it had never existed,
except for the letters etched into stone,
warmed by the sun   30
and at night, lit by a crescent moon.

Considerations for Critical Thinking and Writing

1. **FIRST RESPONSE.** What connotations do you think are associated with
   your own given name?

2. What names do you think are currently in and out of "favor"?

3. Why is the poem about more than just what its title indicates?

4. **CONNECTION TO ANOTHER SELECTION.** How do you think the speaker
   of "Names" would categorize the names in Katharyn Howd Machan's
   "Hazel tells Laverne" (p. 359)?

Mary Oliver (b. 1935)

Oxygen   2005

Everything needs it: bone, muscles, and even,
while it calls the earth its home, the soul.
So the merciful, noisy machine

stands in our house working away in its
lung-like voice. I hear it as I kneel   5
before the fire, stirring with a

stick of iron, letting the logs
lie more loosely. You, in the upstairs room,
are in your usual position, leaning on your

right shoulder which aches   10
all day. You are breathing
patiently; it is a

beautiful sound. It is
your life, which is so close
to my own that I would not know   15

where to drop the knife of
separation. And what does this have to do
with love, except

everything? Now the fire rises
and offers a dozen, singing, deep-red   20
roses of flame. Then it settles

to quietude, or maybe gratitude, as it feeds
as we all do, as we must, upon the invisible gift:
our purest, sweet necessity: the air.

Considerations for Critical Thinking and Writing

1. FIRST RESPONSE. Though this is a poem about someone who is seriously ill, its tone isn't sad. Why not?

2. What is the connection between the loved one's breathing and the fire? How does the speaker's choice of words to describe each connect them?

3. In what sense might this celebration of oxygen be considered a love poem?

Alice Jones (b. 1949)

The Lungs   1997

When I Write "The process of becoming a writer involves recognizing the desire to write, allowing ourselves to take the desire seriously, and then learning to recognize the obstacles we put in our own way." — ALICE JONES

In the tidal flux, the lobed pair avidly
   grasp the invisible.

Along oblique fissures, gnarled vascular roots
   anchor the puffed cushions,

soot-mottled froth, the pink segmented sponges
   that soak up the atmosphere,

then squeezed by the rising dome of the diaphragm's
   muscular bellows, exhale.

Braids of vessels and cartilage descend
   in vanishing smallness,   5

to grape clusters of alveoli, the sheerest
   of membranes, where oxygen

crosses the infinite cellular web, where air turns
   to blood, spirit to flesh,

in a molecular transubstantiation, to bring rich
   food to that red engine,

the heart, which like an equitable mother, pumps
   to each organ and appendage

according to need, so even the cells in the darkest
   corners can breathe.   10

Considerations for Critical Thinking and Writing

1. **First response.** Why do you think the lines in this poem are arranged in pairs? How does the length of the sentences contribute to the poem's meaning?

2. Make a list of words and phrases from the poem that strike you as scientific, and compare those with a list of words that seem poetic. How do they compete or complement each other in terms of how they affect your reading?

3. Comment on the use of personification (see the glossary, p. 929) in the poem.

4. **Connection to another selection.** Compare the diction and the ending in "The Lungs" with those in "The Foot" (p. 455), another poem by Jones.

Gwendolyn Brooks (1917–2000)

We Real Cool

1960

The Pool Players.
Seven at the Golden Shovel.

We real cool. We
Left school. We

Lurk late. We
Strike straight. We

Sing sin. We
Thin gin. We

Jazz June. We
Die soon.

Considerations for Critical Thinking and Writing

1. First Response. How does the speech of the pool players in this poem
    help to characterize them? What is the effect of the pronouns coming at
    the ends of the lines? How would the poem sound if the pronouns came
    at the beginnings of lines?

2. What is the author's attitude toward the players? Is there a change in
    tone in the last line?

3. How is the pool hall's name related to the rest of the poem and its
    theme?

Joan Murray (b. 1945)

We Old Dudes

2006

We old dudes. We
White shoes. We

Golf ball. We
Eat mall. We

Soak teeth. We
Palm Beach; We

Vote red. We
Soon dead.

> When I Read "Reading
> stretches your mind and
> imagination. It lets you
> discover what you like and
> admire. Sometimes after I read
> a poem, I want to write one.
> It's as if someone's speaking
> my language, and I want to
> converse."   — Joan Murray

Considerations for Critical Thinking and Writing

1. First Response. Consider the poem's humor. To what extent does it
    make a serious point?

2. What does the reference to Palm Beach tell you about these "old dudes"?

3. CREATIVE RESPONSE. Write a poem similar in style that characterizes your life as a student.

4. CONNECTION TO ANOTHER SELECTION. Compare the themes of "We Old Dudes" and Brooks's "We Real Cool." How do the two poems speak to each other?

LOUIS SIMPSON (1923–2012)

In the Suburbs   1963

There's no way out.
You were born to waste your life.
You were born to this middleclass life

As others before you
Were born to walk in procession
To the temple, singing.

CONSIDERATIONS FOR CRITICAL THINKING AND WRITING

1. FIRST RESPONSE. Is the title of this poem especially significant? What images does it conjure up for you?

2. What does the repetition in lines 2–3 suggest?

3. Discuss the possible connotative meanings of lines 5 and 6. Who are the "others before you"?

JOHN KEATS (1795–1821)

Ode on a Grecian Urn   1819

I

Thou still unravished bride of quietness,
    Thou foster-child of silence and slow time,
Sylvan° historian, who canst thus express
    A flowery tale more sweetly than our rhyme:
What leaf-fringed legend haunts about thy shape   5
    Of deities or mortals, or of both,
        In Tempe or the dales of Arcady?°
What men or gods are these? What maidens loath?
    What mad pursuit? What struggle to escape?
        What pipes and timbrels? What wild ecstasy?   10

___

3 *Sylvan*: Rustic. The urn is decorated with a forest scene.   7 *Tempe, Arcady*: Beautiful rural valleys in Greece.

II

Heard melodies are sweet, but those unheard
  Are sweeter; therefore, ye soft pipes, play on;
Not to the sensual ear, but, more endeared,
  Pipe to the spirit ditties of no tone:
Fair youth, beneath the trees, thou canst not leave   15
  Thy song, nor ever can those trees be bare;
    Bold Lover, never, never canst thou kiss,
Though winning near the goal — yet, do not grieve;
  She cannot fade, though thou hast not thy bliss,
    For ever wilt thou love, and she be fair!   20

III

Ah, happy, happy boughs! that cannot shed
  Your leaves, nor ever bid the Spring adieu;
And, happy melodist, unwearièd,
  For ever piping songs for ever new;
More happy love! more happy, happy love!   25
  For ever warm and still to be enjoyed,
    For ever panting, and for ever young;
All breathing human passion far above,
  That leaves a heart high-sorrowful and cloyed,
    A burning forehead, and a parching tongue.   30

IV

Who are these coming to the sacrifice?
  To what green altar, O mysterious priest,
Lead'st thou that heifer lowing at the skies,
  And all her silken flanks with garlands drest?
What little town by river or sea shore,   35
  Or mountain-built with peaceful citadel,
    Is emptied of this folk, this pious morn?
And, little town, thy streets for evermore
  Will silent be; and not a soul to tell
    Why thou art desolate, can e'er return.   40

V

O Attic° shape! Fair attitude! with brede°
  Of marble men and maidens overwrought,
With forest branches and the trodden weed;
  Thou, silent form, dost tease us out of thought

41 *Attic*: Possessing classic Athenian simplicity; *brede*: Design.

As doth eternity: Cold Pastoral!   45
   When old age shall this generation waste,
      Thou shalt remain, in midst of other woe
Than ours, a friend to man, to whom thou say'st,
   Beauty is truth, truth beauty — that is all
      Ye know on earth, and all ye need to know.   50

CONSIDERATIONS FOR CRITICAL THINKING AND WRITING

1. FIRST RESPONSE. What does the speaker's diction reveal about his attitude toward the urn in this ode? Does his view develop or change?

2. How is the happiness in stanza 3 related to the assertion in lines 11–12
   that "Heard melodies are sweet, but those unheard / Are sweeter"?

3. What is the difference between the world depicted on the urn and the
   speaker's world?

4. What do lines 49 and 50 suggest about the relation of art to life? Why is
   the urn described as a "Cold Pastoral" (line 45)?

5. Which world does the speaker seem to prefer, the urn's or his own?

6. Describe the overall tone of the poem.

7. CONNECTION TO ANOTHER SELECTION. Write an essay comparing the
   view of time in this ode with that in Marvell's "To His Coy Mistress"
   (p. 363). Pay particular attention to the connotative language in each
   poem.

8. CONNECTION TO ANOTHER SELECTION. Compare the tone and attitude toward life in this ode with those in John Keats's "To Autumn" (p. 392).

14

Images

AP Photo / Rogelio V. Solis.

I think poetry is always a kind of faith. It is the kind that I have.

—NATASHA TRETHEWEY

POETRY'S APPEAL TO THE SENSES

A poet, to borrow a phrase from Henry James, is one on whom nothing is lost. Poets take in the world and give us impressions of what they experience through images. An *image* is language that addresses the senses. The most common images in poetry are visual; they provide verbal pictures of the poets' encounters — real or imagined — with the world. But poets also create images that appeal to our other senses. Li Ho arouses several senses in this excerpt from "A Beautiful Girl Combs Her Hair":

> Awake at dawn
> she's dreaming
> by cool silk curtains
>
> fragrance of spilling hair
> half sandalwood, half aloes
>
> windlass creaking at the well
> singing jade

These vivid images deftly blend textures, fragrances, and sounds that tease out the sensuousness of the moment. Images give us the physical world to experience in our imaginations. Some poems, like the following one, are written to do just that; they make no comment about what they describe.

WILLIAM CARLOS WILLIAMS (1883–1963)

Poem

1934

As the cat
climbed over
the top of

the jamcloset
first the right   5
forefoot

carefully
then the hind
stepped down

into the pit of   10
the empty
flowerpot

This poem defies paraphrase because it is all an image of agile movement. No statement is made about the movement; the title, "Poem" —
really no title — signals Williams's refusal to comment on the movements.
To impose a meaning on the poem, we'd probably have to knock over the
flowerpot.

We experience the image in Williams's "Poem" more clearly because
of how the sentence is organized into lines and groups of lines, or stanzas.
Consider how differently the sentence is read if it is arranged as prose:

As the cat climbed over the top of the jamcloset, first the right forefoot carefully then the hind stepped down into the pit of the empty flowerpot.

The poem's line and stanza division transforms what is essentially an awkward prose sentence into a rhythmic verbal picture. Especially when the
poem is read aloud, this line and stanza division allows us to feel the image
we see. Even the lack of a period at the end suggests that the cat is only
pausing.

Images frequently do more than offer only sensory impressions, however. They also convey emotions and moods, as in the following poem's
view of Civil War troops moving across a river.

WALT WHITMAN (1819–1892)

Cavalry Crossing a Ford

1865

A line in long array where they wind betwixt green islands,
They take a serpentine course, their arms flash in the sun — hark to the
    musical clank,
Behold the silvery river, in it the splashing horses loitering stop to drink,

Behold the brown-faced men, each group, each person, a picture, the
    negligent rest on the saddles,
Some emerge on the opposite bank, others are just entering the
    ford — while,
Scarlet and blue and snowy white,
The guidon flags flutter gaily in the wind.

CONSIDERATIONS FOR CRITICAL THINKING AND WRITING

1. FIRST RESPONSE. Do the colors and sounds establish the mood of this poem? What is the mood?
2. How would the poem's mood have been changed if Whitman had used "look" or "see" instead of "behold" (lines 3–4)?
3. Where is the speaker as he observes this troop movement?
4. Does "serpentine" in line 2 have an evil connotation in this poem? Explain your answer.

Whitman seems to capture momentarily all of the troop's actions, and through carefully chosen, suggestive details — really very few — he succeeds in making "each group, each person, a picture." Specific details, even when few are provided, give us the impression that we see the entire picture; it is as if those are the details we would remember if we had viewed the scene ourselves. Notice, too, that the movement of the "line in long array" is emphasized by the continuous winding syntax of the poem's lengthy lines.

Movement is also central to the next poem, in which action and motion are created through carefully chosen verbs.

DAVID SOLWAY (B. 1941)

Windsurfing   1993

It rides upon the wrinkled hide
of water, like the upturned hull
of a small canoe or kayak
waiting to be righted — yet its law
is opposite to that of boats,   5
it floats upon its breastbone and
brings whatever spine there is to light.
A thin shaft is slotted into place.
Then a puffed right-angle of wind
pushes it forward, out into the bay,   10
where suddenly it glitters into speed,
tilts, knifes up, and for the moment's
nothing but a slim projectile
of cambered fiberglass,
peeling the crests.   15

> WHEN I READ "The good poet always generates a sense of lexical surprise, an openness toward the unexpected, a feeling of novelty and delight."
> — DAVID SOLWAY

                    The man's
clamped to the mast, taut as a guywire.
Part of the sleek apparatus
he controls, immaculate nerve
of balance, plunge and curvet,   20
he clinches all component movements
into single motion.
It bucks, stalls, shudders, yaws, and dips
its hissing sides beneath the surface
that sustains it, tensing   25
into muscle that nude ellipse
of lunging appetite and power.

And now the mechanism's wholly
dolphin, springing toward its prey
of spume and beaded sunlight,   30
tossing spray, and hits the vertex
of the wide, salt glare of distance,
and reverses.

                    Back it comes through
a screen of particles,   35
scalloped out of water, shimmer
and reflection, the wind snapping
and lashing it homeward,
shearing the curve of the wave,
breaking the spell of the caught breath   40
and articulate play of sinew, to enter
the haven of the breakwater
and settle in a rush of silence.

Now the crossing drifts
in the husk of its wake   45
and nothing's the same again
as, gliding elegantly on a film of water,
the man guides
his brash, obedient legend
into shore.   50

CONSIDERATIONS FOR CRITICAL THINKING AND WRITING

1. FIRST RESPONSE. Draw a circle around the verbs that seem especially effective in conveying a strong sense of motion, and explain why they are effective.

2. How is the man made to seem to be one with his board and sail?

3. How does the rhythm of the poem change beginning with line 45?

4. **CONNECTION TO ANOTHER SELECTION.** Consider the effects of the images in "Windsurfing" and the excerpt from Li Ho's "A Beautiful Girl Combs Her Hair" (p. 379). In an essay, explain how these images elicit the emotional responses they do.

"Windsurfing" is awash with images of speed, fluidity, and power. Even the calming aftermath of the breakwater is described as a "rush of silence," adding to the sense of motion that is detailed and expanded throughout the poem.

The tone of the images and mood of the speaker are consistent in Solway's "Windsurfing." In Matthew Arnold's "Dover Beach," however, they shift as the theme is developed.

MATTHEW ARNOLD (1822–1888)

Dover Beach   *1867*

The sea is calm tonight.
The tide is full, the moon lies fair
Upon the straits;—on the French coast the light
Gleams and is gone; the cliffs of England stand,
Glimmering and vast, out in the tranquil bay.   5
Come to the window, sweet is the night-air!
Only, from the long line of spray
Where the sea meets the moon-blanched land,
Listen! you hear the grating roar
Of pebbles which the waves draw back, and fling,   10
At their return, up the high strand,
Begin, and cease, and then again begin,
With tremulous cadence slow, and bring
The eternal note of sadness in.

Sophocles long ago   15
Heard it on the Aegean, and it brought
Into his mind the turbid ebb and flow
Of human misery;° we
Find also in the sound a thought,
Hearing it by this distant northern sea.   20

The Sea of Faith
Was once, too, at the full, and round earth's shore
Lay like the folds of a bright girdle furled.
But now I only hear

15–18 *Sophocles . . . misery*: In *Antigone* (lines 656–77), Sophocles likens the disasters that beset the house of Oedipus to a "mounting tide."

Its melancholy, long, withdrawing roar,   25
Retreating, to the breath
Of the night-wind, down the vast edges drear
And naked shingles° of the world.   *pebble beaches*

Ah, love, let us be true
To one another! for the world, which seems   30
To lie before us like a land of dreams,
So various, so beautiful, so new,
Hath really neither joy, nor love, nor light,
Nor certitude, nor peace, nor help for pain;
And we are here as on a darkling plain   35
Swept with confused alarms of struggle and flight,
Where ignorant armies clash by night.

CONSIDERATIONS FOR CRITICAL THINKING AND WRITING

1. FIRST RESPONSE. Discuss what you consider to be this poem's central point. How do the speaker's descriptions of the ocean work toward making that point?

2. Contrast the images in lines 4–8 and 9–13. How do they reveal the speaker's mood? To whom is he speaking?

3. What is the cause of the "sadness" in line 14? What is the speaker's response to the ebbing "Sea of Faith"? Is there anything to replace his sense of loss?

4. What details of the beach seem related to the ideas in the poem? How is the sea used differently in lines 1–14 and 21–28?

5. Describe the differences in tone between lines 1–8 and 35–37. What has caused the change?

6. CONNECTION TO ANOTHER SELECTION. Explain how the images in Wilfred Owen's "Dulce et Decorum Est" (p. 389) develop further the ideas and sentiments suggested by Arnold's final line concerning "ignorant armies clash[ing] by night."

Consider the appetite for images displayed in the celebration of poetry in the following poem.

RUTH FORMAN (B. 1968)

Poetry Should Ride the Bus   1993

poetry should hopscotch in a polka dot dress
wheel cartwheels
n hold your hand
when you walk past the yellow crackhouse

poetry should wear bright red lipstick
n practice kisses in the mirror
for all the fine young men with fades
shootin craps around the corner

poetry should dress in fine plum linen suits
n not be so educated that it don't stop in
every now n then to sit on the porch
and talk about the comins and goins of the
        world

poetry should ride the bus
in a fat woman's Safeway bag
between the greens n chicken wings
to be served with tuesday's dinner

poetry should drop by a sweet potato pie
ask about the grandchildren
n sit through a whole photo album
on a orange plastic covered lazy boy with no place to go   20

Photograph by Christine Bennett,
www.cbimages.org.

poetry should sing red revolution love songs
that massage your scalp
and bring hope to your blood
when you think you're too old to fight

yeah   25
poetry should whisper electric blue magic
all the years of your life
never forgettin to look you in the soul
every once in a while
n smile   30

CONSIDERATIONS FOR CRITICAL THINKING AND WRITING

1. FIRST RESPONSE. How do the images in each stanza reveal the speaker's
    attitude toward poetry? Do you agree with the poem's ideas about what
    poetry should do and be?

2. What does the poem's diction tell you about the speaker?

3. Discuss the tone of this poem and why you think it does or does not
    work.

4. CONNECTION TO ANOTHER SELECTION. How does Forman's speaker's
    view of poetry compare with that of the speaker in Billy Collins's "Intro-
    duction to Poetry" (p. 341)?

POEMS FOR FURTHER STUDY

ADELAIDE CRAPSEY (1878–1914)

November Night   1913

Listen . . .

With faint dry sound,
Like steps of passing ghosts,
The leaves, frost-crisp'd, break from the trees
And fall.

CONSIDERATIONS FOR CRITICAL THINKING AND WRITING

1. FIRST RESPONSE. Which senses are evoked in the poem? What sort of
   tone do the words produce?

2. Explain whether or not you think "November Night" has a theme.

3. CONNECTION TO ANOTHER SELECTION. Compare the use of images and
   their effects in this poem and in E. E. Cummings's "l(a" (p. 337).

WILLIAM BLAKE (1757–1827)

London   1794

I wander through each chartered° street,   *defined by law*
Near where the chartered Thames does flow,
And mark in every face I meet
Marks of weakness, marks of woe.

In every cry of every man,   5
In every Infant's cry of fear,
In every voice, in every ban,
The mind-forged manacles I hear.

How the Chimney-sweeper's cry
Every black'ning Church appalls;   10
And the hapless Soldier's sigh
Runs in blood down Palace walls.

But most through midnight streets I hear
How the youthful Harlot's curse
Blasts the new-born Infant's tear,   15
And blights with plagues the Marriage hearse.

CONSIDERATIONS FOR CRITICAL THINKING AND WRITING

1. FIRST RESPONSE. What feelings do the visual images in this poem suggest
   to you?

2. What is the predominant sound heard in the poem?

3. What is the meaning of line 8? What is the cause of the problems that the speaker sees and hears in London? Does the speaker suggest additional causes?

4. The image in lines 11 and 12 cannot be read literally. Comment on its effectiveness.

5. How does Blake's use of denotative and connotative language enrich this poem's meaning?

6. An earlier version of Blake's last stanza appeared this way:

> But most the midnight harlot's curse
> From every dismal street I hear,
> Weaves around the marriage hearse
> And blasts the new-born infant's tear.

Examine carefully the differences between the two versions. How do Blake's revisions affect his picture of London life? Which version do you think is more effective? Why?

CHARLES SIMIC (B. 1938)

Fork   *1969*

This strange thing must have crept
Right out of hell.
It resembles a bird's foot.
Worn around the cannibal's neck.

As you hold it in your hand,
As you stab with it into a piece of meat,
It is possible to imagine the rest of the bird:
Its head which like your fist
Is large, bald, beakless, and blind.

CONSIDERATIONS FOR CRITICAL THINKING AND WRITING

1. FIRST RESPONSE. How is the speaker's tone revealed by the images that describe the fork?

2. Explain how the final two lines broaden the poem's themes.

SEAMUS HEANEY (1939–2013)

The Pitchfork   *1991*

Of all implements, the pitchfork was the one
That came near to an imagined perfection:
When he tightened his raised hand and aimed with it,
It felt like a javelin, accurate and light.

So whether he played the warrior or the athlete   5
Or worked in earnest in the chaff and sweat,
He loved its grain of tapering, dark-flecked ash
Grown satiny from its own natural polish.

Riveted steel, turned timber, burnish, grain,
Smoothness, straightness, roundness, length and sheen.   10
Sweat-cured, sharpened, balanced, tested, fitted.
The springiness, the clip and dart of it.

And then when he thought of probes that reached the
        farthest,
He would see the shaft of a pitchfork sailing past
Evenly, imperturbably through space,   15
Its prongs starlit and absolutely soundless —

But has learned at last to follow that simple lead
Past its own aim, out to an other side
Where perfection — or nearness to it — is imagined
Not in the aiming but the opening hand.   20

Considerations for Critical Thinking and Writing

1. FIRST RESPONSE. Provide an alternate title that you think captures the poem's meaning.

2. How do the images make this pitchfork more than merely one of many "implements"?

3. What does the thrower of the pitchfork learn in lines 13–16?

4. CONNECTION TO ANOTHER SELECTION. The images used to describe the pitchfork in this poem and the fork in Charles Simic's "Fork" (p. 387) invest significance in these otherwise ordinary objects. Write an essay that discusses how the images in these two poems give these objects qualities that are not inherent in either pitchforks or forks.

EMILY DICKINSON (1830–1886)

Wild Nights — Wild Nights!   *ca. 1861*

Wild Nights — Wild Nights!
Were I with thee
Wild Nights should be
Our luxury!

Futile — the Winds —   5
To a Heart in port —
Done with the Compass —
Done with the Chart!

Rowing in Eden —
Ah, the Sea!   10
Might I but moor — Tonight —
In Thee!

CONSIDERATIONS FOR CRITICAL THINKING AND WRITING

1. FIRST RESPONSE. Thomas Wentworth Higginson, Dickinson's mentor,
   once said he was afraid that some "malignant" readers might "read into
   [a poem like this] more than that virgin recluse ever dreamed of putting
   there." What do you think?

2. Look up the meaning of *luxury* in a dictionary. Why does this word
   work especially well here?

3. Given the imagery of the final stanza, do you think the speaker is a man
   or a woman? Explain why.

4. CONNECTION TO ANOTHER SELECTION. Write an essay that compares the
   voice, figures of speech, and theme of this poem with those of Margaret
   Atwood's "you fit into me" (p. 396).

WILFRED OWEN (1893–1918)

Dulce et Decorum Est   *1920*

Bent double, like old beggars under sacks,
Knock-kneed, coughing like hags, we cursed through sludge,
Till on the haunting flares we turned our backs,
And towards our distant rest began to trudge.
Men marched asleep. Many had lost their boots,   5
But limped on, blood-shod. All went lame, all blind;
Drunk with fatigue; deaf even to the hoots
Of gas-shells dropping softly behind.

Gas! GAS! Quick, boys! — An ecstasy of fumbling,
Fitting the clumsy helmets just in time,   10
But someone still was yelling out and stumbling
And flound'ring like a man in fire or lime. —
Dim through the misty panes and thick green light,
As under a green sea, I saw him drowning.

In all my dreams before my helpless sight   15
He plunges at me, guttering, choking, drowning.
If in some smothering dreams, you too could pace
Behind the wagon that we flung him in,
And watch the white eyes writhing in his face,
His hanging face, like a devil's sick of sin,   20
If you could hear, at every jolt, the blood

Come gargling from the froth-corrupted lungs
Obscene as cancer, bitter as the cud
Of vile, incurable sores on innocent tongues, —
My friend, you would not tell with such high zest   25
To children ardent for some desperate glory,
The old lie: *Dulce et decorum est*
Pro patria mori.

CONSIDERATIONS FOR CRITICAL THINKING AND WRITING

1. FIRST RESPONSE. The Latin quotation in lines 27 and 28 is from Horace: "It is sweet and fitting to die for one's country." Owen served as a British soldier during World War I and was killed. Is this poem unpatriotic? What is its purpose?

2. Which images in the poem are most vivid? To which senses do they speak?

3. Describe the speaker's tone. What is his relationship to his audience?

4. How are the images of the soldiers in this poem different from the images that typically appear in recruiting posters?

RUTH FAINLIGHT (B. 1931)

Crocuses   2006

Pale, bare, tender stems rising
from the muddy winter-faded grass,

shivering petals the almost luminous
blue and mauve of bruises on the naked

bodies of men, women, children
herded into a forest clearing

before the shouted order, crack of gunfire,
final screams and prayers and moans.

CONSIDERATIONS FOR CRITICAL THINKING AND WRITING

1. FIRST RESPONSE. Comment on Fainlight's choice of title. What effect does it have on your reading of the poem?

2. Trace your response to each image in the poem and describe the poem's tone as it moves from line to line.

3. CREATIVE RESPONSE. Try writing an eight-line poem in the style of Fainlight's based on images that gradually but radically shift in tone.

SALLY CROFT (1935–2006)
Home-Baked Bread   1981

*Nothing gives a household a greater sense of stability and common comfort
than the aroma of cooling bread. Begin, if you like, with a loaf of whole
wheat, which requires neither sifting nor kneading, and go on from there to
more cunning triumphs.*

— The Joy of Cooking

What is it she is not saying?
Cunning triumphs. It rings
of insinuation. Step into my kitchen,
I have prepared a cunning triumph
for you. Spices and herbs   5
sealed in this porcelain jar,

a treasure of my great-aunt
who sat up past midnight
in her Massachusetts bedroom
when the moon was dark. Come,   10
rest your feet. I'll make
you tea with honey and slices

of warm bread spread with peach butter.
I picked the fruit this morning
still fresh with dew. The fragrance   15
is seductive? I hoped you would say that.
See how the heat rises
when the bread opens. Come,

we'll eat together, the small flakes
have scarcely any flavor. What cunning   20
triumphs we can discover in my upstairs room
where peach trees breathe their sweetness
beside the open window and
sun lies like honey on the floor.

CONSIDERATIONS FOR CRITICAL THINKING AND WRITING

1. **FIRST RESPONSE.** Why does the speaker in this poem seize on the phrase
   "cunning triumphs" from the *Joy of Cooking* excerpt?

2. Distinguish between the voice we hear in lines 1–3 and the second voice
   in lines 3–24. Who is the "you" in the poem?

3. Why is the word "insinuation" an especially appropriate choice in line 3?

4. How do the images in lines 20–24 bring together all the senses evoked
   in the preceding lines?

5. **CREATIVE RESPONSE.** Write a paragraph — or stanza — that describes the
   sensuous (and perhaps sensual) qualities of a food you enjoy.

JOHN KEATS (1795–1821)

To Autumn

1819

I

Season of mists and mellow fruitfulness,
   Close bosom-friend of the maturing sun;
Conspiring with him how to load and bless
   With fruit the vines that round the thatch-eves run;
To bend with apples the mossed cottage-trees,   5
   And fill all fruit with ripeness to the core;
     To swell the gourd, and plump the hazel shells
   With a sweet kernel; to set budding more,
And still more, later flowers for the bees,
Until they think warm days will never cease,   10
     For summer has o'er-brimmed their clammy cells.

II

Who hath not seen thee oft amid thy store?
   Sometimes whoever seeks abroad may find
Thee sitting careless on a granary floor,
   Thy hair soft-lifted by the winnowing wind;   15
Or on a half-reaped furrow sound asleep,
   Drowsed with the fume of poppies, while thy hook°   *scythe*
     Spares the next swath and all its twinèd flowers:
And sometimes like a gleaner thou dost keep
   Steady thy laden head across a brook;   20
   Or by a cider-press, with patient look,
     Thou watchest the last oozings hours by hours.

III

Where are the songs of spring? Ay, where are they?
   Think not of them, thou hast thy music too —
While barred clouds bloom the soft-dying day,   25
   And touch the stubble-plains with rosy hue;
Then in a wailful choir the small gnats mourn
   Among the river swallows,° borne aloft   *willows*
     Or sinking as the light wind lives or dies;
And full-grown lambs loud bleat from hilly bourn;°   *territory* 30
   Hedge-crickets sing; and now with treble soft
   The redbreast whistles from a garden-croft,
     And gathering swallows twitter in the skies.

Considerations for Critical Thinking and Writing

1. FIRST RESPONSE. How is autumn made to seem like a person in each stanza of this ode?

2. Which senses are most emphasized in each stanza?

3. How is the progression of time expressed in the ode?

4. How does the imagery convey tone? Which words have especially strong connotative values?

5. What is the speaker's view of death?

Stephen Crane (1871–1900)

The Wayfarer   *1899*

The wayfarer
Perceiving the pathway to truth
Was struck with astonishment.
It was thickly grown with weeds.
"Ha," he said,   5
"I see that none has passed here
"In a long time."
Later he saw that each weed
Was a singular knife.
"Well," he mumbled at last,   10
"Doubtless there are other roads."

Considerations for Critical Thinking and Writing

1. FIRST RESPONSE. How does the metaphor in this poem produce its theme?

2. Why do you think the person is described as a "wayfarer" rather than simply as a "traveler"?

3. CONNECTION TO ANOTHER SELECTION. Discuss how metaphors create meaning in "The Wayfarer" and in Robert Frost's "The Road Not Taken" (p. 542).

Figures of Speech

Like a piece of ice on a hot stove the poem must ride on its own melting.

— ROBERT FROST

Figures of speech are broadly defined as a way of saying one thing in terms of something else. An overeager funeral director might, for example, be described as a vulture. Although figures of speech are indirect, they are designed to clarify, not obscure, our understanding of what they describe. Poets frequently use them because, as Emily Dickinson said, the poet's work is to "tell all the Truth but tell it slant" to capture the reader's interest and imagination. But figures of speech are not limited to poetry. Hearing them, reading them, or using them is as natural as using language itself.

Suppose that in the middle of a class discussion concerning the economic causes of World War II your history instructor introduces a series of statistics by saying, "Let's get down to brass tacks." Would anyone be likely to expect a display of brass tacks for students to examine? Of course not. To interpret the statement literally would be to wholly misunderstand the instructor's point that the time has come for a close look at the economic circumstances leading to the war. A literal response transforms the statement into the sort of hilariously bizarre material often found in a sketch by Stephen Colbert.

The class does not look for brass tacks because, in a nutshell, they understand that the instructor is speaking figuratively. They would understand, too, that in the preceding sentence "in a nutshell" refers to brevity and conciseness rather than to the covering of a kernel of a nut. Figurative language makes its way into our everyday speech and writing as well as into literature because it is a means of achieving color, vividness, and intensity.

Consider the difference, for example, between these two statements:

Literal: The diner strongly expressed anger at the waiter.
Figurative: The diner leaped from his table and roared at the waiter.

The second statement is more vivid because it creates a picture of ferocious anger by likening the diner to some kind of wild animal, such as a lion or tiger. By comparison, "strongly expressed anger" is neither especially strong nor especially expressive; it is flat. Not all figurative language avoids this kind of flatness, however. Figures of speech such as "getting down to brass tacks" and "in a nutshell" are clichés because they lack originality and freshness. Still, they suggest how these devices are commonly used to give language some color, even if that color is sometimes a bit faded.

There is nothing weak about William Shakespeare's use of figurative language in the following passage from *Macbeth*. Macbeth has just learned that his wife is dead, and he laments her loss as well as the course of his own life.

WILLIAM SHAKESPEARE (1564–1616)

From Macbeth *(Act V, Scene v)*   1605–1606

Tomorrow, and tomorrow, and tomorrow
Creeps in this petty pace from day to day
To the last syllable of recorded time;
And all our yesterdays have lighted fools
The way to dusty death. Out, out, brief candle!   5
Life's but a walking shadow, a poor player,
That struts and frets his hour upon the stage,
And then is heard no more. It is a tale
Told by an idiot, full of sound and fury,
Signifying nothing.   10

This passage might be summarized as "life has no meaning," but such a brief paraphrase does not take into account the figurative language that reveals the depth of Macbeth's despair and his view of the absolute meaninglessness of life. By comparing life to a "brief candle," Macbeth emphasizes the darkness and death that surround human beings. The light of life is too brief and unpredictable to be of any comfort. Indeed, life for Macbeth is a "walking shadow," futilely playing a role that is more farcical than dramatic, because life is, ultimately, a desperate story filled with pain and devoid of significance. What the figurative language provides, then, is the emotional force of Macbeth's assertion; his comparisons are disturbing because they are so apt.

The remainder of this chapter discusses some of the most important figures of speech used in poetry. A familiarity with them will help you to understand how poetry achieves its effects.

SIMILE AND METAPHOR

The two most common figures of speech are simile and metaphor. Both compare things that are ordinarily considered unlike each other. A *simile* makes an explicit comparison between two things by using words such as *like, as, than, appears,* or *seems*: "A sip of Mrs. Cook's coffee is like a punch in the stomach." The force of the simile is created by the differences between the two things compared. There would be no simile if the comparison were stated this way: "Mrs. Cook's coffee is as strong as the cafeteria's coffee." This is a literal comparison because Mrs. Cook's coffee is compared with something like it, another kind of coffee. Consider how simile is used in this poem.

MARGARET ATWOOD (B. 1939)

you fit into me   1971

you fit into me
like a hook into an eye

a fish hook
an open eye

© Sophie Bassouls/Sygma/Corbis.

If you blinked on a second reading, you got the point of this poem because you recognized that the simile "like a hook into an eye" gives way to a play on words in the final two lines. There the hook and eye, no longer a pleasant domestic image of a clothing fastener or door latch that fits closely together, become a literal, sharp fishhook and a human eye. The wordplay qualifies the simile and drastically alters the tone of this poem by creating a strong and unpleasant surprise.

A *metaphor*, like a simile, makes a comparison between two unlike things, but it does so implicitly, without words such as *like* or *as*: "Mrs. Cook's coffee is a punch in the stomach." Metaphor asserts the identity of dissimilar things. Macbeth tells us that life *is* a "brief candle," life *is* "a walking shadow," life *is* "a poor player," life *is* "a tale / Told by an idiot." Metaphor transforms people, places, objects, and ideas into whatever the poet imagines them to be, and if metaphors are effective, the reader's experience, understanding, and appreciation of what is described are enhanced. Metaphors are frequently more demanding than similes because they are not signaled by particular words. They are both subtle and powerful.

Here is a poem about presentiment, a foreboding that something terrible is about to happen.

EMILY DICKINSON (1830–1886)

Presentiment — is that long Shadow — on the lawn —

ca. 1863

Presentiment — is that long Shadow — on the lawn —
Indicative that Suns go down —

The notice to the startled Grass
That Darkness — is about to pass —

The metaphors in this poem define the abstraction "Presentiment." The sense of foreboding that Dickinson expresses is identified with a particular moment — the moment when darkness is just about to envelop an otherwise tranquil, ordinary scene. The speaker projects that fear onto the "startled Grass" so that it seems any life must be frightened by the approaching "Shadow" and "Darkness" — two richly connotative words associated with death. The metaphors obliquely tell us ("tell it slant" was Dickinson's motto, remember) that presentiment is related to a fear of death, and, more important, the metaphors convey the feelings that attend that idea.

Some metaphors are more subtle than others because their comparison of terms is less explicit. Notice the difference between the following two metaphors, both of which describe a shaggy derelict refusing to leave the warmth of a hotel lobby: "He was a mule standing his ground" is a quite explicit comparison. The man is a mule; X is Y. But this metaphor is much more covert: "He brayed his refusal to leave." This second version is an *implied metaphor* because it does not explicitly identify the man with a mule. Instead it hints at or alludes to the mule. Braying is associated with mules and is especially appropriate in this context because of the mule's reputation for stubbornness. Implied metaphors can slip by readers, but they offer the alert reader the energy and resonance of carefully chosen, highly concentrated language.

Some poets write extended comparisons in which part or all of the poem consists of a series of related metaphors or similes. Extended metaphors are more common than extended similes. In "Catch" (p. 330), Robert Francis creates an *extended metaphor* that compares poetry to a game of catch. The entire poem is organized around this comparison. Because these comparisons are at work throughout the entire poem, they are called *controlling metaphors.* Extended comparisons can serve as a poem's organizing principle; they are also a reminder that in good poems metaphor and simile are not merely decorative but inseparable from what is expressed.

Notice the controlling metaphor in this poem, published posthumously by a woman whose contemporaries identified her more as a wife and mother than as a poet. Bradstreet's first volume of poetry, *The Tenth Muse*, was published by her brother-in-law in 1650 without her prior knowledge.

ANNE BRADSTREET (CA. 1612–1672)

The Author to Her Book   *1678*

Thou ill-formed offspring of my feeble brain,
Who after birth did'st by my side remain,
Till snatched from thence by friends, less wise than true,
Who thee abroad exposed to public view;
Made thee in rags, halting, to the press to trudge,   5
Where errors were not lessened, all may judge.
At thy return my blushing was not small,
My rambling brat (in print) should mother call;
I cast thee by as one unfit for light,
Thy visage was so irksome in my sight;   10
Yet being mine own, at length affection would
Thy blemishes amend, if so I could:
I washed thy face, but more defects I saw,
And rubbing off a spot, still made a flaw.
I stretched thy joints to make thee even feet,   15
Yet still thou run'st more hobbling than is meet;
In better dress to trim thee was my mind,
But nought save homespun cloth in the house I find.
In this array, 'mongst vulgars may'st thou roam;
In critics' hands beware thou dost not come;   20
And take thy way where yet thou are not known.
If for thy Father asked, say thou had'st none;
And for thy Mother, she alas is poor,
Which caused her thus to send thee out of door.

The extended metaphor likening her book to a child came naturally to Bradstreet and allowed her to regard her work both critically and affectionately. Her conception of the book as her child creates just the right tone of amusement, self-deprecation, and concern.

OTHER FIGURES

Perhaps the humblest figure of speech — if not one of the most familiar — is the pun. A *pun* is a play on words that relies on a word having more than one meaning or sounding like another word. For example, "A fad is in one era and out the other" is the sort of pun that produces obligatory groans. But most of us find pleasant and interesting surprises in puns. Here's one that has a slight edge to its humor.

EDMUND CONTI (B. 1929)

Pragmatist   1985

Apocalypse soon
Coming our way
Ground zero at noon
Halve a nice day.

    Grimly practical under the circumstances, the pragmatist divides the familiar cheerful cliché by half. As simple as this poem is, its tone is mixed because it makes us laugh and wince at the same time.

    Puns can be used to achieve serious effects as well as humorous ones. Although we may have learned to underrate puns as figures of speech, it is a mistake to underestimate their power and the frequency with which they appear in poetry. A close examination, for example, of Robert Frost's "Design" (p. 350) or almost any lengthy passage from a Shakespeare play will confirm the value of puns.

    Synecdoche is a figure of speech in which part of something is used to signify the whole: a neighbor is a "wagging tongue" (a gossip); a criminal is placed "behind bars" (in prison). Less typically, synecdoche refers to the whole used to signify the part: "Germany invaded Poland"; "Princeton won the fencing match." Clearly, certain individuals participated in these activities, not all of Germany or Princeton. Another related figure of speech is **metonymy**, in which something closely associated with a subject is substituted for it: "She preferred the silver screen [motion pictures] to reading." "At precisely ten o'clock the paper shufflers [office workers] stopped for coffee."

    Synecdoche and metonymy may overlap and are therefore sometimes difficult to distinguish. Consider this description of a disapproving minister entering a noisy tavern: "As those pursed lips came through the swinging door, the atmosphere was suddenly soured." The pursed lips signal the presence of the minister and are therefore a synecdoche, but they additionally suggest an inhibiting sense of sin and guilt that makes the bar patrons feel uncomfortable. Hence the pursed lips are also a metonymy, as they are in this context so closely connected with religion. Although the distinction between synecdoche and metonymy can be useful, a figure of speech is usually labeled a metonymy when it overlaps categories.

    Knowing the precise term for a figure of speech is, finally, less important than responding to its use in a poem. Consider how metonymy and synecdoche convey the tone and meaning of the following poem.

Dylan Thomas (1914–1953)
The Hand That Signed the Paper   1936

© Hulton-Deutsch Collection/Corbis.

The hand that signed the paper felled a city;
Five sovereign fingers taxed the breath,
Doubled the globe of dead and halved a
    country;
These five kings did a king to death.

The mighty hand leads to a sloping shoulder,
The finger joints are cramped with chalk;
A goose's quill has put an end to murder
That put an end to talk.

The hand that signed the treaty bred a fever,
And famine grew, and locusts came;   10
Great is the hand that holds dominion over
Man by a scribbled name.

The five kings count the dead but do not soften
The crusted wound nor stroke the brow;
A hand rules pity as a hand rules heaven;   15
Hands have no tears to flow.

The "hand" in this poem is a synecdoche for a powerful ruler because it is a part of someone used to signify the entire person. The "goose's quill" is a metonymy that also refers to the power associated with the ruler's hand. By using these figures of speech, Thomas depersonalizes and ultimately dehumanizes the ruler. The final synecdoche tells us that "Hands have no tears to flow." It makes us see the political power behind the hand as remote and inhuman. How is the meaning of the poem enlarged when the speaker says, "A hand rules pity as a hand rules heaven"?

One of the ways writers energize the abstractions, ideas, objects, and animals that constitute their created worlds is through **personification**, the attribution of human characteristics to nonhuman things: temptation pursues the innocent; trees scream in the raging wind; mice conspire in the cupboard. We are not explicitly told that these things are people; instead, we are invited to see that they behave like people. Perhaps it is human vanity that makes personification a frequently used figure of speech. Whatever the reason, personification, a form of metaphor that connects the nonhuman with the human, makes the world understandable in human terms. Consider this concise example from William Blake's *The Marriage of Heaven and Hell*, a long poem that takes delight in attacking conventional morality: "Prudence is a rich ugly old maid courted by Incapacity." By personifying prudence, Blake transforms what is usually considered a virtue into a comic figure hardly worth emulating.

Often related to personification is another rhetorical figure called *apostrophe*, an address either to someone who is absent and therefore cannot hear the speaker or to something nonhuman that cannot comprehend. Apostrophe provides an opportunity for the speaker of a poem to think aloud, and often the thoughts expressed are in a formal tone. John Keats, for example, begins "Ode on a Grecian Urn" (p. 376) this way: "Thou still unravished bride of quietness." Apostrophe is frequently accompanied by intense emotion that is signaled by phrasing such as "O Life." In the right hands — such as Keats's — apostrophe can provide an intense and immediate voice in a poem, but when it is overdone or extravagant it can be ludicrous. Modern poets are more wary of apostrophe than their predecessors because apostrophizing strikes many self-conscious twenty-first-century sensibilities as too theatrical. Thus modern poets tend to avoid exaggerated situations in favor of less charged though equally meditative moments, as in this next poem, with its amusing, half-serious cosmic twist.

JANICE TOWNLEY MOORE (B. 1939)

To a Wasp   1984

You must have chortled
finding that tiny hole
in the kitchen screen. Right
into my cheese cake batter
you dived,
no chance to swim ashore,
no saving spoon,
the mixer whirring
your legs, wings, stinger,
churning you into such   10
delicious death.
Never mind the bright April day.
Did you not see
rising out of cumulus clouds
That fist aimed at both of us?   15

> **WHEN I WRITE** "I began writing poetry as a freshman in college. I wrote using poetic diction and sometimes rhyme. Then I discovered 'modern poetry.' Seeing what was published in literary magazines quickly changed my style."
> — JANICE TOWNLEY MOORE

Moore's apostrophe "To a Wasp" is based on the simplest of domestic circumstances; there is almost nothing theatrical or exaggerated in the poem's tone until "That fist" in the last line, when exaggeration takes center stage. As a figure of speech, exaggeration is known as **overstatement** or **hyperbole** and adds emphasis without intending to be literally true: "The teenage boy ate everything in the house." Notice how the speaker of

Andrew Marvell's "To His Coy Mistress" (p. 363) exaggerates his devotion in the following overstatement:

> An hundred years should go to praise
> Thine eyes and on thy forehead gaze,
> Two hundred to adore each breast,
> But thirty thousand to the rest:

That comes to 30,500 years. What is expressed here is heightened emotion, not deception.

The speaker also uses the opposite figure of speech, **understatement**, which says less than is intended. In the next section he sums up why he cannot take 30,500 years to express his love:

> The grave's a fine and private place,
> But none, I think, do there embrace.

The speaker is correct, of course, but by deliberately understating — saying "I think" when he is actually certain — he makes his point, that death will overtake their love, all the more emphatic. Another powerful example of understatement appears in the final line of Randall Jarrell's "The Death of the Ball Turret Gunner" (p. 356), when the disembodied voice of the machine-gunner describes his death in a bomber: "When I died they washed me out of the turret with a hose."

Paradox is a statement that initially appears to be self-contradictory but that, on closer inspection, turns out to make sense: "The pen is mightier than the sword." In a fencing match, anyone would prefer the sword, but if the goal is to win the hearts and minds of people, the art of persuasion can be more compelling than swordplay. To resolve the paradox, it is necessary to discover the sense that underlies the statement. If we see that "pen" and "sword" are used as metonymies for writing and violence, then the paradox rings true. **Oxymoron** is a condensed form of paradox in which two contradictory words are used together. Combinations such as "sweet sorrow," "silent scream," "sad joy," and "cold fire" indicate the kinds of startling effects that oxymorons can produce. Paradox is useful in poetry because it arrests a reader's attention by its seemingly stubborn refusal to make sense, and once a reader has penetrated the paradox, it is difficult to resist a perception so well earned. Good paradoxes are knotty pleasures. Here is a simple but effective one.

TAJANA KOVICS (B. 1985)

Text Message

2011

Because I think you're nearly perfect,
I want to love you best:

And since absence makes the heart grow fonder,
We should see each other less.

As the title suggests, the medium is part of the implicit subtext in this quatrain. Consider how the very idea of romantic love is conveyed and built on separation rather than intimacy in this witty paradox.

The following poems are rich in figurative language. As you read and study them, notice how their figures of speech vivify situations, clarify ideas, intensify emotions, and engage your imagination. Although the terms for the various figures discussed in this chapter are useful for labeling the particular devices used in poetry, they should not be allowed to get in the way of your response to a poem. Don't worry about rounding up examples of figurative language. First relax and let the figures work their effects on you. Use the terms as a means of taking you further into poetry, and they will serve your reading well.

POEMS FOR FURTHER STUDY

GARY SNYDER (B. 1930)

How Poetry Comes to Me   *1992*

It comes blundering over the
Boulders at night, it stays
Frightened outside the
Range of my campfire
I go to meet it at the
Edge of the light

> CONSIDERATIONS FOR CRITICAL THINKING AND WRITING
>
> 1. FIRST RESPONSE. How does personification in this poem depict the creative process?
>
> 2. Why do you suppose Snyder makes each successive line shorter?
>
> 3. CREATIVE RESPONSE. How would eliminating the title change your understanding of the poem? Substitute another title that causes you to reinterpret it.

KAY RYAN (B. 1945)

Learning   *1996*

Whatever must be learned
is always on the bottom,

as with the law of drawers
and the necessary item.
It isn't pleasant,
whatever they tell children,
to turn out on the floor
the folded things in them.

CONSIDERATIONS FOR CRITICAL THINKING AND WRITING

1. FIRST RESPONSE. Why does the speaker consider learning to be unpleasant and difficult?

2. Why is unfolding what must be learned an especially apt metaphor?

ERNEST SLYMAN (B. 1946)

Lightning Bugs   1988

In my backyard,
They burn peepholes in the night
And take snapshots of my house.

CONSIDERATIONS FOR CRITICAL THINKING AND WRITING

1. FIRST RESPONSE. Explain why the title is essential to this poem.

2. What makes the description of the lightning bugs effective? How do the second and third lines complement each other?

3. CREATIVE RESPONSE. As Slyman has done, take a simple, common fact of nature and make it vivid by using a figure of speech to describe it.

WILLIAM CARLOS WILLIAMS (1883–1963)

To Waken an Old Lady   1921

Old age is
a flight of small
cheeping birds
skimming
bare trees   5
above a snow glaze.
Gaining and failing
they are buffeted
by a dark wind —
But what?   10
On harsh weedstalks

the flock has rested,
the snow
is covered with broken
seedhusks   15
and the wind tempered
by a shrill
piping of plenty.

CONSIDERATIONS FOR CRITICAL THINKING AND WRITING

1. FIRST RESPONSE. Consider the images and figures of speech in this poem
   and explain why you think it is a positive or negative assessment of
   old age.

2. How does the title relate to the rest of the poem?

WHEN I WRITE "Only on very rare occasions is a poem complete in a first draft. The first draft of a poem can sit for a long time waiting for its other half, or its meaning. Save everything you write, no matter how unhappy you are with it. You often won't see the beauty until later."
— JUDY PAGE HEITZMAN

JUDY PAGE HEITZMAN (B. 1952)

The Schoolroom on the Second Floor of the Knitting Mill   1991

While most of us copied letters out of books,
Mrs. Lawrence carved and cleaned her nails.
Now the red and buff cardinals at my back-room window
make me miss her, her room, her hallway,
even the chimney outside   5
that broke up the sky.

In my memory it is afternoon.
Sun streams in through the door
next to the fire escape where we are lined up
getting our coats on to go out to the playground,   10
the tether ball, its towering height, the swings.
She tells me to make sure the line
does not move up over the threshold.
That would be dangerous.
So I stand guard at the door.   15
Somehow it happens
the way things seem to happen when we're not really looking,

or we are looking, just not the right way.
Kids crush up like cattle, pushing me over the line.

Judy is not a good leader is all Mrs. Lawrence says.   20
She says it quietly. Still, everybody hears.
Her arms hang down like sausages.
I hear her every time I fail.

Considerations for Critical Thinking and Writing

1. **FIRST RESPONSE.** Does your impression of Mrs. Lawrence change from the beginning to the end of the poem? How so?

2. How can line 2 be read as an implied metaphor?

3. Discuss the use of similes in the poem. How do they contribute to the poem's meaning?

Martín Espada (b. 1957)

The Mexican Cabdriver's Poem for His Wife, Who Has Left Him   *2000*

We were sitting in traffic
on the Brooklyn Bridge,
so I asked the poets
in the backseat of my cab
to write a poem for you.   5

They asked
if you are like the moon
or the trees.

I said no,
she is like the bridge   10
when there is so much traffic
I have time
to watch the boats
on the river.

Considerations for Critical Thinking and Writing

1. **FIRST RESPONSE.** What do you think is Espada's attitude toward the cabdriver?

2. Explore the potential meanings of the similes concerning the moon, trees, and the bridge. How does the bridge differ from the other two?

3. **CONNECTION TO ANOTHER SELECTION.** Compare the source of poetry in this poem and in Gary Snyder's "How Poetry Comes to Me" (p. 403).

ROBERT FROST (1874–1963)

Fire and Ice   1923

Some say the world will end in fire,
Some say in ice.
From what I've tasted of desire
I hold with those who favor fire.
But if it had to perish twice,
I think I know enough of hate
To say that for destruction ice
Is also great
And would suffice.

CONSIDERATIONS FOR CRITICAL THINKING AND WRITING

1. FIRST RESPONSE. What characteristics of human behavior does the speaker associate with fire and with ice?

2. What theories about the end of the world are alluded to in lines 1 and 2?

3. How does the speaker's use of understatement and rhyme affect the tone of this poem?

JOHN DONNE (1572–1631)

A Valediction: Forbidding Mourning   1611

As virtuous men pass mildly away,
    And whisper to their souls to go,
While some of their sad friends do say,
    The breath goes now, and some say, no:

So let us melt, and make no noise,   5
    No tear-floods, nor sigh-tempests move;
'Twere profanation of our joys
    To tell the laity our love.

Moving of th' earth° brings harms and fears,   *earthquakes*
    Men reckon what it did and meant,   10
But trepidation of the spheres,°
    Though greater far, is innocent.

Dull sublunary° lovers' love
    (Whose soul is sense) cannot admit
Absence, because it doth remove   15
    Those things which elemented° it.   *composed*

11 *trepidation of the spheres*: According to Ptolemaic astronomy, the planets sometimes moved violently, as in earthquakes, but these movements were not felt by people on Earth. 13 *sublunary*: Under the moon; hence, mortal and subject to change.

But we by a love so much refined,
  That ourselves know not what it is,
Inter-assured of the mind,
  Care less, eyes, lips, and hands to miss.   20

Our two souls therefore, which are one,
  Though I must go, endure not yet
A breach, but an expansion,
  Like gold to airy thinness beat.

If they be two, they are two so   25
  As stiff twin compasses are two;
Thy soul the fixed foot, makes no show
  To move, but doth, if th' other do.

And though it in the center sit,
  Yet when the other far doth roam,   30
It leans, and hearkens after it,
  And grows erect, as that comes home.

Such wilt thou be to me, who must
  Like th' other foot, obliquely run;
Thy firmness makes my circle just,°   35
  And makes me end, where I begun.

35 *circle just*: The circle is a traditional symbol of perfection.

CONSIDERATIONS FOR CRITICAL THINKING AND WRITING

1. **FIRST RESPONSE.** A valediction is a farewell. Donne wrote this poem for his wife before leaving on a trip to France. What kind of "mourning" is the speaker forbidding?

2. Explain how the simile in lines 1–4 is related to the couple in lines 5–8. Who is described as dying?

3. How does the speaker contrast the couple's love to "sublunary lovers' love" (line 13)?

4. Explain the similes in lines 24 and 25–36.

JIM STEVENS (1922–2000)

Schizophrenia   1992

It was the house that suffered most.

It had begun with slamming doors, angry feet scuffing the carpets,
dishes slammed onto the table,
greasy stains spreading on the cloth.

Certain doors were locked at night,   5
feet stood for hours outside them,
dishes were left unwashed, the cloth
disappeared under a hardened crust.

The house came to miss the shouting voices,
the threats, the half-apologies, noisy   10
reconciliations, the sobbing that followed.

Then lines were drawn, borders established,
some rooms declared their loyalties,
keeping to themselves, keeping out the other.
The house divided against itself.   15

Seeing cracking paint, broken windows,
the front door banging in the wind,
the roof tiles flying off, one by one,
the neighbors said it was a madhouse.

It was the house that suffered most.   20

Considerations for Critical Thinking and Writing

1. **FIRST RESPONSE.** What is the effect of personifying the house in this poem?

2. How are the people who live in the house characterized? What does their behavior reveal about them? How does the house respond to them?

3. Comment on the title. If the title were missing, what, if anything, would be missing from the poem? Explain your answer.

LUCILLE CLIFTON (1936–2010)

come home from the movies   *1974*

come home from the movies,
black girls and boys,
the picture be over and the screen
be cold as our neighborhood.
come home from the show,
don't be the show.
take off some flowers and plant them,
pick us some papers and read them,
stop making some babies and raise them.
come home from the movies   10

© Christopher Felver.

black girls and boys,
show our fathers how to walk like men,
they already know how to dance.

CONSIDERATIONS FOR CRITICAL THINKING AND WRITING

1. FIRST RESPONSE. What are the "movies" a metaphor for?
2. What advice does the speaker urge upon "black girls and boys"?
3. Explain the final two lines. Why do they come last?

16

Symbol, Allegory, and Irony

Barbara Savage Cheresh.

Poetry is serious business; literature is the apparatus through which the world tries to keep intact its important ideas and feelings.
—MARY OLIVER

SYMBOL

A *symbol* is something that represents something else. An object, a person, a place, an event, or an action can suggest more than its literal meaning. A handshake between two world leaders might be simply a greeting, but if it is done ceremoniously before cameras, it could be a symbolic gesture signifying unity, issues resolved, and joint policies that will be followed. We live surrounded by symbols. When a $100,000 Mercedes-Benz comes roaring by in the fast lane, we get a quick glimpse of not only an expensive car but also an entire lifestyle that suggests opulence, broad lawns, executive offices, and power. One of the reasons some buyers are willing to spend roughly the cost of five Chevrolets for a single Mercedes-Benz is that they are aware of the car's symbolic value. A symbol is a vehicle for two things at once: it functions as itself, and it implies meanings beyond itself.

The meanings suggested by a symbol are determined by the context in which it appears. The Mercedes could symbolize very different things depending on where it was parked. Would an American political candidate be likely to appear in a Detroit blue-collar neighborhood with such a car? Probably not. Although a candidate might be able to afford the car, it would be an inappropriate symbol for someone seeking votes from all of the people. As a symbol, the German-built Mercedes would backfire if voters perceived it as representing an entity partially responsible for layoffs of automobile workers or, worse, as a sign of decadence and corruption. Similarly, a huge portrait of Mao Tse-tung conveys different meanings to residents of Beijing than it would to farmers in Prairie Center, Illinois. Because symbols depend on contexts for their meaning, literary artists provide those contexts so that the reader has enough information to determine the probable range of meanings suggested by a symbol.

In the following poem, the speaker describes walking at night. How is the night used symbolically?

ROBERT FROST (1874–1963)

Acquainted with the Night   1928

I have been one acquainted with the night.
I have walked out in rain — and back in rain.
I have outwalked the furthest city light.

I have looked down the saddest city lane.
I have passed by the watchman on his beat   5
And dropped my eyes, unwilling to explain.

I have stood still and stopped the sound of feet
When far away an interrupted cry
Came over houses from another street,

But not to call me back or say good-by;   10
And further still at an unearthly height
One luminary clock against the sky

Proclaimed the time was neither wrong nor right.
I have been one acquainted with the night.

In approaching this or any poem, you should read for literal meanings first and then allow the elements of the poem to invite you to symbolic readings, if they are appropriate. Here the somber tone suggests that the lines have symbolic meaning, too. The flat matter-of-factness created by the repetition of "I have" (lines 1–5, 7, 14) understates the symbolic subject matter of the poem, which is, finally, more about the "night" located in the speaker's mind or soul than it is about walking away from a city and back again. The speaker is "acquainted with the night." The importance of this phrase is emphasized by Frost's title and by the fact that he begins and ends the poem with it. Poets frequently use this kind of repetition to alert readers to details that carry more than literal meanings.

The speaker in this poem has personal knowledge of the night but does not indicate specifically what the night means. To arrive at the potential meanings of the night in this context, it is necessary to look closely at its connotations, along with the images provided in the poem. The connotative meanings of night suggest, for example, darkness, death, and grief. By drawing on these connotations, Frost uses a ***conventional symbol*** — something that is recognized by many people to represent certain ideas. Roses conventionally symbolize love or beauty; laurels, fame; spring, growth; the moon, romance. Poets often use conventional symbols to convey tone and meaning.

Frost uses the night as a conventional symbol, but he also develops it into a ***literary*** or ***contextual symbol*** that goes beyond traditional, public meanings. A literary symbol cannot be summarized in a word or two. It tends to be as elusive as experience itself. The night cannot be reduced to or equated with darkness or death or grief, but it evokes those associations and more. Frost took what perhaps initially appears to be an overworked, conventional symbol and prevented it from becoming a cliché by deepening and extending its meaning.

The images in "Acquainted with the Night" lead to the poem's symbolic meaning. Unwilling, and perhaps unable, to explain explicitly to the watchman (and to the reader) what the night means, the speaker nevertheless conveys feelings about it. The brief images of darkness, rain, sad city lanes, the necessity for guards, the eerie sound of a distressing cry coming over rooftops, and the "luminary clock against the sky" proclaiming "the time was neither wrong nor right" all help to create a sense of anxiety in this tight-lipped speaker. Although we cannot know what unnamed personal experiences have acquainted the speaker with the night, the images suggest that whatever the night means, it is somehow associated with insomnia, loneliness, isolation, coldness, darkness, death, fear, and a sense of alienation from humanity and even time. Daylight — ordinary daytime thoughts and life itself — seems remote and unavailable in this poem. The night is literally the period from sunset to sunrise, but, more important, it is an internal state of being felt by the speaker and revealed through the images.

Frost used symbols rather than an expository essay that would explain the conditions that cause these feelings because most readers can provide their own list of sorrows and terrors that evoke similar emotions. Through symbol, the speaker's experience is compressed and simultaneously expanded by the personal darkness that each reader brings to the poem. The suggestive nature of symbols makes them valuable for poets and evocative for readers.

ALLEGORY

Unlike expansive, suggestive symbols, ***allegory*** is a narration or description usually restricted to a single meaning because its events, actions, characters, settings, and objects represent specific abstractions or ideas. Although the elements in an allegory may be interesting in themselves, the emphasis tends to be on what they ultimately mean. Characters may be given names such as Hope, Pride, Youth, and Charity; they have few, if any, personal qualities beyond their abstract meanings. These personifications are a form of extended metaphor, but their meanings are severely restricted. They are not symbols because, for instance, the meaning of a character named Charity is precisely that virtue.

There is little or no room for broad speculation and exploration in allegories. If Frost had written "Acquainted with the Night" as an allegory, he might have named his speaker Loneliness and had him leave the City of Despair to walk the Streets of Emptiness, where Crime, Poverty, Fear, and other characters would define the nature of city life. The literal elements in an allegory tend to be deemphasized in favor of the message. Symbols, however, function both literally and symbolically, so that "Acquainted with the Night" is about both a walk and a sense that something is terribly wrong.

Allegory especially lends itself to **didactic poetry**, which is designed to teach an ethical, moral, or religious lesson. Many stories, poems, and plays are concerned with values, but didactic literature is specifically created to convey a message. "Acquainted with the Night" does not impart advice or offer guidance. If the poem argued that city life is self-destructive or sinful, it would be didactic; instead, it is a lyric poem that expresses the emotions and thoughts of a single speaker.

Although allegory is often enlisted in didactic causes because it can so readily communicate abstract ideas through physical representations, not all allegories teach a lesson. Here is a poem describing a haunted palace while also establishing a consistent pattern that reveals another meaning.

EDGAR ALLAN POE (1809–1849)

The Haunted Palace

1839

I

In the greenest of our valleys,
    By good angels tenanted,
Once a fair and stately palace —
    Radiant palace — reared its head.
In the monarch Thought's dominion —   5
    It stood there!
Never seraph spread a pinion
    Over fabric half so fair.

II

Banners yellow, glorious, golden,
    On its roof did float and flow;   10
(This — all this — was in the olden
    Time long ago)

And every gentle air that dallied,
    In that sweet day,
Along the ramparts plumed and pallid,   15
    A wingèd odor went away.

III

Wanderers in that happy valley
    Through two luminous windows saw
Spirits moving musically
    To a lute's well-tunèd law,   20
Round about a throne, where sitting
    (Porphyrogene!)°   *born to purple, royal*
In state his glory well befitting,
    The ruler of the realm was seen.

IV

And all with pearl and ruby glowing   25
    Was the fair palace door,
Through which came flowing, flowing, flowing
    And sparkling evermore,
A troop of Echoes whose sweet duty
    Was but to sing,   30
In voices of surpassing beauty,
    The wit and wisdom of their king.

V

But evil things, in robes of sorrow,
    Assailed the monarch's high estate;
(Ah, let us mourn, for never morrow   35
    Shall dawn upon him, desolate!)
And, round about his home, the glory
    That blushed and bloomed
Is but a dim-remembered story
    Of the old time entombed.   40

VI

And travelers now within that valley,
    Through the red-litten windows see
Vast forms that move fantastically
    To a discordant melody;
While, like a rapid ghastly river,   45
    Through the pale door,
A hideous throng rush out forever,
    And laugh — but smile no more.

On one level this poem describes how a once happy palace is desolated by "evil things" (line 33). If the reader pays close attention to the diction, however, an allegorical meaning becomes apparent on a second reading. A systematic pattern develops in the choice of words used to describe the palace, so that it comes to stand for a human mind. The palace, banners, windows, door, echoes, and throng are equated with a person's head, hair, eyes, mouth, voice, and laughter. That mind, once harmoniously ordered, is overthrown by evil, haunting thoughts that lead to the mad laughter in the poem's final lines. Once the general pattern is seen, the rest of the details fall neatly into place to strengthen the parallels between the surface description of a palace and the allegorical representation of a disordered mind.

Modern writers generally prefer symbol over allegory because they tend to be more interested in opening up the potential meanings of an experience instead of transforming it into a closed pattern of meaning. Perhaps the major difference is that while allegory may delight a reader's imagination, symbol challenges and enriches it.

IRONY

Another important resource writers use to take readers beyond literal meanings is *irony*, a technique that reveals a discrepancy between what appears to be and what is actually true. Here is a classic example in which appearances give way to the underlying reality.

Edwin Arlington Robinson (1869–1935)

Richard Cory   1897

Whenever Richard Cory went down town,
We people on the pavement looked at him:
He was a gentleman from sole to crown,
Clean favored, and imperially slim.

And he was always quietly arrayed,   5
And he was always human when he talked;
But still he fluttered pulses when he said,
"Good-morning," and he glittered when he walked.

And he was rich — yes, richer than a king —
And admirably schooled in every grace: 10
In fine, we thought that he was everything
To make us wish that we were in his place.

So on we worked, and waited for the light,
And went without the meat, and cursed the bread;
And Richard Cory, one calm summer night,   15
Went home and put a bullet through his head.

Richard Cory seems to have it all. Those less fortunate, the "people on the pavement," regard him as well-bred, handsome, tasteful, and richly endowed with both money and grace. Until the final line of the poem, the reader, like the speaker, is charmed by Cory's good fortune, so quietly expressed in his decent, easy manner. That final, shocking line, however, shatters the appearances of Cory's life and reveals him to have been a desperately unhappy man. While everyone else assumes that Cory represented "everything" to which they aspire, the reality is that he could escape his miserable life only as a suicide. This discrepancy between what appears to be true and what actually exists is known as *situational irony*: what happens is entirely different from what is expected. We are not told why Cory shoots himself; instead, the irony in the poem shocks us into the recognition that appearances do not always reflect realities.

Words are also sometimes intended to be taken at other than face value. *Verbal irony* is saying something different from what is meant. If after reading "Richard Cory," you said, "That rich gentleman sure was happy," your statement would be ironic. Your tone of voice would indicate that just the opposite was meant; hence verbal irony is usually easy to detect in spoken language. In literature, however, a reader can sometimes take literally what a writer intends ironically. The remedy for this kind of misreading is to pay close attention to the poem's context. There is no formula that can detect verbal irony, but contradictory actions and statements as well as the use of understatement and overstatement can often be signals that verbal irony is present.

Consider how verbal irony is used in this poem.

Kenneth Fearing (1902–1961)

AD   *1938*

Wanted: Men;
Millions of men are *wanted at once* in a big new field;
New, tremendous, thrilling, great.
If you've ever been a figure in the chamber of horrors,
If you've ever escaped from a psychiatric ward,   5
If you thrill at the thought of throwing poison into wells, have heavenly
    visions of people, by the thousands, dying in flames —

You are the very man we want
We mean business and our business is *you*
Wanted: A race of brand-new men.

Apply: Middle Europe;   10
No skill needed;
No ambition required; no brains wanted and no character allowed;

Take a permanent job in the coming profession
Wages: *Death.*

This poem was written as Nazi troops stormed across Europe at the start of World War II. The advertisement suggests on the surface that killing is just an ordinary job, but the speaker indicates through understatement that there is nothing ordinary about the "business" of this *"coming profession."* Fearing uses verbal irony to indicate how casually and mindlessly people are prepared to accept the horrors of war.

"AD" is a *satire*, an example of the literary art of ridiculing a folly or vice in an effort to expose or correct it. The object of satire is usually some human frailty; people, institutions, ideas, and things are all fair game for satirists. Fearing satirizes the insanity of a world mobilizing itself for war: his irony reveals the speaker's knowledge that there is nothing *"New, tremendous, thrilling,* [or] *great"* about going off to kill and be killed. The implication of the poem is that no one should respond to advertisements for war. The poem serves as a satiric corrective to those who would troop off armed with unrealistic expectations: wage war, and the wages consist of death.

Dramatic irony is used when a writer allows a reader to know more about a situation than a character does. This creates a discrepancy between what a character says or thinks and what the reader knows to be true. Dramatic irony is often used to reveal character. In the following poem the speaker delivers a public address that ironically tells us more about him than it does about the patriotic holiday he is commemorating.

E. E. CUMMINGS (1894–1962)

next to of course god america i   1926

"next to of course god america i
love you land of the pilgrims' and so forth oh
say can you see by the dawn's early my
country 'tis of centuries come and go
and are no more what of it we should worry   5
in every language even deafanddumb
thy sons acclaim your glorious name by gorry
by jingo by gee by gosh by gum
why talk of beauty what could be more beauti-
ful than these heroic happy dead   10
who rushed like lions to the roaring slaughter
they did not stop to think they died instead
then shall the voice of liberty be mute?"

He spoke. And drank rapidly a glass of water

This verbal debauch of chauvinistic clichés (notice the run-on phrases and lines) reveals that the speaker's relationship to God and country is not, as he claims, one of love. His public address suggests a hearty mindlessness that leads to "roaring slaughter" rather than to reverence or patriotism. Cummings allows the reader to see through the speaker's words to their dangerous emptiness. What the speaker means and what Cummings means are entirely different. Like Fearing's "AD," this poem is a satire that invites the reader's laughter and contempt in order to deflate the benighted attitudes expressed in it.

When a writer uses God, destiny, or fate to dash the hopes and expectations of a character or humankind in general, it is called **cosmic irony**. In "The Convergence of the Twain" (p. 369), for example, Thomas Hardy describes how "The Immanent Will" brought together the *Titanic* and a deadly iceberg. Technology and pride are no match for "the Spinner of the Years." Here's a painfully terse version of cosmic irony.

STEPHEN CRANE (1871–1900)

A Man Said to the Universe   1899

A man said to the universe:
"Sir, I exist!"
"However," replied the universe,
"The fact has not created in me
A sense of obligation."

Unlike in "The Convergence of the Twain," there is the slightest bit of humor in Crane's poem, but the joke is on us.

Irony is an important technique that allows a writer to distinguish between appearances and realities. In situational irony a discrepancy exists between what we expect to happen and what actually happens; in verbal irony a discrepancy exists between what is said and what is meant; in dramatic irony a discrepancy exists between what a character believes and what the reader knows to be true; and in cosmic irony a discrepancy exists between what a character aspires to and what universal forces provide. With each form of irony, we are invited to move beyond surface appearances and sentimental assumptions to see the complexity of experience. Irony is often used in literature to reveal a writer's perspective on matters that previously seemed settled.

POEMS FOR FURTHER STUDY

BOB HICOK (B. 1960)

Making it in poetry   2004

The young teller
at the credit union
asked why so many
small checks
from universities?   5

Because I write
poems I said. Why
haven't I heard
of you? Because
I write poems   10
I said.

CONSIDERATIONS FOR CRITICAL THINKING AND WRITING

1. FIRST RESPONSE. Explain how the speaker's verbal irony is central to the
   poem's humor.
2. What sort of portrait of the poet-speaker emerges from this very brief
   poem?

KEVIN PIERCE (B. 1958)

Proof of Origin   2005

*NEWSWIRE — A U.S. judge ordered a Georgia school district to remove
from textbooks stickers challenging the theory of evolution.*

Though close to their hearts is the version that starts
With Adam and Eve and no clothes,
What enables their grip as the stickers they strip
Is Darwinian thumbs that oppose.

CONSIDERATIONS FOR CRITICAL THINKING AND WRITING

1. FIRST RESPONSE. How do the rhymes contribute to the humorous tone?
2. Discuss the levels of irony in the poem.
3. How do you read the title? Can it be explained in more than one way?

CARL SANDBURG (1878–1967)

A Fence   1916

Now the stone house on the lake front is finished and the workmen
    are beginning the fence.
The palings are made of iron bars with steel points that can stab the
    life out of any man who falls on them.
As a fence, it is a masterpiece, and will shut off the rabble and all
    vagabonds and hungry men and all wandering children looking
    for a place to play.
Passing through the bars and over the steel points will go nothing
    except Death and the Rain and Tomorrow.

Considerations for Critical Thinking and Writing

1. **FIRST RESPONSE.** What is the effect of the capital letters in the final line?

2. Discuss the symbolic meaning of the fence and whether you think the symbolism is too spelled out or not.

JANE KENYON (1947–1995)

Not Writing   1993

A wasp rises to its papery
nest under the eaves
where it daubs

at the gray shape,
but seems unable
to enter its own house.

Donald Hall.

Considerations for Critical Thinking and Writing

1. **FIRST RESPONSE.** Why is the title crucial to an understanding of this poem?

2. Which words serve to reinforce the symbolic meaning that concerns writing?

JIM TILLEY (B. 1950)

Boys   2010

My friends and I couldn't buy cherry bombs
on our weekly allowances. We hoped
that plain firecrackers would be enough
to tear off arms and legs, a private's, not ours.
We were the generals — we ran the war,
decided where to plant soldiers in trenches
we sculpted in mounds left by bulldozers
on the construction site. After the flap
about the Curry boy losing an eye,
we imposed a ceasefire for a week.
Then came the all-out surge to do some
serious damage, the kind that requires you
to eat two bowls of cornflakes every day
to build your army from cereal-box toys.

10

> **WHEN I WRITE** "When I'm creating a story, I try to keep writing until I finish a draft — same for a poem, but I don't set aside a specific block of time. When the inkling of a poem is there, I write. When it's not, I go for a walk until it arrives." — JIM TILLEY

Considerations for Critical Thinking and Writing

1. FIRST RESPONSE. How does the speaker's diction and tone influence your impressions about the boys' play?

2. Despite the seemingly casual qualities of these lines, what formal elements of a sonnet does this poem employ?

3. How might you read this poem differently if it were titled "War" rather than "Boys"?

Alden Nowlan (1933–1983)

The Bull Moose   1962

Down from the purple mist of trees on the mountain,
lurching through forests of white spruce and cedar,
stumbling through tamarack swamps,
came the bull moose
to be stopped at last by a pole-fenced pasture.   5

Too tired to turn or, perhaps, aware
there was no place left to go, he stood with the cattle.
They, scenting the musk of death, seeing his great head
like the ritual mask of a blood god, moved to the other end
of the field, and waited.   10

The neighbors heard of it, and by afternoon
cars lined the road. The children teased him
with alder switches and he gazed at them
like an old, tolerant collie. The women asked
if he could have escaped from a Fair.   15

The oldest man in the parish remembered seeing
a gelded moose yoked with an ox for plowing.
The young men snickered and tried to pour beer
down his throat, while their girl friends took their pictures.

The bull moose let them stroke his tick-ravaged flanks,   20
let them pry open his jaws with bottles, let a giggling girl
plant a little purple cap
of thistles on his head.

When the wardens came, everyone agreed it was a shame
to shoot anything so shaggy and cuddlesome.   25
He looked like the kind of pet
women put to bed with their sons.

So they held their fire. But just as the sun dropped in the river
the bull moose gathered his strength
like a scaffolded king, straightened and lifted his horns   30
so that even the wardens backed away as they raised their rifles.

When he roared, people ran to their cars. All the young men
leaned on their automobile horns as he toppled.

CONSIDERATIONS FOR CRITICAL THINKING AND WRITING

1. FIRST RESPONSE. How does the speaker present the moose and the
   townspeople? How are the moose and townspeople contrasted? Discuss
   specific lines to support your response.

2. Explain how the symbols in this poem point to a conflict between
   humanity and nature. What do you think the speaker's attitude toward
   this conflict is?

JULIO MARZÁN (B. 1946)
Ethnic Poetry   1994

> WHEN I WRITE "Words you are sure convey your truest feelings or thoughts may record only sentiment, not a line of poetry, while another arrangement, different words in another tone or rhythm, unlock and reveal what you really wanted to say." — JULIO MARZÁN

The ethnic poet said: "The earth is maybe
a huge maraca / and the sun a trombone /
and life / is to move your ass / to slow beats."
The ethnic audience roasted a suckling pig.

The ethnic poet said: "Oh thank Goddy, Goddy /   5
I be me, my toenails curled downward /
deep, deep, deep into Mama earth."
The ethnic audience shook strands of sea shells.

The ethnic poet said: "The sun was created black /
so we should imagine light / and also dream /   10
a walrus emerging from the broken ice."
The ethnic audience beat on sealskin drums.

The ethnic poet said: "Reproductive organs /
Eagles nesting California redwoods /
Shut up and listen to my ancestors."   15
The ethnic audience ate fried bread and honey.

The ethnic poet said: "Something there is that
doesn't love a wall / That sends
the frozen-ground-swell under it."
The ethnic audience deeply understood humanity.   20

CONSIDERATIONS FOR CRITICAL THINKING AND WRITING

1. FIRST RESPONSE. What is the implicit definition of *ethnic poetry* in this
   poem?

2. The final stanza quotes lines from Robert Frost's "Mending Wall." Find
   and read the entire poem. Why do you think Marzán chooses these
   lines and this particular poem as one kind of ethnic poetry?

3. What is the poem's central irony? Pay particular attention to the final
   line. What is being satirized here?

4. **CONNECTION TO ANOTHER SELECTION.** Write an essay that discusses the speakers' ideas about what poetry should be in "Ethnic Poetry" and in Ruth Forman's "Poetry Should Ride the Bus" (p. 384).

Paul Muldoon (b. 1951)

Symposium   1998

You can lead a horse to water but you can't make it hold
its nose to the grindstone and hunt with the hounds.
Every dog has a stitch in time. Two heads? You've been sold
one good turn. One good turn deserves a bird in the hand.

A bird in the hand is better than no bread.   5
To have your cake is to pay Paul.
Make hay while you can still hit the nail on the head.
For want of a nail the sky might fall.

People in glass houses can't see the wood
for the new broom. Rome wasn't built between two stools.   10
Empty vessels wait for no man.

A hair of the dog is a friend indeed.
There's no fool like the fool
who's shot his bolt. There's no smoke after the horse is gone.

Considerations for Critical Thinking and Writing

1. **FIRST RESPONSE.** What meanings can you draw from the poem on a first reading? Do the lines mean more to you after subsequent readings? Why or why not?

2. To what extent are these bits of clichés and aphorisms connected to each other? Explain why you find the poem coherent or not.

3. Look up the meaning and origin of *symposium* in a dictionary. Why is this an apt title for this poem?

4. **CONNECTION TO ANOTHER SELECTION.** Discuss the use of irony in this poem and in E. E. Cummings's "next to of course god america i" (p. 418).

Mark Halliday (b. 1949)

Graded Paper   1991

On the whole this is quite successful work:
your main argument about the poet's ambivalence—

how he loves the very things he attacks —
is mostly persuasive and always engaging.

At the same time,   5
                there are spots
where your thinking becomes, for me,
alarmingly opaque, and your syntax seems to jump
backwards through unnecessary hoops,
as on p. 2 where you speak of "precognitive awareness   10
not yet disestablished by the shell that encrusts
each thing that a person actually says"
or at the top of p. 5 where your discussion of
"subverbal undertow miming the subversion of self-belief
woven counter to desire's outreach"   15
leaves me groping for firmer footholds.
(I'd have said it differently,
or rather, said something else.)
And when you say that women "could not fulfill themselves" (p. 6)
"in that era" (only forty years ago, after all!)   20
are you so sure that the situation is so different today?
Also, how does Whitman bluff his way into
your penultimate paragraph? He is the *last* poet
I would have quoted in this context!
What plausible way of behaving   25
does the passage you quote represent? Don't you think
literature should ultimately reveal possibilities for *action*?

Please notice how I've repaired your use of semicolons.

And yet, despite what may seem my cranky response,
I do admire the freshness of   30
your thinking and your style; there is
a vitality here; your sentences thrust themselves forward
with a confidence as impressive as it is cheeky. . . .
You are not
                me, finally,   35
and though this is an awkward problem, involving
the inescapable fact that you are so young, so young
it is also a delightful provocation.

Considerations for Critical Thinking and Writing

1. **First response.** How do you characterize the grader of this paper based on the comments about the paper?

2. Is the speaker a man or a woman? What makes you think so? Does the gender of the speaker affect your reading of the poem? How?

3. Explain whether or not you think the teacher's comments on the paper are consistent with the grade awarded it. How do you account for the grade?

4. **CONNECTION TO ANOTHER SELECTION.** Compare the ways in which Halliday reveals the speaker's character in this poem with the strategies used by Robert Browning in "My Last Duchess" (below).

ROBERT BROWNING (1812–1889)

My Last Duchess   1842

© Corbis.

Ferrara°

That's my last Duchess painted on the wall,
Looking as if she were alive. I call
That piece a wonder, now: Frà Pandolf's° hands
Worked busily a day, and there she stands.
Will't please you sit and look at her? I said
"Frà Pandolf" by design, for never read
Strangers like you that pictured countenance,
The depth and passion of its earnest glance,
But to myself they turned (since none puts by
The curtain I have drawn for you, but I)   10
And seemed as they would ask me, if they durst,
How such a glance came there; so, not the first
Are you to turn and ask thus. Sir, 'twas not
Her husband's presence only, called that spot
Of joy into the Duchess' cheek: perhaps   15
Frà Pandolf chanced to say "Her mantle laps
Over my lady's wrist too much," or "Paint
Must never hope to reproduce the faint
Half-flush that dies along her throat": such stuff
Was courtesy, she thought, and cause enough   20
For calling up that spot of joy. She had
A heart — how shall I say? — too soon made glad,
Too easily impressed; she liked whate'er
She looked on, and her looks went everywhere.
Sir, 'twas all one! My favor at her breast,   25
The dropping of the daylight in the West,
The bough of cherries some officious fool
Broke in the orchard for her, the white mule
She rode with round the terrace — all and each

Ferrara: In the sixteenth century, the duke of this Italian city arranged to marry a second time after the mysterious death of his very young first wife.   3 *Frà Pandolf:* A fictitious artist.

Would draw from her alike the approving speech,   30
Or blush, at least. She thanked men, — good! but thanked
Somehow — I know not how — as if she ranked
My gift of a nine-hundred-years-old name
With anybody's gift. Who'd stoop to blame
This sort of trifling? Even had you skill   35
In speech — which I have not — to make your will
Quite clear to such an one, and say, "Just this
Or that in you disgusts me; here you miss,
Or there exceed the mark" — and if she let
Herself be lessoned so, nor plainly set   40
Her wits to yours, forsooth, and made excuse,
— E'en then would be some stooping; and I choose
Never to stoop. Oh sir, she smiled, no doubt,
Whene'er I passed her; but who passed without
Much the same smile? This grew; I gave commands;   45
Then all smiles stopped together. There she stands
As if alive. Will't please you rise? We'll meet
The company below, then. I repeat,
The Count your master's known munificence
Is ample warrant that no just pretense   50
Of mine for dowry will be disallowed;
Though his fair daughter's self, as I avowed
At starting, is my object. Nay, we'll go
Together down, sir. Notice Neptune, though,
Taming a sea-horse, thought a rarity,   55
Which Claus of Innsbruck° cast in bronze for me!

Considerations for Critical Thinking and Writing

1. FIRST RESPONSE. What do you think happened to the duchess?

2. To whom is the duke addressing his remarks about the duchess in this poem? What is ironic about the situation?

3. Why was the duke unhappy with his first wife? What does this reveal about him? What does the poem's title suggest about his attitude toward women in general?

4. What seems to be the visitor's response (lines 53–54) to the duke's account of his first wife?

5. CONNECTION TO ANOTHER SELECTION. Write an essay describing the ways in which the speakers of "My Last Duchess" and Katharyn Howd Machan's "Hazel Tells LaVerne" (p. 359) inadvertently reveal themselves.

56 *Claus of Innsbruck:* Also a fictitious artist.

WILLIAM BLAKE (1757–1827)

A Poison Tree

1794

I was angry with my friend:
I told my wrath, my wrath did end.
I was angry with my foe:
I told it not, my wrath did grow.

And I water'd it in fears,   5
Night & morning with my tears;
And I sunned it with smiles,
And with soft deceitful wiles.

And it grew both day and night,
Till it bore an apple bright.   10
And my foe beheld it shine,
And he knew that it was mine,

And into my garden stole,
When the night had veild the pole;
In the morning glad I see   15
My foe outstretched beneath the tree.

CONSIDERATIONS FOR CRITICAL THINKING AND WRITING

1. FIRST RESPONSE. Considering the "apple bright" allusion in the third
   stanza, how can "A Poison Tree" be read as more than a meditation on a
   personal relationship gone bad?

2. What is the speaker's attitude toward anger and revenge? What do you
   think the speaker wants the reader's attitude to be?

17

Sounds

In a poem the words should be as pleasing to the ear as the meaning is to the mind.

— MARIANNE MOORE

© Bettmann/Corbis.

LISTENING TO POETRY

Poems yearn to be read aloud. Much of their energy, charm, and beauty come to life only when they are heard. Poets choose and arrange words for their sounds as well as for their meanings. Most poetry is best read with your lips, teeth, and tongue because they serve to articulate the effects that sound may have in a poem. When a voice is breathed into a good poem, there is pleasure in the reading, the saying, and the hearing.

The earliest poetry — before writing and painting — was chanted or sung. The rhythmic quality of such oral performances served two purposes: it helped the chanting bard remember the lines and it entertained audiences with patterned sounds of language, which were sometimes accompanied by musical instruments. Poetry has always been closely related to music. Indeed, as the word suggests, lyric poetry evolved from songs. "Western Wind" (p. 338), an anonymous Middle English lyric, survived as song long before it was written down. Had Robert Frost lived in a nonliterate society, he probably would have sung some version — a very different version to be sure — of "Acquainted with the Night" (p. 412) instead of writing it down. Even though Frost creates a speaking rather than a singing voice, the speaker's anxious tone is distinctly heard in any careful reading of the poem.

Like lyrics, early narrative poems were originally part of an anonymous oral folk tradition. A **ballad** such as "Bonny Barbara Allan" (p. 533) told a story that was sung from one generation to the next until it was finally transcribed. Since the eighteenth century, this narrative form has sometimes been imitated by poets who write **literary ballads**, a more complex and sophisticated reflection of the original ballad traditions that developed in the fifteenth century and earlier. In considering poetry as sound, we should not forget that poetry traces its beginnings to song.

Of course, reading a ballad is not the same as hearing it. Like the lyrics of a song, many poems must be heard — or at least read with listening eyes — before they can be fully understood and enjoyed. The sounds of words are a universal source of music for human beings. This has been so from ancient tribes to bards to the two-year-old child in a bakery gleefully chanting "Cuppitycake, cuppitycake!"

Listen to the sound of this poem as you read it aloud. How do the words provide, in a sense, their own musical accompaniment?

JOHN UPDIKE (1932–2009)

Player Piano   *1958*

My stick fingers click with a snicker
And, chuckling, they knuckle the keys;
Light-footed, my steel feelers flicker
And pluck from these keys melodies.

My paper can caper; abandon   5
Is broadcast by dint of my din,
And no man or band has a hand in
The tones I turn on from within.

At times I'm a jumble of rumbles,
At others I'm light like the moon,   10
But never my numb plunker fumbles,
Misstrums me, or tries a new tune.

The speaker in this poem is a piano that can play automatically by means of a mechanism that depresses keys in response to signals on a perforated roll. Notice how the speaker's voice approximates the sounds of a piano. In each stanza a predominant sound emerges from the carefully chosen words. How is the sound of each stanza tuned to its sense?

Like Updike's "Player Piano," this next poem also employs sounds to reinforce meanings.

EMILY DICKINSON (1830–1886)

A Bird came down the Walk —   *ca. 1862*

A Bird came down the Walk —
He did not know I saw —
He bit an Angleworm in halves
And ate the fellow, raw,

And then he drank a Dew   5
From a convenient Grass —
And then hopped sidewise to the Wall
To let a Beetle pass —

He glanced with rapid eyes
That hurried all around —   10
They looked like frightened Beads, I thought —
He stirred his Velvet Head

Like one in danger, Cautious,
I offered him a Crumb
And he unrolled his feathers   15
And rowed him softer home —

Than Oars divide the Ocean,
Too silver for a seam —
Or Butterflies, off Banks of Noon
Leap, plashless as they swim.   20

This description of a bird offers a close look at how differently a bird moves when it hops on the ground than when it flies in the air. On the ground the bird moves quickly, awkwardly, and irregularly as it plucks up a worm, washes it down with dew, and then hops aside to avoid a passing beetle. The speaker recounts the bird's rapid, abrupt actions from a somewhat superior, amused perspective. By describing the bird in human terms (as if, for example, it chose to eat the worm "raw"), the speaker is almost condescending. But when the attempt to offer a crumb fails and the frightened bird flies off, the speaker is left looking up instead of down at the bird.

With that shift in perspective the tone shifts from amusement to awe in response to the bird's graceful flight. The jerky movements of lines 1 to 13 give way to the smooth motion of lines 15 to 20. The pace of the first three stanzas is fast and discontinuous. We tend to pause at the end of each line, and this reinforces a sense of disconnected movements. In contrast, the final six lines are to be read as a single sentence in one flowing movement, lubricated by various sounds.

Read again the description of the bird flying away. Several *o*-sounds contribute to the image of the serene, expansive, confident flight, just as the *s*-sounds serve as smooth transitions from one line to the next. Notice how these sounds are grouped in the following vertical columns:

unrolled	softer	Too	his	Ocean	Banks
rowed	Oars	Noon	feathers	silver	plashless
home	Or		softer	seam	as
Ocean	off		Oars	Butterflies	swim

This blending of sounds (notice how "Leap, plashless" brings together the *p*- and *l*-sounds without a ripple) helps convey the bird's smooth grace in the air. Like a feathered oar, the bird moves seamlessly in its element.

The repetition of sounds in poetry is similar to the function of the tones and melodies that are repeated, with variations, in music. Just as the patterned sounds in music unify a work, so do the words in poems, which have been carefully chosen for the combinations of sounds they create. These sounds are produced in a number of ways.

The most direct way in which the sound of a word suggests its meaning is through **onomatopoeia**, which is the use of a word that resembles the sound it denotes: *quack, buzz, rattle, bang, squeak, bowwow, burp, choo-choo, ding-a-ling, sizzle*. The sound and sense of these words are closely related, but such words represent a very small percentage of the words available to us. Poets usually employ more subtle means for echoing meanings.

Onomatopoeia can consist of more than just single words. In its broadest meaning the term refers to lines or passages in which sounds help to convey meanings, as in these lines from Updike's "Player Piano":

> My stick fingers click with a snicker
> And, chuckling, they knuckle the keys.

The sharp, crisp sounds of these two lines approximate the sounds of a piano; the syllables seem to "click" against one another. Contrast Updike's rendition with the following lines:

> My long fingers play with abandon
> And, laughing, they cover the keys.

The original version is more interesting and alive because the sounds of the words are pleasurable and reinforce the meaning through a careful blending of consonants and vowels.

Alliteration is the repetition of the same consonant sounds at the beginnings of nearby words: "*d*escending *d*ewdrops," "*l*uscious *l*emons." Sometimes the term is also used to describe the consonant sounds within words: "tres*p*asser's re*p*roach," "we*dd*ed la*d*y." Alliteration is based on sound rather than spelling. "*K*een" and "*c*ar" alliterate, but "car" does not alliterate with "cite." Rarely is heavy-handed alliteration effective. Used too self-consciously, it can be distracting instead of strengthening meaning or emphasizing a relation between words. Consider the relentless *h*'s in this line: "Horrendous horrors haunted Helen's happiness." Those *h*'s certainly suggest that Helen is being pursued, but they have a more comic than serious effect because they are overdone.

Assonance is the repetition of the same vowel sound in nearby words: "as*lee*p under a tr*ee*," "*ti*me and *ti*de," "h*au*nt" and "*aw*esome," "*ea*ch *eve*ning." Both alliteration and assonance help to establish relations among words in a line or a series of lines. Whether the effect is **euphony** (lines that are musically pleasant to the ear and smooth, like the final lines of Dickinson's "A Bird came down the Walk—") or **cacophony** (lines that are discordant and difficult to pronounce, like the claim that "never my numb plunker fumbles" in Updike's "Player Piano"), the sounds of words in poetry can be as significant as the words' denotative or connotative meanings.

RHYME

Like alliteration and assonance, **rhyme** is a way of creating sound patterns. Rhyme, broadly defined, consists of two or more words or phrases that repeat the same sounds: *happy* and *snappy*. Rhyme words often have similar spellings, but that is not a requirement of rhyme; what matters is that the words sound alike: *vain* rhymes with *reign* as well as *rain*. Moreover, words may look alike but not rhyme at all. In **eye rhyme** the spellings are similar, but the pronunciations are not, as with *bough* and *cough*, or *brow* and *blow*.

Not all poems use rhyme. Many great poems have no rhymes, and many weak verses use rhyme as a substitute for poetry. These are especially apparent in commercial messages and greeting-card lines. At its worst, rhyme is merely a distracting decoration that can lead to dullness and predictability. But used skillfully, rhyme creates lines that are memorable and musical.

Here is a poem using rhyme that you might remember the next time you are in a restaurant.

RICHARD ARMOUR (1906–1989)

Going to Extremes   1954

Shake and shake
  The catsup bottle
None'll come —
  And then a lot'll.

The experience recounted in Armour's poem is common enough, but the rhyme's humor is special. The final line clicks the poem shut — an effect that is often achieved by the use of rhyme. That click provides a sense of a satisfying and fulfilled form. Rhymes have a number of uses: they can emphasize words, direct a reader's attention to relations between words, and provide an overall structure for a poem.

Rhyme is used in the following poem to imitate the sound of cascading water.

ROBERT SOUTHEY (1774–1843)

From "The Cataract of Lodore"   1820

"How does the water
Come down at Lodore?"

· · · · · · · · · · · · · · · · · · · ·

From its sources which well
In the tarn on the fell;
From its fountains   5
In the mountains,
Its rills and its gills;
Through moss and through brake,
It runs and it creeps
For awhile, till it sleeps   10
In its own little lake.
And thence at departing,
Awakening and starting,
It runs through the reeds
And away it proceeds,   15
Through meadow and glade,
In sun and in shade,
And through the wood-shelter,
Among crags in its flurry,
Helter-skelter,   20
Hurry-scurry.
Here it comes sparkling,
And there it lies darkling;
Now smoking and frothing
Its tumult and wrath in,   25
Till in this rapid race
On which it is bent,
It reaches the place
Of its steep descent.

· · · · · · · · · · · · · · · · · · · ·

Dividing and gliding and sliding,   30
And falling and brawling and sprawling,
And driving and riving and striving,

And sprinkling and twinkling and wrinkling,
And sounding and bounding and rounding,
And bubbling and troubling and doubling,   35
And grumbling and rumbling and tumbling,
And clattering and battering and shattering;
Retreating and beating and meeting and sheeting,
Delaying and straying and playing and spraying,
Advancing and prancing and glancing and dancing,   40
Recoiling, turmoiling and toiling and boiling,
And gleaming and streaming and steaming and beaming,
And rushing and flushing and brushing and gushing,
And flapping and rapping and clapping and slapping,
And curling and whirling and purling and twirling,   45
And thumping and plumping and bumping and jumping,
And dashing and flashing and splashing and clashing;
And so never ending, but always descending,
Sounds and motions forever and ever are blending,
All at once and all o'er, with a mighty uproar;   50
And this way the water comes down at Lodore.

    This deluge of rhymes consists of "Sounds and motions forever and ever . . . blending" (line 49). The pace quickens as the water creeps from its mountain source and then descends in rushing cataracts. As the speed of the water increases, so do the number of rhymes, until they run in fours: "dashing and flashing and splashing and clashing" (line 47). Most rhymes meander through poems instead of flooding them; nevertheless, Southey's use of rhyme suggests how sounds can flow with meanings. "The Cataract of Lodore" has been criticized, however, for overusing onomatopoeia. Some readers find the poem silly; others regard it as a brilliant example of sound effects. What do you think?

    A variety of types of rhyme is available to poets. The most common form, **end rhyme**, comes at the ends of lines (lines 14–17).

> It runs through the reeds
>   And away it proceeds,
> Through meadow and glade,
>   In sun and in shade.

Internal rhyme places at least one of the rhymed words within the line, as in "Dividing and gliding and sliding" (line 30) or, more subtly, in the fourth and final words of "In mist or cloud, on mast or shroud."

    The rhyming of single-syllable words such as *glade* and *shade* is known as **masculine rhyme**, as we see in these lines from A. E. Housman:

> Loveliest of trees, the cherry now
> Is hung with bloom along the bough.

Rhymes using words of more than one syllable are also called masculine when the same sound occurs in a final stressed syllable, as in *defend*, *contend*; *betray*, *away*. A ***feminine rhyme*** consists of a rhymed stressed syllable followed by one or more rhymed unstressed syllables, as in *butter*, *clutter*; *gratitude*, *attitude*; *quivering*, *shivering*. This rhyme is evident in John Millington Synge's verse:

> Lord confound this surly sister,
> Blight her brow and blotch and blister.

All of the examples so far have been ***exact rhymes*** because they share the same stressed vowel sounds as well as any sounds that follow the vowel. In ***near rhyme*** (also called ***off rhyme***, ***slant rhyme***, and ***approximate rhyme***), the sounds are almost but not exactly alike. There are several kinds of near rhyme. One of the most common is ***consonance***, an identical consonant sound preceded by a different vowel sound: *home*, *same*; *worth*, *breath*; *trophy*, *daffy*. Near rhyme can also be achieved by using different vowel sounds with identical consonant sounds: *sound*, *sand*; *kind*, *conned*; *fellow*, *fallow*. The dissonance of *blade* and *blood* in the following lines from Wilfred Owen helps to reinforce their grim tone:

> Let the boy try along this bayonet-blade
> How cold steel is, and keen with hunger of blood.

Near rhymes greatly broaden the possibility for musical effects in English, a language that, compared with Spanish or Italian, contains few exact rhymes. Do not assume, however, that a near rhyme represents a failed attempt at exact rhyme. Near rhymes allow a musical subtlety and variety and can avoid the sometimes overpowering jingling effects that exact rhymes may create.

These basic terms hardly exhaust the ways in which the sounds in poems can be labeled and discussed, but the terms can help you to describe how poets manipulate sounds for effect. Read the following poem aloud and try to determine how the sounds of the lines contribute to their sense.

Andrew Hudgins (b. 1951)

The Ice-Cream Truck   2009

From blocks away the music floats
to my enchanted ears.
It builds. It's here! And then it fades —
and I explode in tears.

I kick the TV set, and scream,   5
sobbing to extort her,
while Mom stares at *One Life to Live*,
and won't give me a quarter.

I pause, change tactics, snatch a coin
from the bottom of her purse,   10
then race to catch the ice-cream truck,
ignoring Mama's curse.

I stop the truck, I start to choose —
then see I won't be eating.
I stare down at a goddamn dime,   15
and trudge home to my beating.

Considerations for Critical Thinking and Writing

1. FIRST RESPONSE. Describe the tone of each stanza. How do the rhymes serve to establish the tone?

2. Characterize the speaker. How do you reconcile what is said in the first stanza with the description in the final stanza?

3. This poem appeared in a collection by Hudgins titled *Shut Up, You're Fine: Poems for Very, Very Bad Children*. How does that context affect your reading of it?

4. CREATIVE RESPONSE. Add a four-line stanza in Hudgins's style that rhymes and concludes back at home.

POEMS FOR FURTHER STUDY

Lewis Carroll (Charles Lutwidge Dodgson/1832–1898)

Jabberwocky   *1871*

'Twas brillig, and the slithy toves
   Did gyre and gimble in the wabe:
All mimsy were the borogoves,
   And the mome raths outgrabe.

"Beware the Jabberwock, my son!   5
   The jaws that bite, the claws that catch!
Beware the Jubjub bird, and shun
   The frumious Bandersnatch!"

He took his vorpal sword in hand;
   Long time the manxome foe he sought —   10
So rested he by the Tumtum tree,
   And stood awhile in thought.

And, as in uffish thought he stood,
   The Jabberwock, with eyes of flame,
Came whiffling through the tulgey wood,   15
   And burbled as it came!

One, two! One, two! And through and through
  The vorpal blade went snicker-snack!
He left it dead, and with its head
  He went galumphing back.   20

"And hast thou slain the Jabberwock?
  Come to my arms, my beamish boy!
O frabjous day! Callooh, Callay!"
  He chortled in his joy.

'Twas brillig, and the slithy toves   25
  Did gyre and gimble in the wabe:
All mimsy were the borogoves,
  And the mome raths outgrabe.

CONSIDERATIONS FOR CRITICAL THINKING AND WRITING

1. **FIRST RESPONSE.** What happens in this poem? Does it have any meaning?

2. Not all of the words used in this poem appear in dictionaries. In *Through the Looking-Glass*, Humpty Dumpty explains to Alice that "'slithy' means 'lithe and slimy.' 'Lithe' is the same as 'active.' You see it's like a portmanteau — there are two meanings packed up into one word." Are there any other portmanteau words in the poem?

3. Which words in the poem sound especially meaningful, even if they are devoid of any denotative meanings?

4. **CONNECTION TO ANOTHER SELECTION.** Compare Carroll's strategies for creating sound and meaning with those used by Updike in "Player Piano" (p. 430).

KAY RYAN (B. 1945)

Dew   *1996*

As neatly as peas
in their green canoe,
as discretely as beads
strung in a row,
sit drops of dew
along a blade of grass.
But unattached and
subject to their weight,
they slip if they accumulate.
Down the green tongue
out of the morning sun
into the general damp,
they're gone.

© Christopher Felver/Corbis.

1. FIRST RESPONSE. How does reading the poem aloud affect your under-standing of Ryan's use of rhyme to create a particular tone?

2. Explain whether the images in the poem are simply descriptive or are presented as a means of producing a theme. What is the role of the title?

EMILY DICKINSON (1830–1886)

I heard a Fly buzz — when I died —   *ca. 1862*

I heard a Fly buzz — when I died —
The Stillness in the Room
Was like the Stillness in the Air —
Between the Heaves of Storm —

The Eyes around — had wrung them dry —   5
And Breaths were gathering firm
For that last Onset — when the King
Be witnessed — in the Room —

I willed my Keepsakes — Signed away
What portion of me be   10
Assignable — and then it was
There interposed a Fly —

With Blue — uncertain stumbling Buzz —
Between the light — and me —
And then the Windows failed — and then   15
I could not see to see —

1. FIRST RESPONSE. What was expected to happen "when the King" was "witnessed" (lines 7–8)? What happened instead?

2. Why do you think Dickinson chooses a fly rather than perhaps a bee or gnat?

3. What is the effect of the last line? Why not end the poem with "I could not see" instead of the additional "to see"?

4. Discuss the sounds in the poem. Are there any instances of onomatopoeia?

ROBERT FROST (1874–1963)

Stopping by Woods on a Snowy Evening   *1923*

Whose woods these are I think I know.
His house is in the village, though;

He will not see me stopping here
To watch his woods fill up with snow.

My little horse must think it queer   5
To stop without a farmhouse near
Between the woods and frozen lake
The darkest evening of the year.

He gives his harness bells a shake
To ask if there is some mistake.   10
The only other sound's the sweep
Of easy wind and downy flake.

The woods are lovely, dark and deep,
But I have promises to keep,
And miles to go before I sleep,   15
And miles to go before I sleep.

CONSIDERATIONS FOR CRITICAL THINKING AND WRITING

1. FIRST RESPONSE. What is the significance of the setting in this poem? How is tone conveyed by the images?

2. Although the last two lines are identical, they are not read at the same speed. Why the difference? What is achieved by the repetition?

3. What is the poem's rhyme scheme? What is the effect of the rhyme in the final stanza?

WILLIAM HEYEN (B. 1940)

The Trains   1984

Signed by Franz Paul Stangl, Commandant,
there is in Berlin a document,
an order of transmittal from Treblinka:

248 freight cars of clothing,
400,000 gold watches,   5
25 freight cars of women's hair.

Some clothing was kept, some pulped for paper.
The finest watches were never melted down.
All the women's hair was used for mattresses, or dolls.

Would these words like to use some of that same paper? 10
One of those watches may pulse in your own wrist.
Does someone you know collect dolls, or sleep on human hair?

He is dead at last, Commandant Stangl of Treblinka,
but the camp's three syllables still sound like freight cars
straining around a curve, Treblinka,   15

Treblinka. Clothing, time in gold watches,
women's hair for mattresses and dolls' heads.
Treblinka. The trains from Treblinka.

CONSIDERATIONS FOR CRITICAL THINKING AND WRITING

1. FIRST RESPONSE. How does the sound of the word *Treblinka* inform your understanding of the poem?
2. Why does the place name of Treblinka continue to resonate over time? To learn more about Treblinka, search the Web, perhaps starting at ushmm .org, the site of the United States Holocaust Memorial Museum.
3. Why do you suppose Heyen uses the word *in* instead of *on* in line 11?
4. Why is sound so important for establishing the tone of this poem? In what sense do "the camp's three syllables still sound like freight cars" (line 14)?

JEAN TOOMER (1894–1967)

Unsuspecting   *ca. 1929*

© Bettmann/Corbis.

There is a natty kind of mind
That slicks its thoughts,
Culls its oughts,
Trims its views,
Prunes its trues,
And never suspects it is a rind.

CONSIDERATIONS FOR CRITICAL THINKING AND WRITING

1. FIRST RESPONSE. What sort of person do you think is described by the speaker?
2. Comment on the poem's diction and use of rhyme. Which word (or words) do you think are the most crucial for determining the poem's central idea?
3. CONNECTION TO ANOTHER SELECTION. Discuss the tone and themes in "Unsuspecting" and in Stephen Crane's "The Wayfarer" (p. 393).

JOHN DONNE (1572–1631)

Song   *1633*

Go and catch a falling star,
  Get with child a mandrake root,°

2 *mandrake root:* This V-shaped root resembles the lower half of the human body.

Tell me where all past years are,
  Or who cleft the Devil's foot,
Teach me to hear mermaids singing,   5
  Or to keep off envy's stinging,
        And find
        What wind
Serves to advance an honest mind.

If thou be'st borne to strange sights,   10
  Things invisible to see,
Ride ten thousand days and nights,
  Till age snow white hairs on thee,
Thou, when thou return'st, wilt tell me
  All strange wonders that befell thee,   15
        And swear
        Nowhere
Lives a woman true, and fair.

If thou findst one, let me know,
  Such a pilgrimage were sweet —   20
Yet do not, I would not go,
  Though at next door we might meet;
Though she were true, when you met her,
  And last, till you write your letter,
        Yet she   25
        Will be
False, ere I come, to two or three.

CONSIDERATIONS FOR CRITICAL THINKING AND WRITING

1. **FIRST RESPONSE.** What is the speaker's tone in this poem? What is his
   view of a woman's love? What does the speaker's use of hyperbole reveal
   about his emotional state?

2. Do you think Donne wants the speaker's argument to be taken seriously? Is there any humor in the poem?

3. Most of these lines end with masculine rhymes. What other kinds of
   rhymes are used for end rhymes?

PAUL HUMPHREY (1915–2001)

Blow   1983

Her skirt was lofted by the gale;
When I, with gesture deft,
Essayed to stay her frisky sail
She luffed, and laughed, and left.

CONSIDERATIONS FOR CRITICAL THINKING AND WRITING

1. FIRST RESPONSE. How do alliteration and assonance contribute to the euphonic effects in this poem?
2. What is the poem's controlling metaphor? Why is it especially appropriate?
3. Explain the ambiguity of the title.

ROBERT FRANCIS (1901–1987)

The Pitcher   *1953*

His art is eccentricity, his aim
How not to hit the mark he seems to aim at,

His passion how to avoid the obvious,
His technique how to vary the avoidance.

The others throw to be comprehended. He   5
Throws to be a moment misunderstood.

Yet not too much. Not errant, arrant, wild,
But every seeming aberration willed.

Not to, yet still, still to communicate
Making the batter understand too late.   10

CONSIDERATIONS FOR CRITICAL THINKING AND WRITING

1. FIRST RESPONSE. Explain how each pair of lines in this poem works together to describe the pitcher's art.
2. Consider how the poem itself works the way a good pitcher does. Which lines illustrate what they describe?
3. Comment on the effects of the poem's rhymes. How are the final two lines different in their rhyme from the previous lines? How does sound echo sense in lines 9–10?
4. Write an essay that examines "The Pitcher" as an extended metaphor for talking about poetry. How well does the poem characterize strategies for writing poetry as well as pitching?

HELEN CHASIN (1938–2015)

The Word Plum   *1968*

The word *plum* is delicious

pout and push, luxury of
self-love, and savoring murmur

full in the mouth and falling
like fruit   5

taut skin
pierced, bitten, provoked into
juice, and tart flesh

question
and reply, lip and tongue   10
of pleasure.

CONSIDERATIONS FOR CRITICAL THINKING AND WRITING

1. FIRST RESPONSE. What is the effect of the repetitions of the alliteration and assonance throughout the poem? How does it contribute to the poem's meaning?

2. Which sounds in the poem are like the sounds one makes while eating a plum?

3. Discuss the title. Explain whether you think this poem is more about the word *plum* or about the plum itself. Can the two be separated in the poem?

18

Patterns of Rhythm

I would define, in brief, the Poetry of words as the Rhythmical Creation of Beauty. Its sole arbiter is Taste.

— EDGAR ALLAN POE

The rhythms of everyday life surround us in regularly recurring movements and sounds. As you read these words, your heart pulsates while somewhere else a clock ticks, a cradle rocks, a drum beats, a dancer sways, a foghorn blasts, a wave recedes, or a child skips. We may tend to overlook rhythm because it is so tightly woven into the fabric of our experience, but it is there nonetheless, one of the conditions of life. Rhythm is also one of the conditions of speech because the voice alternately rises and falls as words are stressed or unstressed and as the pace quickens or slackens. In poetry *rhythm* refers to the recurrence of stressed and unstressed sounds. Depending on how the sounds are arranged, this can result in a pace that is fast or slow, choppy or smooth.

SOME PRINCIPLES OF METER

Poets use rhythm to create pleasurable sound patterns and to reinforce meanings. "Rhythm," Edith Sitwell once observed, "might be described as, to the world of sound, what light is to the world of sight. It shapes

445

and gives new meaning." Prose can use rhythm effectively too, but prose that does so tends to be an exception. The following exceptional lines are from a speech by Winston Churchill to the House of Commons after Allied forces lost a great battle to German forces at Dunkirk during World War II:

> We shall not flag or fail. We shall go on to the end. We shall fight in France, we shall fight on the seas and oceans, we shall fight with growing confidence and growing strength in the air, we shall defend our island, whatever the cost may be, we shall fight on the beaches, we shall fight on the landing grounds, we shall fight in the fields and in the streets, we shall fight in the hills; we shall never surrender.

The stressed repetition of "we shall" bespeaks the resolute singleness of purpose that Churchill had to convey to the British people if they were to win the war. Repetition is also one of the devices used in poetry to create rhythmic effects. In the following excerpt from "Song of the Open Road," Walt Whitman urges the pleasures of limitless freedom on his reader:

> Allons!° the road is before us!   *Let's go!*
> It is safe — I have tried it — my own feet have
>   tried it well — be not detain'd!
> Let the paper remain on the desk unwritten,
>   and the book on the shelf unopen'd!
> Let the tools remain in the workshop! Let the
>   money remain unearn'd!
> Let the school stand! mind not the cry of the
>   teacher!   5
> Let the preacher preach in his pulpit! Let
>   the lawyer plead in the court, and the
>   judge expound the law.
>
> Camerado,° I give you my hand!   *friend*
> I give you my love more precious than
>   money,
> I give you myself before preaching or law;
> Will you give me yourself? will you come
>   travel with me?   10
> Shall we stick by each other as long as we live?

These rhythmic lines quickly move away from conventional values to the open road of shared experiences. Their recurring sounds are created not by rhyme or alliteration and assonance (see Chapter 17) but by the repetition of words and phrases.

Although the repetition of words and phrases can be an effective means of creating rhythm in poetry, the more typical method consists of patterns of accented or unaccented syllables. Words contain syllables that are either stressed or unstressed. A **stress** (or **accent**) places more emphasis on one syllable than on another. We say "*syl*lable" not "syl*lable*," "*em*phasis" not "em*pha*sis." We routinely stress syllables when we speak: "*Is* she con*tent* with the *con*tents of the *yel*low *pack*age?" To distinguish between two people we might say "Is *she* con*tent* . . . ?" In this way stress can be used to emphasize a particular word in a sentence. Poets often arrange words so that the desired meaning is suggested by the rhythm; hence emphasis is controlled by the poet rather than left entirely to the reader.

When a rhythmic pattern of stresses recurs in a poem, the result is **meter**. Taken together, all the metrical elements in a poem make up what is called the poem's **prosody**. **Scansion** consists of measuring the stresses in a line to determine its metrical pattern. Several methods can be used to mark lines. One widely used system uses ´ for a stressed syllable and ˘ for an unstressed syllable. In a sense, the stress mark represents the equivalent of tapping one's foot to a beat:

> Híckŏrў, díckŏrў, dóck,
>
> Thĕ móuse răn úp thĕ clóck.
>
> Thĕ clóck strŭck ŏne,
>
> Ănd dowń hĕ ruń,
>
> Híckŏrў, díckŏrў, dóck.

In the first two lines and the final line of this familiar nursery rhyme we hear three stressed syllables. In lines 3 and 4, where the meter changes for variety, we hear just two stressed syllables. The combination of stresses provides the pleasure of the rhythm we hear.

To hear the rhythms of "Hickory, dickory, dock" does not require a formal study of meter. Nevertheless, an awareness of the basic kinds of meter that appear in English poetry can enhance your understanding of how a poem achieves its effects. Understanding the sound effects of a poem and having a vocabulary with which to discuss those effects can intensify your pleasure in poetry. Although the study of meter can be extremely technical, the terms used to describe the basic meters of English poetry are relatively easy to comprehend.

The **foot** is the metrical unit by which a line of poetry is measured. A foot usually consists of one stressed and one or two unstressed syllables. A vertical line is used to separate the feet: "Thĕ clóck | strŭck óne" consists of two feet. A foot of poetry can be arranged in a variety of patterns; here are five of the chief ones:

Foot	Pattern	Example
iamb	˘ ´	ăwáy

trochee	´ ˘	lóvel̆y
anapest	˘ ˘ ´	ŭndĕrstánd
dactyl	´ ˘ ˘	déspĕratĕ
spondee	´ ´	déad sét

The most common lines in English poetry contain meters based on iambic feet. However, even lines that are predominantly iambic will often include variations to create particular effects. Other important patterns include trochaic, anapestic, and dactylic feet. The spondee is not a sustained meter but occurs for variety or emphasis.

Iambic
    Whăt képt | hĭs eyés | frŏm gív | ĭng báck | thĕ gáze
Trochaic
    Hé wăs | loúdĕr | thán thĕ | préachĕr
Anapestic
    Ĭ am̆ callĕd | tŏ thĕ frónt | ŏf thĕ roóm
Dactylic
    Sin̆g it̆ all | mérrĭly̆

These meters have different rhythms and can create different effects. Iambic and anapestic are known as **rising meters** because they move from unstressed to stressed sounds, while trochaic and dactylic are known as **falling meters**. Anapests and dactyls tend to move more lightly and rapidly than iambs or trochees. Although no single kind of meter can be considered always better than another for a given subject, it is possible to determine whether the meter of a specific poem is appropriate for its subject. A serious poem about a tragic death would most likely not be well served by lilting rhythms. Keep in mind, too, that though one or another of these four basic meters might constitute the predominant rhythm of a poem, variations can occur within lines to change the pace or call attention to a particular word.

A **line** is measured by the number of feet it contains. Here, for example, is an iambic line with three feet: "Ĭf shĕ | shŏuld wrĭte | ă nóte." These are the names for line lengths:

monometer: one foot	pentameter: five feet
dimeter: two feet	hexameter: six feet
trimeter: three feet	heptameter: seven feet
tetrameter: four feet	octameter: eight feet

By combining the name of a line length with the name of a foot, we can describe the metrical qualities of a line concisely. Consider, for example, the pattern of feet and length of this line:

I didn't want the boy to hit the dog.

The iambic rhythm of this line falls into five feet; hence it is called *iambic pentameter*. Iambic is the most common pattern in English poetry because its rhythm appears so naturally in English speech and writing. Unrhymed iambic pentameter is called *blank verse*; Shakespeare's plays are built on such lines.

Less common than the iamb, trochee, anapest, or dactyl is the *spondee*, a two-syllable foot in which both syllables are stressed (´´). Note the effect of the spondaic foot at the beginning of this line:

Déad sét | ăgaińst | thĕ pĺan | hĕ wént | ăwáy.

Spondees can slow a rhythm and provide variety and emphasis, particularly in iambic and trochaic lines. Also less common is a pyrrhic foot, which consists of two unstressed syllables, as in Shakespeare's "A horse! A horse! My kingdom for a horse!" Pyrrhic feet are typically variants for iambic verse rather than predominant patterns in lines. A line that ends with a stressed syllable is said to have a *masculine ending*, whereas a line that ends with an extra unstressed syllable is said to have a *feminine ending*. Consider, for example, these two lines from Timothy Steele's "Waiting for the Storm" (the entire poem appears on p. 452):

feminine: Thĕ sánd | ăt m̆y féet | grŏw cóld | eř,

masculine: Thĕ dam̆p | aír chíll | ănd spréad.

The effects of English meters are easily seen in the following lines by Samuel Taylor Coleridge, in which the rhythm of each line illustrates the meter described in it:

Samuel Taylor Coleridge (1772–1834)

Mnemonic   1803

Trochee trips from long to short;
From long to long in solemn sort
Slow Spondee stalks; strong foot yet ill able
Ever to come up with Dactylic trisyllable.
Iambics march from short to long —
With a leap and a bound the swift Anapests throng.

CONSIDERATIONS FOR CRITICAL THINKING AND WRITING

1. FIRST RESPONSE. Scan each of the lines and see how this little handbook of a poem works.

2. Memorize this poem (Coleridge wrote it for his son). By doing so, you will have learned from a master.

The speed of a line is also affected by the number of pauses in it. A pause within a line is called a *caesura* and is indicated by a double vertical line (||). A caesura can occur anywhere within a line and need not be indicated by punctuation:

> Camerado, || I give you my hand!
> I give you my love || more precious than
> money.

A slight pause occurs within each of these lines and at its end. Both kinds of pauses contribute to the lines' rhythm.

When a line has a pause at its end, it is called an ***end-stopped line***. Such pauses reflect normal speech patterns and are often marked by punctuation. A line that ends without a pause and continues into the next line for its meaning is called a ***run-on line***. Running over from one line to another is also called ***enjambment***. The first and eighth lines of the following poem are run-on lines; the rest are end-stopped.

WILLIAM WORDSWORTH (1770–1850)

My Heart Leaps Up   1807

My heart leaps up when I behold
  A rainbow in the sky:
So was it when my life began;
So is it now I am a man;
So be it when I shall grow old,
  Or let me die!
The child is father of the Man;
And I could wish my days to be
Bound each to each by natural piety.

Run-on lines have a different rhythm from end-stopped lines. Lines 3 and 4 and lines 8 and 9 are iambic, but the effect of their two rhythms is very different when we read these lines aloud. The enjambment of lines 8 and 9 reinforces their meaning; just as the "days" are bound together, so are the lines.

The rhythm of a poem can be affected by several devices: the kind and number of stresses within lines, the length of lines, and the kinds of pauses that appear within lines or at their ends. In addition, as we saw in Chapter 17, the sound of a poem is affected by alliteration, assonance, rhyme, and consonance. These sounds help to create rhythms by controlling our pronunciations, as in the following lines excerpted from "An Essay on Criticism," a poem by Alexander Pope:

> Soft is the strain when Zephyr gently blows,
> And the smooth stream in smoother
>   numbers flows;
> But when loud surges lash the sounding
>   shore,
> The hoarse, rough verse should like the
>   torrent roar.

These lines are effective because their rhythm and sound work with their meaning.

Suggestions for Scanning a Poem

These suggestions should help you in talking about a poem's meter.

1. After reading the poem through, read it aloud and mark the stressed syllables in each line. Then mark the unstressed syllables.

2. From your markings, identify what kind of foot is dominant (iambic, trochaic, dactylic, or anapestic) and divide the lines into feet, keeping in mind that the vertical line marking a foot may come in the middle of a word as well as at its beginning or end.

3. Determine the number of feet in each line. Remember that there may be variations; some lines may be shorter or longer than the predominant meter. What is important is the overall pattern. Do not assume that variations represent the poet's inability to fulfill the overall pattern. Notice the effects of variations and whether they emphasize words and phrases or disrupt your expectation for some other purpose.

4. Listen for pauses within lines and mark the caesuras; many times there will be no punctuation to indicate them.

5. Recognize that scansion does not always yield a definitive measurement of a line. Even experienced readers may differ over the scansion of a given line. What is important is not a precise description of the line but an awareness of how a poem's rhythms contribute to its effects.

The following poem demonstrates how you can use an understanding of meter and rhythm to gain a greater appreciation for what a poem is saying.

TIMOTHY STEELE (B. 1948)

Waiting for the Storm   1986

Bréeze sént | ă wrínk | lǐng dárk | nĕss
Acróss | thĕ bay. || Ĭ knélt
Bĕnéath | ăn úp | turnĕd bóat,
Ănd, mó | mĕnt bў mó | mĕnt, félt

Thĕ sánd | ăt mў féet | grŏw cóld | ĕr,
Thĕ damp | áir chíll | ănd spréad.
Thĕn thĕ | fírst ráin | drŏps sóund | ĕd
Ŏn thĕ húll | ăbóve | mў héad.

The predominant meter of this poem is iambic trimeter, but there is plenty of variation as the storm rapidly approaches and finally begins to pelt the sheltered speaker. The emphatic spondee ("Breeze sent") pushes the darkness quickly across the bay while the caesura at the end of the sentence in line 2 creates a pause that sets up a feeling of suspense and expectation that is measured in the ticking rhythm of line 4, a run-on line that brings us into the chilly sand and air of the second stanza. Perhaps the most impressive sound effect used in the poem appears in the second syllable of "sounded" in line 7. That "ed" precedes the sound of the poem's final word, "head," just as if it were the first drop of rain hitting the hull above the speaker. The visual, tactile, and auditory images make "Waiting for the Storm" an intense sensory experience.

This next poem also reinforces meanings through its use of meter and rhythm.

WILLIAM BUTLER YEATS (1865-1939)

That the Night Come   1912

Shĕ líved | ĭn stórm | ănd strífe,
Hĕr soúl | hăd súch | dĕsíre
Fŏr whát | proŭd déath | măy bríng
Thăt ĭt | coŭld nót | ĕndúre

Thĕ cóm | mŏn goód | ŏf life,   5

Bŭt livéd | aš 'twére | ă kíng

Thăt packéd | hĭs már | rĭăge dáy

Wĭ thn bán | nĕrét | ănd pén | nŏn,

Trúmpĕt | ănd két | tlĕdrŭm,

Ănd thĕ | oŭtrág | eoŭs cán | nŏn,   10

Tŏ bún | dlĕ timĕ | ăwáy

Thăt thĕ | night comĕ.

Scansion reveals that the predominant meter here is iambic trimeter: each line contains three stressed and unstressed syllables that form a regular, predictable rhythm through line 7. That rhythm is disrupted, however, when the speaker compares the woman's longing for what death brings to a king's eager anticipation of his wedding night. The king packs the day with noisy fanfares and celebrations to fill up time and distract himself. Unable to accept "The common good of life," the woman fills her days with "storm and strife." In a determined effort "To bundle time away," she, like the king, impatiently awaits the night.

Lines 8–10 break the regular pattern established in the first seven lines. The extra unstressed syllable in lines 8 and 10 along with the trochaic feet in lines 9 ("Trúmpĕt") and 10 ("Ănd thĕ") interrupt the basic iambic trimeter and parallel the woman's and the king's frenetic activity. These lines thus echo the inability of the woman and king to "endure" regular or normal time. The last line is the most irregular in the poem. The final two accented syllables sound like the deep resonant beats of a kettledrum or a cannon firing. The words "night come" dramatically remind us that what the woman anticipates is not a lover but the mysterious finality of death. The meter serves, then, in both its regularity and variations to reinforce the poem's meaning and tone.

The following poems are especially rich in their rhythms and sounds. As you read and study them, notice how patterns of rhythm and the sounds of words reinforce meanings and contribute to the poems' effects. And, perhaps most important, read the poems aloud so that you can hear them.

POEMS FOR FURTHER STUDY

JOHN MALONEY (B. 1947)

Good!   *1999*

The ball goes up off glass and rebounded
down the court, outlet flung to the quick guard
like clicking seconds: he dribbles, hounded

by hands, calls the play, stops short, looking hard
for a slant opening, fakes it twice, passes   5
into the center — he lobs to the small
forward, top of the key, a pick: asses
crash (the pick-and-roll), he cuts, bumps, the ball
reaches him as he turns, dribbles, sends it
back to the baseline, forward back to him,   10
jump — and in midair, twisting, he bends it
over a tangle of arms — SHOOTS, the rim
rattles as it jerks against the back joints,
and into the net, trippingly drop two points.

CONSIDERATIONS FOR CRITICAL THINKING AND WRITING

1. FIRST RESPONSE. Comment on the effects of the lines' rhythms.

2. Notice the precise pattern of rhyme. How is that related to the action in the poem?

3. CONNECTION TO ANOTHER SELECTION. Compare the diction and tone in "Good!" and in Jim Tilley's "Boys" (p. 421).

WILLIAM TROWBRIDGE (B. 1941)

Drumming behind You in the High School Band   1989

Rehearsing in street clothes after school,
we measured off the football field
in the spice and chill of early fall.
Through roll-off, counterpoint, and turn,
by the grunt and pop of blocking drill,   5
I marked the cadence of switching hips
no martial air could ever hold.
How left was left, how right was right!
We had a rhythm all our own
and made them march to it, slowing "The Stars   10
and Stripes Forever" as the sun stretched
our shadows toward the rising moon
and my heart kept stepping on my heels.

CONSIDERATIONS FOR CRITICAL THINKING AND WRITING

1. FIRST RESPONSE. Describe the various "cadences" of this poem.

2. How are the rhythms of the lines related to their meaning?

3. Using the images from the poem to make your point, discuss whether the speaker is simply an ogling cad or something else.

Virginia Hamilton Adair (1913–2004)

Pro Snake   1998

Some say the Bible teaches fear of women, snakes,
and God, who killed his manchild for our sakes
and puts a mark beside our least mistakes,
and beats us all until our spirit breaks.

Must we believe his godly finger shakes
at Eve for every apple pie she bakes?
I'd rather take my chances with the snakes.

Considerations for Critical Thinking and Writing

1. FIRST RESPONSE. Scan the poem, marking the stressed and unstressed
   syllables. Which words are particularly stressed? Why?
2. Every line ends with the same rhyme. Why do you suppose Adair chose
   that scheme? How does it affect the tone of the poem?
3. Is there a serious theme coiled in the humor of "Pro Snake"?

Alice Jones (b. 1949)

The Foot   1993

Our improbable support, erected
on the osseous architecture
of the calcaneus, talus, cuboid,
navicular, cuneiforms, metatarsals,
phalanges, a plethora of hinges,   5

all strung together by gliding
tendons, covered by the pearly
plantar fascia, then fat-padded
to form the sole, humble surface
of our contact with earth.   10

Here the body's broadest tendon
anchors the heel's fleshy base,
the finely wrinkled skin stretches
forward across the capillaried arch,
to the ball, a balance point.   15

A wide web of flexor tendons
and branched veins maps the dorsum,
fades into the stub-laden bone

splay, the stuffed sausage sacks
of toes, each with a tuft   20

of proximal hairs to introduce
the distal nail, whose useless
curve remembers an ancestor,
the vanished creature's wild
and necessary claw.   25

CONSIDERATIONS FOR CRITICAL THINKING AND WRITING

1. FIRST RESPONSE. What is the effect of the diction? What sort of tone is
   established by the use of anatomical terms? How do the terms affect the
   rhythm?

2. Jones has described the form of "The Foot" as "five stubby stanzas." Explain why the lines of this poem may or may not warrant this description of the stanzas.

ROBERT HERRICK (1591–1674)

Delight in Disorder   1648

A sweet disorder in the dress
Kindles in clothes a wantonness.
A lawn° about the shoulders thrown   *linen scarf*
Into a fine distraction;
An erring lace, which here and there   5
Enthralls the crimson stomacher,
A cuff neglectful, and thereby
Ribbons to flow confusedly;
A winning wave, deserving note,
In the tempestuous petticoat;   10
A careless shoestring, in whose tie
I see a wild civility;
Do more bewitch me than when art
Is too precise in every part.

CONSIDERATIONS FOR CRITICAL THINKING AND WRITING

1. FIRST RESPONSE. Why does the speaker in this poem value "disorder" so
   highly? How do the poem's organization and rhythmic order relate to its
   theme? Are they "precise in every part" (line 14)?

2. Which words in the poem indicate disorder? Which words indicate the
   speaker's response to that disorder? What are the connotative meanings
   of each set of words? Why are they appropriate? What do they suggest
   about the woman and the speaker?

3. Write a short essay in which you agree or disagree with the speaker's
   views on dress.

E. E. CUMMINGS (1894–1962)

O sweet spontaneous   1920

O sweet spontaneous
earth how often have
the
doting

   fingers of   5
prurient philosophers pinched
and
poked

thee
, has the naughty thumb   10
of science prodded
thy

   beauty   .how
often have religions taken
thee upon their scraggy knees   15
squeezing and

buffeting thee that thou mightest conceive
gods
   (but
true   20

to the incomparable
couch of death thy
rhythmic
lover

   thou answerest   25

them only with

  spring)

CONSIDERATIONS FOR CRITICAL THINKING AND WRITING

1. FIRST RESPONSE. What is the controlling metaphor that Cummings uses to characterize philosophers, scientists, and theologians? How is the earth portrayed?

2. In what sense is spring the answer to the issues raised in the poem?

3. To what extent does the arrangement of lines on the page serve to establish rhythm?

WILLIAM BLAKE (1757–1827)

The Lamb   *1789*

© Corbis.

    Little Lamb, who made thee?
    Dost thou know who made thee?
Gave thee life, and bid thee feed
By the stream and o'er the mead;
Gave thee clothing of delight,
Softest clothing, wooly, bright;
Gave thee such a tender voice,
Making all the vales rejoice?
    Little Lamb, who made thee?
    Dost thou know who made thee?   10

    Little Lamb, I'll tell thee,
    Little Lamb, I'll tell thee:
He is callèd by thy name,
For he calls himself a Lamb.
He is meek, and he is mild;   15
He became a little child.
I a child, and thou a lamb,
We are callèd by his name.
    Little Lamb, God bless thee!
    Little Lamb, God bless thee!   20

CONSIDERATIONS FOR CRITICAL THINKING AND WRITING

1. **FIRST RESPONSE.** This poem is from Blake's *Songs of Innocence*. Describe its tone. How do the meter, rhyme, and repetition help to characterize the speaker's voice?

2. Why is it significant that the animal addressed by the speaker is a lamb? What symbolic value would be lost if the animal were, for example, a doe?

3. How does the second stanza answer the question raised in the first? What is the speaker's view of the creation?

WILLIAM BLAKE (1757–1827)

The Tyger   *1794*

Tyger! Tyger! burning bright
In the forests of the night,
What immortal hand or eye
Could frame thy fearful symmetry?

In what distant deeps or skies   5
Burnt the fire of thine eyes?

On what wings dare he aspire?
What the hand dare seize the fire?

And what shoulder, and what art,
Could twist the sinews of thy heart?   10
And when thy heart began to beat,
What dread hand? and what dread feet?

What the hammer? what the chain?
In what furnace was thy brain?
What the anvil? what dread grasp   15
Dare its deadly terrors clasp?

When the stars threw down their spears,
And watered heaven with their tears,
Did he smile his work to see?
Did he who made the Lamb make thee?   20

Tyger! Tyger! burning bright
In the forests of the night,
What immortal hand or eye
Dare frame thy fearful symmetry?

Considerations for Critical Thinking and Writing

1. **FIRST RESPONSE.** This poem from Blake's *Songs of Experience* is often paired with "The Lamb." Describe the poem's tone. Is the speaker's voice the same here as in "The Lamb"? Which words are repeated, and how do they contribute to the tone?

2. What is revealed about the nature of the tiger by the words used to describe its creation? What do you think the tiger symbolizes?

3. Unlike in "The Lamb," more than one question is raised in "The Tyger." What are these questions? Are they answered?

4. **CONNECTION TO ANOTHER SELECTION.** Compare the rhythms in "The Lamb" and "The Tyger." Each basically uses a seven-syllable line, but the effects are very different. Why?

5. **CONNECTION TO ANOTHER SELECTION.** Using these two poems as the basis of your discussion, describe what distinguishes innocence from experience.

Robert Frost (1874–1963)

"Out, Out —"°   *1916*

The buzz-saw snarled and rattled in the yard
And made dust and dropped stove-length sticks of wood,
Sweet-scented stuff when the breeze drew across it.

"*Out, Out—*": From Act V, Scene v, of Shakespeare's *Macbeth*. See page 395.

And from there those that lifted eyes could count
Five mountain ranges one behind the other   5
Under the sunset far into Vermont.
And the saw snarled and rattled, snarled and rattled,
As it ran light, or had to bear a load.
And nothing happened: day was all but done.
Call it a day, I wish they might have said   10
To please the boy by giving him the half hour
That a boy counts so much when saved from work.
His sister stood beside them in her apron
To tell them "Supper." At the word, the saw,
As if to prove saws knew what supper meant,   15
Leaped out at the boy's hand, or seemed to leap—
He must have given the hand. However it was,
Neither refused the meeting. But the hand!
The boy's first outcry was a rueful laugh,
As he swung toward them holding up the hand   20
Half in appeal, but half as if to keep
The life from spilling. Then the boy saw all—
Since he was old enough to know, big boy
Doing a man's work, though a child at heart—
He saw all spoiled. "Don't let him cut my hand off—   25
The doctor, when he comes. Don't let him, sister!"
So. But the hand was gone already.
The doctor put him in the dark of ether.
He lay and puffed his lips out with his breath.
And then—the watcher at his pulse took fright.   30
No one believed. They listened at his heart.
Little—less—nothing!—and that ended it.
No more to build on there. And they, since they
Were not the one dead, turned to their affairs.

CONSIDERATIONS FOR CRITICAL THINKING AND WRITING

1. **FIRST RESPONSE.** This narrative poem is about the accidental death of
   a Vermont boy. What is the purpose of the story? Some readers have
   argued that the final lines reveal the speaker's callousness and indifference. What do you think?

2. How does Frost's allusion to *Macbeth* contribute to the meaning of this
   poem? Does the speaker seem to agree with the view of life expressed in
   Macbeth's lines?

3. Explain how the rhythm of lines 30–31 is related to the action they
   describe.

4. **CONNECTION TO ANOTHER SELECTION.** Compare the tone and theme
   of "'Out, Out—'" with those of Stephen Crane's "A Man Said to the
   Universe" (p. 419).

19

Poetic Forms

William Hathaway.

Writing a poem is like repacking a small suitcase for a long trip over and over. The balance of want and need.

—WILLIAM HATHAWAY

Poems come in a variety of shapes. Although the best poems always have their own unique qualities, many of them also conform to traditional patterns. Frequently the *form* of a poem — its overall structure or shape — follows an already established design. A poem that can be categorized by the patterns of its lines, meter, rhymes, and stanzas is considered a *fixed form* because it follows a prescribed model such as a sonnet. However, poems written in a fixed form do not always fit models precisely; writers sometimes work variations on traditional forms to create innovative effects.

Not all poets are content with variations on traditional forms. Some prefer to create their own structures and shapes. Poems that do not conform to established patterns of meter, rhyme, and stanza are called *free verse* or *open form* poetry. (See Chapter 20 for further discussion of open forms.) This kind of poetry creates its own ordering principles through the careful arrangement of words and phrases in line lengths that embody rhythms appropriate to the meaning. Modern and contemporary poets in particular have learned to use the blank space on the page as a significant functional element (for a vivid example, see E. E. Cummings's "l(a," p. 337). Good poetry

461

of this kind is structured in ways that can be as demanding, interesting, and satisfying as fixed forms. Open and fixed forms represent different poetic styles, but they are identical in the sense that both use language in concentrated ways to convey meanings, experiences, emotions, and effects.

SOME COMMON POETIC FORMS

A familiarity with some of the most frequently used fixed forms of poetry is useful because it allows for a better understanding of how a poem works. Classifying patterns allows us to talk about the effects of established rhythm and rhyme and to recognize how significant variations from them affect the pace and meaning of the lines. An awareness of form also allows us to anticipate how a poem is likely to proceed. As we shall see, a sonnet creates a different set of expectations in a reader from those of, say, a limerick. A reader isn't likely to find in limericks the kind of serious themes that often make their way into sonnets. The discussion that follows identifies some of the important poetic forms frequently encountered in English poetry.

The shape of a fixed-form poem is often determined by the way in which the lines are organized into stanzas. A *stanza* consists of a grouping of lines, set off by a space, that usually has a set pattern of meter and rhyme. This pattern is ordinarily repeated in other stanzas throughout the poem. What is usual is not obligatory, however; some poems may use a different pattern for each stanza, somewhat like paragraphs in prose.

Traditionally, though, stanzas do share a common **rhyme scheme**, the pattern of end rhymes. We can map out rhyme schemes by noting patterns of rhyme with lowercase letters: the first rhyme sound is designated *a*, the second becomes *b*, the third *c*, and so on. Using this system, we can describe the rhyme scheme in the following poem this way: *aabb, ccdd, eeff*.

A. E. HOUSMAN (1859–1936)

Loveliest of trees, the cherry now   1896

Loveliest of trees, the cherry now	*a*
Is hung with bloom along the bough,	*a*
And stands about the woodland ride	*b*
Wearing white for Eastertide.	*b*
Now, of my threescore years and ten,	*c*
Twenty will not come again,	*c*
And take from seventy springs a score,	*d*
It only leaves me fifty more.	*d*
And since to look at things in bloom	*e*
Fifty springs are little room,	*e*
About the woodlands I will go	*f*
To see the cherry hung with snow.	*f*

5

10

Considerations for Critical Thinking and Writing

1. FIRST RESPONSE. What is the speaker's attitude in this poem toward time and life?
2. Why is spring an appropriate season for the setting rather than, say, winter?
3. Paraphrase each stanza. How do the images in each reinforce the poem's themes?
4. Lines 1 and 12 are not intended to rhyme, but they are close. What is the effect of the near rhyme of "now" and "snow"? How does the rhyme enhance the theme?

Poets often create their own stanzaic patterns; hence there is an infinite number of kinds of stanzas. One way of talking about stanzaic forms is to describe a given stanza by how many lines it contains.

A *couplet* consists of two lines that usually rhyme and have the same meter; couplets are frequently not separated from each other by space on the page. A *heroic couplet* consists of rhymed iambic pentameter. Here is an example from Alexander Pope's "Essay on Criticism":

> One science only will one genius fit;   *a*
>
> So vast is art, so narrow human wit: *a*
>
> Not only bounded to peculiar arts,   *b*
>
> But oft in those confined to single parts.   *b*

A *tercet* is a three-line stanza. When all three lines rhyme, they are called a *triplet*. Two triplets make up this captivating poem.

ROBERT HERRICK (1591–1674)

Upon Julia's Clothes   *1648*

Whenas in silks my Julia goes,   *a*
Then, then, methinks, how sweetly flows   *a*
That liquefaction of her clothes.   *a*

Next, when I cast mine eyes, and see   *b*
That brave vibration, each way free,   *b*
O, how that glittering taketh me!   *b*

Considerations for Critical Thinking and Writing

1. FIRST RESPONSE. What purpose does alliteration serve in this poem?
2. Comment on the effect of the meter. How is it related to the speaker's description of Julia's clothes?
3. Look up the word *brave* in the *Oxford English Dictionary*. Which of its meanings is appropriate to describe Julia's movement? Some readers

interpret lines 4–6 to mean that Julia has no clothes on. What do you think?

4. CONNECTION TO ANOTHER SELECTION. Compare the tone of this poem with that of Paul Humphrey's "Blow" (p. 442). Are the situations and speakers similar? Is there any difference in tone between these two poems?

Terza rima consists of an interlocking three-line rhyme scheme: *aba, bcb, cdc, ded*, and so on. Dante's *Divine Comedy* uses this pattern, as does Robert Frost's "Acquainted with the Night" (p. 412).

A *quatrain*, or four-line stanza, is the most common stanzaic form in the English language and can have various meters and rhyme schemes (if any). The most common rhyme schemes are *aabb, abba, aaba*, and *abcb*. This last pattern is especially characteristic of the popular **ballad stanza**, which consists of alternating eight- and six-syllable lines. Samuel Taylor Coleridge adopted this pattern in "The Rime of the Ancient Mariner"; here is one representative stanza:

> All in a hot and copper sky
> The bloody Sun, at noon,
> Right up above the mast did stand,
> No bigger than the Moon.

There are a number of longer stanzaic forms, and the list of types of stanzas could be extended considerably, but knowing these three most basic patterns should prove helpful to you in talking about the form of a great many poems. In addition to stanzaic forms, there are fixed forms that characterize entire poems. Lyric poems can be, for example, sonnets, villanelles, sestinas, or epigrams.

Sonnet

The **sonnet** has been a popular literary form in English since the sixteenth century, when it was adopted from the Italian *sonnetto*, meaning "little song." A sonnet consists of fourteen lines, usually written in iambic pentameter. Because the sonnet has been such a favorite form, writers have experimented with many variations on its essential structure. Nevertheless, there are two basic types of sonnets: the Italian and the English.

The **Italian sonnet** (also known as the **Petrarchan sonnet**, from the fourteenth-century Italian poet Petrarch) divides into two parts. The first eight lines (the **octave**) typically rhyme *abbaabba*. The final six lines (the **sestet**) may vary; common patterns are *cdecde, cdcdcd*, and *cdccdc*. Very often the octave presents a situation, an attitude, or a problem that the sestet comments upon or resolves, as in John Keats's "On First Looking into Chapman's Homer."

JOHN KEATS (1795–1821)

On First Looking into Chapman's Homer°   *1816*

© Corbis.

Much have I traveled in the realms of gold,
    And many goodly states and kingdoms
        seen;
    Round many western islands have I been
Which bards in fealty to Apollo° hold.
Oft of one wide expanse had I been told
    That deep-browed Homer ruled as his
        demesne;
    Yet did I never breathe its pure serene°   *atmosphere*
Till I heard Chapman speak out loud and bold:
Then felt I like some watcher of the skies
    When a new planet swims into his ken;   10
Or like stout Cortez° when with eagle eyes
    He stared at the Pacific — and all his men
Looked at each other with a wild surmise —
    Silent, upon a peak in Darien.

Chapman's Homer: Before reading George Chapman's (ca. 1560–1634) poetic Elizabethan translations of Homer's *Iliad* and *Odyssey*, Keats had known only stilted and pedestrian eighteenth-century translations.   4 *Apollo:* Greek god of poetry. 11 *Cortez:* Vasco Núñez de Balboa, not Hernando Cortés, was the first European to sight the Pacific from Darien, a peak in Panama.

CONSIDERATIONS FOR CRITICAL THINKING AND WRITING

1. FIRST RESPONSE. How do the images shift from the octave to the sestet? How does the tone change? Does the meaning change as well?

2. What is the controlling metaphor of this poem?

3. What is it that the speaker discovers?

4. How does the rhythm of the lines change between the octave and the sestet? How does that change reflect the tones of both the octave and the sestet?

5. Does Keats's mistake concerning Cortés and Balboa affect your reading of the poem? Explain why or why not.

The Italian sonnet pattern is also used in the next sonnet, but notice that the thematic break between octave and sestet comes within line 9 rather than between lines 8 and 9. This unconventional break helps to reinforce the speaker's impatience with the conventional attitudes he describes.

WILLIAM WORDSWORTH (1770–1850)

The World Is Too Much with Us   1807

The world is too much with us; late and soon,
Getting and spending, we lay waste our powers;
Little we see in Nature that is ours;
We have given our hearts away, a sordid boon!
This Sea that bares her bosom to the moon;   5
The winds that will be howling at all hours,
And are up-gathered now like sleeping flowers;
For this, for everything, we are out of tune;
It moves us not. — Great God! I'd rather be
A Pagan suckled in a creed outworn;   10
So might I, standing on this pleasant lea,
Have glimpses that would make me less forlorn;
Have sight of Proteus rising from the sea;
Or hear old Triton blow his wreathèd horn.

CONSIDERATIONS FOR CRITICAL THINKING AND WRITING

1. FIRST RESPONSE. What is the speaker's complaint in this sonnet? How do the conditions described affect him?

2. Look up "Proteus" and "Triton." What do these mythological allusions contribute to the sonnet's tone?

3. What is the effect of the personification of the sea and wind in the octave?

4. CONNECTION TO ANOTHER SELECTION. Compare the theme of this sonnet with that of Sherman Alexie's "The Facebook Sonnet" (p. 469).

The **English sonnet**, more commonly known as the **Shakespearean sonnet**, is organized into three quatrains and a couplet, which typically rhyme *abab cdcd efef gg*. This rhyme scheme is more suited to English poetry because English has fewer rhyming words than Italian. English sonnets, because of their four-part organization, also have more flexibility about where thematic breaks can occur. Frequently, however, the most pronounced break or turn comes with the concluding couplet.

In the following Shakespearean sonnet, the three quatrains compare the speaker's loved one to a summer's day and explain why the loved one is even more lovely. The couplet bestows eternal beauty and love upon both the loved one and the sonnet.

WILLIAM SHAKESPEARE (1564–1616)

Shall I compare thee to a summer's day?   *1609*

Shall I compare thee to a summer's day?
Thou art more lovely and more temperate:
Rough winds do shake the darling buds of May,
And summer's lease hath all too short a date.
Sometime too hot the eye of heaven shines,   5
And often is his gold complexion dimmed;
And every fair from fair sometime declines,
By chance, or nature's changing course, untrimmed.
But thy eternal summer shall not fade,
Nor lose possession of that fair thou ow'st°   *possess*   10
Nor shall death brag thou wand'rest in his shade,
When in eternal lines to time thou grow'st.
    So long as men can breathe or eyes can see,
    So long lives this, and this gives life to thee.

CONSIDERATIONS FOR CRITICAL THINKING AND WRITING

1. FIRST RESPONSE. Describe the shift in tone and subject matter that begins in line 9.
2. Why is the speaker's loved one more lovely than a summer's day? What qualities does he admire in the loved one?
3. What does the couplet say about the relation between art and love?
4. Which syllables are stressed in the final line? How do these syllables relate to the line's meaning?

Sonnets have been the vehicles for all kinds of subjects, including love, death, politics, and cosmic questions. Although most sonnets tend to treat their subjects seriously, this fixed form does not mean a fixed expression; humor is also possible in it. Compare this next Shakespearean sonnet with "Shall I compare thee to a summer's day?" They are, finally, both love poems, but their tones are markedly different.

WILLIAM SHAKESPEARE (1564–1616)

My mistress' eyes are nothing like the sun   *1609*

My mistress' eyes are nothing like the sun;
Coral is far more red than her lips' red;
If snow be white, why then her breasts are dun;
If hairs be wires, black wires grow on her head.

I have seen roses damasked red and white,   5
But no such roses see I in her cheeks;
And in some perfumes is there more delight
Than in the breath that from my mistress reeks.
I love to hear her speak, yet well I know
That music hath a far more pleasing sound;   10
I grant I never saw a goddess go:
My mistress, when she walks, treads on the ground.
     And yet, by heaven, I think my love as rare
     As any she,° belied with false compare.   *lady*

CONSIDERATIONS FOR CRITICAL THINKING AND WRITING

1. FIRST RESPONSE. What does "mistress" mean in this sonnet? Write a description of this particular mistress based on the images used in the sonnet.

2. What sort of person is the speaker? Does he truly love the woman he describes?

3. In what sense are this sonnet and "Shall I compare thee to a summer's day?" about poetry as well as love?

R. S. GWYNN (B. 1948)
Shakespearean Sonnet   2010

With a first line taken from the tv listings

A man is haunted by his father's ghost.
Boy meets girl while feuding families fight.
A Scottish king is murdered by his host.
Two couples get lost on a summer night.
A hunchback murders all who block his way.   5
A ruler's rivals plot against his life.
A fat man and a prince make rebels pay.
A noble Moor has doubts about his wife.
An English king decides to conquer France.
A duke learns that his best friend is a she.   10
A forest sets the scene for this romance.
An old man and his daughters disagree.
A Roman leader makes a big mistake.
A sexy queen is bitten by a snake.

CONSIDERATIONS FOR CRITICAL THINKING AND WRITING

1. FIRST RESPONSE. How many Shakespearean plays can you identify from the fourteen encapsulated plots that make up this poem?

2. Discuss the significance of the title.

3. CREATIVE RESPONSE. Try your hand at creating a poem — a sonnet or another form — in whole or in part from TV listings.

THOMAS HARDY (1840–1928)

At the Altar-Rail

1914

"My bride is not coming, alas!" says the groom,
And the telegram shakes in his hand. "I own
It was hurried! We met at a dancing-room
When I went to the Cattle-Show alone,
And then, next night, where the Fountain leaps,   5
And the Street of the Quarter-Circle sweeps.

"Ay, she won me to ask her to be my wife —
'Twas foolish perhaps! — to forsake the ways
Of the flaring town for a farmer's life.
She agreed. And we fixed it. Now she says: 10
It's sweet of you, dear, to prepare me a nest,
But a swift, short, gay life suits me best.
What I really am you have never gleaned;
I had eaten the apple ere you were weaned."

CONSIDERATIONS FOR CRITICAL THINKING AND WRITING

1. FIRST RESPONSE. To what extent are the reader's expectations disrupted by the content of the poem in relation to its title?

2. Describe the type of sonnet Hardy has written here.

3. What is the speaker's tone? Consider whether or not that is also the tone Hardy creates for the reader.

SHERMAN ALEXIE (B. 1966)

The Facebook Sonnet

2011

Welcome to the endless high-school
Reunion. Welcome to past friends
And lovers, however kind or cruel.
Let's undervalue and unmend

The present. Why can't we pretend   5
Every stage of life is the same?
Let's exhume, resume, and extend
Childhood. Let's all play the games

That occupy the young. Let fame
And shame intertwine. Let one's search   10
For God become public domain.
Let church.com become our church.

Let's sign up, sign in, and confess
Here at the altar of loneliness.

Considerations for Critical Thinking and Writing

1. FIRST RESPONSE. Why does a fixed form rather than an open form seem especially appropriate for the themes of this poem?
2. What type of sonnet is this?
3. How might Facebook be regarded as the "altar of loneliness" (line 14)? Explain why you agree or disagree with the speaker's assessment.

Villanelle

The **villanelle** is a fixed form consisting of nineteen lines of any length divided into six stanzas: five tercets and a concluding quatrain. The first and third lines of the initial tercet rhyme; these rhymes are repeated in each subsequent tercet (*aba*) and in the final two lines of the quatrain (*abaa*). Moreover, line 1 appears in its entirety as lines 6, 12, and 18, while line 3 appears as lines 9, 15, and 19. This form may seem to risk monotony, but in competent hands a villanelle can create haunting echoes, as in Dylan Thomas's "Do Not Go Gentle into That Good Night."

Dylan Thomas (1914–1953)

Do Not Go Gentle into That Good Night   1952

Do not go gentle into that good night,
Old age should burn and rave at close of day;
Rage, rage against the dying of the light.

Though wise men at their end know dark is right,
Because their words had forked no lightning they   5
Do not go gentle into that good night.

Good men, the last wave by, crying how bright
Their frail deeds might have danced in a green bay,
Rage, rage against the dying of the light.

Wild men who caught and sang the sun in flight,   10
And learn, too late, they grieved it on its way,
Do not go gentle into that good night.

Grave men, near death, who see with blinding sight
Blind eyes could blaze like meteors and be gay,
Rage, rage against the dying of the light.   15

And you, my father, there on the sad height,
Curse, bless, me now with your fierce tears, I pray.
Do not go gentle into that good night.
Rage, rage against the dying of the light.

Considerations for Critical Thinking and Writing

1. FIRST RESPONSE. How does Thomas vary the meanings of the poem's two
   refrains: "Do not go gentle into that good night" and "Rage, rage against
   the dying of the light"?
2. Thomas's father was close to death when this poem was written. How
   does the tone contribute to the poem's theme?
3. How is "good" used in line 1?
4. Characterize the men who are "wise" (line 4), "Good" (7), "Wild" (10),
   and "Grave" (13).
5. What do figures of speech contribute to this poem?
6. Discuss this villanelle's sound effects.

Sestina

Although the *sestina* usually does not rhyme, it is perhaps an even more
demanding fixed form than the villanelle. A sestina consists of thirty-nine
lines of any length divided into six six-line stanzas and a three-line concluding stanza called an *envoy*. The difficulty lies in repeating the six words at
the ends of the first stanza's lines at the ends of the lines in the other five six-
line stanzas as well. Those words must also appear in the final three lines,
where they often resonate important themes. The sestina originated in the
Middle Ages, but contemporary poets continue to find it a fascinating and
challenging form.

Florence Cassen Mayers (b. 1940)

All-American Sestina   1996

One nation, indivisible
two-car garage
three strikes you're out
four-minute mile
five-cent cigar   5
six-string guitar

six-pack Bud
one-day sale
five-year warranty
two-way street   10
fourscore and seven years ago
three cheers

three-star restaurant
sixty-
four-dollar question   15
one-night stand
two-pound lobster
five-star general

five-course meal
three sheets to the wind   20
two bits
six-shooter
one-armed bandit
four-poster

four-wheel drive   25
five-and-dime
hole in one
three-alarm fire
sweet sixteen
two-wheeler   30

two-tone Chevy
four rms, hi flr, w/vu
six-footer
high five
three-ring circus   35
one-room schoolhouse

two thumbs up, five-karat diamond
Fourth of July, three-piece suit
six feet under, one-horse town

CONSIDERATIONS FOR CRITICAL THINKING AND WRITING

1. **FIRST RESPONSE.** Discuss the significance of the title; what is "All-American" about this sestina?

2. How is the structure of this poem different from that of a conventional sestina? (What structural requirement does Mayers add for this sestina?)

3. Do you think important themes are raised by this poem, as is traditional for a sestina? If so, what are they? If not, what is being played with by using this convention?

4. **CONNECTION TO ANOTHER SELECTION.** Describe and compare the strategy used to create meaning in "All-American Sestina" with that used by E. E. Cummings in "next to of course god america i" (p. 418).

Epigram

An *epigram* is a brief, pointed, and witty poem. Although most rhyme and they are often written in couplets, epigrams take no prescribed form. Instead, they are typically polished bits of compressed irony, satire, or paradox. Here is an epigram that defines itself.

SAMUEL TAYLOR COLERIDGE (1772–1834)

What Is an Epigram? 1802

What is an epigram? A dwarfish whole;
Its body brevity, and wit its soul.

These additional examples by David McCord and Paul Laurence Dunbar satisfy Coleridge's definition.

DAVID MCCORD (1897–1997)

Epitaph on a Waiter 1954

By and by
God caught his eye.

PAUL LAURENCE DUNBAR (1872–1906)

Theology 1896

There is a heaven, for ever, day by day,
The upward longing of my soul doth tell
    me so.
There is a hell, I'm quite as sure; for pray,
If there were not, where would my
        neighbors go?

© Corbis.

CONSIDERATIONS FOR CRITICAL THINKING AND WRITING

1. **FIRST RESPONSE.** In what sense is each of these two epigrams, as Coleridge puts it, a "dwarfish whole"?

2. Explain how all three epigrams, in addition to being witty, make a serious point.

3. CREATIVE RESPONSE. Try writing a few epigrams that say something memorable about whatever you choose to focus on.

Limerick

The *limerick* is always light and humorous. Its usual form consists of five predominantly anapestic lines rhyming *aabba*; lines 1, 2, and 5 contain three feet, while lines 3 and 4 contain two. Limericks have delighted everyone from schoolchildren to sophisticated adults, and they range in subject matter from the simply innocent and silly to the satiric or obscene. The sexual humor helps to explain why so many limericks are written anonymously. Here is one that is more concerned with physics than physiology.

ARTHUR HENRY REGINALD BULLER (1874–1944)

There was a young lady named Bright   1923

There was a young lady named Bright,
Whose speed was far faster than light,
    She set out one day,
    In a relative way,
And returned home the previous night.

This next one is a particularly clever definition of a limerick.

LAURENCE PERRINE (1915–1995)

The limerick's never averse   1982

The limerick's never averse
To expressing itself in a terse
    Economical style,
    And yet, all the while,
The limerick's *always* a verse.

CONSIDERATIONS FOR CRITICAL THINKING AND WRITING

1. FIRST RESPONSE. How does this limerick differ from others you know? How is it similar?

2. Scan Perrine's limerick. How do the lines measure up to the traditional fixed metrical pattern?

3. **CREATIVE RESPONSE.** Try writing a limerick. Use the following basic pattern.

    ◡ ◡ ◜   ◡ ◡ ◜   ◡ ◡ ◜
    ◡ ◡ ◜   ◡ ◡ ◜   ◡ ◡ ◜
               ◡ ◡ ◜   ◡ ◡ ◜
               ◡ ◡ ◜   ◡ ◡ ◜
    ◡ ◡ ◜   ◡ ◡ ◜   ◡ ◡ ◜

You might begin with a friend's name or the name of your school or town. Your instructor is, of course, fair game, too, provided your tact matches your wit.

Haiku

Another brief fixed poetic form, borrowed from the Japanese, is the *haiku*. A haiku is usually described as consisting of seventeen syllables organized into three unrhymed lines of five, seven, and five syllables. Owing to language difference, however, English translations of haiku are often only approximated, because a Japanese haiku exists in time (Japanese syllables have duration). The number of syllables in our sense is not as significant as the duration in Japanese. These poems typically present an intense emotion or vivid image of nature, which, in the Japanese, is also designed to lead to a spiritual insight.

MATSUO BASHŌ (1644–1694)

Under cherry trees
date unknown

Under cherry trees
Soup, the salad, fish and all . . .
Seasoned with petals.

CAROLYN KIZER (1925–2014)

After Bashō
1984

Tentatively, you
slip onstage this evening,
pallid, famous moon.

AMY LOWELL (1874–1925)

Last night it rained

1921

Last night it rained.
Now, in the desolate dawn,
Crying of blue jays.

GARY SNYDER (B. 1930)

A Dent in a Bucket

2004

Hammering a dent out of a bucket
  a woodpecker
     answers from the woods

CONSIDERATIONS FOR CRITICAL THINKING AND WRITING

1. FIRST RESPONSE. What different emotions do these four haiku evoke?
2. What differences and similarities are there between the effects of a haiku and those of an epigram?
3. CREATIVE RESPONSE. Compose a haiku. Try to make it as allusive and suggestive as possible.

Elegy

An elegy in classical Greek and Roman literature was written in alternating hexameter and pentameter lines. Since the seventeenth century, however, the term *elegy* has been used to describe a lyric poem written to commemorate someone who is dead. The word is also used to refer to a serious meditative poem produced to express the speaker's melancholy thoughts. Elegies no longer conform to a fixed pattern of lines and stanzas, but their characteristic subject is related to death and their tone is mournfully contemplative.

BEN JONSON (1573–1637)

On My First Son

1603

Farewell, thou child of my right hand,° and joy.
My sin was too much hope of thee, loved boy;
Seven years thou wert lent to me, and I thee pay,
Exacted by thy fate, on the just day.°   *his birthday*
Oh, could I lose all father° now. For why   *fatherhood* 5
Will man lament the state he should envy? —

---

1 *child of my right hand:* This phrase translates the Hebrew name "Benjamin," Jonson's son.

To have so soon 'scaped world's and flesh's rage,
And, if no other misery, yet age.
Rest in soft peace, and asked, say, "Here doth lie
Ben Jonson his best piece of poetry,"   10
For whose sake henceforth all his vows be such
As what he loves may never like too much.

Considerations for Critical Thinking and Writing

1. **First Response.** Describe the tone of this elegy. What makes it so emotionally convincing?

2. In what sense is Jonson's son "his best piece of poetry" (line 10)?

3. Interpret the final two lines. Do they seem consistent with the rest of the poem? Why or why not?

Andrew Hudgins (b. 1951)

Elegy for My Father, Who Is Not Dead   *1991*

One day I'll lift the telephone
and be told my father's dead. He's ready.
In the sureness of his faith, he talks
about the world beyond this world
as though his reservations have   5
been made. I think he wants to go,
a little bit — a new desire
to travel building up, an itch
to see fresh worlds. Or older ones.
He thinks that when I follow him   10
he'll wrap me in his arms and laugh,
the way he did when I arrived
on earth. I do not think he's right.
He's ready. I am not. I can't
just say good-bye as cheerfully   15
as if he were embarking on a trip
to make my later trip go well.
I see myself on deck, convinced
his ship's gone down, while he's convinced
I'll see him standing on the dock   20
and waving, shouting, Welcome back.

Considerations for Critical Thinking and Writing

1. **First Response.** Why does this speaker elegize his father if the father "is not dead"?

2. How does the speaker's view of immortality differ from his father's?

3. Explain why you think this is an optimistic or a pessimistic poem — or explain why these two categories fail to describe the poem.

4. In what sense can this poem be regarded as an elegy?

5. CONNECTION TO ANOTHER SELECTION. Write an essay comparing attitudes toward death in this poem and in Dylan Thomas's "Do Not Go Gentle into That Good Night" (p. 470). Both speakers invoke their fathers, nearer to death than they are; what impact does this invocation have?

Ode

An **ode** is characterized by a serious topic and formal tone, but no prescribed formal pattern describes all odes. In some odes the pattern of each stanza is repeated throughout, while in others each stanza introduces a new pattern. Odes are lengthy lyrics that often include lofty emotions conveyed by a dignified style. Typical topics include truth, art, freedom, justice, and the meaning of life. Frequently such lyrics tend to be more public than private, and their speakers often use apostrophe.

ALEXANDER POPE (1688–1744)

Ode on Solitude   1700

Happy the man, whose wish and care
A few paternal acres bound,
Content to breathe his native air,
   In his own ground.

Whose herds with milk, whose fields with bread,   5
Whose flocks supply him with attire,
Whose trees in summer yield him shade,
   In winter fire.

Blest, who can unconcernedly find
Hours, days, and years slide soft away,   10
In health of body, peace of mind,
   Quiet by day,

Sound sleep by night; study and ease,
Together mixed; sweet recreation;
And innocence, which most does please,   15
   With meditation.

Thus let me live, unseen, unknown;
Thus unlamented let me die;
Steal from the world, and not a stone
   Tell where I lie.   20

Considerations for Critical Thinking and Writing

1. FIRST RESPONSE. This poem is singularly populated. What implicit distinction does the speaker make between solitude and loneliness?

2. Explain why "Ode on Solitude" can be accurately described as an ode.

3. How does the happy contentment expressed by the language in the first stanza anticipate the resolute wish expressed in the final stanza?

4. CONNECTION TO ANOTHER SELECTION. Write an essay comparing the themes of "Ode on Solitude" and Sherman Alexie's "The Facebook Sonnet" (p. 469).

Parody

A *parody* is a humorous imitation of another, usually serious, work. It can take any fixed or open form because parodists imitate the tone, language, and shape of the original. While a parody may be teasingly close to a work's style, it typically deflates the subject matter to make the original seem absurd. Parody can be used as a kind of literary criticism to expose the defects in a work, but it is also very often an affectionate acknowledgment that a well-known work has become both institutionalized in our culture and fair game for some fun. Read Robert Frost's "The Road Not Taken" (p. 542) and then study this parody.

Blanche Farley (b. 1937)

The Lover Not Taken   1984

Committed to one, she wanted both
And, mulling it over, long she stood,
Alone on the road, loath
To leave, wanting to hide in the undergrowth.
This new guy, smooth as a yellow wood   5

Really turned her on. She liked his hair,
His smile. But the other, Jack, had a claim
On her already and she had to admit, he did wear
Well. In fact, to be perfectly fair,
He understood her. His long, lithe frame   10

Beside hers in the evening tenderly lay.
Still, if this blond guy dropped by someday,
Couldn't way just lead on to way?
No. For if way led on and Jack
Found out, she doubted if he would ever come back.   15

Oh, she turned with a sigh.
Somewhere ages and ages hence,

She might be telling this. "And I —"
She would say, "stood faithfully by."
But by then who would know the difference?   20

With that in mind, she took the fast way home,
The road by the pond, and phoned the blond.

WHEN I WRITE "Keep your work, even if it is unfinished or not to your liking. It can be revised or even rewritten in another form. Maybe the original idea is what will prove valuable. Most importantly, despite all else going on in your life, despite rejection or feelings of discouragement, keep writing." —BLANCHE FARLEY

CONSIDERATIONS FOR CRITICAL THINKING AND WRITING

1. **FIRST RESPONSE.** To what degree does this poem duplicate Frost's style? How does it differ?

2. Does this parody seem successful to you? Explain what you think makes a successful parody.

3. **CREATIVE RESPONSE.** Choose a poet whose work you know reasonably well or would like to know better and determine what is characteristic about his or her style. Then choose a poem to parody. It's probably best to attempt a short poem or a section of a long work. If you have difficulty selecting an author, you might consider Herrick, Blake, Keats, Dickinson, Whitman, Hughes, or Frost, as a number of their works are included in this book.

Perspective

ELAINE MITCHELL (1924–2012)

Form

1994

Is it a corset
or primal wave?
Don't try to force it.

Even endorse it
to shape and deceive.
Ouch, too tight a corset.   5

Take it off. No remorse. It
's an ace up your sleeve.
No need to force it.

Can you make a horse knit?
Who would believe?
Consider. Of course, it   10

might be a resource. Wit,
your grateful slave.
Form. Sometimes you force it,   15

sometimes divorce it
to make it behave.
So don't try to force it.
Respect a good corset.

Considerations for Critical Thinking and Writing

1. **FIRST RESPONSE.** What is the speaker's attitude toward form?
2. Explain why you think the form of this poem does or does not conform to the speaker's advice.
3. Why is the metaphor of a corset an especially apt image for this poem?

Picture Poem

By arranging lines into particular shapes, poets can sometimes organize typography into *picture poems* of what they describe. Words have been arranged into all kinds of shapes, from apples to light bulbs. Notice how the shape of this next poem embodies its meaning.

WHEN I WRITE "I've shared my poems with a friend, who's also a poet, for decades now. He marks them up and gives them back; I do the same for him. You need a sympathetic critic who is not you, to help make your poetry as strong and clear as possible to readers who are not you." —MICHAEL MCFEE

Michael McFee (b. 1954)

In Medias Res°

1985

His waist
like the plot
thickens, wedding
pants now breathtaking,
belt no longer the cinch   5
it once was, belly's cambium
expanding to match each birthday,
his body a wad of anonymous tissue
swung in the same centrifuge of years
that separates a house from its foundation,   10
undermining sidewalks grim with joggers
and loose-filled graves and families
and stars collapsing on themselves,
no preservation society capable
of plugging entropy's dike,   15
under his zipper's sneer
a belly hibernation-
soft, ready for
the kill.

In Medias Res: A Latin term for a story that begins "in the middle of things."

Considerations for Critical Thinking and Writing

1. **First Response.** Explain how the title is related to this poem's shape and meaning.

2. Identify the puns. How do they work in the poem?

3. What is "cambium" (line 6)? Why is the phrase "belly's cambium" especially appropriate?

4. What is the tone of this poem? Is it consistent throughout?

20

Open Form

I'm not very good at communicating verbally. I'm somebody who listens more than talks. I like to listen and absorb. But when I need to connect with people and I need to reach out, I write.

—RUTH FORMAN

Photograph by Christine Bennett, www.cbimages.org.

Many poems, especially those written in the past century, are composed of lines that cannot be scanned for a fixed or predominant meter. Moreover, very often these poems do not rhyme. Known as *free verse* (from the French, *vers libre*), such lines can derive their rhythmic qualities from the repetition of words, phrases, or grammatical structures; the arrangement of words on the printed page; or some other means. In recent years the term *open form* has been used in place of *free verse* to avoid the erroneous suggestion that this kind of poetry lacks all discipline and shape.

Although the following poem does not use measurable meters, it does have rhythm.

WALT WHITMAN (1819–1892)

From "I Sing the Body Electric"   1855

O my body! I dare not desert the likes of you in other men and women, nor
    the likes of the parts of you,
I believe the likes of you are to stand or fall with the likes of the soul, (and
    that they are the soul,)

I believe the likes of you shall stand or fall with my
    poems, and that they are my poems.

Man's, woman's, child's, youth's, wife's, husband's,
    mother's, father's, young man's, young
    woman's poems.

Head, neck, hair, ears, drop and tympan of the
    ears.

Eyes, eye-fringes, iris of the eye, eyebrows, and the
    waking or sleeping of the lids,

Mouth, tongue, lips, teeth, roof of the mouth, jaws,
    and the jaw-hinges,

Nose, nostrils of the nose, and the partition,

Library of Congress, Prints and
Photographs Division.

Cheeks, temples, forehead, chin, throat, back of the
    neck, neck-slue,

Strong shoulders, manly beard, scapula, hind-shoulders, and the ample
    side-round of the chest,   10

Upper-arm, armpit, elbow-socket, lower-arm, arm-sinews, arm-bones,

Wrist and wrist-joints, hand, palm, knuckles, thumb, forefinger, finger-joints,
    finger-nails,

Broad breast-front, curling hair of the breast, breast-bone, breast-side,

Ribs, belly, backbone, joints of the backbone,

Hips, hip-sockets, hip-strength, inward and outward round, man-balls,
    man-root,   15

Strong set of thighs, well carrying the trunk above,

Leg-fibers, knee, knee-pan, upper-leg, under-leg,

Ankles, instep, foot-ball, toes, toe-joints, the heel;

All attitudes, all the shapeliness, all the belongings of my or your body
    or of any one's body, male or female,

The lung-sponges, the stomach-sac, the bowels sweet and clean,   20

The brain in its folds inside the skull-frame,

Sympathies, heart-valves, palate-valves, sexuality, maternity,

Womanhood, and all that is a woman, and the man that comes from woman,

The womb, the teats, nipples, breast-milk, tears, laughter, weeping, love-looks,
    love-perturbations and risings,

The voice, articulation, language, whispering, shouting aloud,   25

Food, drink, pulse, digestion, sweat, sleep, walking, swimming,

Poise on the hips, leaping, reclining, embracing, arm-curving and tightening,

The continual changes of the flex of the mouth, and around the eyes,

The skin, the sunburnt shade, freckles, hair,

The curious sympathy one feels when feeling with the hand the naked meat
    of the body,   30

The circling rivers the breath, and breathing it in and out,

The beauty of the waist, and thence of the hips, and thence downward
    toward the knees,

The thin red jellies within you or within me, the bones and the marrow in
    the bones,

The exquisite realization of health;
O I say these are not the parts and poems of the body only, but of the soul,   35
O I say now these are the soul!

CONSIDERATIONS FOR CRITICAL THINKING AND WRITING

1. FIRST RESPONSE. What informs this speaker's attitude toward the human body?
2. Read the poem aloud. Is it simply a tedious enumeration of body parts, or do the lines achieve some kind of rhythmic cadence?

Open form poetry is sometimes regarded as formless because it is unlike the strict fixed forms of a sonnet, villanelle, or sestina. But even though open form poems may not employ traditional meters and rhymes, they still rely on an intense use of language to establish rhythms and relations between meaning and form. Open form poems use the arrangement of words and phrases on the printed page, pauses, line lengths, and other means to create unique forms that express their particular meaning and tone.

The excerpt from Whitman's "I Sing the Body Electric" demonstrates how rhythmic cadences can be aligned with meaning, but there is one kind of open form poetry that doesn't even look like poetry on a page. A ***prose poem*** is printed as prose and represents, perhaps, the most clear opposite of fixed forms. Here are two brief examples.

DAVID SHUMATE (B. 1950)

Shooting the Horse   2004

I unlatch the stall door, step inside, and stroke the silky neck of the old mare like a lover about to leave. I take an ear in hand, fold it over, and run my fingers across her muzzle. I coax her head up so I can blow into those nostrils. All part of the routine we taught each other long ago. I turn a half turn, pull a pistol from my coat, raise it to that long brow with the white blaze and place it between her sleepy eyes. I clear my throat. A sound much louder than it should be. I squeeze the trigger and the horse's feet fly out from under her as gravity gives way to a force even more austere, which we have named mercy.

CONSIDERATIONS FOR CRITICAL THINKING AND WRITING

1. FIRST RESPONSE. Describe the range of emotions that this poem produces for you.
2. Think of other words that could be substituted for *mercy* in the final line. How does your choice change the tone and theme of the poem?
3. Rearrange the poem so that its words, phrases, and sentences are set up to use the white space on the page to convey tone and meaning. Which version do you prefer? Why?

William Carlos Williams (1883–1963)
The Red Wheelbarrow   *1923*

so much depends
upon

a red wheel
barrow

glazed with rain
water

beside the white
chickens.

Considerations for Critical Thinking and Writing

1. **First response.** What "depends upon" the things mentioned in the poem? What is the effect of these images? Do they have a particular meaning?
2. Do these lines have any kind of rhythm?
3. How does this poem resemble a haiku? How is it different?

Much of the poetry published today is written in open form; however, many poets continue to take pleasure in the requirements imposed by fixed forms. Some write both fixed form and open form poetry. Each kind offers rewards to careful readers as well. Here are several more open form poems that establish their own unique patterns.

Michael Ryan (b. 1946)
I   *2013*

When did I learn the word "I"?
What a mistake. For some,
   it may be a placeholder,
    for me it's a contagion.
For some, it's a thin line, a bare wisp,   5
   just enough to be somewhere
    among the gorgeous troublesome you's.
For me, it's a thorn, a spike, its slimness
   a deceit, camouflaged like a stick insect:
    touch it and it becomes what it is: 10
ravenous slit, vertical cut, little boy
   standing upright in his white
    communion suit and black secret.

CONSIDERATIONS FOR CRITICAL THINKING AND WRITING

1. FIRST RESPONSE. What do you think the speaker is suggesting by regarding his identity as a "contagion"?

2. Explain how the poem's images evoke its subject matter.

3. What emotion do you think lines 11–13 produce in the speaker?

4. CONNECTION TO ANOTHER SELECTION. Compare the sense of one's self in "I" and in the excerpt from Walt Whitman's "I Sing the Body Electric" (p. 483).

JULIO MARZÁN (B. 1946)

The Translator at the Reception for Latin American Writers

1997

Air-conditioned introductions,
then breezy Spanish conversation
fan his curiosity to know
what country I come from.
"Puerto Rico and the Bronx."   5

Spectacled downward eyes
translate disappointment
like a poison mushroom
puffed in his thoughts as if,
after investing a sizable   10
intellectual budget, transporting
a huge cast and camera crew
to film on location
Mayan pyramid grandeur,
indigenes whose ancient gods   15
and comet-tail plumage
inspire a glorious epic
of revolution across a continent,
he received a lurid script
for a social documentary   20
rife with dreary streets
and pathetic human interest,
meager in the profits of high culture.

Understandably he turns,
catches up with the hostess,   25
praising the uncommon quality
of her offerings of cheese.

CONSIDERATIONS FOR CRITICAL THINKING AND WRITING

1. FIRST RESPONSE. What is the speaker's attitude toward the person he meets at the reception? What lines in particular lead you to that conclusion?

2. Why is that person so disappointed about the answer, "Puerto Rico and the Bronx" (line 5)?

3. Explain lines 6–23. How do they reveal both the speaker and the person encountered at the reception?

4. Why is the setting of this poem significant?

ANONYMOUS

The Frog   *date unknown*

What a wonderful bird the frog are!
When he stand he sit almost;
When he hop he fly almost.
He ain't got no sense hardly;
He ain't got no tail hardly either.
When he sit, he sit on what he ain't got almost.

CONSIDERATIONS FOR CRITICAL THINKING AND WRITING

1. FIRST RESPONSE. How is the poem a description of the speaker as well as of a frog?

2. Though this poem is ungrammatical, it does have a patterned structure. How does the pattern of sentences create a formal structure?

Charles Harper Webb (b. 1952)

Descent   *1998*

For my son

Let
there be
amino acids,
and there were: a slop
of molecules in ancient seas,
building cell walls to keep their
distance, dividing, replicating, starting
to diversify, one growing oars, one rotors, one
a wiry tail, lumping into clusters — cyanobacteria, sea-
worms, medusae, trilobites, lobe-finned fish dragging onto
land, becoming thrinaxodon, protoceratops, growing larger —
diplodocus, gorgosaurus — dying out — apatosaurus, tyrannosaurus —
mammals evolving from shrew-like deltatheridium into hyenadon, eohippus,
mammoth, saber-tooth, dire wolf, australopithecus rising on two feet, homo erectus
tramping from Africa into Europe and Asia, thriving like a weed that will grow anywhere —
jungle, desert, snow-pack — the genetic rivers flowing downhill now: a husband's skull crushed
in the Alps, a Tartar raping a green-eyed girl who dies in childbirth, whose daughter falls in
love with a Viking who takes her to Istanbul, a Celt who marries a Saxon, a weaver
who abducts the daughter of a witch, a son who steals his father's gold, a girl
who loses one eye leaping from a tree, dozens who die of smallpox,
cholera, black plague, a knight, a prostitute, thieves, carpenters,
farmers, poachers, blacksmiths, seamstresses, peddlers of
odds and ends, an Irishman who sells his family into
servitude, a Limey who jumps ship in New York,
Jews who flee Hungary, a midwife, an X-ray
machine repairman, a psychologist,
a writer, all flowing down,
converging on the great
delta, the point
of all this:
you.

Considerations for Critical Thinking and Writing

1. **FIRST RESPONSE.** What do you make of the shape of this poem? Given its content, why is the shape appropriate?

2. Describe the significance of the change in diction from the first half of the poem to the second half.

3. Why do you think Webb titled the poem "Descent" rather than "Ascent"?

4. **CONNECTION TO ANOTHER SELECTION.** Compare the themes in "Descent" with those in Robert Frost's "Design" (p. 350).

NATASHA TRETHEWEY (B. 1966)

On Captivity   2007

Being all Stripped as Naked as We were Born, and endeavoring to hide our Nakedness, these Cannaballs took [our] Books, and tearing out the Leaves would give each of us a Leaf to cover us . . .

— *Jonathan Dickinson, 1699*

At the hands now
     of their captors, those
          they've named *savages*,
     do they say the word itself
savagely — hissing   5

that first letter,
     the serpent's image,
          releasing
     thought into speech?
For them now,

everything is flesh
     as if their thoughts, made
          suddenly corporeal,
     reveal even more
their nakedness —

AP Photo/Rogelio V. Solis.

the shame of it:
     their bodies rendered
          plain as the natives' —
     homely and pale,
their ordinary sex,   20

the secret illicit hairs
     that do not (cannot)
          cover enough.
     This is how they are brought,
naked as newborns,   25

to knowledge. Adam and Eve
     in the New World,
          they have only the Bible
     to cover them. Think of it:
a woman holding before her   30

the torn leaves of *Genesis*,
     and a man covering himself
          with the Good Book's
     frontispiece — his own name
inscribed on the page.   35

Considerations for Critical Thinking and Writing

1. **First response.** Trethewey has written about the sources of her epigraph: "Because the conquerors made use of the written word to claim land [in North America] inhabited by native people, I found the detail of settlers forced to cover themselves with pages torn from books a compelling irony" (*The Best American Poetry 2008*, p. 182). How does this comment contribute to the central irony in the poem?

2. Discuss Trethewey's use of alliteration in lines 1–9.

3. In what sense are the captors "brought, / naked as newborns, / to knowledge" (lines 24–26)?

David Hernandez (b. 1971)

All-American   2012

I'm this tiny, this statuesque, and everywhere
in between, and everywhere in between
bony and overweight, my shadow cannot hold
one shape in Omaha, in Tuscaloosa, in Aberdeen.
My skin is mocha brown, two shades darker   5
than taupe, your question is racist, nutmeg, beige,
I'm not offended by your question at all.
Penis or vagina? Yes and yes. Gay or straight?
Both boxes. Bi, not bi, who cares, stop
fixating on my sex life, Jesus never leveled   10
his eye to a bedroom's keyhole. I go to church
in Tempe, in Waco, the one with the exquisite
stained glass, the one with a white spire
like the tip of a Klansman's hood. Churches
creep me out, I never step inside one,   15
never utter hymns, Sundays I hide my flesh
with camouflage and hunt. I don't hunt
but wish every deer wore a bulletproof vest
and fired back. It's cinnamon, my skin,
it's more sandstone than any color I know.   20
I voted for Obama, McCain, Nader, I was too
apathetic to vote, too lazy to walk one block,
two blocks to the voting booth. For or against
a woman's right to choose? Yes, for and against.
For waterboarding, for strapping detainees   25
with snorkels and diving masks. Against burning
fossil fuels, let's punish all those smokestacks
for eating the ozone, bring the wrecking balls,
but build more smokestacks, we need jobs
here in Harrisburg, here in Kalamazoo. Against   30
gun control, for cotton bullets, for constructing

a better fence along the border, let's raise
concrete toward the sky, why does it need
all that space to begin with? For creating
holes in the fence, adding ladders, they're not   35
here to steal work from us, no one dreams
of crab walking for hours across a lettuce field
so someone could order the Caesar salad.
No one dreams of sliding a squeegee down
the cloud-mirrored windows of a high-rise,   40
but some of us do it. Some of us sell flowers.
Some of us cut hair. Some of us carefully
steer a mower around the cemetery grounds.
Some of us paint houses. Some of us monitor
the power grid. Some of us ring you up   45
while some of us crisscross a parking lot
to gather the shopping carts into one long,
rolling, clamorous and glittering backbone.

Considerations for Critical Thinking and Writing

1. FIRST RESPONSE. How does the arrangement of lines communicate a sense of energy and vitality?

2. How does the speaker characterize the United States?

3. Discuss the tone and thematic significance of the final image in lines 46–48.

4. CONNECTION TO ANOTHER SELECTION. How does Hernandez's description of what is "All-American" compare with Julio Marzán's in "The Translator at the Reception for Latin American Writers" (p. 487)?

E. E. Cummings (1894–1962)

old age sticks   1958

old age sticks
up Keep
Off
signs)&

youth yanks them   5
down(old
age
cries No

Tres)&(pas)
youth laughs   10
(sing
old age

scolds Forbid
den Stop
Must   15
n't Don't

&)youth goes
right on
gr
owing old   20

Considerations for Critical Thinking and Writing

1. **first response.** What distinctions does the speaker make between age and youth?
2. Paraphrase each stanza. What gets lost in the process if you write out these lines as you would write an ordinary prose sentence?
3. How does the final stanza complicate the poem's central idea?

Found Poem

This next selection is a ***found poem***, unintentional verse discovered in a nonpoetic context, such as a conversation, a news story, or an advertisement. Found poems are playful reminders that the words in poems are very often the language we use every day. Whether such found language should be regarded as a poem is an issue left for you to consider.

Donald Justice (1925–2004)

Order in the Streets   *1969*

(From instructions printed on a child's toy, Christmas 1968, as reported in the New York Times)

1. 2. 3.
Switch on.

Jeep rushes
to the scene
of riot   5

Jeep goes
in all directions
by mystery action.

Jeep stops periodically
to turn hood over   10

machine gun appears
with realistic
shooting noise.

After putting down riot,
jeep goes   15
back to the headquarters.

CONSIDERATIONS FOR CRITICAL THINKING AND WRITING

1. FIRST RESPONSE. What is the effect of arranging these instructions in discrete lines? How are the language and meaning enhanced by this arrangement?

2. How does this poem connect upon the many riots that occurred throughout the United States during the late sixties?

3. CREATIVE RESPONSE. Look for phrases or sentences in ads, textbooks, labels, or directions — in anything that might inadvertently contain provocative material that would be revealed by arranging the words in verse lines. You may even discover some patterns of rhyme and rhythm. After arranging the lines, explain why you organized them as you did.

Poetry in Depth

21

A Study of Billy Collins: The Author Reflects on Five Poems

More interesting to me than what a poem means is how it travels. In the classroom, I like to substitute for the question, "What is the meaning of the poem?" other questions: "How does this poem go?" or "How does this poem travel through itself in search of its own ending?"

— BILLY COLLINS

© Lynn Goldsmith / Corbis.

Billy Collins selected the five poems presented in this chapter and provided commentaries for each so that readers of this anthology might gain a sense of how he, a former poet laureate and teacher, writes and thinks about poetry. In his perspectives on the poems, Collins explores a variety of literary elements ranging from the poems' origins, allusions, images, metaphors, symbols, and tone to his strategies for maintaining his integrity and sensitivity to both language and the reader. Be advised, however, that these discussions do not constitute CliffsNotes to the poems; Collins does not interpret a single one of them for us. Instead of "beating it with a hose / to find out what it really means," as he writes in his poem "Introduction to Poetry" (p. 341), he "hold[s] it up to the light" so that we can see more clearly how each poem works. He explains that the purpose of his discussions is to have students "see how a poem gets written from the opening lines, through the shifts and maneuvers of the body to whatever closure the poem manages to achieve . . . to make the process of writing a poem less mysterious without taking away the mystery that is at the heart of every good poem."

Along with Collins's illuminating and friendly tutorial, the chapter also provides some additional contexts, such as photos from the poet's personal collection; a screen shot that offers a look at his unique — and dynamic — Web presence, which includes a collection of short animated films set to his work; a draft manuscript page; and an interview with Michael Meyer.

A BRIEF BIOGRAPHY AND AN INTRODUCTION TO HIS WORK

Born in New York City in 1941, Billy Collins grew up in Queens, the only child of a nurse and an electrician. His father had hoped that he might go to the Harvard Business School, but following his own lights, after graduating from Holy Cross College, he earned a Ph.D. at the University of California, Riverside, in Romantic poetry, and then began a career in the English department at Lehman College, City University of New York, where he taught writing and literature for more than thirty years. He has also tutored writers at the National University of Ireland at Galway, Sarah Lawrence University, Arizona State University, Columbia University, and Rollins College. Along the way, he wrote poems that eventually earned him a reputation among many people as the most popular living poet in America.

Among his numerous collections of poetry are *Aimless Love* (2013), *Horoscopes for the Dead* (2011), *Ballistics* (2008), *The Trouble with Poetry* (2005), *Nine Horses* (2002), *Sailing Alone Around the Room* (2001), *Picnic, Lightning* (1998), *The Art of Drowning* (1995), *Questions About Angels* (1991), and *The Apple That Astonished Paris* (1988). Collins also edited two anthologies of contemporary poetry designed to entice high school students: *Poetry 180: A Turning Back to Poetry* (2003) and *180 More: Extraordinary Poems for Every Day* (2005). His many honors include fellowships from the New York Foundation for the Arts, the National Endowment for the Arts, and the Guggenheim Foundation. *Poetry* magazine has awarded him the Oscar Blumenthal Prize, the Bess Hokin Prize, the Frederick Bock Prize, and the Levinson Prize.

Collins characterizes himself as someone who was once a professor who wrote poems but who is now a poet who occasionally teaches. This transformation was hard earned because he didn't publish his first complete book of poems until he was in his early forties, with no expectation that twenty years later he would be named United States poet laureate (a gift of hope to writers everywhere). Just as writing poetry has been good for Billy Collins, he has been good for poetry. Both their reputations have risen simultaneously

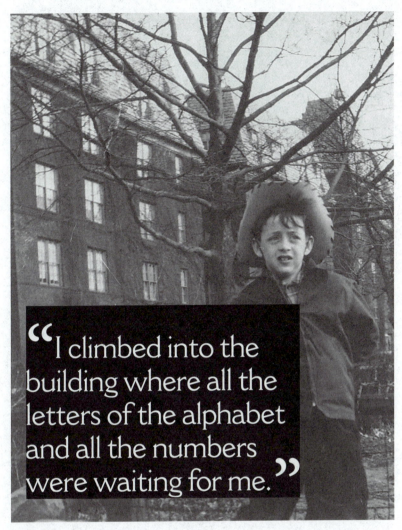

"I climbed into the building where all the letters of the alphabet and all the numbers were waiting for me."

Billy Collins on his first day as a student at St. Joan of Arc School, Jackson Heights, New York, 1948.
Reprinted with permission by Chris Calhoun Agency, © Billy Collins.

owing to his appeal to audiences that pack high school auditoriums, college halls, and public theaters all over the country. His many popular readings — including broadcasts on National Public Radio — have helped to make him a best-selling poet, a phrase that is ordinarily an oxymoron in America.

Unlike many poetry readings, Collins's are attended by readers and fans who come to whoop, holler, and cheer after nearly every poem, as well as

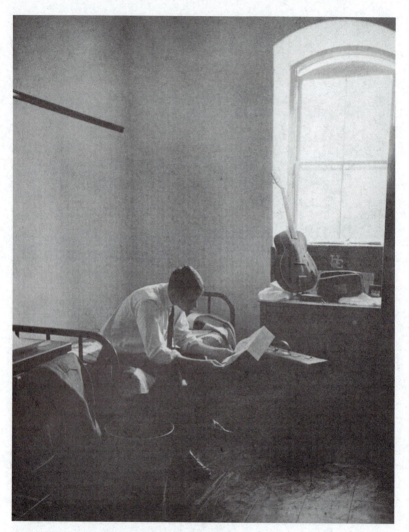

Billy Collins on his first day at Holy Cross College, 1959.
Reprinted with permission by Chris Calhoun Agency, © Billy Collins.

to laugh out loud. His audiences are clearly relieved to be in the presence of a poet who speaks to (not down to) them without a trace of pretension, superiority, or presumption. His work is welcoming and readable because he weaves observations about the commonplace materials of our lives — the notes we write in the margins of our books, the food we eat, the way we speak, even the way we think of death — into startling, evocative insights that open our eyes wider than they were before.

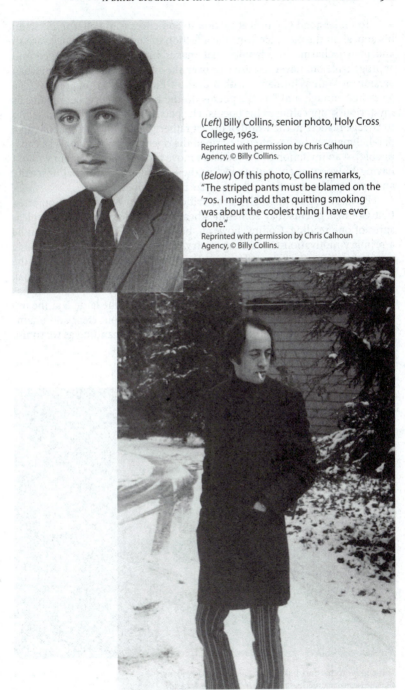

(*Left*) Billy Collins, senior photo, Holy Cross College, 1963.
Reprinted with permission by Chris Calhoun Agency, © Billy Collins.

(*Below*) Of this photo, Collins remarks, "The striped pants must be blamed on the '70s. I might add that quitting smoking was about the coolest thing I have ever done."
Reprinted with permission by Chris Calhoun Agency, © Billy Collins.

To understand Collins's attraction to audiences is to better understand his appeal on the page. He wins the affection of audiences with his warmth and genial charm, an affability that makes him appear unreserved and approachable but never intrusive or over-the-top. He is a quieter, suburban version of Walt Whitman — with a dash of Emily Dickinson's reserve. He gives just enough and lets the poems do the talking so that he remains as mysteriously appealing as his poems. His persona is well crafted and serves to engage readers in the world of his art rather than in his personal life. In a parallel manner, he has often described the openings of his poems as "hospitable" — an invitation to the reader to move further into the poem without having to worry about getting lost in the kind of self-referential obscurity and opacity that sometimes characterize modern poetry.

Perhaps not surprisingly, some critics and fellow poets have objected that Collins's poems may sometimes bear up to little more than the pleasures of one reading. Collins, however, believes immediate pleasure can be a primary motivation for reading poetry, and he argues that a poem using simple language should not be considered simpleminded. In his work the ordinary, the everyday, and the familiar often become curious, unusual, and surprising the more closely the poems are read. In interviews, he has compared a first reading of his poems to a reading of the large *E* at the top of an eye chart in an optometrist's office. What starts out clear and unambiguous gradually becomes more complicated and demanding as we squint

The poet with his dog, Luke. Scarsdale, New York, 1970s.
Reprinted with permission by Chris Calhoun Agency, © Billy Collins.

to make our way to the end. That big *E*—it might be read as "enter"—welcomes us in and gives us the confidence to enjoy the experience, but it doesn't mean that there aren't challenges ahead. The casual, "easy" read frequently becomes a thought-provoking compound of humor, irony, and unconventional wisdom. Humor is such an essential part of Collins's work that in 2004 he was the first recipient of the Poetry Foundation's Mark Twain Award for Humor in Poetry. Given this remarkable trifecta of humor, popularity, and book sales, it is hardly to be unexpected that Collins gives some of his colleagues—as Mark Twain might have put it—the "fantods," but his audiences and readers eagerly anticipate whatever poetic pleasures he will offer them next. In any case, Whitman made the point more than 150 years ago in his preface to *Leaves of Grass*: "The proof of a poet is that his country absorbs him as affectionately as he has absorbed it."

Billy Collins, in his office at Lehman College, 1984.
Reprinted with permission by Chris Calhoun Agency, © Billy Collins.

BILLY COLLINS

"How Do Poems Travel?"   2008

Asking a poet to examine his or her own work is a bit like trying to get a puppy interested in looking in a mirror. Parakeets take an interest in their own reflections but not puppies, who are too busy smelling everything and tumbling over themselves to have time for self-regard. Maybe the difficulty is that most imaginative poems issue largely from the intuitive right side of the brain, whereas literary criticism draws on the brain's more rational, analytic left side. So, writing about your own writing involves getting up, moving from one room of the brain to another, and taking all the furniture with you. When asked about the source of his work, one contemporary poet remarked that if he knew where his poems came from, he would go there and never come back. What he was implying is that much of what goes on in the creative moment takes place on a stealthy level beneath the writer's conscious awareness. If creative work did not offer access to this somewhat mysterious, less than rational region, we would all be writing annual reports or law briefs, not stories, plays, and poems.

Just because you don't know what you are doing doesn't mean you are not doing it; so let me say what I do know about the writing process. While writing a poem, I am also listening to it. As the poem gets underway, I am pushing it forward — after all, I am the one holding the pencil — but I am also ready to be pulled in the direction that the poem seems to want to go. I am willfully writing the poem, but I am also submitting to the poem's will. Emerson once compared writing poetry to ice-skating. I think he meant that both the skater on a frozen pond and the poet on the page might end up going places they didn't intend to go. And Mario Andretti, the Grand Prix driver, once remarked that "If you think everything is under control, you're just not driving fast enough."

Total control over any artistic material eliminates the possibility of surprise. I would not bother to start a poem if I already knew how it was going to end. I try to "maintain the benefits of my ignorance," as another poet put it, letting the poem work toward an understanding of itself (and of me) as I go along. In a student essay, the idea is to stick to the topic. In much imaginative poetry, the pleasure lies in finding a way to escape the initial topic, to transcend the subject and ride the poem into strange, unforeseen areas. As poet John Ashbery put it: "In the process of writing, all sorts of unexpected things happen that shift the poet away from his plan; these accidents are really what we mean whenever we talk about Poetry." Readers of poetry see only the finished product set confidently on the page; but the process of writing a poem involves uncertainty, ambiguity, improvisation, and surprise.

I think of poetry as the original travel literature in that a poem can take me to an imaginative place where I have never been. A good poem often progresses by a series of associative leaps, including sudden shifts in time and space, all of which results in a kind of mental journey. I never know the ending of the poem when I set out, but I am aware that I am moving the poem toward some destination, and when I find the ending, I recognize it right away. More interesting to me than what a poem means is how it travels. In the classroom, I like to substitute for the question, "What is the meaning of the poem?" other questions: "How does this poem go?" or "How does this poem travel through itself in search of its own ending?" Maybe a few of my poems that follow will serve as illustrations, and I hope what I have said so far will help you articulate how poems go and how they find their endings.

BILLY COLLINS

Osso Buco°   1995

I love the sound of the bone against the plate
and the fortress-like look of it
lying before me in a moat of risotto,
the meat soft as the leg of an angel
who has lived a purely airborne existence.   5
And best of all, the secret marrow,
the invaded privacy of the animal
prized out with a knife and swallowed down
with cold, exhilarating wine.

I am swaying now in the hour after dinner,   10
a citizen tilted back on his chair,
a creature with a full stomach —
something you don't hear much about in poetry,
that sanctuary of hunger and deprivation.
You know: the driving rain, the boots by the door,   15
small birds searching for berries in winter.

But tonight, the lion of contentment
has placed a warm, heavy paw on my chest,
and I can only close my eyes and listen
to the drums of woe throbbing in the distance   20
and the sound of my wife's laughter
on the telephone in the next room,
the woman who cooked the savory osso buco,
who pointed to show the butcher the ones she wanted.
She who talks to her faraway friend   25
while I linger here at the table
with a hot, companionable cup of tea,
feeling like one of the friendly natives,
a reliable guide, maybe even the chief's favorite son.

Osso Buco: An Italian veal dish; translated as "hole [buco] bone [osso]."

Somewhere, a man is crawling up a rocky hillside   30
on bleeding knees and palms, an Irish penitent
carrying the stone of the world in his stomach;
and elsewhere people of all nations stare
at one another across a long, empty table.
But here, the candles give off their warm glow,   35
the same light that Shakespeare and Izaak Walton wrote by,
the light that lit and shadowed the faces of history.
Only now it plays on the blue plates,
the crumpled napkins, the crossed knife and fork.

In a while, one of us will go up to bed   40
and the other one will follow.
Then we will slip below the surface of the night
into miles of water, drifting down and down
to the dark, soundless bottom
until the weight of dreams pulls us lower still,   45
below the shale and layered rock,
beneath the strata of hunger and pleasure,
into the broken bones of the earth itself,
into the marrow of the only place we know.

BILLY COLLINS

On Writing "Osso Buco"   *2008*

The critic Terry Eagleton pointed out that "writing is just language which can function perfectly well in the physical absence of its author." In other words, the author does not have to accompany his or her writing into the world to act as its interpreter or chaperone. One way for a poem to achieve that kind of independence is to exhibit a certain degree of clarity, at least in the opening lines. The ideal progression of a poem is from the clear to the mysterious. A poem that begins simply can engage the reader by establishing a common ground and then lead the reader into more challenging, less familiar territory. Robert Frost's poems are admirable models of this process of deepening. Of course, if the initial engagement is not made early, it's hard to see how the participation of a reader can be counted on.

"Osso Buco" opens with a gourmand's appreciation of a favorite dish, one commonly served up in Italian restaurants. The one thing I knew at the outset was that the poem was going to be a meditation on the subject of contentment. Misery, despondency, melancholy, and just plain human wretchedness are more likely to be the moods of poetry. Indeed, happiness in serious literature is often mistaken for a kind of cowlike stupidity. I thought I would address that imbalance by taking on the challenge of writing about the pleasures of a full stomach. Even the gloomiest of philosophers admits that there are occasional interruptions in the despondency that is the human lot; so why not pay those moments some poetic attention?

To me, the image of "the lion of contentment" suggested a larger set of metaphors connected to African exploration that might add glue to the poem. A metaphor can be deployed in one line of a poem and then dropped, but other times the poem develops an interest in its own language and a metaphor can be extended and explored. The result can bind together a number of disparate thoughts by giving them a common vocabulary. Thus, in this extended metaphor that begins with "the lion of contentment," "drums of woe" are heard "throbbing in the distance," and later the speaker feels like "one of the friendly natives" or "even the chief's favorite son."

In the fourth stanza, the camera pulls back from the domestic scene of the poem and its mood of contentment to survey examples of human suffering taking place elsewhere. The man with bleeding knees is a reference to the religious pilgrims who annually climb Croagh Patrick, a rocky mountain in the west of Ireland. The image of the "long, empty table" is meant to express the condition of world hunger and famine. But the poem offers those images only in contrast to its insistent theme: satisfaction. Back in the kitchen, there is the candle-lit scene of pleasures recently taken. The mention of Shakespeare and Izaak Walton, who wrote *The Compleat Angler*, a whimsical book on the pleasures of fly-fishing, adds some historic perspective and shows the speaker to be a person of some refinement, an appreciator of literature, history, and, of course, food.

The poem so far has made two noticeable maneuvers, shifting to a global then a historical perspective, but in the final stanza the poem takes its biggest turn when it hits upon the resolving metaphor of geology. The couple retires to bed—another pleasure—descends into sleep, then deeper into dreams, then deeper still through the layers of the earth and into its very center, a "marrow" which harkens back to the bone marrow of the eaten calf. Thus the poem travels from the domestic setting of a kitchen to the plains of Africa, a mountain in Ireland, then back to the kitchen before boring into the core of the earth itself—a fairly extensive journey for a poem of only fifty lines, but not untypical of the kind of ground a lyric poem can quickly cover.

BILLY COLLINS

Nostalgia   1991

Remember the 1340s? We were doing a dance called
    the Catapult.
You always wore brown, the color craze of the decade,
and I was draped in one of those capes that were popular,
the ones with unicorns and pomegranates in needlework.
Everyone would pause for beer and onions in the afternoon,   5
and at night we would play a game called "Find the Cow."
Everything was hand-lettered then, not like today.

Where has the summer of 1572 gone? Brocade and sonnet
marathons were the rage. We used to dress up in the flags

of rival baronies and conquer one another in cold rooms
    of stone.   10
Out on the dance floor we were all doing the Struggle
while your sister practiced the Daphne all alone in her room.
We borrowed the jargon of farriers for our slang.
These days language seems transparent, a badly broken code.

The 1790s will never come again. Childhood was big.   15
People would take walks to the very tops of hills
and write down what they saw in their journals without
    speaking.
Our collars were high and our hats were extremely soft.
We would surprise each other with alphabets made of twigs.
It was a wonderful time to be alive, or even dead.   20

I am very fond of the period between 1815 and 1821.
Europe trembled while we sat still for our portraits.
And I would love to return to 1901 if only for a moment,
time enough to wind up a music box and do a
    few dance steps,
or shoot me back to 1922 or 1941, or at least let me   25
recapture the serenity of last month when we picked
berries and glided through afternoons in a canoe.

Even this morning would be an improvement over
    the present.
I was in the garden then, surrounded by the hum of bees
and the Latin names of flowers, watching the early light   30
flash off the slanted windows of the greenhouse
and silver the limbs on the rows of dark hemlocks.

As usual, I was thinking about the moments of the past,
letting my memory rush over them like water
rushing over the stones on the bottom of a stream.   35
I was even thinking a little about the future, that place
where people are doing a dance we cannot imagine,
a dance whose name we can only guess.

Billy Collins

On Writing "Nostalgia"   *2008*

"Nostalgia" offers me the opportunity to say something about poetic form.
Broadly speaking, *form* can mean any feature of a poem that keeps it
together and gives it unity. Form is the nails and glue that hold the emotions
and thoughts of a poem in place. Naturally, poets are in the business of self-
expression, but paradoxically they are always looking for limits. Form can be

inherited — the sonnet is an enduring example — or the poet may make up his own rules as he goes along. He might even decide at some point to break the very rules he just imposed upon himself. In either case, formal rules give the poet an enclosed space in which to work, and they keep the poem from descending into chaos or tantrum. As poet Stephen Dunn put it, "form is the pressure that an artist puts on his material in order to see what it will bear."

The Irish poet W. B. Yeats felt that "all that is personal will rot unless it is packed in ice and salt." For a formalist poet like Yeats, "ice and salt," which were common food preservatives of his day, probably meant rhyme and meter. After Walt Whitman showed in *Leaves of Grass* (1855) that poems could be written without those two traditional supporting pillars, poets still had many other formal devices at their disposal. Just because poets could now write poems without a design of rhyme words at the ends of lines or a regular meter such as iambic pentameter did not mean they had abandoned form. Some of these alternative formal strategies would include line length, stanza choice, repetition, rhetorical development (beginning–middle–end), and thematic recurrence as well as patterns of sound and imagery. Focusing on form allows us to see that poetry can combine a high level of imaginative freedom with the imposition of boundaries and rules of procedure. For the reader, the coexistence of these two contrary elements — liberty and restriction — may be said to create a pleasurable tension found to a higher degree in poetry than in any other literary genre.

An apparent formal element in "Nostalgia," besides its use of stanza breaks, is the chronological sequence it obediently follows. After the absurd opening question (to which the only answer is no), the poem moves forward from the Middle Ages (the 1340s would place us smack in the middle of the Black Death) to the Renaissance, to the beginnings of English Romanticism, that being 1798, when the first edition of *Lyrical Ballads*, a poetic collaboration between Wordsworth and Coleridge, was published. The poem then continues to travel forward in time, but now more whimsically with dates that seem plucked out of the air — 1901, 1922, 1941 — before arriving rather abruptly at "last month" and then "this morning." If nothing else, the poem demonstrates poetry's freedom from normal time constraints as it manages to travel more than 600 years from the Middle Ages to the present in only twenty-eight lines.

When the poem does arrive at the present, the speaker morphs from a kind of thousand-year-old man into an actual person, a sympathetic fellow who likes to garden and who appreciates the sounds and sights of the natural world. The imaginary historical journey of the poem ends amid the bees and flowers of the speaker's garden, where he continues to dwell nostalgically on the past until his attention turns to the future, really the only place left for him to go. Having relinquished his power as an eyewitness to centuries of human civilization, the speaker trails off in a dreamy speculation about the unknowable dance crazes of the future.

The poem takes a lot of imaginative liberties in the oddness of its premise and its free-ranging images, yet, formally speaking, it is held together by a strict chronological line drawn from the distant historical past right through the present moment and into the future.

I don't recall how a lot of my poems got started, but I do remember that this poem arose out of a kind of annoyance. Just as a grain of sand can irritate an oyster into producing a pearl by coating it with a smooth surface, so a poem may be irked into being. What was bugging me in this case was the popular twentieth-century habit of breaking the past into decades ("the fifties," "the sixties," and so forth), constructs which amounted to little more than a collage of stereotypes. What a gross simplification of this mysterious, invisible thing we call the past, I thought. Even worse, each decade was so sentimentalized as to make one feel that its passing was cause for feelings of melancholy and regret. "Nostalgia," then, is a poem with a motive, that is, to satirize that kind of enforced nostalgia.

BILLY COLLINS

Questions About Angels   1991

Of all the questions you might want to ask
about angels, the only one you ever hear
is how many can dance on the head of a pin.

No curiosity about how they pass the eternal time
besides circling the Throne chanting in Latin   5
or delivering a crust of bread to a hermit on earth
or guiding a boy and girl across a rickety wooden bridge.

Do they fly through God's body and come out singing?
Do they swing like children from the hinges
of the spirit world saying their names backwards and
        forwards?   10
Do they sit alone in little gardens changing colors?

What about their sleeping habits, the fabric of their robes,
their diet of unfiltered divine light?
What goes on inside their luminous heads? Is there a wall
these tall presences can look over and see hell?   15

If an angel fell off a cloud, would he leave a hole
in a river and would the hole float along endlessly
filled with the silent letters of every angelic word?

If an angel delivered the mail, would he arrive
in a blinding rush of wings or would he just assume   20
the appearance of the regular mailman and
whistle up the driveway reading the postcards?

No, the medieval theologians control the court.
The only question you ever hear is about

the little dance floor on the head of a pin   25
where halos are meant to converge and drift invisibly.

It is designed to make us think in millions,
billions, to make us run out of numbers and collapse
into infinity, but perhaps the answer is simply one:
one female angel dancing alone in her stocking feet,   30
a small jazz combo working in the background.

She sways like a branch in the wind, her beautiful
eyes closed, and the tall thin bassist leans over
to glance at his watch because she has been dancing
forever, and now it is very late, even for musicians.   35

Billy Collins

On Writing "Questions About Angels"   *2008*

I find that it doesn't take much to get a poem going. A poem can start casually with something trivial and then develop significance along the way. The
first inkling may act as a keyhole that allows the poet to look into an imaginary room. When I started to write "Questions About Angels," I really had
nothing on my mind except that odd, speculative question: How many angels
can dance on the head of a pin? Seemingly unanswerable, the question originated as an attempt to mock certain medieval philosophers (notably Thomas
Aquinas) who sought to solve arcane theological mysteries through the sheer
application of reason. I had first heard the question when I was studying theology at a Jesuit college, but well before that, the phrase had made its way into
the mainstream of modern parlance. It was typical of me to want to begin
a poem with something everyone knows and then proceed from there. The
poem found a direction to go in when it occurred to me to open up the discussion to include other questions. At that point, it was "Game on."

My investigation really begins in the second stanza, which draws on
traditional images of angels in religious art, either worshipping God or paying helpful visits to earth, assisting the poor and protecting the innocent.
Then the questions become more fanciful — off-the-wall, really: "Do they fly
through God's body and come out singing?" No doubt you could come up
with questions of your own about angel behavior; clearly, that has become the
poem's game — an open inquiry into the spirit life of these creatures.

After the poem's most bizarre question, which involves a hole that a
fallen angel has left in a river, the interrogation descends into the everyday
with the image of an angel delivering mail, not gloriously "in a blinding rush
of wings" but just like "the regular mailman." After a reminder of the monopoly "the medieval theologians" seem to have on questions about angels, the
poem makes a sudden turn (one I did not see coming) by offering a simple,
irreducible answer to that unanswerable question. On the little word "but"

(line 29), the poem drops down abruptly from "billions" to "one," and the scene shrinks from heaven to a jazz club located in eternity.

In the process of composing a poem, the poet is mentally juggling many concerns, one of the most dominant and persistent being how the poem is going to find a place to end, a point where the journey of the poem was meant to stop, a point where the poet does not want to say any more, and the reader has heard just enough. In this case, the moment she appeared — rather miraculously, as I remember — I knew that this beautiful angel "dancing alone in her stocking feet" was how the poem would close. She was the hidden destination the poem was moving toward all along without my knowing it. I had only to add the detail of the bored bassist and the odd observation that even musicians playing in eternity cannot be expected to stay awake forever.

Billy Collins

Litany

2002

> *You are the bread and the knife,*
> *The crystal goblet and the wine.*
> — *Jacques Crickillon*

You are the bread and the knife,
the crystal goblet and the wine.
You are the dew on the morning grass,
and the burning wheel of the sun.
You are the white apron of the baker,   5
and the marsh birds suddenly in flight.

However, you are not the wind in the orchard,
the plums on the counter,
or the house of cards.
And you are certainly not the pine-scented air.   10
There is no way you are the pine-scented air.

It is possible that you are the fish under the bridge,
maybe even the pigeon on the general's head,
but you are not even close
to being the field of cornflowers at dusk.   15

And a quick look in the mirror will show
that you are neither the boots in the corner
nor the boat asleep in its boathouse.

It might interest you to know,
speaking of the plentiful imagery of the world,   20
that I am the sound of rain on the roof.

I also happen to be the shooting star,
the evening paper blowing down an alley,
and the basket of chestnuts on the kitchen table.

I am also the moon in the trees   25
and the blind woman's teacup.
But don't worry, I am not the bread and the knife.
You are still the bread and the knife.
You will always be the bread and the knife,
not to mention the crystal goblet and — somehow —
         the wine.   30

Billy Collins
On Writing "Litany"   *2008*

As the epigraph to this poem indicates, "Litany" was written in reaction to
another poem, a love poem I came across in a literary magazine by a poet I
had not heard of. What struck me about his poem was its reliance on a strategy that had its heyday in the love sonnets of the Elizabethan age, namely, the
convention of flattering the beloved by comparing her to various aspects of
nature. Typically, her eyes were like twin suns, her lips red as coral or rubies,
her skin pure as milk, and her breath as sweet as flowers or perfume. Such
exaggerations were part of the overall tendency to idealize women who were
featured in the courtly love poetry of the time, each of whom was as unat-
tainable as she was beautiful and as cruel as she was fair. It took Shakespeare
to point out the ridiculousness of these hyperboles, questioning in one of his
sonnets the very legitimacy of comparisons ("Shall I compare thee to a summer's day?" [p. 467]), then drenching the whole process with the cold water
of realism ("My mistress' eyes are nothing like the sun" [p. 467]). You might
think that would have put an end to the practice, but the habit of appealing
to women's vanity through comparisons persists even in the poetry of today.
That poem in the magazine prompted me to respond.

  Starting with the same first two lines, "Litany" seeks to rewrite the earlier
poem by offering a corrective. It aims to point out the latent silliness in such
comparisons and perhaps the potential absurdity at the heart of metaphor
itself. The poem even wants us to think about the kind of romantic relationships that would permit such discourse.

  The poem opens by adding some new metaphors (morning dew, baker's
apron, marsh birds) to the pile, but in the second stanza, the poem reverses
direction by trading in flattery for a mock-serious investigation of what this
woman might be and what she is not. Instead of appealing to her sense of her
own beauty, the speaker is perfectly willing to insult her by bringing up her
metaphoric shortcomings. By the time he informs her that "There is no way
you are the pine-scented air" and "you are not even close / to being the field

of cornflowers at dusk," we know that this is a different kind of love poem altogether.

The second big turn comes in the fifth stanza when the speaker unexpectedly begins comparing himself to such things as "the sound of rain on the roof." Notice that the earlier comparisons were not all positive. The "pigeon on the general's head" should remind us of an equestrian statue in a park, and we all know what pigeons like to do to statues. But the speaker is not the least bit ashamed to flatter himself with a string of appealing images including a "shooting star," a "basket of chestnuts," and "the moon in the trees." Turning attention away from the "you" of the poem to the speaker is part of the poem's impertinence — the attentive lover turns into an egomaniac — but it echoes a strategy used by Shakespeare himself. Several of his sonnets begin by being about the beloved but end by being about the poet, specifically about his power to bestow immortality on the beloved through his art. Thus, what begins as a love poem ends as a self-love poem.

The last thing to notice is that "Litany" has a circular structure: It ends by swinging back to its beginning, to the imagery of the epigraph. True to the cheekiness of the speaker, his last words are devoted to tossing the woman a bit of false reassurance that she is still and will always be "the bread and the knife." For whatever that's worth.

BILLY COLLINS

Building with Its Face Blown Off   *2005*

How suddenly the private
is revealed in a bombed-out city,
how the blue and white striped wallpaper

of a second story bedroom is now
exposed to the lightly falling snow   5
as if the room had answered the explosion

wearing only its striped pajamas.
Some neighbors and soldiers
poke around in the rubble below

and stare up at the hanging staircase,   10
the portrait of a grandfather,
a door dangling from a single hinge.

And the bathroom looks almost embarrassed
by its uncovered ochre walls,
the twisted mess of its plumbing,   15

the sink sinking to its knees,
the ripped shower curtain,
the torn goldfish trailing bubbles.

It's like a dollhouse view   20
as if a child on its knees could reach in
and pick up the bureau, straighten a picture.

Or it might be a room on a stage
in a play with no characters,
no dialogue or audience,

no beginning, middle and end —   25
just the broken furniture in the street,
a shoe among the cinder blocks,

a light snow still falling
on a distant steeple, and people
crossing a bridge that still stands.   30

And beyond that — crows in a tree,
the statue of a leader on a horse,
and clouds that look like smoke,

and even farther on, in another country
on a blanket under a shade tree,   35
a man pouring wine into two glasses

and a woman sliding out
the wooden pegs of a wicker hamper
filled with bread, cheese, and several kinds of olives.

Perspective

On "Building with Its Face Blown Off": Michael Meyer Interviews Billy Collins   *2009*

Meyer: The subject matter of your poetry is well known for being typically about the patterns and rhythms of everyday life, along with its delights, humor, ironies, and inevitable pain. "Building with Its Face Blown Off," however, explicitly concerns war and is implicitly political. What prompted this minority report in your writing?

Collins: It's true that I usually steer away from big historical subjects in my poems. I don't want to assume a level of authority beyond what a reader might trust, nor do I want to appear ridiculous by taking a firm stand against some moral horror that any other humane person would naturally oppose. A few years back, I consciously avoided joining the movement called "Poets against the War" because I thought it was as self-obviating as "Generals for the War." A direct approach to subjects as enormous as war or slavery or genocide carries the risk that the poet will be smothered under the weight of the topic. Plus, readers are already morally wired to respond in a certain way to such things. As a writer, you want to *create* an emotion, not merely activate one that already exists in the reader. And who wants to preach to the choir? I have come across few readers of poetry who are all for war; and, besides, poets have enough work to do without trying to convert the lost. William Butler Yeats put it best in his "On Being Asked for a War Poem":

> I think it better that in times like these
> A poet's mouth be silent, for in truth
> We have no gift to set a statesman right;
> He has had enough of meddling who can please
> A young girl in the indolence of her youth,
> Or an old man upon a winter's night.

Before poetry can be political, it must be personal.

That's my dim view of poems that do little more than declare that the poet, walking the moral high road, is opposed to ethically reprehensible acts. But the world does press in on us, and I was stopped in my tracks one morning when I saw in a newspaper still another photograph of a bombed-out building, which echoed all the similar images I had seen for too many decades in too many conflicts around the world in Dresden, Sarajevo, or Baghdad, wherever shells happen to fall. That photograph revealed one personal aspect of the war: the apartment of a family blown wide open for all to see. "Building with Its Face Blown Off" was my response.

Meyer: The images in the poem have a photojournalistic quality, but they are snapped through the lens of personification rather than a camera. Isn't a picture better than a thousand words?

Collins: I wanted to avoid the moralistic antiwar rhetoric that the underlying subject invites, so I stuck to the visual. A photojournalist once observed that to capture the horrors of war, you don't have to go to the front lines and photograph actual armed conflict: just take a picture of a child's shoe lying on a road. That picture would be worth many words, but as a poet I must add, maybe not quite a thousand. In this poem, I wanted to downplay the horrible violence of the destruction by treating the event as a mere social embarrassment, an invasion of domestic privacy. As Chekhov put it, if you want to get the reader emotionally involved, write cold. For the same reason, I deployed nonviolent metaphors such as the dollhouse and the theater, where the fourth wall is absent. The poem finds a way to end by withdrawing from the scene like a camera pulling back to reveal a larger world. Finally, we are looking down as from a blimp on another country, one where the absence of war provides the tranquility that allows a man and a woman to have a picnic.

A reader once complimented me for ending this poem with olives, the olive branch being a traditional symbol of peace. Another reader heard an echo of Ernest Hemingway's short story "In Another Country," which concerns World War I. Just between you and me, neither of these references had ever occurred to me; but I am always glad to take credit for such happy accidents even if it is similar to drawing a target around a bullet hole. No writer can — or should want to — have absolute control over the reactions of his readers.

Meyer: In your essay on writing "Nostalgia," you point out that "formal rules give the poet an enclosed space in which to work, and they keep the poem from descending into chaos or tantrum" (p. 509). How does form in "Building with Its Face Blown Off" prevent its emotions and thoughts from being reduced to a prose bumper sticker such as "War is hell"?

Collins: I hope what keeps this poem from getting carried away with its traumatic subject is its concentration on the photograph so that the poem maintains a visual, even cinematic, focus throughout. You could think of the poem as a one-minute movie — a short subject about a big topic. Another sign of apparent form here is the division of the poem into three-line stanzas, or tercets, which slow down the reader's progress through the poem. Just as readers should pause slightly at the end of every poetic line (even an unpunctuated one — the equivalent of half a comma), they should also observe a little pause between stanzas. Poetry is famous for condensing large amounts of mental and emotional material into small packages, and it also encourages us to slow down from the speed at which we usually absorb information. The stanzas give the poem a look of regularity, and some of them make visible the grammatical structure of the poem's sentences. Regular stanzas suggest that the poem comes in sections, and they remind us that poetry is a spatial arrangement of words on the page. Think of such stanzas as stones in a stream; the reader steps from one to the next to get to the other side.

Meyer: In a classroom discussion of the final two stanzas, one of my students read the couple's picnic scene as "offering an image of hope and peace in contrast to the reckless destruction that precedes it," while another student countered that the scene appeared to be a depiction of "smug indifference and apathy to suffering." Care to comment?

Collins: I find it fascinating that such contrary views of the poem's ending could exist. Probably the most vexing question in poetry studies concerns interpretation. One thing to keep in mind is that readers of poetry, students especially, are much more preoccupied with "meaning" than poets are. While I am writing, I am not thinking about the poem's meaning; I am only trying to write a good poem, which involves securing the form of the poem and getting the poem to hold together so as to stay true to itself.

Thinking about what my poem means would only distract me from the real work of poetry. Neurologically speaking, I am trying to inhabit the intuitive side of the brain, not the analytical side where critical thought and "study questions" come from. "Meaning," if I think of it at all, usually comes as an afterthought.

But the question remains: How do poets react to interpretations of their work? Generally speaking, once a poem is completed and then published, it is out of the writer's hands. I'm disposed to welcome interpretations that I did not consciously intend — that doesn't mean my unconscious didn't play a role — as long as those readings do not twist the poem out of shape. In "Building with Its Face Blown Off," I added the picnicking couple simply as a sharp contrast to the scene of destruction in the war-torn city. The man and woman are free to enjoy the luxury of each other's company, the countryside, wine, cheese, and even a choice of olives. Are they a sign of hope? Well, yes, insofar as they show us that the whole world is not at war. Smugness? Not so much to my mind, even though that strikes me as a sensible reaction. But if a reader claimed that the couple represented Adam and Eve, or more absurdly, Antony and Cleopatra, or Donny and Marie Osmond, then I would question the person's common sense or sanity. I might even ring for Security. Mainly, the couple is there simply to show us what is no longer available to the inhabitants of the beleaguered city and to give me a place to end the poem.

Considerations for Critical Thinking and Writing

1. In his commentary on "Osso Buco," Collins observes that "happiness in serious literature is often mistaken for a kind of cowlike stupidity" (p. 506). How does the language of the poem maneuver around that kind of sentimental quicksand?

2. What other "formal strategies" can you find in "Nostalgia" (p. 507) in addition to the use of stanza breaks and the chronological sequence that Collins discusses? What other poetic elements serve to unify this satiric poem?

3. CREATIVE RESPONSE. Collins explains that he began "Questions About Angels" by setting out to mock the medieval speculative question of how many angels can dance on the head of a pin. He also describes his discovery of how to end the poem in line 29 after the word "but" (pp. 511–12) with the image of the female angel dancing by herself in a jazz club. That was his solution. Try writing your own final six lines as you discover them from the preceding twenty-nine.

4. As Collins indicates, the speaker in "Litany" writes a parodic love poem that "ends as a self-love poem" (p. 514). Is the "cheekiness" in his language appealing to you? Explain why or why not.

5. In his final paragraph in "On 'Building with Its Face Blown Off'" (above), Collins offers some commonsense observations about literary interpretation and how to read a poem sensitively and sensibly. He also acknowledges that wild misreadings might cause him to "ring for Security." Write an essay on "How Not to Interpret a Poem" that articulates what you think are some of the most important problems to avoid.

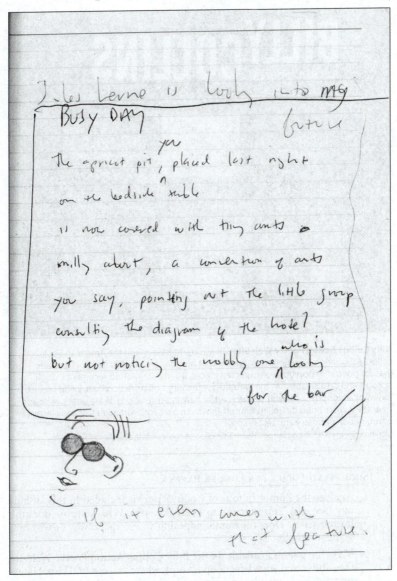

A draft of the unpublished poem "Busy Day" from an undated page of Collins's notebooks.
Reprinted with permission by Chris Calhoun Agency, © Billy Collins.

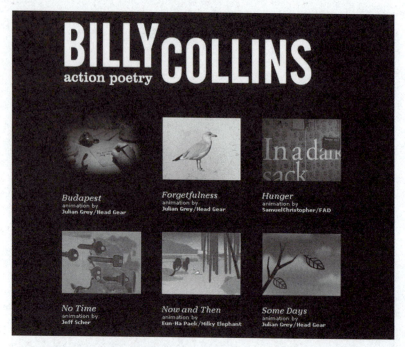

Billy Collins Action Poetry Web Site. In a 2003 interview with the American Book-sellers Association, Billy Collins explained that his goal as United States poet laureate was for poetry "to pop up in unexpected places, like the daily announcement in high schools and on airplanes." At the Web site for the Billy Collins Action Poetry film project (www.bcactionpoet.org), you can view artful new interpretations of the poet's work and hear them read aloud by Collins himself, in what makes for an imaginative and elegant combination of poetry and technology.

Library of Congress (Produced by the J. Walter Thompson ad agency and the Sundance Channel).

SUGGESTED TOPICS FOR LONGER PAPERS

1. Analyze the humor in four of Collins's poems included in this anthology (see also "Introduction to Poetry," p. 341). What purpose does the humor serve? Does the humor appeal to you? Explain why or why not, giving examples.

2. View the poems available on the Billy Collins Action Poetry Web site (see above and www.bcactionpoet.org), where you can find visual interpretations of individual poems and hear Collins read the poems aloud. Choose three of the poems and write an analysis of how the visual and auditory representations affect your response to the poems' language. Explain why you think this approach enhances or diminishes — or is simply different from — reading the poem on a page.

Questions for Writing about an Author in Depth

As you read multiple works by the same author, you're likely to be struck by the similarities and differences in those selections. You'll begin to recognize situations, events, characters, issues, perspectives, styles, and strategies—even recurring words or phrases—that provide a kind of signature, making the poems in some way identifiable with that particular writer.

The following questions can help you to respond to multiple works by the same author. They should help you to listen to how a writer's works can speak to one another and to you.

1. What topics reappear in the writer's work? What seem to be the major concerns of the author?

2. Does the author have a definable worldview that can be discerned from work to work? Is, for example, the writer liberal, conservative, apolitical, or religious?

3. What social values come through in the author's work? Does he or she seem to identify with a particular group or social class?

4. Is there a consistent voice or point of view from work to work? Is it a persona or the author's actual self?

5. How much of the author's own life experiences and historical moments make their way into the works?

6. Does the author experiment with style from work to work, or are the works mostly consistent with one another?

7. Can the author's work be identified with a literary tradition, such as *carpe diem* poetry, that aligns his or her work with that of other writers?

8. What is distinctive about the author's writing? Is the language innovative? Are the themes challenging? Are the voices conventional? Is the tone characteristic?

9. Could you identify another work by the same author without a name being attached to it? What are the distinctive features that allow you to do so?

10. Do any of the writer's works seem *not* to be by that writer? Why?

11. What other writers are most like this author in style and content? Why?

12. Has the writer's work evolved over time? Are there significant changes or developments? Are there new ideas and styles, or do the works remain largely the same?

13. How would you characterize the author's writing habits? Is it possible to anticipate what goes on in different works, or are you surprised by their content or style?

14. Can difficult or ambiguous passages in a work be resolved by referring to a similar passage in another work?

15. What does the writer say about his or her own work? Do you trust the teller or the tale? Which do you think is more reliable?

22

A THEMATIC CASE STUDY
The World of Work

Chris Maddaloni/Getty Images.

> I'd like to be on record as saying that anybody can write a poem that nobody can understand. That's really easy. On the other hand, it might be really hard to write a poem that everyone in a room found meaning in.
>
> —TED KOOSER

This chapter offers some contemporary poems that are thematically connected to business and labor. The vicissitudes associated with making a living are not typically the subject matter chosen by poets, who have traditionally and historically preferred to write about less mundane matters, such as love, nature, spirituality, grief, death, or almost any other side of life that isn't set at a job site or in an office. However much this view of poets may be a stereotype, by the time President Calvin Coolidge confidently declared in 1925 that "the business of America is business," there was an impressive record of objections to such a narrow materialistic assertion. Consider, for example, Henry David Thoreau's assessment in this nineteenth-century journal entry: "In my experience nothing is

so opposed to poetry — not crime — as business. It is a negation of life"
(June 29, 1852).

Not many poems replicate the kind of exuberant optimism about the
business of work to be found in this excerpt from Walt Whitman's "I Hear
America Singing" (1867):

> I hear America singing, the varied carols I hear,
> Those of mechanics, each one singing his as
>   it should be blithe and strong,
> The carpenter singing his as he measures his
>   plank or beam,
> The mason singing his as he makes ready for
>   work, or leaves off work,
> The boatman singing what belongs to him in
>   his boat, the deckhand singing on the
>   steamboat deck,
> The shoemaker singing as he sits on his bench,
>   the hatter singing as he stands. . . .

Whitman's poem celebrates the energy he perceived in workers and business:
"In modern times the new word *Business*, has been brought to the front & now
dominates individuals and nations. . . . Business shall be, nay is, the word of
the modern hero." In recent times in the face of economic turmoil, crushing
debt, and widespread unemployment, however, Thoreau's negative critique
seems to resonate more than does Whitman's cheerful expectations.

The world of work — the business of earning a living — seems to be in
sharper and more problematic focus these days because it is necessarily on
most people's minds, including the imaginations of many poets. The chapter's focus is not just about earning money, though the first poem, "Money,"
by former business executive and now poet Dana Gioia, certainly acknowledges how obsessively central money can be. The following poems about
earning a living are also about personal integrity, working conditions, and
the meaning of life, topics that are explored from a variety of perspectives
and that evoke the misery and joy, as well as the despair and satisfaction,
that going to work can pay out.

DANA GIOIA (B. 1950)

Money   *1991*

Money is a kind of poetry.   — *Wallace Stevens*

Money, the long green,
cash, stash, rhino, jack
or just plain dough.

Chock it up, fork it over,
shell it out. Watch it   5
burn holes through pockets.

To be made of it! To have it
to burn! Greenbacks, double eagles,
megabucks and Ginnie Maes.

It greases the palm, feathers a nest,   10
holds heads above water,
makes both ends meet.

Money breeds money.
Gathering interest, compounding daily.
Always in circulation.   15

Money. You don't know where it's been,
but you put it where your mouth is.
And it talks.

Considerations for Critical Thinking and Writing

1. **FIRST RESPONSE.** Explain whether the poem supports or challenges Stevens's epigraph.

2. How does money "talk" through Gioia's choice of diction?

3. Research Wallace Stevens's biography in terms of his relationship to business. Why is he an especially appropriate source for the quotation that begins the poem?

WHEN I READ "My advice is to read a lot of poetry; to begin with the contemporary and get an ear for contemporary poetic speech; then read your way gradually into the past. Form a strong attachment to a poet whose work you love, and immerse yourself in the work. Then find another." —TONY HOAGLAND

TONY HOAGLAND (B. 1953)

America   2003

Then one of the students with blue hair and a tongue stud
Says that America is for him a maximum-security prison

Whose walls are made of RadioShacks and Burger Kings, and
        MTV episodes
Where you can't tell the show from the commercials,

And as I consider how to express how full of shit I think he is,   5
He says that even when he's driving to the mall in his Isuzu

Trooper with a gang of his friends, letting rap music pour over them
Like a boiling Jacuzzi full of ballpeen hammers, even then he feels

Buried alive, captured and suffocated in the folds
Of the thick satin quilt of America   10

And I wonder if this is a legitimate category of pain,
Or whether he is just spin doctoring a better grade,

And then I remember that when I stabbed my father in the dream
        last night,
It was not blood but money

That gushed out of him, bright green hundred-dollar bills   15
Spilling from his wounds, and — this is the weird part —,

He gasped, "Thank god — those Ben Franklins were
Clogging up my heart —

And so I perish happily,
Freed from that which kept me from my liberty" —   20

Which is when I knew it was a dream, since my dad
Would never speak in rhymed couplets,

And I look at the student with his acne and cell phone and phony
        ghetto clothes
And I think, "I am asleep in America too,

And I don't know how to wake myself either,"   25
And I remember what Marx said near the end of his life:

"I was listening to the cries of the past,
When I should have been listening to the cries of the future."

But how could he have imagined 100 channels of 24-hour cable
Or what kind of nightmare it might be   30

When each day you watch rivers of bright merchandise run past you
And you are floating in your pleasure boat upon this river

Even while others are drowning underneath you
And you see their faces twisting in the surface of the waters

And yet it seems to be your own hand   35
Which turns the volume higher?

Considerations for Critical Thinking and Writing

1. **first response.** This poem consists of two sentences. How do they differ
   in tone and meaning?

2. Discuss the humor embedded in this serious poem.

3. To what extent does this poem reflect your own views about American
   life?

4. **connection to another selection.** Compare the perspective offered
   on money in "America" with that in Dana Gioia's "Money" (p. 523).

Jan Beatty (b. 1952)

My Father Teaches Me to Dream   1996

You want to know what work is?
I'll tell you what work is:
Work is work.
You get up. You get on the bus.
You don't look from side to side.   5
You keep your eyes straight ahead.
That way nobody bothers you — see?
You get off the bus. You work all day.
You get back on the bus at night. Same thing.
You go to sleep. You get up.   10
You do the same thing again.
Nothing more. Nothing less.
There's no handouts in this life.
All this other stuff you're looking for —
it ain't there.   15
Work is work.

Considerations for Critical Thinking and Writing

1. **FIRST RESPONSE.** How likely is it that the son or daughter of this father actually asked for a definition of work? What do you imagine prompted the start of this explanation?

2. Discuss the effect of the use of repeated words and phrases. How are they related to the father's message?

3. Consider what the title reveals about the "you" of the poem.

Michael Chitwood (b. 1958)

Men Throwing Bricks   2007

The one on the ground lofts two at
        a time
with just the right lift for them to
        finish
their rise as the one on the scaffold
        turns
to accept them like a gift and place
        them
on the growing stack. They chime
        slightly
on the catch. You'd have to do this daily,
morning and afternoon, not to marvel.

Derek Anderson.

Considerations for Critical Thinking and Writing

1. FIRST RESPONSE. Explain the title's ironic surprise.

2. Discuss the sounds in the poem. How does it "chime"?

3. Why is "marvel" a better choice to describe the men throwing bricks than the phrase "be impressed"?

4. CONNECTION TO ANOTHER SELECTION. Compare Chitwood's treatment of these working men with Joyce Sutphen's perspective on the men and their work in "Guys Like That" (p. 527).

David Ignatow (1914–1997)

The Jobholder   1998

I stand in the rain waiting for my bus
and in the bus I wait for my stop.
I get let off and go to work
where I wait for the day to end
and then go home, waiting for the bus,   5
of course, and my stop.

And at home I read and wait
for my hour to go to bed
and I wait for the day I can retire
and wait for my turn to die.   10

Considerations for Critical Thinking and Writing

1. FIRST RESPONSE. How do the effects of repetition and brevity contribute to the theme of this poem?

2. Characterize the speaker's attitude toward work and life.

3. CONNECTION TO ANOTHER SELECTION. Compare Ignatow's representation of work with Jan Beatty's in "My Father Teaches Me to Dream" (p. 526).

Joyce Sutphen (b. 1949)

Guys Like That   2007

Drive very nice cars, and from
where you sit in your dented
last-century version of the
most ordinary car in America, they

look dark-suited and neat and fast.   5
Guys like that look as if they are thinking

about wine and marble floors, but
really they are thinking about TiVo

and ESPN. Women think that guys
like that are different from the guys   10
driving the trucks that bring cattle
to slaughter, but guys like that are

planning worse things than the death
of a cow. Guys who look like that —
so clean and cool — are quietly moving   15
money across the border, cooking books,

making deals that leave some people
rich and some people poorer
than they were before guys like that
robbed them at the pump and on   20

their electricity bills, and even
now, guys like that are planning how
to divide up that little farm they just
passed, the one you used to call home.

CONSIDERATIONS FOR CRITICAL THINKING AND WRITING

1. FIRST RESPONSE. How does the phrase "Guys Like That" take on different meanings as the poem progresses?

2. Discuss the poem as a critique of American business practices.

3. Why do you think Sutphen writes this poem specifically from a woman's point of view?

4. CONNECTION TO ANOTHER SELECTION. Consider the treatment of men's relationship to domestic life in "Guys Like That" and in Florence Cassen Mayers's "All-American Sestina" (p. 471).

TED KOOSER (B. 1939)

Laundry   1985

A pink house trailer,
scuffed and rusted, sunken
in weeds. On the line,

five pale blue workshirts
up to their elbows   5
in raspberry canes —

a good, clean crew
of pickers, out early,
sleeves wet with dew,

Chris Maddaloni / Getty Images.

and near them, a pair   10
of bright yellow panties
urging them on.

CONSIDERATIONS FOR CRITICAL THINKING AND WRITING

1. FIRST RESPONSE. Discuss how Kooser uses color to create tonal effects.

2. Just beyond the simplicity of "Laundry," there are some ideas about work suspended from the lines. What are they?

3. CONNECTION TO ANOTHER SELECTION. Discuss the relationship between home and work in "Laundry" and in David Ignatow's "The Jobholder" (p. 527).

MARGE PIERCY (B. 1936)

To be of use   1973

The people I love the best
jump into work head first
without dallying in the shallows
and swim off with sure strokes almost out of sight.
They seem to become natives of that element,   5
the black sleek heads of seals
bouncing like half-submerged balls.

I love people who harness themselves, an ox to a heavy cart,
who pull like water buffalo, with massive patience,
who strain in the mud and the muck to move things forward,   10
who do what has to be done, again and again.

I want to be with people who submerge
in the task, who go into the fields to harvest
and work in a row and pass the bags along,
who are not parlor generals and field deserters   15
but move in a common rhythm
when the food must come in or the fire be put out.

The work of the world is common as mud.
Botched, it smears the hands, crumbles to dust.
But the thing worth doing well done   20
has a shape that satisfies, clean and evident.
Greek amphoras for wine or oil,
Hopi vases that held corn, are put in museums
but you know they were made to be used.
The pitcher cries for water to carry   25
and a person for work that is real.

Considerations for Critical Thinking and Writing

1. FIRST RESPONSE. How does the poem's figurative language suggest the sort of worker the speaker admires?

2. What do you consider to be "work that is real" (line 26)?

3. What is the significance of the title?

4. CONNECTION TO ANOTHER SELECTION. Compare the sense of what constitutes meaningful work in this poem with that in Jan Beatty's "My Father Teaches Me to Dream" (p. 526).

Suggested Topics for Longer Papers

1. There are many contemporary songs about work. Choose one of the poems in this chapter and in terms of poetic elements — such as diction, tone, imagery, figures of speech, sound, and rhythm — compare its themes with the lyrics of a song you admire.

2. Choose one of the writers represented in this chapter and read more poems in his or her collections. Choose five poems that you think make an interesting and coherent thematic grouping and write an analysis that reveals important elements of the poet's style and characteristic concerns.

A Collection
of Poems

23

Poems for Further Reading

Now the role of poetry is not simply to hold understanding in place but to help create and hold a realm of experience. Poetry has become a kind of tool for knowing the world in a particular way.

— JANE HIRSHFIELD

ANONYMOUS (TRADITIONAL SCOTTISH BALLAD)

Bonny Barbara Allan   *date unknown*

It was in and about the Martinmas° time,
    When the green leaves were afalling,
That Sir John Graeme, in the West Country,
    Fell in love with Barbara Allan.

He sent his men down through the town,   5
    To the place where she was dwelling:
"Oh haste and come to my master dear,
    Gin° ye be Barbara Allan."   *if*

O hooly,° hooly rose she up,   *slowly*
    To the place where he was lying,   10

---

1 *Martinmas:* St. Martin's Day, November 11.

And when she drew the curtain by:
    "Young man, I think you're dying."

"O it's I'm sick, and very, very sick,
    And 'tis a' for Barbara Allan." —
"O the better for me ye's never be,   15
    Tho your heart's blood were aspilling."

"O dinna ye mind,° young man," she said,   *don't you remember*
    "When ye was in the tavern adrinking,
That ye made the health° gae round and round,   *toasts*
    And slighted Barbara Allan?"   20

He turned his face unto the wall,
    And death was with him dealing:
"Adieu, adieu, my dear friends all,
    And be kind to Barbara Allan."

And slowly, slowly raise her up,   25
    And slowly, slowly left him,
And sighing said she could not stay,
    Since death of life had reft him.

She had not gane a mile but twa,
    When she heard the dead-bell ringing,   30
And every jow° that the dead-bell geid,   *stroke*
    It cried, "Woe to Barbara Allan!"

"O mother, mother, make my bed!
    O make it saft and narrow!
Since my love died for me today,   35
    I'll die for him tomorrow."

Aphra Behn (1640–1689)

Song: Love Armed   *1684*

Love in fantastic triumph sate,
    Whilst bleeding hearts around him flowed,
For whom fresh pains he did create,
    And strange tyrannic power he showed:
From thy bright eyes he took his fire,   5
    Which round about in sport he hurled;
But 'twas from mine he took desire,
    Enough to undo the amorous world.

From me he took his sighs and tears;
    From thee, his pride and cruelty;   10
From me, his languishments and fears;
    And every killing dart from thee.

Thus thou and I the god have armed
    And set him up a deity;
But my poor heart alone is harmed,   15
    Whilst thine the victor is, and free.

WILLIAM BLAKE (1757–1827)

Infant Sorrow   *1794*

My mother groand! my father wept.
Into the dangerous world I leapt:
Helpless naked piping loud:
Like a fiend hid in a cloud.

Struggling in my father's hands:
Striving against my swadling bands
Bound and weary I thought best
To sulk upon my mother's breast.

ELIZABETH BARRETT BROWNING (1806–1861)

How Do I Love Thee? Let Me Count the Ways   *1850*

How do I love thee? Let me count the ways.
I love thee to the depth and breadth and height
My soul can reach, when feeling out of sight
For the ends of being and ideal grace.
I love thee to the level of every day's   5
Most quiet need, by sun and candle-light.
I love thee freely, as men strive for right.
I love thee purely, as they turn from praise.
I love thee with the passion put to use
In my old griefs, and with my childhood's faith.   10
I love thee with a love I seemed to lose
With my lost saints. I love thee with the breath,
Smiles, tears, of all my life; and, if God choose,
I shall but love thee better after death.

ROBERT BURNS (1759–1796)

A Red, Red Rose   *1799*

O my luve's like a red, red rose
That's newly sprung in June;
O my luve's like the melodie
That's sweetly played in tune.

As fair art thou, my bonny lass,   5
So deep in luve am I;
And I will luve thee still my dear,
Till a' the seas gang° dry —   *go*

Till a' the seas gang dry, my dear,
And the rocks melt wi' the sun: 10
O I will luve thee still, my dear,
While the sands o' life shall run.

And fare thee weel, my only luve,
And fare thee weel awhile!
And I will come again, my luve,   15
Though it were a thousand mile.

EMILY DICKINSON (1830–1886)

Much Madness is divinest Sense —   *ca. 1862*

Much Madness is divinest Sense —
To a discerning Eye —
Much Sense — the starkest Madness —
'Tis the Majority
In this, as All, prevail —
Assent — and you are sane —
Demur — you're straightway dangerous —
And handled with a Chain —

PAUL LAURENCE DUNBAR (1872–1906)

Sympathy   *1893*

I know what the caged bird feels, alas!
    When the sun is bright on the upland slopes;
When the wind stirs soft through the springing grass,
    And the river flows like a stream of glass;
    When the first bird sings and the first bud opens,   5
And the faint perfume from its chalice steals —
I know what the caged bird feels!

I know why the caged bird beats his wing
    Till its blood is red on the cruel bars;
For he must fly back to his perch and cling   10
When he fain° would be on the bough a-swing;   *rather*
    And a pain still throbs in the old, old scars
And they pulse again with a keener sting —
I know why he beats his wing!

I know why the caged bird sings, ah me,   15
   When his wing is bruised and his bosom sore, —
When he beats his bars and he would be free;
It is not a carol of joy or glee,
   But a prayer that he sends from his heart's deep core,
But a plea, that upward to Heaven he flings —   20
I know why the caged bird sings!

GEORGE ELIOT (MARY ANN EVANS / 1819–1880)

In a London Drawingroom   1865

The sky is cloudy, yellowed by the smoke.
For view there are the houses opposite,
Cutting the sky with one long line of wall
Like solid fog: far as the eye can stretch
Monotony of surface and of form   5
Without a break to hang a guess upon.
No bird can make a shadow as it flies,
For all its shadow, as in ways o'erhung
By thickest canvas, where the golden rays
Are clothed in hemp. No figure lingering   10
Pauses to feed the hunger of the eye
Or rest a little on the lap of life.
All hurry on and look upon the ground
Or glance unmarking at the passersby.
The wheels are hurrying, too, cabs, carriages   15
All closed, in multiplied identity.
The world seems one huge prison-house and court
Where men are punished at the slightest cost,
With lowest rate of color, warmth, and joy.

T. S. ELIOT (1888–1965)

The Love Song of J. Alfred Prufrock   1917

S'io credesse che mia risposta fosse
A persona che mai tornasse al mondo,
Questa fiamma staria senza più scosse.
Ma perciocchè giammai di questo fondo
Non tornò vivo alcun, s'i'odo il vero,
Senza tema d'infamia ti rispondo.°

Epigraph: *S'io credesse . . . rispondo*: Dante's *Inferno*, 27:58–63. In the Eighth Chasm of
the Inferno, Dante and Virgil meet Guido da Montefeltro, one of the False Counselors, who
is punished by being enveloped in an eternal flame. When Dante asks Guido to tell his life

Let us go then, you and I,
When the evening is spread out against the sky
Like a patient etherized upon a table;
Let us go, through certain half-deserted streets,
The muttering retreats   5
Of restless nights in one-night cheap hotels
And sawdust restaurants with oyster-shells:
Streets that follow like a tedious argument
Of insidious intent
To lead you to an overwhelming question . . .   10

Oh, do not ask, "What is it?"
Let us go and make our visit.

In the room the women come and go
Talking of Michelangelo.

The yellow fog that rubs its back upon the window panes,   15
The yellow smoke that rubs its muzzle on the window panes
Licked its tongue into the corners of the evening,
Lingered upon the pools that stand in drains,
Let fall upon its back the soot that falls from chimneys,
Slipped by the terrace, made a sudden leap,   20
And seeing that it was a soft October night,
Curled once about the house, and fell asleep.

And indeed there will be time°
For the yellow smoke that slides along the street,
Rubbing its back upon the window panes;   25
There will be time, there will be time
To prepare a face to meet the faces that you meet;
There will be time to murder and create,
And time for all the works and days° of hands
That lift and drop a question on your plate: 30
Time for you and time for me,
And time yet for a hundred indecisions,
And for a hundred visions and revisions,
Before the taking of a toast and tea.

In the room the women come and go   35
Talking of Michelangelo.

And indeed there will be time
To wonder, "Do I dare?" and, "Do I dare?" —

story, the spirit replies: "If I thought that my answer were to one who might ever return to
the world, this flame would shake no more; but since from this depth none ever returned
alive, if what I hear is true, I answer you without fear of infamy."   23 *there will be time*: An
allusion to Ecclesiastes 3:1–8: "To everything there is a season, and a time to every purpose
under heaven. . . ."   29 *works and days*: Hesiod's eighth-century B.C. poem *Works and
Days* gives practical advice on how to conduct one's life in accordance with the seasons.

Time to turn back and descend the stair,
With a bald spot in the middle of my hair —   40
(They will say: "How his hair is growing thin!")
My morning coat, my collar mounting firmly to the chin,
My necktie rich and modest, but asserted by a simple pin —
(They will say: "But how his arms and legs are thin!")
Do I dare   45
Disturb the universe?
In a minute there is time
For decisions and revisions which a minute will reverse.

　　For I have known them all already, known them all:
Have known the evenings, mornings, afternoons,   50
I have measured out my life with coffee spoons;
I know the voices dying with a dying fall
Beneath the music from a farther room.
　　So how should I presume?

　　And I have known the eyes already, known them all —   55
The eyes that fix you in a formulated phrase.
And when I am formulated, sprawling on a pin,
When I am pinned and wriggling on the wall,
Then how should I begin
To spit out all the butt-ends of my days and ways?   60
　　And how should I presume?

　　And I have known the arms already, known them all —
Arms that are braceleted and white and bare
(But in the lamplight, downed with light brown hair!)
　　Is it perfume from a dress   65
　　That makes me so digress?
Arms that lie along a table, or wrap about a shawl.
　　And should I then presume?
　　And how should I begin?

　　Shall I say, I have gone at dusk through narrow streets,   70
And watched the smoke that rises from the pipes
Of lonely men in shirtsleeves, leaning out of windows? . . .

I should have been a pair of ragged claws
Scuttling across the floors of silent seas.

　　And the afternoon, the evening, sleeps so peacefully!   75
Smoothed by long fingers,
Asleep . . . tired . . . or it malingers,
Stretched on the floor, here beside you and me.
Should I, after tea and cakes and ices,
Have the strength to force the moment to its crisis?   80
But though I have wept and fasted, wept and prayed,

Though I have seen my head (grown slightly bald) brought in upon a platter,°
I am no prophet — and here's no great matter;
I have seen the moment of my greatness flicker,
And I have seen the eternal Footman hold my coat, and snicker,   85
    And in short, I was afraid.

    And would it have been worth it, after all,
After the cups, the marmalade, the tea,
Among the porcelain, among some talk of you and me,
Would it have been worth while   90
To have bitten off the matter with a smile,
To have squeezed the universe into a ball°
To roll it toward some overwhelming question,
To say: "I am Lazarus,° come from the dead,
Come back to tell you all, I shall tell you all" —   95
If one, settling a pillow by her head,
    Should say: "That is not what I meant at all;
        That is not it, at all."

    And would it have been worth it, after all,
Would it have been worth while,   100
After the sunsets and the dooryards and the sprinkled streets,
After the novels, after the teacups, after the skirts that trail along the floor —
And this, and so much more? —
It is impossible to say just what I mean!
But as if a magic lantern threw the nerves in patterns on a screen: 105
Would it have been worth while
If one, settling a pillow or throwing off a shawl,
And turning toward the window, should say:
    "That is not it at all,
        That is not what I meant, at all."   110

No! I am not Prince Hamlet, nor was meant to be;
Am an attendant lord,° one that will do
To swell a progress,° start a scene or two,   *state procession*
Advise the prince: withal, an easy tool,
Deferential, glad to be of use,   115
Politic, cautious, and meticulous;
Full of high sentence, but a bit obtuse;
At times, indeed, almost ridiculous —
Almost, at times, the Fool.

82 *head . . . upon a platter*: At Salome's request, Herod had John the Baptist decapi-
tated and had the severed head delivered to her on a platter (see Matt. 14:1–12 and Mark
6:17–29).   92 *squeezed the universe into a ball*: See Andrew Marvell's "To His Coy Mistress" (p. 363), lines 41–42: "Let us roll all our strength and all / Our sweetness up into one
ball."   94 *Lazarus*: The brother of Mary and Martha who was raised from the dead by
Jesus (John 11:1–44). In Luke 16:19–31, a rich man asks that another Lazarus return from
the dead to warn the living about their treatment of the poor.   112 *attendant lord*: Like
Polonius in Shakespeare's *Hamlet*.

I grow old . . . I grow old . . .   120
I shall wear the bottoms of my trousers rolled.

    Shall I part my hair behind? Do I dare to eat a peach?
I shall wear white flannel trousers, and walk upon the beach.
I have heard the mermaids singing, each to each.

I do not think that they will sing to me.   125

I have seen them riding seaward on the waves,
Combing the white hair of the waves blown back
When the wind blows the water white and black.

We have lingered in the chambers of the sea
By seagirls wreathed with seaweed red and brown,   130
Till human voices wake us, and we drown.

Ralph Waldo Emerson (1803–1882)

Days   1867

Daughters of Time, the hypocritic° Days,
Muffled and dumb like barefoot dervishes,
And marching single in an endless file,
Bring diadems and fagots in their hands.
To each they offer gifts after his will,   5
Bread, kingdom, stars, and sky that holds them all.
I, in my pleachéd garden,° watched the pomp,
Forgot my morning wishes, hastily
Took a few herbs and apples, and the Day
Turned and departed silent. I, too late,   10
Under her solemn fillet° saw the scorn.   *headband*

1 *hypocritic*: The archaic meaning of *hypocrite* is "one who plays a part." The days are
being compared to actors in a pomp, or procession.   7 *pleachéd garden*: A garden containing trees whose branches are artificially bent and interwoven.

Robert Frost (1874–1963)

Dust of Snow   1923

The way a crow
Shook down on me
The dust of snow
From a hemlock tree

Has given my heart
A change of mood
And saved some part
Of a day I had rued.

ROBERT FROST (1874–1963)

The Road Not Taken   1916

Two roads diverged in a yellow wood,
And sorry I could not travel both
And be one traveler, long I stood
And looked down one as far as I could
To where it bent in the undergrowth;   5

Then took the other, as just as fair,
And having perhaps the better claim,
Because it was grassy and wanted wear;
Though as for that the passing there
Had worn them really about the same,   10

And both that morning equally lay
In leaves no step had trodden black.
Oh, I kept the first for another day!
Yet knowing how way leads on to way,
I doubted if I should ever come back.   15

I shall be telling this with a sigh
Somewhere ages and ages hence:
Two roads diverged in a wood, and I —
I took the one less traveled by,
And that has made all the difference.   20

THOMAS HARDY (1840–1928)

I Looked Up from My Writing   1916

I looked up from my writing,
    And gave a start to see,
As if rapt in my inditing,
    The moon's full gaze on me.

Her meditative misty head   5
    Was spectral in its air,
And I involuntarily said,
    "What are you doing there?"

"Oh, I've been scanning pond and hole
    And waterway hereabout   10
For the body of one with a sunken soul
    Who has put his life-light out.

"Did you hear his frenzied tattle?
  It was sorrow for his son
Who is slain in brutish battle,   15
  Though he has injured none.

"And now I am curious to look
  Into the blinkered mind
Of one who wants to write a book
  In a world of such a kind."   20

Her temper overwrought me,
  And I edged to shun her view,
For I felt assured she thought me
  One who should drown him too.

FRANCES E. W. HARPER (1825–1911)

Learning to Read   1872

Very soon the Yankee teachers
  Came down and set up school;
But oh! how the Rebs did hate it, —
  It was agin' their rule

Our masters always tried to hide   5
  Book learning from our eyes;
Knowledge did'nt agree with slavery —
  'Twould make us all too wise.

But some of us would try to steal
  A little from the book,   10
And put the words together,
  And learn by hook or crook.

I remember Uncle Caldwell,
  Who took pot-liquor fat
And greased the pages of his book,   15
  And hid it in his hat.

And had his master ever seen
  The leaves upon his head,
He'd have thought them greasy papers,
  But nothing to be read.   20

And there was Mr. Turner's Ben
  Who heard the children spell,
And picked the words right up by heart,
  And learned to read 'em well.

Well the Northern folks kept sending   25
    The Yankee teachers down
And they stood right up and helped us,
    Though Rebs did sneer and frown,

And, I longed to read my Bible,
    For precious words it said;   30
But when I begun to learn it,
    Folks just shook their heads,

And said there is no use trying,
    Oh! Chloe, you're too late;
But as I was rising sixty,   35
    I had no time to wait.

So I got a pair of glasses,
    And straight to work I went,
And never stopped till I could read
    The hymns and Testament.   40

Then I got a little cabin —
    A place to call my own —
And I felt as independent
    As the queen upon her throne.

GERARD MANLEY HOPKINS (1844–1889)

Spring and Fall   1880

To a Young Child

Márgarét áre you gríeving
Over Goldengrove unleaving?
Leáves, like the things of man, you
With your fresh thoughts care for, can you?
Áh! ás the heart grows older   5
It will come to such sights colder
By and by, nor spare a sigh
Though worlds of wanwood° leafmeal° lie;
And yet you wíll weep and know why.
Now no matter, child, the name: 10
Sórrow's spríngs áre the same.
Nor mouth had, no nor mind, expressed
What heart heard of, ghost° guessed: *soul*
It ís the blight man was born for,
It is Margaret you mourn for.   15

8 *wanwood*: Gloomy woods; *leafmeal*: Leaves broken up piecemeal.

Langston Hughes (1902–1967)

Harlem   *1951*

What happens to a dream deferred?

>Does it dry up
>like a raisin in the sun?
>Or fester like a sore —
>And then run?   5
>Does it stink like rotten meat?
>Or crust and sugar over —
>like a syrupy sweet?
>
>Maybe it just sags
>like a heavy load.   10
>
>*Or does it explode?*

Georgia Douglas Johnson (1877–1966)

Prejudice   *1922*

These fell miasmic rings of mist with ghoulish menace bound,
Like noose-horizons tightening my little world around.
They still the soaring will to wing, to dance, to speed away,
And fling the soul insurgent back into its shell of clay.
Beneath incrusted silences, a seething Etna° lies,   *Sicilian volcano*
The fire of whose furnaces may sleep, but never dies!

Ben Jonson (1573–1637)

To Celia   *1616*

Drink to me only with thine eyes,
    And I will pledge with mine;
Or leave a kiss but in the cup,
    And I'll not ask for wine.
The thirst that from the soul doth rise   5
    Doth ask a drink divine;
But might I of Jove's nectar sup,
    I would not change for thine.

I sent thee late a rosy wreath,
    Not so much honoring thee   10
As giving it a hope that there
    It could not withered be.

But thou thereon didst only breathe,
    And sent'st it back to me;
Since when it grows, and smells, I swear,   15
    Not of itself but thee.

JOHN KEATS (1795–1821)

Bright star, would I were steadfast as thou art —   1819

Bright star, would I were steadfast as thou art —
    Not in lone splendor hung aloft the night
And watching, with eternal lids apart,
    Like nature's patient, sleepless Eremite,
The moving waters at their priestlike task   5
    Of pure ablution round earth's human shores,
Or gazing on the new soft fallen mask
    Of snow upon the mountains and the moors —
No — yet still steadfast, still unchangeable,
    Pillowed upon my fair love's ripening breast,   10
To feel forever its soft fall and swell,
    Awake forever in a sweet unrest,
Still, still to hear her tender-taken breath,
And so live ever — or else swoon to death.

JOHN KEATS (1795–1821)

Written in Disgust of Vulgar Superstition   1816

The church bells toll a melancholy round,
    Calling the people to some other prayers,
    Some other gloominess, more dreadful cares,
More hearkening to the sermon's horrid sound.
Surely the mind of man is closely bound   5
    In some black spell; seeing that each one tears
    Himself from fireside joys, and Lydian° airs,
And converse high of those with glory crown'd.
Still, still they toll, and I should feel a damp, —
    A chill as from a tomb, did I not know
That they are dying like an outburnt lamp;   10
    That 'tis their sighing, wailing ere they go
    Into oblivion; — that fresh flowers will grow,
And many glories of immortal stamp.

---

7 *Lydian*: Soft, sweet music.

D. H. LAWRENCE (1885–1930)

How Beastly the Bourgeois Is   1909

How beastly the bourgeois is
especially the male of the species —

Presentable, eminently presentable —
shall I make you a present of him?

Isn't he handsome? isn't he healthy? isn't he a fine specimen?   5
doesn't he look the fresh clean Englishman, outside?
Isn't it god's own image? tramping his thirty miles a day
after partridges, or a little rubber ball?
wouldn't you like to be like that, well off, and quite the thing?

Oh, but wait!   10
Let him meet a new emotion, let him be faced with another
        man's need,
let him come home to a bit of moral difficulty, let life face
        him with a new demand on his understanding
and then watch him go soggy, like a wet meringue.
Watch him turn into a mess; either a fool or a bully.
Just watch the display of him, confronted with a new demand
        on his intelligence,   15
a new life-demand.

How beastly the bourgeois is
especially the male of the species —

Nicely groomed , like a mushroom
standing there so sleek and erect and eyeable —   20
and like a fungus, living on the remains of bygone life
sucking his life out of the dead leaves of greater life than his own.

And even so, he's stale, he's been there too long.
Touch him, and you'll find he's all gone inside
just like an old mushroom, all wormy inside, and hollow   25
under a smooth skin and an upright appearance.

Full of seething, wormy, hollow feelings
rather nasty —
How beastly the bourgeois is!

Standing in their thousands, these appearances, in damp England   30
what a pity they can't all be kicked over
like sickening toadstools, and left to melt back, swiftly
into the soil of England.

EMMA LAZARUS (1849–1887)

The New Colossus   1883

Not like the brazen giant of Greek fame,
With conquering limbs astride from land to land;
Here at our sea-washed, sunset gates shall stand
A mighty woman with a torch, whose flame
Is the imprisoned lightning, and her name   5
Mother of Exiles. From her beacon-hand
Glows world-wide welcome; her mild eyes command
The air-bridged harbor that twin cities frame.
"Keep, ancient lands, your storied pomp!" cries she
With silent lips. "Give me your tired, your poor,   10
Your huddled masses yearning to breathe free,
The wretched refuse of your teeming shore.
Send these, the homeless, tempest-tost to me,
I lift my lamp beside the golden door!"

CLAUDE McKAY (1889–1948)

The Lynching   1920

His spirit is smoke ascended to high heaven.
His father, by the cruelest way of pain,
Had bidden him to his bosom once again;
The awful sin remained still unforgiven.
All night a bright and solitary star   5
(Perchance the one that ever guided him,
Yet gave him up at last to Fate's wild whim)
Hung pitifully o'er the swinging char.
Day dawned, and soon the mixed crowds came to view
The ghastly body swaying in the sun.   10
The women thronged to look, but never a one
Showed sorrow in her eyes of steely blue.

And little lads, lynchers that were to be,
Danced round the dreadful thing in fiendish glee.

JOHN MILTON (1608–1674)

When I consider how my light is spent

ca. 1655

When I consider how my light is spent,°
    Ere half my days in this dark world and wide,
    And that one talent° which is death to hide
Lodged with me useless, though my soul more bent
To serve therewith my Maker, and present   5
    My true account, lest He returning chide;
    "Doth God exact day-labor, light denied?"
I fondly° ask. But Patience, to prevent   *foolishly*
That murmur, soon replies, "God doth not need
    Either man's work or His own gifts. Who best   10
    Bear His mild yoke, they serve Him best. His state
Is kingly: thousands at His bidding speed,
    And post o'er land and ocean without rest;
    They also serve who only stand and wait."

1 *how my light is spent*: Milton had been totally blind since 1651.   3 *that one talent*: Refers to Jesus's parable of the talents (units of money), in which a servant entrusted with a talent buries it rather than invests it and is punished on his master's return (Matt. 25:14–30).

EDGAR ALLAN POE (1809–1849)

To Helen

1823

Helen, thy beauty is to me
    Like those Nicéan barks° of yore,   *Byzantine ships*
That gently, o'er a perfumed sea,
    The weary, way-worn wanderer bore
    To his own native shore.   5

On desperate seas long wont to roam,
    Thy hyacinth hair, thy classic face,
Thy Naiad° airs have brought me home   *water nymph*
    To the glory that was Greece
And the grandeur that was Rome.   10

Lo! in yon brilliant window-niche
    How statue-like I see thee stand,
    The agate lamp within thy hand!
Ah! Psyche,° from the regions which
    Are Holy Land!   15

14 *Psyche*: A princess in Greek mythology loved by Cupid.

CHRISTINA GEORGINA ROSSETTI (1830–1894)
Uphill   *1861*

Does the road wind uphill all the way?
    Yes, to the very end.
Will the day's journey take the whole long day?
    From morn to night, my friend.

But is there for the night a resting place?   5
    A roof for when the slow dark hours begin.
May not the darkness hide it from my face?
    You cannot miss that inn.

Shall I meet other wayfarers at night?
    Those who have gone before.   10
Then must I knock, or call when just in sight?
    They will not keep you standing at that door.

Shall I find comfort, travel-sore and weak?
    Of labor you shall find the sum.
Will there be beds for me and all who seek?   15
    Yea, beds for all who come.

WILLIAM SHAKESPEARE (1564–1616)
That time of year thou mayst in me behold   *1609*

That time of year thou mayst in me behold
When yellow leaves, or none, or few, do hang
Upon those boughs which shake against the cold,
Bare ruined choirs, where late the sweet birds sang.
In me thou see'st the twilight of such day   5
As after sunset fadeth in the west;
Which by and by black night doth take away,
Death's second self,° that seals up all in rest.   *sleep*
In me thou see'st the glowing of such fire,
That on the ashes of his youth doth lie,   10
As the deathbed whereon it must expire,
Consumed with that which it was nourished by.
    This thou perceiv'st, which makes thy love more strong,
    To love that well which thou must leave ere long.

WILLIAM SHAKESPEARE (1564–1616)
When forty winters shall besiege thy brow   *1609*

When forty winters shall besiege thy brow
And dig deep trenches in thy beauty's field,

Thy youth's proud livery, so gazed on now,
Will be a tattered weed,° of small worth held.   *garment*
Then being asked where all thy beauty lies,   5
Where all the treasure of thy lusty days,
To say within thine own deep-sunken eyes
Were an all-eating shame and thriftless praise.
How much more praise deserved thy beauty's use
If thou couldst answer, "This fair child of mine   10
Shall sum my count and make my old excuse,"
Proving his beauty by succession thine.
    This were to be new made when thou art old,
    And see thy blood warm when thou feel'st it cold.

PERCY BYSSHE SHELLEY (1792–1822)

Ozymandias°   1818

I met a traveler from an antique land
Who said: Two vast and trunkless legs of stone
Stand in the desert. . . . Near them, on the sand,
Half sunk, a shattered visage lies, whose frown,
And wrinkled lip, and sneer of cold command,   5
Tell that its sculptor well those passions read
Which yet survive, stamped on these lifeless things,
The hand that mocked them, and the heart that fed:
And on the pedestal these words appear:
"My name is Ozymandias, King of Kings: 10
Look on my works, ye Mighty, and despair!"
Nothing beside remains. Round the decay
Of that colossal wreck, boundless and bare
The lone and level sands stretch far away.

Ozymandias: Greek name for Ramses II, pharaoh of Egypt for sixty-seven years during the thirteenth century B.C. His colossal statue lies prostrate in the sands of Luxor. Napoleon's soldiers measured it (56 feet long, ear 3½ feet long, weight 1,000 tons). Its inscription, according to the Greek historian Diodorus Siculus, was "I am Ozymandias, King of Kings; if anyone wishes to know what I am and where I lie, let him surpass me in some of my exploits."

LYDIA HUNTLEY SIGOURNEY (1791–1865)

Indian Names   1834

*"How can the red men be forgotten, while so many of
our states and territories, bays, lakes and rivers, are
indelibly stamped by names of their giving?"*

Ye say they all have passed away,
　　That noble race and brave,
That their light canoes have vanished
　　From off the crested wave;
That 'mid the forests where they roamed   5
　　There rings no hunter shout,
But their name is on your waters,
　　Ye may not wash it out.

'Tis where Ontario's billow
　　Like Ocean's surge is curled,
Where strong Niagara's thunders wake   10
　　The echo of the world.
Where red Missouri bringeth
　　Rich tribute from the west,
And Rappahannock sweetly sleeps   15
　　On green Virginia's breast.

Ye say their cone-like cabins,
　　That clustered o'er the vale,
Have fled away like withered leaves
　　Before the autumn gale,   20
But their memory liveth on your hills,
　　Their baptism on your shore,
Your everlasting rivers speak
　　Their dialect of yore.

Old Massachusetts wears it,   25
　　Within her lordly crown,
And broad Ohio bears it,
　　Amid his young renown;
Connecticut hath wreathed it
　　Where her quiet foliage waves,   30
And bold Kentucky breathed it hoarse
　　Through all her ancient caves.

Wachuset hides its lingering voice
　　Within his rocky heart,
And Alleghany graves its tone   35
　　Throughout his lofty chart;
Monadnock on his forehead hoar
　　Doth seal the sacred trust,
Your mountains build their monument,
　　Though ye destroy their dust.   40

Ye call these red-browed brethren
　　The insects of an hour,

Crushed like the noteless worm amid
    The regions of their power;
Ye drive them from their father's lands,   45
    Ye break of faith the seal,
But can ye from the court of Heaven
    Exclude their last appeal?

Ye see their unresisting tribes,
    With toilsome step and slow,   50
On through the trackless desert pass,
    A caravan of woe;
Think ye the Eternal's ear is deaf?
    His sleepless vision dim?
Think ye the *soul's blood* may not cry   55
    From that far land to him?

ALFRED, LORD TENNYSON (1809–1892)

Ulysses°   1833

    It little profits that an idle king,
By this still hearth, among these barren crags,
Matched with an agèd wife,° I mete and dole   *Penelope*
Unequal laws unto a savage race,
That hoard, and sleep, and feed, and know not me.   5
    I cannot rest from travel; I will drink
Life to the less. All times I have enjoyed
Greatly, have suffered greatly, both with those
That loved me, and alone; on shore, and when
Through scudding drifts the rainy Hyades°   10
Vexed the dim sea. I am become a name;
For always roaming with a hungry heart
Much have I seen and known – cities of men
And manners, climates, councils, governments,
Myself not least, but honored of them all –   15
And drunk delight of battle with my peers,
Far on the ringing plains of windy Troy.
I am a part of all that I have met;
Yet all experience is an arch wherethrough
Gleams that untraveled world, whose margin fades   20
For ever and for ever when I move.

Ulysses: Ulysses, the hero of Homer's epic poem the *Odyssey*, is presented by Dante in *The Inferno*, XXVI, as restless after his return to Ithaca and eager for new adventures. 10 *Hyades*: Five stars in the constellation Taurus, supposed by the ancients to predict rain when they rose with the sun.

How dull it is to pause, to make an end,
To rust unburnished, not to shine in use!
As though to breathe were life. Life piled on life
Were all too little, and of one to me   25
Little remains; but every hour is saved
From that eternal silence, something more,
A bringer of new things; and vile it were
For some three suns to store and hoard myself,
And this gray spirit yearning in desire   30
To follow knowledge like a sinking star,
Beyond the utmost bound of human thought.

    This is my son, mine own Telemachus,
To whom I leave the scepter and the isle —
Well-loved of me, discerning to fulfill   35
This labor, by slow prudence to make mild
A rugged people, and through soft degrees
Subdue them to the useful and the good.
Most blameless is he, centered in the sphere
Of common duties, decent not to fail   40
In offices of tenderness, and pay
Meet adoration to my household gods,
When I am gone. He works his work, I mine.

    There lies the port; the vessel puffs her sail:
There gloom the dark, broad seas. My mariners,   45
Souls that have toiled, and wrought, and thought with me —
That ever with a frolic welcome took
The thunder and the sunshine, and opposed
Free hearts, free foreheads — you and I are old;
Old age hath yet his honor and his toil.   50
Death closes all; but something ere the end,
Some work of noble note, may yet be done,
Not unbecoming men that strove with Gods.
The lights begin to twinkle from the rocks;
The long day wanes; the slow moon climbs; the deep   55
Moans round with many voices. Come, my friends.
'Tis not too late to seek a newer world.
Push off, and sitting well in order smite
The sounding furrows; for my purpose holds
To sail beyond the sunset, and the baths   60
Of all the western stars, until I die.
It may be that the gulfs will wash us down;
It may be we shall touch the Happy Isles,°
And see the great Achilles,° whom we knew.

---

63 *Happy Isles*: Elysium, the home after death of heroes and others favored by the gods. It was thought by the ancients to lie beyond the sunset in the uncharted Atlantic.   64 *Achilles*: The hero of Homer's *Iliad*.

Though much is taken, much abides; and though   65
We are not now that strength which in old days
Moved earth and heaven, that which we are, we are:
One equal temper of heroic hearts,
Made weak by time and fate, but strong in will
To strive, to seek, to find, and not to yield.   70

WALT WHITMAN (1819–1892)

When I Heard the Learn'd Astronomer   1865

When I heard the learn'd astronomer,
When the proofs, the figures, were ranged in columns before me,
When I was shown the charts and diagrams, to add, divide, and measure them,
When I sitting heard the astronomer where he lectured with much applause
    in the lecture-room,
How soon unaccountable I became tired and sick,
Till rising and gliding out I wandered off by myself,
In the mystical moist night-air, and from time to time,
Looked up in perfect silence at the stars.

WILLIAM WORDSWORTH (1770–1850)

I Wandered Lonely as a Cloud   1807

I wandered lonely as a cloud
That floats on high o'er vales and hills,
When all at once I saw a crowd,
A host, of golden daffodils,
Beside the lake, beneath the trees,   5
Fluttering and dancing in the breeze.

Continuous as the stars that shine
And twinkle on the milky way,
They stretched in never-ending line
Along the margin of a bay;   10
Ten thousand saw I at a glance,
Tossing their heads in sprightly dance.

The waves beside them danced, but they
Outdid the sparkling waves in glee;
A poet could not but be gay,   15
In such a jocund company;
I gazed — and gazed — but little thought
What wealth the show to me had brought:

For oft, when on my couch I lie
In vacant or in pensive mood,   20
They flash upon that inward eye
Which is the bliss of solitude;
And then my heart with pleasure fills,
And dances with the daffodils.

WILLIAM WORDSWORTH (1770–1850)

Mutability   1822

From low to high doth dissolution climb,
And sink from high to low, along a scale
Of awful° notes, whose concord shall not fail;   *awe-filled*
A musical but melancholy chime,
Which they can hear who meddle not with crime,   5
Nor avarice, nor over-anxious care.
Truth fails not; but her outward forms that bear
The longest date do melt like frosty rime,
That in the morning whitened hill and plain
And is no more; drop like the tower sublime   10
Of yesterday, which royally did wear
His crown of weeds, but could not even sustain
Some casual shout that broke the silent air,
Or the unimaginable touch of Time.

WILLIAM BUTLER YEATS (1865–1939)

The Lake Isle of Innisfree°   1892

I will arise and go now, and go to Innisfree,
And a small cabin build there, of clay and
        wattles made:
Nine bean-rows will I have there, a hive for
        the honey-bee,
And live alone in the bee-loud glade.

And I shall have some peace there, for peace
        comes dropping slow,   5
Dropping from the veils of the morning to
        where the cricket sings;

© Hulton-Deutsch Collection / Corbis.

The Lake Isle of Innisfree: An island in Lough (or Lake) Gill, in western Ireland.

There midnight's all a glimmer, and noon a purple glow,
And evening full of the linnet's wings.

I will arise and go now, for always night and day
I hear lake water lapping with low sounds by the shore: 10
While I stand on the roadway, or on the pavements grey,
I hear it in the deep heart's core.

WILLIAM BUTLER YEATS (1865–1939)

Leda and the Swan°   *1924*

A sudden blow: the great wings beating still
Above the staggering girl, her thighs caressed
By the dark webs, her nape caught in his bill,
He holds her helpless breast upon his breast.

How can those terrified vague fingers push   5
The feathered glory from her loosening thighs?
And how can body, laid in that white rush,
But feel the strange heart beating where it lies?

A shudder in the loins engenders there
The broken wall, the burning roof and tower   10
And Agamemnon dead.
                    Being so caught up,
So mastered by the brute blood of the air,
Did she put on his knowledge with his power
Before the indifferent beak could let her drop?   15

Leda and the Swan: In Greek myth, Zeus in the form of a swan seduced Leda and fathered
Helen of Troy (whose abduction started the Trojan War) and Clytemnestra, Agamemnon's
wife and murderer. Yeats thought of Zeus's appearance to Leda as a type of annunciation,
like the angel appearing to Mary.

DRAMA

The Study
of Drama

24

Reading Drama

I regard the theater as serious business, one that makes or should make man more human, which is to say, less alone.
— ARTHUR MILLER

© Corbis.

There are people who ask why we need the arts. It's an intangible quality that the arts are teaching. People always want to quantify it, and you can't quantify the arts.
— NILAJA SUN

Thos Robinson/Getty Images.

READING DRAMA RESPONSIVELY

The publication of a short story, novel, or poem represents for most writers the final step in a long creative process that might have begun with an idea, issue, emotion, or question that demanded expression. *Playwrights* — writers who make plays — may begin a work in the same way as other writers, but rarely are they satisfied with only its publication because most dramatic literature — what we call *plays* — is written to be performed by actors on a stage before an audience. Playwrights typically create a play keeping in mind not only readers but also actors, producers, directors, costumers, designers, technicians, and a theater full of other support staff who have a hand in presenting the play to a live audience.

563

Drama is literature equipped with arms, legs, tears, laughs, whispers, shouts, and gestures that are alive and immediate. Indeed, the word *drama* derives from the Greek word *dran*, meaning "to do" or "to perform." The text of many plays — the *script* — may come to life fully only when the written words are transformed into a performance. Although there are plays that do not invite production, they are relatively few. Such plays, written to be read rather than performed, are called *closet dramas*. In this kind of work (primarily associated with nineteenth-century English literature), literary art outweighs all other considerations. The majority of playwrights, however, view the written word as the beginning of a larger creation and hope that a producer will deem their scripts worthy of production.

Given that most playwrights intend their works to be performed, it might be argued that reading a play is a poor substitute for seeing it acted on a stage — perhaps something like reading a recipe without having access to the ingredients and a kitchen. This analogy is tempting, but it overlooks the literary dimensions of a script; the words we hear on a stage were written first. Read from a page, these words can feed an imagination in ways that a recipe cannot satisfy a hungry cook. We can fill in a play's missing faces, voices, actions, and settings in much the same way that we imagine these elements in a short story or novel. Like any play director, we are free to include as many ingredients as we have an appetite for.

Trifles

In the following play, Susan Glaspell skillfully draws on many dramatic elements and creates an intense story that is as effective on the page as it is in the theater. Glaspell wrote *Trifles* in 1916 for the Provincetown Players on Cape Cod, in Massachusetts. Their performance of the work helped her develop a reputation as a writer sensitive to feminist issues. The year after *Trifles* was produced, Glaspell transformed the play into a short story titled "A Jury of Her Peers."

Glaspell's life in the Midwest provided her with the setting for *Trifles*. Born and raised in Davenport, Iowa, she graduated from Drake University in 1899 and then worked for a short time as a reporter on

Provided courtesy of the Lear Center for Special Collections & Archives, Connecticut College.

the *Des Moines News*, until her short stories were accepted in magazines such as *Harper's* and *Ladies' Home Journal*. Glaspell moved to the Northeast when she was in her early thirties to continue writing fiction and drama. She published novels, some twenty plays, and more than forty short stories. *Alison's House*, based on Emily Dickinson's life, earned her a Pulitzer Prize for drama in 1931. *Trifles* and "A Jury of Her Peers" remain, however, Glaspell's best-known works.

Glaspell wrote *Trifles* to complete a bill that was to feature several one-act plays by Eugene O'Neill. In *The Road to the Temple* (1926), she recalls how the play came to her as she sat in the theater looking at a bare stage. First, "the stage became a kitchen. . . . Then the door at the back opened, and people all bundled up came in — two or three men. I wasn't sure which, but sure enough about the two women, who hung back, reluctant to enter that kitchen. When I was a newspaper reporter out in Iowa, I was sent down-state to do a murder trial, and I never forgot going to the kitchen of a woman who had been locked up in town."

As you read the play, keep track of your responses to the characters and note in the margin the moments when Glaspell reveals how men and women respond differently to the evidence before them. What do those moments suggest about the kinds of assumptions these men and women make about themselves and each other? How do their assumptions compare with your own?

Susan Glaspell (1882–1948)

Trifles   *1916*

CHARACTERS

George Henderson, county attorney
Henry Peters, sheriff
Lewis Hale, a neighboring farmer
Mrs. Peters
Mrs. Hale

SCENE: The kitchen in the now abandoned farmhouse of John Wright, a gloomy kitchen, and left without having been put in order — unwashed pans under the sink, a loaf of bread outside the breadbox, a dish towel on the table — other signs of incompleted work. At the rear the outer door opens and the Sheriff comes in followed by the County Attorney and Hale. The Sheriff and Hale are men in middle life, the County Attorney is a young man; all are much bundled up and go at once to the stove. They are followed by the two women — the Sheriff's wife first; she is a slight wiry woman, a thin nervous face. Mrs. Hale is larger and would ordinarily be called more comfortable looking, but she is disturbed now and looks fearfully about as she enters. The women have come in slowly, and stand close together near the door.

County Attorney (rubbing his hands): This feels good. Come up to the fire, ladies.
Mrs. Peters (after taking a step forward): I'm not — cold.

Sheriff (unbuttoning his overcoat and stepping away from the stove as if to mark the beginning of official business): Now, Mr. Hale, before we move things about, you explain to Mr. Henderson just what you saw when you came here yesterday morning.

County Attorney: By the way, has anything been moved? Are things just as you left them yesterday?

Sheriff (looking about): It's just about the same. When it dropped below zero last night I thought I'd better send Frank out this morning to make a fire for us — no use getting pneumonia with a big case on, but I told him not to touch anything except the stove — and you know Frank.

County Attorney: Somebody should have been left here yesterday.

Sheriff: Oh — yesterday. When I had to send Frank to Morris Center for that man who went crazy — I want you to know I had my hands full yesterday. I knew you could get back from Omaha by today and as long as I went over everything here myself —

County Attorney: Well, Mr. Hale, tell just what happened when you came here yesterday morning.

Hale: Harry and I had started to town with a load of potatoes. We came along the road from my place and as I got here I said, "I'm going to see if I can't get John Wright to go in with me on a party telephone." I spoke to Wright about it once before and he put me off, saying folks talked too much anyway, and all he asked was peace and quiet — I guess you know about how much he talked himself; but I thought maybe if I went to the house and talked about it before his wife, though I said to Harry that I didn't know as what his wife wanted made much difference to John —

County Attorney: Let's talk about that later, Mr. Hale. I do want to talk about that, but tell now just what happened when you got to the house.

Hale: I didn't hear or see anything; I knocked at the door, and still it was all quiet inside. I knew they must be up, it was past eight o'clock. So I knocked again, and I thought I heard somebody say, "Come in." I wasn't sure, I'm not sure yet, but I opened the door — this door *(indicating the door by which the two women are still standing)* and there in that rocker — *(pointing to it)* sat Mrs. Wright. *(They all look at the rocker.)*

County Attorney: What — was she doing?

Hale: She was rockin' back and forth. She had her apron in her hand and was kind of — pleating it.

County Attorney: And how did she — look?

Hale: Well, she looked queer.

County Attorney: How do you mean — queer?

Hale: Well, as if she didn't know what she was going to do next. And kind of done up.

County Attorney: How did she seem to feel about your coming?

Hale: Why, I don't think she minded — one way or other. She didn't pay much attention. I said, "How do, Mrs. Wright, it's cold, ain't it?" And she said, "Is it?" — and went on kind of pleating at her apron. Well, I was surprised; she didn't ask me to come up to the stove, or to set down, but just sat there, not even looking at me, so I said, "I want to see John." And then she — laughed. I guess you would call it a laugh. I thought of Harry and the team outside, so I said a little sharp: "Can't I see John?" "No," she says, kind o' dull like. "Ain't he home?" says I. "Yes," says she, "he's home." "Then why can't I see him?" I asked her, out of patience. "'Cause he's dead," says she. "*Dead?*" says I. She just nodded her head, not getting a bit excited, but rockin' back and forth. "Why — where is he?" says I, not knowing what to say. She just pointed upstairs — like that *(himself pointing to the room above)*. I started for the stairs, with the idea of going up there. I walked from there to here — then I says, "Why, what did he die of?" "He died of a rope round his neck," says she, and just went on pleatin' at her apron. Well, I went out and called Harry. I thought I might — need help. We went upstairs and there he was lyin' —

County Attorney: I think I'd rather have you go into that upstairs, where you can point it all out. Just go on now with the rest of the story.

Hale: Well, my first thought was to get that rope off. It looked . . . *(stops; his face twitches)* . . . but Harry, he went up to him, and he said, "No, he's dead all right, and we'd better not touch anything." So we went back downstairs. She was still sitting that same way. "Has anybody been notified?" I asked. "No," says she, unconcerned. "Who did this, Mrs. Wright?" said Harry. He said it businesslike — and she stopped pleatin' of her apron. "I don't know," she says. "You don't *know?*" says Harry. "No," says she. "Weren't you sleepin' in the bed with him?" says Harry. "Yes," says she, "but I was on the inside." "Somebody slipped a rope round his neck and strangled him and you didn't wake up?" says Harry. "I didn't wake up," she said after him. We must 'a' looked as if we didn't see how that could be, for after a minute she said, "I sleep sound." Harry was going to ask her more questions but I said maybe we ought to let her tell her story first to the coroner, or the sheriff, so Harry went fast as he could to Rivers' place, where there's a telephone.

County Attorney: And what did Mrs. Wright do when she knew that you had gone for the coroner?

Hale: She moved from the rocker to that chair over there *(pointing to a small chair in the corner)* and just sat there with her hands held together and looking down. I got a feeling that I ought to make some conversation, so I said I had come in to see if John wanted to put in a telephone, and at that she started to laugh, and then she stopped and looked at me — scared. *(The County Attorney, who has had his notebook out, makes a note.)* I dunno, maybe it wasn't scared. I wouldn't like to say it was. Soon Harry got back, and then Dr. Lloyd came and you, Mr. Peters, and so I guess that's all I know that you don't.

County Attorney *(looking around)*: I guess we'll go upstairs first — and then out to the barn and around there. *(To the Sheriff.)* You're convinced that there was nothing important here — nothing that would point to any motive?

Sheriff: Nothing here but kitchen things. *(The County Attorney, after again looking around the kitchen, opens the door of a cupboard closet. He gets up on a chair and looks on a shelf. Pulls his hand away, sticky.)*

County Attorney: Here's a nice mess. *(The women draw nearer.)*

Mrs. Peters (to the other woman): Oh, her fruit; it did freeze. *(To the Lawyer.)* She worried about that when it turned so cold. She said the fire'd go out and her jars would break.

Sheriff (rises): Well, can you beat the woman! Held for murder and worryin' about her preserves.

County Attorney: I guess before we're through she may have something more serious than preserves to worry about.

Hale: Well, women are used to worrying over trifles. *(The two women move a little closer together.)*

County Attorney (with the gallantry of a young politician): And yet, for all their worries, what would we do without the ladies? *(The women do not unbend. He goes to the sink, takes a dipperful of water from the pail, and pouring it into a basin, washes his hands. Starts to wipe them on the roller towel, turns it for a cleaner place.)* Dirty towels! *(Kicks his foot against the pans under the sink.)* Not much of a housekeeper, would you say, ladies?

Mrs. Hale (stiffly): There's a great deal of work to be done on a farm.

County Attorney: To be sure. And yet *(with a little bow to her)* I know there are some Dickson county farmhouses which do not have such roller towels. *(He gives it a pull to expose its full length again.)*

Mrs. Hale: Those towels get dirty awful quick. Men's hands aren't always as clean as they might be.

County Attorney: Ah, loyal to your sex, I see. But you and Mrs. Wright were neighbors. I suppose you were friends, too.

Mrs. Hale (shaking her head): I've not seen much of her of late years. I've not been in this house — it's more than a year.

County Attorney: And why was that? You didn't like her?

Mrs. Hale: I liked her all well enough. Farmers' wives have their hands full, Mr. Henderson. And then —

County Attorney: Yes — ?

Mrs. Hale (looking about): It never seemed a very cheerful place.

County Attorney: No — it's not cheerful. I shouldn't say she had the homemaking instinct.

Mrs. Hale: Well, I don't know as Wright had, either.

County Attorney: You mean that they didn't get on very well?

Mrs. Hale: No, I don't mean anything. But I don't think a place'd be any cheerfuller for John Wright's being in it.

County Attorney: I'd like to talk more of that a little later. I want to get the lay of things upstairs now. *(He goes to the left where three steps lead to a stair door.)*

Sheriff: I suppose anything Mrs. Peters does'll be all right. She was to take in some clothes for her, you know, and a few little things. We left in such a hurry yesterday.

County Attorney: Yes, but I would like to see what you take, Mrs. Peters, and keep an eye out for anything that might be of use to us.

Mrs. Peters: Yes, Mr. Henderson. *(The women listen to the men's steps on the stairs, then look about the kitchen.)*

Mrs. Hale: I'd hate to have men coming into my kitchen, snooping around and criticizing. *(She arranges the pans under sink which the Lawyer had shoved out of place.)*

Mrs. Peters: Of course it's no more than their duty.

Mrs. Hale: Duty's all right, but I guess that deputy sheriff that came out to make the fire might have got a little of this on. *(Gives the roller towel a pull.)* Wish I'd thought of that sooner. Seems mean to talk about her for not having things slicked up when she had to come away in such a hurry.

Mrs. Peters (who has gone to a small table in the left rear corner of the room, and lifted one end of a towel that covers a pan): She had bread set. *(Stands still.)*

Mrs. Hale (eyes fixed on a loaf of bread beside the breadbox, which is on a low shelf at the other side of the room. Moves slowly toward it.): She was going to put this in there. *(Picks up loaf, then abruptly drops it. In a manner of returning to familiar things.)* It's a shame about her fruit. I wonder if it's all gone. *(Gets up on the chair and looks.)* I think there's some here that's all right, Mrs. Peters. Yes — here; *(holding it toward the window)* this is cherries, too. *(Looking again.)* I declare I believe that's the only one. *(Gets down, bottle in her hand. Goes to the sink and wipes it off on the outside.)* She'll feel awful bad after all her hard work in the hot weather. I remember the afternoon I put up my cherries last summer. *(She puts the bottle on the big kitchen table, center of the room. With a sigh, is about to sit down in the rocking-chair. Before she is seated realizes what chair it is; with a slow look at it, steps back. The chair which she has touched rocks back and forth.)*

Mrs. Peters: Well, I must get those things from the front room closet. *(She goes to the door at the right, but after looking into the other room, steps back.)* You coming with me, Mrs. Hale? You could help me carry them. *(They go in the other room; reappear, Mrs. Peters carrying a dress and skirt, Mrs. Hale following with a pair of shoes.)* My, it's cold in there. *(She puts the clothes on the big table, and hurries to the stove.)*

Mrs. Hale (examining the skirt): Wright was close. I think maybe that's why she kept so much to herself. She didn't even belong to the Ladies' Aid. I suppose she felt she couldn't do her part, and then you don't enjoy things when you feel shabby. I heard she used to wear pretty clothes and be lively, when she was Minnie Foster, one of the town girls singing in the choir. But that — oh, that was thirty years ago. This all you want to take in?

Mrs. Peters: She said she wanted an apron. Funny thing to want, for there isn't much to get you dirty in jail, goodness knows. But I suppose just to make her feel more natural. She said they was in the top drawer in this cupboard. Yes, here. And then her little shawl that always hung behind the door. (*Opens stair door and looks.*) Yes, here it is. (*Quickly shuts door leading upstairs.*)

Mrs. Hale (*abruptly moving toward her*): Mrs. Peters?

Mrs. Peters: Yes, Mrs. Hale?

Mrs. Hale: Do you think she did it?

Mrs. Peters (*in a frightened voice*): Oh, I don't know.

Mrs. Hale: Well, I don't think she did. Asking for an apron and her little shawl. Worrying about her fruit.

Mrs. Peters (*starts to speak, glances up, where footsteps are heard in the room above. In a low voice*): Mr. Peters says it looks bad for her. Mr. Henderson is awful sarcastic in a speech and he'll make fun of her sayin' she didn't wake up.

Mrs. Hale: Well, I guess John Wright didn't wake when they was slipping that rope under his neck.

Mrs. Peters: No, it's strange. It must have been done awful crafty and still. They say it was such a — funny way to kill a man, rigging it all up like that.

Mrs. Hale: That's just what Mr. Hale said. There was a gun in the house. He says that's what he can't understand.

Mrs. Peters: Mr. Henderson said coming out that what was needed for the case was a motive; something to show anger, or — sudden feeling.

Mrs. Hale (*who is standing by the table*): Well, I don't see any signs of anger around here. (*She puts her hand on the dish towel which lies on the table, stands looking down at table, one-half of which is clean, the other half messy.*) It's wiped to here. (*Makes a move as if to finish work, then turns and looks at loaf of bread outside the breadbox. Drops towel. In that voice of coming back to familiar things.*) Wonder how they are finding things upstairs. I hope she had it a little more red-up up there. You know, it seems kind of *sneaking*. Locking her up in town and then coming out here and trying to get her own house to turn against her!

Mrs. Peters: But, Mrs. Hale, the law is the law.

Mrs. Hale: I s'pose 'tis. (*Unbuttoning her coat.*) Better loosen up your things, Mrs. Peters. You won't feel them when you go out. (*Mrs. Peters takes off her fur tippet, goes to hang it on hook at back of room, stands looking at the under part of the small corner table.*)

Mrs. Peters: She was piecing a quilt. (*She brings the large sewing basket and they look at the bright pieces.*)

Mrs. Hale: It's a log cabin pattern. Pretty, isn't it? I wonder if she was goin' to quilt it or just knot it? (*Footsteps have been heard coming down the stairs. The Sheriff enters followed by Hale and the County Attorney.*)

Sheriff: They wonder if she was going to quilt it or just knot it! (*The men laugh, the women look abashed.*)

County Attorney (*rubbing his hands over the stove*): Frank's fire didn't do much up there, did it? Well, let's go out to the barn and get that cleared up. (*The men go outside.*)

Mrs. Hale (resentfully): I don't know as there's anything so strange, our takin' up our time with little things while we're waiting for them to get the evidence. *(She sits down at the big table smoothing out a block with decision.)* I don't see as it's anything to laugh about.

Mrs. Peters (apologetically): Of course they've got awful important things on their minds. *(Pulls up a chair and joins Mrs. Hale at the table.)*

Mrs. Hale (examining another block): Mrs. Peters, look at this one. Here, this is the one she was working on, and look at the sewing! All the rest of it has been so nice and even. And look at this! It's all over the place! Why, it looks as if she didn't know what she was about! *(After she has said this they look at each other, then start to glance back at the door. After an instant Mrs. Hale has pulled at a knot and ripped the sewing.)*

Mrs. Peters: Oh, what are you doing, Mrs. Hale?

Mrs. Hale (mildly): Just pulling out a stitch or two that's not sewed very good. *(Threading a needle.)* Bad sewing always made me fidgety.

Mrs. Peters (nervously): I don't think we ought to touch things.

Mrs. Hale: I'll just finish up this end. *(Suddenly stopping and leaning forward.)* Mrs. Peters?

Mrs. Peters: Yes, Mrs. Hale?

Mrs. Hale: What do you suppose she was so nervous about?

Mrs. Peters: Oh—I don't know. I don't know as she was nervous. I sometimes sew awful queer when I'm just tired. *(Mrs. Hale starts to say something, looks at Mrs. Peters, then goes on sewing.)* Well, I must get these things wrapped up. They may be through sooner than we think. *(Putting apron and other things together.)* I wonder where I can find a piece of paper, and string. *(Rises.)*

Mrs. Hale: In that cupboard, maybe.

Mrs. Peters (looking in cupboard): Why, here's a bird-cage. *(Holds it up.)* Did she have a bird, Mrs. Hale?

Mrs. Hale: Why, I don't know whether she did or not—I've not been here for so long. There was a man around last year selling canaries cheap, but I don't know as she took one; maybe she did. She used to sing real pretty herself.

Mrs. Peters (glancing around): Seems funny to think of a bird here. But she must have had one, or why would she have a cage? I wonder what happened to it?

Mrs. Hale: I s'pose maybe the cat got it.

Mrs. Peters: No, she didn't have a cat. She's got that feeling some people have about cats—being afraid of them. My cat got in her room and she was real upset and asked me to take it out.

Mrs. Hale: My sister Bessie was like that. Queer, ain't it?

Mrs. Peters (examining the cage): Why, look at this door. It's broke. One hinge is pulled apart.

Mrs. Hale (looking too): Looks as if someone must have been rough with it.

Mrs. Peters: Why, yes. *(She brings the cage forward and puts it on the table.)*

Mrs. Hale: I wish if they're going to find any evidence they'd be about it. I don't like this place.

Mrs. Peters: But I'm awful glad you came with me, Mrs. Hale. It would be lonesome for me sitting here alone.

Mrs. Hale: It would, wouldn't it? *(Dropping her sewing.)* But I tell you what I do wish, Mrs. Peters. I wish I had come over sometimes when *she* was here. I — *(looking around the room)* — wish I had.

Mrs. Peters: But of course you were awful busy, Mrs. Hale — your house and your children.

Mrs. Hale: I could've come. I stayed away because it weren't cheerful — and that's why I ought to have come. I — I've never liked this place. Maybe because it's down in a hollow and you don't see the road. I dunno what it is, but it's a lonesome place and always was. I wish I had come over to see Minnie Foster sometimes. I can see now — *(Shakes her head.)*

Mrs. Peters: Well, you mustn't reproach yourself, Mrs. Hale. Somehow we just don't see how it is with other folks until — something turns up.

Mrs. Hale: Not having children makes less work — but it makes a quiet house, and Wright out to work all day, and no company when he did come in. Did you know John Wright, Mrs. Peters?

Mrs. Peters: Not to know him; I've seen him in town. They say he was a good man.

Mrs. Hale: Yes — good; he didn't drink, and kept his word as well as most, I guess, and paid his debts. But he was a hard man, Mrs. Peters. Just to pass the time of day with him — *(Shivers.)* Like a raw wind that gets to the bone. *(Pauses, her eye falling on the cage.)* I should think she would 'a' wanted a bird. But what do you suppose went with it?

Mrs. Peters: I don't know, unless it got sick and died. *(She reaches over and swings the broken door, swings it again, both women watch it.)*

Mrs. Hale: You weren't raised round here, were you? *(Mrs. Peters shakes her head.)* You didn't know — her?

Mrs. Peters: Not till they brought her yesterday.

Mrs. Hale: She — come to think of it, she was kind of like a bird herself — real sweet and pretty, but kind of timid and — fluttery. How — she — did — change. *(Silence: then as if struck by a happy thought and relieved to get back to everyday things.)* Tell you what, Mrs. Peters, why don't you take the quilt in with you? It might take up her mind.

Mrs. Peters: Why, I think that's a real nice idea, Mrs. Hale. There couldn't possibly be any objection to it, could there? Now, just what would I take? I wonder if her patches are in here — and her things. *(They look in the sewing basket.)*

Mrs. Hale: Here's some red. I expect this has got sewing things in it. *(Brings out a fancy box.)* What a pretty box. Looks like something somebody would give you. Maybe her scissors are in here. *(Opens box. Suddenly puts her hand to her nose.)* Why — *(Mrs. Peters bends nearer, then turns her face away.)* There's something wrapped up in this piece of silk.

Mrs. Peters: Why, this isn't her scissors.

Mrs. Hale (lifting the silk): Oh, Mrs. Peters — it's — *(Mrs. Peters bends closer.)*

Mrs. Peters: It's the bird.

Mrs. Hale (jumping up): But, Mrs. Peters — look at it! Its neck! Look at its neck! It's all — other side *to*.

Mrs. Peters: Somebody — wrung — its — neck. *(Their eyes meet. A look of growing comprehension, of horror. Steps are heard outside. Mrs. Hale slips box under quilt pieces, and sinks into her chair. Enter Sheriff and County Attorney. Mrs. Peters rises.)*

County Attorney (as one turning from serious things to little pleasantries): Well, ladies, have you decided whether she was going to quilt it or knot it?

Mrs. Peters: We think she was going to — knot it.

County Attorney: Well, that's interesting, I'm sure. *(Seeing the bird-cage.)* Has the bird flown?

Mrs. Hale (putting more quilt pieces over the box): We think the — cat got it.

County Attorney (preoccupied): Is there a cat? *(Mrs. Hale glances in a quick covert way at Mrs. Peters.)*

Mrs. Peters: Well, not *now*. They're superstitious, you know. They leave.

County Attorney (to Sheriff Peters, continuing an interrupted conversation): No sign at all of anyone having come from the outside. Their own rope. Now let's go up again and go over it piece by piece. *(They start upstairs.)* It would have to have been someone who knew just the — *(Mrs. Peters sits down. The two women sit there not looking at one another, but as if peering into something and at the same time holding back. When they talk now it is in the manner of feeling their way over strange ground, as if afraid of what they are saying, but as if they cannot help saying it.)*

Mrs. Hale: She liked the bird. She was going to bury it in that pretty box.

Mrs. Peters (in a whisper): When I was a girl — my kitten — there was a boy took a hatchet, and before my eyes — and before I could get there — *(Covers her face an instant.)* If they hadn't held me back I would have — *(catches herself, looks upstairs where steps are heard, falters weakly)* — hurt him.

Mrs. Hale (with a slow look around her): I wonder how it would seem never to have had any children around. *(Pause.)* No, Wright wouldn't like the bird — a thing that sang. She used to sing. He killed that, too.

Mrs. Peters (moving uneasily): We don't know who killed the bird.

Mrs. Hale: I knew John Wright.

Mrs. Peters: It was an awful thing was done in this house that night, Mrs. Hale. Killing a man while he slept, slipping a rope around his neck that choked the life out of him.

Mrs. Hale: His neck. Choked the life out of him. *(Her hand goes out and rests on the bird-cage.)*

Mrs. Peters (with rising voice): We don't know who killed him. We don't know.

Mrs. Hale (her own feeling not interrupted): If there'd been years and years of nothing, then a bird to sing to you, it would be awful — still, after the bird was still.

Mrs. Peters (something within her speaking): I know what stillness is. When we homesteaded in Dakota, and my first baby died — after he was two years old, and me with no other then —

Mrs. Hale (moving): How soon do you suppose they'll be through looking for the evidence?

Mrs. Peters: I know what stillness is. *(Pulling herself back.)* The law has got to punish crime, Mrs. Hale.

Mrs. Hale (not as if answering that): I wish you'd seen Minnie Foster when she wore a white dress with blue ribbons and stood up there in the choir and sang. *(A look around the room.)* Oh, I *wish* I'd come over here once in a while! That was a crime! That was a crime! Who's going to punish that?

Mrs. Peters (looking upstairs): We mustn't — take on.

Mrs. Hale: I might have known she needed help! I know how things can be — for women. I tell you, it's queer, Mrs. Peters. We live close together and we live far apart. We all go through the same things — it's all just a different kind of the same thing. *(Brushes her eyes, noticing the bottle of fruit, reaches out for it.)* If I was you I wouldn't tell her her fruit was gone. Tell her it *ain't.* Tell her it's all right. Take this in to prove it to her. She — she may never know whether it was broke or not.

Mrs. Peters (takes the bottle, looks about for something to wrap it in; takes petticoat from the clothes brought from the other room, very nervously begins winding this around the bottle. In a false voice): My, it's a good thing the men couldn't hear us. Wouldn't they just laugh! Getting all stirred up over a little thing like a — dead canary. As if that could have anything to do with — with — wouldn't they *laugh!* (*The men are heard coming down stairs.*)

Mrs. Hale (under her breath): Maybe they would — maybe they wouldn't.

County Attorney: No, Peters, it's all perfectly clear except a reason for doing it. But you know juries when it comes to women. If there was some definite thing. Something to show — something to make a story about — a thing that would connect up with this strange way of doing it — (*The women's eyes meet for an instant. Enter Hale from outer door.*)

Hale: Well, I've got the team around. Pretty cold out there.

County Attorney: I'm going to stay here a while by myself. *(To the Sheriff.)* You can send Frank out for me, can't you? I want to go over everything. I'm not satisfied that we can't do better.

Sheriff: Do you want to see what Mrs. Peters is going to take in? *(The Lawyer goes to the table, picks up the apron, laughs.)*

County Attorney: Oh, I guess they're not very dangerous things the ladies have picked out. *(Moves a few things about, disturbing the quilt pieces which cover the box. Steps back.)* No, Mrs. Peters doesn't need supervising. For that matter, a sheriff's wife is married to the law. Ever think of it that way, Mrs. Peters?

Mrs. Peters: Not — just that way.

Sheriff (chuckling): Married to the law. *(Moves toward the other room.)* I just want you to come in here a minute, George. We ought to take a look at these windows.

County Attorney (scoffingly): Oh, windows!

Sheriff: We'll be right out, Mr. Hale. (*Hale goes outside. The Sheriff follows the County Attorney into the other room. Then Mrs. Hale rises, hands tight together, looking intensely at Mrs. Peters, whose eyes make a slow turn, finally meeting Mrs. Hale's. A moment Mrs. Hale holds her, then her own eyes point the way to where the box is concealed. Suddenly Mrs. Peters throws back quilt pieces and tries to put the box in the bag she is wearing. It is too big. She opens box, starts to take bird out, cannot touch it, goes to pieces, stands there helpless. Sound of a knob turning in the other room. Mrs. Hale snatches the box and puts it in the pocket of her big coat. Enter County Attorney and Sheriff.*)

County Attorney (facetiously): Well, Henry, at least we found out that she was not going to quilt it. She was going to — what is it you call it, ladies?

Mrs. Hale (her hand against her pocket): We call it — knot it, Mr. Henderson.

Curtain

CONSIDERATIONS FOR CRITICAL THINKING AND WRITING

1. FIRST RESPONSE. Describe the setting of this play. What kind of atmosphere is established by the details in the opening scene? Does the atmosphere change through the course of the play?

2. Characterize John Wright. Why did his wife kill him?

3. Why do the men fail to see the clues that Mrs. Hale and Mrs. Peters discover?

4. How do the men's conversations and actions reveal their attitudes toward women?

5. What is the significance of the play's last line, spoken by Mrs. Hale: "We call it — knot it, Mr. Henderson"? Explain what you think the tone of Mrs. Hale's voice is when she says this line. What is she feeling? What are you feeling?

6. CONNECTION TO ANOTHER SELECTION. Write an essay comparing the views of marriage in *Trifles* and in Kate Chopin's short story "The Story of an Hour" (p. 15). What similarities do you find in the themes of these two works? Are there any significant differences between the works?

A SAMPLE CLOSE READING

An Annotated Section of Trifles

As you read a play for the first time, highlight lines, circle or underline words, and record your responses in the margins. These responses will allow you to retrieve initial reactions and questions that in subsequent readings you can pursue and resolve. Just as the play is likely to have layered meanings, so too will your own readings as you gradually piece together a variety of elements such as exposition, plot, and character that will lead you toward their thematic significance. The following annotations for an excerpt from *Trifles* offer an interpretation that was produced by several readings of the play. Of course, your annotations could be quite different, depending upon your own approach to the play.

The following excerpt appears about two pages into this nine-page play and is preceded by a significant amount of exposition that establishes the bleak midwestern farm setting and some details about Mrs. Wright, who is the prime suspect in the murder of her husband. Prior to this dialogue, only the male characters speak as they try to discover a motive for the crime.

The Sheriff unknowingly announces a major conflict in the play that echoes the title: from a male point of view, there is nothing of any importance to be found in the kitchen — or in women's domestic lives. Mr. Hale confirms this by pronouncing such matters "trifles."

The County Attorney weighs in with his assessment of this "sticky" situation by calling it a "mess," from which he pulls away.

As the Attorney pulls away, the women move closer together (sides are slowly being drawn), and Mrs. Peters says more than she realizes when she observes, "Oh, her fruit; it did freeze." This anticipates our understanding of the cold, fruitless life that drove Mrs. Wright to murder.

The Sheriff's exasperation about women worrying about "preserves" will ironically help preserve the secret of Mrs. Wright — a woman who was beaten down by her husband but who cannot be beaten by these male authorities.

County Attorney *(looking around)*: I guess we'll go upstairs first — and then out to the barn and around there. *(To the Sheriff.)* You're convinced that there was nothing important here — nothing that would point to any motive?

Sheriff: Nothing here but kitchen things. *(The County Attorney, after again looking around the kitchen, opens the door of a cupboard closet. He gets up on a chair and looks on a shelf. Pulls his hand away, sticky.)*

County Attorney: Here's a nice mess. *(The women draw nearer.)*

Mrs. Peters *(to the other woman)*: Oh, her fruit; it did freeze. *(To the Lawyer.)* She worried about that when it turned so cold. She said the fire'd go out and her jars would break.

Sheriff *(rises)*: Well, can you beat the woman! Held for murder and worryin' about her preserves.

County Attorney: I guess before we're through she may have something more serious than preserves to worry about.

Hale: Well, women are used to worrying over trifles. *(The two women move a little closer together.)*

County Attorney *(with the gallantry of a young politician)*: And yet, for all their worries, what would we do without the ladies? *(The women do not unbend. He goes to the sink, takes a dipperful of water from the pail, and pouring it into a basin, washes his hands. Starts to wipe them on the roller towel, turns it for a cleaner place.)*

Dirty towels! *(Kicks his foot against the pans under the sink.)* Not much of a housekeeper, would you say, ladies?

Mrs. Hale (stiffly): There's a great deal of work to be done on a farm.

County Attorney: To be sure. And yet *(with a little bow to her)* I know there are some Dickson county farmhouses which do not have such roller towels. *(He gives it a pull to expose its full length again.)*

Mrs. Hale: Those towels get dirty awful quick. Men's hands aren't always as clean as they might be.

County Attorney: Ah, loyal to your sex, I see. But you and Mrs. Wright were neighbors. I suppose you were friends, too.

Mrs. Hale (shaking her head): I've not seen much of her of late years. I've not been in this house — it's more than a year.

County Attorney: And why was that? You didn't like her?

Mrs. Hale: I liked her all well enough. Farmers' wives have their hands full, Mr. Henderson. And then —

County Attorney: Yes — ?

Mrs. Hale (looking about): It never seemed a very cheerful place.

The Attorney has an eye for dirty towels but not for the real "dirt" embedded in the Wrights' domestic life.

The female characters are identified as "Mrs.," which emphasizes their roles as wives, while the men are autonomous and identified by their professions.

Mrs. Hale's comment begins a process of mitigating Mrs. Wright's murder of her husband. He — husbands, men — must share some of the guilt, too.

In contrast to men (a nice irony), farmers' wives' hands are full of responsibilities for which they receive little credit owing to the males' assumption that they fill their lives with trifles.

ELEMENTS OF DRAMA

Trifles is a **one-act play**; in other words, the entire play takes place in a single location and unfolds as one continuous action. As in a short story, the characters in a one-act play are presented economically, and the action is sharply focused. In contrast, full-length plays can include many characters as well as different settings in place and time. The main divisions of a full-length play are typically **acts**; their ends are indicated by lowering a curtain or turning up the houselights. Playwrights frequently employ acts to accommodate changes in time, setting, characters on stage, or mood. In many full-length plays, such as Shakespeare's *Hamlet*, acts are further divided into **scenes**; according to tradition a scene changes when the location of the action changes or when a new character enters. Acts and scenes are **conventions** that are understood and accepted by audiences because they have come, through usage and time, to be recognized as familiar techniques. The major convention of a one-act play is that it typically consists of only a single scene; nevertheless, one-act plays contain many of the elements of drama that characterize their full-length counterparts.

One-act plays create their effects through compression. They especially lend themselves to modestly budgeted productions with limited stage facilities, such as those put on by little theater groups. However, the potential of a one-act play to move audiences and readers is not related to its length. As *Trifles* shows, one-acts represent a powerful form of dramatic literature.

The single location that composes the **setting** for *Trifles* is described at the very beginning of the play; it establishes an atmosphere that will later influence our judgment of Mrs. Wright. The "gloomy" kitchen is disordered, bare, and sparsely equipped with a stove, a sink, a rocker, a cupboard, two tables, some chairs, three doors, and a window. These details are just enough to allow us to imagine the stark, uninviting place where Mrs. Wright spent most of her time. Moreover, "signs of incompleted work," coupled with the presence of the sheriff and county attorney, create an immediate tension by suggesting that something is terribly wrong. Before a single word is spoken, **suspense** is created as the characters enter. This suspenseful situation causes an anxious uncertainty about what will happen next.

The setting is further developed through the use of **exposition**, a device that provides the necessary background information about the characters and their circumstances. For example, we immediately learn through **dialogue** — the verbal exchanges between characters — that Mr. Henderson, the county attorney, is just back from Omaha. This establishes the setting as somewhere in the Midwest, where winters can be brutally cold and barren. We also find out that John Wright has been murdered and that his wife has been arrested for the crime.

Even more important, Glaspell deftly characterizes the Wrights through exposition alone. Mr. Hale's conversation with Mr. Henderson explains how Mr. Wright's body was discovered, but it also reveals that Wright was a noncommunicative man, who refused to share a "party telephone" and who did not consider "what his wife wanted." Later Mrs. Hale adds to this characterization when she tells Mrs. Peters that though Mr. Wright was an honest, good man who paid his bills and did not drink, he was a "hard man" and "Like a raw wind that gets to the bone." Mr. Hale's description of Mrs. Wright sitting in the kitchen dazed and disoriented gives us a picture of a shattered, exhausted woman. But it is Mrs. Hale who again offers further insights when she describes how Minnie Foster, a sweet, pretty, timid young woman who sang in the choir, was changed by her marriage to Mr. Wright and by her childless, isolated life on the farm.

This information about Mr. and Mrs. Wright is worked into the dialogue throughout the play in order to suggest the nature of the **conflict** or struggle between them, a motive, and, ultimately, a justification for the murder. In the hands of a skillful playwright, exposition is not merely a mechanical device; it can provide important information while simultaneously developing characterizations and moving the action forward.

The action is shaped by the *plot*, the author's arrangement of incidents in the play that gives the story a particular focus and emphasis. Plot involves more than simply what happens; it involves how and why things happen. Glaspell begins with a discussion of the murder. Why? She could have begun with the murder itself: the distraught Mrs. Wright looping the rope around her husband's neck. The moment would be dramatic and horribly vivid. We neither see the body nor hear very much about it. When Mr. Hale describes finding Mr. Wright's body, Glaspell has the county attorney cut him off by saying, "I think I'd rather have you go into that upstairs, where you can point it all out. Just go on now with the rest of the story." It is precisely the "rest of the story" that interests Glaspell. Her arrangement of incidents prevents us from sympathizing with Mr. Wright. We are, finally, invited to see Mrs. Wright instead of her husband as the victim.

Mr. Henderson's efforts to discover a motive for the murder appear initially to be the play's focus, but the real conflicts are explored in what seems to be a *subplot*, a secondary action that reinforces or contrasts with the main plot. The discussions between Mrs. Hale and Mrs. Peters and the tensions between the men and the women turn out to be the main plot because they address the issues that Glaspell chooses to explore. Those issues are not about murder but about marriage and how men and women relate to each other.

The *protagonist* of *Trifles*, the central character with whom we tend to identify, is Mrs. Hale. The *antagonist*, the character who is in some kind of opposition to the central character, is the county attorney, Mr. Henderson. These two characters embody the major conflicts presented in the play because each speaks for a different set of characters who represent disparate values. Mrs. Hale and Mr. Henderson are developed less individually than as representative types.

Mrs. Hale articulates a sensitivity to Mrs. Wright's miserable life as well as an awareness of how women are repressed in general by men; she also helps Mrs. Peters to arrive at a similar understanding. When Mrs. Hale defends Mrs. Wright's soiled towels from Mr. Henderson's criticism, Glaspell has her say more than the county attorney is capable of hearing. The *stage directions*, the playwright's instructions about how the actors are to move and behave, indicate that Mrs. Hale responds "stiffly" to Mr. Henderson's disparagements: "Men's hands aren't always as clean as they might be." Mrs. Hale eventually comes to see that the men are, in a sense, complicit because it was insensitivity like theirs that drove Mrs. Wright to murder.

Mr. Henderson, on the other hand, represents the law in a patriarchal, conventional society that blithely places a minimal value on the concerns of women. In his attempt to gather evidence against Mrs. Wright, he implicitly defends men's severe dominance over women. He also patronizes Mrs. Hale and Mrs. Peters. Like Sheriff Peters and Mr. Hale, he regards the women's world as nothing more than "kitchen things" and "trifles." Glaspell, however, patterns the plot so that the women see more about Mrs. Wright's motives than the men do and shows that the women have a deeper understanding of justice.

Many plays are plotted in what has come to be called a *pyramidal pattern*, because the plot is divided into three essential parts. Such plays begin with a *rising action*, in which complication creates conflict for the protagonist. The resulting tension builds to the second major division, known as the *climax*, when the action reaches a final *crisis*, a turning point that has a powerful effect on the protagonist. The third part consists of *falling action*; here the tensions are diminished in the *resolution* of the plot's conflicts and complications (the resolution is also referred to as the conclusion or *dénouement*, a French word meaning "unknotting"). These divisions may occur at different times. There are many variations to this pattern. The terms are helpful for identifying various moments and movements within a given plot, but they are less useful if seen as a means of reducing dramatic art to a formula.

Because *Trifles* is a one-act play, this pyramidal pattern is less elaborately worked out than it might be in a full-length play, but the basic elements of the pattern can still be discerned. The complication consists mostly of Mrs. Hale's refusal to assign moral or legal guilt to Mrs. Wright's murder of her husband. Mrs. Hale is able to discover the motive in the domestic details that are beneath the men's consideration. The men fail to see the significance of the fruit jars, messy kitchen, and badly sewn quilt.

At first Mrs. Peters seems to voice the attitudes associated with the men. Unlike Mrs. Hale, who is "more comfortable looking," Mrs. Peters is "a slight wiry woman" with "a thin nervous face" who sounds like her husband, the sheriff, when she insists, "the law is the law." She also defends the men's patronizing attitudes, because "they've got awful important things on their minds." But Mrs. Peters is a *foil*—a character whose behavior and values contrast with the protagonist's—only up to a point. When the most telling clue is discovered, Mrs. Peters suddenly understands, along with Mrs. Hale, the motive for the killing. Mrs. Wright's caged life was no longer tolerable to her after her husband had killed the bird (which was the one bright spot in her life and which represents her early life as the young Minnie Foster). This revelation brings about the climax, when the two women must decide whether to tell the men what they have discovered. Both women empathize with Mrs. Wright as they confront this crisis, and their sense of common experience leads them to withhold the evidence.

This resolution ends the play's immediate conflicts and complications. Presumably, without a motive the county attorney will have difficulty prosecuting Mrs. Wright—at least to the fullest extent of the law. However, the larger issues related to the *theme*, the central idea or meaning of the play, are left unresolved. The men have both missed the clues and failed to perceive the suffering that acquits Mrs. Wright in the minds of the two women. The play ends with Mrs. Hale's ironic answer to Mr. Henderson's question about quilting. When she says "knot it," she gives him part of the evidence he needs to connect Mrs. Wright's quilting with the knot used to strangle her husband. Mrs. Hale knows—and we know—that Mr. Henderson will miss the clue she offers because he is blinded by his own self-importance and assumptions.

Though brief, *Trifles* is a masterful representation of dramatic elements working together to keep both audiences and readers absorbed in its characters and situations.

Quiet Torrential Sound

A successful playwright, screenwriter, journalist, and actress, Joan Ackermann is also cofounder and artistic director of the three-decade-old Mixed Company Theater in Great Barrington, Massachusetts. She has published and produced more than a dozen of her plays around the country in such venues as the Guthrie Theater, Circle Rep, Cleveland Playhouse, Shakespeare & Company, and the Atlantic Theatre Company. Her plays include *Off the Map* (1994), which was adapted and released as a motion picture at the Sundance Film Festival in 2003; *The Batting Cage* (1996); *Marcus Is Walking* (1999); and *Ice Glen* (2005). Ackermann was also a longtime writer and producer of the television series **Arli$$**. In addition to writing articles for the *Atlantic, Esquire,* and *Time,*

Courtesy of Joan Ackermann.

she had a seven-year stint as a special contributor to *Sports Illustrated. Quiet Torrential Sound* is set in the Berkshires, where Ackermann resides and takes pleasure in being a part-time hiking guide and leading audiences on dramatic adventures.

JOAN ACKERMANN (B. 1951)

Quiet Torrential Sound   1995

CHARACTERS

Monica, late thirties
Claire, early thirties
Waiter

TIME & PLACE: The Present. Cafe table with two chairs.

Monica and Claire enter, dressed up, from a concert.

Monica: Well, isn't this charming.
Claire: Mmm.

Monica: How about this cute little table right here? My. Aren't these flowers delightful.

Claire: Mmm.

Monica: A little past their prime but . . . such a precious little vase.

Claire: Mmmm.

Monica: (*Sighs.*) Beethoven. Beethoven. I feel so . . . renewed, don't you? That was the greatest classical experience of my life.

Claire: Mm-mm.

Monica: Claire, I believe I've expressed this to you before. I wish you would make more of an effort to expand your vocabulary. No one would ever think that you're a junior college graduate if all you do is go around hmmmming things. (*Beat.*) And another thing. I wouldn't tell you this if we weren't sisters and the best of friends, but quite frankly, that blouse does very little for you. Blue is your color, Claire. Keep away from the pastels. They tend to wash you out. You don't have very strong features so you need more vibrancy of color to perk you up. Do you feel a draft?

Claire: I like this blouse.

Monica: It's not a question of liking it or not. As far as blouses go that one is perfectly acceptable. It's just pointless to wear something that does absolutely nothing for you. Clothes should make us appear as attractive as possible. Like wrapping paper. (*Waiter enters.*) Would you rather receive a gift in a plain brown paper bag or in nice cheerful paper with a bright colorful bow?

Waiter: Hi, my name is Nathan. Can I help you?

Monica: Nathan. At long last. Where have you been? I would like a cup of decaf, please, Nathan. Your freshest pot. With some Sweet and Low.

Waiter: Right-y-o. Anything to eat?

Monica: We've just been to the outdoor concert at Tanglewood. Beethoven's Seventh Symphony. So lovely, sitting out on the lawn.

Waiter: That's nice. Do you want something to eat?

Monica: I'm only telling you because I'm sure we smell of Avon Skin So Soft. For the bugs. It's an excellent bug repellent. Not completely effective, but . . . can you smell it?

Waiter: I smell something.

Monica: Avon Skin So Soft. Do you ever go to Tanglewood, Nathan? To hear the classical concerts?

Waiter: No.

Monica: I thought not. Pardon me for asking, but is your decaf truly decaf?

Waiter: Yes, we brew our own.

Monica: I'm so glad. I have ordered decaf before and received real coffee instead. The effects are not pleasant. My digestive system; I won't go into detail. Is there a fan on in here?

Waiter: No.

Monica: Could you turn it off, please?

Waiter: Sure.

Claire: I'd like a Coke and a hot fudge sundae.

Monica: Claire, dear. Really. A Coke and a hot fudge sundae? We were only just moments ago discussing your figure in the car.

Claire: Oh. Well, make it Diet Coke.

Waiter: Right-y-o. *(Starts to leave.)*

Monica: You're sure now about that decaf?

Waiter: Yes, m'am.

Monica: Thank you so very much. I appreciate your courtesy. *(Waiter exits.)* What a charming waiter. Doesn't seem to have been to the dentist recently but I'm sure he has a heart of gold. My, we are having a splendid little vacation aren't we, Claire? I never dreamed that the Berkshires held so many cultural attractions. I am so looking forward to the Norman Rockwell Museum this afternoon, aren't you?

Claire: Mmm. *(Then quickly:)* Yes, I am. Monica. I am. Looking forward.

Monica: I really should get subscription tickets to the Boston Symphony. I've been telling myself that for years. When I get home I will, I will, I'm going to, I'm making myself a promise right now, you're a witness. There's something about classical music, especially live classical music . . . something so pure, so humane, so . . . *honest.* There's no such thing as dishonest classical music — Claire, please don't pick at your face — it simply doesn't exist. You can see why it takes a certain intellect, a certain upbringing to appreciate it. An uncultivated mind could never appreciate classical music. Couldn't. Our waiter, for instance, Nathan. Classical music would just wash right over Nathan. Like rain on a duck. So. Do you have any observations from this morning you'd care to share with me?

Claire: Oh. I enjoyed the concert.

Monica: Yes?

Claire: Huh-huh. Yes. I did.

Monica: And what about it did you enjoy in particular?

Claire: Uh . . .

Monica: Was it the lovely outdoor setting? The view of distant rolling hills? The harmonious marriage between the natural beauty and Beethoven's Seventh Symphony? Was it the thrilling final movement?

Claire: I thought the conductor was exceptional.

Monica: Exceptional? Interesting choice of words. You're picking at your face again. Perhaps if you used a different moisturizer it wouldn't break out so. I'll give you some of mine when we get back to the hotel. In what way exceptional?

Claire: In the way he conducted. *(Clears throat.)* His musicians.

Monica: Ah . . . how astute of you, Claire. You know I think your hair is due for a trim. You're looking rather mousey of late, though you do have a strange glow about you I can't quite figure. *(Waiter enters.)* Maybe after the museum we can find a beauty shop.

Waiter: Here you go. *(Serves both and exits.)*

Monica: Why thank you so much, Nathan. *(Eyeing Claire's sundae.)* Oh my. I'm not saying a word. *(Takes Sweet and Low, shakes it hard, pours and watches it settle.)* Ah, it is decaf, I can tell by the way the Sweet and Low penetrates. Real coffee offers more resistance.

Claire: Monica . . .

Monica: You know what I find hard to believe, Claire, what I'll never understand, is how it could be, how it could come to pass that a man like Beethoven, a man blessed with such extraordinary gifts, such a superhuman capacity to paint with sound, paint giant murals of sound, how such a genius could actually become deaf. Did you know he became deaf in later years? He did. Such a tragedy. My coffee tastes like Avon Skin So Soft.

(Claire is eating an enormous hot fudge sundae.)

Claire: Monica . . .

Monica: It's hard to imagine what it would be like to be deaf and be Beethoven. To only listen in your mind. Actually, you would be listening in your mind, *to* your mind, to what your mind remembered. Sound was. Just imagine being Beethoven, deaf; listening to all that quiet sound, that quiet torrential sound. Is that real whipped cream? No, honey, I'm counting calories. But you enjoy it. Funny that his ears — of all parts of Beethoven's body — his ears should be the ones to break down. You use a certain part of your body so much, you just plum wear it out. Like a painter going blind. Like Renoir, for instance, going blind. Or Matisse, or Manet, or Monet, or Van Gogh, or Jackson Pollock, or Leonardo da Vinci. Or any of the great impressionists. Going blind. From overuse. The opposite of vestigial. Classical music is so stimulating, isn't it? My brain is full of thoughts.

Claire: Monica . . .

Monica: What?

Claire: *(Eating her sundae.)* You know that workshop on "Human Intimacy" that you suggested I go to a couple months ago?

Monica: No.

Claire: Remember? You gave me this brochure with workshops . . . the Adult Education Center. You had several circled, with an eyebrow pencil?

Monica: Mmm.

Claire: Well, I took one.

Monica: Good for you. *(Wanting more coffee.)* Where is our waiter? Where is Mr. Right-y-o? Imagine, a grown man speaking like that.

Claire: Remember too how we once talked about orgasms and how neither of us had ever had one? *(Pause.)* Remember? That night we got a little tipsy on peach wine coolers at Rose's?

Monica: We are sisters, Claire. We've shared many secrets with each other over the years. Such confidences are quite natural.

Claire: Well, I learned a couple of things at that workshop that really . . . helped.

Monica: I'm so glad. I was thinking of taking a music appreciation class there over the winter session. It's given by a Harvard professor and it's supposed to be excellent.

Claire: Mmm. My teacher was excellent.

Monica: Was he from Harvard?

Claire: No.

Monica: Oh.

Claire: Have you ever heard of multiple orgasms?

Monica: I'm an educated woman, Claire, and an avid magazine reader. I've heard about just about everything under the sun from multiple orgasms to multiple sclerosis. Just because I have experienced neither does not mean I am poorly informed on either topic.

Claire: Well, I'm having them.

Monica: Right now?

Claire: No, not right now.

Monica: *(Pause.)* Truly?

Claire: *(Eating ice cream.)* Huh-huh.

Monica: Well. Bless your heart.

Claire: Lots of them.

Monica: I'm very happy for you, dear. Now. Would you care to hear about the Norman Rockwell Museum? This guide book has been most informative.

Claire: First I figured out how to have them by myself. In the bathtub? Then I started seeing this guy, Jim, I call him Jimbo, sometimes Jumbo, inside joke, he helped me with my tax returns, he works for H&R Block? Monica . . . I can't tell you how wonderful it's been.

Monica: Then don't. Listen to this. "The Corner House in Stockbridge has the largest collection of Rockwell originals in the world, over four hundred. The museum changes its exhibit twice a year with a few exceptional paintings remaining on permanent display (for example, 'Stockbridge at Christmas'). There are six galleries within this beautifully restored 18th-century house, and the tour is a delight. All sorts of colorful information is passed along (such as pointers about the portraits of Grandma Moses and Rockwell's family contained within one painting). Helpful hints are given about how to appreciate Rockwell's attention to detail: 'Notice the ring finger on the old woman's hand; it's been indented by many years of wear . . .'"

(While Monica reads, Claire speaks.)

Claire: I'm thirty-three years old, Monica, and I've finally gotten in touch with my own body.

(Monica continues reading.)

Claire: It's like I've been walking around all these years with this hidden sunken treasure. It was there the whole time! What a feeling, I am telling you. Woo!

(Monica reads louder.)

Claire: I could have died and never even known, Monica, I could have gone my whole life and never known. I mean, I could have been in a car accident last year, I could easily have died in a car accident without ever knowing. What a crying shame that would have been.

(Monica reads louder.)

Claire: And to share that feeling with someone else. Monica. There's just nothing like it. Nothing. Not distant rolling hills. Not Beethoven's Seventh Symphony. *(Monica stops.)* Not even the thrilling final movement. Talk about thrilling final movements!

Monica: SHUT UP!

(Pause.)

Claire: Jimbo likes this blouse, Monica. He likes what's inside it no matter how it's packaged. He thinks it's vibrant.

(Pause. Waiter enters.)

Waiter: Did you call? Did you need something?

Monica: Yes, I need something, I need you to know that I know that that was not decaffeinated coffee, young man, it was not decaffeinated coffee you gave me, there was caffeine in it you assured me there wouldn't be but there was. Caffeine. Am I right, am I? I am. Do you know how many times that happens to me, how many times waiters and waitresses love to intentionally do that to me, just love to intentionally give me straight black coffee all the while smirking inside, insisting oh yes it's decaffeinated? Smirking, do you know? And do you know that as a result I'll be awake all night tonight, I'll be awake with a splitting headache and severe stomach cramps, awake all by myself alone in my bed. Tell me, Nathan, is that a cheerful picture? Is that a cheerful Norman Rockwell Saturday Evening Post cover, a woman alone in bed with a splitting headache and stomach cramps? Jaws clenched?

(Pause.)

Waiter: I'm sorry. I didn't think you would notice.

Monica: You know, Nathan, if you were the sort of person who went to classical concerts, the sort of person who was capable of enjoying classical concerts, capable of sitting there, quietly listening, appreciating, you would not be so cruel. So cruel. It's because I'm a cultured woman, isn't it? That's why, because I'm cultured.

(Silence. He exits.)

Claire: I don't think you were very nice to Nathan.

Monica: Nathan who did not turn off that fan, did willfully not turn off that fan on purpose when I asked him, asked him very cordially, I'll most likely end up with an earache from the draft; lying alone tonight in my bed with an earache and stomach cramps and a headache while my baby sister lies in the next bed . . . glowing. *(Takes a breath.)* Are you ready to leave, Claire? I was planning to have a dish of frozen light yogurt after sitting here watching you eat that Mt. Vesuvius of a hot fudge sundae but quite frankly, the unexpected turn in our conversation has left a disagreeable note in the atmosphere.

Claire: I'm ready to go. *(Looks at bill, opens purse, puts down money.)*

Monica: *(Stands.)* They have tours at the museum every twenty minutes. I plan to buy several postcards and perhaps a poster, if they are reasonably priced. *(Takes another breath.)* I think, Claire, that Stockbridge will be one of the highlights of our trip.

Claire: Mmm.

Monica: And far be it from me to be the one to suggest that there is ample room for you to show a little more appreciation for the fact that I have organized this vacation, this entire vacation, entirely by myself and by a little more appreciation I mean any at all.

Claire: I do. Appreciate.

Monica: How anyone could fathom why you would feel moved to share that kind of information with me at this point in time, at the very peak of our vacation.

Claire: That's why. You were in such a good mood. You just had the greatest classical experience of your life. The information was pretty . . . upbeat. I thought.

Monica: Upbeat.

Claire: I thought it was perfect vacation information. To share with my only living sister.

Monica: *(Starts walking out, turns back.)* Claire?

Claire: Mmm?

Monica: I apologize for my choice of words just then.

Claire: When?

Monica: Back then.

Claire: You mean when you said shut up?

Monica: Mm.

Claire: It's okay.

Monica: It was inappropriate. Uncalled for. The caffeine . . .

Claire: It's all right. Really.

Monica: *(Takes one step and turns back again.)* Claire?

Claire: Yes, Monica.

Monica: If you received any pertinent literature in your workshop — books, pamphlets, diagrams, whatever — I'd venture to say that I'd be willing to peruse whatever material you had.

Claire: All right. *(Smiles.)*

Monica: All right. *(She goes back and puts a bill on the table.)*

Claire: Ten dollars? Geez Louise.

Monica: Claire, don't say "geez Louise." It doesn't become a woman of your age. *(Starts to exit.)*

Claire: Okay.

Monica: *(Sarcastic.)* Or breadth of experience.

(Claire follows Monica off.)

The end

Considerations for Critical Thinking and Writing

1. FIRST RESPONSE. Analyze how Monica's opening conversation with Claire — before Nathan appears — serves to establish her character.

2. Discuss the significance of what the sisters order from Nathan in the café. What do their respective appetites reveal about them?

3. Describe the conflict that exists between Monica and Claire.

4. How is Monica's discussion of Beethoven relevant to the conflict in the play?

5. Comment on Ackermann's strategies for working humor and irony into the dialogue.

6. Consider the play's final scene. How would you characterize the tone of the ending and the sisters' future relationship?

DRAMA IN POPULAR FORMS

Audiences for live performances of plays have been thinned by high ticket prices but perhaps even more significantly by the impact of motion pictures and television. Motion pictures, the original threat to live theater, have in turn been superseded by television (along with DVDs and online streaming), now the most popular form of entertainment in America. Television audiences are measured in the millions. Probably more people have seen a single episode of a top-rated prime-time program such as *Modern Family* in one evening than have viewed a live performance of *Hamlet* in nearly four hundred years.

Though most of us are seated more often before a television than before live actors, our limited experience with the theater presents relatively few obstacles to appreciation because many of the basic elements of drama are similar whether the performance is on a screen or on a stage. Television has undoubtedly seduced audiences that otherwise might have been attracted to the theater, but television obviously satisfies some aspects of our desire for drama and can be seen as a potential introduction to live theater rather than as its irresistible rival.

Significant differences do, of course, exist between television and theater productions. Most obviously, television's special camera effects can capture phenomena such as earthquakes, raging fires, car chases, and space travel that cannot be realistically rendered on a live stage. The presentation of characters and the plotting of action are also handled differently owing to both the possibilities and the limitations of television and the theater. Television's multiple camera angles and close-ups provide a degree of intimacy that cannot be duplicated by actors onstage, yet this intimacy does not achieve the immediacy that live actors create. On commercial television the plot must accommodate itself to breaks in the action so that advertisements can be aired at regular intervals. Beyond these and many other differences, however, there are enough important similarities that the experience of watching television shows can enhance our understanding of a theater production.

Seinfeld

Seinfeld, which aired on NBC, was first produced during the summer of 1989. Although the series ended in the spring of 1998, it remains popular in reruns. No one expected the half-hour situation comedy that evolved from the pilot to draw some twenty-seven million weekly viewers, who avidly watched Jerry Seinfeld playing himself as a standup comic. Nominated for numerous Emmys, the show became one of the most popular programs of the 1990s. Although *Seinfeld* portrays a relatively narrow band of contemporary urban life — four thirtysomething characters living in New York City's Upper West Side — its quirky humor and engaging characters have attracted vast numbers of devoted fans who have conferred on it a kind of cult status. If you haven't watched an episode on television, noticed the T-shirts and posters, or read *Seinlanguage* (a best-selling collection of Seinfeld's monologues), you can catch up with reruns, on Hulu and on TV, and on the Internet, where fans discuss the popularity and merits of the show.

The setting for *Seinfeld* is determined by its subject matter, which is everyday life in Manhattan. Most of the action alternates between two principal locations: Jerry's modest one-bedroom apartment on West 81st Street and the characters' favorite restaurant in the neighborhood. Viewers are often surprised to learn that the show was filmed on a soundstage before a live audience in Studio City, California, because the sights, sounds, and seemingly unmistakable texture of Manhattan appear in background shots so that the city functions almost as a major character in many episodes. If you ever find yourself on the corner of Broadway and 112th Street, you'll recognize the facade of Jerry's favorite restaurant; but don't bother to look for the building that matches the exterior shot of his apartment building because it is in Los Angeles, as are the scenes in which the characters actually appear on the street. The care with which the sets are created suggests how important the illusion of the New York City environment is to the show.

As the central character, Jerry begins and ends each episode with a standup comedy act delivered before a club audience. These monologues (played down in later episodes) are connected to the events in the episodes and demonstrate with humor and insight that ordinary experience — such as standing in line at a supermarket or getting something caught in your teeth — can be a source of genuine humor. For Jerry, life is filled with daily annoyances that he copes with by making sharp humorous observations. Here's a brief instance from "The Pitch" (not reprinted in the excerpt on p. 591) in which Jerry is in the middle of a conversation with friends when he is interrupted by a phone call.

Jerry (into phone): Hello?
Man (v[oice] o[ver]): Hi, would you be interested in switching over to T.M.I. long distance service?
Jerry: Oh gee, I can't talk right now, why don't you give me your home number and I'll call you later?

Man (v[oice] o[ver]): Uh, well I'm sorry, we're not allowed to do that.
Jerry: Oh, I guess you don't want people calling you at home.
Man (v[oice] o[ver]): No.
Jerry: Well now you know how I feel.
Hangs up.

This combination of polite self-assertion and humor is Jerry's first line of defense in his ongoing skirmishes with the irritations of daily life. Unthreatening in his Nikes and neatly pressed jeans, Jerry nonetheless knows how to give it back when he is annoyed. Seinfeld has described his fictional character as a "nice, New York Jewish boy," but his character's bemused and pointed observations reveal a tough-mindedness that is often wittily on target.

Jerry's life and apartment are continually invaded by his three closest friends: George, Kramer, and Elaine. His refrigerator is the rallying point from which they feed each other lines over cardboard takeout cartons and containers of juice. Jerry's success as a standup comic is their cue to enjoy his groceries as well as his company, but they know their intrusions are welcome because the refrigerator is always restocked.

Jerry's closest friend is George Costanza (played by Jason Alexander), a frequently unemployed, balding, pudgy schlemiel. Any straightforward description of his behavior and sensibilities makes him sound starkly unappealing: he is hypochondriacal, usually upset and depressed, inept with women, embarrassingly stingy, and persistently demanding while simultaneously displaying a vain and cocky nature. As intolerable as he can be, he is nonetheless endearing. The pleasure of his character is in observing how he talks his way into trouble and then attempts to talk his way out of it to Jerry's amazement and amusement.

Across the hall from Jerry's apartment lives Kramer (played by Michael Richards), who is strategically located so as to be the mooch in Jerry's life. Known only as Kramer (until an episode later than "The Pitch" reveals his first name to be Cosmo), he amuses viewers with slapstick twitching, tripping, and falling that serve as a visual contrast to all the talking that goes on. His bizarre schemes and eccentric behavior have their physical counterpart in his vertical hair and his outrageous thrift-shop shirts from the 1960s.

Elaine Benes (played by Julia Louis-Dreyfus), on the other hand, is a sharp-tongued, smart, sexy woman who can hold her own and is very definitely a female member of this boys' club. As Jerry's ex-girlfriend, she provides some interesting romantic tension while serving as a sounding board for the relationship issues that George and Jerry obsess about. Employed at a book company at the time of the episode reprinted here, she, like George and Kramer, is also in the business of publishing her daily problems in Jerry's apartment.

The plots of most *Seinfeld* episodes are generated by the comical situations that Jerry and his friends encounter during the course of their daily lives. Minor irritations develop into huge conflicts that are offbeat, irreverent, or even absurd. The characters have plenty of time to create conflicts in their lives over such everyday situations as dealing with parents, finding an apartment, getting a date, riding the subway, ordering a meal, and losing a car in a mall parking garage. The show's screwball plots involve freewheeling misadventures that are played out in unremarkable but hilarious conversations.

© Dan Winters.

The following scenes from *Seinfeld* are from a classic script titled "The Pitch" that concerns Jerry's and George's efforts to develop a television show for NBC. The script is loosely based on events that actually occurred when Jerry Seinfeld and his real-life friend Larry David (the author of "The Pitch") sat down to discuss ideas for the pilot NBC produced in 1989. As brief as these scenes are, they contain some of the dramatic elements found in a play.

LARRY DAVID (B. 1947)

Seinfeld 1992

"THE PITCH"

[The following excerpted scenes do not appear one after the other in the original script but are interspersed through several subplots involving Kramer and Elaine.]

ACT ONE

SCENE A: *Int[erior] comedy club bar — night*

> *Jerry and George are talking. Suits enter, Stu and Jay.*

Stu: Excuse me, Jerry? I'm Stu Chermak. I'm with NBC.
Jerry: Hi.
Stu: Could we speak for a few moments?
Jerry: Sure, sure.
Jay: Hi, Jay Crespi.
Jerry: Hello.
George: C-R-E-S-P-I?

Jay: That's right.

George: I'm unbelievable at spelling last names. Give me a last name.

Jay: Mm, I'm not —

Jerry: George.

George (backing off): Huh? All right, fine.

Stu: First of all, that was a terrific show.

Jerry: Oh thank you very much.

Stu: And basically, I just wanted to let you know that we've been discussing you at some of our meetings and we'd be very interested in doing something.

Jerry: Really? Wow.

Stu: So, if you have an idea for like a TV show for yourself, well, we'd just love to talk about it.

Jerry: I'd be very interested in something like that.

Stu: Well, here, why don't you give us a call and maybe we can develop a series.

> *They start to exit.*

Jerry: Okay. Great. Thanks.

Stu: It was very nice meeting you.

Jerry: Thank you.

Jay: Nice meeting you.

Jerry: Nice meeting you.

> *George returns.*

George: What was that all about?

Jerry: They said they were interested in me.

George: For what?

Jerry: You know, a TV show.

George: Your own show?

Jerry: Yeah, I guess so.

George: They want you to do a TV show?

Jerry: Well, they want me to come up with an idea. I mean, I don't have any ideas.

George: Come on, how hard is that? Look at all the junk that's on TV. You want an idea? Here's an idea. You coach a gymnastics team in high school. And you're married. And your son's not interested in gymnastics and you're pushing him into gymnastics.

Jerry: Why should I care if my son's into gymnastics?

George: Because you're a gymnastics teacher. It's only natural.

Jerry: But gymnastics is not for everybody.

George: I know, but he's your son.

Jerry: So what?

George: All right, forget that idea, it's not for you. . . . Okay, okay, I got it, I got it. You run an antique store.

Jerry: Yeah and . . . ?

George: And people come in the store and you get involved in their lives.

Jerry: What person who runs an antique store gets involved in people's lives?

George: Why not?

Jerry: So someone comes in to buy an old lamp and all of a sudden I'm getting them out of a jam? I could see if I was a pharmacist because a pharmacist knows what's wrong with everybody that comes in.

George: I know, but antiques are very popular right now.

Jerry: No they're not, they used to be.

George: Oh yeah, like you know.

Jerry: Oh like you do.

    Cut to:

ACT ONE

SCENE B: *Int[erior] Jerry's apartment — day*

    Jerry and Kramer.

Kramer: . . . And you're the manager of the circus.

Jerry: A circus?

Kramer: Come on, this is a great idea. Look at the characters. You've got all these freaks on the show. A woman with a moustache? I mean, who wouldn't tune in to see a woman with a moustache? You've got the tallest man in the world; the guy who's just a head.

Jerry: I don't think so.

Kramer: Look Jerry, the show isn't about the circus, it's about watching freaks.

Jerry: I don't think the network will go for it.

Kramer: Why not?

Jerry: Look, I'm not pitching a show about freaks.

Kramer: Oh come on Jerry, you're wrong. People they want to watch freaks. This is a "can't miss."

ACT ONE

SCENE C: *Int[erior] coffee shop — lunchtime — day*

    Jerry and George enter.

George: So, what's happening with the TV show? You come up with anything?

Jerry: No, nothing.

George: Why don't they have salsa on the table?

Jerry: What do you need salsa for?

George: Salsa is now the number one condiment in America.

Jerry: You know why? Because people like to say "salsa." "Excuse me, do you have salsa?" "We need more salsa." "Where is the salsa? No salsa?"

George: You know it must be impossible for a Spanish person to order seltzer and not get salsa. *(Angry.)* "I wanted seltzer, not salsa."

Jerry: "Don't you know the difference between seltzer and salsa? You have the seltzer after the salsa!"

George: See, this should be the show. This is the show.

Jerry: What?

George: This. Just talking.

Jerry (dismissing): Yeah, right.

George: I'm really serious. I think that's a good idea.

Jerry: Just talking? What's the show about?

George: It's about nothing.

Jerry: No story?

George: No, forget the story.

Jerry: You've got to have a story.

George: Who says you gotta have a story? Remember when we were waiting for that table in that Chinese restaurant that time? That could be a TV show.

Jerry: And who is on the show? Who are the characters?

George: I could be a character.

Jerry: You?

George: You could base a character on me.

Jerry: So on the show there's a character named George Costanza?

George: Yeah. There's something wrong with that? I'm a character. People are always saying to me, "You know you're quite a character."

Jerry: And who else is on the show?

George: Elaine could be a character. Kramer.

Jerry: Now he's a character. . . . So, everyone I know is a character on the show.

George: Right.

Jerry: And it's about nothing?

George: Absolutely nothing.

Jerry: So you're saying, I go in to NBC and tell them I got this idea for a show about nothing.

George: *We* go into NBC.

Jerry: We? Since when are you a writer?

George: Writer. We're talking about a sit-com.

Jerry: You want to go with me to NBC?

George: Yeah, I think we really got something here.

Jerry: What do we got?

George: An idea.

Jerry: What idea?

George: An idea for the show.

Jerry: I still don't know what the idea is.

George: It's about nothing.

Jerry: Right.

George: Everybody's doing something, we'll do nothing.

Jerry: So we go into NBC, we tell them we've got an idea for a show about nothing.

George: Exactly.

Jerry: They say, "What's your show about?" I say, "Nothing."

George: There you go.

   A beat.

Jerry: I think you may have something there.

   Cut to:

ACT ONE

Scene D: *Int[erior] Jerry's apartment — day*

   Jerry and Kramer.

Jerry: So it would be about my real life. And one of the characters would be based on you.

Kramer (thinks): No. I don't think so.

Jerry: What do you mean you don't think so?

Kramer: I don't like it.

Jerry: I don't understand. What don't you like about it?

Kramer: I don't like the idea of a character based on me.

Jerry: Why not?

Kramer: Doesn't sit well.

Jerry: You're my neighbor. There's got to be a character based on you.

Kramer: That's your problem, buddy.

Jerry: I don't understand what the big deal is.

Kramer: Hey I'll tell you what, you can do it on one condition.

Jerry: Whatever you want.

Kramer: I get to play Kramer.

Jerry: You can't play Kramer.

Kramer: I am Kramer.

Jerry: But you can't act.

ACT ONE

Scene G: *Int[erior] NBC reception area — day*

   Jerry and George.

Jerry (to himself): Salsa, seltzer. Hey excuse me, you got any salsa? No not seltzer, salsa. *(George doesn't react.)* What's the matter?

George (nervous): Nothing.

Jerry: You sure? You look a little pale.

George: No, I'm fine. I'm good. I'm fine. I'm very good.

Jerry: What are you, nervous?

George: No, not nervous. I'm good, very good. *(A beat, then: explodes.)* I can't do this! Can't do this!

Jerry: What?

George: I can't do this! I can't do it. I have tried. I'm here. It's impossible.

Jerry: This was your idea.

George: What idea? I just said something. I didn't know you'd listen to me.

Jerry: Don't worry about it. They're just TV executives.

George: They're men with jobs, Jerry! They wear suits and ties. They're married, they have secretaries.

Jerry: I told you not to come.

George: I need some water. I gotta get some water.

Jerry: They'll give us water inside.

George: Really? That's pretty good. . . .

> *Receptionist enters.*

Receptionist: They're ready for you.

George: Okay, okay, look, you do all the talking, okay?

Jerry: Relax. Who are they?

George: Yeah, they're not better than me.

Jerry: Course not.

George: Who are they?

Jerry: They're nobody.

George: What about me?

Jerry: What about you?

George: Why them? Why not me?

Jerry: Why not you?

George: I'm as good as them.

Jerry: Better.

George: You really think so?

Jerry: No.

> *Door opens, Jerry and George P.O.V., the four execs stand up.*

> *Fade out.*

ACT TWO

Scene G: *Int[erior] NBC president's office — day*

> *The mood is jovial. Stu Chermak is there — along with Susan Ross, Jay Crespi, and Russell Dalrymple, the head of the network.*

Stu (to Jerry): The bit, the bit I really liked was where the parakeet flew into the mirror. Now that's funny.

George: The parakeet in the mirror. That is a good one, Stu.

Jerry: Yeah, it's one of my favorites.

Russell: What about you George, have you written anything we might know?

George: Well, possibly. I wrote an off-Broadway show, "La Cocina." . . . Actually it was off-off-Broadway. It was a comedy about a Mexican chef.

Jerry: Oh it was very funny. There was one great scene with the chef — what was his name?

George: Pepe.

Jerry: Oh Pepe, yeah Pepe. And, uh, he was making tamales.

Susan: Oh, he actually cooked on the stage?

George: No, no, he mimed it. That's what was so funny about it.

Russell: So what have you two come up with?

Jerry: Well we've thought about this in a variety of ways. But the basic idea is I will play myself.

George (interrupting, to Jerry): May I?

Jerry: Go ahead.

George: I think I can sum up the show for you with one word. NOTHING.

Russell: Nothing?

George: Nothing.

Russell: What does that mean?

George: The show is about nothing.

Jerry (to George): Well, it's not about nothing.

George (to Jerry): No, it's about nothing.

Jerry: Well, maybe in philosophy. But even nothing is something.

Jerry and George glare at each other. Receptionist sticks her head in.

Receptionist: Mr. Dalrymple, your niece is on the phone.

Russell: I'll call back.

George: D-A-L-R-I-M-P-E-L.

Russell: Not even close.

George: Is it with a "y"?

Russell: No.

Susan: What's the premise?

Jerry: . . . Well, as I was saying, I would play myself. And as a comedian, living in New York, and I have a friend and a neighbor and an ex-girlfriend, which is all true.

George: Yeah, but nothing happens on the show. You see, it's just like life. You know, you eat, you go shopping, you read. You eat, you read, you go shopping.

Russell: You read? You read on the show?

Jerry: Well I don't know about the reading. We didn't discuss the reading.

Russell: All right, tell me, tell me about the stories. What kind of stories?

George: Oh no, no stories.

Russell: No stories? So what is it?

George: What'd you do today?

Russell: I got up and came to work.

George: There's a show. That's a show.

Russell (confused): How is that a show?

Jerry: Well, uh, maybe something happens on the way to work.

George: No, no, no. Nothing happens.

Jerry: Well, something happens.

Russell: Well why am I watching it?

George: Because it's on TV.

Russell: Not yet.

George: Okay, uh, look, if you want to just keep on doing the same old thing, then maybe this idea is not for you. I for one will not compromise my artistic integrity. And I'll tell you something else. This is the show and we're not going to change it. *(To Jerry.)* Right?

Jerry: How about this? I manage a circus . . .

Considerations for Critical Thinking and Writing

1. **FIRST RESPONSE.** What does George mean when he says the proposed show should be about "nothing"? Why is George's idea both a comic and a serious proposal?

2. How does the stage direction "Suits enter" serve to characterize Stu and Jay? Write a description of how you think they would look.

3. What is revealed about George's character when he spells Crespi's and Dalrymple's names?

4. Discuss Kramer's assertion that people "want to watch freaks." Do you think this line could be used to sum up accurately audience responses to *Seinfeld*?

5. Choose a scene, and explain how humor is worked into it. What other emotions are evoked in the scene?

6. View an episode of *Seinfeld*. How does reading a script compare with watching the show? Which do you prefer? Why?

7. **CONNECTION TO ANOTHER SELECTION.** In an essay explain whether you think David Ives's play *Moby-Dude, Or: The Three-Minute Whale* (p. 846) fills George's prescription that a story should be about "nothing."

Like those of many plays, the settings for these scenes are not detailed. Jerry's apartment and the coffee shop are, to cite only two examples, not described at all. We are told only that it is lunchtime in the coffee shop. Even without a set designer's version of these scenes, we readily create a mental picture of these places that provides a background for the characters. In the coffee shop scene we can assume that Jerry and George are having lunch, but we must supply the food, the plates and cutlery, the tables and chairs, and the other customers. For the television show sets were used that repli-cated the details of a Manhattan coffee shop, right down to the menus and cash register. If the scene were presented on a stage, a set designer might use minimal sets and props to suggest the specific location. The director of such a production would rely on the viewers' imagination to create the details of the setting.

As brief as they are, these scenes include some exposition to provide the necessary background about the characters and their circumstances. We learn through dialogue, for example, that George is not a writer and that he doesn't think it takes very much talent to write a sitcom even though he's unemployed. These bits of information help to characterize George and allow an audience to place his attitudes and comments in a larger context that will be useful for understanding how other characters read them. Rather than dramatizing background information, the script-writer arranges incidents to create a particular focus and effect while work-ing in the necessary exposition through dialogue.

The plot in these scenes shapes the conflicts to emphasize humor. As in any good play, incidents are carefully arranged to achieve a particular effect. In the first scene we learn that NBC executives are interested in hav-ing Jerry do his own television show. We also learn, through his habit of spelling people's last names when he meets them, that George is a poten-tial embarrassment. The dialogue between Jerry and George quickly estab-lishes the conflict. The NBC executives would like to produce a TV show with Jerry provided that he can come up with an idea for the series; Jerry, however, has no ideas (here's the complication of the pyramidal plot pat-tern discussed in Elements of Drama, p. 577). This complication sets up a conflict for Jerry because George assumes that he can help Jerry develop an idea for the show, which, after all, shouldn't be any more difficult than spelling a stranger's name. As George says, "How hard is that? Look at all the junk that's on TV."

All of a sudden everyone is an expert on scriptwriting. George's off-the-wall suggestions that the premise for the show be Jerry's running an antique shop or teaching gymnastics are complemented by Kramer's idea that Jerry be "the manager of the circus" because "people they want to watch freaks." As unhelpful as Kramer's suggestion is, there is some truth here as well as humor, given his own freakish behavior. However, it is George who comes through with the most intriguing suggestion. As a result of the exuberantly funny riff he and Jerry do on "the difference between seltzer and salsa," George suddenly realizes that the show should be "about nothing"—that it should consist of nothing more than Jerry talking and hanging out with his friends George, Elaine, and Kramer. Jerry's initial skepticism gives way as he seriously considers George's proposal and is intrigued enough to bring George with him to the NBC offices to make the pitch. His decision to bring George to the meeting can only, of course, complicate matters further.

Before the meeting with the NBC executives, George is stricken with one of his crises of confidence when he compares himself to the "men with jobs" who are married and have secretaries. Characteristically, George's temporary lack of confidence shifts to an equally ill-timed arrogance once the meeting begins. He usurps Jerry's role and makes the pitch himself: "Nothing happens on the show. You see, it's just like life. You know, you eat, you go shopping, you read. You eat, you read, you go shopping." The climax occurs when George refuses even to consider any of the reservations the executives have about "nothing" happening on the show. George's insistence that he not compromise his "artistic integrity" creates a crisis for Jerry, a turning point that makes him realize that George's ridiculous arrogance might cost him his opportunity to have a TV show. Jerry's final lines to the executives — "How about this? I manage a circus . . ." — work two ways: he resignedly acknowledges that something — not "nothing" — has just happened and that George is, indeed, something of a freak.

The falling action and resolution typical of a pyramidal plot are not present in "The Pitch" because the main plot is not resolved until a later episode. "The Pitch" also contains several subplots not included in the scenes excerpted in this book. Like the main plot, these subplots involving Elaine, Kramer, and a few minor characters are not resolved until later episodes. Self-contained series episodes are increasingly rare on television, as programmers attempt to hook viewers week after week by creating suspense once associated with serialized stories that appeared weekly or monthly in magazines.

The theme of "The Pitch" is especially interesting because it self-reflexively comments on the basic premise of *Seinfeld* scripts: they are all essentially about "nothing" in that they focus on the seemingly trivial details of the four main characters' lives. The unspoken irony of this theme is that such details are in fact significant because it is just such small, everyday activities that constitute most people's lives.

25

Sophocles
and Greek Drama

© Corbis.

I depict men as they ought to be . . .
— SOPHOCLES

Not all things are to be discovered;
many are better concealed.
— SOPHOCLES

Sophocles lived a long, productive life (496?–406 B.C.) in Athens. During his life Athens became a dominant political and cultural power after the Persian Wars, but before he died, Sophocles witnessed the decline of Athens as a result of the Peloponnesian Wars and the city's subsequent surrender to Sparta. He saw Athenian culture reach remarkable heights as well as collapse under enormous pressures.

Sophocles embodied much of the best of Athenian culture; he enjoyed success as a statesman, general, treasurer, priest, and, of course, prize-winning dramatist. Although surviving fragments indicate that he wrote over 120 plays, only a handful remain intact. Those that survive consist of the three plays he wrote about Oedipus and his children — *Oedipus the King*, *Oedipus at Colonus*, and *Antigone* — and four additional tragedies: *Philoctetes*, *Ajax*, *Maidens of Trachis*, and *Electra*.

His plays won numerous prizes at festival competitions because of his careful, subtle plotting and the sense of inevitability with which their action is charged. Moreover, his development of character is richly complex. Instead of relying on the extreme situations and exaggerated actions that earlier tragedians used, Sophocles created powerfully motivated characters who even today fascinate audiences with their psychological depth.

In addition to crafting sophisticated tragedies for the Greek theater, Sophocles introduced several important innovations to the stage. Most important, he broke the tradition of using only two actors; adding a third resulted in more complicated relationships and intricate dialogue among characters. As individual actors took center stage more often, Sophocles reduced the role of the chorus (discussed on p. 603). This shift placed even more emphasis on the actors, although the chorus remained important as a means of commenting on the action and establishing its tone. Sophocles was also the first dramatist to write plays with specific actors in mind, a development that many later playwrights, including Shakespeare, exploited usefully. But without question Sophocles' greatest contribution to drama was *Oedipus the King*, which, it has been argued, is the most influential drama ever written.

Map of Ancient Greece. During Sophocles' time, the city-state of Athens (roughly in the center of this map) was the leading cultural and intellectual center of Greece — until the Peloponnesian Wars (431–404 B.C.) and Athens's defeat in 404 B.C. by the city-state of Sparta (below Athens, to the left).
Steven Wright/Shutterstock.

THEATRICAL CONVENTIONS OF GREEK DRAMA

© Corbis.

More than twenty-four hundred years have passed since 430 B.C., when Sophocles' *Oedipus the King* was probably first produced on a Greek stage. We inhabit a vastly different planet than Sophocles' audience did, yet concerns about what it means to be human in a world that frequently runs counter to our desires and aspirations have remained relatively constant. The ancient Greeks continue to speak to us. But inexperienced readers or viewers may have some initial difficulty understanding the theatrical conventions used in classical Greek tragedies such as *Oedipus the King* and *Antigone*. If Sophocles were alive today, he would very likely need some sort of assistance with the conventions of an Arthur Miller play or a television production of *Seinfeld*.

Classical Greek drama developed from religious festivals that paid homage to Dionysus, the god of wine and fertility. Most of the details of these festivals have been lost, but we do know that they included dancing and singing that celebrated legends about Dionysus. From these choral songs developed stories of both Dionysus and mortal culture-heroes. These heroes became the subject of playwrights whose works were produced in contests at the festivals. The Dionysian festivals lasted more than five hundred years, but relatively few of their plays have survived. Among the works of the three great writers of tragedy, only seven plays each by Sophocles and Aeschylus (525?–456 B.C.) and nineteen plays by Euripides (480?–406 B.C.) survive.

Plays were such important events in Greek society that they were partially funded by the state. The Greeks associated drama with religious and community values as well as entertainment. In a sense, their plays celebrate their civilization; in approving the plays, audiences applauded their own culture. The enormous popularity of the plays is indicated by the size of surviving amphitheaters. Although information about these theaters is sketchy, we do know that most of them had a common form. They were built into hillsides with rising rows of seats accommodating more than fourteen thousand people. These seats partially encircled an *orchestra* or "dancing place," where the *chorus* of a dozen or so men chanted lines and danced.

Tradition credits the Greek poet Thespis with adding an actor who was separate from the choral singing and dancing of early performances. A second actor was subsequently included by Aeschylus and a third, as noted earlier, by Sophocles. These additions made possible the conflicts and complicated relationships that evolved into the dramatic art we know today. The two or three male actors who played all the roles appeared behind

Classical Greek Theater in Delphi, Greece. This photo represents the features typical of a classical theater.
© Kevin Schafer/Corbis.

the orchestra in front of the *skene*, a stage building that served as dressing rooms. As Greek theater evolved, a wall of the skene came to be painted to suggest a palace or some other setting, and the roof was employed to indicate, for instance, a mountain location. Sometimes gods were lowered from the roof by mechanical devices to set matters right among the mortals below. This method of rescuing characters from complications beyond their abilities to resolve was known in Latin as *deus ex machina* ("god from the machine"), a term now used to describe any improbable means by which an author provides a too-easy resolution for a story.

Inevitably, the conventions of the Greek theaters affected how plays were presented. Few if any scene changes occurred because the amphitheater stage was set primarily for one location. If an important event happened somewhere else, it was reported by a minor character, such as a messenger. The chorus also provided necessary background information. In *Oedipus the King* and *Antigone*, the choruses, acting as townspeople, also assess the characters' strengths and weaknesses, praising them for their virtues, chiding them for their rashness, and giving them advice. The reactions of the chorus provide a connection between the actors and audience because the chorus is at once a participant in and an observer of the action. In addition, the chorus helps structure the action by indicating changes in scene or mood. Thus the chorus could be used in a variety of ways to shape the audience's response to the play's action and characters.

Actors in classical Greek amphitheaters faced considerable challenges. An intimate relationship with the audience was impossible because many spectators would have been too far away to see a facial expression or subtle gesture. Indeed, some in the audience would have had difficulty even hearing the voices of individual actors. To compensate for these disadvantages, actors wore large masks that extravagantly expressed the major characters' emotions or identified the roles of minor characters. The masks also allowed the two or three actors in a performance to play all the characters without confusing the audience. Each mask was fitted so that the mouthpiece amplified the actor's voice. The actors were further equipped with padded costumes and elevated shoes (*cothurni* or *buskins*) that made them appear larger than life.

As a result of these adaptive conventions, Greek plays tend to emphasize words — formal, impassioned speeches — more than physical action. We are invited to ponder actions and events rather than to see all of them enacted. Although the stark simplicity of Greek theater does not offer an audience realistic detail, the classical tragedies that have survived present characters in dramatic situations that transcend theatrical conventions. Tragedy, it seems, has always been compelling for human beings, regardless of the theatrical forms it has taken.

A Greek tragedy is typically divided into five parts: prologue, parodos, episodia, stasimon, and exodus. Understanding these terms provides a sense of the overall rhythm of a Greek play. The opening speech or dialogue is known as the ***prologue*** and usually gives the exposition necessary to follow the subsequent action. In the *parodos* the chorus makes its first entrance and gives its perspective on what the audience has learned in the prologue. Several *episodia*, or episodes, follow, in which characters engage in dialogue that frequently consists of heated debates dramatizing the play's conflicts. Following each episode is a choral ode or *stasimon*, in which the chorus responds to and interprets the preceding dialogue. The *exodus*, or last scene, follows the final episode and stasimon; in it the resolution occurs and the characters leave the stage.

The effect of alternating dialogues and choral odes has sometimes been likened to that of opera. Greek tragedies were written in verse, and the stasima were chanted or sung as the chorus moved rhythmically, so the plays have a strong musical element that is not always apparent on the printed page. If we remember their musical qualities, we are less likely to forget that no matter how terrifying or horrific the conflicts they describe, these plays are stately, measured, and dignified works that reflect a classical Greek sense of order and proportion.

TRAGEDY

Newspapers are filled with daily reports of tragedies: a child is struck and injured by a car; an airplane plunges into a suburban neighborhood; a volcano erupts and kills thousands. These unexpected instances of suffering are commonly and accurately described as tragic, but they are not tragedies in the literary sense of the term. A literary *tragedy* presents courageous individuals who confront powerful forces within or outside themselves with a dignity that reveals the breadth and depth of the human spirit in the face of failure, defeat, and even death.

Aristotle (384–322 B.C.), in his *Poetics*, defined *tragedy* on the basis of the plays contemporary to him. His definition has generated countless variations, qualifications, and interpretations, but we still derive our literary understanding of this term from Aristotle.

The protagonist of a Greek tragedy is someone regarded as extraordinary rather than typical: a great man or woman brought from happiness to agony. The character's stature is important because it makes his or her fall all the more terrifying. The protagonist also carries mythic significance for the audience. Oedipus and Antigone, for example, are not only human beings but legendary figures from a distant, revered past. Although the gods do not appear onstage in either *Oedipus the King* or *Antigone*, their power is ever present as the characters invoke their help or attempt to defy them. In addition, Greek tragedy tends to be public rather than private. The fate of the community — the state — is often linked with that of the protagonist, as when Thebes suffers a plague as a result of Oedipus's mistaken actions.

The protagonists of classical Greek tragedies (and of those of Shakespeare) are often rulers of noble birth who represent the monarchical values of their periods, but in modern tragedies the protagonists are more likely to reflect democratic values that make it possible for anyone to be a suitable subject. What is finally important is not so much the protagonist's social stature as a greatness of character that steadfastly confronts suffering, whether it comes from supernatural, social, or psychological forces. Although Greek tragic heroes were aristocrats, the nobility of their characters was more significant than their inherited titles and privileges.

The protagonist's eminence and determination to complete some task or goal make him or her admirable in Greek tragedy, but that does not free the protagonist from what Aristotle described as "some error or frailty" that brings about his or her misfortune. The term Aristotle used for this weakness is *hamartia*. This word has frequently been interpreted to mean that the protagonist's fall is the result of an internal *tragic flaw*, such as an excess of pride, ambition, passion, or some other character trait that leads directly to disaster.

Sometimes, however, misfortunes are the result not of a character flaw but of misunderstood events that overtake and thwart the protagonist's best intentions. Thus, virtue can lead to tragedy too. *Hamartia* has also been interpreted to mean "wrong act" — a mistake based not on a personal failure but on circumstances outside the protagonist's personality and control. Many readers find that a combination of these two interpretations sheds the most light on the causes of the tragic protagonist's fall. Both internal and external forces can lead to downfall because the protagonist's personality may determine crucial judgments that result in mistaken actions.

However the idea of tragic flaw is understood, it is best not to use it as a means of reducing the qualities of a complex character to an adjective or two that labels Oedipus as guilty of "overweening pride" (the Greek term for which is *hubris* or *hybris*) or Antigone as "fated." The protagonists of tragedies require more careful characterization than a simplistic label can provide.

Whatever the causes of the tragic protagonist's downfall, he or she accepts responsibility for it. Hence, even in his or her encounter with failure (and possibly death) the tragic protagonist displays greatness of character. Perhaps it is the witnessing of this greatness, which seems both to accept and to transcend human limitations, that makes audiences feel relief rather than hopelessness at the end of a tragedy. Aristotle described this response as a *catharsis*, or purgation of the emotions of "pity and fear." We are faced with the protagonist's misfortune, which often seems out of proportion to his or her actions, and so we are likely to feel compassionate pity. Simultaneously, we may experience fear because the failure of the protagonist, who is so great in stature and power, is a frightening reminder of our own vulnerabilities. Ultimately, however, both these negative emotions are purged because the tragic protagonist's suffering is an affirmation of human values — even if they are not always triumphant — rather than a despairing denial of them.

Nevertheless, tragedies are disturbing. Instead of coming away with the reassurance of a happy ending, we must take solace in the insight produced by the hero's suffering. And just as our expectations are changed, so are the protagonist's. Aristotle described the moment in the plot when this change occurs as a *reversal* (*peripeteia*), the point when the hero's fortunes turn in an unexpected direction. He more specifically defined this term as meaning an action performed by a character that has the opposite of its intended effect. An example cited by Aristotle is the messenger's attempts to relieve Oedipus's anxieties about his relationship to his father and mother. Instead, the messenger reveals previously unknown information that eventually results in a *recognition* (*anagnorisis*); Oedipus discovers the terrible truth that he has killed his father and married his mother.

Tragedy is typically filled with ironies because there are so many moments in the plot when what seems to be turns out to be radically different from what actually is. Because of this, a particular form of irony called *dramatic irony* is also known as *tragic irony*. In dramatic irony, the meaning of a character's words or actions is understood by the audience but not by the character. Audiences of Greek tragedy shared with the playwrights a knowledge of the stories on which many tragic plots were based. Consequently, they frequently were aware of what was going to happen before the characters were. When Oedipus declares that he will seek out the person responsible for the plague that ravishes his city, the audience already knows that the person Oedipus pursues is himself.

Oedipus the King

A familiarity with the Oedipus legend allows modern readers to appreciate the series of ironies that unfolds in Sophocles' *Oedipus the King*. As an infant, Oedipus had been abandoned by his parents, Laius and Jocasta, the king and queen of Thebes, because a prophecy warned that their son would kill his father and marry his mother. They instructed a servant to leave him on a mountain to die. The infant's feet were pierced and pinned together, but he was not left on the mountain; instead the servant, out of pity, gave him to a shepherd, who in turn presented him to the king and queen of Corinth. They named him Oedipus (for "swollen foot") and raised him as their own son.

On reaching manhood, Oedipus learned from an oracle that he would kill his father and marry his mother; to avoid this horrendous fate, he left Corinth forever. In his travels, Oedipus found his way blocked by a chariot at a crossroads; in a fit of anger, he killed the servants and their passenger. That passenger, unknown to Oedipus, was his real father. In Thebes, Oedipus successfully answered the riddle of the Sphinx, a winged lion with a woman's head. The reward for defeating this dreaded monster was both the crown and the dead king's wife. Oedipus and Jocasta had four children and prospered. But when the play begins, Oedipus's rule is troubled by a plague that threatens to destroy Thebes, and he is determined to find the cause of the plague in order to save the city again.

Oedipus the King is widely recognized as the greatest of the surviving Greek tragedies. Numerous translations are available. The highly regarded translation of *Oedipus the King* by David Grene is the choice here. The play has absorbed readers for centuries because Oedipus's character — his intelligence, confidence, rashness, and suffering — represents powers and limitations that are both exhilarating and chastening. Although no reader or viewer is likely to identify with Oedipus's extreme circumstances, anyone can appreciate his heroic efforts to find the truth about himself. In that sense, he is one of us — at our best.

SOPHOCLES (496?–406 B.C.)

Oedipus the King   *ca. 430 B.C.*

TRANSLATED BY DAVID GRENE

CHARACTERS

Oedipus, King of Thebes
Jocasta, His Wife
Creon, His Brother-in-Law
Teiresias, an Old Blind Prophet

A Priest
First Messenger
Second Messenger
A Herdsman
Chorus of Old Men of Thebes

SCENE: In front of the palace of Oedipus at Thebes. To the right of the stage near the altar stands the Priest with a crowd of children. Oedipus emerges from the central door.

Oedipus: Children, young sons and daughters of old Cadmus,°
    why do you sit here with your suppliant crowns?
    The town is heavy with a mingled burden
    of sounds and smells, of groans and hymns and incense;
    I did not think it fit that I should hear   5
    of this from messengers but came myself, —
    I Oedipus whom all men call the Great.   *(He turns to the Priest.)*
    You're old and they are young; come, speak for them.
    What do you fear or want, that you sit here
    suppliant? Indeed I'm willing to give all   10
    that you may need; I would be very hard
    should I not pity suppliants like these.
Priest: O ruler of my country, Oedipus,
    you see our company around the altar;
    you see our ages; some of us, like these,   15
    who cannot yet fly far, and some of us
    heavy with age; these children are the chosen
    among the young, and I the priest of Zeus.
    Within the market place sit others crowned
    with suppliant garlands, at the double shrine   20
    of Pallas° and the temple where Ismenus
    gives oracles by fire. King, you yourself
    have seen our city reeling like a wreck
    already; it can scarcely lift its prow
    out of the depths, out of the bloody surf.   25
    A blight is on the fruitful plants of the earth,
    A blight is on the cattle in the fields,
    a blight is on our women that no children
    are born to them; a God that carries fire,
    a deadly pestilence, is on our town,   30
    strikes us and spares not, and the house of Cadmus
    is emptied of its people while black Death
    grows rich in groaning and in lamentation.

---

1 *Cadmus:* Founder and first king of Thebes.   21 *Pallas:* Pallas Athene, goddess of wisdom and daughter of Zeus.

We have not come as suppliants to this altar
because we thought of you as of a God, 35
but rather judging you the first of men
in all the chances of this life and when
we mortals have to do with more than man.
You came and by your coming saved our city,
freed us from tribute which we paid of old 40
to the Sphinx,° cruel singer. This you did
in virtue of no knowledge we could give you,
in virtue of no teaching; it was God
that aided you, men say, and you are held
with God's assistance to have saved our lives. 45
Now Oedipus, Greatest in all men's eyes,
here falling at your feet we all entreat you,
find us some strength for rescue.
Perhaps you'll hear a wise word from some God,
perhaps you will learn something from a man 50
(for I have seen that for the skilled of practice
the outcome of their counsels live the most).
Noblest of men, go, and raise up our city,
go, — and give heed. For now this land of ours
calls you its savior since you saved it once. 55
So, let us never speak about your reign
as of a time when first our feet were set
secure on high, but later fell to ruin.
Raise up our city, save it and raise it up.
Once you have brought us luck with happy omen; 60
be no less now in fortune.
If you will rule this land, as now you rule it,
better to rule it full of men than empty.
For neither tower nor ship is anything
when empty, and none live in it together. 65

Oedipus: I pity you, children. You have come full of longing,
but I have known the story before you told it
only too well. I know you are all sick,
yet there is not one of you, sick though you are,
that is as sick as I myself. 70
Your several sorrows each have single scope
and touch but one of you. My spirit groans
for city and myself and you at once.
You have not roused me like a man from sleep;

---

41 *Sphinx:* A mythical creature with the body of a lion, wings of a bird, and the face of
a woman. The Sphinx stumped Thebans with her riddle and killed those that could not
answer it. Oedipus solved the riddle, the Sphinx killed herself, and Oedipus became king
of Thebes.

know that I have given many tears to this,   75
gone many ways wandering in thought,
but as I thought I found only one remedy
and that I took. I sent Menoeceus' son
Creon, Jocasta's brother, to Apollo,°
to his Pythian temple,   80
that he might learn there by what act or word
I could save this city. As I count the days,
it vexes me what ails him; he is gone
far longer than he needed for the journey.
But when he comes, then, may I prove a villain,   85
if I shall not do all the God commands.

Priest: Thanks for your gracious words. Your servants here
    signal that Creon is this moment coming.

Oedipus: His face is bright. O holy Lord Apollo,
    grant that his news too may be bright for us   90
    and bring us safety.

Priest: It is happy news,
    I think, for else his head would not be crowned
    with sprigs of fruitful laurel.

Oedipus: We will know soon,
    he's within hail. Lord Creon, my good brother,   95
    what is the word you bring us from the God?   *(Creon enters.)*

Creon: A good word, — for things hard to bear themselves
    if in the final issue all is well
    I count complete good fortune.

Oedipus: What do you mean?
    What you have said so far   100
    leaves me uncertain whether to trust or fear.

Creon: If you will hear my news before these others
    I am ready to speak, or else to go within.

Oedipus: Speak it to all;
    the grief I bear, I bear it more for these   105
    than for my own heart.

Creon: I will tell you, then,
    what I heard from the God.
    King Phoebus° in plain words commanded us
    to drive out a pollution from our land,
    pollution grown ingrained within the land;   110
    drive it out, said the God, not cherish it,
    till it's past cure.

Oedipus: What is the rite
    of purification? How shall it be done?

---

79 *Apollo:* Oracular god of the sun, light, and truth, and son of Zeus.   108 *King Phoebus:* Apollo.

Creon: By banishing a man, or expiation
    of blood by blood, since it is murder guilt 115
    which holds our city in this destroying storm.
Oedipus: Who is this man whose fate the God pronounces?
Creon: My Lord, before you piloted the state
    we had a king called Laius.°
Oedipus: I know of him by hearsay. I have not seen him. 120
Creon: The God commanded clearly: let some one
    punish with force this dead man's murderers.
Oedipus: Where are they in the world? Where would a trace
    of this old crime be found? It would be hard
    to guess where.
Creon: The clue is in this land; 125
    that which is sought is found;
    the unheeded thing escapes:
    so said the God.
Oedipus: Was it at home,
    or in the country that death came upon him,
    or in another country travelling? 130
Creon: He went, he said himself, upon an embassy,
    but never returned when he set out from home.
Oedipus: Was there no messenger, no fellow traveller
    who knew what happened? Such a one might tell
    something of use. 135
Creon: They were all killed save one. He fled in terror
    and he could tell us nothing in clear terms
    of what he knew, nothing, but one thing only.
Oedipus: What was it?
    If we could even find a slim beginning 140
    in which to hope, we might discover much.
Creon: This man said that the robbers they encountered
    were many and the hands that did the murder
    were many; it was no man's single power.
Oedipus: How could a robber dare a deed like this 145
    were he not helped with money from the city,
    money and treachery?
Creon: That indeed was thought.
    But Laius was dead and in our trouble
    there was none to help.
Oedipus: What trouble was so great to hinder you 150
    inquiring out the murder of your king?
Creon: The riddling Sphinx induced us to neglect
    mysterious crimes and rather seek solution
    of troubles at our feet.

119 *Laius:* Former king of Thebes.

Oedipus: I will bring this to light again. King Phoebus   155
    fittingly took this care about the dead,
    and you too fittingly.
    And justly you will see in me an ally,
    a champion of my country and the God.
    For when I drive pollution from the land   160
    I will not serve a distant friend's advantage,
    but act in my own interest. Whoever
    he was that killed the king may readily
    wish to dispatch me with his murderous hand;
    so helping the dead king I help myself.   165
    Come, children, take your suppliant boughs and go;
    up from the altars now. Call the assembly
    and let it meet upon the understanding
    that I'll do everything. God will decide
    whether we prosper or remain in sorrow.   170
Priest: Rise, children — it was this we came to seek,
    which of himself the king now offers us.
    May Phoebus who gave us the oracle
    come to our rescue and stay the plague.   *(Exeunt° all but the Chorus.)*

Chorus (Strophe°): What is the sweet spoken word of God from the
      shrine of Pytho° rich in gold   175
    that has come to glorious Thebes?
    I am stretched on the rack of doubt, and terror and trembling hold
    my heart, O Delian Healer,° and I worship full of fears
    for what doom you will bring to pass, new or renewed in the revolving years.
    Speak to me, immortal voice,   180
    child of golden Hope.

    (Antistrophe°) First I call on you, Athene, deathless daughter of Zeus,
    and Artemis, Earth Upholder,
    who sits in the midst of the market place in the throne which men
      call Fame,
    and Phoebus, the Far Shooter, three averters of Fate,   185
    come to us now, if ever before, when ruin rushed upon the state,
    you drove destruction's flame away
    out of our land.

    (Strophe) Our sorrows defy number;
    all the ship's timbers are rotten;   190

Exeunt: Stage direction indicating that the characters have left the stage.   *Strophe:* The song sung by the Chorus, dancing from stage right to stage left.   175 *shrine
of Pytho:* Delphi, site of the oracle and shrine dedicated to Apollo.   178 *Delian
Healer:* Apollo.   *Antistrophe:* The song sung after the strophe by the Chorus, dancing
back from stage left to stage right.

taking of thought is no spear for the driving away of the plague.
There are no growing children in this famous land;
there are no women bearing the pangs of childbirth.
You may see them one with another, like birds swift on the wing,
quicker than fire unmastered,   195
speeding away to the coast of the Western God.

(*Antistrophe*) In the unnumbered deaths
of its people the city dies;
those children that are born lie dead on the naked earth
unpitied, spreading contagion of death; and grey haired mothers
    and wives   200
everywhere stand at the altar's edge, suppliant, moaning;
the hymn to the healing God rings out but with it the wailing
    voices are blended.
From these our sufferings grant us, O golden Daughter of Zeus,
glad-faced deliverance.

(*Strophe*) There is no clash of brazen shields but our fight is with
    the War God,   205
a War God ringed with the cries of men, a savage God who burns us;
grant that he turn in racing course backwards out of our country's
    bounds
to the great palace of Amphitrite° or where the waves of the Thracian sea
deny the stranger safe anchorage.
Whatsoever escapes the night   210
at last the light of day revisits;
so smite the War God, Father Zeus,
beneath your thunderbolt,
for you are the Lord of the lightning, the lightning that carries fire.

(*Antistrophe*) And your unconquered arrow shafts, winged by
    the golden corded bow,   215
Lycean King,° I beg to be at our side for help;
and the gleaming torches of Artemis with which she scours the Lycean hills,
and I call on the God with the turban of gold, who gave his name to
    this country of ours,
the Bacchic God° with the wind flushed face,
Evian One, who travel   220
with the Maenad company,°
combat the God that burns us
with your torch of pine;
for the God that is our enemy is a God unhonoured among the Gods.

(*Oedipus returns.*)

---

208 *Amphitrite:* Sea goddess and wife of Poseidon.   216 *Lycean King:* Apollo.
219 *Bacchic God:* Bacchus, also known as Dionysus, god of wine and wild celebration.
221 *Maenad company:* Female followers of Bacchus.

Oedipus: For what you ask me — if you will hear my words,   225
and hearing welcome them and fight the plague,
you will find strength and lightening of your load.

Hark to me; what I say to you, I say
as one that is a stranger to the story
as stranger to the deed. For I would not   230
be far upon the track if I alone
were tracing it without a clue. But now,
since after all was finished, I became
a citizen among you, citizens —
now I proclaim to all the men of Thebes: 235
who so among you knows the murderer
by whose hand Laius, son of Labdacus,
died — I command him to tell everything
to me, — yes, though he fears himself to take the blame
on his own head; for bitter punishment   240
he shall have none, but leave this land unharmed.
Or if he knows the murderer, another,
a foreigner, still let him speak the truth.
For I will pay him and be grateful, too.
But if you shall keep silence, if perhaps   245
some one of you, to shield a guilty friend,
or for his own sake shall reject my words —
hear what I shall do then:
I forbid that man, whoever he be, my land,
my land where I hold sovereignty and throne;   250
and I forbid any to welcome him
or cry him greeting or make him a sharer
in sacrifice or offering to the Gods,
or give him water for his hands to wash.
I command all to drive him from their homes,   255
since he is our pollution, as the oracle
of Pytho's God proclaimed him now to me.
So I stand forth a champion of the God
and of the man who died.
Upon the murderer I invoke this curse —   260
whether he is one man and all unknown,
or one of many — may he wear out his life
in misery to miserable doom!
If with my knowledge he lives at my hearth
I pray that I myself may feel my curse.   265
On you I lay my charge to fulfill all this
for me, for the God, and for this land of ours
destroyed and blighted, by the God forsaken.

Even were this no matter of God's ordinance
it would not fit you so to leave it lie,   270

unpurified, since a good man is dead
and one that was a king. Search it out.
Since I am now the holder of his office,
and have his bed and wife that once was his,
and had his line not been unfortunate   275
we would have common children — (fortune leaped
upon his head) — because of all these things,
I fight in his defence as for my father,
and I shall try all means to take the murderer
of Laius the son of Labdacus   280
the son of Polydorus and before him
of Cadmus and before him of Agenor.°
Those who do not obey me, may the Gods
grant no crops springing from the ground they plough
nor children to their women! May a fate   285
like this, or one still worse than this consume them!
For you whom these words please, the other Thebans,
may Justice as your ally and all the Gods
live with you, blessing you now and for ever!

Chorus: As you have held me to my oath, I speak: 290
    I neither killed the king nor can declare
    the killer; but since Phoebus set the quest
    it is his part to tell who the man is.

Oedipus: Right; but to put compulsion on the Gods
    against their will — no man can do that.   295

Chorus: May I then say what I think second best?

Oedipus: If there's a third best, too, spare not to tell it.

Chorus: I know that what the Lord Teiresias
    sees, is most often what the Lord Apollo
    sees. If you should inquire of this from him   300
    you might find out most clearly.

Oedipus: Even in this my actions have not been sluggard.
    On Creon's word I have sent two messengers
    and why the prophet is not here already
    I have been wondering.

Chorus: His skill apart   305
    there is besides only an old faint story.

Oedipus: What is it?
    I look at every story.

Chorus: It was said
    that he was killed by certain wayfarers.

Oedipus: I heard that, too, but no one saw the killer.   310

---

282 *Labdacus, Polydorus, Cadmus, and Agenor:* Referring to the father, grandfather,
great-grandfather, and great-great-grandfather of Laius.

Chorus: Yet if he has a share of fear at all,
　　　his courage will not stand firm, hearing your curse.
Oedipus: The man who in the doing did not shrink
　　　will fear no word.
Chorus:　　　　　　　Here comes his prosecutor:
　　　led by your men the godly prophet comes   315
　　　in whom alone of mankind truth is native.

　　　　　　　　　　(Enter Teiresias, led by a little boy.)

Oedipus: Teiresias, you are versed in everything,
　　　things teachable and things not to be spoken,
　　　things of the heaven and earth-creeping things.
　　　You have no eyes but in your mind you know   320
　　　with what a plague our city is afflicted.
　　　My lord, in you alone we find a champion,
　　　in you alone one that can rescue us.
　　　Perhaps you have not heard the messengers,
　　　but Phoebus sent in answer to our sending   325
　　　an oracle declaring that our freedom
　　　from this disease would only come when we
　　　should learn the names of those who killed King Laius,
　　　and kill them or expel from our country.
　　　Do not begrudge us oracles from birds,°   330
　　　or any other way of prophecy
　　　within your skill; save yourself and the city,
　　　save me; redeem the debt of our pollution
　　　that lies on us because of this dead man.
　　　We are in your hands; pains are most nobly taken   335
　　　to help another when you have means and power.
Teiresias: Alas, how terrible is wisdom when
　　　it brings no profit to the man that's wise!
　　　This I knew well, but had forgotten it,
　　　else I would not have come here.
Oedipus:　　　　　　　　　What is this?   340
　　　How sad you are now you have come!
Teiresias:　　　　　　　　Let me
　　　go home. It will be easiest for us both
　　　to bear our several destinies to the end
　　　if you will follow my advice.
Oedipus:　　　　　　　You'd rob us
　　　of this your gift of prophecy? You talk   345
　　　as one who had no care for law nor love
　　　for Thebes who reared you.

---

330 *oracles from birds:* Bird flight, a method by which prophets predicted the future
using the flight of birds.

Teiresias: Yes, but I see that even your own words
 miss the mark; therefore I must fear for mine.
Oedipus: For God's sake if you know of anything,   350
 do not turn from us; all of us kneel to you,
 all of us here, your suppliants.
Teiresias: All of you here know nothing. I will not
 bring to the light of day my troubles, mine —
 rather than call them yours.
Oedipus: What do you mean?   355
 You know of something but refuse to speak.
 Would you betray us and destroy the city?
Teiresias: I will not bring this pain upon us both,
 neither on you nor on myself. Why is it
 you question me and waste your labour? I   360
 will tell you nothing.
Oedipus: You would provoke a stone! Tell us, you villain,
 tell us, and do not stand there quietly
 unmoved and balking at the issue.
Teiresias: You blame my temper but you do not see   365
 your own that lives within you; it is me
 you chide.
Oedipus: Who would not feel his temper rise
 at words like these with which you shame our city?
Teiresias: Of themselves things will come, although I hide them   370
 and breathe no word of them.
Oedipus: Since they will come
 tell them to me.
Teiresias: I will say nothing further.
 Against this answer let your temper rage
 as wildly as you will.
Oedipus: Indeed I am
 so angry I shall not hold back a jot   375
 of what I think. For I would have you know
 I think you were complotter° of the deed
 and doer of the deed save in so far
 as for the actual killing. Had you had eyes
 I would have said alone you murdered him.   380
Teiresias: Yes? Then I warn you faithfully to keep
 the letter of your proclamation and
 from this day forth to speak no word of greeting
 to these nor me; you are the land's pollution.
Oedipus: How shamelessly you started up this taunt!   385
 How do you think you will escape?

---

377 *complotter:* One who is part of a plot or conspiracy.

Teiresias: I have.
   I have escaped; the truth is what I cherish
   and that's my strength.
Oedipus: And who has taught you truth?
   Not your profession surely!
Teiresias: You have taught me,
   for you have made me speak against my will.   390
Oedipus: Speak what? Tell me again that I may learn it better.
Teiresias: Did you not understand before or would you
   provoke me into speaking?
Oedipus: I did not grasp it,
   not so to call it known. Say it again.
Teiresias: I say you are the murderer of the king   395
   whose murderer you seek.
Oedipus: Not twice you shall
   say calumnies like this and stay unpunished.
Teiresias: Shall I say more to tempt your anger more?
Oedipus: As much as you desire; it will be said
   in vain.
Teiresias: I say that with those you love best   400
   you live in foulest shame unconsciously
   and do not see where you are in calamity.
Oedipus: Do you imagine you can always talk
   like this, and live to laugh at it hereafter?
Teiresias: Yes, if the truth has anything of strength.   405
Oedipus: It has, but not for you; it has no strength
   for you because you are blind in mind and ears
   as well as in your eyes.
Teiresias: You are a poor wretch
   to taunt me with the very insults which
   every one soon will heap upon yourself.   410
Oedipus: Your life is one long night so that you cannot
   hurt me or any other who sees the light.
Teiresias: It is not fate that I should be your ruin,
   Apollo is enough; it is his care
   to work this out.
Oedipus: Was this your own design   415
   or Creon's?
Teiresias: Creon is no hurt to you,
   but you are to yourself.
Oedipus: Wealth, sovereignty and skill outmatching skill
   for the contrivance of an envied life!
   Great store of jealousy fill your treasury chests,   420
   if my friend Creon, friend from the first and loyal,
   thus secretly attacks me, secretly
   desires to drive me out and secretly

suborns this juggling, trick devising quack,
this wily beggar who has only eyes   425
for his own gains, but blindness in his skill.
For, tell me, where have you seen clear, Teiresias,
with your prophetic eyes? When the dark singer,
the sphinx, was in your country, did you speak
word of deliverance to its citizens?   430
And yet the riddle's answer was not the province
of a chance comer. It was a prophet's task
and plainly you had no such gift of prophecy
from birds nor otherwise from any God
to glean a word of knowledge. But I came,   435
Oedipus, who knew nothing, and I stopped her.
I solved the riddle by my wit alone.
Mine was no knowledge got from birds. And now
you would expel me,
because you think that you will find a place   440
by Creon's throne. I think you will be sorry,
both you and your accomplice, for your plot
to drive me out. And did I not regard you
as an old man, some suffering would have taught you
that what was in your heart was treason.   445
Chorus: We look at this man's words and yours, my king,
and we find both have spoken them in anger.
We need no angry words but only thought
how we may best hit the God's meaning for us.
Teiresias: If you are king, at least I have the right   450
no less to speak in my defence against you.
Of that much I am master. I am no slave
of yours, but Loxias', and so I shall not
enroll myself with Creon for my patron.
Since you have taunted me with being blind,   455
here is my word for you.
You have your eyes but see not where you are
in sin, nor where you live, nor whom you live with.
Do you know who your parents are? Unknowing
you are an enemy to kith and kin   460
in death, beneath the earth, and in this life.
A deadly footed, double striking curse,
from father and mother both, shall drive you forth
out of this land, with darkness on your eyes,
that now have such straight vision. Shall there be   465
a place will not be harbour to your cries,
a corner of Cithaeron° will not ring

---

467 *Cithaeron:* Mountain in Greece and the location where Oedipus was abandoned as a baby.

in echo to your cries, soon, soon, —
when you shall learn the secret of your marriage,
which steered you to a haven in this house, —   470
haven no haven, after lucky voyage?
And of the multitude of other evils
establishing a grim equality
between you and your children, you know nothing.
So, muddy with contempt my words and Creon's!   475
Misery shall grind no man as it will you.

Oedipus: Is it endurable that I should hear
such words from him? Go and a curse go with you!
Quick, home with you! Out of my house at once!

Teiresias: I would not have come either had you not called me.   480

Oedipus: I did not know then you would talk like a fool —
or it would have been long before I called you.

Teiresias: I am a fool then, as it seems to you —
but to the parents who have bred you, wise.

Oedipus: What parents? Stop! Who are they of all the world?   485

Teiresias: This day will show your birth and will destroy you.

Oedipus: How needlessly your riddles darken everything.

Teiresias: But it's in riddle answering you are strongest.

Oedipus: Yes. Taunt me where you will find me great.

Teiresias: It is this very luck that has destroyed you.   490

Oedipus: I do not care, if it has saved this city.

Teiresias: Well, I will go. Come, boy, lead me away.

Oedipus: Yes, lead him off. So long as you are here,
you'll be a stumbling block and a vexation;
once gone, you will not trouble me again.

Teiresias: I have said   495
what I came here to say not fearing your
countenance: there is no way you can hurt me.
I tell you, king, this man, this murderer
(whom you have long declared you are in search of,
indicting him in threatening proclamation   500
as murderer of Laius) — he is here.
In name he is a stranger among citizens
but soon he will be shown to be a citizen
true native Theban, and he'll have no joy
of the discovery: blindness for sight   505
and beggary for riches his exchange,
he shall go journeying to a foreign country
tapping his way before him with a stick.
He shall be proved father and brother both
to his own children in his house; to her   510
that gave him birth, a son and husband both;
a fellow sower in his father's bed
with that same father that he murdered.

Go within, reckon that out, and if you find me
mistaken, say I have no skill in prophecy.   515

(Exeunt separately Teiresias and Oedipus.)

Chorus (Strophe): Who is the man proclaimed
by Delphi's prophetic rock
as the bloody handed murderer,
the doer of deeds that none dare name?
Now is the time for him to run   520
with a stronger foot
than Pegasus
for the child of Zeus leaps in arms upon him
with fire and the lightning bolt,
and terribly close on his heels   525
are the Fates that never miss.

(Antistrophe) Lately from snowy Parnassus°
clearly the voice flashed forth,
bidding each Theban track him down,
the unknown murderer.   530
In the savage forests he lurks and in
the caverns like
the mountain bull.
He is sad and lonely, and lonely his feet
that carry him far from the navel of earth;   535
but its prophecies, ever living,
flutter around his head.

(Strophe) The augur has spread confusion,
terrible confusion;
I do not approve what was said   540
nor can I deny it.
I do not know what to say;
I am in a flutter of foreboding;
I never heard in the present
nor past of a quarrel between   545
the sons of Labdacus and Polybus,
that I might bring as proof
in attacking the popular fame
of Oedipus, seeking
to take vengeance for undiscovered   550
death in the line of Labdacus.

(Antistrophe) Truly Zeus and Apollo are wise
and in human things all knowing;
but amongst men there is no

527 *Parnassus:* Mountain in Greece that was sacred to Apollo.

distinct judgment, between the prophet   555
and me — which of us is right.
One man may pass another in wisdom
but I would never agree
with those that find fault with the king
till I should see the word   560
proved right beyond doubt. For once
in visible form the Sphinx
came on him and all of us
saw his wisdom and in that test
he saved the city. So he will not be condemned by my mind.   565

> *(Enter Creon.)*

Creon: Citizens, I have come because I heard
deadly words spread about me, that the king
accuses me. I cannot take that from him.
If he believes that in these present troubles
he has been wronged by me in word or deed   570
I do not want to live on with the burden
of such a scandal on me. The report
injures me doubly and most vitally —
for I'll be called a traitor to my city
and traitor also to my friends and you.   575

Chorus: Perhaps it was a sudden gust of anger
that forced that insult from him, and no judgment.

Creon: But did he say that it was in compliance
with schemes of mine that the seer told him lies?

Chorus: Yes, he said that, but why, I do not know.   580

Creon: Were his eyes straight in his head? Was his mind right
when he accused me in this fashion?

Chorus: I do not know; I have no eyes to see
what princes do. Here comes the king himself. *(Enter Oedipus.)*

Oedipus: You, sir, how is it you come here? Have you so much   585
brazen-faced daring that you venture in
my house although you are proved manifestly
the murderer of that man, and though you tried,
openly, highway robbery of my crown?
For God's sake, tell me what you saw in me,   590
what cowardice or what stupidity,
that made you lay a plot like this against me?
Did you imagine I should not observe
the crafty scheme that stole upon me or
seeing it, take no means to counter it?   595
Was it not stupid of you to make the attempt,
to try to hunt down royal power without
the people at your back or friends? For only
with the people at your back or money can

the hunt end in the capture of a crown.   600
Creon: Do you know what you're doing? Will you listen
　　to words to answer yours, and then pass judgment?
Oedipus: You're quick to speak, but I am slow to grasp you,
　　for I have found you dangerous, — and my foe.
Creon: First of all hear what I shall say to that.   605
Oedipus: At least don't tell me that you are not guilty.
Creon: If you think obstinacy without wisdom
　　a valuable possession, you are wrong.
Oedipus: And you are wrong if you believe that one,
　　a criminal, will not be punished only   610
　　because he is my kinsman.
Creon:　　　　　　　　　　　This is but just —
　　but tell me, then, of what offense I'm guilty?
Oedipus: Did you or did you not urge me to send
　　to this prophetic mumbler?
Creon:　　　　　　　　　　　I did indeed,
　　and I shall stand by what I told you.   615
Oedipus: How long ago is it since Laius. . . .
Creon: What about Laius? I don't understand.
Oedipus: Vanished — died — was murdered?
Creon:　　　　　　　　　　　　　　　It is long,
　　a long, long time to reckon.
Oedipus:　　　　　　　　　　Was this prophet
　　in the profession then?
Creon:　　　　　　　　He was, and honoured   620
　　as highly as he is today.
Oedipus: At that time did he say a word about me?
Creon: Never, at least when I was near him.
Oedipus: You never made a search for the dead man?
Creon: We searched, indeed, but never learned of anything.   625
Oedipus: Why did our wise old friend not say this then?
Creon: I don't know; and when I know nothing, I
　　usually hold my tongue.
Oedipus:　　　　　　　　　You know this much,
　　and can declare this much if you are loyal.
Creon: What is it? If I know, I'll not deny it.   630
Oedipus: That he would not have said that I killed Laius
　　had he not met you first.
Creon:　　　　　　　　　　　You know yourself
　　whether he said this, but I demand that I
　　should hear as much from you as you from me.
Oedipus: Then hear, — I'll not be proved a murderer.   635
Creon: Well, then. You're married to my sister.
Oedipus:　　　　　　　　　　　　　　　Yes,
　　that I am not disposed to deny.

Creon: You rule
    this country giving her an equal share
    in the government?
Oedipus: Yes, everything she wants
    she has from me.
Creon: And I, as thirdsman to you,   640
    am rated as the equal of you two?
Oedipus: Yes, and it's there you've proved yourself false friend.
Creon: Not if you will reflect on it as I do.
    Consider, first, if you think any one
    would choose to rule and fear rather than rule   645
    and sleep untroubled by a fear if power
    were equal in both cases. I, at least,
    I was not born with such a frantic yearning
    to be a king — but to do what kings do.
    And so it is with every one who has learned   650
    wisdom and self-control. As it stands now,
    the prizes are all mine — and without fear.
    But if I were the king myself, I must
    do much that went against the grain.
    How should despotic rule seem sweeter to me   655
    than painless power and an assured authority?
    I am not so besotted yet that I
    want other honours than those that come with profit.
    Now every man's my pleasure; every man greets me;
    now those who are your suitors fawn on me, —   660
    success for them depends upon my favour.
    Why should I let all this go to win that?
    My mind would not be traitor if it's wise;
    I am no treason lover, of my nature,
    nor would I ever dare to join a plot.   665
    Prove what I say. Go to the oracle
    at Pytho and inquire about the answers,
    if they are as I told you. For the rest,
    if you discover I laid any plot
    together with the seer, kill me, I say,   670
    not only by your vote but by my own.
    But do not charge me on obscure opinion
    without some proof to back it. It's not just
    lightly to count your knaves as honest men,
    nor honest men as knaves. To throw away   675
    an honest friend is, as it were, to throw
    your life away, which a man loves the best.
    In time you will know all with certainty;
    time is the only test of honest men,
    one day is space enough to know a rogue.   680

Chorus: His words are wise, king, if one fears to fall.
  Those who are quick of temper are not safe.
Oedipus: When he that plots against me secretly
  moves quickly, I must quickly counterplot.
  If I wait taking no decisive measure   685
  his business will be done, and mine be spoiled.
Creon: What do you want to do then? Banish me?
Oedipus: No, certainly; kill you, not banish you.
Creon: I do not think that you've your wits about you.
Oedipus: For my own interests, yes.
Creon: But for mine, too,   690
  you should think equally.
Oedipus: You are a rogue.
Creon: Suppose you do not understand?
Oedipus: But yet
  I must be ruler.
Creon: Not if you rule badly.
Oedipus: O, city, city!
Creon: I too have some share
  in the city; it is not yours alone.   695
Chorus: Stop, my lords! Here — and in the nick of time
  I see Jocasta coming from the house;
  with her help lay the quarrel that now stirs you.   *(Enter Jocasta.)*
Jocasta: For shame! Why have you raised this foolish squabbling
  brawl? Are you not ashamed to air your private   700
  griefs when the country's sick? Go in, you, Oedipus,
  and you, too, Creon, into the house. Don't magnify
  your nothing troubles.
Creon: Sister, Oedipus,
  your husband, thinks he has the right to do
  terrible wrongs — he has but to choose between   705
  two terrors: banishing or killing me.
Oedipus: He's right, Jocasta; for I find him plotting
  with knavish tricks against my person.
Creon: That God may never bless me! May I die
  accursed, if I have been guilty of   710
  one tittle of the charge you bring against me!
Jocasta: I beg you, Oedipus, trust him in this,
  spare him for the sake of this his oath to God,
  for my sake, and the sake of those who stand here.
Chorus: Be gracious, be merciful,   715
  we beg of you.
Oedipus: In what would you have me yield?
Chorus: He has been no silly child in the past.
  He is strong in his oath now.
  Spare him.   720

Oedipus: Do you know what you ask?

Chorus: Yes.

Oedipus: Tell me then.

Chorus: He has been your friend before all men's eyes; do not cast him
away dishonoured on an obscure conjecture.   725

Oedipus: I would have you know that this request of yours
really requests my death or banishment.

Chorus: May the Sun God, king of Gods, forbid! May I die without
God's blessing, without friends'. help, if I had any such thought. But
my spirit is broken by my unhappiness for my wasting country; and   730
this would but add troubles amongst ourselves to the other troubles.

Oedipus: Well, let him go then — if I must die ten times for it,
or be sent out dishonoured into exile.
It is your lips that prayed for him I pitied,
not his; wherever he is, I shall hate him.   735

Creon: I see you sulk in yielding and you're dangerous
when you are out of temper; natures like yours
are justly heaviest for themselves to bear.

Oedipus: Leave me alone! Take yourself off, I tell you.

Creon: I'll go, you have not known me, but they have,   740
and they have known my innocence.   *(Exit.)*

Chorus: Won't you take him inside, lady?

Jocasta: Yes, when I've found out what was the matter.

Chorus: There was some misconceived suspicion of a story, and on
the other side the sting of injustice.   745

Jocasta: So, on both sides?

Chorus: Yes.

Jocasta: What was the story?

Chorus: I think it best, in the interests of the country, to leave it where
it ended.   750

Oedipus: You see where you have ended, straight of judgment
although you are, by softening my anger.

Chorus: Sir, I have said before and I say again — be sure that I would
have been proved a madman, bankrupt in sane council, if I
should put you away, you who steered the country I love safely   755
when she was crazed with troubles. God grant that now, too, you
may prove a fortunate guide for us.

Jocasta: Tell me, my lord, I beg of you, what was it
that roused your anger so?

Oedipus: Yes, I will tell you.
I honour you more than I honour them.   760
It was Creon and the plots he laid against me.

Jocasta: Tell me — if you can clearly tell the quarrel —

Oedipus: Creon says
that I'm the murderer of Laius.

Jocasta: Of his own knowledge or on information?

Oedipus: He sent this rascal prophet to me, since   765
    he keeps his own mouth clean of any guilt.

Jocasta: Do not concern yourself about this matter;
    listen to me and learn that human beings
    have no part in the craft of prophecy.
    Of that I'll show you a short proof.   770
    There was an oracle once that came to Laius,—
    I will not say that it was Phoebus' own,
    but it was from his servants—and it told him
    that it was fate that he should die a victim
    at the hands of his own son, a son to be born   775
    of Laius and me. But, see now, he,
    the king, was killed by foreign highway robbers
    at a place where three roads meet—so goes the story;
    and for the son—before three days were out
    after his birth King Laius pierced his ankles   780
    and by the hands of others cast him forth
    upon a pathless hillside. So Apollo
    failed to fulfill his oracle to the son,
    that he should kill his father, and to Laius
    also proved false in that the thing he feared,   785
    death at his son's hands, never came to pass.
    So clear in this case were the oracles,
    so clear and false. Give them no heed, I say;
    what God discovers need of, easily
    he shows to us himself.

Oedipus: O dear Jocasta,   790
    as I hear this from you, there comes upon me
    a wandering of the soul—I could run mad.

Jocasta: What trouble is it, that you turn again
    and speak like this?

Oedipus: I thought I heard you say
    that Laius was killed at a crossroads.   795

Jocasta: Yes, that was how the story went and still
    that word goes round.

Oedipus: Where is this place, Jocasta,
    where he was murdered?

Jocasta: Phocis is the country
    and the road splits there, one of two roads from Delphi,
    another comes from Daulia.

Oedipus: How long ago is this?   800

Jocasta: The news came to the city just before
    you became king and all men's eyes looked to you.
    What is it, Oedipus, that's in your mind?

Oedipus: What have you designed, O Zeus, to do with me?

Jocasta: What is the thought that troubles your heart?   805

Oedipus: Don't ask me yet — tell me of Laius —
    How did he look? How old or young was he?
Jocasta: He was a tall man and his hair was grizzled
    already — nearly white — and in his form
    not unlike you.
Oedipus: O God, I think I have   810
    called curses on myself in ignorance.
Jocasta: What do you mean? I am terrified
    when I look at you.
Oedipus: I have a deadly fear
    that the old seer had eyes. You'll show me more
    if you can tell me one more thing.
Jocasta: I will.   815
    I'm frightened, — but if I can understand,
    I'll tell you all you ask.
Oedipus: How was his company?
    Had he few with him when he went this journey,
    or many servants, as would suit a prince?
Jocasta: In all there were but five, and among them   820
    a herald; and one carriage for the king.
Oedipus: It's plain — it's plain — who was it told you this?
Jocasta: The only servant that escaped safe home.
Oedipus: Is he at home now?
Jocasta: No, when he came home again
    and saw you king and Laius was dead,   825
    he came to me and touched my hand and begged
    that I should send him to the fields to be
    my shepherd and so he might see the city
    as far off as he might. So I
    sent him away. He was an honest man,   830
    as slaves go, and was worthy of far more
    than what he asked of me.
Oedipus: O, how I wish that he could come back quickly!
Jocasta: He can. Why is your heart so set on this?
Oedipus: O dear Jocasta, I am full of fears   835
    that I have spoken far too much; and therefore
    I wish to see this shepherd.
Jocasta: He will come;
    but, Oedipus, I think I'm worthy too
    to know what it is that disquiets you.
Oedipus: It shall not be kept from you, since my mind   840
    has gone so far with its forebodings. Whom
    should I confide in rather than you, who is there
    of more importance to me who have passed
    through such a fortune?
    Polybus was my father, king of Corinth,   845

and Merope,° the Dorian, my mother.
I was held greatest of the citizens
in Corinth till a curious chance befell me
as I shall tell you — curious, indeed,
but hardly worth the store I set upon it. 850
There was a dinner and at it a man,
a drunken man, accused me in his drink
of being bastard. I was furious
but held my temper under for that day.
Next day I went and taxed my parents with it; 855
they took the insult very ill from him,
the drunken fellow who had uttered it.
So I was comforted for their part, but
still this thing rankled always, for the story
crept about widely. And I went at last 860
to Pytho, though my parents did not know.
But Phoebus sent me home again unhonoured
in what I came to learn, but he foretold
other and desperate horrors to befall me,
that I was fated to lie with my mother, 865
and show to daylight an accursed breed
which men would not endure, and I was doomed
to be murderer of the father that begot me.
When I heard this I fled, and in the days
that followed I would measure from the stars 870
the whereabouts of Corinth — yes, I fled
to somewhere where I should not see fulfilled
the infamies told in that dreadful oracle.
And as I journeyed I came to the place
where, as you say, this king met with his death. 875
Jocasta, I will tell you the whole truth.
When I was near the branching of the crossroads,
going on foot, I was encountered by
a herald and a carriage with a man in it,
just as you tell me. He that led the way 880
and the old man himself wanted to thrust me
out of the road by force. I became angry
and struck the coachman who was pushing me.
When the old man saw this he watched his moment,
and as I passed he struck me from his carriage, 885
full on the head with his two pointed goad.
But he was paid in full and presently
my stick had struck him backwards from the car
and he rolled out of it. And then I killed them

---

846 *Polybus and Merope:* King and queen that adopted and raised Oedipus.

all. If it happened there was any tie   890
of kinship twixt this man and Laius,
who is then now more miserable than I,
what man on earth so hated by the Gods,
since neither citizen nor foreigner
may welcome me at home or even greet me,   895
but drive me out of doors? And it is I,
I and no other have so cursed myself.
And I pollute the bed of him I killed
by the hands that killed him. Was I not born evil?
Am I not utterly unclean? I had to fly   900
and in my banishment not even see
my kindred nor set foot in my own country,
or otherwise my fate was to be yoked
in marriage with my mother and kill my father,
Polybus who begot me and had reared me.   905
Would not one rightly judge and say that on me
these things were sent by some malignant God?
O no, no, no — O holy majesty
of God on high, may I not see that day!
May I be gone out of men's sight before   910
I see the deadly taint of this disaster
come upon me.

Chorus: Sir, we too fear these things. But until you see this man face to
face and hear his story, hope.

Oedipus: Yes, I have just this much of hope — to wait until the herdsman comes.   915

Jocasta: And when he comes, what do you want with him?

Oedipus: I'll tell you; if I find that his story is the same as yours, I at least
will be clear of this guilt.

Jocasta: Why what so particularly did you learn from my story?

Oedipus: You said that he spoke of highway *robbers* who killed Laius. Now   920
if he uses the same number, it was not I who killed him. One man
cannot be the same as many. But if he speaks of a man travelling
alone, then clearly the burden of the guilt inclines towards me.

Jocasta: Be sure, at least, that this was how he told the story. He cannot unsay
it now, for everyone in the city heard it — not I alone. But, Oedipus, even   925
if he diverges from what he said then, he shall never prove that the murder of Laius squares rightly with the prophecy — for Loxias declared
that the king should be killed by his own son. And that poor creature
did not kill him surely, — for he died himself first. So as far as prophecy
goes, henceforward I shall not look to the right hand or the left.   930

Oedipus: Right. But yet, send some one for the peasant to bring him
here; do not neglect it.

Jocasta: I will send quickly. Now let me go indoors. I will do nothing
except what pleases you.   *(Exeunt.)*

Chorus (Strophe): May destiny ever find me   935

pious in word and deed
prescribed by the laws that live on high:
laws begotten in the clear air of heaven,
whose only father is Olympus;
no mortal nature brought them to birth,   940
no forgetfulness shall lull them to sleep;
for God is great in them and grows not old.

(*Antistrophe*) Insolence breeds the tyrant, insolence
if it is glutted with a surfeit, unseasonable, unprofitable,
climbs to the roof-top and plunges   945
sheer down to the ruin that must be,
and there its feet are no service.
But I pray that the God may never
abolish the eager ambition that profits the state.
For I shall never cease to hold the God as our protector.   950

(*Strophe*) If a man walks with haughtiness
of hand or word and gives no heed
to Justice and the shrines of Gods
despises — may an evil doom
smite him for his ill-starred pride of heart!—   955
he reaps gains without justice
and will not hold from impiety
and his fingers itch for untouchable things.
When such things are done, what man shall contrive
to shield his soul from the shafts of the God?   960
When such deeds are held in honour,
why should I honour the Gods in the dance?

(*Antistrophe*) No longer to the holy place,
to the navel of earth I'll go
to worship, nor to Abae   965
nor to Olympia,
unless the oracles are proved to fit,
for all men's hands to point at.
O Zeus, if you are rightly called
the sovereign lord, all-mastering,   970
let this not escape you nor your ever-living power!
The oracles concerning Laius
are old and dim and men regard them not.
Apollo is nowhere clear in honour; God's service perishes.

(Enter Jocasta, carrying garlands.)

Jocasta: Princes of the land, I have had the thought to go   975
to the Gods' temples, bringing in my hand
garlands and gifts of incense, as you see.

For Oedipus excites himself too much
at every sort of trouble, not conjecturing,
like a man of sense, what will be from what was,   980
but he is always at the speaker's mercy,
when he speaks terrors. I can do no good
by my advice, and so I came as suppliant
to you, Lycaean Apollo, who are nearest.
These are the symbols of my prayer and this   985
my prayer: grant us escape free of the curse.
Now when we look to him we are all afraid;
he's pilot of our ship and he is frightened.   *(Enter Messenger.)*

Messenger: Might I learn from you, sirs, where is the house of
  Oedipus? Or best of all, if you know, where is the king himself?   990
Chorus: This is his house and he is within doors. This lady is his wife
  and mother of his children.
Messenger: God bless you, lady, and God bless your household! God
  bless Oedipus' noble wife!
Jocasta: God bless you, sir, for your kind greeting! What do you want   995
  of us that you have come here? What have you to tell us?
Messenger: Good news, lady. Good for your house and for your husband.
Jocasta: What is your news? Who sent you to us?
Messenger: I come from Corinth and the news I bring will give you
  pleasure. Perhaps a little pain too.   1000
Jocasta: What is this news of double meaning?
Messenger: The people of the Isthmus will choose Oedipus to be
  their king. That is the rumour there.
Jocasta: But isn't their king still old Polybus?
Messenger: No. He is in his grave. Death has got him.   1005
Jocasta: Is that the truth? Is Oedipus' father dead?
Messenger: May I die myself if it be otherwise!
Jocasta (to a servant): Be quick and run to the King with the news!
  O oracles of the Gods, where are you now? It was from this man
  Oedipus fled, lest he should be his murderer! And now he is dead, 1010
  in the course of nature, and not killed by Oedipus.   *(Enter Oedipus.)*
Oedipus: Dearest Jocasta, why have you sent for me?
Jocasta: Listen to this man and when you hear reflect what is the
  outcome of the holy oracles of the Gods.
Oedipus: Who is he? What is his message for me?   1015
Jocasta: He is from Corinth and he tells us that your father Polybus
  is dead and gone.
Oedipus: What's this you say, sir? Tell me yourself.
Messenger: Since this is the first matter you want clearly told: Polybus
  has gone down to death. You may be sure of it.   1020
Oedipus: By treachery or sickness?
Messenger: A small thing will put old bodies asleep.

Oedipus: So he died of sickness, it seems, — poor old man!
Messenger: Yes, and of age — the long years he had measured.
Oedipus: Ha! Ha! O dear Jocasta, why should one   1025
    look to the Pythian hearth?° Why should one look
    to the birds screaming overhead? They prophesied
    that I should kill my father! But he's dead,
    and hidden deep in earth, and I stand here
    who never laid a hand on spear against him, —   1030
    unless perhaps he died of longing for me,
    and thus I am his murderer. But they,
    the oracles, as they stand — he's taken them
    away with him, they're dead as he himself is,
    and worthless.
Jocasta: That I told you before now.   1035
Oedipus: You did, but I was misled by my fear.
Jocasta: Then lay no more of them to heart, not one.
Oedipus: But surely I must fear my mother's bed?
Jocasta: Why should man fear since chance is all in all
    for him, and he can clearly foreknow nothing?   1040
    Best to live lightly, as one can, unthinkingly.
    As to your mother's marriage bed, — don't fear it.
    Before this, in dreams too, as well as oracles,
    many a man has lain with his own mother.
    But he to whom such things are nothing bears   1045
    his life most easily.
Oedipus: All that you say would be said perfectly
    if she were dead; but since she lives I must
    still fear, although you talk so well, Jocasta.
Jocasta: Still in your father's death there's light of comfort?   1050
Oedipus: Great light of comfort; but I fear the living.
Messenger: Who is the woman that makes you afraid?
Oedipus: Merope, old man, Polybus' wife.
Messenger: What about her frightens the queen and you?
Oedipus: A terrible oracle, stranger, from the Gods.   1055
Messenger: Can it be told? Or does the sacred law
    forbid another to have knowledge of it?
Oedipus: O no! Once on a time Loxias said
    that I should lie with my own mother and
    take on my hands the blood of my own father.   1060
    And so for these long years I've lived away
    from Corinth; it has been to my great happiness;
    but yet it's sweet to see the face of parents.
Messenger: This was the fear which drove you out of Corinth?
Oedipus: Old man, I did not wish to kill my father.   1065

1026 *Pythian hearth:* Delphi.

Messenger: Why should I not free you from this fear, sir,
    since I have come to you in all goodwill?
Oedipus: You would not find me thankless if you did.
Messenger: Why, it was just for this I brought the news, —
    to earn your thanks when you had come safe home.   1070
Oedipus: No, I will never come near my parents.
Messenger: Son,
    it's very plain you don't know what you're doing.
Oedipus: What do you mean, old man? For God's sake, tell me.
Messenger: If your homecoming is checked by fears like these.
Oedipus: Yes, I'm afraid that Phoebus may prove right.   1075
Messenger: The murder and the incest?
Oedipus: Yes, old man;
    that is my constant terror.
Messenger: Do you know
    that all your fears are empty?
Oedipus: How is that,
    if they are father and mother and I their son?
Messenger: Because Polybus was no kin to you in blood.   1080
Oedipus: What, was not Polybus my father?
Messenger: No more than I but just so much.
Oedipus: How can
    my father be my father as much as one
    that's nothing to me?
Messenger: Neither he nor I
    begat you.
Oedipus: Why then did he call me son?   1085
Messenger: A gift he took you from these hands of mine.
Oedipus: Did he love so much what he took from another's hand?
Messenger: His childlessness before persuaded him.
Oedipus: Was I a child you bought or found when I
    was given to him?
Messenger: On Cithaeron's slopes   1090
    in the twisting thickets you were found.
Oedipus: And why
    were you a traveller in those parts?
Messenger: I was
    in charge of mountain flocks.
Oedipus: You were a shepherd?
    A hireling vagrant?
Messenger: Yes, but at least at that time
    the man that saved your life, son.   1095
Oedipus: What ailed me when you took me in your arms?
Messenger: In that your ankles should be witnesses.
Oedipus: Why do you speak of that old pain?
Messenger: I loosed you;

the tendons of your feet were pierced and fettered, —

Oedipus: My swaddling clothes brought me a rare disgrace.   1100

Messenger: So that from this you're called your present name.°

Oedipus: Was this my father's doing or my mother's?
For God's sake, tell me.

Messenger: I don't know, but he
who gave you to me has more knowledge than I.

Oedipus: You yourself did not find me then? You took me   1105
from someone else?

Messenger: Yes, from another shepherd.

Oedipus: Who was he? Do you know him well enough
to tell?

Messenger: He was called Laius' man.

Oedipus: You mean the king who reigned here in the old days?

Messenger: Yes, he was that man's shepherd.

Oedipus: Is he alive   1110
still, so that I could see him?

Messenger: You who live here
would know that best.

Oedipus: Do any of you here
know of this shepherd whom he speaks about
in town or in the fields? Tell me. It's time
that this was found out once for all.   1115

Chorus: I think he is none other than the peasant
whom you have sought to see already; but
Jocasta here can tell us best of that.

Oedipus: Jocasta, do you know about this man
whom we have sent for? Is he the man he mentions?   1120

Jocasta: Why ask of whom he spoke? Don't give it heed;
nor try to keep in mind what has been said.
It will be wasted labour.

Oedipus: With such clues
I could not fail to bring my birth to light.

Jocasta: I beg you — do not hunt this out — I beg you,   1125
if you have any care for your own life.
What I am suffering is enough.

Oedipus: Keep up
your heart, Jocasta. Though I'm proved a slave,
thrice slave, and though my mother is thrice slave,
you'll not be shown to be of lowly lineage.   1130

Jocasta: O be persuaded by me, I entreat you;
do not do this.

Oedipus: I will not be persuaded to let be
the chance of finding out the whole thing clearly.

1101 *name:* Oedipus literally translates to "swollen foot."

Jocasta: It is because I wish you well that I   1135
    give you this counsel — and it's the best counsel.
Oedipus: Then the best counsel vexes me, and has
    for some while since.
Jocasta: O Oedipus, God help you!
    God keep you from the knowledge of who you are!
Oedipus: Here, some one, go and fetch the shepherd for me;   1140
    and let her find her joy in her rich family!
Jocasta: O Oedipus, unhappy Oedipus!
    that is all I can call you, and the last thing
    that I shall ever call you.   *(Exit.)*
Chorus: Why has the queen gone, Oedipus, in wild   1145
    grief rushing from us? I am afraid that trouble
    will break out of this silence.
Oedipus: Break out what will! I at least shall be
    willing to see my ancestry, though humble.
    Perhaps she is ashamed of my low birth,   1150
    for she has all a woman's high-flown pride.
    But I account myself a child of Fortune,
    beneficent Fortune, and I shall not be
    dishonoured. She's the mother from whom I spring;
    the months, my brothers, marked me, now as small,   1155
    and now again as mighty. Such is my breeding,
    and I shall never prove so false to it,
    as not to find the secret of my birth.
Chorus (Strophe): If I am a prophet and wise of heart
    you shall not fail, Cithaeron,   1160
    by the limitless sky, you shall not! —
    to know at tomorrow's full moon
    that Oedipus honours you,
    as native to him and mother and nurse at once;
    and that you are honoured in dancing by us, as finding   1165
      favour in sight of our king.
    Apollo, to whom we cry, find these things pleasing!

(Antistrophe) Who was it bore you, child? One of
    the long-lived nymphs who lay with Pan —
    the father who treads the hills?   1170
    Or was she a bride of Loxias, your mother? The grassy slopes
    are all of them dear to him. Or perhaps Cyllene's king
    or the Bacchants' God that lives on the tops
    of the hills received you a gift from some
    one of the Helicon Nymphs, with whom he mostly plays?   1175
        (Enter an old man, led by Oedipus' servants.)
Oedipus: If some one like myself who never met him
    may make a guess, — I think this is the herdsman,

whom we were seeking. His old age is consonant
with the other. And besides, the men who bring him
I recognize as my own servants. You   1180
perhaps may better me in knowledge since
you've seen the man before.

Chorus: You can be sure
I recognize him. For if Laius
had ever an honest shepherd, this was he.

Oedipus: You, sir, from Corinth, I must ask you first,   1185
is this the man you spoke of?

Messenger: This is he
before your eyes.

Oedipus: Old man, look here at me
and tell me what I ask you. Were you ever
a servant of King Laius?

Herdsman: I was,—
no slave he bought but reared in his own house.   1190

Oedipus: What did you do as work? How did you live?

Herdsman: Most of my life was spent among the flocks.

Oedipus: In what part of the country did you live?

Herdsman: Cithaeron and the places near to it.

Oedipus: And somewhere there perhaps you knew this man?   1195

Herdsman: What was his occupation? Who?

Oedipus: This man here,
have you had any dealings with him?

Herdsman: No—
not such that I can quickly call to mind.

Messenger: That is no wonder, master. But I'll make him remember
what he does not know. For I know, that he well knows the   1200
country of Cithaeron, how he with two flocks, I with one kept
company for three years — each year half a year — from spring
till autumn time and then when winter came I drove my flocks
to our fold home again and he to Laius' steadings. Well — am I
right or not in what I said we did?   1205

Herdsman: You're right — although it's a long time ago.

Messenger: Do you remember giving me a child
to bring up as my foster child?

Herdsman: What's this?
Why do you ask this question?

Messenger: Look old man,
here he is — here's the man who was that child!   1210

Herdsman: Death take you! Won't you hold your tongue?

Oedipus: No, no,
do not find fault with him, old man. Your words
are more at fault than his.

Herdsman: O best of masters,
    how do I give offense?
Oedipus: When you refuse
    to speak about the child of whom he asks you.   1215
Herdsman: He speaks out of his ignorance, without meaning.
Oedipus: If you'll not talk to gratify me, you
    will talk with pain to urge you.
Herdsman: O please, sir,
    don't hurt an old man, sir.
Oedipus (to the servants):   Here, one of you,
    twist his hands behind him.
Herdsman: Why, God help me, why?   1220
    What do you want to know?
Oedipus: You gave a child
    to him, — the child he asked you of?
Herdsman: I did.
    I wish I'd died the day I did.
Oedipus: You will
    unless you tell me truly.
Herdsman: And I'll die
    far worse if I should tell you.
Oedipus: This fellow   1225
    is bent on more delays, as it would seem.
Herdsman: O no, no! I have told you that I gave it.
Oedipus: Where did you get this child from? Was it your own or did you
    get it from another?
Herdsman: Not
    my own at all; I had it from some one.   1230
Oedipus: One of these citizens? or from what house?
Herdsman: O master, please — I beg you, master, please
    don't ask me more.
Oedipus: You're a dead man if I
    ask you again.
Herdsman: It was one of the children
    of Laius.
Oedipus: A slave? Or born in wedlock?   1235
Herdsman: O God, I am on the brink of frightful speech.
Oedipus: And I of frightful hearing. But I must hear.
Herdsman: The child was called his child; but she within,
    your wife would tell you best how all this was.
Oedipus: She gave it to you?
Herdsman: Yes, she did, my lord.   1240
Oedipus: To do what with it?
Herdsman: Make away with it.
Oedipus: She was so hard — its mother?

Herdsman: Aye, through fear
   of evil oracles.
Oedipus: Which?
Herdsman: They said that he
   should kill his parents.
Oedipus: How was it that you
   gave it away to this old man?
Herdsman: O master,   1245
   I pitied it, and thought that I could send it
   off to another country and this man
   was from another country. But he saved it
   for the most terrible troubles. If you are
   the man he says you are, you're bred to misery.   1250
Oedipus: O, O, O, they will all come,
   all come out clearly! Light of the sun, let me
   look upon you no more after today!
   I who first saw the light bred of a match
   accursed, and accursed in my living   1255
   with them I lived with, cursed in my killing.

                                 (Exeunt all but the Chorus.)

Chorus (Strophe): O generations of men, how I
   count you as equal with those who live
   not at all!
   What man, what man on earth wins more   1260
   of happiness than a seeming
   and after that turning away?
   Oedipus, you are my pattern of this,
   Oedipus, you and your fate!
   Luckless Oedipus, whom of all men   1265
   I envy not at all.

   (Antistrophe) In as much as he shot his bolt
   beyond the others and won the prize
   of happiness complete —
   O Zeus — and killed and reduced to nought   1270
   the hooked taloned maid of the riddling speech,
   standing a tower against death for my land:
   hence he was called my king and hence
   was honoured the highest of all
   honours; and hence he ruled   1275
   in the great city of Thebes.

   (Strophe) But now whose tale is more miserable?
   Who is there lives with a savager fate?
   Whose troubles so reverse his life as his?

O Oedipus, the famous prince   1280
for whom a great haven
the same both as father and son
sufficed for generation,
how, O how, have the furrows ploughed
by your father endured to bear you, poor wretch,   1285
and hold their peace so long?

(*Antistrophe*) Time who sees all has found you out
against your will; judges your marriage accursed,
begetter and begot at one in it.

O child of Laius,   1290
would I had never seen you.
I weep for you and cry
a dirge of lamentation.

To speak directly, I drew my breath
from you at the first and so now I lull   1295
my mouth to sleep with your name.   (*Enter a second messenger.*)

Second Messenger: O Princes always honoured by our country,
what deeds you'll hear of and what horrors see,
what grief you'll feel, if you as true born Thebans
care for the house of Labdacus's sons.   1300
Phasis nor Ister cannot purge this house,
I think, with all their streams, such things
it hides, such evils shortly will bring forth
into the light, whether they will or not;
and troubles hurt the most   1305
when they prove self-inflicted.

Chorus: What we had known before did not fall short
of bitter groaning's worth; what's more to tell?

Second Messenger: Shortest to hear and tell — our glorious queen
Jocasta's dead.

Chorus: Unhappy woman! How?   1310

Second Messenger: By her own hand. The worst of what was done
you cannot know. You did not see the sight.
Yet in so far as I remember it
you'll hear the end of our unlucky queen.
When she came raging into the house she went   1315
straight to her marriage bed, tearing her hair
with both her hands, and crying upon Laius
long dead — Do you remember, Laius,
that night long past which bred a child for us
to send you to your death and leave   1320
a mother making children with her son?
And then she groaned and cursed the bed in which

she brought forth husband by her husband, children
by her own child, an infamous double bond.
How after that she died I do not know, —   1325
for Oedipus distracted us from seeing.
He burst upon us shouting and we looked
to him as he paced frantically around,
begging us always: Give me a sword, I say,
to find this wife no wife, this mother's womb,   1330
this field of double sowing whence I sprang
and where I sowed my children! As he raved
some god showed him the way — none of us there.
Bellowing terribly and led by some
invisible guide he rushed on the two doors, —   1335
wrenching the hollow bolts out of their sockets,
he charged inside. There, there, we saw his wife
hanging, the twisted rope around her neck.
When he saw her, he cried out fearfully
and cut the dangling noose. Then, as she lay,   1340
poor woman, on the ground, what happened after,
was terrible to see. He tore the brooches —
the gold chased brooches fastening her robe —
away from her and lifting them up high
dashed them on his own eyeballs, shrieking out   1345
such things as: they will never see the crime
I have committed or had done upon me!
Dark eyes, now in the days to come look on
forbidden faces, do not recognize
those whom you long for — with such imprecations   1350
he struck his eyes again and yet again
with the brooches. And the bleeding eyeballs gushed
and stained his beard — no sluggish oozing drops
but a black rain and bloody hail poured down.

So it has broken — and not on one head   1355
but troubles mixed for husband and for wife.
The fortune of the days gone by was true
good fortune — but today groans and destruction
and death and shame — of all ills can be named
not one is missing.   1360
Chorus: Is he now in any ease from pain?
Second Messenger: He shouts
for some one to unbar the doors and show him
to all the men of Thebes, his father's killer,
his mother's — no I cannot say the word,
it is unholy — for he'll cast himself,   1365
out of the land, he says, and not remain
to bring a curse upon his house, the curse

he called upon it in his proclamation. But
he wants for strength, aye, and some one to guide him;
his sickness is too great to bear. You, too,   1370
will be shown that. The bolts are opening.
Soon you will see a sight to waken pity
even in the horror of it.   *(Enter the blinded Oedipus.)*

Chorus: This is a terrible sight for men to see!
I never found a worse!   1375
Poor wretch, what madness came upon you!
What evil spirit leaped upon your life
to your ill-luck — a leap beyond man's strength!
Indeed I pity you, but I cannot
look at you, though there's much I want to ask   1380
and much to learn and much to see.
I shudder at the sight of you.

Oedipus: O, O,
where am I going? Where is my voice
borne on the wind to and fro?   1385
Spirit, how far have you sprung?

Chorus: To a terrible place whereof men's ears
may not hear, nor their eyes behold it.

Oedipus: Darkness!
Horror of darkness enfolding, resistless, unspeakable visitant
sped by an ill wind in haste!   1390
madness and stabbing pain and memory
of evil deeds I have done!

Chorus: In such misfortunes it's no wonder
if double weighs the burden of your grief.

Oedipus: My friend,   1395
you are the only one steadfast, the only one that attends on me;
you still stay nursing the blind man.
Your care is not unnoticed. I can know
your voice, although this darkness is my world.

Chorus: Doer of dreadful deeds, how did you dare   1400
so far to do despite to your own eyes?
what spirit urged you to it?

Oedipus: It was Apollo, friends, Apollo,
that brought this bitter bitterness, my sorrows to completion.
But the hand that struck me   1405
was none but my own.
Why should I see
whose vision showed me nothing sweet to see?

Chorus: These things are as you say.

Oedipus: What can I see to love?   1410
What greeting can touch my ears with joy?
Take me away, and haste — to a place out of the way!
Take me away, my friends, the greatly miserable,

the most accursed, whom God too hates
above all men on earth!   1415
Chorus: Unhappy in your mind and your misfortune,
would I had never known you!
Oedipus: Curse on the man who took
the cruel bonds from off my legs, as I lay in the field.
He stole me from death and saved me,   1420
no kindly service.
Had I died then
I would not be so burdensome to friends.
Chorus: I, too, could have wished it had been so.
Oedipus: Then I would not have come   1425
to kill my father and marry my mother infamously.
Now I am godless and child of impurity,
begetter in the same seed that created my wretched self.
If there is any ill worse than ill,
that is the lot of Oedipus.   1430
Chorus: I cannot say your remedy was good;
you would be better dead than blind and living.
Oedipus: What I have done here was best done — don't tell me
otherwise, do not give me further counsel.
I do not know with what eyes I could look   1435
upon my father when I die and go
under the earth, nor yet my wretched mother —
those two to whom I have done things deserving
worse punishment than hanging. Would the sight
of children, bred as mine are, gladden me?   1440
No, not these eyes, never. And my city,
its towers and sacred places of the Gods,
of these I robbed my miserable self
when I commanded all to drive *him* out,
the criminal since proved by God impure   1445
and of the race of Laius.
To this guilt I bore witness against myself —
with what eyes shall I look upon my people?
No. If there were a means to choke the fountain
of hearing I would not have stayed my hand   1450
from locking up my miserable carcase,
seeing and hearing nothing; it is sweet
to keep our thoughts out of the range of hurt.

Cithaeron, why did you receive me? why
having received me did you not kill me straight?   1455
And so I had not shown to men my birth.

O Polybus and Corinth and the house,
the old house that I used to call my father's —

what fairness you were nurse to, and what foulness
festered beneath! Now I am found to be   1460
a sinner and a son of sinners. Crossroads,
and hidden glade, oak and the narrow way
at the crossroads, that drank my father's blood
offered you by my hands, do you remember
still what I did as you looked on, and what   1465
I did when I came here? O marriage, marriage!
you bred me and again when you had bred
bred children of your child and showed to men
brides, wives and mothers and the foulest deeds
that can be in this world of ours.   1470

Come — it's unfit to say what is unfit
to do. — I beg of you in God's name hide me
somewhere outside your country, yes, or kill me,
or throw me into the sea, to be forever
out of your sight. Approach and deign to touch me   1475
for all my wretchedness, and do not fear.
No man but I can bear my evil doom.
Chorus: Here Creon comes in fit time to perform
or give advice in what you ask of us.
Creon is left sole ruler in your stead.   1480
Oedipus: Creon! Creon! What shall I say to him?
How can I justly hope that he will trust me?
In what is past I have been proved towards him
an utter liar.   *(Enter Creon.)*
Creon: Oedipus, I've come   1485
not so that I might laugh at you nor taunt you
with evil of the past. But if you still
are without shame before the face of men
reverence at least the flame that gives all life,
our Lord the Sun, and do not show unveiled
to him pollution such that neither land   1490
nor holy rain nor light of day can welcome.   *(To a servant)*
Be quick and take him in. It is most decent
that only kin should see and hear the troubles
of kin.
Oedipus: I beg you, since you've torn me from   1495
my dreadful expectations and have come
in a most noble spirit to a man
that has used you vilely — do a thing for me.
I shall speak for your own good, not for my own.
Creon: What do you need that you would ask of me?   1500
Oedipus: Drive me from here with all the speed you can
to where I may not hear a human voice.

Creon: Be sure, I would have done this had not I
wished first of all to learn from the God the course
of action I should follow.

Oedipus: But his word   1505
has been quite clear to let the parricide,°
the sinner, die.

Creon: Yes, that indeed was said.
But in the present need we had best discover
what we should do.

Oedipus: And will you ask about
a man so wretched?

Creon: Now even you will trust   1510
the God.

Oedipus: So. I command you — and will beseech you —
to her that lies inside that house give burial
as you would have it; she is yours and rightly
you will perform the rites for her. For me —
never let this my father's city have me   1515
living a dweller in it. Leave me live
in the mountains where Cithaeron is, that's called
my mountain, which my mother and my father
while they were living would have made my tomb.
So I may die by their decree who sought   1520
indeed to kill me. Yet I know this much:
no sickness and no other thing will kill me.
I would not have been saved from death if not
for some strange evil fate. Well, let my fate
go where it will.

                    Creon, you need not care   1525
about my sons; they're men and so wherever
they are, they will not lack a livelihood.
But my two girls — so sad and pitiful —
whose table never stood apart from mine,
and everything I touched they always shared —   1530
O Creon, have a thought for them! And most
I wish that you might suffer me to touch them
and sorrow with them.

                    (Enter Antigone and Ismene, Oedipus' two daughters.)
O my lord! O true noble Creon! Can I
really be touching them, as when I saw?   1535
What shall I say?
Yes, I can hear them sobbing — my two darlings!
and Creon has had pity and has sent me

1506 *parricide:* One who kills his parent or another close relative.

what I loved most?
Am I right?   1540
Creon: You're right: it was I gave you this
    because I knew from old days how you loved them
    as I see now.
Oedipus: God bless you for it, Creon,
    and may God guard you better on your road
    than he did me!
              O children,   1545
where are you? Come here, come to my hands,
a brother's hands which turned your father's eyes,
those bright eyes you knew once, to what you see,
a father seeing nothing, knowing nothing,
begetting you from his own source of life.   1550
I weep for you — I cannot see your faces —
I weep when I think of the bitterness
there will be in your lives, how you must live
before the world. At what assemblages
of citizens will you make one? to what   1555
gay company will you go and not come home
in tears instead of sharing in the holiday?
And when you're ripe for marriage, who will he be,
the man who'll risk to take such infamy
as shall cling to my children, to bring hurt   1560
on them and those that marry with them? What
curse is not there? "Your father killed his father
and sowed the seed where he had sprung himself
and begot you out of the womb that held him."
These insults you will hear. Then who will marry you?   1565
No one, my children; clearly you are doomed
to waste away in barrenness unmarried.
Son of Menoeceus,° since you are all the father
left these two girls, and we, their parents, both
are dead to them — do not allow them wander   1570
like beggars, poor and husbandless.
They are of your own blood.
And do not make them equal with myself
in wretchedness; for you can see them now
so young, so utterly alone, save for you only.   1575
Touch my hand, noble Creon, and say yes.
If you were older, children, and were wiser,
there's much advice I'd give you. But as it is,
let this be what you pray: give me a life
wherever there is opportunity   1580

1568 *Son of Menoeceus:* Creon.

to live, and better life than was my father's.

Creon: Your tears have had enough of scope; now go within the house.

Oedipus: I must obey, though bitter of heart.

Creon: In season, all is good.

Oedipus: Do you know on what conditions I obey?

Creon: You tell me them,   1585
and I shall know them when I hear.

Oedipus: That you shall send me out
to live away from Thebes.

Creon: That gift you must ask of the God.

Oedipus: But I'm now hated by the Gods.

Creon: So quickly you'll obtain your
prayer.

Oedipus: You consent then?

Creon: What I do not mean, I do not use to say.

Oedipus: Now lead me away from here.

Creon: Let go the children, then,
and come.   1590

Oedipus: Do not take them from me.

Creon: Do not seek to be master in
everything, for the things you mastered did not follow you
throughout your life.

                              (As Creon and Oedipus go out.)

Chorus: You that live in my ancestral Thebes, behold this Oedipus, —
him who knew the famous riddles and was a man most masterful;
not a citizen who did not look with envy on his lot —   1595
see him now and see the breakers of misfortune swallow him!
Look upon that last day always. Count no mortal happy till
he has passed the final limit of his life secure from pain.

CONSIDERATIONS FOR CRITICAL THINKING AND WRITING

1. FIRST RESPONSE. Is it possible for a twenty-first-century reader to identify with Oedipus's plight? What philosophic issues does he confront?

2. In the opening scene what does the priest's speech reveal about how Oedipus has been regarded as a ruler of Thebes?

3. What do Oedipus's confrontations with Teiresias and Creon indicate about his character?

4. Aristotle defined a tragic flaw as consisting of "error and frailties." What errors does Oedipus make? What are his frailties?

5. What causes Oedipus's downfall? Is he simply a pawn in a predetermined game played by the gods? Can he be regarded as responsible for the suffering and death in the play?

6. Locate instances of dramatic irony in the play. How do they serve as foreshadowings?

7. Describe the function of the Chorus. How does the Chorus's view of life and the gods differ from Jocasta's?

8. Trace the images of vision and blindness throughout the play. How are they related to the theme? Why does Oedipus blind himself instead of joining Jocasta in suicide?

9. What is your assessment of Oedipus at the end of the play? Was he foolish? Heroic? Fated? To what extent can your emotions concerning him be described as "pity and fear"?

10. **CONNECTION TO ANOTHER SELECTION.** Consider the endings of *Oedipus the King* and Shakespeare's *Othello* (p. 660). What feelings do you have about these endings? Are they irredeemably unhappy? Is there anything that suggests hope for the future at the ends of these plays?

26

William Shakespeare
and Elizabethan Drama

Shakespeare — the nearest thing
in incarnation to the eye of God.
— SIR LAURENCE OLIVIER

© Corbis.

All the world's a stage,
And all the men and women
merely players:
They have their exits and their
entrances;
And one man in his time plays
many parts . . .
— WILLIAM SHAKESPEARE

By permission of the Folger
Shakespeare Library.

Although relatively little is known about William Shakespeare's life, his writings reveal him to have been an extraordinary man. His vitality, compassion, and insights are evident in his broad range of characters, who have fascinated generations of audiences, and his powerful use of the English language, which has been celebrated since his death nearly four centuries ago. Ben Jonson, his contemporary, rightly claimed that "he was not of an age, but for all time!" Shakespeare's plays have been produced so often and his writings read so widely that quotations from them have woven their way into our everyday conversations. If you have ever experienced "fear and trembling" because there was "something in the wind" or discovered that it was "a foregone conclusion" that you would "make a virtue of necessity," then it wouldn't be quite accurate for you to say that Shakespeare "was Greek to me" because these phrases come, respectively, from his plays *Much Ado about Nothing*, *Comedy of Errors*, *Othello*, *The Two Gentlemen of Verona*, and *Julius*

"First Folio" portrait (top). The image of William Shakespeare above is a portrait included on the *First Folio*, a collected edition of Shakespeare's plays published seven years after his death.

"Chandos" portrait engraving (middle). This engraving is of an image painted during Shakespeare's lifetime known as the "Chandos portrait," rumored to have been painted by Shakespeare's friend and fellow actor Richard Burbage.

Shakespeare's signature (bottom). The signature shown here is one of the bard's six authenticated signatures in existence and is from his last will and testament.

Top image: Reprinted by permission of the Folger Shakespeare Library. *Middle image:* HIP/Art Resource, NY. *Bottom image:* Courtesy of the National Archives, United Kingdom.

Caesar. Many more examples could be cited, but it is enough to say that Shakespeare's art endures. His words may give us only an oblique glimpse of his life, but they continue to give us back the experience of our own lives.

Shakespeare was born in Stratford-on-Avon on or about April 23, 1564. His father, an important citizen who held several town offices, married a woman from a prominent family; however, when their son was only a teenager, the family's financial situation became precarious. Shakespeare probably attended the Stratford grammar school, but no records of either his schooling or his early youth exist. As limited as his education was, it is clear that he was for his time a learned man. At the age of eighteen, he struck out on his own and married the twenty-six-year-old Anne Hathaway, who bore him a daughter in 1583 and twins, a boy and a girl, in 1585. Before he was twenty-one, Shakespeare had a wife and three children to support.

What his life was like for the next seven years is not known, but there is firm evidence that by 1592 he was in London enjoying some success as both an actor and a playwright. By 1594 he had also established himself as a poet with two lengthy poems, *Venus and Adonis* and *The Rape of Lucrece.* But it was in the theater that he made his living and his strongest reputation. He was well connected with a successful troupe first known as the Lord Chamberlain's Men; they built the famous Globe Theatre in 1599. Later this company, because of the patronage of King James, came to be known as the King's Men. Writing plays for this company throughout his career, Shakespeare also became one of its principal shareholders, an arrangement that allowed him to prosper in London as well as in his native Stratford, where in 1597 he bought a fine house called New Place. About 1611 he retired there with his family, although he continued writing plays. He died on April 23, 1616, and was buried at Holy Trinity Church in Stratford.

The documented details of Shakespeare's life provide barely enough information for a newspaper obituary. But if his activities remain largely unknown, his writings — among them thirty-seven plays and 154 sonnets — more than compensate for that loss. Plenty of authors have produced more work, but no writer has created so much literature that has been so universally admired. Within twenty-five years Shakespeare's dramatic works included *Hamlet, Macbeth, King Lear, Othello, Julius Caesar, Richard III, 1 Henry IV, Romeo and Juliet, Love's Labour's Lost, A Midsummer Night's Dream, The Tempest, Twelfth Night,* and *Measure for Measure.* These plays represent a broad range of characters and actions conveyed in poetic language that reveals human nature as well as the author's genius.

SHAKESPEARE'S THEATER

Drama languished in Europe after the fall of Rome during the fifth and sixth centuries. From about A.D. 400 to 900 almost no record of dramatic productions exists except for those of minstrels and other entertainers, such as acrobats and jugglers, who traveled through the countryside.

The Catholic church was instrumental in suppressing drama because the theater — represented by the excesses of Roman productions — was seen as subversive. No state-sponsored festivals brought people together in huge theaters the way they had in Greek and Roman times.

In the tenth century, however, the church helped revive theater by incorporating dialogues into the Mass as a means of dramatizing portions of the Gospels. These brief dialogues developed into more elaborate mystery plays, miracle plays, and morality plays, anonymous works that were created primarily to inculcate religious principles rather than to entertain. But these works also marked the reemergence of relatively large dramatic productions.

Mystery plays dramatize stories from the Bible, such as the Creation, the Fall of Adam and Eve, or the Crucifixion. The most highly regarded surviving example is *The Second Shepherd's Play* (ca. 1400), which dramatizes Christ's nativity. *Miracle plays* are based on the lives of saints. An extant play of the late fifteenth century, for example, is titled *Saint Mary Magdalene*. *Morality plays* present allegorical stories in which virtues and vices are personified to teach humanity how to achieve salvation. *Everyman* (ca. 1500), the most famous example, has as its central conflict every person's struggle to avoid the sins that lead to hell and practice the virtues that are rewarded in heaven.

The clergy who performed these plays gave way to trade guilds that presented them outside the church on stages featuring scenery and costumed characters. The plays' didactic content was gradually abandoned in favor of broad humor and worldly concerns. Thus by the sixteenth century religious drama had been replaced largely by secular drama.

Because theatrical productions were no longer sponsored and financed by the church or trade guilds during Shakespeare's lifetime, playwrights had to figure out ways to draw audiences willing to pay for entertainment. This necessitated some simple but important changes. Somehow, people had to be prevented from seeing a production unless they paid. Hence an enclosed space with controlled access was created. In addition, the plays had to change frequently enough to keep audiences returning, and this resulted in more experienced actors and playwrights sensitive to their audiences' tastes and interests. Plays compelling enough to attract audiences had to employ powerful writing brought to life by convincing actors in entertaining productions. Shakespeare always wrote his dramas for the stage — for audiences who would see and hear the characters. The conventions of the theater for which he wrote are important, then, for appreciating and understanding his plays. Detailed information about Elizabethan theater (theater during the reign of Elizabeth I, from 1558 to 1603) is less than abundant, but historians have pieced together a good sense of what theaters were like from sources such as drawings, building contracts, and stage directions.

Early performances of various kinds took place in the courtyards of inns and taverns. These secular entertainments attracted people of all classes. To the dismay of London officials, such gatherings were also settings for the illegal activities of brawlers, thieves, and prostitutes. To avoid licensing regulations, some theaters were constructed outside the city's limits. The Globe, for instance, built by the Lord Chamberlain's company, with which Shakespeare was closely associated, was located on the south bank of the Thames River. Regardless of the play, an Elizabethan theatergoer was likely to have an exciting time. Playwrights understood the varied nature of their audiences, so the plays appealed to a broad range of sensibilities and tastes. Philosophy and poetry rubbed shoulders with violence and sexual jokes, and somehow all were made compatible.

Physically, Elizabethan theaters resembled the courtyards where they originated, but the theaters could accommodate more people — perhaps as many as twenty-five hundred. The exterior of a theater building was many-sided or round and enclosed a yard that was only partially roofed over, to take advantage of natural light. The interior walls consisted of three galleries of seats looking onto a platform stage that extended from the rear wall. These seats were sheltered from the weather and more comfortable than the area in front of the stage, which was known as the *pit*. Here "groundlings" paid a penny to stand and watch the performance. Despite the large number

A Conjectural Reconstruction of the Globe Theatre, 1599–1613. Drawing by C. Walter Hodges from his *Globe Restored*, Oxford University Press. Folger Shakespeare Library. ART Box H688 no.12 pt.1.

By permission of the Folger Shakespeare Library.

of spectators, the theater created an intimate atmosphere because the audience closely surrounded the stage on three sides.

This arrangement produced two theatrical conventions: asides and soliloquies. An *aside* is a speech directed only to the audience. It makes the audience privy to a character's thoughts, allowing them to perceive ironies and intrigues that other characters know nothing about. In a large performing space, such as a Greek amphitheater, asides would be unconvincing because they would have to be declaimed loudly to be heard, but they were well suited to Elizabethan theaters. A *soliloquy* is a speech delivered while an actor is alone on the stage; like an aside, it reveals a character's state of mind. Hamlet's "To be or not to be" speech is the most famous example of a soliloquy.

The Elizabethan platform stage was large enough — approximately twenty-five feet deep and forty feet wide — to allow a wide variety of actions, ranging from festive banquets to bloody battles. Sections of the floor could be opened or removed to create, for instance, the gravediggers' scene in *Hamlet* or to allow characters to exit through trapdoors. At the rear of the platform an inner stage was covered by curtains that could be drawn to reveal an interior setting, such as a bedroom or tomb. The curtains were also a natural location for a character to hide in order to overhear conversations. On each side of the curtains were doors through which characters entered and exited. An upper stage could be used as a watchtower, a castle wall, or a balcony. Although most of the action occurred on the main platform stage, there were opportunities for fluid movements from one acting area to another, providing a variety of settings.

These settings were not, however, elaborately indicated by scenery or props. A scene might change when one group of characters left the stage and another entered. A table and some chairs could be carried on quickly to suggest a tavern. But the action was not interrupted for set changes. Instead, the characters' speeches often identify the location of a scene. (In modern editions of Shakespeare's plays, editors indicate in brackets the scene breaks, settings, and movements of actors not identified in the original manuscripts to help readers keep track of things.) Today's performances of the plays frequently use more elaborate settings and props. But Shakespeare's need to paint his scenery with words resulted in many poetic descriptions. Here is one of moonlight from *Merchant of Venice*:

> How sweet the moonlight sleeps upon this bank!
> Here will we sit and let the sounds of music
> Creep in our ears. Soft stillness and the night
> Become the touches of sweet harmony.

Although the settings were scant and the props mostly limited to what an actor carried onto the stage (a sword, a document, a shovel), Elizabethan costuming was an elaborate visual treat that identified the characters. Moreover, because women were not permitted to act in the theater, their roles were played by boys dressed in female costumes. In addition, elaborate sound effects were used to create atmosphere. A flourish of trumpets might accompany the entrance of a king; small cannons might be heard during a battle; thunder might punctuate a storm. In short, Elizabethan theater was alive with sights and sounds, but at the center of the stage was the play-wright's language; that's where the magic began.

THE RANGE OF SHAKESPEARE'S DRAMA: HISTORY, COMEDY, AND TRAGEDY

Shakespeare's plays fall into three basic categories: histories, comedies, and tragedies. Broadly speaking, a history play is any drama based on historical materials. In this case, Shakespeare's *Antony and Cleopatra* and *Julius Caesar* would fit the definition, since they feature historical figures. More specifi-cally, though, a history play is a British play based primarily on Raphael Holinshed's *Chronicles of England, Scotland, and Ireland* (1578). This acc-ount of British history was popular toward the end of the sixteenth century because of the patriotic pride that was produced by the British defeat of the Spanish Armada in 1588, and it was an important source for a series of plays Shakespeare wrote treating the reigns of British kings from Richard II to Henry VIII. The political subject matter of these plays both entertained audiences and instructed them in virtues and vices involved in England's past efforts to overcome civil war and disorder. Ambition, deception, and treason were of more than historical interest. Shakespeare's audiences saw these plays about the fifteenth century as ways of sorting through the mean-ings of both the calamities of the past and the uncertainties of the present.

Although Shakespeare used Holinshed's *Chronicles* as a source, he did not hesitate to make changes for dramatic purposes. In *1 Henry IV*, for example, he ages Henry IV to contrast him with the youthful Prince Hal, and he makes Hotspur younger than he actually was to have him serve as a foil to the prince. The serious theme of Hal's growth into the kind of man who would make an ideal king is counterweighted by Shakespeare's comic creation of Falstaff, that good-humored "huge hill of flesh" filled with delightful contradictions. Fal-staff had historic antecedents, but the true source of his identity is the imagi-nation of Shakespeare, a writer who was, after all, a dramatist first.

Comedy is a strong element in *1 Henry IV*, but the play's overall tone is se-rious. Falstaff's behavior ultimately gives way to the measured march of English history. While Shakespeare encourages us to laugh at some of the participants, we are not invited to laugh at the history of English monar-chies. Comedy even appears in Shakespeare's tragedies, as in Hamlet's jests with the gravediggers or in Emilia's biting remarks in *Othello*. This use of comedy is called **comic relief**, a humorous scene or incident that alleviates tension in an otherwise serious work. In many instances these moments enhance the thematic significance of the story in addition to pro-viding laughter. When Hamlet jokes with the gravediggers, we laugh, but something hauntingly serious about the humor also intensifies our more serious emotions.

A true comedy, however, lacks a tragedy's sense that some great disaster will finally descend on the protagonist. There are conflicts and obstacles that must be confronted, but in comedy the characters delight us by overcoming whatever initially thwarts them. We can laugh at their misfortunes because we are confident that everything will turn out fine in the end. Shakespearean comedy tends to follow this general principle; it begins with problems and ends with their resolution.

Shakespeare's comedies are called **romantic comedies** because they typically involve lovers whose hearts are set on each other but whose lives are complicated by disapproving parents, deceptions, jealousies, illusions, confused identities, disguises, or other misunderstandings. Conflicts are present, but they are more amusing than threatening. This lightness is apparent in some of the comedies' titles: The conflict in a play such as *A Midsummer Night's Dream* is, in a sense, *Much Ado about Nothing* — *As You Like It* in a comedy. Shakespeare orchestrates the problems and confusion that typify the initial plotting of a romantic comedy into harmonious wedding arrangements in the final scenes. In these comedies life is a celebration, a feast that always satisfies, because the generosity of the humor leaves us with a revived appetite for life's surprising possibilities. Discord and misunderstanding give way to concord and love. Marriage symbolizes a pledge that life itself is renewable, so we are left with a sense of new beginnings.

Although a celebration of life, comedy is also frequently used as a vehicle for criticizing human affairs. **Satire** casts a critical eye on vices and follies by holding them up to ridicule — usually to point out an absurdity so that it can be avoided or corrected. In *Twelfth Night* Malvolio is satirized for his priggishness and pomposity. He thinks himself better than almost everyone around him, but Shakespeare reveals him to be comic as well as pathetic. We come to understand what Malvolio will apparently never comprehend: that no one can take him as seriously as he takes himself. Polonius is subjected to a similar kind of scrutiny in *Hamlet*.

Malvolio's ambitious efforts to attract Olivia's affections are rendered absurd by Shakespeare's use of both high and low comedy. **High comedy** consists of verbal wit, while **low comedy** is generally associated with physical action and is less intellectual. Through puns and witty exchanges, Shakespeare's high comedy displays Malvolio's inconsistencies of character. His self-importance is deflated by low comedy. We are treated to a **farce**, a form of humor based on exaggerated, improbable incongruities, when the staid Malvolio is tricked into wearing bizarre clothing and behaving like a fool to win Olivia. Our laughter is Malvolio's pain, but though he has been "notoriously abus'd," vowing in the final scene to be "reveng'd on the whole pack" of laughing conspirators who have tricked him, the play ends on a light note. Indeed, it concludes with a song, the last line of which reminds us of the predominant tone of the play as well as the nature of comedy: "And we'll strive to please you every day."

Tragedy, in contrast, does not promise peace and contentment. The basic characteristics of tragedy have already been outlined in the context of Greek drama (see Chapter 25). Like Greek tragic heroes, Shakespeare's protagonists are exceptional human beings whose stature makes their misfortune all the more dramatic. These characters pay a high price for their actions. Oedipus's search for the killer of Laius, Hamlet's agonized conviction that "The time is out of joint," and Othello's willingness to doubt his wife's fidelity all lead to irreversible results. Comic plots are largely free of this sense of inevitability. Instead of the festive mood that prevails once the characters in a comedy recognize their true connection to each other, tragedy gives us dark reflections that emanate from suffering. The laughter of comedy is a shared experience, a recognition of human likeness, but suffering estranges tragic heroes from the world around them.

Some of the wrenching differences between comedy and tragedy can be experienced in *Othello*. Although this play is a tragedy, Shakespeare includes in its plot many of the ingredients associated with comedy. For a time it seems possible that Othello and Desdemona will overcome the complications of a disapproving father, along with the seemingly minor deceptions, awkward misperceptions, and tender illusions that hover around them. But in *Othello* marriage is not a sign of concord displacing discord; instead, love and marriage mark the beginning of the tragic action.

A NOTE ON READING SHAKESPEARE

Readers who have had no previous experience with Shakespeare's language may find it initially daunting. They might well ask whether people ever talked the way, for example, Hamlet does in his most famous soliloquy:

> To be, or not to be: that is the question:
> Whether 'tis nobler in the mind to suffer
> The slings and arrows of outrageous fortune,
> Or to take arms against a sea of troubles,
> And by opposing end them?

People did not talk like this in Elizabethan times. Hamlet speaks in poetry. Shakespeare might have had him say something like this: "The most important issue one must confront is whether the pain that life inevitably creates should be passively accepted or resisted." But Shakespeare chose poetry to reveal the depth and complexity of Hamlet's experience. This heightened language is used to clarify rather than obscure his characters' thoughts. Shakespeare has Hamlet, as well as many other characters, speak in prose too, but in general his plays are written in poetry. If you keep in mind that Shakespeare's dialogue is not typically intended to imitate everyday speech, it should be easier to understand that his language is more than simply a vehicle for expressing the action of the play.

Here are a few practical suggestions to enhance your understanding of and pleasure in reading Shakespeare's plays.

1. Keep track of the characters by referring to the *dramatis personae* (characters) listed and described at the beginning of each play.
2. Remember that poetic language deserves to be read slowly and carefully. A difficult passage can sometimes be better understood if it's read aloud. Don't worry if every line isn't absolutely clear to you.
3. Pay attention to the annotations, which explain unfamiliar words, phrases, and allusions in the text. These can be distracting, but they are sometimes necessary to determine the basic meaning of a passage.
4. As you read each scene, try to imagine how it would be played on a stage.
5. If you find the reading especially difficult, try listening to a recording of the play. (Most college libraries have recordings of Shakespeare's plays.) Allowing professional actors to do the reading aloud for you can enrich your imaginative reconstruction of the action and characters. Hearing a play can help you with subsequent readings of it.
6. After reading the play, view a film or DVD recording of a performance. It is important to view the performance *after* your reading, though, so that your own mental re-creation of the play is not short-circuited by a director's production.

And finally, to quote Hamlet, "Be not too tame . . . let your own discretion be your tutor." Read Shakespeare's work as best you can; it warrants such careful attention not because the language and characters are difficult to understand but because they offer so much to enjoy.

Othello, the Moor of Venice

Othello has compelled audiences since it was first produced in 1604. Its power is as simple and as complex as the elemental emotions it dramatizes; the play ebbs and flows with the emotional energy derived from the characters' struggles with love and hatred, good and evil, trust and jealousy, appearance and reality. These conflicts are played out on a domestic scale rather than on some metaphysical level. Anyone who has ever been in love will empathize with Othello and Desdemona. They embody a love story gone horribly — tragically — wrong.

Although the plot of *Othello* is filled with Iago's intrigues and a series of opaque mysteries for Othello, it moves swiftly and precisely to its catastrophic ending as the tragedy relentlessly claims its victims. On one level the plot is simple. As the Moorish general of the Venetian army, Othello chooses Cassio to serve as his lieutenant, a selection Iago resents and decides to subvert. To discredit Cassio, Iago poisons Othello's faith in his wife, Desdemona, by falsely insinuating that she and Cassio are having an affair. Through a series of cleverly demonic manipulations, Iago succeeds in convincing Othello of his wife's infidelity and his lieutenant's betrayal. Believing these lies, Othello insists upon taking his revenge.

If the plot of *Othello* is relatively direct and simple in its focus on Iago's manipulation of events, the play's major characters are considerably more complex. Love and jealousy are central in *Othello*. The Moor's virtues of openness and trust cause him to experience betrayal as intensely as he does love. He is distinguished by his nobility, bravery, strength, and deep sense of honor, but he is also vulnerable to the doubts Iago raises owing to his race ("I am black") and marginal status in Venetian society.

Iago, whose motivations are much deeper and more mysterious than his maneuvering for a coveted lieutenancy, personifies a nearly inexplicable evil in the play. Just as Desdemona's nature seems to be all goodness, Iago's is malignant destruction. His profound villainy both horrifies and fascinates us: How can he be what he is? He thrives on ambition, envy, deception, jealousy, and doubt. Although he commands absolutely no respect, he holds our attention because of his cunning duplicity.

The play is finally, however, Othello's story. As we watch him be seduced by Iago's veiled hints and seeming confidences, we see how his trusting nature is inextricably related to his propensity to suspect Desdemona. Iago plays on the complexity and paradox of Othello's character and manipulates those tensions to keep him off balance and blind to the truth of Desdemona's faithfulness. Ultimately, though, Othello must take responsibility for the destruction of his love, a responsibility that is both his tragedy and redemption.

WILLIAM SHAKESPEARE (1564–1616)
Othello, the Moor of Venice   *1604*

THE NAMES OF THE ACTORS

Othello, the Moor
Brabantio, [a Venetian senator,] father to Desdemona
Cassio, an honorable lieutenant [to Othello]
Iago, [Othello's ancient,] a villain
Roderigo, a gulled gentleman
Duke of Venice
Senators [of Venice]
Montano, governor of Cyprus
Lodovico and Gratiano, [kinsmen to Brabantio,] two noble Venetians
Sailors
Clowns
Desdemona, wife to Othello
Emilia, wife to Iago
Bianca, a courtesan
[Messenger, Herald, Officers, Venetian Gentlemen, Musicians, Attendants

SCENE: *Venice and Cyprus]*

ACT I

SCENE I: *A street in Venice.*

Enter Roderigo and Iago.

Roderigo: Tush, never tell me! I take it much unkindly
    That thou, Iago, who hast had my purse
    As if the strings were thine, shouldst know of this.°
Iago: 'Sblood,° but you'll not hear me!
    If ever I did dream of such a matter,   5
    Abhor me.
Roderigo: Thou told'st me thou didst hold him in thy hate.
Iago: Despise me if I do not. Three great ones of the city,
    In personal suit to make me his lieutenant,
    Off-capped to him;° and, by the faith of man,   10
    I know my price; I am worth no worse a place.
    But he, as loving his own pride and purposes,
    Evades them with a bombast circumstance.°
    Horribly stuffed with epithets of war;
    [And, in conclusion,]   15
    Nonsuits° my mediators; for, "Certes," says he,
    "I have already chose my officer."
    And what was he?
    Forsooth, a great arithmetician,°
    One Michael Cassio, a Florentine   20
    (A fellow almost damned in a fair wife°)
    That never set a squadron in the field,
    Nor the division of a battle knows
    More than a spinster; unless the bookish theoric,
    Wherein the togèd consuls can propose   25
    As masterly as he. Mere prattle without practice
    Is all his soldiership. But he, sir, had th' election;
    And I (of whom his eyes had seen the proof
    At Rhodes, at Cyprus, and on other grounds
    Christian and heathen) must be belee'd and calmed°   30
    By debitor and creditor; this counter-caster,°
    He, in good time, must his lieutenant be,
    And I — God bless the mark! — his Moorship's ancient.°
Roderigo: By heaven, I rather would have been his hangman.
Iago: Why, there's no remedy; 'tis the curse of service.   35

Act I, Scene I. 3 *this:* i.e., Desdemona's elopement. 4 *'Sblood:* By God's blood.
10 *him:* i.e., Othello. 13 *a bombast circumstance:* Pompous circumlocutions.
16 *Nonsuits:* Rejects. 19 *arithmetician:* Theoretician. 21 *almost . . . wife:* (An obscure
allusion; Cassio is unmarried, but see IV.i.114). 30 *belee'd and calmed:* Left in the
lurch. 31 *counter-caster:* Bookkeeper. 33 *ancient:* Ensign.

Preferment goes by letter and affection,°
And not by old gradation, where each second
Stood heir to th' first. Now, sir, be judge yourself,
Whether I in any just term am affined°
To love the Moor.

Roderigo: I would not follow him then.   40

Iago: O, sir, content you;
I follow him to serve my turn upon him.
We cannot all be masters, nor all masters
Cannot be truly followed. You shall mark
Many a duteous and knee-crooking knave   45
That, doting on his own obsequious bondage,
Wears out his time, much like his master's ass,
For naught but provender; and when he's old, cashiered.°
Whip me such honest knaves! Others there are
Who, trimmed° in forms and visages of duty,   50
Keep yet their hearts attending on themselves;
And, throwing but shows of service on their lords,
Do well thrive by them, and when they have lined their coats,
Do themselves homage. These fellows have some soul;
And such a one do I profess myself. For, sir,   55
It is as sure as you are Roderigo,
Were I the Moor, I would not be Iago.
In following him, I follow but myself;
Heaven is my judge, not I for love and duty,
But seeming so, for my peculiar end;   60
For when my outward action doth demonstrate
The native act and figure of my heart°
In compliment extern,° 'tis not long after
But I will wear my heart upon my sleeve
For daws to peck at; I am not what I am.   65

Roderigo: What a full fortune does the thick-lips° owe°
If he can carry't thus!

Iago: Call up her father,
Rouse him. Make after him, poison his delight,
Proclaim him in the streets. Incense her kinsmen,
And though he in a fertile climate dwell,   70
Plague him with flies; though that his joy be joy,
Yet throw such changes of vexation on't
As it may lose some color.

Roderigo: Here is her father's house. I'll call aloud.

---

36 *affection:* Favoritism.   39 *affined:* Obliged.   48 *cashiered:* Turned off.   50 *trimmed:*
Dressed up.   62 *The . . . heart:* What I really believe and intend.   63 *compliment
extern:* Outward appearance.   66 *thick-lips:* An Elizabethan epithet for blacks, including
Moors; *owe:* Own.

Iago: Do, with like timorous° accent and dire yell   75
     As when, by night and negligence, the fire
     Is spied in populous cities.
Roderigo: What, ho, Brabantio! Signior Brabantio, ho!
Iago: Awake! What, ho, Brabantio! Thieves! thieves! thieves!
     Look to your house, your daughter, and your bags!   80
     Thieves! thieves!

     Brabantio at a window.°

Brabantio (above): What is the reason of this terrible summons?
     What is the matter there?
Roderigo: Signior, is all your family within?
Iago: Are your doors locked?
Brabantio: Why, wherefore ask you this?   85
Iago: Zounds, sir, y' are robbed! For shame, put on your gown!
     Your heart is burst; you have lost half your soul.
     Even now, now, very now, an old black ram
     Is tupping your white ewe. Arise, arise!
     Awake the snorting° citizens with the bell.   90
     Or else the devil will make a grandsire of you.
     Arise, I say!
Brabantio: What, have you lost your wits?
Roderigo: Most reverend signior, do you know my voice?
Brabantio: Not I. What are you?   95
Roderigo: My name is Roderigo.
Brabantio: The worser welcome!
     I have charged thee not to haunt about my doors.
     In honest plainness thou hast heard me say
     My daughter is not for thee; and now, in madness,
     Being full of supper and distemp'ring draughts,   100
     Upon malicious knavery dost thou come
     To start my quiet.
Roderigo: Sir, sir, sir —
Brabantio: But thou must needs be sure
     My spirit and my place have in them power   105
     To make this bitter to thee.
Roderigo: Patience, good sir.
Brabantio: What tell'st thou me of robbing? This is Venice;
     My house is not a grange.°
Roderigo: Most grave Brabantio,
     In simple and pure soul I come to you.
Iago: Zounds, sir, you are one of those that will not serve God if the   110
     devil bid you. Because we come to do you service, and you think

---

75 *timorous:* Terrifying.   *Brabantio at a window:* (added from quarto).   90 *snorting:*
Snoring.   108 *grange:* Isolated farmhouse.

we are ruffians, you'll have your daughter covered with a Barbary
horse; you'll have your nephews° neigh to you; you'll have cours-
ers for cousins, and gennets for germans.°

Brabantio: What profane wretch art thou?   115

Iago: I am one, sir, that comes to tell you your daughter and the Moor
are now making the beast with two backs.

Brabantio: Thou are a villain.

Iago: You are — a senator.

Brabantio: This thou shalt answer. I know thee, Roderigo.

Roderigo: Sir, I will answer anything. But I beseech you,   120
If 't be your pleasure and most wise consent,
As partly I find it is, that your fair daughter,
At this odd-even° and dull watch o' th' night,
Transported, with no worse nor better guard
But with a knave of common hire, a gondolier,   125
To the gross clasps of a lascivious Moor —
If this be known to you, and your allowance,°
We then have done you bold and saucy wrongs;
But if you know not this, my manners tell me
We have your wrong rebuke. Do not believe   130
That, from the sense° of all civility,
I thus would play and trifle with your reverence.
Your daughter, if you have not given her leave,
I say again, hath made a gross revolt,
Tying her duty, beauty, wit, and fortunes   135
In an extravagant and wheeling° stranger
Of here and everywhere. Straight satisfy yourself.
If she be in her chamber, or your house,
Let loose on me the justice of the state
For thus deluding you.

Brabantio: Strike on the tinder, ho!   140
Give me a taper! Call up all my people!
This accident° is not unlike my dream.
Belief of it oppresses me already.
Light, I say! light!   *Exit [above].*

Iago: Farewell, for I must leave you.
It seems not meet, nor wholesome to my place,   145
To be produced — as, if I stay, I shall —
Against the Moor. For I do know the state,
However this may gall him with some check,°
Cannot with safety cast° him; for he's embarked

---

113 *nephews:* i.e., grandsons. 114 *gennets for germans:* Spanish horses for near kinsmen. 123 *odd-even:* Between night and morning. 127 *allowance:* Approval. 131 *from
the sense:* In violation. 136 *extravagant and wheeling:* Expatriate and roving.
142 *accident:* Occurrence. 148 *check:* Reprimand. 149 *cast:* Discharge.

With such loud reason to the Cyprus wars,   150
Which even now stand in act,° that for their souls
Another of his fathom° they have none
To lead their business; in which regard,
Though I do hate him as I do hell-pains,
Yet, for necessity of present life,   155
I must show out a flag and sign of love,
Which is indeed but sign. That you shall surely find him,
Lead to the Sagittary° the raisèd search;
And there will I be with him. So farewell.   *Exit.*

Enter [below] Brabantio in his nightgown,° and Servants with torches.

Brabantio: It is too true an evil. Gone she is;   160
And what's to come of my despisèd time
Is naught but bitterness. Now, Roderigo,
Where didst thou see her? — O unhappy girl! —
With the Moor, say'st thou? — Who would be a father? —
How didst thou know 'twas she! — O, she deceives me   165
Past thought! — What said she to you? — Get moe° tapers!
Raise all my kindred! — Are they married, think you?
Roderigo: Truly I think they are.
Brabantio: O heaven! How got she out? O treason of the blood!
Fathers, from hence trust not your daughters' minds   170
By what you see them act. Is there not charms
By which the property° of youth and maidhood
May be abused? Have you not read, Roderigo,
Of some such thing?
Roderigo: Yes, sir, I have indeed.
Brabantio: Call up my brother. — O, would you had had her! —   175
Some one way, some another. — Do you know
Where we may apprehend her and the Moor?
Roderigo: I think I can discover him, if you please
To get good guard and go along with me.
Brabantio: I pray you lead on. At every house I'll call;   180
I may command at most. — Get weapons, ho!
And raise some special officers of night. —
On, good Roderigo; I'll deserve° your pains.   *Exeunt.*

SCENE II: *Before the lodgings of Othello.*

Enter Othello, Iago, and Attendants with torches.

Iago: Though in the trade of war I have slain men,
Yet do I hold it very stuff o' th' conscience

---

151 *stand in act:* Are going on. 152 *fathom:* Capacity. 158 *Sagittary:* An inn. *night-gown:* Dressing gown. 166 *moe:* More. 172 *property:* Nature. 183 *deserve:* Show gratitude for.

To do no contrived murther. I lack iniquity
Sometimes to do me service. Nine or ten times
I had thought t' have yerked° him here under the ribs.   5
Othello: 'Tis better as it is.
Iago: Nay, but he prated,
And spoke such scurvy and provoking terms
Against your honor
That with the little godliness I have
I did full hard forbear him. But I pray you, sir,   10
Are you fast° married? Be assured of this,
That the magnifico° is much beloved,
And hath in his effect a voice potential°
As double° as the Duke's. He will divorce you,
Or put upon you what restraint and grievance   15
The law, with all his might to enforce it on,
Will give him cable.
Othello: Let him do his spite.
My services which I have done the signiory°
Shall out-tongue his complaints. 'Tis yet to know° —
Which, when I know that boasting is an honor,   20
I shall promulgate — I fetch my life and being
From men of royal siege;° and my demerits°
May speak unbonneted to as proud a fortune
As this that I have reached.° For know, Iago,
But that I love the gentle Desdemona,   25
I would not my unhoused° free condition
Put into circumscription and confine
For the sea's worth. But look what lights come yond?
Iago: Those are the raisèd father and his friends.
You were best go in.
Othello: Not I; I must be found.   30
My parts, my title, and my perfect soul°
Shall manifest me rightly. Is it they?
Iago: By Janus, I think no.

Enter Cassio, with torches, Officers.

Othello: The servants of the Duke, and my lieutenant.
The goodness of the night upon you, friends!   35
What is the news?
Cassio: The Duke does greet you, general;

Scene II.   5 *yerked:* Stabbed.   11 *fast:* Securely.   12 *magnifico:* Grandee (Brabantio).
13 *potential:* Powerful.   14 *double:* Doubly   influential.   18 *signiory:* Venetian government.   19 *yet to know:* Still not generally known.   22 *siege:* Rank; *demerits:*
Deserts.   23–4 *May speak . . . reached:* Are equal, I modestly assert, to those of Desdemona's family.   26 *unhoused:* Unrestrained.   31 *perfect soul:* Stainless conscience.

And he requires your haste-post-haste appearance
Even on the instant.
Othello: What's the matter, think you?
Cassio: Something from Cyprus, as I may divine.
It is a business of some heat. The galleys   40
Have sent a dozen sequent° messengers
This very night at one another's heels,
And many of the consuls, raised and met,
Are at the Duke's already. You have been hotly called for;
When, being not at your lodging to be found,   45
The Senate hath sent about three several quests
To search you out.
Othello: 'Tis well I am found by you.
I will but spend a word here in the house,
And go with you.   *[Exit]*
Cassio: Ancient, what makes he here?
Iago: Faith, he to-night hath boarded a land carack.°   50
If it prove lawful prize, he's made for ever.
Cassio: I do not understand.
Iago: He's married.
Cassio: To who?

     [Enter Othello.]

Iago: Marry, to — Come, captain, will you go?
Othello: Have with you.
Cassio: Here comes another troop to seek for you.

     Enter Brabantio, Roderigo, and others with lights and weapons.

Iago: It is Brabantio. General, be advised.   55
He comes to bad intent.
Othello: Holla! stand there!
Roderigo: Signior, it is the Moor.
Brabantio: Down with him, thief!

     [They draw on both sides.]

Iago: You, Roderigo! Come, sir, I am for you.
Othello: Keep up° your bright swords, for the dew will rust them.
Good signior, you shall more command with years   60
Than with your weapons.
Brabantio: O thou foul thief, where hast thou stowed my daughter?
Damned as thou art, thou hast enchanted her!
For I'll refer me to all things of sense,
If she in chains of magic were not bound,   65
Whether a maid so tender, fair, and happy,
So opposite to marriage that she shunned

41 *sequent:* Consecutive.   50 *carack:* Treasure ship.   59 *Keep up:* i.e., sheath.

The wealthy curlèd darlings of our nation,
Would ever have, t' incur a general mock,
Run from her guardage to the sooty bosom   70
Of such a thing as thou — to fear, not to delight.
Judge me the world if 'tis not gross in sense°
That thou hast practiced on her with foul charms,
Abused her delicate youth with drugs or minerals
That weaken motion.° I'll have't disputed on;   75
'Tis probable, and palpable to thinking.
I therefore apprehend and do attach° thee
For an abuser of the world, a practicer
Of arts inhibited and out of warrant.
Lay hold upon him. If he do resist,   80
Subdue him at his peril.
Othello: Hold your hands,
Both you of my inclining and the rest.
Were it my cue to fight, I should have known it
Without a prompter. Where will you that I go
To answer this your charge?
Brabantio: To prison, till fit time   85
Of law and course of direct session°
Call thee to answer.
Othello: What if I do obey?
How may the Duke be therewith satisfied,
Whose messengers are here about my side
Upon some present business of the state   90
To bring me to him?
Officer: 'Tis true, most worthy signior.
The Duke's in council, and your noble self
I am sure is sent for.
Brabantio: How? The Duke in council?
In this time of the night? Bring him away.
Mine's not an idle° cause. The Duke himself,   95
Or any of my brothers of the state,
Cannot but feel this wrong as 'twere their own;
For if such actions may have passage free,
Bondslaves and pagans shall our statesmen be.   *Exeunt.*

SCENE III: *The Venetian Senate Chamber.*

Enter Duke and Senators, set at a table, with lights and Attendants.

Duke: There is no composition° in these news
That gives them credit.

---

72 *gross in sense:* Obvious.   75 *motion:* Perception.   77 *attach:* Arrest.   86 *direct session:* Regular trial.   95 *idle:* Trifling.   **Scene III.**   1 *composition:* Consistency.

1. Senator: Indeed they are disproportioned.
    My letters say a hundred and seven galleys.
Duke: And mine a hundred forty.
2. Senator: And mine two hundred.
    But though they jump° not on a just account —   5
    As in these cases where the aim° reports
    'Tis oft with difference — yet do they all confirm
    A Turkish fleet, and bearing up to Cyprus.
Duke: Nay, it is possible enough to judgment.
    I do not so secure me° in the error   10
    But the main article° I do approve°
    In fearful sense.
Sailor (within):   What, ho! what, ho! what, ho!
Officer: A messenger from the galleys.

    Enter Sailor.

Duke: Now, what's the business?
Sailor: The Turkish preparation makes for Rhodes.
    So was I bid report here to the state   15
    By Signior Angelo.
Duke: How say you by this change?
1. Senator: This cannot be
    By no assay° of reason. 'Tis a pageant
    To keep us in false gaze.° When we consider
    Th' importancy of Cyprus to the Turk,   20
    And let ourselves again but understand
    That, as it more concerns the Turk than Rhodes,
    So may he with more facile question bear° it,
    For that it stands not in such warlike brace,°
    But altogether lacks th' abilities   25
    That Rhodes is dressed in — if we make thought of this,
    We must not think the Turk is so unskillful
    To leave that latest which concerns him first,
    Neglecting an attempt of ease and gain
    To wake and wage° a danger profitless.   30
Duke: Nay, in all confidence, he's not for Rhodes.
Officer: Here is more news.

    Enter a Messenger.

Messenger: The Ottomites, reverend and gracious,
    Steering with due course toward the isle of Rhodes,
    Have there injointed them with an after fleet.   35

---

5 *jump:* Agree.   6 *aim:* Conjecture.   10 *so secure me:* Take such comfort.   11 *article:* Substance; *approve:* Accept.   18 *assay:* Test.   19 *in false gaze:* Looking the wrong way.   23 *with . . . bear:* More easily capture.   24 *brace:* Posture of defense.   30 *wake and wage:* Rouse and risk.

1. Senator: Ay, so I thought. How many, as you guess?
Messenger: Of thirty sail; and now they do restem°
    Their backward course, bearing with frank appearance
    Their purposes toward Cyprus, Signior Montano,
    Your trusty and most valiant servitor,   40
    With his free duty recommends you thus,
    And prays you to believe him.
Duke: 'Tis certain then for Cyprus.
    Marcus Luccicos,° is not he in town?
1. Senator: He's now in Florence.   45
Duke: Write from us to him; post, post-haste dispatch.
1. Senator: Here comes Brabantio and the valiant Moor.

    Enter Brabantio, Othello, Cassio, Iago, Roderigo, and Officers.

Duke: Valiant Othello, we must straight employ you
    Against the general enemy Ottoman.   *[To Brabantio.]*
    I did not see you. Welcome, gentle signior.   50
    We lacked your counsel and your help to-night.
Brabantio: So did I yours. Good your grace, pardon me.
    Neither my place, nor aught I heard of business,
    Hath raised me from my bed; nor doth the general care
    Take hold on me; for my particular grief   55
    Is of so floodgate° and o'erbearing nature
    That it engluts° and swallows other sorrows,
    And it is still itself.
Duke: Why, what's the matter?
Brabantio: My daughter! O, my daughter!
All: Dead?
Brabantio: Ay, to me.
    She is abused, stol'n from me, and corrupted   60
    By spells and medicines bought of mountebanks;
    For nature so prepost'rously to err,
    Being not deficient,° blind, or lame of sense,
    Sans witchcraft could not.
Duke: Whoe'er he be that in this foul proceeding   65
    Hath thus beguiled your daughter of herself,
    And you of her, the bloody book of law
    You shall yourself read in the bitter letter
    After your own sense; yea, though our proper° son
    Stood in your action.°
Brabantio: Humbly I thank your grace.   70
    Here is the man — this Moor, whom now, it seems,

---

37 *restem:* Steer again.   44 *Marcus Luccicos:* (Presumably a Venetian envoy).   56 *flood-gate:* Torrential.   57 *engluts:* Devours.   63 *deficient:* Feeble-minded.   69 *our proper:* My own.   70 *Stood in your action:* Were accused by you.

Your special mandate for the state affairs
Hath hither brought.
All: We are very sorry for't.
Duke [to Othello]: What, in your own part, can you say to this?
Brabantio: Nothing, but this is so.   75
Othello: Most potent, grave, and reverend signiors,
My very noble, and approved° good masters,
That I have ta'en away this old man's daughter,
It is most true; true I have married her.
The very head and front of my offending   80
Hath this extent, no more. Rude° am I in my speech,
And little blessed with the soft phrase of peace;
For since these arms of mine had seven years' pith°
Till now some nine moons wasted, they have used
Their dearest action in the tented field;   85
And little of this great world can I speak
More than pertains to feats of broil and battle;
And therefore little shall I grace my cause
In speaking for myself. Yet, by your gracious patience,
I will a round° unvarnished tale deliver   90
Of my whole course of love — what drugs, what charms,
What conjuration, and what mighty magic
(For such proceeding am I charged withal)
I won his daughter.
Brabantio: A maiden never bold;
Of spirit so still and quiet that her motion   95
Blushed° at herself; and she — in spite of nature,
Of years, of country, credit, everything —
To fall in love with what she feared to look on!
It is a judgment maimed and most imperfect
That will confess perfection so could err   100
Against all rules of nature, and must be driven
To find out practices° of cunning hell
Why this should be. I therefore vouch° again
That with some mixtures pow'rful o'er the blood,°
Or with some dram, conjured to this effect,   105
He wrought upon her.
Duke: To vouch this is no proof,
Without more certain and more overt test
Than these thin habits° and poor likelihoods
Of modern seeming° do prefer against him.

---

77 *approved:* Tested by experience.   81 *Rude:* Unpolished.   83 *pith:* Strength.
90 *round:* Plain.   95–6 *her motion Blushed:* Her own emotions caused her to
blush.   102 *practices:* Plots.   103 *vouch:* Assert.   104 *blood:* Passions.   108 *thin habits:*
Slight appearances.   109 *modern seeming:* Everyday supposition.

1. Senator: But, Othello, speak.   110
    Did you by indirect and forcèd° courses
    Subdue and poison this young maid's affections?
    Or came it by request, and such fair question°
    As soul to soul affordeth?
Othello: I do beseech you,
    Send for the lady to the Sagittary   115
    And let her speak of me before her father.
    If you do find me foul in her report,
    The trust, the office, I do hold of you
    Not only take away, but let your sentence
    Even fall upon my life.
Duke: Fetch Desdemona hither.   120
Othello: Ancient, conduct them; you best know the place.
               Exit [Iago, with] two or three [Attendants].
    And till she come, as truly as to heaven
    I do confess the vices of my blood,
    So justly to your grave ears I'll present
    How I did thrive in this fair lady's love,   125
    And she in mine.
Duke: Say it, Othello.
Othello: Her father loved me, oft invited me;
    Still° questioned me the story of my life
    From year to year — the battles, sieges, fortunes   130
    That I have passed.
    I ran it through, even from my boyish days
    To th' very moment that he bade me tell it.
    Wherein I spoke of most disastrous chances,
    Of moving accidents by flood and field;   135
    Of hairbreadth scapes i' th' imminent deadly breach;
    Of being taken by the insolent foe
    And sold to slavery; of my redemption thence
    And portance° in my travels' history;
    Wherein of anters° vast and deserts idle,   140
    Rough quarries, rocks, and hills whose heads touch heaven,
    It was my hint° to speak — such was the process;
    And of the Cannibals that each other eat,
    The Anthropophagi,° and men whose heads
    Do grow beneath their shoulders. This to hear   145
    Would Desdemona seriously incline;
    But still the house affairs would draw her thence;
    Which ever as she could with haste dispatch,
    She'ld come again, and with a greedy ear
    Devour up my discourse. Which I observing,   150

---

111 *forcèd:* Violent. 113 *question:* Conversation. 129 *Still:* Continually. 139 *portance:*
Behavior. 140 *anters:* Caves. 142 *hint:* Occasion. 144 *Anthropophagi:* Man-eaters.

Took once a pliant° hour, and found good means
To draw from her a prayer of earnest heart
That I would all my pilgrimage dilate,°
Whereof by parcels° she had something heard,
But not intentively.° I did consent,   155
And often did beguile her of her tears
When I did speak of some distressful stroke
That my youth suffered. My story being done,
She gave me for my pains a world of sighs.
She swore, i' faith, 'twas strange, 'twas passing strange;   160
'Twas pitiful, 'twas wondrous pitiful.
She wished she had not heard it; yet she wished
That heaven had made her such a man. She thanked me;
And bade me, if I had a friend that loved her,
I should but teach him how to tell my story,   165
And that would woo her. Upon this hint° I spake.
She loved me for the dangers I had passed,
And I loved her that she did pity them.
This only is the witchcraft I have used.
Here comes the lady. Let her witness it.   170

Enter Desdemona, Iago, Attendants.

Duke: I think this tale would win my daughter too.
Good Brabantio,
Take up this mangled matter at the best.
Men do their broken weapons rather use
Than their bare hands.
Brabantio: I pray you hear her speak.   175
If she confess that she was half the wooer,
Destruction on my head if my bad blame
Light on the man! Come hither, gentle mistress.
Do you perceive in all this noble company
Where most you owe obedience?
Desdemona: My noble father,   180
I do perceive here a divided duty.
To you I am bound for life and education;°
My life and education both do learn me
How to respect you: you are the lord of duty;
I am hitherto your daughter. But here's my husband;   185
And so much duty as my mother showed
To you, preferring you before her father,
So much I challenge° that I may profess
Due to the Moor my lord.

---

151 *pliant:* Propitious.   153 *dilate:* Recount in full.   154 *parcels:* Portions.   155 *intentively:*
With full attention.   166 *hint:* Opportunity.   182 *education:* Upbringing.   188 *challenge:*
Claim the right.

Brabantio: God be with you! I have done.
  Please it your grace, on to the state affairs.   190
  I had rather to adopt a child than get° it.
  Come hither, Moor.
  I here do give thee that with all my heart
  Which, but thou hast already, with all my heart
  I would keep from thee. For your sake,° jewel,   195
  I am glad at soul I have no other child;
  For thy escape° would teach me tyranny,
  To hang clogs on them. I have done, my lord.
Duke: Let me speak like yourself° and lay a sentence°
  Which, as a grise° or step, may help these lovers   200
  [Into your favor.]
  When remedies are past, the griefs are ended
  By seeing the worst, which late on hopes depended.
  To mourn a mischief that is past and gone
  Is the next way to draw new mischief on.   205
  What cannot be preserved when fortune takes,
  Patience her injury a mock'ry makes.
  The robbed that smiles steals something from the thief;
  He robs himself that spends a bootless grief.
Brabantio: So let the Turk of Cyprus us beguile: 210
  We lose it not so long as we can smile.
  He bears the sentence well that nothing bears
  But the free comfort which from thence he hears;
  But he bears both the sentence and the sorrow
  That to pay grief must of poor patience borrow.   215
  These sentences, to sugar, or to gall,
  Being strong on both sides, are equivocal.
  But words are words. I never yet did hear
  That the bruisèd heart was piercèd through the ear.
  Beseech you, now to the affairs of state.   220
Duke: The Turk with a most mighty preparation makes for Cyprus.
  Othello, the fortitude° of the place is best known to you; and
  though we have there a substitute of most allowed° sufficiency,
  yet opinion,° a more sovereign mistress of effects, throws a more
  safer voice on you. You must therefore be content to slubber° the   225
  gloss of your new fortunes with this more stubborn and boist'rous
  expedition.
Othello: The tyrant custom, most grave senators,
  Hath made the flinty and steel couch of war

---

191 *get:* Beget. 195 *For your sake:* Because of you. 197 *escape:* Escapade. 199 *like yourself:* As you should; *sentence:* Maxim. 200 *grise:* Step. 222 *fortitude:* Fortification. 223 *allowed:* Acknowledged. 224 *opinion:* Public opinion. 225 *slubber:* Sully.

My thrice-driven bed of down. I do agnize   230
A natural and prompt alacrity
I find in hardness;° and do undertake
These present wars against the Ottomites.
Most humbly, therefore, bending to your state,
I crave fit disposition for my wife,   235
Due reference of place, and exhibition,°
With such accommodation and besort°
As levels° with her breeding.
Duke: If you please,
Be't at her father's.
Brabantio: I will not have it so.
Othello: Nor I.
Desdemona: Nor I. I would not there reside,   240
To put my father in impatient thoughts
By being in his eye. Most gracious Duke,
To my unfolding lend your prosperous° ear,
And let me find a charter in your voice,
T' assist my simpleness.°   245
Duke: What would you, Desdemona?
Desdemona: That I did love the Moor to live with him,
My downright violence, and storm of fortunes,
May trumpet to the world. My heart's subdued
Even to the very quality of my lord.   250
I saw Othello's visage in his mind,
And to his honors and his valiant parts
Did I my soul and fortunes consecrate.
So that, dear lords, if I be left behind,
A moth of peace, and he go to the war,   255
The rites for which I love him are bereft me,
And I a heavy interim shall support
By his dear absence. Let me go with him.
Othello: Let her have your voice.
Vouch with me, heaven, I therefore beg it not   260
To please the palate of my appetite,
Not to comply with heat° — the young affects°
In me defunct — and proper satisfaction;
But to be free and bounteous to her mind;
And heaven defend your good souls that you think   265
I will your serious and great business scant

230–32 *agnize . . . hardness:* Recognize in myself a natural and easy response to hardship.   236 *exhibition:* Allowance of money.   237 *besort:* Suitable company.   238 *levels:* Corresponds.   243 *prosperous:* Favorable.   245 *simpleness:* Lack of skill.   262 *heat:* Passions;   *young affects:* Tendencies of youth.

When she is with me. No, when light-winged toys
Of feathered Cupid seel° with wanton dullness
My speculative and officed instruments,°
That° my disports corrupt and taint my business,   270
Let housewives make a skillet of my helm,
And all indign° and base adversities
Make head against my estimation!°

Duke: Be it as you shall privately determine,
Either for her stay or going. Th' affair cries haste,   275
And speed must answer it.

1. Senator: You must away to-night.

Othello: With all my heart.

Duke: At nine i' th' morning here we'll meet again.
Othello, leave some officer behind,
And he shall our commission bring to you,   280
With such things else of quality and respect
As doth import° you.

Othello: So please your grace, my ancient;
A man he is of honesty and trust
To his conveyance I assign my wife,
With what else needful your good grace shall think   285
To be sent after me.

Duke: Let it be so.
Good night to every one.
    [To Brabantio.]   And, noble signior,
If virtue no delighted° beauty lack,
Your son-in-law is far more fair than black.

1. Senator: Adieu, brave Moor. Use Desdemona well.   290

Brabantio: Look to her, Moor, if thou hast eyes to see:
She has deceived her father, and may thee.

                          Exeunt [Duke, Senators, Officers, &c.].

Othello: My life upon her faith! — Honest Iago,
My Desdemona must I leave to thee.
I prithee let thy wife attend on her,   295
And bring them after in the best advantage.°
Come, Desdemona. I have but an hour
Of love, of worldly matters and direction,
To spend with thee. We must obey the time.

                          Exit Moor and Desdemona.

Roderigo: Iago, —   300

Iago: What say'st thou, noble heart?

Roderigo: What will I do, think'st thou?

---

268 *seel:* Blind.   269 *My . . . instruments:* My perceptive and responsible faculties.
270 *That:* So that.   272 *indign:* Unworthy.   273 *estimation:* Reputation.   282 *import:*
Concern.   288 *delighted:* Delightful.   296 *in the best advantage:* At the best opportunity.

Iago: Why, go to bed and sleep.

Roderigo: I will incontinently° drown myself.

Iago: If thou dost, I shall never love thee after. Why, thou silly   305
gentleman!

Roderigo: It is silliness to live when to live is torment; and then have
we a prescription to die when death is our physician.

Iago: O villainous! I have looked upon the world for four times seven
years; and since I could distinguish betwixt a benefit and an in-   310
jury, I never found man that knew how to love himself. Ere I
would say I would drown myself for the love of a guinea hen, I
would change my humanity with a baboon.

Roderigo: What should I do? I confess it is my shame to be so fond,
but it is not in my virtue to amend it.   315

Iago: Virtue? a fig! 'Tis in ourselves that we are thus or thus. Our
bodies are our gardens, to which our wills are gardeners; so
that if we will plant nettles or sow lettuce, set hyssop and weed
up thyme, supply it with one gender° of herbs or distract it with
many — either to have it sterile with idleness or manured with in-   320
dustry — why, the power and corrigible authority° of this lies in
our wills. If the balance of our lives had not one scale of reason to
poise° another of sensuality, the blood and baseness° of our natures would conduct us to most preposterous conclusions. But we
have reason to cool our raging motions,° our carnal strings, our   325
unbitted° lusts; whereof I take this that you call love to be a sect
or scion.°

Roderigo: It cannot be.

Iago: It is merely a lust of the blood and a permission of the will.
Come, be a man! Drown thyself? Drown cats and blind pup-   330
pies! I have professed me thy friend, and I confess me knit to
thy deserving with cables of perdurable toughness. I could never
better stead thee than now. Put money in thy purse. Follow thou
the wars; defeat thy favor° with an usurped beard. I say, put
money in thy purse. It cannot be that Desdemona should long   335
continue her love to the Moor — put money in thy purse — nor
he his to her. It was a violent commencement in her, and thou
shalt see an answerable sequestration° — put but money in
thy purse. These Moors are changeable in their wills — fill thy
purse with money. The food that to him now is as luscious as   340
locusts shall be to him shortly as bitter as coloquintida.° She
must change for youth: when she is sated with his body, she will
find the error of her choice. [She must have change, she must.]

---

304 *incontinently:* Forthwith.   319 *gender:* Species.   321 *corrigible authority:* Corrective
power.   323 *poise:* Counter-balance;   *blood and baseness:* Animal instincts.   325 *motions:*
Appetites.   326 *unbitted:* Uncontrolled.   327 *sect or scion:* Offshoot, cutting.   334 *defeat
thy favor:* Spoil thy appearance.   338 *sequestration:* Estrangement.   341 *coloquintida:*
A medicine.

Therefore put money in thy purse. If thou wilt needs damn thyself, do it a more delicate way than drowning. Make° all the money thou canst. If sanctimony and a frail vow betwixt an erring° barbarian and a supersubtle Venetian be not too hard for my wits and all the tribe of hell, thou shalt enjoy her. Therefore make money. A pox of drowning thyself! 'Tis clean out of the way. Seek thou rather to be hanged in compassing thy joy than to be drowned and go without her.   345   350

Roderigo: Wilt thou be fast to my hopes, if I depend on the issue?

Iago: Thou art sure of me. Go, make money. I have told thee often, and I retell thee again and again, I hate the Moor. My cause is hearted;° thine hath no less reason. Let us be conjunctive in our revenge against him. If thou canst cuckold him, thou dost thyself a pleasure, me a sport. There are many events in the womb of time, which will be delivered. Traverse,° go, provide thy money! We will have more of this to-morrow. Adieu.   355

Roderigo: Where shall we meet i' th' morning?   360

Iago: At my lodging.

Roderigo: I'll be with thee betimes.

Iago: Go to, farewell — Do you hear, Roderigo?

[*Roderigo:* What say you?

Iago: No more of drowning, do you hear?   365

Roderigo: I am changed.

Iago: Go to, farewell. Put money enough in your purse.]

Roderigo: I'll sell all my land.   *Exit.*

Iago: Thus do I ever make my fool my purse;
For I mine own gained knowledge should profane   370
If I would time expend with such a snipe°
But for my sport and profit. I hate the Moor;
And it is thought abroad that 'twixt my sheets
H'as done my office. I know not if't be true;
But I, for mere suspicion in that kind,   375
Will do as if for surety. He holds me well;°
The better shall my purpose work on him.
Cassio's a proper man. Let me see now:
To get his place, and to plume up° my will
In double knavery — How, how? — Let's see: —   380
After some time, to abuse Othello's ears
That he is too familiar with his wife.
He hath a person and a smooth dispose°
To be suspected — framed to make women false.
The Moor is of a free° and open nature   385

---

345 *Make:* Raise.   346–47 *erring:* Wandering.   354–55 *My cause is hearted:* My heart is in it.   358 *Traverse:* Forward march.   371 *snipe:* Fool.   376 *well:* In high regard.   379 *plume up:* Gratify.   383 *dispose:* Manner.   385 *free:* Frank.

That thinks men honest that but seem to be so;
And will as tenderly be led by th' nose
As asses are.
I have't! It is engend'red! Hell and night
Must bring this monstrous birth to the world's light.   *Exit.*   390

ACT II

Scene I: *An open place in Cyprus, near the harbor.*

Enter Montano and two Gentlemen.

Montano: What from the cape can you discern at sea?
1. Gentleman: Nothing at all: it is a high-wrought flood.
  I cannot 'twixt the heaven and the main
  Descry a sail.
Montano: Methinks the wind hath spoke aloud at land;   5
  A fuller blast ne'er shook our battlements.
  If it hath ruffianed so upon the sea,
  What ribs of oak, when mountains melt on them,
  Can hold the mortise?° What shall we hear of this?
2. Gentleman: A segregation° of the Turkish fleet.   10
  For do but stand upon the foaming shore,
  The chidden billow seems to pelt the clouds;
  The wind-shaked surge, with high and monstrous mane,
  Seems to cast water on the burning Bear
  And quench the Guards° of th' ever-fixèd pole.°   15
  I never did like molestation° view
  On the enchafèd flood.
Montano: If that the Turkish fleet
  Be not ensheltered and embayed, they are drowned;
  It is impossible to bear it out.

  Enter a third Gentleman.

3. Gentleman: News, lads! Our wars are done.   20
  The desperate tempest hath so banged the Turks
  That their designment halts.° A noble ship of Venice
  Hath seen a grievous wrack and sufferance°
  On most part of their fleet.
Montano: How? Is this true?

Act II, Scene I.   9 *hold the mortise:* Hold their joints together.   10 *segregation:* Scattering.   15 *Guards:* Stars near the North Star; *pole:* Polestar.   16 *molestation:* Tumult.   22 *designment halts:* Plan is crippled.   23 *sufferance:* Disaster.

3. Gentleman: The ship is here put in,   25
     A Veronesa;° Michael Cassio,
     Lieutenant to the warlike Moor Othello,
     Is come on shore; the Moor himself at sea,
     And is in full commission here for Cyprus.
Montano: I am glad on't. 'Tis a worthy governor.   30
3. Gentleman: But his same Cassio, though he speak of comfort
     Touching the Turkish loss, yet he looks sadly
     And prays the Moor be safe, for they were parted
     With foul and violent tempest.
Montano: Pray heaven he be;
     For I have served him, and the man commands   35
     Like a full soldier. Let's to the seaside, ho!
     As well to see the vessel that's come in
     As to throw out our eyes for brave Othello,
     Even till we make the main and th' aerial blue
     An indistinct regard.°
3. Gentleman: Come, let's do so;   40
     For every minute is expectancy
     Of more arrivance.

     Enter Cassio.

Cassio: Thanks, you the valiant of this warlike isle,
     That so approve the Moor! O, let the heavens
     Give him defense against the elements,   45
     For I have lost him on a dangerous sea!
Montano: Is he well shipped?
Cassio: His bark is stoutly timbered, and his pilot
     Of very expert and approved allowance;
     Therefore my hopes, not surfeited to death,°   50
     Stand in bold cure.°
          (Within.)   A sail, a sail, a sail!   *Enter a messenger.*
Cassio: What noise?
Messenger: The town is empty; on the brow o' th' sea
     Stand ranks of people, and they cry "A sail!"
Cassio: My hopes do shape him for the governor.   55

     A shot.

2. Gentleman: They do discharge their shot of courtesy:
     Our friends at least.
Cassio: I pray you, sir, go forth
     And give us truth who 'tis that is arrived.

---

26 *Veronesa:* Ship furnished by Verona.   40 *An indistinct regard:* Indistinguishable.
50 *surfeited to death:* Overindulged.   51 *in bold cure:* A good chance of fulfillment.

2. Gentleman: I shall.   *Exit.*
Montano: But, good lieutenant, is your general wived?   60
Cassio: Most fortunately. He hath achieved a maid
     That paragons° description and wild fame;
     One that excels the quirks° of blazoning° pens,
     And in th' essential vesture of creation
     Does tire the ingener.°

Enter Second Gentleman.

                              How now? Who has put in?   65
2. Gentleman: 'Tis one Iago, ancient to the general.
Cassio: H'as had most favorable and happy speed:
     Tempests themselves, high seas, and howling winds,
     The guttered° rocks and congregated sands,
     Traitors ensteeped° to clog the guiltless keel,   70
     As having sense of beauty, do omit
     Their mortal° natures, letting go safely by
     The divine Desdemona.
Montano: What is she?
Cassio: She that I spake of, our great captain's captain,
     Left in the conduct of the bold Iago,   75
     Whose footing° here anticipates our thoughts
     A se'nnight's° speed. Great Jove, Othello guard,
     And swell his sail with thine own pow'rful breath,
     That he may bless this bay with his tall ship,
     Make love's quick pants in Desdemona's arms,   80
     Give renewed fire to our extinct spirits,
     [And bring all Cyprus comfort!]

Enter Desdemona, Iago, Roderigo, and Emilia [with Attendants].

                              O, behold!
     The riches of the ship is come on shore!
     You men of Cyprus, let her have your knees.°
     Hail to thee, lady! and the grace of heaven,   85
     Before, behind thee, and on every hand,
     Enwheel thee round!
Desdemona: I thank you, valiant Cassio.
     What tidings can you tell me of my lord?
Cassio: He is not yet arrived; nor know I aught
     But that he's well and will be shortly here.   90
Desdemona: O but I fear! How lost you company?

---

62 *paragons:* Surpasses. 63 *quirks:* Ingenuities; *blazoning:* Describing. 64–5 *And . . .
ingener:* Merely to describe her as God made her exhausts her praiser. 69 *guttered:*
Jagged. 70 *ensteeped:* Submerged. 72 *mortal:* Deadly. 76 *footing:* Landing.
77 *se'nnight's:* Week's. 84 *knees:* i.e., kneeling.

Cassio: The great contention of the sea and skies
    Parted our fellowship.
        (Within.)   *A sail, a sail! [A shot.]*
                                But hark. A sail!
2. Gentleman: They give their greeting to the citadel;
    This likewise is a friend.
Cassio: See for the news.   95

                                [Exit Gentleman.]

    Good ancient, you are welcome.
        [To Emilia.]   Welcome, mistress. —
    Let it not gall your patience, good Iago,
    That I extend my manners. 'Tis my breeding
    That gives me this bold show of courtesy.
        [Kisses Emilia.°]

Iago: Sir, would she give you so much of her lips   100
    As of her tongue she oft bestows on me,
    You would have enough.
Desdemona: Alas, she has no speech!
Iago: In faith, too much.
    I find it still when I have list to sleep.
    Marry, before your ladyship, I grant,   105
    She puts her tongue a little in her heart
    And chides with thinking.
Emilia: You have little cause to say so.
Iago: Come on, come on! You are pictures out of doors,
    Bells in your parlors, wildcats in your kitchens,   110
    Saints in your injuries, devils being offended,
    Players in your housewifery,° and housewives° in your beds.
Desdemona: O, fie upon thee, slanderer!
Iago: Nay, it is true, or else I am a Turk:
    You rise to play, and go to bed to work.   115
Emilia: You shall not write my praise.
Iago: No, let me not.
Desdemona: What wouldst thou write of me, if thou shouldst
    praise me?
Iago: O gentle lady, do not put me to't,
    For I am nothing if not critical.
Desdemona: Come on, assay.° — There's one gone to the harbor?   120
Iago: Ay, madam.
Desdemona: I am not merry; but I do beguile
    The thing I am by seeming otherwise. —
    Come, how wouldst thou praise me?

Kisses Emilia: (Kissing was a common Elizabethan form of social courtesy).
112 *housewifery:* Housekeeping; *housewives:* Hussies. 120 *assay:* Try.

Iago: I am about it; but indeed my invention   125
    Comes from my pate as birdlime° does from frieze° —
    It plucks out brains and all. But my Muse labors,
    And thus she is delivered:
    If she be fair and wise, fairness and wit —
    The one's for use, the other useth it.   130
Desdemona: Well praised! How if she be black° and witty?
Iago: If she be black, and thereto have a wit,
    She'll find a white that shall her blackness fit.
Desdemona: Worse and worse!
Emilia: How if fair and foolish?   135
Iago: She never yet was foolish that was fair,
    For even her folly° helped her to an heir.
Desdemona: These are old fond° paradoxes to make fools laugh
    i' th' alehouse. What miserable praise hast thou for her that's
    foul° and foolish?   140
Iago: There's none so foul, and foolish thereunto,
    But does foul pranks which fair and wise ones do.
Desdemona: O heavy ignorance! Thou praisest the worst best. But
    what praise couldst thou bestow on a deserving woman indeed —
    one that in the authority of her merit did justly put on the vouch°   145
    of very malice itself?
Iago: She that was ever fair, and never proud;
    Had tongue at will, and yet was never loud;
    Never lacked gold, and yet went never gay;
    Fled from her wish, and yet said "Now I may";   150
    She that, being ang'red, her revenge being nigh,
    Bade her wrong stay, and her displeasure fly;
    She that in wisdom never was so frail
    To change the cod's head for the salmon's tail;°
    She that could think, and ne'er disclose her mind;   155
    See suitors following, and not look behind:
    She was a wight (if ever such wight were) —
Desdemona: To do what?
Iago: To suckle fools and chronicle small beer.°
Desdemona: O most lame and impotent conclusion! Do not learn of   160
    him, Emilia, though he be thy husband. How say you, Cassio? Is
    he not a most profane and liberal° counsellor?
Cassio: He speaks home,° madam. You may relish him more in the
    soldier than in the scholar.

---

126 *birdlime:* A sticky paste; *frieze:* Rough cloth. 131 *black:* Brunette. 137 *folly:*
Wantonness. 138 *fond:* Foolish. 140 *foul:* Ugly. 145 *put on the vouch:* Compel the
approval. 154 *To ... tail:* i.e., to exchange the good for the poor but expensive.
159 *chronicle small beer:* Keep petty household accounts. 162 *profane and liberal:*
Worldly and licentious. 163 *home:* Bluntly.

Iago [aside]: He takes her by the palm. Ay, well said, whisper! With as   165
    little a web as this will I ensnare as great a fly as Cassio. Ay, smile
    upon her, do! I will gyve thee in thine own courtship.° — You
    say true; 'tis so, indeed! — If such tricks as these strip you out
    of your lieutenantry, it had been better you had not kissed your
    three fingers so oft — which now again you are most apt to play   170
    the sir° in. Very good! well kissed! an excellent courtesy! 'Tis
    so, indeed. Yet again your fingers to your lips? Would they were
    clyster pipes° for your sake! *(Trumpet within.)*
    The Moor! I know his trumpet.

Cassio: 'Tis truly so.   175
Desdemona: Let's meet him and receive him.
Cassio: Lo, where he comes.

    Enter Othello and Attendants.

Othello: O my fair warrior!
Desdemona: My dear Othello!
Othello: It gives me wonder great as my content
    To see you here before me. O my soul's joy!   180
    If after every tempest come such calms,
    May the winds blow till they have wakened death!
    And let the laboring bark climb hills of seas
    Olympus-high, and duck again as low
    As hell's from heaven! If it were now to die,   185
    'Twere now to be most happy;° for I fear
    My soul hath her content so absolute
    That not another comfort like to this
    Succeeds in unknown fate.
Desdemona: The heavens forbid
    But that our loves and comforts should increase   190
    Even as our days do grow.
Othello: Amen to that, sweet powers!
    I cannot speak enough of this content;
    It stops me here; it is too much of joy.
    And this, and this, the greatest discords be

    They kiss.

    That e'er our hearts shall make!
Iago [aside]:   O, you are well tuned now!   195
    But I'll set down° the pegs that make this music,
    As honest as I am.
Othello: Come, let us to the castle.
    News, friends! Our wars are done; the Turks are drowned.
    How does my old acquaintance of this isle? —

---

167 *gyve . . . courtship:* Manacle you by means of your courtly manners.   171 *sir:*
Courtly gentleman.   173 *clyster pipes:* Syringes.   186 *happy:* Fortunate.   196 *set down:*
Loosen.

Honey, you shall be well desired° in Cyprus;   200
I have found great love amongst them. O my sweet,
I prattle out of fashion, and I dote
In mine own comforts. I prithee, good Iago,
Go to the bay and disembark my coffers.
Bring thou the master° to the citadel;   205
He is a good one, and his worthiness
Does challenge° much respect. — Come, Desdemona,
Once more well met at Cyprus.

Exit Othello [with all but Iago and Roderigo].

Iago [to an Attendant, who goes out]: Do thou meet me presently at the
harbor. *[To Roderigo.]* Come hither. If thou be'st valiant (as they say   210
base men being in love have then a nobility in their natures more
than is native to them), list me. The lieutenant to-night watches
on the court of guard.° First, I must tell thee this: Desdemona is
directly in love with him.

Roderigo: With him? Why, 'tis not possible.   215

Iago: Lay thy finger thus,° and let thy soul be instructed. Mark me
with what violence she first loved the Moor, but for bragging
and telling her fantastical lies; and will she love him still for
prating? Let not thy discreet heart think it. Her eye must be fed;
and what delight shall she have to look on the devil? When the   220
blood is made dull with the act of sport, there should be, again
to inflame it and to give satiety a fresh appetite, loveliness in
favor, sympathy in years, manners, and beauties; all which the
Moor is defective in. Now for want of these required conve-
niences,° her delicate tenderness will find itself abused, begin   225
to heave the gorge,° disrelish and abhor the Moor. Very nature
will instruct her in it and compel her to some second choice.
Now, sir, this granted — as it is a most pregnant° and unforced
position — who stands so eminent in the degree of this fortune
as Cassio does? A knave very voluble; no further conscionable°   230
than in putting on the mere form of civil and humane° seeming for the better compassing of his salt° and most hidden loose
affection? Why, none! why, none! A slipper° and subtle knave;
a finder-out of occasions; that has an eye can stamp and counterfeit advantages, though true advantage never present itself;   235
a devilish knave! Besides, the knave is handsome, young, and
hath all those requisites in him that folly and green minds
look after. A pestilent complete knave! and the woman hath found
him already.

---

200 *well desired:* Warmly welcomed.   205 *master:* Ship captain.   207 *challenge:*
Deserve.   213 *court of guard:* Headquarters.   216 *thus:* i.e., on your lips.   224–25 *con-
veniences:* Compatibilities.   226 *heave the gorge:* Be nauseated.   228 *pregnant:* Evident.
230 *conscionable:* Conscientious.   231 *humane:* Polite.   232 *salt:* Lecherous.   233 *slipper:*
Slippery.

Roderigo: I cannot believe that in her; she's full of most blessed   240
condition.°

Iago: Blessed fig's-end! The wine she drinks is made of grapes. If she
had been blessed, she would never have loved the Moor. Blessed
pudding! Didst thou not see her paddle with the palm of his
hand? Didst not mark that?   245

Roderigo: Yes, that I did; but that was but courtesy.

Iago: Lechery, by this hand! an index and obscure prologue to the
history of lust and foul thoughts. They met so near with their
lips that their breaths embraced together. Villainous thoughts,
Roderigo! When these mutualities° so marshal the way, hard at   250
hand comes the master and main exercise, th' incorporate° conclusion. Pish! But, sir, be you ruled by me: I have brought you
from Venice. Watch you to-night; for the command, I'll lay't
upon you. Cassio knows you not. I'll not be far from you: do you
find some occasion to anger Cassio, either by speaking too loud,   255
or tainting° his discipline, or from what other course you please
which the time shall more favorably minister.

Roderigo: Well.

Iago: Sir, he's rash and very sudden in choler,° and haply with his
truncheon may strike at you. Provoke him that he may; for even   260
out of that will I cause these of Cyprus to mutiny; whose qualifi-
cation° shall come into no true taste° again but by the displant-
ing of Cassio. So shall you have a shorter journey to your desires
by the means I shall then have to prefer° them; and the impedi-
ment most profitably removed without the which there were no   265
expectation of our prosperity.

Roderigo: I will do this if you can bring it to any opportunity.

Iago: I warrant thee. Meet me by and by at the citadel; I must fetch
his necessaries ashore. Farewell.

Roderigo: Adieu.   *Exit.*   270

Iago: That Cassio loves her, I do well believe't;
That she loves him, 'tis apt° and of great credit.
The Moor, howbeit that I endure him not,
Is of a constant, loving, noble nature,
And I dare think he'll prove to Desdemona   275
A most dear husband. Now I do love her too;
Not out of absolute lust, though peradventure
I stand accountant° for as great a sin,
But partly led to diet° my revenge,
For that I do suspect the lusty Moor   280

---

241 *condition:* Character. 250 *mutualities:* Exchanges. 251 *incorporate:* Carnal.
256 *tainting:* Discrediting. 259 *sudden in choler:* Violent in anger. 261–62
qualification: Appeasement. 262 *true taste:* Satisfactory state. 264 *prefer:* Advance.
272 *apt:* Probable. 278 *accountant:* Accountable. 279 *diet:* Feed.

Hath leaped into my seat; the thought whereof
Doth, like a poisonous mineral, gnaw my inwards;
And nothing can or shall content my soul
Till I am evened with him, wife for wife;
Or failing so, yet that I put the Moor   285
At least into a jealousy so strong
That judgment cannot cure. Which thing to do,
If this poor trash of Venice, whom I trash°
For° his quick hunting, stand the putting on,°
I'll have our Michael Cassio on the hip,°   290
Abuse him to the Moor in the rank garb°
(For I fear Cassio with my nightcap too),
Make the Moor thank me, love me, and reward me
For making him egregiously an ass
And practicing upon° his peace and quiet   295
Even to madness. 'Tis here, but yet confused:
Knavery's plain face is never seen till used.   *Exit.*

SCENE II: *A street in Cyprus.*

Enter Othello's Herald, with a proclamation.

Herald: It is Othello's pleasure, our noble and valiant general, that,
upon certain tidings now arrived, importing the mere perdi-
tion° of the Turkish fleet, every man put himself into triumph;
some to dance, some to make bonfires, each man to what sport
and revels his addiction leads him. For, besides these beneficial   5
news, it is the celebration of his nuptial. So much was his pleasure should be proclaimed. All offices° are open, and there is
full liberty of feasting from the present hour of five till the bell
have told eleven. Heaven bless the isle of Cyprus and our noble
general Othello!   *Exit.*   10

SCENE III: *The Cyprian Castle.*

Enter Othello, Desdemona, Cassio, and Attendants.

Othello: Good Michael, look you to the guard to-night.
Let's teach ourselves that honorable stop,
Not to outsport discretion.
Cassio: Iago hath direction what to do;
But not withstanding, with my personal eye   5
Will I look to't.

---

288 *I trash:* I weight down (in order to keep under control).   289 *For:* In order
to develop; *stand the putting on:* Responds to my inciting.   290 *on the hip:* At
my mercy.   291 *rank garb:* Gross manner.   295 *practicing upon:* Plotting against.
Scene II. 2–3 *mere perdition:* Complete destruction.   7 *offices:* Kitchens and storerooms.

Othello: Iago is most honest.
        Michael, good night. To-morrow with your earliest
        Let me have speech with you.
                [To Desdemona.]   Come, my dear love.
        The purchase made, the fruits are to ensue;
        That profit 's yet to come 'tween me and you. —   10
        Good night.

                Exit [Othello with Desdemona and Attendants].

Enter Iago.

Cassio: Welcome, Iago. We must to the watch.
Iago: Not this hour, lieutenant; 'tis not yet ten o' th' clock. Our general
        cast° us thus early for the love of his Desdemona; who let us not
        therefore blame. He hath not yet made wanton the night with her,   15
        and she is sport for Jove.
Cassio: She's a most exquisite lady.
Iago: And, I'll warrant her, full of game.
Cassio: Indeed, she's a most fresh and delicate creature.
Iago: What an eye she has! Methinks it sounds a parley to provocation.   20
Cassio: An inviting eye; and yet methinks right modest.
Iago: And when she speaks, is it not an alarum to love?
Cassio: She is indeed perfection.
Iago: Well, happiness to their sheets! Come, lieutenant, I have a
        stoup° of wine, and here without are a brace of Cyprus gallants that   25
        would fain have a measure to the health of black Othello.
Cassio: Not to-night, good Iago. I have very poor and unhappy brains
        for drinking; I could well wish courtesy would invent some other
        custom of entertainment.
Iago: O, they are our friends. But one cup! I'll drink for you.   30
Cassio: I have drunk but one cup to-night, and that was craftily
        qualified° too; and behold what innovation° it makes here. I
        am unfortunate in the infirmity and dare not task my weakness
        with any more.
Iago: What, man! 'Tis a night of revels: the gallants desire it.   35
Cassio: Where are they?
Iago: Here at the door; I pray you call them in.
Cassio: I'll do't, but it dislikes me.   *Exit.*
Iago: If I can fasten but one cup upon him
        With that which he hath drunk to-night already,   40
        He'll be as full of quarrel and offense
        As my young mistress' dog. Now my sick fool Roderigo,
        Whom love hath turned almost the wrong side out,
        To Desdemona hath to-night caroused

Scene III. 14 *cast:* Dismissed.   25 *stoup:* Two-quart tankard.   32 *qualified:* Diluted;
innovation: Disturbance.

Potations pottle-deep;° and he's to watch.   45
Three lads of Cyprus — noble swelling spirits,
That hold their honors in a wary distance,°
The very elements° of this warlike isle —
Have I to-night flustered with flowing cups,
And they watch too. Now, 'mongst this flock of drunkards   50
Am I to put our Cassio in some action
That may offend the isle.

Enter Cassio, Montano, and Gentlemen [; Servants following with wine].

                                    But here they come.
If consequence do but approve my dream,
My boat sails freely, both with wind and stream.
Cassio: 'Fore God, they have given me a rouse° already.   55
Montano: Good faith, a little one; not past a pint, as I am a soldier.
Iago: Some wine, ho!
    [Sings.]   And let me the canakin clink, clink;
                And let me the canakin clink
                    A soldier's a man;   60
                    A life's but a span,
                Why then, let a soldier drink.
    Some wine, boys!
Cassio: 'Fore God, an excellent song!
Iago: I learned it in England, where indeed they are most potent   65
    in potting. Your Dane, your German, and your swag-bellied
    Hollander — Drink, ho! — are nothing to your English.
Cassio: Is your Englishman so expert in his drinking?
Iago: Why, he drinks you with facility your Dane dead drunk; he
    sweats not to overthrow your Almain; he gives your Hollander a   70
    vomit ere the next pottle can be filled.
Cassio: To the health of our general!
Montano: I am for it, lieutenant, and I'll do you justice.
Iago: O sweet England!
    [Sings.]   King Stephen was a worthy peer;   75
                His breeches cost him but a crown;
                He held 'em sixpence all too dear,
                    With that he called the tailor lown.°
                He was a wight of high renown,
                    And thou art but of low degree.   80
                'Tis pride that pulls the country down;
                    Then take thine auld cloak about thee.
    Some wine, ho!
Cassio: 'Fore God, this is a more exquisite song than the other.

---

45 *pottle-deep:* Bottoms up.   47 *That . . . distance:* Very sensitive about their honor.
48 *very elements:* True representatives.   55 *rouse:* Bumper.   78 *lown:* Rascal.

Iago: Will you hear't again?   85

Cassio: No, for I hold him to be unworthy of his place that does those
   things.° Well, God's above all; and there be souls must be saved, and
   there be souls must not be saved.

Iago: It's true, good lieutenant.

Cassio: For mine own part — no offense to the general, nor any man   90
   of quality — I hope to be saved.

Iago: And so do I too, lieutenant.

Cassio: Ay, but, by your leave, not before me. The lieutenant is to be
   saved before the ancient. Let's have no more of this; let's to our
   affairs. — God forgive us our sins! — Gentlemen, let's look to our   95
   business. Do not think, gentlemen, I am drunk. This is my ancient; this is my right hand, and this is my left. I am not drunk
   now. I can stand well enough, and I speak well enough.

All: Excellent well!

Cassio: Why, very well then. You must not think then that I am   100
   drunk.   *Exit.*

Montano: To th' platform, masters. Come, let's set the watch.

Iago: You see this fellow that is gone before.
   He's a soldier fit to stand by Caesar
   And give direction; and do but see his vice.   105
   'Tis to his virtue a just equinox,°
   The one as long as th' other. 'Tis pity of him.
   I fear the trust Othello puts him in,
   On some odd time of his infirmity,
   Will shake this island.

Montano: But is he often thus?   110

Iago: 'Tis evermore his prologue to his sleep:
   He'll watch the horologe a double set°
   If drink rock not his cradle.

Montano: It were well
   The general were put in mind of it.
   Perhaps he sees it not, or his good nature   115
   Prizes the virtue that appears in Cassio
   And looks not on his evils. Is not this true?

   Enter Roderigo.

Iago [aside to him]: How now, Roderigo?
   I pray you after the lieutenant, go!

                                                            Exit Roderigo.

Montano: And 'tis great pity that the noble Moor   120
   Should hazard such a place as his own second
   With one of an ingraft° infirmity.

86–7 *does those things:* i.e., behaves in this fashion.   106 *just equinox:* Exact equivalent.
112 *watch . . . set:* Stay awake twice around the clock.   122 *ingraft:* i.e., ingrained.

It were an honest action to say
So to the Moor.

Iago: Not I, for this fair island!
I do love Cassio well and would do much   125
To cure him of this evil.
          (Within.) Help! help!
                         But hark! What noise?

Enter Cassio, driving in Roderigo.

Cassio: Zounds, you rogue! you rascal!
Montano: What's the matter, lieutenant?
Cassio: A knave to teach me my duty?
I'll beat the knave into a twiggen° bottle.   130
Roderigo: Beat me?
Cassio: Dost thou prate, rogue? *[Strikes him.]*
Montano: Nay, good lieutenant!
                                   [Stays him.]

I pray you, sir, hold your hand.
Cassio: Let me go, sir,
Or I'll knock you o'er the mazzard.°
Montano: Come, come, you're drunk!
Cassio: Drunk?

     They fight.

Iago [aside to Roderigo]: Away, I say! Go out and cry a mutiny!   135
                              Exit Roderigo.

Nay, good lieutenant. God's will, gentlemen!
Help, ho! — lieutenant — sir — Montano — sir —
Help, masters! — Here's a goodly watch indeed!

A bell rung.

Who's that which rings the bell? Diablo, ho!
The town will rise.° God's will, lieutenant, hold!   140
You'll be shamed for ever.

Enter Othello and Gentlemen with weapons.

Othello: What is the matter here?
Montano: Zounds, I bleed still. I am hurt to th' death.
     He dies!
Othello: Hold for your lives!
Iago: Hold, hold! Lieutenant — sir — Montano — gentlemen!   145
Have you forgot all sense of place and duty?
Hold! The general speaks to you. Hold, for shame!
Othello: Why, how now ho? From whence ariseth this?
Are we turned Turks, and to ourselves do that

---

130 *twiggen:* Wicker-covered.   133 *mazzard:* Head.   140 *rise:* Grow riotous.

Which heaven hath forbid the Ottomites? 150
For Christian shame put by this barbarous brawl!
He that stirs next to carve for° his own rage
Holds his soul light; he dies upon his motion.
Silence that dreadful bell! It frights the isle
From her propriety.° What is the matter, masters? 155
Honest Iago, that looks dead with grieving,
Speak. Who began this? On thy love, I charge thee.

Iago: I do not know. Friends all, but now, even now,
In quarter,° and in terms like bride and groom
Devesting them for bed; and then, but now — 160
As if some planet had unwitted men —
Swords out, and tilting one at other's breast
In opposition bloody. I cannot speak
Any beginning to this peevish odds,°
And would in action glorious I had lost 165
Those legs that brought me to a part of it!

Othello: How comes it, Michael, you are thus forgot?

Cassio: I pray you pardon me; I cannot speak.

Othello: Worthy Montano, you were wont to be civil;
The gravity and stillness of your youth 170
The world hath noted, and your name is great
In months of wisest censure.° What's the matter
That you unlace° your reputation thus
And spend your rich opinion° for the name
Of a night-brawler? Give me answer to it. 175

Montano: Worthy Othello, I am hurt to danger.
Your officer, Iago, can inform you,
While I spare speech, which something now offends° me,
Of all that I do know; nor know I aught
By me that's said or done amiss this night, 180
Unless self-charity be sometimes a vice,
And to defend ourselves it be a sin
When violence assails us.

Othello: Now, by heaven,
My blood° begins my safer guides to rule,
And passion, having my best judgment collied,° 185
Assays° to lead the way. If I once stir
Or do but lift this arm, the best of you
Shall sink in my rebuke. Give me to know
How this foul rout began, who set it on;

---

152 *carve for:* Indulge.   155 *propriety:* Proper self.   159 *quarter:* Friendliness.   164 *peevish odds:* Childish quarrel.   172 *censure:* Judgment.   173 *unlace:* Undo.   174 *rich opinion:* High reputation.   178 *offends:* Pains.   184 *blood:* Passion.   185 *collied:* Darkened. 186 *Assays:* Tries.

And he that is approved in° this offense,   190
Though he had twinned with me, both at a birth,
Shall lose me. What! in a town of war,
Yet wild, the people's hearts brimful of fear,
To manage° private and domestic quarrel?
In night, and on the court and guard of safety?   195
'Tis monstrous. Iago, who began't?
Montano: If partially affined, or leagued in office,°
Thou dost deliver more or less than truth,
Thou art no soldier.
Iago: Touch me not so near.
I had rather have this tongue cut from my mouth   200
Than it should do offense to Michael Cassio;
Yet I persuade myself, to speak the truth
Shall nothing wrong him. This it is, general.
Montano and myself being in speech,
There comes a fellow crying out for help,   205
And Cassio following him with determined sword
To execute° upon him. Sir, this gentleman
Steps in to Cassio and entreats his pause.
Myself the crying fellow did pursue,
Lest by his clamor — as it so fell out —   210
The town might fall in fright. He, swift of foot,
Outran my purpose; and I returned then rather
For that I heard the clink and fall of swords,
And Cassio high in oath;° which till to-night
I ne'er might say before. When I came back —   215
For this was brief — I found them close together
At blow and thrust, even as again they were
When you yourself did part them.
More of this matter cannot I report;
But men are men; the best sometimes forget.   220
Though Cassio did some little wrong to him,
As men in rage strike those that wish them best,
Yet surely Cassio I believe received
From him that fled some strange indignity,
Which patience could not pass.°
Othello: I know, Iago,   225
Thy honesty and love doth mince this matter,
Making it light to Cassio. Cassio, I love thee;
But never more be officer of mine.

---

190 *approved in:* Proved guilty of.   194 *manage:* Carry on.   197 *partially ... office:*
Prejudiced by comradeship or official relations.   207 *execute:* Work his will.   214 *high
in oath:* Cursing.   225 *pass:* Pass over, ignore.

Enter Desdemona, attended.

Look if my gentle love be not raised up!
I'll make thee an example.

Desdemona: What's the matter?   230

Othello: All's well now, sweeting; come away to bed.
[To Montano.]
Sir, for your hurts, myself will be your surgeon.
Lead him off.

[Montano is led off.]

Iago, look with care about the town
And silence those whom this vile brawl distracted.°   235
Come, Desdemona; 'tis the soldiers' life
To have their balmy slumbers waked with strife.

Exit [with all but Iago and Cassio].

Iago: What, are you hurt, lieutenant?

Cassio: Ay, past all surgery.

Iago: Marry, God forbid!   240

Cassio: Reputation, reputation, reputation! O, I have lost my reputation! I have lost the immortal part of myself, and what remains is
bestial. My reputation, Iago, my reputation!

Iago: As I am an honest man, I thought you had received some
bodily wound. There is more sense in that than in reputation.   245
Reputation is an idle and most false imposition; oft got without
merit and lost without deserving. You have lost no reputation at
all unless you repute yourself such a loser. What, man! there are
ways to recover° the general again. You are but now cast in his
mood° — a punishment more in policy than in malice, even so as   250
one would beat his offenseless dog to affright an imperious lion.
Sue to him again, and he's yours.

Cassio: I will rather sue to be despised than to deceive so good a
commander with so slight, so drunken, and so indiscreet an officer. Drunk! and speak parrot!° and squabble! swagger! swear!   255
and discourse fustian° with one's own shadow! O thou invisible
spirit of wine, if thou hast no name to be known by, let us call
thee devil!

Iago: What was he that you followed with your sword? What had he
done to you?   260

Cassio: I know not.

Iago: Is't possible?

Cassio: I remember a mass of things, but nothing distinctly; a
quarrel, but nothing wherefore. O God, that men should put

---

235 *distracted:* Excited.   249 *recover:* Regain favor with.   249–50 *in his mood:* Dismissed because of his anger.   255 *parrot:* Meaningless phrases.   256 *fustian:* Bombastic
nonsense.

an enemy in their mouths to steal away their brains! that we   265
should with joy, pleasance, revel, and applause° transform ourselves into beasts!

Iago: Why, but you are now well enough. How came you thus
recovered?

Cassio: It hath pleased the devil drunkenness to give place to the devil   270
wrath. One unperfectness shows me another, to make me frankly
despise myself.

Iago: Come, you are too severe a moraler. As the time, the place, and
the condition of this country stands, I could heartily wish this
had not so befall'n; but since it is as it is, mend it for your own   275
good.

Cassio: I will ask him for my place again: he shall tell me I am a drunkard! Had I as many mouths as Hydra,° such an answer would stop
them all. To be now a sensible man, by and by a fool, and presently a beast! O strange! Every inordinate cup is unblest, and the   280
ingredient° is a devil.

Iago: Come, come, good wine is a good familiar creature if it be well
used. Exclaim no more against it. And, good lieutenant, I think
you think I love you.

Cassio: I have well approved° it, sir. I drunk!   285

Iago: You or any man living may be drunk at some time, man. I'll tell
you what you shall do. Our general's wife is now the general. I
may say so in this respect, for that he hath devoted and given up
himself to the contemplation, mark, and denotement of her parts
and graces. Confess yourself freely to her; importune her help to   290
put you in your place again. She is of so free,° so kind, so apt,
so blessed a disposition she holds it a vice in her goodness not
to do more than she is requested. This broken joint between you
and her husband entreat her to splinter;° and my fortunes against
any lay° worth naming, this crack of your love shall grow stronger   295
than it was before.

Cassio: You advise me well.

Iago: I protest, in the sincerity of love and honest kindness.

Cassio: I think it freely; and betimes in the morning will I beseech
the virtuous Desdemona to undertake for me. I am desperate of   300
my fortunes if they check me here.

Iago: You are in the right. Good night, lieutenant; I must to the watch.

Cassio: Good night, honest Iago.   *Exit Cassio.*

Iago: And what's he then that says I play the villain,
When this advice is free I give and honest,   305
Probal° to thinking, and indeed the course
To win the Moor again? For 'tis most easy

---

266 *applause:* Desire to please.   278 *Hydra:* Monster with many heads.   281 *ingredi-*
ent: Contents.   285 *approved:* Proved.   291 *free:* Bounteous.   294 *splinter:* Bind up
with splints.   295 *lay:* Wager.   306 *Probal:* Probable.

Th' inclining Desdemona to subdue°
In an honest suit; she's framed as fruitful
As the free elements. And then for her   310
To win the Moor — were't to renounce his baptism,
All seals and symbols of redeemèd sin —
His soul is so enfettered to her love
That she may make, unmake, do what she list,
Even as her appetite shall play the god   315
With his weak function. How am I then a villain
To counsel Cassio to this parallel° course,
Directly to his good? Divinity° of hell!
When devils will the blackest sins put on,°
They do suggest at first with heavenly shows,   320
As I do now. For whiles this honest fool
Plies Desdemona to repair his fortunes,
And she for him pleads strongly to the Moor,
I'll pour this pestilence into his ear,
That she repeals him° for her body's lust;   325
And by how much she strives to do him good,
She shall undo her credit with the Moor.
So will I turn her virtue into pitch,
And out of her own goodness make the net
That shall enmesh them all.

Enter Roderigo.

                        How, now, Roderigo?   330
Roderigo: I do follow here in the chase, not like a hound that hunts, but
    one that fills up the cry.° My money is almost spent; I have been to-
    night exceedingly well cudgelled; and I think the issue will be — I shall
    have so much experience for my pains; and so, with no money at all,
    and a little more wit, return again to Venice.   335
Iago: How poor are they that have not patience!
    What wound did ever heal but by degrees?
    Thou know'st we work by wit, and not by witchcraft;
    And wit depends on dilatory time.
    Does't not go well? Cassio hath beaten thee,   340
    And thou by that small hurt hast cashiered Cassio.°
    Though other things grow fair against the sun,
    Yet fruits that blossom first will first be ripe.
    Content thyself awhile. By the mass, 'tis morning!
    Pleasure and action make the hours seem short.   345
    Retire thee; go where thou art billeted.

---

308 *subdue:* Persuade.   317 *parallel:* Corresponding.   318 *Divinity:* Theology.   319 *put on:* Incite.   325 *repeals him:* Seeks his recall.   332 *cry:* Pack.   341 *cashiered Cassio:* Maneuvered Cassio's discharge.

Away, I say! Thou shalt know more hereafter.
Nay, get thee gone!   *Exit Roderigo.*
                    Two things are to be done:
My wife must move for Cassio to her mistress;
I'll set her on;   350
Myself the while to draw the Moor apart
And bring him jump° when he may Cassio find
Soliciting his wife. Ay, that's the way!
Dull no device by coldness and delay.   *Exit.*

ACT III

SCENE I: *Before the chamber of Othello and Desdemona.*

Enter Cassio, with Musicians and the Clown.

Cassio: Masters, play here, I will content° your pains:
Something that's brief; and bid "Good morrow, general."

[They play.]

Clown: Why, masters, ha' your instruments been in Naples,° that
they speak i' th' nose thus?
Musician: How, sir, how?   5
Clown: Are these, I pray you, called wind instruments?
Musician: Ay, marry, are they, sir.
Clown: O, thereby hangs a tail.
Musician: Whereby hangs a tail, sir?
Clown: Marry, sir, by many a wind instrument that I know. But, masters,   10
here's money for you; and the general so likes your music that he
desires you, for love's sake, to make no more noise with it.
Musician: Well, sir, we will not.
Clown: If you have any music that may not be heard, to't again: but, as
they say, to hear music the general does not greatly care.   15
Musician: We have none such, sir.
Clown: Then put up your pipes in your bag, for I'll away. Go, vanish
into air, away!   *Exit Musician [with his fellows].*
Cassio: Dost thou hear, my honest friend?
Clown: No, I hear not your honest friend. I hear you.   20
Cassio: Prithee keep up thy quillets.° There's a poor piece of gold for
thee. If the gentlewoman that attends the general's wife be stirring,

---

352 *jump:* At the exact moment. **Act III, Scene I.** 1 *content:* Reward. 3 *Naples:*
(Notorious for its association with venereal disease). 21 *quillets:* Quips.

tell her there's one Cassio entreats her a little favor of speech. Wilt
thou do this?

Clown: She is stirring sir. If she will stir hither, I shall seem to notify   25
unto her.

Cassio: [Do, good my friend.]   *Exit Clown.*

    Enter Iago.

                         In happy time,° Iago.

Iago: You have not been abed then?

Cassio: Why, no; the day had broke
Before we parted. I have made bold, Iago,   30
To send in to your wife: my suit to her
Is that she will to virtuous Desdemona
Procure me some access.

Iago: I'll send her to you presently;
And I'll devise a mean to draw the Moor
Out of the way, that your converse and business   35
May be more free.

Cassio: I humbly thank you for't.   *Exit [Iago].*
                    I never knew
A Florentine° more kind and honest.

    Enter Emilia.

Emilia: Good morrow, good lieutenant. I am sorry
For your displeasure: but all will sure be well.   40
The general and his wife are talking of it,
And she speaks for you stoutly. The Moor replied
That he you hurt is of great fame in Cyprus
And great affinity,° and that in wholesome wisdom
He might not but refuse you; but he protests he loves you,   45
And needs no other suitor but his likings
[To take the safest occasion° by the front°]
To bring you in again.

Cassio: Yet I beseech you,
If you think fit, or that it may be done,
Give me advantage of some brief discourse   50
With Desdemona alone.

Emilia: Pray you come in.
I will bestow you where you shall have time
To speak your bosom° freely.

Cassio: I am much bound to you.   *Exeunt.*

---

27 *In happy time:* Well met.   38 *Florentine:* i.e., even a Florentine (like Cassio;
Iago was a Venetian).   44 *affinity:* Family connections.   47 *occasion:* Opportunity; *front:* Forelock.   53 *your bosom:* Your inmost thoughts.

Scene II: *The castle.*

Enter Othello, Iago, and Gentlemen.

Othello: These letters give, Iago, to the pilot
    And by him do my duties to the Senate.
    That done, I will be walking on the works;°
    Repair there to me.
Iago: Well, my good lord, I'll do't.
Othello: This fortification, gentlemen, shall we see't?   5
Gentlemen: We'll wait upon your lordship.   *Exeunt.*

Scene III: *The castle grounds.*

Enter Desdemona, Cassio, and Emilia.

Desdemona: Be thou assured, good Cassio, I will do
    All my abilities in thy behalf.
Emilia: Good madam, do. I warrant it grieves my husband
    As if the cause were his.
Desdemona: O, that's an honest fellow. Do not doubt, Cassio,   5
    But I will have my lord and you again
    As friendly as you were.
Cassio: Bounteous madam,
    Whatever shall become of Michael Cassio,
    He's never anything but your true servant.
Desdemona: I know't; I thank you. You do love my lord;   10
    You have known him long; and be you well assured
    He shall in strangeness° stand no farther off
    Than in a politic distance.°
Cassio: Ay, but, lady,
    That policy may either last so long,
    Or feed upon such nice and waterish diet,°   15
    Or breed itself so out of circumstance,
    That, I being absent, and my place supplied,
    My general will forget my love and service.
Desdemona: Do not doubt° that; before Emilia here
    I give thee warrant of thy place. Assure thee,   20
    If I do vow a friendship, I'll perform it
    To the last article. My lord shall never rest;
    I'll watch him tame° and talk him out of patience;
    His bed shall seem a school, his board a shrift;°

Scene II. 3 *works:* Fortifications. **Scene III.** 12 *strangeness:* Aloofness. 13 *Than . . . distance:* Than wise policy requires. 15 *Or . . . diet:* Or be continued for such slight reasons. 19 *doubt:* Fear. 23 *watch him tame:* Keep him awake until he gives in. 24 *shrift:* Confessional.

I'll intermingle everything he does   25
With Cassio's suit. Therefore be merry, Cassio,
For thy solicitor shall rather die
Than give thy cause away.

Enter Othello and Iago [at a distance].

Emilia: Madam, here comes my lord.
Cassio: Madam, I'll take my leave.   30
Desdemona: Why, stay, and hear me speak.
Cassio: Madam, not now: I am very ill at ease,
  Unfit for mine own purposes.
Desdemona: Well, do your discretion.   *Exit Cassio.*
Iago: Ha! I like not that.
Othello: What dost thou say?   35
Iago: Nothing, my lord; or if — I know not what.
Othello: Was not that Cassio parted from my wife?
Iago: Cassio, my lord? No, sure, I cannot think it,
  That he would steal away so guilty-like,
  Seeing your coming.
Othello: I do believe 'twas he.   40
Desdemona: How now, my lord?
  I have been talking with a suitor here,
  A man that languishes in your displeasure.
Othello: What is't you mean?
Desdemona: Why, your lieutenant, Cassio. Good my lord,   45
  If I have any grace or power to move you,
  His present° reconciliation take;
  For if he be not one that truly loves you,
  That errs in ignorance, and not in cunning,
  I have no judgment in an honest face,   50
  I prithee call him back.
Othello: Went he hence now?
Desdemona: Yes, faith; so humbled
  That he hath left part of his grief with me
  To suffer with him. Good love, call him back.
Othello: Not now, sweet Desdemon; some other time.   55
Desdemona: But shall't be shortly?
Othello: The sooner, sweet, for you.
Desdemona: Shall't be to-night at supper?
Othello: No, not to-night.
Desdemona: To-morrow dinner then?
Othello: I shall not dine at home;
  I meet the captains at the citadel.

47 *present:* Immediate.

Desdemona: Why then, to-morrow night, or Tuesday morn,   60
On Tuesday noon or night, or Wednesday morn.
I prithee name the time, but let it not
Exceed three days. I' faith, he's penitent;
And yet his trespass, in our common reason
(Save that, they say, the wars must make examples   65
Out of their best), is not almost° a fault
T' incur a private check.° When shall he come?
Tell me, Othello. I wonder in my soul
What you could ask me that I should deny
Or stand so mamm'ring on.° What? Michael Cassio,   70
That came a-wooing with you, and so many a time,
When I have spoke of you dispraisingly,
Hath ta'en your part — to have so much to do
To bring him in? By'r Lady, I could do much —
Othello: Prithee no more. Let him come when he will!   75
I will deny thee nothing.
Desdemona: Why, this is not a boon;
'Tis as I should entreat you wear your gloves,
Or feed on nourishing dishes, or keep you warm,
Or sue to you to do a peculiar profit
To your own person. Nay, when I have a suit   80
Wherein I mean to touch your love indeed,
It shall be full of poise and difficult weight,
And fearful° to be granted.
Othello: I will deny thee nothing!
Whereon I do beseech thee grant me this,
To leave me but a little to myself.   85
Desdemona: Shall I deny you? No. Farewell, my lord.
Othello: Farewell, my Desdemon: I'll come to thee straight.
Desdemona: Emilia, come. — Be as your fancies teach you;
Whate'er you be, I am obedient.   *Exit [with Emilia].*
Othello: Excellent wretch!° Perdition catch my soul   90
But I do love thee! and when I love thee not,
Chaos is come again.
Iago: My noble lord —
Othello: What dost thou say, Iago?
Iago: Did Michael Cassio, when you wooed my lady,
Know of your love?   95
Othello: He did, from first to last. Why dost thou ask?

---

66 *not almost:* Hardly.   67 *a private check:* Even a private reprimand.   70 *mamm'ring on:* Hesitating about.   83 *fearful:* Dangerous.   90 *wretch:* (A term of endearment).

Iago: But for a satisfaction of my thought;
   No further harm.
Othello: Why of thy thought, Iago?
Iago: I did not think he had been acquainted with her.
Othello: O, yes, and went between us° very oft.   100
Iago: Indeed?
Othello: Indeed? Ay, indeed! Discern'st thou aught in that?
   Is he not honest?
Iago: Honest, my lord?
Othello: Honest. Ay, honest.
Iago: My lord, for aught I know.
Othello: What dost thou think?
Iago: Think, my lord?
Othello: Think, my lord?   105
   By heaven, he echoes me,
   As if there were some monster in his thought
   Too hideous to be shown. Thou dost mean something:
   I heard thee say even now, thou lik'st not that,
   When Cassio left my wife. What didst not like?   110
   And when I told thee he was of my counsel
   In my whole course of wooing, thou cried'st "Indeed?"
   And didst contract and purse thy brow together,
   As if thou then hadst shut up in thy brain
   Some horrible conceit.° If thou dost love me,   115
   Show me thy thought
Iago: My lord, you know I love you.
Othello: I think thou dost;
   And, for I know thou'rt full of love and honesty
   And weigh'st thy words before thou giv'st them breath,
   Therefore these stops of thine fright me the more;   120
   For such things in a false disloyal knave
   Are tricks of custom; but in a man that's just
   They are close dilations, working from the heart
   That passion cannot rule.°
Iago: For Michael Cassio,
   I dare be sworn I think that he is honest.   125
Othello: I think so too.
Iago: Men should be what they seem;
   Or those that be not, would they might seem none!°
Othello: Certain, men should be what they seem.
Iago: Why then, I think Cassio's an honest man.

---

100 *went between us:* (i.e., as messenger).   115 *conceit:* Fancy.   123–24 *close dilations . . . rule:* Secret emotions which well up in spite of restraint.   127 *seem none:* i.e., not pretend to be men when they are really monsters.

Othello: Nay, yet there's more in this.   130
    I prithee speak to me as to thy thinkings,
    As thou dost ruminate, and give thy worst of thoughts
    The worst of words.
Iago: Good my lord, pardon me:
    Though I am bound to every act of duty,
    I am not bound to that all slaves are free to.°   135
    Utter my thoughts? Why, say they are vile and false,
    As where's that palace whereinto foul things
    Sometimes intrude not? Who has a breast so pure
    But some uncleanly apprehensions
    Keep leets and law days,° and in Sessions sit   140
    With meditations lawful?
Othello: Thou dost conspire against thy friend, Iago,
    If thou but think'st him wronged, and mak'st his ear
    A stranger to thy thoughts.
Iago: I do beseech you —
    Though I perchance am vicious in my guess   145
    (As I confess it is my nature's plague
    To spy into abuses, and oft my jealousy°
    Shapes faults that are not), that your wisdom yet
    From one that so imperfectly conjects°
    Would take no notice, nor build yourself a trouble   150
    Out of his scattering and unsure observance.
    It were not for your quiet nor your good,
    Nor for my manhood, honesty, and wisdom,
    To let you know my thoughts.
Othello: What dost thou mean?
Iago: Good name in man and woman, dear my lord,   155
    Is the immediate° jewel of their souls.
    Who steals my purse steals trash; 'tis something, nothing;
    'Twas mine, 'tis his, and has been slave to thousands;
    But he that filches from me my good name
    Robs me of that which not enriches him   160
    And makes me poor indeed.
Othello: By heaven, I'll know thy thoughts!
Iago: You cannot, if my heart were in your hand;
    Nor shall not whilst 'tis in my custody.
Othello: Ha!
Iago: O, beware, my lord, of jealousy!   165
    It is the green-eyed monster, which doth mock°

---

135 *bound . . . free to:* Bound to tell that which even slaves are allowed to keep to themselves. 140 *leets and law days:* Sittings of the courts. 147 *jealousy:* Suspicion. 149 *conjects:* Conjectures. 156 *immediate:* Nearest the heart. 166 *mock:* Play with, like a cat with a mouse.

The meat it feeds on. That cuckold lives in bliss
Who, certain of his fate, loves not his wronger;
But O, what damnèd minutes tells he o'er
Who dotes, yet doubts — suspects, yet strongly loves!   170
Othello: O misery!
Iago: Poor and content is rich, and rich enough;
But riches fineless° is as poor as winter
To him that ever fears he shall be poor.
Good God, the souls of all my tribe defend   175
From jealousy!
Othello: Why, why is this?
Think'st thou I'ld make a life of jealousy,
To follow still the changes of the moon
With fresh suspicions? No! To be once in doubt
Is once to be resolved. Exchange me for a goat   180
When I shall turn the business of my soul
To such exsufflicate and blown° surmises,
Matching this inference. 'Tis not to make me jealous
To say my wife is fair, feeds well, loves company,
Is free of speech, sings, plays, and dances;   185
Where virtue is, these are more virtuous.
Nor from mine own weak merits will I draw
The smallest fear or doubt of her revolt,°
For she had eyes, and chose me. No, Iago;
I'll see before I doubt; when I doubt, prove;   190
And on the proof there is no more but this —
Away at once with love or jealousy!
Iago: I am glad of this; for now I shall have reason
To show the love and duty that I bear you
With franker spirit. Therefore, as I am bound,   195
Receive it from me. I speak not yet of proof.
Look at your wife; observe her well with Cassio;
Wear your eyes thus, not jealous nor secure:°
I would not have your free and noble nature,
Out of self-bounty,° be abused. Look to't.   200
I know our country disposition well:
In Venice they do let God see the pranks
They dare not show their husbands; their best conscience
Is not to leave't undone, but keep't unknown.
Othello: Dost thou say so?   205
Iago: She did deceive her father, marrying you;
And when she seemed to shake and fear your looks,
She loved them most.

---

173 *fineless:* Unlimited.   182 *exsufflicate and blown:* Spat out and flyblown.   188 *revolt:*
Unfaithfulness.   198 *secure:* Overconfident.   200 *self-bounty:* Natural goodness.

Othello: And so she did.
Iago: Why, go to then!
    She that, so young, could give out such a seeming
    To seel° her father's eyes up close as oak° —   210
    He thought 'twas witchcraft — but I am much to blame.
    I humbly do beseech you of your pardon
    For too much loving you.
Othello: I am bound to thee for ever.
Iago: I see this hath a little dashed your spirits.
Othello: Not a jot, not a jot.
Iago: I' faith, I fear it has.   215
    I hope you will consider what is spoke
    Comes from my love. But I do see y' are moved.
    I am to pray you not to strain my speech
    To grosser issues° nor to larger reach
    Than to suspicion.   220
Othello: I will not.
Iago: Should you do so, my lord,
    My speech should fall into such vile success°
    As my thoughts aim not at. Cassio's my worthy friend —
    My lord, I see y' are moved.
Othello: No, not much moved:
    I do not think but Desdemona's honest.°   225
Iago: Long live she so! and long live you to think so!
Othello: And yet, how nature erring from itself —
Iago: Ay, there's the point! as (to be bold with you)
    Not to affect many proposèd matches
    Of her own clime, complexion, and degree,   230
    Whereto we see in all things nature tends —
    Foh! one may smell in such a will most rank,
    Foul disproportions, thought unnatural —
    But pardon me — I do not in position°
    Distinctly speak of her; though I may fear   235
    Her will, recoiling° to her better judgment,
    May fall to match° you with her country forms,
    And happily° repent.
Othello: Farewell, farewell!
    If more thou dost perceive, let me know more.
    Set on thy wife to observe. Leave me, Iago.   240
Iago: My lord, I take my leave.   *[Going.]*

---

210 *seel:* Close; *oak:* Oak grain.   219 *To grosser issues:* To mean something more monstrous.   222 *vile success:* Evil outcome.   225 *honest:* Chaste.   234 *position:* Definite assertion.   236 *recoiling:* Reverting.   237 *fall to match:* Happen to compare. 238 *happily:* Haply, perhaps.

Othello: Why did I marry? This honest creature doubtless
    Sees and knows more, much more, than he unfolds.
Iago [returns]: My lord, I would I might entreat your honor
    To scan this thing no further: leave it to time.   245
    Although 'tis fit that Cassio have his place,
    For sure he fills it up with great ability,
    Yet, if you please to hold off a while,
    You shall by that perceive him and his means.
    Note if your lady strain his entertainment°   250
    With any strong or vehement importunity;
    Much will be seen in that. In the mean time
    Let me be thought too busy° in my fears
    (As worthy cause I have to fear I am)
    And hold her free,° I do beseech your honor.   255
Othello: Fear not my government.°
Iago: I once more take my leave.   *Exit.*
Othello: This fellow's of exceeding honesty,
    And knows all qualities,° with a learned spirit
    Of° human dealings. If I do prove her haggard,°   260
    Though that her jesses° were my dear heartstrings,
    I'd whistle her off and let her down the wind
    To prey at fortune.° Haply, for I am black
    And have not those soft parts of conversation°
    That chamberers° have, or for I am declined   265
    Into the vale of years — yet that's not much —
    She's gone. I am abused, and my relief
    Must be to loathe her. O curse of marriage,
    That we can call these delicate creatures ours,
    And not their appetites! I had rather be a toad   270
    And live upon the vapor of a dungeon
    Than keep a corner in the thing I love
    For others' uses. Yet 'tis the plague of great ones;°
    Prerogatived° are they less than the base.
    'Tis destiny unshunnable, like death.   275
    Even then this forkèd plague° is fated to us
    When we do quicken.° Look where she comes.

---

250 *strain his entertainment:* Urge his recall. 253 *busy:* Meddlesome. 255 *hold her free:* Consider her guiltless. 256 *government:* Self-control. 259 *qualities:* Natures. 259–60 *learned spirit Of:* Mind informed about. 260 *haggard:* A wild hawk. 261 *jesses:* Thongs for controlling a hawk. 262–63 *whistle . . . fortune:* Turn her out and let her take care of herself. 264 *soft . . . conversation:* Ingratiating manners. 265 *chamberers:* Courtiers. 273 *great ones:* Prominent men. 274 *Prerogatived:* Privileged. 276 *forkèd plague:* i.e., horns of a cuckold. 277 *do quicken:* Are born.

Enter Desdemona and Emilia.

If she be false, O, then heaven mocks itself!
I'll not believe't.
Desdemona: How now, my dear Othello?
Your dinner, and the generous° islanders   280
By you invited, do attend your presence.
Othello: I am to blame.
Desdemona: Why do you speak so faintly?
Are you not well?
Othello: I have a pain upon my forehead, here.
Desdemona: Faith, that's with watching;° 'twill away again.   285
Let me but bind it hard, within this hour
It will be well.
Othello: Your napkin° is too little;

[*He pushes the handkerchief from him, and it falls unnoticed.*]

Let it° alone. Come, I'll go in with you.
Desdemona: I am very sorry that you are not well. *Exit [with Othello].*
Emilia: I am glad I have found this napkin;   290
This was her first remembrance from the Moor,
My wayward husband hath a hundred times
Wooed me to steal it; but she so loves the token
(For he conjured her she should ever keep it)
That she reserves it evermore about her   295
To kiss and talk to. I'll have the work ta'en out°
And give't Iago.
What he will do with it heaven knows, not I;
I nothing but to please his fantasy.°

Enter Iago.

Iago: How now? What do you here alone?   300
Emilia: Do not you chide; I have a thing for you.
Iago: A thing for me? It is a common thing —
Emilia: Ha?
Iago: To have a foolish wife.
Emilia: O, is that all? What will you give me now   305
For that same handkerchief?
Iago: What handkerchief?
Emilia: What handkerchief!
Why, that the Moor first gave to Desdemona;
That which so often you did bid me steal.
Iago: Hast stol'n it from her?   310

---

280 *generous:* Noble. 285 *watching:* Working late. 287 *napkin:* Handkerchief. 288 *it:* i.e., his forehead. 296 *work ta'en out:* Pattern copied. 299 *fantasy:* Whim.

Emilia: No, faith; she let it drop by negligence,
　　And to th' advantage,° I, being here, took't up.
　　Look, here it is.
Iago:　　　　　　　A good wench! Give it me.
Emilia: What will you do with't, that you have been so earnest
　　To have me filch it?
Iago:　　　　　　　Why, what is that to you?　　　　　　315

　　　[*Snatches it.*]

Emilia: If it be not for some purpose of import,°
　　Give't me again. Poor lady, she'll run mad
　　When she shall lack it.
Iago: Be not acknown on't;° I have use for it.
　　Go, leave me.　　　　　　　　　　　*Exit Emilia.*　　320
　　I will in Cassio's lodgings lose this napkin
　　And let him find it. Trifles light as air
　　Are to the jealous confirmations strong
　　As proofs of holy writ. This may do something.
　　The Moor already changes with my poison:　　　　　325
　　Dangerous conceits° are in their nature poisons,
　　Which at the first are scarce found to distaste,
　　But with a little act upon the blood
　　Burn like the mines of sulphur.

Enter Othello.

　　　　　　　　　　　　I did say so.
　　Look where he comes! Not poppy nor mandragora,°　　330
　　Nor all the drowsy syrups of the world,
　　Shall ever med'cine thee to that sweet sleep
　　Which thou owedst yesterday.
Othello:　　　　　　　Ha! ha! false to me?
Iago: Why, how now, general? No more of that!
Othello: Avaunt! be gone! Thou hast set me on the rack.　　335
　　I swear 'tis better to be much abused
　　Than but to know't a little.
Iago:　　　　　　　How now, my lord?
Othello: What sense had I of her stol'n hours of lust?
　　I saw't not, thought it not, it harmed not me;
　　I slept the next night well, fed well, was free° and merry;　　340
　　I found not Cassio's kisses on her lips
　　He that is robbed, not wanting° what is stol'n,
　　Let him not know't, and he's not robbed at all.

---

312 *to th' advantage:* Opportunely.　316 *import:* Importance.　319 *Be . . . on't:* Do not acknowledge it.　326 *conceits:* Ideas.　330 *mandragora:* A narcotic.　340 *free:* Carefree.　342 *wanting:* Missing.

Iago: I am sorry to hear this.

Othello: I had been happy if the general camp,   345
    Pioneers° and all, had tasted her sweet body,
    So I had nothing known. O, now for ever
    Farewell the tranquil mind! farewell content!
    Farewell the plumèd troop, and the big° wars
    That make ambition virtue! O, farewell!   350
    Farewell the neighing steed and the shrill trump,
    The spirit-stirring drum, th' ear-piercing fife,
    The royal banner, and all quality,
    Pride, pomp, and circumstance° of glorious war!
    And O you mortal engines° whose rude throats   355
    Th' immortal Jove's dread clamors counterfeit,°
    Farewell! Othello's occupation's gone!

Iago: Is't possible, my lord?

Othello: Villain, be sure thou prove my love a whore!
    Be sure of it; give me the ocular proof;   360
    Or, by the worth of mine eternal soul,
    Thou hadst been better have been born a dog
    Than answer my waked wrath!

Iago: Is't come to this?

Othello: Make me to see't; or at the least so prove it
    That the probation° bear no hinge nor loop   365
    To hang a doubt on — or woe upon thy life!

Iago: My noble lord —

Othello: If thou dost slander her and torture me,
    Never pray more; abandon all remorse;
    On horror's head horrors accumulate;   370
    Do deeds to make heaven weep, all earth amazed;
    For nothing canst thou to damnation add
    Greater than that.

Iago: O grace! O heaven forgive me!
    Are you a man? Have you a soul or sense? —
    God b' wi' you! take mine office. O wretched fool,   375
    That liv'st to make thine honesty a vice!
    O monstrous world! Take note, take note, O world,
    To be direct and honest is not safe.
    I thank you for this profit;° and from hence
    I'll love no friend, sith love breeds such offense.   380

Othello: Nay, stay. Thou shouldst be honest.

Iago: I should be wise; for honesty's a fool
    And loses that it works for.

---

346 *Pioneers:* Sappers, laborers.   349 *big:* Stately.   354 *circumstance:* Pageantry.
355 *mortal engines:* Deadly artillery.   356 *counterfeit:* Imitate.   365 *probation:* Proof.
379 *profit:* Profitable lesson.

Othello: By the world,
I think my wife be honest, and think she is not;
I think that thou art just, and think thou art not.   385
I'll have some proof. Her name, that was as fresh
As Dian's visage, is now begrimed and black
As mine own face. If there be cords, or knives,
Poison, or fire, or suffocating streams,
I'll not endure it. Would I were satisfied!°   390

Iago: I see, sir, you are eaten up with passion:
I do repent me that I put it to you.
You would be satisfied?

Othello: Would? Nay, I will.

Iago: And may; but how? how satisfied, my lord?
Would you, the supervisor,° grossly gape on?   395
Behold her topped?

Othello: Death and damnation! O!

Iago: It were a tedious difficulty, I think,
To bring them to that prospect. Damn them then,
If ever mortal eyes do see them bolster°
More than their own! What then? How then?   400
What shall I say? Where's satisfaction?
It is impossible you should see this,
Were they as prime° as goats, as hot as monkeys,
As salt° as wolves in pride,° and fools as gross
As ignorance made drunk. But yet, I say,   405
If imputation and strong circumstances
Which lead directly to the door of truth
Will give you satisfaction, you may have't.

Othello: Give me a living reason she's disloyal.

Iago: I do not like the office.   410
But sith I am ent'red in this cause so far,
Pricked to't by foolish honesty and love,
I will go on. I lay with Cassio lately,
And being troubled with a raging tooth,
I could not sleep.   415
There are a kind of men so loose of soul
That in their sleeps will mutter their affairs.
One of this kind is Cassio.
In sleep I heard him say, "Sweet Desdemona,
Let us be wary, let us hide our loves!"   420
And then, sir, would he gripe and wring my hand,
Cry "O sweet creature!" and then kiss me hard,
As if he plucked up kisses by the roots

---

390 *satisfied:* Completely informed.   395 *supervisor:* Spectator.   399 *bolster:* Lie
together.   403 *prime:* Lustful.   404 *salt:* Lecherous; *pride:* Heat.

That grew upon my lips; then laid his leg
Over my thigh, and sighed, and kissed, and then   425
Cried "Cursèd fate that gave thee to the Moor!"
Othello: O monstrous! monstrous!
Iago: Nay, this was but his dream.
Othello: But this denoted a foregone conclusion;°
'Tis a shrewd doubt,° though it be but a dream.
Iago: And this may help to thicken other proofs   430
That do demonstrate thinly.
Othello: I'll tear her all to pieces!
Iago: Nay, but be wise. Yet we see nothing done;
She may be honest yet. Tell me but this —
Have you not sometimes seen a handkerchief
Spotted with strawberries in your wife's hand?   435
Othello: I gave her such a one; 'twas my first gift.
Iago: I know not that; but such a handkerchief —
I am sure it was your wife's — did I to-day
See Cassio wipe his beard with.
Othello: If it be that —
Iago: If it be that, or any that was hers,   440
It speaks against her with the other proofs.
Othello: O, that the slave had forty thousand lives!
One is too poor, too weak for my revenge.
Now do I see 'tis true. Look here, Iago:
All my fond love thus do I blow to heaven.   445
'Tis gone.
Arise, black vengeance, from the hollow hell!
Yield up, O love, thy crown and hearted throne
To tyrannous hate! Swell, bosom, with thy fraught,°
For 'tis of aspics'° tongues!
Iago: Yet be content.   450
Othello: O, blood, blood, blood!
Iago: Patience, I say. Your mind perhaps may change.
Othello: Never, Iago. Like to the Pontic sea,°
Whose icy current and compulsive course
Ne'er feels retiring ebb, but keeps due on   455
To the Propontic and the Hellespont,
Even so my bloody thoughts, with violent pace,
Shall ne'er look back, ne'er ebb to humble love,
Till that a capable° and wide revenge
Swallow them up.
(He kneels.)   Now, by yond marble heaven,   460

---

428 *foregone conclusion:* Previous experience.   429 *a shrewd doubt:* Cursedly suspicious.   449 *fraught:* Burden.   450 *aspics:* Deadly poisonous snakes.   453 *Pontic sea:* Black Sea.   459 *capable:* All-embracing.

In the due reverence of a sacred vow
I here engage my words.
Iago: Do not rise yet.
   (Iago kneels.)
   Witness, you ever-burning lights above,
   You elements that clip° us round about,
   Witness that here Iago doth give up   465
   The execution° of his wit,° hands, heart
   To wronged Othello's service! Let him command,
   And to obey shall be in me remorse,°
   What bloody business ever.

   [They rise.]

Othello: I greet thy love,
   Not with vain thanks but with acceptance bounteous,   470
   And will upon the instant put thee to't.
   Within these three days let me hear thee say
   That Cassio's not alive.
Iago: My friend is dead; 'tis done at your request.
   But let her live.   475
Othello: Damn her, lewd minx! O, damn her! damn her!
   Come, go with me apart. I will withdraw
   To furnish me with some swift means of death
   For the fair devil. Now art thou my lieutenant.
Iago: I am your own forever.   *Exeunt.*   480

SCENE IV: *The environs of the castle.*

Enter Desdemona, Emilia, and Clown.

Desdemona: Do you know, sirrah, where Lieutenant Cassio lies?°
Clown: I dare not say he lies anywhere.
Desdemona: Why, man?
Clown: He's a soldier, and for me to say a soldier lies is stabbing.
Desdemona: Go to. Where lodges he?   5
Clown: To tell you where he lodges is to tell you where I lie.
Desdemona: Can anything be made of this?
Clown: I know not where he lodges; and for me to devise a lodging,
   and say he lies here or he lies there, were to lie in mine own throat.
Desdemona: Can you enquire him out, and be edified by report?   10
Clown: I will catechize the world for him; that is, make questions,
   and by them answer.
Desdemona: Seek him, bid him come hither. Tell him I have moved°
   my lord on his behalf and hope all will be well.

---

464 *clip:* Encompass. 466 *execution:* Activities; *wit:* Mind. 468 *remorse:* Pity.
Scene IV. 1 *lies:* Lives, lodges. 13 *moved:* Made proposals to.

Clown: To do this is within the compass of man's wit, and therefore   15
    I'll attempt the doing of it.   *Exit.*
Desdemona: Where should I lose that handkerchief, Emilia?
Emilia: I know not, madam.
Desdemona: Believe me, I had rather have lost my purse
    Full of crusadoes;° and but my noble Moor   20
    Is true of mind, and made of no such baseness
    As jealous creatures are, it were enough
    To put him to ill thinking.
Emilia: Is he not jealous?
Desdemona: Who? he? I think the sun where he was born
    Drew all such humors° from him.

    Enter Othello.

Emilia: Look where he comes.   25
Desdemona: I will not leave him now till Cassio
    Be called to him — How is't with you, my lord?
Othello: Well, my good lady. *[Aside.]* O, hardness to dissemble! —
    How do you, Desdemona?
Desdemona: Well, my good lord.
Othello: Give me your hand. This hand is moist, my lady.   30
Desdemona: It yet hath felt no age nor known no sorrow.
Othello: This argues fruitfulness and liberal heart.
    Hot, hot, and moist. This hand of yours requires
    A sequester° from liberty, fasting and prayer,
    Much castigation, exercise devout;   35
    For here's a young and sweating devil here
    That commonly rebels. 'Tis a good hand,
    A frank one.
Desdemona: You may, indeed, say so;
    For 'twas that hand that gave away my heart.   40
Othello: A liberal hand! The hearts of old gave hands;
    But our new heraldry° is hands, not hearts.
Desdemona: I cannot speak of this. Come now, your promise!
Othello: What promise, chuck?
Desdemona: I have sent to bid Cassio come speak with you.   45
Othello: I have a salt and sorry rheum° offends me.
    Lend me thy handkerchief.
Desdemona: Here, my lord.
Othello: That which I gave you.
Desdemona: I have it not about me.
Othello: Not?
Desdemona: No, faith, my lord.

---

20 *crusadoes:* Portuguese gold coins.   25 *humors:* Inclinations.   34 *sequester:* Removal.
42 *heraldry:* Heraldic symbolism.   46 *salt . . . rheum:* Distressing head cold.

Othello: That's a fault.
    That handkerchief   50
    Did an Egyptian° to my mother give.
    She was a charmer,° and could almost read
    The thoughts of people. She told her, while she kept it,
    'Twould make her amiable° and subdue my father
    Entirely to her love; but if she lost it   55
    Or made a gift of it, my father's eye
    Should hold her loathèd, and his spirits should hunt
    After new fancies. She, dying, gave it me,
    And bid me, when my fate would have me wive;
    To give it her. I did so; and take heed on't;   60
    Make it a darling like your precious eye.
    To lose't or give't away were such perdition°
    As nothing else could match.
Desdemona: Is't possible?
Othello: 'Tis true. There's magic in the web of it.
    A sibyl that had numb'red in the world   65
    The sun to course two hundred compasses,°
    In her prophetic fury sewed the work;
    The worms were hallowed that did breed the silk;
    And it was dyed in mummy° which the skillful
    Conserved of maidens' hearts.
Desdemona: I' faith? Is't true?   70
Othello: Most veritable. Therefore look to't well.
Desdemona: Then would to God that I had never seen't!
Othello: Ha! Wherefore?
Desdemona: Why do you speak so startingly and rash?
Othello: Is't lost? Is't gone? Speak, is it out o' th' way?   75
Desdemona: Heaven bless us!
Othello: Say you?
Desdemona: It is not lost. But what an if it were?
Othello: How?
Desdemona: I say it is not lost.
Othello: Fetch't, let me see't!   80
Desdemona: Why, so I can, sir; but I will not now.
    This is a trick to put° me from my suit:
    Pray you let Cassio be received again.
Othello: Fetch me the handkerchief! My mind misgives.
Desdemona: Come, come!   85
    You'll never meet a more sufficient man.

---

51 *Egyptian:* Gypsy. 52 *charmer:* Sorceress. 54 *amiable:* Lovable. 62 *perdition:*
Disaster. 66 *compasses:* Annual rounds. 69 *mummy:* A drug made from mummies.
82 *put:* Divert.

Othello: The handkerchief!
    [*Desdemona:*   I pray talk me of Cassio.
Othello: The handkerchief!]
Desdemona: A man that all his time°
    Hath founded his good fortunes on your love,
    Shared dangers with you —   90
Othello: The handkerchief!
Desdemona: I' faith, you are to blame.
Othello: Zounds!   *Exit Othello.*
Emilia: Is not this man jealous?
Desdemona: I ne'er saw this before.   95
    Sure there's some wonder in this handkerchief;
    I am most unhappy in the loss of it.
Emilia: 'Tis not a year or two shows us a man.
    They are all but stomachs, and we all but food;
    They eat us hungerly, and when they are full,   100
    They belch us.

    Enter Iago and Cassio.

          Look you — Cassio and my husband!
Iago: There is no other way; 'tis she must do't.
    And lo the happiness!° Go and importune her.
Desdemona: How now, good Cassio? What's the news with you?
Cassio: Madam, my former suit. I do beseech you   105
    That by your virtuous means I may again
    Exist, and be a member of his love
    Whom I with all the office of my heart
    Entirely honor. I would not be delayed.
    If my offense be of such mortal kind   110
    That neither service past, nor present sorrows,
    Nor purposed merit in futurity,
    Can ransom me into his love again,
    But to know so must be my benefit.
    So shall I clothe me in a forced content,   115
    And shut myself up in° some other course,
    To fortune's alms.
Desdemona: Alas, thrice-gentle Cassio!
    My advocation° is not now in tune.
    My lord is not my lord; nor should I know him,
    Were he in favor° as in humor altered.   120
    So help me every spirit sanctified
    As I have spoken for you all my best

---

88 *all his time:* During his whole career. 103 *happiness:* Good luck. 116 *shut myself up in:* Confine myself to. 118 *advocation:* Advocacy. 120 *favor:* Appearance.

And stood within the blank° of his displeasure
For my free speech! You must a while be patient.
What I can do I will; and more I will   125
Than for myself I dare. Let that suffice you.

Iago: Is my lord angry?

Emilia: He went hence but now,
And certainly in strange unquietness.

Iago: Can he be angry? I have seen the cannon
When it hath blown his ranks into the air   130
And, like the devil, from his very arm
Puffed his own brother — and is he angry?
Something of moment then. I will go meet him.
There's matter in't indeed if he be angry.

Desdemona: I prithee do so.   *Exit [Iago].*
                                   Something sure of state,°   135
Either from Venice or some unhatched practice°
Made demonstrable here in Cyprus to him,
Hath puddled° his clear spirit; and in such cases
Men's natures wrangle with inferior things,
Though great ones are their object. 'Tis even so;   140
For let our finger ache, and it endues°
Our other, healthful members even to a sense
Of pain. Nay, we must think men are not gods,
Nor of them look for such observancy
As fits the bridal. Beshrew me much, Emilia,   145
I was, unhandsome warrior° as I am,
Arraigning his unkindness with my soul;°
But now I find I had suborned the witness,
And he's indicted falsely.

Emilia: Pray heaven it be state matters, as you think,   150
And no conception nor no jealous toy°
Concerning you.

Desdemona: Alas the day! I never gave him cause.

Emilia: But jealous souls will not be answered so;
They are not ever jealous for the cause,   155
But jealous for they're jealous. 'Tis a monster
Begot upon itself,° born on itself.

Desdemona: Heaven keep that monster from Othello's mind!

Emilia: Lady, amen.

Desdemona: I will go seek him. Cassio, walk here about: 160
If I do find him fit, I'll move your suit
And seek to effect it to my uttermost.

---

123 *blank:* Bull's-eye of the target.   135 *state:* Public affairs.   136 *unhatched practice:*
Budding plot.   138 *puddled:* Muddied.   141 *endues:* Brings.   146 *unhandsome
warrior:* Inadequate soldier.   147 *Arraigning . . . soul:* Indicting his unkindness
before the bar of my soul.   151 *toy:* Fancy.   157 *Begot upon itself:* Self-engendered.

Cassio: I humbly thank your ladyship.

Exeunt Desdemona and Emilia.

Enter Bianca.

Bianca: Save you, friend Cassio!
Cassio: What make you from home?
   How is't with you, my most fair Bianca?   165
   I' faith, sweet love, I was coming to your house.
Bianca: And I was going to your lodging, Cassio.
   What, keep a week away? seven days and nights?
   Eightscore eight hours? and lovers' absent hours,
   More tedious than the dial° eightscore times?   170
   O weary reck'ning!
Cassio: Pardon me, Bianca:
   I have this while with leaden thoughts been pressed;
   But I shall in a more continuate° time
   Strike off this score of absence. Sweet Bianca,

   [Gives her Desdemona's handkerchief.]

   Take me this work out.°
Bianca: O Cassio, whence came this?   175
   This is some token from a newer friend
   To the felt absence now I feel a cause.
   Is't come to this? Well, well.
Cassio: Go to, woman!
   Throw your vile guesses in the devil's teeth,
   From whence you have them. You are jealous now   180
   That this is from some mistress, some remembrance.
   No, by my faith, Bianca.
Bianca: Why, whose is it?
Cassio: I know not, sweet; I found it in my chamber.
   I like the work° well; ere it be demanded,
   As like enough it will, I'd have it copied.   185
   Take it and do't, and leave me for this time.
Bianca: Leave you? Wherefore?
Cassio: I do attend here on the general
   And think it no addition, nor my wish,
   To have him see me womaned.
Bianca: Why, I pray you?   190
Cassio: Not that I love you not.
Bianca: But that you do not love me!
   I pray you bring me on the way a little,
   And say if I shall see you soon at night.

---

170 *dial:* Clock.   173 *continuate:* Uninterrupted.   175 *Take . . . out:* Copy this embroidery for me.   184 *work:* Needlework.

Cassio: 'Tis but a little way that I can bring you,
For I attend here; but I'll see you soon.   195
Bianca: 'Tis very good. I must be circumstanced.°   *Exeunt.*

ACT IV

Scene I: *The environs of the castle.*

Enter Othello and Iago.

Iago: Will you think so?
Othello: Think so, Iago?
Iago: What,
To kiss in private?
Othello: An unauthorized kiss.
Iago: Or to be naked with her friend in bed
An hour or more, not meaning any harm?
Othello: Naked in bed, Iago, and not mean harm?   5
It is hypocrisy against the devil.°
They that mean virtuously, and yet do so,
The devil their virtue tempts, and they tempt heaven.
Iago: So they do nothing, 'tis a venial slip.
But if I give my wife a handkerchief—   10
Othello: What then?
Iago: Why, then 'tis hers, my lord; and being hers,
She may, I think, bestow't on any man.
Othello: She is protectress of her honor too;
May she give that?   15
Iago: Her honor is an essence that's not seen;
They have it very oft that have it not.
But for the handkerchief—
Othello: By heaven, I would most gladly have forgot it!
Thou said'st—O, it comes o'er my memory   20
As doth the raven o'er the infected° house,
Boding to all!—he had my handkerchief.
Iago: Ay, what of that?
Othello: That's not so good now.
Iago: What
If I had said I had seen him do you wrong?
Or heard him say—as knaves be such abroad   25
Who having, by their own importunate suit,

---

196 *circumstanced:* Governed by circumstances. **Act IV, Scene I.** 6 *hypocrisy . . .
devil:* i.e., feigned sin instead of feigned virtue.   21 *infected:* Plague-stricken.

Or voluntary dotage of some mistress,
Convincèd or supplied° them, cannot choose
But they must blab —
Othello: Hath he said anything?
Iago: He hath, my lord; but be you well assured,   30
No more than he'll unswear.
Othello: What hath he said?
Iago: Faith, that he did — I know not what he did.
Othello: What? what?
Iago: Lie —
Othello: With her?
Iago: With her, on her; what you will.   35
Othello: Lie with her? lie on her? — We say lie on her when they belie
her. — Lie with her! Zounds, that's fulsome. — Handkerchief —
confessions — handkerchief! — To confess, and be hanged for
his labor — first to be hanged, and then to confess! I tremble
at it. Nature would not invest herself in such shadowing pas-   40
sion without some instruction.° It is not words that shakes me
thus. — Pish! Noses, ears, and lips? Is't possible? — Confess? —
Handkerchief? — O devil!

(Falls in a trance.)

Iago: Work on,
My med'cine, work! Thus credulous fools are caught,   45
And many worthy and chaste dames even thus
All guiltless, meet reproach. — What, ho! my lord!
My lord, I say! Othello!
Enter Cassio.   How now, Cassio?
Cassio: What's the matter?
Iago: My lord is fall'n into an epilepsy.   50
This is his second fit; he had one yesterday.
Cassio: Rub him about the temples.
Iago: No, forbear.
The lethargy° must have his quiet course.
If not, he foams at mouth, and by and by
Breaks out to savage madness. Look, he stirs.   55
Do you withdraw yourself a little while.
He will recover straight. When he is gone,
I would on great occasion speak with you.   *[Exit Cassio.]*
How is it, general? Have you not hurt your head?
Othello: Dost thou mock me?

---

28 *Convincèd or supplied*: Overcome or gratified.   40–41 *Nature ... instruction*: My natural faculties would not be so overcome by passion without reason.   53 *lethargy*: Coma.

Iago: I mock you? No, by heaven.   60
    Would you would bear your fortune like a man!
Othello: A hornèd man's° a monster and a beast.
Iago: There's many a beast then in a populous city,
    And many a civil monster.
Othello: Did he confess it?
Iago: Good sir, be a man.   65
    Think every bearded fellow that's but yoked
    May draw with you. There's millions now alive
    That nightly lie in those unproper° beds
    Which they dare swear peculiar:° your case is better.
    O, 'tis the spite of hell, the fiend's arch-mock,   70
    To lip a wanton in a secure° couch,
    And to suppose her chaste! No, let me know;
    And knowing what I am, I know what she shall be.
Othello: O, thou art wise! 'Tis certain.
Iago: Stand you awhile apart;
    Confine yourself but in a patient list.°   75
    Whilst you were here, o'erwhelmèd with your grief —
    A passion most unsuiting such a man —
    Cassio came hither. I shifted him away
    And laid good 'scuse upon your ecstasy;°
    Bade him anon return, and here speak with me;   80
    The which he promised. Do but encave° yourself
    And mark the fleers, the gibes, and notable scorns
    That dwell in every region of his face;
    For I will make him tell the tale anew —
    Where, how, how oft, how long ago, and when   85
    He hath, and is again to cope° your wife.
    I say, but mark his gesture. Marry, patience!
    Or I shall say y'are all in all in spleen,°
    And nothing of a man.
Othello: Dost thou hear, Iago?
    I will be found most cunning in my patience;   90
    But — dost thou hear? — most bloody.
Iago: That's not amiss:
    But yet keep time in all. Will you withdraw?

                               [Othello retires.]

    Now will I question Cassio of Bianca,
    A huswife° that by selling her desires
    Buys herself bread and clothes. It is a creature   95

---

62 *hornèd man:* Cuckold. 68 *unproper:* Not exclusively their own. 69 *peculiar:* Exclusively their own. 71 *secure:* Free from fear of rivalry. 75 *in a patient list:* Within the limits of self-control. 79 *ecstasy:* Trance. 81 *encave:* Conceal. 86 *cope:* Meet. 88 *all in all in spleen:* Wholly overcome by your passion. 94 *huswife:* Hussy.

That dotes on Cassio, as 'tis the strumpet's plague
To beguile many and be beguiled by one.
He, when he hears of her, cannot refrain
From the excess of laughter. Here he comes.

Enter Cassio.

As he shall smile, Othello shall go mad;   100
And his unbookish° jealousy must conster°
Poor Cassio's smiles, gestures, and light behavior
Quite in the wrong. How do you now, lieutenant?
Cassio: The worser that you give me the addition°
Whose want even kills me.   105
Iago: Ply Desdemona well, and you are sure on't.
Now, if this suit lay in Bianca's power,
How quickly should you speed!
Cassio: Alas, poor caitiff!°
Othello: Look how he laughs already!
Iago: I never knew a woman love man so.   110
Cassio: Alas, poor rogue! I think, i' faith, she loves me.
Othello: Now he denies it faintly, and laughs it out.
Iago: Do you hear, Cassio?
Othello: Now he importunes him
To tell it o'er. Go to! Well said, well said!
Iago: She gives out that you shall marry her.   115
Do you intend it?
Cassio: Ha, ha, ha!
Othello: Do you triumph, Roman? Do you triumph?
Cassio: I marry her? What, a customer?° Prithee bear some charity to
my wit; do not think it so unwholesome. Ha, ha, ha!   120
Othello: So, so, so, so! They laugh that win!
Iago: Faith, the cry goes that you shall marry her.
Cassio: Prithee say true.
Iago: I am a very villain else.
Othello: Have you scored me?° Well.   125
Cassio: This is the monkey's own giving out. She is persuaded I will
marry her out of her own love and flattery, not out of my promise.
Othello: Iago beckons° me; now he begins the story.
Cassio: She was here even now; she haunts me in every place. I was
t' other day talking on the sea bank with certain Venetians, and   130
thither comes the bauble,° and, by this hand, she falls me thus
about my neck —

---

101 *unbookish:* Uninstructed; *conster:* Construe, interpret. 104 *addition:* Title.
108 *caitiff:* Wretch. 119 *customer:* Prostitute. 125 *scored me:* Settled my account (?).
128 *beckons:* Signals. 131 *bauble:* Plaything.

Othello: Crying "O dear Cassio!" as it were. His gesture imports it.

Cassio: So hangs, and lolls, and weeps upon me; so shakes and pulls
    me! Ha, ha, ha!   135

Othello: Now he tells how she plucked him to my chamber. O, I see
    that nose of yours, but not that dog I shall throw it to.

Cassio: Well, I must leave her company.

    Enter Bianca.

Iago: Before me! Look where she comes.

Cassio: 'Tis such another fitchew!° marry, a perfumed one. What do   140
    you mean by this haunting of me?

Bianca: Let the devil and his dam haunt you! What did you mean by
    that same handkerchief you gave me even now? I was a fine fool
    to take it. I must take out the whole work? A likely piece of work
    that you should find it in your chamber and know not who left it   145
    there! This is some minx's token, and I must take out the work?
    There! Give it your hobby-horse.° Wheresoever you had it, I'll
    take out no work on't.

Cassio: How now, my sweet Bianca? How now? how now?

Othello: By heaven, that should be my handkerchief!   150

Bianca: An you'll come to supper to-night, you may; an you will not,
    come when you are next prepared for.   *Exit.*

Iago: After her, after her!

Cassio: Faith, I must; she'll rail in the street else.

Iago: Will you sup there?   155

Cassio: Yes, I intend so.

Iago: Well, I may chance to see you; for I would very fain speak with
    you.

Cassio: Prithee come. Will you?

Iago: Go to! say no more.   *Exit Cassio.* 160

Othello [comes forward]: How shall I murder him, Iago?

Iago: Did you perceive how he laughed at his vice?°

Othello: O Iago!

Iago: And did you see the handkerchief?

Othello: Was that mine?   165

Iago: Your, by this hand! And to see how he prizes° the foolish
    woman your wife! She gave it him, and he hath giv'n it his
    whore.

Othello: I would have him nine years a-killing — A fine woman! a fair
    woman! a sweet woman!   170

Iago: Nay, you must forget that.

Othello: Ay, let her rot, and perish, and be damned to-night; for she
    shall not live. No, my heart is turned to stone; I strike it, and it

---

140 *fitchew:* Polecat (slang for *whore*). 147 *hobby-horse:* Harlot. 162 *vice:* i.e.,
vicious conduct. 166 *prizes:* Values.

hurts my hand. O, the world hath not a sweeter creature! She
might lie by an emperor's side and command him tasks.   175

Iago: Nay, that's not your way.

Othello: Hang her! I do but say what she is. So delicate with her needle!
an admirable musician! O, she will sing the savageness out of a bear!
Of so high and plenteous wit and invention° —

Iago: She's the worse for all this.   180

Othello: O, a thousand thousand times! And then, of so gentle a
condition!°

Iago: Ay, too gentle.

Othello: Nay, that's certain. But yet the pity of it, Iago! O Iago, the pity
of it, Iago!   185

Iago: If you are so fond over her iniquity, give her patent° to offend;
for if it touch not you, it comes near nobody.

Othello: I will chop her into messes! Cuckold me!

Iago: O, 'tis foul in her.

Othello: With mine officer!   190

Iago: That's fouler.

Othello: Get me some poison, Iago, this night. I'll not expostulate
with her, lest her body and beauty unprovide° my mind again.
This night, Iago!

Iago: Do it not with poison. Strangle her in her bed, even the bed she   195
hath contaminated.

Othello: Good, good! The justice of it pleases. Very good!

Iago: And for Cassio, let me be his undertaker;° you shall hear more
by midnight.

Othello: Excellent good!   200

A trumpet.

What trumpet is that same?

Iago: I warrant something from Venice.

Enter Lodovico, Desdemona, and Attendants.

'Tis Lodovico.
This comes from the Duke; and see, your wife is with him.

Lodovico: God save you, worthy general!

Othello: With all my heart, sir.

Lodovico: The Duke and senators of Venice greet you.   205

[Gives him a letter.]

Othello: I kiss the instrument of their pleasures.

[Opens the letter and reads.]

Desdemona: And what's the news, good cousin Lodovico?

179 *invention:* Imagination. 182 *condition:* Disposition. 186 *patent:* License.
193 *unprovide:* Disarm. 198 *be his undertaker:* Undertake to deal with him.

Iago: I am very glad to see you, signior.
    Welcome to Cyprus.
Lodovico: I thank you. How does Lieutenant Cassio?
Iago: Lives, sir.   210
Desdemona: Cousin, there's fall'n between him and my lord
    An unkind breach; but you shall make all well.
Othello: Are you sure of that?
Desdemona: My lord?
Othello [reads]: "This fail you not to do, as you will —"   215
Lodovico: He did not call; he's busy in the paper.
    Is there division 'twixt thy lord and Cassio?
Desdemona: A most unhappy one. I would do much
    T' atone° them, for the love I bear to Cassio.
Othello: Fire and brimstone!
Desdemona: My lord?
Othello: Are you wise?   220
Desdemona: What, is he angry?
Lodovico: May be the letter moved him;
    For, as I think, they do command him home,
    Deputing Cassio in his government.
Desdemona: By my troth, I am glad on't.
Othello: Indeed?
Desdemona: My lord?
Othello: I am glad to see you mad.°
Desdemona: Why, sweet Othello —   225
Othello: Devil!

    [Strikes her.]

Desdemona: I have not deserved this.
Lodovico: My lord, this would not be believed in Venice,
    Though I should swear I saw't. 'Tis very much.
    Make her amends; she weeps.
Othello: O devil, devil!   230
    If that the earth could teem° with woman's tears,
    Each drop she falls would prove a crocodile.°
    Out of my sight!
Desdemona: I will not stay to offend you.   *[Going.]*
Lodovico: Truly, an obedient lady.
    I do beseech your lordship call her back.   235
Othello: Mistress!
Desdemona: My lord?
Othello: What would you with her, sir?
Lodovico: Who? I, my lord?
Othello: Ay! You did wish that I would make her turn.

---

219 *atone:* Reconcile. 225 *mad:* i.e., waggish. 231 *teem:* Breed. 232 *crocodile:* (Crocodiles were supposed to shed hypocritical tears to lure men to destruction).

Sir, she can turn, and turn, and yet go on   240
And turn again; and she can weep, sir, weep;
And she's obedient; as you say, obedient,
Very obedient. — Proceed you in your tears. —
Concerning this, sir — O well-painted passion!° —
I am commanded home. — Get you away;   245
I'll send for you anon. — Sir, I obey the mandate
And will return to Venice. — Hence, avaunt!

                          [Exit Desdemona.]

Cassio shall have my place. And, sir, to-night
I do entreat that we may sup together.
You are welcome, sir, to Cyprus — Goats and monkeys!   *Exit.*   250

Lodovico: Is this the noble Moor whom our full Senate
  Call all in all sufficient? Is this the nature
  Whom passion could not shake? whose solid virtue
  The shot of accident nor dart of chance
  Could neither graze nor pierce?

Iago: He is much changed.   255

Lodovico: Are his wits safe? Is he not light of brain?

Iago: He's that he is; I may not breathe my censure.
  What he might be — if what he might he is not —
  I would to heaven he were!

Lodovico: What, strike his wife?

Iago: Faith, that was not so well; yet would I knew   260
  That stroke would prove the worst!

Lodovico: Is it his use?°
  Or did the letters work upon his blood
  And new-create this fault?

Iago: Alas, alas!
  It is not honesty in me to speak
  What I have seen and known. You shall observe him,   265
  And his own courses will denote him so
  That I may save my speech. Do but go after
  And mark how he continues.

Lodovico: I am sorry that I am deceived in him.   *Exeunt.*

Scene II: *Within the castle.*

  Enter Othello and Emilia.

Othello: You have seen nothing then?

Emilia: Nor ever heard, nor ever did suspect.

Othello: Yes, you have seen Cassio and she together.

Emilia: But then I saw no harm, and then I heard
  Each syllable that breath made up between them.   5

Othello: What, did they never whisper?

---

244 *passion:* Grief.   261 *use:* Custom.

Emilia: Never, my lord.
Othello: Nor send you out o' th' way?
Emilia: Never.
Othello: To fetch her fan, her gloves, her mask, nor nothing?
Emilia: Never, my lord.   10
Othello: That's strange.
Emilia: I durst, my lord, to wager she is honest,
        Lay down my soul at stake. If you think other,
        Remove your thought; it doth abuse your bosom.°
        If any wretch have put this in your head,   15
        Let heaven requite it with the serpent's curse!°
        For if she be not honest, chaste, and true,
        There's no man happy; the purest of their wives
        Is foul as slander.
Othello: Bid her come hither. Go.   *Exit Emilia.*
        She says enough; yet she's a simple bawd   20
        That cannot say as much. This is a subtle whore,
        A closet lock and key of villainous secrets;
        And yet she'll kneel and pray; I have seen her do't.

        Enter Desdemona and Emilia.

Desdemona: My lord, what is your will?
Othello: Pray, chuck, come hither.
Desdemona: What is your pleasure?
Othello: Let me see your eyes.   25
        Look in my face.
Desdemona: What horrible fancy's this?
Othello [to Emilia]: Some of your function, mistress.
        Leave procreants° alone and shut the door;
        Cough or cry hem if anybody come.
        Your mystery, your mystery!° Nay, dispatch!   30
                                                        Exit Emilia.
Desdemona: Upon my knees, what doth your speech import?
        I understand a fury in your words,
        [But not the words.]
Othello: Why, what art thou?
Desdemona: Your wife, my lord; your true
        And loyal wife.
Othello: Come, swear it, damn thyself;   35
        Lest, being like one of heaven,° the devils themselves
        Should fear to seize thee. Therefore be double-damned —
        Swear thou art honest.°

Scene II. 14 *abuse your bosom:* Deceive your heart. 16 *serpent's curse:* (cf. Genesis
3:14). 28 *procreants:* Mating couples. 30 *mystery:* Trade, occupation. 36 *being . . .
heaven:* Looking like an angel. 38 *honest:* Chaste.

Desdemona: Heaven doth truly know it.
Othello: Heaven truly knows that thou art false as hell.
Desdemona: To whom, my lord? With whom? How am I false?   40
Othello: Ah, Desdemona! away! away! away!
Desdemona: Alas the heavy day! Why do you weep?
    Am I the motive of these tears, my lord?
    If haply you my father do suspect
    An instrument° of this your calling back,   45
    Lay not your blame on me. If you have lost him,
    Why, I have lost him too.
Othello: Had it pleased heaven
    To try me with affliction, had they rained
    All kinds of sores and shames on my bare head,
    Steeped me in poverty to the very lips,   50
    Given to captivity me and my utmost hopes,
    I should have found in some place of my soul
    A drop of patience. But, alas, to make me
    A fixèd figure for the time of scorn°
    To point his slow unmoving finger at!   55
    Yet could I bear that too; well, very well.
    But there where I have garnered up my heart,
    Where either I must live or bear no life,
    The fountain from the which my current runs
    Or else dries up — to be discarded thence,   60
    Or keep it as a cistern for foul toads
    To knot and gender in — turn thy complexion there,°
    Patience, thou young and rose-lipped cherubin!
    Ay, there look grim as hell!
Desdemona: I hope my noble lord esteems me honest.   65
Othello: O, ay; as summer flies are in the shambles,°
    That quicken° even with blowing. O thou weed,
    Who art so lovely fair, and smell'st so sweet,
    That the sense aches at thee, would thou hadst ne'er been born!
Desdemona: Alas, what ignorant sin have I committed?   70
Othello: Was this fair paper, this most goodly book,
    Made to write "whore" upon? What committed?
    Committed? O thou public commoner!°
    I should make very forges of my cheeks
    That would to cinders burn up modesty,   75
    Did I but speak thy deeds. What committed?
    Heaven stops the nose at it, and the moon winks;°

---

45 *An instrument:* To be the cause.   54 *time of scorn:* Scornful world.   62 *turn thy complexion there:* Change thy color at that point.   66 *shambles:* Slaughterhouse.   67 *quicken:* Come to life.   73 *commoner:* Harlot.   77 *winks:* Closes her eyes.

The bawdy wind, that kisses all it meets,
Is hushed within the hollow mine of earth
And will not hear it. What committed?   80
Impudent strumpet!
Desdemona: By heaven, you do me wrong!
Othello: Are not you a strumpet?
Desdemona: No, as I am a Christian!
If to preserve this vessel for my lord
From any other foul unlawful touch
Be not to be a strumpet, I am none.   85
Othello: What, not a whore?
Desdemona: No, as I shall be saved!
Othello: Is't possible?
Desdemona: O, heaven forgive us!
Othello: I cry you mercy° then.
I took you for that cunning whore of Venice
That married with Othello. — *[Calling.]* You, mistress,   90
That have the office opposite to Saint Peter
And keep the gate of hell!

    Enter Emilia.

                         You, you, ay, you!
We have done our course; there's money for your pains:
I pray you turn the key, and keep our counsel.   *Exit.*
Emilia: Alas, what does this gentleman conceive?   95
How do you, madam? How do you, my good lady?
Desdemona: Faith, half asleep.°
Emilia: Good madam, what's the matter with my lord?
Desdemona: With who?
Emilia: Why, with my lord, madam.   100
Desdemona: Who is thy lord?
Emilia: He that is yours, sweet lady.
Desdemona: I have none. Do not talk to me, Emilia.
I cannot weep; nor answer have I none
But what should go by water. Prithee to-night
Lay on my bed my wedding sheets, remember;   105
And call thy husband hither.
Emilia: Here's a change indeed!   *Exit.*
Desdemona: 'Tis meet I should be used so, very meet.
How have I been behaved, that he might stick
The small'st opinion° on my least misuse?°

    Enter Iago and Emilia.

---

88 *cry you mercy:* Beg your pardon. 97 *half asleep:* i.e., stunned. 109 *small'st
opinion:* Least suspicion; *least misuse:* Slightest misconduct.

Iago: What is your pleasure, madam? How is't with you?   110
Desdemona: I cannot tell. Those that do teach young babes
    Do it with gentle means and easy tasks:
    He might have chid me so; for, in good faith,
    I am a child to chiding.
Iago: What is the matter, lady?
Emilia: Alas, Iago, my lord hath so bewhored her,   115
    Thrown such despite and heavy terms upon her
    As true hearts cannot bear.
Desdemona: Am I that name, Iago?
Iago: What name, fair lady?
Desdemona: Such as she said my lord did say I was.
Emilia: He called her whore. A beggar in his drink   120
    Could not have laid such terms upon his callet.°
Iago: Why did he so?
Desdemona: I do not know; I am sure I am none such.
Iago: Do not weep, do not weep. Alas the day!
Emilia: Hath she forsook so many noble matches,   125
    Her father and her country, and her friends,
    To be called whore? Would it not make one weep?
Desdemona: It is my wretched fortune.
Iago: Beshrew him for't!
    How comes this trick° upon him?
Desdemona: Nay, heaven doth know.
Emilia: I will be hanged if some eternal villain,   130
    Some busy and insinuating rogue,
    Some cogging, cozening° slave, to get some office,
    Have not devised this slander. I'll be hanged else.
Iago: Fie, there is no such man! It is impossible.
Desdemona: If any such there be, heaven pardon him!   135
Emilia: A halter pardon him! and hell gnaw his bones!
    Why should he call her whore? Who keeps her company?
    What place? what time? what form? what likelihood?
    The Moor 's abused by some most villainous knave,
    Some base notorious knave, some scurvy fellow.   140
    O heaven, that such companions° thou 'dst unfold,°
    And put in every honest hand a whip
    To lash the rascals naked through the world
    Even from the east to th' west!
Iago: Speak within door.°
Emilia: O, fie upon them! Some such squire he was   145
    That turned your wit the seamy side without

---

121 *callet:* Whore.   129 *trick:* Freakish behavior.   132 *cogging, cozening:* Cheating, defrauding.   141 *companions:* Rogues;   *unfold:* Expose.   144 *within door:* With restraint.

And made you to suspect me with the Moor.
Iago: You are a fool. Go to.
Desdemona: Alas, Iago,
    What shall I do to win my lord again?
    Good friend, go to him; for, by this light of heaven,   150
    I know not how I lost him. Here I kneel:
    If e'er my will did trespass 'gainst his love
    Either in discourse° of thought or actual deed,
    Or that mine eyes, mine ears, or any sense
    Delighted them in any other form,   155
    Or that I do not yet, and ever did,
    And ever will (though he do shake me off
    To beggarly divorcement) love him dearly,
    Comfort forswear° me! Unkindness may do much;
    And his unkindness may defeat° my life,   160
    But never taint my love. I cannot say "whore."
    It does abhor me now I speak the word;
    To do the act that might the addition earn
    Not the world's mass of vanity could make me.
Iago: I pray you be content. 'Tis but his humor.   165
    The business of the state does him offense,
    [And he does chide with you.]
Desdemona: If 'twere no other —
Iago: 'Tis but so, I warrant.

    [Trumpets within.]

    Hark how these instruments summon you to supper.
    The messengers of Venice stay the meat: 170
    Go in, and weep not. All things shall be well.
                    Exeunt Desdemona and Emilia.

    Enter Roderigo.

    How now, Roderigo?
Roderigo: I do not find that thou deal'st justly with me.
Iago: What in the contrary?
Roderigo: Every day thou daff'st me with some device,° Iago, and   175
    rather, as it seems to me now, keep'st from me all conveniency°
    than suppliest me with the least advantage of hope. I will indeed
    no longer endure it; nor am I yet persuaded to put up in peace
    what already I have foolishly suffered.
Iago: Will you hear me, Roderigo?   180

---

153 *discourse:* Course.   159 *Comfort forswear:* Happiness forsake.   160 *defeat:*
Destroy.   175 *thou . . . device:* You put me off with some trick.   176 *conveniency:*
Favorable opportunities.

Roderigo: Faith, I have heard too much; for your words and performances are no kin together.

Iago: You charge me most unjustly.

Roderigo: With naught but truth. I have wasted myself out of my
means. The jewels you have had from me to deliver to Desde-   185
mona would half have corrupted a votarist.° You have told me she
hath received them, and returned me expectations and comforts
of sudden respect° and acquaintance; but I find none.

Iago: Well, go to; very well.

Roderigo: Very well! go to! I cannot go to, man; nor 'tis not very   190
well. By this hand, I say 'tis very scurvy, and begin to find myself
fopped° in it.

Iago: Very well.

Roderigo: I tell you 'tis not very well. I will make myself known to
Desdemona. If she will return me my jewels, I will give over my   195
suit and repent my unlawful solicitation; if not, assure yourself I
will seek satisfaction of you.

Iago: You have said now.

Roderigo: Ay, and said nothing but what I protest intendment of
doing.   200

Iago: Why, now I see there's mettle in thee; and even from this instant
do build on thee a better opinion than ever before. Give me thy
hand, Roderigo. Thou has taken against me a most just exception;
but yet I protest I have dealt most directly° in thy affair.

Roderigo: It hath not appeared.   205

Iago: I grant indeed it hath not appeared, and your suspicion is not
without wit and judgment. But, Roderigo, if thou hast that in thee
indeed which I have greater reason to believe now than ever, I
mean purpose, courage, and valor, this night show it. If thou the
next night following enjoy not Desdemona, take me from this   210
world with treachery and devise engines for° my life.

Roderigo: Well, what is it? Is it within reason and compass?

Iago: Sir, there is especial commission come from Venice to depute
Cassio in Othello's place.

Roderigo: Is that true? Why, then Othello and Desdemona return   215
again to Venice.

Iago: O, no; he goes into Mauritania and takes away with him
the fair Desdemona, unless his abode be lingered here° by some
accident; wherein none can be so determinate° as the removing
of Cassio.   220

Roderigo: How do you mean removing of him?

Iago: Why, by making him uncapable of Othello's place — knocking
out his brains.

---

186 *votarist:* Nun.   188 *sudden respect:* Immediate notice.   192 *fopped:* Duped.
204 *directly:* Straightforwardly.   211 *engines for:* Plots against.   218 *abode ... here:*
Stay here be extended.   219 *determinate:* Effective.

Roderigo: And that you would have me to do?

Iago: Ay, if you dare do yourself a profit and a right. He sups to-night   225
with a harlotry, and thither will I go to him. He knows not yet of
his honorable fortune. If you will watch his going thence, which I
will fashion to fall out between twelve and one, you may take him
at your pleasure. I will be near to second your attempt, and he
shall fall between us. Come, stand not amazed at it, but go along   230
with me. I will show you such a necessity in his death that you
shall think yourself bound to put it on him. It is now high supper
time, and the night grows to waste. About it!

Roderigo: I will hear further reason for this.

Iago: And you shall be satisfied.   *Exeunt.*   235

SCENE III: *Within the castle.*

    Enter Othello, Lodovico, Desdemona, Emilia, and Attendants.

Lodovico: I do beseech you, sir, trouble yourself no further.

Othello: O, pardon me; 'twill do me good to walk.

Lodovico: Madam, good night. I humbly thank your ladyship.

Desdemona: Your honor is most welcome.

Othello: Will you walk, sir?
    O, Desdemona —   5

Desdemona: My lord?

Othello: Get you to bed on th' instant; I will be returned forthwith.
    Dismiss your attendant there. Look't be done.

Desdemona: I will, my lord.

    Exit [Othello, with Lodovico and Attendants].

Emilia: How goes it now? He looks gentler than he did.   10

Desdemona: He says he will return incontinent.°
    He hath commanded me to go to bed,
    And bade me to dismiss you.

Emilia: Dismiss me?

Desdemona: It was his bidding; therefore, good Emilia,
    Give me my nightly wearing, and adieu.   15
    We must not now displease him.

Emilia: I would you had never seen him!

Desdemona: So would not I. My love doth so approve him
    That even his stubbornness,° his checks,° his frowns —
    Prithee unpin me — have grace and favor in them.   20

Emilia: I have laid those sheets you bade me on the bed.

Desdemona: All's one. Good faith, how foolish are our minds!
    If I do die before thee, prithee shroud me
    In one of those same sheets.

Scene III.   11 *incontinent:* At once.   19 *stubbornness:* Roughness;   *checks:* Rebukes.

Emilia: Come, come! You talk.

Desdemona: My mother had a maid called Barbary.   25
    She was in love; and he she loved proved mad°
    And did forsake her. She had a song of "Willow";
    An old thing 'twas; but it expressed her fortune,
    And she died singing it. That song to-night
    Will not go from my mind; I have much to do   30
    But to go hang my head all at one side
    And sing it like poor Barbary. Prithee dispatch.

Emilia: Shall I go fetch your nightgown?°

Desdemona: No, unpin me here.
    This Lodovico is a proper man.

Emilia: A very handsome man.   35

Desdemona: He speaks well.

Emilia: I know a lady in Venice would have walked barefoot to
    Palestine for a touch of his nether lip.

Desdemona (sings): "The poor soul sat sighing by a sycamore tree
      Sing all a green willow;   40
   Her hand on her bosom, her head on her knee,
      Sing willow, willow, willow.
   The fresh streams ran by her and murmured her moans;
      Sing willow, willow, willow;
   Her salt tears fell from her, and soft'ned the stones" —   45
    Lay by these.
      "Sing willow, willow, willow" —
    Prithee hie thee;° he'll come anon.
      "Sing all a green willow must be my garland.
   Let nobody blame him; his scorn I approve" —   50
    Nay, that's not next. Hark! who is't that knocks?

Emilia: It's the wind.

Desdemona (sings): "I call my love false love; but what said he then?
      Sing willow, willow, willow:
   If I court moe women, you'll couch with moe men."   55
    So get thee gone; good night. Mine eyes do itch.
    Doth that bode weeping?

Emilia: 'Tis neither here nor there.

Desdemona: I have heard it said so. O, these men, these men!
    Dost thou in conscience think — tell me, Emilia —
    That there be women do abuse their husbands   60
    In such gross kind?

Emilia: There be some such, no question.

Desdemona: Wouldst thou do such a deed for all the world?

Emilia: Why, would not you?

---

26 *mad:* Wild, faithless.   33 *nightgown:* Dressing gown.   48 *hie thee:* Hurry.

Desdemona: No, by this heavenly light!
Emilia: Nor I neither by this heavenly light.
    I might do't as well i' th' dark.   65
Desdemona: Wouldst thou do such a deed for all the world?
Emilia: The world's a huge thing; it is a great price for a small vice.
Desdemona: In troth, I think thou wouldst not.
Emilia: In troth, I think I should; and undo't when I had done it.
    Marry, I would not do such a thing for a joint-ring,° nor for mea-   70
    sures of lawn, nor for gowns, petticoats, nor caps, nor any petty
    exhibition;° but, for all the whole world — 'Ud's pity! who would
    not make her husband a cuckold to make him a monarch? I
    should venture purgatory for't.
Desdemona: Beshrew me if I would do such a wrong   75
    For the whole world.
Emilia: Why, the wrong is but a wrong i' th' world; and having the
    world for your labor, 'tis a wrong in your own world, and you might
    quickly make it right.
Desdemona: I do not think there is any such woman.   80
Emilia: Yes, a dozen; and as many to th' vantage° as
    would store° the world they played for.
    But I do think it is their husbands' faults
    If wives do fall. Say that they slack their duties
    And pour our treasures into foreign laps;   85
    Or else break out in peevish° jealousies,
    Throwing restraint upon us; or say they strike us,
    Or scant our former having° in despite —
    Why, we have galls;° and though we have some grace,
    Yet have we some revenge. Let husbands know   90
    Their wives have sense like them. They see, and smell,
    And have their palates both for sweet and sour,
    As husbands have. What is it that they do
    When they change us for others? Is it sport?
    I think it is. And doth affection breed it?   95
    I think it doth. Is't frailty that thus errs?
    It is so too. And have not we affections,
    Desires for sport, and frailty, as men have?
    Then let them use us well; else let them know,
    The ills we do, their ills instruct us so.   100
Desdemona: Good night, good night. God me such usage° send,
    Not to pick bad from bad, but by bad mend!   *Exeunt.*

---

70 *joint-ring:* Ring made in separable halves.   72 *exhibition:* Gift.   81 *to th' vantage:*
Besides.   82 *store:* Populate.   86 *peevish:* Senseless.   88 *having:* Allowance.   89 *galls:*
Spirits to resent.   101 *usage:* Habits.

ACT V

Scene I: *A street in Cyprus.*

Enter Iago and Roderigo.

Iago: Here, stand behind this bulk;° straight will he come.
Wear thy good rapier bare, and put it home.
Quick, quick! Fear nothing; I'll be at thy elbow.
It makes us, or it mars us — think on that,
And fix most firm thy resolution.   5
Roderigo: Be near at hand; I may miscarry in't.
Iago: Here, at thy hand. Be bold, and take thy stand.

[Stands aside.]

Roderigo: I have no great devotion to the deed,
And yet he hath given me satisfying reasons.
'Tis but a man gone. Forth my sword! He dies!   10
Iago: I have rubbed this young quat° almost to the sense,°
And he grows angry. Now whether he kill Cassio,
Or Cassio him, or each do kill the other,
Every way makes my gain. Live Roderigo,
He calls me to a restitution large   15
Of gold and jewels that I bobbed° from him
As gifts to Desdemona.
It must not be. If Cassio do remain,
He hath a daily beauty in his life
That makes me ugly; and besides, the Moor   20
May unfold me to him; there stand I in much peril.
No, he must die. Be't so! I hear him coming.

Enter Cassio.

Roderigo: I know his gait. 'Tis he. Villain, thou diest!

[Makes a pass at Cassio.]

Cassio: That thrust had been mine enemy indeed
But that my coat° is better than thou know'st.   25
I will make proof of thine.

[Draws, and wounds Roderigo.]

Roderigo: O, I am slain!

[Iago darts from concealment behind Cassio, wounds him in the leg, and exit.]

Act V, Scene I. 1 *bulk:* Projecting shop-front.   11 *quat:* Pimple;   *sense:* Quick.
16 *bobbed:* Swindled.   25 *coat:* Undershirt of mail.

Cassio: I am maimed for ever. Help, ho! Murder! murder!

> [*Falls.*]
> *Enter Othello.*

Othello: The voice of Cassio. Iago keeps his word.

Roderigo: O, villain that I am!

Othello: It is even so.

Cassio: O, help, ho! light! a surgeon!   30

Othello: 'Tis he. O brave Iago, honest and just,
That hast such noble sense of thy friend's wrong!
Thou teachest me. Minion,° your dear lies dead,
And your unblest fate hies.° Strumpet, I come.
Forth of my heart those charms, thine eyes, are blotted.   35
Thy bed, lust-stained, shall with lust's blood be spotted.

> *Exit Othello.*

> *Enter Lodovico and Gratiano.*

Cassio: What, ho? No watch? No passage?° Murder! murder!

Gratiano: 'Tis some mischance. The cry is very direful.

Cassio: O, help!

Lodovico: Hark!   40

Roderigo: O wretched villain!

Lodovico: Two or three groan. It is a heavy° night.
These may be counterfeits. Let's think't unsafe
To come in to the cry without more help.

Roderigo: Nobody come? Then shall I bleed to death.   45

Lodovico: Hark!

> *Enter Iago, with a light.*

Gratiano: Here's one comes in his shirt, with light and weapons.

Iago: Who's there? Whose noise is this that cries on° murder?

Lodovico: We do not know.

Iago: Did not you hear a cry?

Cassio: Here, here! For heaven's sake, help me!

Iago: What's the matter?   50

Gratiano: This is Othello's ancient, as I take it.

Lodovico: The same indeed, a very valiant fellow.

Iago: What are you here that cry so grievously?

Cassio: Iago? O, I am spoiled, undone by villains!
Give me some help.   55

Iago: O me, lieutenant! What villains have done this?

Cassio: I think that one of them is hereabout
And cannot make° away.

---

33 *Minion:* Mistress.   34 *hies:* Hurries on.   37 *passage:* Passersby.   42 *heavy:* Cloudy, dark.   48 *cries on:* Raises the cry of.   58 *make:* Get.

Iago: O treacherous villains!

   [To Lodovico and Gratiano.]

  What are you there? Come in, and give some help.

Roderigo: O, help me here!   60

Cassio: That's one of them.

Iago: O murd'rous slave! O villain!

   [Stabs Roderigo.]

Roderigo: O damned Iago! O inhuman dog!

Iago: Kill men i' th' dark? — Where be these bloody thieves? —

  How silent is this town! — Ho! murder! murder! —

  What may you be? Are you of good or evil?   65

Lodovico: As you shall prove us, praise us.

Iago: Signior Lodovico?

Lodovico: He, sir.

Iago: I cry you mercy. Here's Cassio hurt by villains.

Gratiano: Cassio?   70

Iago: How is't, brother?

Cassio: My leg is cut in two.

Iago: Marry,° heaven forbid!

  Light, gentlemen. I'll bind it with my shirt.

   Enter Bianca.

Bianca: What is the matter, ho? Who is't that cried?

Iago: Who is't that cried?   75

Bianca: O my dear Cassio! my sweet Cassio!

  O Cassio, Cassio, Cassio!

Iago: O notable strumpet! — Cassio, may you suspect

  Who they should be that have thus mangled you?

Cassio: No.   80

Gratiano: I am sorry to find you thus. I have been to seek you.

Iago: Lend me a garter. So. O for a chair°

  To bear him easily hence!

Bianca: Alas, he faints! O Cassio, Cassio, Cassio!

Iago: Gentlemen all, I do suspect this trash   85

  To be a party in this injury. —

  Patience a while, good Cassio. — Come, come!

  Lend me a light. Know we this face or no?

  Alas, my friend and my dear countryman

  Roderigo? No — Yes, sure. — O heaven, Roderigo!   90

Gratiano: What, of Venice?

Iago: Even he, sir. Did you know him?

Gratiano: Know him? Ay.

---

72 *Marry:* (From "By Mary").   82 *chair:* Litter.

Iago: Signior Gratiano? I cry your gentle pardon.
     These bloody accidents must excuse my manners
     That so neglected you.
Gratiano: I am glad to see you.   95
Iago: How do you, Cassio? — O, a chair, a chair!
Gratiano: Roderigo?
Iago: He, he, 'tis he!

     [A chair brought in.]

     O, that's well said;° the chair.
     Some good man bear him carefully from hence.   100
     I'll fetch the general's surgeon. *[To Bianca.]* For you, mistress,
     Save you your labor. — He that lies slain here, Cassio,
     Was my dear friend. What malice was between you?
Cassio: None in the world; nor do I know the man.
Iago [to Bianca]: What, look you pale? — O, bear him out o' th' air.   105

          [Cassio and Roderigo are borne off.]

     Stay you, good gentlemen. — Look you pale, mistress? —
     Do you perceive the gastness° of her eye? —
     Nay, if you stare, we shall hear more anon.
     Behold her well; I pray you look upon her.
     Do you see, gentlemen? Nay, guiltiness will speak.   110
     Though tongues were out of use.

     Enter Emilia.

Emilia: 'Las, what's the matter? What's the matter, husband?
Iago: Cassio hath here been set on in the dark
     By Roderigo, and fellows that are scaped.
     He's almost slain, and Roderigo dead.   115
Emilia: Alas, good gentlemen! alas, good Cassio!
Iago: This is the fruits of whoring. Prithee, Emilia,
     Go know of Cassio where he supped to-night.

     [To Bianca.]

     What, do you shake at that?
Bianca: He supped at my house; but I therefore shake not.   120
Iago: O, did he so? I charge you go with me.
Emilia: Fie, fie upon thee, strumpet!
Bianca: I am no strumpet, but of life as honest°
     As you that thus abuse me.
Emilia: As I? Foh! fie upon thee!
Iago: Kind gentlemen, let's go see poor Cassio dressed.   125

---

99 *well said:* Well done.   107 *gastness:* Terror.   123 *honest:* Chaste.

[To Bianca.]

Come, mistress, you must tell 's another tale.
Emilia, run you to the citadel
And tell my lord and lady what hath happed.

                                                            [Exit Emilia.]

Will you go on afore?   *Exeunt [all but Iago].*
                        This is the night
That either makes me or fordoes° me quite.   *[Exit.]* 130

SCENE II: *A bedchamber in the castle.*

Desdemona [asleep] in her bed. Enter Othello with a light.

Othello: It is the cause, it is the cause,° my soul.
Let me not name it to you, you chaste stars!
It is the cause. Yet I'll not shed her blood,
Nor scar that whiter skin of hers than snow,
And smooth as monumental alabaster.   5
Yet she must die, else she'll betray more men.
Put out the light, and then put out the light.
If I quench thee, thou flaming minister,°
I can again thy former light restore,
Should I repent me; but once put out thy light,   10
Thou cunning'st pattern of excelling nature,
I know not where is that Promethean heat°
That can thy light relume.° When I have plucked the rose,
I cannot give it vital growth again;
It needs must wither. I'll smell thee on the tree.   15

(He kisses her.)

O balmy breath, that dost almost persuade
Justice to break her sword! One more, one more!
Be thus when thou art dead, and I will kill thee,
And love thee after. One more, and that's the last!
So sweet was ne'er so fatal. I must weep,   20
But they are cruel tears. This sorrow's heavenly;
It strikes where it doth love. She wakes.
Desdemona: Who's there? Othello?
Othello: Ay, Desdemona.
Desdemona: Will you come to bed, my lord?
Othello: Have you prayed to-night, Desdemon?
Desdemona: Ay, my lord.   25

---

130 *fordoes:* Destroys. **Scene II.** 1 *cause:* Cause of justice. 8 *minister:* Servant.
12 *Promethean heat:* Divine fire. 13 *relume:* Relight.

Othello: If you bethink yourself of any crime°
 Unreconciled as yet to heaven and grace,
 Solicit for it straight.
Desdemona: Alack, my lord, what may you mean by that?
Othello: Well, do it, and be brief; I will walk by.   30
 I would not kill thy unpreparèd spirit.
 No, heaven forfend!° I would not kill thy soul.
Desdemona: Talk you of killing?
Othello: Ay, I do.
Desdemona: Then heaven
 Have mercy on me!
Othello: Amen, with all my heart!
Desdemona: If you say so, I hope you will not kill me.   35
Othello: Hum!
Desdemona: And yet I fear you; for you're fatal then
 When your eyes roll so. Why I should fear I know not,
 Since guiltiness I know not; but yet I feel I fear.
Othello: Think on thy sins.
Desdemona: They are loves I bear to you.   40
Othello: Ay, and for that thou diest.
Desdemona: That death's unnatural that kills for loving.
 Alas, why gnaw you so your nether lip?
 Some bloody passion shakes your very frame.
 These are portents,° but yet I hope, I hope,   45
 They do not point on me.
Othello: Peace and be still!
Desdemona: I will so. What's the matter?
Othello: That handkerchief which I so loved and gave thee
 Thou gav'st to Cassio.
Desdemona: No, by my life and soul!
 Send for the man and ask him.
Othello: Sweet soul, take heed,   50
 Take heed of perjury; thou art on thy deathbed.
Desdemona: Ay, but not yet to die.
Othello: Yes, presently.°
 Therefore confess thee freely of thy sin;
 For to deny each article with oath
 Cannot remove nor choke the strong conception°   55
 That I do groan withal. Thou art to die.
Desdemona: Then Lord have mercy on me!
Othello: I say amen.

---

26 *crime:* Sin. 32 *forfend:* Forbid. 45 *portents:* Signs of impending violence.
52 *presently:* At once. 55 *conception:* Belief.

Desdemona: And have you mercy too! I never did
    Offend° you in my life; never loved Cassio
    But with such general warranty of heaven   60
    As I might love. I never gave him token.
Othello: By heaven, I saw my handkerchief in's hand!
    O perjured woman! thou dost stone my heart,°
    And mak'st me call what I intend to do
    A murder, which I thought a sacrifice.   65
    I saw the handkerchief.
Desdemona: He found it then.
    I never gave it him. Send for him hither.
    Let him confess a truth.
Othello: He hath confessed.
Desdemona: What, my lord?
Othello: That he hath used thee.
Desdemona: How? Unlawfully?
Othello: Ay.   70
Desdemona: He will not say so.
Othello: No, his mouth is stopped.
    Honest Iago hath ta'en order° for't.
Desdemona: O, my fear interprets. What, is he dead?
Othello: Had all his hairs been lives, my great revenge
    Had stomach for them all.   75
Desdemona: Alas, he is betrayed, and I undone!
Othello: Out, strumpet! Weep'st thou for him to my face?
Desdemona: O, banish me, my lord, but kill me not!
Othello: Down, strumpet!
Desdemona: Kill me to-morrow; let me live to-night!   80
Othello: Nay, if you strive —
Desdemona: But half an hour!
Othello: Being done, there is no pause.
Desdemona: But while I say one prayer!
Othello: It is too late.

    (Smothers her.)

[*Desdemona:* O Lord, Lord, Lord!]

    Emilia at the door.

Emilia (calls within): My lord, my lord! What, ho! my lord, my lord!   85
Othello: What noise is this? Not dead? not yet quite dead?
    I that am cruel am yet merciful;

---

59 *Offend:* Wrong.   63 *stone my heart:* Turn my heart to stone.   72 *ta'en order:* Taken measures.

I would not have thee linger in thy pain.
So, so.
Emilia (within): What, ho! my lord, my lord!
Othello: Who's there?   90
Emilia (within): O, good my lord, I would speak a word with you!
Othello: Yes, 'tis Emilia. — By and by.° — She's dead. —
'Tis like she comes to speak of Cassio's death.
The noise was here. Ha! no more moving?
Still as the grave. — Shall she come in? Were't good! —   95
I think she stirs again. No. — What's best to do?
If she come in, she'll sure speak to my wife.
My wife! my wife! what wife? I have no wife.
O, insupportable! O heavy hour!
Methinks it should be now a huge eclipse   100
Of sun and moon, and that th' affrighted globe
Should yawn° at alteration.
Emilia (within):   I do beseech you
That I may speak with you, O good my lord!
Othello: I had forgot thee. O, come in, Emilia.
Soft, by and by. — Let me the curtains draw. —   105

[Closes the bed-curtains.]

Where art thou?

[Opens the door.]
Enter Emilia.

                        What's the matter with thee now?
Emilia: O my good lord, yonder's foul murder done!
Othello: What? Now?
Emilia: But now, my lord.
Othello: It is the very error° of the moon.   110
She comes more nearer earth than she was wont
And makes men mad.
Emilia: Cassio, my lord, hath killed a young Venetian
Called Roderigo.
Othello: Roderigo killed?
And Cassio killed?
Emilia: No, Cassio is not killed.   115
Othello: Not Cassio killed? Then murder's out of tune,
And sweet revenge grows harsh.
Desdemona: O, falsely, falsely murdered?
Emilia: O, Lord! what cry is that?
Othello: That? What?

---

92 *By and by:* Just a moment (addressed to Emilia). 102 *yawn:* Open, as in an earthquake. 110 *error:* Straying off course.

Emilia: Out and alas! that was my lady's voice.   120
    Help! help, ho! help! O lady, speak again!
    Sweet Desdemona! O sweet mistress, speak!
Desdemona: A guiltless death I die.
Emilia: O, who hath done this deed?
Desdemona: Nobody — I myself. Farewell.   125
    Commend° me to my kind lord. O, farewell!

    (She dies.)

Othello: Why, how should she be murd'red?
Emilia: Alas, who knows?
Othello: You heard her say herself, it was not I.
Emilia: She said so. I must needs report the truth.
Othello: She's like a liar gone to burning hell!   130
    'Twas I that killed her.
Emilia: O, the more angel she,
    And you the blacker devil!
Othello: She turned to folly, and she was a whore.
Emilia: Thou dost belie her, and thou art a devil.
Othello: She was false as water.°
Emilia: Thou art rash as fire to say   135
    That she was false. O, she was heavenly true!
Othello: Cassio did top her. Ask thy husband else.
    O, I were damned beneath all depth in hell
    But that I did proceed upon just grounds
    To this extremity. Thy husband knew it all.   140
Emilia: My husband?
Othello: Thy husband.
Emilia: That she was false to wedlock?
Othello: Ay, with Cassio. Nay, had she been true,
    If heaven would make me such another world   145
    Of one entire and perfect chrysolite,°
    I'ld not have sold her for it.
Emilia: My husband?
Othello: Ay 'twas he that told me first.
    An honest man he is, and hates the slime
    That sticks on filthy deeds.
Emilia: My husband?   150
Othello: What needs this iterance,° woman? I say thy husband.
Emilia: O mistress, villainy hath made mocks with love!
    My husband say that she was false?
Othello: He, woman.
    I say, thy husband. Dost understand the word?

---

126 *Commend:* Remember.   135 *water:* (Which is yielding).   146 *chrysolite:* (Precious topaz).   151 *iterance:* Repetition.

My friend, thy husband; honest, honest Iago.   155
Emilia: If he say so, may his pernicious soul
    Rot half a grain a day! he lies to th' heart.
    She was too fond of her most filthy bargain.
Othello: Ha!
Emilia: Do thy worst.   160
    This deed of thine is no more worthy heaven
    Than thou wast worthy her.
Othello: Peace, you were best.
Emilia: Thou hast not half the power to do me harm
    As I have to be hurt.° O gull! O dolt!
    As ignorant as dirt! thou hast done a deed —   165
    I care not for thy sword; I'll make thee known,
    Though I lost twenty lives. Help! help! Ho! help!
    The Moor hath killed my mistress! Murder! murder!

Enter Montano, Gratiano, Iago, and others.

Montano: What is the matter? How now, general?
Emilia: O, are you come, Iago? You have done well,   170
    That men must lay their murders on your neck.
Gratiano: What is the matter?
Emilia: Disprove this villain, if thou be'st a man.
    He says thou told'st him that his wife was false.
    I know thou didst not; thou'rt not such a villain.   175
    Speak, for my heart is full.
Iago: I told him what I thought, and told no more
    Than what he found himself was apt and true.
Emilia: But did you ever tell him she was false?
Iago: I did.   180
Emilia: You told a lie, an odious damnèd lie!
    Upon my soul, a lie! a wicked lie!
    She false with Cassio? Did you say with Cassio?
Iago: With Cassio, mistress. Go to, charm° your tongue.
Emilia: I will not charm my tongue; I am bound to speak: 185
    My mistress here lies murdered in her bed —
All: O heavens forfend!
Emilia: And your reports have set the murder on.
Othello: Nay, stare not, masters. It is true indeed.
Gratiano: 'Tis a strange truth.   190
Montano: O monstrous act!
Emilia: Villainy, villainy, villainy!
    I think upon't — I think I smell't! — O villainy!
    I thought so then. — I'll kill myself for grief. —
    O villainy, villainy!

---

164 *to be hurt:* To endure hurt.   184 *charm:* Cast a spell on.

Iago: What, are you mad? I charge you get you home.   195
Emilia: Good gentlemen, let me have leave to speak.
 'Tis proper I obey him, but not now.
 Perchance, Iago, I will ne'er go home.
Othello: O! O! O!   *(Falls on the bed.)*
Emilia: Nay, lay thee down and roar!
 For thou hast killed the sweetest innocent   200
 That e'er did lift up eye.
Othello: O, she was foul!

 [Rises.]

 I scarce did know you, uncle. There lies your niece,
 Whose breath, indeed, these hands have newly stopped.
 I know this act shows° horrible and grim.
Gratiano: Poor Desdemon! I am glad thy father's dead.   205
 Thy match was mortal to him, and pure grief
 Shore his old thread in twain. Did he live now,
 This sight would make him do a desperate turn;°
 Yea, curse his better angel from his side,
 And fall to reprobation.°   210
Othello: 'Tis pitiful; but yet Iago knows
 That she with Cassio hath the act of shame
 A thousand times committed. Cassio confessed it;
 And she did gratify° his amorous works
 With that recognizance° and pledge of love   215
 Which I first gave her. I saw it in his hand.
 It was a handkerchief, an antique token
 My father gave my mother.
Emilia: O God! O heavenly God!
Iago: Zounds, hold your peace!
Emilia: 'Twill out, 'twill out! I peace?   220
 No, I will speak as liberal as the north,°
 Let heaven and men and devils, let them all,
 All, all, cry shame against me, yet I'll speak.
Iago: Be wise, and get you home.
Emilia: I will not.

 [Iago draws and threatens Emilia.]

Gratiano: Fie!
 Your sword upon a woman?   225
Emilia: O thou dull Moor, that handkerchief thou speak'st of
 I found by fortune, and did give my husband;
 For often with a solemn earnestness —

---

204 *shows:* Appears. 208 *turn:* Act. 210 *reprobation:* Rejection by God, damnation. 214 *gratify:* Reward. 215 *recognizance:* Token. 221 *liberal as the north:* Unchecked as the north wind blows.

More than indeed belonged to such a trifle —
He begged of me to steal't.

Iago: Villainous whore!   230

Emilia: She give it Cassio? No, alas, I found it,
And I did give't my husband.

Iago: Filth, thou liest!

Emilia: By heaven, I do not, I do not, gentlemen.
O murd'rous coxcomb! what should such a fool
Do with so good a wife?

Othello: Are there no stones° in heaven   235
But what serves for the thunder? Precious villain!

The Moor runs at Iago [but is disarmed by Montano].
Iago kills his wife.

Gratiano: The woman falls. Sure he hath killed his wife.

Emilia: Ay, ay. O, lay me by my mistress' side.   *Exit Iago.*

Gratiano: He's gone, but his wife's killed.

Montano: 'Tis a notorious° villain. Take you this weapon,   240
Which I have here recovered from the Moor.
Come, guard the door without. Let him not pass,
But kill him rather. I'll after that same villain,
For 'tis a damnèd slave.

Exit [Montano, with all but Othello and Emilia].

Othello: I am not valiant neither;
But every puny whipster° gets my sword.   245
But why should honor outlive honesty?
Let it go all.

Emilia: What did thy song bode, lady?
Hark, canst thou hear me? I will play the swan,
And die in music. *[Sings.]* "Willow, willow, willow."
Moor, she was chaste. She loved thee, cruel Moor: 250
So come my soul to bliss as I speak true.
So speaking as I think, alas, I die.

(She dies.)

Othello: I have another weapon in this chamber;
It is a sword of Spain, the ice brook's° temper.
O, here it is. — Uncle, I must come forth.   255

Gratiano (within): If thou attempt it, it will cost thee dear.
Thou hast no weapon, and perforce must suffer.

Othello: Look in upon me then and speak with me,
Or, naked° as I am, I will assault thee.

---

235 *stones:* Bolts like those used for thunderbolts.   240 *notorious:* Notable.   245 *puny*
whipster: Whippersnapper.   254 *ice brook:* i.e., a Spanish blade, tempered in cold
running water.   259 *naked:* Disarmed.

[Enter Gratiano.]

Gratiano: What is the matter?

Othello: Behold, I have a weapon;   260
A better never did itself sustain
Upon a soldier's thigh. I have seen the day
That with this little arm and this good sword
I have made my way through more impediments
Than twenty times your stop.° But O vain boast!   265
Who can control his fate? 'Tis not so now.
Be not afraid, though you do see me weaponed.
Here is my journey's end, here is my butt,°
And very seamark° of my utmost sail:
Do you go back dismayed? 'Tis a lost° fear.   270
Man but a rush° against Othello's breast,
And he retires. Where should Othello go?
Now, how dost thou look now? O ill-starred wench!
Pale as thy smock! When we shall meet at compt,°
This look of thine will hurl my soul from heaven,   275
And fiends will snatch at it. Cold, cold, my girl?
Even like thy chastity.
O cursèd, cursèd slave! Whip me, ye devils,
From the possession of this heavenly sight!
Blow me about in winds! roast me in sulphur!   280
Wash me in steep-down gulfs of liquid fire!
Oh Desdemon! dead Desdemon! dead! Oh! Oh!

Enter Lodovico, Montano, Iago [as prisoner], and Officers; Cassio in a chair.

Lodovico: Where is this rash and most unfortunate man?

Othello: That's he that was Othello. Here I am.

Lodovico: Where is that viper? Bring the villain forth.   285

Othello: I look down towards his feet° — but that's a fable.
If that thou be'st a devil, I cannot kill thee.

[Wounds Iago.]

Lodovico: Wrench his sword from him.

[Othello is disarmed.]

Iago: I bleed, sir, but not killed.

Othello: I am not sorry neither. I'ld have thee live;
For in my sense, 'tis happiness to die.   290

---

265 *stop:* Power to stop. 268 *butt:* Limit. 269 *seamark:* Beacon, destination.
270 *lost:* Wasted. 271 *Man but a rush:* Wield only a reed. 274 *compt:* Final
accounting, Last Judgment. 286 *I . . . feet:* i.e., to see if they are cloven, like the Devil's.

Lodovico: O thou Othello that wert once so good,
    Fall'n in the practice° of a damnèd slave,
    What shall be said to thee?
Othello: Why, anything;
    An honorable murderer, if you will;
    For naught did I in hate, but all in honor.   295
Lodovico: This wretch hath part confessed his villainy.
    Did you and he consent in° Cassio's death?
Othello: Ay.
Cassio: Dear general, I never gave you cause.
Othello: I do believe it, and I ask your pardon.   300
    Will you, I pray, demand that demi-devil
    Why he hath thus ensnared my soul and body?
Iago: Demand me nothing. What you know, you know.
    From this time forth I never will speak word.
Lodovico: What, not to pray?
Gratiano: Torments will ope your lips.   305
Othello: Well, thou dost best.
Lodovico: Sir, you shall understand what hath befall'n,
    Which, as I think, you know not. Here is a letter
    Found in the pocket of the slain Roderigo;
    And here another. The one of them imports   310
    The death of Cassio to be undertook
    By Roderigo.
Othello: O villain!
Cassio: Most heathenish and most gross!
Lodovico: Now here's another discontented paper
    Found in the pocket too; and this, it seems,   315
    Roderigo meant t' have sent this damnèd villain;
    But that, belike, Iago in the nick°
    Came in and satisfied him.
Othello: O thou pernicious caitiff! —
    How came you, Cassio, by that handkerchief
    That was my wife's?
Cassio: I found it in my chamber;   320
    And he himself confessed but even now
    That there he dropped it for a special purpose
    Which wrought to his desire.
Othello: O fool! fool! fool!
Cassio: There is besides in Roderigo's letter,
    How he upbraids Iago that he made him   325
    Brave me upon the watch; whereon it came
    That I was cast;° and even but now he spake,

---

292 *practice:* Plot.   297 *consent in:* Agree upon.   317 *nick:* Nick of time.   327 *cast:* Dismissed.

After long seeming dead — Iago hurt him,
Iago set him on.
Lodovico: You must forsake this room and go with us.   330
Your power and your command is taken off,
And Cassio rules in Cyprus. For this slave,
If there be any cunning cruelty
That can torment him much and hold him long,
It shall be his. You shall close prisoner rest   335
Till that the nature of your fault be known
To the Venetian state. Come, bring away.
Othello: Soft you! a word or two before you go.
I have done the state some service, and they know't.
No more of that. I pray you, in your letters,   340
When you shall these unlucky° deeds relate,
Speak of me as I am. Nothing extenuate,
Nor set down aught in malice. Then must you speak
Of one that loved not wisely, but too well;
Of one not easily jealous, but, being wrought,   345
Perplexed° in the extreme; of one whose hand,
Like the base Judean,° threw a pearl away
Richer than all his tribe; of one whose subdued° eyes,
Albeit unusèd to the melting mood,
Drop tears as fast as the Arabian trees   350
Their med'cinable gum. Set you down this.
And say besides that in Aleppo once,
Where a malignant and a turbaned Turk
Beat a Venetian and traduced the state,
I took by th' throat the circumcisèd dog   355
And smote him — thus.

(He stabs himself.)

Lodovico: O bloody period!°
Gratiano: All that's spoke is marred.
Othello: I kissed thee ere I killed thee. No way but this,
Killing myself, to die upon a kiss.

(He [falls upon the bed and] dies.)

Cassio: This did I fear, but thought he had no weapon;   360
For he was great of heart.
Lodovico [to Iago]:   O Spartan dog,
More fell° than anguish, hunger, or the sea!
Look on the tragic loading of this bed.

---

341 *unlucky:* Fatal.   346 *Perplexed:* Distracted.   347 *Judean:* Judas Iscariot (?) (quarto reads "Indian").   348 *subdued:* i.e., conquered by grief.   357 *period:* Ending.   362 *fell:* Cruel.

This is thy work. The object poisons sight;
Let it be hid.° Gratiano, keep the house,   365
And seize upon° the fortunes of the Moor,
For they succeed on you. To you, lord governor,
Remains the censure° of this hellish villain,
The time, the place, the torture. O, enforce it!
Myself will straight aboard, and to the state   370
This heavy act with heavy heart relate.

Exeunt.

365 *Let it be hid:* i.e., draw the bed curtains.   366 *seize upon:* Take legal possession
of.   368 *censure:* Judicial sentence.

Considerations for Critical Thinking and Writing

1. **FIRST RESPONSE.** Characterize Othello. In what ways is he presented
   as having a jealous disposition as well as a noble one? Why is he so
   vulnerable to Iago's villainy?

2. Explain how Iago presents himself to the world. What is beneath the
   surface of his public identity? Why does he hate Othello so passionately? What makes Iago so effective at manipulating people? What do
   other characters, besides Othello, think of him?

3. Explain why you think Othello's racial background does or doesn't
   affect events in the play.

4. How does Othello change during the course of the play? Do you feel
   the same about him from beginning to end? Trace your response to his
   character as it develops, paying particular attention to Othello's final
   speech.

5. Consider how women — Desdemona, Emilia, and Bianca — are presented in the play. What characteristics do they have in common? How
   do they relate to the men in their lives?

6. Despite its grinding emotional impact and bleak ending, *Othello* does
   have its humorous moments. Locate a scene that includes humor and
   describe its tone and function in the play.

7. **CONNECTION TO ANOTHER SELECTION.** Here's a long reach but a potentially interesting one: Write an essay that considers Desdemona as
   a wife alongside Nora in Henrik Ibsen's *A Doll's House* (p. 755). How
   responsible are they to themselves and to others? Can they be discussed
   in the same breath, or are they from such different worlds that nothing useful can be said about comparing them? Either way, explain your
   response.

27

Henrik Ibsen
and Modern Drama

A play should give you something to think about. When I see a play and understand it the first time, then I know it can't be much good.

—T. S. ELIOT

MS Am 2560 (177). By permission of the Houghton Library, Harvard University.

REALISM

Realism is a literary technique that attempts to create the appearance of life as it is actually experienced. Characters in modern realistic plays (written during and after the last quarter of the nineteenth century) speak dialogue that we might hear in our daily lives. These characters are not larger than life but representative of it; they seem to speak the way we do rather than in highly poetic language, formal declarations, asides, or soliloquies. It is impossible to imagine a heroic figure such as Oedipus inhabiting a comfortably furnished living room and chatting about his wife's household budget the way Torvald Helmer does in Henrik Ibsen's *A Doll's House*. Realism brings into focus commonplace, everyday life rather than the extraordinary kinds of events that make up Sophocles' *Oedipus the King* or Shakespeare's *Othello*.

Realistic characters can certainly be heroic, but like Nora Helmer, they find that their strength and courage are tested in the context of events ordinary people might experience. Work, love, marriage, children, and death are often the focus of realistic dramas. These subjects can also constitute much of the material in nonrealistic plays, but modern realistic dramas present such material in the realm of the probable. Conflicts in realistic plays are likely to reflect problems in our own lives. Hence, making ends meet takes precedence over saving a kingdom; middle- and lower-class individuals take center stage as primary characters in main plots rather than being secondary characters in subplots. Thus we can see why the nineteenth-century movement toward realism paralleled the rise of a middle class eagerly seeking representations of its concerns in the theater.

Before the end of the nineteenth century, however, few attempts were made in the theater to present life as it is actually lived. The chorus's role in Sophocles' *Oedipus the King*, the allegorical figures in morality plays, the remarkable mistaken identities in Shakespeare's comedies, or the rhymed couplets spoken in seventeenth-century plays such as Molière's *Tartuffe* represent theatrical conventions rather than life. Theatergoers have understood and appreciated these conventions for centuries — and still do — but in the nineteenth century social, political, and industrial revolutions helped create an atmosphere in which some playwrights found it necessary to create works that more directly reflected their audiences' lives.

Playwrights such as Henrik Ibsen and Anton Chekhov refused to join the ranks of their romantic contemporaries, who they felt falsely idealized life. The most popular plays immediately preceding the works of these realistic writers consisted primarily of love stories and action-packed plots. Such **melodramas** offer audiences thrills and chills as well as happy endings. They typically include a virtuous individual struggling under the tyranny of a wicked oppressor, who is defeated only at the last moment. Suspense is reinforced by a series of pursuits, captures, and escapes that move the plot quickly and de-emphasize character or theme. These representations of extreme conflicts enjoyed wide popularity in the nineteenth century — indeed, they still do — because their formula was varied enough to be entertaining yet their outcomes were always comforting to the audience's sense of justice. From the realists' perspective, melodramas were merely escape fantasies that distorted life by refusing to examine the real world closely and objectively. But an indication of the popularity of such happy endings can be seen in Chekhov's farcical comedies, such as *The Proposal*, a one-act play filled with exaggerated characters and action. Despite his realist's values, Chekhov was also sometimes eager to please audiences.

Realists attempted to open their audiences' eyes; to their minds, the only genuine comfort was in knowing the truth. Many of their plays concern controversial issues of the day and focus on people who fall prey to indifferent societal institutions. English dramatist John Galsworthy (1867–1933) examined social values in *Strife* (1909) and *Justice* (1910), two plays whose titles broadly suggest the nature of his concerns. British playwright George Bernard Shaw (1856–1950) often used comedy and irony as a means of awakening his audiences to contemporary problems: *Arms and the Man* (1894) satirizes romantic attitudes toward war, and *Mrs. Warren's Profession* (1898) indicts a social and economic system that drives a woman to prostitution. Chekhov's major plays are populated by characters frustrated by their social situations and their own sensibilities; they are ordinary people who long for happiness but become entangled in everyday circumstances that limit their lives. Ibsen also took a close look at his characters' daily lives. His plays attack social conventions and challenge popular attitudes toward marriage; he stunned audiences by dramatizing the suffering of a man dying of syphilis.

With these kinds of materials, Ibsen and his contemporaries popularized the **problem play**, a drama that represents a social issue in order to awaken the audience to it. These plays usually reject romantic plots in favor of holding up a mirror that reflects not simply what audiences want to see but what the playwright sees in them. Nineteenth-century realistic theater was no refuge from the social, economic, and psychological problems that melodrama ignored or sentimentalized.

THEATRICAL CONVENTIONS OF MODERN DRAMA

The picture-frame stage that is often used for realistic plays typically reproduces the setting of a room in some detail. Within the stage, framed by a proscenium arch (from which the curtain hangs), scenery and props are used to create an illusion of reality. Whether the "small book-case with well-bound books" described in the opening setting of Ibsen's *A Doll's House* is only painted scenery or an actual case with books, it will probably look real to the audience. Removing the fourth wall of a room so that an audience can look in fosters the illusion that the actions onstage are real events happening before unseen spectators. The texture of Nora's life is communicated by the set as well as by what she says and does. That doesn't happen in a play like Sophocles' *Oedipus the King*. Technical effects can make us believe there is wood burning in a fireplace or snow falling outside a window. Outdoor settings are made similarly realistic by props and painted sets. In one of Chekhov's full-length plays, for example, the second act opens in a meadow with the faint outline of a city on the horizon.

In addition to lifelike sets, a particular method of acting is used to create a realistic atmosphere. Actors address each other instead of directing formal speeches toward the audience; they act within the setting, not merely before it. At the beginning of the twentieth century Konstantin Stanislavsky (1863–1938), a Russian director, teacher, and actor, developed a system of acting that was an important influence in realistic theater. He trained actors to identify with the inner emotions of the characters they played. They were encouraged to recall from their own lives emotional responses similar to those they were portraying. The goal was to present a role truthfully by first feeling and then projecting the character's situation. Among Stanislavsky's early successes in this method were the plays of Chekhov.

There are, however, degrees of realism on the stage. Tennessee Williams's *The Glass Menagerie* (1945), for example, is a partially realistic portrayal of characters whose fragile lives are founded on illusions. Williams's dialogue rings true, and individual scenes resemble the kind of real-life action we would imagine such vulnerable characters engaging in, but other elements of the play are nonrealistic. For instance, Williams uses Tom as a major character in the play as well as narrator and stage manager. Here is part of Williams's stage directions: "The narrator is an undisguised convention of the play. He takes whatever license with dramatic convention as is convenient to his purposes." Although this play can be accurately described as including realistic elements, Williams, like many other contemporary playwrights, does not attempt an absolute fidelity to reality. He uses flashbacks — as does Arthur Miller in *Death of a Salesman* — to present incidents that occurred before the opening scene because the past impinges so heavily on the present. Most playwrights don't attempt to duplicate reality, since that can now be done so well by motion pictures.

Realism needn't lock a playwright into a futile attempt to make everything appear as it is in life. There is no way to avoid theatrical conventions: actors impersonate characters in a setting that is, after all, a stage. Indeed, even the dialogue in a realistic play is quite different from the pauses, sentence fragments, repetitions, silences, and incoherencies that characterize the way people usually speak. Realistic dialogue may seem like ordinary speech, but it, like Shakespeare's poetic language, is constructed. If we remember that realistic drama represents only the appearance of reality and that what we read on a page or see and hear onstage is the result of careful selecting, editing, and even distortion, then we are more likely to appreciate the playwright's art.

A Doll's House

Henrik Ibsen was born in Skien, Norway, to wealthy parents, who lost their money while he was a young boy. His early experiences with small-town life and genteel poverty sensitized him to the problems that he subsequently dramatized in a number of his plays. At age sixteen he was apprenticed to a druggist; he later thought about studying medicine, but by his early twenties he was earning a living writing and directing plays in various Norwegian cities. By the time of his death he enjoyed an international reputation for his treatment of social issues related to middle-class life.

Time Life Pictures/Mansell/Getty Images.

Ibsen's earliest dramatic works were historical and romantic plays, some in verse. His first truly realistic work was *The Pillars of Society* (1877), whose title ironically hints at the corruption and hypocrisy exposed in it. The realistic social-problem plays for which he is best known followed. These dramas at once fascinated and shocked international audiences. Among his most produced and admired works are *A Doll's House* (1879), *Ghosts* (1881), *An Enemy of the People* (1882), *The Wild Duck* (1884), and *Hedda Gabler* (1890). The common denominator in many of Ibsen's dramas is his interest in individuals struggling for an authentic identity in the face of tyrannical social conventions. This conflict often results in his characters' being divided between a sense of duty to themselves and their responsibility to others.

Ibsen used such external and internal conflicts to propel his plays' action. Like many of his contemporaries who wrote realistic plays, he adopted the form of the **well-made play**. A dramatic structure popularized in France by Eugène Scribe (1791–1861) and Victorien Sardou (1831–1908), the well-made play employs conventions including plenty of suspense created by meticulous plotting. Extensive exposition explains past events that ultimately lead to an inevitable climax. Tension is released when a secret that reverses the protagonist's fortunes is revealed. Ibsen, having directed a number of Scribe's plays in Norway, knew their cause-to-effect plot arrangements and used them for his own purposes in his problem plays.

A Doll's House dramatizes the tensions of a nineteenth-century middle-class marriage in which a wife struggles to step beyond the limited identity imposed on her by her husband and society.

HENRIK IBSEN (1828–1906)

A Doll's House   1879

TRANSLATED BY R. FARQUHARSON SHARP

DRAMATIS PERSONAE

Torvald Helmer
Nora, his wife
Doctor Rank
Mrs. Linde
Nils Krogstad
Helmer's three small children
Anne, their nurse
A Housemaid
A Porter

SCENE: The action takes place in Helmer's house.

ACT I

SCENE: *A room furnished comfortably and tastefully, but not extravagantly. At the back, a door to the right leads to the entrance-hall, another to the left leads to Helmer's study. Between the doors stands a piano. In the middle of the left-hand wall is a door, and beyond it a window. Near the window are a round table, arm-chairs, and a small sofa. In the right-hand wall, at the farther end, another door; and on the same side, nearer the footlights, a stove, two easy chairs, and a rocking-chair; between the stove and the door, a small table. Engravings on the walls; a cabinet with china and other small objects; a small book-case with well-bound books. The floors are carpeted, and a fire burns in the stove. It is winter.*

A bell rings in the hall; shortly afterwards the door is heard to open. Enter Nora, humming a tune and in high spirits. She is in outdoor dress and carries a number of parcels; these she lays on the table to the right. She leaves the outer door open after her, and through it is seen a Porter who is carrying a Christmas Tree and a basket, which he gives to the Maid who has opened the door.

Nora: Hide the Christmas Tree carefully, Helen. Be sure the children do not see it until this evening, when it is dressed. *(To the Porter, taking out her purse.)* How much?

Porter: Sixpence.

Nora: There is a shilling. No, keep the change. *(The Porter thanks her, and goes out. Nora shuts the door. She is laughing to herself, as she takes off her hat and coat. She takes a packet of macaroons from her pocket and eats one or two; then goes cautiously to her husband's door and listens.)* Yes, he is in. *(Still humming, she goes to the table on the right.)*

Helmer (calls out from his room): Is that my little lark twittering out there?

Nora (busy opening some of the parcels): Yes, it is!

Helmer: Is it my little squirrel bustling about?

Nora: Yes!

Helmer: When did my squirrel come home?

Nora: Just now. *(Puts the bag of macaroons into her pocket and wipes her mouth.)* Come in here, Torvald, and see what I have bought.

Helmer: Don't disturb me. *(A little later, he opens the door and looks into the room, pen in hand.)* Bought, did you say? All these things? Has my little spendthrift been wasting money again?

Nora: Yes but, Torvald, this year we really can let ourselves go a little. This is the first Christmas that we have not needed to economise.

Helmer: Still, you know, we can't spend money recklessly.

Nora: Yes, Torvald, we may be a wee bit more reckless now, mayn't we? Just a tiny wee bit! You are going to have a big salary and earn lots and lots of money.

Helmer: Yes, after the New Year; but then it will be a whole quarter before the salary is due.

Nora: Pooh! we can borrow until then.

Helmer: Nora! *(Goes up to her and takes her playfully by the ear.)* The same little featherhead! Suppose, now, that I borrowed fifty pounds to-day, and you spent it all in the Christmas week, and then on New Year's Eve a slate fell on my head and killed me, and —

Nora (putting her hands over his mouth): Oh! don't say such horrid things.

Helmer: Still, suppose that happened, — what then?

Nora: If that were to happen, I don't suppose I should care whether I owed money or not.

Helmer: Yes, but what about the people who had lent it?

Nora: They? Who would bother about them? I should not know who they were.

Helmer: That is like a woman! But seriously, Nora, you know what I think about that. No debt, no borrowing. There can be no freedom or beauty about a home life that depends on borrowing and debt. We two have kept bravely on the straight road so far, and we will go on the same way for the short time longer that there need be any struggle.

Nora (moving towards the stove): As you please, Torvald.

Helmer (following her): Come, come, my little skylark must not droop her wings. What is this! Is my little squirrel out of temper? *(Taking out his purse.)* Nora, what do you think I have got here?

Nora (turning round quickly): Money!

Helmer: There you are. *(Gives her some money.)* Do you think I don't know what a lot is wanted for housekeeping at Christmas-time?

Nora (counting): Ten shillings — a pound — two pounds! Thank you, thank you, Torvald; that will keep me going for a long time.

Helmer: Indeed it must.

Nora: Yes, yes, it will. But come here and let me show you what I have bought. And all so cheap! Look, here is a new suit for Ivar, and a sword; and a horse and a trumpet for Bob; and a doll and dolly's bedstead for Emmy, — they are very plain, but anyway she will soon break them in pieces. And here are dress-lengths and handkerchiefs for the maids; old Anne ought really to have something better.

Helmer: And what is in this parcel?

Nora (crying out): No, no! you mustn't see that until this evening.

Helmer: Very well. But now tell me, you extravagant little person, what would you like for yourself?

Nora: For myself? Oh, I am sure I don't want anything.

Helmer: Yes, but you must. Tell me something reasonable that you would particularly like to have.

Nora: No, I really can't think of anything — unless, Torvald —

Helmer: Well?

Nora (playing with his coat buttons, and without raising her eyes to his): If you really want to give me something, you might — you might —

Helmer: Well, out with it!

Nora (speaking quickly): You might give me money, Torvald. Only just as much as you can afford; and then one of these days I will buy something with it.

Helmer: But, Nora —

Nora: Oh, do! dear Torvald; please, please do! Then I will wrap it up in beautiful gilt paper and hang it on the Christmas Tree. Wouldn't that be fun?

Helmer: What are little people called that are always wasting money?

Nora: Spendthrifts — I know. Let us do as you suggest, Torvald, and then I shall have time to think what I am most in want of. That is a very sensible plan, isn't it?

Helmer (smiling): Indeed it is — that is to say, if you were really to save out of the money I give you, and then really buy something for yourself. But if you spend it all on the housekeeping and any number of unnecessary things, then I merely have to pay up again.

Nora: Oh but, Torvald —

Helmer: You can't deny it, my dear little Nora. *(Puts his arm round her waist.)* It's a sweet little spendthrift, but she uses up a deal of money. One would hardly believe how expensive such little persons are!

Nora: It's a shame to say that. I do really save all I can.

Helmer (laughing): That's very true, — all you can. But you can't save anything!

Nora (smiling quietly and happily): You haven't any idea how many expenses we skylarks and squirrels have, Torvald.

Helmer: You are an odd little soul. Very like your father. You always find some new way of wheedling money out of me, and, as soon as you have got it, it seems to melt in your hands. You never know where it has gone. Still, one must take you as you are. It is in the blood; for indeed it is true that you can inherit these things, Nora.

Nora: Ah, I wish I had inherited many of papa's qualities.

Helmer: And I would not wish you to be anything but just what you are, my sweet little skylark. But, do you know, it strikes me that you are looking rather — what shall I say — rather uneasy today?

Nora: Do I?

Helmer: You do, really. Look straight at me.

Nora (looks at him): Well?

Helmer (wagging his finger at her): Hasn't Miss Sweet Tooth been breaking rules in town today?

Nora: No; what makes you think that?

Helmer: Hasn't she paid a visit to the confectioner's?

Nora: No, I assure you, Torvald —

Helmer: Not been nibbling sweets?

Nora: No, certainly not.

Helmer: Not even taken a bite at a macaroon or two?

Nora: No, Torvald, I assure you really —

Helmer: There, there, of course I was only joking.

Nora (going to the table on the right): I should not think of going against your wishes.

Helmer: No, I am sure of that; besides, you gave me your word — *(Going up to her.)* Keep your little Christmas secrets to yourself, my darling. They will all be revealed to-night when the Christmas Tree is lit, no doubt.

Nora: Did you remember to invite Doctor Rank?

Helmer: No. But there is no need; as a matter of course he will come to dinner with us. However, I will ask him when he comes in this morning. I have ordered some good wine. Nora, you can't think how I am looking forward to this evening.

Nora: So am I! And how the children will enjoy themselves, Torvald!

Helmer: It is splendid to feel that one has a perfectly safe appointment, and a big enough income. It's delightful to think of, isn't it?

Nora: It's wonderful!

Helmer: Do you remember last Christmas? For a full three weeks beforehand you shut yourself up every evening until long after midnight, making ornaments for the Christmas Tree, and all the other fine things that were to be a surprise to us. It was the dullest three weeks I ever spent!

Nora: I didn't find it dull.

Helmer (smiling): But there was precious little result, Nora.

Nora: Oh, you shouldn't tease me about that again. How could I help the cat's going in and tearing everything to pieces?

Helmer: Of course you couldn't, poor little girl. You had the best of intentions to please us all, and that's the main thing. But it is a good thing that our hard times are over.

Nora: Yes, it is really wonderful.

Helmer: This time I needn't sit here and be dull all alone, and you needn't ruin your dear eyes and your pretty little hands —

Nora (clapping her hands): No, Torvald, I needn't any longer, need I! It's wonderfully lovely to hear you say so! *(Taking his arm.)* Now I will tell you how I have been thinking we ought to arrange things, Torvald. As soon as Christmas is over — *(A bell rings in the hall.)* There's the bell. *(She tidies the room a little.)* There's some one at the door. What a nuisance!

Helmer: If it is a caller, remember I am not at home.

Maid (in the doorway): A lady to see you, ma'am, — a stranger.

Nora: Ask her to come in.

Maid (to Helmer): The doctor came at the same time, sir.

Helmer: Did he go straight into my room?

Maid: Yes, sir.

> *Helmer goes into his room. The Maid ushers in Mrs. Linde, who is in travelling dress, and shuts the door.*

Mrs. Linde (in a dejected and timid voice): How do you do, Nora?

Nora (doubtfully): How do you do —

Mrs. Linde: You don't recognise me, I suppose.

Nora: No, I don't know — yes, to be sure, I seem to — *(Suddenly.)* Yes! Christine! Is it really you?

Mrs. Linde: Yes, it is I.

Nora: Christine! To think of my not recognising you! And yet how could
    I — *(In a gentle voice.)* How you have altered, Christine!

Mrs. Linde: Yes, I have indeed. In nine, ten long years —

Nora: Is it so long since we met? I suppose it is. The last eight years have been
    a happy time for me, I can tell you. And so now you have come into the
    town, and have taken this long journey in winter — that was plucky of you.

Mrs. Linde: I arrived by steamer this morning.

Nora: To have some fun at Christmas-time, of course. How delightful! We
    will have such fun together! But take off your things. You are not cold,
    I hope. *(Helps her.)* Now we will sit down by the stove, and be cosy. No,
    take this arm-chair; I will sit here in the rocking-chair. *(Takes her hands.)*
    Now you look like your old self again; it was only the first moment —
    You are a little paler, Christine, and perhaps a little thinner.

Mrs. Linde: And much, much older, Nora.

Nora: Perhaps a little older; very, very little; certainly not much. *(Stops sud-
    denly and speaks seriously.)* What a thoughtless creature I am, chattering
    away like this. My poor, dear Christine, do forgive me.

Mrs. Linde: What do you mean, Nora?

Nora (gently): Poor Christine, you are a widow.

Mrs. Linde: Yes; it is three years ago now.

Nora: Yes, I knew; I saw it in the papers. I assure you, Christine, I meant
    ever so often to write to you at the time, but I always put it off and some-
    thing always prevented me.

Mrs. Linde: I quite understand, dear.

Nora: It was very bad of me, Christine. Poor thing, how you must have suf-
    fered. And he left you nothing?

Mrs. Linde: No.

Nora: And no children?

Mrs. Linde: No.

Nora: Nothing at all, then.

Mrs. Linde: Not even any sorrow or grief to live upon.

Nora (looking incredulously at her): But, Christine, is that possible?

Mrs. Linde (smiles sadly and strokes her hair): It sometimes happens, Nora.

Nora: So you are quite alone. How dreadfully sad that must be. I have three
    lovely children. You can't see them just now, for they are out with their
    nurse. But now you must tell me all about it.

Mrs. Linde: No, no; I want to hear about you.

Nora: No, you must begin. I mustn't be selfish today; today I must only
    think of your affairs. But there is one thing I must tell you. Do you know
    we have just had a great piece of good luck?

Mrs. Linde: No, what is it?

Nora: Just fancy, my husband has been made manager of the Bank!

Mrs. Linde: Your husband? What good luck!

Nora: Yes, tremendous! A barrister's profession is such an uncertain
    thing, especially if he won't undertake unsavoury cases; and naturally

Torvald has never been willing to do that, and I quite agree with him. You may imagine how pleased we are! He is to take up his work in the Bank at the New Year, and then he will have a big salary and lots of commissions. For the future we can live quite differently — we can do just as we like. I feel so relieved and so happy, Christine! It will be splendid to have heaps of money and not need to have any anxiety, won't it?

Mrs. Linde: Yes, anyhow I think it would be delightful to have what one needs.

Nora: No, not only what one needs, but heaps and heaps of money.

Mrs. Linde (smiling): Nora, Nora, haven't you learned sense yet? In our schooldays you were a great spendthrift.

Nora (laughing): Yes, that is what Torvald says now. *(Wags her finger at her.)* But "Nora, Nora" is not so silly as you think. We have not been in a position for me to waste money. We have both had to work.

Mrs. Linde: You too?

Nora: Yes; odds and ends, needlework, crotchet-work, embroidery, and that kind of thing. *(Dropping her voice.)* And other things as well. You know Torvald left his office when we were married? There was no prospect of promotion there, and he had to try and earn more than before. But during the first year he over-worked himself dreadfully. You see, he had to make money every way he could, and he worked early and late; but he couldn't stand it, and fell dreadfully ill, and the doctors said it was necessary for him to go south.

Mrs. Linde: You spent a whole year in Italy, didn't you?

Nora: Yes. It was no easy matter to get away, I can tell you. It was just after Ivar was born; but naturally we had to go. It was a wonderfully beautiful journey, and it saved Torvald's life. But it cost a tremendous lot of money, Christine.

Mrs. Linde: So I should think.

Nora: It cost about two hundred and fifty pounds. That's a lot, isn't it?

Mrs. Linde: Yes, and in emergencies like that it is lucky to have the money.

Nora: I ought to tell you that we had it from papa.

Mrs. Linde: Oh, I see. It was just about that time that he died, wasn't it?

Nora: Yes; and, just think of it, I couldn't go and nurse him. I was expecting little Ivar's birth every day and I had my poor sick Torvald to look after. My dear, kind father — I never saw him again, Christine. That was the saddest time I have known since our marriage.

Mrs. Linde: I know how fond you were of him. And then you went off to Italy?

Nora: Yes; you see we had money then, and the doctors insisted on our going, so we started a month later.

Mrs. Linde: And your husband came back quite well?

Nora: As sound as a bell!

Mrs. Linde: But — the doctor?

Nora: What doctor?

Mrs. Linde: I thought your maid said the gentleman who arrived here just as I did, was the doctor?

Nora: Yes, that was Doctor Rank, but he doesn't come here professionally. He is our greatest friend, and comes in at least once everyday. No, Torvald has not had an hour's illness since then, and our children are strong and healthy and so am I. *(Jumps up and claps her hands.)* Christine! Christine! it's good to be alive and happy! — But how horrid of me; I am talking of nothing but my own affairs. *(Sits on a stool near her, and rests her arms on her knees.)* You mustn't be angry with me. Tell me, is it really true that you did not love your husband? Why did you marry him?

Mrs. Linde: My mother was alive then, and was bedridden and helpless, and I had to provide for my two younger brothers; so I did not think I was justified in refusing his offer.

Nora: No, perhaps you were quite right. He was rich at that time, then?

Mrs. Linde: I believe he was quite well off. But his business was a precarious one; and, when he died, it all went to pieces and there was nothing left.

Nora: And then? —

Mrs. Linde: Well, I had to turn my hand to anything I could find — first a small shop, then a small school, and so on. The last three years have seemed like one long working-day, with no rest. Now it is at an end, Nora. My poor mother needs me no more, for she is gone; and the boys do not need me either; they have got situations and can shift for themselves.

Nora: What a relief you must feel it —

Mrs. Linde: No, indeed; I only feel my life unspeakably empty. No one to live for anymore. *(Gets up restlessly.)* That was why I could not stand the life in my little backwater any longer. I hope it may be easier here to find something which will busy me and occupy my thoughts. If only I could have the good luck to get some regular work — office work of some kind —

Nora: But, Christine, that is so frightfully tiring, and you look tired out now. You had far better go away to some watering-place.

Mrs. Linde (walking to the window): I have no father to give me money for a journey, Nora.

Nora (rising): Oh, don't be angry with me!

Mrs. Linde (going up to her): It is you that must not be angry with me, dear. The worst of a position like mine is that it makes one so bitter. No one to work for, and yet obliged to be always on the lookout for chances. One must live, and so one becomes selfish. When you told me of the happy turn your fortunes have taken — you will hardly believe it — I was delighted not so much on your account as on my own.

Nora: How do you mean? — Oh, I understand. You mean that perhaps Torvald could get you something to do.

Mrs. Linde: Yes, that was what I was thinking of.

Nora: He must, Christine. Just leave it to me; I will broach the subject very cleverly — I will think of something that will please him very much. It will make me so happy to be of some use to you.

Mrs. Linde: How kind you are, Nora, to be so anxious to help me! It is doubly kind in you, for you know so little of the burdens and troubles of life.

Nora: I — ? I know so little of them?

Mrs. Linde (smiling): My dear! Small household cares and that sort of thing! — You are a child, Nora.

Nora (tosses her head and crosses the stage): You ought not to be so superior.

Mrs. Linde: No?

Nora: You are just like the others. They all think that I am incapable of anything really serious —

Mrs. Linde: Come, come —

Nora: — that I have gone through nothing in this world of cares.

Mrs. Linde: But, my dear Nora, you have just told me all your troubles.

Nora: Pooh! — those were trifles. *(Lowering her voice.)* I have not told you the important thing.

Mrs. Linde: The important thing? What do you mean?

Nora: You look down upon me altogether, Christine — but you ought not to. You are proud, aren't you, of having worked so hard and so long for your mother?

Mrs. Linde: Indeed, I don't look down on anyone. But it is true that I am both proud and glad to think that I was privileged to make the end of my mother's life almost free from care.

Nora: And you are proud to think of what you have done for your brothers?

Mrs. Linde: I think I have the right to be.

Nora: I think so, too. But now, listen to this; I too have something to be proud and glad of.

Mrs. Linde: I have no doubt you have. But what do you refer to?

Nora: Speak low. Suppose Torvald were to hear! He mustn't on any account — no one in the world must know, Christine, except you.

Mrs. Linde: But what is it?

Nora: Come here. *(Pulls her down on the sofa beside her.)* Now I will show you that I too have something to be proud and glad of. It was I who saved Torvald's life.

Mrs. Linde: "Saved"? How?

Nora: I told you about our trip to Italy. Torvald would never have recovered if he had not gone there —

Mrs. Linde: Yes, but your father gave you the necessary funds.

Nora (smiling): Yes, that is what Torvald and all the others think, but —

Mrs. Linde: But —

Nora: Papa didn't give us a shilling. It was I who procured the money.

Mrs. Linde: You? All that large sum?

Nora: Two hundred and fifty pounds. What do you think of that?

Mrs. Linde: But, Nora, how could you possibly do it? Did you win a prize in the Lottery?

Nora (contemptuously): In the Lottery? There would have been no credit in that.

Mrs. Linde: But where did you get it from, then?

Nora (humming and smiling with an air of mystery): Hm, hm! Aha!

Mrs. Linde: Because you couldn't have borrowed it.

Nora: Couldn't I? Why not?

Mrs. Linde: No, a wife cannot borrow without her husband's consent.

Nora (tossing her head): Oh, if it is a wife who has any head for business — a wife who has the wit to be a little bit clever —

Mrs. Linde: I don't understand it at all, Nora.

Nora: There is no need you should. I never said I had borrowed the money. I may have got it some other way. *(Lies back on the sofa.)* Perhaps I got it from some other admirer. When anyone is as attractive as I am —

Mrs. Linde: You are a mad creature.

Nora: Now, you know you're full of curiosity, Christine.

Mrs. Linde: Listen to me, Nora dear. Haven't you been a little bit imprudent?

Nora (sits up straight): Is it imprudent to save your husband's life?

Mrs. Linde: It seems to me imprudent, without his knowledge, to —

Nora: But it was absolutely necessary that he should not know! My goodness, can't you understand that? It was necessary he should have no idea what a dangerous condition he was in. It was to me that the doctors came and said that his life was in danger, and that the only thing to save him was to live in the south. Do you suppose I didn't try, first of all, to get what I wanted as if it were for myself? I told him how much I should love to travel abroad like other young wives; I tried tears and entreaties with him; I told him that he ought to remember the condition I was in, and that he ought to be kind and indulgent to me; I even hinted that he might raise a loan. That nearly made him angry, Christine. He said I was thoughtless, and that it was his duty as my husband not to indulge me in my whims and caprices — as I believe he called them. Very well, I thought, you must be saved — and that was how I came to devise a way out of the difficulty —

Mrs. Linde: And did your husband never get to know from your father that the money had not come from him?

Nora: No, never. Papa died just at that time. I had meant to let him into the secret and beg him never to reveal it. But he was so ill then — alas, there never was any need to tell him.

Mrs. Linde: And since then have you never told your secret to your husband?

Nora: Good Heavens, no! How could you think so? A man who has such strong opinions about these things! And besides, how painful and humiliating it would be for Torvald, with his manly independence, to know that he owed me anything! It would upset our mutual relations altogether; our beautiful happy home would no longer be what it is now.

Mrs. Linde: Do you mean never to tell him about it?

Nora (meditatively, and with a half smile): Yes — someday, perhaps, after many years, when I am no longer as nice-looking as I am now. Don't laugh at me! I mean, of course, when Torvald is no longer as devoted to me as he is now; when my dancing and dressing-up and reciting have palled on him; then it may be a good thing to have something in reserve — *(Breaking off.)* What nonsense! That time will never come. Now, what do you think of my great secret, Christine? Do you still think I am of no use? I can tell you, too, that this affair has caused me a lot of worry. It has been by no means easy for me to meet my engagements punctually. I may tell you that there is something that is called, in business, quarterly interest, and another thing called payment in installments, and it is always so dreadfully difficult to manage them. I have had to save a little here and there, where I could, you understand. I have not been able to put aside much from my housekeeping money, for Torvald must have a good table. I couldn't let my children be shabbily dressed; I have felt obliged to use up all he gave me for them, the sweet little darlings!

Mrs. Linde: So it has all had to come out of your own necessaries of life, poor Nora?

Nora: Of course. Besides, I was the one responsible for it. Whenever Torvald has given me money for new dresses and such things, I have never spent more than half of it; I have always bought the simplest and cheapest things. Thank Heaven, any clothes look well on me, and so Torvald has never noticed it. But it was often very hard on me, Christine — because it is delightful to be really well dressed, isn't it?

Mrs. Linde: Quite so.

Nora: Well, then I have found other ways of earning money. Last winter I was lucky enough to get a lot of copying to do; so I locked myself up and sat writing every evening until quite late at night. Many a time I was desperately tired; but all the same it was a tremendous pleasure to sit there working and earning money. It was like being a man.

Mrs. Linde: How much have you been able to pay off in that way?

Nora: I can't tell you exactly. You see, it is very difficult to keep an account of a business matter of that kind. I only know that I have paid every penny that I could scrape together. Many a time I was at my wits' end. (Smiles.) Then I used to sit here and imagine that a rich old gentleman had fallen in love with me —

Mrs. Linde: What! Who was it?

Nora: Be quiet! — that he had died; and that when his will was opened it contained, written in big letters, the instruction: "The lovely Mrs. Nora Helmer is to have all I possess paid over to her at once in cash."

Mrs. Linde: But, my dear Nora — who could the man be?

Nora: Good gracious, can't you understand? There was no old gentleman at all; it was only something that I used to sit here and imagine, when I couldn't think of any way of procuring money. But it's all the same now; the tiresome old person can stay where he is, as far as I am concerned; I don't care about him or his will either, for I am free from care now. (Jumps up.) My goodness, it's delightful to think of, Christine! Free from care! To be able to be free from care, quite free from care; to be able to play and romp with the children; to be able to keep the house beautifully and have everything just as Torvald likes it! And, think of it, soon the spring will come and the big blue sky! Perhaps we shall be able to take a little trip — perhaps I shall see the sea again! Oh, it's a wonderful thing to be alive and be happy. (*A bell is heard in the hall.*)

Mrs. Linde (rising): There is the bell; perhaps I had better go.

Nora: No, don't go; no one will come in here; it is sure to be for Torvald.

Servant (at the hall door): Excuse me, ma'am — there is a gentleman to see the master, and as the doctor is with him —

Nora: Who is it?

Krogstad (at the door): It is I, Mrs. Helmer (*Mrs. Linde starts, trembles, and turns to the window.*)

Nora (takes a step towards him, and speaks in a strained, low voice): You? What is it? What do you want to see my husband about?

Krogstad: Bank business — in a way. I have a small post in the Bank, and I hear your husband is to be our chief now —

Nora: Then it is —

Krogstad: Nothing but dry business matters, Mrs. Helmer; absolutely nothing else.

Nora: Be so good as to go into the study, then. (*She bows indifferently to him and shuts the door into the hall; then comes back and makes up the fire in the stove.*)

Mrs. Linde: Nora — who was that man?

Nora: A lawyer, of the name of Krogstad.

Mrs. Linde: Then it really was he.

Nora: Do you know the man?

Mrs. Linde: I used to — many years ago. At one time he was a solicitor's clerk in our town.

Nora: Yes, he was.

Mrs. Linde: He is greatly altered.

Nora: He made a very unhappy marriage.

Mrs. Linde: He is a widower now, isn't he?

Nora: With several children. There now, it is burning up. (*Shuts the door of the stove and moves the rocking-chair aside.*)

Mrs. Linde: They say he carries on various kinds of business.

Nora: Really! Perhaps he does; I don't know anything about it. But don't let us think of business; it is so tiresome.

Doctor Rank (comes out of Helmer's study. Before he shuts the door he calls to him): No, my dear fellow, I won't disturb you; I would rather go in to your wife for a little while. (*Shuts the door and sees Mrs. Linde.*) I beg your pardon; I am afraid I am disturbing you too.

Nora: No, not at all. (*Introducing him.*) Doctor Rank, Mrs. Linde.

Rank: I have often heard Mrs. Linde's name mentioned here. I think I passed you on the stairs when I arrived, Mrs. Linde?

Mrs. Linde: Yes, I go up very slowly; I can't manage stairs well.

Rank: Ah! some slight internal weakness?

Mrs. Linde: No, the fact is I have been overworking myself.

Rank: Nothing more than that? Then I suppose you have come to town to amuse yourself with our entertainments?

Mrs. Linde: I have come to look for work.

Rank: Is that a good cure for overwork?

Mrs. Linde: One must live, Doctor Rank.

Rank: Yes, the general opinion seems to be that it is necessary.

Nora: Look here, Doctor Rank — you know you want to live.

Rank: Certainly. However wretched I may feel, I want to prolong the agony as long as possible. All my patients are like that. And so are those who are morally diseased; one of them, and a bad case too, is at this very moment with Helmer —

Mrs. Linde (sadly): Ah!

Nora: Whom do you mean?

Rank: A lawyer of the name of Krogstad, a fellow you don't know at all. He suffers from a diseased moral character, Mrs. Helmer; but even he began talking of its being highly important that he should live.

Nora: Did he? What did he want to speak to Torvald about?

Rank: I have no idea; I only heard that it was something about the Bank.

Nora: I didn't know this — what's his name — Krogstad had anything to do with the Bank.

Rank: Yes, he has some sort of appointment there. *(To Mrs. Linde.)* I don't know whether you find also in your part of the world that there are certain people who go zealously snuffing about to smell out moral corruption, and, as soon as they have found some, put the person concerned into some lucrative position where they can keep their eye on him. Healthy natures are left out in the cold.

Mrs. Linde: Still I think the sick are those who most need taking care of.

Rank (shrugging his shoulders): Yes, there you are. That is the sentiment that is turning Society into a sick-house.

Nora, who has been absorbed in her thoughts, breaks out into smothered laughter and claps her hands.

Rank: Why do you laugh at that? Have you any notion what Society really is?

Nora: What do I care about tiresome Society? I am laughing at something quite different, something extremely amusing. Tell me, Doctor Rank, are all the people who are employed in the Bank dependent on Torvald now?

Rank: Is that what you find so extremely amusing?

Nora (smiling and humming): That's my affair! *(Walking about the room.)* It's perfectly glorious to think that we have — that Torvald has so much power over so many people. *(Takes the packet from her pocket.)* Doctor Rank, what do you say to a macaroon?

Rank: What, macaroons? I thought they were forbidden here.

Nora: Yes, but these are some Christine gave me.

Mrs. Linde: What! I? —

Nora: Oh, well, don't be alarmed! You couldn't know that Torvald had forbidden them. I must tell you that he is afraid they will spoil my teeth.

But, bah! — once in a way — That's so, isn't it, Doctor Rank? By your leave! *(Puts a macaroon into his mouth.)* You must have one too, Christine. And I shall have one, just a little one — or at most two. *(Walking about.)* I am tremendously happy. There is just one thing in the world now that I should dearly love to do.

Rank: Well, what is that?

Nora: It's something I should dearly love to say, if Torvald could hear me.

Rank: Well, why can't you say it?

Nora: No, I daren't; it's so shocking.

Mrs. Linde: Shocking?

Rank: Well, I should not advise you to say it. Still, with us you might. What is it you would so much like to say if Torvald could hear you?

Nora: I should just love to say — Well, I'm damned!

Rank: Are you mad?

Mrs. Linde: Nora, dear — !

Rank: Say it, here he is!

Nora (hiding the packet): Hush! Hush! Hush! *(Helmer comes out of his room, with his coat over his arm and his hat in his hand.)*

Nora: Well, Torvald dear, have you got rid of him?

Helmer: Yes, he has just gone.

Nora: Let me introduce you — this is Christine, who has come to town.

Helmer: Christine — ? Excuse me, but I don't know —

Nora: Mrs. Linde, dear; Christine Linde.

Helmer: Of course. A school friend of my wife's, I presume?

Mrs. Linde: Yes, we have known each other since then.

Nora: And just think, she has taken a long journey in order to see you.

Helmer: What do you mean?

Mrs. Linde: No, really, I —

Nora: Christine is tremendously clever at book-keeping, and she is frightfully anxious to work under some clever man, so as to perfect herself —

Helmer: Very sensible, Mrs. Linde.

Nora: And when she heard you had been appointed manager of the Bank — the news was telegraphed, you know — she travelled here as quick as she could. Torvald, I am sure you will be able to do something for Christine, for my sake, won't you?

Helmer: Well, it is not altogether impossible. I presume you are a widow, Mrs. Linde?

Mrs. Linde: Yes.

Helmer: And have had some experience of book-keeping?

Mrs. Linde: Yes, a fair amount.

Helmer: Ah! well, it's very likely I may be able to find something for you —

Nora (clapping her hands): What did I tell you? What did I tell you?

Helmer: You have just come at a fortunate moment, Mrs. Linde.

Mrs. Linde: How am I to thank you?

Helmer: There is no need. *(Puts on his coat.)* But to-day you must excuse me —

Rank: Wait a minute; I will come with you. (*Brings his fur coat from the hall and warms it at the fire.*)

Nora: Don't be long away, Torvald dear.

Helmer: About an hour, not more.

Nora: Are you going too, Christine?

Mrs. Linde (putting on her cloak): Yes, I must go and look for a room.

Helmer: Oh, well then, we can walk down the street together.

Nora (helping her): What a pity it is we are so short of space here; I am afraid it is impossible for us —

Mrs. Linde: Please don't think of it! Good-bye, Nora dear, and many thanks.

Nora: Good-bye for the present. Of course you will come back this evening. And you too, Dr. Rank. What do you say? If you are well enough? Oh, you must be! Wrap yourself up well. (*They go to the door all talking together. Children's voices are heard on the staircase.*)

Nora: There they are! There they are! (*She runs to open the door. The Nurse comes in with the children.*) Come in! Come in! (*Stoops and kisses them.*) Oh, you sweet blessings! Look at them, Christine! Aren't they darlings?

Rank: Don't let us stand here in the draught.

Helmer: Come along, Mrs. Linde; the place will only be bearable for a mother now!

> *Rank, Helmer, and Mrs. Linde go downstairs. The Nurse comes forward with the children; Nora shuts the hall door.*

Nora: How fresh and well you look! Such red cheeks like apples and roses. (*The children all talk at once while she speaks to them.*) Have you had great fun? That's splendid! What, you pulled both Emmy and Bob along on the sledge? — both at once? — that was good. You are a clever boy, Ivar. Let me take her for a little, Anne. My sweet little baby doll! (*Takes the baby from the Maid and dances it up and down.*) Yes, yes, mother will dance with Bob too. What! Have you been snowballing? I wish I had been there too! No, no, I will take their things off, Anne; please let me do it, it is such fun. Go in now, you look half frozen. There is some hot coffee for you on the stove.

> *The Nurse goes into the room on the left. Nora takes off the children's things and throws them about, while they all talk to her at once.*

Nora: Really! Did a big dog run after you? But it didn't bite you? No, dogs don't bite nice little dolly children. You mustn't look at the parcels, Ivar. What are they? Ah, I daresay you would like to know. No, no — it's something nasty! Come, let us have a game! What shall we play at? Hide and Seek? Yes, we'll play Hide and Seek. Bob shall hide first. Must I hide? Very well, I'll hide first. (*She and the children laugh and shout, and romp in and out of the room; at last Nora hides under the table, the children rush in and out for her, but do not see her; they hear her smothered laughter, run to the table, lift up the cloth and find her. Shouts of laughter. She crawls forward and pretends to frighten them. Fresh laughter. Meanwhile there has been a knock at the hall door, but none of them has noticed it. The door is half opened, and Krogstad appears. He waits a little; the game goes on.)*

Krogstad: Excuse me, Mrs. Helmer.

Nora (with a stifled cry, turns round and gets up on to her knees): Ah! what do you want?

Krogstad: Excuse me, the outer door was ajar; I suppose someone forgot to shut it.

Nora (rising): My husband is out, Mr. Krogstad.

Krogstad: I know that.

Nora: What do you want here, then?

Krogstad: A word with you.

Nora: With me? — *(To the children, gently.)* Go in to nurse. What? No, the strange man won't do mother any harm. When he has gone we will have another game. *(She takes the children into the room on the left, and shuts the door after them.)* You want to speak to me?

Krogstad: Yes, I do.

Nora: To-day? It is not the first of the month yet.

Krogstad: No, it is Christmas Eve, and it will depend on yourself what sort of a Christmas you will spend.

Nora: What do you mean? To-day it is absolutely impossible for me —

Krogstad: We won't talk about that until later on. This is something different. I presume you can give me a moment?

Nora: Yes — yes, I can — although —

Krogstad: Good. I was in Olsen's Restaurant and saw your husband going down the street —

Nora: Yes?

Krogstad: With a lady.

Nora: What then?

Krogstad: May I make so bold as to ask if it was a Mrs. Linde?

Nora: It was.

Krogstad: Just arrived in town?

Nora: Yes, to-day.

Krogstad: She is a great friend of yours, isn't she?

Nora: She is. But I don't see —

Krogstad: I knew her too, once upon a time.

Nora: I am aware of that.

Krogstad: Are you? So you know all about it; I thought as much. Then I can ask you, without beating about the bush — is Mrs. Linde to have an appointment in the Bank?

Nora: What right have you to question me, Mr. Krogstad? — You, one of my husband's subordinates! But since you ask, you shall know. Yes, Mrs. Linde *is* to have an appointment. And it was I who pleaded her cause, Mr. Krogstad, let me tell you that.

Krogstad: I was right in what I thought, then.

Nora (walking up and down the stage): Sometimes one has a tiny little bit of influence, I should hope. Because one is a woman, it does not necessarily follow that — . When anyone is in a subordinate position, Mr. Krogstad, they should really be careful to avoid offending anyone who — who —

Krogstad: Who has influence?

Nora: Exactly.

Krogstad (changing his tone): Mrs. Helmer, you will be so good as to use your influence on my behalf.

Nora: What? What do you mean?

Krogstad: You will be so kind as to see that I am allowed to keep my subordinate position in the Bank.

Nora: What do you mean by that? Who proposes to take your post away from you?

Krogstad: Oh, there is no necessity to keep up the pretence of ignorance. I can quite understand that your friend is not very anxious to expose herself to the chance of rubbing shoulders with me; and I quite understand, too, whom I have to thank for being turned off.

Nora: But I assure you —

Krogstad: Very likely; but, to come to the point, the time has come when I should advise you to use your influence to prevent that.

Nora: But, Mr. Krogstad, I *have* no influence.

Krogstad: Haven't you? I thought you said yourself just now —

Nora: Naturally I did not mean you to put that construction on it. What should make you think I have any influence of that kind with my husband?

Krogstad: Oh, I have known your husband from our student days. I don't suppose he is any more unassailable than other husbands.

Nora: If you speak slightingly of my husband, I shall turn you out of the house.

Krogstad: You are bold, Mrs. Helmer.

Nora: I am not afraid of you any longer. As soon as the New Year comes, I shall in a very short time be free of the whole thing.

Krogstad (controlling himself): Listen to me, Mrs. Helmer. If necessary, I am prepared to fight for my small post in the Bank as if I were fighting for my life.

Nora: So it seems.

Krogstad: It is not only for the sake of the money; indeed, that weighs least with me in the matter. There is another reason — well, I may as well tell you. My position is this. I daresay you know, like everybody else, that once, many years ago, I was guilty of an indiscretion.

Nora: I think I have heard something of the kind.

Krogstad: The matter never came into court; but every way seemed to be closed to me after that. So I took to the business that you know of. I had to do something; and, honestly, I don't think I've been one of the worst. But now I must cut myself free from all that. My sons are growing up; for their sake I must try and win back as much respect as I can in the town. This post in the Bank was like the first step up for me — and now your husband is going to kick me downstairs again into the mud.

Nora: But you must believe me, Mr. Krogstad; it is not in my power to help you at all.

Krogstad: Then it is because you haven't the will; but I have means to compel you.

Nora: You don't mean that you will tell my husband that I owe you money?

Krogstad: Hm! — suppose I were to tell him?

Nora: It would be perfectly infamous of you. *(Sobbing.)* To think of his learning my secret, which has been my joy and pride, in such an ugly, clumsy way — that he should learn it from you! And it would put me in a horribly disagreeable position —

Krogstad: Only disagreeable?

Nora (impetuously): Well, do it, then! — and it will be the worse for you. My husband will see for himself what a blackguard you are, and you certainly won't keep your post then.

Krogstad: I asked you if it was only a disagreeable scene at home that you were afraid of?

Nora: If my husband does get to know of it, of course he will at once pay you what is still owing, and we shall have nothing more to do with you.

Krogstad (coming a step nearer): Listen to me, Mrs. Helmer. Either you have a very bad memory or you know very little of business. I shall be obliged to remind you of a few details.

Nora: What do you mean?

Krogstad: When your husband was ill, you came to me to borrow two hundred and fifty pounds.

Nora: I didn't know anyone else to go to.

Krogstad: I promised to get you that amount —

Nora: Yes, and you did so.

Krogstad: I promised to get you that amount, on certain conditions. Your mind was so taken up with your husband's illness, and you were so anxious to get the money for your journey, that you seem to have paid no attention to the conditions of our bargain. Therefore it will not be amiss if I remind you of them. Now, I promised to get the money on the security of a bond which I drew up.

Nora: Yes, and which I signed.

Krogstad: Good. But below your signature there were a few lines constituting your father a surety for the money; those lines your father should have signed.

Nora: Should? He did sign them.

Krogstad: I had left the date blank; that is to say, your father should himself have inserted the date on which he signed the paper. Do you remember that?

Nora: Yes, I think I remember —

Krogstad: Then I gave you the bond to send by post to your father. Is that not so?

Nora: Yes.

Krogstad: And you naturally did so at once, because five or six days afterwards you brought me the bond with your father's signature. And then I gave you the money.

Nora: Well, haven't I been paying it off regularly?

Krogstad: Fairly so, yes. But — to come back to the matter in hand — that must have been a very trying time for you, Mrs. Helmer.

Nora: It was, indeed.

Krogstad: Your father was very ill, wasn't he?

Nora: He was very near his end.

Krogstad: And he died soon afterwards?

Nora: Yes.

Krogstad: Tell me, Mrs. Helmer, can you by any chance remember what day your father died? — on what day of the month, I mean.

Nora: Papa died on the 29th of September.

Krogstad: That is correct; I have ascertained it for myself. And, as that is so, there is a discrepancy *(taking a paper from his pocket)* which I cannot account for.

Nora: What discrepancy? I don't know —

Krogstad: The discrepancy consists, Mrs. Helmer, in the fact that your father signed this bond three days after his death.

Nora: What do you mean? I don't understand —

Krogstad: Your father died on the 29th of September. But, look here; your father has dated his signature the 2nd of October. It is a discrepancy, isn't it? *(Nora is silent.)* Can you explain it to me? *(Nora is still silent.)* It is a remarkable thing, too, that the words "2nd of October," as well as the year, are not written in your father's handwriting but in one that I think I know. Well, of course it can be explained; your father may have forgotten to date his signature, and someone else may have dated it haphazard before they knew of his death. There is no harm in that. It all depends on the signature of the name; and *that* is genuine, I suppose, Mrs. Helmer? It was your father himself who signed his name here?

Nora (after a short pause, throws her head up and looks defiantly at him): No, it was not. It was I that wrote papa's name.

Krogstad: Are you aware that is a dangerous confession?

Nora: In what way? You shall have your money soon.

Krogstad: Let me ask you a question; why did you not send the paper to your father?

Nora: It was impossible; papa was so ill. If I had asked him for his signature, I should have had to tell him what the money was to be used for; and when he was so ill himself I couldn't tell him that my husband's life was in danger — it was impossible.

Krogstad: It would have been better for you if you had given up your trip abroad.

Nora: No, that was impossible. That trip was to save my husband's life; I couldn't give that up.

Krogstad: But did it never occur to you that you were committing a fraud on me?

Nora: I couldn't take that into account; I didn't trouble myself about you at all. I couldn't bear you, because you put so many heartless difficulties in my way, although you knew what a dangerous condition my husband was in.

Krogstad: Mrs. Helmer, you evidently do not realise clearly what it is that you have been guilty of. But I can assure you that my one false step, which lost me all my reputation, was nothing more or nothing worse than what you have done.

Nora: You? Do you ask me to believe that you were brave enough to run a risk to save your wife's life?

Krogstad: The law cares nothing about motives.

Nora: Then it must be a very foolish law.

Krogstad: Foolish or not, it is the law by which you will be judged, if I produce this paper in court.

Nora: I don't believe it. Is a daughter not to be allowed to spare her dying father anxiety and care? Is a wife not to be allowed to save her husband's life? I don't know much about law; but I am certain that there must be laws permitting such things as that. Have you no knowledge of such laws — you who are a lawyer? You must be a very poor lawyer, Mr. Krogstad.

Krogstad: Maybe. But matters of business — such business as you and I have had together — do you think I don't understand that? Very well. Do as you please. But let me tell you this — if I lose my position a second time, you shall lose yours with me. *(He bows, and goes out through the hall.)*

Nora (appears buried in thought for a short time, then tosses her head): Nonsense! Trying to frighten me like that! — I am not so silly as he thinks. *(Begins to busy herself putting the children's things in order.)* And yet — ? No, it's impossible! I did it for love's sake.

Children (in the doorway on the left): Mother, the stranger man has gone out through the gate.

Nora: Yes, dears, I know. But, don't tell anyone about the stranger man. Do you hear? Not even papa.

Children: No, mother; but will you come and play again?

Nora: No, no, — not now.

Children: But, mother, you promised us.

Nora: Yes, but I can't now. Run away in; I have such a lot to do. Run away in, my sweet little darlings. *(She gets them into the room by degrees and shuts the door on them; then sits down on the sofa, takes up a piece of needlework and sews a few stitches, but soon stops.)* No! *(Throws down the work, gets up, goes to the hall door and calls out.)* Helen! bring the Tree in. *(Goes to the table on the left, opens a drawer, and stops again.)* No, no! it is quite impossible!

Maid (coming in with the Tree): Where shall I put it, ma'am?

Nora: Here, in the middle of the floor.

Maid: Shall I get you anything else?

Nora: No, thank you. I have all I want.   *(Exit Maid.)*

Nora (begins dressing the tree): A candle here — and flowers here —. The horrible man! It's all nonsense — there's nothing wrong. The Tree shall be splendid! I will do everything I can think of to please you, Torvald! — I will sing for you, dance for you — *(Helmer comes in with some papers under his arm.)* Oh! are you back already?

Helmer: Yes. Has anyone been here?

Nora: Here? No.

Helmer: That is strange. I saw Krogstad going out of the gate.

Nora: Did you? Oh yes, I forgot, Krogstad was here for a moment.

Helmer: Nora, I can see from your manner that he has been here begging you to say a good word for him.

Nora: Yes.

Helmer: And you were to appear to do it of your own accord; you were to conceal from me the fact of his having been here; didn't he beg that of you too?

Nora: Yes, Torvald, but —

Helmer: Nora, Nora, and you would be a party to that sort of thing? To have any talk with a man like that, and give him any sort of promise? And to tell me a lie into the bargain?

Nora: A lie — ?

Helmer: Didn't you tell me no one had been here? *(Shakes his finger at her.)* My little song-bird must never do that again. A song-bird must have a clean beak to chirp with — no false notes! *(Puts his arm around her waist.)* That is so, isn't it? Yes, I am sure it is. *(Lets her go.)* We will say no more about it. *(Sits down by the stove.)* How warm and snug it is here! *(Turns over his papers.)*

Nora (after a short pause, during which she busies herself with the Christmas Tree): Torvald!

Helmer: Yes.

Nora: I am looking forward tremendously to the fancy-dress ball at the Stenborgs' the day after to-morrow.

Helmer: And I am tremendously curious to see what you are going to surprise me with.

Nora: It was very silly of me to want to do that.

Helmer: What do you mean?

Nora: I can't hit upon anything that will do; everything I think of seems so silly and insignificant.

Helmer: Does my little Nora acknowledge that at last?

Nora (standing behind his chair with her arms on the back of it): Are you very busy, Torvald?

Helmer: Well —

Nora: What are all those papers?

Helmer: Bank business.

Nora: Already?

Helmer: I have got authority from the retiring manager to undertake the necessary changes in the staff and in the rearrangement of the work; and I must make use of the Christmas week for that, so as to have everything in order for the new year.

Nora: Then that was why this poor Krogstad —

Helmer: Hm!

Nora (leans against the back of his chair and strokes his hair): If you hadn't been so busy I should have asked you a tremendously big favour, Torvald.

Helmer: What is that? Tell me.

Nora: There is no one has such good taste as you. And I do so want to look nice at the fancy-dress ball. Torvald, couldn't you take me in hand and decide what I shall go as, and what sort of a dress I shall wear?

Helmer: Aha! so my obstinate little woman is obliged to get someone to come to her rescue?

Nora: Yes, Torvald, I can't get along a bit without your help.

Helmer: Very well, I will think it over, we shall manage to hit upon something.

Nora: That is nice of you. *(Goes to the Christmas Tree. A short pause.)* How pretty the red flowers look — . But, tell me, was it really something very bad that this Krogstad was guilty of?

Helmer: He forged someone's name. Have you any idea what that means?

Nora: Isn't it possible that he was driven to do it by necessity?

Helmer: Yes; or, as in so many cases, by imprudence. I am not so heartless as to condemn a man altogether because of a single false step of that kind.

Nora: No, you wouldn't, would you, Torvald?

Helmer: Many a man has been able to retrieve his character, if he has openly confessed his fault and taken his punishment.

Nora: Punishment — ?

Helmer: But Krogstad did nothing of that sort; he got himself out of it by a cunning trick, and that is why he has gone under altogether.

Nora: But do you think it would — ?

Helmer: Just think how a guilty man like that has to lie and play the hypocrite with every one, how he has to wear a mask in the presence of those near and dear to him, even before his own wife and children. And about the children — that is the most terrible part of it all, Nora.

Nora: How?

Helmer: Because such an atmosphere of lies infects and poisons the whole life of a home. Each breath the children take in such a house is full of the germs of evil.

Nora (coming nearer him): Are you sure of that?

Helmer: My dear, I have often seen it in the course of my life as a lawyer. Almost everyone who has gone to the bad early in life has had a deceitful mother.

Nora: Why do you only say — mother?

Helmer: It seems most commonly to be the mother's influence, though naturally a bad father's would have the same result. Every lawyer is familiar with the fact. This Krogstad, now, has been persistently poisoning his own children with lies and dissimulation; that is why I say he has lost all moral character. *(Holds out his hands to her.)* That is why my sweet little

Nora must promise me not to plead his cause. Give me your hand on it. Come, come, what is this? Give me your hand. There now, that's settled. I assure you it would be quite impossible for me to work with him; I literally feel physically ill when I am in the company of such people.

Nora (takes her hand out of his and goes to the opposite side of the Christmas Tree): How hot it is in here; and I have such a lot to do.

Helmer (getting up and putting his papers in order): Yes, and I must try and read through some of these before dinner; and I must think about your costume, too. And it is just possible I may have something ready in gold paper to hang up on the Tree. *(Puts his hand on her head.)* My precious little singing-bird! *(He goes into his room and shuts the door after him.)*

Nora (after a pause, whispers): No, no — it isn't true. It's impossible; it must be impossible.

The Nurse opens the door on the left.

Nurse: The little ones are begging so hard to be allowed to come in to mamma.

Nora: No, no, no! Don't let them come in to me! You stay with them, Anne.

Nurse: Very well, ma'am. *(Shuts the door.)*

Nora (pale with terror): Deprave my little children? Poison my home? *(A short pause. Then she tosses her head.)* It's not true. It can't possibly be true.

ACT II

THE SAME SCENE: *The Christmas Tree is in the corner by the piano, stripped of its ornaments and with burnt-down candle-ends on its dishevelled branches. Nora's cloak and hat are lying on the sofa. She is alone in the room, walking about uneasily. She stops by the sofa and takes up her cloak.*

Nora (drops her cloak): Someone is coming now! *(Goes to the door and listens.)* No — it is no one. Of course, no one will come to-day, Christmas Day — nor to-morrow either. But, perhaps — *(opens the door and looks out).* No, nothing in the letter-box; it is quite empty. *(Comes forward.)* What rubbish! of course he can't be in earnest about it. Such a thing couldn't happen; it is impossible — I have three little children.

Enter the Nurse from the room on the left, carrying a big cardboard box.

Nurse: At last I have found the box with the fancy dress.

Nora: Thanks; put it on the table.

Nurse (doing so): But it is very much in want of mending.

Nora: I should like to tear it into a hundred thousand pieces.

Nurse: What an idea! It can easily be put in order — just a little patience.

Nora: Yes, I will go and get Mrs. Linde to come and help me with it.

Nurse: What, out again? In this horrible weather? You will catch cold, ma'am, and make yourself ill.

Nora: Well, worse than that might happen. How are the children?

Nurse: The poor little souls are playing with their Christmas presents, but —

Nora: Do they ask much for me?

Nurse: You see, they are so accustomed to have their mamma with them.

Nora: Yes, but, nurse, I shall not be able to be so much with them now as I was before.

Nurse: Oh well, young children easily get accustomed to anything.

Nora: Do you think so? Do you think they would forget their mother if she went away altogether?

Nurse: Good heavens! — went away altogether?

Nora: Nurse, I want you to tell me something I have often wondered about — how could you have the heart to put your own child out among strangers?

Nurse: I was obliged to, if I wanted to be little Nora's nurse.

Nora: Yes, but how could you be willing to do it?

Nurse: What, when I was going to get such a good place by it? A poor girl who has got into trouble should be glad to. Besides, that wicked man didn't do a single thing for me.

Nora: But I suppose your daughter has quite forgotten you.

Nurse: No, indeed she hasn't. She wrote to me when she was confirmed, and when she was married.

Nora (putting her arms round her neck): Dear old Anne, you were a good mother to me when I was little.

Nurse: Little Nora, poor dear, had no other mother but me.

Nora: And if my little ones had no other mother, I am sure you would — What nonsense I am talking! *(Opens the box.)* Go in to them. Now I must — . You will see to-morrow how charming I shall look.

Nurse: I am sure there will be no one at the ball so charming as you, ma'am. *(Goes into the room on the left.)*

Nora (begins to unpack the box, but soon pushes it away from her): If only I dared go out. If only no one would come. If only I could be sure nothing would happen here in the meantime. Stuff and nonsense! No one will come. Only I mustn't think about it. I will brush my muff. What lovely, lovely gloves! Out of my thoughts, out of my thoughts! One, two, three, four, five, six — *(Screams.)* Ah! there is someone coming — . *(Makes a movement towards the door, but stands irresolute.)*

Enter Mrs. Linde from the hall, where she has taken off her cloak and hat.

Nora: Oh, it's you, Christine. There is no one else out there, is there? How good of you to come!

Mrs. Linde: I heard you were up asking for me.

Nora: Yes, I was passing by. As a matter of fact, it is something you could help me with. Let us sit down here on the sofa. Look here. To-morrow evening there is to be a fancy-dress ball at the Stenborgs', who live above us;

and Torvald wants me to go as a Neapolitan fisher-girl, and dance the Tarantella that I learned at Capri.

Mrs. Linde: I see; you are going to keep up the character.

Nora: Yes, Torvald wants me to. Look, here is the dress; Torvald had it made for me there, but now it is all so torn, and I haven't any idea —

Mrs. Linde: We will easily put that right. It is only some of the trimming come unsewn here and there. Needle and thread? Now then, that's all we want.

Nora: It *is* nice of you.

Mrs. Linde (sewing): So you are going to be dressed up to-morrow, Nora. I will tell you what — I shall come in for a moment and see you in your fine feathers. But I have completely forgotten to thank you for a delightful evening yesterday.

Nora (gets up, and crosses the stage): Well, I don't think yesterday was as pleasant as usual. You ought to have come to town a little earlier, Christine. Certainly Torvald does understand how to make a house dainty and attractive.

Mrs. Linde: And so do you, it seems to me; you are not your father's daughter for nothing. But tell me, is Doctor Rank always as depressed as he was yesterday?

Nora: No; yesterday it was very noticeable. I must tell you that he suffers from a very dangerous disease. He has consumption of the spine, poor creature. His father was a horrible man who committed all sorts of excesses; and that is why his son was sickly from childhood, do you understand?

Mrs. Linde (dropping her sewing): But, my dearest Nora, how do you know anything about such things?

Nora (walking about): Pooh! When you have three children, you get visits now and then from — from married women, who know something of medical matters, and they talk about one thing and another.

Mrs. Linde (goes on sewing. A short silence): Does Doctor Rank come here everyday?

Nora: Everyday regularly. He is Torvald's most intimate friend, and a great friend of mine too. He is just like one of the family.

Mrs. Linde: But tell me this — is he perfectly sincere? I mean, isn't he the kind of man that is very anxious to make himself agreeable?

Nora: Not in the least. What makes you think that?

Mrs. Linde: When you introduced him to me yesterday, he declared he had often heard my name mentioned in this house; but afterwards I noticed that your husband hadn't the slightest idea who I was. So how could Doctor Rank — ?

Nora: That is quite right, Christine. Torvald is so absurdly fond of me that he wants me absolutely to himself, as he says. At first he used to seem almost jealous if I mentioned any of the dear folk at home, so naturally I gave up doing so. But I often talk about such things with Doctor Rank, because he likes hearing about them.

Mrs. Linde: Listen to me, Nora. You are still very like a child in many things, and I am older than you in many ways and have a little more experience. Let me tell you this — you ought to make an end of it with Doctor Rank.

Nora: What ought I to make an end of?

Mrs. Linde: Of two things, I think. Yesterday you talked some nonsense about a rich admirer who was to leave you money —

Nora: An admirer who doesn't exist, unfortunately! But what then?

Mrs. Linde: Is Doctor Rank a man of means?

Nora: Yes, he is.

Mrs. Linde: And has no one to provide for?

Nora: No, no one; but —

Mrs. Linde: And comes here everyday?

Nora: Yes, I told you so.

Mrs. Linde: But how can this well-bred man be so tactless?

Nora: I don't understand you at all.

Mrs. Linde: Don't prevaricate, Nora. Do you suppose I don't guess who lent you the two hundred and fifty pounds?

Nora: Are you out of your senses? How can you think of such a thing! A friend of ours, who comes here everyday! Do you realise what a horribly painful position that would be?

Mrs. Linde: Then it really isn't he?

Nora: No, certainly not. It would never have entered into my head for a moment. Besides, he had no money to lend then; he came into his money afterwards.

Mrs. Linde: Well, I think that was lucky for you, my dear Nora.

Nora: No, it would never have come into my head to ask Doctor Rank. Although I am quite sure that if I had asked him —

Mrs. Linde: But of course you won't.

Nora: Of course not. I have no reason to think it could possibly be necessary. But I am quite sure that if I told Doctor Rank —

Mrs. Linde: Behind your husband's back?

Nora: I must make an end of it with the other one, and that will be behind his back too. I *must* make an end of it with him.

Mrs. Linde: Yes, that is what I told you yesterday, but —

Nora (walking up and down): A man can put a thing like that straight much easier than a woman —

Mrs. Linde: One's husband, yes.

Nora: Nonsense! *(Standing still.)* When you pay off a debt you get your bond back, don't you?

Mrs. Linde: Yes, as a matter of course.

Nora: And can tear it into a hundred thousand pieces, and burn it up — the nasty dirty paper!

Mrs. Linde (looks hard at her, lays down her sewing and gets up slowly): Nora, you are concealing something from me.

Nora: Do I look as if I were?

Mrs. Linde: Something has happened to you since yesterday morning. Nora, what is it?

Nora (going nearer to her): Christine! *(Listens.)* Hush! there's Torvald come home. Do you mind going in to the children for the present? Torvald can't bear to see dressmaking going on. Let Anne help you.

Mrs. Linde (gathering some of the things together): Certainly — but I am not going away from here until we have had it out with one another. *(She goes into the room on the left, as Helmer comes in from the hall.)*

Nora (going up to Helmer): I have wanted you so much, Torvald dear.

Helmer: Was that the dressmaker?

Nora: No, it was Christine; she is helping me to put my dress in order. You will see I shall look quite smart.

Helmer: Wasn't that a happy thought of mine, now?

Nora: Splendid! But don't you think it is nice of me, too, to do as you wish?

Helmer: Nice? — because you do as your husband wishes? Well, well, you little rogue, I am sure you did not mean it in that way. But I am not going to disturb you; you will want to be trying on your dress, I expect.

Nora: I suppose you are going to work.

Helmer: Yes. *(Shows her a bundle of papers.)* Look at that. I have just been into the bank. *(Turns to go into his room.)*

Nora: Torvald.

Helmer: Yes.

Nora: If your little squirrel were to ask you for something very, very prettily — ?

Helmer: What then?

Nora: Would you do it?

Helmer: I should like to hear what it is, first.

Nora: Your squirrel would run about and do all her tricks if you would be nice, and do what she wants.

Helmer: Speak plainly.

Nora: Your skylark would chirp about in every room, with her song rising and falling —

Helmer: Well, my skylark does that anyhow.

Nora: I would play the fairy and dance for you in the moonlight, Torvald.

Helmer: Nora — you surely don't mean that request you made to me this morning?

Nora (going near him): Yes, Torvald, I beg you so earnestly —

Helmer: Have you really the courage to open up that question again?

Nora: Yes, dear, you *must* do as I ask; you *must* let Krogstad keep his post in the bank.

Helmer: My dear Nora, it is his post that I have arranged Mrs. Linde shall have.

Nora: Yes, you have been awfully kind about that; but you could just as well dismiss some other clerk instead of Krogstad.

Helmer: This is simply incredible obstinacy! Because you chose to give him a thoughtless promise that you would speak for him, I am expected to —

Nora: That isn't the reason, Torvald. It is for your own sake. This fellow writes in the most scurrilous newspapers; you have told me so yourself. He can do you an unspeakable amount of harm. I am frightened to death of him —

Helmer: Ah, I understand; it is recollections of the past that scare you.

Nora: What do you mean?

Helmer: Naturally you are thinking of your father.

Nora: Yes — yes, of course. Just recall to your mind what these malicious creatures wrote in the papers about papa, and how horribly they slandered him. I believe they would have procured his dismissal if the Department had not sent you over to inquire into it, and if you had not been so kindly disposed and helpful to him.

Helmer: My little Nora, there is an important difference between your father and me. Your father's reputation as a public official was not above suspicion. Mine is, and I hope it will continue to be so, as long as I hold my office.

Nora: You never can tell what mischief these men may contrive. We ought to be so well off, so snug and happy here in our peaceful home, and have no cares — you and I and the children, Torvald! That is why I beg you so earnestly —

Helmer: And it is just by interceding for him that you make it impossible for me to keep him. It is already known at the Bank that I mean to dismiss Krogstad. Is it to get about now that the new manager has changed his mind at his wife's bidding —

Nora: And what if it did?

Helmer: Of course! — if only this obstinate little person can get her way! Do you suppose I am going to make myself ridiculous before my whole staff, to let people think that I am a man to be swayed by all sorts of outside influence? I should very soon feel the consequences of it, I can tell you! And besides, there is one thing that makes it quite impossible for me to have Krogstad in the Bank as long as I am manager.

Nora: Whatever is that?

Helmer: His moral failings I might perhaps have overlooked, if necessary —

Nora: Yes, you could — couldn't you?

Helmer: And I hear he is a good worker, too. But I knew him when we were boys. It was one of those rash friendships that so often prove an incubus in afterlife. I may as well tell you plainly, we were once on very intimate terms with one another. But this tactless fellow lays no restraint on himself when other people are present. On the contrary, he thinks it gives him the right to adopt a familiar tone with me, and every minute it is "I say, Helmer, old fellow!" and that sort of thing. I assure you it is extremely painful for me. He would make my position in the Bank intolerable.

Nora: Torvald, I don't believe you mean that.

Helmer: Don't you? Why not?

Nora: Because it is such a narrow-minded way of looking at things.

Helmer: What are you saying? Narrow-minded? Do you think I am narrow-minded?

Nora: No, just the opposite, dear — and it is exactly for that reason.

Helmer: It's the same thing. You say my point of view is narrow-minded, so I must be so too. Narrow-minded! Very well — I must put an end to this. *(Goes to the hall door and calls.)* Helen!

Nora: What are you going to do?

Helmer (looking among his papers): Settle it. *(Enter Maid.)* Look here; take this letter and go downstairs with it at once. Find a messenger and tell him to deliver it, and be quick. The address is on it, and here is the money.

Maid: Very well, sir. *(Exit with the letter.)*

Helmer (putting his papers together): Now then, little Miss Obstinate.

Nora (breathlessly): Torvald — what was that letter?

Helmer: Krogstad's dismissal.

Nora: Call her back, Torvald! There is still time. Oh Torvald, call her back! Do it for my sake — for your own sake — for the children's sake! Do you hear me, Torvald? Call her back! You don't know what that letter can bring upon us.

Helmer: It's too late.

Nora: Yes, it's too late.

Helmer: My dear Nora, I can forgive the anxiety you are in, although really it is an insult to me. It is, indeed. Isn't it an insult to think that I should be afraid of a starving quill-driver's vengeance? But I forgive you nevertheless, because it is such eloquent witness to your great love for me. *(Takes her in his arms.)* And that is as it should be, my own darling Nora. Come what will, you may be sure I shall have both courage and strength if they be needed. You will see I am man enough to take everything upon myself.

Nora (in a horror-stricken voice): What do you mean by that?

Helmer: Everything, I say —

Nora (recovering herself): You will never have to do that.

Helmer: That's right. Well, we will share it, Nora, as man and wife should. That is how it shall be. *(Caressing her.)* Are you content now? There! there! — not these frightened dove's eyes! The whole thing is only the wildest fancy! — Now, you must go and play through the Tarantella and practise with your tambourine. I shall go into the inner office and shut the door, and I shall hear nothing; you can make as much noise as you please. *(Turns back at the door.)* And when Rank comes, tell him where he will find me. *(Nods to her, takes his papers and goes into his room, and shuts the door after him.)*

Nora (bewildered with anxiety, stands as if rooted to the spot, and whispers): He was capable of doing it. He will do it. He will do it in spite of everything. — No, not that! Never, never! Anything rather than that! Oh, for some help, some way out of it! *(The door-bell rings.)* Doctor Rank! Anything rather than that — anything, whatever it is! *(She puts her hands over*

her face, pulls herself together, goes to the door and opens it. Rank is stand-
ing without, hanging up his coat. During the following dialogue it begins to
grow dark.)

Nora: Good-day, Doctor Rank. I knew your ring. But you mustn't go in to
   Torvald now; I think he is busy with something.

Rank: And you?

Nora (brings him in and shuts the door after him): Oh, you know very well I
   always have time for you.

Rank: Thank you. I shall make use of as much of it as I can.

Nora: What do you mean by that? As much of it as you can?

Rank: Well, does that alarm you?

Nora: It was such a strange way of putting it. Is anything likely to happen?

Rank: Nothing but what I have long been prepared for. But I certainly
   didn't expect it to happen so soon.

Nora (gripping him by the arm): What have you found out? Doctor Rank,
   you must tell me.

Rank (sitting down by the stove): It is all up with me. And it can't be helped.

Nora (with a sigh of relief): Is it about yourself?

Rank: Who else? It is no use lying to one's self. I am the most wretched of
   all my patients, Mrs. Helmer. Lately I have been taking stock of my internal economy. Bankrupt! Probably within a month I shall lie rotting
   in the churchyard.

Nora: What an ugly thing to say!

Rank: The thing itself is cursedly ugly, and the worst of it is that I shall have
   to face so much more that is ugly before that. I shall only make one
   more examination of myself; when I have done that, I shall know pretty
   certainly when it will be that the horrors of dissolution will begin. There
   is something I want to tell you. Helmer's refined nature gives him an
   unconquerable disgust at everything that is ugly; I won't have him in my
   sick-room.

Nora: Oh, but, Doctor Rank —

Rank: I won't have him there. Not on any account. I bar my door to him.
   As soon as I am quite certain that the worst has come, I shall send
   you my card with a black cross on it, and then you will know that the
   loathsome end has begun.

Nora: You are quite absurd to-day. And I wanted you so much to be in a
   really good humour.

Rank: With death stalking beside me? — To have to pay this penalty for another man's sin? Is there any justice in that? And in every single family, in one way or another, some such inexorable retribution is being
   exacted —

Nora (putting her hands over her ears): Rubbish! Do talk of something
   cheerful.

Rank: Oh, it's a mere laughing matter, the whole thing. My poor innocent
   spine has to suffer for my father's youthful amusements.

Nora (sitting at the table on the left): I suppose you mean that he was too
   partial to asparagus and pâté de foie gras, don't you?

Rank: Yes, and to truffles.

Nora: Truffles, yes. And oysters too, I suppose?

Rank: Oysters, of course, that goes without saying.

Nora: And heaps of port and champagne. It is sad that all these nice things should take their revenge on our bones.

Rank: Especially that they should revenge themselves on the unlucky bones of those who have not had the satisfaction of enjoying them.

Nora: Yes, that's the saddest part of it all.

Rank (with a searching look at her): Hm! —

Nora (after a short pause): Why did you smile?

Rank: No, it was you that laughed.

Nora: No, it was you that smiled, Doctor Rank!

Rank (rising): You are a greater rascal than I thought.

Nora: I am in a silly mood to-day.

Rank: So it seems.

Nora (putting her hands on his shoulders): Dear, dear Doctor Rank, death mustn't take you away from Torvald and me.

Rank: It is a loss you would easily recover from. Those who are gone are soon forgotten.

Nora (looking at him anxiously): Do you believe that?

Rank: People form new ties, and then —

Nora: Who will form new ties?

Rank: Both you and Helmer, when I am gone. You yourself are already on the high road to it, I think. What did that Mrs. Linde want here last night?

Nora: Oho! — you don't mean to say you are jealous of poor Christine?

Rank: Yes, I am. She will be my successor in this house. When I am done for, this woman will —

Nora: Hush! don't speak so loud. She is in that room.

Rank: To-day again. There, you see.

Nora: She has only come to sew my dress for me. Bless my soul, how unreasonable you are! *(Sits down on the sofa.)* Be nice now, Doctor Rank, and to-morrow you will see how beautifully I shall dance, and you can imagine I am doing it all for you — and for Torvald too, of course. *(Takes various things out of the box.)* Doctor Rank, come and sit down here, and I will show you something.

Rank (sitting down): What is it?

Nora: Just look at those!

Rank: Silk stockings.

Nora: Flesh-coloured. Aren't they lovely? It is so dark here now, but to-morrow —. No, no, no! you must only look at the feet. Oh well, you may have leave to look at the legs too.

Rank: Hm! —

Nora: Why are you looking so critical? Don't you think they will fit me?

Rank: I have no means of forming an opinion about that.

Nora (looks at him for a moment): For shame! *(Hits him lightly on the ear with the stockings.)* That's to punish you. *(Folds them up again.)*

Rank: And what other nice things am I to be allowed to see?

Nora: Not a single thing more, for being so naughty. *(She looks among the things, humming to herself.)*

Rank (after a short silence): When I am sitting here, talking to you as intimately as this, I cannot imagine for a moment what would have become of me if I had never come into this house.

Nora (smiling): I believe you do feel thoroughly at home with us.

Rank (in a lower voice, looking straight in front of him): And to be obliged to leave it all —

Nora: Nonsense, you are not going to leave it.

Rank (as before): And not be able to leave behind one the slightest token of one's gratitude, scarcely even a fleeting regret — nothing but an empty place which the first comer can fill as well as any other.

Nora: And if I asked you now for a — ? No!

Rank: For what?

Nora: For a big proof of your friendship —

Rank: Yes, yes!

Nora: I mean a tremendously big favour.

Rank: Would you really make me so happy for once?

Nora: Ah, but you don't know what it is yet.

Rank: No — but tell me.

Nora: I really can't, Doctor Rank. It is something out of all reason; it means advice, and help, and a favour —

Rank: The bigger a thing it is the better. I can't conceive what it is you mean. Do tell me. Haven't I your confidence?

Nora: More than anyone else. I know you are my truest and best friend, and so I will tell you what it is. Well, Doctor Rank, it is something you must help me to prevent. You know how devotedly, how inexpressibly deeply Torvald loves me; he would never for a moment hesitate to give his life for me.

Rank (leaning towards her): Nora — do you think he is the only one — ?

Nora (with a slight start): The only one — ?

Rank: The only one who would gladly give his life for your sake.

Nora (sadly): Is that it?

Rank: I was determined you should know it before I went away, and there will never be a better opportunity than this. Now you know it, Nora. And now you know, too, that you can trust me as you would trust no one else.

Nora (rises, deliberately and quietly): Let me pass.

Rank (makes room for her to pass him, but sits still): Nora!

Nora (at the hall door): Helen, bring in the lamp. *(Goes over to the stove.)* Dear Doctor Rank, that was really horrid of you.

Rank: To have loved you as much as anyone else does? Was that horrid?

Nora: No, but to go and tell me so. There was really no need —

Rank: What do you mean? Did you know — ? *(Maid enters with lamp, puts it down on the table, and goes out.)* Nora — Mrs. Helmer — tell me, had you any idea of this?

Nora: Oh, how do I know whether I had or whether I hadn't? I really can't tell you — To think you could be so clumsy, Doctor Rank! We were getting on so nicely.

Rank: Well, at all events you know now that you can command me, body and soul. So won't you speak out?

Nora (looking at him): After what happened?

Rank: I beg you to let me know what it is.

Nora: I can't tell you anything now.

Rank: Yes, yes. You mustn't punish me in that way. Let me have permission to do for you whatever a man may do.

Nora: You can do nothing for me now. Besides, I really don't need any help at all. You will find that the whole thing is merely fancy on my part. It really is so — of course it is! *(Sits down in the rocking-chair, and looks at him with a smile.)* You are a nice sort of man, Doctor Rank! — don't you feel ashamed of yourself, now the lamp has come?

Rank: Not a bit. But perhaps I had better go — for ever?

Nora: No, indeed, you shall not. Of course you must come here just as before. You know very well Torvald can't do without you.

Rank: Yes, but you?

Nora: Oh, I am always tremendously pleased when you come.

Rank: It is just that, that put me on the wrong track. You are a riddle to me. I have often thought that you would almost as soon be in my company as in Helmer's.

Nora: Yes — you see there are some people one loves best, and others whom one would almost always rather have as companions.

Rank: Yes, there is something in that.

Nora: When I was at home, of course I loved papa best. But I always thought it tremendous fun if I could steal down into the maids' room, because they never moralised at all, and talked to each other about such entertaining things.

Rank: I see — it is *their* place I have taken.

Nora (jumping up and going to him): Oh, dear, nice Doctor Rank, I never meant that at all. But surely you can understand that being with Torvald is a little like being with papa —

Enter Maid from the hall.

Maid: If you please, ma'am. *(Whispers and hands her a card.)*

Nora (glancing at the card): Oh! *(Puts it in her pocket.)*

Rank: Is there anything wrong?

Nora: No, no, not in the least. It is only something — it is my new dress —

Rank: What? Your dress is lying there.

Nora: Oh, yes, that one; but this is another. I ordered it. Torvald mustn't know about it —

Rank: Oho! Then that was the great secret.

Nora: Of course. Just go in to him; he is sitting in the inner room. Keep him as long as —

Rank: Make your mind easy; I won't let him escape. *(Goes into Helmer's room.)*

Nora (to the Maid): And he is standing waiting in the kitchen?

Maid: Yes; he came up the back stairs.

Nora: But didn't you tell him no one was in?

Maid: Yes, but it was no good.

Nora: He won't go away?

Maid: No; he says he won't until he has seen you, ma'am.

Nora: Well, let him come in — but quietly. Helen, you mustn't say anything about it to anyone. It is a surprise for my husband.

Maid: Yes, ma'am, I quite understand. *(Exit.)*

Nora: This dreadful thing is going to happen! It will happen in spite of me! No, no, no, it can't happen — it shan't happen! *(She bolts the door of Helmer's room. The Maid opens the hall door for Krogstad and shuts it after him. He is wearing a fur coat, high boots and a fur cap.)*

Nora (advancing towards him): Speak low — my husband is at home.

Krogstad: No matter about that.

Nora: What do you want of me?

Krogstad: An explanation of something.

Nora: Make haste then. What is it?

Krogstad: You know, I suppose, that I have got my dismissal.

Nora: I couldn't prevent it, Mr. Krogstad. I fought as hard as I could on your side, but it was no good.

Krogstad: Does your husband love you so little, then? He knows what I can expose you to, and yet he ventures —

Nora: How can you suppose that he has any knowledge of the sort?

Krogstad: I didn't suppose so at all. It would not be the least like our dear Torvald Helmer to show so much courage —

Nora: Mr. Krogstad, a little respect for my husband, please.

Krogstad: Certainly — all the respect he deserves. But since you have kept the matter so carefully to yourself, I make bold to suppose that you have a little clearer idea, than you had yesterday, of what it actually is that you have done?

Nora: More than you could ever teach me.

Krogstad: Yes, such a bad lawyer as I am.

Nora: What is it you want of me?

Krogstad: Only to see how you were, Mrs. Helmer. I have been thinking about you all day long. A mere cashier, a quill-driver, a — well, a man like me — even he has a little of what is called feeling, you know.

Nora: Show it, then; think of my little children.

Krogstad: Have you and your husband thought of mine? But never mind about that. I only wanted to tell you that you need not take this matter too seriously. In the first place there will be no accusation made on my part.

Nora: No, of course not; I was sure of that.

Krogstad: The whole thing can be arranged amicably; there is no reason why anyone should know anything about it. It will remain a secret between us three.

Nora: My husband must never get to know anything about it.

Krogstad: How will you be able to prevent it? Am I to understand that you can pay the balance that is owing?

Nora: No, not just at present.

Krogstad: Or perhaps that you have some expedient for raising the money soon?

Nora: No expedient that I mean to make use of.

Krogstad: Well, in any case, it would have been of no use to you now. If you stood there with ever so much money in your hand, I would never part with your bond.

Nora: Tell me what purpose you mean to put it to.

Krogstad: I shall only preserve it — keep it in my possession. No one who is not concerned in the matter shall have the slightest hint of it. So that if the thought of it has driven you to any desperate resolution —

Nora: It has.

Krogstad: If you had it in your mind to run away from your home —

Nora: I had.

Krogstad: Or even something worse —

Nora: How could you know that?

Krogstad: Give up the idea.

Nora: How did you know I had thought of *that*?

Krogstad: Most of us think of that at first. I did, too — but I hadn't the courage.

Nora (faintly): No more had I.

Krogstad (in a tone of relief): No, that's it, isn't it — you hadn't the courage either?

Nora: No, I haven't — I haven't.

Krogstad: Besides, it would have been a great piece of folly. Once the first storm at home is over — . I have a letter for your husband in my pocket.

Nora: Telling him everything?

Krogstad: In as lenient a manner as I possibly could.

Nora (quickly): He mustn't get the letter. Tear it up. I will find some means of getting money.

Krogstad: Excuse me, Mrs. Helmer, but I think I told you just now —

Nora: I am not speaking of what I owe you. Tell me what sum you are asking my husband for, and I will get the money.

Krogstad: I am not asking your husband for a penny.

Nora: What do you want, then?

Krogstad: I will tell you. I want to rehabilitate myself, Mrs. Helmer; I want to get on; and in that your husband must help me. For the last year and a half I have not had a hand in anything dishonourable, and all that time I have been struggling in most restricted circumstances. I was content to work my way up step by step. Now I am turned out, and I am not going to be satisfied with merely being taken into favour again. I want to get on, I tell you. I want to get into the Bank again, in a higher position. Your husband must make a place for me —

Nora: That he will never do!

Krogstad: He will; I know him; he dare not protest. And as soon as I am in there again with him, then you will see! Within a year I shall be the manager's right hand. It will be Nils Krogstad and not Torvald Helmer who manages the Bank.

Nora: That's a thing you will never see!

Krogstad: Do you mean that you will — ?

Nora: I have courage enough for it now.

Krogstad: Oh, you can't frighten me. A fine, spoilt lady like you —

Nora: You will see, you will see.

Krogstad: Under the ice, perhaps? Down into the cold, coal-black water? And then, in the spring, to float up to the surface, all horrible and unrecognisable, with your hair fallen out —

Nora: You can't frighten me.

Krogstad: Nor you me. People don't do such things, Mrs. Helmer. Besides, what use would it be? I should have him completely in my power all the same.

Nora: Afterwards? When I am no longer —

Krogstad: Have you forgotten that it is I who have the keeping of your reputation? *(Nora stands speechlessly looking at him.)* Well, now, I have warned you. Do not do anything foolish. When Helmer has had my letter, I shall expect a message from him. And be sure you remember that it is your husband himself who has forced me into such ways as this again. I will never forgive him for that. Good-bye, Mrs. Helmer. *(Exit through the hall.)*

Nora (goes to the hall door, opens it slightly and listens): He is going. He is not putting the letter in the box. Oh no, no! that's impossible! *(Opens the door by degrees.)* What is that? He is standing outside. He is not going downstairs. Is he hesitating? Can he — ? *(A letter drops into the box; then Krogstad's footsteps are heard, till they die away as he goes downstairs. Nora utters a stifled cry, and runs across the room to the table by the sofa. A short pause.)*

Nora: In the letter-box. *(Steals across to the hall door.)* There it lies — Torvald, Torvald, there is no hope for us now!

Mrs. Linde comes in from the room on the left, carrying the dress.

Mrs. Linde: There, I can't see anything more to mend now. Would you like to try it on — ?

Nora (in a hoarse whisper): Christine, come here.

Mrs. Linde (throwing the dress down on the sofa): What is the matter with you? You look so agitated!

Nora: Come here. Do you see that letter? There, look — you can see it through the glass in the letter-box.

Mrs. Linde: Yes, I see it.

Nora: That letter is from Krogstad.

Mrs. Linde: Nora — it was Krogstad who lent you the money!

Nora: Yes, and now Torvald will know all about it.

Mrs. Linde: Believe me, Nora, that's the best thing for both of you.

Nora: You don't know all. I forged a name.

Mrs. Linde: Good heavens —!

Nora: I only want to say this to you, Christine — you must be my witness.

Mrs. Linde: Your witness? What do you mean? What am I to —?

Nora: If I should go out of my mind — and it might easily happen —

Mrs. Linde: Nora!

Nora: Or if anything else should happen to me — anything, for instance, that might prevent my being here —

Mrs. Linde: Nora! Nora! you are quite out of your mind.

Nora: And if it should happen that there were some one who wanted to take all the responsibility, all the blame, you understand —

Mrs. Linde: Yes, yes — but how can you suppose —?

Nora: Then you must be my witness, that it is not true, Christine. I am not out of my mind at all! I am in my right senses now, and I tell you no one else has known anything about it; I, and I alone, did the whole thing. Remember that.

Mrs. Linde: I will, indeed. But I don't understand all this.

Nora: How should you understand it? A wonderful thing is going to happen!

Mrs. Linde: A wonderful thing?

Nora: Yes, a wonderful thing! — But it is so terrible, Christine; it *mustn't* happen, not for all the world.

Mrs. Linde: I will go at once and see Krogstad.

Nora: Don't go to him; he will do you some harm.

Mrs. Linde: There was a time when he would gladly do anything for my sake.

Nora: He?

Mrs. Linde: Where does he live?

Nora: How should I know —? Yes *(feeling in her pocket)*, here is his card. But the letter, the letter —!

Helmer (calls from his room, knocking at the door): Nora!

Nora (cries out anxiously): Oh, what's that? What do you want?

Helmer: Don't be so frightened. We are not coming in; you have locked the door. Are you trying on your dress?

Nora: Yes, that's it. I look so nice, Torvald.

Mrs. Linde (who has read the card): I see he lives at the corner here.

Nora: Yes, but it's no use. It is hopeless. The letter is lying there in the box.

Mrs. Linde: And your husband keeps the key?

Nora: Yes, always.

Mrs. Linde: Krogstad must ask for his letter back unread, he must find some pretence —

Nora: But it is just at this time that Torvald generally —

Mrs. Linde: You must delay him. Go in to him in the meantime. I will come back as soon as I can. *(She goes out hurriedly through the hall door.)*

Nora (goes to Helmer's door, opens it and peeps in): Torvald!

Helmer (from the inner room): Well? May I venture at last to come into my own room again? Come along, Rank, now you will see — *(Halting in the doorway.)* But what is this?

Nora: What is what, dear?

Helmer: Rank led me to expect a splendid transformation.

Rank (in the doorway): I understood so, but evidently I was mistaken.

Nora: Yes, nobody is to have the chance of admiring me in my dress until to-morrow.

Helmer: But, my dear Nora, you look so worn out. Have you been practising too much?

Nora: No, I have not practised at all.

Helmer: But you will need to —

Nora: Yes, indeed I shall, Torvald. But I can't get on a bit without you to help me; I have absolutely forgotten the whole thing.

Helmer: Oh, we will soon work it up again.

Nora: Yes, help me, Torvald. Promise that you will! I am so nervous about it — all the people —. You must give yourself up to me entirely this evening. Not the tiniest bit of business — you mustn't even take a pen in your hand. Will you promise, Torvald dear?

Helmer: I promise. This evening I will be wholly and absolutely at your service, you helpless little mortal. Ah, by the way, first of all I will just — *(Goes towards the hall door.)*

Nora: What are you going to do there?

Helmer: Only see if any letters have come.

Nora: No, no! don't do that, Torvald!

Helmer: Why not?

Nora: Torvald, please don't. There is nothing there.

Helmer: Well, let me look. *(Turns to go to the letter-box. Nora, at the piano, plays the first bars of the Tarantella. Helmer stops in the doorway.)* Aha!

Nora: I can't dance tomorrow if I don't practise with you.

Helmer (going up to her): Are you really so afraid of it, dear?

Nora: Yes, so dreadfully afraid of it. Let me practise at once; there is time now, before we go to dinner. Sit down and play for me, Torvald dear; criticise me, and correct me as you play.

Helmer: With great pleasure, if you wish me to. *(Sits down at the piano.)*

Nora (takes out of the box a tambourine and a long variegated shawl. She hastily drapes the shawl round her. Then she springs to the front of the stage and calls out): Now play for me! I am going to dance!

Helmer plays and Nora dances. Rank stands by the piano behind Helmer, and looks on.

Helmer (as he plays): Slower, slower!

Nora: I can't do it any other way.

Helmer: Not so violently, Nora!

Nora: This is the way.

Helmer (stops playing): No, no — that is not a bit right.

Nora (laughing and swinging the tambourine): Didn't I tell you so?

Rank: Let me play for her.

Helmer (getting up): Yes, do. I can correct her better then.

Rank sits down at the piano and plays. Nora dances more and more wildly. Helmer has taken up a position beside the stove, and during her dance gives her frequent instructions. She does not seem to hear him; her hair comes down and falls over her shoulders; she pays no attention to it, but goes on dancing. Enter Mrs. Linde.

Mrs. Linde (standing as if spell-bound in the doorway): Oh! —

Nora (as she dances): Such fun, Christine!

Helmer: My dear darling Nora, you are dancing as if your life depended on it.

Nora: So it does.

Helmer: Stop, Rank; this is sheer madness. Stop, I tell you! *(Rank stops playing, and Nora suddenly stands still. Helmer goes up to her.)* I could never have believed it. You have forgotten everything I taught you.

Nora (throwing away the tambourine): There, you see.

Helmer: You will want a lot of coaching.

Nora: Yes, you see how much I need it. You must coach me up to the last minute. Promise me that, Torvald!

Helmer: You can depend on me.

Nora: You must not think of anything but me, either to-day or to-morrow; you mustn't open a single letter — not even open the letter-box —

Helmer: Ah, you are still afraid of that fellow —

Nora: Yes, indeed I am.

Helmer: Nora, I can tell from your looks that there is a letter from him lying there.

Nora: I don't know; I think there is; but you must not read anything of that kind now. Nothing horrid must come between us until this is all over.

Rank (whispers to Helmer): You mustn't contradict her.

Helmer (taking her in his arms): The child shall have her way. But to-morrow night, after you have danced —

Nora: Then you will be free. *(The Maid appears in the doorway to the right.)*

Maid: Dinner is served, ma'am.

Nora: We will have champagne, Helen.

Maid: Very good, ma'am.   [*Exit.*]

Helmer: Hullo! — are we going to have a banquet?

Nora: Yes, a champagne banquet until the small hours. *(Calls out.)* And a few macaroons, Helen — lots, just for once!

Helmer: Come, come, don't be so wild and nervous. Be my own little skylark, as you used.

Nora: Yes, dear, I will. But go in now and you too, Doctor Rank. Christine, you must help me to do up my hair.

Rank (whispers to Helmer as they go out): I suppose there is nothing — she is not expecting anything?

Helmer: Far from it, my dear fellow; it is simply nothing more than this childish nervousness I was telling you of. *(They go into the right-hand room.)*

Nora: Well!

Mrs. Linde: Gone out of town.

Nora: I could tell from your face.

Mrs. Linde: He is coming home to-morrow evening. I wrote a note for him.

Nora: You should have let it alone; you must prevent nothing. After all, it is splendid to be waiting for a wonderful thing to happen.

Mrs. Linde: What is it that you are waiting for?

Nora: Oh, you wouldn't understand. Go in to them, I will come in a moment. (*Mrs. Linde goes into the dining-room. Nora stands still for a little while, as if to compose herself. Then she looks at her watch.*) Five o'clock. Seven hours until midnight; and then four-and-twenty hours until the next midnight. Then the Tarantella will be over. Twenty-four and seven? Thirty-one hours to live.

Helmer (from the doorway on the right): Where's my little skylark?

Nora (going to him with her arms outstretched): Here she is!

ACT III

THE SAME SCENE: *The table has been placed in the middle of the stage, with chairs round it. A lamp is burning on the table. The door into the hall stands open. Dance music is heard in the room above. Mrs. Linde is sitting at the table idly turning over the leaves of a book; she tries to read, but does not seem able to collect her thoughts. Every now and then she listens intently for a sound at the outer door.*

Mrs. Linde (looking at her watch): Not yet — and the time is nearly up. If only he does not — . (*Listens again.*) Ah, there he is. (*Goes into the hall and opens the outer door carefully. Light footsteps are heard on the stairs. She whispers.*) Come in. There is no one here.

Krogstad (in the doorway): I found a note from you at home. What does this mean?

Mrs. Linde: It is absolutely necessary that I should have a talk with you.

Krogstad: Really? And is it absolutely necessary that it should be here?

Mrs. Linde: It is impossible where I live; there is no private entrance to my rooms. Come in; we are quite alone. The maid is asleep, and the Helmers are at the dance upstairs.

Krogstad (coming into the room): Are the Helmers really at a dance to-night?

Mrs. Linde: Yes, why not?

Krogstad: Certainly — why not?

Mrs. Linde: Now, Nils, let us have a talk.

Krogstad: Can we two have anything to talk about?

Mrs. Linde: We have a great deal to talk about.

Krogstad: I shouldn't have thought so.

Mrs. Linde: No, you have never properly understood me.

Krogstad: Was there anything else to understand except what was obvious to all the world — a heartless woman jilts a man when a more lucrative chance turns up?

Mrs. Linde: Do you believe I am as absolutely heartless as all that? And do you believe that I did it with a light heart?

Krogstad: Didn't you?

Mrs. Linde: Nils, did you really think that?

Krogstad: If it were as you say, why did you write to me as you did at the time?

Mrs. Linde: I could do nothing else. As I had to break with you, it was my duty also to put an end to all that you felt for me.

Krogstad (wringing his hands): So that was it. And all this — only for the sake of money!

Mrs. Linde: You must not forget that I had a helpless mother and two little brothers. We couldn't wait for you, Nils; your prospects seemed hopeless then.

Krogstad: That may be so, but you had no right to throw me over for anyone else's sake.

Mrs. Linde: Indeed I don't know. Many a time did I ask myself if I had the right to do it.

Krogstad (more gently): When I lost you, it was as if all the solid ground went from under my feet. Look at me now — I am a shipwrecked man clinging to a bit of wreckage.

Mrs. Linde: But help may be near.

Krogstad: It *was* near; but then you came and stood in my way.

Mrs. Linde: Unintentionally, Nils. It was only to-day that I learned it was your place I was going to take in the Bank.

Krogstad: I believe you, if you say so. But now that you know it, are you not going to give it up to me?

Mrs. Linde: No, because that would not benefit you in the least.

Krogstad: Oh, benefit, benefit — I would have done it whether or no.

Mrs. Linde: I have learned to act prudently. Life, and hard, bitter necessity have taught me that.

Krogstad: And life has taught me not to believe in fine speeches.

Mrs. Linde: Then life has taught you something very reasonable. But deeds you must believe in?

Krogstad: What do you mean by that?

Mrs. Linde: You said you were like a shipwrecked man clinging to some wreckage.

Krogstad: I had good reason to say so.

Mrs. Linde: Well, I am like a shipwrecked woman clinging to some wreckage — no one to mourn for, no one to care for.

Krogstad: It was your own choice.

Mrs. Linde: There was no other choice — then.

Krogstad: Well, what now?

Mrs. Linde: Nils, how would it be if we two shipwrecked people could join forces?

Krogstad: What are you saying?

Mrs. Linde: Two on the same piece of wreckage would stand a better chance than each on their own.

Krogstad: Christine!

Mrs. Linde: What do you suppose brought me to town?

Krogstad: Do you mean that you gave me a thought?

Mrs. Linde: I could not endure life without work. All my life, as long as I can remember, I have worked, and it has been my greatest and only pleasure. But now I am quite alone in the world — my life is so dreadfully empty and I feel so forsaken. There is not the least pleasure in working for one's self. Nils, give me someone and something to work for.

Krogstad: I don't trust that. It is nothing but a woman's overstrained sense of generosity that prompts you to make such an offer of yourself.

Mrs. Linde: Have you ever noticed anything of the sort in me?

Krogstad: Could you really do it? Tell me — do you know all about my past life?

Mrs. Linde: Yes.

Krogstad: And do you know what they think of me here?

Mrs. Linde: You seemed to me to imply that with me you might have been quite another man.

Krogstad: I am certain of it.

Mrs. Linde: Is it too late now?

Krogstad: Christine, are you saying this deliberately? Yes, I am sure you are. I see it in your face. Have you really the courage, then — ?

Mrs. Linde: I want to be a mother to someone, and your children need a mother. We two need each other. Nils, I have faith in your real character — I can dare anything together with you.

Krogstad (grasps her hands): Thanks, thanks, Christine! Now I shall find a way to clear myself in the eyes of the world. Ah, but I forgot —

Mrs. Linde (listening): Hush! The Tarantella! Go, go!

Krogstad: Why? What is it?

Mrs. Linde: Do you hear them up there? When that is over, we may expect them back.

Krogstad: Yes, yes — I will go. But it is all no use. Of course you are not aware what steps I have taken in the matter of the Helmers.

Mrs. Linde: Yes, I know all about that.

Krogstad: And in spite of that have you the courage to — ?

Mrs. Linde: I understand very well to what lengths a man like you might be driven by despair.

Krogstad: If I could only undo what I have done!

Mrs. Linde: You cannot. Your letter is lying in the letter-box now.

Krogstad: Are you sure of that?

Mrs. Linde: Quite sure, but —

Krogstad (with a searching look at her): Is that what it all means? — that you want to save your friend at any cost? Tell me frankly. Is that it?

Mrs. Linde: Nils, a woman who has once sold herself for another's sake, doesn't do it a second time.

Krogstad: I will ask for my letter back.

Mrs. Linde: No, no.

Krogstad: Yes, of course I will. I will wait here until Helmer comes; I will tell him he must give me my letter back — that it only concerns my dismissal — that he is not to read it —

Mrs. Linde: No, Nils, you must not recall your letter.

Krogstad: But, tell me, wasn't it for that very purpose that you asked me to meet you here?

Mrs. Linde: In my first moment of fright, it was. But twenty-four hours have elapsed since then, and in that time I have witnessed incredible things in this house. Helmer must know all about it. This unhappy secret must be disclosed; they must have a complete understanding between them, which is impossible with all this concealment and falsehood going on.

Krogstad: Very well, if you will take the responsibility. But there is one thing I can do in any case, and I shall do it at once.

Mrs. Linde (listening): You must be quick and go! The dance is over; we are not safe a moment longer.

Krogstad: I will wait for you below.

Mrs. Linde: Yes, do. You must see me back to my door.

Krogstad: I have never had such an amazing piece of good fortune in my life! *(Goes out through the outer door. The door between the room and the hall remains open.)*

Mrs. Linde (tidying up the room and laying her hat and cloak ready): What a difference! what a difference! Some-one to work for and live for — a home to bring comfort into. That I will do, indeed. I wish they would be quick and come — *(Listens.)* Ah, there they are now. I must put on my things. *(Takes up her hat and cloak. Helmer's and Nora's voices are heard outside; a key is turned, and Helmer brings Nora almost by force into the hall. She is in an Italian costume with a large black shawl around her; he is in evening dress, and a black domino° which is flying open.)*

Nora (hanging back in the doorway, and struggling with him): No, no, no! — don't take me in. I want to go upstairs again; I don't want to leave so early.

Helmer: But, my dearest Nora —

Nora: Please, Torvald dear — please, *please* — only an hour more.

Helmer: Not a single minute, my sweet Nora. You know that was our agreement. Come along into the room; you are catching cold standing there. *(He brings her gently into the room, in spite of her resistance.)*

Mrs. Linde: Good-evening.

Nora: Christine!

Helmer: You here, so late, Mrs. Linde?

Mrs. Linde: Yes, you must excuse me; I was so anxious to see Nora in her dress.

Nora: Have you been sitting here waiting for me?

---

domino: A loose cloak, worn with a mask for the upper part of the face at masquerades.

Mrs. Linde: Yes, unfortunately I came too late, you had already gone up-stairs; and I thought I couldn't go away again without having seen you.

Helmer (taking off Nora's shawl): Yes, take a good look at her. I think she is worth looking at. Isn't she charming, Mrs. Linde?

Mrs. Linde: Yes, indeed she is.

Helmer: Doesn't she look remarkably pretty? Everyone thought so at the dance. But she is terribly self-willed, this sweet little person. What are we to do with her? You will hardly believe that I had almost to bring her away by force.

Nora: Torvald, you will repent not having let me stay, even if it were only for half an hour.

Helmer: Listen to her, Mrs. Linde! She had danced her Tarantella, and it had been a tremendous success, as it deserved — although possibly the per-formance was a trifle too realistic — a little more so, I mean, than was strictly compatible with the limitations of art. But never mind about that! The chief thing is, she had made a success — she had made a tre-mendous success. Do you think I was going to let her remain there after that, and spoil the effect? No, indeed! I took my charming little Capri maiden — my capricious little Capri maiden, I should say — on my arm; took one quick turn round the room; a curtsey on either side, and, as they say in novels, the beautiful apparition disappeared. An exit ought always to be effective, Mrs. Linde; but that is what I cannot make Nora understand. Pooh! this room is hot. *(Throws his domino on a chair, and opens the door of his room.)* Hullo! it's all dark in here. Oh, of course — excuse me —. *(He goes in, and lights some candles.)*

Nora (in a hurried and breathless whisper): Well?

Mrs. Linde (in a low voice): I have had a talk with him.

Nora: Yes, and —

Mrs. Linde: Nora, you must tell your husband all about it.

Nora (in an expressionless voice): I knew it.

Mrs. Linde: You have nothing to be afraid of as far as Krogstad is concerned; but you must tell him.

Nora: I won't tell him.

Mrs. Linde: Then the letter will.

Nora: Thank you, Christine. Now I know what I must do. Hush —!

Helmer (coming in again): Well, Mrs. Linde, have you admired her?

Mrs. Linde: Yes, and now I will say good-night.

Helmer: What, already? Is this yours, this knitting?

Mrs. Linde (taking it): Yes, thank you, I had very nearly forgotten it.

Helmer: So you knit?

Mrs. Linde: Of course.

Helmer: Do you know, you ought to embroider.

Mrs. Linde: Really? Why?

Helmer: Yes, it's far more becoming. Let me show you. You hold the em-broidery thus in your left hand, and use the needle with the right — like this — with a long, easy sweep. Do you see?

Mrs. Linde: Yes, perhaps—

Helmer: But in the case of knitting—that can never be anything but ungraceful; look here—the arms close together, the knitting-needles going up and down—it has a sort of Chinese effect—. That was really excellent champagne they gave us.

Mrs. Linde: Well,—good-night, Nora, and don't be self-willed any more.

Helmer: That's right, Mrs. Linde.

Mrs. Linde: Good-night, Mr. Helmer.

Helmer (accompanying her to the door): Good-night, good-night. I hope you will get home all right. I should be very happy to—but you haven't any great distance to go. Good-night, good-night. *(She goes out; he shuts the door after her, and comes in again.)* Ah!—at last we have got rid of her. She is a frightful bore, that woman.

Nora: Aren't you very tired, Torvald?

Helmer: No, not in the least.

Nora: Nor sleepy?

Helmer: Not a bit. On the contrary, I feel extraordinarily lively. And you?— you really look both tired and sleepy.

Nora: Yes, I am very tired. I want to go to sleep at once.

Helmer: There, you see it was quite right of me not to let you stay there any longer.

Nora: Everything you do is quite right, Torvald.

Helmer (kissing her on the forehead): Now my little skylark is speaking reasonably. Did you notice what good spirits Rank was in this evening?

Nora: Really? Was he? I didn't speak to him at all.

Helmer: And I very little, but I have not for a long time seen him in such good form. *(Looks for a while at her and then goes nearer to her.)* It is delightful to be at home by ourselves again, to be all alone with you—you fascinating, charming little darling!

Nora: Don't look at me like that, Torvald.

Helmer: Why shouldn't I look at my dearest treasure?—at all the beauty that is mine, all my very own?

Nora (going to the other side of the table): You mustn't say things like that to me to-night.

Helmer (following her): You have still got the Tarantella in your blood, I see. And it makes you more captivating than ever. Listen—the guests are beginning to go now. *(In a lower voice.)* Nora—soon the whole house will be quiet.

Nora: Yes, I hope so.

Helmer: Yes, my own darling Nora. Do you know, when I am out at a party with you like this, why I speak so little to you, keep away from you, and only send a stolen glance in your direction now and then?—do you know why I do that? It is because I make believe to myself that we are secretly in love, and you are my secretly promised bride, and that no one suspects there is anything between us.

Nora: Yes, yes—I know very well your thoughts are with me all the time.

Helmer: And when we are leaving, and I am putting the shawl over your beautiful young shoulders — on your lovely neck — then I imagine that you are my young bride and that we have just come from the wedding, and I am bringing you for the first time into our home — to be alone with you for the first time — quite alone with my shy little darling! All this evening I have longed for nothing but you. When I watched the seductive figures of the Tarantella, my blood was on fire; I could endure it no longer, and that was why I brought you down so early —

Nora: Go away, Torvald! You must let me go. I won't —

Helmer: What's that? You're joking, my little Nora! You won't — you won't? Am I not your husband — ? *(A knock is heard at the outer door.)*

Nora (starting): Did you hear — ?

Helmer (going into the hall): Who is it?

Rank (outside): It is I. May I come in for a moment?

Helmer (in a fretful whisper): Oh, what does he want now? *(Aloud.)* Wait a minute! *(Unlocks the door.)* Come, that's kind of you not to pass by our door.

Rank: I thought I heard your voice, and felt as if I should like to look in. *(With a swift glance round.)* Ah, yes! — these dear familiar rooms. You are very happy and cosy in here, you two.

Helmer: It seems to me that you looked after yourself pretty well upstairs too.

Rank: Excellently. Why shouldn't I? Why shouldn't one enjoy everything in this world? — at any rate as much as one can, and as long as one can. The wine was capital —

Helmer: Especially the champagne.

Rank: So you noticed that too? It is almost incredible how much I managed to put away!

Nora: Torvald drank a great deal of champagne to-night too.

Rank: Did he?

Nora: Yes, and he is always in such good spirits afterwards.

Rank: Well, why should one not enjoy a merry evening after a well-spent day?

Helmer: Well spent? I am afraid I can't take credit for that.

Rank (clapping him on the back): But I can, you know!

Nora: Doctor Rank, you must have been occupied with some scientific investigation to-day.

Rank: Exactly.

Helmer: Just listen! — little Nora talking about scientific investigations!

Nora: And may I congratulate you on the result?

Rank: Indeed you may.

Nora: Was it favourable, then?

Rank: The best possible, for both doctor and patient — certainty.

Nora (quickly and searchingly): Certainty?

Rank: Absolute certainty. So wasn't I entitled to make a merry evening of it after that?

Nora: Yes, you certainly were, Doctor Rank.

Helmer: I think so too, so long as you don't have to pay for it in the morning.

Rank: Oh well, one can't have anything in this life without paying for it.

Nora: Doctor Rank — are you fond of fancy-dress balls?

Rank: Yes, if there is a fine lot of pretty costumes.

Nora: Tell me — what shall we two wear at the next?

Helmer: Little featherbrain! — are you thinking of the next already?

Rank: We two? Yes, I can tell you. You shall go as a good fairy —

Helmer: Yes, but what do you suggest as an appropriate costume for that?

Rank: Let your wife go dressed just as she is in everyday life.

Helmer: That was really very prettily turned. But can't you tell us what you will be?

Rank: Yes, my dear friend, I have quite made up my mind about that.

Helmer: Well?

Rank: At the next fancy-dress ball I shall be invisible.

Helmer: That's a good joke!

Rank: There is a big black hat — have you never heard of hats that make you invisible? If you put one on, no one can see you.

Helmer (suppressing a smile): Yes, you are quite right.

Rank: But I am clean forgetting what I came for. Helmer, give me a cigar — one of the dark Havanas.

Helmer: With the greatest pleasure. *(Offers him his case.)*

Rank (takes a cigar and cuts off the end): Thanks.

Nora (striking a match): Let me give you a light.

Rank: Thank you. *(She holds the match for him to light his cigar.)* And now good-bye!

Helmer: Good-bye, good-bye, dear old man!

Nora: Sleep well, Doctor Rank.

Rank: Thank you for that wish.

Nora: Wish me the same.

Rank: You? Well, if you want me to sleep well! And thanks for the light. *(He nods to them both and goes out.)*

Helmer (in a subdued voice): He has drunk more than he ought.

Nora (absently): Maybe. *(Helmer takes a bunch of keys out of his pocket and goes into the hall.)* Torvald! what are you going to do there?

Helmer: Empty the letter-box; it is quite full; there will be no room to put the newspaper in to-morrow morning.

Nora: Are you going to work to-night?

Helmer: You know quite well I'm not. What is this? Someone has been at the lock.

Nora: At the lock —?

Helmer: Yes, someone has. What can it mean? I should never have thought the maid —. Here is a broken hairpin. Nora, it is one of yours.

Nora (quickly): Then it must have been the children —

Helmer: Then you must get them out of those ways. There, at last I have got it open. *(Takes out the contents of the letter-box, and calls to the kitchen.)*

Helen! — Helen, put out the light over the front door. *(Goes back into the room and shuts the door into the hall. He holds out his hand full of letters.)* Look at that — look what a heap of them there are. *(Turning them over.)* What on earth is that?

Nora (at the window): The letter — No! Torvald, no!

Helmer: Two cards — of Rank's.

Nora: Of Doctor Rank's?

Helmer (looking at them): Doctor Rank. They were on the top. He must have put them in when he went out.

Nora: Is there anything written on them?

Helmer: There is a black cross over the name. Look there — what an uncomfortable idea! It looks as if he were announcing his own death.

Nora: It is just what he is doing.

Helmer: What? Do you know anything about it? Has he said anything to you?

Nora: Yes. He told me that when the cards came it would be his leave-taking from us. He means to shut himself up and die.

Helmer: My poor old friend! Certainly I knew we should not have him very long with us. But so soon! And so he hides himself away like a wounded animal.

Nora: If it has to happen, it is best it should be without a word — don't you think so, Torvald?

Helmer (walking up and down): He had so grown into our lives. I can't think of him as having gone out of them. He, with his sufferings and his loneliness, was like a cloudy background to our sunlit happiness. Well, perhaps it is best so. For him, anyway. *(Standing still.)* And perhaps for us too, Nora. We two are thrown quite upon each other now. *(Puts his arms round her.)* My darling wife, I don't feel as if I could hold you tight enough. Do you know, Nora, I have often wished that you might be threatened by some great danger, so that I might risk my life's blood, and everything, for your sake.

Nora (disengages herself, and says firmly and decidedly): Now you must read your letters, Torvald.

Helmer: No, no; not to-night. I want to be with you, my darling wife.

Nora: With the thought of your friend's death —

Helmer: You are right, it has affected us both. Something ugly has come between us — the thought of the horrors of death. We must try and rid our minds of that. Until then — we will each go to our own room.

Nora (hanging on his neck): Good-night, Torvald — Good-night!

Helmer (kissing her on the forehead): Good-night, my little singing-bird. Sleep sound, Nora. Now I will read my letters through. *(He takes his letters and goes into his room, shutting the door after him.)*

Nora (gropes distractedly about, seizes Helmer's domino, throws it round her, while she says in quick, hoarse, spasmodic whispers): Never to see him again. Never! Never! *(Puts her shawl over her head.)* Never to see my children again either — never again. Never! Never! — Ah! the icy, black water — the unfathomable depths — If only it were over! He has got it now — now he is reading it. Good-bye, Torvald and my children! *(She is about to rush out through the hall, when Helmer opens his door hurriedly and stands with an open letter in his hand.)*

Helmer: Nora!

Nora: Ah! —

Helmer: What is this? Do you know what is in this letter?

Nora: Yes, I know. Let me go! Let me get out!

Helmer (holding her back): Where are you going?

Nora (trying to get free): You shan't save me, Torvald!

Helmer (reeling): True? Is this true, that I read here? Horrible! No, no — it is impossible that it can be true.

Nora: It is true. I have loved you above everything else in the world.

Helmer: Oh, don't let us have any silly excuses.

Nora (taking a step towards him): Torvald — !

Helmer: Miserable creature — what have you done?

Nora: Let me go. You shall not suffer for my sake. You shall not take it upon yourself.

Helmer: No tragedy airs, please. *(Locks the hall door.)* Here you shall stay and give me an explanation. Do you understand what you have done? Answer me! Do you understand what you have done?

Nora (looks steadily at him and says with a growing look of coldness in her face): Yes, now I am beginning to understand thoroughly.

Helmer (walking about the room): What a horrible awakening! All these eight years — she who was my joy and pride — a hypocrite, a liar — worse, worse — a criminal! The unutterable ugliness of it all! — For shame! For shame! *(Nora is silent and looks steadily at him. He stops in front of her.)* I ought to have suspected that something of the sort would happen. I ought to have foreseen it. All your father's want of principle — be silent! — all your father's want of principle has come out in you. No religion, no morality, no sense of duty — . How I am punished for having winked at what he did! I did it for your sake, and this is how you repay me.

Nora: Yes, that's just it.

Helmer: Now you have destroyed all my happiness. You have ruined all my future. It is horrible to think of! I am in the power of an unscrupulous man; he can do what he likes with me, ask anything he likes of me, give me any orders he pleases — I dare not refuse. And I must sink to such miserable depths because of a thoughtless woman!

Nora: When I am out of the way, you will be free.

Helmer: No fine speeches, please. Your father had always plenty of those ready, too. What good would it be to me if you were out of the way, as you say? Not the slightest. He can make the affair known everywhere; and if he does, I may be falsely suspected of having been a party to your criminal action. Very likely people will think I was behind it all — that it was I who prompted you! And I have to thank you for all this — you whom I have cherished during the whole of our married life. Do you understand now what it is you have done for me?

Nora (coldly and quietly): Yes.

Helmer: It is so incredible that I can't take it in. But we must come to some understanding. Take off that shawl. Take it off, I tell you. I must try and appease him some way or another. The matter must be hushed up at any cost. And as for you and me, it must appear as if everything between us were just as before — but naturally only in the eyes of the world. You will still remain in my house, that is a matter of course. But I shall not allow you to bring up the children; I dare not trust them to you. To think that I should be obliged to say so to one whom I have loved so dearly, and whom I still —. No, that is all over. From this moment happiness is not the question; all that concerns us is to save the remains, the fragments, the appearance —

A ring is heard at the front-door bell.

Helmer (with a start): What is that? So late! Can the worst —? Can he —? Hide yourself, Nora. Say you are ill.

Nora stands motionless. Helmer goes and unlocks the hall door.

Maid (half-dressed, comes to the door): A letter for the mistress.

Helmer: Give it to me. *(Takes the letter, and shuts the door.)* Yes, it is from him. You shall not have it; I will read it myself.

Nora: Yes, read it.

Helmer (standing by the lamp): I scarcely have the courage to do it. It may mean ruin for both of us. No, I must know. *(Tears open the letter, runs his eye over a few lines, looks at a paper enclosed, and gives a shout of joy.)* Nora! *(She looks at him questioningly.)* Nora! — No, I must read it once again —. Yes, it is true! I am saved! Nora, I am saved!

Nora: And I?

Helmer: You too, of course; we are both saved, both you and I. Look, he sends you your bond back. He says he regrets and repents — that a happy change in his life — never mind what he says! We are saved, Nora! No one can do anything to you. Oh, Nora, Nora! — no, first I must destroy these hateful things. Let me see —. *(Takes a look at the bond.)* No, no, I won't look at it. The whole thing shall be nothing but a bad dream to me. *(Tears up the bond and both letters, throws them all into the stove, and watches them burn.)* There — now it doesn't exist any longer. He says that since Christmas Eve you —. These must have been three dreadful days for you, Nora.

Nora: I have fought a hard fight these three days.

Helmer: And suffered agonies, and seen no way out but —. No, we won't call any of the horrors to mind. We will only shout with joy, and keep saying, "It's all over! It's all over!" Listen to me, Nora. You don't seem to realise that it is all over. What is this? — such a cold, set face! My poor little Nora, I quite understand; you don't feel as if you could believe that

I have forgiven you. But it is true, Nora, I swear it; I have forgiven you everything. I know that what you did, you did out of love for me.

Nora: That is true.

Helmer: You have loved me as a wife ought to love her husband. Only you had not sufficient knowledge to judge of the means you used. But do you suppose you are any the less dear to me, because you don't understand how to act on your own responsibility? No, no; only lean on me; I will advise you and direct you. I should not be a man if this womanly helplessness did not just give you a double attractiveness in my eyes. You must not think anymore about the hard things I said in my first moment of consternation, when I thought everything was going to overwhelm me. I have forgiven you, Nora; I swear to you I have forgiven you.

Nora: Thank you for your forgiveness. (*She goes out through the door to the right.*)

Helmer: No, don't go — . (*Looks in.*) What are you doing in there?

Nora (from within): Taking off my fancy dress.

Helmer (standing at the open door): Yes, do. Try and calm yourself, and make your mind easy again, my frightened little singing-bird. Be at rest, and feel secure; I have broad wings to shelter you under. (*Walks up and down by the door.*) How warm and cosy our home is, Nora. Here is shelter for you; here I will protect you like a hunted dove that I have saved from a hawk's claws; I will bring peace to your poor beating heart. It will come, little by little, Nora, believe me. To-morrow morning you will look upon it all quite differently; soon everything will be just as it was before. Very soon you won't need me to assure you that I have forgiven you; you will yourself feel the certainty that I have done so. Can you suppose I should ever think of such a thing as repudiating you, or even reproaching you? You have no idea what a true man's heart is like, Nora. There is something so indescribably sweet and satisfying, to a man, in the knowledge that he has forgiven his wife — forgiven her freely, and with all his heart. It seems as if that had made her, as it were, doubly his own; he has given her a new life, so to speak; and she has in a way become both wife and child to him. So you shall be for me after this, my little scared, helpless darling. Have no anxiety about anything, Nora; only be frank and open with me, and I will serve as will and conscience both to you — . What is this? Not gone to bed? Have you changed your things?

Nora (in everyday dress): Yes, Torvald, I have changed my things now.

Helmer: But what for? — so late as this.

Nora: I shall not sleep to-night.

Helmer: But, my dear Nora —

Nora (looking at her watch): It is not so very late. Sit down here, Torvald. You and I have much to say to one another. (*She sits down at one side of the table.*)

Helmer: Nora — what is this? — this cold, set face?

Nora: Sit down. It will take some time; I have a lot to talk over with you.

Helmer (sits down at the opposite side of the table): You alarm me, Nora! — and I don't understand you.

Nora: No, that is just it. You don't understand me, and I have never understood you either — before to-night. No, you mustn't interrupt me. You must simply listen to what I say. Torvald, this is a settling of accounts.

Helmer: What do you mean by that?

Nora (after a short silence): Isn't there one thing that strikes you as strange in our sitting here like this?

Helmer: What is that?

Nora: We have been married now eight years. Does it not occur to you that this is the first time we two, you and I, husband and wife, have had a serious conversation?

Helmer: What do you mean by serious?

Nora: In all these eight years — longer than that — from the very beginning of our acquaintance, we have never exchanged a word on any serious subject.

Helmer: Was it likely that I would be continually and forever telling you about worries that you could not help me to bear?

Nora: I am not speaking about business matters. I say that we have never sat down in earnest together to try and get at the bottom of anything.

Helmer: But, dearest Nora, would it have been any good to you?

Nora: That is just it; you have never understood me. I have been greatly wronged, Torvald — first by papa and then by you.

Helmer: What! By us two — by us two, who have loved you better than anyone else in the world?

Nora (shaking her head): You have never loved me. You have only thought it pleasant to be in love with me.

Helmer: Nora, what do I hear you saying?

Nora: It is perfectly true, Torvald. When I was at home with papa, he told me his opinion about everything, and so I had the same opinions; and if I differed from him I concealed the fact, because he would not have liked it. He called me his doll-child, and he played with me just as I used to play with my dolls. And when I came to live with you —

Helmer: What sort of an expression is that to use about our marriage?

Nora (undisturbed): I mean that I was simply transferred from papa's hands into yours. You arranged everything according to your own taste, and so I got the same tastes as you — or else I pretended to, I am really not quite sure which — I think sometimes the one and sometimes the other. When I look back on it, it seems to me as if I had been living here like a poor woman — just from hand to mouth. I have existed merely to perform tricks for you, Torvald. But you would have it so. You and papa have committed a great sin against me. It is your fault that I have made nothing of my life.

Helmer: How unreasonable and how ungrateful you are, Nora! Have you not been happy here?

Nora: No, I have never been happy. I thought I was, but it has never really been so.

Helmer: Not — not happy!

Nora: No, only merry. And you have always been so kind to me. But our home has been nothing but a playroom. I have been your doll-wife, just as at home I was papa's doll-child; and here the children have been my dolls. I thought it great fun when you played with me, just as they thought it great fun when I played with them. That is what our marriage has been, Torvald.

Helmer: There is some truth in what you say — exaggerated and strained as your view of it is. But for the future it shall be different. Playtime shall be over, and lesson-time shall begin.

Nora: Whose lessons? Mine, or the children's?

Helmer: Both yours and the children's, my darling Nora.

Nora: Alas, Torvald, you are not the man to educate me into being a proper wife for you.

Helmer: And you can say that!

Nora: And I — how am I fitted to bring up the children?

Helmer: Nora!

Nora: Didn't you say so yourself a little while ago — that you dare not trust me to bring them up?

Helmer: In a moment of anger! Why do you pay any heed to that?

Nora: Indeed, you were perfectly right. I am not fit for the task. There is another task I must undertake first. I must try and educate myself — you are not the man to help me in that. I must do that for myself. And that is why I am going to leave you now.

Helmer (springing up): What do you say?

Nora: I must stand quite alone, if I am to understand myself and everything about me. It is for that reason that I cannot remain with you any longer.

Helmer: Nora, Nora!

Nora: I am going away from here now, at once. I am sure Christine will take me in for the night —

Helmer: You are out of your mind! I won't allow it! I forbid you!

Nora: It is no use forbidding me anything any longer. I will take with me what belongs to myself. I will take nothing from you, either now or later.

Helmer: What sort of madness is this!

Nora: To-morrow I shall go home — I mean, to my old home. It will be easiest for me to find something to do there.

Helmer: You blind, foolish woman!

Nora: I must try and get some sense, Torvald.

Helmer: To desert your home, your husband and your children! And you don't consider what people will say!

Nora: I cannot consider that at all. I only know that it is necessary for me.

Helmer: It's shocking. This is how you would neglect your most sacred duties.

Nora: What do you consider my most sacred duties?

Helmer: Do I need to tell you that? Are they not your duties to your husband and your children?

Nora: I have other duties just as sacred.

Helmer: That you have not. What duties could those be?

Nora: Duties to myself.

Helmer: Before all else, you are a wife and a mother.

Nora: I don't believe that any longer. I believe that before all else I am a reasonable human being, just as you are — or, at all events, that I must try and become one. I know quite well, Torvald, that most people would think you right, and that views of that kind are to be found in books; but I can no longer content myself with what most people say, or with what is found in books. I must think over things for myself and get to understand them.

Helmer: Can you not understand your place in your own home? Have you not a reliable guide in such matters as that? — have you no religion?

Nora: I am afraid, Torvald, I do not exactly know what religion is.

Helmer: What are you saying?

Nora: I know nothing but what the clergyman said, when I went to be confirmed. He told us that religion was this, and that, and the other. When I am away from all this, and am alone, I will look into that matter too. I will see if what the clergyman said is true, or at all events if it is true for me.

Helmer: This is unheard of in a girl of your age! But if religion cannot lead you aright, let me try and awaken your conscience. I suppose you have some moral sense? Or — answer me — am I to think you have none?

Nora: I assure you, Torvald, that is not an easy question to answer. I really don't know. The thing perplexes me altogether. I only know that you and I look at it in quite a different light. I am learning, too, that the law is quite another thing from what I supposed; but I find it impossible to convince myself that the law is right. According to it a woman has no right to spare her old dying father, or to save her husband's life. I can't believe that.

Helmer: You talk like a child. You don't understand the conditions of the world in which you live.

Nora: No, I don't. But now I am going to try. I am going to see if I can make out who is right, the world or I.

Helmer: You are ill, Nora; you are delirious; I almost think you are out of your mind.

Nora: I have never felt my mind so clear and certain as to-night.

Helmer: And is it with a clear and certain mind that you forsake your husband and your children?

Nora: Yes, it is.

Helmer: Then there is only one possible explanation.

Nora: What is that?

Helmer: You do not love me anymore.

Nora: No, that is just it.

Helmer: Nora! — and you can say that?

Nora: It gives me great pain, Torvald, for you have always been so kind to me, but I cannot help it. I do not love you any more.

Helmer (regaining his composure): Is that a clear and certain conviction too?

Nora: Yes, absolutely clear and certain. That is the reason why I will not stay here any longer.

Helmer: And can you tell me what I have done to forfeit your love?

Nora: Yes, indeed I can. It was to-night, when the wonderful thing did not happen; then I saw you were not the man I had thought you.

Helmer: Explain yourself better. I don't understand you.

Nora: I have waited so patiently for eight years; for, goodness knows, I knew very well that wonderful things don't happen every day. Then this horrible misfortune came upon me; and then I felt quite certain that the wonderful thing was going to happen at last. When Krogstad's letter was lying out there, never for a moment did I imagine that you would consent to accept this man's conditions. I was so absolutely certain that you would say to him: Publish the thing to the whole world. And when that was done —

Helmer: Yes, what then? — when I had exposed my wife to shame and disgrace?

Nora: When that was done, I was so absolutely certain, you would come forward and take everything upon yourself, and say: I am the guilty one.

Helmer: Nora —!

Nora: You mean that I would never have accepted such a sacrifice on your part? No, of course not. But what would my assurances have been worth against yours? That was the wonderful thing which I hoped for and feared; and it was to prevent that, that I wanted to kill myself.

Helmer: I would gladly work night and day for you, Nora — bear sorrow and want for your sake. But no man would sacrifice his honour for the one he loves.

Nora: It is a thing hundreds of thousands of women have done.

Helmer: Oh, you think and talk like a heedless child.

Nora: Maybe. But you neither think nor talk like the man I could bind myself to. As soon as your fear was over — and it was not fear for what threatened me, but for what might happen to you — when the whole thing was past, as far as you were concerned it was exactly as if nothing at all had happened. Exactly as before, I was your little skylark, your doll, which you would in future treat with doubly gentle care, because it was so brittle and fragile. *(Getting up.)* Torvald — it was then it dawned upon me that for eight years I had been living here with a strange man, and had borne him three children —. Oh, I can't bear to think of it! I could tear myself into little bits!

Helmer (sadly): I see, I see. An abyss has opened between us — there is no denying it. But, Nora, would it not be possible to fill it up?

Nora: As I am now, I am no wife for you.

Helmer: I have it in me to become a different man.

Nora: Perhaps — if your doll is taken away from you.

Helmer: But to part! — to part from you! No, no, Nora, I can't understand that idea.

Nora (going out to the right): That makes it all the more certain that it must be done. *(She comes back with her cloak and hat and a small bag which she puts on a chair by the table.)*

Helmer: Nora, Nora, not now! Wait until to-morrow.

Nora (putting on her cloak): I cannot spend the night in a strange man's room.

Helmer: But can't we live here like brother and sister — ?

Nora (putting on her hat): You know very well that would not last long. *(Puts the shawl round her.)* Good-bye, Torvald. I won't see the little ones. I know they are in better hands than mine. As I am now, I can be of no use to them.

Helmer: But some day, Nora — some day?

Nora: How can I tell? I have no idea what is going to become of me.

Helmer: But you are my wife, whatever becomes of you.

Nora: Listen, Torvald. I have heard that when a wife deserts her husband's house, as I am doing now, he is legally freed from all obligations towards her. In any case, I set you free from all your obligations. You are not to feel yourself bound in the slightest way, any more than I shall. There must be perfect freedom on both sides. See, here is your ring back. Give me mine.

Helmer: That too?

Nora: That too.

Helmer: Here it is.

Nora: That's right. Now it is all over. I have put the keys here. The maids know all about everything in the house — better than I do. To-morrow, after I have left her, Christine will come here and pack up my own things that I brought with me from home. I will have them sent after me.

Helmer: All over! All over! — Nora, shall you never think of me again?

Nora: I know I shall often think of you, the children, and this house.

Helmer: May I write to you, Nora?

Nora: No — never. You must not do that.

Helmer: But at least let me send you —

Nora: Nothing — nothing —

Helmer: Let me help you if you are in want.

Nora: No. I can receive nothing from a stranger.

Helmer: Nora — can I never be anything more than a stranger to you?

Nora (taking her bag): Ah, Torvald, the most wonderful thing of all would have to happen.

Helmer: Tell me what that would be!

Nora: Both you and I would have to be so changed that — . Oh, Torvald, I don't believe any longer in wonderful things happening.

Helmer: But I will believe in it. Tell me! So changed that — ?

Nora: That our life together would be a real wedlock. Good-bye. *(She goes out through the hall.)*

Helmer (sinks down on a chair at the door and buries his face in his hands): Nora! Nora! *(Looks round, and rises.)* Empty. She is gone. *(A hope flashes across his mind.)* The most wonderful thing of all — ?

The sound of a door shutting is heard from below.

CONSIDERATIONS FOR CRITICAL THINKING AND WRITING

1. FIRST RESPONSE. What is the significance of the play's title?

2. Why is Nora "pale with terror" at the end of Act I? What is the significance of the description of the Christmas tree now "stripped of its ornaments and with burnt-down candle-ends on its dishevelled branches" that opens Act II? What other symbols are used in the play?

3. What is Doctor Rank's purpose in the play?

4. How does the relationship between Krogstad and Mrs. Linde serve to emphasize certain qualities in the Helmers' marriage?

5. Would you describe the ending as essentially happy or unhappy? Is the play more like a comedy or a tragedy?

6. Ibsen believed that a "dramatist's business is not to answer questions, but only to ask them." What questions are raised in the play? Does Ibsen propose any specific answers?

7. CONNECTION TO ANOTHER SELECTION. Explain how Torvald's attitude toward Nora is similar to the men's attitudes toward women in Susan Glaspell's *Trifles* (p. 565). Write an essay exploring how the assumptions the men make about women in both plays contribute to the plays' conflicts.

Plays for Further Reading

28

A Collection of Short Plays

© Michal Daniel.

I've found that the more culturally specific you are, the more universal the work is. There's no conflict between wanting to reach a large audience and being particular and culturally accurate.

— DAVID HENRY HWANG

Tender Offer

Born in Brooklyn, New York, in 1950, Wendy Wasserstein studied at Mount Holyoke College, City College of New York, and the Yale School of Drama. She was a resident playwright off-Broadway, at New York's Playwrights Horizon Theatre, where

Jack Mitchell/Getty Images.

many of her plays were performed before audiences receptive to Wasserstein's humorous treatment of feminist issues. Among her plays are *Uncommon Women* (1977), *Isn't It Romantic* (1980), *The Sisters Rosenzweig* (1993), and the enormously successful *The Heidi Chronicles* (1988), which won numerous honors including a Tony Award, a Pulitzer Prize, and the New York Drama Critics' Circle Award. In 1990 her book of essays, *Bachelor Girl*, was published. Her last play, *Third* (2005), explores the politics of academic life. She received National Endowment for the Arts and Guggenheim grants in support of her work.

Tender Offer, which appeared in a special issue of one-act plays in the Spring 1991 *Antaeus*, is a brief but absorbing treatment of the tentative relationship between a father and daughter. Characteristic of Wasserstein's work, this play uses humor deftly to present a serious moment that requires a "good deal" to resolve it.

WENDY WASSERSTEIN (1950–2006)
Tender Offer   1991

> *A girl of around nine is alone in a dance studio. She is dressed in traditional leotards and tights. She begins singing to herself, "Nothing Could Be Finer Than to Be in Carolina." She maps out a dance routine, including parts for the chorus. She builds to a finale. A man, Paul, around thirty-five, walks in. He has a sweet, though distant, demeanor. As he walks in, Lisa notices him and stops.*

Paul: You don't have to stop, sweetheart.

Lisa: That's okay.

Paul: Looked very good.

Lisa: Thanks.

Paul: Don't I get a kiss hello?

Lisa: Sure.

Paul (embraces her): Hi, Tiger.

Lisa: Hi, Dad.

Paul: I'm sorry I'm late.

Lisa: That's okay.

Paul: How'd it go?

Lisa: Good.

Paul: Just good?

Lisa: Pretty good.

Paul: "Pretty good." You mean you got a lot of applause or "pretty good" you could have done better?

Lisa: Well, Courtney Palumbo's mother thought I was pretty good. But you know the part in the middle when everybody's supposed to freeze and the big girl comes out. Well, I think I moved a little bit.

Paul: I thought what you were doing looked very good.

Lisa: Daddy, that's not what I was doing. That was tap-dancing. I made that up.

Paul: Oh. Well it looked good. Kind of sexy.

Lisa: Yuch!

Paul: What do you mean "yuch"?

Lisa: Just yuch!

Paul: You don't want to be sexy?

Lisa: I don't care.

Paul: Let's go, Tiger. I promised your mother I'd get you home in time for dinner.

Lisa: I can't find my leg warmers.

Paul: You can't find your what?

Lisa: Leg warmers. I can't go home till I find my leg warmers.

Paul: I don't see you looking for them.

Lisa: I was waiting for you.

Paul: Oh.

Lisa: Daddy.

Paul: What?

Lisa: Nothing.

Paul: Where do you think you left them?

Lisa: Somewhere around here. I can't remember.

Paul: Well, try to remember, Lisa. We don't have all night.

Lisa: I told you. I think somewhere around here.

Paul: I don't see them. Let's go home now. You'll call the dancing school tomorrow.

Lisa: Daddy, I can't go home till I find them. Miss Judy says it's not professional to leave things.

Paul: Who's Miss Judy?

Lisa: She's my ballet teacher. She once danced the lead in *Swan Lake*, and she was a June Taylor dancer.

Paul: Well, then, I'm sure she'll understand about the leg warmers.

Lisa: Daddy, Miss Judy wanted to know why you were late today.

Paul: Hmmmmmmmm?

Lisa: Why were you late?

Paul: I was in a meeting. Business. I'm sorry.

Lisa: Why did you tell Mommy you'd come instead of her if you knew you had business?

Paul: Honey, something just came up. I thought I'd be able to be here. I was looking forward to it.

Lisa: I wish you wouldn't make appointments to see me.

Paul: Hmmmmmmm.

Lisa: You shouldn't make appointments to see me unless you know you're going to come.

Paul: Of course I'm going to come.

Lisa: No, you're not. Talia Robbins told me she's much happier living without her father in the house. Her father used to come home late and go to sleep early.

Paul: Lisa, stop it. Let's go.

Lisa: I can't find my leg warmers.

Paul: Forget your leg warmers.

Lisa: Daddy.

Paul: What is it?

Lisa: I saw this show on television, I think it was WPIX Channel 11. Well, the father was crying about his daughter.

Paul: Why was he crying? Was she sick?

Lisa: No. She was at school. And he was at business. And he just missed her, so he started to cry.

Paul: What was the name of this show?

Lisa: I don't know. I came in in the middle.

Paul: Well, Lisa, I certainly would cry if you were sick or far away, but I know that you're well and you're home. So no reason to get maudlin.

Lisa: What's maudlin?

Paul: Sentimental, soppy. Frequently used by children who make things up to get attention.

Lisa: I am sick! I am sick! I have Hodgkin's disease and a bad itch on my leg.

Paul: What do you mean you have Hodgkin's disease? Don't say things like that.

Lisa: Swoosie Kurtz, she had Hodgkin's disease on a TV movie last year, but she got better and now she's on *Love Sidney.*

Paul: Who is Swoosie Kurtz?

Lisa: She's an actress named after an airplane. I saw her on *Live at Five.*

Paul: You watch too much television; you should do your homework. Now, put your coat on.

Lisa: Daddy, I really do have a bad itch on my leg. Would you scratch it?

Paul: Lisa, you're procrastinating.

Lisa: Why do you use words I don't understand? I hate it. You're like Daria Feldman's mother. She always talks in Yiddish to her husband so Daria won't understand.

Paul: *Procrastinating* is not Yiddish.

Lisa: Well, I don't know what it is.

Paul: Procrastinating means you don't want to go about your business.

Lisa: I don't go to business. I go to school.

Paul: What I mean is you want to hang around here until you and I are late for dinner and your mother's angry and it's too late for you to do your homework.

Lisa: I do not.

Paul: Well, it sure looks that way. Now put your coat on and let's go.

Lisa: Daddy.

Paul: Honey, I'm tired. Really, later.

Lisa: Why don't you want to talk to me?

Paul: I do want to talk to you. I promise when we get home we'll have a nice talk.

Lisa: No, we won't. You'll read the paper and fall asleep in front of the news.

Paul: Honey, we'll talk on the weekend, I promise. Aren't I taking you to the theater this weekend? Let me look. (*He takes out appointment book.*)

Yes; Sunday. *Joseph and the Amazing Technicolor Raincoat* with Lisa. Okay, Tiger?

Lisa: Sure. It's *Dreamcoat.*

Paul: What?

Lisa: Nothing. I think I see my leg warmers. (*She goes to pick them up, and an odd-looking trophy.*)

Paul: What's that?

Lisa: It's stupid. I was second best at the dance recital, so they gave me this thing. It's stupid.

Paul: Lisa.

Lisa: What?

Paul: What did you want to talk about?

Lisa: Nothing.

Paul: Was it about my missing your recital? I'm really sorry, Tiger. I would have liked to have been here.

Lisa: That's okay.

Paul: Honest?

Lisa: Daddy, you're prostrastinating.

Paul: I'm procrastinating. Sit down. Let's talk. So. How's school?

Lisa: Fine.

Paul: You like it?

Lisa: Yup.

Paul: You looking forward to camp this summer?

Lisa: Yup.

Paul: Is Daria Feldman going back?

Lisa: Nope.

Paul: Why not?

Lisa: I don't know. We can go home now. Honest, my foot doesn't itch anymore.

Paul: Lisa, you know what you do in business when it seems like there's nothing left to say? That's when you really start talking. Put a bid on the table.

Lisa: What's a bid?

Paul: You tell me what you want and I'll tell you what I've got to offer. Like Monopoly. You want Boardwalk, but I'm only willing to give you the Railroads. Now, because you are my daughter I'd throw in Water Works and Electricity. Understand, Tiger?

Lisa: No. I don't like board games. You know, Daddy, we could get Space Invaders for our home for thirty-five dollars. In fact, we could get Osborne System for two thousand. Daria Feldman's parents . . .

Paul: Daria Feldman's parents refuse to talk to Daria, so they bought a computer to keep Daria busy so they won't have to speak in Yiddish. Daria will probably grow up to be a homicidal maniac lesbian prostitute.

Lisa: I know what that word *prostitute* means.

Paul: Good. (*Pause.*) You still haven't told me about school. Do you still like your teacher?

Lisa: She's okay.

Paul: Lisa, if we're talking try to answer me.

Lisa: I am answering you. Can we go home now, please?

Paul: Damn it, Lisa, if you want to talk to me . . . Talk to me!

Lisa: I can't wait till I'm old enough so I can make my own money and never have to see you again. Maybe I'll become a prostitute.

Paul: Young lady, that's enough.

Lisa: I hate you, Daddy! I hate you! (*She throws her trophy into the trash bin.*)

Paul: What'd you do that for?

Lisa: It's stupid.

Paul: Maybe I wanted it.

Lisa: What for?

Paul: Maybe I wanted to put it where I keep your dinosaur and the picture you made of Mrs. Kimbel with the chicken pox.

Lisa: You got mad at me when I made that picture. You told me I had to respect Mrs. Kimbel because she was my teacher.

Paul: That's true. But she wasn't my teacher. I liked her better with the chicken pox. (*Pause.*) Lisa, I'm sorry. I was very wrong to miss your recital, and you don't have to become a prostitute. That's not the type of profession Miss Judy has in mind for you.

Lisa (mumbles): No.

Paul: No. (*Pause.*) So Talia Robbins is really happy her father moved out?

Lisa: Talia Robbins picks open the eighth-grade lockers during gym period. But she did that before her father moved out.

Paul: You can't always judge someone by what they do or what they don't do. Sometimes you come home from dancing school and run upstairs and shut the door, and when I finally get to talk to you, everything is "okay" or "fine." Yup or nope?

Lisa: Yup.

Paul: Sometimes, a lot of times, I come home and fall asleep in front of the television. So you and I spend a lot of time being a little scared of each other. Maybe?

Lisa: Maybe.

Paul: Tell you what. I'll make you a tender offer.

Lisa: What?

Paul: I'll make you a tender offer. That's when one company publishes in the newspaper that they want to buy another company. And the company that publishes is called the Black Knight because they want to gobble up the poor little company. So the poor little company needs to be rescued. And then a White Knight comes along and makes a bigger and better offer so the shareholders won't have to tender shares to the Big Black Knight. You with me?

Lisa: Sort of.

Paul: I'll make you a tender offer like the White Knight. But I don't want to own you. I just want to make a much better offer. Okay?

Lisa (sort of understanding): Okay. (*Pause. They sit for a moment.*) Sort of, Daddy, what do you think about? I mean, like when you're quiet what do you think about?

Paul: Oh, business usually. If I think I made a mistake or if I think I'm doing okay. Sometimes I think about what I'll be doing five years from now and if it's what I hoped it would be five years ago. Sometimes I think about what your life will be like, if Mount Saint Helens will erupt again. What you'll become if you'll study penmanship or word processing. If you speak kindly of me to your psychiatrist when you are in graduate school. And how the hell I'll pay for your graduate school. And sometimes I try and think what it was I thought about when I was your age.

Lisa: Do you ever look out your window at the clouds and try to see which kinds of shapes they are? Like one time, honest, I saw the head of Walter Cronkite in a flower vase. Really! Like look don't those kinda look like if you turn it upside down, two big elbows or two elephant trunks dancing?

Paul: Actually still looks like Walter Cronkite in a flower vase to me. But look up a little. See the one that's still moving? That sorta looks like a whale on a thimble.

Lisa: Where?

Paul: Look up. To your right.

Lisa: I don't see it. Where?

Paul: The other way.

Lisa: Oh, yeah! There's the head and there's the stomach. Yeah! (*Lisa picks up her trophy.*) Hey, Daddy.

Paul: Hey, Lisa.

Lisa: You can have this thing if you want it. But you have to put it like this, because if you put it like that it is gross.

Paul: You know what I'd like? So I can tell people who come into my office why I have this gross stupid thing on my shelf, I'd like it if you could show me your dance recital.

Lisa: Now?

Paul: We've got time. Mother said she won't be home till late.

Lisa: Well, Daddy, during a lot of it I freeze and the big girl in front dances.

Paul: Well, how 'bout the number you were doing when I walked in?

Lisa: Well, see, I have parts for a lot of people in that one, too.

Paul: I'll dance the other parts.

Lisa: You can't dance.

Paul: Young lady, I played Yvette Mimieux in a *Hasty Pudding Show.*

Lisa: Who's Yvette Mimieux?

Paul: Watch more television. You'll find out. (*Paul stands up.*) So I'm ready. (*He begins singing.*) "Nothing could be finer than to be in Carolina."

Lisa: Now I go. In the morning. And now you go. Dum-da.

Paul (obviously not a tap dancer): Da-da-dum.

Lisa (whines): Daddy!

Paul (mimics her): Lisa! Nothing could be finer . . .

Lisa: That looks dumb.

Paul: Oh, yeah? You think they do this better in *The Amazing Minkcoat*? No way! Now you go — da da da dum.

Lisa: Da da da dum.

Paul: If I had Aladdin's lamp for only a day, I'd make a wish . . .

Lisa: Daddy, that's maudlin!

Paul: I know it's maudlin. And here's what I'd say:

Lisa and Paul: I'd say that "nothing could be finer than to be in Carolina in the moooooooooooornin'."

Naked Lunch

Born in Lancaster, Pennsylvania, Michael Hollinger earned a B.A. in music at Oberlin Conservatory and a master of arts degree in theater from Villanova University, where he now teaches theater. His comedies and dramas have been widely produced in the United States and abroad. Among his plays are *An Empty Plate in the Café Du Grand Boeuf* (1994), *Red Herring* (1996), *Hot Air* (1997), *Tiny Island* (1998), *Eureka* (1999), *Opus* (2006), *Ghost-Writer* (2011), *Hope and Gravity (2014),* and *Under the Skin* (2015). He has also written three short films and coauthored *Philadelphia Diary* with Bruce Graham and Sonia Sanchez for PBS. His writing awards include the Roger

Courtesy of Michael Hollinger.

L. Stevens Award from the Kennedy Center's Fund for Outstanding New American Plays, the Barrymore Award for Outstanding New Play, and the Otto Haas Award for Emerging Theatre Artist. Hollinger's extensive music background strongly influences his work as a playwright. He has said about his own work, "Plays are music to me; characters are instruments, scenes are movements; tempo, rhythm and dynamics are critical; and melody and counterpoint are always set in relief by rests — beats, pauses, the spaces between." *Naked Lunch* (2003) is one of a group of sixteen plays written by various playwrights for *Trepidation Nation: A Phobic Anthology,* which was produced at the 2002–2003 Humana Festival by Actors Theatre of Louisville.

WHEN I WRITE "Conflict is the source of all drama, so I always return to the key questions when writing: Who wants what? What gets in the way? Why is it so important? Opposing forces engage our curiosity about outcome — a crucial element for an art form that requires such focused, sustained attention." —MICHAEL HOLLINGER

Michael Hollinger (b. 1962)

Naked Lunch   *2003*

Lights up on Vernon and Lucy sitting at a small dining-room table, eating. There's a small vase with too many flowers in it, or a large vase with too few. A bottle of wine has been opened. Vernon regales Lucy as he vigorously devours a steak. Lucy discreetly nibbles on her corn-on-the-cob.

Vernon: Larry thinks the whole show's a fake. He says the guy's just an actor and all the crocs are trained. I said, you can't train a crocodile! It's not like some poodle you can teach to ride a bike. It's got this reptile brain, a million years old. All it knows, or wants to know, is whether or not you're juicy. Anyway, this one show the guy's sneaking up on a mother protecting her nest. And she's huge — I mean, this thing could swallow a Buick. And the guy's really playing it up: *(Australian accent.)* "Amazing — look at the size of those teeth!" But just —

(He stops, looking at Lucy. Pause. She looks up from her corn.)

Lucy: What.
Vernon: What's the matter?
Lucy: I'm listening.
Vernon: You're not eating your steak.
Lucy: Oh. No.
Vernon: How come?
Lucy: I'll just eat the corn.

> *(She returns to nibbling.)*

Vernon: What's wrong with the steak?
Lucy: Nothing.
Vernon: Then eat it. It's good.
Lucy: I'd . . . rather not.
Vernon: Why not?

> *(Pause.)*

Lucy: I'm vegetarian.

> *(Beat.)*

Vernon: What?
Lucy: I don't eat meat anymore.
Vernon: Since when?
Lucy: Since we, you know. Broke up.

> *(Pause.)*

Vernon: Just like that?
Lucy: Well —
Vernon: You break up with me and boom next day you start eating tofu?

Lucy: I'd been thinking about it for a while.

Vernon: First I ever heard of it.

Lucy: Well, I'd been thinking. *(Pause. Lucy picks up her corn again, guiding him back to the story:)* So anyway, the guy's sneaking up on the mother . . .

Vernon: Was it because of me?

Lucy: No . . .

Vernon: Something I said, or did . . .

Lucy: It's nothing like that.

Vernon: You were always fond of cataloguing the careless things I said and did . . .

Lucy: I just did some soul-searching, that's all.

(Beat.)

Vernon: Soul-searching.

Lucy: About a lot of things.

Vernon: And your soul said to you "no more meat."

Lucy: You make it sound silly when you say it like that.

Vernon: Then what, what did your soul tell you?

(Beat. Lucy exhales heavily and sets down her corn.)

Lucy: I decided I didn't want to eat anything with a face.

(Beat.)

Vernon: A *face*?

(He gets up, stands behind her and looks at her plate.)

Lucy: Vern . . .

Vernon: I don't see any face . . .

Lucy: This doesn't have to be a big deal . . .

Vernon: I don't see a face. Do you see a face?

(He lifts the plate toward her face.)

Lucy: There's other reasons.

Vernon: No face.

(He sets the plate down again.)

Lucy: I've been reading things.

Vernon: What things?

Lucy: You know, health reports . . .

Vernon: You can't believe that stuff.

Lucy: What do you mean?

Vernon: You can't! One day they say bran's good for you — "Want to live forever? Eat more bran." — the next day they find out bran can kill you.

Lucy: Whatever.

Vernon: Too much bran boom you're dead.

Lucy: There are diseases you can get from meat.

Vernon: Like what?

Lucy: Well, listeria . . .

Vernon: That's chicken. Chicken and turkey.

Lucy: Or Mad Cow.

Vernon: Mad Cow? Did you — That's not even — that's *English*, they have that in *England*. This isn't English meat, this is from, I don't know, Kansas, or . . . *Wyoming*.

Lucy: Even so, —

Vernon: No. Now you're making stuff up.

Lucy: I'm not; I saw an article —

Vernon: You're just being paranoid, this whole . . . You know what this is? Do you?

Lucy: What.

Vernon: Carnophobia.

Lucy: "Carnophobia"?

Vernon: It's a word, look it up.

Lucy: It's not like I'm scared of meat . . .

Vernon: How do you think this makes me feel?

Lucy: Look, let's just drop it.

Vernon: Huh?

Lucy: We were doing so well . . .

Vernon: I invite you over, cook a nice steak, set out flowers, napkins, the whole nine yards . . .

Lucy: I appreciate the napkins.

Vernon: . . . figure I'll open a bottle of wine, apologize . . . maybe we'll get naked, be like old times.

Lucy: So let's start over.

Vernon: Then you get *carnophobic* on me.

Lucy: Can we?

Vernon: Throw it in my face.

Lucy: Please?

Vernon: Start *cataloguing* what's wrong with everything . . .

Lucy: I never meant this to be a big deal. *(Beat. She puts her hand on his. He looks at her.)* I really didn't.

> *(Long pause.)*

Vernon: Then eat it.

> *(Beat.)*

Lucy: Vern . . . *(He picks up her fork, jams it into her steak, and cuts off a bite with his knife.)* Why do you always have to —

> *(He extends the piece of meat toward Lucy's mouth.)*

Vernon: Eat the meat.

Lucy: I don't want to.

Vernon: Eat the meat.

Lucy: Vernon . . .

Vernon: I SAID EAT THE MEAT! *(They are locked in a struggle, he menacing, she terrified. Long pause. Finally, Lucy opens her mouth and* takes the bite into it. Pause.) Chew. (She chews for fifteen or twenty seconds.) Swallow. (She swallows. Cheerfully, without malice:) Good, isn't it. (Lucy nods obediently.) Nice and juicy. (He stabs his fork into his own steak, cuts off a bite and lifts it.) See, nothing to be afraid of.

(He pops it into his mouth and begins cutting another. After a moment, Lucy goes back to her corn. They eat in absolute silence. Lights fade.)

"Naked Lunch — *a frozen moment when everyone sees what is on the end of every fork.*" — William S. Burroughs

Mistaken Identity

Sharon E. Cooper is an award-winning playwright and teacher whose work has been produced in India, Germany, England, and Hungary and across the United States. Her work has appeared in *Laugh Lines: Short Comic Plays* and in the 2010 and 2014 editions of *The Best Ten-Minute Plays.* Cooper is an English tutor, a writing coach, a fitness instructor, a screenwriter, a resident playwright at the CRY HAVOC Company in New York City, and a member of the Dramatists Guild. Her full-length screenplay *The Golden Age of Kali* was inspired by *Mistaken Identity.* *Mistaken Identity* starts the way a good many shaky blind dates begin but then takes an interesting turn.

Virginia Zapar.

WHEN I WRITE "Don't be scared to write the truth as you know it and as you see it. Find like-minded, thoughtful people — people you can trust, who will listen and help you write the story you want to write. But if someone tries to rewrite or 'fix' your story, stop listening." — SHARON E. COOPER

SHARON E. COOPER (B. 1975)

Mistaken Identity

2004
(2008 Revised)

CHARACTERS

Kali Patel, 29. Single lesbian Hindu of Indian heritage; social worker who works as much as possible; lives in Leicester, England.

Steve Dodd, 32. Single straight guy, desperate to marry, raised Baptist but attends church only on Christmas and Easter; studying abroad for his final year as an undergraduate.

SETTING: The Castle, a pub in Kirby Muxlowe in Leicester, England.

TIME: The present.

> *(Lights up on Steve and Kali in a busy pub on their first date. They are in the middle of dinner.)*

Steve: You must get tired of fish and chips all the time. Why do y'all call them "chips"? When they're french fries, I mean. And you ever notice when people swear, they say, "Excuse my French." Not me. Nope. I have nothing against the French.

Kali: Right, well, I'm not French, Steve, now am I?

Steve: I just didn't want you to think I was prejudiced against the French or *anyone else*. . . . They're like your neighbors, the French. And your neighbors are like my neighbors. And like a good neighbor, State Farm is there. Have you heard that commercial?

Kali: What? No. Steve —

Steve: It's for insurance. Y'all must not play it here. *(Pause.)* So I know that you all do the "arranged marriage thing." Rashid and I had a long talk about it. Of course, Rashid and I wanted you to approve, too, Kali.

Kali: How twenty-first century of you and my brother. Steve . . .

Kali: I'm gay. / *Steve:* Will you marry me?

Kali: Come again? / *Steve:* What?

Kali: How could you ask me to . . . / *Steve:* Well, I can't believe this.

Kali: Bloody hell, stop talking while I'm talking . . . / *Steve:* This is very strange.

Kali: So — what?

Steve: This new information is, well, new, and changes things, I guess.

Kali: You guess? What the hell is wrong with you? I'm sorry, Steve, you just happened to show up at the end of a very long line of a lot of very bad dates. You know, movies where the bloke negotiates holding your hand while you're just trying to eat popcorn; running across De Montfort University in the pouring rain; dropping a bowling ball on the bloke's pizza.

Steve: You had me until the bowling ball. Kali, this doesn't make sense. I invite you out on a lovely date. We eat fish and chips — when I would rather be eating a burger or lasagna —

Kali: Steve, I'm sorry.

Steve: I figured we would have a nice long traditional wedding with the colorful tents. All of my family would be there. We're more of the Christmas/Easter Christians, so we'd do your religion and I would wear —

Kali: *(Overlapping.)* You don't know anything about my people. What are you —

Steve: *(Overlapping.)* Ooohhh, yes, I do. I saw *Monsoon Wedding.* And the director's cut! And I saw *Slumdog Millionaire* like three times. Three times. Unbelievable!

Kali: Yes, this makes loads of sense at the end of the day. I am a lesbian who has to date every Hindu bloke in England until her brother gets so desperate that he sets her up with a cowboy —

Steve: I take offense to that.

Kali: *(Overlapping.)* But I should feel sorry for *you* because *you* watched *two,* count them, *two* movies about Indian people in your entire life and ordered fish when there are hamburgers on the menu! Forgive *me* for being so insensitive.

Steve: I ordered fish because I wanted you to like me. And I'm sure I've seen other Asian movies. Like all those fighting movies. You know, the ones where women are jumping through the air —

Kali: Aaahhh! Do you see how all of this is a moot point now?

Steve: I'm confused. Let's review.

Kali: Please, no, bloody hell, let's not review. Let's get the waiter. Haven't you had enough?

(She gets up. He follows.)

Steve: *(Overlapping.)* Why is your brother setting up his *lesbian* sister —

Kali: *(Overlapping.)* Will you please keep your voice down?

Steve: *(Overlapping.)* — up on dates for marriage and tricking well-meaning men — specifically me — into proposing to her? I'm here to finish my business degree, but I wasn't born yesterday. So I took a few years off and changed careers a few times, was a fireman —

Kali: *(Overlapping.)* What does that have to do with anything?

Steve: And I'm thirty-two years old, but that doesn't mean —

Kali: Mate, are you going to keep on and on?

Steve: Why did your brother put me through this? This isn't one of those new reality shows: "Little Brothers Set Up Their Lesbian Sisters." Is there a camera under the table? *(He looks.)* Let's talk about this. *(He sits back down.)* I'm a good listener. Go ahead. *(Pause.)* I'm listening. *(Pause.)* You have to say something if you want this to continue with what we call in America, a conversation.

Kali: Are you done?

Steve: Go ahead.

(She sits.)

Kali: I guess I was hoping you wouldn't tell Rashid.

Steve: He doesn't know?

Kali: You are finishing your bachelor's degree, is that right?

Steve: If you're so "bloody" smart, I'm wondering why you would tell me, a man that is friends with your brother and sits next to him twice a week in eight A.M. classes — why would you tell *me* you're a lesbian and *not* your brother?

Kali: Maybe for the same reason you would ask a woman you've never met before to marry you.

Steve: Your brother made it sound like it would be easy. I've been looking for that.

Kali: *(Overlapping.)* Look, you seem very nice, you do.

Steve: I am very nice.

Kali: And at the end of the day, I hope you find someone you like.

Steve: I like how you say "at the end of the day" and I like how you say "bloke" and "mate." It's so endearing. And you're beautiful and small and your hair falls on your back so.

Kali: Steve, being a lesbian is not negotiable. And don't start with how sexy it would be to be with me or to watch me and another woman —

Steve: *(Overlapping.)* Kali, I didn't say any of that.

Kali: You didn't have to. Up until a few minutes ago, you thought I was a quiet, subservient Asian toy for sale from her brother. Steve, go get a doll. She can travel with you to America whenever you want. In the meantime, I'll continue to be a loud, abrasive *(Whispering.)* lesbian while my brother sets me up with every bloke on the street — and they don't even have to be Hindu anymore! Do you have any idea what that's like? *(Pause.)* How would you know?

Steve: You're right. I wouldn't.

Kali: Steve, why did you want to be with me? I mean, before.

Steve: I figured that we would have visited my family in the winter when it's so cold here. I would have been willing to stay here when I'm done with school and we would get a nice little place by the —

Kali: Steve, we hadn't even shared dessert yet.

Steve: Don't blame me for all of this. Five minutes ago, we were on a date.

Kali: We're just two people in a pub.

Steve: Kali, do you remember the last time someone — man, woman, I don't care — had their hand down the small of your back or leaned into you like it didn't matter where you ended and they began?

Kali: Yes, I do remember that. And that was strangely poetic.

Steve: You don't have to sound so surprised. Anyway, I remember that feeling. Three years ago, at a Fourth of July celebration — you know, that's the holiday —

Kali: Yes, Steve, I know the holiday.

Steve: She was the only woman I ever really loved. I knew it was ending. Could taste it. I just held her as the fireworks went off and the dust got in our skin. Figured I would hold on, hoping that would keep me for a while. You know how they say babies will die if they're left alone too long. Always wondered if it's true for bigger people, too. Like how long would we last? . . . She left with her Pilates mat and Snoopy slippers a few days later. I bet it hasn't been three years for you.

Kali: No, it hasn't. But you wouldn't want to hear about that.

Steve: Why not?

Kali: Come on, Steve, I'm not here for your fantasies —

Steve: This thing where you assume you know what I'm thinking — it's gettin' old.

Kali: I'm . . . sorry. I do have a woman in my life, Michele — She's a teacher for people that are deaf. We've been together for eleven months. The longest we were away from each other was this one time for three weeks. She was at a retreat where they weren't allowed to talk — you know, total immersion. So she would call and I would say, "Is it beautiful there, love?" and she would hit a couple of buttons. Sometimes she would leave me messages: "beep, beep, beep beep beep beep." It didn't matter that she didn't say anything . . . But I can't take her home for Diwali.

Steve: What's that?

Kali: It's a festival of lights where —

Steve: You mean like Hanukkah.

Kali: No, like Diwali. It's a New Year's celebration where we remember ancestors, family, and friends. And reflect back and look to the future.

Steve: It sounds nice. You know, my mother has been asking me for grandchildren since I turned twenty-seven. Every year at Christmas, it's the same: "I can't wait to hang another stocking for my grandchildren, if I ever get to have them."

Kali: Now, imagine that same conversation, well, not about Christmas, and what if you could never give that to them — could never bring someone home for any holiday for the rest of your life?

Steve: Then why don't you just tell them the truth?

Kali: I can't say, Mum, Daddy, Rashid, I've chosen women over men — it's not a hamburger over fish. You just don't know how they'll react. I'd run the risk of not being allowed to see my nieces. I'm so exhausted from hiding, I can barely breathe.

Steve: So stop hiding.

Kali: Have you been listening to what I've been saying?

Steve: Have you?

Kali: Are you going to tell my brother?

Steve: Do you want me to?

Kali: I don't know.

Steve: I've never thought about that thing that you said.

Kali: Which thing would that be?

Steve: The one where maybe you can't see your nieces 'cause you're gay. That must suck.

Kali: Yes, well, thanks for trying to make me feel better.

Steve: Listen, you get to decide what you tell your family and when. As far as I'm concerned, I'll tell Rashid tomorrow that we're getting married. Or I can tell him you're a lesbian, and if he doesn't let you be with his kids anymore, I'll punch him in the face. That was me kidding.

Kali: You're funny. *(Pause.)* Maybe I told you because somewhere deep down, I do want him to know. But I don't know if I can take the risk.

Steve: You don't have to rush.

Kali: I just wish it could be more simple. Like, why can't what I want be part of the whole picket-fence thing? That's pretty ridiculous, huh?

Steve: We're all looking for that. My grandparents met before World War II, dated for seven days in a row, and my grandfather asked my grandmother to go with him to Louisiana, where he'd be stationed. She said, "Is that a proposal?" And he said, "Of course it is." And they've been together ever since. And I just want that, too. Huh — asking you to marry me on a first date! You must think I'm pretty desperate, huh?

Kali: Not any more than the rest of us . . . Oh, hell, do you want to have some dessert?

Steve: Oh, hell, sure. You know, we're going to share dessert.

Kali: Hey, mate, no one said anything about sharing.

Steve: I would go home with you for Diwali. I mean, as friends. If you ever wanted one around. You're a nice girl, Kali. I mean woman, mate, bloke. I mean —

Kali: Sssshhhh. Let's just get some dessert.

(Lights fade as they motion for the waiter. Blackout.)

Playwriting 101: The Rooftop Lesson

Born in Chicago, Rich Orloff graduated from Oberlin College in 1973 and has built a successful career as a comedic playwright. He has written fifteen full-length plays, seven collections of one-act plays, and more than seventy short plays, seven of which have appeared in *Best American Short Plays*. His works are produced throughout the United States and have won a number of awards, including the 2002–03 Dramatists Guild Playwriting Fellowship. On his Web site <www.richorloff.com> Orloff explains what prompted him to write *Playwriting 101: The Rooftop Lesson:*

Photo by Rick Tormone.

"The play was originally produced as part of a series of short plays produced on an actual rooftop in Manhattan. When I was invited to submit to the festival, every idea I came up with seemed completely clichéd. So I gathered the clichés into one story and satirized them. Voila, an original play!"

WHEN I WRITE "One of the joys of writing plays is knowing that it's always a draft. I keep revising until I sense the play is connecting well with an audience, that they're laughing at the funny parts and are engaged in the story." —RICHARD ORLOFF

Rich Orloff (b. 1951)

Playwriting 101: The Rooftop Lesson   2000

NOTE: The characters [the Teacher, the Jumper, and the Good Samaritan] can
be of either sex, but the Jumper and Good Samaritan should be of the same sex.
References are written as if the characters are male, but that can be changed.
TIME: The present.
PLACE: The rooftop of a large urban building.

> *(As the play begins, The Jumper is on the ledge of the roof and is about to
> jump.)*

The Jumper: I'm going to jump, and nobody can stop me!

> *(The Good Samaritan enters quickly.)*

The Good Samaritan: Don't!!!!!

> *(The Teacher enters and stands to the side. The Teacher points a clicker at
> the others and clicks, freezing the action.)*

The Teacher (addressing the audience): A typical dramatic scenario: Two
people in conflict — at least one in deep inner conflict — with high
stakes, suspense, and affordable cast size. How will this situation
play out? That depends, of course, on the level of craft and creativity
in that remarkable art form known as playwriting. Let's rewind from
the start — *(The Teacher clicks, and The Jumper and Good Samaritan
return to their places at the top of the play, quickly reversing their initial
movements.)* And see what happens.

> *(The Teacher clicks again to resume the action. The Jumper is on the ledge
> of the roof and is about to jump.)*

The Jumper: I'm going to jump, and nobody can stop me!

> *(The Good Samaritan enters quickly.)*

The Good Samaritan: Don't!!!!!
The Jumper: Okay.

> *(The Teacher clicks to freeze the action.)*

The Teacher: Not very satisfying, is it? Where's the suspense? Where's the
tension? And what audience member will want to pay today's ticket
prices for a play whose conflict resolves in forty-five seconds? But most
importantly, where can you go from here?

> *(The Teacher clicks to unfreeze the action.)*

The Good Samaritan: Gee, you could've hurt yourself.
The Jumper: Gosh, you're right.
The Good Samaritan: Want to grab a brew?
The Jumper: Sure.

(The Teacher clicks to freeze the action.)

The Teacher: Without intense oppositional desires, more commonly known as "conflict," there is no play. When Nora leaves in *A Doll's House,* nobody wants her husband to reply — *(upbeat)* "Call when you get work!" So let's start this scene over — *(The Teacher clicks. The Jumper and Good Samaritan rewind to their initial places.)* maintaining conflict.

(The Teacher clicks again.)

The Jumper: I'm going to jump, and nobody can stop me!

(The Good Samaritan enters quickly.)

The Good Samaritan: Don't!!!!!
The Jumper: Fuck you!
The Good Samaritan *(giving an obscene gesture):* No, you asshole, fuck you!

(The Teacher clicks and freezes the action.)

The Teacher: Let's rise above profanity, shall we? It alienates conservatives and makes liberals think you're second-rate David Mamet. *(Clicks.)* Rewind . . . And again: *(Clicks.)*
The Jumper: I'm going to jump, and nobody can stop me!

(The Good Samaritan enters quickly.)

The Good Samaritan: Don't!!!!!
The Jumper: Why not?!!!

(The Teacher clicks.)

The Teacher: Oooo, you can just feel the suspense rising now, can't you?

(The Teacher clicks again.)

The Good Samaritan: Because suicide is a sin!

(The Teacher clicks.)

The Teacher: Big deal. Theatre is written by sinners about sinners for sinners. Nobody goes to *Othello* to hear, "Iago, you're so naughty!" Always let the audience form their own judgments. Rewind a bit. *(Clicks.)* Now let's try a different tack. *(Clicks.)*
The Jumper: Why not?!
The Good Samaritan: Because I love you.
The Jumper: I didn't know!

(The Teacher clicks.)

The Teacher: I don't care! Let's see if we can find something less clichéd.

(The Teacher clicks again.)

The Jumper: Why not?!
The Good Samaritan: Because if you jump there, you'll land on my little girl's lemonade stand. And my little girl!

(The Jumper looks over the ledge and moves over two feet.)

The Jumper: Is this better?

(*The Teacher clicks.*)

The Teacher: Now what have we gained? Be wary of minor obstacles. Unless, of course, you need to fill time. Again.

(*The Teacher clicks again.*)

The Jumper: Why not?!
The Good Samaritan: Because life is worth living.
The Jumper: Mine isn't!

(*The Teacher clicks.*)

The Teacher: Excellent. We don't just have a plot anymore, we have a theme. Theme, the difference between entertainment and art. No theme, add a car chase and sell it to the movies. But with theme, you have the potential to create something meaningful, something memorable, something college students can write term papers about. So let's rewind a bit and see where this thematically rich drama goes now.

(*The Teacher clicks to rewind and clicks again to resume.*)

The Good Samaritan: Because life is worth living!
The Jumper: Mine isn't!
The Good Samaritan: Gosh. Tell me all about it.

(*The Teacher clicks.*)

The Teacher: Some expositional subtlety, please.

(*The Teacher clicks again.*)

The Good Samaritan: Because life is worth living!
The Jumper: Mine isn't!
The Good Samaritan: Are you sure?

(*The Teacher clicks.*)

The Teacher: Better.

(*The Teacher clicks again.*)

The Jumper: Yes, I'm sure. I'm broke, I have no friends, and I see no reason to continue.
The Good Samaritan: Look, so you're broke and friendless. All experiences are transient. Detach, as the Buddha once did.

(*The Teacher clicks.*)

The Teacher: Of all the world's great religions, Buddhism is the least entertaining. Let's try again.

(*The Teacher clicks again.*)

The Good Samaritan: So you're broke and you're friendless. Why not try Prozac?

(*The Teacher clicks.*)

The Teacher: The popularity and effectiveness of modern antidepressants is one of the great challenges of contemporary dramaturgy. We no more want Willy Loman to solve his problems with Prozac than we want Stanley and Stella Kowalski to get air-conditioning. How can today's playwright deal with today's medicinal deus ex machinas? Let's see.

(The Teacher clicks again.)

The Jumper: I tried Prozac once, and it made my mouth really dry.

(The Teacher clicks.)

The Teacher: Not great, but we'll let it slide.

(The Teacher clicks again.)

The Good Samaritan: Let me help you.
The Jumper: It's too late.
The Good Samaritan: No, it's not.
The Jumper: You don't understand. I haven't told you the worst.

(The Teacher clicks.)

The Teacher: Fictional characters are rarely straightforward.

(The Teacher clicks again.)

The Jumper: You see, until a few weeks ago, I was in love. Deep love. True love. I was involved with two of the most wonderful gals in the world. One was sexy, rich, generous and caring. The other was streetwise, daring and even sexier. Between the two of them, I had everything. Then they found out about each other, and they both dumped me. Not just one, but both.

(The Teacher clicks.)

The Teacher: Excellent playwriting. Here's a heartbreaking situation with which we can all identify. Maybe not in the specifics, but in the universal experience of rejection.

(The Teacher clicks again.)

The Good Samaritan: At least you've had two exciting affairs. I haven't gotten laid in a year.

(The Teacher clicks.)

The Teacher: A superb response. Another situation with which, um, well, we've all had friends who've had that problem.

(The Teacher clicks again.)

The Jumper: So what are you telling me? That life can get *worse*? That's supposed to get me off this ledge?
The Good Samaritan: Hey, I'm just trying to help!
The Jumper: Well, you're doing a lousy job.

The Good Samaritan: At least I've got some money in the bank!
The Jumper: You've also got rocks in your head!

(*The Teacher clicks.*)

The Teacher: A common beginner's mistake. Two characters in hostile disagreement isn't conflict, it's just bickering. We don't go to the theatre to hear petty, puerile antagonism; that's why we have families. Let's hope this goes somewhere interesting, or I'll have to rewind.

(*The Teacher clicks again.*)

The Jumper: You've only got money in the bank because you're cheap.
The Good Samaritan: I am not.
The Jumper: Well, you certainly dress like you are.
The Teacher: Now this is really degenerating.

(*The Teacher clicks, but the action continues.*)

The Good Samaritan: Listen, you stupid twerp —
The Jumper: At least I'm a twerp with a decent sex life.
The Good Samaritan: And if it was decent for *them,* maybe you'd still have a sex life.

(*The Teacher continues to click, but the action continues.*)

The Teacher (as the action continues): Now stop it . . . Stop it! . . . Stop it!! (*Etc.*)

(*Shouting above The Teacher's "Stop it"s, which they ignore:*)

The Jumper: Loser!
The Good Samaritan: Pervert!
The Jumper: Cheapskate!
The Good Samaritan: Cretin!
The Jumper: Asshole!
The Good Samaritan: Imbecile!
The Jumper: Shithead!
The Teacher (clicking in vain): Stop it!!!!

(*The Good Samaritan takes out a clicker and freezes The Teacher.*)

The Good Samaritan: Notice how organically the teacher's frustration has increased. What began as a minor irritation became unbearable when the human desire to control was thwarted.

(*The Good Samaritan clicks again.*)

The Teacher: What are you doing?! I hold the clicker around here. How dare —

(*The Good Samaritan clicks. The Teacher freezes.*)

The Good Samaritan: See how frustration becomes "anger"? Although the real life stakes are minor, the character's emotional investment is intense. That's good playwriting.

(The Good Samaritan clicks again.)

The Teacher: Stop that. What do you think this is, a Pirandello° play?

The Good Samaritan: Well, how do you think *we* feel? We can't say more than two lines without being interrupted by your self-important pronouncements. How'd you like it if I did that to you?

The Teacher: You have no dra — *(The Good Samaritan clicks and stops/ starts The Teacher during the following:)* matically vi — able rea — son to inter — rupt me. Damn it, will you get back in the play?

The Good Samaritan: No, and you can't make me!

(The Good Samaritan clicks at The Teacher, who dodges the clicker.)

The Teacher: Aha, missed. You superficial stereotype!

(The Teacher clicks at The Good Samaritan and vice versa during the following, both successfully dodging the other.)

The Good Samaritan: Control freak!

The Teacher: Cliché!

The Good Samaritan: Semi-intellectual!

The Teacher: Contrivance!

The Good Samaritan: Academic tapeworm!

The Teacher: First draft mistake!

(The Jumper, who has been watching this, takes out a gun and shoots it into the air.)

The Jumper: Hey!!! I'm the one with the problem. This play's supposed to be about me.

The Good Samaritan: Tough. The well-made play died with Ibsen.

The Teacher (to The Good Samaritan): Damn it, get back into the play!

The Good Samaritan: Don't tell me what to do. Ever since I was a kid, everyone's told me how I'm supposed to behave. When I was five, my mom sent me to my room *(The Teacher starts clicking manically at The Good Samaritan.)* four thousand times because I wouldn't be the kid she wanted me —

The Teacher: This monologue is not justified!

The Good Samaritan: Tough shit, it's my life!

The Teacher: It's bad drama!

The Good Samaritan: I'll show you bad drama!

(The Good Samaritan and The Teacher begin to fight.)

The Jumper: Stop it! Come on, stop it, you're pulling focus.

The Teacher: Butt out!

(The Jumper tries to break up the fight.)

The Jumper: Come on, guys, cool it!

The Good Samaritan: Get away from us!

The Jumper: Just stop it!

Luigi Pirandello (1867–1936): Italian playwright famous for exploring illusion and reality in his plays.

The Good Samaritan: Leave us alone!

(*The three of them are in a tight cluster. We hear a gunshot. The Teacher pulls away. There's blood on The Teacher's chest.*)

The Teacher: I just got tenure.

(*The Teacher collapses.*)

The Good Samaritan: Oh my God.
The Jumper: He's dead.

(*The Good Samaritan looks at The Jumper.*)

The Good Samaritan: How horrible. Is that good playwriting or bad playwriting?
The Jumper: I, I don't know. It just happened.

(*The Good Samaritan and The Jumper look at The Teacher.*)

The Jumper and The Good Samaritan (simultaneously): Hmmmmmmm.

(*The Good Samaritan and The Jumper begin to exit.*)

The Good Samaritan: Gee, you could've hurt yourself.
The Jumper: Gosh, you're right.
The Good Samaritan: Want to grab a brew?
The Jumper: Sure.

(*The Teacher comes to life for a moment, clicks into the air and: Blackout.*)

Trying to Find Chinatown

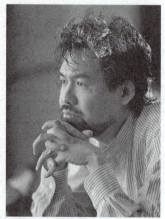

© Michal Daniel.

Born in Los Angeles, David Henry Hwang is the son of immigrant Chinese American parents; his father worked as a banker, and his mother was a professor of piano. Educated at Stanford University, from which he earned his B.A. in English in 1979, he became interested in theater after attending plays at the American Conservatory in San Francisco. His marginal interest in a law career quickly gave way to his involvement in the engaging world of live theater. By his senior year, he had written and produced his first play, *FOB* (an acronym for "fresh off the boat"), which marked the beginning of a meteoric rise as a playwright.

Although Hwang was successful in having additional plays produced in the mid-1980s and won prestigious fellowships from the Guggenheim Foundation and the National Endowment for the Arts, it was not until

1988, when *M. Butterfly* — a complex treatment of social, political, racial, cultural, and sexual issues — was produced on Broadway, that he achieved astonishing commercial success as well as widespread acclaim. His awards for this play include the Outer Critics Circle Award for best Broadway play, the Drama Desk Award for best new play, the John Gassner Award for best American play, and the Tony Award for best play of the year. By the end of 1988, Hwang was regarded by many critics as the most talented young playwright in the United States. One of his recent plays, *Chinglish* (2011), is a humorous treatment of an American businessman in China. *Trying to Find Chinatown* is a brief but complicated confrontation between two young men who argue about racial identity in unexpected ways. Hwang's strategy is to challenge the polemical stereotyping that often passes for discussions of ethnic and cultural heritage in the United States.

DAVID HENRY HWANG (B. 1957)

Trying to Find Chinatown   1996

CHARACTERS

Benjamin, Caucasian male, early twenties.
Ronnie, Asian-American male, mid-twenties.

TIME AND PLACE A street corner on the Lower East Side, New York City. The present.

NOTE ON MUSIC Obviously, it would be foolish to require that the actor portraying Ronnie perform the specified violin music live. The score of this play can be played on tape over the house speakers, and the actor can feign playing the violin using a bow treated with soap. However, in order to effect a convincing illusion, it is desirable that the actor possess some familiarity with the violin or another stringed instrument.

> *Darkness. Over the house speakers, sound fades in: Hendrix-like virtuoso rock 'n' roll riffs — heavy feedback, distortion, phase shifting, wah-wah — amplified over a tiny Fender pug-nose.*
>
> *Lights fade up to reveal that the music's being played over a solid-body electric violin by Ronnie, a Chinese-American male in his mid-twenties; he is dressed in retro-'60s clothing and has a few requisite '90s body mutilations. He's playing on a sidewalk for money, his violin case open before him; change and a few stray bills have been left by previous passersby.*
>
> *Benjamin enters; he's in his early twenties, blond, blue-eyed, a Midwestern tourist in the big city. He holds a scrap of paper in his hands, scanning street signs for an address. He pauses before Ronnie, listens for a while. With a truly bravura run, Ronnie concludes the number and falls to his knees, gasping. Benjamin applauds.*

Benjamin: Good. That was really great. *(Pause)* I didn't ... I mean, a
   fiddle ... I mean, I'd heard them at square dances, on country stations
   and all, but I never ... wow, this must really be New York City!

   *(Benjamin applauds, starts to walk on. Still on his knees, Ronnie clears
   his throat loudly.)*

   Oh, I ... you're not just doing this for your health, right?

   *(Benjamin reaches in his pocket, pulls out a couple of coins. Ronnie clears
   his throat again.)*

   Look, I'm not a millionaire, I'm just ...

   *(Benjamin pulls out his wallet, removes a dollar bill. Ronnie nods
   his head and gestures toward the violin case as he takes out a pack of
   cigarettes, lights one.)*

Ronnie: And don't call it a "fiddle," OK?

Benjamin: Oh. Well, I didn't mean to —

Ronnie: You sound like a wuss. A hick. A dipshit.

Benjamin: It just slipped out. I didn't really —

Ronnie: If this was a fiddle, I'd be sitting here with a cob pipe, stomping
   my cowboy boots and kicking up hay. Then I'd go home and fuck my
   cousin.

Benjamin: Oh! Well, I don't really think —

Ronnie: Do you see a cob pipe? Am I fucking my cousin?

Benjamin: Well, no, not at the moment, but —

Ronnie: All right. Then this is a violin, now you give me your money, and I
   ignore the insult. Herein endeth the lesson.

   (Pause.)

Benjamin: Look, a dollar's more than I've ever given to a ... to someone
   asking for money.

Ronnie: Yeah, well, this is New York. Welcome to the cost of living.

Benjamin: What I mean is, maybe in exchange, you could help me — ?

Ronnie: Jesus Christ! Do you see a sign around my neck reading "Big Apple
   Fucking Tourist Bureau"?

Benjamin: I'm just looking for an address, I don't think it's far from here,
   maybe you could ... ?

   (Benjamin holds out his scrap of paper, Ronnie snatches it away.)

Ronnie: You're lucky I'm such a goddamn softy. *(He looks at the paper)* Oh,
   fuck you. Just suck my dick, you and the cousin you rode in on.

Benjamin: I don't get it! What are you — ?

Ronnie: Eat me. You know exactly what I —

Benjamin: I'm just asking for a little —

Ronnie: "13 Doyers Street"? Like you don't know where that is?

Benjamin: Of course I don't know! That's why I'm asking —

Ronnie: C'mon, you trailer-park refugee. You don't know that's Chinatown?

Benjamin: Sure I know that's Chinatown.

Ronnie: I know you know that's Chinatown.

Benjamin: So? That doesn't mean I know where Chinatown —

Ronnie: So why is it that you picked *me*, of all the street musicians in the city — to point you in the direction of Chinatown? Lemme guess — is it the earring? No, I don't think so. The Hendrix riffs? Guess again, you fucking moron.

Benjamin: Now, wait a minute. I see what you're —

Ronnie: What are you gonna ask me next? Where you can find the best dim sum in the city? Whether I can direct you to a genuine opium den? Or do I happen to know how you can meet Miss Saigon for a night of nookie-nookie followed by a good old-fashioned ritual suicide? Now, get your white ass off my sidewalk. One dollar doesn't even begin to make up for all this aggravation. Why don't you go back home and race bullfrogs, or whatever it is you do for — ?

Benjamin: Brother, I can absolutely relate to your anger. Righteous rage, I suppose, would be a more appropriate term. To be marginalized, as we are, by a white racist patriarchy, to the point where the accomplishments of our people are obliterated from the history books, this is cultural genocide of the first order, leading to the fact that you must do battle with all of Euro-America's emasculating and brutal stereotypes of Asians — the opium den, the sexual objectification of the Asian female, the exoticized image of a tourist's Chinatown which ignores the exploitation of workers, the failure to unionize, the high rate of mental illness and tuberculosis — against these, each day, you rage, no, not as a victim, but as a survivor, yes, brother, a glorious warrior survivor!

(Silence.)

Ronnie: Say what?

Benjamin: So, I hope you can see that my request is not —

Ronnie: Wait, wait.

Benjamin: — motivated by the sorts of racist assumptions —

Ronnie: But, but where . . . how did you learn all that?

Benjamin: All what?

Ronnie: All that — you know — oppression stuff — tuberculosis . . .

Benjamin: It's statistically irrefutable. TB occurs in the community at a rate —

Ronnie: Where did *you* learn it?

Benjamin: I took Asian-American studies. In college.

Ronnie: Where did you go to college?

Benjamin: University of Wisconsin. Madison.

Ronnie: Madison, Wisconsin?

Benjamin: That's not where the bridges are, by the way.

Ronnie: Huh? Oh, right . . .

Benjamin: You wouldn't believe the number of people who —

Ronnie: They have Asian-American studies in Madison, Wisconsin? Since when?

Benjamin: Since the last Third World Unity hunger strike. *(Pause)* Why do you look so surprised? We're down.

Ronnie: I dunno. It just never occurred to me, the idea of Asian students in the Midwest going on a hunger strike.

Benjamin: Well, a lot of them had midterms that week, so they fasted in shifts. *(Pause)* The administration never figured it out. The Asian students put that "They all look alike" stereotype to good use.

Ronnie: OK, so they got Asian-American studies. That still doesn't explain —

Benjamin: What?

Ronnie: Well . . . what *you* were doing taking it?

Benjamin: Just like everyone else. I wanted to explore my roots. And, you know, the history of oppression which is my legacy. After a lifetime of assimilation, I wanted to find out who I really am.

(Pause.)

Ronnie: And did you?

Benjamin: Sure. I learned to take pride in my ancestors who built the railroads, my Popo who would make me a hot bowl of jok with thousand-day-old eggs when the white kids chased me home yelling, "Gook! Chink! Slant-eyes!"

Ronnie: OK, OK, that's enough!

Benjamin: Painful to listen to, isn't it?

Ronnie: I don't know what kind of bullshit ethnic studies program they're running over in Wuss-consin, but did they bother to teach you that in order to find your Asian "roots," it's a good idea to first be Asian?

(Pause.)

Benjamin: Are you speaking metaphorically?

Ronnie: No! Literally! Look at your skin!

Benjamin: You know, it's very stereotypical to think that all Asian skin tones conform to a single hue.

Ronnie: You're white! Is this some kind of redneck joke or something? Am I the first person in the world to tell you this?

Benjamin: Oh! Oh! Oh!

Ronnie: I know real Asians are scarce in the Midwest, but . . . Jesus!

Benjamin: No, of course, I . . . I see where your misunderstanding arises.

Ronnie: Yeah. It's called, "You white."

Benjamin: It's just that — in my hometown of Tribune, Kansas, and then at school — see, everyone knows me — so this sort of thing never comes up. *(He offers his hand)* Benjamin Wong. I forget that a society wedded to racial constructs constantly forces me to explain my very existence.

Ronnie: Ronnie Chang. Otherwise known as "The Bow Man."

Benjamin: You see, I was adopted by Chinese-American parents at birth. So, clearly, I'm an Asian-American —

Ronnie: Even though you're blond and blue-eyed.

Benjamin: Well, you can't judge my race by my genetic heritage alone.

Ronnie: If genes don't determine race, what does?

Benjamin: Perhaps you'd prefer that I continue in denial, masquerading as a white man?

Ronnie: You can't just wake up and say, "Gee, I *feel* black today."

Benjamin: Brother, I'm just trying to find what you've already got.

Ronnie: What do I got?

Benjamin: A home. With your people. Picketing with the laundry workers. Taking refuge from the daily slights against your masculinity in the noble image of Gwan Gung.

Ronnie: Gwan who?

Benjamin: C'mon — the Chinese god of warriors and — what do you take me for? There're altars to him up all over the community.

Ronnie: I dunno what community you're talking about, but it's sure as hell not mine.

(*Pause.*)

Benjamin: What do you mean?

Ronnie: I mean, if you wanna call Chinatown *your* community, OK, knock yourself out, learn to use chopsticks, big deal. Go ahead, try and find your "roots" in some dim sum parlor with headless ducks hanging in the window. Those places don't tell you a thing about who *I* am.

Benjamin: Oh, I get it.

Ronnie: You get what?

Benjamin: You're one of those self-hating, *assimilated* Chinese-Americans, aren't you?

Ronnie: Oh, Jesus.

Benjamin: You probably call yourself "Oriental," huh? Look, maybe I can help you. I have some books I can —

Ronnie: Hey, I read all those Asian identity books when you were still slathering on industrial-strength sunblock. (*Pause*) Sure, I'm Chinese. But folks like you act like that means something. Like, all of a sudden, you know who I am. You think identity's that simple? That you can wrap it all up in a neat package and say, "I have ethnicity, therefore I am"? All you fucking ethnic fundamentalists. Always settling for easy answers. You say you're looking for identity, but you can't begin to face the real mysteries of the search. So instead, you go skin-deep, and call it a day. (*Pause. He turns away from Benjamin and starts to play his violin — slow and bluesy.*)

Benjamin: So what are you? "Just a human being"? That's like saying you *have* no identity. If you asked me to describe my dog, I'd say more than, "He's just a dog."

Ronnie: What — you think if I deny the importance of my race, I'm nobody? There're worlds out there, worlds you haven't even begun to understand. Open your eyes. Hear with your ears.

(Ronnie holds his violin at chest level, but does not attempt to play during the following monologue. As he speaks, rock and jazz violin tracks fade in and out over the house speakers, bringing to life the styles of music he describes.)

I concede — it was called a fiddle long ago — but that was even before the birth of jazz. When the hollering in the fields, the rank injustice of human bondage, the struggle of God's children against the plagues of the devil's white man, when all these boiled up into that bittersweet brew, called by later generations, the blues. That's when fiddlers like Son Sims held their chin rests at their chests, and sawed away like the hillbillies still do today. And with the coming of ragtime appeared the pioneer Stuff Smith, who sang as he stroked the catgut, with his raspy, Louis Armstrong–voice — gruff and sweet like the timber of horsehair riding south below the fingerboard — and who finally sailed for Europe to find ears that would hear. Europe — where Stephane Grappelli initiated a magical French violin, to be passed from generation to generation — first he, to Jean-Luc Ponty, then Ponty to Didier Lockwood. Listening to Grappelli play "A Nightingale Sang in Berkeley Square" is to understand not only the song of birds, but also how they learn to fly, fall in love on the wing, and finally falter one day, to wait for darkness beneath a London street lamp. And Ponty — he showed how the modern violin man can accompany the shadow of his own lead lines, which cascade, one over another, into some nether world beyond the range of human hearing. Joe Venuti. Noel Pointer. Sven Asmussen. Even the Kronos Quartet, with their arrangement of "Purple Haze." Now, tell me, could any legacy be more rich, more crowded with mythology and heroes to inspire pride? What can I say if the banging of a gong or the clinking of a pickax on the Transcontinental Railroad fails to move me even as much as one note, played through a violin MIDI controller by Michael Urbaniak? *(He puts his violin to his chin, begins to play a jazz composition of his own invention)* Does it have to sound like Chinese opera before people like you decide I know who I am?

(Benjamin stands for a long moment, listening to Ronnie play. Then, he drops his dollar into the case, turns and exits right. Ronnie continues to play a long moment. Then Benjamin enters downstage left, illuminated in his own spotlight. He sits on the floor of the stage, his feet dangling off the lip. As he speaks, Ronnie continues playing his tune, which becomes underscoring for Benjamin's monologue. As the music continues, does it slowly begin to reflect the influence of Chinese music?)

Benjamin: When I finally found Doyers Street, I scanned the buildings for Number 13. Walking down an alley where the scent of freshly steamed char siu bao lingered in the air, I felt immediately that I had entered a world where all things were finally familiar. *(Pause)* An old woman bumped me with her shopping bag — screaming to her friend in Cantonese, though they walked no more than a few inches apart. Another man—shouting to a vendor in Sze-Yup. A youth, in white undershirt, perhaps a recent newcomer, bargaining with a grocer in Hokkien. I walked through this ocean of dialects, breathing in the richness with deep gulps, exhilarated by the energy this symphony brought to my step. And when I finally saw the number 13, I nearly wept at my good fortune. An old tenement, paint peeling, inside walls no doubt thick with a century of grease and broken dreams—and yet, to me, a temple—the house where my father was born. I suddenly saw it all: Gung Gung, coming home from his sixteen-hour days pressing shirts he could never afford to own, bringing with him candies for my father, each sweet wrapped in the hope of a better life. When my father left the ghetto, he swore he would never return. But he had, this day, in the thoughts and memories of his son, just six months after his death. And as I sat on the stoop, I pulled a hua-moi° from my pocket, sucked on it, and felt his spirit returning. To this place where his ghost, and the dutiful hearts of all his descendants, would always call home. *(He listens for a long moment)* And I felt an ache in my heart for all those lost souls, denied this most important of revelations: to know who they truly are.

(Benjamin sucks his salted plum and listens to the sounds around him. Ronnie continues to play. The two remain oblivious of one another. Lights fade slowly to black.)

End of play

Hua-moi: A dry, sour plum that is a Cantonese specialty food.

Moby-Dude, Or: The Three-Minute Whale

Born in Chicago and educated at Northwestern University and the Yale School of Drama, David Ives writes for television, film, and opera. A recipient of a Guggenheim Fellowship in playwriting, he has created a number of one-act plays for the annual comedy festival called Manhattan Punch Line. Many of his one-act plays are available in *All in the Timing* (1994), *Lives of the Saints* (2000), and *Time Flies*

Peter Sumner Walton Bellamy.

and Other Short Plays (2001); his full-length plays are collected in *Polish Joke and Other Plays* (2004). *Venus in Fur*, another full-length play, is an erotic comic drama that opened in 2010. *Moby-Dude, Or: The Three-Minute Whale* is a very brief play about a student trying to convince his teacher that he actually completed reading a very long novel. In the introduction to *Talk to Me: Monologue Plays*, from which *Moby-Dude* is reprinted, the editors, Nina Shengold and Eric Lane, offer a valuable perspective on the nature of monologue plays by describing them as a "modern form of that most ancient of human entertainments, storytelling. Our paleolithic ancestors listened to hunters enacting their sagas in front of a campfire, and members of every human community since have stood up in front of their peers and performed their tales." Here's Ives's updated version of classic storytelling.

> **WHEN I WRITE** "I have worked on writing schedules covering every hour of the day. All schedules are good. All rituals are good. All writing superstitions are good. The point is not to have a writing schedule; the point is to write." —DAVID IVES

DAVID IVES (B. 1950)

Moby-Dude, Or: The Three-Minute Whale 2004

SFX: sound of waves and gulls. Distant ship's bell.
Our Narrator is a stoned-out surfer of seventeen.

Our Narrator: Call me Ishmael, dude. Yes, Mrs. Podgorski, I *did* read *Moby-Dick* over the summer like I was supposed to. It was bohdacious. Actually, y'know, it's "*Moby-hyphen-Dick.*" The title's got a little hyphen before the "Dick." And what is the meaning of this dash before the "Dick"? *WHOAAA!* Another mystery in this awesome American masterpiece, a peerless allegorical saga of mortal courage, metaphysical ambiguity and maniacal obsession! *What*, Mrs. Podgorski? You don't believe I really *read* Herman Melville's *Moby-Dick Or The Whale*? Five hundred sixty-two pages, fourteen ounces, published 1851, totally tanked its first weekend, rereleased in the 1920s as one of the world's gnarliest works of Art? You think I copped all this like off the back of the tome or by watching the crappy 1956 film starring Gregory Peck? Mrs. P., you been chasing my tail since middle school, do *I* get all testy? Do *I* say, what is the plot in under two minutes — besides a whale and a hyphen? *Moby-Dick* in two minutes, huh? Okay, kyool. Let's rip.

(SFX: ship's bell, close up and sharp, to signal the start and a ticking watch, underneath. Very fast.)

Fade in the boonies of Massachusetts, eighteen-something. Young dude possibly named Ishmael, like the Bible, meets-cute with, TAA-DAA!, *Queequeg*, a South Sea cannibal with a heart of gold.

(SFX: cutesy voice going, "Awwww.")

Maybe they're gay.

(SFX: tongue slurp.)

Or maybe they represent some east-west, pagan-Christian duality action. Anyway, the two newfound bros go to Mass and hear a sermon about Jonah . . .

(SFX: one second of church organ.)

Biblical tie-in, then ship out on Christmas Day (*could be symbolical!*) aboard the USS *Pequod* with its mysterious wacko Captain Ahab . . .

(SFX: madman laughter.)

. . . who — *backstory* — is goofyfoot because the equally mysterious momboosaloid white whale Moby-like-the-singer Dick bit his leg off.

(SFX: chomp.)

Freudian castration action. I mean he's big and he's got sperm and his last name is "Dick," right? Moby is also a metaphor for God, Nature, Truth, obsessisical love, the world, the past, and white people. Check out Pip the Negro cabin boy who by a *fluke* . . .

(SFX: rimshot.)

. . . goes wacko too. Ahab says,

(SFX: echo effect.)

"Bring me the head of the Great White Whale and you win this prize!"

(SFX: echo effect out, cash register sound.)

The crew is stoked, by *NOT* first-mate like-the-coffee-Starbuck. Ahab wants the big one, Starbuck wants the whale juice. Idealism versus capitalism.

(SFX: an impressed "Whoo.")

Radical. Queequeg tells the carpenter to build him a coffin shaped like a canoe.

(SFX: theremin.)

Foreshadowing! Then lots of chapters everybody skips about the scientology of whales.

(SFX: yawn.)

Cut to . . .

(SFX: trumpet fanfare.)

Page 523, the Pacific Ocean. *"Surf's up!"* Ahab sights the Dick. He's totally amped. The boards hit the waves, the crew snakes the Dick for three whole days, bottom of the third Ahab is ten-toes-on-the-nose, he's aggro, Moby goes aerial, Ahab's in the zone, he fires his choicest harpoon, the rope does a 360 round his neck, Ahab crushes out, Moby totals the *Pequod*, everybody eats it 'cept our faithful narrator Ishmael who boogies to safety on Queequeg's coffin . . .

(SFX: resounding echo effect, deeper voice.)

"AND I ONLY AM ESCAPED ALONE TO TELL THEE!"

(Resume normal voice.)

Roll final credits. The End.

(SFX: ship's bell to signal end of fight. End ticking watch.)

So what do you say, Mrs. Podgorski? You want to like hang and catch a cup of Starbucks sometime . . . ? — *Tubular!*

End of play

Rodeo

Jane Martin is a pseudonym. The author's identity is known only to a handful of present and former administrators at Actors Theatre of Louisville for productions and reprints of the play. *Rodeo* is one of eleven monologues in *Talking With . . .* Martin has also published other plays conveniently grouped in two volumes: *Jane Martin: Collected Plays 1980–1995* (1996) and *Jane Martin: Collected Plays, Volume 2, 1996–2001* (2001).

Although only one character appears in *Rodeo*, the monologue is surprisingly moving as she describes what the rodeo once was, how it has changed, and what it means to her. At first glance the subject matter may not seem very promising for drama, but the character's energy, forthrightness, and colorful language transform seemingly trivial details into significant meanings.

JANE MARTIN

Rodeo   1981

A young woman in her late twenties sits working on a piece of tack. Beside her is a Lone Star beer in the can. As the lights come up we hear the last verse of a Tanya Tucker song or some other female country-western vocalist. She is wearing old worn jeans and boots plus a long-sleeved workshirt with the sleeves rolled up. She works until the song is over and then speaks.

Big Eight: Shoot — Rodeo's just goin' to hell in a handbasket. Rodeo used to be somethin'. I loved it. I did. Once Daddy an' a bunch of 'em was foolin' around with some old bronc over to our place and this ol' red nose named Cinch got bucked off and my Daddy hooted and said he had him a nine-year-old girl, namely me, wouldn't have no damn trouble cowboyin' that horse. Well, he put me on up there, stuck that ridin' rein in my hand, gimme a kiss, and said, "Now there's only one thing t' remember Honey Love, if ya fall off you jest don't come home." Well I stayed up. You gotta stay on a bronc eight seconds. Otherwise the ride don't count. So from that day on my daddy called me Big Eight. Heck! That's all the name I got anymore . . . Big Eight.

Used to be fer cowboys, the rodeo did. Do it in some open field, folks would pull their cars and pick-ups round it, sit on the hoods, some ranch hand'd bulldog him some rank steer and everybody'd wave their hats and call him by name. Ride us some buckin' stock, rope a few calves, git throwed off a bull, and then we'd jest git us to a bar and tell each other lies about how good we were.

Used to be a family thing. Wooly Billy Tilson and Tammy Lee had them five kids on the circuit. Three boys, two girls and Wooly and Tammy. Wasn't no two-beer rodeo in Oklahoma didn't have a Tilson entered. Used to call the oldest girl Tits. Tits Tilson. Never seen a girl that top-heavy could ride so well. Said she only fell off when the gravity got her. Cowboys used to say if she landed face down you could plant two young trees in the holes she'd leave. Ha! Tits Tilson.

Used to be people came to a rodeo had a horse of their own back home. Farm people, ranch people—lord, they *knew* what they were lookin' at. Knew a good ride from a bad ride, knew hard from easy. You broke some bones er spent the day eatin' dirt, at least ya got appreciated.

Now they bought the rodeo. Them. Coca-Cola, Pepsi Cola, Marlboro damn cigarettes. You know the ones I mean. Them. Hire some New York faggot t' sit on some ol' stuffed horse in front of a sagebrush photo n' smoke that junk. Hell, tobacco wasn't made to smoke, honey, it was made to chew. Lord wanted ya filled up with smoke he would've set ya on fire. Damn it gets me!

There's some guy in a banker's suit runs the rodeo now. Got him a pinky ring and a digital watch, honey. Told us we oughta have a watchamacallit, choriographus or somethin', some ol' ballbuster used to be with the Ice damn Capades. Wants us to ride around dressed up like Mickey Mouse, Pluto, crap like that. Told me I had to haul my butt through the barrel race done up like Minnie damn Mouse in a tu-tu. Huh uh, honey! Them people is so screwed-up they probably eat what they run over in the road.

Listen, they got the clowns wearin' Astronaut suits! I ain't lyin'. You know what a rodeo clown does! You go down, fall off whatever—the clown runs in front of the bull so's ya don't git stomped. Pin-stripes, he got 'em in space suits tellin' jokes on a microphone. First horse see 'em, done up like the Star Wars went crazy. Best buckin' horse on the circuit, name of Piss 'N' Vinegar, took one look at them clowns, had him a heart attack and died. Cowboy was ridin' him got hisself squashed. Twelve hundred pounds of coronary arrest jes fell right through 'em. Blam! Vio con dios. Crowd thought that was funnier than the astronauts. I swear it won't be long before they're strappin' ice-skates on the ponies. Big crowds now. Ain't hardly no ranch people, no farm people, nobody I know. Buncha disco babies and dee-vorce lawyers—designer jeans and day-glo Stetsons. Hell, the whole bunch of 'em wears French perfume. Oh it smells like money now!

Got it on the cable T and V — hey, you know what, when ya rodeo yer just bound to kick yerself up some dust — well now, seems like that fogs up the ol' TV camera, so they told us a while back that from now on we was gonna ride on some new stuff called Astro-dirt. Dust free. Artificial damn dirt, honey. Lord have mercy.

Banker Suit called me in the other day said "Lurlene . . ." "Hold it," I said, "Who's this Lurlene? Round here they call me Big Eight." "Well, Big Eight," he said, "My name's Wallace." "Well that's a real surprise t' me," I said, "Cause aroun' here everybody jes calls you Dumb-ass." My, he laughed real big, slapped his big ol' desk, an' then he said I wasn't suitable for the rodeo no more. Said they was lookin' fer another type, somethin' a little more in the showgirl line, like the Dallas Cowgirls maybe. Said the ridin' and ropin' wasn't the thing no more. Talked on about floats, costumes, dancin' choreog-aphy. If I was a man I woulda pissed on his shoe. Said he'd give me a lifetime pass though. Said I could come to his rodeo any time I wanted.

Rodeo used to be people ridin' horses for the pleasure of people who rode horses — made you feel good about what you could do. Rodeo wasn't worth no money to nobody. Money didn't have nothing to do with it! Used to be seven Tilsons riding in the rodeo. Wouldn't none of 'em dress up like Donald damn Duck so they quit. That there's the law of gravity!

There's a bunch of assholes in this country sneak around until they see ya havin' fun and then they buy the fun and start in sellin' it. See, they figure if ya love it, they can sell it. Well you look out, honey! They want to make them a dollar out of what you love. Dress *you* up like Minnie Mouse. Sell your rodeo. Turn *yer* pleasure into Ice damn Capades. You hear what I'm sayin'? You're jus' merchandise to them, sweetie. You're jus' merchandise to them.

Blackout.

The Reprimand

Writer and director Jane Anderson started her career as an actor. She left college at the age of nineteen to pursue acting and was cast in the David Mamet hit play *Sexual Perversity in Chicago*. The experience familiarized Anderson with scriptwriting, and eventually she founded a writing group called New York Writers' Block. She later wrote and performed in a number of one-woman comedic plays, whose success afforded her the opportunity to write for the television sitcoms *The Facts of Life* and *The Wonder Years*.

Photo by permission of Jilly Wendell.

In 1986, Anderson wrote the play *Defying Gravity*, a composite of monologues about the space shuttle *Challenger* explosion. Her first screenplay, *The Positively True Adventures of the Alleged Texas Cheerleader-Murdering Mom*, was a satirical look at the true story of a Texas mother who tried to hire a contract killer to murder her daughter's rival (and her mother) for the junior high school cheerleading squad. The HBO movie starred Holly Hunter and gave Anderson instant notoriety as a screenwriter. She has written the screenplays for a number of movies since, including *The Baby Dance*, starring Jody Foster, and *When Billie Beat Bobby*, the story of tennis champion Billie Jean King beating an aging Bobby Riggs. In 2009 she was nominated for the Writer's Guild of America Award for Best Dramatic Series for her writing on the second season of the television series *Mad Men*, and in 2015 she won Emmy Awards for writing and coproducing the HBO miniseries *Olive Kitteridge*.

The Reprimand was one of five "phone plays" that premiered in February 2000 at the annual Humana Festival of New American Plays held at Actors Theatre in Louisville, Kentucky. The phone call is a traditional stage convention that consists of an actor providing one side of a conversation, but for the Humana Festival performances, the actors conversed offstage and the audience heard both sides of the three-minute conversation. In *The Reprimand*, the overheard conversation reveals a complicated power struggle between two women.

Jane Anderson (b. 1954)

The Reprimand   *2000*

CHARACTERS

Rhona
Mim

Rhona: . . . we need to talk about what you did in the meeting this morning.
Mim: My God, what?
Rhona: That reference you made about my weight.
Mim: What reference?
Rhona: When we came into the room and Jim was making the introductions, you said, "Oh Rhona, why don't you take the bigger chair."
Mim: But that was — I thought since this was your project that you should sit in the better chair.
Rhona: But you didn't say better, you said bigger.
Mim: I did? Honest to God, that isn't what I meant. I'm so sorry if it hurt your feelings.
Rhona: You didn't hurt my feelings. This has nothing to do with my feelings. What concerns me — and concerns Jim by the way — is how this could have undermined the project.

Mim: Jim said something about it?

Rhona: Yes.

Mim: What did he say?

Rhona: He thought your comment was inappropriate.

Mim: Really? How? I was talking about a chair.

Rhona: Mim, do you honestly think anyone in that room was really listening to what I had to say after you made that comment?

Mim: I thought they were very interested in what you had to say.

Rhona: Honey, there was a reason why Dick and Danny asked you all the follow-up questions.

Mim: But that's because I hadn't said anything up to that point. Look, I'm a little confused about Jim's reaction, because after the meeting he said he liked what I did with the follow-up.

Rhona: He should acknowledge what you do. And I know the reason why he's finally said something is because I've been telling him that you deserve more credit.

Mim: Oh, thank you. But I think Jim already respects what I do.

Rhona: He should respect you. But from what I've observed, I think — because you're an attractive woman — that he still uses you for window dressing. Especially when you're working with me. You know what I'm saying?

Mim: Well, if that's the case, Jim is a jerk.

Rhona: I know that. And I know you know that. But I think you still have a lot of anger about the situation and sometimes it really shows.

Mim: I don't mean it to show.

Rhona: I know that. Look, I consider you — regardless of what Jim thinks — I think you're really talented and I really love working with you.

Mim: And I enjoy working with you.

Rhona: Thank you. And that's why I want to keep things clear between us. Especially when we're working for men like Jim.

Mim: No, I agree, absolutely.

Rhona: *(To someone off-phone.)* Tell him I'll be right there. *(Back to Mim.)* Mim, sorry — I have Danny on the phone.

Mim: Oh — do you want to conference me in?

Rhona: I can handle it, but thank you. Mim, I'm so glad we had this talk.

Mim: Well, thank you for being so honest with me.

Rhona: And thank you for hearing me. I really appreciate it. Let's talk later?

Mim: Sure. *(Rhona hangs up. A beat.) (Mumbling.)* Fat pig. *(Hangs up.)*

CRITICAL THINKING AND WRITING

Credits, clockwise from top left: © Bettmann/Corbis; © Bettmann/CORBIS; © Beth Gwinn; Everett Collection/Newscom; © Michael Nicholson/CORBIS; Boston Globe/Getty Images.

29

Reading and the Writing Process

I can't write five words but that I change seven.

—DOROTHY PARKER

© Bettmann/Corbis.

THE PURPOSE AND VALUE OF WRITING ABOUT LITERATURE

Introductory literature courses typically include three components — reading, discussion, and writing. Students usually find the readings a pleasure, the class discussions a revelation, and the writing assignments — at least initially — a little intimidating. Writing an analysis of Melville's use of walls in "Bartleby, the Scrivener" (p. 99), for example, may seem considerably more daunting than making a case for animal rights or analyzing a campus newspaper editorial that calls for grade reforms. Like Bartleby, you might want to respond with "I would prefer not to." Literary topics are not, however, all that different from the kinds of papers assigned in English composition courses; many of the same skills are required for both. Regardless of the type of paper, you must develop a thesis and support it with evidence in language that is clear and persuasive.

Whether the subject matter is a marketing survey, a political issue, or a literary work, writing is a method of communicating information and perceptions. Writing teaches. But before writing becomes an instrument for informing the reader, it serves as a means of learning for the writer. An essay is a process of discovery as well as a record of what has been discovered. One of the chief benefits of writing is that we frequently realize what we want to say only after trying out ideas on a page and seeing our thoughts take shape in language.

More specifically, writing about a literary work encourages us to be better readers because it requires a close examination of the elements of a short story, poem, or play. To determine how plot, character, setting, point of view, style, tone, irony, or any number of other literary elements function in a work, we must study them in relation to one another as well as separately. Speed-reading won't do. To read a text accurately and validly — neither ignoring nor distorting significant details — we must return to the work repeatedly to test our responses and interpretations. By paying attention to details and being sensitive to the author's use of language, we develop a clearer understanding of how the work conveys its effects and meanings.

READING THE WORK CLOSELY

Know the piece of literature you are writing about before you begin your essay. Think about how the work makes you feel and how it is put together. The more familiar you are with how the various elements of the text convey effects and meanings, the more confident you will be explaining whatever perspective on it you ultimately choose. Do not insist that everything make sense on a first reading. Relax and enjoy yourself; you can be attentive and still allow the author's words to work their magic on you. With subsequent readings, however, go more slowly and analytically as you try to establish relations between characters, actions, images, or whatever else seems important. Ask yourself why you respond as you do. Think as you read, and notice how the parts of a work contribute to its overall nature. Whether the work is a short story, poem, or play, you will read relevant portions of it over and over, and you will very likely find more to discuss in each review if the work is rich.

ANNOTATING THE TEXT
AND JOURNAL NOTE TAKING

As you read, get in the habit of annotating your texts. Whether you write marginal notes, highlight, underline, or draw boxes and circles around important words and phrases, you'll eventually develop a system that allows you to retrieve significant ideas and elements from the text. Another way to record your impressions of a work — as with any other experience — is to keep a journal. By writing down your reactions to characters, images, language, actions, and other matters in a reading journal, you can often determine why you like or dislike a work or feel sympathetic or antagonistic to an author or discover paths into a work that might have eluded you if you hadn't preserved your impressions. Your journal notes and annotations may take whatever form you find useful; full sentences and grammatical correctness are not essential (unless they are to be handed in and your instructor requires that), though they might allow you to make better sense of your own reflections days later. The point is simply to put in writing thoughts that you can retrieve when you need them for class discussion or a writing assignment. Consider the following student annotation of the first twenty-four lines of Andrew Marvell's "To His Coy Mistress" (p. 363) and the journal entry that follows it:

Annotated Text

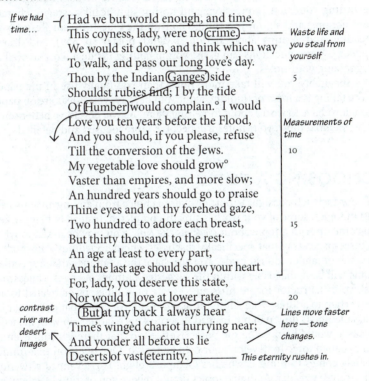

If we had time...

Had we but world enough, and time,
This coyness, lady, were no (crime.) ——— *Waste life and you steal from yourself*
We would sit down, and think which way
To walk, and pass our long love's day.
Thou by the Indian (Ganges) side   5
Shouldst rubies find; I by the tide
Of (Humber) would complain.° I would
Love you ten years before the Flood,   *Measurements of time*
And you should, if you please, refuse
Till the conversion of the Jews.   10
My vegetable love should grow°
Vaster than empires, and more slow;
An hundred years should go to praise
Thine eyes and on thy forehead gaze,
Two hundred to adore each breast,   15
But thirty thousand to the rest:
An age at least to every part,
And the last age should show your heart.
For, lady, you deserve this state,
Nor would I love at lower rate.   20
(But) at my back I always hear   *Lines move faster here — tone changes.*
Time's wingèd chariot hurrying near;
And yonder all before us lie
(Deserts) of vast (eternity.) ——— *This eternity rushes in.*

contrast river and desert images

Journal Note

He'd be patient and wait for his "mistress" if they had the time — sing songs, praise her, adore her, etc. But they don't have that much time according to him. He *seems* to be patient but he actually begins by calling patience — her coyness — a "crime." Looks to me like he's got his mind made up from the beginning of the poem. Where's her response? I'm not sure about him.

This journal note responds to some of the effects noted in the annotations of the poem; it's an excellent beginning for making sense of the speaker's argument in the poem.

Taking notes will preserve your initial reactions to the work. Many times first impressions are the best. Your response to a peculiar character in a story, a striking phrase in a poem, or a subtle bit of stage business in a play might lead to larger perceptions. You should take detailed notes only after you've read through the work. If you write too many notes during the first reading, you're likely to disrupt your response. Moreover, until you have a sense of the entire work, it will be difficult to determine how connections can be made among its various elements. In addition to recording your first impressions and noting significant passages, characters, actions, and so on, you should consult the Questions for Responsive Reading and Writing about fiction (p. 869), poetry (p. 877), and drama (p. 892). These questions can assist you in getting inside a work as well as organizing your notes.

Inevitably you will take more notes than you finally use in the paper. Note taking is a form of thinking aloud, but because your ideas are on paper you don't have to worry about forgetting them. As you develop a better sense of a potential topic, your notes will become more focused and detailed.

CHOOSING A TOPIC

If your instructor assigns a topic or offers a choice from among an approved list of topics, some of your work is already completed. Instead of being asked to come up with a topic about *Oedipus the King,* you may be asked to write a three-page essay that specifically discusses whether Oedipus's downfall is a result of fate or foolish pride. You also have the assurance that a specified topic will be manageable within the suggested number of pages. Unless you ask your instructor for permission to write on a different or related topic, be certain to address yourself to the assignment. An essay that does not discuss Oedipus's downfall but instead describes his relationship with his wife, Jocasta, would be missing the point. Notice too that there is room even in an assigned topic to develop your own approach. One question that immediately comes to mind is whether Oedipus's plight is relevant to a twenty-first-century reader. Assigned topics do not relieve you of thinking about an aspect of a work, but they do focus your thinking.

At some point during the course, you may have to begin an essay from scratch. You might, for example, be asked to write about a short story that somehow impressed you or that seemed particularly well written or filled with insights. Before you start considering a topic, you should have a sense of how long the paper will be because the assigned length can help to determine the extent to which you should develop your topic. Ideally, the paper's length should be based on how much space you deem necessary to present your discussion clearly and convincingly, but if you have any doubts and no specific guidelines have been indicated, ask. The question is important; a topic that might be appropriate for a three-page paper could be too narrow for ten pages. Three pages would probably be adequate for a discussion of why Emily murders Homer in Faulkner's "A Rose for Emily." Conversely, it would be futile to try to summarize Faulkner's use of the South in his fiction in even ten pages; this would have to be narrowed to something like "Images of the South in 'A Rose for Emily." Be sure that the topic you choose can be adequately covered in the assigned number of pages.

DEVELOPING A THESIS

When you are satisfied that you have something interesting to say about a work and that your notes have led you to a focused topic, you can formulate a *thesis*, the central idea of the paper. Whereas the topic indicates what the paper focuses on (the setting in "A & P"), the thesis explains what you have to say about the topic (because the intolerant setting of "A & P" is the antagonist in the story, it is crucial to our understanding of Sammy's decision to quit his job). The thesis should be a complete sentence (though sometimes it may require more than one sentence) that establishes your argument in clear, unambiguous language. The thesis may be revised as you get further into the argument and discover what you want to say about it, but once the thesis is firmly established, it will serve as a guide for you and your reader because all the information and observations in your essay should be related to the thesis.

One student on an initial reading of Andrew Marvell's "To His Coy Mistress" saw that the male speaker of the poem urges a woman to love now before time runs out for them. This reading gave him the impression that the poem is a simple celebration of the pleasures of the flesh, but on subsequent readings he underlined or noted these images: "Time's wingèd chariot hurrying near"; "Deserts of vast eternity"; "marble vault"; "worms"; "dust"; "ashes"; and these two lines: "The grave's a fine and private place, / But none, I think, do there embrace."

By listing these images associated with time and death, he established an inventory that could be separated from the rest of his notes on point of view, character, sounds, and other subjects. Inventorying notes allows patterns to emerge that you might have only vaguely perceived otherwise. Once these images are grouped, they call attention to something darker and more complex in Marvell's poem than a first impression might suggest.

These images may create a different feeling about the poem, but they still don't explain very much. One simple way to generate a thesis about a literary work is to ask the question "why?" Why do these images appear in the poem? Why is Othello swayed by Iago's insinuations? Why does Hemingway choose the Midwest as the setting of "Soldier's Home"? Your responses to these kinds of questions can lead to a thesis.

Writers sometimes use freewriting to help themselves explore possible answers to such questions. It can be an effective way of generating ideas. Freewriting is exactly that: the technique calls for nonstop writing without concern for mechanics or editing of any kind. Freewriting for ten minutes or so on a question will result in fragments and repetitions, but it can also produce some ideas. Here's an example of a student's response to the question about the images in "To His Coy Mistress":

He wants her to make love. Love poem. There's little time. Her crime. He exaggerates.
Sincere? Sly? What's he want? She says nothing — he says it all. What about deserts,
ashes, graves, and worms? Some love poem. Sounds like an old Vincent Price movie. Full of
sweetness but death creeps in. Death — hurry hurry! Tear pleasures. What passion! Where's
death in this? How can a love poem be so ghoulish? She does nothing. Maybe frightened?
Convinced? Why death? Love and death — time — death.

This freewriting contains several ideas; it begins by alluding to the poem's plot and speaker, but the central idea seems to be death. A paper that merely pointed out the death images in "To His Coy Mistress" would not contain a thesis, but a paper that attempted to make a case for the death imagery as a grim reminder of how vulnerable flesh is would involve persuasion. In developing a thesis, remember that you are expected not merely to present information but to argue a point.

ARGUING ABOUT LITERATURE

An argumentative essay is designed to make persuasive your interpretation of a work. Arguing about literature doesn't mean that you're engaged in an angry, antagonistic dispute (though controversial topics do sometimes engender heated debates). Instead, argumentation requires that you present your interpretation of a work (or a portion of it) by supporting your discussion with clearly defined terms, ample evidence, and a detailed analysis of relevant portions of the text.

If you have a choice, it's generally best to write about a topic that you feel strongly about. If you're not fascinated by the haunting presence of the title character in Melville's "Bartleby, the Scrivener," then perhaps you'll find chilling Emily Grierson's behavior in Faulkner's "A Rose for Emily," or maybe you can explain why Bartleby's character is so excruciatingly boring to you. If your essay is to be interesting and convincing, what is important is that it be written from a strong point of view that persuasively argues your evaluation, analysis, and interpretation of a work. It is not enough to say that you like or dislike a work; instead you must give your reader some ideas and evidence that can be accepted or rejected based on the quality of the answers to the questions you raise.

ORGANIZING A PAPER

After you have chosen a manageable topic and developed a thesis, a central idea about it, you can begin to organize your paper. Your thesis, even if it is still somewhat tentative, should help you decide what information will need to be included and provide you with a sense of direction.

Consider this sample thesis:

On the surface, "To His Coy Mistress" is a celebration of the pleasures of the flesh, but this witty seduction is tempered by a chilling recognition of the reality of death.

This thesis indicates that the paper can be divided into two parts — the pleasures of the flesh and the reality of death. It also indicates an order: because the central point is to show that the poem is more than a simple celebration, the pleasures of the flesh should be discussed first so that another, more complex, reading of the poem can follow. If the paper began with the reality of death, its point would be anticlimactic.

Having established such a broad and informal outline, you can draw on your underlinings, margin notations, and notes for the subheadings and evidence required to explain the major sections of your paper. This next level of detail would look like the following:

1. Pleasures of the flesh
    Part of the traditional tone of love poetry
2. Recognition of death
    Ironic treatment of love
        Diction
        Images
        Figures of speech
        Symbols
        Tone

This list was initially a jumble of terms, but the student arranged the items so that each of the two major sections leads to a discussion of tone. (The student also found it necessary to drop some biographical information from his notes because it was irrelevant to the thesis.) The list indicates that the first part of the paper will establish the traditional tone of love poetry that celebrates the pleasures of the flesh, while the second part will present a more detailed discussion about the ironic recognition of death. The emphasis is on the latter because that is the point to be argued in the paper. Hence, the thesis has helped to organize the parts of the paper, establish an order, and indicate the paper's proper proportions.

The next step is to fill in the subheadings with information from your notes. Many experienced writers find that making lists of information to be included under each subheading is an efficient way to develop paragraphs. For a longer paper (perhaps a research paper), you should be able to develop a paragraph or more on each subheading. On the other hand, a shorter paper may require that you combine several subheadings in a paragraph. You may also discover that while an informal list is adequate for a brief paper, a ten-page assignment could require a more detailed outline. Use the method that is most productive for you.

WRITING A DRAFT

Be flexible. Your outline should smoothly conduct you from one point to the next, but do not permit it to railroad you. If a relevant and important idea occurs to you now, work it into the draft. By using the first draft as a means of thinking about what you want to say, you will very likely discover more than your notes originally suggested. Plenty of good writers don't use outlines at all but discover ordering principles as they write. Do not attempt to compose a perfectly correct draft the first time around. Grammar, punctuation, and spelling can wait until you revise. Concentrate on what you are saying. Good writing most often occurs when you are in hot pursuit of an idea rather than in a nervous search for errors.

Once you have a first draft on paper, you can delete material that is unrelated to your thesis and add material necessary to illustrate your points and make your paper convincing. The student who wrote "John Updike's 'A & P' as a State of Mind" (p. 871) wisely dropped a paragraph that questioned whether Sammy displays chauvinistic attitudes toward women. Although this is an interesting issue, it has nothing to do with the thesis, which explains how the setting influences Sammy's decision to quit his job. Instead of including that paragraph, she added one that described Lengel's crabbed response to the girls so that she could lead up to the A & P "policy" he enforces.

Remember that your initial draft is only that. You should go through the paper many times — and then again — working to substantiate and clarify your ideas. You may even end up with several entire versions of the paper. Rewrite. The sentences within each paragraph should be related to a single topic. Transitions should connect one paragraph to the next so that there are no abrupt or confusing shifts. Awkward or wordy phrasing or unclear sentences and paragraphs should be mercilessly poked and prodded into shape.

Writing the Introduction and Conclusion

After you have clearly and adequately developed the body of your paper, pay particular attention to the introductory and concluding paragraphs. It's probably best to write the introduction — at least the final version of it — last, after you know precisely what you are introducing. Because this paragraph is crucial for generating interest in the topic, it should engage the reader and provide a sense of what the paper is about. There is no formula for writing effective introductory paragraphs because each writing situation is different — depending on the audience, topic, and approach — but if you pay attention to the introductions of the essays you read, you will notice a variety of possibilities. The introductory paragraph to "John Updike's 'A & P' as a State of Mind," for example, is a straightforward explanation of why the story's setting is important for understanding Updike's treatment of the antagonist. The rest of the paper then offers evidence to support this point.

Concluding paragraphs demand equal attention because they leave the reader with a final impression. The conclusion should provide a sense of closure instead of starting a new topic or ending abruptly. In the final paragraph about the significance of the setting in "A & P," the student brings together the reasons Sammy quit his job by referring to his refusal to accept Lengel's store policies. At the same time she makes this point, she also explains the significance of Sammy ringing up the "No Sale" mentioned in her introductory paragraph. Thus, we are brought back to where we began, but we now have a greater understanding of why Sammy quits his job. Of course, the body of your paper is the most important part of your presentation, but do remember that first and last impressions have a powerful impact on readers.

Using Quotations

Quotations can be a valuable means of marshaling evidence to illustrate and support your ideas. A judicious use of quoted material will make your points clearer and more convincing. Here are some guidelines that should help you use quotations effectively.

Brief and lengthy quotations

Brief quotations (four lines or fewer of prose or three lines or fewer of poetry) should be carefully introduced and integrated into the text of your paper with quotation marks around them:

According to the narrator, Bertha "had a reputation for strictness." He tells us that she always "wore dark clothes, dressed her hair simply, and expected contrition and obedience from her pupils."

For brief poetry quotations, use a slash to indicate a division between lines:

The concluding lines of Blake's "The Tyger" pose a disturbing question: "What immortal hand or eye / Dare frame thy fearful symmetry?"

Lengthy quotations should be separated from the text of your paper. More than three lines of poetry should be double spaced and indent half an inch from the left margin. More than four lines of prose should be double spaced and indented half an inch from the left margin, with the right margin the same as for the text. Do *not* use quotation marks for the passage; the indentation indicates that the passage is a quotation. Lengthy quotations should not be used in place of your own writing. Use them only if they are absolutely necessary.

Brackets and ellipses

If any words are added to a quotation, use brackets to distinguish your addition from the original source:

"He [Young Goodman Brown] is portrayed as self-righteous and disillusioned."

Any words inside quotation marks and not in brackets must be precisely those of the author. Brackets can also be used to change the grammatical structure of a quotation so that it fits into your sentence:

Smith argues that Chekhov "present[s] the narrator in an ambivalent light."

If you drop any words from the source, use ellipses to indicate the omission:

"Early to bed . . . makes a man healthy, wealthy, and wise."

Use ellipses following a period to indicate an omission at the end of a sentence:

"Early to bed and early to rise makes a man healthy. . . ."

Use a single line of spaced periods to indicate the omission of a line or more of poetry or more than one paragraph of prose:

Nothing would sleep in that cellar, dank as a ditch,
Bulbs broke out of boxes hunting for chinks in the dark,
. . . .
Nothing would give up life:
Even the dirt kept breathing a small breath.

Punctuation

You will be able to punctuate quoted material accurately and confidently if you observe these conventions.

Place commas and periods inside quotation marks:

"Even the dirt," Roethke insists, "kept breathing a small breath."

Even though a comma does not appear after "dirt" in the original quotation, it is placed inside the quotation mark. The exception to this rule occurs when a parenthetical reference to a source follows the quotation:

"Even the dirt," Roethke insists, "kept breathing a small breath" (11).

Punctuation marks other than commas or periods go outside the quotation marks unless they are part of the material quoted:

What does Roethke mean when he writes that "the dirt kept breathing a small breath"?

Yeats asked, "How can we know the dancer from the dance?"

REVISING AND EDITING

Put some distance — a day or so if you can — between yourself and each draft of your paper. The phrase that seemed just right on Wednesday may be revealed as all wrong on Friday. You'll have a better chance of detecting lumbering sentences and thin paragraphs if you plan ahead and give yourself the time to read your paper from a fresh perspective. Through the process of revision, you can transform a competent paper into an excellent one.

Begin by asking yourself if your approach to the topic requires any rethinking. Is the argument carefully thought out and logically presented? Are there any gaps in the presentation? How well is the paper organized? Do the paragraphs lead into one another? Does the body of the paper deliver what the thesis promises? Is the interpretation sound? Are any relevant and important elements of the work ignored or distorted to advance the thesis? Are the points supported with evidence? These large questions should be addressed before you focus on more detailed matters. If you uncover serious problems as a result of considering these questions, you'll probably have quite a lot of rewriting to do, but at least you will have the opportunity to correct the problems — even if doing so takes several drafts.

The following checklist offers questions to ask about your paper as you revise and edit it. Most of these questions will be familiar to you; however, if you need help with any of them, ask your instructor or review the appropriate section in a composition handbook.

Questions for Writing: A Revision Checklist

1. Is the topic manageable? Is it too narrow or too broad?
2. Is the thesis clear? Is it based on a careful reading of the work?
3. Is the paper logically organized? Does it have a firm sense of direction?
4. Is your argument persuasive?
5. Should any material be deleted? Do any important points require further illustration or evidence?
6. Does the opening paragraph introduce the topic in an interesting manner?

(continued)

7. Are the paragraphs developed, unified, and coherent? Are any too short or long?

8. Are there transitions linking the paragraphs?

9. Does the concluding paragraph provide a sense of closure?

10. Is the tone appropriate? Is it unduly flippant or pretentious?

11. Is the title engaging and suggestive?

12. Are the sentences clear, concise, and complete?

13. Are a mix of simple, complex, and compound sentences used for variety?

14. Have technical terms been used correctly? Are you certain of the meanings of all the words in the paper? Are they spelled correctly?

15. Have you documented any information borrowed from books, articles, or other sources? Have you quoted too much instead of summarizing or paraphrasing secondary material?

16. Have you used a standard format for citing sources (see p. 905)?

17. Have you followed your instructor's guidelines for the manuscript format of the final draft?

18. Have you carefully proofread the final draft?

When you proofread your final draft, you may find a few typographical errors that must be corrected but do not warrant reprinting an entire paper. Provided there are not more than a handful of such errors throughout the paper, they can be corrected as shown in the following passage. This example condenses a short paper's worth of errors; no single passage should be this shabby in your essay:

To add a letter or word, use a caret on the line where the addition $\stackrel{is}{\wedge}$ needed. To delete a

word draw a single line through ~~through~~ it. Run-on words are separated by a vertical⌇line,

and inadvertent spaces are closed like t͡his. Transposed letters are indicated this w⟋a⟍y.

New paragraphs are noted with the sign ¶ in front of where the next paragraph is to

begin.¶ Unless you . . .

You can minimize these sorts of errors by proofreading on the screen and simply entering your corrections as you go along.

TYPES OF WRITING ASSIGNMENTS

The types of papers most frequently assigned in literature classes are *explication*, *analysis*, and *comparison and contrast*. Most writing about literature involves some combination of these skills. For genre-based assignments, see the following sample papers: for analysis (Chapter 30, "Writing about Fiction," p. 873), for explication (Chapter 31, "Writing about Poetry," p. 884), and for comparison and contrast (Chapter 32, "Writing about Drama," p. 896). For a sample research paper that demonstrates a variety of strategies for documenting outside sources, see page 911.

30

Writing about Fiction

Jason Doiy.

Write every day. Even if it's just a paragraph, start writing! Then keep writing every day so that it becomes like eating or breathing, a part of your life that you can't live without.

— MAY-LEE CHAI

FROM READING TO WRITING

There's no question about it: writing about fiction is a different experience than reading it. The novelist William Styron amply concedes that writing for him is not so much about pleasure as it is about work: "Let's face it, writing is hell." Although Styron's lament concerns his own feelings about writing prose fiction, he no doubt speaks for many other writers, including essayists. Writing is, of course, work, but it is also a pleasure when it goes well—when ideas feel solid and the writing is fluid. You can experience that pleasure as well if you approach writing as an intellectual and emotional opportunity rather than merely a vexing sentence.

Just as reading fiction requires an imaginative, conscious response, so does writing about fiction. Composing an essay is not just recording your interpretive response to a work because the act of writing can change your response as you explore, clarify, and discover relationships you hadn't previously considered or recognized. Most writers discover new ideas and connections as they move through the process of rereading and annotating the text, taking notes, generating ideas, developing a thesis, and organizing an argumentative essay (these matters are detailed in Chapter 29, "Reading and the Writing Process"). To become more conscious of the writing process, first study the following questions specifically aimed at sharpening your response to reading and writing about fiction. Then examine the student's analysis of John Updike's short story "A & P."

Questions for Responsive Reading and Writing

The following questions can help you consider important elements of fiction that reveal your responses to a story's effects and meanings. The questions are general, so they will not always be relevant to a particular story. Many of them, however, should prove useful for thinking, talking, and writing about a work of fiction.

PLOT

1. Does the plot conform to a formula? Is it like those of any other stories you have read? Did you find it predictable?

2. What is the source and nature of the conflict for the protagonist? Was your major interest in the story based on what happens next or on some other concern? What does the title reveal now that you've finished the story?

3. Is the story told chronologically? If not, in what order are its events told, and what is the effect of that order on your response to the action?

4. What does the exposition reveal? Are flashbacks used? Did you see any foreshadowings? Where is the climax?

5. Is the conflict resolved at the end? Would you characterize the ending as happy, unhappy, or somewhere in between?

6. Is the plot unified? Is each incident somehow related to some other element in the story?

CHARACTER

7. Do you identify with the protagonist? Who (or what) is the antagonist?

8. Did your response to any characters change as you read? What do you think caused the change? Do any characters change and develop in the course of the story? How?

9. Are round, flat, or stock characters used? Is their behavior motivated and plausible?

10. How does the author reveal characters? Are they directly described or indirectly presented? Are the characters' names used to convey something about them?

11. What is the purpose of the minor characters? Are they individualized, or do they primarily represent ideas or attitudes?

SETTING

12. Is the setting important in shaping your response? If it were changed, would your response to the story's action and meaning be significantly different?

(continued)

13. Is the setting used symbolically? Are the time, place, and atmosphere related to the theme?

14. Is the setting used as an antagonist?

POINT OF VIEW

15. Who tells the story? Is it a first-person or third-person narrator? Is it a major or minor character or one who does not participate in the action at all? How much does the narrator know? Does the point of view change at all in the course of the story?

16. Is the narrator reliable and objective? Does the narrator appear too innocent, emotional, or self-deluded to be trusted?

17. Does the author directly comment on the action?

18. If it were told from a different point of view, how would your response to the story change? Would anything be lost?

SYMBOLISM

19. Did you notice any symbols in the story? Are they actions, characters, settings, objects, or words?

20. How do the symbols contribute to your understanding of the story?

THEME

21. Did you find a theme? If so, what is it?

22. Is the theme stated directly, or is it developed implicitly through the plot, characters, or some other element?

23. Is the theme a confirmation of your values, or does it challenge them?

STYLE, TONE, AND IRONY

24. Do you think the style is consistent and appropriate throughout the story? Do all the characters use the same kind of language, or did you hear different voices?

25. Would you describe the level of diction as formal or informal? Are the sentences short and simple, long and complex, or some combination?

26. How does the author's use of language contribute to the tone of the story? Did it seem, for example, intense, relaxed, sentimental, nostalgic, humorous, angry, sad, or remote?

27. Do you think the story is worth reading more than once? Does the author's use of language bear close scrutiny so that you feel and experience more with each reading?

Analysis

An *analysis* usually examines only a single element — such as plot, character, point of view, symbol, tone, or irony — and relates it to the entire work. An analytic topic separates the work into parts and focuses on a specific one; you might, for example, consider "Point of View in 'A Rose for Emily.'" The specific element must be related to the work as a whole or it will appear irrelevant. Whether an analytic paper is just a few pages or many, it cannot attempt to discuss everything about the work it is considering. Only those elements that are relevant to the topic can be treated. This kind of focusing makes the topic manageable; this is why most papers that you write will probably be some form of analysis.

A SAMPLE STUDENT ANALYSIS

John Updike's "A & P" as a State of Mind

The following paper by Nancy Lager analyzes the setting in John Updike's "A & P" (the story appears on p. 149). The assignment simply asked for an essay of approximately 750 words on a short story written in the twentieth century. The approach was left to the student.

The idea for this essay began with Lager asking herself why Updike used "A & P" as the title. The initial answer to the question was that "the setting is important in this story." This answer was the rough beginning of a tentative thesis. What still had to be explained, though, was how the setting is important. To determine the significance of the setting, Lager jotted down some notes based on her underlinings and marginal notations:

A & P
"usual traffic"
lights and tile
"electric eye"
shoppers like "sheep," "houseslaves," "pigs"
"Alexandrov and Petrooshki" — Russia

New England Town	*Lengel*
typical: bank, church, etc.	"manager"
traditional	"doesn't miss that much" (like lady shopper)
conservative	Sunday school
proper	"It's our policy"
near Salem — witch trials	spokesman for A & P values
puritanical	
intolerant	

From these notes Lager saw that Lengel serves as the voice of the A & P. He is, in a sense, a personification of the intolerant atmosphere of the setting. This insight led to another version of her thesis statement: "The setting of 'A & P' is the antagonist of the story." That explained at least some of the setting's importance. By seeing Lengel as a spokesman for "A & P" policies, she could view him as a voice that articulates the morally smug atmosphere created by the setting. Finally, she considered why it is significant that the setting is the antagonist, and this generated her last thesis: "Because the intolerant setting of 'A & P' is the antagonist in the story, it is crucial to our understanding of Sammy's decision to quit his job." This thesis sentence does not appear precisely in these words in the essay, but it is the backbone of the introductory paragraph.

The remaining paragraphs consist of details that describe the A & P in the second paragraph, the New England town in the third, Lengel in the fourth, and Sammy's reasons for quitting in the concluding paragraph. Paragraphs 2, 3, and 4 are largely based on Lager's notes, which she used as an outline once her thesis was established. The essay is sharply focused, well organized, and generally well written. In addition, it suggests a number of useful guidelines for analytic papers:

1. Only the points related to the thesis are included. In another type of paper the role of the girls in the bathing suits, for example, might have been considerably more prominent.

2. The analysis keeps the setting in focus while at the same time indicating how it is significant in the major incident in the story — Sammy's quitting.

3. The title is a useful lead into the paper; it provides a sense of what the topic is. In addition, the title is drawn from a sentence (the final one of the first paragraph) that clearly explains its meaning.

4. The introductory paragraph is direct and clearly indicates the paper will argue that the setting serves as the antagonist of the story.

5. Brief quotations are deftly incorporated into the text of the paper to illustrate points. We are told what we need to know about the story as evidence is provided to support ideas. There is no unnecessary plot summary. Even though "A & P" is only a few pages in length, page numbers are included after quoted phrases. If the story were longer, page numbers would be especially helpful for the reader.

6. The paragraphs are well developed, unified, and coherent. They flow naturally from one to another. Notice, for example, the smooth transition worked into the final sentence of the third paragraph and the first sentence of the fourth paragraph.

7. Lager makes excellent use of her careful reading and notes by finding revealing connections among the details she has observed. The store's "electric eye," for instance, is related to the woman's and Lengel's watchfulness.

8. As events are described, the present tense is used. This avoids awkward tense shifts and lends an immediacy to the discussion.

9. The concluding paragraph establishes the significance of why the setting should be seen as the antagonist and provides a sense of closure by referring again to Sammy's "No Sale," which has been mentioned at the end of the first paragraph.

10. In short, Lager has demonstrated that she has read the work closely, has understood the relation of the setting to the major action, and has argued her thesis convincingly by using evidence from the story.

Nancy Lager
Professor Taylor
English 102-12
2 April 2016

John Updike's "A & P" as a State of Mind

The setting of John Updike's "A & P" is crucial to our understanding of Sammy's decision to quit his job. Although Sammy is the central character in the story and we learn that he is a principled, good-natured nineteen-year-old with a sense of humor, Updike seems to invest as much effort in describing the setting as he does in Sammy. The setting is the antagonist and plays a role that is as important as Sammy's. The title, after all, is not "Youthful Rebellion" or "Sammy Quits" but "A & P." Even though Sammy knows that his quitting will make life more difficult for him, he instinctively insists on rejecting what the A & P comes to represent in the story. When he rings up a "No Sale" and "saunter[s]" (Updike 154) out of the store, he leaves behind not only a job but the rigid state of mind associated with the A & P.

Sammy's descriptions of the A & P present a setting that is ugly, monotonous, and rigidly regulated. The fluorescent light is as blandly cool as the "checker-board green-and-cream rubber-tile floor" (151). We can see the uniformity Sammy describes because we have all been in chain stores. The "usual traffic" moves in one direction (except for the swimsuited girls, who move against it), and everything is neatly ordered and categorized in tidy aisles. The dehumanizing routine of this environment is suggested by Sammy's offhand references to the typical shoppers as "sheep" (151), "houseslaves" (151), and "pigs" (153). They seem to pace through the store in a stupor; as Sammy tells us, not even dynamite could move them.

The A & P is appropriately located "right in the middle" (151) of a proper, conservative, traditional New England town north of Boston. This location, coupled with the fact that the town is only five miles from Salem, the site of the famous seventeenth-century witch trials, suggests a narrow, intolerant social atmosphere in which there is no room for stepping beyond the boundaries of what is regarded as normal and proper. The importance of this setting can be appreciated even more if we imagine the action taking place in, say, a mellow suburb of southern California. In this prim New England setting, the girls in their bathing suits are bound to offend somebody's sense of propriety.

As soon as Lengel sees the girls, the inevitable conflict begins. He embodies the dull conformity represented by the A & P. As "manager" (152), he is both the guardian and enforcer of "policy" (153). When he gives the girls "that sad Sunday-school-superintendent stare" (152), we know we are in the presence of the A & P version of a dreary bureaucrat who "doesn't miss that much" (152). He is as unsympathetic and unpleasant as the woman "with rouge on her cheekbones and no eyebrows" (149) who pounces on Sammy for ringing up her "HiHo crackers" twice. Like the "electric eye" (154) in the doorway, her vigilant eyes allow nothing to escape their notice. For Sammy the logical extension of Lengel's "policy" is the half-serious notion that one day the A & P might be known as the "Great Alexandrov and Petrooshki Tea Company" (151). Sammy's connection between what he regards as mindless "policy" (153) and Soviet oppression is obviously an exaggeration, but the reader is invited to entertain the similarities anyway.

The reason Sammy quits his job has less to do with defending the girls than with his own sense of what it means to be a decent human being. His decision is not an easy one. He doesn't want to make trouble or disappoint his parents, and he knows his independence and self-reliance (the other side of New England tradition) will make life more complex for him. In spite of his own hesitations, he finds himself blurting out "Fiddle-de-doo" (153) to Lengel's policies and in doing so knows that his grandmother "would have been pleased" (153). Sammy's "No Sale" rejects the crabbed perspective on life that Lengel represents as manager of the A & P. This gesture is more than just a negative, however, for as he punches in that last entry on the cash register, "the machine whirs 'pee-pul'" (154). His decision to quit his job at the A & P is an expression of his refusal to regard policies as more important than people.

Work Cited

Updike, John. "A & P." *Literature to Go*, edited by Michael Meyer, 3rd ed.,
Bedford/St. Martin's, 2017, pp. 149-54.

— 31 —

Writing about Poetry

Derek Anderson.

Many people, especially beginning writers, think that writing is mostly inspiration. The muse tosses down a lightning bolt and you write something good. I think writing is mostly perspiration. You go to your chair or desk, and you stay there.
— MICHAEL CHITWOOD

FROM READING TO WRITING

Writing about poetry can be a rigorous means of testing the validity of your own reading of a poem. Anyone who has been asked to write several pages about a fourteen-line poem knows how intellectually challenging this exercise is, because it means paying close attention to language. Such scrutiny of words, however, sensitizes you not only to the poet's use of language but also to your own use of language. At first you may feel intimidated by having to compose a paper that is longer than the poem you're writing about, but a careful reading will reveal that there's plenty to write about what the poem says and how it says it. Keep in mind that your job is not to produce a definitive reading of the poem — even Carl Sandburg once confessed that "I've written some poetry I don't understand myself." It is enough to develop an interesting thesis and to present it clearly and persuasively.

An interesting thesis will come to you if you read and reread, take notes, annotate the text, and generate ideas (for a discussion of this process, see Chapter 29, "Reading and the Writing Process"). Although it requires energy to read closely and to write convincingly about the charged language found in poetry, there is nothing mysterious about such reading and writing. This chapter provides a set of questions designed to sharpen your reading and writing about poetry. Following these questions are two sample papers that offer explication of John Donne's "Death Be Not Proud" and Emily Dickinson's "There's a certain Slant of light."

Questions for Responsive Reading and Writing

The following questions can help you respond to important elements that reveal a poem's effects and meanings. The questions are general, so not all of them will necessarily be relevant to a particular poem. Many, however, should prove useful for thinking, talking, and writing about each poem in this collection.

Before addressing these questions, read the poem you are studying in its entirety. Don't worry about interpretation on a first reading; allow yourself the pleasure of enjoying whatever makes itself apparent to you. Then on subsequent readings, use the questions to understand and appreciate how the poem works.

1. Who is the speaker? Is it possible to determine the speaker's age, sex, sensibilities, level of awareness, and values?

2. Is the speaker addressing anyone in particular?

3. How do you respond to the speaker? Favorably? Negatively? What is the situation? Are there any special circumstances that inform what the speaker says?

4. Is there a specific setting of time and place?

5. Does reading the poem aloud help you to understand it?

6. Does a paraphrase reveal the basic purpose of the poem?

7. What does the title emphasize?

8. Is the theme presented directly or indirectly?

9. Do any allusions enrich the poem's meaning?

10. How does the diction reveal meaning? Are any words repeated? Do any carry evocative connotative meanings? Are there any puns or other forms of verbal wit?

11. Are figures of speech used? How does the figurative language contribute to the poem's vividness and meaning?

12. Do any objects, persons, places, events, or actions have allegorical or symbolic meanings? What other details in the poem support your interpretation?

13. Is irony used? Are there any examples of situational irony, verbal irony, or dramatic irony? Is understatement or paradox used?

14. What is the tone of the poem? Is the tone consistent?

15. Does the poem use onomatopoeia, assonance, consonance, or alliteration? How do these sounds affect you?

(continued)

16. What sounds are repeated? If there are rhymes, what is their effect? Do they seem forced or natural? Is there a rhyme scheme? Do the rhymes contribute to the poem's meaning?

17. Do the lines have a regular meter? What is the predominant meter? Are there significant variations? Does the rhythm seem appropriate for the poem's tone?

18. Does the poem's form—its overall structure—follow an established pattern? Do you think the form is a suitable vehicle for the poem's meaning and effects?

19. Is the language of the poem intense and concentrated? Do you think it warrants more than one or two close readings?

20. Did you enjoy the poem? What, specifically, pleased or displeased you about what was expressed and how it was expressed?

21. How might biographical information about the author help to determine the poem's central concerns?

22. How might historical information about the poem provide a useful context for interpretation?

23. To what extent do your own experiences, values, beliefs, and assumptions inform your interpretation?

24. What kinds of evidence from the poem are you focusing on to support your interpretation? Does your interpretation leave out any important elements that might undercut or qualify your interpretation?

EXPLICATION

The purpose of this approach to a literary work is to make the implicit explicit. *Explication* is a detailed explanation of a passage of poetry or prose. Because explication is an intensive examination of a text line by line, it is mostly used to interpret a short poem in its entirety or a brief passage from a long poem, short story, or play. Explication can be used in any kind of paper when you want to be specific about how a writer achieves a certain effect. An explication pays careful attention to language—the connotations of words, allusions, figurative language, irony, symbol, rhythm, sound, and so on. These elements are examined in relation to one another and to the overall effect and meaning of the work.

The simplest way to organize an explication is to move through the passage line by line, explaining whatever seems significant. It is wise to avoid, however, an assembly-line approach that begins each sentence with "In line one (two, three) . . ." Instead, organize your paper in whatever way best serves your thesis. You might find that the right place to start is with the final lines, working your way back to the beginning of the poem or passage. The sample explication on Dickinson's "There's a certain Slant of light," beginning on page 887 in this chapter, does just that. The student's opening paragraph refers to the final line of the poem in order to present her thesis. She explains that though the poem begins with an image of light, it is not a bright or cheery poem but one concerned with "the look of Death." Since the last line prompted her thesis, that is where she begins the explication.

You might also find it useful to structure a paper by discussing various elements of literature. The following sample explication on John Donne's "Death Be Not Proud" is organized in this manner. However your paper is organized, keep in mind that the aim of an explication is not simply to summarize the passage but to comment on the effects and meanings produced by the author's use of language in it. An effective explication (the Latin word *explicare* means "to unfold") displays a text to reveal how it works and what it signifies. Although writing an explication requires some patience and sensitivity, it is an excellent method for coming to understand and appreciate the elements and qualities that constitute literary art.

A SAMPLE PAPER-IN-PROGRESS
Mapping a Poem

When you write about a poem, you are, in some ways, providing a guide for a place that might otherwise seem unfamiliar and remote. Put simply, writing enables you to chart a work so that you can comfortably move around in it to discuss or write about what interests you. Your paper represents a record and a map of your intellectual journey through the poem, pointing out the things worth noting and your impressions about them. Your role as writer is to offer insights into the challenges, pleasures, and discoveries that the poem harbors. These insights are a kind of sightseeing as you navigate the various elements of the poem to make some overall point about it.

This section shows you how one student, Rose Bostwick, moves through the stages of writing about how a poem's elements combine for a final effect. Included here are Rose's first response, her informal outline, and the final draft of an explication of John Donne's "Death Be Not Proud." After reviewing the elements of poetry covered in Chapters 12 through 20, Rose read the poem (which follows) several times, paying careful attention to diction, figurative language, irony, symbol, rhythm, sound, and so on. Her final paper is more concerned with the overall effect of the combination of elements than with a line-by-line breakdown. As you read and reread "Death Be Not Proud," keep notes on how *you* think the elements of this poem work together and to what overall effect.

JOHN DONNE (1572–1631)

Death Be Not Proud   *1611*

Death be not proud, though some have
    callèd thee
Mighty and dreadful, for thou art not so;
For those whom thou think'st thou dost
    overthrow
Die not, poor Death, nor yet canst thou
    kill me.
From rest and sleep, which but thy
    pictures° be,   *images*
Much pleasure; then from thee much
    more must flow,
And soonest our best men with thee
    do go,

© Michael Nicholson/CORBIS.

Rest of their bones, and soul's delivery.°   *deliverance*
Thou art slave to Fate, Chance, kings, and desperate men,
And dost with Poison, War, and Sickness dwell;   10
And poppy or charms can make us sleep as well,
And better than thy stroke; why swell'st° thou then?   *swell with pride*
One short sleep past, we wake eternally
And death shall be no more; Death, thou shalt die.

Asking Questions about the Elements

After reading a poem, use the Questions for Responsive Reading and Writing (pp. 877–78) to help you think, talk, and write about it. Before you do, though, be sure that you have read the poem several times without worrying actively about interpretation. With poetry, as with all literature, it's important to allow yourself the pleasure of enjoying whatever makes itself apparent to you. On subsequent readings, use the questions to understand and appreciate how the poem works; remember to keep in mind that not all questions will necessarily be relevant to a particular poem. A good starting point is to ask yourself what elements are exemplified in the parts of the poem that especially interest you. Then ask the Questions for Responsive Reading and Writing that relate to those elements. Finally, as you begin to get a sense of what elements are important to the poem and how those elements fit together, it often helps to put your impressions on paper.

A SAMPLE FIRST RESPONSE

First Response to John Donne's "Death Be Not Proud"

After Rose carefully read "Death Be Not Proud" and had a sense of how the elements work, she took the first step toward a formal explication by writing informally about the relevant elements and addressing the question *Why doesn't the speaker fear death? Explain why you find the argument convincing or not.* Note that at this point, she was not as concerned with textual evidence and detail as she would need to be in her final paper.

Rose Bostwick

English 101

Professor Hart

28 January 2016

First Response to John Donne's "Death Be Not Proud"

I've read the poem "Death Be Not Proud" by John Donne a few times now, and I have a sense of how it works. The poem is a sonnet, and each of the three quatrains presents a piece of the argument that Death should not be proud, because it is not really all-powerful, and may even be a source of pleasure. As a reader, I resist this seeming paradox at first, but I know it must be a trick, a riddle of some sort that the poem will proceed to untangle. I think one of the reasons the poem comes off as such a powerful statement is that Donne at first seems to be playful and paradoxical in his characterizations of Death. He's almost teasing Death. But beneath the teasing tone you feel the strong foundation of the real reason Death should not be proud—Donne's faith in the immortality of the soul. The poem begins to feel more solemn as it progresses, as the hints at the idea of immortality become more clearly articulated.

Donne utilizes two literary conventions to increase the effect of this poem: he uses the convention of personifying death, so that he can address it directly, and he uses the metaphor of death as a kind of sleep. These two things determine the tone and the progression from playful to solemn in the poem.

The last clause of the poem (line 14) plays with the paradoxical-seeming character of what he's been declaring. Ironically, it seems the only thing susceptible to death is death itself. Or, when death becomes powerless is when it only has power over itself.

Organizing Your Thoughts

Showing in a paper how different elements of a particular poem work together is often quite challenging. While you may have a clear intuitive sense of what elements are important to the poem and how they complement one another, it is important to organize your thoughts in such a way as to make the relationships clear to your audience. The simplest way is to go line by line, but that can quickly become rote for writer and reader. Because you will want to organize your paper in the way that best serves your thesis, it may help to write an informal outline that charts how you think the argument moves. You may find, for example, that the argument is not persuasive if you start with the final lines and go back to the beginning of the poem or passage. However you decide to organize your argument, keep in mind that a single idea, or thesis, will have to run throughout the entire paper.

A SAMPLE INFORMAL OUTLINE

Proposed Outline for Paper on John Donne's "Death Be Not Proud"

In her informal outline (following), Rose discovers that her argument works best if she begins at the beginning. Note that, though her later paper concerns itself with how several elements of poetry contribute to the poem's theme and message, her informal outline concerns itself much more with what that message is and how it develops as the poem progresses. She will fill in the details later.

Bostwick 1

Rose Bostwick

English 101

Professor Hart

6 February 2016

Proposed Outline for Paper on

John Donne's "Death Be Not Proud"

Thesis: From the very first word, addressing "Death" directly, Donne uses the literary conventions of personifying death and comparing it to sleep to begin an argument that Death should not be proud of its might or dreadfulness.

Bostwick 2

But these two elements of his argument come to be seen as the superficial points when the true reason for death's powerlessness becomes clear. The Christian belief in the immortality of the soul is the reason for death's powerlessness and likeness to sleep.

Body of essay: Show how argument proceeds by quatrains from playful address to Death, and statement that Death is much like sleep, its "picture," to statement that Death is "slave" to other forces (and so should not be proud of being the mightiest), to the couplet, which articulates clearly the idea of immortality and gives the final paradox, "Death, thou shalt die."

Conclusion: Donne's faith in the immortality of the soul enables him to "prove" in this argument that Death is truly like its metaphorical representation, sleep. Faith allows him to derive a source for this conventional trope, and it allows him to state his truth in paradoxes. He relies on the conventional idea that death is an end, and a conqueror, and the only all-powerful force, to make the paradoxes that lend his argument the force of mystery—the mystery of faith.

The Elements and Theme

As you create an informal outline, your understanding of the poem will grow, change, and finally, solidify. You will develop a much clearer sense of what the poem's elements combine to create, and you will have chosen a scheme for organizing your argument. The next step before drafting is to determine the paper's thesis, which will not only keep your paper focused but will also help you center your thoughts. For papers that discuss how the elements of poetry come together, the thesis is a single and concise statement of what the elements combine to create—the idea around which all the elements revolve. In Robert Herrick's "Delight in Disorder," for example, the two elements, rhythm and rhyme, work together to create the speaker's self-directed irony. To state this as a thesis, we might say that by making his own rhythm and rhyme "too precise," Herrick's speaker is making fun of himself while complimenting a certain type of woman. (You may ask yourself if he's doing a little flirting.)

Once you understand how all of the elements of a poem fit together and have articulated your understanding in the thesis statement, the next step is to flesh out your argument. By including quotations from the poem to illustrate the points you will be making, you will better explain exactly how each element relates to the others and, more specifically, to your thesis, and you will have created a finished paper that helps readers navigate the poem's geography.

FINAL PAPER: A SAMPLE EXPLICATION

The Use of Conventional Metaphors for Death in John Donne's "Death Be Not Proud"

In Rose's final draft, she focuses on the use of metaphor in "Death Be Not Proud." Her essay provides a coherent reading that relates each line of the poem to the speaker's intense awareness of death. Although the essay discusses each stanza in order, the introductory paragraph provides a brief overview explaining how the poem's metaphors and arguments contribute to its total meaning. In addition, Rose does not hesitate to discuss a line out of sequence when it can be usefully connected to another phrase. She also works quotations into her sentences to support her points. When she adds something to a quotation to clarify it, she encloses her words in brackets so that they will not be mistaken for the poet's, and she uses a slash to indicate line divisions: "soonest . . . with thee do go, / [for] Rest of their bones, and soul's delivery." Finally, Rose cites the line numbers for direct quotations from the poem (though MLA does not require this if the poem occupies a page or less of your source). As you read through her final draft, remember that the word *explication* comes from the Latin *explicare*, "to unfold." How successful do you think Rose is at unfolding this poem to reveal how its elements—here ranging from metaphor to structure, meter, personification, paradox, irony, and theme—contribute to its meaning?

Rose Bostwick

English 101

Professor Hart

24 February 2016

The Use of Conventional Metaphors for Death

in John Donne's "Death Be Not Proud"

In the sonnet that begins "Death be not proud . . ." John Donne argues that death is not "mighty and dreadful" but is more like its metaphorical representation, sleep. Death, Donne puts forth, is even a source of pleasure and rest. The poet builds this argument on two foundations. One is made up of the metaphors and literary conventions for death: Death is compared with sleep and is often personified so that it can be addressed directly. The poem is an address to death that at first seems paradoxical and somewhat playful, but which then rises in all the emotion of faith as it reveals the second foundation of the argument—the Christian belief in the immortality of the soul. Seen against the backdrop of this belief, death loses its powerful threat and is seen as only a metaphorical sleep, or rest.

> Thesis providing interpretation of the poem's use of metaphor and how it contributes to the poem's central argument.

The poem is an ironic argument that proceeds according to the structure of the sonnet form. Each quatrain contains a new development or aspect of the argument, and the final couplet serves as a conclusion. The metrical scheme is mainly iambic pentameter, but in several places in the poem, the stress pattern is altered for emphasis. For example, the first foot of the poem is inverted, so that "Death," the first word, receives the stress. This announces to us right away that Death is being personified and addressed. This inversion also serves to begin the poem energetically and forcefully. The second line behaves in the same way. The first syllable of "Mighty" receives the stress, emphasizing the meaning of the word and its assumed relation to Death.

> Discussion of how form and meter contribute to the poem's central argument.

This first quatrain offers the first paradox and sets up the argument that death has been conventionally personified with the wrong attributes, might and dreadfulness. The poet tells death not to be proud, "though some have called thee / Mighty and dreadful," because, he says, death is "not so" (lines 1-2). Donne will turn this conventional characterization of death on its head with the paradox of the third and fourth lines: he says the people overthrown by death (as if by a conqueror) "Die not, poor Death, nor yet canst thou kill me." These lines establish the paradox of death not being able to cause death.

> Discussion of how personification contributes to the poem's central argument.

The next quatrain will not begin to answer the question of why this paradox is so, but will posit another slight paradox—the idea of death as pleasurable. In lines 5-8, Donne uses the literary convention of describing death as a metaphorical sleep, or rest, to construct the argument that death must give pleasure: "From rest and sleep, which but thy pictures be, / Much pleasure; then from thee much more must flow" (5-6). At this point, the argument seems almost playful, but is carefully hinting at the solemnity of

> Discussion of how metaphor of sleep and idea of immortality support the poem's central argument.

the deeper foundation of the belief in immortality. The metaphor of sleep for death includes the idea of waking; one doesn't sleep forever. The next two lines put forth the idea that death is pleasurable enough to be desired by "our best men" who "soonest . . . with thee do go, / [for] Rest of their bones, and soul's delivery" (7-8). This last line comes closer to announcing the true reason for death's powerlessness and pleasure: it is the way to the "soul's delivery" from the body and life on earth, and implicitly, into another, better realm.

A new reason for death's powerlessness arises in the next four lines. The poet says to death:

Thou art slave to Fate, Chance, kings, and desperate men,

And dost with Poison, War, and Sickness dwell;

And poppy or charms can make us sleep as well,

And better than thy stroke; why swell'st thou then? (9-12)

Donne argues here that there are forces more powerful than death that actually control it. Fate and chance determine when death occurs, and to whom it comes. Kings, with the powers of law and war, can summon death and throw it on whom they wish. And desperate men, murderers or suicides, can also summon death with the strength of their emotions. In lines 11 and 12, Donne again uses the metaphor of death as a kind of sleep, but says that drugs or "charms" give one a better sleep than death. And he asks playfully why death should be so proud, after all these illustrations of its weakness have been given: "why swell'st thou then?" (12).

Finally, with the last couplet, Donne reveals the true, deeper reason behind his argument that death should not be proud of its power. These lines also offer an explanation of the metaphor for death of sleep, or rest: "One short sleep past, we wake eternally / And death shall be no more; Death, thou shalt die" (13-14). After death, the soul lives on, according to Christian theology and belief. In the Christian heaven, where the soul is immortal, death will no longer exist, and so this last paradox, "Death, thou shalt die," becomes true. Again in this line, a significant inversion of metrical stress occurs. "Death," in the second clause, receives the stress, recalling the first line, emphasizing that it is an address and giving the clause a forceful sense of finality. His belief in the immortality of the soul enables Donne to "prove" in this argument that death is in actuality like its metaphorical representation, sleep. His faith allows him to derive a source for this conventional metaphor and to "disprove" the

> Discussion of how language and tone contribute to the poem's central argument.

> Discussion of function of religious faith in the poem and how word order and meter create emphasis.

Bostwick 4

metaphor of death as an all-powerful conqueror. His Christian beliefs also allow him to state his truth in paradoxes, the mysteries that are justified by the mystery of faith.

> Conclusion supporting thesis in context of poet's beliefs.

Bostwick 5

Work Cited

Donne, John. "Death Be Not Proud." *Literature to Go*, edited by Michael Meyer, 3rd ed., Bedford/St. Martin's, 2017, p. 880.

A SAMPLE STUDENT EXPLICATION

A Reading of Emily Dickinson's "There's a certain Slant of light"

The sample paper by Bonnie Katz is the result of an assignment calling for an explication of about 750 words on any poem by Emily Dickinson. Katz selected "There's a certain Slant of light."

EMILY DICKINSON (1830–1886)

There's a certain Slant of light   ca. 1861

There's a certain Slant of light,
Winter Afternoons —
That oppresses, like the Heft
Of Cathedral Tunes —

Heavenly Hurt, it gives us —   5
We can find no scar,
But internal difference,
Where the Meanings, are —

None may teach it — Any —
'Tis the Seal Despair —   10
An imperial affliction
Sent us of the Air —

When it comes, the Landscape listens —
Shadows — hold their breath —
When it goes, 'tis like the Distance   15
On the look of Death —

Bonnie Katz's essay comments on every line of the poem and provides a coherent reading that relates each line to the speaker's intense awareness of death. Although the essay discusses each stanza in the order that it appears, the introductory paragraph provides a brief overview explaining how the poem's images contribute to its total meaning. In addition, the student does not hesitate to discuss a line out of sequence when it can be usefully connected to another phrase. This is especially apparent in the third paragraph, in her discussion of stanzas 2 and 3. The final paragraph describes some of the formal elements of the poem. It might be argued that this discussion could have been integrated into the previous paragraphs rather than placed at the end, but the student does make a connection in her concluding sentence between the pattern of language and its meaning.

Several other matters are worth noticing. The student works quotations into her own sentences to support her points. She quotes exactly as the words appear in the poem, even Dickinson's irregular use of capital letters. When something is added to a quotation to clarify it, it is enclosed in brackets so that the essayist's words will not be mistaken for the poet's: "Seal [of] Despair." A slash is used to indicate line divisions as in "imperial affliction / Sent us of the Air."

Katz 1

Bonnie Katz
Professor Quiello
English 109–2
23 March 2016

A Reading of Emily Dickinson's
"There's a certain Slant of light"

Because Emily Dickinson did not provide titles for her poetry, editors follow the customary practice of using the first line of a poem as its title. However, a more appropriate title for "There's a certain Slant of light," one that

Thesis providing overview of explication.

suggests what the speaker in the poem is most concerned about, can be drawn from the poem's last line, which ends with "the look of Death" (line 16). Although the first line begins with an image of light, nothing bright, carefree, or cheerful appears in the poem. Instead, the predominant mood and images are darkened by a sense of despair resulting from the speaker's awareness of death.

In the first stanza, the "certain Slant of light" is associated with "Winter Afternoons" (2), a phrase that connotes the end of a day, a season, and even life itself. Such light is hardly warm or comforting. Not a ray or beam, this slanting light suggests something unusual or distorted and creates in the speaker a certain slant on life that is consistent with the cold, dark mood that winter afternoons can produce. Like the speaker, most of us have seen and felt this sort of light: it "oppresses" (3) and pervades our sense of things when we encounter it. Dickinson uses the senses of hearing and touch as well as sight to describe the overwhelming oppressiveness that the speaker experiences. The light is transformed into sound by a simile that tells us it is "like the Heft / Of Cathedral Tunes" (3-4). Moreover, the "Heft" of that sound—the slow, solemn measures of tolling church bells and organ music—weighs heavily on our spirits. Through the use of shifting imagery, Dickinson evokes a kind of spiritual numbness that we keenly feel and perceive through our senses.

By associating the winter light with "Cathedral Tunes," Dickinson lets us know that the speaker is concerned about more than the weather. Whatever it is that "oppresses" is related by connotation to faith, mortality, and God. The second and third stanzas offer several suggestions about this connection. The pain caused by the light is a "Heavenly Hurt" (5). This "imperial affliction / Sent us of the Air" (11-12) apparently comes from God above, and yet it seems to be part of the very nature of life. The oppressiveness we feel is in the air, and it can neither be specifically identified at this point in the poem nor be eliminated, for "None may teach it — Any" (9). All we know is that existence itself seems depressing under the weight of this "Seal [of] Despair" (10). The impression left by this "Seal" is stamped within the mind or soul rather than externally. "We can find no scar" (6), but once experienced this oppressiveness challenges our faith in life and its "Meanings" (8).

The final stanza does not explain what those "Meanings" are, but it does make clear that the speaker is acutely aware of death. As the winter

Line-by-line explication of first stanza, focusing on connotations of words and imagery, in relation to mood and meaning of poem as a whole; supported with references to the text.

Explication of second, third, and fourth stanzas, focusing on connotations of words and imagery in relation to mood and meaning of poem as a whole. Supported with references to the text.

daylight fades, Dickinson projects the speaker's anxiety onto the surrounding landscape and shadows, which will soon be engulfed by the darkness that follows this light: "the Landscape listens — /Shadows — hold their breath" (13-14). This image firmly aligns the winter light in the first stanza with darkness. Paradoxically, the light in this poem illuminates the nature of darkness. Tension is released when the light is completely gone, but what remains is the despair that the "imperial affliction" has imprinted on the speaker's sensibilities, for it is "like the Distance / On the look of Death — " (15-16). There can be no relief from what that "certain Slant of light" has revealed because what has been experienced is permanent — like the fixed stare in the eyes of someone who is dead.

The speaker's awareness of death is conveyed in a thoughtful, hushed tone. The lines are filled with fluid *l* and smooth *s* sounds that are appropriate for the quiet, meditative voice in the poem. The voice sounds tentative and uncertain — perhaps a little frightened. This seems to be reflected in the slightly irregular meter of the lines. The stanzas are trochaic with the second and fourth lines of each stanza having five syllables, but no stanza is identical because each works a slight variation on the first stanza's seven syllables in the first and third lines. The rhymes also combine exact patterns with variations. The first and third lines of each stanza are not exact rhymes, but the second and fourth lines are exact so that the paired words are more closely related: *Afternoons, Tunes; scar, are; Despair, Air;* and *breath, Death.* There is a pattern to the poem, but it is unobtrusively woven into the speaker's voice in much the same way that "the look of Death" (16) is subtly present in the images and language of the poem.

> Explication of the elements of rhythm and sound throughout poem.

> Conclusion tying explication of rhythm and sound with explication of words and imagery in previous paragraphs.

Work Cited

Dickinson, Emily. "There's a certain Slant of light." *Literature to Go*, edited by Michael Meyer, 3rd ed., Bedford/St. Martin's, 2017, pp. 887-88.

32

Writing about Drama

When you create drama, you look for the best conflict.
— JANE ANDERSON

Photo by permission of Jilly
Wendell.

FROM READING TO WRITING

Because dramatic literature is written to be performed, writing about reading a play may seem twice removed from what playwrights intend the experience of drama to be: a live audience responding to live actors. Although reading a play creates distance between yourself and a performance of it, reading a play can actually bring you closer to understanding that what supports a stage production of any play is the literary dimension of a script. Writing about that script—examining carefully how the language of the stage directions, setting, exposition, dialogue, plot, and other dramatic elements serve to produce effects and meanings—can enhance an imaginative re-creation of a performance. In a sense, writing about a play gauges your own interpretative response as an audience member—the difference, of course, is that instead of applauding, you are typing.

"There's the rub," as Hamlet might say, because you're working with the precision of your fingertips rather than with the hearty response of your palms. Composing an essay about drama records more than your response to a play; writing also helps you explore, clarify, and discover dimensions of the play you may not have perceived by simply watching a performance

891

of it. Writing is work, of course, but it's the kind of work that brings you closer to your own imagination as well as to the play. That process is more accessible if you read carefully, take notes, and annotate the text to generate ideas (for a discussion of this process, see Chapter 29, "Reading and the Writing Process"). This chapter offers a set of questions to help you read and write about drama and includes a sample paper that compares and contrasts Henrik Ibsen's play *A Doll's House* with James Joyce's short story "Eveline."

Questions for Responsive Reading and Writing

The questions below can help you consider important elements that reveal a play's effects and meanings. These questions are general and will not, therefore, always be relevant to a particular play. Many of them, however, should prove to be useful for thinking, talking, and writing about drama.

1. Did you enjoy the play? What, specifically, pleased or displeased you about what was expressed and how it was expressed?

2. What is the significance of the play's title? How does it suggest the author's overall emphasis?

3. What information do the stage directions provide about the characters, action, and setting? Are these directions primarily descriptive, or are they also interpretive?

4. How is the exposition presented? What does it reveal? How does the playwright's choice *not* to dramatize certain events on stage help to determine what the focus of the play is?

5. In what ways is the setting important? Would the play be altered significantly if the setting were changed?

6. Are foreshadowings used to suggest what is to come? Are flashbacks used to dramatize what has already happened?

7. What is the major conflict the protagonist faces? What complications constitute the rising action? Where is the climax? Is the conflict resolved?

8. Are one or more subplots used to qualify or complicate the main plot? Is the plot unified so that each incident somehow has a function that relates it to some other element in the play?

9. Does the author purposely avoid a pyramidal plot structure of rising action, climax, and falling action? Is the plot experimental? Is the plot logically and chronologically organized, or is it fantastical or absurd? What effects are produced by the plot? How does it reflect the author's view of life?

10. Who is the protagonist? Who (or what) is the antagonist?

11. By what means does the playwright reveal character? What do the characters' names, physical qualities, actions, and words convey about them? What do the characters reveal about each other?

12. What is the purpose of the minor characters? Are they individualized, or do they primarily represent ideas or attitudes? Are any character foils used?

13. Do the characters all use the same kind of language, or is their speech differentiated? Is it formal or informal? How do the characters' diction and manner of speaking serve to characterize them?

14. Does your response to the characters change in the course of the play? What causes the change?

15. Are words and images repeated in the play so that they take on special meanings? Which speeches seem particularly important? Why?

16. How does the playwright's use of language contribute to the tone of the play? Is the dialogue, for example, predominantly light, humorous, relaxed, sentimental, sad, angry, intense, or violent?

17. Are any symbols used in the play? Which actions, characters, settings, objects, or words convey more than their literal meanings?

18. Are any unfamiliar theatrical conventions used that present problems in understanding the play? How does knowing more about the nature of the theater from which the play originated help to resolve these problems?

19. Is the theme stated directly, or is it developed implicitly through the plot, characters, or some other element? Does the theme confirm or challenge most people's values?

20. How does the play reflect the values of the society in which it is set and in which it was written?

21. How does the play reflect or challenge your own values?

22. Is there a recording, film, or DVD of the play available in your library or media center or online? How does this version compare with your own reading?

23. How would you produce the play on a stage? Consider scenery, costumes, casting, and characterizations. What would you emphasize most in your production?

24. How might biographical information about the author help the reader to grasp the central concerns of the play?

25. How might historical information about the play provide a useful context for interpretation?

26. To what extent do your own experiences, values, beliefs, and assumptions inform your interpretation?

27. What kinds of evidence from the play are you focusing on to support your interpretation? Does your interpretation leave out any important elements that might undercut or qualify your interpretation?

28. Given that there are a variety of ways to interpret the play, which one seems the most useful to you?

Comparison and Contrast

Essay assignments in literature courses often require you to write about similarities and differences between or within works. You might be asked to discuss "How Sounds Express Meanings in Kay Ryan's 'Dew' and Lewis Carroll's 'Jabberwocky,'" or "Sammy's and Stokesie's Attitudes about Conformity in Updike's 'A & P.'" A *comparison* of either topic would emphasize their similarities, while a *contrast* would stress their differences. It is possible, of course, to include both perspectives in a paper if you find significant likenesses and differences. A comparison of Andrew Marvell's "To His Coy Mistress" and Ann Lauinger's "Marvell Noir" would, for example, yield similarities because each poem describes a man urging his lover to make the most of their precious time together; however, important differences also exist in the tone and theme of each poem that would constitute a contrast. (You should, incidentally, be aware that the term *comparison* is sometimes used inclusively to refer to both similarities and differences. If you are assigned a comparison of two works, be sure that you understand what your instructor's expectations are; you may be required to include both approaches in the essay.)

There is no single way to organize comparative papers since each topic is likely to have its own particular issues to resolve, but it is useful to be aware of two basic patterns that can be helpful with a comparison, a contrast, or a combination of both. One method that can be effective for relatively short papers consists of dividing the paper in half, first discussing one work and then the other. Here, for example, is a partial informal outline for a discussion of Sophocles' *Oedipus the King* and Shakespeare's *Othello*; the topic is a comparison and contrast: "Oedipus and Othello as Tragic Figures."

1. Oedipus
   a. The nature of the conflict
   b. Strengths and stature
   c. Weaknesses and mistakes
   d. What is learned
2. Othello
   a. The nature of the conflict
   b. Strengths and stature
   c. Weaknesses and mistakes
   d. What is learned

This organizational strategy can be effective provided that the second part of the paper combines the discussion of Othello with references to Oedipus so that the thesis is made clear and the paper unified without being repetitive. If the two characters were treated entirely separately, then the discussion would be merely parallel rather than integrated. In a lengthy paper, this organization probably would not work well because a reader would have difficulty remembering the points made in the first half as he or she reads on.

Thus, for a longer paper it is usually better to create a more integrated structure that discusses both works as you take up each item in your outline. Here is the second basic pattern using the elements in the partial outline just cited:

1. The nature of the conflict
   a. Oedipus
   b. Othello
2. Strengths and stature
   a. Oedipus
   b. Othello
3. Weaknesses and mistakes
   a. Oedipus
   b. Othello
4. What is learned
   a. Oedipus
   b. Othello

This pattern allows you to discuss any number of topics without requiring your reader to recall what you first said about the conflict Oedipus confronts before you discuss Othello's conflicts fifteen pages later. However you structure your comparison or contrast paper, make certain that a reader can follow its elements and keep track of its thesis.

A SAMPLE STUDENT COMPARISON

The Struggle for Women's Self-Definition in Henrik Ibsen's A Doll's House *and James Joyce's "Eveline"*

The following paper was written in response to an assignment that required a comparison and contrast — about 750 words — of two works of literature. The student chose to write an analysis of how the women in each work respond to being defined by men.

Monica Casis

Professor Matthews

English 105-4

4 February 2016

The Struggle for Women's Self-Definition

in Henrik Ibsen's *A Doll's House* and

James Joyce's "Eveline"

Although Henrik Ibsen's *A Doll's House* (1879) and James Joyce's "Eveline" (1914) were written more than thirty years apart and portray radically different characters and circumstances, both works raise similar questions about the role of women and how they are defined in their respective worlds. Each work presents a woman who conforms to society's ideas of gender in an effort to be accepted and loved. While both Ibsen's Nora Helmer and Joyce's Eveline are intelligent and resourceful, Nora is able to break free of society's hold; Eveline cannot. Nevertheless, these narratives show the emergence of each woman's identity — Nora's refusal to be a submissive and belittled housewife and Eveline's awareness of the constraints placed upon her by her father and community. From the beginning, these women are more intelligent and self-aware than the people who oppress them; unfortunately, that does not necessarily lead to complete autonomy.

In *A Doll's House*, Nora is treated as her father's, then her husband's, doll. She is called "squirrel," "spendthrift," and "lark" and is admonished for such things as eating sweets or asking her husband to take her ideas into consideration (758). Torvald's concept of the ideal woman is a showpiece who can dress up, recite, and dance. As a mother, Nora only plays with her children; it is Anne Marie who takes care of them. As a housewife, she has no control over the household finances; her husband gives her an allowance.

Although Nora continually conforms to her husband's expectations, she has the strength and courage to borrow money for a trip to Italy to save his life and does odd jobs to pay the debt that she has committed forgery to secure. She is proud of her sacrifice for her family. At the same time, she plays the role of a frivolous, helpless, dependent woman in order to coax her husband into giving her money and to keep him away from Krogstad's incriminating letter; she lies in order to keep him happy. Though Nora appears to be a woman trapped within her husband's expectations of her, she does have a will of her own. Once she sees and understands Torvald's superficiality and selfishness — that he is concerned only with what threatens him — Nora realizes she must abandon him and the role he has defined for her. Eveline, who submits to her overbearing father for most of Joyce's story, ultimately sees the need for change—the need to break out of her current life. However, unlike Nora, Eveline does not imagine an independent life; she sees marriage to Frank as her only way out. It is marriage that she believes will bring respect, happiness, and a kind of freedom: "People would treat her with respect then. She would not be treated as her mother had been" (310).

The turning points in *A Doll's House* and in "Eveline" occur when the women protagonists are faced with the choice of whether to leave the men in their lives. Nora is convinced that she will corrupt her children and home with the guilt she bears—for being with a man whom she no longer respects. When Torvald learns the truth from Krogstad, he regards her as liar, hypocrite, and criminal and therefore repudiates her. Once Nora realizes the selfishness of her husband, she knows she cannot stay with him. She must leave him and her children in order to search for her own identity.

Eveline's turning point, on the other hand, results in inaction. She cannot bring herself to leave her home or her father, however unpleasant her daily life. The reasons are not entirely clear, but we can assume that her reluctance stems from the fear of such overwhelming change. Leaving her home and the people she has known her entire life is understandably daunting, especially for such a young person. However, there is also the possibility that Eveline recognizes the problem with her plan. Relocating and marrying Frank will only substitute one dependence with another. Leaving would force her to, once again, rely on the male presence in her life. As a married woman she would never truly gain her own identity.

When Nora and Eveline come to terms with themselves, their situations are no less problematic than when they falsely fulfilled the expectations imposed on them by the men in their lives. Nora leaves to pursue what may seem to be selfish desires, yet this bold move is necessary to gain independence and self-reliance. Eveline, however, cannot free herself from her father's control or leave Dublin with Frank, because her fear and guilt entrap her "like a helpless animal" (312). She lacks Nora's strength and determination to embark on a new life of risky possibilities; instead, Eveline remains passive and unable to choose a different life for herself.

At the end of the works, both women face the struggles that will inform the rest of their lives, but whereas Nora's circumstances might be understood as potentially hopeful, Eveline's condition almost certainly must be considered as hopeless.

Works Cited

Ibsen, Henrik, *A Doll's House*. *Literature to Go*, edited by Michael Meyer, 3rd ed.,
     Bedford/St. Martin's, 2017, pp. 755–811.

Joyce, James, "Eveline." *Literature to Go*, edited by Michael Meyer, 3rd ed.,
     Bedford/St. Martin's, 2017, pp. 309–12.

33

The Literary Research Paper

Does anyone know a good poet who's a vegetarian?
—DONALD HALL

Nancy Crampton.

A close reading of a primary source such as a short story, poem, or play can give insights into a work's themes and effects, but sometimes you will want to know more. A published commentary by a critic who knows the work well and is familiar with the author's life and times can provide insights that otherwise may not be available. Such comments and interpretations — known as *secondary sources* — are, of course, not a substitute for the work itself, but they often can take you into a work further than if you made the journey by yourself.

After imagination, good sense, and energy, perhaps the next most important quality for writing a research paper is the ability to organize material. A research paper on a literary topic requires a writer to take account of quite a lot at once: the text, ideas, sources, and documentation techniques all make demands on one's efforts to present a topic clearly and convincingly.

The following list should give you a sense of what goes into creating a research paper. Although some steps on the list can be folded into one another, they offer an overview of the work that is required:

1. Choosing a topic
2. Finding sources
3. Evaluating sources
4. Taking notes
5. Developing a thesis
6. Organizing an outline

899

7. Writing drafts
8. Revising
9. Documenting sources
10. Preparing the final draft and proofreading

Even if you have never written a research paper, you most likely have already had experience choosing a topic, developing a thesis, organizing an outline, and writing a draft that you then revised, proofread, and handed in. Those skills represent six of the ten items on the list. This chapter briefly reviews some of these steps and focuses on the remaining tasks, unique to research paper assignments.

CHOOSING A TOPIC

Chapter 29 discussed the importance of reading a work closely and taking careful notes as a means of generating topics for writing about literature. If you know a work well and record your understanding of it in notes, you'll have impressions and ideas to choose from for potential topics.

The student author of the sample research paper "How William Faulkner's Narrator Cultivates a Rose for Emily" (p. 911) was asked to write a five-page paper that demonstrated some familiarity with published critical perspectives on a Faulkner story of his choice. Before looking into critical discussions of the story, he read "A Rose for Emily" several times, taking notes and making comments in the margin of his textbook on each reading.

What prompted his choice of "A Rose for Emily" was a class discussion in which many of his classmates found the story's title inappropriate or misleading because they could not understand how and why the story constituted a tribute to Emily given that she murdered a man and slept with his dead body over many years. The gruesome surprise ending revealing Emily as a murderer and necrophiliac hardly seemed to warrant a rose and a tribute for the central character. Why did Faulkner use such a title? Only after having thoroughly examined the story did the student go to the library to see what professional critics had to say about this question.

FINDING SOURCES

Whether your college library is large or small, its reference librarians can usually help you locate secondary sources about a particular work or author. Unless you choose a very recently published story, poem, play, or essay about which little or nothing has been written, you should be able to find out more about a literary work efficiently and quickly. Even if a work has been published recently, you can probably find relevant information on the Internet (see Electronic Sources, following).

Electronic Sources

Researchers can locate materials in a variety of sources, including library online catalogs, specialized encyclopedias, bibliographies, and indexes to periodicals. Libraries also provide online databases that you can access from home. This can be an efficient way to establish a bibliography on a specific topic. Consult a reference librarian about how to use your library's online resources and to determine how they will help you research your topic.

In addition to the many electronic databases available, including your library's computerized holdings, the Internet also connects millions of sites with primary sources (the full texts of stories, poems, plays, and essays) and secondary sources (biography or criticism). If you have not had practice with academic research on the Web, it is a good idea to get guidance from your instructor or a librarian, and by using your library's home page as a starting point. Browsing on the Internet can be absorbing as well as informative, but unless you have plenty of time to spare, don't wait until the last minute to locate your electronic sources. You might find yourself trying to find reliable, professional sources among thousands of sites if you enter too-general search terms such as "Charles Dickens." Following are several especially useful electronic databases that will provide you with bibliographic information in literature studies. Your school's English Department home page may offer online support as well.

Internet Public Library Online Criticism. This site provides links to literary criticism by author, work, country, or period, up through June 2015.

JSTOR. An index that also offers abstracts of journal articles on language and literature.

MLA International Bibliography. This is a standard resource for articles and books on literary subjects that allows topical and keyword searches.

Voice of the Shuttle. Maintained by the University of California, Santa Barbara, this site is a wide-ranging resource for British and American literary studies.

Do remember that your own college library offers a broad range of electronic sources. If you're feeling uncertain or intimidated, your reference librarians are there to help you to get started.

EVALUATING SOURCES AND TAKING NOTES

Evaluate your sources for their reliability and the quality of their evidence. Check to see whether an article or book has been superseded by later studies; try to use up-to-date sources. A popular magazine article will probably not be as authoritative as an article in a scholarly journal. Sources that are well documented with primary and secondary materials usually indicate that the author has done his or her homework. Books printed by university presses and established trade presses are preferable to books privately printed. But there are always exceptions. If you are uncertain about how to assess a book, try to find out something about the author. Are there any other books listed in the online catalog that indicate the author's expertise? What do book reviews say about the work? Three valuable indexes to book reviews of literary studies are *Book Review Digest*, *Book Review Index*, and *An Index to Book Reviews in the Humanities*. Your reference librarian can show you how to use these important tools for evaluating books. Reviews can be a quick means to gain a broad perspective on writers and their works because reviewers often survey previous approaches to the topic under discussion.

A cautionary note: Assessing online sources can be more problematic than evaluating print sources because anyone with a computer and online access can publish on the Internet. Be sure to determine the nature of your sources and their authority. Is the site the work of a professional or an amateur? Is the information likely to be reliable? Is it documented? Before placing your trust in an Internet source, make sure that it warrants your confidence.

As you prepare a list of reliable sources relevant to your topic, record the necessary bibliographic information so that it will be available when you make up the list of works cited for your paper. For a book, include the author, complete title, place of publication, publisher, and date. For an article, include author, complete title, name of periodical, volume number, date of issue, and page numbers. For an Internet source, include the author, complete title, database title, periodical or site name, date of posting of the site (or last update), name of the institution or organization, date when you accessed the source, and its URL.

Once you have assembled a tentative bibliography, you will need to take notes on your readings. Be sure to keep track of where particular information comes from by noting the author's name and page number. If you use more than one work by the same author, include a brief title as well as the author's name.

DEVELOPING A THESIS AND ORGANIZING THE PAPER

As the notes on "A Rose for Emily" accumulated, the student sorted them into topics:

1. Publication history of the story
2. Faulkner on the title of "A Rose for Emily"
3. Is Emily simply insane?
4. The purpose of Emily's servant
5. The narrator
6. The townspeople's view of Emily

7.   The surprise ending
8.   Emily's admirable qualities
9.   Homer's character

The student quickly saw that items 1, 4, and 9 were not directly related to his topic concerning the significance of the story's title. The remaining numbers (2, 3, 5, 6, 7, 8) are the topics taken up in the paper. The student had begun his reading of secondary sources with a tentative thesis that stemmed from his question about the appropriateness of the title. That "why" shaped itself into the expectation that he would have a thesis something like this: "The title justifies Emily's murder of Homer because . . ."

The assumption was that he would find information that indicated some specific reason. But the more he read, the more he discovered that it was possible to speak only about how the narrator prevents the reader from making a premature judgment about Emily rather than justifying her actions. Hence, he wisely changed his tentative thesis to this final statement — "The narrator describes incidents and withholds information in such a way as to cause the reader to sympathize with Emily before her crime is revealed." This thesis helped the student explain why the title is accurate and useful rather than misleading.

Because the assignment was relatively brief, the student did not write up a formal outline but instead organized his notes and proceeded to write the first draft from them.

REVISING

After writing your first draft, you should review the advice and revision checklist on pages 865–66 so that you can read your paper with an objective eye. Two days after writing his next-to-last draft, the writer of "How William Faulkner's Narrator Cultivates a Rose for Emily" realized that he had allotted too much space for critical discussions of the narrator that were not directly related to his approach. He wanted to demonstrate a familiarity with these studies, but it was not essential that he summarize or discuss them. He corrected this by consolidating parenthetical references: "Though a number of studies discuss the story's narrator (see, for example, Curry; Kempton; Sullivan; and Watkins) . . ." His earlier draft had included summaries of these studies that were tangential to his argument. The point is that he saw this himself after he took some time to approach the paper from a fresh perspective.

DOCUMENTING SOURCES AND AVOIDING PLAGIARISM

You must acknowledge the use of a source when you (1) quote someone's exact words, (2) summarize or borrow someone's opinions or ideas, or (3) use information and facts that are not considered to be common knowledge. The purpose of this documentation is to acknowledge your sources, to demonstrate that you are familiar with what others have thought about the topic, and to provide your reader access to the same sources. If your paper is not adequately documented, it will be vulnerable to a charge of *plagiarism* — the presentation of someone else's work as your own. Conscious plagiarism is easy to avoid; honesty takes care of that for most people. However, there is a more problematic form of plagiarism that is often inadvertent. Whether inadequate documentation is conscious or not, plagiarism is a serious matter and must be avoided. Papers can be evaluated only by what is on the page, not by their writers' intentions.

Let's look more closely at what constitutes plagiarism. Consider the following passage quoted from John Gassner's introduction to *Four Great Plays by Henrik Ibsen* (Bantam, 1959, p. viii):

> Today it seems incredible that *A Doll's House* should have created the furor it did. In exploding Victorian ideals of feminine dependency the play seemed revolutionary in 1879. When its heroine Nora left her home in search of self-development it seemed as if the sanctity of marriage had been flouted by a playwright treading the stage with cloven-feet.

Now read this plagiarized version:

A Doll's House created a furor in 1879 by blowing up Victorian ideals about a woman's place in the world. Nora's search for self-fulfillment outside her home appeared to be an attack on the sanctity of marriage by a cloven-footed playwright.

Though the writer has shortened the passage and made some changes in the wording, this paragraph is basically the same as Gassner's. Indeed, several of his phrases are lifted almost intact. Even if a parenthetical reference had been included at the end of the passage and the source included in "Works Cited," the language of this passage would still be plagiarism because it is presented as the writer's own. Both language and ideas must be acknowledged.

Here is an adequately documented version of the passage:

John Gassner has observed how difficult it is for today's readers to comprehend the intense reaction against *A Doll's House* in 1879. When Victorian audiences watched Nora walk out of her stifling marriage, they assumed that Ibsen was expressing a devilish contempt for the "sanctity of marriage" (viii).

This passage makes absolutely clear that the observation is Gassner's, and it is written in the student's own language with the exception of one quoted phrase. Had Gassner not been named in the passage, the parenthetical reference would have included his name: (Gassner viii).

Some mention should be made of the notion of common knowledge before we turn to the standard format for documenting sources. Observations and facts that are widely known and routinely included in many of your sources do not require documentation. It is not necessary to cite a source for the fact that Alfred, Lord Tennyson was born in 1809 or that Ernest Hemingway loved to fish and hunt. Sometimes it will be difficult for you to determine what common knowledge is for a topic that you know little about. If you are in doubt, the best strategy is to supply a reference.

There are two basic ways to document sources. Traditionally, sources have been cited in footnotes at the bottom of each page or in endnotes grouped together at the end of the paper. Here is how a portion of the sample paper would look if footnotes were used instead of parenthetical documentation:

As Heller points out, before we learn of Emily's bizarre behavior we see her as a sympathetic — if antiquated — figure in a town whose life and concerns have passed her by; hence, "we are disposed to see Emily as victimized."[1]

[1]Terry Heller, "The Telltale Hair: A Critical Study of William Faulkner's 'A Rose for Emily,'" *Arizona Quarterly*, vol. 28, no. 4, 1972, p. 306.

Unlike endnotes, which are double spaced throughout under the title of "Notes" on separate pages at the end of the paper, footnotes appear four spaces below the text. They are single spaced with double spaces between notes.

No doubt you will have encountered these documentation methods in your reading. A different style is recommended, however, in the Modern Language Association's *MLA Handbook*, Eighth Edition (MLA, 2016). This style employs parenthetical references within the text of the paper; these are keyed to an alphabetical list of works cited at the end of the paper. This method is designed to be less distracting for the reader. Unless you are instructed to follow the footnote or endnote style for documentation, use the parenthetical method explained in the next section.

The List of Works Cited

Items in the list of works cited are arranged alphabetically according to the author's last name and indented a half inch after the first line. This allows the reader to locate quickly the complete bibliographic information for the author's name cited within the parenthetical reference in the text. The following are common entries for literature papers and should be used as models. If some of your sources are of a different nature, consult the *MLA Handbook*, Eighth Edition (MLA, 2016); or, for the latest updates, check MLA's Web site at style.mla.org.

The following entries include examples to follow when citing electronic sources. For electronic sources, include as many of the following elements as apply and as are available:

- Author's name
- Title of the work (if it's a book, italicize the title; if it's a short work, such as an article or a poem, use quotation marks)
- Title of the site (or of the publication, if you're citing an online periodical, for example), italicized

- Sponsor or publisher of the site (if not named as the author)
- Date of publication or last update
- URL

A book by one author

Hendrickson, Robert. *The Literary Life and Other Curiosities*. Viking Press, 1981.

An online book

Frost, Robert. *A Boy's Will*. Henry Holt, 1915. *Bartleby.com: Great Books Online*, 1999, www
   .bartleby.com/117/.

Part of an online book

Frost, Robert. "Into My Own." *A Boy's Will*. Henry Holt, 1915. *Bartleby.com: Great Books
   Online*, 1999, www.bartleby.com/117/.

Notice that the author's name is in reverse order. This information, along with the full title, publisher, and date, should be taken from the title and copyright pages of the book. The title is italicized and is also followed by a period. Use the publication date on the title page; if none appears there, use the copyright date (after ©) on the back of the title page.

A book by two authors

Horton, Rod W., and Herbert W. Edwards. *Backgrounds of American Literary Thought*. 3rd ed.,
   Prentice-Hall, 1974.

Only the first author's name is given in reverse order. The edition number appears after the title.

A book with more than two authors or editors

Gates, Henry Louis, Jr., et al., eds. *The Norton Anthology of African American Literature*. 3rd ed.,
   W. W. Norton, 2014.

(Note: The abbreviation *et al.* means "and others.")

A work in a collection by the same author

O'Connor, Flannery. "Greenleaf." *The Complete Stories*, by Flannery O'Connor, Farrar, Straus
   and Giroux, 1971, pp. 311-34.

Page numbers are given because the reference is to only a single story in the collection.

A work in a collection by a different writer

Frost, Robert. "Design." *Literature to Go*, edited by Michael Meyer, 3rd ed., Bedford/
   St. Martin's, 2017, p. 350.

Sophocles. *Oedipus the King*. *Literature to Go*, edited by Michael Meyer, 3rd ed., Bedford/
   St. Martin's, 2017, pp. 608-48.

The titles of poems and short stories are enclosed in quotation marks; plays
and novels are italicized.

Cross-reference to a collection

Frost, Robert. "Design." Meyer, pp. 350.

Meyer, Michael, editor. *Literature to Go*. 3rd ed., Bedford/St. Martin's, 2017.

O'Connor, Flannery. "A Good Man Is Hard to Find." Meyer, pp. 242-53.

Sophocles. *Oedipus the King*. Meyer, pp. 608-48.

When citing more than one work from the same collection, use a cross-reference
to avoid repeating the same bibliographic information that appears in the main
entry for the collection.

A translated book

Grass, Günter. *The Tin Drum*. Translated by Ralph Manheim, Pantheon Books, 1962.

An introduction, preface, foreword, or afterword

Johnson, Thomas H. Introduction. *Final Harvest: Emily Dickinson's Poems*, by Emily
   Dickinson, Little, Brown, 1961, pp. vii-xiv.

This cites the introduction by Johnson. Notice that a colon is used between
the book's main title and subtitle. To cite a poem in this book, use this
method:

Dickinson, Emily. "A Tooth upon Our Peace." *Final Harvest: Emily Dickinson's Poems*, edited
   by Thomas H. Johnson, Little, Brown, 1961, p. 110.

An entry in an encyclopedia

Robinson, Lisa Clayton. "Harlem Writers Guild." *Africana: The Encyclopedia of the African and
   African American Experience*. 2nd ed., Oxford UP, 2005.

An article in a magazine

Morrow, Lance. "Scribble, Scribble, Eh, Mr. Toad?" *Time*, 24 Feb. 1986, p. 84.

An article from an online magazine

Wasserman, Elizabeth. "The Byron Complex." *TheAtlantic.com*, 1 Oct. 2002, www.theatlantic
   .com/entertainment/archive/2002/10/the-byron-complex/378504/.

The citation for an unsigned article would begin with the title and be
alphabetized by the first word of the title other than "a," "an," or "the."

An article in a scholarly journal with continuous pagination beyond a single issue

Fuqua, Amy. " 'The Furrow of His Brow': Providence and Pragmatism in Toni Morrison's
   Paradise." *Midwest Quarterly*, vol. 54, no. 1, Autumn 2012, pp. 38-52.

Regardless of whether the journal uses continuous pagination or separate pagination for each issue, it is necessary to include the volume number and the issue number for every entry. If a journal does not offer an issue number, use only the volume number, as in the next entry. If a journal uses *only* issue numbers, use that in place of the volume number.

An article in a scholarly journal with separate pagination for each issue

Updike, John. "The Cultural Situation of the American Writer." *American Studies
   International,* vol. 15, 1977, pp. 19-28.

In the following citation, noting the winter issue helps a reader find the correct article among all of the articles published by the online journal in 2004.

An article from an online scholarly journal

Mamet, David. "Secret Names." *The Threepenny Review*, vol. 96, Winter 2004, www
   .threepennyreview.com/samples/mamet_w04.html.

The following citation indicates that the article appears on page 1 of section 7 and continues onto another page.

An article in a newspaper

Ziegler, Philip. "The Lure of Gossip, the Rules of History." *The New York Times,* 23 Feb. 1986,
   sec. 7, pp. 1+.

An article from an online newspaper

Brantley, Ben. "Souls Lost and Doomed Enliven London Stages." *The New York Times*, 4 Feb.
   2004, www.nytimes.com/2004/02/04/theater/critic-s-notebook-souls-lost-and
   -doomed-enliven-london-stages.html.

A lecture

Tilton, Robert. "The Beginnings of American Studies." English 270 class lecture, University
   of Connecticut, Storrs, 12 Mar. 2016. Lecture.

Letter, e-mail, or interview

Vellenga, Carolyn. Letter to the author. 9 Oct. 2015.

Harter, Stephen P. E-mail to the author. 28 Nov. 2015.

McConagha, Bill. Personal interview. 9 May 2016.

Following are additional examples for citing electronic sources.

Work from a subscription service

Libraries pay for access to databases such as *Lexis-Nexis*, *ProQuest Direct*, and *Expanded Academic ASAP*. When you retrieve an article or other work from a subscription database, cite your source based on this model:

Macari, Anne Marie. "Lyric Impulse in a Time of Extinction." *American Poetry Review*,

    vol. 44, no. 4, July/Aug. 2015, pp. 11-14. General OneFile, go.galegroup.com/.

Vendler, Helen Hennessey. "The Passion of Emily Dickinson." *New Republic,* 3 Aug. 1992,

    pp. 34-8. *Expanded Academic ASAP,* go.galegroup.com.

A document from a Web site

When citing sources from the Internet, include as much publication information as possible (see guidelines on pp. 905–06). The entry below provides the author, title of the document, title of the site, the URL, and the date of access.

Perdue, David. "Dickens in America." *David Perdue's Charles Dickens Page,* 13 Apr. 2016,

    charlesdickenspage.com/america.html.

An entire Web site

Perdue, David. *David Perdue's Charles Dickens Page,* 13 Apr. 2016, charlesdickenspage.com.

An online posting

Bedford English. "Stacey Cochran explores Reflective Writing in the classroom and

    as a writer: http://ow.ly/YkjVB." *Facebook,* 15 Feb. 2016, www.facebook.com/

    BedfordEnglish/posts/10153415001259607.

Parenthetical References

A list of works cited is not an adequate indication of how you have used sources in your paper. You must also provide the precise location of quotations and other information by using parenthetical references within the text of the paper. You do this by citing the author's last name (or the source's title if the work is anonymous) and the page number:

Collins points out that "Nabokov was misunderstood by early reviewers of his work" (28).

or

Nabokov's first critics misinterpreted his stories (Collins 28).

Either way a reader will find the complete bibliographic entry in the list of works cited under Collins's name and know that the information cited in the paper appears on page 28. Notice that the end punctuation comes after the parentheses.

If you have listed more than one work by the same author, you would add a brief title to the parenthetical reference to distinguish between them. You could also include the full title in your text:

Nabokov's first critics misinterpreted his stories (Collins, "Early Reviews" 28).

or

Collins points out in "Early Reviews of Nabokov's Fiction" that Nabokov's early work was misinterpreted by reviewers (28).

For electronic sources, provide the author's name. Unless your online source is a stable, paginated document (such as a pdf file), do not include page numbers in your parenthetical references. The following example shows an in-text citation to William Faulkner's acceptance speech for the Nobel Prize in Literature, found at the Nobel Web site.

William Faulkner believed that it was his duty as a writer to "help man endure by lifting his heart" (Faulkner).

This reference would appear in the works cited list as follows:

Faulkner, William. "Banquet Speech: The Nobel Prize in Literature." *Nobelprize.org*, 10 Dec. 1950, nobelprize.org/nobel_prizes/literature/laureates/1949/faulkner-speech.html.

There can be many variations on what is included in a parenthetical reference, depending on the nature of the entry in the list of works cited. But the general principle is simple enough: provide enough parenthetical information for a reader to find the work in "Works Cited." Examine the following sample research paper for more examples of works cited and strategies for including parenthetical references. If you are puzzled by a given situation, refer to the *MLA Handbook*.

A SAMPLE STUDENT RESEARCH PAPER

How William Faulkner's Narrator Cultivates a Rose for Emily

The following research paper by Tony Groulx follows the format described in the *MLA Handbook*, Eighth Edition (2016). Though the sample paper is short, it illustrates many of the techniques and strategies useful for writing an essay that includes secondary sources. (Faulkner's "A Rose for Emily" is reprinted on p. 54.)

Groulx 1

Tony Groulx

Professor Hugo

English 109-3

4 February 2016

How William Faulkner's Narrator

Cultivates a Rose for Emily

William Faulkner's "A Rose for Emily" is an absorbing mystery story whose chilling ending contains a gruesome surprise. When we discover, along with the narrator and townspeople, what was left of Homer Barron's body, we may be surprised or not, depending on how carefully we have been reading the story and keeping track of details such as Emily Grierson's purchase of rat poison and Homer's disappearance. Probably most readers anticipate finding Homer's body at the end of the story because Faulkner carefully prepares the groundwork for the discovery as the townspeople force their way into that mysterious upstairs room where a "thin, acrid pall as of the tomb seemed to lie everywhere" (60). But very few readers, if any, are prepared for the story's final paragraph, when we realize that the strand of "iron-gray hair" (the last three words of the story) on the second pillow indicates that Emily has slept with Homer since she murdered him. This last paragraph produces the real horror in the story and an extraordinary revelation about Emily's character.

Reference to text of the story.

The final paragraph seems like the right place to begin a discussion of this story because the surprise ending not only creates a powerful emotional effect in us but also raises an important question about what we are to think of Emily. Is this isolated, eccentric woman simply mad? All the circumstantial evidence indicates that she is a murderer and necrophiliac, and yet Faulkner titles the story "A Rose for Emily," as if she is due some kind of tribute. The title somehow qualifies the gasp of horror that the story leads up to in the final paragraph. Why would anyone offer this woman a "rose"? What's behind the title?

Groulx 2

Faulkner was once directly asked the meaning of the title and replied:

> Oh it's simply the poor woman had had no life at all. Her father had kept
> her more or less locked up and then she had a lover who was about to quit
> her, she had to murder him. It was just "A Rose for Emily" — that's all.
> (qtd. in Gwynn and Blotner 87-88)

Reference to
secondary
source
(Gwynn and
Blotner).

This reply explains some of Emily's motivation for murdering Homer, but it
doesn't actually address the purpose and meaning of the title. If Emily killed
Homer out of a kind of emotional necessity — out of a fear of abandonment —
how does that explain the fact that the title seems to suggest that the story is a
way of paying respect to Emily? The question remains.

Whatever respect the story creates for Emily cannot be the result of
her actions. Surely there can be no convincing excuse made for murder and
necrophilia; there is nothing to praise about what she does. Instead, the tribute
comes in the form of how her story is told rather than what we are told about
her. To do this Faulkner uses a narrator who tells Emily's story in such a way as
to maximize our sympathy for her. The grim information about Emily's "iron-gray
hair" on the pillow is withheld until the very end and not only to produce a
surprise but to permit the reader to develop a sympathetic understanding of her
before we are shocked and disgusted by her necrophilia.

Significantly, the narrator begins the story with Emily's death rather
than Homer's. Though a number of studies discuss the story's narrator (see, for
example, Curry; Kempton; Sullivan; and Watkins), Terry Heller's is one of the most
comprehensive in its focus on the narrator's effects on the readers' response to
Emily. As Heller points out, before we learn of Emily's bizarre behavior we see
her as a sympathetic — if antiquated — figure in a town whose life and concerns
have passed her by; hence, "we are disposed to see Emily as victimized" (306).
Her refusal to pay her taxes is an index to her isolation and eccentricity, but
this incident also suggests a degree of dignity and power lacking in the town
officials who fail to collect her taxes. Her encounters with the officials of
Jefferson — whether in the form of the sneaking aldermen who try to cover
up the smell around her house or the druggist who unsuccessfully tries to get
her to conform to the law when she buys arsenic — place her in an admirable
light because her willfulness is based on her personal strength. Moreover,
it is relatively easy to side with Emily when the townspeople are described
as taking pleasure in her being reduced to poverty as a result of her father's
death because "now she too would know the old thrill and the old despair
of a penny more or less" (Faulkner 57). The narrator's account of their

Reference to
secondary
sources
(Curry;
Kempton;
Sullivan;
Watkins)
with signal
phrase for
Heller.

Reference to
secondary
source
(Heller)
with signal
phrase ("As
Heller points
out ...").

pettiness, jealousy, and inability to make sense of Emily causes the reader to sympathize with Emily's eccentricities before we must judge her murderous behavior. We admire her for taking life on her own terms, and the narrator makes sure this response is in place prior to our realization that she also takes life.

> Reference to text of the story.

We don't really know much about Emily because the narrator arranges the details of her life so that it's difficult to know what she's been up to. We learn, for example, about the smell around the house before she buys the poison and Homer disappears, so that the cause-and-effect relationship among these events is a bit slippery (for a detailed reconstruction of the chronology, see McGlynn and Nebecker's revision of McGlynn's work), but the effect is to suspend judgment of Emily. By the time we realize what she has done, we are already inclined to see her as outside community values almost out of necessity. That's not to say that the murdering of Homer is justified by the narrator, but it is to say that her life maintains its private—though no longer secret—dignity. Despite the final revelation, Emily remains "dear, inescapable, impervious, tranquil, and perverse" (Faulkner 60).

> Reference to secondary sources (McGlynn and Nebecker).

> References to text of the story.

The narrator's "rose" to Emily is his recognition that Emily is all these things—including "perverse." She evokes "a sort of respectful affection for a fallen monument" (Faulkner 54). She is, to be sure, "fallen," but she is also somehow central—a "monument"—to the life of the community. Faulkner does not offer a definitive reading of Emily, but he does have the narrator pay tribute to her by attempting to provide a complex set of contexts for her actions—contexts that include a repressive father, resistance to a changing South and impinging North, the passage of time and its influence on the present, and relations between men and women as well as relations between generations. Robert Crosman discusses the narrator's efforts to understand Emily:

> The narrator is himself a "reader" of Emily's story, trying to put together from fragments a complete picture, trying to find the meaning of her life in its impact upon an audience, the citizens of Jefferson, of which he is a member. (212)

> Reference to secondary source (Crosman).

The narrator refuses to dismiss Emily as simply mad or to treat her life as merely a grotesque, sensational horror story. Instead, his narrative method brings us into her life before we too hastily reject her, and in doing so it offers us a complex imaginative treatment of fierce determination and strength coupled with illusions and shocking eccentricities. The narrator's rose for Emily is paying her the tribute of placing that "long strand of iron-gray hair" in the context of her entire life.

Works Cited

Crosman, Robert. "How Readers Make Meaning." *College Literature*, vol. 9, no. 3, 1982, pp. 207-15.

Curry, Renee R. "Gender and Authorial Limitation in Faulkner's 'A Rose for Emily.'" *The Mississippi Quarterly*, vol. 47, no. 3, 1994, pp. 391-402. *Expanded Academic ASAP*, connection.ebscohost.com/c/literary-criticism/9502231814/gender-authorial-limitation-faulkners-rose-emily.

Faulkner, William. "A Rose for Emily." *Literature to Go*, edited by Michael Meyer, 3rd ed., Bedford/St. Martin's, 2017, pp. 54-61.

Gwynn, Frederick, and Joseph Blotner, editors. *Faulkner in the University: Class Conferences at the University of Virginia, 1957-58.* U of Virginia P, 1959.

Heller, Terry. "The Telltale Hair: A Critical Study of William Faulkner's 'A Rose for Emily.' " *Arizona Quarterly*, vol. 28, no. 4, 1972, pp. 301-18.

Kempton, K. P. *The Short Story.* Harvard UP, 1954, pp. 104-06.

McGlynn, Paul D. "The Chronology of 'A Rose for Emily.' " *Studies in Short Fiction*, vol. 6, no. 4, 1969, pp. 461-62.

Nebecker, Helen E. "Chronology Revised." *Studies in Short Fiction*, vol. 8, no. 4, 1971, pp. 471-73.

Sullivan, Ruth. "The Narrator in 'A Rose for Emily.' " *Journal of Narrative Technique*, vol. 1, no. 3, 1971, pp. 159-78.

Watkins, F. C. "The Structure of 'A Rose for Emily.'" *Modern Language Notes*, vol. 69, no. 6, 1954, pp. 508-10.

Glossary of Literary Terms

Accent The emphasis, or stress, given a syllable in pronunciation. We say "*syl*lable" not "syl*lable*," "*em*phasis" not "em*phasis*." Accents can also be used to emphasize a particular word in a sentence: *Is* she con*tent* with the *con*tents of the *yel*low *pack*age? See also METER.

Act A major division in the action of a play. The ends of acts are typically indicated by lowering the curtain or turning up the houselights. Playwrights frequently employ acts to accommodate changes in time, setting, characters onstage, or mood. In many full-length plays, acts are further divided into scenes, which often mark a point in the action when the location changes or when a new character enters. See also SCENE.

Allegory A narration or description usually restricted to a single meaning because its events, actions, characters, settings, and objects represent specific abstractions or ideas. Although the elements in an allegory may be interesting in themselves, the emphasis tends to be on what they ultimately mean. Characters may be given names such as Hope, Pride, Youth, and Charity; they have few if any personal qualities beyond their abstract meanings. These personifications are not symbols because, for instance, the meaning of a character named Charity is precisely that virtue. See also SYMBOL.

Alliteration The repetition of the same consonant sounds in a sequence of words, usually at the beginning of a word or stressed syllable: "*descend*ing *d*ew *d*rops"; "*l*uscious *l*emons." Alliteration is based on the sounds of letters, rather than the spelling of words; for example, "*k*een" and "*c*ar" alliterate, but "*c*ar" and "*c*ite" do not. Used sparingly, alliteration can intensify ideas by emphasizing key words, but when used too self-consciously, it can be distracting, even ridiculous, rather than effective. See also ASSONANCE, CONSONANCE.

Allusion A brief reference to a person, a place, a thing, an event, or an idea in history or literature. Allusions conjure up biblical authority, scenes from Shakespeare's plays, historic figures, wars, great love stories, and anything else that might enrich an author's work. Allusions imply reading and cultural experiences shared by the writer and the reader, functioning as a kind of shorthand whereby the recalling of something outside the work supplies an emotional or intellectual context, such as a poem about current racial struggles calling up the memory of Abraham Lincoln.

915

Ambiguity Allows for two or more simultaneous interpretations of a word, a phrase, an action, or a situation, all of which can be supported by the context of a work. Deliberate ambiguity can contribute to the effectiveness and richness of a work, for example, in Randall Jarrell's poem "The Death of the Ball Turret Gunner." However, unintentional ambiguity obscures meaning and can confuse readers.

Anagram A word or phrase made from the letters of another word or phrase, as "heart" is an anagram of "earth." Anagrams have often been considered merely an exercise of one's ingenuity, but sometimes writers use anagrams to conceal proper names or veiled messages, or to suggest important connections between words, as in "hated" and "death."

Anapestic meter See FOOT.

Antagonist The character, force, or collection of forces in fiction or drama that opposes the PROTAGONIST and gives rise to the conflict of the story; an opponent of the protagonist, such as Iago in Shakespeare's play *Othello*. See also CHARACTER, CONFLICT.

Antihero A protagonist who has the opposite of most of the traditional attributes of a hero. He or she may be bewildered, ineffectual, deluded, or merely pathetic. Often what antiheroes learn, if they learn anything at all, is that the world isolates them in an existence devoid of God and absolute values. Yossarian from Joseph Heller's *Catch-22* is an example of an antihero. See also CHARACTER.

Apostrophe An address, either to someone who is absent and therefore cannot hear the speaker or to something nonhuman that cannot comprehend. Apostrophe often provides a speaker the opportunity to think aloud.

Approximate rhyme See RHYME.

Aside In drama, a speech directed to the audience that supposedly is not audible to the other characters onstage at the time. Iago's asides in *Othello*, for example, serve to reveal his sinister character. See also SOLILOQUY.

Assonance The repetition of internal vowel sounds in nearby words that do not end the same, for example, "asleep under a tree," or "each evening." Similar endings result in rhyme, as in "asleep in the deep." Assonance is a strong means of emphasizing important words in a line. See also ALLITERATION, CONSONANCE.

Ballad Traditionally, a ballad is a song, transmitted orally from generation to generation, that tells a story and that eventually is written down. As such, ballads usually cannot be traced to a particular author or group of authors. Typically, ballads are dramatic, condensed, and impersonal narratives, such as "Bonny Barbara Allan." **A literary ballad** is a narrative poem that is written in deliberate imitation of the language, form, and spirit of the traditional ballad. See also BALLAD STANZA, QUATRAIN.

Ballad stanza A four-line stanza, known as a QUATRAIN, consisting of alternating eight- and six-syllable lines. Usually only the second and fourth lines rhyme (an *abcb* pattern). Coleridge adopted the ballad stanza in "The Rime of the Ancient Mariner."

All in a hot and copper sky
The bloody Sun, at noon,
Right up above the mast did stand,
No bigger than the Moon.

See also BALLAD.

Blank verse Unrhymed iambic pentameter. Blank verse is the English verse form closest to the natural rhythms of English speech and therefore is the most common pattern found in traditional English narrative and dramatic poetry from Shakespeare to the early twentieth century. Shakespeare's plays use blank verse extensively. See also IAMBIC PENTAMETER.

Cacophony Language that is discordant and difficult to pronounce, such as this line from John Updike's "Player Piano": "never my numb plunker fumbles." Cacophony ("bad sound") may be unintentional in the writer's sense of music, or it may be used consciously for deliberate dramatic effect. See also EUPHONY.

Caesura A pause within a line of poetry that contributes to the rhythm of the line. A caesura can occur anywhere within a line and need not be indicated by punctuation. In scanning a line, caesuras are indicated by a double vertical line (‖). See also METER, RHYTHM, SCANSION.

Canon Those works generally considered by scholars, critics, and teachers to be the most important to read and study, which collectively constitute the "masterpieces" of literature. Since the 1960s, the traditional English and American literary canon, consisting mostly of works by white male writers, has been rapidly expanding to include many female writers and writers of varying ethnic backgrounds.

Carpe diem The Latin phrase meaning "seize the day." This is a very common literary theme, especially in lyric poetry, which emphasizes that time is fleeting and that one should make the most of present pleasures. Robert Herrick's poem "To the Virgins, to Make Much of Time" employs the *carpe diem* theme.

Catharsis Meaning "purgation," *catharsis* describes the release of the emotions of pity and fear by the audience at the end of a tragedy. In his *Poetics*, Aristotle discusses the importance of catharsis. The audience faces the misfortunes of the protagonist, which elicit compassionate pity. Simultaneously, the audience experiences fear as it confronts the failure of the protagonist, thus receiving a frightening reminder of human limitations and frailties. Ultimately, however, both these negative emotions are purged, because the tragic protagonist's suffering is an affirmation of human values rather than a despairing denial of them. See also TRAGEDY.

Character, characterization A character is a person presented in a dramatic or narrative work, and characterization is the process by which a writer makes that character seem real to the reader. A **hero** or **heroine**, often called the PROTAGONIST, is the central character who engages the reader's interest and empathy. The ANTAGONIST is the character, force, or collection of forces that stands directly opposed to the protagonist and gives rise to the conflict of the story. A **static character** does not change throughout the work, and the reader's knowledge of that character does not grow, whereas a **dynamic character** undergoes some kind of change because of the action in the plot. **Flat characters** embody one or two qualities, ideas, or traits that can be readily described in a brief summary. They are not psychologically complex characters and therefore are readily accessible to readers. Some flat characters are recognized as **stock characters**; they embody stereotypes such as the "dumb blonde" or the "mean stepfather." They become types rather than individuals. **Round characters** are more complex than flat or stock characters, and often display the inconsistencies and internal conflicts found in most real people. They are more fully developed, and therefore are harder to summarize. Authors have two major methods of presenting characters: **showing** and **telling**. **Showing** allows the author to present a character talking and acting, and lets the reader infer what kind of person the character is. In **telling**, the author intervenes to describe and sometimes evaluate the character for the reader. Characters can be convincing whether they are presented by showing or by telling, as long as their actions are motivated. **Motivated action** by the characters occurs when the reader or audience is offered reasons for how the characters behave, what they say, and the decisions they make. **Plausible action** is action by a character in a story that seems reasonable, given the motivations presented. See also PLOT.

Chorus In Greek tragedies (especially those of Aeschylus and Sophocles), a group of people who serve mainly as commentators on the characters and events. They add to the audience's understanding of the play by expressing traditional moral, religious, and social attitudes. The role of the chorus in dramatic works evolved through the sixteenth century, and the chorus occasionally is still used by modern playwrights such as T. S. Eliot in *Murder in the Cathedral*. See also DRAMA.

Cliché An idea or expression that has become tired and trite from overuse, its freshness and clarity having worn off. Clichés often anesthetize readers and are usually a sign of weak writing. See also SENTIMENTALITY, STOCK RESPONSES.

Climax See PLOT.

Closet drama A play that is written to be read rather than performed onstage. In this kind of drama, literary art outweighs all other considerations. See also DRAMA.

Colloquial Refers to a type of informal diction that reflects casual, conversational language and often includes slang expressions. See also DICTION.

Comedy A work intended to interest, involve, and amuse the reader or audience, in which no terrible disaster occurs and that ends happily for the main characters. **High comedy** refers to verbal wit, such as puns, whereas **low comedy** is generally associated with physical action and is less intellectual. **Romantic comedy** involves a love affair that meets with various obstacles (like disapproving parents, mistaken identities, deceptions, or other sorts of misunderstandings) but overcomes them to end in a blissful union. Shakespeare's comedies, such as *A Midsummer Night's Dream*, are considered romantic comedies.

Comic relief A humorous scene or incident that alleviates tension in an otherwise serious work. In many instances these moments enhance the thematic significance of the story in addition to providing laughter. In *Othello*, Desdemona's brief encounter with the clown reveals her gullible nature (III.i).

Conflict The struggle within the plot between opposing forces. The PROTAGONIST engages in the conflict with the ANTAGONIST, which may take the form of a character, society, nature, or an aspect of the protagonist's personality. See also CHARACTER, PLOT.

Connotation Associations and implications that go beyond the literal meaning of a word, which derive from how the word has been commonly used and the associations people make with it. For example, the word *eagle* connotes ideas of liberty and freedom that have little to do with the word's literal meaning. See also DENOTATION.

Consonance A common type of near rhyme that consists of identical consonant sounds preceded by different vowel sounds: *home, same; worth, breath.* See also RHYME.

Contextual symbol See SYMBOL.

Controlling metaphor See METAPHOR.

Convention A characteristic of a literary genre (often unrealistic) that is understood and accepted by audiences because it has come, through usage and time, to be recognized as a familiar technique. For example, the division of a play into acts and scenes is a dramatic convention, as are soliloquies and asides. FLASHBACKS and FORESHADOWING are examples of literary conventions.

Conventional symbol See SYMBOL.

Cosmic irony See IRONY.

Couplet Two consecutive lines of poetry that usually rhyme and have the same meter. A **heroic couplet** is a couplet written in rhymed iambic pentameter.

Crisis A turning point in the action of a story that has a powerful effect on the protagonist. Opposing forces come together decisively to lead to the climax of the plot. See also PLOT.

Dactylic meter See FOOT.

Denotation The dictionary meaning of a word. See also CONNOTATION.

Dénouement A French term meaning "unraveling" or "unknotting," used to describe the resolution of the plot following the climax. See also PLOT, RESOLUTION.

Dialect A type of informational diction. Dialects are spoken by definable groups of people from a particular geographic region, economic group, or social class. Writers use dialect to contrast and express differences in educational, class, social, and regional backgrounds of their characters. See also DICTION.

Dialogue The verbal exchanges between characters. Dialogue makes the characters seem real to the reader or audience by revealing firsthand their thoughts, responses, and emotional states. See also DICTION.

Diction A writer's choice of words, phrases, sentence structures, and figurative language, which combine to help create meaning. **Formal diction** consists of a dignified, impersonal, and elevated use of language; it follows the rules of syntax exactly and is often characterized by complex words and lofty tone. **Middle diction** maintains correct language usage, but is less elevated than formal diction; it reflects the way most educated people speak. **Informal diction** represents the plain language of everyday use, and often includes idiomatic expressions, slang, contractions, and many simple, common words. **Poetic diction** refers to the way poets sometimes employ an elevated diction that deviates significantly from the common speech and writing of their time, choosing words for their supposedly inherent poetic qualities. Since the eighteenth century, however, poets have been incorporating all kinds of diction in their work, and so there is no longer an automatic distinction between the language of a poet and the language of everyday speech. See also DIALECT, JARGON.

Didactic poetry Poetry designed to teach an ethical, moral, or religious lesson. John Donne's poem "Death Be Not Proud" is an example of didactic poetry.

Doggerel A derogatory term used to describe poetry whose subject is trite and whose rhythm and sounds are monotonously heavy-handed.

Drama Derived from the Greek word *dran*, meaning "to do" or "to perform," the term *drama* may refer to a single play, a group of plays ("Jacobean drama"), or to all plays ("world drama"). Drama is designed for performance in a theater; actors take on the roles of characters, perform indicated actions, and speak the dialogue written in the script. **Play** is a general term for a work of dramatic literature, and a **playwright** is a writer who makes plays.

Dramatic irony See IRONY.

Dramatic monologue A type of lyric poem in which a character (the speaker) addresses a distinct but silent audience imagined to be present in the poem in such a way as to reveal a dramatic situation and, often unintentionally, some aspect of his or her temperament or personality. See also LYRIC.

Dynamic character See CHARACTER.

Editorial omniscience See NARRATOR.

Elegy A mournful, contemplative lyric poem written to commemorate someone who is dead, often ending in a consolation; see, for example, Ben Jonson's "On My First Son." *Elegy* may also refer to a serious meditative poem produced to express the speaker's melancholy thoughts. See also LYRIC.

End rhyme See RHYME.

End-stopped line A poetic line that has a pause at the end. End-stopped lines reflect normal speech patterns and are often marked by punctuation. The first line of Keats's "Endymion" is an example of an end-stopped line; the natural pause coincides with the end of the line, and is marked by a period:

A thing of beauty is a joy forever.

English sonnet See SONNET.

Enjambment In poetry, when one line ends without a pause and continues into the next line for its meaning. This is also called a **run-on line**. The transition between the first two lines of Wordsworth's poem "My Heart Leaps Up" demonstrates enjambment:

My heart leaps up when I behold
  A rainbow in the sky:

Envoy See SESTINA.

Epic A long narrative poem, told in a formal, elevated style, that focuses on a serious subject and chronicles heroic deeds and events important to a culture or nation. Milton's *Paradise Lost*, which attempts to "justify the ways of God to man," is an epic. See also NARRATIVE POEM.

Epigram A brief, pointed, and witty poem that usually makes a satiric or humorous point. Epigrams are most often written in couplets, but take no prescribed form.

Epiphany In fiction, when a character suddenly experiences a deep realization about himself or herself; a truth that is grasped in an ordinary rather than a melodramatic moment.

Escape literature See FORMULA FICTION.

Euphony *Euphony* ("good sound") refers to language that is smooth and musically pleasant to the ear. See also CACOPHONY.

Exact rhyme See RHYME.

Exposition A narrative device, often used at the beginning of a work, that provides necessary background information about the characters and their circumstances. Exposition explains what has gone on before, the relationships between characters, the development of a theme, and the introduction of a conflict. See also FLASHBACK.

Extended metaphor See METAPHOR.

Eye rhyme See RHYME.

Falling action See PLOT.

Falling meter See METER.

Farce A form of humor based on exaggerated, improbable incongruities. Farce involves rapid shifts in action and emotion, as well as slapstick comedy and extravagant dialogue. Malvolio in Shakespeare's *Twelfth Night* is a farcical character.

Feminine rhyme See RHYME.

Figures of speech Ways of using language that deviate from the literal, denotative meanings of words in order to suggest additional meanings or effects. Figures of speech say one thing in terms of something else, such as when an overeager funeral director is described as a vulture. See also METAPHOR, SIMILE.

First-person narrator See NARRATOR.

Fixed form A poem that may be categorized by the patterns of its lines, meter, rhymes, and stanzas. A sonnet is a fixed form of poetry because by definition it must have fourteen lines. Other fixed forms include LIMERICK, SESTINA, and VILLANELLE. However, poems written in a fixed form may not always fit into categories precisely, because writers sometimes vary traditional forms to create innovative effects. See also OPEN FORM.

Flashback A narrated scene that marks a break in the narrative in order to inform the reader or audience member about events that took place before the opening scene of a work. See also EXPOSITION.

Flat character See CHARACTER.

Foil A character in a work whose behavior and values contrast with those of another character in order to highlight the distinctive temperament of that character (usually the protagonist). In Shakespeare's *Hamlet*, Laertes acts as a foil to Hamlet, because his willingness to act underscores Hamlet's inability to do so.

Foot The metrical unit by which a line of poetry is measured. A foot usually consists of one stressed and one or two unstressed syllables. An *iambic foot*, which consists of one unstressed syllable followed by one stressed syllable ("away"), is the most common metrical foot in English poetry. A *trochaic foot* consists of one stressed syllable followed by an unstressed syllable ("lovely"). An *anapestic foot* is two unstressed syllables followed by one stressed one ("understand"). A *dactylic foot* is one stressed syllable followed by two unstressed ones ("desperate"). A *spondee* is a foot consisting of two stressed syllables ("dead set"), but is not a sustained metrical foot and is used mainly for variety or emphasis. See also IAMBIC PENTAMETER, LINE, METER.

Foreshadowing The introduction early in a story of verbal and dramatic hints that suggest what is to come later.

Form The overall structure or shape of a work, which frequently follows an established design. Forms may refer to a literary type (narrative form, short story form) or to patterns of meter, lines, and rhymes (stanza form, verse form). See also FIXED FORM, OPEN FORM.

Formal diction See DICTION.

Formula fiction Often characterized as escape literature, formula fiction follows a pattern of conventional reader expectations. Romance novels, westerns, science fiction, and detective stories are all examples of formula fiction; while the details of individual stories vary, the basic ingredients of each kind of story are the same. Formula fiction offers happy endings (the hero "gets the girl," the detective cracks the case), entertains wide audiences, and sells tremendously well.

Found poem An unintentional poem discovered in a nonpoetic context, such as a conversation, a news story, or an advertisement. Found poems serve as reminders that everyday language often contains what can be considered poetry, or that poetry is definable as any text read as a poem.

Free verse Also called OPEN FORM poetry, *free verse* refers to poems characterized by their nonconformity to established patterns of meter, rhyme, and stanza. Free verse uses elements such as speech patterns, grammar, emphasis, and breath pauses to decide line breaks, and usually does not rhyme.

Genre A French word meaning "kind" or "type." The major genres in literature are poetry, fiction, drama, and essays. Genre can also refer to more specific types of literature such as comedy, tragedy, epic poetry, or science fiction.

Haiku A style of lyric poetry borrowed from the Japanese that typically presents an intense emotion or vivid image of nature, which, traditionally, is designed to lead to a spiritual insight. Haiku is a fixed poetic form, consisting of seventeen syllables organized into three unrhymed lines of five, seven, and five syllables. Today, however, many poets vary the syllabic count in their haiku. See also FIXED FORM.

Hamartia A term coined by Aristotle to describe "some error or frailty" that brings about misfortune for a tragic hero. The concept of *hamartia* is closely related to that of the tragic flaw: both lead to the downfall of the protagonist in a tragedy. *Hamartia* may be interpreted as an internal weakness in a character (like greed or passion or HUBRIS); however, it may also refer to a mistake that a character makes that is based not on a personal failure but on circumstances outside the protagonist's personality and control. See also TRAGEDY.

Hero, heroine See CHARACTER.

Heroic couplet See COUPLET.

High comedy See COMEDY.

Hubris or hybris Excessive pride or self-confidence that leads a protagonist to disregard a divine warning or to violate an important moral law. In tragedies, hubris is a very common form of *hamartia*. See also HAMARTIA, TRAGEDY.

Hyperbole A boldly exaggerated statement that adds emphasis without intending to be literally true, as in the statement "He ate everything in the house." Hyperbole (also called **overstatement**) may be used for serious, comic, or ironic effect. See also FIGURES OF SPEECH.

Iambic meter See FOOT.

Iambic pentameter A metrical pattern in poetry that consists of five iambic feet per line. (An iamb, or iambic foot, consists of one unstressed syllable followed by a stressed syllable.) See also BLANK VERSE, FOOT, METER.

Image A word, phrase, or figure of speech (especially a SIMILE or a METAPHOR) that addresses the senses, suggesting mental pictures of sights, sounds, smells, tastes, feelings, or actions. Images offer sensory impressions to the reader and also convey emotions and moods through their verbal pictures. See also FIGURES OF SPEECH.

Implied metaphor See METAPHOR.

In medias res See PLOT.

Informal diction See DICTION.

Internal rhyme See RHYME.

Irony A literary device that uses contradictory statements or situations to reveal a reality different from what appears to be true. It is ironic for a firehouse to burn down or for a police station to be burglarized. **Verbal irony** is a figure of speech that occurs when a person says one thing but means the opposite. **Sarcasm** is a strong form of verbal irony that is calculated to hurt someone through, for example, false praise. **Dramatic irony** creates a discrepancy between what a character believes or says and what the reader or audience member knows to be true. **Tragic irony** is a form of dramatic irony found in tragedies such as *Oedipus the King*, in which Oedipus searches for the person responsible for the plague that ravishes his city and ironically ends up hunting himself. **Situational irony** exists when there is an incongruity between what is expected to happen and what actually happens due to forces beyond human comprehension or control. The suicide of the seemingly successful main character in Edwin Arlington Robinson's poem "Richard Cory" is an example of situational irony. **Cosmic irony** occurs when a writer uses God, destiny, or fate to dash the hopes and expectations of a character or of humankind in general. In cosmic irony, a discrepancy exists between what a character aspires to and what universal forces provide. Stephen Crane's poem "A Man Said to the Universe" is a good example of cosmic irony, because the universe acknowledges no obligation to the man's assertion of his own existence.

Italian sonnet See SONNET.

Jargon Language used by a trade or profession such as the jargon used in Sally Croft's "Home-Baked Bread."

Limerick A light, humorous style of fixed form poetry. Its usual form consists of five lines with the rhyme scheme *aabba*; lines 1, 2, and 5 contain three feet, while lines 3 and 4 usually contain two feet. Limericks range in subject matter from the silly to the obscene, and since Edward Lear popularized them in the nineteenth century, children and adults have enjoyed these comic poems. See also FIXED FORM.

Limited omniscient narrator See NARRATOR.

Line A sequence of words printed as a separate entity on the page. In poetry, lines are usually measured by the number of feet they contain. The names for various line lengths are as follows:

monometer: one foot	pentameter: five feet
dimeter: two feet	hexameter: six feet
trimeter: three feet	heptameter: seven feet
tetrameter: four feet	octameter: eight feet

The number of feet in a line, coupled with the name of the foot, describes the metrical qualities of that line. See also END-STOPPED LINE, ENJAMBMENT, FOOT, METER.

Literary ballad See BALLAD.

Literary symbol See SYMBOL.

Low comedy See COMEDY.

Lyric A type of brief poem that expresses the personal emotions and thoughts of a single speaker. It is important to realize, however, that although the lyric is uttered in the first person, the speaker is not necessarily the poet. There are many varieties of lyric poetry, including the DRAMATIC MONOLOGUE, ELEGY, HAIKU, ODE, and SONNET forms.

Masculine rhyme See RHYME.

Melodrama A term applied to any literary work that relies on implausible events and sensational action for its effect. The conflicts in melodramas typically arise out of plot rather than characterization; often a virtuous individual must somehow confront and overcome a wicked oppressor. Usually, a melodramatic story ends happily, with the protagonist defeating the antagonist at the last possible moment. Thus, melodramas entertain the reader or audience with exciting action while still conforming to a traditional sense of justice. See also SENTIMENTALITY.

Metafiction The literary term used to describe a work that explores the nature, structure, logic, status, and function of storytelling.

Metaphor A metaphor is a figure of speech that makes a comparison between two unlike things, without using the word *like* or *as*. Metaphors assert the identity of dissimilar things, as when Macbeth asserts that life *is* a "brief candle." Metaphors can be subtle and powerful, and can transform people, places, objects, and ideas into whatever the writer imagines them to be. An **implied metaphor** is a more subtle comparison; the terms being compared are not so specifically explained. For example, to describe a stubborn man unwilling to leave, one could say that he was "a mule standing his ground." This is a fairly explicit metaphor; the man is being compared to a mule. But to say that the man "brayed his refusal to leave" is to create an implied metaphor, because the subject (the man) is never overtly identified as a mule. Braying is associated with the mule, a notoriously stubborn creature, and so the comparison between the stubborn man and the mule is sustained. Implied metaphors can slip by inattentive readers who are not sensitive to such carefully chosen, highly concentrated language. An **extended metaphor** is a sustained comparison in which part or all of a poem consists of a series of related metaphors. Robert Francis's poem "Catch" relies on an extended metaphor that compares poetry to playing catch. A **controlling metaphor** runs through an entire work and determines the form or nature of that work. The controlling metaphor in Anne Bradstreet's poem "The Author to Her Book" likens her book to a child. **Synecdoche** is a kind of metaphor in which a part of something is used to signify the whole, as when a gossip is called a "wagging tongue," or when ten ships are called "ten sails." Sometimes, synecdoche refers to the whole being used to signify the part, as in the phrase "Boston won the baseball game." Clearly, the entire city of Boston did not participate in the game; the whole of Boston is being used to signify the individuals who played and won the game. **Metonymy** is a type of metaphor in which something closely associated with a subject is substituted for it. In this way, we speak of the "silver screen" to mean motion pictures, "the crown" to stand for the king, "the White House" to stand for the activities of the president. See also FIGURES OF SPEECH, PERSONIFICATION, SIMILE.

Meter When a rhythmic pattern of stresses recurs in a poem, it is called *meter*. Metrical patterns are determined by the type and number of feet in a line of verse; combining the name of a line length with the name of a foot concisely describes the meter of a line. **Rising meter** refers to metrical feet that move from unstressed to stressed sounds, such as the iambic foot and the anapestic foot. **Falling meter** refers to metrical feet that move from stressed to unstressed sounds, such as the trochaic foot and the dactylic foot. See also ACCENT, FOOT, IAMBIC PENTAMETER, LINE.

Metonymy See METAPHOR.

Middle diction See DICTION.

Motivated action See CHARACTER.

Naive narrator See NARRATOR.

Narrative poem A poem that tells a story. A narrative poem may be short or long, and the story it relates may be simple or complex. See also BALLAD, EPIC.

Narrator The voice of the person telling the story, not to be confused with the author's voice. With a **first-person narrator**, the *I* in the story presents the point of view of only one character. The reader is restricted to the perceptions, thoughts, and feelings of that single character. For example, in Melville's "Bartleby, the Scrivener," the lawyer is the first-person narrator of the story. First-person narrators can play either a major or a minor role in the story they are telling. An **unreliable narrator** reveals an interpretation of events that is somehow different from the author's own interpretation of those events. Often, the unreliable narrator's perception of plot, characters, and setting becomes the actual subject of the story, as in Melville's "Bartleby, the Scrivener." Narrators can be unreliable for a number of reasons: they might lack self-knowledge (like Melville's lawyer), they might be inexperienced, or they might even be insane. **Naive narrators** such as Mark Twain's Huck Finn or J. D. Salinger's Holden Caulfield are usually characterized by youthful innocence. An **omniscient narrator** is an all-knowing narrator who is not a character in the story and who can move from place to place and pass back and forth through time, slipping into and out of characters as no human being possibly could in real life. Omniscient narrators can report the thoughts and feelings of the characters as well as their words and actions. The narrator of *The Scarlet Letter* is an omniscient narrator. **Editorial omniscience** refers to an intrusion by the narrator in order to evaluate a character for a reader, as when the narrator of *The Scarlet Letter* describes Hester's relationship to the Puritan community. Narration that allows the characters' actions and thoughts to speak for themselves is called **neutral omniscience**. Most modern writers use neutral omniscience so that readers can reach their own conclusions. **Limited omniscience** occurs when an author restricts a narrator to the single perspective of either a major or a minor character. The way people, places, and events appear to that character is the way they appear to the reader. Sometimes a limited omniscient narrator can see into more than one character, particularly in a work that focuses on two characters alternately from one chapter to the next. Short stories, however, are frequently limited to a single character's point of view. See also PERSONA, POINT OF VIEW, STREAM-OF-CONSCIOUSNESS TECHNIQUE.

Near rhyme See RHYME.

Neutral omniscience See NARRATOR.

Objective point of view See POINT OF VIEW.

Octave A poetic stanza of eight lines, usually forming one part of a sonnet. See also SONNET, STANZA.

Ode A relatively lengthy lyric poem that often expresses lofty emotions in a dignified style. Odes are characterized by a serious topic, such as truth, art, freedom, justice, or the meaning of life; their tone tends to be formal. There is no prescribed pattern that defines an ode; some odes repeat the same pattern in each stanza, while others introduce a new pattern in each stanza. See also LYRIC.

Off rhyme See RHYME.

Omniscient narrator See NARRATOR.

One-act play A play that takes place in a single location and unfolds as one continuous action. The characters in a one-act play are presented economically, and the action is sharply focused. See also DRAMA.

Onomatopoeia A term referring to the use of a word that resembles the sound it denotes. *Buzz, rattle, bang,* and *sizzle* all reflect onomatopoeia. Onomatopoeia can also consist of more than one word; writers sometimes create lines or whole passages in which the sound of the words helps to convey their meanings.

Open form Sometimes called FREE VERSE, open form poetry does not conform to established patterns of METER, RHYME, and STANZA. Such poetry derives its rhythmic qualities from the repetition of words, phrases, or grammatical structures; the arrangement of words on the printed page; or by some other means. The poet E. E. Cummings wrote open form poetry; his poems do not have measurable meters, but they do have rhythm. See also FIXED FORM.

Organic form Refers to works whose formal characteristics are not rigidly predetermined but follow the movement of thought or emotion being expressed. Such works are said to grow like living organisms, following their own individual patterns rather than external fixed rules that govern, for example, the form of a SONNET.

Overstatement See HYPERBOLE.

Oxymoron A condensed form of paradox in which two contradictory words are used together, as in "sweet sorrow" or "original copy." See also PARADOX.

Paradox A statement that initially appears to be contradictory but then, on closer inspection, turns out to make sense. For example, John Donne ends his sonnet "Death, Be Not Proud" with the paradoxical statement "Death, thou shalt die." To resolve the paradox, it is necessary to discover the sense that underlies the statement. Paradox is useful in poetry because it arrests a reader's attention by its seemingly stubborn refusal to make sense.

Paraphrase A prose restatement of the central ideas of a poem in your own language.

Parody A humorous imitation of another, usually serious, work. It can take any fixed or open form, because parodists imitate the tone, language, and shape of the original in order to deflate the subject matter, making the original work seem absurd. Parody may also be used as a form of literary criticism to expose the defects in a work. But sometimes parody becomes an affectionate acknowledgment that a well-known work has become both institutionalized in our culture and fair game for some fun. For example, Ann Lauinger's "Marvell Noir" gently mocks Andrew Marvell's "To His Coy Mistress." See also SATIRE.

Persona Literally, a *persona* is a mask. In literature, a *persona* is a speaker created by a writer to tell a story or to speak in a poem. A persona is not a character in a story or narrative, nor does a persona necessarily directly reflect the author's personal voice. A persona is a separate self, created by and distinct from the author, through which he or she speaks. See also NARRATOR.

Personification A form of metaphor in which human characteristics are attributed to nonhuman things. Personification offers the writer a way to give the world life and motion by assigning familiar human behaviors and emotions to animals, inanimate objects, and abstract ideas. For example, in Keats's "Ode on a Grecian Urn," the speaker refers to the urn as an "unravished bride of quietness." See also METAPHOR.

Petrarchan sonnet See SONNET.

Picture poem A type of open form poetry in which the poet arranges the lines of the poem so as to create a particular shape on the page. The shape of the poem embodies its subject; the poem becomes a picture of what the poem is describing. Michael McFee's "In Medias Res" is an example of a picture poem. See also OPEN FORM.

Plausible action See CHARACTER.

Play See DRAMA.

Playwright See DRAMA.

Plot An author's selection and arrangement of incidents in a story to shape the action and give the story a particular focus. Discussions of plot include not just what happens but also how and why things happen the way they do. Stories that are written in a **pyramidal pattern** divide the plot into three essential parts. The first part is the **rising action**, in which complication creates some sort of conflict for the protagonist. The second part is the **climax**, the moment of greatest emotional tension in a narrative, usually marking a turning point in the plot at which the **rising action** reverses to become the falling action. The third part, the **falling action** (or RESOLUTION), is characterized by diminishing tensions and the resolution of the plot's conflicts and complications. ***In medias res*** is a term used to describe the common strategy of beginning a story in the middle of the action. In this type of plot, we enter the story on the verge of some important moment. See also CHARACTER, CRISIS, RESOLUTION, SUBPLOT.

Poetic diction   See DICTION.

Point of view   Refers to who tells us a story and how it is told. What we know and how we feel about the events in a work are shaped by the author's choice of a point of view. The teller of the story, the narrator, inevitably affects our understanding of the characters' actions by filtering what is told through his or her own perspective. The various points of view that writers draw on can be grouped into two broad categories: (1) the third-person narrator uses *he, she,* or *they* to tell the story and does not participate in the action; and (2) the first-person narrator uses *I* and is a major or minor participant in the action. A second-person narrator, *you,* is also possible but is rarely used because of the awkwardness in thrusting the reader into the story, as in "You are minding your own business on a park bench when a drunk steps out and demands your lunch bag." An **objective point of view** employs a third-person narrator who does not see into the mind of any character. From this detached and impersonal perspective, the narrator reports action and dialogue without telling us directly what the characters think and feel. Since no analysis or interpretation is provided by the narrator, this point of view places a premium on dialogue, actions, and details to reveal character to the reader. See also NARRATOR, STREAM-OF-CONSCIOUSNESS TECHNIQUE.

Problem play   Popularized by Henrik Ibsen, a problem play is a type of drama that presents a social issue in order to awaken the audience to it. These plays usually reject romantic plots in favor of holding up a mirror that reflects not simply what the audience wants to see but what the playwright sees in them. Often, a problem play will propose a solution to the problem that does not coincide with prevailing opinion. The term is also used to refer to certain Shakespeare plays that do not fit the categories of tragedy, comedy, or romance. See also DRAMA.

Prologue   The opening speech or dialogue of a play, especially a classic Greek play, that usually gives the exposition necessary to follow the subsequent action. Today the term also refers to the introduction to any literary work. See also DRAMA, EXPOSITION.

Prose poem   A kind of open form poetry that is printed as prose and represents the most clear opposite of fixed form poetry. Prose poems are densely compact and often make use of striking imagery and figures of speech. See also FIXED FORM, OPEN FORM.

Prosody The overall metrical structure of a poem. See also METER.

Protagonist The main character of a narrative; its central character who engages the reader's interest and empathy. See also CHARACTER.

Pun A play on words that relies on a word having more than one meaning or sounding like another word. Shakespeare and other writers use puns extensively, for serious and comic purposes; in *Romeo and Juliet* (III.i.101), the dying Mercutio puns, "Ask for me tomorrow and you shall find me a grave man." Puns have serious literary uses, but since the eighteenth century, puns have been used almost purely for humorous effect. See also COMEDY.

Pyramidal pattern See PLOT.

Quatrain A four-line stanza. Quatrains are the most common stanzaic form in the English language; they can have various meters and rhyme schemes. See also METER, RHYME, STANZA.

Recognition The moment in a story when previously unknown or withheld information is revealed to the protagonist, resulting in the discovery of the truth of his or her situation and, usually, a decisive change in course for that character. In *Oedipus the King*, the moment of recognition comes when Oedipus finally realizes that he has killed his father and married his mother.

Resolution The conclusion of a plot's conflicts and complications. The resolution, also known as the **falling action**, follows the climax in the plot. See also DÉNOUEMENT, PLOT.

Reversal The point in a story when the protagonist's fortunes turn in an unexpected direction. See also PLOT.

Rhyme The repetition of identical or similar concluding syllables in different words, most often at the ends of lines. Rhyme is predominantly a function of sound rather than spelling; thus, words that end with the same vowel sounds rhyme, for instance, *day, prey, bouquet, weigh,* and words with the same consonant ending rhyme, for instance, *vain, feign, rein, lane.* Words do not have to be spelled the same way or look alike to rhyme. In fact, words may look alike but not rhyme at all. This is called **eye rhyme**, as with *bough* and *cough*, or *brow* and *blow*. **End rhyme** is the most common form of rhyme in poetry; the rhyme comes at the end of the lines:

It runs through the reeds
   And away it proceeds,
Through meadow and glade,
   In sun and in shade.

The **rhyme scheme** of a poem describes the pattern of end rhymes. Rhyme schemes are mapped out by noting patterns of rhyme with small letters: the first rhyme sound is designated *a*, the second becomes *b*, the third *c*, and so on. Thus, the rhyme scheme of the stanza above is *aabb*. **Internal rhyme** places at least one of the rhymed words within the line, as in "Dividing and gliding and sliding" or "In mist or cloud, on mast or shroud." **Masculine rhyme** describes the rhyming of single-syllable words, such as *grade* and *shade*. Masculine rhyme also occurs in rhyming words of more than one syllable when the same sound occurs in a final stressed syllable, as in *defend* and *contend* or *betray* and *away*. **Feminine rhyme** consists of a rhymed stressed syllable followed by one or more identical unstressed syllables, as in *butter*, *clutter*; *gratitude*, *attitude*; *quivering*, *shivering*. All the examples so far have illustrated **exact rhymes**, because they share the same stressed vowel sounds as well as sharing sounds that follow the vowel. In **near rhyme** (also called **off rhyme**, **slant rhyme**, and **approximate rhyme**), the sounds are almost but not exactly alike. A common form of near rhyme is CONSONANCE, which consists of an identical consonant sound preceded by different vowel sounds: *home*, *same*; *worth*, *breath*.

Rhyme scheme See RHYME.

Rhythm A term used to refer to the recurrence of stressed and unstressed sounds in poetry. Depending on how sounds are arranged, the rhythm of a poem may be fast or slow, choppy or smooth. Poets use rhythm to create pleasurable sound patterns and to reinforce meanings. Rhythm in prose arises from pattern repetitions of sounds and pauses that create looser rhythmic effects. See also METER.

Rising action See PLOT.

Rising meter See METER.

Romantic comedy See COMEDY.

Round character See CHARACTER.

Run-on line See ENJAMBMENT.

Sarcasm See IRONY.

Satire The literary art of ridiculing a folly or vice in order to expose or correct it. The object of satire is usually some human frailty; people, institutions, ideas, and things are all fair game for satirists. Satire evokes attitudes of amusement, contempt, scorn, or indignation toward its faulty subject in the hope of somehow improving it. See also IRONY, PARODY.

Scansion The process of measuring the stresses in a line of verse in order to determine the metrical pattern of the line. See also LINE, METER.

Scene In drama, a scene is a subdivision of an ACT. In modern plays, scenes usually consist of units of action in which there are no changes in the setting or breaks in the continuity of time. According to traditional conventions, a scene changes when the location of the action shifts or when a new character enters. See also ACT, CONVENTION, DRAMA.

Script The written text of a play, which includes the dialogue between characters, stage directions, and often other expository information. See also DRAMA, EXPOSITION, PROLOGUE, STAGE DIRECTIONS.

Sentimentality A pejorative term used to describe the effort by an author to induce emotional responses in the reader that exceed what the situation warrants. Sentimentality especially pertains to such emotions as pathos and sympathy; it cons readers into falling for the mass murderer who is devoted to stray cats, and it requires that readers do not examine such illogical responses. Clichés and stock responses are the key ingredients of sentimentality in literature. See also CLICHÉ, STOCK RESPONSES.

Sestet A stanza consisting of exactly six lines. See also STANZA.

Sestina A type of fixed form poetry consisting of thirty-nine lines of any length divided into six sestets and a three-line concluding stanza called an **envoy**. The six words at the end of the first sestet's lines must also appear at the ends of the lines in the other five sestets, in varying order, and they must appear in the envoy, where they often resonate important themes. An example of this highly demanding form of poetry is Florence Cassen Mayers's "All-American Sestina." See also SESTET.

Setting The physical and social context in which the action of a story occurs. The major elements of setting are the time, the place, and the social environment that frames the characters. Setting can be used to evoke a mood or an atmosphere that will prepare the reader for what is to come, as in the excerpt from Edgar Rice Burroughs's *Tarzan of the Apes*. Sometimes, writers choose a particular setting because of traditional associations with that setting that are closely related to the action of a story. For example, stories filled with adventure or romance often take place in exotic locales.

Shakespearean sonnet See SONNET.

Showing See CHARACTER.

Simile A common figure of speech that makes an explicit comparison between two things by using words such as *like, as, than, appears,* or *seems*: "A sip of Mrs. Cook's coffee is like a punch in the stomach." The effectiveness of this simile is created by the differences between the two things compared. There would be no simile if the comparison were stated this way: "Mrs. Cook's coffee is as strong as the cafeteria's coffee." This is a literal comparison because Mrs. Cook's coffee is compared with something like it — another kind of coffee. See also FIGURES OF SPEECH, METAPHOR.

Situational irony See IRONY.

Slant rhyme See RHYME.

Soliloquy A dramatic convention by means of which a character, alone onstage, utters his or her thoughts aloud. Playwrights use soliloquies as a convenient way to inform the audience about a character's motivations and state of mind. Shakespeare's Hamlet delivers perhaps the best known of all soliloquies, which begins: "To be or not to be." See also ASIDE, CONVENTION.

Sonnet A fixed form of lyric poetry that consists of fourteen lines, usually written in iambic pentameter. There are two basic types of sonnets, the Italian and the English. The **Italian sonnet**, also known as the **Petrarchan sonnet**, is divided into an octave, which typically rhymes *abbaabba*, and a sestet, which may have varying rhyme schemes. Common rhyme patterns in the sestet are *cdecde*, *cdcdcd*, and *cdccdc*. Very often the octave presents a situation, an attitude, or a problem that the sestet comments upon or resolves, as in John Keats's "On First Looking into Chapman's Homer." The **English sonnet**, also known as the **Shakespearean sonnet**, is organized into three quatrains and a couplet, which typically rhyme *abab cdcd efef gg*. This rhyme scheme is more suited to English poetry because English has fewer rhyming words than Italian. English sonnets, because of their four-part organization, also have more flexibility with respect to where thematic breaks can occur. Frequently, however, the most pronounced break or turn comes with the concluding couplet, as in Shakespeare's "Shall I compare thee to a summer's day?" See also COUPLET, IAMBIC PENTAMETER, LINE, OCTAVE, QUATRAIN, SESTET.

Speaker The voice used by an author to tell a story or speak a poem. The speaker is often a created identity and should not automatically be equated with the author's self. See also NARRATOR, PERSONA, POINT OF VIEW.

Spondee See FOOT.

Stage directions A playwright's written instructions about how the actors in a play are to move and behave. They explain in which direction characters should move, what facial expressions they should assume, and so on. See also DRAMA, SCRIPT.

Stanza In poetry, *stanza* refers to a grouping of lines, set off by a space, that usually has a set pattern of meter and rhyme. See also LINE, METER, RHYME.

Static character See CHARACTER.

Stock character See CHARACTER.

Stock responses Predictable, conventional reactions to language, characters, symbols, or situations. The flag, motherhood, puppies, God, and peace are some objects commonly used to elicit stock responses from unsophisticated audiences. See also CLICHÉ, SENTIMENTALITY.

Stream-of-consciousness technique The most intense use of a central consciousness in narration. The stream-of-consciousness technique takes a reader inside a character's mind to reveal perceptions, thoughts, and feelings on a conscious or unconscious level. This technique suggests the flow of thought as well as its content; hence, complete sentences may give way to fragments as the character's mind makes rapid associations free of conventional logic or transitions. James Joyce's novel *Ulysses* makes extensive use of this narrative technique. See also NARRATOR, POINT OF VIEW.

Stress The emphasis, or accent, given a syllable in pronunciation. See also ACCENT.

Style The distinctive and unique manner in which a writer arranges words to achieve particular effects. Style essentially combines the idea to be expressed with the individuality of the author. These arrangements include individual word choices as well as matters such as the length of sentences, their structure, tone, and use of irony. See also DICTION, IRONY, TONE.

Subplot The secondary action of a story, complete and interesting in its own right, that reinforces or contrasts with the main plot. There may be more than one subplot, and sometimes as many as three, four, or even more, running through a piece of fiction. Subplots are generally either analogous to the main plot, thereby enhancing our understanding of it, or extraneous to the main plot, to provide relief from it. See also PLOT.

Suspense The anxious anticipation of a reader or an audience as to the outcome of a story, especially concerning the character or characters with whom sympathetic attachments are formed. Suspense helps to secure and sustain the interest of the reader or audience throughout a work.

Symbol A person, object, image, word, or event that evokes a range of additional meaning beyond and usually more abstract than its literal significance. Symbols are economical devices for evoking complex ideas without having to resort to painstaking explanations that would make a story more like an essay than an experience. **Conventional symbols** have meanings that are widely recognized by a society or culture. Some conventional symbols are the Christian cross, the Star of David, a swastika, or a nation's flag. Writers use conventional symbols to reinforce meanings. Kate Chopin, for example, emphasizes the spring setting in "The Story of an Hour" as a way of suggesting the renewed sense of life that Mrs. Mallard feels when she thinks herself free from her husband. A **literary** or **contextual symbol** can be a setting, character, action, object, name, or anything else in a work that maintains its literal significance while suggesting other meanings. Such symbols go beyond conventional symbols; they gain their symbolic meaning within the context of a specific story. For example, the white whale in Melville's *Moby-Dick* takes on multiple symbolic meanings in the work, but these meanings do not automatically carry over into other stories about whales. The meanings suggested by Melville's whale are specific to that text; therefore, it becomes a contextual symbol. See also ALLEGORY.

Synecdoche See METAPHOR.

Syntax The ordering of words into meaningful verbal patterns such as phrases, clauses, and sentences. Poets often manipulate syntax, changing conventional word order, to place certain emphasis on particular words. Emily Dickinson, for instance, writes about being surprised by a snake in her poem "A narrow Fellow in the Grass," and includes this line: "His notice sudden is." In addition to creating the alliterative hissing *s*-sounds here, Dickinson also effectively manipulates the line's syntax so that the verb *is* appears unexpectedly at the end, making the snake's hissing presence all the more "sudden."

Telling See CHARACTER.

Tercet A three-line stanza. See also STANZA, TRIPLET.

Terza rima An interlocking three-line rhyme scheme: *aba, bcb, cdc, ded,* and so on. Dante's *Divine Comedy* and Frost's "Acquainted with the Night" are written in *terza rima*. See also RHYME, TERCET.

Theme The central meaning or dominant idea in a literary work. A theme provides a unifying point around which the plot, characters, setting, point of view, symbols, and other elements of a work are organized. It is important not to mistake the theme for the actual subject of the work; the theme refers to the abstract concept that is made concrete through the images, characterization, and action of the text. In nonfiction, however, the theme generally refers to the main topic of the discourse.

Thesis The central idea of an essay. The thesis is a complete sentence (although sometimes it may require more than one sentence) that establishes the topic of the essay in clear, unambiguous language.

Tone The author's implicit attitude toward the reader or the people, places, and events in a work as revealed by the elements of the author's style. Tone may be characterized as serious or ironic, sad or happy, private or public, angry or affectionate, bitter or nostalgic, or any other attitudes and feelings that human beings experience. See also STYLE.

Tragedy A story that presents courageous individuals who confront powerful forces within or outside themselves with a dignity that reveals the breadth and depth of the human spirit in the face of failure, defeat, and even death. Tragedies recount an individual's downfall; they usually begin high and end low. Shakespeare is known for his tragedies, including *Macbeth, King Lear, Othello*, and *Hamlet*. A **tragic flaw** is an error or a defect in the tragic hero that leads to his downfall, such as greed, pride, or ambition. This flaw may be a result of bad character, bad judgment, an inherited weakness, or any other defect of character. **Tragic irony** is a form of dramatic irony found in tragedies such as *Oedipus the King*, in which Oedipus ironically ends up hunting himself. See also COMEDY, DRAMA.

Tragic flaw See TRAGEDY.

Tragic irony See IRONY, TRAGEDY.

Triplet A tercet in which all three lines rhyme. See also TERCET.

Trochaic meter See FOOT.

Understatement The opposite of hyperbole, understatement (or litotes) refers to a figure of speech that says less than is intended. Understatement usually has an ironic effect and sometimes may be used for comic purposes, as in Mark Twain's statement, "The reports of my death are greatly exaggerated." See also HYPERBOLE, IRONY.

Unreliable narrator See NARRATOR.

Verbal irony See IRONY.

Verse A generic term used to describe poetic lines composed in a measured rhythmical pattern that are often, but not necessarily, rhymed. See also LINE, METER, RHYME, RHYTHM.

Villanelle A type of fixed-form poetry consisting of nineteen lines of any length divided into six stanzas: five tercets and a concluding quatrain. The first and third lines of the initial tercet rhyme; these rhymes are repeated in each subsequent tercet (*aba*) and in the final two lines of the quatrain (*abaa*). Line 1 appears in its entirety as lines 6, 12, and 18, while line 3 reappears as lines 9, 15, and 19. Dylan Thomas's "Do Not Go Gentle into That Good Night" is a villanelle. See also FIXED FORM, QUATRAIN, RHYME, TERCET.

Well-made play A realistic style of play that employs conventions including plenty of suspense created by meticulous plotting. Well-made plays are tightly and logically constructed and lead to a logical resolution that is favorable to the protagonist. This dramatic structure was popularized in France by Eugène Scribe (1791–1861) and Victorien Sardou (1831–1908) and was adopted by Henrik Ibsen. See also CHARACTER, PLOT.

POETRY

Collins. Copyright © 1991. Reprinted by permission of the University of Pittsburgh Press. "On 'Building with Its Face Blown Off,'" "On Writing 'Litany,'" "On Writing 'Nostalgia,'" "On Writing 'Osso Buco,'" "On Writing 'Questions About Angels,'" copyright © Billy Collins. Reprinted by permission of the Chris Calhoun Agency. "Osso Buco" from *The Art of Drowning* by Billy Collins. Copyright © 1995. Reprinted by permission of the University of Pittsburgh Press. "Questions About Angels" from *Questions About Angels* by Billy Collins. Copyright © 1991. Reprinted by permission of the University of Pittsburgh Press.

Edmund Conti. "Pragmatist" from *Light Year '86*. Reprinted by permission of the author.

Sally Croft. "Home-Baked Bread" from *Light Year '86*. Reprinted by permission of Bruce Croft.

E. E. Cummings. "l(a," copyright © 1958, 1986, 1991 by the Trustees for the E. E. Cummings Trust. "next to of course god america i," copyright © 1926, 1954, © 1991 by the Trustees for the E. E. Cummings Trust. Copyright © 1985 by George James Firmage. "old age sticks" copyright © 1948, © 1976, 1991 by the Trustees for the E. E. Cummings Trust. Copyright © 1979 by George J. Firmage. All selections from *Complete Poems: 1904–1962* by E. E. Cummings, edited by George J. Firmage. Copyright 1923, 1925, 1926, 1931, 1935, 1938, 1939, 1940, 1944, 1945, 1946, 1947, 1948, 1949, 1950, 1951, 1952, 1953, 1954, © 1955, 1956, 1957, 1958, 1959, 1960, 1961, 1962, 1963, 1966, 1967, 1968, 1972, 1973, 1974, 1975, 1976, 1977, 1978, 1979, 1980, 1981, 1982, 1983, 1984, 1985, 1986, 1987, 1988, 1989, 1990, 1991 by the Trustees for the E. E. Cummings Trust. Copyright © 1973, 1976, 1978, 1979, 1981, 1983, 1985, 1991 by George James Firmage. Used by permission of Liveright Publishing Corporation.

Emily Dickinson. "A Bird came down the Walk —," "I heard a Fly buzz — when I died —," "Much Madness is divinest Sense —," "A narrow Fellow in the Grass," and "There's a certain Slant of light." Reprinted by permission of the publishers and the Trustees of Amherst College from *The Poems of Emily Dickinson*, edited by Thomas H. Johnson, Cambridge, Mass.: The Belknap Press of Harvard University Press. Copyright © 1951, 1955 by the President and Fellows of Harvard College. Copyright © renewed 1979, 1983 by the President and Fellows of Harvard College. Copyright © 1914, 1918, 1919, 1924, 1929, 1930, 1932, 1935, 1937, 1942 by Martha Dickinson Bianchi. Copyright © 1952, 1957, 1958, 1963, 1965 by Mary L. Hampson.

Cornelius Eady. "The Supremes" from *The Gathering of My Name*. Copyright © 1991 by Cornelius Eady. Reprinted with the permission of The Permissions Company, Inc., on behalf of Carnegie Mellon University Press.

Martín Espada. "Latin Night at the Pawn Shop" from *Rebellion Is the Circle of a Lover's Hands / Rebelión es el giro de manos del amante* by Martín Espada. Copyright © 1990 by Martín Espada. Translation copyright © by Camilo Pérez-Bustillo and Martín Espada. First printed in 1990 by Curbstone Press. Reprinted with the permission of the author and Northwestern University Press. "The Mexican Cabdriver's Poem for His Wife, Who Has Left Him" from *A Mayan Astronomer in Hell's Kitchen* by Martín Espada. Copyright © 2000 by Martín Espada. Used by permission of the author and W. W. Norton & Company, Inc.

Ruth Fainlight. "Crocuses" from *New & Collected Poems* by Ruth Fainlight (Bloodaxe Books, 2010). Copyright © 2010 by Ruth Fainlight. Reprinted with permission of Bloodaxe Books on behalf of the author. www.bloodaxebooks.com.

Blanche Farley. "The Lover Not Taken" from *Light Year '86*. Reprinted by permission of the author.

Kenneth Fearing. "AD" from *Kenneth Fearing Complete Poems*, ed. by Robert Ryely (Orono, ME: National Poetry Foundation, 1997). Copyright © 1938 by Kenneth Fearing, renewed in 1966 by the Estate of Kenneth Fearing. Reprinted by permission of Russell & Volkening as agents for the author.

Ruth Forman. "Poetry Should Ride the Bus." From *We Are the Young Magicians* (Boston: Beacon Press, 1993). Copyright © 1993 by Ruth Forman. Reprinted with the permission of the author.

Robert Francis. "Catch" and "The Pitcher" from *The Orb Weaver*. Copyright © 1960 by Robert Francis. Reprinted with permission of Wesleyan University Press.

Robert Frost. "Acquainted with the Night," "Design," "Dust of Snow," "Fire and Ice," and "Stopping by Woods on a Snowy Evening," from *The Poetry of Robert Frost*, edited by Edward Connery Lathem. Copyright © 1923, 1928, 1942, 1956, 1969 by Henry Holt and Company, copyright © 1936, 1951, 1956 by Robert Frost, copyright © 1964, 1970 by Lesley Frost Ballantine. Reprinted by permission of Henry Holt and Company, LLC. All rights reserved.

Dana Gioia. "Money" from *The Gods of Winter*. Copyright © 1991 by Dana Gioia. Reprinted with the permission of The Permissions Company, Inc., on behalf of Graywolf Press, Minneapolis, Minnesota, www.graywolfpress.org.

R. S. Gwynn. "Shakespearean Sonnet." Originally appeared in *Formalist* 12.2 (2001). Copyright © 2001 by R. S. Gwynn. Reprinted by permission of the author.

Mark Halliday. "Graded Paper," *Michigan Quarterly Review*. Reprinted by permission of the author.

William Hathaway. "Oh, Oh" from *Light Year '86*. This poem was originally published in the *Cincinnati Poetry Review*. Reprinted by permission of the author.

Robert Hayden. "Those Winter Sundays," copyright © 1966 by Robert Hayden, from *Collected Poems of Robert Hayden* by Robert Hayden, edited by Frederick Glaysher. Used by permission of Liveright Publishing Corporation.

Seamus Heaney. "The Pitchfork" from *Opened Ground: Selected Poems 1966–1996* by Seamus Heaney. Copyright © 1998 by Seamus Heaney. Reprinted by permission of Farrar, Straus and Giroux, LLC, and Faber and Faber, Ltd.

Judy Page Heitzman. "The Schoolroom on the Second Floor of the Knitting Mill." Copyright © 1991 by Judy Page Heitzman. Originally appeared in the *New Yorker,* December 2, 1992, p. 102. Reprinted by permission of the author.

David Hernandez. "All-American," *Southern Review* 48.4 (Autumn 2012). Copyright © 2012 by David Hernandez. Used by permission of the author.

William Heyen. "The Trains" from *The Host: Selected Poems 1965–1990* by William Heyen. Copyright © 1994 by Time Being Press. Reprinted by permission of the author.

Bob Hicok. "Making it in poetry," copyright © 2004 by Bob Hicok. "Making it in poetry" first appeared in the *Georgia Review* 58.2 (Summer 2004), and is reprinted here with the acknowledgment of the editors and the permission of the author.

Tony Hoagland. "America" from *What Narcissism Means to Me.* Copyright © 2003 by Tony Hoagland. Reprinted with the permission of The Permissions Company, Inc., on behalf of Graywolf Press, Minneapolis, Minnesota, www.graywolfpress.org.

Andrew Hudgins. "Elegy for My Father, Who Is Not Dead" from *The Never-Ending: New Poems* by Andrew Hudgins. Copyright © 1991 by Andrew Hudgins. Reprinted by permission of Houghton Mifflin Harcourt Publishing Company. All rights reserved. "The Ice-Cream Truck" from *Shut Up, You're Fine! Poems for Very, Very Bad Children* by Andrew Hudgins. Copyright © 2009 by Andrew Hudgins. Reprinted by permission of the author.

Langston Hughes. "Harlem," from *The Collected Poems of Langston Hughes* by Langston Hughes, edited by Arnold Rampersad with David Roessel, Associate Editor. Copyright © 1994 by the Estate of Langston Hughes. Used by permission of Alfred A. Knopf, an imprint of the Knopf Doubleday Publishing Group, a division of Penguin Random House LLC. All rights reserved. Any third party use of this material, outside of this publication, is prohibited. Interested parties must apply directly to Penguin Random House LLC for permission.

Paul Humphrey. "Blow" from *Light Year '86.* Reprinted with the permission of Eleanor Humphrey.

David Ignatow. "The Jobholder" from *At My Ease: Uncollected Poems of the Fifties and Sixties.* Copyright © 1998 by the Estate of David Ignatow. Reprinted with the permission of The Permissions Company, Inc., on behalf of BOA Editions Ltd., www.boaeditions.org.

Randall Jarrell. "The Death of the Ball Turret Gunner" from *The Complete Poems* by Randall Jarrell. Copyright © 1969, renewed 1997 by Mary von S. Jarrell. Reprinted by permission of Farrar, Straus and Giroux, LLC.

Alice Jones. "The Foot" and "The Lungs," from *Anatomy* by Alice Jones (San Francisco: Bullnettle Press, 1997). Copyright © 1997 by Alice Jones. Reprinted by permission of the author.

Donald Justice. "Order in the Streets" from *Losers Weepers: Poems Found Practically Everywhere,* edited by George Hitchcock. Reprinted by permission of Jean Ross Justice.

Jane Kenyon. "Not Writing" from *Collected Poems.* Copyright © 2005 by the Estate of Jane Kenyon. Reprinted with the permission of The Permissions Company, Inc., on behalf of Graywolf Press, Minneapolis, Minnesota, www.graywolfpress.org.

Carolyn Kizer. "After Bashô" from *Cool, Calm & Collected: Poems 1960–2000.* Copyright © 2001 by Carolyn Kizer. Reprinted with the permission of The Permissions Company, Inc., on behalf of Copper Canyon Press, www.coppercanyonpress.org.

Ted Kooser. "Laundry" from *One World at a Time* by Ted Kooser. Copyright © 1985. Reprinted by permission of the University of Pittsburgh Press. "Selecting a Reader" from *Sure Signs: New and Selected Poems* by Ted Kooser. Copyright © 1980. Reprinted by permission of the University of Pittsburgh Press.

Danusha Laméris. "Names" from *The Moons of August* by Danusha Laméris. Copyright © 2014 by Danusha Laméris. Reprinted with the permission of The Permissions Company, Inc., on behalf of Autumn House Press, www.autumnhouse.org.

Philip Larkin. "A Study of Reading Habits" from *The Complete Poems of Philip Larkin* by Philip Larkin, edited by Archie Burnett. Copyright © 2012 by the Estate of Philip Larkin. Reprinted by permission of Farrar, Straus and Giroux, LLC, and Faber and Faber, Ltd.

Ann Lauinger. "Marvell Noir." First appeared in *Parnassus: Poetry in Review* 28, no. 1 & 2 (2005). Copyright © 2005 by Ann Lauinger. Reprinted by permission of the author.

Katharyn Howd Machan. "Hazel Tells LaVerne" from *Light Year '85.* Copyright © 1977 by Katharyn Howd Machan. Reprinted by permission of the author.

John Maloney. "Good!" from *Proposal* by John Maloney. Zoland Books, 1999. Copyright © 1999 by John Maloney. Reprinted by permission of the author.

Julio Marzán. "Ethnic Poetry." Originally appeared in *Parnassus: Poetry in Review.* "The Translator at the Reception for Latin American Writers." Reprinted by permission of the author.

Florence Cassen Mayers. "All-American Sestina," © 1996 Florence Cassen Mayers, as first published in the *Atlantic Monthly.* Reprinted with permission of the author.

David McCord. "Epitaph on a Waiter" from *Odds Without Ends,* copyright © 1954 by David T. W. McCord. Reprinted by permission of the estate of David T. W. McCord.

Michael McFee. "In Medias Res" from *Colander* by Michael McFee. Copyright © 1996 by Michael McFee. Reprinted by permission of Michael McFee. "Spitwads" from *Shinemaster.* Copyright © 2006 by Michael McFee. Reprinted with the permission of The Permissions Company, Inc., on behalf of Carnegie Mellon University Press, www.cmu.edu/universitypress.

Elaine Mitchell. "Form" from *Light 9* (Spring 1994). Reprinted by permission of the Literary Estate of Elaine Mitchell.

Janice Townley Moore. "To a Wasp" first appeared in *Light Year,* Bits Press. Reprinted by permission of the author.

Robert Morgan. "Mountain Graveyard" from *Sigodlin.* Copyright © 1990 by Robert Morgan. Reprinted by permission of the author.

Paul Muldoon. "Symposium" from *Poems: 1968–1998* by Paul Muldoon. Copyright © 2001 by Paul Muldoon. Reprinted by permission of Farrar, Straus and Giroux, LLC.

Joan Murray. "We Old Dudes," copyright © 2006 by Joan Murray. First appeared in the July/August 2006 issue of *Poetry* magazine. Reprinted by permission of the author.

John Frederick Nims. "Love Poem" from *Selected Poems.* Copyright © 1982 by the University of Chicago. Reprinted by permission of the University of Chicago Press.

Alden Nowlan. "The Bull Moose" from *Alden Nowlan: Selected Poems* by Alden Nowlan. Copyright © 1967. Reprinted by permission of the Estate of Alden Nowlan.

Angela Alaimo O'Donnell. "Messenger" from *Waking My Mother* by Angela Alaimo O'Donnell, published in 2013 by Word Poetry, Cincinnati, Ohio. Copyright © 2013 by Angela Alaimo O'Donnell.

Sharon Olds. "Last Night" from *The Wellspring: Poems* by Sharon Olds. Copyright © 1996 by Sharon Olds. Used by permission of Alfred A. Knopf, an imprint of the Knopf Doubleday Publishing Group, a division of Penguin Random House LLC. All rights reserved. Any third party use of this material, outside of this publication, is prohibited. Interested parties must apply directly to Penguin Random House LLC for permission.

Mary Oliver. "Oxygen" and "The Poet with His Face in His Hands," from *New and Selected Poems, Volume Two* by Mary Oliver. Published by Beacon Press, Boston. Copyright © 2005 by Mary Oliver. Reprinted by permission of the Charlotte Sheedy Literary Agency, Inc.

Lisa Parker. "Snapping Beans" from the collection *This Gone Place* by Lisa Parker. Originally appeared in *Parnassus* 23, no. 2 (1998). Reprinted by permission of the author.

Laurence Perrine. "The limerick's never averse." Copyright © Laurence Perrine. Reprinted by permission of Douglas Perrine.

Kevin Pierce. "Proof of Origin" from *Light 50* (Autumn 2005). Copyright © 2005 by Kevin Pierce. Reprinted with the permission of the author.

Marge Piercy. "To be of use" from *Circles on the Water* by Marge Piercy. Copyright © 1982 by Middlemarsh, Inc. Used by permission of Alfred A. Knopf, an imprint of the Knopf Doubleday Publishing Group, a division of Penguin Random House LLC. Any third party use of this material, outside of this publication, is prohibited. Interested parties must apply directly to Penguin Random House LLC, for permission.

Alberto Ríos. "Seniors" from *Five Indiscretions.* Copyright © 1985 by Alberto Ríos. Reprinted by permission of the author.

Kay Ryan. "Dew" and "Learning," from *Elephant Rocks* by Kay Ryan. Copyright © 1996 by Kay Ryan. Used by permission of Grove/Atlantic, Inc. Any third party use of this material, outside of this publication, is prohibited.

Michael Ryan. "I" from *Poetry* 202.4 (July/August 2013). Copyright © 2013 by Michael Ryan. Reprinted with the permission of the author.

David Shumate. "Shooting the Horse" from *High Water Mark: Prose Poems* by David Shumate. Copyright © 2004. Reprinted by permission of the University of Pittsburgh Press.

Charles Simic. "Fork" from *Selected Early Poems* by Charles Simic. Copyright © 1999 by Charles Simic. Reprinted with the permission of George Braziller, Inc., www.georgebraziller.com.

Louis Simpson. "In the Suburbs" from *The Owner of the House: New Collected Poems, 1940–2001.* Copyright © 1963, 2001 by Louis Simpson. Reprinted with the permission of The Permissions Company, Inc., on behalf of BOA Editions Ltd., www.boaeditions.org.

David R. Slavitt. "Titanic" from *Change of Address: Poems New and Selected* by David R. Slavitt. Copyright © 2005 by David R. Slavitt. Reprinted by permission of Louisiana State University Press.

Ernest Slyman. "Lightning Bugs" from *Sometime the Cow Kick Your Head, Light Year 88/89.* Reprinted by permission of the author.

Gary Snyder. "A Dent in the Bucket" from *Danger on Peaks* by Gary Snyder. Copyright © 2004 by Gary Snyder. Reprinted by permission of Counterpoint. "How Poetry Comes to Me" from *No Nature* by Gary Snyder. Copyright © 1992 by Gary Snyder. Used by permission of Pantheon Books, an imprint of the Knopf

David Solway. "Windsurfing." Reprinted by permission of the author.

Timothy Steele. "Waiting for the Storm" from *Sapphics and Uncertainties: Poems, 1970–1986*. Copyright © 1986, 1995 by Timothy Steele. Reprinted with the permission of The Permissions Company, Inc., on behalf of the University of Arkansas Press, www.uapress.com.

Jim Stevens. "Schizophrenia." Originally appeared in *Light: The Quarterly of Light Verse* (Spring 1992). Copyright © 1992 by Jim Stevens. Reprinted by permission.

Joyce Sutphen. "Guys Like That" from *The Writer's Almanac* online, January 7, 2007. Copyright © 2007 by Joyce Sutphen. Reprinted by permission of the author.

Dylan Thomas. "Do not go gentle into that good night" from *The Poems of Dylan Thomas*. Copyright © 1952 by Dylan Thomas. "The Hand That Signed the Paper" from *The Poems of Dylan Thomas*. Copyright © 1939 by New Directions Publishing Corp. Both selections reprinted by permission of New Directions Publishing Corp.

Jean Toomer. "Unsuspecting." Reprinted from the Jean Toomer Papers, James Weldon Johnson Memorial Collection, Beinecke Rare Book and Manuscript Library, with the permission of the Yale Committee on Literary Property on behalf of Yale University as owner of the literary property rights.

Natasha Trethewey. "On Captivity" from *Thrall: Poems* by Natasha Trethewey. Copyright © 2012 by Natasha Trethewey. Reprinted by permission of Houghton Mifflin Harcourt Publishing Company. All rights reserved.

William Trowbridge. "Drumming Behind You in the High School Band" from *Enter Dark Stranger*. Copyright © 1989 by William Trowbridge. Reprinted with the permission of The Permissions Company, Inc., on behalf of the University of Arkansas Press, www.uapress.com.

John Updike. "Dog's Death" and "Player Piano," from *Collected Poems, 1953–1993* by John Updike. Copyright © 1993 by John Updike. Used by permission of Alfred A. Knopf, an imprint of the Knopf Doubleday Publishing Group, a division of Penguin Random House LLC. All rights reserved. Any third party use of this material, outside of this publication, is prohibited. Interested parties must apply directly to Penguin Random House LLC for permission.

Charles Harper Webb. "Descent" from *Liver* by Charles Harper Webb. Copyright © 1999 The Board of Regents of the University of Wisconsin System. Reprinted by permission of the University of Wisconsin Press.

William Carlos Williams. "Poem" and "The Red Wheelbarrow," from *The Collected Poems: Volume 1, 1909–1939*. Copyright © 1938 by New Directions Publishing Corp. Reprinted by permission of New Directions Publishing Corp.

William Butler Yeats. "Leda and the Swan" from *The Collected Works of W. B. Yeats, Volume I: The Poems, Revised*, by W. B. Yeats, edited by Richard J. Finneran. Copyright © 1928 by the Macmillan Company, renewed © 1956 by Georgie Yeats. All rights reserved. Reprinted with the permission of Scribner, a division of Simon & Schuster, Inc.

DRAMA

Joan Ackermann. *Quiet Torrential Sound* from *Ten-Minute Plays: Volume 3* from Actors Theatre Of Louisville, ed. by Michael Bigelow Dixon and Michele Volansky (New York: Samuel French, 1995). Copyright © 1994 by Joan Ackermann. Reprinted by permission of Bret Adams Ltd.

Jane Anderson. *The Reprimand*. Copyright © 2000 by Jane Anderson. Reprinted by permission of William Morris Endeavor Entertainment, LLC, on behalf of the author.

Sharon E. Cooper. *Mistaken Identity*. Copyright © 2003, 2009 by Sharon E. Cooper. Originally published by Vintage Press in the anthology *Laugh Lines: Short Comic Plays*, ed. by Eric Lane and Nina Shengold. Reprinted by permission of the author. For inquiries regarding producing, please contact the author at secooper1@yahoo.com, or visit her Web site, www.sharonecooper.com.

Larry David. Episode entitled "The Pitch" from the television series *Seinfeld* © 1992 Castle Rock Entertainment, written by Larry David. All Rights Reserved. Reprinted by permission of Castle Rock Entertainment.

Michael Hollinger. *Naked Lunch* from *Humana Festival 2003*, ed. Tanya Palmer and Amy Wegener. Copyright © 2003 by Michael Hollinger. Reprinted by permission.

David Henry Hwang. *Trying to Find Chinatown*. Published in *Trying to Find Chinatown: The Selected Plays of David Henry Hwang*. Copyright © 2000 by David Henry Hwang. Published by Theatre Communications Group. Used by permission of Theatre Communications Group.

David Ives. *Moby-Dude, or: The Three-Minute Whale* from *Talk to Me: Monologue Plays*, ed. Nina Shengold and Eric Lane. Copyright © 2004 by David Ives. Reprinted by permission of Abrams Artists Agency.

Jane Martin. *Rodeo*. Copyright © 1982 by Alexander Speer, as Trustee. Reprinted by permission. CAUTION: Professionals and amateurs are hereby warned that *Rodeo* is subject to a royalty. It is fully

Index of First Lines

Index of Authors and Titles

Index of Terms

Boldface numbers refer to the Glossary of Literary Terms.

957